NAMES AND NUMBERS

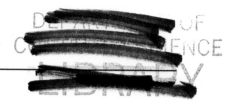

QUICK REFERENCE CONTENTS
(IN ALPHABETICAL ORDER)

The complete table of contents begins on page xi. An index, including detailed subject area entries, begins on page 519

HOW TO USE THIS BOOK—see page xiii

NAMES AND NUMBERS

NAMES AND NUMBERS

A Journalist's Guide to the Most Needed
Information Sources and Contacts

ROD NORDLAND
The Philadelphia Inquirer
Philadelphia, Pennsylvania

A Wiley-Interscience Publication
JOHN WILEY & SONS, New York · Chichester · Brisbane · Toronto

NAMES AND NUMBERS

STAFF

Carole Ann Jacobs
Chief Researcher

Curtis T. Reeve
Researcher

Cathy L. Landis
Researcher

Dusty Harding
Researcher

Published by John Wiley & Sons, Inc.

Library of Congress Cataloging in Publication Data

Nordland, Rod.
  Names and numbers.

  "A Wiley-Interscience publication."
  Includes index.
  1. Associations, institutions, etc.—United
States—Directories. 2. Associations, institutions,
etc.—Directories. I. Title.
AS22.N67   061'.3   78-18903
ISBN 0-471-03994-2

Printed in the United States of America

10 9 8 7 6 5 4 3 2

TO

CYNTHIA LYNN AND CRISTA LEE

PREFACE

Names and Numbers: A Journalist's Guide to the Most Needed Information Sources and Contacts was developed as a professional tool for the working press, and it is intended to fulfill the serious need for a national directory of information sources and contacts. Its more than 20,000 listings form a sort of master national card file in annotated form, with contact information for governments, businesses, institutions, organizations, and people in all walks of life. The book places at the journalist's fingertips the names and telephone numbers of people and places he may need to reach; the sources of specialized information, comment, and background; and the outlets for documents, records, and advice.

There have been many directories of the news media for the benefit of news makers; this is a directory of news makers for the benefit of the news media, and as such it is long overdue. Gaining quick and ready access to information is often simply a matter of knowing the right name and the right number. Wherever practical, this book gives names and direct-line telephone numbers for the key contact people in each listing; often, it also includes alternative contacts and emergency and home telephone numbers. Many of the numbers and names in this book will not be found in telephone books, even if one had a current national collection of them. And it would take dozens of specialized directories to duplicate even a portion of this directory.

In compiling the book, the aim has been to address the needs of both generalists and specialists. One can find the home number of his or her own congressman here, or the home number of a nuclear physicist. Much of the information will prove useful to a lay person—airline reservation numbers, for instance. Other information, such as the list of meteorological institutes, will be most useful to people who are well versed in the field. The result is a book that should be a valuable reference work for information-gatherers of many types: students, researchers, public relations and advertising people, businessmen, marketing experts, salesmen, and even tourists—anyone who may need quick access to information sources.

The book is broadly arranged in three parts: Useful Logistics, Information Sources and Contacts, and The Media. The first part provides practical, often hard-to-find information on the logistics of getting around, that is, toll-free airline reservation numbers, unpublished airport numbers, international telephone calling instructions, hotel reservation numbers, and so on.

The bulk of the book, however, is devoted to Part Two, Information Sources and Contacts. Here are research and information services, many of which perform work free or at cost; colleges and universities, arranged alphabetically on a national basis; and federal agency contacts—even direct lines into the President's office.

This is the place to find, for instance, where the nearest Red Cross chapter is located and what its director's home and office numbers are. How does one reach Jackie Onassis, Richard Petty, Arnold Palmer, or Robert Heilbroner? Where is the International Air Transport Association, or the Insurance Services Office, or the Disease Detection Information Center, or even the Ku Klux Klan? The answers to these and thousands of similar questions are all in this part.

Part Three, The Media, is included in recognition of the fact that often a journalist's most useful initial source is a colleague. All daily newspapers and AP and UPI wire service bureaus are listed, as well as networks, radio and television stations, book publishers, magazines, and press clubs.

We live in a mass information society, but its very mass can render information useless unless one knows how to identify and locate sources. This directory gathers, organizes, and classifies that mass in a way that will help news people and communications specialists to do their jobs more easily and more thoroughly.

Every effort was made to ensure that the information in this book was up-to-date and accurate at the time that compilation was completed, but it is always possible that some details may have changed during the book's production. I welcome being advised of changes that have occurred or may occur in any listing. I also welcome the reader's suggestions for expansions, additions, and improvements to future editions of *Names and Numbers*. Address editorial comments to P.O. Box 12808, Commerce Station, Philadelphia, PA 19108.

ROD NORDLAND

Philadelphia, Pennsylvania
July 1978

ACKNOWLEDGMENTS

My debt to my researchers, who worked diligently and long and with relatively little recompense, is self-evident. I am grateful as well to the thousands of people who made the research manageable by freely and forthrightly answering the questionnaires on which so much of this book is based; their cooperation more than made up for the many difficulties encountered. I also thank the following editors at *The Philadelphia Inquirer* for their understanding acceptance of the disruption the project caused in my normal duties and for their eleventh-hour grant of enough leave to enable me to finish it in a timely fashion: Charles Layton, Gene Foreman, Lois G. Wark, and Eugene L. Roberts, Jr. I am indebted too to many of my colleagues, both at *The Inquirer* and elsewhere, whose assistance was often the mortar filling in the chinks in my own knowledge: these include, but are not limited to, Jay Searcy, Larry Williams, James H. McCartney, Steve Neal, William Vance, Robert S. Boyd, Steve Rubin, Larry Moskowitz, Anita Myette, Harry Gould, James Steele, Donald Barlett, Don Clippinger, John V. R. Bull, Arthur R. H. Morrow, Michael Leary, Bill Lambert, Peter Falchetta, Joe DiMarino, Joe Keeley, and Burr Van Atta. A special note of thanks is due to my colleague, Tom Masland, and my agent and attorney, Nicholas Trott Long, particularly for their early recognition of the value of the project and their encouragement throughout. I am grateful as well to Richard P. Zeldin, Ruth Flohn, Valda Aldzeris, and Jacky Philpotts at John Wiley & Sons; and William Strassheim, Frances Heffner, Jean Reeve, Vilma Wallis, Marie Bertolette, Jimmy Green, Alison McFall, Jan McClay, Rita Brian, Karen Bruno, and Maureen Nester. My greatest debt of all, however, is to the Nordlands: Darrell, Darlene, Cynthia, Craig, Gary, Susan, and Lorine, each of whom made generous donations of logistic and material assistance, without which the project would not have been conducted on the scale it needed and concluded in the short time it demanded.

RN

CONTENTS

PART THREE: THE MEDIA

HOW TO USE THIS BOOK

The complete table of contents begins on page xi. The index begins on page 519

Listings

The listings are the basic units of this book, and although they vary greatly in content depending on the section, the typical one contains several basic pieces of information:

> **ORGANIZATIONAL NAME.** (Abbreviated name, if in common use) (Former or popular name) Street address (mailing address), city, state, zip code. Main or headquarters **telephone number**. Night line **telephone number**. Chief executive's name and office **telephone number** [if different]. Press contact's name, office **telephone number** [if different] and home **telephone number**.

Typically, listings also include information on alternate press contacts, information officers, public relations counsel, regional or branch offices and contacts, as well as a description of an organization's activities, function or purpose, and special services provided to the press.

Locating Organizations

The quickest way to find what you want among the more than 20,000 organizational listings in this book will usually be to consult the index, which begins on page 519. The index combines entries for subject, organizational proper name, and organizational classified name. Throughout the book, organizations and agencies are arranged alphabetically by their proper names within the appropriate sections. If you already know the full, proper name, you can just turn to the right section and look up the name in sequence. But as so often happens, an organization or agency may be known by variant names, or the exact name may not be known. In such instances, you can consult the index under the keyword in an organizational name; for instance, "American Association of Retired Persons" would be found in SPECIAL INTERESTS under "A," and it would of course be indexed in the "A's." But it would also be indexed under the keyword, "Retired," in an entry that would appear thus: "Retired Persons, American Association of."

If the title of an organization or agency does not contain a readily identifiable keyword, it would still be found listed under this system; for instance, "Operation PUSH" would be found indexed under both the "O's" and the "P's," and there would also be a keyword index entry, "(Civil rights) Operation PUSH," located under the "C's."

This system not only enables you rapidly to locate contacts and sources you already know about, but also to browse and to search for contacts you might expect to be available.

If you are not looking for a specific private association, consult the several chapters in the book that include numerous organizations arranged in broad categories.

SPECIAL INTERESTS includes the bulk of private and semiprivate organizations: lobbyists and special interest groups; trade, professional, and fraternal associations; medical and health groups; service and public interest organizations; minor political parties; and other nongovernmental organizations. The following exceptions, that is, private or semiprivate associations *not* listed under SPECIAL INTERESTS, should be noted.

EDUCATION includes associations composed of *educators*; organizations whose functions are *educational* will generally be found in SPECIAL INTERESTS or other chapters.

SCIENCE AND TECHNOLOGY includes associations whose functions or membership are highly technical or esoteric.

INFORMATION AND RESEARCH SERVICES includes associations whose primary functions are to provide information to others.

SPORTS includes athletic associations, as well as teams, leagues, and regulatory bodies.

WORLD includes foreign and international associations that emphasize activities outside the US.

MEDIA ORGANIZATIONS includes associations composed of journalists or communicators, as well as groups whose activities concentrate on the media.

Locating People

Space does not permit indexing of the approximately 30,000 individuals listed in this book, but sections of the book that include prominent people are self-indexed. The PEOPLE chapter itself lists 1200 of the most prominent Americans, and this section is in alphabetical order. Congressmen are listed alphabetically in THE FEDERAL GOVERNMENT. Governors and mayors are listed by state and city, respectively, and officials of agencies, organizations, and businesses can be found listed with their organizations. Some prominent individuals are listed in two or more places in the book. In such cases you may wish to consult alternate listings to obtain the fullest contact information. Brief contact information for a state's governor is given, for instance, if he or she makes the list of the most prominent Americans in PEOPLE; fuller details, including the name of the governor's press secretary and night contacts, are given in STATE GOVERNMENTS.

Alphabetizing

Because the material in the 45 chapters of this book varies so greatly, the alphabetizing of listings and entries differs somewhat in many chapters. Where the system employed is not self-evident, an explanatory note is given at the beginning of the chapter or section. In all cases, the effort has been to employ the system that would be most practical and useful to the reader. Colleges, for example, are alphabetized by their names (disregarding the words "college" and "university") on a nationwide basis, since one may know the name of a particular college without knowing the state or city in which it is located. Congressmen are listed both alphabetically and by state. Newspapers are listed alphabetically by city and state. Federal cabinet-level departments are grouped together and listed alphabetically, rather than hierarchially as is usually done in government manuals. Independent federal agencies are grouped alphabetically in a separate list.

While the systems vary, the rules of alphabetizing are uniform and follow the dictionary method: names are alphabetized by letter up to the first comma, regardless of how many words there are in the name. Abbreviations are alphabetized as if spelled out in full. Thus US would be alphabetized as United States. Company and organizational names that consist of a given name followed by surname are alphabetized by the surname. John Hancock Mutual Life Insurance Co., for instance, would be under the "H's." Articles and superfluous words, or words repeated constantly in the same list, are generally ignored for the purpose of alphabetizing. Thus *Department of the Treasury* would be arranged on the basis of the word *Treasury*.

Abbreviations

In the interest of clarity abbreviations are used as little as possible in this book except in addresses. Other exceptions include

    AA—administrative assistant
¬ (h)—home telephone number
    LA—legislative assistant
    NL—no telephone number listed
    NP—nonpublished telephone number
    US—United States

The standard postal abbreviations are used for the names of states:

Alabama	AL	Massachusetts	MA
Alaska	AK	Michigan	MI
Arizona	AZ	Minnesota	MN
Arkansas	AR	Mississippi	MS
American Samoa	AS	Missouri	MO
California	CA	Montana	MT
Canal Zone	CZ	Nebraska	NE
Colorado	CO	Nevada	NV
Connecticut	CT	New Hampshire	NH
Delaware	DE	New Jersey	NJ
District of Columbia	DC	New Mexico	NM
Florida	FL	New York	NY
Georgia	GA	North Carolina	NC
Guam	GU	North Dakota	ND
Hawaii	HI	Ohio	OH
Idaho	ID	Oklahoma	OK
Illinois	IL	Oregon	OR
Indiana	IN	Pennsylvania	PA
Iowa	IA	Puerto Rico	PR
Kansas	KS	Rhode Island	RI
Kentucky	KY	South Carolina	SC
Louisiana	LA	South Dakota	SD
Maine	ME	Tennessee	TN
Maryland	MD	Trust Territories	TT

Texas. . . . . TX	Washington. . . . . WA
Utah. . . . . UT	West Virginia. . . . . WV
Vermont. . . . . VT	Wisconsin. . . . . .WI
Virginia. . . . . .VA	Wyoming. . . . . WY
Virgin Islands. VI	

PART ONE
USEFUL LOGISTICS

AIRLINES

This section includes reservation and, where available, press contact information for all major airlines operating in the US. Toll-free numbers are also included for those airlines that make them available. Note that in lists of reservations numbers, one calls the number for the city in which one is located—not for the city to which one is traveling. If no area code is listed, the number is intended for local use and is not toll free if called long distance. Direct-dial toll-free numbers with 800 area codes; ask the local operator for Zenith (ZE), Enterprise (EN), and WX toll-free numbers. Foreign place names in the lists below are given alphabetically in the same sequence as states of the US.

AER LINGUS (IRISH INTERNATIONAL AIRLINES). 564 5th Ave, New York, NY 10036. **212-575-8400.** *Reservations.* **212-575-8400**

AEROFLOT SOVIET AIRLINES. 545 5th Ave, New York, NY 10017. **212-661-4050**

AEROMEXICO. 500 5th Ave, New York, NY 10036. **212-221-8700.** *Reservations.* **212-279-9700**

AIR CANADA. 600 Madison Ave, New York, NY 10022. **1-800-223-5010.** *Press contact.* Steve Pisni, **212-935-7653**

Reservations

Alabama. 1-800-621-6464

Alberta (Canada)
Banff. **762-3516**
Lethbridge. **329-4120**
Red Deer. **343-0900**
All other points north of Red Deer. **ZE 0-7177**
All other points south of Red Deer. **ZE 0-7260**

Arizona
Phoenix. **1-800-621-6464**

British Columbia (Canada)
Abassiz. **ZE 6293**
Abbotsford. **ZE 6293**
Albert Bay. **800-663-3721**
Aldergrove. **ZE 6293**
Alta Lake. **ZE 6293**

Armstrong. **800-663-3721**
Ashcroft. **800-663-3721**
Beaver Cove. **800-663-3721**
Boston Bar. **ZE 6293**
Britannia Beach. **ZE 6293**
Burns Lake. **800-663-3721**
Campbell River. **ZE 6293**
Castlegar. **800-663-3721**
Chemainus. **ZE 6293**
Chilliwack. **ZE 6293**
Cortez Island. **ZE 6293**
Courtenay. **ZE 6293**
Cranbrook. **ZE 0-7260**
Cumberland. **ZE 6293**
Enderby. **800-663-3721**
Fernie. **ZE 0-7260**
Gabriola. **ZE 6293**
Gibsons. **ZE 6293**
Golden. **ZE 0-7260**
Gold River. **ZE 6293**
Grand Forks. **800-663-3721**
Haney. **ZE 6293**
Holberg. **800-663-3721**
Hope. **ZE 6293**
Houston. **800-663-3721**
Invermere. **ZE 0-7260**
Kamloops. **800-663-3721**
Kelowna. **800-663-3721**
Keremeos. **800-663-3721**
Kimberley. **ZE 0-7260**
Kinnard. **800-663-3721**
Kitimat. **800-663-3721**
Ladysmith. **ZE 6293**
Lytton. **800-663-3721**
Merritt. **800-663-3721**
Mission. **ZE 6293**
Nanaimo. **ZE 6293**
Nelson. **800-663-3721**
Oliver. **800-663-3721**
Osoyoos. **800-663-3721**
Oyster Bay. **ZE 6293**
Parksville. **ZE 6293**
Peachland. **800-663-3721**
Pender Harbour. **ZE 6293**
Penticton. **800-663-3721**
Port Alberni. **ZE 6293**
Port Alice. **800-663-3721**

Port Hardy. **800-663-3721**
Port McNeil. **800-663-3721**
Port Mellon. **ZE 6293**
Powell River. **ZE 6293**
Prince George. **800-663-3721**
Prince Rupert. **800-663-3721**
Princeton. **800-663-3721**
Quesnel. **800-663-3721**
Radium Hot Springs. **ZE 0-7260**
Revelstoke. **800-663-3721**
Rossland. **800-663-3721**
Rutland. **800-663-3721**
Salmo. **800-663-3721**
Salmon Arm. **800-663-3721**
Sayward. **ZE 6293**
Sechelt. **ZE 6293**
Smithers. **800-663-3721**
Sointula. **800-663-3721**
Squamish. **ZE 6293**
Summerland. **800-663-3721**
Tahsis. **ZE 6293**
Terrace. **800-663-3721**
Tofino. **ZE 6293**
Trail. **800-663-3721**
Ucluelet. **ZE 6293**
Vananda. **ZE 6293**
Vanderhoof. **800-663-3721**
Vernon. **800-663-3721**
Williams Lake. **800-663-3721**
Winfield. **800-663-3721**
Woodfibre. **ZE 6293**
Youbou. **ZE 6293**

California
Beverly Hills. **986-4200**
Burbank. **776-7000**
Compton. **639-6615**
Glendale. **776-7000**
Hollywood. **776-7000**
Inglewood. **646-7100**
Norwalk. **639-6615**
Pasadena. **776-7000**
Santa Monica. **646-7100**
Van Nuys. **986-4200**
All other cities. **1-800-634-6351**

Colorado
Denver. **800-621-6464**

Connecticut. 800-223-5010

Delaware. 800-223-5010

Florida. 800-432-3561 (except Miami and Miami Beach)

Georgia. 800-621-6464

Idaho
Boise. **800-634-6351**

Illinois. 800-972-6484 (except Chicago)

Indiana
Anderson. **800-621-8030**
Bloomington. **800-621-8030**
East Chicago. **800-621-8030**
Elkhart. **800-621-8030**
Evansville. **800-621-8030**
Fort Wayne. **800-621-8030**
Gary. **800-621-8030**
Hammond. **800-621-8030**
Hishawaka. **1-800-621-8030**
Indianapolis. **1-800-621-8030**
Lafayette. **1-800-621-8030**
South Bend. **1-800-621-8030**
Terre-Haute. **1-800-621-8030**

Iowa. 1-800-621-8030

Kentucky. 800-621-8030

Maine. 1-800-621-6464

Maryland
Baltimore. **EN 9-2132**

Massachusetts. 800-223-5010 (except Boston)

Michigan
Alma. **EN 7747**
Ann Arbour. **EN 7747**
Auburn Heights. **EN 7747**
Battle Creek. **EN 7747**
Bay City. **EN 7747**
Belleville. **EN 7747**
Benton Harbour. **EN 7747**
Brighton. **EN 7747**
Cadillac. **EN 7747**
Caro. **EN 7747**
Commerce. **EN 7747**
Drayton Plains. **EN 7747**
Escanaba. **EN 6602**
Flatrock. **EN 7747**
Flint. **EN 7747**

Grand Haven. **EN 7747**
Grand Rapids. **EN 7747**
Greenville. **EN 7747**
Holland. **EN 7747**
Ishpeming. **EN 6602**
Jackson. **EN 7747**
Kalamazoo. **EN 7747**
Lansing. **EN 7747**
Ludington. **EN 7747**
Manistee. **EN 7747**
Marquette. **EN 6602**
Midland. **EN 7747**
Mount Clemens. **EN 7747**
Mount Pleasant. **EN 7747**
Muskegon. **EN 7747**
New Boston. **EN 7747**
Niles. **EN 7747**
Northville. **EN 7747**
Owosso. **EN 7747**
Paw Paw. **EN 7747**
Petoskey. **EN 6602**
Plymouth. **EN 7747**
Pontiac. **EN 7747**
Port Huron. **EN 7747**
Rochester. **EN 7747**
Rockwood. **EN 7747**
Saginaw. **EN 7747**
St Joseph. **EN 7747**
Sault Ste Marie. **EN 6602**
Sturgis. **EN 7747**
Traverse City. **EN 7747**
Utica. **EN 7747**
Walled Lake. **EN 7747**
Ypsilanti. **EN 7747**

Minnesota
Duluth. **800-621-8030**
Hibbing. **800-621-8030**
Minneapolis. **800-621-8030**
Rochester. **800-621-8030**
St Paul. **800-621-8030**
Thief River Falls. **EN 3400**

Mississippi. 1-800-621-6464

Missouri
Columbia. **800-621-8030**
Jefferson City. **800-621-8030**
St Louis. **800-621-8030**
Springfield. **800-621-8030**

Montana
Great Falls. **ZE 0-7260**
Kalispell. **ZE 0-7260**

Nevada
Carson City. **1-8188**
Las Vegas. **EN 4204**
Reno. **1-8188**
Virginia City. **1-8188**

New Brunswick (Canada)
Bath. **1-800-222-9660**
Bathurst. **1-800-332-3926**
Bouctouche. **1-800-332-3926**
Campbellton. **1-800-332-3926**
Cap Pele. **1-800-332-3926**
Caraquet. **1-800-332-3926**
Centreville. **1-800-222-9660**
Chatham. **1-800-332-3926**
Dalhousie. **1-800-332-3926**
Edmundston. **1-800-222-9660**
Florenceville. **1-800-222-9660**
Glassville. **1-800-222-9660**
Grand Falls. **1-800-222-9660**
Hartland. **1-800-222-9660**
Newcastle. **1-800-332-3926**
Richibucto. **1-800-332-3926**
Sackville. **536-2482**
St Andrew. **1-800-222-9660**
St Stephen. **1-800-222-9660**
Shippengan. **1-800-332-3926**
Sussex. **1-800222-9660**
Tracadie. **1-800-332-3926**
Woodstock. **1-800-222-9660**

Newfoundland (Canada)
Bay Roberts. **ZE 0-7006**
Bell Island. **ZE 0-7006**
Bonavista. **ZE 0-7006**
Botwood. **ZE 0-7006**
Carbonear. **ZE 0-7006**
Freshwater. **ZE 0-7006**
Grand Bank. **ZE 0-7006**
Lewisport. **ZE 0-7006**
Marystown. **ZE 0-7006**
Port aux Basques. **ZE 0-7006**
Springdale. **ZE 0-7006**

New Hampshire. 800-223-5010

New Jersey
Atlantic City. **800-223-5010**
Bergen County. **800-223-5010**
Clifton. **800-223-5010**
East Orange. **800-233-5010**
Fort Lee. **800-233-5010**
Jersey City. **800-233-5010**
Livingston. **800-223-5010**

Morristown. **800-223-5010**
Newark. **621-1710**
New Brunswick. **800-223-5010**
Passaic. **800-233-5010**
Paterson. **800-223-5010**
Plainfield. **800-223-5010**
Princeton. **800-223-5010**
Somerville. **800-223-5010**
Trenton. **800-223-5010**
Wayne. **800-223-5010**
Westfield. **800-223-5010**

New York
Albany. **434-1742**
Batavia. **EN 8800**
Buffalo. **854-5911**
Geneva. **EN 8800**
Glens Falls. **800-442-5914**
Jamestown. **EN 8800**
Lake Placid. **800-442-5914**
Lockport. **EN 8800**
Long Island
   Suffolk County. **543-4444**
   Nassau County. **561-2744**
Malone. **800-442-5914**
Massena. **800-442-5914**
Niagara Falls. **EN 8800**
Olean. **EN 8800**
Plattsburgh. **561-6120**
Potsdam. **800-442-5914**
Rochester. **EN 8800**
Schenectady. **434-1742**
Syracuse. **800-442-5914**
Troy. **434-1742**
Watertown. **800-442-5914**
Westchester. **428-4994**

North Carolina. 1-800-621-6464

North Dakota
Grand Forks. **EN 3400**
Minot. **EN 3400**

Nova Scotia (Canada)
Amhurst. **ZE 07-716**
Digby. **ZE 57-777**
North Sydney. **794-4761**
Port Hawkesbury. **625-1483**
Shelburne. **ZE 57-777**
All other cities. **1-800-565-7121**

Ohio. 1-800-621-8030 (except Cleveland)

Oklahoma. 1-800-621-6464

Ontario (Canada)

Alliston. **1-800-261-7240**
Arnprior. **1-800-361-8620**
Aurora. **1-800-261-7240**
Aylmer. **1-800-261-7240**
Barrie. **1-800-261-7240**
Belleville. **1-800-261-7240**
Blenheim. **1-800-261-7240**
Blind River. **1-800-461-7170**
Bracebridge. **1-800-261-7240**
Bradford. **1-800-261-7240**
Brantford. **1-800-261-7240**
Breslau. **1-800-261-7240**
Brockville. **1-800-361-8620**
Cambridge. **1-800-261-7240**
Camp Borden. **1-800-261-7240**
Capreol. **675-3311**
Carleton Place. **1-800-361-8620**
Chalk River. **1-800-361-8620**
Charlton. **1-800-461-7170**
Chapeau. **1-800-461-7240**
Chatham. **1-800-261-7240**
Cobalt. **1-800-461-7170**
Cobourg. **1-800-261-7240**
Collingwood. **1-800-261-7240**
Cookstown. **1-800-261-7240**
Cornwall. **1-800-361-8620**
Deep River. **1-800-361-8620**
Delhi. **1-800-261-7240**
Dundas. **528-7061**
Earlton. **1-800-461-7170**
Elliot Lake. **1-800-461-7170**
Englehart. **1-800-461-7170**
Espanola. **1-800-461-7170**
Fergus. **1-800-261-7240**
Fort Erie. **1-800-261-7240**
French River. **1-800-461-7170**
Georgetown. **1-800-261-7240**
Goderich. **1-800-261-7240**
Gogama. **1-800-461-7170**
Gore Bay. **1-800-461-7170**
Gravenhurst. **1-800-261-7240**
Grimsby. **1-800-261-7240**
Guelph. **1-800-261-7240**
Haileybury. **1-800-461-7170**
Hanover. **1-800-261-7240**
Hawkesbury. **1-800-361-8620**
Huntsville. **1-800-261-7240**
Ingersoll. **1-800-261-7240**
Killarney. **1-800-461-7170**
King City. **1-800-261-7240**
Kingston. **1-800-361-8620**

Kirkland Lake. **1-800-461-7170**
Kitchener. **1-800-261-7240**
Latchford. **1-800-461-7170**
Leamington. **1-800-261-7240**
Lindsay. **1-800-261-7240**
Little Current. **1-800-461-7170**
Maitland. **1-800-361-8620**
Massey. **1-800-461-7170**
Midland. **1-800-261-7240**
Milton. **1-800-261-7240**
Mount Forest. **1-800-261-7240**
Napanee. **1-800-261-7240**
New Liskeard. **1-800-461-7170**
Newmarket. **1-800-261-7240**
Niagara Falls. **1-800-261-7240**
Niagara-on-the-Lake. **1-800-261-7240**
Oak Ridges. **1-800-261-7240**
Orangeville. **1-800-261-7240**
Orillia. **1-800-261-7240**
Owen Sound. **1-800-261-7240**
Parry Sound. **1-800-261-7240**
Pembroke. **1-800-361-8620**
Perth. **1-800-361-8620**
Peterborough. **1-800-261-7240**
Port Colborne. **1-800-261-7240**
Port Hope. **1-800-261-7240**
Prescott. **1-800-261-7240**
Princeton. **1-800-261-7240**
Renfrew. **1-800-361-8620**
Ridgetown. **1-800-261-7240**
St Catharines. **1-800-261-7240**
St Thomas. **1-800-261-7240**
Sarnia. **1-800-261-7240**
Schomberg. **1-800-261-7240**
Simcoe. **1-800-261-7240**
Smiths Falls. **1-800-361-8620**
Stratford. **1-800-261-7240**
Sturgeon Falls. **1-800-461-7170**
Thorold. **1-800-261-7240**
Tillsonburg. **1-800-261-7240**
Tottenham. **1-800-261-7240**
Trenton. **1-800-261-7240**
Wallaceburg. **1-800-261-7240**
Waterloo. **1-800-261-7240**
Welland. **1-800-261-7240**
Whitby. **1-800-261-7240**
Woodstock. **1-800-261-7240**

Oregon
Eugene. **1-800-634-6351**
Portland. **1-800-634-6351**
Salem. **1-800-634-6351**

Pennsylvania
Erie. **800-621-6464**
Harrisburg. **800-223-5010**
Philadelphia. **800-223-5010**
Pittsburgh. **800-621-6464**

Prince Edward Island (Canada)
Charlottetown. **800-561-3933**

Quebec (Canada). **1-800-361-8620**

Rhode Island. 800-223-5010

Saskatchewan (Canada)
Estevan. **1-800-552-8395**
Melville. **1-800-552-8395**
Moose Jaw. **1-800-552-8395**
Regina Rural. **1-800-552-8395**
Swift Current. **1-800-552-8395**
Seyburn. **1-800-552-8395**
Yorkton. **1-800-552-8395**

South Carolina. 1-800-621-6464

South Dakota
Sioux Falls. **800-621-6464**

Tennessee. 1-800-621-6464

Texas. 800-621-6464

Utah
Salt Lake City. **1-800-634-6351**

Vermont. 800-223-5010

Washington
Aberdeen. **ZE 9255**
Anacortes. **ZE 9255**
Belleveu. **244-2300**
Bellingham. **733-4889**
Bremerton. **ZE 9255**
Everett. **259-0821**
Hoquiam. **ZE 9255**
Kelso. **ZE 9255**
Longview. **ZE 9255**
Lynden. **ZE 9255**
Mount Vernon. **ZE 9255**
Oak Harbor. **ZE 9255**
Olympia. **ZE 9255**
Port Angeles. **ZE 9255**
Richland. **ZE 9255**
Sedro Woolley. **ZE 9255**
Spokane. **838-4421**
Tacoma. **383-3757**

Walla Walla. **ZE 9255**
Wenatchee. **ZE 9255**
Yakima. **ZE 9255**

West Virginia. 800-621-6464

Wisconsin. 1-800-621-8030

AIR FRANCE. 683 5th Ave, New York, NY 10022. **212-758-6300**

AIR-INDIA. 345 Park Ave, New York, NY 10022. **212-935-7500.** *Reservations.* **212-751-6300**

AIR JAMAICA. 19 E 49th St, New York, NY 10017. **212-935-2336.** *Reservations.* **212-421-9750**

AIR MIDWEST. Municipal Airport, Wichita, KS 67209. **316-942-8321.** Gary Adamson, president. *Reservations from Wichita.* **316-942-1223.** Kansas toll-free number: **800-362-2070**

AIR NEW ENGLAND, INC. Logan International Airport, East Boston, MA. 02128. **617-569-5650.** Charles F Butler, president. Edward Smick, vice-president, sales.
Reservations
Boston. MA. 617-569-5510
Other Massachusetts cities. 800-732-3450
Other New England states, New York, and New Jersey. 800-225-3640
Mid-Atlantic. 800-225-3900

ALASKA AIRLINES, INC.. Box 68900, Seattle-Tacoma International Airport, Seattle, WA. 98188. **800-426-0333.** Ross W Anderson, president

ALITALIA. 666 5th Ave, New York, NY 10019. **212-262-4480**

Atlanta, GA. 225 Peachtree St NE: *Reservations.* **800-223-9770.** *Sales office.* 577-1320. *Cargo office.* **800-221-9870**
Baltimore, MD. *Reservations.* **800-223-9770.** *Sales office.* **685-3020.** *Cargo office.* **800-221-9870**
Boston, MA. 535 Boylston St: *Reservations.* **542-9060.** *Sales office.* **267-4600.** *Cargo office.* **800-221-9870.** Logan International Airport: *Reservations.* **567-7740.** *Sales office.* 567-7740. *Cargo office.* **567-1200**
Buffalo, NY. 627 Statler Hilton Bldg: *Reservations.* **800-442-5860.** *Sales office.* **854-7454.** *Cargo office.* **800-522-6050**
Chicago, IL. 138 S Michigan Ave: *Reservations.* **427-4720.** *Sales office.* **781-0540.** *Cargo*

office. **800-221-9870.** Mid-Continental Plaza, 55 E Monroe St: *Reservations.* **800-223-9770.** *Sales office.* **781-0545.** *Cargo office.* **800-221-9870**
Cleveland, OH. 1422 Euclid Ave: *Reservations.* **800-223-9770.** *Sales office.* **861-3615.** *Cargo office.* **800-221-9870**
Dallas, TX. 8350 Central Expy: *Reservations.* **800-223-5730.** *Sales office.* **692-8761.** *Cargo office.* **800-221-4745**
Detroit, MI. 2840 Book Bldg: *Reservations.* **800-223-9770.** *Sales office.* **963-0030.** *Cargo office.* **800-221-9870**
East Meadow, NY. See New York.
Hartford, CT. 60 Washington St: *Reservations.* **800-223-5090,** 527-7237. *Sales office.* **525-5691.** *Cargo office.* **800-221-9870**
Los Angeles, CA. 5959 W Century Blvd: *Reservations.* **800-223-5730.** *Cargo office.* 221-4745. 5758 W Century Blvd: *Reservations.* **800-223-5730.** *Sales office.* **776-5611.** *Cargo office.* **776-2626, 646-7330**
Mexico City, Mexico. Calle Niza 12 1° Piso: *Reservations.* **533-12-40.** *Sales office.* **553-55-90**
Miami, FL. 150 SE 2nd Ave: *Reservations.* **800-223-5730.** *Sales office.* **377-1401.** *Cargo office.* **800-221-4745**
Minneapolis, MN. 801 Nicollet Mall: *Reservations.* **800-223-5730.** *Sales office.* **335-7625.** *Cargo office.* **800-221-4745**
Montreal, Que (Canada). 2055 Peel St: *Reservations.* **842-5201.** *Sales office.* **842-8241.** *Cargo office.* **842-8241.** International Airport: *Reservations.* **476-3702.** *Sales office.* **467-3702.** *Cargo office.* **476-3709**
New York, NY. 666 5th Ave 10019: *Reservations.* **582-8900.** *Sales office.* **262-4480.** *Cargo office.* **262-4455.** East Meadow, Long Island, 1900 Hempstead Tpke: *Sales office.* **794-6444.** Kennedy International Airport: *Reservations.* **656-2720.** *Arrivals.* **656-2787.** *Departures.* **656-2820.** *Import.* **656-2730.** *Export.* **656-2755**
Ottawa, Ont (Canada). *Reservations.* **237-1460.** *Sales office.* **521-2694.** *Cargo office.* **237-1461**
Philadelphia, PA. 1704 Kennedy Blvd: *Reservations.* **568-5444.** *Sales office.* **569-1122.** 1819 Kennedy Blvd: *Reservations.* **568-5444.** *Sales office.* **569-1122.** *Cargo office.* **800-221-9870**
Pittsburgh, PA. 320 Fort Duquesne Blvd: *Reservations.* **800-223-5730.** *Sales office.* **391-6882.** *Cargo office.* **800-221-9870**
St Paul, MN. 801 Nicollet Mall: *Reservations.* **800-223-5730.** *Sales office.* **335-7625.** *Cargo office.* **800-221-4745**

San Francisco, CA. 421 Powell St: *Reservations.* **800-223-5730.** *Sales office.* **397-4855.** *Cargo office.* **800-221-4745**

Toronto, Ont (Canada). 85 Richmond St W: *Reservations.* **363-2001.** *Sales office.* **363-1348.** *Cargo office.* **363-1347.** Malton Airport: *Sales office.* **676-2884.** *Cargo office.* **676-3360**

Union, NJ. 1435 Morris Ave: *Reservations.* **800-223-5090, 643-4222.** *Sales office.* **964-4520.** *Cargo office.* **212-656-2720**

Vancouver, BC (Canada). 700 W Georgia St: *Reservations.* **800-361-8171.** *Sales office.* **682-7876.** *Cargo office.* **682-7876**

Washington, DC. 1001 Connecticut Ave NW: *Reservations.* **393-2829.** *Sales office.* **331-1383.** *Cargo office.* **800-221-9870**

Winnipeg, Man (Canada). 15 Greenmouth Rd: *Reservations.* **800-361-8050.** *Sales office.* **256-8373.** *Cargo office.* **256-8373**

Reservations by States

Alabama. **800-223-5730**
Alberta (Canada). **800-361-8060**
Arizona. **800-223-5730**
Arkansas. **800-223-5730**
British Columbia (Canada). **800-361-8171**
California. **800-223-5730**
Colorado. **800-223-5730**
Connecticut. **800-223-5090**
Delaware. **800-223-5090**
Florida. **800-223-5730**
Georgia. **800-223-9770**
Idaho. **800-223-5730**
Illinois. **800-223-9770**
Indiana. **800-223-9770**
Iowa. **800-223-5730**
Kansas. **800-223-5730**
Kentucky. **800-223-9770**
Labrador (Canada). **800-361-8058**
Louisiana. **800-223-5730**
Maine. **800-223-9770**
Manitoba (Canada). **800-361-8050**
Maryland. **800-223-9770**
Massachusetts. **800-223-5090**
Michigan. **800-223-9770**
Minnesota. **800-223-5730**
Mississippi. **800-223-5730**
Missouri. **800-223-5730**
Montana. **800-223-5730**
Nebraska. **800-223-5730**
Nevada. **800-223-5730**
New Brunswick (Canada). **800-361-8336**
Newfoundland (Canada). **800-361-8050**
New Hampshire. **800-223-5090**

New Jersey. **800-223-5090**
New Mexico. **800-223-5730**
New York. **800-442-5869** (except Nassau and Westchester. **EN 6955**
North Carolina. **800-223-9770**
North Dakota. **800-223-5730**
Nova Scotia (Canada). **800-361-8336**
Ohio. **800-223-9770**
Oklahoma. **800-223-5730**
Ontario (Canada) **(eastern).** **800-361-8336**
Ontario (Canada) **(western).** **800-361-8050**
Oregon. **800-223-5730**
Pennsylvania (eastern). **800-223-5090**
Pennsylvania (western). **800-223-9770**
Prince Edward Island (Canada). **800-361-8336**
Quebec (Canada). **800-361-8336**
Rhode Island. **800-223-5090**
Saskatchewan (Canada). **800-361-8660**
South Carolina. **800-223-9770**
South Dakota. **800-223-5730**
Tennessee. **800-223-9770**
Texas. **800-223-5730**
Utah. **800-223-5730**
Vermont. **800-223-5090**
Virginia. **800-223-9770**
Washington. **800-223-5730**
Wisconsin. **800-223-9770**
Wyoming. **800-223-5730**

ALLEGHENY AIRLINES. Washington International Airport, Washington, DC 20001. **703-892-7096.** *Press contact.* David Shipley, **703-892-7096.** (h) **703-569-4198.**

Reservations

Akron, OH. **762-9211**
Albany, NY. **462-5881**
Allentown, PA. **437-9801**
Altoona, PA. **695-9813**
Anderson, IN. **288-3629**
Ashland, KY. **800-245-1640**
Atlantic City, NY. **344-7104**
Baltimore, MD. **727-0825**
Bellefonte, PA. **238-8414**
Bethlehem, PA. **437-9801**
Binghamton, NY. **729-6111**
Bloomington, IN. **336-1136**
Boston, MA. **482-3160**
Bradford, PA. **362-3551**
Bridgeport, CT. **334-5545**
Bristol, TN. **323-2177**
Bristol, VA. **323-2177**

Brookville, PA. **800-448-2970**
Buffalo, NY. **632-3000**
Burlington, VT. **862-9611**
Camden, NJ. **800-448-2970**
Canton, OH. **499-5154**
Cape May, NJ. **800-448-2970**
Charleston, WV. **622-4350**
Chesapeake, VA. **622-4350**
Chicago, IL. **726-1201**
Cincinnati, OH. **621-9220**
Clarksburg, WV. **842-3531**
Clearfield, PA. **342-1670**
Cleveland, OH. **696-8050**
Columbus, OH. **228-4564**
Corning, NY. **562-8482**
Cornwall, Ont (Canada). **ZE 0-2540**
Cortland, NY. **800-245-2200**
Danville, IL. **446-4727**
Dayton, OH. **228-6134**
Detroit, MI. **963-8340**
DuBois, PA. **371-2477**
Easton, PA. **437-9801**
Elkins, WV. **800-245-2200**
Elmira, NY. **739-3656**
Endicott, NY. **729-6111**
Erie, PA. **452-6951**
Evansville, IN. **423-7746**
Fairmont, WV. **800-245-2200**
Frankfort, KY. **800-245-1640**
Franklin, PA. **437-6115**
Groton, CT. **445-7405**
Grove City, PA. **800-445-2970**
Hagerstown, MD. **733-6700**
Hamilton, Ont (Canada). **526-6020**
Hampton, VA. **877-9205**
Harrisburg, PA. **236-5001**
Hartford, CT. **522-2161**
Hazen, PA. **800-448-2970**
Huntington, WV. **529-3346**
Indianapolis, IN. **248-1211**
Ironton, OH. **800-245-2200**
Islip, NY. **273-1300**
Jamestown, NY. **484-1118**
Johnson City, NY. **729-6111**
Johnson City, TN. **800-245-1640**
Johnstown, PA. **535-6704**
Keene, NH. **800-448-2970**
Kingsport, TN. **323-2177**
Lafayette, IN. **742-1175**
Lake Placid, NY. **800-245-2200**
Lancaster, PA. **569-0461**
Lexington, KY. **255-8511**

Louisville, KY. 584-0354
Mansfield, OH. 800-245-2200
Marietta, OH. 800-245-2200
Martinsburg, PA. 695-9813
Martinsburg, WV. 800-245-2200
Massena, NY. 800-245-2200
Memphis, TN. 526-7691
Milwaukee, WI. 278-8689
Minneapolis, MN. 338-5841
Montreal, Que (Canada). 871-0017
Morgantown, WV. 292-3301
Muncie, IN. 288-3629
Nashville, TN. 256-1944
Newark, NJ. 622-3201
New Castle, IN. 288-3629
New Haven, CT. 787-4137
New London, CT. 445-7405
Newport News, VA. 877-9205
New York City, NY. 736-3200
Norfolk, VA. 622-4350
North Philadelphia, PA. 563-8055
Ocean City, MD. 749-7105
Ocean City, NJ. 344-7104
Ogdensburg, NY. 800-245-2200
Oil City, PA. 437-6115
Olean, NY. 800-245-2200
Oneida, NY. 800-245-2200
Parkersburg, WV. 485-4541
Philadelphia, PA. 563-8055
Philipsburg, PA. 243-1670
Pittsburgh, PA. 922-7500
Plattsburgh, NY. 561-4160
Portsmouth, VA. 622-4350
Prescott, Ont (Canada). ZE 0-2540
Preston, Ont (Canada). 653-1191
Providence, RI. 274-5600
Reading, PA. 375-4553
Rochester, NY. 546-4660
Rome, NY. 337-7000
Rutland, VT. 1-800-448-2970
St Louis, MO. 421-1018
St Paul, MN. 338-5841
Salisbury, MD. 749-7105
Saranac Lake, NY. 800-245-2200
Schenectady, NY. 462-5881
Scranton, PA. 346-7311
Sharon, PA. 800-448-2970
Springfield, MA. 736-6374
Stamford, CT. 324-9271
State College, PA. 238-8414
Syracuse, NY. 422-1121
Terre Haute, IN. 235-6143

Toledo, OH. 243-8211
Toronto, Ont (Canada). 361-1560
Trenton, NJ. 882-4100
Troy, NY. 462-5881
Utica, NY. 736-5252
Valley Stream, NY. 561-1360
Virginia Beach, VA. 622-4350
Warren, OH. 800-245-2200
Warren, PA. 800-448-2970
Washington, DC. 783-4500
Watertown, NY. 639-6221
Waynesboro, PA. 733-6700
Westfield, MA. 736-6374
White Plains, NY. 761-7227
Wildwood, NJ. 800-448-2970
Wilkes-Barre, PA. 825-5641
Williamsburg, VA. 877-9205
Williamsport, PA. 326-2011
Wilmington, DE. 654-7743
Worcester, MA. 800-448-2970
York, PA. 846-8507
Yorktown, VA. 877-9205
Youngstown, OH. 744-5053

ALTAIR AIRLINES. Scott Plz 2, Philadelphia, PA 19113. **215-521-4300.** *Press contact.* Jack Tucker, **215-WA 3-5400**

AMERICAN AIRLINES. 633 3rd Ave, New York, NY 10017. **212-557-6286.** David Fralley, vice-president, public relations

BRANIFF AIRWAYS, INC. Braniff International Exchange Park (PO Box 3500), Dallas, TX 75235. **214-358-6011.** Jeri L Cox, public relations, **214-358-8577**

Reservations
Alabama. 800-527-4000

Alaska
Anchorage. **274-6666**
Fairbanks. **452-1661**

Arizona. 800-527-4000

Arkansas
Fort Smith. **785-2341**
Little Rock. **372-7321**
All other cities. **800-527-4000**

California
Los Angeles. **680-2202**
San Francisco. **981-7202**
All other cities. **800-527-4000**

Canada
Hamilton, Ont. **ZE 56820**
Montreal, Que. **ZE 56820**
Ottawa, Ont. **ZE 56820**
Quebec, Que. **ZE 56820**
Toronto, Ont. **ZE 56820**
Vancouver, BC. **ZE 9838**
Winnipeg, Man. **ZE 27000**

Colorado
Colorado Springs. **473-3920**
Denver. **825-1111**
All other cities. **800-527-4000**

Connecticut. 800-527-4000

Delaware. 800-527-4000

District of Columbia. 296-2400

Florida
Clearwater. **822-3896**
Fort Lauderdale. **525-8401**
Miami. **358-9400**
St Petersburg. **822-3896**
Tampa. **223-7871**
All other cities. **800-527-4000**

Georgia
Atlanta. **577-7700**
All other cities. **800-527-4000**

Hawaii
Honolulu. **922-3311**
All other cities and islands. **EN 7500**

Idaho. 800-527-4000

Illinois
Chicago. **372-8900**
All other cities. **800-527-4000**

Indiana. 800-527-4000

Iowa
Des Moines. **243-1234**
All other cities. **800-527-4000**

Kansas
Kansas City. **753-1740**
Wichita. **267-0211**
All other cities. **800-527-4000**

Kentucky. 800-527-4000

Louisiana
New Orleans. **523-9011**

Shreveport. **221-4155**
All other cities. **800-527-4000**

Maine. 800-527-4000

Maryland. 800-527-4000

Massachusetts. 800-527-4000

Michigan
Detroit. **964-5710**
All other cities. **800-527-4000**

Minnesota
Minneapolis. **339-3131**
St Paul. **339-3131**
All other cities. **800-527-4000**

Mississippi. 800-527-4000

Missouri
Kansas City. **753-1740**
St Louis. **436-6500**
All other cities. **800-527-4000**

Montana. 800-527-4000

Nebraska
Omaha. **422-6300**
All other cities. **800-527-4000**

Nevada. 800-527-4000

New Hampshire. 800-527-4000

New Jersey
Newark. **621-6411**
All other cities. **800-527-4000**

New Mexico. 800-527-4000

New York
New York City. **687-8200**
White Plains. **527-4000**
All other cities. **800-527-4000**

North Carolina. 800-527-4000

North Dakota. 800-527-4000

Ohio. 800-527-4000

Oklahoma
Oklahoma City. **235-8531**
Tulsa. **584-1311**
All other cities. **800-527-4000**

Oregon
Portland. **224-5030**
All other cities. **800-527-4000**

Pennsylvania. 800-527-4000

Rhode Island. 800-527-4000

South Carolina. 800-527-4000

South Dakota. 800-527-4000

Tennessee
Memphis. **278-5700**
Nashville. **244-4560**
All other cities. **800-527-4000**

Texas
Amarillo. **372-3401**
Austin. **476-4631**
Brownsville. **542-9141**
Corpus Christi. **884-3081**
Dallas. **357-9511**
Fort Worth. **335-5811**
Houston. **621-3111**
Lubbock. **763-7981**
San Antonio. **224-4941**
All other cities. **800-492-4300**

Utah. 800-527-4000

Vermont. 800-527-4000

Virginia. 800-527-4000

Washington
Seattle. **623-2390**
Tacoma. **927-2252**
All other cities. **800-527-4000**

West Virginia. 800-527-4000

Wisconsin. 800-527-4000

Wyoming. 800-527-4000

BRITISH AIRWAYS. 245 Park Ave, New York, NY 10017. **212-983-3113.** *Reservations in New York* **212-687-1600**

BRITISH CALEDONIAN AIRWAYS. 415 Madison Ave, New York, NY 10017. **212-832-6250.** *Reservations* **212-697-3200**

CONTINENTAL AIRLINES. Los Angeles International Airport, Los Angeles, CA 90009. **213-646-3885.** Joseph A Daley, vice-president and public relations director

DELTA AIR LINES, INC. Hartsfield Atlanta International Airport, Atlanta, GA 30320. **404-346-6011.** W T Beebe, chairman of the board and chief executive officer, **404-762-2454.** George E Shedd, assistant vice-president, public relations, **404-762-2533.** Night line: **404-346-6011.** W D Berry, public relations manager, Western Region, **404-762-2533.** R J Jones, public relations manager, Eastern Region, **404-762-2534.** James E Ewing, manager, national news media relations, **404-762-2532.** (h) **404-394-3248**
Reservations

Alabama
Birmingham. **328-2000**
Huntsville. **534-6457**
Mobile. **433-5511**
Montgomery. **262-6451**
All other cities. **800-241-1200**

Arkansas
Hot Springs. **624-5335**
Little Rock. **376-6211**
West Memphis. **396-7200**
All other cities. **800-527-6510**

Arizona
Chandler. **258-5930**
Glendale. **258-5930**
Litchfield. **258-5930**
Mesa. **258-5930**
Phoenix. **258-5930**
Scottsdale. **258-5930**
Sun City. **258-5930**
Tempe. **258-5930**
All other cities. **800-421-0194**

Bahamas
Freeport. **352-8371**
Nassau. **2-1911**
West End. **352-8371**

Bermuda
Hamilton. **3-2000**

California
Albany. **483-7271**
Alhambra. **442-2100**
Anaheim. **534-8468**
Arcadia. **422-2100**
Belvedere. **626-6500**
Berkeley. **483-7271**
Beverly Hills. **386-5510**
Brea. **534-8468**

Buena Park. **534-8468**
Burbank. **247-0700**
Canoga Park. **782-7551**
Compton. **639-4000**
Concord. **937-6520**
Covina. **442-2100**
Crescenta. **247-0700**
Culver City. **386-5510**
Danville. **937-6520**
Downey. **639-4000**
Dublin. **937-6520**
El Monte. **442-2100**
El Segundo. **675-1124**
Fullerton. **534-8468**
Garden Grove. **534-8468**
Glendale. **247-0700**
Hawthorne. **675-1124**
Hayward. **483-7271**
Hollywood. **386-5510**
Huntington Beach. **534-8468**
Inglewood. **675-1124**
Lafayette. **937-6520**
Lomita. **639-4000**
Long Beach. **639-4000**
Los Altos. **328-3011**
Los Angeles. **386-5510**
Martinez. **937-6520**
Marin County. **453-6022**
Monrovia. **442-2100**
Montebello. **442-2100**
Moraga. **483-7271**
Mountain View. **328-3011**
Newport Beach. **534-8468**
North Hollywood. **782-7551**
Oakland. **626-9313**
Orange. **534-8468**
Orinda. **937-6520**
Palo Alto. **328-3011**
Pasadena. **247-0700**
Placentia. **534-8468**
Redondo. **675-1124**
Redwood City. **328-3011**
Reseda. **782-7551**
Sacramento. **927-4211**
San Carlos. **342-1434**
San Diego. **239-3431**
San Fernando. **782-7551**
San Francisco. **552-5700**
San Jose. **287-1313**
San Leandro. **483-7271**
San Mateo. **342-1434**
San Pedro. **639-4000**

San Rafeal. **453-6022**
Santa Ana. **534-8468**
Santa Monica. **782-7551**
Sausalito. **626-6500**
Sierra Madre. **442-2100**
South San Francisco. **588-4517**
Sunnyvale. **287-1313**
Sun Valley. **782-7551**
Torrance. **675-1124**
Tujunga. **247-0700**
Van Nuys. **782-7551**
Walnut Creek. **937-6520**
West Los Angeles. **782-7551**
Westminister. **534-8468**
Whittier. **442-2100**
Other cities in area codes 805, 213, and 714.
800-252-9121
Other cities in area codes 707, 916, 415, 408, and 209. **800-652-1330**

Canada
New Brunswick. **800-361-8464**
Nova Scotia. **800-361-8464**
Ontario
    Ottawa. **236-0431**
    Toronto. **868-1717**
    Windsor. **256-5445**
    Other cities in area codes 519, 416, and 705. **800-361-8464**
    Other cities in area code 613.
800-361-8863
Prince Edward Island. **800-361-8464**
Quebec
    Hull. **236-0431**
    Montreal. **931-9351**
    Quebec. **694-9416**
    All other cities. **800-361-8863**

Colorado
Colorado Springs. **599-5333**
Denver. **623-1400**
All other cities. **800-527-3950**

Connecticut
Branford. **772-4020**
Bridgeport. **334-9495**
Canton. **527-1811**
Cheshire. **772-4020**
Darien. **359-3941**
Fairfield. **334-9495**
Farmington. **527-1811**
Glastonbury. **527-1811**
Greenwich. **359-3941**

Hartford. **527-1811**
Huntington. **334-9495**
Manchester. **527-1811**
Milford. **772-4020**
New Canaan. **359-3941**
New Haven. **772-4020**
Newington. **527-1811**
Old Greenwich. **359-3941**
Simsbury. **527-1811**
Stamford. **359-3941**
Stratford. **334-9495**
Trumbull. **334-9495**
Wallingford. **772-4020**
Windsor. **527-1811**
All other cities. **800-225-3600**

Delaware
Wilmington. **652-3011**
All other cities. **800-225-3600**

District of Columbia. 920-5500

Florida
Auburndale. **682-2163**
Bartow. **682-2163**
Boca Raton. **276-0381**
Boynton Beach. **276-0381**
Bradenton. **955-2205**
Clearwater. **894-1861**
Cocoa. **636-3144**
Cocoa Beach. **773-5500, 636-3144**
Coral Gables. **448-7000**
Daytona Beach. **252-9661**
Deerfield Beach. **276-0381**
Delray Beach. **276-0381**
Fort Lauderdale. **763-2211**
Fort Myers. **334-1014**
Gainesville. **378-2547**
Hollywood. **763-2211**
Homestead. **373-0441**
Jacksonville. **298-3011**
Kennedy Space Center.
773-5500, 636-3144
Key West. **294-9503**
Lakeland. **682-2163**
Marathon. **743-9461**
Melbourne. **773-5500**
Merritt Island. **636-3144**
Miami. **448-7000**
Miami Beach. **448-7000**
Mulberry. **682-2163**
Orlando. **849-6400**
Pensacola. **432-9871**

Plant City. **682-2163**
Polk City. **682-2163**
Pompano Beach. **763-2211**
St Petersburg. **894-1861**
Sarasota. **955-2205**
Tampa. **879-5800**
West Palm Beach. **655-5300**
Winter Haven. **682-2163**
All other cities. **800-282-9153**

Georgia
Atlanta. **349-3100**
Augusta. **724-2641**
Brunswick. **264-2200**
Columbus. **324-0131**
Macon. **788-6680**
Savannah. **234-1221**
All other cities. **800-282-9310**

Hawaii
Honolulu. **521-7598**

Idaho. 800-227-4586

Illinois
Champaign. **359-2310**
Chicago and metropolitan area. **346-5300**
East St Louis. **421-2600**
Peoria. **674-3101**
Rockford. **968-1800**
Springfield. **523-4513**
Urbana. **359-2310**
All other cities. **800-972-9005**

Indiana
Evansville. **426-1211**
Fort Wayne. **422-8511**
Indianapolis. **634-3200**
Louisville metropolitan area. **584-6151**
South Bend. **287-7201**
All other cities. **800-621-9425**

Iowa. 800-621-9425

Jamaica
Montego Bay. **952-5560**

Kansas
Kansas City. **471-1828**
Overland Park. **471-1828**
All other cities. **800-527-6510**

Kentucky
Cincinnati metropolitan area. **721-7000**
Lexington. **252-4411**
Louisville. **584-6151**
Paducah. **443-8791**

All other cities. **800-543-7220**

Louisiana
Alexandria. **448-3581**
Baton Rouge. **356-4361**
Lafayette. **235-5211**
Lake Charles. **439-8833**
Leesville. **239-4568**
Monroe. **387-1900**
New Orleans. **529-2431**
Shreveport. **424-6311**
All other cities. **800-527-6510**

Maine
Auburn. **783-2031**
Augusta. **622-9381**
Bangor. **947-0161**
Houlton. **225-3660**
Lewiston. **783-2031**
Portland. **774-3941**
Presque Isle. **764-3711**
All other cities. **800-225-3660**

Maryland
Annapolis. **768-9000**
Baltimore. **768-9000**
All other cities. **800-336-4940**

Massachusetts
Boston. **567-4100**
Chicopee. **785-1605**
Holyoke. **785-1605**
Hyannis. **775-1800**
Lawrence. **686-9401**
Springfield. **785-1605**
Westfield. **785-1605**
Worcester. **799-4431**
All other cities. **800-962-3500**

Michigan
Ann Arbor. **455-9200**
Battle Creek. **962-5481**
Bay City. **695-5511**
Benton Harbor. **925-0649**
Detroit. **355-3200**
Escanaba. **EN 7221**
Flint. **767-3840**
Freeland. **695-5511**
Garden City. **455-9200**
Grand Rapids. **459-1159**
Hancock. **EN 7221**
Houghton. **EN 7221**
Iron Mountain. **EN 7221**
Ironwood. **EN 7221**

Ishpeming. **EN 7221**
Jackson. **787-4700**
Kalamazoo. **342-0171**
Lansing. **371-1420**
Livonia. **455-9200**
Marquette. **EN 7221**
Midland. **695-5511**
Negaunee. **EN 7221**
Northville. **455-9200**
Plymouth. **455-9200**
Saginaw. **695-5511**
Sault Ste Marie. **EN 7221**
Southfield. **355-3200**
South Lyon. **455-9200**
Wayne. **455-9200**
Westland. **455-9200**
Ypsilanti. **455-9200**
All other cities (except those with area code 906). **800-621-9425**

Minnesota
Duluth. **ZE 7477**
Minneapolis. **339-7477**
Rochester. **ZE 7477**
St Paul. **339-7477**

Mississippi
Biloxi. **864-6111**
Gulfport. **864-6111**
Jackson. **939-5200**
Meridian. **483-9266**
All other cities. **800-241-1200**

Missouri
Kansas City. **471-1828**
St Louis. **421-2600**
Springfield. **866-1951**
All other cities. **800-527-6510**

Nebraska
Lincoln. **EN 6430**
Omaha. **422-6430**
All other cities. **800-527-3950**

Nevada
Boulder City. **736-6161**
Henderson. **736-3131**
Las Vegas. **385-3000**
All other cities. **800-227-4586**

New Hampshire
Concord. **225-3600**
Manchester. **623-7201**
All other cities. **800-225-3600**

New Jersey
Atlantic City. **348-4841**
Elizabeth. **201-622-2111**
Jersey City. **201-622-2111**
Newark. **201-622-2111**
New Brunswick. **545-8600**
Ocean City. **348-4841**
Union City. **201-622-2111**
All other cities. **800-223-6190**

New Mexico. 800-421-0194

New York
Albany. **518-463-2181**
Nassau County. **516-292-1555**
New York. **212-239-0700**
White Plains. **914-948-0303**
All other cities. **800-442-7038**

North Carolina
Arden. **684-2211**
Asheville. **252-7601**
Charlotte. **372-3000**
Durham. **688-9311**
Fayetteville. **485-8746**
Greensboro. **294-2100**
Hendersonville. **684-2211**
High Point. **883-6187**
Raleigh. **833-7371**
Thomasville. **883-6187**
Winston-Salem. **725-0536**
All other cities. **800-241-1200**

Ohio
Cincinnati. **721-7000**
Cleveland. **781-8800**
Columbus. **228-6000**
Dayton. **223-7141**
Toledo. **241-4156**
All other cities. **800-582-3900**

Oklahoma
Tulsa. **582-6500**
All other cities. **800-527-6510**

Oregon. 800-227-4586

Pennsylvania
Harrisburg. **238-1745**
Philadelphia. **928-1700**
Pittsburgh. **566-2100**
Reading. **376-7431**
Other cities in area codes
412 and 814. **800-336-4940**

Other cities in area codes
717 and 215. **800-223-6190**

Puerto Rico
Aquadilla. **WX 200**
Arecibo. **WX 200**
Fajardo. **WX 200**
Mayaguez. **823-9340, 9346**
Ponce. **843-9343, 9243**
San Juan. **724-0655**

Rhode Island
Pawtucket. **861-2850**
Providence. **861-2850**
All other cities. **800-225-3600**

South Carolina
Charleston. **577-3230**
Columbia. **779-4300**
Greenville. **242-1033**
Hilton Head. **785-5232**
All other cities. **800-241-1200**

South Dakota. 800-527-3950

Tennessee
Chattanooga. **756-2411**
Jackson. **422-1611**
Knoxville. **546-5050**
Maryville. **982-0871**
Memphis. **345-7200**
Nashville. **244-9860**
All other cities. **800-241-1200**

Texas
Abilene. **673-5261**
Austin. **477-5911**
Beaumont. **722-3471**
Corpus Christi. **883-2533**
Dallas. **630-3200**
Fort Worth. **336-8341**
Galveston. **762-8426**
Houston. **623-6000**
Lamarque. **762-8426**
Longview. **757-2140**
Orange. **735-5332**
Port Arthur. **722-3471**
San Antonio. **222-2354**
Texas City. **762-8426**
Tyler. **595-0781**
Waco. **753-4521**
Wichita Falls. **723-2135**
All other cities. **800-492-6780**

Utah. 800-227-4586

Venezuela
Caracas. **71-97-56**
Maracaibo. **78945, 78036**

Virgin Islands
St Croix. **774-2503**
St John. **774-2504**
St Thomas. **774-2504**

Vermont
Burlington. **658-2515**
Montpelier. **225-3600**
All other cities. **800-225-3600**

Virginia
Washington metropolitan area. **920-5500**
All other cities. **800-572-4920**

Washington. 800-572-4586

West Virginia. 800-543-7220

Wisconsin
Green Bay. **435-5281**
Madison. **257-7111**
Milwaukee. **342-7252**
Oshkosh. **235-8700**
All other cities. **800-621-9425**

Wyoming. 800-527-3950

EASTERN AIRLINES. 10 Rockefeller Plz,
New York, NY 10020. **212-956-7982.**
Miami. Robert V Christian, vice-president,
public relations, **305-873-3975.**

Public Relations Staff

New York. Gil Perlroth, 10 Rockefeller Plz,
New York, NY 10020. **212-956-7982**
Northern. June Farrell, 300 N Washington
St, Alexandria, VA 22314. **202-347-2176**
Southern. Carolyn Lee Wills, 47 Perimeter
Ctr NE, Suite 103, Atlanta, GA 30346.
404-394-0306
Midwest. Robert Raynesford, 1111 Touhy
Ave, Des Plains, IL 60018. **312-686-5411**
Miami. Julie Gangler, Miami International
Airport, Miami, FL 33148. **305-873-2352**
San Juan. Felix Forestieri, Eastern Airlines
Bldg, Santurce, PR 00911. **809-724-8524**
Reservations
Alabama
Birmingham/Bessemer. **328-9851**
Huntsville. **883-1660**
Mobile. **438-3461**

Montgomery. **262-7361**
All other cities. **800-241-1440**

Arizona. 800-323-7323

Arkansas
West Memphis. **527-2241**
All other cities. **800-323-7323**

Bahamas
Freeport. **352-2311**
Nassau. **322-1461**

Bermuda
Hamilton. **2-5900**

California
Los Angeles (central). **380-2070**
All other cities. **800-323-7323**

Canada
British Columbia
   Coquitian. **ZE 8980**
   Ladner. **ZE 8980**
   New Westminister. **ZE 8980**
   North Vancouver. **ZE 8980**
   Richmond. **ZE 8980**
   Vancouver. **ZE 8980**
   Victoria. **ZE 8980**
   West Vancouver. **ZE 8980**
   White Rock. **ZE 8980**
Ontario
   Ottawa. **733-5430**
   Toronto. **362-7561**
   Other cities (except area
code 807). **800-361-8530**
Quebec
   Montreal. **931-8211**
   All other cities. **800-361-8530**

Colorado. 800-323-7323

Connecticut
Hartford. **525-0141**
New Canaan. **838-4831**
New Haven. **469-1301**
Norwalk. **838-4831**
All other cities. **800-631-5720**

Delaware
Wilmington. **658-9101**
All other cities. **800-631-5720**

District of Columbia (metropolitan area).
202-393-4000

Dominican Republic
Santo Domingo. **682-3131**

Florida
Cocoa. **632-3110**
Daytona Beach. **253-6541**
Delray Beach. **276-2001**
Fort Lauderdale/Hollywood. **463-1515**
Fort Myers. **334-4191**
Gainesville. **376-4411**
Jacksonville. **355-7392**
Lakeland. **688-5531**
Melbourne. **773-1270**
Miami. **873-3000**
   Spanish desk. **873-3780**
Orlando. **843-7280**
Pensacola. **432-0261**
St Petersburg/Clearwater. **896-7631**
Sarasota/Bradenton. **366-9200**
Tallahassee. **224-4121**
Tampa. **877-8811**
Vero Beach. **567-3456**
West Palm Beach/Palm Beach. **655-3111**
Winter Park. **843-7280**
All other cities. **800-432-5401**

Georgia
Atlanta. **435-1111**
Augusta. **722-4684**
Columbus. **324-4781**
Macon. **746-0273**
All other cities. **800-282-8960**

Guadeloupe
Pointe-à-Pitre. **82-1211**

Idaho. 800-323-7323

Illinois
Chicago. **467-2900**
Peoria. **673-6151**
Springfield. **525-1506**
All other cities. **800-942-3010**

Indiana
Evansville. **425-2451**
Indianapolis. **639-6611**
South Bend. **232-7913**
All other cities. **800-323-7323**

Iowa. 800-323-7323

Jamaica
Montego Bay. **952-4460**

Kansas
Kansas City. **471-4353**
All other cities. **800-323-7323**

Kentucky
Lexington. **254-2701**
Louisville. **587-7551**
Owensboro. **684-9671**
All other cities. **800-323-7323**

Louisiana
Baton Rouge. **356-3301**
New Orleans. **524-4211**
All other cities. **800-323-7323**

Maine. 800-526-4220

Martinique
Fort-de-France. **74-11-26**

Maryland
Baltimore. **768-3100**
All other cities. **800-631-5720**

Massachusetts
Boston. **262-3700**
Springfield. **781-1160**
Worcester. **756-1523**
All other cities. **800-631-5720**

Mexico
Acapulco. **4-63-63**
Mexico City. **5-35-78-50**

Michigan
Ann Arbor. **453-0800**
Detroit. **965-8200**
Flint. **742-3500**
Kalamazoo. **382-0760**
Lansing. **372-5530**
Plymouth. **453-0800**
All other cities. **800-323-7323**

Minnesota
Minneapolis/St Paul. **335-9541**
All other cities. **800-323-7323**

Mississippi
Gulfport/Biloxi. **864-8571**
All other cities. **800-241-1440**

Missouri
Kansas City. **471-4353**
St Louis. **621-8900**
All other cities. **800-323-7323**

Montana. 800-323-7323

Nebraska
Omaha. **422-6500**
All other cities. **800-323-7323**

Netherlands Antilles
St Maarten. **2244, 4244**

Nevada. 800-323-7323

New Hampshire. 800-631-5720

New Jersey
Atlantic City. **348-9161**
Camden (Philadelphia north). **923-3500**
Metuchen. **548-8100**
Newark. **621-2121**
  International desk. **621-9450**
  Spanish desk. **621-9450**
Trenton. **989-7500**
Woodbridge. **548-8100**
All other cities. **800-572-2610**

New Mexico. 800-323-7323

New York
Albany. **436-4721**
Buffalo. **852-3170**
Nassau County. **489-9042**
Newburg. **471-1510**
New York City. **986-5000**
  International desk. **661-3500**
  Spanish desk. **661-3500**
Poughkeepsie. **471-1510**
Rochester. **325-2840**
Schenectady. **436-4721**
Syracuse. **472-5541**
Troy. **436-4721**
Utica. **724-9885**
White Plains. **946-1166**
All other cities. **800-631-5720**

North Carolina
Burlington. **228-8338**
Chapel Hill. **942-4182**
Charlotte. **366-6131**
Durham. **682-5621**
Fayetteville. **485-7141**
Greensboro. **299-3221**
High Point. **885-5141**
Raleigh. **828-1390**
Winston-Salem. **725-2344**
All other cities. **800-432-7700**

North Dakota. 800-323-7323

Ohio
Akron. **762-2471**
Canton. **454-8899**
Cincinnati. **241-6800**
Cleveland. **861-7300**
Columbus. **228-2061**
Toledo. **242-8451**
Youngstown. **746-6381**
All other cities. **800-323-7323**

Oklahoma. 800-323-7323

Oregon
Portland. **224-7550**
All other cities. **800-323-7323**

Pennsylvania
Allentown/Bethlehem. **821-8860**
Harrisburg. **236-5013**
Philadelphia. **923-3500**
Pittsburgh. **391-6600**
Scranton. **346-7461**
Wilkes-Barre. **825-6416**
All other cities. **800-631-5720**

Port of Spain
Trinidad. **625-1661**

Puerto Rico
Ponce. **843-3131**
San Juan. **725-3131**

Rhode Island
Pawtucket/Providence. **831-4460**
All other cities. **800-631-5720**

South Carolina
Charleston. **723-7851**
Columbia. **794-1520**
Greenville. **232-3571**
Spartanburg. **585-9121**
All other cities. **800-438-5510**

South Dakota. 800-323-7323

Tennessee
Chattanooga. **265-2351**
Memphis. **527-2241**
Nashville. **244-3780**
All other cities. **800-241-1440**

Texas
Austin. **477-9661**
Beaumont/Port Arthur. **722-4351**

Corpus Christi. **882-5511**
Dallas. **453-0231**
Fort Worth. **435-0231**
Galveston. **763-3491**
Houston. **621-8100**
San Antonio. **222-2461**
All other cities. **800-323-7323**

Utah. 800-323-7323

Vermont. 800-631-5720

Virginia
Norfolk. **625-0316**
Richmond. **644-3481**
Roanoke. **366-7661**
All other cities. **800-438-5510**

Virgin Islands
St Croix/St Thomas. **774-3131**

Washington
Seattle. **622-1881**
Tacoma. **927-5600**
All other cities. **800-438-5510**

West Indies
Antigua. **2-0323**
Barbados. **8-8002**
St Lucia. **3131**

West Virginia. 800-438-5510

Wisconsin
Madison. **256-2641**
Milwaukee. **344-7910**
All other cities. **800-323-7323**

Wyoming. 800-323-7323

EL AL ISRAEL AIRLINES. John F.
Kennedy International Airport, Jamaica,
NY 11430. **212-656-2911.** *Reservations.*
212-486-2600

FRONTIER AIRLINES, INC. 8250 Smith
Rd, Denver, CO. 80209. **303-398-5151.**
Robert Schulman, public relations director

HUGHES AIRWEST. San Francisco International Airport, San Francisco, CA 94128.
415-573-4000. Russell V Stephenson, general
manager. Larry Litchfield, manager, public
relations, **415-573-4747. (h) 415-573-0226**

ICELANDIC AIRLINES. 630 5th Ave, New
York, NY 10020. **800-223-5080.** *Press
contact.* George McGrath, **212-975-1242**

IBERIA. 97-71 Queens Blvd, Rego Park, NY 11374. **212-793-5000, 800-221-9640.** *Press contact.* W Corraro
Reservations
Boston, MA. 617-426-8335, 800-221-9640

Chicago, IL. 312-332-0694, 800-221-9640

Miami, Fl. 305-358-8800, 800-221-9741

Montreal, Que (Canada). **861-7211, 861-9531**

Philadelphia, PA. 215-568-7166, 800-221-9640

Toronto, Ont (Canada). **966-6645**

Washington, DC. 202-293-1452, 800-221-9640

JAPAN AIRLINES. 655 5th Ave, New York, NY 10022. **800-223-5030.** Morris Simoncelli, deputy director, public relations, **212-758-8850**
Reservations
Alabama. 800-223-5405

Alberta (Canada). **800-663-3316**

Arizona. 800-421-8262

Arkansas. 800-621-8353

British Columbia (Canada)
Cranbrook. **ZE 6800**
Kamloops. **ZE 6800**
Kelowna. **ZE 6800**
Nanaimo. **ZE 6800**
Penticton. **ZE 6800**
Victoria. **ZE 6800**

California (except San Francisco and Los Angeles). **800-252-0071**

Colorado. 800-421-8262

Connecticut. 800-223-5030

Delaware. 800-223-5405

District of Columbia. 800-223-5405

Florida. 800-223-5405

Georgia. 800-223-5405

Hawaii
Hawaii. **EN 6300**
Kauai. **EN 6300**
Mauai. **EN 6300**

Idaho. 800-421-8262

Illinois
Champaign. **EN 6612**
Moline. **EN 6612**
Peoria. **EN 6612**
Rockford. **EN 6612**
Springfield. **EN 6612**

Indiana. 800-621-8353

Iowa. 800-621-8353

Kansas. 800-621-8353

Kentucky. 800-621-8353

Louisiana. 800-621-8353

Maine. 800-223-5405

Manitoba (Canada)
Winnipeg. **ZE 5-4250**

Maryland. 800-223-5405

Massachusetts. 800-223-5030

Michigan. 800-621-8353

Minnesota. 800-621-8353

Mississippi. 800-223-5405

Missouri. 800-621-8353

Montana
Billings. **EN 949**
Great Falls. **EN 949**
All other cities. **800-421-8262**

Nebraska. 800-621-8353

Nevada. 800-421-8262

New Brunswick (Canada)
Moncton. **ZE 0-4840**
St John. **ZE 0-4840**

Newfoundland (Canada)
St John's. **ZE 0-4840**

New Hampshire. 800-223-5030

New Jersey. 800-223-5030

New Mexico. 800-421-8262

New York
Albany. **EN 6037**

Binghampton. **EN 6037**
Buffalo. **716-854-7960**
Ithaca. **EN 6037**
Nassau County. **EN 6037**
Niagara Falls. **EN 6037**
Rochester. **EN 6037**
Schenectady. **EN 6037**
South Westchester. **EN 6037**
Syracuse. **EN 6037**
Troy. **EN 6037**
Utica. **EN 6037**

North Carolina. 800-223-5405

North Dakota. 800-621-8353

Nova Scotia (Canada)
Halifax. **ZE 0-4840**

Ohio. 800-621-8353

Oklahoma. 800-621-8353

Ontario (Canada)
Brantford. **ZE 0-4840**
Guelph. **ZE 0-4840**
Hamilton. **ZE 0-4840**
Kingston. **ZE 0-4840**
Kitchener. **ZE 0-4840**
London. **ZE 0-4840**
Niagara Falls. **ZE 0-4840**
North Bay. **ZE 0-4840**
Ottawa. **ZE 0-4840**
Sarnia. **ZE 0-4840**
Sudbury. **ZE 0-4840**
Thunderbay. **ZE 0-4840**
Windsor. **ZE 5-4102**

Oregon. 800-421-8262

Pennsylvania
Eastern. **800-223-5030**
Western. **800-621-8353**

Quebec (Canada)
Montreal. **514-861-1521**
Quebec. **ZE 0-4840**

Rhode Island. 500-223-5030

Saskatchewan (Canada)
Regina. **ZE 6800**
Saskatoon. **ZE 6800**

South Carolina. 800-223-5405

South Dakota. 800-621-8353

Tennessee. 800-223-5405

Texas (except El Paso County).
800-621-8353
El Paso County. 800-421-8262

Utah. 800-421-8262

Vermont. 800-223-5030

Virginia. 800-223-5405

Washington. 800-421-8262

West Virginia. 800-621-8353

Wisconsin. 800-621-8353

Wyoming. 800-421-8262

KLM AIRLINES. 609 5th Ave, New York, NY 10017. **212-759-2400** or **800-631-1935.** Hans Fischer, advertising manager
Reservations
Albany, NY. 800-631-7933
Anchorage, AK. 907-277-1414
Atlanta, GA. 800-223-5322
Baltimore, MD. 800-223-5322
Boston, MA. 800-223-5007
Buffalo, NY. 800-631-7933
Charlotte, NC. 800-223-5322
Chicago, Il. 312-686-6070, 312-346-3635
Cincinnati, OH. 800-223-5322
Cleveland, OH. 800-223-5322
Dallas, TX. 800-392-3366
Denver, CO. 800-231-2164
Des Moines, IA. 800-621-1121
Detroit, MI. 800-621-1121
Fort Lauderdale, FL. 800-221-2080
Hartford, CT. 800-223-5007
Houston, TX. 713-658-1781
Indianapolis, IN. 800-621-1121
Kansas City, MO. 800-621-1121
Los Angeles, CA. 800-231-2164
Miami, FL. 800-221-2080
Milwaukee, WI. 800-621-1121
Minneapolis, MN. 800-621-1121
Montreal, Que (Canada). 514-844-2011
New Haven, CT. 800-223-5007
New Orleans, LA. 800-231-1831
New York, NY. 212-759-3600
Ottawa, Ont (Canada). 613-237-0650
Philadelphia, PA. 800-223-5007
Phoenix, AZ. 800-231-2164
Pittsburgh, PA. 800-223-5322

St Louis, MO. 800-621-1121
Salt Lake City, UT. 800-231-2164
San Antonio, TX. 800-392-3366
San Francisco, CA. 800-231-2164
Seattle, WA. 800-231-2164
Syracuse, NY. 800-631-7933
Toronto, Ont (Canada). 416-366-9041
Tulsa, OK. 800-231-1831
Washington, DC. 800-223-5322

LUFTHANSA GERMAN AIRLINES. 1640 Hempstead Tpke, East Meadow, NY, 11554. **516-794-2020.** Karl H Koepcke, public relations manager, North and Central America, Ext 207. Lucille M Hoshabjian, press relations manager, New York, **212-397-9272**
Reservations
Anchorage, AK. 907-243-1598
Atlanta, GA. 800-645-3880
Baltimore, MD. 800-645-3880
Beverly Hills, CA. 800-645-3880
Boston, MA. 800-645-3860
Buffalo, NY. 800-632-3770
Charlotte, NC. 800-645-3880
Chicago, IL. 800-645-3880
Cincinnati, OH. 800-645-3880
Cleveland, OH. 800-645-3880
Dallas, TX. 800-645-3880
Denver, CO. 800-645-3880
Detroit, MI. 800-645-3880
Honolulu, HI. 923-1303
Houston, TX. 800-645-3880
Long Island, NY. 516-794-3930
Los Angeles, CA. 800-645-3880
Miami, FL. 800-645-3880
Milwaukee, WI. 800-645-3880
Minneapolis, MN. 800-645-3880
Montreal, Que (Canada). 514-861-1661
New Orleans, LA. 800-645-3880
New York, NY. 212-357-8400
Ottawa, Ont (Canada). 613-238-8905
Pennsylvania. (area codes 412 and 814). 800-645-3880
Philadelphia, PA. (area codes 215 and 717). 800-645-3860
Phoenix, AZ. 800-645-3880
Pittsburgh, PA. 800-645-3880
St Louis, MO. 800-645-3880
San Diego, CA. 800-645-3880
San Francisco, CA. 800-645-3880
Seattle, WA. 800-645-3880
Toronto, Ont (Canada). 416-362-5911
Washington, DC. 800-645-3880

MEXICANA AIRLINES. Suite 600, 851 Burlway Rd, Burlingame, CA. 94010. **800-421-8301.** Thomas C Brown, vice-president, public relations, J Walter Thompson, Alcoa Bldg, 1 Maritime Plz, San Francisco, CA 94111, **415-421-3510**
Reservations
Mexico City, Mexico. 905-585-2666
Los Angeles (metropolitan area). 213-487-6950
California (intrastate only). 800-252-0251
Continental United States. 800-421-8301

NATIONAL AIRLINES. PO Box 592055, Miami, FL 33159. **305-874-4111.** E F Dolansky, president. J B Andersen, vice-president, marketing, **305-874-3636**
Reservations
Alabama
Mobile Airport Terminal. **432-7503**
All other cities. **800-535-6764**

Arizona. 800-421-0195

Arkansas. 800-535-6764

California
Agoura. **786-5950**
Alameda. **626-6600**
Alhambra. **579-0200**
Anaheim (Disneyland Hotel). **534-7245**
Arcadia. **579-0200**
Atherton. **369-4686**
Azusa. **579-0200**
Belmont. **369-4686**
Beverly Hills (Beverly Hilton Hotel, Century Plaza Hotel). **381-5777**
Burbank. **845-7618**
Burlingame. **871-4863**
Campbell. **286-5700**
Canoga Park. **786-5950**
Compton. **638-0358**
Concord. **934-5446**
Covina. **579-0200**
Culver City. **381-5777**
Daly City. **626-6600**
Downey. **638-0358**
El Monte. **579-0200**
El Segundo. **679-0336**
Emeryville. **626-6600**
Gardena. **638-0358**
Garden Grove. **534-7245**
Glendale. **381-5777**
Hawthorne. **679-0336**
Hollywood (6203 Sunset Blvd). **381-5777**

Inglewood (Los Angeles Airport Terminal). **679-0336**

La Crescenta. **845-7618**

Lomita. **638-0358**

Long Beach (438 W Ocean Blvd). **638-0358**

Los Alamitos. **638-0358**

Los Altos. **286-5700**

Los Angeles
  Reservations and information. **381-5777**
  Airport Terminal. **381-5777**
  Beverly Hilton Hotel. **381-5777**
  Biltmore Hotel. **381-5777**
  Century Plaza Hotel. **381-5777**
  6203 Sunset Blvd, Hollywood. **381-5777**

Martinez. **934-5446**

Mar Vista. **679-0336**

Menlo Park. **369-4686**

Millbrae (San Francisco Airport Terminal). **871-4863**

Monrovia. **579-0200**

Montebello. **579-0200**

Moraga. **934-5446**

Mountain View. **286-5700**

North Hollywood. **845-7618**

Oakland (2150 Franklin St). **626-6600**

Palo Alto. **369-4686**

Pasadena. **579-0200**

Piedmont. **626-6600**

Redondo Beach. **679-0336**

Redwood City. **369-4686**

Reseda. **786-5950**

San Bruno (San Francisco Airport Terminal). **871-4863**

San Diego
  Airport Terminal. **239-3036**
  West Gate Plaza. **239-3036**

San Fernando. **786-5950**

San Francisco
  Airport Terminal. **626-6600**
  427 Post St. **626-6600**
  Sheraton Palace Hotel. **626-6600**

San Gabriel. **579-0200**

San Jose
  San Jose Municipal Airport. **286-5700**
  1 Town and Country Village. **286-5700**

San Mateo. **871-4863**

San Pedro. **638-0358**

Santa Ana. **534-7245**

Santa Clara. **286-5700**

Santa Monica. **786-5950**

Sausalito. **626-6600**

South San Francisco. **871-4863**

Sunland-Tujunga. **845-7618**

Sunnyvale. **286-5700**

Tiburon. **626-6600**

Torrance. **638-0358**

Van Nuys. **786-5950**

Walnut Creek. **934-5446**

West Hollywood. **786-5950**

West Los Angeles (Century Plaza Hotel). **786-5950**

Whittier. **579-0200**

Canada

Montreal, Que. **878-3566**

Toronto, Ont. **364-6174**

Connecticut, 800-223-5160

Delaware. 800-336-3082

District of Columbia. 202-549-7633

Florida

Boca Raton
  Domestic. **800-432-9431**
  International. **800-432-9761**

Bradenton
  Domestic. **958-9771**
  International. **800-432-9761**
  Airport Terminal. **958-9771**

Clearwater
  Domestic. **822-4261**
  International. **800-432-9761**

Coral Gables
  Domestic. **874-5000**
  International. **874-3160**
  Airport Terminal. **874-5000**

Daytona Beach
  Domestic. **252-0563**
  International. **800-432-9761**
  Airport Terminal. **252-0563**

Delray Beach
  Domestic. **800-432-9431**
  International. **800-432-9761**

Fort Lauderdale
  Domestic. **462-6600**
  International. **800-463-3609**
  Airport Terminal. **462-6600**
  10 S Federal Hwy. **462-6600**

Fort Myers
  Domestic. **334-2141**
  International. **800-462-9761**
  Airport Terminal. **334-2141**

Hollywood
  Domestic. **462-6600**
  International. **800-432-9761**

Homestead
  Domestic. **874-5000**
  International. **874-3160**

Jacksonville
  Domestic. **354-1785**
  International. **800-432-9761**
  Airport Terminal. **354-1785**
  Hilton Hotel. **354-1785**
  Robert Meyer Hotel. **354-1785**

Key West
  Domestic. **800-432-9431**
  International. **800-432-9761**

Lakeland
  Domestic. **800-432-9431**
  International. **800-432-9761**

Melbourne
  Domestic. **800-432-9431**
  International. **800-432-9761**
  Airport Terminal. **800-432-9431**

Miami
  Domestic. **874-5000**
  International. **874-3160**
  Airport Terminal. **874-5000**
  1626 Collins Ave. **874-5000**
  7101 Collins Ave. **874-5000**

Orlando
  Domestic. **422-0701**
  International. **800-432-9761**
  Airport Terminal. **422-0701**
  243 S Orange Ave. **422-0701**

Palm Beach
  Domestic. **683-2500**
  International. **800-432-9761**
  Airport Terminal. **683-2500**
  First National Bank Bldg. **683-2500**

Palmetto
  Domestic. **800-432-9431**
  International. **800-432-9761**

Panama City (Airport Terminal). **763-1791**

Pensacola
  Airport Terminal. **432-9841**
  Naval Air Station. **432-9841**

Perrine
  Domestic. **874-5000**
  International. **874-3160**

Pompano Beach
  Domestic. **462-6600**
  International. **800-432-9761**

St Petersburg
  Domestic. **822-4261**
  International. **800-432-9761**
  42 4th St N. **822-4261**

Sarasota
  Domestic. 958-9771
  International. 800-432-9761
  Airport Terminal. 958-9771
Tallahassee (Airport Terminal). 224-0792
Tampa
  Domestic. 229-0951
  International. 800-432-9761
  402 Tampa St. 229-0951
  Airport Terminal. 229-0951
Titusville
  Domestic. 800-432-9431
  International. 800-432-9761
Venice
  Domestic. 958-9771
  International. 800-432-9761
West Palm Beach
  Domestic. 683-2500
  International. 800-432-9761
  Airport Terminal. 683-2500
  Holiday Inn of West Palm Beach. 683-2500
All other cities
  Domestic. 800-432-9431
  International. 800-432-9761

Georgia
Albany. WX 9534
Athens. WX 9534
Atlanta. 688-9534
Augusta. WX 9534
Brunswick. 638-2571
Columbus. WX 9534
Dalton. WX 9534
Gainesville. WX 9534
Macon. WX 9534
Rome. WX 9534
St Simon Island. 638-2571
Savannah (Airport Terminal). 232-0256
Thomasville. WX 2121
Warner Robins. WX 9534
All other cities. 800-327-4490

Hawaii
Honolulu. 2342 Kalakaua Ave. 955-5938

Kentucky. 800-336-3082

Louisiana
Baton Rouge. 387-5944
New Orleans
  Airport Terminal. 529-5192
  Fairmont Hotel. 529-5192
  Grand Hotel. 529-5192

Hyatt Regency Hotel. 529-5192
  Marriott Hotel. 529-5192
All other cities. 800-362-6790

Maine. EN 6634

Maryland
Baltimore
  Airport Terminal. 539-7250
  Hilton Hotel. 539-7250
All other cities. 800-336-3082

Massachusetts
Boston (Airport Terminal). 269-4120
All other cities. 800-223-5160

Michigan
Detroit. 800-963-0112

Mississippi. 800-535-6764

Nevada
Las Vegas
  Airport Terminal. 385-1181
  Riviera Hotel. 385-1181
All other cities. 800-421-0195

New Hampshire. 800-223-5160

New Jersey
Newark (Airport Terminal). 624-1300
Trenton. 800-336-3082
All other cities in area code 201. 800-223-5160
All other cities in area code 609. 800-336-3082

New Mexico. 800-421-0195

New York
Amityville. EN 6199
Ardsley Dobbs Ferry. EN 6562
Bronxville Tuckahoe. EN 6562
Brooklyn (200 Livingston St). 697-9000
Elmsford. EN 6562
Harrison. EN 6562
Hastings. EN 6562
Irvington. EN 6562
Larchmont. EN 6562
Mamaroneck. EN 6562
Mount Vernon. EN 6562
Nassau County. 485-2211
New Rochelle. EN 6562
New York City
  Airport Terminals. 697-9000
  100 E 42nd St. 697-9000

120 Broadway. 697-9000
Statler Hilton Hotel. 697-9000
620 5th Ave. 697-9000
200 Livingston St. **Brooklyn.** 697-9000
1 E 59th St. 697-9000
1 World Trade Ctr. 697-9000
Pelham. EN 6562
Port Chester. EN 6562
Rye. EN 6562
Scarsdale. EN 6562
Tarrytown. EN 6562
White Plains (175 Main St). 946-1515
Yonkers. EN 6562
All other cities. 800-442-5896

North Carolina. 800-336-3082

Ohio. 800-336-3082

Oklahoma. 800-535-6764

Oregon. 800-421-0195

Pennsylvania
Philadelphia (Airport Terminal). 923-1860
York. 800-336-3082
All other cities. 800-336-3082

Rhode Island
Providence (Airport Terminal). 521-5400
All other cities. 800-223-5160

South Carolina
Charleston
  Airport Terminal. 577-5000
  Francis Marion Hotel. 577-5000
All other cities. 800-336-3082

Tennessee. 800-336-3082

Texas
Houston
  Airport Terminal. 224-9011
  821 Walker St. 224-9011
  Shamrock Hilton Hotel. 224-9011
Webster. 224-9011
All other cities except area codes 806 and 915. 800-535-6764

Utah. 800-421-0195

Vermont. 800-223-5160

Virginia
Alexandria. 549-7633
Chesapeake. 622-1301

Dulles Airport. **800-572-4695**
Hampton (Airport Terminal) (Newport News). **877-0201**
Manassas. **800-572-4965**
Newport News. **877-0201**
Norfolk
   Airport Terminal. **622-1301**
   Holiday Inn—Scope. **622-1301**
   Naval Operating Base. **622-1301**
Portsmouth. **622-1301**
Quantico. **800-572-4695**
Triangle. **800-572-4695**
Virginia Beach. **622-1301**
Williamsburg. **877-0201**
All other cities. **800-572-4695**

West Virginia. 800-336-3082

NORTHWEST ORIENT AIRLINES.
19th floor, 2 Penn Plz, New York, NY
212-564-2300. Roy K Erickson, vice-president, public relations, **612-726-2331**
Reservations
Alabama. 800-327-4511

Alaska
Anchorage. **243-1123**
All other cities. **ZEN 8277**

Alberta (Canada)
Calgary. **263-8755**
Edmonton. **429-5781**

Arizona. 800-421-8282

Arkansas. 800-328-7120

British Columbia (Canada)
Abbotsford. **ZEN 6770**
Chilliwack. **ZEN 6770**
Duncan. **ZEN 6770**
Kamloops. **ZEN 6770**
Kelowna. **ZEN 6770**
Nanaimo. **ZEN 6770**
Penticton. **ZEN 6770**
Port Alberni. **ZEN 6770**
Trail. **ZEN 6770**
Vancouver area. **683-8281**
Victoria. **386-6321**

California
Northern California
   Central Contra Costa County. **939-7930**
   Marin County. **456-5921**
   Palo Alto area. **327-4311**

Sacramento. **922-7173**
San Francisco/Oakland. **391-8440**
San Jose. **289-8420**
San Mateo County. **697-7910**
All other cities (from area Codes 415, 707, 916, 408, and 209). **800-792-0764**
Southern California
   Compton/Long Beach/San Pedro area. **537-3333**
   Glendale/Pasadena area. **247-3323**
   Inglewood/Santa Monica area. **644-8633**
   Los Angeles. **380-1511**
   Orange County area. **530-6333**
   San Diego area. **239-0488**
   San Gabriel Valley area. **444-4531**
   Van Nuys/San Fernando Valley area. **986-3733**
All other cities (from area codes 213, 714, and 805). **800-252-9041**

Colorado
Denver. **534-2349**
All other cities. **800-328-7120**

Connecticut
Hartford. **522-3251**
New Haven. **787-7491**
All other cities. **800-221-7300**

Delaware. 800-424-9380

District of Columbia
Washington (metropolitan area). **202-337-0611**
International reservations. **202-337-0666**

Florida
Clearwater. **896-3131**
Fort Lauderdale/Hollywood. **525-7204**
Miami/Miami Beach. **377-0311**
St Petersburg. **896-3131**
Tampa. **229-7761**
West Palm Beach. **833-6485**
All other cities. **800-432-1210**

Georgia
Atlanta area. **577-3271**
All other cities. **800-327-4511**

Hawaii
Hawaii. **935-5275**
Kauai. **245-4731**
Maui. **244-3933**
Molokai. **ENT 7004**
Oahu. **955-2255**

Idaho
Lewiston. **746-1309**
All other cities. **800-426-0380**

Illinois
Chicago area. **346-4900**
International reservations. **346-6570**
All other cities. **800-972-9008**

Indiana
Indianapolis. **634-1944**
South Bend. **289-5584**
All other cities. **800-621-7311**

Iowa. 800-328-7120

Kansas
Kansas City area. **842-3788**
All other cities. **800-328-7120**

Kentucky. 800-328-7120

Louisiana
New Orleans area. **566-1100**
All other cities. **800-327-4511**

Maine. 800-328-7120

Manitoba (Canada)
Winnipeg. **475-2730**

Maryland
Baltimore. **837-6663**
All other cities. **800-424-9380**

Massachusetts
Boston area. **267-4885**
All other cities. **800-221-7300**

Michigan
Ann Arbor/Ypsilanti. **453-2120**
Battle Creek. **965-5173**
Detroit
   Domestic. **962-2002**
   International. **962-7241**
Flint. **239-8621**
Grand Rapids. **459-4349**
Jackson. **789-7113**
Kalamazoo. **381-3390**
Lansing. **484-5361**
Plymouth. **453-2120**
Pontiac. **335-0550**
All other cities with area codes 616, 517, and 313. **800-621-7311**
Cities with area code 906. **800-328-7120**

Minnesota
Duluth. **727-2525**
Minneapolis/St Paul area
    Domestic. **726-1234**
    International. **726-3369**
Moorhead. **237-5400**
Rochester. **288-1821**
All other cities. **800-552-1290**

Mississippi. 800-327-4511

Missouri
Kansas City area. **842-3788**
St Louis area. **241-2151**
All other cities. **800-328-7120**

Montana
Billings. **248-7301**
Bozeman. **587-4591**
Butte. **792-8341**
Great Falls. **761-8310**
Helena. **442-9586**
Missoula. **728-1400**
All other cities. **800-426-0380**

Nebraska
Omaha. **341-7474**
All other cities. **800-328-7120**

Nevada. 800-421-8282

New Hampshire. 800-221-7300

New Jersey
Newark area. **643-8555**
Trenton. **392-6133**
All other cities. **800-221-7300**

New Mexico. 800-421-8282

New York
Buffalo. **853-5186**
Hempstead. **485-0200**
New York City
    Domestic. **564-2300**
    International. **563-7200**
White Plains area. **946-1183**
All other cities. **800-522-2177**

North Carolina. 800-327-4511

North Dakota
Bismarck. **255-3054**
Fargo. **237-5400**
Grand Forks. **775-2504**
Jamestown. **252-1310**
All other cities. **800-328-7120**

Ohio
Akron. **762-9201**
Cincinnati. **241-6444**
Cleveland
    Domestic. **267-0515**
    International. **267-0549**
Columbus. **228-6507**
Toledo. **241-1287**
Youngstown. **747-1943**
All other cities. **800-362-2122**

Oklahoma. 800-328-7120

Ontario (Canada)
Blenheim. **ZEN 18120**
Chatham. **ZEN 18120**
Leamington. **ZEN 18120**
London. **ZEN 18120**
Sarnia. **ZEN 18120**
Toronto. **362-2613**
Windsor-Tecumseh. **313-962-2002**

Oregon
Eugene. **342-5165**
Portland
    Domestic. **226-3211**
    International. **226-6091**
Salem. **581-5215**
All other cities. **800-426-0380**

Pennsylvania
Philadelphia. **922-2900**
Pittsburgh. **391-8484**
All other cities with area codes 215 and 717.
800-221-7300
All other cities with area codes 412 and 814.
800-424-9380

Quebec (Canada)
Montreal. **861-2611**

Rhode Island. 800-221-7300

Saskatchewan (Canada)
Moose Jaw. **ZEN 07566**
Regina. **ZEN 07566**
Saskatoon. **ZEN 07566**

South Carolina. 800-327-4511

South Dakota. 800-328-7120

Tennessee. 800-327-4511

Texas. 800-327-4511

Utah
Salt Lake City. **355-7489**
All other cities. **800-421-8282**

Vermont. 800-221-7300

Virginia
Norfolk. **625-0347**
Richmond. **643-0111**
All other cities. **800-424-9380**

Washington
Bellingham. **676-8950**
Bremerton. **479-1521**
Everett. **259-6064**
Olympia. **943-0480**
Pasco. **547-3304**
Seattle area
    Domestic. **433-3500**
    International. **433-3678**
Spokane
    Domestic. **838-4741**
    International. **838-5296**
Tacoma area. **927-7100**
Vancouver. **696-4663**
Walla Walla. **529-4790**
Yakima. **457-6131**
All other cities. **800-552-0775**

West Virginia. 800-424-9380

Wisconsin
Green Bay. **435-4477**
Kenosha. **658-1668**
Madison. **255-6711**
Milwaukee
    Domestic. **272-8920**
    International. **278-7422**
Oshkosh. **233-2800**
Racine. **637-6191**
Superior. **727-2525**
All other cities. **800-621-7311**

Wyoming. 800-328-7120

OLYMPIC AIRWAYS. 647 5th Ave, New York, NY 10022. **212-750-7900**
International on-line offices
Chicago, IL. 312-329-0200
Montreal, Que (Canada). 514-878-3891
New York, NY. 212-750-7900, 212-838-3600
Atlanta, GA. 404-237-4631
Boston, MA. 617-542-5810
Cleveland, OH. 216-621-2550
Dallas, TX. 800-392-1994

Detroit, MI. 313-354-4646
Hartford, CT. 203-525-2187
Houston, TX. 713-659-6760
Los Angeles, CA. 213-624-6441
Miami, FL. 305-374-0500
Philadelphia, PA. 215-629-0970
San Francisco, CA. 415-982-0692
Toronto, Ont (Canada). 416-363-7012
Washington, DC. 202-659-2525

OZARK AIR LINES, INC. Box 10007, Lambert Field, St Louis, MO 63145. 314-895-6600. Edward J Crane, president. Charles R Ehlert, manager, public relations, 314-895-6784. *New York public relations.* 212-695-5885. *New York reservations.* 212-586-3612

PAN AM (PAN AMERICAN WORLD AIRWAYS). 200 Park Ave, New York, NY. 10017. 212-973-3820., Brad Dressler, staff vice-president. *Press contact.* James Arey, 212-973-3820

Reservations
Albany, NY. 436-4816
Atlanta, GA. 688-9830
Baltimore, MD. 685-2115
Beverly Hills, CA. 274-9935
Boston, MA. 482-6910
Buffalo, NY. 856-1393
Chicago, IL. 236-4494
Cincinnati, OH. 1-800-621-2909
Cleveland, OH. 1-800-621-2909
Denver, CO. 629-0251
Detroit, MI. 354-0500
Hartford, CT. 249-9651
Honolulu, HI. 955-9111
Houston, TX. 659-3333
Indianapolis, IN. 1-800-621-2909
Lake Success, NY. 294-9550
Las Vegas, NV. 800-421-0105
Long Beach, CA. 639-7440
Los Angeles, CA. 629-3292
Miami, FL. 637-6444
Milwaukee, WI. 800-621-2909
Minneapolis/St Paul, MN. 800-621-2909
Montreal, Que (Canada). 514-861-3601
Newark, NJ. 201-643-0010
New Orleans, LA. 838-6475
New York, NY. 973-4000; for arrival and departure information, 973-7500
Oakland, CA. 835-2900
Ontario, CA. 800-252-9081
Orange, CA. 800-252-9081
Philadelphia, PA. 569-1300

Phoenix. AZ. 252-6747
Pittsburgh, PA. 261-5811
St Louis, MO. 800-621-2909
San Diego, CA. 234-7321
San Francisco, CA. 397-5200
Seattle, WA. 206-624-2121
Tampa, FL. 223-4442
Toronto, Ont (Canada). 368-2941
Washington, DC. 833-1000
White Plains, NY. 914-428-6640

PIEDMONT AVIATION, INC. Box 2720, Smith Reynolds Airport, Winston-Salem, NC 27102. T H Davis, president, 919-767-5100. *Reservations.* 919-768-5171. Betsy Allen, public relations, press information, 919-767-5454. (h) 919-945-5382.

SAS/SCANDINAVIAN AIRLINES. North American Division Headquarters, 138-02 Queens Blvd, Jamaica, NY 11435. 212-520-5500. B John Heistein, vice-president and general manager

Headquarters press contacts. SAS Public Relations, Suite 1465, 630 5th Ave, New York, NY 10020. S Ralph Cohen, director, public relations, and Raymond R Chambers, manager, news bureau, 212-977-2640 or 2645; night line, 212-520-5500

Field press contacts
Midwest US. Marj Abrams, of Marj Abrams Public Relations, 505 N Michigan Ave, Chicago, IL 60611. 312-467-6989
Southwest US. Jeanne Parry, of David Parry & Associates, Suite 2110, 5900 Wilshire Blvd, Los Angeles, CA 90036. 213-938-7138
Northwest US and Western Canada. Helen Bonds, of Jay Rockey Public Relations, 212 5th Ave, Seattle, WA 98121. 206-624-8525
Eastern Canada. Eric Kuutti of SAS, Suite 1420, 1200 McGill College Ave, Montreal, Que, Canada H3B 4G7, 514-861-8317
Reservations
New York City. 212-657-7700
Elsewhere in New York State. 800-522-0450
East of the Mississippi (except Florida). 800-221-2350
Los Angeles. 213-655-8600
Elsewhere in California. 800-252-0161
West of the Mississippi (including Florida). 800-421-0850

SEABOARD WORLD AIRLINES. John F Kennedy International Airport, Jamaica, NY 11430. 212-632-7400. Stephen Moran, director, public relations, 212-632-7759

Air freight information
Atlanta, GA. 800-231-3847
Baltimore, MD. 800-221-8900
Boston, MA. 567-7544
Charlotte, NC. 800-221-8900
Dallas, TX. 214-453-0554
Detroit, MI. 283-3844
Houston, TX. 688-9200
Los Angeles, CA. 646-9344
Minneapolis, MN. 726-5885
New York, NY. 682-1000, 632-7400
Philadelphia, PA. 365-8228
San Francisco, CA. 589-1627
Washington, DC. 800-221-8900

SOUTHERN AIRWAYS, INC. Airport Station, Hartsfield, Atlanta International Airport, Atlanta, GA 30320. 404-768-4000. Graydon Hall, president. Redmond Tyler, director, public relations, Ext. 578

TEXAS INTERNATIONAL AIRLINES, INC. Box 12788, Houston, TX 77017. 713-644-3471. Francisco A Lorenzo, president.

TRANS WORLD AIRLINES. 605 3rd Ave, New York, NY 10016. 212-695-6000. *Press contact.* Richard Greenberg, 212-557-6107
Reservations
Albany, NY. 462-6711
Albuquerque, NM
  Domestic. 243-8611
  International. 800-421-8210
Amarillo, TX. 376-6326
Anaheim, CA. 534-8252
Annapolis MD. 301-768-6300
Atlanta, GA. 522-5738
Atlantic City, NJ. 348-0126
Baltimore, MD. 301-768-6300
Beverly Hills, CA. 274-7506
Binghamton, NY. 729-1517
Boston, MA. 742-8800
Burbank, CA. 247-3600
Chicago, IL. 332-7600
Cincinnati, OH. 381-1600
Clearwater, FL. 898-3131
Cleveland, OH
  Domestic. 781-2700
  International. 781-7950
Columbus, OH
  Domestic. 221-6411
  International. 221-7531
Dallas, TX. 741-6741
Dayton, OH
  Domestic. 226-2600
  International. 223-3955

Denver, CO
Domestic. 292-6620
International. 292-6150
Des Moines, IA. 282-0243
Detroit, MI. 962-8650
Endicott, NY. 729-1571
Evanston, IL. 332-7600
Harrisburg, PA. 800-462-2990
Hartford, CT. 278-7710
Hollywood, CA. 483-1100
Honolulu, HI. 946-0295
Houston, TX. 222-7273
Indianapolis, IN. 635-4381
Johnson City, NY. 729-1571
Kansas City, MO/KS.
Domestic. 842-4000
International. 842-2100
Las Vegas, NV
Domestic. 385-1000
International. 800-421-8210
Long Beach, CA. 639-8000
Los Angeles, CA
Domestic. 483-1100
International. 483-1200
Louisville, KY. 584-8101
Miami, FL. 371-7471
Milwaukee, WI. 933-8292
Minneapolis, MN. 333-6543
Montreal, Que (Canada). 878-3687
Nashville, TN. 254-7741
Newark, NJ. 643-7650
Newport Beach, CA. 534-8252
New Orleans, LA. 529-2585
New York, NY. 695-6000
Oakland, CA. 863-2120
Oklahoma City, OK. 232-3511
Ontario, CA. 800-252-9001
Palo Alto, CA. 323-1323
Panorama City, CA. 781-0200
Pasadena, CA. 247-3600
Peoria, IL. 800-972-8020
Philadelphia, PA. 923-2000
Phoenix, AZ
Domestic. 252-7711
International. 800-421-8210
Pittsburgh, PA
Domestic. 391-3600
International. 391-2277
Rockford, IL. 800-972-8020
Sacramento, CA. 800-792-0742
St Louis, MO
Domestic. 291-7500
International. 291-7575
St Paul, MN. 333-6543
St Petersburg, FL. 898-3131

San Diego, CA. 800-252-9001
San Francisco, CA. 626-5600
San Jose, CA. 298-6600
San Mateo, CA. 877-4222
Schenectady, NY. 462-6711
South Bend, IN. 232-3057
Springfield, MA. 800-322-4883
Tampa, FL. 299-7961
Terre Haute, IN. 234-3718
Troy, NY. 462-6711
Tucson, AZ
Domestic. 624-2771
International. 800-421-8210
Tulsa, OK. 584-3471
Washington, DC. 659-1000
White Plains, NY. 948-7282
Wichita, KS
Domestic. 267-5231
International. 267-4256
Woodland Hills, CA. 884-0630

UNITED AIRLINES. PO Box 66100, Chicago, IL 60666. **312-952-4000.** Jim Kennedy, public relations director, **312-952-4324.** *New York.* Chuck Novak, **212-764-2841.** *West Coast.* Mardy Leaver, **415-876-5321**

WESTERN AIRLINES. 6060 Avion Dr, Los Angeles, CA 90045. **800-328-4990.** *Press contact.* Linda Cole, **213-646-2389**

Reservations

Anaheim, CA. 714-534-0881
Anchorage, AK. 907-243-1311
Annette, AK. 907-882-3611
Atlanta, GA. 800-328-4990
Bellingham, WA. 207-733-4440
Beverly Hills, CA. 213-273-8310
Billings, MT. 406-248-2101
Bremerton, WA. 206-479-3900
Burbank, CA. 213-246-7311
Butte, MT. 406-494-3030
Casper, WY. 307-235-2721
Cheyenne, WY. 307-638-8916
Chicago, IL. 312-782-8296
City of Commerce, CA. 213-776-2311
Colorado Springs, CO. 303-636-2303
Compton, CA. 213-537-4705
Dallas, TX. 214-823-2002
Denver, CO. 303-398-3400
Detroit, MI. 313-965-4972
Downey, CA. 213-537-4705
Duluth, MN. 218-727-6567
Edmonton, Alta (Canada). 403-426-5990
El Monte, CA. 213-443-0261

Fairbanks, AK. 907-452-1643
Fort Lauderdale, FL. 305-467-8777
Fresno, CA. 800-453-5330
Garden Grove, CA. 714-534-0881
Glendale, CA. 213-246-7311
Grand Junction, CO. 800-453-5330
Great Falls, MT. 406-453-4355
Hawthorne, CA. 213-646-4311
Hayward, CA. 800-632-4630
Helena, MT. 406-442-8550
Hilo, HI. 808-935-9741
Hollywood, CA. 213-776-2311
Honolulu, HI. 808-946-7711
Huntington Park, CA. 213-776-2311
Idaho Falls, ID. 208-522-8161
Inglewood, CA. 231-646-4311
Juneau, AK. ZE 6000
Kansas City, MO. 816-453-2055
Kauai, HI. 808-245-4705
Ketchikan, AK. ZE 6000
Kodiak, AK. 907-486-3178
Kenai, AK. 907-776-8197
Las Vegas, NV. 702-731-3111
Lead-Deadwood, SD. 605-578-1507
Logan, UT. 800-277-0224
Long Beach CA. 213-537-4705
Los Angeles, CA. 213-776-2311, 213-273-8310, 213-776-4872 (Spanish)
Marin County, CA. 415-388-2775
Maui, HI. 808-244-3956
Miami, FL. 305-526-6700
Minneapolis, MN. 612-726-4141
Modesto, CA. 800-453-5330
New York, NY. 212-966-1646
Norwalk, CA. 213-537-3354
Oakland, CA. 415-834-9080
Ogden, UT. 801-773-0343
Oklahoma City, OK. 800-328-4990
Olympia, WA. 206-943-3010
Ontario, CA. 714-983-1881
Palm Springs, CA. 714-327-1491
Palo Alto, CA. 415-324-4451
Pasadena, CA. 213-246-7311
Phoenix, AZ. 602-257-8881
Pierre, SD. 605-224-7372
Pocatello, ID. 208-232-8654
Portland, OR. 503-225-0830
Provo, UT. 801-375-2411
Pueblo, CO. 303-545-8880
Rapid City, SC. 605-342-7110
Redondo Beach, CA. 213-646-4311
Redwood City, CA. 415-324-4451
Reno, NV. 702-323-1661

Riverside, CA. 714-682-0137
Rochester, MN. 507-289-0080
Sacramento, CA. 916-446-3464
Salt Lake City, UT. 801-268-1155
San Bernardino, CA. 714-884-5356
San Carlos, CA. 415-877-1106
San Diego, CA. 714-223-8040
San Francisco, CA. 415-761-3300
San Jose, CA. 408-298-3456
San Mateo, CA. 415-877-1106
Santa Monica, CA. 213-788-6020

Seattle, WA. 206-433-4711
Sheridan, WY. 307-672-2424
Sherman Oaks, CA. 213-788-6020
Sioux Falls, SC. 605-336-1410
South San Francisco, CA. 415-877-1106
Stockton, CA. 800-453-5330
St Paul, MN. 612-726-4141
Tacoma, WA. 206-927-6550
Tracy, CA. 800-453-5330
Tucson, AZ. 602-623-6455
Valdez, AK. 907-835-4346

Vallejo, CA. 800-632-4630
Vancouver, BC (Canada). 604-682-5933
Vancouver, WA. 206-256-4401
Van Nuys, CA. 213-788-6020
Victoria, BC (Canada). 604-386-8711
Walnut Creek, CA. 415-939-1633
Washington, DC. 202-737-4825
West Yellowstone, MT. 406-646-7396

WORLD AIRWAYS, INC. 1100 Airport Dr, Oakland, CA 94614. **415-577-2000.** Tom Wheeler, vice-president, public relations

INTERNATIONAL AIRPORTS

Alabama

BIRMINGHAM. Birmingham Airport. 205-325-3764

MOBILE. Bates Field. 205-690-2111

MONTGOMERY. Dannelly Airport. 205-325-3764

Alaska

ANCHORAGE. Anchorage International Airport. 907-274-9611

COLD BAY. Cold Bay Airport. 907-565-7216

EAGLE. Eagle Airport.

FAIRBANKS. Fairbanks International Airport. 907-452-3307

HAINES. Haines Airport. 907-766-2741

JUNEAU. Juneau Airport. 907-586-7211

KETCHIKAN. Ketchikan International Airport. 907-225-2254

KODIAK. Kodiak Airport. 907-274-9611

NORTHWAY. Northway Airport. 907-888-2605

SITKA. Sitka Airport. 907-747-3374

SKAGWAY. Skagway Airport. 907-983-2325

WRANGELL. Wrangell Airport. 907-844-3415

Arizona

DOUGLAS. Bisbee-Douglas International Airport. 602-364-8486, 602-364-8458

NOGALES. Nogales International Airport. 602-287-2562, 5161

PHOENIX. Sky Harbor International Airport. 602-261-4295

TUCSON. Tucson International Airport. 602-287-2562

YUMA. Yuma International Airport. 602-726-2595, 2601

Arkansas

LITTLE ROCK. Adams Field. 501-378-6353

California

CALEXICO. Calexico International Airport. 714-357-1195, 714-352-8740

EUREKA. Eureka Airport. 707-442-4822

FRESNO. Fresno Airport. 209-487-5460

LOS ANGELES. Los Angeles International Airport. 213-536-6218, 6189, 6124

MONTEREY. Monterey Airport. 408-372-1155

OAKLAND. Metropolitan Oakland International Airport. 415-876-2811

SACRAMENTO. Sacramento Metropolitan Airport. 916-981-1628

SAN DIEGO. Brown Field. 714-428-7202, 714-293-5530

SAN DIEGO. San Diego International Airport. 714-428-7207, 714-293-5530

SAN FRANCISCO. San Francisco International Airport. 415-876-2811

SAN JOSE. San Jose Airport. 408-275-7533

Colorado

DENVER. Stapleton International Airport. 303-837-4023

Connecticut

BRIDGEPORT. Bridgeport Airport. 203-366-7851, Ext 4207 or 4219, 203-377-9660

GROTON. Trumbull Airport. 203-442-7123, 203-596-0725

NEW HAVEN. Tweed-New Haven Airport. 203-432-2040, 203-372-3973

WINDSOR LOCKS. Bradley International Airport. **203-244-2680** or **3189, 203-658-0686**

Delaware

WILMINGTON. Greater Wilmington Airport. **302-571-6191**

District of Columbia

WASHINGTON. Dulles International Airport. **703-661-8282, 703-471-5885**

Florida

FORT LAUDERDALE. Executive Airport. **305-776-5160**

FORT LAUDERDALE. Fort Lauderdale Hollywood International Airport. **305-522-3218**

FORT PIERCE. St Lucie County Airport. **305-461-1200**

JACKSONVILLE. Jacksonville International Airport. **904-791-2775**

KEY WEST. Key West International Airport. **305-296-5411**

MARATHON. Marathon Airport. **305-743-6054;** if no answer call **305-872-2915**

MELBOURNE. Melbourne Regional Airport. **305-494-4443**

MIAMI. Miami International Airport. **305-526-2875**

MIAMI. Opa-Locka Airport. **305-526-2875**

ORLANDO. Herndon Airport

PANAMA CITY. Panama City-Bay County Airport. **904-785-4688**

PENSACOLA. Pensacola Airport. **904-432-6811**

ST PETERSBURG. St Petersburg-Clearwater Airport. **813-446-7161,** Ext. 131 (days), **7178** (nights)

TAMPA. Tampa International Airport. **813-228-7711,** Ext. 112

WEST PALM BEACH. Palm Beach International Airport. **305-683-1806**

Georgia

ATLANTA. Charlie Brown County Airport. **404-526-5956**

ATLANTA. Dekalb-Peachtree Airport. **404-526-5956**

ATLANTA. William B Hartsfield International Airport. **404-526-7248**

BRUNSWICK. Malcolm-Mckinnon Airport. **912-265-1955**

SAVANNAH. Savannah Airport. **912-232-4321**

Hawaii

HILO. Gen Lyman Field. **808-935-6976**

HONOLULU. Honolulu International Airport. **808-841-8568**

KAHULUI. Kahului Airport. **808-877-6013**

NAWILIWILI (HANAPEPE). Nawiliwili-Port Allen Airport. **808-822-5521**

Idaho

PORTHILL. Eckhart International Airport. **208-267-7535**

Illinois

CHICAGO. Chicago Midway Airport. **312-767-2270**

CHICAGO. Chicago-O'Hare International Airport. **312-686-2133**

CHICAGO. Meigs Field. **312-767-2270**

PEORIA. Greater Peoria Airport. **309-673-9061**

Indiana

INDIANAPOLIS. Weir Cook Airport. **317-269-7223**

Iowa

DES MOINES. Des Moines International Airport. **515-862-4403**

Kansas

WICHITA. Mid-Continent Airport. **316-942-2233**

Kentucky

LOUISVILLE. Bowman Field. **502-582-5183**

LOUISVILLE. Standiford Field. **502-582-5183**

Louisiana

BATON ROUGE. Ryan Airport. **504-348-0181**

LAKE CHARLES. Lake Charles Airport. **318-439-5512**

NEW ORLEANS. New Orleans International Airport (Moisant Field). **504-729-4011**

Maine

BANGOR. Bangor International Airport. **207-942-8271,** Ext 343

BAR HARBOR. Bar Harbor Airport. **207-288-4675**

BARING. St Croix Airport. **207-454-3621**

CARIBOU. Caribou Airport. **207-473-7474**

FORT FAIRFIELD. Fort Fairfield Airport. **207-473-7474, 207-532-2475**

HOULTON. Houlton International Airport. **207-532-2131, 2475**

JACKMAN. Newton Field. **207-668-3711**

OLD TOWN. Old Town Airport (DeWitt Field). **207-942-8271,** Ext 343; **207-827-4010**

PORTLAND. Portland International Airport. **207-775-3131,** Ext 328; **207-775-0602**

PRESQUE ISLE. Presque Isle Airport. **207-473-7474, 207-532-2475**

PRINCETON. Princeton Airport. **207-454-3621**

Maryland

BALTIMORE. Baltimore-Washington International Airport. **301-962-3170**

Massachusetts

BEDFORD. Hanscom Field. **617-686-1363** (Methun), **617-223-6530**

BEVERLY. Beverly Airport. **617-223-6530**

BOSTON. Logan International Airport. **617-223-6530, 617-569-0620**

LAWRENCE. Lawrence Airport. **617-686-1363, 617-223-6530**

NEW BEDFORD. New Bedford Airport. **617-997-0721,** Ext 257; **617-223-6530**

WESTFIELD. Barnes Airport. **413-781-2365, 617-223-6530**

WORCESTER. Worcester Airport. **617-223-6530**

Michigan

ALPENA. Phelps-Collins Airport. **517-595-2413, 517-354-2293**

BATTLE CREEK. Kellogg Airport. **616-722-2913, 616-894-4301**

BAY CITY. Clements Airport. **517-753-3571, 517-793-3799**

DETROIT. Detroit City Airport. **313-226-3140**

DETROIT. Detroit Metropolitan-Wayne County Airport. **313-226-3140**

GRAND RAPIDS. Kent County Airport. **616-722-2913**

HANCOCK. Houghton County Airport. **906-482-2210, 0810**

KALAMAZOO. Kalamazoo Airport. **616-722-2913, 616-894-4301**

MARQUETTE. Marquette County Airport. **906-475-4082, 9421**

MENOMINEE. Menominee County Airport. **414-432-4311,** Ext 4210

MUSKEGON. Muskegon County Airport. **616-722-2913, 616-894-4301**

PORT HURON. Baker's Field. **313-985-9541**

PORT HURON. St Clair County Airport. **313-985-9541**

SAGINAW. Tri-City Airport. **517-753-3571, 517-793-3799**

SAULT STE MARIE. Sault Ste Marie City-County Airport. **906-632-7221**

Minnesota

BAUDETTE. Baudette International Airport. **218-634-3661**

DULUTH. Duluth International Airport. **218-727-6692,** Ext 203

DULUTH. Sky Harbor Airport. **218-727-6692,** Ext 203

ELY. Ely Airport. **218-365-3262**

GRAND MARAIS. Grand Marais-Devil Track Airport. **218-387-1750**

INTERNATIONAL FALLS. Falls International Airport. **218-283-2541**

MINNEAPOLIS. Minneapolis-St Paul International Airport (Wold Chamberlain Field). **612-725-3689**

PINECREEK. Pinecreek Airport. **612-463-1952**

WARROAD. Warroad Airport. **218-386-1676**

Mississippi

GULFPORT. Gulfport Airport. **601-863-6794**

PASCAGOULA. Jackson County Airport. **601-762-7311**

Missouri

KANSAS CITY. Kansas City International Airport. **816-374-3958**

KANSAS CITY. Municipal Airport. **816-374-3958**

ST LOUIS. Lambert-St Louis Airport. **314-425-3142**

Montana

BILLINGS. Logan International Airport. **406-453-7631**

CUT BANK. Cut Bank Airport. **406-453-7631**

GLASGOW. Glasgow International Airport. **406-453-7631**

GREAT FALLS. Great Falls International Airport. **406-452-1318**

HAVRE. Havre City-County Airport. **406-453-7631**

KALISPELL. Glacier Park International Airport. **406-453-7631**

MORGAN-LORING. Morgan Airport. **406-674-3451**

SCOBEY. East Poplar International Airport. **406-783-2212**

SWEETGRASS. Ross International Airport. **406-335-2434**

Nebraska

OMAHA. Eppley Airfield. **402-221-4661**

Nevada

LAS VEGAS. McCarran International Airport. **702-385-6480**

RENO. Reno International Airport. **702-784-5585**

New Jersey

NEWARK. Newark International Airport. **201-645-6105, 2679**

TETERBORO. Teterboro Airport. **201-645-3084**

New Mexico

ALBUQUERQUE. Albuquerque International Airport. **505-766-2621**

COLUMBUS. Columbus Airport. **505-531-2686**

New York

ALBANY. Albany County Airport. **518-472-3457**

BUFFALO. Greater Buffalo International Airport. **716-632-4727**

MASSENA. Richards Field. 315-769-3091

NEWBURGH. Stewart Airport.
914-564-6353, 7200

NEW YORK. John F Kennedy International
Airport. 212-995-7008

NEW YORK. La Guardia Airport.
212-995-9144

NIAGARA FALLS. Niagara Falls International Airport. 716-694-6617

OGDENSBURG. Ogdensburg Harbor Airport. 315-393-1390

OGDENSBURG. Ogdensburg International
Airport. 315-393-1390

ROCHESTER. Rochester-Monroe County
Airport. 716-328-6340

SCHENECTADY. Schenectady County
Airport. 518-472-3457

SYRACUSE. Syracuse Hancock International Airport. 315-475-9904, 2470

WATERTOWN. Watertown New York
International Airport. 315-482-2261

WHITE PLAINS. Westchester County
Airport. 914-428-7858, 914-946-9000

North Carolina

CHARLOTTE. Coughlas Airport.
704-392-9328

GREENSBORO. Greensboro Highpoint
Winston-Salem Regional Airport.
919-723-9211, Ext 324

RALEIGH-DURHAM. Raleigh-Durham
Airport. 919-286-0411, Ext 456

WILMINGTON. New Hanover County
Airport. 919-763-9971, Ext 425 or 415

WINSTON-SALEM. Smith Reynolds International Airport. 919-723-9211, Ext 324

North Dakota

DUNSEITH. International Peace Garden
Airport. 701-263-4513

GRAND FORKS. Grand Forks International Airport. 701-772-3301

MINOT. Minot International Airport. 701-838-6704

NOONAN. Border International Airport.
701-925-6154

PEMBINA. Pembina Airport. 701-825-6551

PORTAL. Portal Airport. 701-926-4411

WILLISTON. Sloulin Field International
Airport. 701-572-2197

Ohio

AKRON. Akron-Canton Airport.
216-375-5499

CINCINNATI. Cincinnati-Lunken Field.
513-684-3528

CINCINNATI (Covington, KY). Greater
Cincinnati Airport. 513-684-3598

CLEVELAND. Burke Lakefront Airport.
216-522-4437

CLEVELAND. Cleveland Hopkins International Airport. 216-267-3135

COLUMBUS. Port Columbus International
Airport. 614-469-6670

DAYTON. Cox-Dayton Airport.
513-461-5276

KENT. West Paton of Kent State University
Airport. 216-375-5400, Ext 2367 or 2373

SANDUSKY. Griffing-Sandusky Airport.
419-625-0033, 1602

TOLEDO. Toledo Express Airport.
419-259-6424

Oklahoma

OKLAHOMA CITY. Will Rogers World
Airport. 405-231-4347

TULSA. Tulsa International Airport.
918-835-7631

Oregon

PORTLAND. Portland International Airport. 503-284-1935

Pennsylvania

ERIE. Erie International Airport.
814-438-3742

HARRISBURG. Harrisburg International
Airport. 717-782-4510

PHILADELPHIA. Philadelphia International Airport. 215-596-1972, 1973

PITTSBURGH. Allegheny County Airport.
412-644-3592

PITTSBURGH. Greater Pittsburgh International Airport. 412-644-3592

WILKES-BARRE/SCRANTON. Wilkes-Barre/Scranton Airport. 717-457-8357

Puerto Rico

CULEBRA. Culebra Airport. 809-741-2291

ISLA DE VIEQUES. Vieques (Mosquito)
Airport. 809-741-3991

MAYAGUEZ. Mayaguez Airport.
809-832-0308

PONCE. Mercedita Airport. 809-842-1030

SAN JUAN. Puerto Rico International
Airport. 809-791-0222

SAN JUAN. San Juan-Isla Grand Airport.
809-725-6911

Rhode Island

PROVIDENCE. T F Green State Airport.
401-528-4384, 401-941-7543, 401-861-2595,
401-942-0506, 401-934-0288

South Carolina

CHARLESTON. Charleston Airport.
803-744-0712

GREER. Greenville-Spartanburg Airport.
803-877-8006

Tennessee

CHATTANOOGA. Lovell Field.
615-266-3151

KNOXVILLE. McGhee Tyson Airport.
615-637-9300, Ext 1338

MEMPHIS. Memphis International Airport.
901-534-3558

NASHVILLE. Nashville Airport.
615-749-5861

Texas

AMARILLO. Amarillo Air Terminal.
806-376-2347

BEAUMONT. Jefferson County Airport.
713-982-2832

BROWNSVILLE. Brownsville International
Airport. **512-542-4232**

CORPUS CHRISTI. Corpus Christi International Airport. **512-888-3352**

DALLAS. Dallas-Fort Worth Regional
Airport. **214-574-2136**

DALLAS. Love Field. **214-749-3705**

DEL RIO. Del Rio International Airport.
512-775-8502

EAGLE PASS. Eagle Pass Airport.
512-843-2231

EL PASO. El Paso International Airport.
915-543-7430

GALVESTON. Scholes Field. **713-763-1211,**
Ext 6623

HOUSTON. Houston Intercontinental Airport. **713-443-4356**

HOUSTON. W P Hobby Airport.
713-921-4107

LAREDO. Laredo International Airport.
512-722-1113

LUBBOCK. Lubbock Airport. **806-762-7458**

McALLEN. Miller International Airport.
512-542-4232

SAN ANTONIO. San Antonio International
Airport. **512-822-0471, 512-225-4266**

Utah

SALT LAKE CITY. Salt Lake International
Airport. **801-524-5093**

Vermont

BURLINGTON. Burlington International
Airport. **802-864-5181, 802-878-3393**

HIGHGATE. Franklin County Regional
Airport. **802-868-3341**

NEWPORT. Newport State Airport.
802-873-3219

Virginia

CHANTILLY. Dulles International Airport
(Washington, DC). **703-661-8282,**
703-471-5885

NEWPORT NEWS. Patrick Henry International Airport. **804-247-5836, 804-244-1931**

NORFOLK. Norfolk International Airport.
804-441-6741, 6779, 804-411-6731

RICHMOND. Byrd International Airport.
804-782-2552

Virgin Islands

ST CROIX. A Hamilton Airport.
809-773-0216

ST THOMAS. H S Truman Airport.
809- 774-1719

Washington

ANACORTES. Anacortes Airport.
206-293-2331

BELLINGHAM. Bellingham International
Airport. **206-734-5460**

BLAINE. Blaine Airport. **206-332-5771**

EVERETT. Snohomish County Airport.
206-259-0246

FRIDAY HARBOR. Friday Harbor Airport.
206-378-2080

HOQUIAM. Boverman Field. **206-532-2030**

KELSO. Kelso-Longview Airport.
206-425-3710

NORTHPORT. J A Lowry Airport.
509-732-4418

OLYMPIA. Olympia Airport. **206-593-6338**

OROVILLE. D Scott Airport. **509-476-3514**

PORT ANGELES. Fairchild International
Airport. **206-457-4311**

PORT ANGELES. Port Angeles Marine
Dock Airport. **206-457-4311**

PORT TOWNSEND. Jefferson County
International Airport. **206-385-3777**

SEATTLE. Kenmore Air Harbor Airport.
206-246-8805

SEATTLE. King County International Airport. **206-246-8805**

SEATTLE. Kurtzer's Flying Service Airport.
206-246-8805

SEATTLE. Lake Union Air Service Airport.
206-246-8805

SEATTLE. Seattle-Tacoma International
Airport. **206-246-8805**

SPOKANE. Felts Field. **509-456-4661**

SPOKANE. Spokane International Airport.
509-456-4691

TACOMA. Tacoma Industrial Airport.
206-593-6338

West Virginia

CHARLESTON. Kanawha Airport.
304-343-6181, Ext 423 or 424

Wisconsin

APPLETON. Outagamie County Airport.
414-465-3923

GREEN BAY. Austin Strabel Airport.
414-465-3923

MILWAUKEE. Mitchell Field.
414-224-3932

OSHKOSH. Wittman Field. **414-465-3923**

RACINE. Horlick-Racine Airport.
414-633-0286

SHEBOYGAN. Sheboygan County Airport.
414-465-3923

SUPERIOR. Bong Airport. **218-727-6692,**
Ext 203

Wyoming

CASPER. Natrona County International
Airport. **406-453-7561**

PASSENGER RAILROADS

AMTRAK (NATIONAL RAIL PASSENGER CORPORATION).
955 L'Enfant Plz SW, Washington, DC 20024. **202-484-7220.** For contact information, *see* BUSINESS.

Reservations
Alabama. **800-874-2800**
Arizona. **800-421-8320**
Arkansas. **800-874-2775**
California
Los Angeles. **213-624-0171**
All other cities. **800-648-3850**
Colorado. **800-421-8320**
Connecticut. **800-523-5720**
Delaware. **800-523-5700**
District of Columbia. **800-523-5720**
Florida. **800-342-2520**
Georgia. **800-874-2800**
Idaho. **800-421-8320**
Illinois
Chicago. **312-786-1333**
All other cities. **800-972-9147**
Indiana. **800-621-0353**
Iowa. **800-621-0353**
Kansas. **800-421-8320**
Kentucky. **800-874-2775**
Louisiana. **800-874-2800**
Maine. **800-523-5731**
Maryland. **800-523-5700**
Massachusetts. **800-523-5720**
Michigan
Northern Michigan (area code 906).
800-621-0317
All other cities. **800-621-0353**
Minnesota. **800-621-0317**
Mississippi. **800-874-2800**
Missouri. **800-621-0317**
Montana. **800-421-8320**
Nebraska. **800-421-8320**
Nevada. **800-421-8320**
New Hampshire. **800-523-5720**
New Jersey. **800-523-5700**
New Mexico. **800-421-8320**
New York
Buffalo area (area code 716). **800-523-5720**
New York City. **212-736-4545**
All other cities. **800-523-5700**

North Carolina. **800-874-2800**
North Dakota. **800-421-8320**
Ohio. **800-621-0317**
Oklahoma. **800-421-8320**
Oregon. **800-421-8320**
Pennsylvania
Philadelphia. **215-824-1600**
All other cities. **800-562-5380**
Rhode Island. **800-523-5720**
South Carolina. **800-874-2800**
South Dakota. **800-421-8320**
Tennessee. **800-874-2800**
Texas. **800-421-8320**
Utah. **800-421-8320**
Vermont. **800-523-5720**
Virginia. **800-874-2775**
Washington. **800-421-8320**
West Virginia. **800-874-2775**
Wisconsin. **800-621-0353**
Wyoming. **800-421-8320**

CHICAGO, ROCK ISLAND & PACIFIC RAILROAD.
332 S Michigan Ave, Chicago, IL 60604. **312-435-7300.** Theodore Zirbes, manager of public relations, **312-435-7481.** Reservations and passenger information are handled by the AMTRAK system; consult AMTRAK listings.

DENVER & RIO GRANDE WESTERN RAILROAD.
1531 Stout St., Denver, CO 80202. **303-629-5533.** Reservations and passenger information are handled by the AMTRAK system; consult AMTRAK listings.

SOUTHERN RAILWAY CO.
920 15th St., NW, Washington, DC 20013. **202-628-4460.** For contact information, see BUSINESS. Reservations and passenger information are handled by the AMTRAK system; consult AMTRAK listings.

TRAIN ARRIVAL AND DEPARTURE INFORMATION

Albany/Rensselaer, NY. **518-434-1693**
Buffalo, NY. **716-856-6568**

Carbondale, IL. **618-457-3388**
Chicago, IL. **312-443-8610**
Colonie/Schenectady, NY. **518-456-3556**
Dallas, TX. **214-653-1101**
Denver, CO. **303-534-2371**
Detroit, MI. **313-965-0314**
Fort Lauderdale, FL. **305-463-8251**
Fort Worth, TX. **817-332-2931**
Fresno, CA. **209-486-7651**
Fullerton, CA. **714-992-0530**
Glenview, IL. **312-724-2530**
Harrisburg, PA. **717-236-7902**
Houston, TX. **713-224-1577**
Hudson, NY. **518-828-3379**
Indianapolis, IN. **317-269-6728**
Jacksonville, FL. **904-768-1553**
Joliet, IL. **815-727-9279**
Kansas City, MO. **816-421-3622**
Lancaster, PA. **717-394-9341**
Los Angeles, CA. **213-683-6987**
Miami, FL. **305-324-4121**
Minneapolis, MN. **612-336-1621**
New Haven, CT. **203-497-2222**
New London, CT. **203-442-5813**
New Orleans, LA. **504-586-0027**
New York, NY. **212-239-6334**
Orlando, FL. **305-843-7611**
Paoli, PA. **215-644-4825**
Philadelphia, PA
30th St Station. **215-382-7242**
North Philadelphia. **215-382-7242,
215-597-2291.**
Richmond, VA. **804-264-9194**
Rochester, NY. **716-454-2894**
St Petersburg, FL. **813-522-9475**
San Diego, CA. **714-239-9021**
Springfield, IL. **217-753-2013**
Stamford, CT. **203-324-3173**
Syracuse, NY. **315-463-1135**
Tacoma, WA. **206-627-8141**
Tampa, FL. **813-229-2473**
Utica, NY. **315-797-8962**
Washington, DC. **202-484-7876**

BUS LINES

CONTINENTAL TRAILWAYS. 1500 Jackson St, Dallas, TX 75201. **214-655-7711.** For contact information, *see* BUSINESS.

GREYHOUND LINES. Greyhound Tower, Phoenix, AZ 85077. **602-248-5000.** Agents' toll-free number: **800-528-6055.** For contact information, *see* BUSINESS.

AUTOMOBILE RENTAL COMPANIES

AIRWAYS RENT-A-CAR SYSTEMS, INC. **800-648-5656** (except Nevada)

ALFA RENT-A-CAR. 800-528-0535

AMERICAN INTERNATIONAL RENT-A-CAR. 800-527-6346 (except Texas)

AUTO EUROPE. 800-223-5740 (except New York). **800-223-5125** (New York and New England)

AVIS CAR RENTAL. 800-331-1212 (except Oklahoma and New York). **800-632-1200** (New York). **800-482-4554** (Oklahoma)

BROOKS RENT-A-CAR. 800-634-6721 (except Nevada)

BUDGET RENT-A-CAR. 800-228-9650 (except Nebraska). **800-642-9910** (Nebraska)

DOLLAR-A-DAY RENT-A-CAR. 800-327-6362 (eastern US only)

ECONO CAR RENTAL. 800-874-5000 (except Florida). **800-342-5628** (Florida)

GREYHOUND RENT-A-CAR. 800-327-2501 (except Florida)

HERTZ CAR RENTAL. 800-654-3131 (except Oklahoma). **800-522-3711** (Oklahoma)

NATIONAL CAR RENTAL. 800-328-4567 (except Minnesota)

SEARS RENT-A-CAR. 800-228-2800 (except Nebraska)

THRIFTY RENT-A-CAR. 800-331-4200 (except Oklahoma)

HOTEL AND MOTEL CHAINS

BEST WESTERN MOTELS, HOTELS, AND RESORTS. Best Western Way, Box 10203, Phoenix AZ 85064. **602-957-4200.** *Credit cards.* Master Charge, BankAmericard/Visa, American Express, Carte Blanche, Diner's Club, Exxon and Sohio, Boron, and Pacific 66 (Canada) *Reservations.* **800-528-1234** (except Arizona). **800-352-1222** (Arizona, except Phoenix). **602-279-7600** (Phoenix)

HILTON HOTELS CORPORATION. 9880 Wilshire Blvd, Beverly Hills, CA 90210. **213-278-4321.** Hilton Hotels International Co, 301 Park Ave, New York, NY 10022. **212-688-2240.** Major credit cards
Reservations
Alabama. 800-241-5838

Alaska
Anchorage. **272-7411**
Juneau. **586-6900**

Alberta (Canada). 800-261-9275

Arizona
Phoenix. **264-2566**
All other cities. **800-352-6096**

Arkansas. 800-325-4620

California
Area Codes 209, 408, 707, and 916. **800-792-0775**
Area Code 805. **800-542-6101**
Long Beach. **437-1818**
Los Angeles. **628-6231**
San Diego. **276-6000**

San Francisco. **771-1200**
Van Nuys. **990-5365**

Colorado
Denver. **292-3600**
All other cities. **800-332-3074**

Connecticut. 800-225-2400

Delaware. 800-523-4183

District of Columbia. 483-3700

Florida
Miami. **379-3426**
All other cities. **800-432-5141**

Georgia
Atlanta. **659-1515**
All other cities. **800-282-5806**

Hawaii
Honolulu. 949-4321
Kona. 329-3111

Idaho. 800-426-5350

Illinois
Chicago. 346-2772
All other cities. 800-325-4620

Indiana
Indianapolis. 636-2371
All other cities. 800-382-1510

Iowa. 800-328-9155

Kansas. 800-325-4620

Kentucky. 800-446-3811

Louisiana
New Orleans. 721-2381
All other cities. 800-452-8702

Maine. 800-225-1546

Manitoba (Canada). 800-261-9275

Maryland
Baltimore. 837-5454
All other cities. 800-446-3811

Massachusetts
Boston. 357-8320
All other cities. 800-882-1653

Michigan
Detroit. 524-2300
All other cities. 800-482-3940

Minnesota
Minneapolis/St Paul. 227-8921
Duluth/Rochester. ZE 2662

Mississippi. 800-241-4385

Missouri
St Louis. 726-2666
All other cities. 800-392-5838

Montana. 800-426-5350

Nebraska
Omaha. 344--4231
All other cities. 800-642-9927

Nevada. 800-528-0313

Newfoundland (Canada). 800-361-6140

New Hampshire. 800-225-2400

New Jersey
Area code 201. 643-7150
Area code 609. 800-523-4183

New Mexico. 800-528-0313

New York
Area codes 315, 518, and 607. 800-462-1083
Buffalo. 856-2811
Nassau County. 212-594-4500
New York City. 212-594-4500
Rochester. 454-4610
Suffolk County. 549-4180
Tonawanda. 692-1000
Westchester County. 946-0580

North Carolina. 800-462-1083

North Dakota. 800-328-9155

Nova Scotia (Canada). 800-361-6140

Ohio
Cincinnati. 381-6240
All other cities. 800-582-3920

Oklahoma
Tulsa. 622-7730
All other cities. 800-482-2705

Ontario (Canada)
Area code 613. 800-361-7171
Area codes 519 and 705. 800-261-9343
Area code 807. 800-261-9275
Toronto. 362-3771

Oregon
Portland. 226-7047
All other cities. 800-452-7682

Pennsylvania
Area code 717. 800-222-9280
Area code 814. 800-242-0541
Philadelphia. 382-7665
Pittsburgh. 261-5600

Prince Edward Island (Canada).
800-361-6140

Quebec (Canada)
Area codes 418 and 819. 800-361-6140
Montreal. 861-3301

Rhode Island. 800-225-2400

Saskatchewan (Canada). 800-261-9275

South Carolina. 800-241-5838

South Dakota. 800-328-9155

Tennessee. 800-446-3811

Texas
Austin. 472-4091
Dallas. 747-8011
Fort Worth. 263-0737
Houston. 667-9141
San Antonio. 223-9191
All other cities. 800-492-6993

Utah. 800-528-0313

Vermont. 800-225-2400

Virginia
Richmond. 282-9716
All other cities. 800-552-9910

Washington
Seattle. 244-4884
All other cities. 800-562-8853

West Virginia. 800-446-3811

Wisconsin
Milwaukee. 383-5911
All other cities. 800-328-9155

Wyoming. 800-525-6009

HOLIDAY INNS, INC. 3742 Lamar Ave,
Memphis, TN 38118. **901-362-4001**
Credit cards. American Express, Bank
Americard/Visa, Master Charge, Diners
Club, Amoco Torch Club, Gulf Travel, and
Gulf Oil of Canada

Reservations
Atlanta, GA. 800-238-5400
Baltimore, MD. 800-238-5400
Birmingham, AL. 800-238-5400
Boston, MA. 800-243-2350
Buffalo, NY. 800-243-2350
Charleston, SC. 800-238-5400
Charlotte, NC. 800-238-5400
Chicago, IL. 654-2700
Cincinnati, OH. 800-323-9050
Cleveland, OH. 800-323-9050
Columbus, OH. 800-323-9050
Dallas/Fort Worth, TX. 800-453-5555
Denver, CO. 800-453-5555
Detroit, MI. 800-323-9050
Hartford, CT. 243-2975
Houston, TX. 800-453-5555

Indianapolis, IN. 800-323-9050
Jacksonville, FL. 800-238-5400
Kansas City, KS. 800-453-5555
Kansas City, MO. 800-323-9050
Los Angeles/Long Beach, CA. 800-453-5555
Memphis, TN. 363-3400
Miami/Fort Lauderdale, FL. 800-238-5400
Milwaukee, WI. 800-323-9050
Minneapolis/St Paul, MN. 800-323-9050
Nashville, TN. 800-323-9050
Newark, NJ. 800-243-2350
New Haven, CT. 800-842-1650
New Orleans, LA. 800-238-5400
New York, NY. 212-736-4800
Oklahoma City, OK. 800-453-5555
Philadelphia, PA. 800-243-2350
Pittsburgh, PA. 800-243-2350
Salt Lake City, UT. 521-6200
San Antonio, TX. 800-453-5555
San Diego, CA. 800-453-5555

San Francisco, CA. 800-453-5555
St Louis, MO. 800-323-9050
St Petersburg/Tampa, FL. 800-238-5400
Washington, DC. 800-238-5400

HOWARD JOHNSON COMPANY. 220 Forbes Rd, Braintree, MA 02184. 617-848-2350. Howard B Johnson, chairman of the board and president. Evelyn G Sullivan, manager, public relations
Credit cards. Master Charge, American Express, BankAmericard/Visa, Diners Club, Carte Blanche, Amoco, and Exxon
Reservations. 800-654-2000 (except Canada and Oklahoma). 800-522-9041 (Oklahoma). 405-848-8611 (Canada; call collect)

MARRIOTT HOTELS. 5161 River Rd, Washington, DC 20016. 301-986-5000. Major credit cards
Reservations. 800-228-9290 (US). 800-261-6222 (eastern Canada, except

Toronto). 416-446-2231 (Toronto). 800-261-6362 (western Canada)

SHERATON HOTELS AND INNS. 470 Atlantic Ave, Boston, MA 02210. 617-482-1250. *Telex:* 940998
Credit cards. BankAmericard/Visa, Barclay Card, Chargex, Master Charge, Eurocard, American Express, Carte Blanche, Diners Club, Access, and American Torch Club
Reservations. 800-325-3535 (except Missouri). 800-392-3500 (Missouri). *Group Rooms Availability Bank:* 800-621-5727 (except Illinois). 800-972-8282 (Illinois)

TRAVELODGE INTERNATIONAL, INC. TraveLodge Dr, El Cajon, CA 92090. 714-442-0311
Credit cards. TraveLodge Travel Card, BankAmericard/Visa, Chargex, Barclay, InterBank, Master Charge, and Euro Card
Reservations. 800-255-3050 (except Kansas). 800-332-4350 (Kansas). 800-261-3330 (Canada)

MISCELLANY

PEOPLES TRANS-SHARE. 258 SW Alder St (PO Box 40303), Portland, OR 97240. 503-227-2419. Toll-free number (except Oregon): 800-547-0933. A membership service that arranges cost-sharing cross-country transportation by car or private plane.

NEW YORK HOTEL AND MOTEL RESERVATIONS. 212-782-4364.

US TRAVEL SERVICE. Washington, DC 20230. 202-377-4752. Maintains a nationwide, toll-free travelers' information line that can provide tourists with information on activities, events, travel conditions, transportation, and so on anywhere in the country. Basically, it is a travel service without a commission, but there is only one

hitch. The service is intended for foreign visitors. As a result, whenever the toll-free number is publicized, the service changes it —and does not list it in this country. In 1978 the number was 800-323-4180. If it has been changed, the new number can be obtained sometimes by calling the US Travel Service's number in Washington.

MONEY ORDER COMPANIES

FEDERAL EXPRESS. 800-238-5355 (except Alaska, Hawaii, Tennessee). 800-542-5171 (Tennessee)

Travelers Express Co, Inc. 800-328-4800 (except Alaska, Hawaii, and Minnesota). 800-257-8418 (northeastern states)

WESTERN UNION, TELEGRAPHS, AND TELEX

WESTERN UNION

Western Union Corporation. 1 Lake St, Upper Saddle River, NJ 07458. **201-825-5000.** For corporate contact information, see BUSINESS.

Regional Offices

ATLANTA AREA (Alabama, Florida, Georgia, Kentucky except Boone, Campbell, and Kenton counties, Mississippi, South Carolina, and Tennessee). 56 Marietta St NW, Atlanta, GA 30303. **404-688-9820.** *Telex:* **5414.** *TWX:* **810-751-8449**

BOSTON AREA (Connecticut, Maine, Massachusetts, New Hampshire, New York except New York City and all of Long Island, Rhode Island, and Vermont). 40 William St, Wellesley, MA 02181. **617-237-2580.** *Telex:* **940381.** *TWX:* **710-383-0293**

CHICAGO AREA (Illinois). 427 S La Salle St, Chicago, IL 60605. **312-435-1500.** *Telex:* **254008**

DALLAS AREA (Louisiana and Texas). Suite 234, Northpoint Business Campus, 9229 LBJ Pkwy, Dallas, TX 75243. **214-690-0071.** *Telex:* **732416.** *TWX:* **910-861-4988**

DETROIT AREA (Indiana, Michigan, and Ohio, plus the three Kentucky counties of Boone, Campbell, and Kenton). Suite 200, 23100 Providence Dr, Southfield, MI 48075. **313-559-7850.** *Telex:* **235265.** *TWX:* **810-224-4993**

KANSAS CITY AREA (Arkansas, Colorado, Kansas, Missouri, New Mexico, and Oklahoma). Rm 777, Tenmain Ctr, Kansas City, MO 64105. **816-474-4330.** *Telex:* **42364**

LOS ANGELES AREA (Arizona, the southern third of California, and the county of Clark, NV). 745 S Flower St, Los Angeles, CA 90017. **213-627-4321.** *Telex:* **674240**

MINNEAPOLIS AREA (Iowa, Minnesota, Nebraska, North Dakota, South Dakota, and Wisconsin). 317 2nd Ave S, Minneapolis, MN 55401. **612-332-4242.** *Telex:* **290664**

NEW YORK AREA (New York City, all of Long Island, and Hudson County, NJ). Rm 2300, 60 Hudson St, New York, NY 10013. **212-577-4190.** *Telex:* **126400**

PHILADELPHIA AREA (Delaware, New Jersey except Hudson County, and Pennsylvania). 950 Kings Hwy N, Cherry Hill, NJ 08034. **215-928-0300.** *Telex:* **834452**

SAN FRANCISCO AREA (northern two thirds of California, Nevada except Clark County, and Utah). 303 Hegenberger Rd, Oakland, CA 94621. **415-568-6126;** **415-781-4321** (nights, weekends, and holidays). *Telex:* **340517.** *TWX:* **910-366-7330**

SEATTLE AREA (Idaho, Montana, Oregon, Washington, and Wyoming). 655 Orcas St, Seattle, WA. 96108. **206-764-4511.** *Telex:* **320115**

WASHINGTON DC, AREA (District of Columbia, Maryland, North Carolina, Virginia, and West Virginia). Western Union Bldg, 7916 W Park Dr, McLean, VA 22101. **703-790-2274.** *Telex:* **892316**

TELEX AND TWX INFORMATION

For the US, directory assistance is provided by computer.
Telex: **7931,** DIRECTORY
TWX: **910-221-5151** (four-row keyboard) or **312-431-1525** (three-row keyboard), DIRECTORY

For Canada, Mexico, and Puerto Rico, directory assistance is provided by an operator.
Telex: **4119**
TWX: **610-555-1212.** For information on Telex subscribers, **910-555-1212**

INFOMASTER ASSISTANCE (Domestic). *Telex:* **6161.** *TWX:* **910-420-1212.**

INFOMASTER ASSISTANCE (International). *Telex:* **4114.** *TWX:* **710-822-1953**

MAILGRAM AND TELEGRAM NUMBERS

ALABAMA. 800-325-5300

ARIZONA. 800-648-4100

ARKANSAS. 800-325-5100

CALIFORNIA. 800-648-4100

COLORADO. 800-325-5400

CONNECTICUT. 800-257-2211

DELAWARE. 800-257-2211

DISTRICT OF COLUMBIA. 800-257-2211

FLORIDA. 800-325-5500

GEORGIA. 800-257-2231

IDAHO. 800-648-4100

ILLINOIS. 800-325-5100

INDIANA. 800-325-5200

IOWA. 800-325-5100

KANSAS. 800-325-5100

KENTUCKY. 800-325-5100

LOUISIANA. 800-325-5300

MAINE. 800-257-2231

MARYLAND. 800-257-2211

MASSACHUSETTS. 800-257-2221

MICHIGAN. 800-325-5300

MINNESOTA. 800-325-5300

MISSISSIPPI. 800-325-5200

MISSOURI. 800-342-5700

MONTANA. 800-325-5500

NEBRASKA. 800-325-5100

NEVADA. 800-992-5700

NEW HAMPSHIRE. 800-257-2221

NEW JERSEY. 800-632-2271

NEW MEXICO. 800-325-5400

NEW YORK
Area codes 315, 518, 607, and 716.
800-257-2221
Area codes 212, 516, and 914. 800-257-2211

NORTH CAROLINA. 800-257-2231

NORTH DAKOTA. 800-325-5400

OHIO. 800-325-5300

OKLAHOMA. 800-325-5100

OREGON. 800-648-4100

PENNSYLVANIA
Eastern (area codes 215 and 717).
800-257-2211
Western (area codes 412 and 814).
800-257-2221

RHODE ISLAND. 800-257-2221

SOUTH CAROLINA. 800-257-2231

SOUTH DAKOTA. 800-325-5300

TENNESSEE. 800-325-5100

TEXAS. 800-325-5300

UTAH. 800-648-4100

VERMONT. 800-257-2221

VIRGINIA. 800-257-2221

WASHINGTON. 800-648-4500

WEST VIRGINIA. 800-257-2221

WISCONSIN. 800-325-5200

WYOMING. 800-648-4500

TELEX TELEGRAMS

Telex users can send hand-delivered telegrams from their own machines to addresses within each of the cities listed below by dialing the number given.

ALEXANDRIA, VA. 8929

ATLANTA, GA. 5412

BALTIMORE, MD. 8712

BEVERLY HILLS, CA. 6777

BIRMINGHAM, AL. 5912

BOSTON, MA. 94-0112

BRIDGEPORT, CT. 96-4231

BROOKLINE, MA (via Boston). 94-0112

BUFFALO, NY. 9112

BURLINGAME, CA (via San Francisco). 3412

CAMBRIDGE, MA. 92-1412

CAMDEN, NJ (via Philadelphia). 8-3912

CEDAR RAPIDS, IA (via Minneapolis). 29-0112

CHELSEA, MA (via Boston). 94-0112

CHICAGO, IL. 2512

CINCINNATI, OH. 21-4112

CLAYTON, MO (via St. Louis). 4412

CLEVELAND, OH. 98-0112

COLUMBUS, OH. 24-5412

DALLAS, TX. 73-0112

DAYTON, OH. 28-8012

DENVER, CO. 4512

DETROIT, MI. 23-0112

DULUTH, MN. 29-4412

EDINA, MN (via Minneapolis). 29-0112

ELIZABETH, NJ. 13-8112

ERIE, PA (via Pittsburgh). 86-6112

EVANSTON, IL. 2-5391

FORT WAYNE, IN (via Indianapolis). 2712

FORT WORTH, TX. 75-8012

GREENSBORO, NC 57-4412

HAMILTON, OH (via Cincinnati). 21-4112

HARTFORD, CT. 9912

HOUSTON, TX. 76-2112

HUNTINGTON PARK, CA (via Los Angeles). 6712

INDIANAPOLIS, IN. 2712

JACKSON, MS. 58-5412

JACKSONVILLE, FL. 5612

KANSAS CITY, MO. 4212

LOS ANGELES CA. 6712

LOUISVILLE, KY. 20-4312

MAYWOOD, IL. 72-8412

MEMPHIS, TN. 5312

MIAMI, FL. 51-9112

MIAMI BEACH, FL. 51-9112

MILWAUKEE, WI. 2612

MINNEAPOLIS, MN. 29-0112

NASHVILLE, TN. 55-4412

NEW ORLEANS, LA. 5812

NEW YORK, NY. 1212

OAKLAND, CA. 33-5412

OAK PARK, IL (via Chicago). 2512

OKLAHOMA CITY, OK. 74-7112

OMAHA, NE. 48-4412

PALO ALTO, CA. 34-8412

PASADENA, CA. 6779

PATERSON, NJ. 13-0412

PEORIA, IL. 40-4412

PHILADELPHIA, PA. 84-5112

PHOENIX, AZ. 66-7412

PITTSBURGH, PA. 86-6112

PORTLAND, OR. 36-0112

PROVIDENCE, RI. 92-7612

RICHMOND, VA. 82-7412

SACRAMENTO, CA. 37-7412

ST LOUIS, MO. 4412

ST PAUL, MN. 29-7012

SALT LAKE CITY, UT. 38-8412

SAN DIEGO, CA. 69-5012

SAN FRANCISCO, CA. 3412

SEATTLE, WA. 32-0322

SILVER SPRING, MD. 8928

SOMERVILLE, MA (via Boston). 94-0112

SPRINGFIELD, MA. 95-5412

STAMFORD, CT. 96-5931

TAMPA FL. 5212

TOLEDO, OH. 28-6012

TULSA, OK. 49-2412

WASHINGTON, DC. 8912
Messages to US Senators 8-9554

Messages to members of the House of Representatives 8-9555

WORCESTER, MA. 92-0412

INTERNATIONAL TELEGRAM SERVICE

Through Western Union. Toll-Free
Telex: **6161**
TWX: **910-420-1212**

Through Other Carriers, Toll-Free

FRENCH TELEGRAPH CABLE CO.
Telex: **1045.** *TWX:* **810-621-0477**

ITT WORLD COMMUNICATIONS.
Telex: **1041.** *TWX:* **810-621-7800**

RCA GLOBAL COMMUNICATIONS.
Telex: **1042.** *TWX:* **810-621-7850**

TRT TELECOMMUNICATIONS. *Telex:* **6044.** *TWX:* **810-621-0524**

WESTERN UNION INTERNATIONAL.
Telex: **1043.** *TWX:* **810-621-7860**

NO PREFERENCE. *Telex:* **1044.** *TWX:* **810-621-7870**

Carriers' Telephone Numbers

RCA GLOBAL COMMUNICATIONS. 30 Rockefeller Plz, New York, NY 10020. **212-247-5525**

TRT TELECOMMUNICATIONS. 630 3rd Ave, New York, NY 10017. **212-986-2250**

WESTERN UNION INTERNATIONAL. 1 Western Union International Plz, New York, NY 10004. **212-363-6400**. Toll-free number: **800-835-2246** (all states except Kansas)

AMERICAN EXPRESS

AMERICAN EXPRESS COMPANY.
American Express Plz, New York, NY 10004. **212-480-2000**. For contact information, *see* BUSINESS.

Customer service. **800-528-8000** (except New York, Alaska, and Hawaii). **800-522-3350** (New York)

Applications. **800-528-8000** (except Arizona). **800-352-3000** (Arizona)

Information, Accounts, Billings

ALABAMA. **800-327-4300**

ARIZONA. **800-352-1500**

ARKANSAS. **800-327-4300**

CALIFORNIA. **800-528-1000**

COLORADO. **800-528-1000**

CONNECTICUT. **800-221-3000**

DELAWARE. **800-327-4300**

DISTRICT OF COLUMBIA. **800-327-4300**

FLORIDA. **800-432-4100**

GEORGIA. **800-327-4300**

IDAHO. **800-528-1000**

ILLINOIS. **800-528-4800**

INDIANA. **800-528-4800**

IOWA. **800-528-4800**

KANSAS. **800-528-1000**

KENTUCKY. **800-327-4300**

LOUISIANA. **800-327-4300**

MAINE. **800-221-3070**

MARYLAND. **800-327-4300**

MASSACHUSETTS. **800-221-3000**

MICHIGAN. **800-528-4800**

MINNESOTA. **800-528-4800**

MISSISSIPPI. **800-327-4300**

MISSOURI. **800-528-4800**

MONTANA. **800-528-1000**

NEBRASKA. **800-528-1000**

NEVADA. **800-528-1000**

NEW HAMPSHIRE. **800-221-3000**

NEW JERSEY. **800-221-3000**

NEW MEXICO. **800-528-1000**

NEW YORK. **800-522-3350**

NORTH CAROLINA. **800-327-4300**

NORTH DAKOTA. **800-528-4800**

OHIO. **800-327-4300**

OKLAHOMA. 800-528-1000

OREGON. 800-528-1000

PENNSYLVANIA. 800-327-4300

RHODE ISLAND. 800-221-3000

SOUTH CAROLINA. 800-327-4300

SOUTH DAKOTA. 800-528-1000

TENNESSEE. 800-327-4300

TEXAS. 800-528-1000

UTAH. 800-528-1000

VERMONT. 800-221-3000

VIRGINIA. 800-327-4300

WASHINGTON. 800-528-1000

WEST VIRGINIA. 800-327-4300

WISCONSIN. 800-528-4800

WYOMING. 800-528-1000

INTERNATIONAL TELEPHONE CALLS

Direct-dialing is now possible to 36 countries, including most of the major ones, with no assitance from operators in the US or in the country being called.

To place such a call, first dial the international access code, 011, which is the same for all countries. Then dial the two- or three-digit country code, followed by the city routing code (from one to five digits), and then the local telephone number.

For instance, to call the local number 123456 in Hiroshima, Japan, dial 011 (international access code) + 81 (country code) + 822 (city routing code) + 123456 (local number). If using a Touch-Tone telephone, press the (#) key after having dialed the entire number; this will help to make the connection more quickly.

When overseas telephone numbers appear in original sources, such as foreign telephone books, letterheads, and publications, they often include extraneous information that should not be used when dialing from the US. Usually, in the original source the numbers are given with a national access code used only within the country in question. For instance, a typical number may appear this way: (02) 123456. The 0 is a national access code, which is dropped. The remaining number is the city routing code + the local number. In this instance, dialing 011 + country code + 2 + 123456 should make the connection. When in doubt, compare the number to a list such as the following. It includes the 36 countries that can be dialed directly, along with country and city routing codes, and the number of digits to be expected in the local number.

ANDORRA. Country code 33. *City route codes.* All points, 078. **Local numbers, five digits**

AUSTRALIA. Country code 61
City Route Codes
Adelaide, 8
Belgrave, 3
Brisbane, 7
Canberra, 62
Chelsea, 3
Culcairn, 60
Finley, 58
Hobart, 02
Melbourne, 3
Newcastle, 49
Perth, 92
Southport, 75
Sydney, 2
Townsville, 77
Whyalla, 86
Wonga Park, 3
Local numbers, five to seven digits

AUSTRIA. Country code 43
City Route Codes
Baden bei Wien, 2252
Badgastein, 6434
Bludenz, 5552
Graz, 3122
Innsbruck, 5222
Kitzbuhel, 5356
Klagenfurt, 4222
Linz, Donau, 7222
Lofer, 6248
Neunkirchen, 2635
Salzburg, 6222
Thuringen, 5550
Vienna, 222
Villach, 4242
Wels, 7242
Local numbers, three to seven digits

BELGIUM. Country code 32
City Route Codes
Antwerp, 31
Bruges, 50
Brussels, 2
Charleroi, 56

Chent, 91
Hasselt, 11
La Louviere, 64
Libramont, 61
Liege, 41
Louvain, 16
Malines, 15
Mons, 65
Namur, 81
Ostend, 59
Verviers, 87
Local numbers, six to seven digits

BRAZIL. Country code 55
City Route Codes
Belem, 912
Belo Horizonta, 31
Brasilia, 612
Curitiba, 412
Fortaleza, 852
Goiania, 622
Niteroi, 21
Pelotas, 532
Porto Alegre, 512
Recife, 812
Rio de Janeiro, 21
Salvadore, 712
Santo Andre, 11
Santos, 132
Sao Paulo, 11
Vitoria, 272
Local numbers, four to seven digits

CHILE. Country code 56
City Route Codes
Chiquayante, 42
Concepcion, 42
Recreo, 31
San Bernardo, 2
Santiago, 2
Talcahuano, 42
Valparaiso, 31
Vina del Mar, 31
Local numbers, four to six digits

CHINA, REPUBLIC OF. Country code 86.
City Route Codes
Changhua, 47
Chunan, 36
Chungli, 34
Fengyuan, 45
Hsinying, 66
Hualien, 38
Kaohsiung, 7
Keelung, 32
Lotung, 39
Pingtung, 87
Taichung, 42
Tainan, 62
Taipei, 2
Taitung, 89
Taoyuan, 33
Local numbers, four to seven digits

COSTA RICA. Country code 506. City
routing codes not required. **Local numbers,
six digits**

DENMARK. Country code 45
City Route Codes
Aalborg, 8
Aarhus, 6
Allerod, 3
Ansager, 5
Assens, 9
Billund, 5
Borre, 3
Copenhagen, 1 or 2
Esbjerg, 5
Gelsted, 9
Haderslev, 4
Korsor, 3
Nykobing, 3
Odense, 9
Randers, 6
Vorgod, 7
Local numbers, four to six digits

EL SALVADOR. Country code 503. City
routing codes not required. **Local numbers,
six digits**

FRANCE. Country code 33
City Route Codes
Aix-en-Provence, 91
Bordeaux, 56
Cannes, 93
Chauvigny, 49
Cherbourg, 33
Grenoble, 76
Le Havre, 35
Lourdes, 62
Lyon, 78
Marseille, 91
Nancy, 28
Nice, 93
Paris, 1

Rouen, 35
Roulouse, 61
Rours, 47
Local numbers, six to seven digits

GERMANY, FEDERAL REPUBLIC OF.
Country code 49
City Route Codes
Bad Homburg, 6172
Berlin, 30
Bonn, 2221
Bremen, 421
Cologne, 221
Dusseldorf, 211
Essen, 201
Frankfurt, 611
Hamburg, 40
Heidelberg, 6221
Koblenz, 261
Mannheim, 621
Munich, 89
Nurnberg, 911
Stuttgart, 711
Wiesbaden, 6121
Local numbers, two to seven digits

GREECE. Country code 30
City Route Codes
Archanai, 81
Athens, 21
Candia, Crete, 81
Corinth, 741
Elefsis, 21
Hydra, 298
Kavala, 51
Larissa, 41
Naxos, 285
Oraiokastron, 31
Piraeus, 21
Rhodes, 241
Salonica, 31
Sparta, 731
Volos, 421
Zagora, 426
Local numbers, three to seven digits

GUATEMALA. Country code 502
City Route Codes
Amatitian, 33
Antigua, 32
Guatemala City, 2
Quatzaltenango, 61
Villa Nueva, 31
Local numbers, two to six digits

HONG KONG. Country code 852
City Route Codes
Castle Peak, 12
Cheung Chau, 5
Fan Ling, 12
Hong Kong, 5
Howloon, 3

Kwai Chung, 12
Lamma, 5
Ma Wan, 5
Peng Chau, 5
Sek Kong, 12
Sha Tin, 12
Silvermine Bay, 5
Tai-o, 5
Tai Po, 12
Ting Kau, 12
Tsun Wan, 12
Local numbers, five to seven digits

IRELAND, REPUBLIC OF. Country code
353.
City Route Codes
Arklow, 402
Cork, 21
Drogheda, 41
Dublin, 1
Dundalk, 42
Ennis, 65
Galway, 91
Kildare, 45
Kilkenny, 56
Killarney, 64
Sligo, 71
Tipperary, 62
Tralee, 66
Tullamore, 506
Waterford, 51
Wexford, 53
Local numbers, three to six digits

ISRAEL. Country code 972.
City Route Codes
Afula, 65
Akko, 4
Ashqeion, 51
Bat Yam, 3
Beer Sheva, 57
Dimona, 57
Hadera, 63
Haifa, 4
Holon, 3
Jerusalem, 2
Nazareth, 65
Netanya, 53
Rehovot, 3
Tel Aviv, 3
Tiberias, 67
Zefat, 67
Local numbers, four to six digits

ITALY. Country code 39
City Route Codes
Bari, 80
Bologna, 51
Brindisi, 831
Capri, 81
Como, 31
Florence, 55

Genoa, 10
Milan, 2
Naples, 81
Padua, 49
Palermo, 91
Piza, 50
Rome, 6
Trieste, 40
Venice, 41
Verona, 45
Local numbers, four to seven digits

JAPAN. Country code 81.
City Route Codes
Gifu, 582
Hiroshima, 822
Kanazawa, 762
Kanda, 93
Kobe, 78
Kyoto, 75
Nagoya, 52
Niigata, 252
Osaka, 6
Sapporo, 11
Sasebo, 956
Tachikawa, 425
Tokyo, 3
Toyota, 565
Yokohama, 45
Yokosuka, 468
Local numbers, four to seven digits

LIECHTENSTEIN. Country code 41. *City route codes:* All points, 75. **Local numbers, five to six digits**

LUXEMBOURG. Country code 352. City routing codes not required. **Local numbers, four to nine digits**

MONACO. Country code 33. *City route codes:* All points, 93. **Local numbers, six to seven digits.**

NETHERLANDS. Country code 31
City Route Codes
Amsterdam, 20
Arnhem, 85
Eindhoven, 40
Groningen, 50
Haarlem, 23
Heemstede, 23
Hillegersberg, 10
Hoensbroek, 45
Hoogkerk, 50
Hoogvliet, 10
Loosduinen, 70
Nijmegen, 80
Oud Zuilen, 30
Rotterdam, 10
The Hague, 70
Ultrecht, 30
Local numbers, three to seven digits

NEW ZEALAND. Country code 64.
City route codes
Auckland, 9
Christchurch, 3
Dunedin, 24
Hamilton, 71
Hastings, 70
Invercargill, 21
Napier, 70
Nelson, 54
New Plymouth, 67
Palmerston North, 63
Rotorua, 73
Tauranga, 75
Wanganui, 64
Wellington, 4
Whangerei, 89
Local numbers, three to seven digits

NORWAY. Country code 47
City route codes
Arendal, 41
Bergen, 5
Drammen, 2
Fredrikstad, 32
Haugesund, 47
Kongsvinger, 66
Kristiansund, 73
Larvik, 34
Moss, 32
Narvik, 82
Oslo, 2
Sarpsborg, 31
Skien, 35
Stavanger, 45
Tonsberg, 33
Trondheim, 75
Local numbers, five to six digits

PERU. Country code 51
City route codes
Arequipa, 542
Ayacucho, 6492
Callao, 14
Chiclayo, 7423
Chimbote, 4432
Cuzco, 8423
Huancavelica, 6495
Huancayo, 6423
Ica, 3423
Lima, 14
Piura, 7432
Tacna, 5472
Trujillo, 4423
Local numbers, four to six digits

PHILIPPINES. Country code 63
City route codes
Angeles, 40
Bacolod, 34
Bagulo, 442
Cebu, 32
Clark Field, 7

Cotabato, 325
Dagupan, 48
Davao, 35
Iloilo, 33
Lucena, 42
Manila, 2
San Fernando, La Union, 46
San Pablo, 41
Subic Bay, 8884
Tarlac, 47
Local numbers, four to seven digits

SAN MARINO. Country code 39. *City route codes:* All points, 541. **Local numbers, four to six digits**

SINGAPORE. Country code 65. City routing codes not required. **Local numbers, five to seven digits**

SOUTH AFRICA. Country code 27
City route codes
Bloemfontein, 51
Cape Town, 21
De Aar, 571
Durban, 31
East London, 431
Gordons Bay, 24
Johannesburg, 11
La Lucia, 31
Pietermaritzburg, 331
Port Elizabeth, 41
Pretoria, 12
Richards Bay, 351
Sasolburg, 16
Somerset West, 24
Uitenhage, 442
Welkom, 17
Local numbers, three to seven digits

SPAIN. Country code 34
City route codes
Barcelona, 3
Balboa, 4
Cadiz, 56
Ceuta (Morocco), 56
Granada, 58
Igualada, 3
Las Palmas (Canary Islands), 28
Leon, 87
Madrid, 1
Malaga, 52
Palma de Mallorca, 71
Santander, 42
Seville, 54
Valencia, 6
Local numbers, six to seven digits

SWEDEN. Country code 46
City route codes
Alingsas, 322
Boras, 33
Eskilstuna, 16

Gamleby, 493
Goteborg, 31
Helsingborg, 42
Karlstad, 54
Linkoping, 13
Lund, 46
Malmo, 40
Norrkoping, 11
Stockholm, 8
Sundsvall, 60
Trelleborg, 410
Uppsala, 18
Vasteras, 21

Local numbers, five to seven digits

SWITZERLAND. Country code 41
City route codes
Baden, 56
Basel, 61
Berne, 31
Bavos, 83
Fribourg, 37
Geneva, 22
Interlaken, 36
Lausanne, 21
Lucerne, 41

Lugano, 91
Montreux, 21
Neuchatel, 38
St Gallen, 71
St Moritz, 82
Winterthur, 52
Zurich, 1

Local numbers, five to six digits

UNITED KINGDOM. Country code 44
City route codes
Belfast (Northern Ireland), 232
Birmingham, 21
Bournemouth, 202
Cardiff (Wales), 222
Durham, 385
Edinburgh (Scotland), 31
Glasgow (Scotland), 41
Gloucester, 452
Ipswich, 473
Liverpool, 51
London, 1
Manchester, 61
Nottingham, 602
Prestwick (Scotland), 292

Sheffield, 742
Southhampton, 703

Local numbers, three to seven digits

VATICAN CITY. Country code 39. *City route code:* All points, 6

VENEZUELA. Country code 58
City route codes
Barquisimeto, 51
Cabimas, 64
Caracas, 2
Coro, 68
Guanare, 57
Maiquetia, 31
Maracaibo, 61
Maracay, 43
Merida, 74
Puerto Cabello, 42
Punto Fijo, 69
San Cristobal, 76
San Juan de los Morros, 46
Valencia, 41
Zaraza, 38

Local numbers, four to six digits

TRAVELERS AID SOCIETIES

Alabama

TRAVELERS AID SOCIETY. Greyhound Bus Lines, Birmingham, AL. **205-322-5426.** Daily, 8 am–4:30 pm

California

TRAVELERS AID SOCIETY. Greyhound Bus Station, Long Beach, CA. **213-432-3485.** Mon–Fri, 9 am–4 pm

TRAVELERS AID SOCIETY. Greyhound Bus Lines, Sacramento, CA. **916-443-1719.** "Crisis hot lines": 24 hours a day

TRAVELERS AID SOCIETY. Lindbergh Field, San Diego, CA. **714-297-4314.** Daily, 9 am–10 pm

TRAVELERS AID SOCIETY. Greyhound Bus Depot and International Airport, 38 Mason St, San Francisco, CA. **415-781-6738**

Colorado

TRAVELERS AID SERVICES. Stapleton International Airport, Denver, CO. **303-222-0829.** Mon–Fri, 9 am–6:30 pm; Sat and Sun, 9 am–5 pm

District of Columbia

TRAVELERS AID SOCIETY. Union Station, Washington, DC. **202-347-0101.** Mon–Fri, 10 am–7 pm. Sat, 10 am–4 pm Washington National Airport, Washington, DC. **202-347-0101.** Mon–Sat, 10 am–9 pm; Sun, 1 pm–9 pm

Georgia

TRAVELERS AID OF METROPOLITAN ATLANTA. International Airport, Atlanta, GA. **404-523-0585.** Mon–Fri, 9 am–5:30 pm

Illinois

TRAVELERS AID SOCIETY. Union Station, Chicago, IL. **312-435-4500.** Mon–Fri, 8:30 am–5 pm. O'Hare International Airport, Chicago, IL. **312-686-7562.** Mon–Fri, 8:30 am–5 pm. Telephone answering service for emergencies at night and on weekends: **312-686-7562**

Kentucky

TRAVELERS AID SERVICE. Family and Children's Agency, 1115 Garvin Pl, Louisville, KY 40203. **502-583-1741.** Mon–Fri, 9am–5 pm

TRAVELERS AID OF NORTHERN KENTUCKY. City-County Bldg, 303 E Court St, Covington, KY. **606-292-2358**

Maine

TRAVELERS AID DIVISION, COMMUNITY COUNSELING CENTER. Greyhound Bus Terminal, Portland, ME. Mon–Fri, 8:30 am–5 pm; Sat, 9 am–12:30 pm

Massachusetts

TRAVELERS AID SOCIETY. Greyhound Bus Terminal, Boston, MA. **617-542-7286.** Mon–Sat, 11 am–7 pm. Logan International Airport, Boston, MA. **617-542-7286.** Mon–Fri, 12:30 pm–7 pm

Michigan

TRAVELERS AID SOCIETY. Metropolitan Airport, Detroit, MI. 313-962-8251. Sun only, 2:00 pm–10 pm; Mon–Sat, irregular coverage

Minnesota

TRAVELERS AID, COMMUNITY IN-FORMATION AND REFERRAL SERVICE. Minneapolis-St Paul International Airport, Minneapolis, MN. 612-340-7431. Mon–Sat, 9 am–9 pm; Sat, 10 am–6 pm

TRAVELERS AID-FAMILY SERVICE. Minneapolis-St Paul International Airport, St Paul, MN. 612-222-0311. Mon–Sat, 9 am–9 pm; Sun, 10 am–6 pm

Missouri

MULLANPHY TRAVELERS AID. Greyhound Bus Terminal, St Louis, MO. 314-241-5820. Mon–Sat, 9 am–5 pm

New York

CAPITAL DISTRICT TRAVELERS AID SOCIETY. Albany Trailways Bus Terminal, Albany, NY. 518-463-2124. Mon–Fri, 9 am–5 pm. Schenectady Travel Center, Albany, NY. 518-463-2124. Mon–Fri, 9 am–5 pm

TRAVELERS AID SOCIETY. Main office, Suite 656, Ellicott Sq Bldg; branch office, Metro Transportation Ctr, 181 Ellicott, Buffalo, NY. 716-854-8661. Mon–Fri, 9 am–4:30 pm, 6 pm–9 pm; Sat, 9 am–4:30 pm. Buffalo Airport, Buffalo, NY. 716-854-8661. 24-Hour service

TRAVELERS AID SOCIETY. Central office, 204 E 39th St, New York, NY. 212-679-0200. Mon–Fri, 9 am–5 pm. Port Authority Bus Terminal, New York, NY. 212-679-0200. Mon–Fri, 10 am–6 pm. John F. Kennedy International Airport, New York, NY. 212-679-0200. Mon–Fri, 10 am–10 pm

TRAVELERS AID INTERNATIONAL. 345 E 46th St, New York, NY. 212-254-1700

Ohio

TRAVELERS AID-INTERNATIONAL INSTITUTE. Rm 307, 700 Walnut St, Cincinnati, OH. 513-721-7660. Mon–Fri, 8:30 am–4:30 pm. Greyhound Bus Terminal, Court and Gilbert Sts, Cincinnati, OH. 513-651-1652

TRAVELERS AID SERVICES. Greyhound Bus Terminal, Cleveland, OH. 216-241-5861. Mon–Fri, 8:30 am–5 pm

Oklahoma

TRAVELERS AID SOCIETY. Union Bus Station, Oklahoma City, OK. 405-232-5507. Mon–Fri, 9 am–noon, 1 pm–4:30 pm; Sat, 9 am–5 pm. Will Rogers World Airport, Oklahoma City, OK. 405-232-5507. Mon–Fri, 10 am–5 pm, 6 pm–10 pm.

TRAVELERS AID SOCIETY. Bus Terminal, Tulsa, OK. 918-582-9231. Mon–Fri, 3:30 pm–6 pm; Sat, 2 pm–6:30 pm. Tulsa International Airport, Tulsa, OK. 918-835-2573. Mon–Sat, 9 am–5 pm. No-answer and night line: 918-582-4993

Pennsylvania

TRAVELERS AID SOCIETY. Philadelphia International Airport, Philadelphia, PA. 215-922-0950. Mon and Fri, 10 am–6 pm; Tues and Thurs, 9 am–5 pm

TRAVELERS AID OF GREATER PITTS-BURGH. International Airport, Pittsburgh, PA. 412-264-7110. Mon–Fri, 9 am–5 pm

Rhode Island

TRAVELERS AID SOCIETY. Bonanza Bus Terminal, Providence, RI. 401-521-2255. Mon–Fri, 9 am–5 pm

Tennessee

TRAVELERS AID DIVISION. Greyhound Bus Station, Chattanooga, TN. 615-267-9543. Mon–Fri, 9 am–5 pm

TRAVELERS AID SOCIETY. Greyhound Terminal, Memphis, TN. 901-525-5466. Mon–Fri, 8:30 am–4:30 pm

Texas

TRAVELERS AID SOCIETY. Greyhound Bus Station, Houston, TX. 713-522-3846. Mon–Fri, 10 am–4:45 pm, 6 pm–10 pm; Sat and Sun, 1 pm–5 pm, 6 pm–10 pm. Intercontinental Airport, Houston, TX. 713-522-3846. Mon–Fri, 9 am–5 pm; 7 pm–10 pm

Utah

TRAVELERS AID SOCIETY. Greyhound Bus Terminal, Salt Lake City, UT. 801-328-8996. Mon–Fri, 8:30 am–4:30 pm; Sat, 8:30 am–noon. International Airport, Salt Lake City, UT. 801-328-8996. Mon–Fri, 9 am–9 pm

Washington

TRAVELERS AID SOCIETY. Seattle-Tacoma Airport, Seattle, WA. 206-447-3888. Mon–Fri, 10 am–10 pm; Sat and Sun, noon–8 pm

TRAVELERS AID SOCIETY. Rm 630, 909 4th Ave, Seattle, WA 98104. 206-447-3888. Mon–Fri, 8:30 am–9 pm; Sat, Sun, and holidays, 2 pm–6 pm

PART TWO
INFORMATION SOURCES AND CONTACTS

INFORMATION AND RESEARCH SERVICES

The following is a list of businesses, private organizations, and government agencies that specialize in providing information—in some cases for a fee and in others at cost or no charge. Many other organizations and agencies provide information and referral as a secondary activity, and these are described in several other chapters (*see*, e.g., THE FEDERAL GOVERNMENT, SPECIAL INTERESTS, SPORTS, SCIENCE AND TECHNOLOGY, WORLD, AND EDUCATION). Of special interest to any researcher of current affairs is the Library of Congress, which handles numerous types of queries by telephone and by mail; details can be found in THE FEDERAL GOVERNMENT.

AMERICAN ANTIQUARIAN SOCIETY. 185 Salisbury St, Worcester, MA 01609. **617-755-5221.** Marcus A McCorison, director and librarian. Mary V C Callahan, development officer. A research library specializing in printed Americana from the colonial period to 1877, with 650,000 volumes and four million printed items, including three million early American newspaper numbers

AMMINET. (Automated Mortgage Market Information Network). Suite 710, 400 1st St NW, Washington, DC 20001. **202-624-7190.** Morgan Moore, executive vice-president. Dorothy Godwin, information coordinator. **202-624-7140.** "The primary source in the nation for accurate, instantaneous information on who has mortgage investments to sell and who is in the market to buy them"

AUTEX TRADING INFORMATION SYSTEM. 55 William St, Wellesley, MA 02181. **617-235-1940.** *New York office:* 90 Broad St, New York, N Y 10004. **212-952-7060**

BUREAU OF SOCIAL SCIENCE RESEARCH, INC. 1990 M St N W, Washington, DC 20036. **202-223-4300.** Robert T Bower, director. Purisima K Tan, administrative assistant, publications, Ext 202. An independent, nonprofit organization "devoted to the development of social science knowledge for its application to contemporary social problems"

CELEBRITY SERVICE, INC. 171 W 57th St, New York, N Y 10019. **212-757-7979.** Earl Blackwell, president. Roslyn M Lipps, manager

Branch offices
Hollywood. 8746 Sunset Blvd, Hollywood, CA 90069. **213-652-1700**
Atlanta. P O Box 11710, Atlanta, GA 30305. **404-237-6116**
London. 10 Dover St, London W.1. Grosvenor **8511** and **8512**
Paris. 7, rue Jean Gouion, 75008 Paris, France. **225-02-47, 225-02-,37**
Rome. Via Poggio Moiano, 34, 00199 Rome, Italy. **88-88-096**

Celebrity Service provides subscribers with contact information for celebrities—defined as anyone whose name is generally recognizable. Although the emphasis is on entertainment figures, the service is not limited to these. Contact information can range from home and office numbers for the individual, to names and contacts at his agent or publisher. Background information is also supplied. It is the major service of its kind (there is one other, much smaller such service; see Roz Starr, Inc, in this chapter). "Much of the information supplied by Celebrity Service cannot be obtained from any other source as it is in great measure supplied to us exclusively," according to a Celebrity Service brochure.

The service also issues a regular Celebrity Bulletin detailing scheduled arrivals in New York. Here is a typical entry, from the March 14, 1977, bulletin, for Geraldine Fitzgerald: "returns from club engagement in California 3/21 to prepare for 3/31 Broadway opening of 'Shadow Box.' PR: Alan Eichler, **929-1130**; Agt: ICM (Milton Goldman), **556-5600**; PR Con: Bettly Lee Hunt, **354-0880**."

In addition the service publishes *Celebrity Register*, issued every several years with biographies of celebrities; the *Celebrity Service International Contact Book*, issued every few years and described as a "trade directory of the entertainment industry"; and a Theatrical Calendar, "listing current and future activities in New York's theatre."

CENTER FOR INTERNATIONAL ENVIRONMENT INFORMATION.
300 E 42nd St, New York, NY 10017. **212-697-3232.** Dr Whitman Bassow, executive director. Night line: **212-876-0265.**

A nonprofit, educational organization established by the United Nations Association of the US and supported by the US State Department and the Environmental Protection Agency, the center is "devoted to reporting on worldwide environmental developments through correspondents in 60 countries." Among its other services, it provides "a query service for the communications media on all aspects of international environment issues and developments."

CENTER FOR SHORT-LIVED PHENOMENA, INC. 129 Mount Auburn St, Cambridge, MA 02138. **617-492-3310.** Richard Golob, director, *See* SPECIAL INTERESTS for more detail.

CHINESE INFORMATION SERVICE. 159 Lexington Ave, New York, NY 10016. **212-725-4950.** I-cheng Loh, director, **212-725-4957** or **212-725-4950**, Ext 37. T C Chiang, deputy director, Ext 36. Night line: **212-725-4950** before 9 pm, **212-291-5954** thereafter. C Y Chang, audiovisual officer, **212-725-4950**, Ext 40. Shih-hung Liu, news editor, Ext 23.

COMMERCE CLEARING HOUSE, INC. *Editorial offices.* 425 13th St NW, Washington, DC 20004. **202-347-1555.** *Corporate offices.* 4025 W Peterson, Chicago, IL 60646. **312-267-9010.** Issues specialized publications on regulatory matters.

COMMITTEE FOR ENVIRONMENTAL INFORMATION (CEI). 560 Trinity Ave, St Louis, MO 63130. **314-863-6560.** John M Newman, president, **314-421-5061.** Sarah J Miller, director, information services, **314-863-6560**

The purpose of CEI is the dissemination of scientific information on the environment; it publishes *Environment Magazine*. CEI "would be glad to handle inquiries from environmental writers or science writers. Their inquiries might be answered with referrals to reading sources or to other experts, but wherever possible answers will be submitted by CEI."

THE CONFERENCE BOARD, INC. 845 3rd Ave, New York, NY 10022. **212-759-0900.** Kenneth A Randall, president. Joseph L Naar, director, public information, (h) **914-941-1345.** Randall E Poe, assistant director, public information.

The Conference Board, a nonprofit business and economic research organization supported by its subscribers, conducts conferences and seminars and distributes more than three million research documents and periodicals annually. The purpose "is to promote broader understanding of business and the economy for the enlightenment both of those who manage business enterprises and of the society which shapes the business system." The fruits of its research and seminar activities are available to researchers and media, and the board "encourages reporters, editors, and broadcasters to draw upon the Board's staff of experts and pool of information when facts are needed."

CONSTRUCTION INDUSTRY RESEARCH BOARD. Suite 804, 1625 W Olympic Blvd, Los Angeles, CA 90015. **213-381-6544.** Ben Bartolotto, research director, (h) **213-761-6924.** A nonprofit, industry-sponsored organization specializing in research involving land-use, environmental, employment, and economic issues related to the construction and development industry

CORPORATE INFORMATION CENTER. 475 Riverside Dr, New York, NY 10027. **212-870-2293.** *See* Interfaith Center *under* SPECIAL INTERESTS.

DATA RESOURCES, INC. 29 Hartwell Ave, Lexington, MA 02173. **617-861-0165.** Otto Eckstein, president and chief executive officer. David Kelley, general company information. Edward Siegfried, financial information.

Branch office contacts
California. Chris Snyder. **415-956-4050**
New York. Tom Flaherty. **212-233-7755**
Chicago, IL. Peter Zeismer. **312-440-2400**
Washington, DC. Joe Kasputys.
202-862-3700
Pittsburgh, PA. Harvey Cohen. **412-288-0573**
Canada. 416-961-9323

Provides econometric model building and economic forecasting of the US and other principal industrial economies (eg, Canada, the United Kingdom, Germany) and specific industries (petrochemicals, steel, automobiles, energy, etc)

DATA USE AND ACCESS LABORATORIES, INC. (DUALabs) Suite 900, 1601 N Kent St, Arlington, VA 22209. **703-525-1480.** John C Beresford, president. Joy F Reamy, director, administration. Syl Morrison, publications manager. Night line:

703-525-1480. A nonprofit, tax-exempt corporation established in 1970 for the purpose of assisting users of publicly available statistical data files produced by government agencies and other organizations

DISEASE DETECTION INFORMATION BUREAU. 3553 W Peterson, Chicago, IL 60659. **312-267-7184**

EDUCATIONAL RESOURCES INFORMATION CENTER (ERIC). 19th and M Sts, Washington, DC 20208. **202-254-6050**

Operated by the National Institute of Education, ERIC is the parent body of a nationwide network of clearinghouses in various fields of education. ERIC itself, through the Document Reproduction Service, provides copies of reports, publications, journal abstracts, curriculum guides, and similar materials. The various clearinghouses produce bibliographies and gather and disseminate material in their areas of interest. A list of the ERIC clearinghouses follows.

Clearinghouse on Career Education. Center for Vocational Education, 1960 Kenny Rd, Columbus, OH 43210. **614-486-3655**

Clearinghouse on Counseling and Personnel Services. School of Education, University of Michigan, Ann Arbor, MI 48104. **313-764-9492**

Clearinghouse on Early Childhood Education. University of Illinois, 805 W Pennsylvania Ave, Urbana, IL 61801. **217-333-1386**

Clearinghouse on Handicapped and Gifted Children. The Council for Exceptional Children, 1920 Association Dr, Reston, VA 22091. **703-620-3660**

Clearinghouse on Higher Education. George Washington University, Suite 630, 1 Dupont Cir, Washington, DC 20036. **202-296-2597**

Clearinghouse for Information Resources. Syracuse University, School of Education, Syracuse, NY 13210. **314-423-3640**

Clearinghouse on Junior Colleges. University of California, Los Angeles, Rm 96, Powell Library, 405 Hilgard Ave, Los Angeles, CA 90024. **213-825-3931**

Clearinghouse on Reading and Communication Skills. National Council of Teachers of English, 1111 Kenyon Rd, Urbana, IL 61801. **217-328-3870**

Clearinghouse on Rural Education and Small Schools. New Mexico State University, Box 3-AR, Las Croces, NM 88003. **505-646-2628**

Clearinghouse for Science, Mathematics, and Environmental Education. Ohio State University, 1200 Chambers Rd, Columbus, OH 43212. **614-422-6717**

Clearinghouse for Social Studies. 855 Broadway, Boulder, CO 80302. **303-492-8434**

Clearinghouse on Teacher Education. Suite 616, 1 Dupont Cir NW, Washington, DC 20036. **202-293-7280**

Clearinghouse on Tests, Measurement, and Evaluation. Educational Testing Service, Rosedale Rd, Princeton, NJ 08540. **609-921-9000**

Clearinghouse on Urban Education. Columbia University, Teachers College, Horace Mann-Lincoln Institute, 525 W 120th St (Box 40), New York, NY 10027. **212-678-3437**

ENVIRONMENT INFORMATION CENTER, INC. 292 Madison Ave, New York, NY 10017. **212-949-9494.** James G Kollegger, president and publisher, **212-949-9480.** Karen Ziegler, special projects director, **212-949-9479.**

EIC is an independent research and publishing organization specializing in energy and environmental information. "We maintain computerized data bases monitoring documents, laws and regulations, organizations and people, and miscellaneous sources such as conferences, books, and films."

ENVIRONMENTAL DATA SERVICE. Washington, DC 20235. **202-634-7306.** Thomas S Austin, director, **202-634-7318.** Patrick Hughes, chief, publications and media staff, **202-634-7306,** night line: (h), **202-529-2569.** James F Lander, deputy director, national geophysical and solar-terrestrial data center, **303-323-6474.** Keith D Butson, executive officer, national climatic center, **704-672-0289.** Dr Norton Strommen, director, center for climatic and environmental assessment, **314-276-3261.**

EDS, an agency of the National Atmospheric and Oceanic Administration, disseminates global environmental data and information packaged to meet the needs of the general public, users in commerce, industry, and agriculture, the scientific and engineering communities, and federal, state, and local governments. EDS also assesses the impact of environmental fluctuations on food and energy production, distribution, and use; environmental quality; and other vital national areas; and provides data management for large-scale environmental programs. *See also* WEATHER.

EQUIFAX, INC. 1600 Peachtree Rd NW, Atlanta, GA 30309. **404-875-8321.** Night line: **404-875-1958.** W Lee Burge, chairman and president. Hal Arnold, director, public relations, (h) **404-451-4997.** "Provides insurance, financial control, claim, and personal selection reports to businesses for business decisions"

EUTHROPHICATION INFORMATION PROGRAM. *See* WATER RESOURCES INFORMATION PROGRAM.

FEDERAL INFORMATION CENTER PROGRAM OFFICE. General Services Administration, Rm 6018, 18th and F Sts NW, Washington, DC 20405. **202-566-1937.** Don Knenlein, national coordinator. For a complete list of the Federal Information Centers around the country *see* REGIONAL GOVERNMENT OFFICES.

FINANCIAL INFORMATION SERVICE. 5454 Beethoven St, Los Angeles, CA 90066. **213-398-2761.** A subscriber service that provides instantaneous stock market information through an on-line data base system

FIND/SVP. *See* INFORMATION CLEARING HOUSE, INC.

FOREIGN BROADCAST INFORMATION SERVICE. PO 2604, Washington DC 20013. **703-527-2368.** A CIA-run operation that digests and monitors radio broadcasts throughout the world; subscriptions available from National Technical Information Service

THE FOUNDATION CENTER. 888 7th Ave, New York, NY 10019. **212-975-1120.** Thomas R Buckman, president, **212-975-1132.** Carol M Kurzig, director, library services, **212-975-1128**
Washington, DC, office. 1001 Connecticut Ave NW, Washington, DC 20036. **202-331-1400**
Chicago. Donor's Forum of Chicago, 208 S La Salle St, Chicago, Ill. 60604. **312-726-4879**

"The Foundation Center is the only nonprofit organization devoted solely to the gathering, analysis, and dissemination of information on foundations and their grant-making activities. It is the foremost authority in the area of statistics and factual information on the universe of 27,000 private foundations in the U.S."

The Foundation Center, supported largely by foundations, has libraries in New York and Washington, DC, with collections of foundation materials, and there is a system of 64 cooperating collections at libraries in 45 states. The center maintains, in New York, Washington, and Chicago, a full collection of the information returns that private foundations must file annually with the IRS. The collections are open to the public without charge. Each cooperating collection around the country also usually maintains copies of the information returns for foundations in its general geographic area.

Center publications include *The Foundation Directory*, *The Foundation Grants Index*, and *The Foundation Center Source Book*. Associates of the center—those who pay a $200 annual fee—can obtain toll-free telephone reference services and toll-free taped bulletins, as well as information updates and computer coverage of information available in foundations.

FREE INFORMATION BUREAU. 1799 Lexington Ave, New York, NY 10029. **212-876-3688**

FUNDING SOURCES CLEARINGHOUSE, INC. Suite 1000, 760 Market St, San Francisco, CA 94102. **415-548-5880.** A centralized source of information on philanthropy and funding, including the private and public grant programs of private foundations, government agencies, businesses, and associations

FUTURES INFORMATION NETWORK. World Institute, 777 United Nations Plz, New York, NY 10017. **201-661-0884**

GALE READER SERVICE BUREAU. Gale Research Co, Book Tower, Detroit, MI 48226. **313-961-2242.** *Contact.* Denise Akey

Gale Research Co publishes the thorough and useful *Encyclopedia of Associations* and similar reference publications, which contain addresses and phone numbers in addition to background information. The reader service provides users of the *Encyclopedia* with updated contact information for organizations that have moved since the latest annual edition was published, and is extremely helpful and cooperative.

THE INFORMATION BANK. Mount Pleasant Office Park, 1719A Route 10, Parsippany, NJ 07054. **201-539-5850.** James L Bauer, vice-president. Toll-free line for customers: **800-631-8056**

Branch Offices

New York. Suite 86011, 1 World Trade Ctr, New York, NY 10048. **212-775-0552**
Washington. Suite 207, 1909 K St NW, Washington, DC 20036. **202-833-3291**
Chicago. Suite 500, 625 N Michigan Ave, Chicago, IL 60611. **312-664-6536**
San Francisco. Suite 901, 1390 Market St, San Francisco, CA 94012. **415-552-2600**

The Information Bank, a subsidiary of the New York Times Company, is a computerized information storage and retrieval service that indexes and provides abstracts of articles published in the *New York Times* (late city edition) and other major newspapers and periodicals (for a complete list, see the introduction to PEOPLE). The service numbers its subscribers at over 500—including libraries, newspapers, research services, and government agencies. Many on-line subscribers, in turn, make the service available to the public at cost or, in some cases for limited searches, at no charge. The location of the nearest such subscriber can be obtained by calling the Information Bank at **201-539-5850**, or the nearest branch office. On-line subscribers have a terminal connected directly to the Information Bank, and a printer that will provide abstracts of indexed articles in particular subject areas. There is also an on-demand service for special projects and for users who do not have the on-line service.

INFORMATION FOR BUSINESS. 18th Floor F, 8 W 40th St, New York, NY 10018. **212-867-7030.** A research service for subscribers

INFORMATION CLEARING HOUSE, INC. 500 5th Ave, New York, NY 10036. **212-354-2424.** Andrew P Garvin, chairman and chief executive officer. A research service for subscribers, primarily businesses; distributes *Management Contents*, a biweekly publication that reprints the tables of contents of business periodicals and journals

INFORMATION INDUSTRY ASSOCIATION. 4720 Montgomery Ln, Bethesda, MD 20014. **301-654-4150.** Paul G Zurkowski, president. Helena M Strauch, communications director. A trade association for the information industry; publishes a directory of members, *Information Sources*, and can provide referrals to companies and organizations in the information field, as well as information about services provided by IIA members

INFORMATION UNLIMITED.
2510 Channing 3, Berkeley, CA 94708.
415-841-5861. Sue Rugge, co-owner

Information Unlimited, a research service for subscribers, also has a useful document delivery service that can photocopy and send materials from major information centers. The service promises daily access at the University of California's Berkeley, Davis, San Francisco, and Los Angeles campuses, the Countway Library of Medicine, San Francisco Public Library, Linda Hall Library, Library of Congress, and National Library of Medicine

INFOSEARCH, INC. PO Box 1110, Albany, NY 12201. **800-833-9848**

INTERCONTINENTAL RESEARCH ASSOCIATES. 111 W Washington Ave, Chicago, IL 60602. **312-236-6123**

INTERFILE. See World Trade Information Center

INTERNATIONAL ASSOCIATION OF CONVENTION AND VISITOR BUREAUS. See SPECIAL INTERESTS

INTERNATIONAL ASSOCIATION FOR IDENTIFICATION. PO Box 139, Utica, NY 13503. **315-732-2897.** Walter G Hoetzer, secretary-treasurer. Joseph J Musial, 1920 SW 33rd Ave, Miami, FL 33145. Law enforcement oriented; provides scientific and educational services for persons working in the fields of fingerprint identification, questioned documents, firearm and toolmark identification, photography, etc—that is, the forensic and identification sciences

KIPLINGER WASHINGTON EDITORS, INC. 1729 H St NW, Washington, DC 20006. **202-298-6400.** Austin H Kiplinger, president and publisher. Gwen A Fitzpatrick, promotion director. Night line: **301-656-6270.** Publishes *Changing Times* magazine and six newsletters: *The Kiplinger Washington Letter, Tax Letter, Agricultural Letter, Florida Letter, California Letter,* and *European Letter.*

MOORLAND-SPINGARN RESEARCH CENTER. Howard University. 500 Howard Place NW, Washington, DC 20059. **202-636-7239.** Dr Michael R Winston, director, 202-636-7241, Night line: **202-829-4085.** Millie P Baker, Administrative assistant, **202-636-7240.** Collects, preserves, makes available for study, and reproduces thou-

sands of items in its specialty area: black culture and history

NATIONAL ASSOCIATION FOR MENTAL HEALTH. 1800 N Kent St, Arlington, VA 22209. **703-528-6405.** Serves as a clearinghouse for information on mental illness, for both the public and the profession

NATIONAL ASSOCIATION FOR STATE INFORMATION SYSTEMS. Iron Works Pike (PO Box 11910), Lexington, KY 40578. **606-252-2291.** Carl Vorlander, executive director

NATIONAL AUTOMOBILE THEFT BUREAU. 17 John St, New York, NY 10038. **212-233-1400.** James B Allen, manager, Eastern Division.

A voluntary, nonprofit association of member insurance companies, the bureau cooperates with "duly authorized" law enforcement agencies in the identification and tracing of stolen motor vehicles, as well as with motor vehicle manufacturers and motor vehicle departments. It maintains a nationwide computer file on stolen vehicles.

NATIONAL BUSINESS INTELLIGENCE CORPORATION (NBI). 26th Floor, 200 Park Ave, New York, NY 10017. **212-972-1770.** John R Dallas, Jr, president

NBI serves many of the world's largest corporations with high-priority information-handling systems, services, and programs, mostly of a financial nature. It owns and operates a computer-assisted editorial process providing virtually concurrent production of transcripts of proceedings transmitted from around the world to its New York City Document Processing Center.

This system is used by companies when presidents and other principal spokesmen are addressing key audiences. Reports and transcripts of such presentations are produced by NBI. The system is also used by the media (ABC, CBS, NBC, and PBS) for high-priority transcription of major boradcasts. The system was used to produce the official transcripts of the '76 presidential debates

NATIONAL CLEARING CORPORATION. 1735 K St NW, Washington, DC 20006. **202-833-7150.** *New York office.* 2 Broadway, NY, NY 10004. **212-952-4000.**

NATIONAL CLEARING HOUSE FOR MENTAL HEALTH INFORMATION. Division of Scientific and Public Information, National Institute of Mental Health, 5600 Fishers Ln, Rockville, MD 20857. **301-443-4517.** Carrie Lee Rothgeb, acting chief. Answers inquiries, provides consultation on mental health information, supplies technical assistance, makes referrals to other sources, and distributes single copies of its publications

NATIONAL HEALTH PLANNING INFORMATION CENTER. PO Box 31, Rockville, MD 20850. **301-881-5075.** Frank A Morrone, Jr, chief, **301-436-6736.** Maintains a health planning data base, based on contributions from government agencies and cooperating institutions, answers inquiries, and does searches of its documents in response to topical questions

NATIONAL INFORMATION BUREAU, INC. 419 Park Ave S, New York, NY 10016. **212-532-8595.** M C Van de Workeen, executive director. Jane Pendergast, assistant director.

The bureau prepares evaluative reports on national nonprofit organizations soliciting the public, and helps to maintain sound standards in philanthropy. It evaluates organizations against eight widely accepted standards of ethics and sound management. The bureau publishes the monthly *Wise Giving Guide*, listing agencies on which it reports and giving the current evaluations against its standards.

The *Guide* also lists organizations that have not provided the NIB with adequate information, and pulls no ideological punches. Recent such listees included the Freedoms Foundation at Valley Forge, Nader's Center for the Study of Responsive Law, the Veterans of Foreign Wars, and the Southern Christian Leadership Conference. The bureau also publishes other types of information.

NATIONAL REFERRAL CENTER.
10 1st St SE, Washington DC 20540.
202-426-5670

An agency of the Library of Congress (*see also* THE FEDERAL GOVERNMENT), the National Referral Center is similarly cooperative and efficient in responding, free of charge, to information queries in many areas. Although the emphasis in the past was on scientific and technical subjects, the NRC has broadened its scope and frequently proves valuable to the layman interested in less than esoteric subjects. The NRC welcomes inquiries by either phone or mail. It publishes an informal series of monographs, under the general heading "NRC Switchboard," which give contact information and descriptions of information sources in specific subject areas. The contacts included on a subject such as, say, land use range from highly technical to lay oriented.

NATIONAL TECHNICAL INFORMATION SERVICE. 5285 Port Royal Rd, Springfield, VA 22161. **703-557-4736.** William T Knox, director, **202-724-3374.** Dean Smith, assistant director, marketing, **202-557-4736**

NTIS is an important source of government publications and documents in many areas, although it places principal emphasis on science and technology. The service provides many documents also for sale through the Government Printing Office, but NTIS manages to process and ship them promptly and is generally willing to invoice—two services unknown to the government's printing behemoth.

An agency of the Department of Commerce, NTIS originally was known as the Clearinghouse for Federal Scientific and Technical Information. Its purpose is to provide business, government, and the public with up-to-date information on the fruits of government-sponsored, unclassified research. Since such research goes on in many fields of endeavor, many of which are technical or scientific only in the sense that they are the subject of serious investigation, NTIS often proves useful to the lay person who is in a hurry for a particular publication or document. Other fields covered include social sciences, business, health, law, and urban planning.

NTIS publishes a *Fast Announcement Service*, specially prepared announcements highlighting selected new reports it receives; *Clearinghouse Announcements in Science and Technology*, an abstract service that reviews all scientific and technical reports handled by NTIS (some 40,000 annually); and *US Government Research and Development Reports Index*.

The service also handles inquiries about document availability and, on request, searches for documents in particular subject areas. Publications are provided at cost, and most are available either on paper or on microfiche. Working press can be listed on the NTIS trade announcement list by writing NTIS at Rm 620, 424 13th St NW, Washington, DC 20005, attention: Mary Sutton.

NEWS ELECTION SERVICE. 350 S Figueroa, Los Angeles, CA 90071. **213-623-2421**

A C NIELSON COMPANY. Nielson Plz, Northbrook, IL 60062. **312-498-6300**

Nielson, best known for its television viewing surveys based on recording devices in a cross section of American homes, provides a large variety of information services to business. The largest of its operations is a retail index, which reports on what people are buying in the US and overseas. Other divisions and subsidiaries also provide magazine subscription lists, statistical research, and industrial and marketing analysis. For contact information and further details, see BUSINESS.

OVER-THE-COUNTER INFORMATION BUREAU. 120 Broadway, New York, NY 10005. **212-697-6897.** *See* SPECIAL INTERESTS.

PACKAGED FACTS, INC. 274 Madison Ave, New York, NY 10016. **212-532-5533.** David A Weiss, president. An information service that does library research, back-dated clipping, advertising tear-sheet research, and historical research on a fee basis

PHILANTHROPIC ADVISORY SERVICE. See SPECIAL INTERESTS under the Council of Better Business Bureaus, Inc.

POPULATION REFERENCE BUREAU, INC. 1337 Connecticut Ave NW, Washington, DC 20036. **202-785-4664.** Robert M Avedon, president. Jean van der Tak, senior editor, (h) **202-966-4441.** Phyllis Avedon, editor, INTERCOM, monthly population newsletter, (h), **301-279-9291.** Bruce Knarr, director, library and information services, **202-785-4664.** Lance Canter, assistant librarian, **202-785-4664.**

The bureau gathers, interprets, and publishes information about population trends and their economic, environmental, and social effects. Founded in 1929, it is a private, nonprofit educational organization that is supported by foundation grants, individual and corporate contributions, memberships, and subscriptions. It consults with other groups in the United States and abroad and provides library and information services.

REAL ESTATE DATA, INC. 2398 NW 119th St, Miami, FL 33167. **305-685-5731.** Provides land maps and details on ownership of land, and compiles data on real estate transactions

SCIENCE SERVICE, INC. 1719 N St NW, Washington, DC 20036. **202-785-2255**

SMITHSONIAN SCIENCE INFORMATION EXCHANGE. Rm 300, 1730 M St NW, Washington, DC 20036. **202-381-4211.** Dr David F Hersey, president, Ext 200. Janet D Goldstein, marketing manager, Ext 226

SSIE collects and disseminates prepublication information about scientific projects in progress in all fields of basic and applied research in the life and physical sciences. "A nonprofit corporation of the Smithsonian Institution, it complements the services of technical libraries and documentation centers by providing information about research in progress between the time a project is proposed or started and the time results are made available in published form."

SOCIAL LEGISLATION INFORMATION SERVICE. 1346 Connecticut Ave NW, Washington, DC 20036. **202-223-2396.** William L Pierce, executive editor. Marjorie Kopp, editor. A nonprofit organization and division of the Child Welfare League of America, Inc; promises to report impartially on federal social legislation and the activities of federal agencies affecting children, the elderly, the handicapped, and delinquents, as well as health, education, welfare, housing, employment, and other social welfare conditions

SOLID WASTE RECYCLING INFORMATION SERVICE. *See* SCIENCE AND TECHNOLOGY.

SONG REGISTRATION SERVICE. 6381 Hollywood, Los Angeles, CA. **213-463-7178.** *See* SPECIAL INTERESTS.

ROZ STARR, INC. 227 W 45th St, New York, NY 10036. **212-354-5050.** Roz Starr, president. A celebrity locator service. *See also* Celebrity Services, Inc.

STATE FARM INSURANCE COMPANIES MEDIA INFORMATION SERVICE. Public Relations Department, State Farm Insurance Companies, 1 State Farm Plz, Bloomington, IL 61701. **309-662-2625.**

The service issues, at no charge, a detailed and continuously updated *No Fault Press Reference Manual* that reports on developments in the 50 states in regard to no-fault legislation, including amendments. It also issues "Insurance Backgrounders" on other automobile insurance topics— all, of course, from the point of view of the insurance industry.

TAX ANALYSTS AND ADVOCATES. *See* SPECIAL INTERESTS.

TECHNICAL ASSISTANCE INFORMATION CLEARINGHOUSE. American Council of Voluntary Agencies for Foreign Service, 200 Park Ave S, New York, NY 10003. **212-777-8210.** Provides information on assistance programs overseas conducted by US, nonprofit, religious, and other voluntary organizations

TECHNICAL INFORMATION SERVICE. 750 3rd Ave, New York, NY 10017. **212-867-8300**

TECHREPORT, INC. 299 Broadway, New York, NY 10007. **212-962-3449**

TELEVISION INFORMATION OFFICE. 745 5th Ave, New York, NY 10022. **212-759-6800.** Affiliated with the industry trade organization, the National Association of Broadcasters; the office collects and provides information on the impact of television on American society.

TREATY RESEARCH CENTER. University of Washington, Seattle, WA 98195. **206-543-8030.** Peter H Rohn, director. John L Panettoni, head research assistant. Compiles and provides information on treaties between countries throughout the world

UNITED NATIONS INFORMATION CENTRE. 2101 L St NW, Washington, DC 20037. **202-296-5370.** *See also* WORLD.

URBAN DATA SERVICE. 1140 Connecticut Ave NW, Washington, DC 20036. **202-293-2200**

The service is a joint operation of the International City Management Association and the National Association of Counties. It publishes directories on local government and maintains a data base of statistical information about demographics and other characteristics of local municipalities, government agencies, counties, and so forth.

VITAMIN INFORMATION BUREAU, INC. 664 N Michigan Ave, Chicago, IL 60611. **312-751-2223.** Night line: **312-787-0863.** Caryl M Wright, president. John B Wright, chairman. Provides nutrition education aids, printed and audiovisual, and scientific "backgrounders" on vitamins and minerals

WASHINGTON CRIME NEWS SERVICES. Suite 400, 7620 Little River Tpke, Annandale, VA 22003. **703-941-6600.** R J O'Connell, publisher. Charles A Bailey, Dan Casalaro, and Dick O'Connell, editors. Publishes a series of useful digests of news and developments in criminal justice, among them *Security Systems Digest, Crime Control Digest, Juvenile Justice Digest, Court Systems Digest, Corrections Digest,* and *Narcotics Control Digest*

WASHINGTON SERVICES, INCORPORATED. 908 National Press Bldg, Washington, DC 20045. **202-737-4434.** LeRoy R Chittenden, owner

This is a research service for subscribers; it also distributes news releases in Washington, provides messenger services, and delivers the *Congressional Record* and *Federal Register* on a same-day basis. For a fee, it will pick up and mail publications from the GPO Book Room.

WATER RESOURCES INFORMATION PROGRAM (formerly Euthrophication Information Program). Water Resources Center and Engineering and Physical Sciences Library, University of Wisconsin, 215 N Randell Ave, Madison, WI 53706. **608-262-0561.** Prof LeRoy G Zweifel, di-

rector. *Contact.* John R Luedtke, coordinator. Provides search, referral, and information services on euthrophication and related aspects of the aging or maturing of lakes, reservoirs, and other inland bodies of water

WATER RESOURCES SCIENTIFIC INFORMATION CENTER. 18th and C Sts NW, Washington, DC 20240. **202-343-8435**

The center is operated by the Department of the Interior. It is a computer-based information retrieval and consulting service for scientists and technologists in the water resources field.

WORLD TRADE INFORMATION CENTER. Lobby, 1 World Trade Center, New York, NY 10048. **212-466-3063**

The center provides international business research through the use of a collection of worldwide directories, statistical data, tariffs, regulations, etc., and through searches on its own computerized data bank, "Interfile." It also performs searches on some 50 additional data bases, including the New York Times Information Bank, the Marine Information System, and the data banks accessible through SDC and Lockheed Dialog.

WORLD WIDE INFORMATION SERVICES, INC. 660 1st Ave, New York, NY 10016. **212-679-7240.** Richard W Hubbell, president. Night line: **212-677-8358.**

WWIS was formed by newsmen who lost their jobs as a result of the 1958 merger of United Press and International News Service into UPI. It now provides research and investigative services primarily to the business community from offices throughout the world, through an arrangement in which it says it can call on the services of some 14,000 journalists, whom it catalogues by their specialties. The service is available for fees beginning at $1000.

TOOLS AND SPECIAL SERVICES

CLIPPING BUREAUS

Clipping bureaus are extremely useful services for in-depth research over a long period of time—even in these days of computerized data bases. The cost can run as little as $30 a month plus a charge for each item clipped.

ALLEN'S CLIPPING BUREAU. 657 Mission St, San Francisco, CA 94105. **213-392-2353**

AMERICAN PRESS CLIPPING SERVICE, INC. 119 Nassau, New York, NY 10038. **212-W02-3797**

ATP CLIPPING BUREAU. 5 Beekman St, New York, NY 10038. **212-349-1177**

BACON'S. 14 E Jackson Blvd, Chicago, IL. 60604. **312-922-8419.** Robert H Bacon, Jr, president. Operates Bacon's Clipping Bureau, Bacon's Publishing Co (publishers of *Bacon's Publicity Directories*), and Bacon's Direct Mail Services, Inc.

BURRELLE'S PRESS CLIPPING SERVICE. 75 E Northfield Ave, Livingston, NJ 07039. **800-631-1160.** Arthur V Wynne or Robert V Waggoner, partners, **201-992-6600.** Reads all US daily and weekly newspapers plus 4000 magazines and trade journals for press clipping; also does TV monitoring

LUCE PRESS CLIPPINGS. 420 Lexington Ave, New York, NY 10017. **212-889-6711**

NAMES IN THE NEWS, INC. 31 E 28th St, New York, NY 10016. **212-889-1850**

DETECTIVE AGENCIES

PINKERTON'S, INC. 100 Church St, New York, NY 10007. **212-285-4800.** William C Linn, vice-president, labor, public, and stockholders relations, **212-285-4860.** The largest private detective and security service in the US.

BURNS INTERNATIONAL SECURITY SERVICES, INC. 320 Old Briarcliff Rd,

Briarcliff Manor, NY 10510. **914-762-1000.** Edward W Hyde, president. Ashley W Burner, director, marketing services. Night line: **203-762-7543.** A full-service private security company—guards, investigations, electronics, crowd control at spectator events, management consulting—with 86 branches in the US; "confidential nature of business requires initial clearance through Mr. Burner"

WACKENHUT. 3280 Ponce de Leon Blvd, Coral Gables, FL. 33134. **305-445-1481.** George Wackenhut, president. Lawrence Burnett, vice-president. The third largest security and investigative firm in the US.

LECTURE BUREAUS

AMERICAN PROGRAM BUREAU. 850 Boylston St, Chestnut Hill, MA 02617. **617-731-0500**

KEEDICK LECTURE BUREAU. 475 5th Ave, New York, NY 10017. **212-683-5627**

LEIGH LECTURE BUREAU, INC. 1185 Avenue of the Americas, New York, NY 10036. **212-869-8430**

TELEPHONE ANSWERING SERVICE

NATIONAL COMMUNICATIONS CENTER. 3939 Cambridge Rd, Cameron Park, CA 95682. **800-824-5120** (except California). **800-852-7711** (California)

A national, toll-free answering service that works as follows. For $20 a month, the client purchases a locator service, and leaves word, over the toll-free number, where and when he or she can be reached. Callers also call the toll-free number and receive the information. For $40 a month, the service takes messages from people who call for the client, and passes them on when the client calls in. For $60 a month, both services are available. Special arrangements are made for an entire company to use the service at different rates.

MISCELLANY

EXECUTIVE JET AVIATION. PO Box 19707, Columbus, OH 43219. **614-237-0363.** Jet charters

NY SHOPPING AND DINING INFORMATION, INC. 113 University Pl, New York, NY 10003. **212-675-0900**

WESTERN UNION FYI NEWS SERVICE

FYI NEWS SERVICE. 1 Lake St, Upper Saddle River, NJ 07458. **201-825-5103.** *Telex.* **10-4737.** *Contact* R McCluskie. Any Telex or TWX subscriber can, for a usage charge, obtain regular news summaries, in any or all of 21 subject areas, over his own machine

Telex users dial **8513**
TWX users east of Chicago dial **710-988-5956**
TWX users west of Chicago dial **910-221-2115**

After dialing and receiving the go-ahead, the subscriber enters the name of the news summary desired (the names are given in boldface capitals below).

NEWS. Latest news bulletins, updated hourly from 7:30 am to 8:30 pm

SPORTS. Latest sports news, updated hourly from 8 am to 12 midnight

FINANCE. Latest business bulletins, updated hourly from 9 am to 6:59 pm

MARKET. Latest stock market averages and activity, updated hourly from 11 am to market close at 5 pm with market commentary from 9 am to 10:59 am

ALL4. to request NEWS, SPORTS, FINANCE, and MARKET

CURRENCY. Foreign exchange and domestic money rates, updated every two hours from 9 am to 5 pm

SPECIAL. The big stories of the day, updated at 8 am, 1:30 pm, and 4:30 pm

WEATHER. Two-day forecast for 20 principal cities, updated at 8 am and 8 pm

METAL. Domestic copper, silver, and gold future prices from 10:45 am to 1 pm for metals open and 3:40 pm to 9:44 am for metals close; also London metal market from 9:45 am to 10:44 am for metals first session and 1:01 pm to 3:39 pm for metals second session

GRAIN. Wheat, corn, oats, and soybean commodity future prices from 11 am, updated at 1:30 pm and 3:35 pm, with commentary from 6:45 am to 10:59 am

LIVESTOCK. Cattle, live hog, pork belly, and egg future prices from 10:55 am, updated at 12:45 pm and 2:45 pm, with commentary from 6:45 pm to 10:59 pm

SUGAR. Sugar and coffee commodity future prices from 11:15 am, updated at 12:10 pm, 12:45 pm, 2 pm, and 4:15 pm

GOLD. Gold future prices from 10:30 am, updated at 1:30 pm and 3:40 pm

LUMBER. Lumber and plywood future prices from 11:45 am, updated at 1:30 pm and 3:40 pm

CASH. Cash prices on 22 agricultural products from US Department of Agriculture, updated at 4:30 pm

CONGRESS. Daily report on legislation affecting business from the US Chamber of Commerce at 10 am

Ski Reports in Season

EASTSKI. Ski reports from Pennsylvania, New Jersey, and New York
MIDSKI. Midwestern ski reports from 1 pm
NESKI. New England ski report
ROCKSKI. Rocky Mountain ski reports from 1 pm
WESTSKI. West Coast ski reports from 1 pm

DIAL-A-NUMBER

The telephone company in New York has developed a novel way to increase revenues: a variety of recorded public service and entertainment messages on telephone lines that are not toll-free.

DIAL-A-JOKE (joke of the day by various comedians). **212-999-3838**
DOW JONES REPORT. 212-999-4141
HOROSCOPES-BY-PHONE (Jeanne Dixon).
Aries (Mar 21–Apr 19), **212-936-5050**.
Taurus (Apr 20–May 20), **212-936-5151**.
Gemini (May 21–June 20), **212-936-5252**.
Cancer (June 21–July 22), **212-936-5353**.
Leo (July 23–Aug 22), **212-936-5454**.
Virgo (Aug 23–Sept 22), **212-936-5656**.
Libra (Sept 23–Oct 22), **212-936-5757**.
Scorpio (Oct 23–Nov 21), **212-936-5858**.
Sagittarius (Nov 22–Dec 21), **212-936-5959**.
Capricorn (Dec 22–Jan 19), **212-936-6060**.
Aquarius (Jan 20–Feb 18), **212-936-6161**.
Pisces (Feb 19–Mar 20), **212-936-6262**

MUSICLINE (described as "entertainment at home," including interviews with rock stars, commentary on albums, etc). **212-936-4545**

THE EMPIRE STAKES (NEW YORK STATE WEEKLY LOTTERY). 212-999-6868

SPORTS PHONE (major league results updated several times daily, features, and interviews). **212-999-1313**

OTB RESULTS (thoroughbred and harness racing results from "just about every track OTB covers." Lists scratches, order of finish, and payouts). **212-999-2121**

NEW YORK REPORT (commuter traffic and emergency messages). **212-999-1234**

GOVERNMENT DOCUMENTS

GOVERNMENT PRINTING OFFICE

Published documents, records, monographs, books, maps, periodicals, and similar material issued by the federal Government Printing Office can be obtained through the mail by writing to Superintendant of Documents, US Government Printing Office, Washington, DC 20402.

Orders can be placed by phone, then picked up five days later at the main bookstore in Washington, DC; call **202-783-3238.**

Either way it's a difficult procedure. Mail service is exceedingly slow; many months may pass before an order is fulfilled. Bookstores are frequently out of stock on some items, and many items go out of print quickly. Journalists may get better service through the Special Assistant to the Public Printer. *See* THE FEDERAL GOVERNMENT, Independent Agencies, GPO for contact information.

Publications that are in high demand, and whose rapid public dissemination is essential, can usually be found at the GPO bookstores located around the country (see the list that follows). The surest source of government documents are Regional Depository Libraries; *see* LIBRARIES for full details.

GOVERNMENT PRINTING OFFICE BOOKSTORES

ATLANTA. Rm 100, Federal Bldg, 275 Peachtree St NE, Atlanta, GA 30303. **404-221-6947**

BIRMINGHAM. Rm 102A, 2121 Bldg, 2121 8th Ave N, Birmingham, AL 35203. **205-229-1056**

BOSTON. Rm G25, Federal Bldg, Sudbury St, Boston, MA 02203. **617-223-6071**

CHICAGO. Rm 1463, Federal Bldg, 219 S Dearborn St, Chicago, IL 60604. **312-353-5133**

CLEVELAND. 1st Floor, Federal Bldg, 1240 E 9th St, Cleveland, OH 44114. **216-522-4922**

COLUMBUS. Rm 207, Federal Bldg, 200 N High St, Columbus, OH 43215. **614-469-6956**

DALLAS. Rm 1C46, Federal Bldg, 1100 Commerce St, Dallas, TX 75242. **214-749-1541**

DENVER. RM 1421, Federal Bldg, 1961 Stout St, Denver, CO 80202. **303-837-3964**

DETROIT. Suite 160, Federal Bldg, 477 Michigan Ave, Detroit, MI 48226. **313-226-7816**

HOUSTON. 9319 Gulf Fwy, Houston, TX 77017. **713-226-5453**

JACKSONVILLE. Rm 158, Federal Bldg, 400 W Bay St, Jacksonville, FL 32202. **904-791-3801**

KANSAS CITY. Rm 144, Federal Bldg, 601 E 12th St, Kansas City, MO 64106. **816-374-2160**

LOS ANGELES. Rm 2039, Federal Bldg, 300 N Los Angeles St, Los Angeles, CA 90012. **213-688-5841**

MILWAUKEE. Rm 190, Federal Bldg, 519 E Wisconsin Ave, Milwaukee, WI 53202. **414-291-1304**

NEW YORK. Rm 110, 26 Federal Plz, New York, NY 10007. **212-264-3825**

PHILADELPHIA. Rm 1214 Federal Bldg, 600 Arch St, Philadelphia, PA 19106. **215-597-0677**

PUEBLO. Public Documents Distribution Center, Pueblo Industrial Park, Pueblo, CO 81009. **303-544-3142**

SAN FRANCISCO. Rm 1023, Federal Bldg, 450 Golden Gate Ave, San Francisco, CA 94102. **415-556-6657**

SEATTLE. Rm 194, Federal Bldg, 915 2nd Ave, Seattle, WA 98174. **206-442-4270**

WASHINGTON, DC. *Main GPO.* **202-275-2091.** *USIA Bldg.* **202-632-9668.** *Pentagon.* **202-557-1821.** *Commerce Department.* **202-377-3527.** *State Department.* **202-632-1437**

OTHER GOVERNMENT DOCUMENT SOURCES

AERONAUTICAL CHARTS. NATIONAL OCEAN SURVEY, DISTRIBUTION DIVISION (C-44), RIVERDALE, MD 20804. **301-436-6990.** Also: National Ocean Survey, Chart Sales and Control Data Office, 632 Sixth Ave, Room 405, Anchorage, AK 99501. **907-265-4470.**

CONGRESSIONAL PUBLICATIONS. Secretary of the Senate, The Capitol, Washington, DC 20510. Clerk, House of Representatives, The Capitol, Washington, DC 20515

GAO REPORTS. General Accounting Office, Room 4522, 441 G St NW, Washington, DC 20548. **202-275-6241**

MINERAL INFORMATION. Office of Mineral Information, Bureau of Mines,

2401 E St NW, Washington, DC 20241. **202-634-1004**

NATIONAL ARCHIVES PUBLICATIONS. General Services Administration, Publication Sales Branch (NEPS-G) Washington, DC 20408. **202-523-3164**

NAUTICAL CHARTS. Defense Mapping Agency Depot, Clearfield, UT 84016. **801-777-4436.** Also: Defense Mapping Agency Depot, 5801 Tabor Ave, Philadelphia, PA 19120. **215-697-4262**

NTIS REPORTS AND OTHER GOVERNMENT DOCUMENTS HANDLED BY NTIS. (see also, RESEARCH AND INFORMATION SERVICES): National Technical Information Services, 5285 Port Royal Rd, Springfield, VA 22161. **703-321-8543** or **202-724-3383**

SMITHSONIAN PUBLICATIONS. Smithsonian Institution Press, Publications Distribution Section, 1111 N Capitol St, Washington, DC 20002. **202-381-5021**

TOPOGRAPHIC MAPS. US. Geological Survey, 1200 S Eads St, Arlington, VA 22202, **703-557-2751**

LIBRARIES

REGIONAL DEPOSITORY LIBRARIES

Regional depository libraries are those that have contracted with the Government Printing Office (GPO) to receive and retain one copy of every government publication, and are required to do so. Many other large libraries are designated as depository libraries, meaning that they are given the opportunity to receive all government publications, but are allowed to pick and choose.

This arrangement has been made, according to the GPO, because of chronic difficulties in purchasing documents that may be out of stock or out of print. A complete list of the depository libraries can be obtained from the US Government Printing Office, Public Documents Department, Washington, DC 20402, or from the special assistant to the public printer (*see*

GPO details in THE FEDERAL GOVERNMENT). This publication is not usually out of stock, but it was, in late 1977, out of date.

Alabama

UNIVERSITY OF ALABAMA. Amelia Gayle Gorgas Library. Box S, University, 35486. **205-348-6044**

AUBURN UNIVERSITY AT MONTGOMERY LIBRARY. Montgomery, 36092. **205-279-9110,** Ext. 251. Barbara W Dekle, documents librarian

Arizona

DEPARTMENT OF ADMINISTRATION, LIBRARY, ARCHIVES, AND PUBLIC

RECORDS DIVISION. Capitol Bldg, Phoenix, 85007. **602-271-3701**

UNIVERSITY OF ARIZONA LIBRARY. Tucson, 85721. **602-884-2101**

California

CALIFORNIA STATE LIBRARY. Library-Courts Bldg, Box 2037, Sacramento, 95809. **916-445-4374.** Ethel S Crockett, state librarian, **916-445-2585**

Colorado

UNIVERSITY OF COLORADO LIBRARIES. Norlin Library. Boulder, 80302. **303-492-7159**

DENVER PUBLIC LIBRARY. 1357 Broadway, Denver, 80203. **303-573-5152**

Connecticut

CONNECTICUT STATE LIBRARY. 231 Capitol Ave, Hartford, 06115. **203-566-4971**

Florida

UNIVERSITY OF FLORIDA LIBRARIES. Documents Department, Library W. Gainesville, 32611. **904-392-0367**

Idaho

UNIVERSITY OF IDAHO LIBRARY. Moscow, 83843. **208-885-6344**

Illinois

ILLINOIS STATE LIBRARY. Centennial Bldg, Springfield, 62756. **217-782-5185**

Indiana

INDIANA STATE LIBRARY. 140 N Senate Ave, Indianapolis, 46204. **317-633-5440**

Iowa

UNIVERSITY OF IOWA LIBRARIES. Iowa City, 52242. **319-353-3318**

Kentucky

UNIVERSITY OF KENTUCKY. Margaret I King Library. Lexington, 40506. **606-275-2639**

Louisiana

LOUISIANA STATE UNIVERSITY LIBRARY. Baton Rouge, 70803. **504-388-2570**

LOUISIANA TECH UNIVERSITY. Prescott Memorial Library. Ruston, 71270. **318-257-4962**

Maine

UNIVERSITY OF MAINE. Raymond H Fogler Library. Orono, 04473. **207-581-7178**

Maryland

UNIVERSITY OF MARYLAND. McKeldin Library. College Park, 20742. **301-454-3034**

Massachusetts

BOSTON PUBLIC LIBRARY. Copley Sq, 666 Boylston St (Box 286), Boston, 02117. **617-536-5400**

Michigan

DETROIT PUBLIC LIBRARY. 5201 Woodward Ave, Detroit, 48202. **313-833-1409**

MICHIGAN STATE LIBRARY. 735 E Michigan Ave, Lansing, 48913. **517-373-0640**

Minnesota

UNIVERSITY OF MINNESOTA. O Meredith Wilson Library. Minneapolis, 55455. **612-373-7813**

Mississippi

UNIVERSITY OF MISSISSIPPI LIBRARY. University, 38677. **601-232-7091**

Montana

UNIVERSITY OF MONTANA LIBRARY. Missoula, 59812. **406-243-6700**

Nebraska

NEBRASKA PUBLICATIONS CLEARINGHOUSE. Nebraska Library Commission. 1420 P St, Lincoln, 68508. **402-471-2045**

Nevada

UNIVERSITY OF NEVADA LIBRARY. Reno, 89557. **702-784-6579** or **6570**. Government Publications Department. Joan Chambers, Librarian

New Jersey

NEWARK PUBLIC LIBRARY. 5 Washington St, Newark, 07101. **201-733-7813**

New Mexico

UNIVERSITY OF NEW MEXICO. Zimmerman Library. Albuquerque, 87106. **505-277-5441**

NEW MEXICO STATE LIBRARY. PO Box 1629, Sante Fe, 87503. **505-827-2033**

New York

NEW YORK STATE LIBRARY. Washington Ave, Albany, 12234. **518-474-5563**

North Carolina

UNIVERSITY OF NORTH CAROLINA. Louis Round Wilson Library. Drawer 870, Chapel Hill, 27514. **919-933-1151**

North Dakota

NORTH DAKOTA STATE UNIVERSITY LIBRARY. Fargo, 58102. **701-237-8876**

Ohio

STATE LIBRARY OF OHIO. 65 S Front St, Columbus, 43215. **614-466-2693**

Oklahoma

OKLAHOMA DEPARTMENT OF LIBRARIES. 200 NE 18, Oklahoma City, 73105. **405-521-2502.** Doris Cornell, public information officer. Maryellen Trautman, US Government documents librarian

Oregon

PORTLAND STATE UNIVERSITY LIBRARY. 934 SW Harrison St, Portland, 97207. **503-229-3673**

Pennsylvania

STATE LIBRARY OF PENNSYLVANIA. Box 1601, Walnut St and Commonwealth Ave, Harrisburg, 17126. **717-787-2646**

Texas

TEXAS STATE LIBRARY. 1201 Brazos St, Capitol Station, Austin, 78711. **512-475-2996**

TEXAS TECH UNIVERSITY LIBRARY. Box 4079, Lubbock, 79409. **806-742-2268**

Utah

UTAH STATE UNIVERSITY. Merrill Library and Learning Resources Program. College Hill, Logan, 84322. **801-752-4100**

Virginia

UNIVERSITY OF VIRGINIA. Alderman Library. Charlottesville, 22901. **804-924-3133**

Washington

WASHINGTON STATE LIBRARY. Olympia, 98504. **206-753-4027**

West Virginia

WEST VIRGINIA UNIVERSITY LIBRARY. Morgantown, 26506. **304-293-5440**

Wisconsin

STATE HISTORICAL SOCIETY LIBRARY. 816 State St, Madison, 53706. **608-262-4347**

MILWAUKEE PUBLIC LIBRARY. 814 W Wisconsin Ave, Milwaukee, 53233. **414-278-3000.** Henry E Bates, Jr, city librarian. Ruth Goren, publications; **414-278-3031**

Wyoming

WYOMING STATE LIBRARY. Supreme Court and Library Bldg, Cheyenne, 82002. **307-777-7281**

MAJOR NORTH AMERICAN RESEARCH LIBRARIES

Common or university name is given first, followed by proper name.

ALABAMA UNIVERSITY LIBRARY. Amelia Gayle Gorgas Library. Box S, University, AL 35486. **205-348-5298.** 1,162,712 volumes

ALBERTA UNIVERSITY LIBRARY. Saint-Jean Library. 8406 91 Rue, Edmonton, Alberta, Canada. **403-466-2196.** 1,685,409 volumes

ARIZONA STATE LIBRARY. 1700 W Washington St, Phoenix, AZ 85007. **602-271-3501.** 1,060,080 volumes

ARIZONA UNIVERSITY LIBRARY. Tucson, AZ 85721. **901-884-2101.** 964,427 volumes

BOSTON PUBLIC LIBRARY. 666 Boylston St, Boston, MA 02117. **617-536-5400.** 3,863,786 volumes

BRIGHAM YOUNG UNIVERSITY LIBRARY. Harold B Lee Library. 3080 HBLL, University Hill, Provo, UT 84602. **801-374-1211** Ext, 2905. 1,400,241 volumes

BRITISH COLUMBIA UNIVERSITY LIBRARY. 2075 Wesbrook Mall, Vancouver, BC V6T1W5, Canada. **604-228-3871.** 1,851,380 volumes

BROWN UNIVERSITY LIBRARY. Providence, RI 02912. **401-863-2162.** 1,527,376 volumes

CALIFORNIA STATE UNIVERSITY AT LOS ANGELES LIBRARY. John F Kennedy Memorial Library. 5151 State University Dr, Los Angeles, CA 90032. **213-224-2201.** 690,000 volumes

UNIVERSITY OF CALIFORNIA AT BERKELEY LIBRARY. University Library. Berkeley, CA 94720. **415-642-3773.** 4,917,330 volumes

UNIVERSITY OF CALIFORNIA AT DAVIS LIBRARY. General Library. Davis, CA 95616. **916-752-2110.** 1,299,500 volumes

UNIVERSITY OF CALIFORNIA AT SAN DIEGO LIBRARY. James S Coply Library. Alcala Park, San Diego, CA 92110. **714-291-6480.** 178,753 volumes

UNIVERSITY OF CALIFORNIA AT SANTA BARBARA LIBRARY. Santa Barbara Library. Santa Barbara, CA 93106. **805-961-2674.** 1,100,000 volumes

CASE WESTERN RESERVE LIBRARY. 11161 E Blvd, Cleveland, OH 44106. **216-368-2992.** 1,558,670 volumes. Press contact Sally Brickman, **216-368-2988.** Night line: **216-368-3506**

CENTER FOR RESEARCH LIBRARIES. 5721 Cottage Grove Ave, Chicago, IL 60637. **312-955-4545.** 3,000,000 volumes

CHICAGO UNIVERSITY LIBRARY. Joseph Regenstein Library. 1100 E 57th St, Chicago, IL 60637. **312-753-2977.** 3,622,300 volumes

CINCINNATI UNIVERSITY LIBRARY. Main Library. Cincinnati, OH 45221. **513-475-2535.** 1,009,000 volumes

COLUMBIA UNIVERSITY, LIBRARY. University Library. 535 W 114th St, New York, NY 10027. **212-280-2241.** 4,466,911 volumes

UNIVERSITY OF CONNECTICUT LIBRARY. Greater Hartford Campus. 1800 Asylum Ave, W Hartford, CT. 06117. **203-523-4841**

CORNELL UNIVERSITY LIBRARIES. Ithaca, NY 14853. **607-256-4144.** 3,979,581 volumes

JOHN CRERAR LIBRARY. 35 W 33rd St, Chicago, IL 60616. **312-225-2526.** 1,155,000 volumes

DARTMOUTH COLLEGE LIBRARY. Hanover, NH 03755. **603-646-2235.** 1,240,000 volumes

UNIVERSITY OF DENVER LIBRARY. Penrose Library. 2150 E Evans, Denver, CO. 80208. **303-753-2007.** 1,241,000 volumes

DUKE UNIVERSITY LIBRARY. William R Perkins Library. Durham, NC 27706. **919-684-2034.** 2,622,167 volumes

UNIVERSITY OF FLORIDA LIBRARIES. Gainesville, FL 32611. **904-392-0341.** 1,756,441 volumes total

FLORIDA STATE UNIVERSITY ·LIBRARY. Robert Manning Strozier Library. Tallahassee, FL 32306. **904-644-5211.** 1,126,075 volumes

GEORGETOWN UNIVERSITY LIBRARY. Joseph Mark Lauinger Library. 37th and 0 Sts NW, Washington, DC 20057. **202-625-4173.** 950,000 volumes

UNIVERSITY OF GEORGIA LIBRARIES. Athens, GA 30602. **404-542-2716.** 1,719,178 volumes

HARVARD UNIVERSITY LIBRARY. Cambridge, MA 02138. **617-495-2401.** 9,383,255 volumes

HOWARD UNIVERSITY LIBRARY. Founders Library. 500 Howard Pl NW, Washington, DC 20059. **202-636-7234.** 837,055 volumes

UNIVERSITY OF ILLINOIS AT URBANA–CHAMPAIGN LIBRARY. 230 Library, Wright St, Urbana, IL 61801. **217-333-1031.** 5,494,786 volumes

UNIVERSITY OF INDIANA LIBRARY. University Library. 10th and Jordan Ave, Bloomington, IN 47401. **812-337-3403.** 2,762,582 volumes

UNIVERSITY OF IOWA LIBRARIES. Iowa City, IA 52242. **319-353-4450.** 2,055,581 volumes

IOWA STATE UNIVERSITY LIBRARY. Ames, IA 50011. **515-294-1442.** 1,112,000 volumes

JOHN HOPKINS UNIVERSITY LIBRARY. Milton S Eisenhower Library. Baltimore, MD 21218. **301-336-3000.** 1,717,534 volumes

JOINT UNIVERSITY, NASHVILLE, LIBRARY. 419 21st Ave, Nashville, TN. 37203. **615-322-2834.** 1,301,631 volumes

UNIVERSITY OF KANSAS LIBRARY. Watson Memorial Library. Lawrence, KS 66054. **913-864-3601.** 1,500,158 volumes

LIBRARY OF CONGRESS. Washington, DC 20540. **202-426-5108.** 72,605,909 items, 18,013,089 volumes and pamphlets. See also THE FEDERAL GOVERNMENT, Independent Agencies, Library of Congress

LINDA HALL LIBRARY. 5109 Cherry St, Kansas City, MO 64110. **816-363-4600.** 430,000 volumes

LOUISIANA STATE UNIVERSITY LIBRARY. Baton Rouge, LA 70803. **504-388-2217.** 1,332,891 volumes

MCGILL UNIVERSITY LIBRARIES. 3459 McTavish St, Montreal, Que H3A 1Y1, Canada. **514-392-4948.** 3,600,000 items

UNIVERSITY OF MARYLAND LIBRARY. College Park, MD 20742. **301-454-3011.** 1,231,540 volumes

UNIVERSITY OF MASSACHUSETTS LIBRARY. Amherst Library. Amherst, MA 01003. **413-545-0284.** 1,532,850 volumes

MIT (MASSACHUSETTS INSTITUTE OF TECHNOLOGY) LIBRARY. Cambridge, MA 02139. **617-253-5651.** 1,234,500 volumes

MICHIGAN STATE LIBRARY. 735 E Michigan Ave, East Lansing, MI 48824. **517-355-1855.** 1,003,000 volumes

MICHIGAN UNIVERSITY LIBRARY. Ann Arbor, MI 48109. **313-764-9356.** 3,924,498 volumes

MINNESOTA UNIVERSITY LIBRARY. O Meredith Wilson Library. Minneapolis, MN. 55455. **612-633-4311.** 3,046,982 volumes

MISSOURI UNIVERSITY LIBRARY. Elmer Ellis Library. Columbia, MO 65201. **314-882-4786.** 1,793,896 volumes

NATIONAL AGRICULTURAL LIBRARY. 10301 Baltimore Blvd, Beltsville, MD 20705. **301-344-3778.** 1,548,028 volumes

NATIONAL LIBRARY OF CANADA. 395 Wellingham St, Ottawa, Ont, Canada. **613-995-9481.** 1,270,000 volumes

NATIONAL LIBRARY OF MEDICINE. 8600 Rockville Pike, Bethesda, MD 20014. **301-496-6095.** 1,400,000 volumes

NEBRASKA UNIVERSITY LIBRARY. Don L Love Library. Lincoln, NE 68588. **402-472-2526.** 1,208,451 volumes

NEW YORK PUBLIC LIBRARY. Astor, Lenox, and Tilden Foundations Library. 5th Ave and 42nd St, New York, NY 10018. **212-790-6262.** 8,898,363 volumes

NEW YORK STATE LIBRARY. 31 Washington Ave, New York, NY 12234. **212-474-5930.** 5,000,000 volumes

NEW YORK UNIVERSITY LIBRARY. Elmer Holmes Bobst Library. 70 Washington Sq S, New York, NY 10012. **212-598-2484.** 1,692,000 volumes

NEW YORK, STATE UNIVERSITY OF. See State University of New York

NORTHWESTERN UNIVERSITY LIBRARY. 1935 Sheridan Rd, Evanston, IL 60201. **312-492-7640.** *Information.* **312-492-7658.** 1,947,915 volumes

NOTRE DAME UNIVERSITY LIBRARY. Notre Dame, IN 46556. **219-283-6258.** 1,220,854 volumes

OHIO STATE UNIVERSITY LIBRARY. William Oxley Thompson Memorial Library. 1858 Neil Hall, Columbus, OH 43210. **614-422-6151.** 1,516,566 volumes

OKLAHOMA UNIVERSITY LIBRARY. William Bennett Bizzell Memorial Library. 401 W Brooks St, Norman, OK 73069. **405-325-2611.** 1,141,081 volumes

OREGON UNIVERSITY LIBRARY. Eugene, OR 97403. **503-686-3056.** 1,303,375 volumes

PENNSYLVANIA UNIVERSITY LIBRARIES. 3420 Walnut St, Philadelphia, PA 19174. **215-243-7091.** 2,700,000 volumes

PENNSYLVANIA STATE UNIVERSITY LIBRARIES. Fred Lewis Pattee Library. University Park, PA 16802. **814-865-0401.** 1,476,610 volumes

PITTSBURGH UNIVERSITY LIBRARY. Hillman Library. Pittsburgh, PA 15260. **412-624-4000.** 1,824,472 volumes

PRINCETON UNIVERSITY LIBRARY. Princeton, NJ 08540. **609-452-3180.** 2,910,461 volumes

PURDUE UNIVERSITY LIBRARY. Stewart Ctr, W, Lafayette, IN 47907. **812-749-2571.** 1,300,000 volumes

RICE UNIVERSITY LIBRARY. Fondren Library. 6100 S Main (PO Box 1892), Houston, TX. 77001. **713-527-4022.** 875,877 volumes; 1,000,000 microforms.

ROCHESTER UNIVERSITY LIBRARY. Rush Rhees Library. Rochester, NY 14627. **716-275-4461.** 1,700,000 volumes

RUTGERS UNIVERSITY LIBRARY. College Ave, New Brunswick, NJ 08901. **201-932-7505.** 1,346,460 volumes

ST LOUIS UNIVERSITY LIBRARY. Pius XII Memorial Library. 3655 W Pine Blvd, St Louis, MO 63108. **314-535-3300** Ext 386. 600,000 volumes

SMITHSONIAN INSTITUTION LIBRARIES. Constitution Ave at 10th St NW, Washington, DC 20560. **202-381-5421.** 900,000 volumes

SOUTHERN ILLINOIS UNIVERSITY LIBRARY. Delyte W Morris Library. Carbondale, IL 62091. **618-453-2522.** 1,800,000 volumes

STANFORD UNIVERSITY LIBRARY. University and Coordinate Libraries. Stanford, CA 94305. **415-497-2016.** 4,092,362 volumes

STATE UNIVERSITY OF NEW YORK AT BUFFALO LIBRARY. Lockwood Memorial Library. 3435 Main St, Buffalo, NY 14214. **716-831-2505.** 1,629,078 volumes

SYRACUSE UNIVERSITY LIBRARY. Ernst S Bird Library. 222 Waverly Ave, Syracuse, NY 12310. **315-423-2575.** 1,009,000 volumes

TEMPLE UNIVERSITY LIBRARY. Samuel Paley Library. Berks and 13th Sts, Philadelphia, PA 19122. **215-787-8231.** 1,247,261 volumes

TENNESSEE UNIVERSITY LIBRARY. James D Hopkins Library, Knoxville, TN. 37916. **615-974-0111.** 1,229,423 volumes

UNIVERSITY OF TEXAS AT AUSTIN GENERAL LIBRARIES. Austin, TX. 78712. **512-471-3811.** 3,878,535 volumes

TEXAS A & M UNIVERSITY LIBRARIES. College Station, TX. 77843. **713-845-6111.** 1,100,000 volumes

TORONTO UNIVERSITY LIBRARY. Toronto, Ont, Canada. **416-978-2294.** 273,000 volumes

TULANE UNIVERSITY LIBRARY. Howard-Tilton Memorial Library, New Orleans, LA 70118. **504-865-5131.** 1,217,667 volumes

UTAH UNIVERSITY LIBRARY. Marriot Library. Salt Lake City, UT 84112. **801-581-8558.** 1,130,000 volumes

VIRGINIA UNIVERSITY LIBRARY. Alderman Library. Charlottsville, VA 22901. **804-924-3026.** 2,006,454 volumes

WASHINGTON UNIVERSITY LIBRARIES. Seattle, WA 98195.

206-543-1760. 2,982,308 volumes. Merle N Boylan, director

WASHINGTON STATE UNIVERSITY LIBRARY. Pullman, WA 99164. **509-335-4557**

WASHINGTON UNIVERSITY, ST LOUIS, LIBRARY. John M Olin Library. Skinker and Lindell Blvds, St Louis, MO 63130. **314-863-1000.** 1,543,423 volumes

WAYNE STATE UNIVERSITY LIBRARY. G Flint Purdy Library. Detroit, MI 48202. **313-577-4020.** 1,759,000 volumes

WISCONSIN UNIVERSITY LIBRARY. Memorial Library. 728 State St, Madison, WI 53706. **608-262-3521.** 2,973,300 volumes

YALE UNIVERSITY LIBRARY. 120 High St, New Haven, CT 06520. **203-436-8335.** 6,518,848 volumes

THE FEDERAL GOVERNMENT

JUDICIAL BRANCH

UNITED STATES SUPREME COURT. US Supreme Court Bldg, 1 1st St NE, Washington, DC 20543. **202-252-3000**

Chief Justice. Warren E Burger (Circuit Justice for District of Columbia and Fourth Circuits)

Associate Justices. William J Brennan, Jr (First and Third Circuits), Harry A Blackmun (Eighth Circuit), Potter Stewart (Sixth Circuit), Lewis F Powell, Jr (Fifth Circuit), Byron R White (Tenth Circuit), William H Rehnquist (Ninth Circuit), Thurgood Marshall (Second Circuit), and John Paul Stevens (Seventh Circuit)

Clerk. Michael Rodak, Jr
Marshal. Alfred Wong
Librarian. Betty Clowers (acting)
Reporter of Decisions. Henry Putzel, Jr
Administrative Assistant to the Chief Justice. Mark Cannon

Director of Public Information. Barrett McGurn. **202-393-1640,** Ext 335 or 336, (h) **301-229-7439.** McGurn handles all Supreme Court media requests, including arranging for journalists to attend sessions of the Court.

ADMINISTRATIVE OFFICE OF THE US COURTS. US Supreme Court Bldg, 1 1st St NE, Washington, DC 20544. **202-633-6000**

Director. Rowland F Kirks
Deputy Director. William E Foley
Administrative Services Division. Robert H Hartzell, chief
Bankruptcy Division. Berkeley Wright, Jr, chief
Clerks Division. Robert J Pellicoro, chief
Criminal Justice Act Division. James E Macklin, Jr, chief
Financial Management Division. Edward V Garabedian, chief
Information Systems Division. William E Davis, chief
Magistrates Division. Peter G McCabe, chief
Management Review Division. James B Ueberhorst, chief
Personnel Division. R Glenn Johnson, chief
Probation Division. Wayne P Jackson, chief

The Administrative Office of the US Courts is responsible for the administration of all US courts except the Supreme Court, in addition to handling the personnel and operations of the courts, federal probation officers, public defenders, and magistrates. It is not, however, a centralized administra-

tion in the sense that much line control is exercised by the appellate and district courts over their own operations.

FEDERAL JUDICIAL CENTER. Dolley Madison House, 1520 H Street NW, Washington, DC 20005. **202-633-6011.**

Director. A Leo Levin.
Deputy Director. Joe L Ebersole
Division of Innovations and Systems Development. Charles W Nihan, director
Division of Research. William B Eldridge, director
Division of Continuing Education and Training. Kenneth C Crawford, director
Division of Interjudicial Affairs and Information Services. Alice L O'Donnell, director
Press Contacts. Sue Welsh, information specialist **202-633-6011.** Bob Williams, information officer, **202-633-6374**

The function of the Judicial Center is to research and study the operations of the US courts, and "to stimulate and coordinate such research and study on the part of other public and private persons and agencies," according to the US Government Manual. In consistency with that purpose, the Judicial Center, unlike most court agencies, has a public information staff. However, most of the appellate circuit courts (other than the First Circuit at this writing) now have a circuit executive whom Bob Williams describes as "a highly paid administrator whose responsibilities include public relations."

United States Courts of Appeals

DISTRICT OF COLUMBIA CIRCUIT. US Courthouse, 3rd St and Constitution Ave NW, Washington, DC 20001. **202-426-7118**
Chief Judge. David L Bazelon
Circuit Executive. Charles E Nelson. **202-426-2773**
Clerk. George A Fisher. **202-426-7017**
Senior Law Clerk. Michael E Smith. **202-472-4467**

FIRST CIRCUIT (Maine, Massachusetts, New Hampshire, Puerto Rico, Rhode Island). 104 Federal Bldg, Portland, ME 04112. **207-780-3291**
Chief Judge. Frank M Coffin
Clerk. Dana H Gallup. 1606 John W McCormack Post Office and Courthouse Bldg, Boston, MA 02109. **617-223-2888**
Senior Law Clerk. Marshall D Stein. 1606 John W McCormack Post Office and Courthouse Bldg, Boston, MA. 02109. **617-223-2898**

SECOND CIRCUIT (Connecticut, New York, Vermont). US Courthouse, Foley Sq, New York, NY 10007. **212-791-0915**
Chief Judge. Irving R Kaufman
Circuit Executive. Robert D. Lipscher. **212-791-0982**
Clerk. A Daniel Fusaro. **212-791-0103**
Senior Law Clerk. Nathaniel Fensterstock. **212-791-0981**

THIRD CIRCUIT (Delaware, New Jersey, Pennsylvania, Virgin Islands). Federal Bldg, 844 King St, Wilmington, DE 19801. **302-571-6159**
Chief Judge. Collins J Seitz
Circuit Executive. William A (Pat) Doyle. 20716 US Courthouse, 601 Market St, Philadelphia, PA 19106. **215-597-0718**
Clerk. Thomas F Quinn. **215-597-2995**
Senior Law Clerk. Louise Jacobs. **215-597-2378**

FOURTH CIRCUIT (Maryland, North Carolina, South Carolina, Virginia, West Virginia). Greenville, SC 29603. **803-235-8949**

Chief Judge. Clement F Haynsworth
Circuit Executive. Samuel W Phillips. US Courthouse, 10th and Main Sts (PO Box 6G), Richmond, VA 23214. **804-782-2184**
Clerk. William K Slate II. **804-782-2213**
Senior Law Clerk. Dulcey B Fowler. **804-782-2340**

FIFTH CIRCUIT (Alabama, Canal Zone, Florida, Georgia, Louisiana, Mississippi, Texas). 11501 US Courthouse, Houston, TX 77002. **713-226-4517**
Chief Judge. John R Brown
Circuit Executive. Thomas H Reese. Rm 109, 600 Camp St, New Orleans, LA 70130. **504-589-2730**
Clerk. Edward S Wadsworth. **504-589-6386**
Senior Law Clerk. Henry Hoppe. **504-589-6935**

SIXTH CIRCUIT (Kentucky, Michigan, Ohio, Tennessee). US Courthouse, Nashville, TN. 37203. **615-749-5447**
Chief Judge. Harry Phillips
Circuit Executive. James A Higgins. US Post Office and Courthouse Bldg, Cincinnati, OH 45202. **513-684-3135**
Clerk. John P Hehman. **513-684-2953**
Senior Law Clerk. Kenneth A Howe. **513-684-2953**

SEVENTH CIRCUIT (Illinois, Indiana, Wisconsin). US Courthouse and Federal Office Bldg, 219 S Dearborn St, Chicago, IL 60604. **312-435-5800**
Chief Judge. Thomas E Fairchild
Circuit Executive. Collins T Fitzpatrick. **312-435-5803**
Clerk. Thomas F Strubbe. **312-435-5842**
Senior Law Clerk. John W Cooley. **312-435-5805**

EIGHTH CIRCUIT (Arkansas, Iowa, Minnesota, Missouri, Nebraska, North Dakota, South Dakota). 837 US Courthouse, Kansas City, MO 64106. **816-842-9450**
Chief Judge. Floyd R Gibson
Circuit Executive. R Hanson Lawton. **816-374-2283**
Clerk. Robert C Tucker. 511 US Court and Customs House, St Louis, MO 63101. **314-425-5609**
Senior Law Clerk. Mary J Lyle. **314-425-5669**

NINTH CIRCUIT (Alaska, Arizona, California, Guam, Hawaii, Idaho, Montana, Nevada, Oregon, Washington). US Court of Appeals and Post Office Bldg, PO Box 547,

San Francisco, CA 94101. **415-556-6128**
Chief Judge. James R Browning
Clerk. Emil E Felfi, Jr. **415-556-7340**
Senior Law Clerk. John Naff. **415-556-5844**

TENTH CIRCUIT (Colorado, Kansas, New Mexico, Oklahoma, Utah, Wyoming). 4201 Federal Bldg, Salt Lake City, UT 84138. **801-524-5173**
Chief Judge. David T Lewis
Circuit Executive. Emory G Hatcher. 414 US Courthouse, Denver, CO 80294. **303-837-4118**
Clerk. Howard K Phillips. **303-837-3157**
Senior Law Clerk. Richard J Banta. **303-837-3157**

TEMPORARY EMERGENCY COURT OF APPEALS. US Courthouse, 3rd St and Constitution Ave NW, Washington, DC 20001. **202-426-7666**
Chief Judge. Edward Allen Tamm

Special Courts

US COURT OF CLAIMS. 717 Madison Pl NW, Washington, DC 20005. **202-633-7267**
Chief Trial Judge (Commissioner). Roald A Hogenson
Clerk. Frank T Peartree. **202-633-7257**

US COURT OF CUSTOMS AND PATENT APPEALS. 717 Madison Pl, NW, Washington, DC 20439. **202-783-4619**
Chief Judge. Howard T Markey
Clerk. George E Hutchinson. **202-633-7214**

US CUSTOMS COURT. 1 Federal Plz, New York, NY 10007. **212-264-2800**
Clerk. Joseph E Lombardi. **212-264-2814**

US COURT OF MILITARY APPEALS (not under the Administrative Office of the US courts). 450 E St NW, Washington, DC 20442. **202-693-1904**
Chief Judge. Albert B Fletcher, Jr
Court Executive. Ward Mundy. **202-693-1903**

United States District Courts

In each case the person named is the clerk of the court.

ALABAMA (NORTHERN). 311 Federal Courthouse, Birmingham, 35203. **205-254-1701.** James E Vandegrift

ALABAMA (MIDDLE). PO Box 711, Montgomery, 36101. **205-832-7308.** Jane P Gordon

ALABAMA (SOUTHERN). 213 US Courthouse and Custom House Bldg, Mobile, 36602. **205-690-2371.** William J O'Connor

ALASKA. Rm 166, US Courthouse, 605 W 4th Ave, Anchorage, 99501. **907-276-2650.** JoAnn Myres

ARIZONA. Rm 6218, Federal Bldg, Phoenix, 85025. **602-261-3341.** Wallace J Furstenau

ARKANSAS (EASTERN). PO Box 869, Little Rock, 72203. **501-378-5353.** Woodrow H McClellan

ARKANSAS (WESTERN). PO Box 1523, Fort Smith, 72902. **501-783-6833.** Pat L Graham, Jr

CALIFORNIA (NORTHERN). US Courthouse, PO Box 36060, San Francisco, 94102. **415-556-3031.** William L Whittaker

CALIFORNIA (EASTERN). 2546 US Courthouse, 650 Capitol Mall, Sacramento, 95814. **916-440-2171.** James R Grindstaff

CALIFORNIA, (CENTRAL). US Courthouse, 312 N Spring St, Los Angeles, 90012. **213-688-3535.** Edward M Kritzman

CALIFORNIA (SOUTHERN). Rm 1N20, US Courthouse, 940 Front St, San Diego, 92189. **714-293-5600.** William W Luddy

CANAL ZONE, DISTRICT COURT OF THE. Box 2006, Balboa Heights. **52-7675.** Doris L McClellan

COLORADO. Rm 145, US Courthouse, 1929 Stout St, Denver, 80294. **303-837-3433.** James R Manspeaker

CONNECTICUT. Federal Bldg, 141 Church St, New Haven, 06505. **203-432-2140.** Sylvester A Markowski, Jr

DELAWARE. Lockbox 18, Federal Bldg, 844 King St, Wilmington, 19801. **302-571-6170.** Evan L Barney

DISTRICT OF COLUMBIA. US Courthouse, 3rd St and Constitution Aves NW, Washington, 20001. **202-426-7226.** James F Davey

FLORIDA (NORTHERN). PO Box 958, Tallahassee, 32303. **904-222-8797.** Marvin S Waits

FLORIDA (MIDDLE). PO Box 53558, Jacksonville, 32201. **904-791-2297.** Wesley R Thies

FLORIDA (SOUTHERN). PO Box 010669, Flagler Station, Miami, 33101. **305-350-5212.** Joseph I Bogart

GEORGIA (NORTHERN). Rm 100, US Courthouse, 56 Forsyth St NW, Atlanta, 30303. **404-221-6496.** Ben H Carter

GEORGIA (MIDDLE). PO Box 128, Macon, 31202. **912-742-2161.** Walter F Doyle

GEORGIA (SOUTHERN). PO Box 8286, Savannah, 31402. **912-232-4321,** Ext 281. Louis E Aenchbacher

GUAM, DISTRICT COURT OF. PO Box DC, Agana 96910. **Guam 472-6041.** Edward L G Aguon

HAWAII. PO Box 3193, Honolulu, 96801. **808-546-3162.** Walter A Y H Chinn

IDAHO. US Courthouse, 550 W Fort St (PO Box 039), Boise, 83724. **208-384-1361.** Gerold L Clapp

ILLINOIS (NORTHERN). US Courthouse, 219 S Dearborn St, Chicago, 60604. **312-435-5670.** H Stuart Cunningham

ILLINOIS (EASTERN). PO Box 786, Danville, 61832. **217-442-0402.** John P Ovall

ILLINOIS (SOUTHERN). PO Box 238, Peoria, 61601. **309-671-7117.** Robert J Kauffman

INDIANA (NORTHERN). Federal Bldg, 507 State St (PO Box 645), Hammond 46325. **219-932-5500,** Ext 235. Francis T Grandys

INDIANA (SOUTHERN). Rm 105, US Courthouse, 46 E Ohio St, Indianapolis, 46204. **317-269-6679.** William A Heede

IOWA (NORTHERN). Federal Bldg (PO Box 4411), Cedar Rapids, 52407. **319-366-2411,** Ext 466. Kenneth W Fuelling

IOWA (SOUTHERN). Rm 200, US Courthouse, E 1st and Walnut Sts, Des Moines, 50309. **515-284-4381.** James R Rosenbaum

KANSAS. PO Box 2201, Wichita, 67201. **316-267-6311,** Ext 491. Arthur G Johnson

KENTUCKY (EASTERN). PO Box 741, Lexington, 40501. **606-233-2503.** Davis T McGarvey

KENTUCKY (WESTERN). 230 US Courthouse Bldg, Louisville, 40202. **502-582-5156.** Jesse W Grider

LOUISIANA (EASTERN). Chambers C-151, US Courthouse, 500 Camp St, New Orleans, 70130. **504-589-2946.** Nelson B Jones

LOUISIANA (MIDDLE). Rm 308, Federal Bldg and US Courthouse, 707 Florida Ave, Baton Rouge, 70801. **504-387-0181,** Ext 321. Charles H Banta

LOUISIANA (WESTERN). PO Box 106, Shreveport, 71161. **318-226-5273.** Robert H Shemwell

MAINE. 156 Federal St (PO Box 4820), Portland, 04112. **207-780-3357.** Elizabeth Sax

MARYLAND. US Courthouse, 101 W Lombard St, Baltimore, 21202. **301-962-2600.** Paul R Schlitz

MASSACHUSETTS. McCormack Post Office and Courthouse Bldg, Boston, 02109. **617-223-2845.** George F McGrath

MICHIGAN (EASTERN). Rm 133, Federal Bldg, Detroit, 48226. **313-226-7060.** Henry R Hanssen

MICHIGAN (WESTERN). 458 Federal Bldg, 110 Michigan St NW, Grand Rapids, 49503. **616-456-2381.** Gerald H Liefer

MINNESOTA. 708 Federal Bldg, 316 N Robert St, St Paul, 55101. **612-725-7179.** Harry A Sieben

MISSISSIPPI (NORTHERN). PO Box 727, Oxford, 38655. **601-234-1971.** Norman L Gillespie

MISSISSIPPI (SOUTHERN). PO Box 769, Jackson, 39205. **601-969-4439.** Harvey G Henderson

MISSOURI (EASTERN). US Court and Custom House, 1114 Market St, St Louis, 63101. **314-425-6056.** William D Rund

MISSOURI (WESTERN). Rm 445, US Courthouse, 811 Grand Ave, Kansas City, 64106. **816-374-3321.** Robert F Connor

MONTANA. PO Box 1287, Missoula, 59801. **406-453-3378.** John E Pederson

NEBRASKA. 9000 US Courthouse and Post Office Bldg (PO Box 129, Downtown Station), Omaha, 68101. **402-221-4761.** William L Olson

NEVADA. Rm 3-632, 300 Las Vegas Blvd S, Las Vegas, 89101. **702-385-6351.** Carol C Fitzgerald

NEW HAMPSHIRE. PO Box 1498, Concord, 03301. **603-228-0506.** William H Barry, Jr

NEW JERSEY. US Post Office and Courthouse, Trenton, 08605. **609-989-2068.** Angelo W Locascio

NEW MEXICO. PO Box 689, Albuquerque, 87103. **505-766-2852.** Jesse Casaus

NEW YORK (NORTHERN). Box 950, Post Office and Courthouse Bldg, Albany, 11201. **518-472-5651.** Joseph R Scully

NEW YORK, (SOUTHERN). US Courthouse, Foley Sq, New York 10007. **212-791-0108.** Raymond F Burghardt

NEW YORK (EASTERN). US Courthouse, 225 Cadman Plz E, Brooklyn, 11201. **212-330-7206.** Lewis Orgel

NEW YORK (WESTERN). 604 US Courthouse, Buffalo, 14202. **716-842-3440.** John K Adams

NORTH CAROLINA (EASTERN). PO Box 25670, Raleigh, 27611. **919-755-4370.** John R Whitty

NORTH CAROLINA (MIDDLE). PO Box V-1, Greensboro, 27402. **919-378-5347.** Carmon H Stuart

NORTH CAROLINA (WESTERN). PO Box 92, Post Office Bldg, Asheville, 28802. **704-258-2850,** Ext. 648. J Toliver Davis

NORTH DAKOTA. PO Box 1193, Bismarck, 58501. **701-255-4011.** Cletus J Schmidt

OHIO (NORTHERN). 328 US Courthouse, Cleveland, 44114. **216-522-4359.** Mark Schlachet

OHIO (SOUTHERN). 328 US Courthouse, 85 Marconi Blvd, Columbus, 43215. **614-469-5442.** John D Lyter

OKLAHOMA (NORTHERN). Rm 411, US Courthouse, Tulsa, 74103. **918-581-7796.** Jack C Silver

OKLAHOMA (EASTERN). PO Box 607, US Courthouse, Muskogee, 74401. **918-687-2471.** Lewis L Vaughn

OKLAHOMA (WESTERN). Rm 3210, US Courthouse, Oklahoma City, 73102. **405-235-8491.** Rex B Hawks

OREGON. PO Box 1150, Portland, 97202. **503-223-2201.** Robert M Christ

PENNSYLVANIA (EASTERN). 2609 US Courthouse, Independence Mall W, 601 Market St, Philadelphia, 19106. **215-597-7704.** John J Harding

PENNSYLVANIA (MIDDLE). PO Box 1148, Scranton, 18501. **717-344-7111.** Donald R Berry

PENNSYLVANIA (WESTERN). PO Box 1805, Pittsburgh, 15230. **412-644-3528.** Jack L Wagner

PUERTO RICO. PO Box 3671, San Juan, 00904. **809-724-0843.** Ramon A Alfaro

RHODE ISLAND. US Courthouse, Providence, 02901. **401-528-4883.** Frederick R De Cesaris

SOUTH CAROLINA. PO Box 867, Columbia, 29202. **803-765-5816.** Miller C Foster, Jr

SOUTH DAKOTA. Rm 220, Federal Bldg and US Courthouse, 400 S Phillips Ave, Sioux Falls, 57102. **605-343-4447.** William J Srstka

TENNESSEE (EASTERN). PO Box 2348, Knoxville, 37901. **615-524-0751.** Karl D Saulpaw, Jr

TENNESSEE (WESTERN). 850 Federal Bldg, 167 N Main St, Memphis, 38103. **901-521-3317.** J Franklin Reid

TEXAS (NORTHERN). Rm 15C22, US Courthouse, 1100 Commerce St, Dallas, 75242. **214-749-2986.** Joseph McElroy, Jr

TEXAS (SOUTHERN). PO Box 61010, Houston, 77208. **713-226-4261.** V Bailey Thomas

TEXAS (EASTERN). PO Box 231, Beaumont, 77704. **713-838-0271,** Ext. 323. Murray L Harris

TEXAS (WESTERN). Hemisfair Plz, 655 E Durango Blvd, San Antonio, 78206. **512-229-6550.** Dan W Benedict

UTAH. US Post Office and Courthouse, Salt Lake City, 84101. **801-524-5160.** Paul L Badger

VERMONT. PO Box 945, Federal Bldg, Burlington, 05401. **802-862-6501,** Ext 6302 Edward J Trudell

VIRGIN ISLANDS, DISTRICT COURT OF THE. US Courthouse, Charlotte Amalie, St Thomas, 00801. **809-774-0640.** Leo Penha

VIRGINIA (EASTERN). PO Box 1318, Norfolk, 23501. **804-441-6677.** W Farley Powers, Jr

VIRGINIA (WESTERN). PO Box 1234, US Courthouse, Roanoke, 24006. **703-982-6224.** Joyce F Witt

WASHINGTON (EASTERN). PO Box 1493, Spokane, 99210. **509-456-3728.** J R Fallquist

WASHINGTON (WESTERN). 308 US Courthouse, Seattle, 98104. **206-442-5598.** Edgar Scofield

WEST VIRGINIA (NORTHERN). PO Box 1518, Elkins, 26241. **304-636-1445.** Thomas F Stafford

WEST VIRGINIA (SOUTHERN). PO Box 2546, Charleston, 25329. **304-342-5154.** James A McWhorter

WISCONSIN (EASTERN). Rm 362, US Courthouse, 517 E Wisconsin Ave, Milwaukee, 53202. **414-224-3372.** Ruth W La Fave

WISCONSIN (WESTERN). PO Box 432, Madison, 53701. **608-252-5156.** Joseph W Skupniewitz

WYOMING. PO Box 727, Cheyenne, 82201. **307-778-2220,** Ext 2145. A Marvin Helart

THE NINETY-FIFTH CONGRESS

THE SENATE. The Capitol, Washington, DC 20510. Main telephone number: **202-224-3121**

THE HOUSE OF REPRESENTATIVES. The Capitol, Washington, DC 20515. Main telephone number: **202-224-3121**

The office of any congressman or congressional committee can be reached through the Capitol switchboard. **202-224-3121**

Press Galleries: Senate

PRESS GALLERY. S-316 The Capitol, 20510. **202-224-0241**

Superintendent. Don C Womack. **202-224-0254.**

Also 218B Russell Senate Office Bldg, 205105. **202-224-5540, 5440, 5170,** or **5840**

PERIODICAL PRESS GALLERY. S-320 The Capitol, 20510. **202-224-0265**

Superintendent. Roy L McGhee

Assistant Superintendent. L. Curran Crow

PRESS PHOTOGRAPHERS GALLERY. S-317 The Capitol, 20510. **202-224-6548**

Superintendent. Maurice J Johnson

Assistant Superintendent. Jospeh M Darling
Also 1402 Dirksen Senate Office Bldg, 20510. **202-224-4204**

RADIO TELEVISION GALLERY. S-312 The Capitol, 20510. **202-224-6421**

Superintendent. Max M Barber
Also G-329 Dirksen Senate Office Bldg, 20510. **202-224-4204**

WESTERN UNION-SENATE PRESS GALLERY. 202-224-4330

Press Galleries: House

PERIODICAL PRESS GALLERY. H-304 The Capitol, 20515. **202-224-2941**

PRESS GALLERY. H-315 The Capitol, 20515. **202-225-3945** or **6722**

Superintendent. Benjamin C West (h: 3612 Gramby St, Hyattsville, Md 20784 **301-773-4195)**

RADIO AND TELEVISION GALLERY. H-320 The Capitol, 20515. **202-225-5214**

PRESS PHOTOGRAPHERS GALLERY. (Same as Senate Press Photographers Gallery).

Senate Officers

PRESIDENT OF THE SENATE. Walter F Mondale (Vice-President of the United States). S-212 The Capitol, 20510. **202-224-0636.** (The Vice-President's ceremonial office is in the Capitol. Mondale also

has offices in the Dirksen Senate Office Bldg and the Old Executive Office Bldg.)

Press Secretary. Albert Eisele, Old Executive Office Bldg, 20506. **202-395-6303** or **202-456-6404**

CHIEF OF STAFF. Richard Moe, Old Executive Office Bldg, 20506. **202-456-6606**

PRESIDENT PRO TEMPORE. Senator James O Eastland. 2241 Dirksen Senate Office Bldg, 20510. **202-224-5054**

MAJORITY LEADER. Senator Robert C Byrd. S-208 The Capitol, 20510. **202-224-5556**

Administrative Assistant. Ethel Low

MAJORITY WHIP. Senator Alan Cranston. S-148 The Capitol, 20510. **202-224-2158**

Press Secretary. Murray S Flander

MINORITY LEADER. Senator Howard H Baker, Jr. S-230 The Capitol, 20510. **202-224-3135**

Administrative Assistant. Lamar Alexander

ASSISTANT MINORITY LEADER. Senator Ted Stevens. S-229 The Capitol, 20510. **202-224-2708**

Administrative Assistant. John Ferguson

Executive Secretary. Jan Nichols

SECRETARY OF THE SENATE. J S Kimmitt. S-221 The Capitol, 20510. **202-224-2115.** (h) 6004 Copely Ln, McLean, VA 22101. **703-538-2507**

Chief Reporter of Debates. G Russell Walker. **202-224-3152** or **3153**

SERGEANT AT ARMS. Frank Nordy Hoffmann. S-321 The Capitol, 20510. **202-224-2341.** (h) Montgomery County, MD

SECRETARY FOR THE MAJORITY. James H Duffy. S-309 The Capitol, 20510. **202-224-3735.** (h) 4630 Western Ave Bethesda, MD 20016. **301-229-8133**

SECRETARY FOR THE MINORITY. William F Hildenbrand. S-337 The Capitol, 20510. **202-224-3835.** (h) 700 Seventh St SW 20024. **202-554-3219**

LEGISLATIVE COUNSEL. Harry B Littell, 6123 Dirksen Senate Office Bldg, 20510. **202-224-6461.** (h) 937 N Potomac St, Arlington, VA 22205. **703-534-6653**

DEMOCRATIC POLICY COMMITTEE. S-318 The Capitol, 20510. **202-224-5551**

Chief Counsel. Thomas D Hart. **202-224-5551**

DEMOCRATIC SENATORIAL CAMPAIGN COMMITTEE. 130 Russell Senate Office Bldg 20515. **202-224-2447**

Executive Director. Charlie McBride

REPUBLICAN CONFERENCE. 335 Russell Senate Office Bldg 20515. **202-224-2946**

REPUBLICAN POLICY COMMITTEE. 333 Russell Senate Office Bldg 20515. **202-224-2946**

Secretary and Staff Director. Max L Friedersdorf (h) 7617 Leith Pl, Alexandria, VA 22307

REPUBLICAN SENATORIAL CAMPAIGN COMMITTEE. 445 Russell Senate Office Bldg, 20515. **202-224-2351.**

POLICE DEPARTMENT (Office of the Sergeant at Arms)

Chief. James M Powell, 215 Plaza Hotel, 20510. **202-224-9806,** emergencies: **202-224-0911**

TELEPHONE SERVICE

Chief Operator. Josephine E Collins. **202-224-5105**

House Officers

SPEAKER OF THE HOUSE. Thomas P O'Neill Jr. H-204 The Capitol, 20515. **202-225-5414.** (h) 4982 Sentinel Dr, Sumner, MD 20016

Administrative Assistant. Leo E Diehl (h) 90 Payson Rd, Belmont, MA 02178

Legislative Assistant. Linda Melconian (h) 465 Dwight Rd, Springfield, MA

General Counsel. Charles Ferris (h) 8802 Mansion Farm, Mount Vernon, VA 22121. **703-780-7788**

Personal Secretary. Elanor Kelley (h) 2527 Afton St, Hillcrest Heights, MD. **301-630-9519**

SPEAKER'S ROOMS. H-209 The Capitol, 20515. **202-225-2204**

Administrative Assistant. Gary Hymel (h) 4111 Rosemary St, Chevy Chase, MD

SPEAKER'S CONGRESSIONAL OFFICE. 2231 Rayburn House Office Bldg, 20515. **202-225-5111**

Executive Secretary. Dolores Snow (h) 3804 Needles Pl, Alexandria, VA. **703-360-5846**

PARLIAMENTARIAN. William Holmes Brown. H-209 The Capitol, 20515. **202-225-7373**

MAJORITY LEADER. James C Wright, Jr. H-148 The Capitol, 20515. **202-225-8040**
Administrative Assistant. Marshall L Lynam
Executive Assistant. Craig Raupe
Legislative Aide. Richard C Olson
Executive Secretary. Katy Mitchell

MAJORITY WHIP. John Brademas. H-107 The Capitol, 20515. **202-225-5604**
Assistant. James P Mooney

MINORITY LEADER. John J Rhodes. H-232 The Capitol, 20515. **202-225-0604** (h) 5502 Pollard Rd, Washington, DC 20016
Staff Director. John J Williams (h) 4001 47th St, Washington, DC 20016
Press Assistant. J Brian Smith (h) 2059 Huntington Ave, Alexandria, VA 22203
Executive Secretary. Clara Posey (h) 611 Tennessee Ave, Alexandria, VA 22305

MINORITY WHIP. Robert H Michel. 2112 Rayburn House Office Bldg, 20515. **202-225-6201**
Press Assistant. Michael Johnson. **202-225-6201**

CLERK. Edmund L Henshaw, Jr. H-105 The Capitol, 20515. **202-225-7000.** (h) 9343 Sibelius Dr, Vienna, VA 22180. **703-938-2356**
Records and Registration Chief. Russ Welch. **202-225-1300**

SERGEANT AT ARMS. Kenneth R Harding. H-124 The Capitol, 20515. **202-225-2456**

DOORKEEPER. James T Molloy. H-154 The Capitol, 20515. **202-225-3505.**
House Document Room. H-226 The Capitol, 20515. **202-225-2456**
Superintendent. Gilman G Udell
Publications Distribution Service. B-241 Longworth House Office Bldg, 20515. **202-225-4355**
Chief. Eli S Bjellos

LEGISLATIVE COUNSEL. Ward M Hussey. 136 Cannon House Office Building, 20515. **202-225-6060.** (h) 312 Princeton Blvd, Alexandria, VA 22314. **703-370-1214**

HOUSE CAUCUS ROOM. 202-225-6450

CONGRESSIONAL BLACK CAUCUS. 307 House Office Bldg Annex 2, 20515. **202-225-1691**

CONGRESSIONAL BUDGET OFFICE. House Office Bldg Annex 2, 20515. **202-225-1491**

CONGRESSIONAL RURAL CAUCUS. 309 House Office Bldg Annex 1, 20515. **202-225-5080**

DEMOCRATIC CAUCUS. 1109 Longworth House Office Bldg, 20515. **202-225-9141**

DEMOCRATIC STEERING AND POLICY COMMITTEE. 202-225-7187

HOUSE INFORMATION SYSTEMS. 3624 House Office Bldg Annex 2, 20515. **202-225-9276**
LEGIS Office (Bill Status). Rm 3674. **202-225-1772**

REPUBLICAN CONFERENCE. 1618 Longworth House Office Bldg, 20515. **202-225-5107**

REPUBLICAN POLICY COMMITTEE. 1620 Longworth House Office Bldg, 20515. **202-225-6168**

REPORTERS OF DEBATES. H-132 The Capitol, 20515. **202-225-5621**

REPORTERS TO COMMITTEES. 1718 Longworth House Office Bldg, 20515. **202-225-2627**

Members by State

For detailed contact information, see the alphabetical listings of members in the next section.

ALABAMA
Senators. John J Sparkman (D), Mrs. James B Allen (D)
Representatives (Democrats, 4; Republicans, 3). 1. Jack Edwards (R); 2. William L Dickinson (R); 3. Bill Nichols (D); 4. Tom Bevill (D); 5. Ronnie G Flippo (D); 6. John Buchanan (R); 7. Walter Flowers (D)

ALASKA
Senators. Ted Stevens (R), Mike Gravel (D)
Representative (Republican, 1). At large—Donald E Young (R)

ARIZONA
Senators. Barry Goldwater (R), Dennis Deconcini (D)

Representatives (Democrats, 2; Republicans, 2). 1. John J Rhodes (R); 2. Morris K Udall (D); 3. Bob Stump (D); 4. Eldon D Rudd (R)

ARKANSAS
Senators. John L McClellan (D), Dale Bumpers (D)
Representatives (Democrats, 3; Republican, 1). 1. Bill Alexander (D); 2. James G Tucker, Jr (D); 3. John P Hammerschmidt (R); 4. Ray Thornton (D)

CALIFORNIA
Senators. Alan Cranston (D), S I Hayakawa (R)
Representatives. (Democrats, 29; Republicans, 14). 1. Harold T Johnson (D); 2. Don H Clausen (R); 3. John E Moss (D); 4. Robert L Leggett (D); 5. John Burton (D); 6. Phillip Burton (D); 7. George Miller (D); 8. Ronald V Dellums (D); 9. Fortney H (Pete) Stark (D); 10. Don Edwards (D); 11. Leo J Ryan (D); 12. Paul N (Pete) McCloskey Jr (R); 13. Norman Y Mineta (D); 14. John J McFall (D); 15. B F Sisk (D); 16. Leon E Panetta (D); 17. John Krebs (D); 18. William M Ketchum (R); 19. Robert J Lagomarsino (R); 20. Barry Goldwater, Jr (R); 21. James C Corman (D); 22. Carlos J Moorhead (R); 23. Anthony C Beilenson (D); 24. Henry A Waxman (D); 25. Edward R Roybal (D); 26. John Rousselot (R); 27. Robert K Dornan (R); 28. Yvonne Brathwaite Burke (D); 29. Augustus F (Gus) Hawkins (D); 30. George E Danielson (D); 31. Charles H Wilson (D); 32. Glenn M Anderson (D); 33. Del Clawson (R); 34. Mark W Hannaford (D); 35. Jim Lloyd (D); 36. George E Brown, Jr (D); 37. Shirley N Pettis (R); 38. Jerry M Patterson (D); 39. Charles E Wiggins (R); 40. Robert E Badham (R); 41. Bob Wilson (R); 42. Lionel Van Deerlin (D); 43. Clair W Burgener (R)

COLORADO
Senators. Floyd K Haskell (D), Gary Hart (D)
Representatives (Democrats, 3; Republicans, 2). 1. Patricia Schroeder (D); 2. Timothy E Wirth (D); 3. Frank E Evans (D); 4. James P (Jim) Johnson (R); 5. William L Armstrong (R)

CONNECTICUT
Senators. Abraham A Ribicoff (D), Lowell P Weicker, Jr (R)
Representatives (Democrats, 4; Republicans, 2). 1. William R Cotter (D); 2. Christopher J Dodd (D); 3. Robert N Giaimo (D); 4.

Stewart B McKinney (R); 5. Ronald A Sarasin (R); 6. Toby Moffett (D)

DELAWARE
Senators. William V Roth, Jr (R), Joseph R Biden, Jr (D)

Representative (Republican, 1). At large—Thomas B Evans, Jr (R)

FLORIDA
Senators. Lawton Chiles (D), Richard (Dick) Stone (D)

Representatives (Democrats, 10; Republicans, 5). 1. Robert L F Sikes (D); 2. Don Fuqua (D); 3. Charles E Bennett (D); 4. Bill Chappell, Jr (D); 5. Richard Kelly (R); 6. C W Bill Young (R); 7. Sam M Gibbons (D); 8. Andrew P Ireland (D); 9. Louis Frey, Jr (R); 10. L A (Skip) Bafalis (R); 11. Paul G Rogers (D); 12. J Herbert Burke (R); 13. William Lehman (D); 14. Claude D Pepper (D); 15. Dante B Fascell (D)

GEORGIA
Senators. Herman E Talmadge (D), Sam Nunn (D)

Representatives (Democrats, 9; vacant, 1). 1. Bo Ginn (D); 2. Dawson Mathis (D); 3. Jack Brinkley (D); 5. Elliott H Levitis (D); 5. vacant; 6. John J Flynt, Jr (D); 7. Larry McDonald (D); 8. Billy Lee Evans (D); 9. Edgar L Jenkins (D); 10. D Douglas Barnard, Jr (D)

HAWAII
Senators. Daniel K Inouye (D), Spark M Matsunaga (D)

Representatives (Democrats, 2). 1. Cecil Heftel (D); 2. Daniel K Akaka (D)

IDAHO
Senators. Frank Church (D), James A McClure (R)

Representatives (Republicans, 2). 1. Steven D Symms (R); 2. George Hansen (R)

ILLINOIS
Senators. Charles H Percy (R), Adlai E Stevenson (D)

Representatives (Democrats, 12; Republicans, 12). 1. Ralph H Metcalfe (D); 2. Morgan F Murphy (D); 3. Martin A Russo (D); 4. Edward J Derwinski (R); 5. John G Fary (D); 6. Henry J Hyde (R); 7. Cardiss Collins (D); 8. Dan Rostenkowski (D); 9. Sidney R Yates (D); 10. Abner J Mikva (D); 11. Frank Annunzio (D); 12. Philip M Crane (R); 13. Robert McClory (R); 14. John N Erlenborn (R); 15. Thomas J Corcoran (R); 16. John B Anderson (R); 17. George M

O'Brien (R); 18. Robert H Michel (R); 19. Thomas F Railsback (R); 20. Paul Findley (R); 21. Edward R Madigan (R); 22. George E Shipley (D); 23. Melvin Price (D); 24. Paul Simon (D)

INDIANA
Senators. Birch Bayh (D), Richard G Lugar (R)

Representatives (Democrats, 8; Republicans, 3). 1. Adam Benjamin, Jr (D); 2. Floyd J Fithian (D); 3. John Brademas (D); 4. J Danforth Quayle (R); 5. Elwood Hillis (R); 6. David W Evans (D); 7. John T Myers (R); 8. David L Cornwell (D); 9. Lee H Hamilton (D); 10. Philip R Sharp (D); 11. Andrew Jacobs, Jr (D)

IOWA
Senators. Dick Clark (D), John C Culver (D).

Representatives (Democrats, 4; Republicans, 2). 1. James A S Leach (R); 2. Michael T Blouin (D); 3. Charles E Grassley (R); 4. Neal Smith (D); 5. Tom Harkin (D); 6. Berkley Bedell (D)

KANSAS
Senators. James B Pearson (R), Bob Dole (R)

Representatives (Democrats, 2; Republicans, 3). 1. Keith G Sebelius (R); 2. Martha Keys (D); 3. Larry Winn, Jr (R); 4. Daniel R Glickman (D); 5. Joe Skubitz (R)

KENTUCKY
Senators. Walter (Dee) Huddleston (D), Wendell H Ford (D)

Representatives (Democrats, 5; Republicans, 2). 1. Carroll Hubbard, Jr (D); 2. William H Natcher (D); 3. Romano L Mazzoli (D); 4. M G (Gene) Snyder (R); 5. Tim Lee Carter (R); 6. John Breckinridge (D); 7. Carl D Perkins (D)

LOUISIANA
Senators. Russell B Long (D), J Bennett Johnston, Jr (D)

Representatives (Democrats, 6; Republicans, 2). 1. Richard A Tonry (D); 2. Corinne C (Lindy) Boggs (D); 3. David C Treen (R); 4. Joe D Waggonner, Jr (D); 5. Thomas J Huckaby (D); 6. W Henson Moore (R); 7. John B Breaux (D); 8. Gillis W Long (D)

MAINE
Senators. Edmund S Muskie (D), William D Hathaway (D)

Representatives (Republicans, 2). 1. David F Emmery (R); 2. William S Cohen (R)

MARYLAND
Senators. Charles McC Mathias, Jr (R), Paul S Sarbanes (D)

Representatives (Democrats, 5; Republicans, 3). 1. Robert E Bauman (R); 2. Clarence D Long (D); 3. Barbara A Mikulski (D); 4. Marjorie S Holt (R); 5. Gladys Noon Spellman (D); 6. Goodloe E Byron (D); 7. Parren J Mitchell (D); 8. Newton I Steers, Jr (R)

MASSACHUSETTS
Senators. Edward M Kennedy (D), Edward W Brooke (R)

Representatives (Democrats, 10; Republicans, 2). 1. Silvio O Conta (R); 2. Edward P Boland (D); 3. Joseph D Early (D); 4. Robert F Drinan (D); 5. Paul E Tsongas (D); 6. Michael J Harrington (D); 7. Edward J Markey (D); 8. Thomas P O'Neill, Jr (D); 9. John Joseph Moakley (D); 10. Margaret M Heckler (R); 11. James A Burke (D); 12. Gerry E Studds (D)

MICHIGAN
Senators. Robert P Griffin (R), Donald W Riegle, Jr (D)

Representatives (Democrats, 11; Republicans, 8). 1. John Conyers, Jr (D); 2. Carl D Pursell (R); 3. Garry E Brown (R); 4. David A Stockman (R); 5. Harold S Sawyer (R); 6. Bob Carr (D); 7. Dale E Kildee (D); 8. Bob Traxler (D); 9. Guy Vander Jagt (R); 10. Elford A Cederberg (R); 11. Philip E Ruppe (R); 12. David E Bonjor (D); 13. Charles C Diggs, Jr (D); 14. Lucien N Nedzi (D); 15. William D Ford (D); 16. John D Dingell (D); 17. William M. Brodhead (D); 18. James J Blanchard (D); 19. William S Broomfield (R)

MINNESOTA
Senators. Muriel Buck Humphrey (D), Wendell R Anderson (D)

Representatives (Democrats, 4; Republicans, 4). 1. Albert H Quie (R); 2. Tom Hagedorn (R); 3. Bill Frenzel (R); 4. Bruce F Vento (D); 5. Donald M Fraser (D); 6. Richard Nolan (D); 7. Arlan Strangeland (R); 8. James L Oberstar (D)

MISSISSIPPI
Senators. James O Eastland (D), John C Stennis (D)

Representatives (Democrats, 3; Republicans, 2). 1. Jamie L Whitten (D); 2. David R Bowen (D); 3. G V (Sonny) Montgomery (D); 4. Thad Cochran (R); 5. Trent Lott (R)

MISSOURI
Senators. Thomas F Eagleton (D), John C Danforth (R)

Representatives (Democrats, 8; Republicans, 2). 1. William (Bill) Clay (D); 2. Robert A Young (D); 3. Richard A Gephardt (D); 4. Ike Skelton (D); 5. Richard Bolling (D); 6. E Thomas Coleman (R); 7. Gene Taylor (R); 8. Richard H Ichord (D); 9. Harold L Volkmer (D); 10. Bill D Burlison (D)

MONTANA
Senators. Paul G Hatfield (D), John Melcher (D)

Representatives (Democrat, 1; Republican, 1). 1. Max Baucus (D); 2. Ron Marlenee (R)

NEBRASKA
Senators. Carl T Curtis (R), Edward Zorinsky (D)

Representatives (Democrat, 1; Republicans, 2). 1. Charles Thone (R); 2. John J Cavanaugh (D); 3. Virginia Smith (R)

NEVADA
Senators. Howard W Cannon (D), Paul Laxalt (R)

Representative (Democrat, 1). At large—Jim Santini (D)

NEW HAMPSHIRE
Senators. Thomas J McIntyre (D), John A Durkin (D)

Representatives (Democrat, 1; Republican, 1). 1. Norman E D'Amours (D); 2. James C Cleveland (R)

NEW JERSEY
Senators. Clifford P Case (R), Harrison A Williams, Jr (D)

Representatives (Democrats, 11; Republicans, 4). 1. James J Florio (D); 2. William J Hughes (D); 3. James J Howard (D); 4. Frank Thompson, Jr (D); 5. Millicent Fenwick (R); 6. Edwin B Forsythe (R); 7. Andrew Maguire (D); 8. Robert A Roe (D); 9. Harold C Hollenbeck (R); 10. Peter W Rodino, Jr (D); 11. Joseph G Minish (D); 12. Matthew J Rinaldo (R); 13. Helen S Meyner (D); 14. Joseph A Le Fante (D); 15. Edward J Patten (D)

NEW MEXICO
Senators. Pete V Comenici (R), Harrison H Schmitt (R)

Representatives (Democrat, 1; Republican, 1). 1. Manuel Lujan, Jr (R); 2. Harold Runnels (D)

NEW YORK
Senators. Jacob K Javits (R), Daniel P Moynihan (D)

Representatives (Democrats, 27; Republicans, 12). 1. Otis G Pike (D); 2. Thomas J Downey (D); 3. Jerome A Ambro (D); 4. Norman F Lent (R); 5. John W Wydler (R); 6. Lester L Wolff (D); 7. Joseph P Addabbo (D); 8. Benjamin S Rosenthal (D); 9. James J Delaney (D); 10. Mario Biaggi (D); 11. James H Scheuer (D); 12. Shirley Chisholm (D); 13. Stephen J Solarz (D); 14. Frederick W Richmond (D); 15. Leo C Zeferetti (D); 16. Elizabeth Holtzman (D); 17. John M Murphy (D); 18. William Green (R); 19. Charles B Rangel (D); 20. Ted Weiss (D); 21. Robert Garcia (D); 22. Jonathan B Bingham (D); 23. Bruce F Caputo (R); 24. Richard L Ottinger (D); 25. Hamilton Fish, Jr (R); 26. Benjamin A Gilman (R); 27. Matthew F McHugh (D); 28. Samuel S Stratton (D); 29. Edward W Pattison (D); 30. Robert C McEwen (R); 31. Donald J Mitchell (R); 32. James M Hanley (D); 33. William F Walsh (R); 34. Frank Horton (R); 35. Barber B Conable, Jr (R); 36. John J La Falce (D); 37. Henry J Nowak (D); 38. Jack Kemp (R); 39. Stanley N Lundine (D)

NORTH CAROLINA
Senators. Jesse A Helms (R), Robert Morgan (D)

Representatives (Democrats, 9; Republicans, 2). 1. Walter B Jones (D); 2. L H Fountain (D); 3. Charles O Whitley, Sr (D); 4. Ike F Andrews (D); 5. Stephen L Neal (D); 6. Richardson Preyer (D); 7. Charles Rose (D); 8. W G (Bill) Hefner (D); 9. James G Martin (R); 10. James T Broyhill (R); 11. V Lamar Gudger (D)

NORTH DAKOTA
Senators. Milton R Young (R), Quentin N Burdick (D)

Representative (Republican, 1). At large—Mark Andrews (R)

OHIO
Senators. John Glenn (D), Howard M Metzenbaum (D)

Representatives (Democrats, 10; Republicans, 13). 1. Willis D Gradison, Jr (R); 2. Thomas A Luken (D); 3. Charles W Whalen, Jr (R); 4. Tennyson Guyer (R); 5. Delbert L Latta (R); 6. William H Harsha (R); 7. Clarence J Brown (R); 8. Thomas N Kindness (R); 9. Thomas L Ashley (D); 10. Clarence E Miller (R); 11. J William Stanton (R); 12. Samuel L Devine (R); 13. Donald J Pease (D); 14. John F Seiberling (D); 15. Chalmers P Wylie (R); 16. Ralph S Regula (R); 17. John M. Ashbrook (R); 18. Douglas Applegate (D); 19. Charles J Carney (D); 20. Mary Rose Oakar (D); 21. Louis Stokes (D); 22. Charles A Vanik (D); 23. Ronald M Mottl (D)

OKLAHOMA
Senators. Henry L Bellmon (R), Dewey F Bartlett (R)

Representatives (Democrats, 5; Republican, 1). 1. James R Jones (D); 2. Ted Risenhoover (D); 3. Wesley W Watkins (D); 4. Tom Steed (D); 5. Mickey Edwards (R); 6. Glenn English (D)

OREGON
Senators. Mark O Hatfield (R), Bob Packwood (R)

Representatives (Democrats, 4). 1. Les AuCoin (D); 2. Al Ullman (D); 3. Robert Duncan (D); 4. James Weaver (D)

PENNSYLVANIA
Senators. Richard S Schweiker (R), H John Heinz 3d (R)

Representatives (Democrats, 17; Republicans, 8). 1. Michael O Myers (D); 2. Robert N C Nix (D); 3. Raymond F Lederer (D); 4. Joshua Eilberg (D); 5. Richard T Schultz (R); 6. Gus Yatron (D); 7. Robert W Edgar (D); 8. Peter H Kostmayer (D); 9. E G (Bud) Shuster (R); 10. Joseph M McDade (R); 11. Daniel J Flood (D); 12. John P Murtha (D); 13. Lawrence Coughlin (R); 14. William S Moorhead (D); 15. Fred B Rooney (D); 16. Robert S Walker (R); 17. Allen E Ertel (D); 18. Doug Walgren (D); 19. William F Goodline (R); 20. Joseph M Gaydos (D); 21. John H Dent (D); 22. Austin J Murphy (D); 23. Joseph S Ammerman (D); 24. Marc L Marks (R); 25. Gary A Myers (R)

RHODE ISLAND
Senators. Claiborne Pell (D), John H Chafee (R)

Representatives (Democrats, 2). 1. Fernand J St Germain (D); 2. Edward P Beard (D)

SOUTH CAROLINA
Senators. Strom Thurmond (R), Ernest F Hollings (D)

Representatives (Democrats, 5; Republican, 1). 1. Mendel J Davis (D); 2. Floyd Spence (R); 3. Butler Derrick (D); 4. James R Mann (D); 5. Kenneth L Holland (D); 6. John W Jenrette, Jr (D)

SOUTH DAKOTA
Senators. George McGovern (D), James Abourezk (D)

Representatives (Republicans, 2). 1. Larry Pressler (R); 2. James Abdnor (R)

TENNESSEE
Senators. Howard H Baker, Jr (R), James R Sasser (D)

Representatives (Democrats, 5; Republicans, 3). 1. James H Quillen (R); 2. John J Duncan (R); 3. Marilyn Lloyd (D); 4. Albert A Gore, Jr (D); 5. Clifford R Allen (D); 6. Robin L Beard (R); 7. Ed Jones (D); 8. Harold E Ford (D)

TEXAS
Senators. John G Tower (R), Lloyd M Bentsen (D)

Representatives (Democrats, 22; Republicans, 2). 1. Sam B Hall, Jr (D); 2. Charles Wilson (D); 3. James M Collins (R); 4. Ray Roberts (D); 5. James A Mattox (D); 6. Olin E Teague (D); 7. Bill Archer (R); 8. Bob Eckhardt (D); 9. Jack Brooks (D); 10. J J (Jake) Pickle (D); 11. W R Poage (D); 12. James C Wright, Jr (D); 13. Jack Hightower (D); 14. John Young (D); 15. E (Kika) de la Garza (D); 16. Richard C White (D); 17. Omar Burleson (D); 18. Barbara Jordan (D); 19. George H Mahon (D); 20. Henry B Gonzalez (D); 21. Robert (Bob) Krueger (D); 22. Robert A Gammage (D); 23. Abraham Kazen, Jr (D); 24. Dale Milford (D)

UTAH
Senators. Jake Garn (R), Orrin G Hatch (R)

Representatives (Democrat, 1; Republican, 1). 1. K Gunn McKay (D); 2. David D Marriott (R)

VERMONT
Senators. Robert T Stafford (R), Patrick J Leahy (D)

Representative (Republican, 1). At large—James M Jeffords (R)

VIRGINIA
Senators. Harry F Byrd, Jr (Ind), William Lloyd Scott (R)

Representatives (Democrats, 4; Republicans, 6). 1. Paul S Trible, Jr (R); 2. G William Whitehurst (R); 3. David E Satterfield 3d (D); 4. Robert W Daniel, Jr (R); 5. W C (Dan) Daniel (D); 6. M Caldwell Butler (R); 7. J Kenneth Robinson (R); 8. Herbert E Harris 2d (D); 9. William C Wampler (R); 10. Joseph L Fisher (D)

WASHINGTON
Senators. Warren G Magnuson (D), Henry M Jackson (D)

Representatives (Democrats, 5; Republican, 1; vacant, 1). 1. Joel Pritchard (R); 2. Lloyd Meeds (D); 3. Don Bonker (D); 4. Mike McCormack (D); 5. Thomas S Foley (D); 6. Norman D Dicks (D); 7. vacant

WEST VIRGINIA
Senators. Jennings Randolph (D), Robert C Byrd (D)

Representatives (Democrats, 4). 1. Robert H Mollohan (D); 2. Harley O Staggers (D); 3. John Slack (D); 4. Nick J Rahall 2d (D)

WISCONSIN
Senators. William Proxmire (D), Gaylord Nelson (D)

Representatives (Democrats, 7; Republicans, 2). 1. Les Aspin (D); 2. Robert W Kastenmeier (D); 3. Alvin Baldus (D); 4. Clement J Zablocki (D); 5. Henry S Reuss (D); 6. William A Steiger (R); 7. David R Obey (D); 8. Robert J Cornell (D); 9. Robert W Kasten, Jr (R)

WYOMING
Senators. Clifford P Hansen (R), Malcolm Wallop (R)

Representative (Democrat, 1). At large—Teno Roncalio (D)

DISTRICT OF COLUMBIA
Delegate (Democrat, 1). Walter E Fauntroy (D)

GUAM
Delegate (Democrat, 1). Antonio Borja Won Pat (D)

PUERTO RICO
Resident Commissioner (New Progressive, 1). Baltasar Corrado (New Progressive)

VIRGIN ISLANDS
Delegate (Democrat, 1). Ron de Lugo (D)

United States Senators (Alphabetical)

In this list and in the list of US Representatives that follows, AA stands for "administrative assistant," and LA for "legislative assistant."

ABOUREZK, JAMES (D–SD). 3313 Dirksen Senate Office Bldg, 20510. **202-224-5842.** (h) Rapid City, SD. **605-434-6011**

Committees. Indian Affairs (Select); Budget; Energy and Natural Resource; Judiciary

Press. Ron Kroese. **202-224-5842**

AA. Peter Stavrianos, Rm 3317 (h) 4121

Dunnel Ln, Kensington, MD 20795
Secretary. Sue A Sadler

ALLEN, MRS. JAMES B (D–AL). 6205 Dirksen Senate Office Bldg, 20510. **202-224-5744.** (h) Gadsden, AL. **205-547-7813**

Committees. Agriculture; Rules; Judiciary; Printing (Joint)

Press. Fred Eiland, Rm 6211. **202-224-5744**

AA. Tom E Coker, Rm 6207

Secretary. Charles R Mitchell, Rm 6131. (h) 9628 Carriage Rd, Kensington, MD 20795

ANDERSON, WENDELL R (D–MN). 304 Russell Senate Office Bldg, 20510. **202-224-5641.** (h) St Paul, MN. **612-231-0904**

Committees. Armed Services; Budget; Environment and Public Works

Press. Robert Woodrum or Meg Ravnholt. **202-224-8455**

AA. Peter Gove (h) Apt B-818, 103 G St SW, Washington, DC 20024

Secretary. Norma Sommerdorf (h) 9628 Carriage Rd, Kensington, MD 20795

BAKER, HOWARD H, JR (R–TN). 4123 Dirksen Senate Office Bldg, 20510. **202-224-4944.** (h) Huntsville, TN. **615-663-2255**

Committees. Environment and Public Works; Foreign Relations; Rules and Administration; Intelligence (Joint). *Minority leader*

Press. Ron McMahon. **202-224-4944**

AA. Hugh Branson (h) 1215 Old Stable Rd, McLean, VA 22101. **703-356-2620**

Secretary. Doris Lovett (h) Apt 5, 311 3rd Ave NE, Washington, DC 20002

BARTLETT, DEWEY F (R–OK). 140 Russell Office Bldg, 20510. **202-224-4721.** (h) Tulsa, OK. **918-587-3777.** (h) 3919 Watson Pl, Washington, DC 20016

Committees. Armed Services; Energy and Natural Resources; Indian Affairs (Select); Small Business (Select)

Press. Tony Garrett. **202-224-4721**

AA. Lou Rooker (h) 311 C St SE, Washington, DC 20003. **202-543-6788**

Secretary. Mary Ann Freeman (h) 1811 N Shore Ctr, Reston, VA 22090

BAYH, BIRCH (D–IN). 363 Russel Office Bldg, 20510. **202-224-5623.** (h) Terre Haute, IN. **812-232-5331.** (h) 4701 32nd St, Washington, DC 20008

Committees. Appropriations; Judiciary; Intelligence (Select, Chairman)

Press. Carol Sanger. **202-224-5623.** (h) **202-554-3130**

AA. P A Mack (h) 4701 32nd St, Washington, DC 20008. **202-363-3795**

Secretary. Lynne Mann (h) 326 16th St SE, Washington, DC 20002

BELLMON, HENRY L (R–Ok). 125 Russell Office Bldg, 20510. **202-224-5754.** (h) Red Rock, OK. **405-231-4941.** (h) 1001 S 26th Rd, Arlington, VA 22202

Committees. Agriculture, Nutrition, and Forestry; Appropriations; Budget; Nutrition and Human Needs (Select)

Press. Andrew Tevington. **202-224-5754**

AA. Robert L Haught (h) 1768 Dogwood Dr, Alexandria, VA 22302

Secretary. Cathy Buchanan (h) 4956 Schuyler Dr, Annandale, VA 22003

BENTSEN, LLOYD M (R–TX). 240 Russell Office Bldg, 20510. **202-224-5922.** (h) Brazoria County, TX. **713-798-2745**

Committees. Environmental and Public Works; Finance; Economic (Joint)

Press. Jack De Vore. **202-224-5922**

AA. Gary Bushell

Secretary. Gaye Siverson

BIDEN, JOSEPH R (D–DE). 347 Russell Office Bldg, 20510. **202-224-5042.** (h) Wilmington, DE. **302-571-6345**

Committees. Budget; Foreign Relations; Judiciary; Intelligence (Select)

Press. Mike McAdams. **202-224-5042**

AA. Edward E Kaufman (h) 621 Halstead Rd, Wilmington, DE 19803

Secretary. Edwina R Doran (h) 419 A St NE, Washington, DC 20002

BROOKE, EDWARD W (R–MA). 437 Russell Senate Office Bldg, 20510. **202-224-2742.** (h) Newton, MA. N P

Committees. Appropriations; Banking, Housing, and Urban Affairs; Defense Production (Joint); Aging (Special)

Press. Hap Ellis. **202-224-2742**

LA. Ralph Neas. **202-224--8521**

Secretary. Sheila Crowley (h) 2614 39th St, Washington, DC 20007. **202-338-5116**

BUMPERS, DALE (D–AR). 6243 Dirksen Senate Office Bldg, 20510. **202-224-4843.** (h) Charleston, AR. **501-965-2345**

Committees. Armed Services; Energy and Natural Resources.

Press and AA. Kenneth C Danforth. **202-224-4843.** (h) 7002 Tyndale, McLean, VA 22101

Secretary. Joe Nobles (h) 657 St SE, Washington, DC 20003 **202-543-1321**

BURDICK, QUENTIN (D–ND). 451 Russell Senate Office Bldg, 20510. **202-224-2551.** (h) Fargo, ND. **701-237-4000.** (h) 305 C St NE, Washington, DC 20002

Committees. Appropriations; Environmental and Public Works

Press. Ann Humphrey. **202-224-2551**

AA. Yvonne Eider (h) 35 E St, Washington, DC 20001

Secretary. Geraldine Gaginis (h) 2601 Woodley Pl, Washington, DC 20008. **202-667-8081**

BYRD, HARRY F (Ind–VA). 417 Russell Senate Office Bldg, 20510. **202-224-4024.** (h) Winchester, VA. **703-662-7745**

Committees. Armed Services; Finance

Press. John Brooks. **202-224-4024**

AA. J Phyllis Reberger (h) 8230 The Midway, Annandale, VA 22003. **703-978-2550**

Secretary. Audrey A Jones (h) 2000 S Eads St, Arlington, VA 22202. **703-521-4451**

BYRD, ROBERT C (D–WV). 133 Russell Senate Office Bldg, 20510. **202-224-3954.** (h) Sophia, WV. NP

Committees. Appropriations; Judiciary; Rules and Adminstration; Intelligence (Select). *Majority leader*

Press. Mike Willard. **202-224-3904**

AA. Virginia Yates (h) 1500 Arlington Blvd, Arlington, VA 22209. **703-525-7871**

Secretary. Ethel R Low (h) 5609 37th Ave, Hyattsville, MD 20782. **301-864-2262**

CANNON, HOWARD W (D–NV). 259 Russell Senate Office Bldg, 20510. **202-224-6244.** (h) Las Vegas, NV. **702-385-6278.** (h) McLean, VA 22101

Committees. Rules and Adminstration (chairman); Armed Services; Commerce, Science, and Transportation; Printing (Joint, chairman); Library (Joint)

Press. Mike Vernetti. **202-224-6244**

AA. Chester B Sobsey

Secretary. Janene Assuras

CASE, CLIFFORD B (R–NJ). 315 Russell Senate Office Bldg, 20510. **202-224-3224.** (h) Rahway, NJ. **201-388-2052.** (h) 2728 Dumbarton Ave, Washington, DC 20007

Committees. Appropriations; Foreign Relations; Intelligence (Select)

Press and AA. Frances Henderson. **202-224-3224.** (h) Yonder House, Indian Head, MD 20640. **301-743-3482**

Secretary. Jack Vandenberg (h) 3309 Hemlock Dr, Falls Church, VA 22042. **703-560-9267**

CHAFEE, JOHN H (R–RI). 3105 Dirksen Senate Office Bldg, 20510. **202-224-2921.** (h) Warwick, RI. **401-528-5194**

Committees. Environmental and Public Works; Human Resources; Intelligence (Select)

Press. Jamie Pound. **202-224-2921**

AA. William Roesing (h) 2729 29th St, Washington, DC 20008. **202-234-8937**

Secretary. Hollis Brown (h) 3925 Davis Pl, Washington, DC 20007. **202-338-3167**

CHILES, LAWTON (D–FL). 443 Russell Senate Office Bldg, 20510. **202-224-5274.** (h) Lakeland, FL. **813-688-6681**

Committees. Appropriations; Budget; Governmental Affairs; Congressional Operations (Joint); Aging (Special)

Press. Jack Pridgen. **202-224-5274**

AA. Charles Canady

Secretary. Fran Williams

CHURCH, FRANK (D–ID). 245 Russell Senate Office Bldg, 20510. **202-224-6142.** (h) Boise, ID. **208-384-1700**

Committees. Energy and Natural Resources; Foreign Relations; Aging (Special, chairman)

Press. Cleve Corlett. **202-224-6142**

AA. Mike Weatherell (h) 3815 N 30th St, Arlington, VA 22203

Secretary. Jennie Marie Ward (h) 12507 Kembridge Dr, Bowie, MD 20715

CLARK, DICK (D–IA). 404 Russell Senate Office Bldg, 20510. **202-224-3254.** (h) Marion, IA. **319-366-2411**

Committees. Agriculture, Nutrition, and Forestry; Foreign Relations; Rules and Administration

Press. Pete Smith. **202-224-3254**

AA. Bob Miller (h) 908 Enderby Dr, Alexandria, VA 22302

Secretary. Julie Marshall (h) 4424 Edmunds St, Washington, DC 20007

CRANSTON, ALAN (D–CA). 229 Russell Senate Office Bldg, 20510. **202-224-3553.** (h) Los Angeles, CA. **213-824-7641**

Committees. Veterans Affairs (chairman); Banking, Housing, and Urban; Budget; Human Resources. *Majority whip*

Press. Murray Flander. **202-224-3553**

AA. Roy F Greenaway (h) 2100 Walton Way Rd, Alexandria, VA 22307

Secretary. Mary Louise McNeeley

CULVER, JOHN C (D–IA). 344 Russell Senate Office Bldg, 20510. **202-224-3744.** (h) Cedar Rapids, IA. **319-366-2411.** (h) 6800 Connecticut Ave, Chevy Chase, MD

Committees. Armed Services; Environment and Public Works; Judiciary; Small Business (Select)

Press. Don Brownlee. **202-224-3744**

AA. Park Rinard.

Secretary. Patricia A Sarcone (h) B-1601, 1400 S Joyce St, Arlington, VA 22202. **703-979-5652**

CURTIS, CARL T (R–NE). 2213 Dirksen Senate Office Bldg, 20510. **202-224-4424.** (h) Minden, NE. **308-832-2676.** (h) 6613 31st Pl, Washington, DC 20015

Committees. Agriculture, Nutrition, and Forestry; Finance; Taxation (Joint)

Press. Belinda Neilsen. **202-224-4224**

AA. Don E Shasteen (h) 11704 Judy Pl, Potomac, MD 20854. **301-299-7498**

Secretary. Marilyn Grimm (h) 6501 Westland Rd, Bethesda, MD 20034. **301-530-7284**

DANFORTH, JOHN C (R–MO). 460 Russell Senate Office Bldg, 20510. **202-224-6154.** (h) Flat, MO. NP (h) 3500 Williamsburg Ln, Washington, DC 20008

Committees. Commerce, Science, and Transportation; Finance; Governmental Affairs

Press. Carrie Franke. **202-224-1405**

AA. Alexander Netchvolodoff (h) 5814 Cromwell St, Bethesda, MD 20016

Secretary. Judith A Hollis (h) 7423 Carol Ln, Falls Church, VA 22042. **703-573-6532**

DE CONCINI, DENNIS (D–AZ). 4104 Dirksen Senate Office Bldg, 20510. **202-224-4521.** (h) Tucson, AZ. **602-792-6831**

Committees. Appropriations; Judiciary; Aging (Special)

Press. Robert Maynes. **202-224-4701**

AA. Gene Karp (h) 4428 25th St, Arlington, VA 22202

Secretary. Sharon Nelson (h) 1401 North St 1002, 20005. **202-234-5681**

DOLE, ROBERT (R–KS). 4213Dirksen Senate Office Bldg, 20510. **202-224-6521.** (h) Russell, KS. NP

Committees. Agriculture, Nutrition, and Forestry; Budget; Finance; Nutrition and Human Needs (Select)

Press. Janet Anderson. **202-224-8947**

AA. Bill Wohlford (h) 2801 Westmoreland St, Arlington, VA 22213

Secretary. Betty Meyer (h) 4501 Arlington Blvd, Arlington, VA 22203. **703-524-5929**

DOMENICI, PETE V (R–NM). 405 Russell Senate Office Bldg, 20510. **202-224-6621.** (h) Albuequerque, NM. **505-766-3481.** (h) 11110 Stephalee Ln, Rockville, MD 20852

Committees. Budget; Energy and Natural Resources; Environment and Public Works; Congressional Operations (Joint); Aging (Special)

Press. Steve Bell. **202-224-6621**

AA. Dennis Home (h) 3 Bunker Ctr, Rockville MD 20852

Secretary. Helen R Cameron (h) 3319 Huntley Sq, Temple Hills, MD 20031. **301-630-9495**

DURKIN, JOHN A (D–NH). 3230 Dirksen Senate Office Bldg, 20510. **202-224-3324.** (h) Manchester, NH. **603-666-7791**

Committees. Commerce, Science, and Transportation; Energy and Natural Resources; Veterans' Affairs

Press. Ruth La Brie. **202-224-3324**

AA. Charles Meara

Secretary. Stephanie Pavelic

EAGLETON, THOMAS F (D–MO). 1215 Dirksen Senate Office Bldg, 20510. **202-224-5721.** (h) St Louis, MO. **314-425-5067**

Committees. Appropriations; Governmental Affairs; Human Resources

Press. Mark Abels. **202-224-5721**

AA. H Edward Quick (h) 5611 Mamakagan Rd, Washington, DC 20016

Secretary. Ruth V Herbst (h) 2508 St Johns Pl, Alexandria, VA 22311. **703-931-2542**

EASTLAND, JAMES O (D–MS). 2241 Dirksen Senate Office Bldg, 20510. **202-224-5054.** (h) Doddsville, MS. **601-756-4766.** (h) 5116 Malcomb St, Washington, DC 20016

Committees. Judiciary (chairman); Agriculture, Nutrition, and Forestry. *President pro tempore*

Press. David Lambert. **202-224-5054**

AA. Courtney C Pace (h) 201 Massachusetts Ave NE, Washington, DC 20002

Secretary. Jean Allen (h) 3225 Nealon Dr, Falls Church, VA 22042

FORD, WENDELL H (D–KY). 4107 Dirksen Senate Office Bldg, 20510. **202-224-4343.**

(h) Owensboro, KY. **502-685-5158.** (h) 4974 Sentinel Dr, Sumner, MD 20016

Committees. Commerce, Science, and Transportation; Energy and Natural Resources

Press. Mike Ruehling. **202-224-4343**

AA. James T Fleming (h) 200 C St SE, Washington, DC 20003

Secretary. Helen Price (h) 3705 George Mason Dr, Falls Church, VA 22041

GARN, E J (JAKE) (R–UT). 4203 Dirksen Senate Office Bldg, 20510. **202-224-5444.** (h) Salt Lake City, UT. **801-524-5933.** (h) 7707 Bridle Path Ln, McLean, VA 22101

Committees. Armed Services; Banking; Housing and Urban Affairs; Intelligence (Select)

Press. Don Olsen. **202-224-5444**

AA. Jeff M Bingham (h) 215 Constitution Ave NE, Washington, DC 20002. **202-547-0705**

Secretary. Suzanne De Costa (h) 815 S 18th St, Arlington, VA 22204. **703-521-5703**

GLENN, JOHN H, JR (D–OH). 204 Russell Senate Office Bldg, 20510. **202-224-3353.** (h) Columbus, OH. **614-469-6697**

Committees. Foreign Relations; Governmental Affairs; Aging (Special)

Press. Steve Avakian. **202-224-3353**

AA. William R White

Secretary. Kathy Prosser

GOLDWATER, BARRY (R–AZ). 427 Russell Senate Office Bldg, 20510. **202-224-2235.** (h) Scottsdale, AZ. **602-261-4086**

Committees. Armed Services; Commerce, Science, and Transportation; Intelligence (Select)

Press. Tony Smith. **202-224-2235**

AA. John F Murphy

Secretary. Judy Eisenhower

GRAVEL, MIKE (D–AK). 3121 Dirksen Senate Office Bldg, 20510. **202-224-6665.** (h) Anchorage, AK. **907-277-4591**

Committees. Environment and Public Works; Finance; Congressional Operations (Joint)

Press. Campbell Gardett. **202-224-6665**

AA. Robert Mitchell, 3317 Dirksen Senate Office Bldg, 20510

Secretary. Donna Harlow

GRIFFIN, ROBERT P (R–MI). 353 Russell Senate Office Bldg, 20510. **202-224-6221.** (h) Traverse City, MI. **616-941-7170**

Committees. Commerce, Science, and Transportation; Foreign Relations; Rules and Administration; Congressional Operations (Joint)

Press. Jane Denison. **202-224-9108.** (h) **202-543-2162**

AA. Albert A Applegate (h) 7209 Ashview Dr, Springfield, VA 22153. **703-455-5248**

Secretary. Barbara S Bengtson (h) 2132 N Military Rd, Arlington, VA 22207. **703-524-2482**

HANSEN, CLIFFORD P (R–WY). 3229 Dirksen Senate Office Bldg, 20510. **202-224-3424.** (h) Jackson, WY. **307-733-5656.** (h) 2510 Virginia Ave, Washington, DC 20037

Committees. Energy and Natural Resources; Finance; Veterans' Affairs; Taxation (Joint)

Press. Patty Howe. **202-224-3424**

AA. Paul R Holtz (h) 8234 Toll House Rd, Annandale, VA 22003. **703-978-3999**

Secretary. Carmen Martin (h) 1331 35th St, Washington, DC, 20007

HART, GARY W (D–CO). 254 Russell Senate Office Bldg, 20510. **202-224-5854.** (h) Denver, CO. **303-837-4421**

Committees. Armed Services; Environment and Public Works; Intelligence (Select)

Press. Kathy Bushkin. **202-224-5854**

AA. Tom Hoog

Secretary. Elsie Vance

HASKELL, FLOYD K (D–CO). 452 Russell Senate Office Bldg, 20510. **202-224-5951.** (h) Littleton, CO. **303-837-2411.** (h) 907 6th St SW, Washington, DC 20024

Committees. Energy and Natural Resources; Finance; Small Business (Select)

Press. Darrell Knuffke. **202-224-5941**

AA. John Cevette (h) 2128 N Courthouse Rd, Arlington, VA 22201

Secretary. Mary B Nudd (h) 7424 Colshire Dr, McLean, VA 22101. **703-356-4290**

HATCH, ORRIN G (R–UT). 6313 Dirksen Senate Office Bldg, 20510. **202-224-5251.** Salt Lake City, UT. **801-524-4380.** (h) 2127 Galloping Way, Vienna, VA 22180

Committees. Human Resources; Judiciary; Economic (Joint)

Press. Bill Hendrix. **202-224-5251**

AA. Frank A Madsen (h) 1912 Great Falls St, McLean, VA 22101

Secretary. Sue Brands (h) 3722 S 12th St, Arlington, VA 22204. **703-521-0026**

HATFIELD, MARK O (R–OR). 463 Russell Senate Office Bldg, 20510. **202-224-3753.** (h) Newport, OR. **503-399-5731**

Committees. Appropriations; Energy and Natural Resources; Rules and Administration; Printing (Joint); Indian Affairs (Select)

Press. Walt Evans. **202-224-3753**

AA. Gerald W Frank

Secretary. Marian Bruner

HATFIELD, PAUL G (D–MT). 1121 Dirksen Senate Office Bldg, 20510. **202-224-2651.** (h) Great Falls, MT

Committees. Armed Services; Judiciary

Press. Alec Hanson. **202-224-2651**

Secretary. Mrs Sherry Lincoln

HATHAWAY, WILLIAM D (R–ME). 248 Russell Senate Office Bldg, 20510. **202-224-2523.** (h) Auburn, ME. **207-783-2049.** (h) 6707 Wemberly Way, McLean, VA 22207

Committees. Finance; Human Resources; Intelligence (Select); Small Business (Select)

Press. Bill Fredrick. **202-224-2523**

AA. Edward S King (h) 3502 Taylor St, Chevy Chase, MD 20015. **301-654-4817**

Secretary. Elizabeth Blackshaw (h) 1122 Waverly Way, McLean, VA 22101. **703-356-1123**

HAYAKAWA, S I (R–CA). 6217 Dirksen Senate Office Bldg, 20510. **202-224-3841.** (h) Mill Valley, CA. **415-556-8686**

Committees. Agriculture, Nutrition, and Forestry; Budget; Human Resources

Press. Pat Agnew. **202-224-3841**

AA. Eugene Prat (h) 633 E St SE, Washington, DC 20003. **202-554-2729**

Secretary. Rita Buckingham (h) 4327 Hartford Hills Dr, Silver Hill, MD 20003. **301-423-3294**

HEINZ, H J III (R–PA). 4327 Dirksen Senate Office Bldg, 20510. **202-224-6324.** (h) Pittsburgh, PA. **412-562-0533**

Committees. Banking, Housing, and Urban Affairs; Budget; Governmental Affairs

Press. Larry McCarthy. **202-224-7754**

AA. Geoffrey Garin

Secretary. Dolores Senanis

HELMS, JESSE A (R–NC). 411 Russell Senate Office Bldg, 20510. **202-224-6342.** (h) Raleigh, NC. **919-834-0690**

Committees. Agriculture, Nutrition, and Forestry; Armed Services; Congressional Operations (Joint)

Press and **AA.** Clint Fuller. **202-224-6342.** (h) 3830 N 30th St, Arlington, VA 22207

Secretary. Claire Eastman (h) 915 S Washington St, Alexandria, VA 22314

HOLLINGS, ERNEST F (D–SC). 115 Russell Senate Office Bldg, 20510. **202-224-6121.** (h) Charleston, SC. **803-723-5211**

Committees. Appropriations; Budget; Commerce, Science, and Transportation.

Press. Mary Ellis. **202-224-6121**

AA. Michael J Copps (h) 6916 Baylor Dr, Alexandria, VA 22307. **703-768-2677**

Secretary. Mary Hughes (h) 2500 Q St, Washington, DC 20007. **202-338-1574**

HUDDLESTON, WALTER (D–KY). 3327 Dirksen Senate Office Bldg, 20510. **202-224-2541.** (h) Elizabethtown, KY. **502-769-6316.** (h) 4139 27th St N, Arlington, VA 22207

Committees. Agriculture, Nutrition, Forestry; Appropriations; Intelligence (Select)

Press. Ed Graves. **202-224-2542**

AA. Philip L Swift (h) 6388 Dockscer Ter, Falls Church, VA 22041. **703-256-8990**

Secretary. Kathryn Roberts (h) 11004 Vale Rd, Oakton, VA 22124. **703-620-4663**

HUMPHREY, MURIEL B (D–MN). 2121 Dirksen Senate Office Bldg, 20510. **202-224-3244.** (h) Waverly, MN. **612-725-2632**

Committees. Foreign Relations; Governmental Affairs

Press. Betsy South. **202-224-3244**

AA. Albert Saunders (h) 3420 N George Mason Dr, Arlington, VA 22207. **703-536-6986**

Secretary. Violet W Biglane (h) 4424 Fewsenden St, Washington, DC 20016. **202-244-5911**

INOUYE, DANIEL K (D–HI). 442 Russell Senate Office Bldg, 20510. **202-224-3934.** (h) Honolulu, HI. **808-946-4322.** (h) 8013 Erb Farm Dr, Bethesda, MD 20034

Committees. Appropriations; Commerce, Science, and Transportation; Intelligence (Select, chairman)

Press. Rick Sia. **202-224-3934**

AA. Eiler Ravnholt (h) 3566 Raymoor Rd, Kensington, MD 20795

Secretary. Sharon Yoshimura

JACKSON, HENRY A (D–WA). 137 Russell Senate Office Bldg, 20510. **202-224-9378.** (h) Everett, WA. NP

Committees. Energy and Natural Resources (chairman); Armed Services; Governmental Affairs

Press. Brian Corcoran. **202-224-9378**

Secretary. Erna W Miller (h) 210 A St NE, Washington, DC 20002

JAVITS, JACOB K (R–NY). 321 Russell Senate Office Bldg, 20510. **202-224-6542.** (h) New York, NY. **212-867-7777**

Committees. Foreign Relations; Governmental Affairs; Human Resources; Economic (Joint); Small Business (Select)

Press. Edmund Pinto. **202-224-8352**

AA. Don Kellermann (h) 3001 Veazey Ter, Washington, DC. **202-686-0438**

Secretary. Geraldine Welch (h) 4737 N 14th St, Arlington, VA

JOHNSTON, J BENNETT JR (D–LA). 421 Russell Senate Office Bldg, 20510. **202-224-5824.** (h) Shreveport, LA. **318-226-5085**

Committees. Appropriations; Budget; Energy and Natural Resources

Press. Kirk Melancon. **202-224-5824**

AA. James H Chubbuck (h) 3045 Chestnut St, Washington, DC 20015. **202-686-1218**

Secretary. Laurelie M Wallace (h) 1115 Litton Ln, McLean, VA 22101

KENNEDY, EDWARD M (D–MA). 431 Russell Senate Office Bldg, 20510. **202-224-4543.** (h) Hyannis Port, MA. **617-223-2826.** (h) 636 Chain Bridge Rd, McLean, VA 22101

Committees. Human Resources; Judiciary; Economic (Joint); Nutrition and Human Needs (Select)

Press. Hadley Roff. **202-224-4543**

AA. Edward M Martin (h) 6906 Breezewood Ter, Rockville, MD. **202-881-3058**

Secretary. Angelique Lee (h) 2500 Q St, Washington, DC 20007

LAXALT, PAUL D (R–NV). 326 Russell Senate Office Bldg, 20510. **202-224-3542.** (h) Carson City, NV. **702-883-1930.** (h) 6600 Midhill Pl, Falls Church, VA 20043

Committees. Energy and Natural Resources; Finance; Judiciary; Small Business (Select)

Press. Dave Bethel. **202-224-1053**

AA. David Russell (h) 3003 Van Ness St, Washington, DC 20008. **202-686-9656**

Secretary. Carol Laxalt, 6660 Midhill Pl, Falls Church, VA 22043

LEAHY, PATRICK J (D–VT). 232 Russell Senate Office Bldg, 20510. **202-224-4242.** (h) Burlington, VT. **802-642-3193**

Committees. Agriculture, Nutrition, and Forestry; Appropriations; Nutrition and Human Needs (Select)

Press. David Julyan. **202-224-4242**

AA. Paul A Bruhn

Secretary. Particia McLaughlin, 7517 Ambergate Pl-2, McLean, VA 22101. **703-356-9044**

LONG, RUSSELL B (D–LA). 217 Russell Senate Office Bldg, 20510. **202-224-4623.** (h) Baton Rouge, LA. **504-387-0181**

Committees. Finance (chairman); Commerce, Science, and Transportation; Taxation (Joint)

Press. John Steen. **202-224-0313**

AA. James Guirard, Jr (h) 1129 Cameron Rd, Alexandria, VA 22308. **703-768-3077**

Secretary. Dorothy Turnipseed (h) 1339 30th St, Washington, DC 20007. **703-337-9055**

LUGAR, RICHARD G (R–IN). 5109 Dirksen Senate Office Bldg, 20510. **202-224-4814.** (h) Indianapolis, IN. **317-269-6555**

Committees. Agriculture, Nutrition, and Forestry; Banking, Housing, and Urban Affairs; Intelligence (Select)

Press. Roger Duncan. **202-224-4814**

AA. Mitchell E Daniels, Jr (h) 23 3rd St NE, Washington, DC. **202-543-3492**

Secretary. Erika Lee (h) 5375 Duke St, Alexandria, VA 22304. **703-370-9064**

McCLELLAN, JOHN L (D–AR). 3241 Dirksen Senate Office Bldg, 20510. **202-224-2353.** (h) Little Rock, AR. **501-378-6101.** (h) 2801 New Mexico Ave, Washington, DC 20007

Committees. Appropriations (chairman); Governmental Affairs; Judiciary

Press and **AA.** Buddy Whiteaker. **202-224-7827.** (h) 8415 Thames St, Springfield, VA 22151. **703-978-8936**

Secretary. Margie Nicholson (h) 1600 S Eads St, Arlington, VA 22202

McCLURE, JAMES A (R–ID). 5229 Dirksen Senate Office Bldg, 20510. **202-224-2752.** (h) Payette, ID. NP (h) 3567 N Venice, Arlington, VA 22207

Committees. Budget; Energy and Natural Resources; Environment and Public Works; Economic (Joint)

Press. Todd Neuenschwander. **202-224-2752**

AA. Richard K Thompson (h) 3704 Maryland, Alexandria, VA 22309. **703-360-9442**

Secretary. Ms Bobbie Butler (h) 812 Rittenhouse St, Washington, DC 20011

McGOVERN, GEORGE (D–SD). 4239 Dirksen Senate Office Bldg, 20510. **202-224-2321.** (h) Mitchell, SD. **605-996-7563**

Committees. Agriculture, Nutrition, and Forestry; Foreign Relations; Nutrition and Human Needs (Select, chairman)

Press. Bob McKeithen. **202-224-2321**

AA. George V Cunningham (h) 3918 Calvert St, Washington, DC 20007. **202-337-2036**

Secretary. Patricia J Donovan

McINTYRE, THOMAS J (D–NH). 105 Russell Senate Office Bldg, 20510. **202-224-2841.** (h) Laconia, NH. **603-524-0447.** (h) 2923 Garfield St, Washington, DC 20008

Committees. Armed Services; Banking, Housing, and Urban Affairs; Defense Production (Joint); Small Business (Select)

Press. Edward Dooley. **202-224-2841**

AA. David A Laroche (h) 46 N Fenwick St, Arlington, VA 22201. **703-527-4613**

Secretary. Patricia McHugh (h) 4117 Davis Pl 302, 20007. **202-337-0960**

MAGNUSON, WARREN G (D–WA). 127 Russell Senate Office Bldg, 20510. **202-224-2621.** (h) Seattle, WA. **206-442-5545**

Committees. Commerce, Science, and Transportation (chairman); Appropriations; Budget

Press. Ken Reigner. **202-224-2621**

AA. Michael E Steward (h) 2401 Calvert St, Washington, DC 20008. **202-234-2579**

Secretary. Alma A Hostetler (h) 2853 Ontario Rd, Washington, DC 20009. **202-234-5612**

MATHIAS, CHARLES MC JR (R–MD). 358 Russell Senate Office Bldg, 20510. **202-224-4654.** (h) Frederick, MD. **301-694-8225.** (h) 3808 Leland St, Chevy Chase, MD 20015

Committees. Appropriations; Governmental Affairs; Judiciary; Intelligence (Select)

Press. Charles Cogan. **202-224-8870**

AA. Ed O'Connell

Secretary. Amelia H Graves (h) 1001 Wilson Blvd, Arlington, VA 22209

MATSUNAGA, SPARK M (D–HI). 362 Russell Senate Office Bldg 20510. **202-224-6361.** (h) Honolulu, HI. **808-546-7555**

Committees. Energy and Natural Resources; Finance; Veterans' Affairs

Press. Elma Henderson. **202-224-6361**

AA. Sheri Matano (h) 413 D St SE, Washington, DC 20003. **202-546-6249**

Secretary. Virginia Ing (h) 317 3rd St SE, 6, Washington, DC 20003

MELCHER, JOHN (D–MT) 440 Russell Senate Office Bldg, 20510. **202-224-2644.** (h) Forsyth, Mt. **406-449-5251.** (h) 300 New Jersey Ave, Washington, DC, 20001

Committees. Agriculture, Nutrition, and Forestry; Commerce, Science, and Transportation; Indian Affairs (Select); Aging (Special)

Press. Henry Hicks. **202-224-2644**

AA. Ben Stong (h) 404 W Great Falls Dr, Falls Church, VA 22041

METZENBAUM, HOWARD M (D–OH). 342 Russell Senate Office Bldg, 20510. **202-224-2315.** (h) Shaker Heights, OH. **216-522-7272**

Committees. Energy and Natural Resources; Judiciary; Indian Affairs (Select)

Press. Tom Hall. **202-224-2315**

AA. Mary Jane C Due (h) 608 6th Pl SW, Washington, DC. **202-484-3245**

Secretary. Juanita C Powe (h) Apt 710, 907 6th St SW, Washington, DC 20024

MORGAN, ROBERT B (D–NC). 2107 Dirksen Senate Office Bldg, 20510. **202-224-3154.** (h) Lillington, NC. **919-893-5330**

Committees. Armed Services; Banking, Housing, and Urban Affairs; Ethics (Select); Intelligence (Select)

Press and **AA.** Carroll Leggett. **202-224-3154**

Secretary. Sarah E Stewart

MOYNIHAN, DANIEL P (D–NY). 1109 Dirksen Senate Office Bldg, 20510. **202-224-4451.** (h) New York, NY. **212-661-5150.** (h) 627 G St SE, Washington, DC 20003

Committees. Environment and Public Works; Finance; Intelligence (Select)

Press. Tim Russert. **202-224-4451**

AA. Stuart Gordon (h) 1221 S Washington, Alexandria, VA. **703-524-6385**

Secretary. Florence Roth

MUSKIE, EDMUND S (D–ME). 145 Russell Senate Office Bldg, 20510. **202-224-5344.** (h) Waterville, ME. **207-873-3361**

Committees. Budget (chairman); Environment and Public Works; Governmental Affairs; Aging (Special)

Press. Bob Rose. **202-224-5344**

AA. Charles J Micoleau (h) 3179 Porter St, Washington, DC 20008. **202-362-4549**

NELSON, GAYLORD (D–WI). 221 Russell Senate Office Bldg, 20510. **202-224-5323.** (h) Madison, WI. NL (h) 3611 Calvend Ln, Kensington, MD 20795

Committees. Armed Services; Banking, Housing, and Urban Affairs; Ethics (Select); Intelligence (Select)

Press. Jim McCulla. **202-224-5323**

AA. J Louis Hanson (h) 1435 4th St SW, Washington, DC 20024. **202-554-3246**

Secretary. Joan C Mutz (h) 2516 Tunlaw Rd, Washington, DC 20007

NUNN, SAM (D–GA). 110 Russell Senate Office Bldg, 20510. **202-224-3521.** (h) Perry, GA. NL

Committees. Armed Services; Governmental Affairs; Small Business (Select)

Press. Roland McElroy. **202-224-3521**

AA. Richard B Ray

Secretary. Martha Tate

PACKWOOD, BOB (R–OR). 1317 Dirksen Senate Office Bldg, 20510. **202-224-5244.** (h) Portland, OR. **503-233-4471**

Committees. Commerce, Science, and Transportation; Finance; Small Business (Select)

Press. Mimi Weyforth. **202-224-5244**

AA. Alan F Holmer (h) 7714 Falstaff Ct, McLean, VA. **703-356-5263**

Secretary. Cathy Wagner (h) 416 New Jersey Ave SE, Washington, DC 20003. **202-546-2462**

PEARSON, JAMES B (R–KS). 5313 Dirksen Senate Office Bldg, 20510. **202-224-4774.** (h) Prairie Village, KS. **913-262-0002**

Committees. Commerce, Science, and Transportation; Foreign Relations; Intelligence (Select)

Press. Emerson Lynn. **202-224-4774**

AA. Jerry B Waters (h) 7900 Lynbrook, Bethesda, MD 20014. **301-657-3838**

Secretary. Frances J Cody (h) 6101 Edsall Rd, Alexandria, VA 22304. **703-751-0422**

PELL, CLAIBORNE (D–RI). 325 Russell Senate Office Bldg, 20510. **202-224-4642.** (h) Newport, RI. **401-847-0003.** (h) 3425 Prospect St NW, Washington, DC 20007

Committees. Foreign Relations; Human Resources; Rules and Administration; Library (Joint)

Press. William Bryant. **202-224-4642**

AA. Thomas G Hughes (h) 4478 MacArthur Blvd, Washington, DC 20007. **202-337-3956**

Secretary. Janice H Demers (h) 3252 Prospect St, Washington, DC 20007. **202-337-4084**

PERCY, CHARLES H (R–IL). 4321 Dirksen Senate Office Bldg, 20510. **202-224-2152.** (h) Wilmette, IL. **312-251-4962**

Committees. Foreign Relations; Governmental Affairs; Economic (Joint); Nutrition and Human Needs (Select); Aging (Special)

Press. John Walker. **202-224-2152**

AA. Joseph A Farrell

Secretary. Nadine Jacobsen

PROXMIRE, WILLIAM (D–WI). 5241 Dirksen Senate Office Bldg, 20510. **202-224-5653.** (h) Madison, WI. **608-252-5338.** (h) 3097 Ordway St, Washington, DC 20008

Committees. Banking, Housing, and Urban Affairs (chairman); Appropriations; Defense Production (Joint, chairman); Economic (Joint)

Press and **AA.** Howard Shuman. **202-224-5653**

Secretary. Arlene Branca

RANDOLPH, JENNINGS (D–WV). 5121 Dirksen Senate Office Bldg, 20510. **202-224-6472.** (h) Elkins, WV. **304-636-2000.** (h) 4608 Reservoir Rd, Washington, DC 20007

Committees. Environment and Public Works (chairman); Human Resources; Veterans' Affairs

Press. George Lawless, Jr. **202-224-9840**

AA. Phillip V McGance

Secretary. Stella A Sargent (h) 4002 Belle Rive Ter, Alexandria, VA 22309. **703-780-0147**

RIBICOFF, ABRAHAM A (D–CT). 337 Russell Senate Office Bldg, 20510. **202-224-2823.** (h) Hartford, CT. **203-244-3545**

Committees. Governmental Affairs (chairman); Finance; Taxation (Joint); Economic (Joint); Ethics (Select)

Press. Fred Asselin. **202-224-2823**

AA. Malcolm O Campbell, Jr (h) 602 E Capitol St, Washington, DC 20003. **202-547-0195**

Secretary. Vergie L Cass (h) 4000 Massachusetts Ave, Washington, DC 20016. **202-363-9304**

RIEGLE, DONALD W JR (D–MI). 1207 Dirksen Senate Office Bldg, 20510. **202-224-4822.** (h) Flint, MI. **313-232-7707**

Committees. Banking, Housing, and Urban Affairs; Commerce, Science, and Transportation; Human Resources
Press. Suzanne M Lowery. **202-224-6785.** (h) **202-547-3772**
AA. Carl Blake
Secretary. Janet Howard

ROTH, WILLIAM V JR (R–DE). 4327 Dirksen Senate Office Bldg, 20510. **202-224-2441.** (h) Wilmington, DE. **302-656-8755**
Committees. Finance; Governmental Affairs; Economic (Joint)
Press. Very Hershberg. **202-224-2441**
AA. Dennis Thomas (h) 2600 Nicodemus Rd, Westminster, MD 21157
Secretary. Catherine M Donahoe (h) 3327 Reservoir Rd, Washington, DC 20007

SARBANES, PAUL S (D–MD). 362 Russell Senate Office Bldg, 20510. **202-224-4524.** (h) Baltimore, MD. **301-366-5341**
Committees. Banking, Housing, and Urban Affairs; Foreign Relations
Press. John Baran. **202-224-4524**
AA. Burton V Wides (h) 208 9th St, Washington, DC 20003. **202-546-4498**

SASSER, JAMES R (D–TN). 2106 Dirksen Senate Office Bldg, 20510. **202-224-3344.** (h) Nashville, TN. **615-373-2558.** (h) 2224 Hawthorne, Washington, DC
Committees. Appropriations; Budget; Governmental Affairs
Press. Drucilla Smith. **202-224-3344**
AA. Jerry Grant (h) 2901 S Grant, Arlington, VA 22202
Secretary. Dolores H Stover (h) 2550 N Van Dorn, Alexandria, VA 22302. **703-931-6875**

SCHMITT, HARRISON H (R–NM). 1251 Dirksen Senate Office Bldg, 20510. **202-224-5521.** (h) Silver City, NM. **505-538-2513**
Committees. Banking, Housing, and Urban Affairs; Commerce, Science, and Transportation; Ethics (Select)
Press. Anne Grahan. **202-224-5521**
AA. Tony Payton (h) 907 6th St SW, Washington, DC 20024. **202-554-8795**
Secretary. Diana Griffin (h) 338 8th St SE, Washington, DC 20003. **202-547-6147**

SCHWEIKER, RICHARD S (R–PA). 253 Russell Senate Office Bldg, 20510. **202-224-4254.** (h) Worcester, PA. NL
Committees. Appropriations; Human Resources; Nutrition and Human Needs (Select)

Press. Troy Gustavson. **202-224-9026**
AA. David Newhall III
Secretary. Elsie M May

SCOTT, WILLIAM LLOYD (R–VA). 2313 Dirksen Senate Office Bldg, 20510. **202-224-2023.** (h) Fairfax, VA. **703-971-3800**
Committees. Armed Services; Judiciary
Press. Jim Roberts. **202-224-2023**
AA. John T White II (h) 8905 Stratford Ln, Alexandria, VA 22308. **703-780-8860**
Secretary. Delphine Neiney (h) 9323 Humphries Dr, Burke, VA 22015

SPARKMAN, JOHN J (D–AL). 3203 Dirksen Senate Office Bldg, 20510. **202-224-4124.** (h) Huntsville, AL. **205-534-4363.** (h) 4928 Indian Ln, Washington, DC 20016
Committees. Foreign Relations (chairman); Banking, Housing, and Urban Affairs; Defense Production (Joint); Economic (Joint)
Press. Grover Smith. **202-224-4124**
AA. Octa R Watson (h) 312 Mansion Dr, Alexandria, VA 22308
Secretary. Ellis Stewart (h) 417 A St SE, Washington, DC 20003. **202-547-4643**

STAFFORD, ROBERT T (R–VT). 5219 Dirksen Senate Office Bldg, 20510. **202-224-5141.** (h) Rutland, VT. **802-775-5446.** (h) 3541 Devon Dr, Falls Church, VA 22042
Committees. Environment and Public Works; Human Resources; Veterans' Affairs; Aging (Special)
Press and AA. Neal Houston. **202-224-5141.** (h) 1124 Cameron Rd, Alexandria, VA 22308. **703-505-1718**
Secretary. Jean W Lupton (h) 3421 Spring Dr, Alexandria, VA 22306. **703-765-4173**

STENNIS, JOHN C (D–MS). 205 Russell Senate Office Bldg, 20510. **202-224-6253.** (h) DeKalb, MS. **601-743-2631**
Committees. Armed Services (chairman); Appropriations
Press. Don Fitts. **202-224-6253**
AA. William E Cresswell (h) 1208 Westgrove Blvd, Alexandria, VA 22307. **703-768-2887**
Secretary. Mildred M Ward (h) 2500 Wisconsin Ave, Washington, DC. **202-337-7698**

STEVENS, TED (R–AK). 411 Russell Senate Office Bldg, 20510. **202-224-3004.** (h) Anchorage, AK. **907-272-9561**

Committees. Appropriations; Commerce, Science, and Transportation; Governmental Affairs
AA. Timothy A McKeever
Secretary. Celia B Niemi (h) 700 New Hampshire Ave, Washington, DC. **202-338-0731**

STEVENSON, ADLAI E (D–IL). 456 Russell Senate Office Bldg, 20510. **202-224-2854.** (h) Hanover, IL, NP
Committees. Banking, Housing, and Urban Affairs; Commerce, Science, and Transportation; Ethics (Select, chairman); Intelligence (Select)
Press. Hal Levy. **202-224-2854**
AA. Thomas J Wagner (h) 7707 Glenmore Spring Way, Bethesda, MD 20034
Secretary. Phyllis E Gustafson (h) 1101 New Hampshire Ave, Washington, DC 20037. **202-223-3321**

STONE, RICHARD (DICK)(D–FL) 1327 Dirksen Senate Office Bldg, 20510. **202-224-3041.** (h) Tallahassee, FL. **904-385-8116.** (h) 700 New Hampshire Ave, Washington, DC 20037
Committees. Agriculture, Nutrition, and Forestry; Foreign Relations; Veterans' Affairs
Press. Jean Parvin. **202-224-3041**
AA. Eli Feinberg (h) 4936 Western Ave, Chevy Chase, MD 20016
Secretary. Cecilia Jackson (h) 6036 Westchester Park Dr, College Park, MD 20740

TALMADGE, HERMAN E (D–GA) 109 Russell Senate Office Bldg, 20510. **202-224-3643.** (h) Lovejoy, GA. **404-478-6677**
Committees. Agriculture, Nutrition, and Forestry (chairman); Finance; Veterans' Affairs; Taxation (Joint)
Press. Gordon Roberts. **202-224-3643**
AA. Rogers T Wade
Secretary. Rita Hubler

THURMOND, STROM (R–SC) 209 Russell Senate Office Bldg, 20510. **202-224-5972.** (h) Aiken, SC. **803-648-1959.** (h) McLean, VA
Committees. Armed Services; Judiciary; Veterans' Affairs
Press. Ed Harrill. **202-224-5972.**
Secretary. Sylvia Mitchell (h) College Park, MD

TOWER, JOHN G (R–TX). 142 Russell Senate Office Bldg, 20510. **202-224-2934.** (h) Wichita Falls, TX. NL

Committees. Armed Services; Banking, Housing, and Urban Affairs; Defense Production (Joint); Ethics (Select)

Press. Alan Balch. **202-224-2934**

AA. Carolyn Bacon (h) 950 25th St, Washington, DC 20037. **202-965-0866**

Secretary. Martha Jennison (h) 208 Wilkes, Alexandria, VA 22314

WALLOP, MALCOLM (R–WY). 6327 Dirksen Senate Office Bldg, 20510. **202-224-6441.** (h) Big Horn, WY. **307-674-4311**

Committees. Environment and Public Works; Judiciary; Intelligence (Select)

AA. Becky Lambert (h) 3232 Prospect St, Washington, DC 20007. **202-337-1367**

Secretary. Pat Halcomb (h) 2305 Pennsylvania Ave, Washington, DC 20037

WEICKER, LOWELL P JR (R–CT) 313 Russell Senate Office Bldg, 20510. **202-224-4041.** (h) Greenwich, CT. **203-335-0195.** (h) McLean, VA

Committees. Appropriations; Energy and Natural Resources; Ethics (Select); Small Business (Select)

Press. Fred Mann. **202-224-4041**

AA. Roy E Kinsey (h) 8905 Union Farm Rd, Alexandria, VA 22309

Secretary. Marge Broadbin (h) 1743 N Cliff St, Alexandria, VA 22301. **703-548-5983**

WILLIAMS, HARRISON A JR (D–NJ). 352 Russell Senate Office Bldg, 20510. **202-224-4744.** (h) Bedminster, NJ. NP

Committees. Human Resources (chairman); Banking, Housing, and Urban Affairs; Rules and Administration; Library (Joint); Aging (Special)

Press. Mike McCurry. **202-224-9717**

AA. Walter Ramsay (h) 215 Constitution Ave NE, Washington, DC 20003. **202-543-4131**

Secretary. Jean Jones (h) 3160 Greenway Pl, Alexandria, VA 22302

YOUNG, MILTON R (R–ND). 5205 Dirksen Senate Office Bldg, 20510. **202-224-2043.** (h) La Moure, ND. **701-883-5301.** (h) 3001 Veazey Ter, Washington, DC 20008

Committees. Agriculture, Nutrition, and Forestry; Appropriations

Press. Karen Steidl. **202-224-2043**

AA. Robert J Christman (h) 4153 Novar Dr, Chantilly, VA 22021. **703-378-6716**

Secretary. Patricia B Young (h) 3001 Veazey Ter, Washington, DC 20008

ZORINSKY, EDWARD (D–NE). 1407 Dirksen Senate Office Bldg, 20510. **202-224-6551.** (h) Omaha, NE. **402-221-4381**

Committees. Agriculture, Nutrition, and Forestry; Commerce, Science, and Transportation; Nutrition and Human Needs (Select)

Press. Kent Wolgamott and Rich Fitzsimmons. **202-224-6551**

Secretary. Carolyn M Andrade (h) 1334 31st St, Washington, DC 20007. **202-965-5112**

United States Representatives (Alphabetical)

ABNOR, JAMES (R–SD, 2nd). 1224 Longworth House Office Bldg, 20515. **202-225-5165.** (h) Kennebec, SC. **605-869-2445**

Committees. Public Works; Veterans Affairs; Aging (Select)

Press. Jane Boorman

AA. Walter C Conahan.

Secretary. Dana K Urban

ADDABBO, JOSEPH P (D–NY, 7th). 2440 Rayburn House Office Bldg, 20515. **202-225-3461.** (h) Ozone Park, NY. **212-268-6161**

Committees. Appropriations; Small Business

Press and AA. Helen T MacDonald

LA. Irving Maness

AKAKA, DANIEL K (D–HI, 2nd). 415 Cannon House Office Bldg, 20515. **202-225-4906.** (h) Honolulu, HI. **808-546-8952**

Committees. Agriculture; Merchant Marine

Press. D W Harrington.

AA. John Uchima

Secretary. Arlene Sumimoto

ALEXANDER, BILL (D–AR, 1st). 301 Cannon House Office Bldg, 20515. **202-225-4076.** (h) Osceola, AR, NL

Committee. Appropriations

Press. Henry Woods

AA. William J Miles

Secretary. Julia R Smith

ALLEN, CLIFFORD R (D–TN, 5th). 132 Cannon House Office Bldg, 20515. **202-225-4311.** (h) Nashville, TN. **615-352-3545**

Committees. Banking; Veterans' Affairs

Press. Rilla Woods

AA. Bonnie Cowan

AMBRO, JEROME A (D–NY, 3rd). 1313 Longworth House Office Bldg, 20515. **202-225-3865.** (h) East Northport, NY. **516-864-3593**

Committees. Public Works; Science

Press. Dan Driscoll

AA. Barbara Paley

Secretary. Charlotte Dye

AMMERMAN, JOSEPH S (D–PA, 23rd). 1723 Longworth House Office Bldg, 20515. **202-225-5121.** (h) Curwensville, PA. **814-236-2356**

Committees. Agriculture; House Administration

Press. Alan F Gordon

AA. Neil McAuliffe

Secretary. Colleen J Healy

ANDERSON, GLENN M (D–CA, 32nd). 2410 Rayburn House Office Bldg, 20515. **202-225-6676.** (h) Harbor City, CA. **213-548-2551**

Committees. Merchant Marine; Public Works

AA. Darrel H Sterns

LA. Mark A Theisen

ANDERSON, JOHN B (R–IL, 16th). 1101 Longworth House Office Bldg, 20515. **202-225-5676.** (h) Rockford, IL. **815-962-8807**

Committees. Rules; Assassination (Select)

Press. Michael Vaughn

AA. Michael J Masterson

Secretary. June H Foster

ANDREWS, IKE F (D–NC, 4th). 228 Cannon House Office Bldg, 20515. **202-225-1784.** (h) Research Triangle Park, NC. **919-541-2981**

Committees. Education; Aging (Select)

Press. Robert Auman

AA. Margaret J Sugg

LA. Barbara M Fletcher

ANDREWS, MARK (R–ND, at large). 2470 Rayburn House Office Bldg, 20515. **202-225-2611.** (h) Mapleton, ND. **701-282-0573**

Committee. Appropriations

Press. Donald Jacob

AA. George Stannard

Secretary. Mary Ann Bond

ANNUNZIO, FRANK (D–IL, 11th). 2303 Rayburn House Office Bldg, 20515. **202-225-6661.** (h) Chicago, IL. **312-736-0700**

Committees. Banking; House Administration
AA. Anna Azhderian
Secretary. William Nelson

APPLEGATE, DOUGLAS (D–OH, 18th).
1039 Longworth House Office Bldg, 20515.
202-225-6265. (h) Steubenville, OH.
614-264-1012
Committees. District of Columbia; Public
Works; Veterans' Affairs
Press and LA. Ken Parmelee
Secretary. Pat Wood

ARCHER, BILL (R–TX, 7th). 1024
Longworth House Office Bldg, 20515.
202-225-2571. (h) Houston, TX.
713-226-4941
Committee. Ways and Means
Press. Phillip Moseley
AA. Lloyd O Pierson
Secretary. Jane Uhrig

ARMSTRONG, WILLIAM L (R–CO, 5th).
401 Cannon House Office Bldg, 20515.
202-225-4422. (h) Aurora, CO. 303-837-2655
Committee. Appropriations
Press. Laura Genero
AA. Walt Klein
Secretary. Mary Spaulding

ASHBROOK, JOHN M (R–OH, 17th).
1436 Longworth House Office Bldg, 20515.
202-225-6431. (h) Johnstown, OH.
614-967-5941
Committees. Education; Judiciary; Congressional Operations (Joint)
Press and AA. Ronald Pearson
LA. Donald D Evans

ASHLEY, THOMAS L (D–OH, 9th).
2406 Rayburn House Office Bldg, 20515.
202-225-4146. (h) Toledo, OH.
419-242-9567
Committees. Banking; Budget; Merchant
Marine
Press. William Skow
AA. June G Clendening
Secretary. Sandra Rinck

ASPIN, LES (D–WI, 1st). 439 Cannon
House Office Bldg, 20515. 202-225-3031. (h)
Racine, WI. 414-632-8194 (office)
Committees. Armed Services; Government
Operations
AA. Charles Gonzales
Secretary. Kathy Cooper

AUCOIN, LES (D–OR, 1st). 231 Cannon
House Office Bldg, 20515. 202-225-0855. (h)
Forest Grove, OR. 503-221-2901
Committees. Banking; Merchant Marine
Press. Gene Maudlin
AA. Susan Geoghegan
Secretary. Dayle A Thompson

BADHAM, ROBERT E (R–CA, 40th). 1108
Longworth House Office Bldg, 20515.
202-225-5611. (h) Newport Beach, CA.
714-631-0040
Committees. Armed Services; House
Administration
AA. Brad Hathaway
Secretary. Louise Willett

BAFALIS, L A (SKIP) (R–FL, 10th). 408
Cannon House Office Bldg, 20515.
202-225-2536. (h) Fort Myers Beach, FL.
813-334-4424
Committee. Ways and Means
Press. John J McDavitt
AA. Richard T Nelson
Secretary. Joyce Stone

BALDUS, ALVIN J (D–WI, 3rd). 1424
Longworth House Office Bldg, 20515.
202-225-5506. (h) Menomonie, WI, NL
Committees. Agriculture; Small Business
Press. Joseph E O'Neill
AA. Dave Metzger
Secretary. Margaret Whitford

BARNARD, D DOUGLAS JR (D–GA,
10th). 418 Cannon House Office Bldg,
20515. 202-225-4101. (h) Augusta, GA.
404-724-0739
Committees. Banking; Veterans' Affairs
Press. Becky Thompson
AA. D Mayne Elder
Secretary. Barbara Wyche

BAUCUS, MAX (D–MT, 1st). 226 Cannon
House Office Bldg, 20515. 202-225-3211. (h)
Missoula, MT. 406-728-2043
Committee. Appropriations
Press. Kayle Jackson
AA. Steve Browning
Secretary. Holly Kaleczyc

BAUMAN, ROBERT E (R–MD, 1st). 118
Cannon House Office Bldg, 20515.
202-225-5311. (h) Easton, MD. 301-822-4300
(office)
Committees. Interior; Merchant Marine;
Outer Continental Shelf (Ad Hoc Select)

AA. Richard L Ribbentrop
Secretary. Nancy Howard

BEARD EDWARD P (D–RI, 2nd). 131
Cannon House Office Bldg, 20515.
202-225-2735. (h) Cranston, RI.
401-528-4871
Committees. Education; Veterans' Affairs;
Aging (Select)
Press. Mort Blender
AA. John F Smollins, Jr
Secretary. Beverly L G Moss

BEARD, ROBIN (R–TN, 6th). 124 Cannon
House Office Bldg, 20515. 202-225-2811. (h)
Franklin, TN, NL
Committees. Armed Services; Narcotics
Abuse (Select)
Press. Charles Haber
AA. Gary Sisco
Secretary. Patricia A Madson

BEDELL, BERKLEY W (D–IA, 6th). 316
Cannon House Office Bldg, 20515.
202-225-5476. (h) Spirit Lake, IA.
712-336-2516
Committees. Agriculture; International
Relations; Small Business
Press. Steve Cook
AA. Ken Fredgren
Secretary. Nancy Payne

BEILENSON, ANTHONY C (D–CA, 23rd).
1730 Longworth House Office Bldg, 20515.
202-225-5911. (h) Los Angeles, CA.
213-824-7081
Committees. International Relations;
Judiciary; Science
AA. Jan Faulstich

BENJAMIN, ADAM JR (D–IN, 1st). 1608
Longworth House Office Bldg, 20515.
202-225-2461. (h) Hobart, IN, NP
Committee. Appropriations
Press and AA. Earl Thompson
Secretary. Rose Hammers

BENNETT, CHARLES E (D–FL, 3rd). 2113
Rayburn House Office Bldg. 20515.
202-225-2501. (h) Jacksonville, FL.
904-791-2587
Committees. Armed Services; Conduct
Press and LA. John W Farley
AA. S R (Bart) Johnson

BEVILL, TOM (D–AL, 4th). 2305 Rayburn
House Office Bldg, 20515. 202-225-4876. (h)
Jasper, AL. 205-384-3257

Committee. Appropriations
Press. Steve Bevis
AA. Hank Sweitzer
Secretary. Betty S Johnson

BIAGGI, MARIO (D–NY, 10th). 2421 Rayburn House Office Bldg, 20515. **202-225-2464.** (h) Bronx, NY. **202-792-8000**
Committees. Education; Merchant Marine; Aging (Select)
Press and **AA.** Peter Ilchuk
Secretary. Cyndy Wilkinson

BINGHAM, JONATHAN B (D–NY, 22nd). 2241 Rayburn House Office Bldg, 20515. **202-225-4411.** (h) Bronx, NY. **202-933-2310**
Committees. Interior Affairs; International Relations
Press and **AA.** Gordon C Kerr
Secretary. Paula Altman

BLANCHARD, JAMES J (D–MI, 18th). 330 Cannon House Office Bldg, 20515. **202-225-2101.** (h) Pleasant Ridge, MI. **313-543-1106**
Committees. Banking; Science
Press and **AA.** Susan Laird
Secretary. Celia McCabe

BLOUIN, MICHAEL T (D–IA, 2nd). 213 Cannon House Office Bldg, 20515. **202-225-2911.** (h) Dubuque, IA. **319-556-7575** (office)
Committees. Education; Government Operations; Aging (Select)
Press. Dave Cushing
AA. Roger Woods
Secretary. Susan Glaza

BOGGS, CORINE C (LINDY) (D–LA, 2nd). 1524 Longworth House Office Bldg, 20515. **202-225-6636.** (h) New Orleans, LA. **504-581-1441**
Committee. Appropriations
Press. Mimi Griffith
AA. Barbara A Rathe
LA. Jan Schoonmaker

BOLAND, EDWARD P (D–MA, 2nd). 2426 Rayburn House Office Bldg, 20515. **202-225-5601.** (h) Springfield, MA. **413-734-1739**
Committee. Appropriations
Press. Mike Broman
AA. P Joseph Donoghue
Secretary. Joan Fay Campbell

BOLLING, RICHARD (D–MO, 5th). 2465 Rayburn House Office Bldg, 20515. **202-225-4535.** (h) Kansas City, MO. **816-842-4798**
Committees. Rules; Economic (Joint); Ethics (Select)
Press and **AA.** Nancy R Lowe
Secretary. Gladyce Sumida

BONOIR, DAVID E (D–MI, 12th). 1123 Longworth House Office Bldg, 20515. **202-225-2106.** (h) Mount Clemens, MI. **313-469-3232**
Committees. Merchant Marine; Public Works
AA. James W Vollman

BONKER, DON L (D–WA, 3rd). 1529 Longworth House Office Bldg, 20515. **202-225-3536.** (h) Olympia, WA. **206-753-9528**
Committees. International Relations; Merchant Marine; Aging (Select)
Press. Jim Van Nostrand
AA. David V Yaden
Secretary. Louise D Hardman

BOWEN, DAVID R (D–MS, 2nd). 116 Cannon House Office Bldg, 20515. **202-225-5876.** (h) Cleveland, MS. **601-843-4630**
Committees. Agriculture; Merchant Marine
Press. John Perkins
AA. John Hugh Henry
Secretary. Retha Jeffreys

BRADEMAS, JOHN (D–IN, 3rd). 1236 Longworth House Office Bldg, 20515. **202-225-3915.** (h) South Bend, IN. **219-233-5964**
Committees. Education; House Administration; Library (Joint)
AA. Frank Sullivan, Jr
Secretary. Agnes Ribarich

BREAUX, JOHN B (D–LA, 7th). 2443 Rayburn House Office Bldg, 20515. **202-225-2031.** (h) Crowley, LA. **318-788-1525**
Committees. Merchant Marine; Public Works; Continental Shelf (Ad Hoc Select)
Press. Sandy Branch
AA. Valsin A Marmillion
Secretary. Claudia Henagan

BRECKINRIDGE, JOHN B (D–KY, 6th). 125 Cannon House Office Bldg, 20515. **202-225-4706.** (h) Lexington, KY. **606-253-1501** (office)

Committees. Agriculture; Small Business
AA. Carolyn H Giolito

BRINKLEY, JACK (D–GA, 3rd). 2412 Rayburn House Office Bldg, 20515. **202-225-5901.** (h) Columbus, GA. **404-324-3091** (office)
Committees. Armed Services; Veterans' Affairs
Press. Bob Fort
AA. Larry M Wheeler
Secretary. Dorothy H Miles

BRODHEAD, WILLIAM M (D–MI, 17th). 416 Cannon House Office Bldg, 20515. **202-225-4961.** (h) Detroit, MI, NP
Committee. Ways and Means
Press and **AA.** J Phillip Jourdan
Secretary. Ann Ogden

BROOKS, JACK (D–TX, 9th). 2449 Rayburn House Office Bldg, 20515. **202-225-6565.** (h) Beaumont, TX. **713-832-8539** (office)
Committees. Government Operations; Judiciary; Congressional Operations (Joint)
AA. D Sharon Matts
Secretary. Ginger Heuer

BROOMFIELD, WILLIAM S (R–MI, 19th). 2435 Rayburn House Office Bldg, 20515. **202-225-6135.** (h) Birmingham, MI. **313-642-3800**
Committees. International Relations; Small Business
AA. John R Sinclair
Secretary. Nancy G Comer

BROWN, CLARENCE J (R–OH, 7th). 2242 Rayburn House Office Bldg, 20515. **202-225-4324.** (h) Urbana, OH. **513-653-5555**
Committees. Government Operations; Interstate Commerce; Economic (Joint)
Press. Roger Bolton
AA. James D McIntire
Secretary. Margaret Harpster

BROWN, GARRY (R–MI, 3rd). 2446 Rayburn House Office Bldg, 20515. **202-225-5011.** (h) Schoolcraft, MI. **616-679-5816**
Committees. Banking; Government Operations; Defense (Joint); Economic (Joint)
Press and **AA.** John W Lampmann
Secretary. DeAnna L De Long

BROWN, GEORGE E JR (D–CA, 36th). 2342 Rayburn House Office Bldg, 20515. **202-225-6161.** (h) Colton, CA. **714-825-2472**
Committees. Agriculture; Science; Atomic Energy (Joint)
AA. Thomas H Moss
Secretary. Pat Hester

BROYHILL, JAMES T (R–NC, 10th). 2227 Rayburn House Office Bldg, 20515. **202-225-2576.** (h) Lenoir, NC. **704-754-9564**
Committees. Budget; Interstate Commerce
Press and AA. Don Wilson
Secretary. Lynn Clayton

BUCHANAN, JOHN (R–AL, 6th). 2159 Rayburn House Office Bldg, 20515. **202-225-4921.** (h) Birmingham, AL. **205-251-4455**
Committees. Education; International Relations
AA. Janean L Mann and James T Apple

BURGENER, CLAIR W (R–CA, 43rd). 436 Cannon House Office Bldg, 20515. **202-225-3906.** (h) Rancho Santa Fe, CA. **714-231-1912**
Committees. Appropriations; Budget
Press. Brent Erkman
AA. Harry Compton
Secretary. Jayne Gillenwaters

BURKE, J HERBERT (R–FL, 12th). 2301 Rayburn House Office Bldg, 20515. **202-225-3026.** (h) Hollywood, FL. **305-463-3739**
Committees. House Administration; International Relations; Narcotics Abuse (Select)
AA and Secretary. Lois Blackburn

BURKE, JAMES A (D–MA, 11th). 241 Cannon House Office Bldg, 20515. **202-225-3215.** (h) Milton, MA. **615-472-1314** (office)
Committees. Ways and Means; Taxation (Joint)
AA. Edward J Moore
Secretary. Deborah Swartz

BURKE, YVONNE B (D–CA, 28th). 336 Cannon House Office Bldg, 20515. **202-225-7084.** (h) Los Angeles, CA. **213-678-5424**
Committees. Appropriations; Assassinations (Select)
Press. Julia Mulvaney
AA. Wendell M Hollaway
Secretary. Beverly A King

BURLESON, OMAR (D–TX, 17th). 2369 Rayburn House Office Bldg, 20515. **202-255-6605.** (h) Anson, TX, NL
Committees. Budget; Ways and Means
Press. Levenie Hughes
AA. Judith S Curtis
Secretary. Claudia Sipe

BURLISON, BILL D (D–MO, 10th). 1338 Longworth House Office Bldg, 20515. **202-225-4404.** (h) Cape Girardeau, MO. NL
Committee. Appropriations
Press and AA. Michal Sue Prosser

BURTON, JOHN L (D–CA, 5th). 1714 Longworth House Office Bldg, 20515. **202-225-5161.** (h) San Francisco, CA. **415-457-7272**
Committees. Government Operations; House Administration; Aging (Select)
Press. Ed Siegal

BURTON, PHILLIP (D–CA, 6th). 2454 Rayburn House Office Bldg, 20515. **202-225-4965.** (h) San Francisco, CA. **415-556-4862**
Committees. Education; Interior Affairs
AA. Frank J. Kieliger
Secretary. Nanci Leong

BUTLER, M CALDWELL (R–VA, 6th). 409 Cannon House Office Bldg, 20515. **202-225-5431.** (h) Roanoke, VA. **804-982-6200** (office)
Committees. Judiciary; Small Business
Press. Susan Aheron
AA. Donald W Ruby
Secretary. Lee McKenna

BYRON, GOODLOE E (D–MD, 6th). 1232 Longworth House Office Bldg, 20515. **202-225-2721.** (h) Frederick, MD. **301-662-8622**
Committees. Armed Services; Interior Affairs
Press and AA. Robert H Atkinson
Secretary. Karen E Wakefield

CAPUTO, BRUCE F (R–NY, 23rd). 417 Cannon House Office Bldg, 20515. **202-225-5536.** (h) Yonkers, NY. **914-631-8812**
Committees. Banking; Conduct
Press and AA. Dick Leggitt
Secretary. Regina M Aglietti

CARNEY, CHARLES J (D–OH, 19th). 2235 Rayburn House Office Bldg, 20515.

202-225-5261. (h) Youngstown, OH. **216-746-8071**
Committees. Interstate Commerce; Small Business; Veterans' Affairs.
Press. Phil Ola
AA. Thomas J Keyes
Secretary. Betty Schrinner

CARR, M ROBERT (D–MI, 6th). 332 Cannon House Office Bldg, 20515. **202-225-4872.** (h) East Lansing, MI. **517-489-6517**
Committee. Armed Services; Interior Affairs
Press. Mike Arnett
AA. Bernie Schroeder
Secretary. Kathy Kahn

CARTER, TIM LEE (R–KY, 5th). 2161 Rayburn House Office Building, 20515. **202-225-4601.** (h) Tompkinsville, KY. **502-487-5173**
Committees. Interstate Commerce; Small Business
Press. Johanna Schrambling
AA. and Secretary. Kathleen Dehnel

CAVANAUGH, JOHN J (D–NE, 2nd). 424 Cannon House Office Bldg, 20515. **202-225-4155.** (h) Omaha, NE. **402-221-4117** (office)
Committees. Banking; International Relations
Press. Tom Fogarty
AA. Paul V O'Hara
Secretary. Peg Tentinger

CEDERBERG, ELFORD A (R–MI, 10th). 2306 Rayburn House Office Bldg, 20515. **202-225-3561.** (h) Midland, MI. NL
Committee. Appropriations; Ethics (Select)
Press. Larry Becker
AA. Michael A Forgash
Secretary. Rachelle Rosenberg

CHAPPELL, BILL JR (D–FL, 4th). 2353 Rayburn House Office Bldg, 20515. **202-225-4035.** (h) Ocala, FL. **904-694-3586**
Committee. Appropriations
Press. Bert Otto
AA. H S Matthews
Secretary. Diana K Tully

CHISHOLM, SHIRLEY (D–NY, 12th). 2182 Rayburn House Office Bldg, 20515. **202-225-6231.** (h) Brooklyn, NY. **212-330-7588**
Committee. Rules

Press. Collen O'Connor
AA. and **Secretary.** Carolyn J Smith

CLAUSEN, DON H (R–CA, 2nd). 2336 Rayburn House Office Bldg, 20515. **202-225-3111.** (h) Crescent City, CA. **707-464-3241** (office)
Committees. Interior Affairs; Public Works
Press. John Bovard
AA. Larry Graves
Secretary. Sandra Ball

CLAWSON, DEL (R–CA, 33rd). 2262 Rayburn House Office Bldg, 20515. **202-225-3576.** (h) Downey, CA. **213-923-9200**
Committee. Rules
Press and **AA.** Anita S Charles

CLAY, WILLIAM (D–MO, 1st). 2264 Rayburn House Office Bldg, 20515. **202-225-2406.** (h) St Louis, MO
Committees. Education; Post Office
Press and **AA.** Jerome Williams
LA. Beverly J Schwarz

CLEVELAND, JAMES C (R–NH, 2nd). 2265 Rayburn House Office Bldg, 20515. **202-225-5206.** (h) New London, NH. **603-526-2651**
Committees. House Administration; Public Works; Congressional Operations (Joint)
Press. Kathleen Kaswandik
AA. William R Joslin
Secretary. M Kate Jackson

COCHRAN, THAD (R–MS, 4th). 212 Cannon House Office Bldg, 20515. **202-225-5865.** (h) Jackson, MS. **601-969-1353**
Committees. Public Works; Conduct; Aging (Select); Ethics (Select)
Press. Lynda South
LA. James Lofton
Secretary. Doris Wagley

COHEN, WILLIAM S (R–ME, 2nd). 412 Cannon House Office Bldg, 20515. **202-225-6306.** (h) Bangor, ME. **207-947-6504** (office)
Committees. Judiciary; Small Business; Aging (Select)
Press. Thomas Bright
AA. Thomas A Daffron
Secretary. Linda G Craig

COLEMAN, E THOMAS (R–MO, 6th). 1207 Longworth House Office Bldg, 20515.

202-225-7041. (h) Kansas City, MO. **816-454-1429**
Committees. Agriculture; District of Columbia
Press. Carol Conrow
AA. Dennis E Lambert
Secretary. Marlene Thompson

COLLINS, CARDISS (D–IL, 7th). 113 Cannon House Office Bldg, 20515. **202-225-5006.** (h) Chicago, IL. **312-522-2442**
Committees. District of Columbia; Government Operations; International Relations
LA. Robert Sylvester
Secretary. Dorothy Ross

COLLINS, JAMES M (R–TX, 3rd). 2419 Rayburn House Office Bldg, 20515. **202-225-4201.** (h) Dallas, TX. **214-479-2453** (office)
Committees. Interstate Commerce; Post Office
LA. Shirley Simpson
Secretary. Pam Herath

CONABLE, BARBER B JR (R–NY, 35th). 2228 Rayburn House Office Bldg, 20515. **202-225-3615.** (h) Alexander, NY. **716-343-4030**
Committees. Budget; Ways and Means; Taxation (Joint)
Press and **AA.** Harry K Nicholas
Secretary. Linda McLaughlin

CONTE, SILVIO O (R–MA, 1st). 2300 Rayburn House Office Bldg, 20515. **202-225-5126.** (h) Detroit, MI. **313-861-2569**
Committees. Government Operations; Judiciary
Press. Bill Kirk
AA. Heidi Napper

CORCORAN, THOMAS J (R–IL, 15th). 1107 Longworth House Office Bldg, 20515. **202-225-2976.** (h) Ottawa, IL. **815-434-7176**
Committees. Government Operations; Post Office
Press. Jay Meisenhelder
AA. Don Stephens
Secretary. Mary Cavanaugh

CORMAN, JAMES (D–CA, 21st). 2252 Rayburn House Office Bldg, 20515. **202-225-5811.** (h) Van Nuys, CA. **213-787-1776**
Committees. Small Business; Ways and Means

Press. Michael Orban
AA. Robert C Ruben
Secretary. Colleen Moll

CORNELL, ROBERT J (D–WI, 8th). 1512 Longworth House Office Bldg, 20515. **202-225-5665.** (h) De Pere, WI. **414-465-3931**
Committees. Education; Veterans' Affairs
Press. John Dussling
AA. Elizabeth Ross Withnell
Secretary. Anita Mariana

CORNWELL, DAVID L (D–IN, 8th). 1609 Longworth House Office Bldg, 20515. **202-225-4636.** (h) Paoli, IN. **812-273-4366**
Committee. Public Works
Press. Jane Von Kaenel
AA. Walter Stasey
Secretary. Martha Riester

COTTER, WILLIAM R (D–CT, 1st). 2338 Rayburn House Office Bldg, 20515. **202-225-2265.** (h) Hartford, CT. **203-244-2383** (office)
Committee. Ways and Means
Press. Malcolm O Campbell, Jr
AA. William J Cunningham, Jr
Secretary. Angela A Luzzi

COUGHLIN, LAWRENCE. (R–PA, 13th). 306 Cannon House Office Bldg, 20515. **202-225-6111.** (h) Villanova, PA **215-257-5483**
Committee. Appropriations
Press and **AA.** Mitchell A Rosenfeld
Secretary. Debbie K Williams

CRANE, PHILIP M. (R–IL, 12th). 1406 Longworth House Office Bldg, 20515. **202-225-3711.** (h) Mount Prospect, IL. **312-394-0790**
Committee. Ways and Means
AA. Ed Milne
Secretary. Diana Hoalst

D'AMOURS, NORMAN E (D–NH, 1st). 1503 Longworth House Office Bldg, 20515. **202-225-5456.** (h) Manchester, NH. **603-625-5123**
Committees. Banking; District of Columbia; Merchant Marine
Press. Brad Woodward
AA. John Pfeiffer
Secretary. Sue Beauchesne

DANIEL, ROBERT W, JR (R–VA, 4th). 410 Cannon House Office Bldg, 20515. **202-225-6365.** (h) Spring Grove, VA. **703-866-2200**
Committees. Armed Services; District of Columbia
Press. William Alford
AA. Thad S Murray
Secretary. Barbara J Montgomery

DANIEL, W C (DAN) (D–VA, 5th). 1705 Longworth House Office Bldg, 20515. **202-225-4711.** (h) Danville, VA. **804-384-6719**
Committees. Armed Services; District of Columbia
Press. Terry Hoye
AA. W Fred Fletcher
Press. Vivian Anderson

DANIELSON, GEORGE E (D–CA, 30th). 2447 Rayburn House Office Bldg, 20515. **202-225-5464.** (h) Monterey Park, CA. **213-287-1134**
Committees. International Relations; Judiciary; Veterans' Affairs; Ethics (Select)
Press and **AA.** Ray Sebens
Secretary. Patricia Anderson

DAVIS, MENDEL J (D–SC, 1st). 2442 Rayburn House Office Bldg, 20515. **202-225-3176.** (h) Charleston, SC, NL
Committees. Armed Services; House Administration
AA. W Mullins McLeod
Secretary. Linda G Taylor

DE LA GARZA, E (D–TX, 15th). 1434 Longworth House Office Bldg, 20515. **202-225-2531.** (h) Mission, TX, NL
Committees. Agriculture; International Relations; Merchant Marine; Narcotics Abuse (Select)
AA. Celia Hare Martin

DELANEY, JAMES J (D–NY, 9th). 2267 Longworth House Office Bldg, 20515. **202-225-3965.** (h) Long Island City, NY. **212-793-0729** (office)
Committee. Rules
AA. Dolores Cook

DELLUMS, RONALD V (D–CA, 8th). 1417 Longworth House Office Bldg, 20515. **202-225-2661.** (h) Berkeley, CA. **415-548-7767** (office)
Committees. Armed Services; District of Columbia
Press. Oziel Garza

AA. Barbara Lee Solon
LA. Robert B Brauer

DEVINE, SAMUEL L (R–OH, 12th). 2206 Rayburn House Office Bldg, 20515. **202-225-5355.** (h) Columbus, OH. **614-237-2165**
Committees. House Administration; Interstate Commerce; Library (Joint); Assassinations (Select)
Press. Al Eckes
AA. John S Hoyt
Secretary. Brenda O Vaughn

DICKINSON, WILLIAM L (R–AL, 2nd). 2468 Rayburn House Office Bldg, 20515. **202-225-2901.** (h) Montgomery, AL. **205-832-7292** (office)
Committees. Armed Services; House Administration; Printing (Joint)
Press. Ron Buckhalt
AA. J C Steen
Secretary. Brenda Wambough

DICKS, NORMAN D (D–WA, 6th). 1508 Longworth House Office Bldg, 20515. **202-225-5916.** (h) Bremerton, WA, NL
Committee. Appropriations
Press. Margaret Hollenbeck
Secretary. Shirley A Beck

DIGGS, CHARLES C, JR (D–MI, 13th). 2208 Rayburn House Office Bldg, 20515. **202-225-2261.** (h) Detroit, MI. **313-875-8811** (office)
Committees. District of Columbia; International Relations
Press. Joan Willoughby
AA. Randall Robinson
Secretary. Lorraine McDaniels

DINGELL, JOHN D (D–MI, 16th). 2221 Rayburn House Office Bldg, 20515. **202-225-4071.** (h) Trenton, MI. NP
Committees. Interstate Commerce; Merchant Marine; Small Business
Press. Robert Howard
AA. Marilynne Mikulich
Secretary. Judith Brennan

DODD, CHRISTOPHER J (D–CT, 2nd). 224 Cannon House Office Bldg, 20515. **202-225-2076.** (h) Norwich, CT. **203-886-0139**
Committees. Rules; Continental Shelf (Ad Hoc Select); Assassinations (Select)
Press. Peter Lennon
AA. Beth Provinse
LA. Brice Swinn

DORNAN, ROBERT K (R–CA, 27th). 419 Cannon House Office Bldg, 20515. **202-225-6451.** (h) Santa Monica, CA. **213-824-0222**
Committees. Merchant Marine; Science
AA. Vincent Ryan
Secretary. Linda Love

DOWNEY, THOMAS J (D–NY, 2nd). 326 Cannon House Office Bldg, 20515. **202-225-3335.** (h) West Islip, NY. NL
Committees. Armed Services; Science; Aging (Select)
Press. David Murray
LA. Philip Sparks
Secretary. Hillary Lieber

DRINAN, ROBERT F (D–MA, 4th). 2452 Rayburn House Office Bldg, 20515. **202-225-5931.** (h) Newton, MA. **617-893-1050**
Committees. Government Operations; Judiciary; Aging (Select)
Press and **AA.** Ranny Shuman
Secretary. Mary Anderson

DUNCAN, JOHN J (R–TN, 2nd). 2458 Rayburn House Office Bldg, 20515. **202-225-5435.** (h) Knoxville, TN. **615-246-7577**
Committees. Budget; Ways and Means; Taxation (Joint).
AA. Pat Robinson
LA. Sherry Cook

DUNCAN, ROBERT B (D–OR, 3rd). 440 Cannon House Office Bldg, 20515. **202-225-4811.** (h) Portland, OR. **503-282-0141**
Committee. Appropriations
Press and **AA.** A Conover Spencer
Secretary. Helen Larkin Burton

EARLY, JOSEPH D (D–MA, 3rd). 1032 Longworth House Office Bldg, 20515. **202-225-6101.** (h) Worcester, MA. NL
Committee. Appropriations
Press and **Secretary.** Melanie Markarian
AA. William Rourke

ECKHARDT, BOB (D–TX, 8th). 1741 Longworth House Office Bldg, 20515. **202-225-4901.** (h) Houston, TX. **713-226-4931** (office)
Committees. Interior Affairs; Interstate Commerce
Press and **AA.** Ann K Lower
Secretary. Frances L Gray

EDGAR, ROBERT W (D–PA, 7th).
117 Cannon House Office Bldg, 20515.
202-225-2011. (h) Broomall, PA. NP
Committees. Public Works; Veterans'
Affairs; Assassinations (Select)
Press. Skip Powers
AA. Priscilla Skillman
Secretary. Kathy Keel

EDWARDS, DON (D–CA, 10th).
2329 Rayburn House Office Bldg, 20515.
202-225-3072. (h) San Jose, CA.
408-292-0143
Committees. Judiciary; Veterans' Affairs
Press. Sally Fisher
LA. Gary Fay
Secretary. Doris B Lumpkins

EDWARDS, JACK (R–AL, 1st). 2439
Rayburn House Office Bldg, 20515.
202-225-4931. (h) Mobile, AL. NP
Committee. Appropriations
Press. Clay Swanzy
AA. David C Pruitt III
Secretary. Charlotte C O'Malley

EDWARDS, MICKEY (R–OK, 5th). 1223
Longworth House Office Bldg, 20515.
202-225-2132. (h) Oklahoma City, OK.
405-495-0626
Committees. Education; Interior Affairs
Press. Mick Taylor
LA. Greg Maier
Secretary. Jane Craft

EILBERG, JOSHUA (D–PA, 4th). 2135
Rayburn House Office Bldg, 20515.
202-225-8251. (h) Philadelphia, PA. NL
Committees. Judiciary; Merchant Marine;
Continental Shelf (Ad Hoc Select)
AA. David J Umansky
Secretary. Patricia Gies

EMERY, DAVID F (R–ME, 1st). 425
Cannon House Office Bldg, 20515.
202-225-6116. (h) Rockland, ME.
207-594-4809
Committees. Armed Services; Merchant
Marine
Press. Mike Craig
AA. Charles F Bass
Secretary. Merry Bennett

ENGLISH, GLEN (D–OK, 6th).
109 Cannon House Office Bldg, 20515.
202-225-5565. (h) Cordel, OK.
405-832-2465
Committees. Agriculture; Government Operations; Narcotics Abuse (Select)

Press. Steve Ristow
AA. Gary Dage
Secretary. Judy Dutterer

ERLENBORN, JOHN N (R–IL, 14th).
2236 Rayburn House Office Bldg, 20515.
202-225-3515. (h) Glen Ellyn, IL.
312-668-1417
Committees. Education; Government
Operations
Press. Mike Chapin
AA. Carolyn M Sladek
Secretary. Glenda Zepp

ERTEL, ALLEN E (D–PA, 17th). 1019
Longworth House Office Bldg, 20515.
202-225-4315. (h) Montoursville, PA.
717-323-8491
Committees. Judiciary; Public Works
Press. Bill Brobst
AA. Jon Warren Plebani
Secretary. Margaret Sharkey

EVANS, BILLY LEE (D–GA, 8th).
506 Cannon House Office Bldg, 20515.
202-225-6531. (h) Macon, GA. **912-742-5753**
Committees. Judiciary; Public Works
Press. Carole Amato
AA. Wallace R Wright
Secretary. Martha Parrish

EVANS, DAVID W (D–IN, 6th). 432
Cannon House Office Bldg, 20515.
202-225-2276. (h) Indianapolis, IN.
317-269-7364 (office)
Committees. Banking; Government Opera-
tions; Defense (Joint); Aging (Select)
Press. Dave Lakin
LA. Martin E Tolomeo
Secretary. Sally Battin

EVANS, FRANK E (D–CO, 3rd). 2230
Rayburn House Office Bldg, 20515.
202-225-4761. Pueblo, CO. **303-544-5277**
Committee. Appropriations
Press. Byron Nelson III
AA. Dale Hulshizer
Secretary. Sue Feinthel

EVANS, THOMAS B JR (R–DE, at large).
1113 Longworth House Office Bldg, 20515.
202-225-4165. (h) Wilmington, DE.
302-656-1233
Committees. Banking; Merchant Marine.
AA. William T Kendall
Secretary. Barbara A Andrukitis

FARY, JOHN G (D–IL, 5th). 1116 Longworth House Office Bldg, 20515.

202-225-5701. (h) Chicago, IL. NP
Committee. Public Works
AA. Al Desecki
LA. Tom Campbell

FASCELL, DANTE B (D–FL, 15th). 2256
Rayburn House Office Bldg, 20515.
202-225-4506. (h) Miami, FL. **305-667-3161**
Committees. Government Operations; Inter-
national Relations
Press and Secretary. Barbara Burris, (h)
202-686-0128
AA. Charles R O'Regan

FENWICK, MILLICENT H (R–NJ, 5th).
1427 Longworth House Office Bldg, 20515.
202-225-7300. (h) Bernardsville, NJ.
201-538-7267
Committees. Banking; Small Business;
Conduct
Press. and AA. Hollis McLoughlin
Secretary. Catherine Armstrong

FINDLEY, PAUL (R–IL, 20th). 2133
Rayburn House Office Bldg, 20515.
202-225-5271. (h) Pittsfield, IL. NL.
Committees. Agriculture; International
Relations
AA. Robert J Wichser
Secretary. Karen Cindrich

FISH, HAMILTON JR (R–NY, 25th). 2428
Rayburn House Office Bldg, 20515.
202-225-5441. (h) Millbrook, NY.
914-677-3988
Committees. Judiciary; Science; Continental
Shelf (Ad Hoc Select)
Press. Laurie Buchanan
AA. John D Barry
Secretary. Aya H Ely

FISHER, JOSEPH L (D–VA, 10th). 404
Cannon House Office Bldg, 20515.
202-225-5136. (h) Arlington, VA.
703-777-5859
Committees. Budget; Ways and Means
Press. Jean McDonald
AA. John G Milliken
Secretary. Janice Williams

FITHIAN, FLOYD J (D–IN, 2nd). 1205
Longworth House Office Bldg, 20515.
202-225-5777. (h) Lafayette, IN. NL
Committees. Agriculture; Government Oper-
ations; Assassinations (Select)
Press. Rex Smith
AA. Keith F Abbott
Secretary. Edith M Munro

FLIPPO, RONNIE G (D–AL, 5th). 513 Cannon House Office Bldg, 20515. **202-225-4801.** (h) Florence, AL. **205-764-5302**
Committees. Public Works; Science
Press and **AA.** William E Rasco
Secretary. Linda Sue Jordan

FLOOD, DANIEL J (D–PA, 11th). 108 Cannon House Office Bldg, 20515. **202-225-6511.** (h) Wilkes-Barre, PA. **717-823-3635**
Committee. Appropriations
Press. Larry Casey
AA. Helen M Tomascik

FLORIO, JAMES J (D–NJ, 1st). 1726 Longworth House Office Bldg, 20515. **202-225-6501.** (h) Runnemede, NJ. **609-627-8222** (office)
Committees. Interior Affairs; Interstate Commerce; Aging (Select)
Press and **AA.** Robert C Gatty
Secretary. Gay A Duty

FLOWERS, WALTER (D–AL, 7th). 2434 Rayburn House Office Bldg, 20515. **202-225-2665.** (h) Tuscaloosa, AL. **205-339-2852**
Committees. Judiciary; Science; Conduct; Aging (Select); Ethics (Select)
Press. Joe Keefer
Secretary. Beverly Burns

FLYNT, JOHN J, JR (D–GA, 6th). 2110 Rayburn House Office Bldg, 20515. **202-225-4501.** (h) Griffin, GA. **404-227-2382**
Committees. Conduct; Appropriations; Ethics (Select)
Press. Tom Carter
AA. Clarence L Leathers Jr
Secretary. Mary Lou Locus

FOLEY, THOMAS S (D–WA, 5th). 1201 Longworth House Office Bldg, 20515. **202-225-2006.** (h) Spokane, WA. **509-456-4680**
Committee. Agriculture
Press. William L First
AA. Heather Foley
Secretary. Sandra McElvey

FORD, HAROLD E (D–TN, 8th). 1230 Longworth House Office Bldg, 20515. **202-225-3265.** (h) Memphis, TN. **901-346-7779**
Committees. Ways and Means; Aging (Select); Assassinations (Select)

Press. Mindy McWilliams
AA. Percy Harvey
LA. Marty Foster

FORD, WILLIAM D (D–MI, 15th). 2368 Rayburn House Office Bldg, 20515. **202-225-6261.** (h) Taylor, MI. **313-291-6654**
Committees. Education; Post Office
Press and **AA.** Frank H Rathbun
Secretary. Margaret Borellis

FORSYTHE, EDWIN B (R–NJ, 6th). 303 Cannon House Office Bldg, 20515. **202-225-4765.** (h) Moorestown, NJ. **609-235-6622** (office)
Committees. Merchant Marine; Science; Continental Shelf (Ad Hoc Select)
Press and **AA.** Dan Cryor
Secretary. Mary B McGann

FOUNTAIN, L H (D–NC, 2nd). 2188 Rayburn House Office Bldg, 20515. **202-225-4531.** (h) Tarboro, NC. NL
Committees. Government Operations; International Relations
Press and **LA.** Ted L Daniel
AA. Walter J Pittman

FOWLER, WYCHE JR (D–GA, 5th). 1317 Longworth House Office Bldg, 20515. **202-225-3801**
LA. William Johnstone

FRASER, DONALD M (D–MN, 5th). 2268 Rayburn House Office Bldg, 20515. **202-225-4755.** (h) Minneapolis, MN. **612-725-2081** (office)
Committees. Budget; International Relations
Press and **LA.** Iric Nathanson
Secretary. Elsie Wonneberger

FRENZEL, BILL (R–MN, 3rd). 1026 Longworth House Office Bldg, 20515. **202-225-2871.** (h) Golden Valley, MN. **612-725-2173**
Committees. House Administration; Ways and Means; Ethics (Select)
AA. Dick Willow
Secretary. Pat Eveland

FREY, LOU JR (R–FL, 9th). 2427 Rayburn House Office Bldg, 20515. **202-225-3671.** (h) Winter Park, FL. **305-645-1978**
Committees. Interstate Commerce; Science; Narcotics Abuse (Select)
Press. Ann Wrobleski
AA. Oscar F Juarex
Secretary. Anne C Pickett

FUQUA, DON (D–FL, 2nd). 2266 Rayburn House Office Bldg, 20515. **202-225-5235.** (h) Altha, FL. **904-762-3960**
Committees. Government Operations; Science
Press. Ralph Pugh
AA. Herb Wadsworth
Secretary. Ruth Fisher

GAMMAGE, ROBERT A (D–TX, 22nd). 515 Cannon House Office Bldg, 20515. **202-225-5951.** (h) Houston, TX. **713-644-8011**
Committees. Interstate Commerce; Science
Press and **AA.** Stuart Glass
Secretary. Jan G Taylor

GARCIA, ROBERT (D–NY, 21st). 1723 Longworth House Office Bldg, 20515. **202-225-4361**
Committees. Banking; Post Office and Civil Service
Press. Roberta Weiner
AA. Mary Ann Miller

GAYDOS, JOSEPH M (D–PA, 20th). 2238 Rayburn House Office Bldg, 20515. **202-225-4631.** (h) McKeesport, PA. **412-673-7750**
Committees. Education; House Administration
AA. Bernard A Mandella
Secretary. Phyllis S Jones

GEPHARDT, RICHARD A (D–MO, 3rd). 509 Cannon House Office Bldg, 20515. **202-225-2671.** (h) St Louis, MO. **314-351-5100** (office)
Committee. Ways and Means
Press. Don Foley
AA. John B Crosby
Secretary. Vicki Watt

GIAIMO, ROBERT N (D–CT, 3rd). 2207 Rayburn House Office Bldg, 20515. **202-225-3661.** (h) North Haven, CT. **203-239-7569**
Committees. Budget; Appropriations; Congressional Operations (Joint)
AA. D Eileen Nixon
Secretary. Charlene Abshire

GIBBONS, SAM M (D–FL, 7th). 2209 Rayburn House Office Bldg, 20515. **202-225-3376.** (h) Tampa, FL. **813-228-2101**
Committee. Ways and Means
Press and **AA.** Nell Howlett
Secretary. Patricia Harford

GILMAN, BENJAMIN A (R–NY, 26th). 1226 Longworth House Office Bldg, 20515. **202-225-3776.** (h) Middletown, NY. **914-343-6666** (office)
Committees. International Relations; Post Office; Narcotics Abuse (Select)
Press. Joseph Sutherland
AA. Robert J Becker
Secretary. Geralding Sheflett

GINN, BO (D–GA, 1st). 317 Cannon House Office Bldg, 20515. **202-225-5831.** (h) Millen, GA. **912-482-4022**
Committees. Merchant Marine; Public Works; Continental Shelf (Ad Hoc Select)
Press and **AA.** Robert H Hart
Secretary. Katherine Calhoun

GLICKMAN, DANIEL R (D–KS, 4th). 1128 Longworth House Office Bldg, 20515. **202-225-6216.** (h) Wichita, KS. **316-262-8396**
Committees. Agriculture; Science
Press. Lou Ketchman
AA. Jack Williams
Secretary. Mary Helen Kelly

GOLDWATER, BARRY M, JR (R–CA, 20th). 2240 Rayburn House Office Bldg, 20515. **202-225-4461.** (h) Woodland Hills, CA. **213-883-1233**
Committees. Public Works; Science
Press. Signy Ellerton
AA. Kenneth L Black
Secretary. Jane Havlicek

GONZALEZ, HENRY B (D–TX, 20th). 2312 Rayburn House Office Bldg, 20515. **202-225-3236.** (h) San Antonio, TX. **512-732-9779**
Committees. Banking; Small Business; Assassinations (Select)
Press and **AA.** Gail J Beagle
Secretary. Ella M Wong

GOODLING, WILLIAM F (R–PA, 19th). 1713 Longworth House Office Bldg, 20515. **202-225-5836.** (h) York, PA. **717-428-1839**
Committees. Education; International Relations
Press. Kevin Tally
AA. William A Cornell, Jr
Secretary. Nancy A Newcomer

GORE, ALBERT A, JR (D–TN, 4th). 1725 Longworth House Office Bldg, 20515. **202-225-4231.** (h) Carthage, TN. **615-735-1154**
Committees. Interstate Commerce; Science

Press and **AA.** Kenneth Jost
Secretary. Marcia Webb

GRADISON, WILLIS D, JR (R–OH, 1st). 1519 Longworth House Office Bldg, 20515. **202-225-3164.** (h) Cincinnati, OH. **513-684-2456** (office)
Committee. Ways and Means
Press and **AA.** Ronald R Roberts
Secretary. Victoria D Kirk

GRASSLEY, CHARLES E (R–IA, 3rd). 1227 Longworth House Office Bldg, 20515. **202-225-3301.** (h) New Hartford, IA. **319-983-2458**
Committees. Agriculture; Banking; Aging (Select)
Press. Kris Heine
AA. James B (Pete) Conroy
Secretary. Yvonne R O Goodman

GREEN, WILLIAM (R–NY, 18th). 1213 Longworth House Office Bldg, 20515. **202-225-2436.**
Committee. Banking
AA. Alice Tetelman

GUDGER, V LAMAR (D–NC, 11th). 428 Cannon House Office Bldg, 20515. **202-225-6401.** (h) Asheville, NC. **704-252-5276**
Committees. Interior Affairs; Judiciary
Press. Stover Dunnagan
AA. Ms Tempie Bobrowski
LA. Thomas L Adams

GUYER, TENNYSON (R–OH, 4th). 114 Cannon House Office Bldg, 20515. **202-225-2676.** (h) Findlay, OH. **419-422-6736**
Committees. International Relations; Veterans' Affairs; Narcotics Abuse (Select)
Press. Joe Jansen
AA. M E Monroe
Secretary. Margaret W Hynes

HAGEDORN, THOMAS M (R–MN, 2nd). 325 Cannon House Office Bldg, 20515. **202-225-2472.** (h) Truman, MN. **507-776-7711**
Committees. Agriculture; Public Works
Press. John Enright
AA. George L Berg, Jr
Secretary. B Jean Bell

HALL, SAM B, JR (D–TX, 1st). 318 Cannon House Office Bldg, 20515. **202-225-3035.** (h) Marshall, TX. **214-938-6519**

Committees. Judiciary; Veterans' Affairs
AA. Baron I Shacklette
Secretary. Dorothy F Councill

HAMILTON, LEE H (D–IN, 9th). 2202 Rayburn House Office Bldg, 20515. **202-225-5315.** (h) Columbus, IN. NL
Committees. International Relations; Conduct; Economic (Joint); Ethics (Select)
Press. Sandy Jesse
AA. Rick Stoner
Secretary. Gloria Cherry

HAMMERSCHMIDT, JOHN P (R–AR, 3rd). 2160 Rayburn House Office Bldg, 20515. **202-225-4301.** (h) Harrison, AR. **501-365-6900** (office)
Committees. Public Works; Veterans' Affairs; Aging (Select)
Press. Pam Wehner
AA. Raymond T Teid
Secretary. Pam Wehner

HANLEY, JAMES J (D–NY, 32nd). 239 Cannon House Office Bldg, 20515. **202-225-3701.** (h) Syracuse, NY. **315-423-5657**
Committees. Banking; Post Office; Small Business
Press. Art Sando
AA. J Daniel Costello
Secretary. Norma J Bright

HANNAFORD, MARK W (D–CA, 34th). 315 Cannon House Office Bldg, 20515. **202-225-2415.** (h) Lakewood, CA. **213-925-3983**
Committees. Banking; Veterans' Affairs
Press. Rich Nelson
AA. William H Devine
Secretary. Elizabeth A Stack

HANSEN, GEORGE V (R–ID, 2nd). 1125 Longworth House Office Bldg, 20515. **202-225-5531.** (h) Pacatello, ID. **208-232-0900** (office)
Committees. Banking; Veterans' Affairs
Press. Norm Martin
Secretary. Connie Hansen

HARKIN, THOMAS R (D–IA, 5th). 324 Cannon House Office Bldg, 20515. **202-225-3806.** (h) Ames, IA. **515-232-6111**
Committees. Agriculture; Science
Press. Barry Piatt
AA. John Fitzpatrick
Secretary. Dianna J Baker

HARRINGTON, MICHAEL J (D–MA, 6th). 2423 Rayburn House Office Bldg, 20515. **202-225-8020.** (h) Beverly, MA. **617-922-8113** (office)
Committees. Government Operations; International Relations
AA. Lawrence J Tell
Secretary. Virginia McIntyre

HARRIS, HERBERT E II (D–VA, 8th). 1133 Longworth House Office Bldg, 20515. **202-225-4376.** (h) Alexandria, VA. **703-780-2437**
Committees. District of Columbia; Judiciary; Post Office
Press. Jack Sweeney
AA. Christopher J Spanos
Secretary. Connie O'Reilly

HARSHA, WILLIAM H (R–OH, 6th). 2457 Rayburn House Office Bldg, 20515. **202-225-5705.** (h) Portsmouth, OH. **614-353-4479**
Committees. Public Works
Press. George Noblin
AA. Pamela Jane Richards
LA. Jean Armistead

HAWKINS, AGUSTUS F (D–CA, 29th). 2350 Rayburn House Office Bldg, 20515. **202-225-2201.** (h) Los Angeles, CA. **213-750-0260**
Committees. Education; House Administration; Printing (Joint)
AA. John W Smith
Secretary. Helen K D Bardby

HECKLER, MARGARET M (R–MA, 10th). 343 Cannon House Office Bldg, 20515. **202-225-4335.** (h) Wellesley, MA. **617-235-3356**
Committees. Agriculture; Veterans' Affairs; Economic (Joint); Ethics (Select)
Press. Steven Cohen
AA. Karen Rittinger
Secretary. Glenda Leggitt

HEFNER, W G (BILL) (D–NC, 8th). 328 Cannon House Office Bldg, 20515. **202-225-3715.** (h) Concord, NC. NL
Committees. Public Works; Veterans' Affairs
Press. Jo Stockstill
AA. Bill McEwen
Secretary. Maddie L Young

HEFTEL, CECIL (D–HI, 1st). 322 Cannon House Office Bldg, 20515. **202-225-2726.** (h) Honolulu, HI. **808-373-4308**

Committees. Education; Post Office
Press. Doug Carlson
AA. Bill Brown
Secretary. Barbara Tyres

HIGHTOWER, JACK E (D–TX, 13th). 120 Cannon House Office Bldg, 20515. **202-225-3706.** (h) Vernon, TX. **817-552-7200**
Committees. Agriculture; Government Operations
AA. Ivan Sinclair

HILLIS, ELWOOD H (R–IN, 5th). 2429 Rayburn House Office Bldg, 20515. **202-225-5037.** (h) Kokomo, IN. **317-453-6124**
Committees. Armed Services, Veterans' Affairs
AA. Robert C Junk
Secretary. Barbara A Thoelke

HOLLAND, KENNETH L (D–SC, 5th). 103 Cannon House Office Bldg, 20515. **202-225-5501.** (h) Lugoff, SC. NL
Committee. Ways and Means
AA. Margaret Bethea Phipps
LA. John P Winborn

HOLLENBECK, HAROLD C (R–NJ, 9th). 1221 Longworth House Office Bldg, 20515. **202-225-5061.** (h) East Rutherford, NJ. **201-939-7191**
Committees. Banking; Science
Press. Paul Wickerson
AA. Neil S Newhouse
Secretary. Christine A Daly

HOLT, MARJORIE S (R–MD, 4th). 1510 Longworth House Office Bldg, 20515. **202-225-8090.** (h) Severna Park, MD. NL
Committees. Armed Services; Budget
Press. Roy Gill
AA. Richard H Prendergast
Secretary. Leslie Adlam

HOLTZMAN, ELIZABETH (D–NY, 16th). 1025 Longworth House Office Bldg, 20515. **202-225-6616.** (h) Brooklyn, NY. **212-859-9111**
Committees. Budget; Judiciary
LAs. Anthony Freedman and Leah Wortham

HORTON, FRANK (R–NY, 24th). 2229 Rayburn House Office Bldg, 20515. **202-225-4916.** (h) Rochester, NY. **716-422-4422**
Committee. Government Operations

AA. David A Lovenheim
Secretary. Ruby G Moy

HOWARD, JAMES J (D–NJ, 3rd). 2245 Rayburn House Office Bldg, 20515. **202-225-4671.** (h) Spring Lake Heights, NJ. **201-431-2830**
Committees. Post Office; Public Works
Press and LA. Nancy Blades
AA. Timothy F Sullivan

HUBBARD, CARROLL, JR (D–KY, 1st). 204 Cannon House Office Bldg, 20515. **202-225-3115.** (h) Mayfield, KY. **502-247-7128**
Committees. Banking; Merchant Marine
Press. Jeanne Donohue
LA. Darrell Hotchkiss
Secretary. Vicki L Price

HUCKABY, THOMAS J (D–LA, 5th). 423 Cannon House Office Bldg, 20515. **202-225-2376.** (h) Ringgold, LA. **318-894-9137**
Committees. Agriculture; Interior Affairs
AA. Lou Burnett
Secretary. Billie Thomas

HUGES, WILLIAM J (D–NJ, 2nd). 327 Cannon House Office Bldg, 20515. **202-225-6572.** (h) Ocean City, NJ. **609-339-2251**
Committees. Judiciary; Merchant Marine; Continental Shelf (Ad Hoc Select); Aging (Select)
Press and AA. Michael Petit
Secretary. Mary E Minutes

HYDE, HENRY J (R–IL, 6th) 1206 Longworth House Office Bldg, 20515. **202-225-4561.** (h) Park Ridge, IL. NP
Committees. Banking; Judiciary
Pres. Donna Harper
LA. Jane Fogarty

ICHORD, RICHARD H (D–MO, 8th). 2302 Rayburn House Office Bldg, 20515. **202-225-5155.** (h) Houston, MO. **417-967-2270**
Committees. Armed Services; Small Business
AA. Susan Livingstone
Secretary. Betty Pattie

IRELAND, ANDREW P (D–FL, 8th). 1513 Longworth House Office Bldg, 20515. **202-225-5015.** (h) Winter Haven, FL. **813-294-6047**
Committees. International Relations; Small Business

Press and **LA.** Stephen A Sauls

AA. Alice V Myers

JACOBS, ANDREW, JR (D–IN, 11th). 1501 Longworth House Office Bldg, 20515. **202-225-4011.** (h) Indianapolis, IN. **317-253-0873**

Committee. Ways and Means

AA. Winnie Burrell

Secretary. Mary Kay Anderson

JEFFORDS, JAMES M (R–VT, at large). 429 Cannon House Office Bldg, 20515. **202-225-4115.** (h) Rutland, VT. **802-775-1058**

Committees. Agriculture; Education

Press. Steve Carlson

AA. Robert J Gray

Secretary. Lorraine F Benedini

JENKINS, EDGAR L (D–GA, 9th). 501 Cannon House Office Bldg, 20515. **202-225-5211.** (h) Jasper, GA. **404-692-2059**

Committee. Ways and Means

AA. Terry Miller

Secretary. Elizabeth Fleming

JENRETTE, JOHN W, JR (D–SC, 6th). 426 Cannon House Office Bldg, 20515. **202-225-3315.** (h) North Myrtle Beach, SC. **803-249-1441**

Committees. Agriculture; Government Operations

Press. Bill Carrick

AA. William Keyserling

Secretary. Cookie Miller

JOHNSON, HAROLD T (D–CA, 1st). 2347 Rayburn House Office Bldg, 20515. **202-225-3076.** (h) Roseville, CA. **916-782-4411**

Committee. Public Works

LA. John F Nutter

Secretary. Ellen Gospodnetich

JOHNSON, JAMES P (JIM) (R–CO, 4th). 129 Cannon House Office Bldg, 20515. **202-225-4676.** (h) Fort Collins, CO. **303-482-9178**

Committees. Agriculture; Interior Affairs

AA. William H Cleary

Secretary. Patti J Wilson

JONES, ED (D–TN, 7th). 104 Cannon House Office Bldg, 20515. **202-225-4714.** (h) Yorkville, TN. **901-643-6271** (office)

Committees. Agriculture; House Administration

Press. Kelly Sharbell

AA. Ray H Lancaster

Secretary. Anita Ebersole

JONES, JAMES R (D–OK, 1st). 225 Cannon House Office Bldg, 20515. **202-225-2211.** (h) Tulsa, OK. **918-587-7777**

Committee. Ways and Means

AA. John E Lynn

Secretary. Sandra Webster

JONES, WALTER B (D–NC, 1st). 201 Cannon House Office Bldg, 20515. **202-225-3101.** (h) Farmville, NC. **919-753-3082** (office)

Committees. Agriculture; Merchant Marine

Press. Kelly Sharbell

AA. Floyd J Lupton

Secretary. Gloria Curry

JORDAN, BARBARA (D–TX, 18th). 1534 Longworth House Office Bldg, 20515. **202-225-3816.** (h) Houston, TX. **713-674-8465**

Committees. Government Operations; Judiciary

AA. Rufus (Bud) Myers

KASTEN, ROBERT W JR (R–WI, 9th). 119 Cannon House Office Bldg, 20515. **202-225-5101.** (h) Brookfield, WI. **414-784-1111**

Committees. Government Operations; Small Business

Press. Marcie Powers

AA. James Harff

Secretary. Lynn K Beal

KASTENMEIER, ROBERT W (D–WI, 2nd). 2232 Rayburn House Office Bldg, 20515. **202-225-2906.** (h) Sun Prairie, WI. **608-837-2990**

Committees. Interior Affairs; Judiciary; Ethics (Select)

Press. Judith Carr

AA. Kaz Oshiki

Secretary. Anne Marie Donohoe

KAZEN, ABRAHAM, JR (D–TS, 23rd). 2411 Rayburn House Office Bldg, 20515. **202-225-4511.** (h) Laredo, TX. **512-722-7445**

Committees. Armed Services; Interior Affairs; Continental Shelf (Ad Hoc Select)

AA. Robert H Fleming

Secretary. Patricia A Murray

KELLY, RICHARD (R–FL, 5th). 307 Cannon House Office Bldg, 20515.

202-225-2176. (h) New Port Richey, FL. **813-848-0320** (office)

Committees. Agriculture; Banking

Press. Bill Purvis

AA. John Gartland

Secretary. Nancy Guiden

KEMP, JACK (R-NY, 38th). 2244 Rayburn House Office Bldg, 20515. **202-225-5265.** (h) Hanburg, NY. **716-842-6876**

Committee. Appropriations

Press. Louis Rotterman

AA. Randal C Teague

Secretary. Janet Dorn

KETCHUM, WILLIAM M (R-CA, 18th). 413 Cannon House Office Bldg, 20515. (h) Bakersfield, CA. **805-366-8356**

Committee. Ways and Means

Press. Tracy Smith

AA. Christopher C Seeger

Secretary. Kathy Dignan

KEYS, MARTHA E (D-KS, 2nd). 1502 Longworth House Office Bldg, 20515. **202-225-6601.** (h) Manhattan, KS. **913-776-6281**

Committees. Ways and Means

Press. Gloria O'Dell

AA. Judith Aitken

Secretary. Robbie Nichols

KILDEE, DALE E (D-MI, 7th). 503 Cannon House Office Bldg, 20515. **202-225-3611.** (h) Flint, MI. **313-239-1437**

Committees. Education; Small Business

Press. Dennis Herrick

AA. Thomas W Wagamon

Secretary. Dolores Nouhan

KINDNESS, THOMAS (R-OH, 8th). 1440 Longworth House Office Bldg, 20515. **202-225-6205.** (h) Hamilton, OH. **513-895-5656**

Committees. Government Operations; Judiciary

Press. Bill McKenney

Secretary. Nancy S Scott

KOSTMAYER, PETER H (D-PA, 8th). 1017 Longworth House Office Bldg, 20515. **202-225-4276.** (h) Solebury, PA. **215-862-5618**

Committees. Government Operations; Interior Affairs

Press and **AA.** Edward Mitchell

KREBS, JOHN H (D–CA, 17th). 435 Cannon House Office Bldg, 20515. **202-225-3341.** (h). Fresno, CA. **209-487-5487**
Committees. Agriculture; Interior Affairs
AA. Dennis Gaab

KRUEGER, ROBERT C (D–TX, 21st). 127 Cannon House Office Bldg, 20515. **202-225-4236.** (h) New Braunfels, TX. **512-625-7347**
Committees. Interstate; Science
Press. Jeff Talmadge
AA. Dan Dutko
Secretary. Sara E Hilber

LA FALCE, JOHN J (D–NY, 36th). 230 Cannon House Office Bldg, 20515. **202-225-3231.** (h) Buffalo, NY. **716-842-2880** (office)
Committees. Banking; Small Business
Secretary. Lyn Taecker

LAGOMARSINO, ROBERT J (R–CA, 19th). 1117 Longworth House Office Bldg, 20515. **202-225-3601.** (h) Ventura, CA. **805-643-3830**
Committees. Interior Affairs; International Relations
Press. John Doherty
AA. Montgomery K Winkler
Secretary. Susan Gerrick

LATTA, DELBERT L (R–OH, 5th). 2309 Rayburn House Office Bldg, 20515. **202-225-6405.** (h) Bowling Green, OH. **419-352-8627**
Committees. Budget; Rules
Press. Beverly Hubble
AA. Kaye M Burchell

LEACH, JAMES A S (R–IA, 1st). 1724 Longworth House Office Bldg, 20515. **202-225-6576.** (h) Davenport, IA. **319-326-1841** (office)
Committees. Banking; Post Office
Press. Chris Hurt
AA. Gary Madson
Secretary. Lee Goodell

LEDERER, RAYMOND F (D–Pa, 3rd). 516 Cannon House Office Bldg, 20515. **202-225-6271.** (h) Philadelphia, PA. **215-597-8670**
Committee. Ways and Means
Press. James Albertine
AA. Robert Diamond
Secretary. Estelle M Tyler

LE FANTE, JOSEPH A (D–NJ, 14th). 507 Cannon House Office Bldg, 20515. **202-225-2765.** (h) Bayonne, NJ. **201-823-2900** (office)
Committees. Education; Small Business
Press and AA. James M Dolan
Secretary. Karen F Grube

LEGETT, ROBERT L (D–CA, 4th). 2263 Longworth House Office Bldg, 20515. **202-225-5716.** (h) Suisun, CA. **707-422-7770**
Committees. Armed Services; Budget; Merchant Marine
AA. Owen R Chaffee
Secretary. Dorothy C O'Brien

LEHMAN, WILLIAM (D–FL, 13th). 236 Cannon House Office Bldg, 20515. **202-225-4211.** (h) Miami, FL. **305-945-7518** (office)
Committees. Budget; Post Office
Press. Mark Olman
LA. Lucy McLelland
Secretary. Carolyn Rockymore

LENT, NORMAN F (R–NY, 4th). 341 Cannon House Office Bldg, 20515. **202-225-7896.** (h) East Rockaway, NY. **516-593-4105**
Committees. Interstate Commerce; Merchant Marine
Press. Steve Saunders
AA. Barbara A Morris
Secretary. Donna Malone

LEVITAS, ELLIOT H (D–GA, 4th). 329 Cannon House Office Bldg, 20515. **202-225-4272.** (h) Atlanta, GA. **404-377-1717** (office)
AA. Fred M York, Jr
Secretary. Helen W Morey

LLOYD, JAMES F (D–CA, 35th). 222 Cannon House Office Bldg, 20515. **202-225-2305.** (h) West Covina, CA. **213-339-7356**
Committees. Armed Services; Science
Press. Rita Hunt
AA. Jerry Giovaniello
Secretary. Brigid Davis

LLOYD, MARILYN L (D–TN, 3rd). 208 Cannon House Office Bldg, 20515. **202-225-3271.** (h) Chattanooga, TN. **615-899-0355**
Committees. Public Works; Science; Aging (Select)
Press. Mike Krag

AA. Richard J Ebersole
Secretary. Kathy Becker

LONG, CLARENCE D (D–MD, 2nd). 2304 Rayburn House Office Bldg, 20515. **202-225-3061.** (h) Ruxton, MD. **301-828-6616** (office)
Committee. Appropriations
Press. Jean O'Neil
Press Secretary. Barbara Reno, (h) **202-965-0574**
Secretary. Christy Cole

LONG, GILLIS W (D–LA, 8th). 2445 Rayburn House Office Bldg, 20515. **202-225-4926.** (h) Alexandria, LA. **318-487-0632**
Committees. Rules; Economic (Joint)
Press. Bill Moreau
AA. Patti Birge Tyson
Secretary. Virginia Lee Kinta

LOTT, TRENT (R–MS, 5th). 308 Cannon House Office Bldg, 20515. **202-225-5772.** (h) Pascagoula, MS. **601-762-6435**
Committees. Post Office; Rules
Press. Tom Houston
AA. Tom H Anderson, Jr
Secretary. Susan L Wooten

LUJAN, MANUEL, JR (R–NM, 1st). 1323 Longworth House Office Bldg, 20515. **202-225-6316.** (h) Albuquerque, NM. **505-344-7721**
Committees. Interior Affairs; Science
AA. Jack Crandall

LUKEN, THOMAS A (D–OH, 2nd). 1131 Longworth House Office Bldg, 20515. **202-225-2216.** (h) Cincinnati, OH. **513-541-1322**
Committees. Interstate Commerce; Small Business
Press. Jeff Dinnard
AA. Esther Lane

LUNDINE, STANLEY (D–NY, 39th). 430 Cannon House Office Bldg, 20515. **202-225-3161.** (h) Jamestown, NY. **716-484-0252**
Committees. Banking; Aging (Select)
Press. Steve Sprague
AA. Ann Lewis
Secretary. Joanne Reinauer

MCCLORY, ROBERT (R–IL, 13th). 2469 Rayburn House Office Bldg, 20515. **202-225-5221.** (h) Lake Bluff, IL. NP

Committee. Judiciary
Press. Louise Hutchinson
AA. Geraldean Colevas
Secretary. Jean E Morrow

MCCLOSKEY, PAUL N, JR (R–CA, 12th). 205 Cannon House Office Bldg, 20515. **202-225-5411.** (h) Menlo Park, CA. **415-326-7383**
Committees. Government Operations; Merchant Marine
Press. Bill Johnson
AA. E Amber Scholtz
Secretary. Laurette T Rash

MCCORMACK, MIKE (D–WA, 4th). 1202 Longworth House Office Bldg, 20515. **202-225-5816.** (h) Richland, WA. **509-942-7273** (office)
Committees. Public Works; Science
AA. John Andelin
Secretary. Gail Ingels

MCDADE, JOSEPH M (R–PA, 10th). 2370 Rayburn House Office Bldg, 20515. **202-225-3731.** (h) Clarks Summit, PA. NP
Committees. Appropriations; Small Business
Press and AA. James W Dyer
Secretary. Gertrude L Moser

MCDONALD, LAWRENCE P (D–GA, 7th). 504 Cannon House Office Bldg, 20515. **202-225-2931.** (h) Marietta, GA. **404-973-2614**
Committee. Armed Services
Press. Don Vice
AA. Frederic N Smith
Secretary. Sue Ahearn

MCEWEN, ROBERT C (R–NY, 30th). 2210 Rayburn House Office Bldg, 20515. **202-225-4611.** (h) Ogdensburg, NY. **315-393-1363**
Committee. Appropriations
AA. John E Mellon
Secretary. Donna M Bell

MCFALL, JOHN J (D–CA, 14th). 2346 Rayburn House Office Bldg, 20515. **202-225-2511.** (h) Monteca, CA. **209-239-3568**
Committee. Appropriations
Press. David Edlund
AA. Raymond F Barnes
LA. Samuel A Mabry

MCHUGH, MATTHEW F (D–NY, 27th). 1204 Longworth House Office Bldg, 20515.

202-225-6335. (h) Ithaca, NY. **607-273-7380** (office)
Committees. Agriculture; Interior Affairs
AA. Marvin S Rappaport
LA. Gary Bombardier

MCKAY, K GUNN (D–UT, 1st). 1203 Longworth House Office Bldg, 20515. **202-225-0453.** (h) Huntsville, UT. **801-399-6816** (office)
Committee. Appropriations
Press. Mike Cannon
AA. David B Lee
Secretary. Wanda Scott

MCKINNEY, STEWART B (R–CT, 4th). 106 Cannon House Office Bldg, 20515. **202-225-5541.** (h) Fairfield, CT. **203-259-8595**
Committees. Banking; District of Columbia; Assassinations (Select)
Press. George McKiernan
AA. Joseph J McGee
Secretary. Lynn Lehrman

MADIGAN, EDWARD R (R–IL, 21st). 1514 Longworth House Office Bldg, 20515. **202-225-2371.** (h) Lincoln, IL. **217-732-3888**
Committees. Agriculture; Interstate Commerce
Press and AA. Dan Doran
Secretary. Diane Liesman

MAGUIRE, ANDREW (D–NJ, 7th). 1314 Longworth House Office Bldg, 20515. **202-225-4465.** (h) Ridgewood, NJ. NL
Committees. Government Operations; Interstate Commerce
Press. Steve D'Arazian
AA. Robert Kerr
Secretary. Connie Davis

MAHON, GEORGE H (D–TX, 19th). 2314 Rayburn House Office Bldg, 20515. **202-225-4005.** (h) Lubbock, TX. NL
Committee. Appropriations
AA. Dorothy Martin
LA. Ms Savannah Walker

MANN, JAMES R (D–SC, 4th). 2134 Rayburn House Office Bldg, 20515. **202-225-6030.** (h) Greenville, SC. **803-232-2391**
Committees. District of Columbia; Judiciary; Narcotics Abuse (Select)
Press. Nikki McNamee
AA. Elizabeth A Seeley
Secretary. Elizabeth Byrd

MARKEY, EDWARD J (D–MA, 7th). 319 Cannon House Office Bldg, 20515. **202-225-2836.** (h) Malden, MA. **617-324-0815**
Committees. Interior Affairs; Interstate Commerce
Press. David Hoffman
AA. Dan O'Connell
Secretary. Katie Sullivan

MARKS, MARC L (R–PA, 24th). 1213 Longworth House Office Bldg, 20515. **202-225-5406.** (h) Sharon, PA. **412-347-2481**
Committees. District of Columbia; Interstate Commerce; Aging (Select)
Press. Joe Shafran
AA. Marvin Collins
Secretary. Janet Klinger

MARLENEE, RON (R–MT, 2nd). 128 Cannon House Office Bldg, 20515. **202-225-1555.** (h) Scobey, MT. **406-487-2603**
Committees. Agriculture; Interior Affairs
Press. Bob Ziemer
AA. Herb Williams
LA. Christie Snyder

MARRIOTT, DAVID D (R–UT, 2nd). 1610 Longworth House Office Bldg, 20515. **202-225-3011.** (h) Salt Lake City, UT. **801-524-4394**
Committees. Interior Affairs; Small Business
Press. John Hanks
AA. Barry Nielsen
Secretary. Cristy Valentine

MARTIN, JAMES G (R–NC, 9th). 115 Cannon House Office Bldg, 20515. **202-225-1976.** (h) Davidson, NC. NL
Committee. Ways and Means
Press. Paul Jones
AA. James S Lofton
Secretary. Elizabeth A Naumoff

MATHIS, DAWSON (D–GA, 2nd). 2331 Rayburn House Office Bldg, 20515. **202-225-3631.** (h) Albany, GA. **912-439-8300**
Committees. Agriculture; Interior Affairs
LA. Julian Holland
Secretary. Lexine Rollins

MATTOX, JAMES A (D–TX, 5th). 1130 Longworth House Office Bldg, 20515. **202-225-2231.** (h) Dallas, TX. **214-827-8800**
Committees. Banking; Budget
Press. J D Arnold

AA. John Thorne
Secretary. Jennie Grindberg

MAZZOLI, ROMANO L (D–KY, 3rd).
1212 Longworth House Office Bldg, 20515.
202-225-5401. (h) Louisville, KY.
502-637-9016
Committees. District of Columbia; Judiciary;
Ethics (Select)
AA. T Michael Nevens
Secretary. Olive J Daddario

MEEDS, LLOYD (D–WA, 2nd).
2352 Rayburn House Office Bldg, 20515.
202-225-2605. (h) Lake Stevens, WA.
206-252-3188
Committees. Interior Affairs; Rules; Ethics
(Select)
Press. John O'Leary
AA. Leonard Saari
Secretary. Mary Martinex

METCALFE, RALPH H (D–IL, 1st).
2438 Rayburn House Office Bldg, 20515.
202-225-4372. (h) Chicago, IL.
312-373-7784
Committees. Interstate Commerce; Merchant
Marine; Post Office
Press. Richard C Weston, evening
202-547-9073
AA. Joseph Jacoby
Secretary. Annie M Abbott

MEYNER, HELEN S (D–NJ, 13th).
107 Cannon House Office Bldg, 20515.
202-225-5801. (h) Phillipsburg, NJ.
201-859-1170
Committees. District of Columbia; International Relations; Aging (Select)
Press. Tom Berrigan
AA. Mark S Singel
Secretary. Shirley A Kalich

MICHEL, ROBERT H (R–IL, 18th).
2112 Rayburn House Office Bldg, 20515.
202-225-6201. (h) Peoria, IL.
309-673-6574
Committee. Appropriations
Press. Mike Johnson
AA. Ralph Vinovich
Secretary. Sharon G Yard

MIKULSKI, BARBARA A (D–MD, 3rd).
1004 Longworth House Office Bldg, 20515.
202-225-4016. (h) Baltimore, MD.
301-633-8870
Committees. Interstate Commerce; Merchant
Marine

Press and **AA.** Marilyn Marcosson
Secretary. Mary Jane Small

MIKVA, ABNER J (D–IL, 10th).
403 Cannon House Office Bldg, 20515.
202-225-4835. (h) Evanston, IL.
312-869-6316
Committees. Ways and Means
Press. Sandy Horwitt
AA. Eugenie Ermoyan
Secretary. Zoe Gratsias

MILFORD, DALE (D–TX, 24th).
405 Cannon House Office Bldg, 20515.
202-225-3605. (h) Grand Prairie, TX.
214-263-4520
Committees. Public Works; Science
Press. Lee Ounkleberg
AA. Richard H White, Jr
Secretary. Betty C Gibson

MILLER, CLARENCE E (R–OH, 10th).
2246 Rayburn House Office Bldg, 20515.
202-225-5131. (h) Lancaster, OH.
614-653-4188
Committee. Appropriations
Press. Phil Straw
AA. Dave Brown
Secretary. Linda G Rodercik

MILLER, GEORGE (D–CA, 7th). 1532
Longworth House Office Bldg, 20515.
202-225-2095. (h) Martinez, CA.
415-687-3200
Committees. Education; Interior Affairs;
Continental Shelf (Ad Hoc Select)
LA. John A Lawrence
Secretary. Sylvia Muszalski

MINETA, NORMAN Y (D–CA, 13th).
313 Cannon House Office Bldg, 20515.
202-225-2631. (h) San Jose, CA.
408-984-6045
Committees. Budget; Public Works
Press. Antoinette Durkin
AA. Les Francis
Secretary. Elinore Newland

MINISH, JOSEPH G (D–NJ, 11th). 2162
Rayburn House Office Bldg, 20515.
202-225-5035. (h) West Orange, NJ.
201-736-1684
Committees. Banking; House Administration
Press. Bob Loftus
Secretary. Peggy Stack

MITCHELL, DONALD J (R–NY, 31st).
1527 Longworth House Office Bldg, 20515.

202-225-3665. (h) Herkimer, NY.
315-866-1051
Committee. Armed Services
Press and **AA.** Sherwood Boehlert
Secretary. Vicky a'Becket

MITCHELL, PARREN J (D–MD, 7th).
414 Cannon House Office Bldg, 20515.
202-225-4741. (h) Baltimore, MD.
301-669-6296
Committees. Banking; Budget; Defense
Production (Joint)
AA. George Minor
Secretary. Geraldine Houston

MOAKLEY, JOHN JOSEPH (D–MA,
9th). 238 Cannon House Office Bldg, 20515.
202-225-8273. (h) South Boston, MA.
617-268-7171
Committee. Rules
Press. John Weinfurter
AA. Nelson Hammell
Secretary. Yvonne White

MOFFETT, TOBY (D–CT, 6th). 1007
Longworth House Office Bldg, 20515.
202-225-4476. (h) Unionville, CT. NL
Committees. Government Operations;
Interstate Commerce
Press. William Blacklow
AA. Kathleen I Sadler
Secretary. Anne M Senese

MOLLOHAN, ROBERT H (D–WV, 1st).
339 Cannon House Office Bldg, 20515.
202-225-4172. (h) Fairmont, WV.
304-363-3356
Committees. Armed Services; House
Administration
Press. John Brown
AA. C. Louise Ingram
Secretary. Kathy Snodgrass

MONTGOMERY, GV (SONNY) (D–MS,
3rd). 2367 Rayburn House Office Bldg,
20515. **202-225-5031.** (h) Meridan, MS.
601-485-8876
Committees. Armed Services; Veterans'
Affairs
Press. Andre Clemandot, Jr
AA. Hilton R Vance
Secretary. Anne McGhee

MOORE, W HANSON (D–LA, 6th). 407
Cannon House Office Bldg, 20515.
202-225-3901. (h) Baton Rouge, LA.
504-344-7696 (office)
Committees. Agriculture; Interstate Commerce

Press. Joseph Karpinski
AA. Jay Stone
Secretary. Sue Cornick

MOORHEAD, CARLOS J (R–CA, 22nd).
1208 Longworth House Office Bldg, 20515.
202-225-4176. (h) Glendale, CA.
213-247-8445
Committees. Interstate Commerce; Judiciary.
AA. Alice K Andersen
Secretary. G Maxine Dean

MOORHEAD, WILLIAM S (D–PA, 14th).
2467 Rayburn House Office Bldg, 20515.
202-225-2301. (h) Pittsburgh, PA.
412-644-2870 (office)
Committees. Banking; Government
Operations; Economic (Joint)
Press and **LA.** William R Maloni
AA. Mollie D Cohen

MOSS, JOHN E (D–CA, 3rd). 2354
Rayburn House Office Bldg, 20515.
202-225-7163. (h) Sacramento, CA.
916-440-3543
Committees. Government Operations; Inter-
state Commerce
Press and **AA.** Kathleen Benson
Secretary. Betty Del Vecchio

MOTTL, RONALD M (D–OH, 23rd). 1233
Longworth House Office Bldg, 20515.
202-225-5731. (h) Parma, OH. **216-842-1111**
Committees. Education, Veterans' Affairs
AA. Bob Kitchel
Secretary. Mary Kahoun

MURPHY, AUSTIN J (D–PA, 22nd). 1118
Longworth House Office Bldg, 20515.
202-225-4665. (h) Charleroi, PA.
412-489-4217
Committees. Education; Interior Affairs
Press. Richard Roberts
AA. Fred P McLuckie
Secretary. RoseAnn Tulley

MURPHY, JOHN M (D–NY, 17th). 2187
Rayburn House Office Bldg, 20515.
202-225-3371. (h) Staten Island, NY.
212-981-9800 (office)
Committees. Merchant Marine; Interstate
Commerce; Continental Shelf (Ad Hoc
Select)
AA. Jane Nacke
Secretary. Taddy McAllister

MURPHY, MORGAN F (D–IL, 2nd). 2436
Rayburn House Office Bldg, 20515.

202-225-3406. (h) Chicago, IL.
312-353-5390
Committees. Rules; Narcotics Abuse (Select)
AA. Eugene Callahan
Secretary. Ann Fletcher

MURTHA, JOHN P, JR (D–PA, 12th). 431
Cannon House Office Bldg, 20515.
202-225-2065. (h) Johnstown, PA.
814-536-4611
Committee. Appropriations
Press. Bill Allen
AA. Philip Giomariso
Secretary. Janice Scialabba

MYERS, GARY A (R–PA, 25th). 1711
Longworth House Office Bldg, 20515.
202-225-2565. (h) Butler, PA. **412-285-3649**
Committees. Public Works; Science
Press. Karen Ostrowski
AA. Robert J Ludwiczak
Secretary. Donna J Fry

MYERS, JOHN T (R–IN, 7th). 2448
Rayburn House Office Bldg, 20515.
202-225-5805. (h) Covington, IN.
317-793-3363 (office)
Committees. Appropriations
Press and **AA.** Ronald L Hardman
Secretary. Eunice M Rowe

MYERS, MICHAEL O (D–PA, 1st). 1311
Longworth House Office Bldg, 20515.
202-225-4731. (h) Philadelphia, PA.
215-925-6840 (office)
Committees. Education; Post Office
AA. Michael T Corbett
Secretary. Bonnie Lockett

NATCHER, WILLIAM H (D–KY, 2nd).
2333 Rayburn House Office Bldg, 20515.
202-225-3501. (h) Bowling Green, KY.
502-842-5126
Committee. Appropriations
Secretary. Karen R Gray

NEAL, STEPHEN L (D–NC, 5th). 331
Cannon House Office Bldg, 20515.
202-225-2071. (h) Winston-Salem, NC.
919-761-3125
Committees. Banking; Science
Press. James Taylor
AA. Donald D Abernethy
Secretary. Jackie Brincefield

NEDZI, LUCIEN N (D–MI, 14th). 2418
Rayburn House Office Bldg, 20515.
202-225-6276. (h) Detroit, MI. **313-892-4010**

Committees. Armed Services; House
Administration; Library (Joint)
Press and **AA.** James G Pyrros
Secretary. Mary Flanagan

NICHOLS, BILL (D–AL, 3rd). 2417
Rayburn House Office Bldg, 20515.
202-225-3261. (h) Sylacauga, AL. NL
Committee. Armed Services
Press. Tom Eiland
AA. David Patrick
Secretary. Mary Elva Rice

NIX, ROBERT NC (D–PA, 2nd). 2201
Rayburn House Office Bldg, 20515.
202-225-4001. (h) Philadelphia, PA.
215-912-0156
Committees. Post Office; International
Relations
Press. Greg McGowan
QA. Cyrill Jenious
Secretary. Delois Harding

NOLAN, RICHARD M (D–MN, 6th). 214
Cannon House Office Bldg, 20515.
202-225-2331. (h) Waite Park, MN.
612-252-7580
Committees. Agriculture; Small Business
Press. Steve Johnson
AA. James A DeChaine
Secretary. Ione V Yates

NOWAK, HENRY (D–NY, 37th). 1504
Longworth House Office Building, 20515.
202-225-3306. (h) Buffalo, NY. **716-893-7858**
(office)
Committees. Public Works; Small Business
Press and **AA.** Ronald J Maselka
Secretary. Helen Burton

OAKAR, MARY ROSE (D–OH 20th). 427
Cannon House Office Bldg, 20515.
202-225-5871. (h) Cleveland, OH.
216-522-4927 (office)
Committees. Banking; Aging (Select)
Press and **AA.** Paul A Slimak
Secretary. Virginia F Karas

OBERSTAR, JAMES L (D–MN, 8th). 323
Cannon House Office Bldg, 20515.
202-225-6211. (h) Chisholm, MN.
218-727-7474 (office)
Committees. Merchant Marine; Public
Works; Congressional Operations (Joint)
Press. John H O'Connor
AA. Thomas R Reagan
Secretary. Charlotte Flax

OBEY, DAVID R (D–WI, 7th). 2349 Rayburn House Office Bldg, 20515. **202-225-3365.** (h) Wausau, WI. **715-848-3244**

Committees. Appropriations; Budget; Ethics (Select)

Press. Kathy Martin

AA. Lyle H Stitt

Secretary. Norma Schuster

O'BRIEN, GEORGE M (R–IL, 17th). 434 Cannon House Office Bldg, 20515. **202-225-3635.** (h) Joliet, IL. **815-740-2040**

Committee. Appropriations

AA. Marion Burson

Secretary. Carolyn Groves

O'NEILL, THOMAS P JR (D–MA, 8th). 2231 Rayburn House Office Bldg, 20515. **202-225-5111.** (h) Cambridge, MA. *Speaker of the House*

Press. Gary Hymel

AA. Leo E Kiehl

Secretary. Dolores C Snow

OTTINGER, RICHARD L (D–NY, 24th). 240 Cannon House Office Bldg, 20515. **202-225-6506.** (h) Pleasantville, NY. **914-769-3884**

Committees. Interstate Commerce; Science

Press. Frank Nardozzi

AA. Martin Rogowsky

Secretary. Cynthia Wallquist

PANETTA, LEON E (D–CA, 16th). 437 Cannon House Office Bldg, 20515. **202-225-2861.** (h) Carmel Valley, CA. **408-649-3555** (office)

Committees. Agriculture; House Administration

Press. Larry Bauman

AA. BT (John) Franzen

Secretary. Diana Marino

PATTEN, EDWARD J (D-NJ, 15th). 2332 Rayburn House Office Bldg, 20515. **202-225-6301.** (h) Perth Amboy, NJ. **201-826-0456**

Committee. Appropriations

AA. Stephen G Callis

PATTERSON, JERRY M (D-CA, 38th). 123 Cannon House Office Bldg, 20515. **202-225-2965.** (h) Buena Park, CA. **714-835-3811** (office)

Committees. Banking; Merchant Marine

Press. Shone Cotner

AA. James Cousins

Secretary. Mary Kay McClure

PATTISON, EDWARD W (D-NY, 9th). 1127 Longworth House Office Bldg, 20515. **202-225-5614.** (*.*) West Sand Lake, NY. **518-272-3082**

Committees. Banking; House Administration

AA. Owen Goldfarb

Secretary. Ann Gibson

PEASE, DONALD J (D-OH, 13th). 1641 Longworth House Office Bldg, 20515. **202-225-3401.** (h) Oberlin, OH. **216-774-6855**

Committee. International Relations

AA. Bette Welch

Secretary. Bambi Turner

PEPPER, CLAUDE (D-FL, 14th). 2239 Rayburn House Office Bldg, 20515. **202-225-3931.** (h) Miami, FL. **305-573-2489**

Committees. Rules; Aging (Select)

Press and AA. James F Southerland

Secretary. Charlotte Dickson

PERKINS, CARL D (D-KY, 7th). 2365 Rayburn House Office Bldg, 20515. **202-225-4935.** (h) Hindman, KY. **606-785-5661**

Committee. Education

AA. Ivan Swift

Secretary. Nancy Hirst

PETTIS, SHIRLEY N (R-CA, 37th). 1421 Longworth House Office Bldg, 20515. **202-225-5861.** (h) Loma Linda, CA. **714-862-6030** (office)

Committees. Education; International Relations

Press. Gerrie Skipske

AA. Rose Zamaria

Secretary. Ingrid Schlossberg

PICKLE, J J (JAKE) (D-TX, 10th). 242 Cannon House Office Bldg, 20515. **202-225-4865.** (h) Austin, TX. **512-472-9788**

Committee. Ways and Means

Press. John S Bender

AA. J Michael Keeling

Secretary. Molly Shulman

PIKE, OTIS G (D-NY, 1st). 2308 Rayburn House Office Bldg, 20515. **202-225-3826.** (h) Riverhead, NY. **516-727-0968**

Committees. Budget; Ways and Means; Economic (Joint)

Secretary. Betty L Orr

POAGE, WR (D-TX, 11th). 2107 Rayburn House Office Bldg, 20515. **202-225-6105.** (h) Waco, TX. **817-724-5111**

Committee. Agriculture

AA. C Dayle Henington

Secretary. Ruth Lair

PRESSLER, LARRY (R-SD, 1st). 1132 Longworth House Office Bldg, 20515. **202-225-2801.** (h) Munboldt, SD. **605-363-2763**

Committees. Education; Small Business

Press. Ann Reilly

AA. Jon R Grunseth

Secretary. Eleanor F Rhodes

PREYER, RICHARDSON (D-NC, 6th). 2344 Rayburn House Office Bldg, 20515. **202-225-3065.** (h) Greensboro, NC. **919-272-7178**

Committees. Government Operations; Interstate Commerce; Conduct; Ethics (Select); Assassinations (Select)

Press and AA. Tom Lambeth

Secretary. Bernice Pruitt

PRICE, MELVIN (D-IL, 23rd). 2340 Rayburn House Office Bldg, 20515. **202-225-6311.** (h) Seattle, WA. NL

Committees. Government Operations; Merchant Marine

AA. Robert A Davidson

Secretary. Mary Lou Domres

PURSELL, CARL D (R-MI, 2nd). 1709 Longworth House Office Bldg, 20515. **202-225-4401.** (h) Plymouth, MI. **313-455-0646**

Committees. Education; Science

Press. Bill Kerans

AA. Robert Webber

Secretary. Patsy Semple

QUAYLE, J DANFORTH (R-IN, 4th). 1407 Longworth House Office Bldg, 20515. **202-225-4436.** (h) Huntington, IN. **219-356-6822**

Committees. Government Operations; Small Business

Press. Marion Tuerff

AA. Lester Rosen

Secretary. Cynthia Love

QUIE, ALBERT H (R–MN, 1st). 2185 Rayburn House Office Bldg, 20515. **202-225-2271.** (h) Dennison, MN. **507-288-2384**

Committees. Education; Conduct

Press. Roger Runningen

AA. Keith E Hall

Secretary. Mary C Bradley

QUILLEN, JAMES H (R–TN, 1st). 102 Cannon House Office Bldg, 20515. **202-225-6356.** (h) Kingsport, TN. **615-245-3306**
Committees. Rules; Conduct
Press. Roger Hoover
AA. Frances Light Currie
Secretary. Jane Wooten

RAHALL, NICK J II (D–WV, 4th). 511 Cannon House Office Bldg, 20515. **202-225-3452.** (h) Beckley, WV, NL
Committees. Interior Affairs; Public Works
Press. Michael Serpke
AA. Paula Smith
Secretary. Joan M Kunkel

RAILSBACK, THOMAS F (R–IL, 19th). 2431 Rayburn House Office Bldg, 20515. **202-225-5905.** (h) Moline, IL. **209-794-1681**
Committees. Judiciary; Narcotics Abuse (Select)
Press. Dave Mahsman, **202-225-7839** (h) **301-567-5484**
LA. Pat Wichser
Secretary. Linda G Stephenson

RANGEL, CHARLES B (D–NY, 19th). 2432 Rayburn House Office Bldg, 20515. **202-225-4365.** (h) New York, NY. **212-183-1212**
Committees. Ways and Means; Narcotics Abuse (Select)
Press and **AA.** George A Dalley
Secretary. Patricia O'Bradley

REGULA, RALPH S (R–OH, 16th). 1707 Longworth House Office Bldg, 20515. **202-225-3876.** (h) Navarre, OH. **216-756-2635**
Committees. Appropriations; Budget
Press. Allan Simpson
AA. Thomas Morr

REUSS, HENRY S (D–WI, 5th). 2413 Rayburn House Office Bldg, 20515. **202-225-3571.** (h) Milwaukee, WI, NL
Committees. Banking; Economic (Joint)
Press. Tom Tolan
LA. Joseph Sisk
Secretary. Judith Buechner

RHODES, JOHN J (R–AZ, 1st). 2310 Rayburn House Office Bldg, 20515. **202-225-0600** or **0604.** (h) Mesa, AZ. **602-261-3181** *Minority leader of the House*
Press. J Brian Smith
AA. James R Feltham
Secretary. Clara Posey

RICHMOND, FREDERICK W (D–NY, 14th). 1728 Longworth House Office Bldg, 20515. **202-225-5936.** (h) Brooklyn, NY. **202-522-7121**
Committees. Agriculture; Small Business
Press. Louis Gordon
AA. Timothy E Wyman
Secretary. Deborah S McVicker

RINALDO, MATTHEW J (R–NJ, 12th). 314 Cannon House Office Bldg, 20515. **202-225-5361.** (h) Union, NJ. **201-686-0915**
Committees. Interstate Commerce; Aging (Select)
Press. Charles Oustow
AA. Paul Schlegel
Secretary. Louise Van Duyne

RISENHOOVER, TED (D–OK, 2nd). 1124 Longworth House Office Bldg, 20515. **202-225-2701.** (h) Tahlequah, OK. **918-456-8835**
Committees. District of Columbia; Interior Affairs; Public Works; Aging (Select)
Press. Del Smith
AA. Joe Carter
Secretary. Julia Platt

ROBERTS, RAY (D–TX, 4th). 2184 Rayburn House Office Bldg, 20515. **202-225-6673.** (h) McKinney, TX. **214-542-2617**
Committees. Veterans' Affairs; Public Works
Press. Linda Boyer
LA. Pat Hill
Secretary. Grace Warren

ROBINSON, J KENNETH (R–VA, 7th). 2437 Rayburn House Office Bldg, 20515. **202-225-6561.** (h) Winchester, VA. NL
Committee. Appropriations
Press and **AA.** Chris Mathisen
Secretary. Barbara N Daniel

RODINO, PETER W, JR (D–NJ, 10th). 2462 Rayburn House Office Bldg, 20515. **202-225-3436.** (h) Newark, NJ. **201-645-3213**
Committees. Judiciary; Narcotics Abuse (Select)
Press. Eva Deney
AA. Thomas S Boyd, Jr
Secretary. Sonja L DeChambeau

ROE, ROBERT A (D–NJ, 8th). 2243 Rayburn House Office Bldg, 20515. **202-225-5751.** (h) Wayne, NJ. **201-696-2077**
Committees. Public Works; Science
AA. Kathryn M Marazzo
LA. Glenn D Johnson

ROGERS, PAUL L (D–FL, 11th). 2407 Rayburn House Office Bldg, 20515. **202-225-3001.** (h) West Palm Beach, FL. **305-832-6424**
Committees. Interstate Commerce; Merchant Marine; Narcotics Abuse (Select)
AA. Richard G Lepeska
Secretary. Norman W Reed

RONCALIO, TENO (D–WY, at large). 1134 Longworth House Office Bldg, 20515. **202-225-2311.** (h) Cheyenne, WY. **307-632-1225**
Committees. Interior Affairs; Public Works
Press. Jack Huizenga
AA. Denis Earhart
Secretary. Mary Meyer Cook

ROONEY, FRED B (D–PA, 15th). 2313 Rayburn House Office Bldg, 20515. **202-225-6411.** (h) Bethlehem, PA. **215-866-2219**
Committees. Interstate Commerce; Merchant Marine; Aging (Select)
Press and **AA.** Ray A Huber
Secretary. Marguerite D Noll

ROSE, CHARLES (D–NC, 7th). 218 Cannon House Office Bldg, 20515. **202-225-2731.** (h) Fayetteville, NC. **919-485-3243**
Committees. Agriculture; District of Columbia; House Administration
Secretary. Marion Brickell

ROSENTHAL, BENJAMIN S (D–NY, 8th). 2372 Rayburn House Office Bldg, 20515. **202-225-2601.** (h) Elmhurst, NY. **212-939-8200**
Committees. Government Operations; International Relations
Press. Doug Bloomfield
AA. Mary W Davis
Secretary. Arlene M Hennessey

ROSTENKOWSKI, DAN (D–IL, 8th). 2111 Rayburn House Office Bldg, 20515. **202-225-4061.** (h) Chicago, IL. **312-276-6000**
Committees. Ways and Means; Taxation (Joint)
AA. Joseph K Dowley
Secretary. Virginia Fletcher

ROUSSELOT, JOHN H (R–CA, 26th). 2430 Rayburn House Office Bldg, 20515. **202-225-6235.** (h) Los Angeles, CA. **213-688-4870**
Committees. Appropriations; Aging (Select)

Press. Brent Jaquet
AA. Dan Maldonado
Secretary. Nancy Naylor

RUDD, ELDON D (R–AZ, 4th). 1428 Longworth House Office Bldg, 20515. **202-225-3361.** (h) Scottsdale, AZ. **602-261-4803**
Committees. Interior Affairs; Science
Press and AA. George H Archibald
Secretary. Jean E Robillard

RUNNELS, HAROLD (D–NM, 2nd). 1535 Longworth House Office Bldg, 20515. **202-225-2365.** (h) Lovington, NM. **505-396-2232**
Committees. Armed Services; Interior Affairs
Press. Mike Olquin
AA. Larry Morgan
Secretary. Shirley Dicken

RUPPE, PHILIP E (R–MI, 11th). 203 Cannon House Office Bldg, 20515. **202-225-4735.** (h) Houghton, MI. **906-482-0642**
Committees. Interior Affairs; Merchant Marine
Press. James Storey
AA. Paul Hillegonds
Secretary. Kathy Miller

RUSSO, MARTIN A (D–IL, 3rd). 126 Cannon House Office Bldg, 20515. **202-225-5736.** (h) South Holland, IL. **312-596-8242**
Committees. Interstate Commerce; Small Business; Continental Shelf (Ad Hoc Select); Aging (Select)
Press. Carol Hall
AA. Robert A Macari
Secretary. Nana R Schuring

RYAN, LEO J (D–CA, 11th). 137 Cannon House Office Bldg, 20515. **202-225-3531.** (h) Belmont, CA. **415-349-1978**
Committees. Government Operations; International Relations; Post Office
LA. K Jacqueline Speier

ST GERMAIN, FERNAND J (D–RI, 1st). 2136 Rayburn House Office Bldg, 20515. **202-225-4911.** (h) Woonsocket, RI. **401-528-4323**
Committees. Banking; Government Operations; Small Business
AA. Joseph Scanlon
Secretary. Elizabeth Gallas

SANTINI, JAMES D (D–NV, at large). 1408 Longworth House Office Bldg, 20515. **202-225-5965.** (h) Las Vegas, NV NL
Committees. Interior Affairs; Interstate Commerce; Judiciary; Aging (Select)
Press. Dante Pistone
AA. John Brodeur
Secretary. Kim Short

SARASIN, RONALD A (R–CT, 5th). 229 Cannon House Office Bldg, 20515. **202-225-3822.** (h) Beacon Falls, CT. **203-573-1418**
Committees. Education; Aging (Select)
Press. Charles T Kline, Jr
AA. Marc G Stanley
Secretary. Cindy Fritts

SATTERFIELD, DAVID E III (D—VA, 3rd). 2348 Rayburn House Office Bldg, 20515. **202-225-2815.** (h) Richmond, VA. **804-282-7211**
Committees. Interstate Commerce; Veterans' Affairs
Press. Richard O'Neal
AA. RG Armistead
LA. Jon Jewett

SAWYER, HAROLD S (R–MI, 5th). 508 Cannon House Office Bldg, 20515. **202-225-3831.** (h) Rockford, MI. **616-866-9269**
Committees. Judiciary; Veterans' Affairs; Ethics (Select)
Press. Birge Watkins
AA. Russell Rourke
Secretary. Sylvia Roberts

SCHEUER, JAMES H (D–NY, 11th). 2402 Rayburn House Office Bldg, 20515. **202-225-5471.** (h) Neponsit, NY. **212-634-1575**
Committees. Interstate Commerce; Science; Narcotics Abuse (Select)
Press and AA. Martin Mendelsohn
Secretary. Natalie Ruvell

SCHROEDER, PATRICIA (D–CO, 1st). 1507 Longworth House Office Bldg, 20515. **202-225-4431.** (h) Denver, CO. **303-837-2351**
Committees. Armed Services; Post Office
Press and secretary. Kitty Hearty
AA. Dan Buck

SCHULZE, RICHARD T (R–PA, 5th). 223 Cannon House Office Bldg, 20515. **202-225-5761.** (h) Malvern, PA. **215-644-0507**
Committee. Ways and Means

Press. Laura Broderick
AA. Joe Westner
Secretary. Rita Ann Pfeiffer

SEBELIUS, KEITH G (R–KS, 1st). 1211 Longworth House Office Bldg, 20515. **202-225-2715.** (h) Norton, KS. **913-877-3180**
Committees. Agriculture; Interior Affairs
Press. Dixie Lee Dodd

SEIBERLING, JOHN F (D–OH, 14th). 1225 Longworth House Office Bldg, 20515. **202-225-5231.** (h) Akron, OH. **216-375-5710**
Committees. Interior Affairs; Judiciary; Continental Shelf (Ad Hoc Select)
AA. Donald W Mansfield
Secretary. Wilda E Chisolm

SHARP, PHILIP R (D–IN, 10th). 1234 Longworth House Office Bldg, 20515. **202-225-3021.** (h) Muncie, IN. NP
Committees. Interior Affairs; Interstate Commerce
Press and AA. Jack Riggs
Secretary. Suzanne M Langsdorf

SHIPLEY, GEORGE E (D–IL, 22nd). 237 Cannon House Office Bldg, 20515. **202-225-5001.** (h) Olney, IL. **618-395-2171**
Committee. Appropriations
Press and Secretary. Kathleen Smiley
AA. Goldie Eckl

SHUSTER, EG (BUD) (R–PA, 12th). 1112 Longworth House Office Bldg, 20515. **202-225-2431.** (h) Everett, PA. NL
Committees. Education; Public Works
Press. Joseph La Sala, Jr
AA. Ann Eppard

SIKES, ROBERT LF (D–FL, 1st). 2269 Rayburn House Office Bldg, 20515. **202-225-4136.** (h) Crestview, FL. **904-682-3131**
Committee. Appropriations
AA. Alma D Butler
LA. John H Allen

SIMON, PAUL M (D–IL, 24th). 227 Cannon House Office Bldg, 20515. **202-225-5201.** (h) Carbondale, IL. **618-457-4171.** (h) **301-983-1120**
Committees. Budget; Education
Press. Terry Michael. (h) **202-546-4074**
AA. Margaret Bergin
Secretary. Karen Steele

SISK, BF (D–CA, 15th). 2217 Rayburn House Office Bldg, 20515. **202-225-6131.** (h)

Fresno, CA. **209-487-5004**
Committee. Rules
AA. Tony Coelho
Secretary. Elizabeth Larcombe

SKELTON, IKE (D–MO, 4th). 1404 Longworth House Office Bldg, 20515. **202-225-2876.** (h) Lexington, MO, NL
Committees. Agriculture; Small Business
Press. Dan O'Brien
AA. Gary Edwards
Secretary. Noreen A O'Hagan

SKUBITZ, JOE (R–KS, 5th). 2211 Rayburn House Office Bldg, 20515. **202-225-3911.** (h) Pittsburg, KS. **316-232-2320**
Committees. Interior Affairs; Interstate Commerce
Press. James Rinker
AA. Chuck Pike
Secretary. Janet De Stefano

SLACK, JOHN (D–WV, 3rd). 1536 Longworth House Office Bldg, 20515. **202-225-2711.** (h) Charleston, WV. **204-346-9714**
Committee. Appropriations
AA. Paul H Becker

SMITH, NEAL (D–IA, 4th). 2373 Rayburn House Office Bldg, 20515. **202-225-4426.** (h) Altoona, IA. **515-967-4722**
Committees. Small Business; Appropriations
AA. Tom Dawson
Secretary. Nancy Simplicio

SMITH, VIRGINIA (MRS HAVEN) (R–NE, 3rd). 1105 Longworth House Office Bldg, 20515. **202-225-6435.** (h) Chappell, NE. **308-632-3333**
Committee. Appropriations
Press. Jim Huttenmaier
AA. Robert R Davenport
Secretary. Linda K Lambrecht

SNYDER, MG (GENE) (R–KY, 4th). 2330 Rayburn House Office Bldg, 20515. **202-225-3465.** (h) Louisvville, KY. **502-897-1123**
Committees. Merchant Marine; Public Works
AA. William E Tanner
Secretary. Ann Booth

SOLARZ, STEPHEN J (D–NY, 13th). 1530 Longworth House Office Bldg, 20515. **202-225-2361.** (h) Brooklyn, NY. **212-648-6342**

Committees. International Relations; Post Office
Press. Joshua Horowitz
AA. Michael Lewan
Secretary. Carol Ditta

SPELLMAN, GLADYS NOON (D–MD, 5th). 1110 Longworth House Office Bldg, 20515. **202-225-4131.** (h) Laurel, MD. NL
Committees. Banking; Post Office
Press. Terry Schuette
AA. Gene Kennedy
Secretary. Edna McLellan

SPENCE, FLOYD D (R–SC, 2nd). 2351 Rayburn House Office Bldg, 20515. **202-225-2452.** (h) Lexington, SC. **803-359-6372**
Committees. Armed Services; Conduct
Press. Bob Hodges, Jr
AA. W A Cook
Secretary. Shirley O'Neal

STAGGERS, HARLEY O (D–WV, 2nd). 2366 Rayburn House Office Bldg, 20515. **202-225-4331.** (h) Keyser, WV. **304-788-1298**
Committee. Interstate Commerce
Press. Philip Jordan
AA. Marguerite Furfari
Secretary. Carole A McElvain

STANGELAND, ARLAN (R–MN, 7th). 1518 Longworth House Office Bldg, 20515. **202-225-2165.** (h) Barnesville, MN. **218-493-4385**
Committees. Government Operations; Public Works
AA. Jack Stewart
Secretary. Lane Beard

STANTON, J WILLIAM (R–OH, 11th). 2466 Longworth House Office Bldg, 20515. **202-225-5306.** (h) Painesville, OH. **216-352-6167**
Committees. Banking; Small Business
Press and Secretary. Bob Hardgrove
AA. Shirlee Enders McGloon

STARK, FORTNEY H (PETE) (D–CA, 9th). 1034 Longworth House Office Bldg, 20515. **202-225-5065.** (h) Oakland, CA. **415-635-1092**
Committees. District of Columbia; Ways and Means; Narcotics Abuse (Select)
AA. Edith Wijkie
Secretary. Beth McCann

STEED, TOM (D–OK, 4th). 2405 Rayburn House Office Bldg, 20515. **202-225-6165.** (h)

Shawnee, OK. **405-273-8183**
Committees. Appropriations; Small Business
Press. Vaughn Clark
AA. Truman Richardson
Secretary. Thelma Fogleman

STEERS, NEWTON I, JR (R–MD, 8th). 510 Cannon House Office Bldg, 20515. **202-225-5341.** (h) Bethesda, MD. **301-320-5820**
Committees. Banking; District of Columbia
Press. David Blee
AA. William Grigg
Secretary. Grace Shapiro

STEIGER, WILLIAM A (R–WI, 6th). 1111 Longworth House Office Bldg, 20515. **202-225-2476.** (h) Oshkosh, WI. **414-231-6333** (office)
Committee. Ways and Means
Press. Jim Dykstra
AA. Maureen Drummy
Secretary. Marilyn Monnette

STOCKMAN, DAVID A (R–MI, 4th). 1021 Longworth House Office Bldg, 20515. **202-225-3761.** (h) St Joseph, MI. **616-983-5575**
Committees. House Administration; Interstate Commerce; Library (Joint)
Press. Robert Murphy
AA. David Gerson
Secretary. Mary Ellen Tevoedjre

STOKES, LOUIS (D–OH, 21st). 2455 Rayburn House Office Bldg, 20515. **202-225-7032.** (h) Cleveland, OH. **216-522-4900**
Committees. Appropriations; Budget; Assassinations (Select)
Press. Mary Helen Thompson, **202-225-7034**
AA. James C Harper
Secretary. Jo Ann White

STRATTON, SAMUEL S (D–NY, 28th). 2205 Rayburn House Office Bldg, 20515. **202-225-5076.** (h) Amsterdam, NY. **518-843-3400**
Committees. Armed Services; Ethics (Select)
AA. Roger Mott
Secretary. Mary Leslie

STUDDS, GERRY E (D–MA, 12th). 1511 Longworth House Office Bldg, 20515. **202-225-3111.** (h) Cohasset, MA. **617-783-3400**
Committees. International Relations; Merchant Marine; Continental Shelf (Ad Hoc Select)

AA. Samuel Allis

Secretary. Julia M Miller

STUMP, BOB (D–AZ, 3rd). 211 Cannon House Office Bldg, 20515. **202-225-4576.** (h) Tolleson, AZ. **602-261-6923** (office, Phoenix, AZ)

Committee. Public Works

AA. Charles P Thompson

LA. Lisa Jackson

SYMMS, STEVEN D (R–ID, 1st). 1410 Longworth House Office Bldg, 20515. **202-225-6611.** (h) Caldwell, ID. **208-459-2860**

Committees. Agriculture; Interior Affairs

Press. Rita Vanover

AA. Robert Smith

Secretary. Margaret Lundy

TAYLOR, GENE (R–MO, 7th). 1114 Longworth House Office Bldg, 20515. **202-225-6536.** (h) Sarcoxie, MO. **411-548-7226**

Committees. Post Office; Public Works

AA. Gerald Henson

Secretary. Frances A Watkins

TEAGUE, OLIN E (D–TX, 6th). 2311 Rayburn House Office Bldg, 20515. **202-225-2002.** (h) College Station, TX. **713-779-5744**

Committees. Science; Conduct; Veterans' Affairs

AA. George W Fisher

Secretary. Margaret Bale

THOMPSON, FRANK, JR (D–NJ, 4th). 2109 Rayburn House Office Bldg, 20515. **202-225-3765.** (h) Trenton, NJ. **609-393-4535**

Committees. House Administration; Education; Library (Joint); Printing (Joint); Ethics (Select)

Press and **AA.** William T Deitz

Secretary. Judith H Simmons

THONE, CHARLES (R–NE, 1st). 2433 Rayburn House Office Bldg, 20515. **202-225-4806.** (h) Lincoln, NE. **402-471-5175** (office)

Committees. Agriculture; Government Operations; Assassinations (Select)

Press and **AA.** William H Palmer

LA. Victoria B Peckham

THORNTON, RAY (D–AR, 4th). 1414 Longworth House Office Bldg, 20515. **202-225-3772.** (h) Sheridan, AR. NL

Committees. Agriculture; Science

AA. Julie W McDonald

Secretary. Susan Nash

TONRY, RICHARD A (D–LA, 1st). 422 Cannon House Office Bldg, 20515. **202-225-3015.** (h) Arabi, LA. **504-779-6851**

Committees. Armed Services; Science

Press. Sandy Miller

AA. Frank Massa

Secretary. Joy W Colombo

TRAXLER, BOB (D–MI, 8th). 1526 Longworth House Office Bldg, 20515. **202-225-2806.** (h) Bay City, MI. **517-684-2381**

Committee. Appropriations

AA. Gary R Bachula

Secretary. Aileen L Kizer

TREEN, DAVID C (R–LA, 3rd). 438 Cannon House Office Bldg, 20515. **202-225-4031.** (h) Matarie, LA. **504-889-2303** (office)

Committees. Armed Services; Merchant Marine; Continental Shelf (Ad Hoc Select)

Press. Emile Brinkman

AA. John S Rivers

Secretary. Marihelen Horneman

TRIBLE, PAUL S, JR (R–VA, 1st). 512 Cannon House Office Bldg, 20515. **202-225-4261.** (h) Tappahannock, VA. **804-443-3730**

Committees. Armed Services; Merchant Marine

Press. Rene Stephens

AA. Gus Edwards

Secretary. Beverly P Doerflein

TSONGAS, PAUL E (D–MA, 5th). 217 Cannon House Office Bldg, 20515. **202-225-3411.** (h) Lowell, MA. **617-458-0435**

Committees. Banking; Interior Affairs; Defense Production (Joint)

Press. Fred Faust

LA. Richard Arenberg

Secretary. Marsha McMullin

TUCKER, JAMES G JR (D–AR, 2nd). 1729 Longworth House Office Bldg, 20515. **202-225-2506.** (h) Little Rock, AR. **501-663-2476**

Committee. Ways and Means

AA. Robert L Brown

Secretary. Margaret Shean

UDALL, MORRIS K (D–AZ, 2nd). 235 Cannon House Office Bldg, 20515. **202-225-4065.** (h) Tucson, AZ. **602-792-6404** (office)

Committees. Interior Affairs; Post Office; Continental Shelf (Ad Hoc Select); Ethics (Select)

Press. Bob Neuman

AA. Roger Lewis

Secretary. Dee Jackson

ULLMAN, AL (D–OR, 2nd). 1136 Longworth House Office Bldg, 20515. **202-225-7511.** (h) Baker, OR. NL

Committees. Ways and Means; Taxation (Joint)

AA. Bill Alberger

LA. Bill Robertson

VAN DEERLIN, LIONEL (D–CA, 42nd). 2408 Rayburn House Office Bldg, 20515. **202-225-5672.** (h) Chula Vista, CA. **714-233-8959**

Committees. House Administration; Interstate Commerce

AA. Rudy P Murillo

Secretary. Shirley E Dave

VANDER JAGT, GUY (R–MI, 9th). 2334 Rayburn House Office Bldg, 20515. **202-225-3511.** (h) Luther, MI. **616-797-5445**

Committee. Ways and Means

Press and **AA.** James M Sparling, Jr

Secretary. Margaret L Treanor

VANIK, CHARLES A (D–OH, 22nd). 2108 Rayburn House Office Bldg, 20515. **202-225-6331.** (h) Euclid, OH. **216-522-4253** (office)

Committee. Ways and Means

Press and **LA.** Arnold C Woodrich

Secretary. Dianne E Tomasek

VENTO, BRUCE F (D–MN, 4th). 1330 Longworth House Office Bldg, 20515. **202-225-6631.** (h) St Paul, MN. **612-725-7869** (office)

Committees. Banking; Interior Affairs

AA. Jim Pirius

VOLKMER, HAROLD L (D–MO, 9th). 1228 Longworth House Office Bldg, 20515. **202-225-2956.** (h) Hannibal, MO. **314-221-6106** (office)

Committees. Agriculture; Judiciary

Press. Larry Grewach

AA. Valerie H Davis

Secretary. Jennie Frederick

WAGGONNER, JOE D (D–LA, 4th). 221 Cannon House Office Bldg, 20515. **202-225-2777.** (h) Plain Dealing, LA. NL
Committee. Ways and Means
AA. David L Batt
Secretary. Rene Gibson

WALGREN, DOUG (D–PA, 18th). 1008 Longworth House Office Bldg, 20515. **202-225-2135.** (h) Pittsburgh, PA. **412-391-4016** (office)
Committees. Interstate Commerce; Science
Press. Sandy Glickman
AA. Jan Hogan
Secretary. Florrie Eubanks

WALKER, ROBERT S, (R–PA, 16th). 1028 Longworth House Office Bldg, 20515. **202-225-2411.** (h) East Petersburg, PA. **717-569-3990**
Committees. Government; Science
Press. Thomas Blank
AA. Hugh M Coffman
Secretary. Clara D Tarry

WALSH, WILLIAM F (R–NY, 33rd). 206 Cannon House Office Bldg, 20515. **202-225-3333.** (h) Syracuse, NY. **315-488-3752**
Committees. Public Works; Veterans' Affairs; Aging (Select)
Press. Connie Schreiber
AA. F Gibson Darrison Jr
Secretary. Dorothy Vagnozzi

WAMPLER, WILLIAM C (R–VA, 9th). 2422 Rayburn House Office Bldg, 20515. **202-225-3861.** (h) Bristol, VA. **703-466-9451**
Committees. Agriculture; Aging (Select)
Press. Lynn Ogden
AA. J Ray Dotson
Secretary. Diane Keyser

WATKINS, WESLEY W (D–OK, 3rd). 514 Cannon House Office Bldg, 20515. **202-225-4565.** (h) Ada, OK. **405-436-0000**
Committees. Banking; Science
AA. LeRoy Jackson
Secretary. Marilyn Storn

WAXMAN, HENRY A (D–CA, 24th). 1721 Longworth House Office Bldg, 20515. **202-225-3976.** (h) Los Angeles, CA. **213-652-2095**
Committees. Government Operations; Interstate Commerce; Narcotics Abuse (Select)

AA. Burt Margolin
Secretary. Norah P Lucey

WEAVER, JAMES H (D-OR, 4th). 1238 Longworth House Office Bldg, 20515. **202-225-6416.** (h) Eugene, OR. **503-687-6732**
Committees. Agriculture; Interior Affairs
AA. Phyllis Rock
Secretary. Sandra Schaller

WEISS, TED (D-NY, 20th). 1229 Longworth House Office Bldg, 20515. **202-225-5635.** (h) New York, NY. **212-787-3480**
Committees. Education; Government Operations.
AA. Ralph Andrew
Secretary. James Gottlieb

WHALEN, CHARLES W, JR (R-OH, 3rd). 1035 Longworth House Office Bldg, 20515. **202-225-6465.** (h) Dayton, OH. **513-225-2843**
Committees. District of Columbia; International Relations
Press and **AA.** Bill Steponkus
LA. George Minter Lowrey

WHITE, RICHARD C (D-TX, 16th). 2233 Rayburn House Office Bldg, 20515. **202-225-4831.** (h) El Paso, TX. **915-543-7650**
Committees. Armed Services; Post Office
Press. Maxine Nagel
AA. Hawley Richeson
Secretary. Barbara J Potter

WHITEHURST, G WILLIAM (R-VA, 2nd). 442 Cannon House Office Bldg, 20515. **202-225-4215.** (h) Virginia Beach, VA. **804-428-8781**
Committee. Armed Services
Press. Victor Powell
AA. Charles H Fitzpatrick
Secretary. Kathleen Towers

WHITLEY, CHARLES O, SR (D-NC, 3rd). 502 Cannon House Office Bldg, 20515. **202-225-3415.** (h) Mount Olive, NC. **919-658-2289**
Committees. Agriculture; Armed Services
AA. Lewis Wren
Secretary. Rachel Spears

WHITTEN, JAMIE L (D-MS, 1st). 2328 Rayburn House Office Bldg, 20515. **202-225-4306.** (h) Charleston, MS. **601-647-8449**

Committee. Appropriations
AA. Marion F (Buddy) Bishop
Secretary. Mary Smallwood

WIGGINS, CHARLES E (R-CA, 39th). 2371 Rayburn House Office Bldg, 20515. **202-225-4111.** (h) Fullerton, CA. **714-870-7266**
Committees. House Administration; Judiciary; Continental Shelf (Ad Hoc Select); Ethics (Select)
Press and **AA.** Michael W Blommer
Secretary. Leslie C Marshall

WILSON, BOB (R-CA, 41st). 2307 Rayburn House Office Bldg, 20515. **202-225-3201.** (h) San Diego, CA. **714-231-0957**
Committees. Armed Services; Aging (Select)
Press. Douglas Wilburn
AA. Edward F Tarrar Jr
Secretary. Margaret Young

WILSON, CHARLES (D-TX, 2nd). 1214 Longworth House Office Bldg, 20515. **202-225-2401.** (h) Lufkin, TX. **713-632-2087**
Committee. Appropriations
AA. Charles W Simpson
Secretary. Linda L Sullivan

WILSON, CHARLES H (D–CA, 31st). 2409 Rayburn House Office Bldg, 20515. **202-225-5425.** (h) Hawthorne, CA. **213-531-6644**
Committees. Armed Services; Post Office
Press. Pam Beer
AA. John Pontius
Secretary. Betty Teitgen

WINN, LARRY, JR (R–KS, 3rd). 2416 Rayburn House Office Bldg, 20515. **202-225-2865.** (h) Overland Park, KS. **913-642-5449**
Committees. International Affairs; Science
Press. Meredith Masoner
AA. Richard L Bond
Secretary. Nan Orr Elder

WIRTH, TIMOTHY E (D–CO, 2nd). 312 Cannon House Office Bldg, 20515. **202-225-2161.** (h) Denver, CO. **303-234-5200**
Committees. Interstate; Science
Press. George Gudauskas
LA. Robert Sachs
Secretary. Judith La Drew

WOLFF, LESTER L (D-NY, 6th). 2463 Rayburn House Office Bldg, 20515. **202-225-5956.** (h) Great Neck, NY, NL

Committees. International Affairs; Veterans' Affairs; Narcotics Abuse (Select)

Press. Christopher Nelson

AA. Richard Carro

Secretary. Bonnie Robinson

WRIGHT, JAMES C, JR (D–TX, 12th). 2459 Rayburn House Office Bldg, 20515. **202-225-5071.** (h) Fort Worth, TX, NP

Committee. Budget Majority leader

Press and AA. Marshall Lynam

Secretary. Katherine Mitchell

WYDLER, JOHN W (R–NY, 5th). 2186 Rayburn House Office Bldg, 20515. **202-225-5516.** (h) Garden City, NY. **516-747-0112**

Committees. Government Operations; Science

Press. Babs Raesly

AA. Elizabeth D Hoppel

Secretary. Gloria I Pershing

WYLIE, CHALMERS P (R–OH, 15th). 2335 Rayburn House Office Bldg, 20515. **202-225-2015.** (h) Columbus, OH. **614-469-5614**

Committees. Banking; Veterans' Affairs, Defense (Joint)

Press. Roulhac Hamilton

AA. Jack M Foulk

Secretary. Teresa W Grasso

YATES, SIDNEY R (D–IL, 9th). 2234 Rayburn House Office Bldg, 20515. **202-225-2111.** (h) Chicago, IL. **312-353-4596**

Committee. Appropriations

Press and AA. Mary Bain

Secretary. Vickie L Winpisinger

YATRON, GUS (D–PA, 6th). 2400 Rayburn House Office Bldg, 20515. **202-225-5546.** (h) Reading, PA. **215-376-9123**

Committee. International Relations

AA. Joseph P Gemmell

YOUNG, C W (BILL) (R–FL, 6th). 2453 Rayburn House Office Bldg, 20515. **202-225-5961.** (h) St Petersburg, FL. **813-581-0980**

Committee. Appropriations

AA. Douglas Gregory

Secretary. Mary C Nesbit

YOUNG, DON (R–AK, at large). 1210 Longworth House Office Bldg, 20515. **202-225-5765.** (h) Fort Uykon, AK. **907-456-6949**

Committees. Interior Affairs; Merchant Marine; Continental Shelf (Ad Hoc Select)

Press. Ann Mullens

AA. Jack Ferguson

Secretary. Edith Vivian

YOUNG, JOHN (D–TX, 14th). 2204 Rayburn House Office Bldg, 20515. **202-225-2831.** (h) Corpus Christi, TX. **512-888-3141**

Committee. Rules

Press and AA. Joseph T Prendergast

Secretary. Gail F Hughes

YOUNG, ROBERT A (D–MO, 2nd). 1315 Longworth House Office Bldg, 20515. **202-225-2561.** (h) St Ann, MO. **314-428-6373**

Committee. Public Works

Press. David Nathan

AA. Chris Papagianis

Secretary. Deborah Lamb

ZABLOCKI, CLEMENT J (D–WI, 4th). 2183 Rayburn House Office Bldg, 20515. **202-225-4577.** (h) Milwaukee, WI. **414-383-4000**

Committee. International Relations

AA. Ivo Spalatin

Secretary. Eileen Walley

ZEFERETTI, LEO (D–NY, 15th). 215 Cannon House Office Bldg, 20515. **202-225-4105.** (h) Brooklyn, NY. **212-680-1000**

Committees. Education; Merchant Marine; Continental Shelf (Ad Hoc Select)

AA. Ms Lou B Nelson

LA. Karen Erica Johnson

Senate Committees

Standing Committees

AGRICULTURE, NUTRITION, AND FORESTRY. 322 Russell Senate Office Bldg, 20510. **202-224-2035**

Chairman. Herman E Talmadge (D–Ga)

General Counsel and Staff Director. Michael R McLeod. **202-224-0016**

Chief Clerk and Press Secretary. Nelson Denlinger. **202-224-2003**

Ranking Minority Member. Robert Dole (R–KS)

Minority member. Dale Sherwin. **202-224-0004**

Subcommittees and Chairmen. Environment, Soil Conservation, and forestry (Eastland, MS); Agricultural Credit and Rural Electri-

fication; Agricultural Production (Huddleston, KY); Agricultural Research (Leahy, VT); Rural Development (Clark, IA); Nutrition (McGovern, SD)

APPROPRIATIONS. 1235 Dirkson Senate Office Bldg, 20510. **202-224-3471**

Chairman. John L McClellan (D–AR)

Chief Counsel and Staff Director. James R Calloway. **202-224-7293**

Ranking Minority Member. Milton R Young (R–ND)

Minority Staff Director. Joel E Bonner Jr. **202-224-7255**

Subcommittees and Chairmen. Agriculture (Eagleton, MO); Defense (McClellan, AR); District of Columbia (Leahy, VT); Foreign Operations (Inouye, HI); HUD—Independent Agencies (Proxmire, WI); Interior (Byrd, WV); Labor, HEW (Magnuson, WA); Legislative (Huddleston, KY); Military Construction (Johnston, LA); Public Works (Stennis, MS); State, Justice, Commerce, and the Judiciary (Hollings, SC); Transportation (Bayh, IN); Treasury, Postal Service, and General Government (Chiles, FL)

ARMED SERVICES. 212 Russell Senate Office Bldg, 20510. **202-224-3871**

Chairman. John C Stennis (D–MS)

Staff Director. Francis J Sullivan

General Counsel. John C Roberts

Chief Clerk. John T Ticer

Ranking Minority Member. John Tower (R–TX)

Subcommittees and Chairmen. Intelligence (Byrd, VA); General Procurement (Stennis, MS); Military Construction and Stockpiles (Hart, CO); Arms Control (Jackson, WA); Tactical Air (Cannon, NV); Research and Development (McIntyre, NH); General Legislation (Culver, IA); Manpower and Personnel (Nunn, GA)

BANKING, HOUSING, AND URBAN AFFAIRS. 5300 Dirksen Senate Office Bldg, 20510. **202-224-7391**

Chairman. William Proxmire (D–WI)

Staff Director. Kenneth A McLean

Chief Clerk. Mary de la Pava

Ranking Minority Member. Edward W Brooke (R–MA)

Minority Staff Director. Anthony T Cluff

Subcommittees and Chairmen. Federal Credit Programs (Sarbanes, MD); Housing and Urban Affairs (Sparkman, AL, **202-224-6348**): Financial Institutions (McIntyre, NH); Securities (Williams, NJ);

International Finance (Stevenson, IL); Production and Stabilization (Cranston, CA); Consumer Affairs (Riegle, MI); Rural Housing (Morgan, NC)

BUDGET. 208 Carroll Arms Bldg, 301 1st St NE, 20002. **202-224-0642**

Chairman. Edmund S Muskie (D–ME)

Staff Director. John McEnvoy

Press. Christopher Matthews

Ranking Minority Member. Henry Bellmon (R–OK)

Minority counsel. Robert S Boyd. **202-224-0540**

No subcommittees

COMMERCE, SCIENCE, AND TRANS-PORTATION. 5202 Dirksen Senate Office Bldg, 20510. **202-224-5115**

Chairman. Warren G Magnuson (D–WA)

Staff Director. Edward R Merlis. **202-224-9321**

Chief Counsel. Thomas G Allison. **202-224-9321**

Ranking Minority Member. James B Pearson (R–KS)

Minority Counsel. Malcolm M Sterrett. **202-224-1251**

Subcommittees and Chairmen. Aviation (Cannon, NV); Communications (Hollings, SC); Consumer (Ford, KY); Merchant Marine and Tourism (Inouye, HI); Science, Technology, and Space (Stevenson, IL); Surface Transportation (Long, LA)

ENERGY AND NATURAL RESOURCES. 3105 Dirksen Senate Office Bldg, 20510. **202-224-4971**

Chairman. Henry M Jackson (D–WA)

Staff Director. Grenville Garside. **202-224-7155**

Chief Counsel. Michael Harvey. **202-224-0611**

Ranking Minority Member. Clifford P Hansen (R–WY)

Minority Counsel. Winfred O Craft, Jr. **202-224-3221**

Subcommittees and Chairmen. Public Lands and Resources; Parks and Recreation (Abourezk, SD); Energy Production and Supply (Haskell, CO); Energy Conservation and Regulation (Johnston, LA); Energy Research and Development (Church, ID)

ENVIRONMENT AND PUBLIC WORKS. 4202 Dirksen Senate Office Bldg, 20510. **202-224-6176**

Chairman. Hennings Randolph (D–WV)

Staff Director. John W Yago, Jr. **202-224-7842**

Majority Counsel. Philip T Cummings and Richard M Harris. **202-224-8743**

Ranking Minority Member. Robert T Stafford (R–VT)

Minority Counsel. Rick Herod and Katherine Cudlipp. **202-224-7854**

Subcommittees and Chairmen. Environmental Pollution (Muskie, ME); Water Resources (Gravel, AK); Transportation (Bensten, TX); Regional and Community Development (Burdick, ND); Resource Protection (Culver, IA); Nuclear Regulation (Hart, CO)

FINANCE. 227 Dirksen Senate Office Bldg, 20510. **202-224-4515**

Chairman. Russell B Long (D–LA)

Staff Director. Michael Stern

Tax Counsel. William Morris and Robert N Willan

Ranking Minority Member. Carl T Curtis (R–NE)

Chief Minority Counsel. Gordon Gilman. **202-224-4416**

Subcommittees and Chairmen. Health (Talmadge, GA); International Trade (Ribicoff, CT); Taxation and Debt Management (Byrd, VA); Social Security (Nelson, WI); Energy and Foundations (Gravel, AK); Private Pension Plans and Employee Fringe Benefits (Bentsen, TX); Unemployment Compensation, Revenue Sharing, and Economic Problems (Hathaway, ME); Administration of the Internal Revenue Code (Haskell, CO); Tourism and Sugar (Matsunaga, HI); Public Assistance (Moynihan, NY)

FOREIGN RELATIONS. 4229 Dirksen Senate Office Bldg, 20510. **202-224-4651**

Chairman. John Sparkman (D–AL). **202-224-4124**

Chairman's Administrative Assistant. George Kroloff. **202-224-5381**. (h). **301-340-1869**

Chief of Staff. Norvill Jones. **202-224-4651**

Ranking Minority Member. Clifford P Case (R–NJ)

Minority Staff. Steve Byren. **202-224-5381**

Subcommittees and Chairmen. European affairs (Biden, DE); East Asian and Pacific Affairs (Glenn, OH); International Operations (McGovern, SD); Foreign Economic Policy (Church, ID); Arms Control, Oceans, and International Environment (Pell, RI); Western Hemisphere Affairs (Sarbanes, MD); Near Eastern and South Asian Affairs

(Stone, FL); Foreign Assistance (Humphrey, MN); African Affairs (Clark, IA)

GOVERNMENTAL AFFAIRS. 3308 Dirksen Senate Office Bldg, 20510. **202-224-4751**

Chairman. Abraham A Ribicoff (D–CT)

Chief Counsel and Staff Director. Richard A Wegman

Ranking Minority Member. Charles H Percy (R–IL)

Minority Counsel. John Childers. **202-224-0431**

Subcommittees and Chairmen. Permanent Subcommittee on Investigations (Jackson, WA); Intergovernmental Operations (Muskie, ME); Reports, Accounting, and Management; Governmental Efficiency and District of Columbia (Eagleton, MO); Federal Spending Practices and Open Government (Chiles, FL); Energy, Nuclear Proliferation, and Federal Services (Glenn, OH); Civil Service and General Services (Sasser, TN)

HUMAN RESOURCES. 4320 Dirksen Senate Office Bldg, 20510. **202-224-5375**

Chairman. Harrison A Williams (D–NJ)

General Counsel and Staff Director. Stephen J Paradise. **202-224-7664**

Ranking Minority Member. Jacob K Javits (R–NY)

Minority Counsel. Jay Cutler. **202-224-7692**

Subcommittees and Chairmen. Labor (Williams, NJ); Handicapped (Randolph, WV); Education, Arts, and Humanities (Pell, RI); Employment, Poverty, and Migratory Labor (Nelson, WI); Health and Scientific Research (Kennedy, MA); Aging (Eagleton, MO); Child and Human Development (Cranston, CA); Alcoholism and Drug Abuse (Hathaway, ME)

JUDICIARY. 2226 Dirksen Senate Office Bldg, 20510. **202-224-5225**

Chairman. James O Eastland (D–MS)

Chief Counsel and Staff Director. Francis C Rosenberger

Ranking Minority Member. Strom Thurmond (R–SC)

Minority Chief Counsel. Emory Sneeden. **202-224-5668**

Subcommittees and Chairmen. Administrative Practice and Procedure (Abourezk, SC); Antitrust and Monopoly (Kennedy, MA); Citizen and Shareholder Rights and Interests (Metzenbaum, OH); Constitution (Bayh, IN); Criminal Laws and Procedures (McClellan, AR); Immigration (Eastland, MS); Improvements in Judicial Machinery (DeConcini, AZ); Juvenile Delinquency

(Culver, IA); Penitentiaries and Corrections (Biden, DE); Separation of Powers

RULES AND ADMINISTRATION. 305 Russell Senate Office Bldg, 20510. **202-224-6352**

Chairman. Howard W Cannon (D–NV)

Staff Director. William McWhorter Cochrane. **202-224-0275**

Chief Counsel. Chester H Smith. **202-224-0279**

Ranking Minority Member. Mark O Hatfield (R–OR)

Minority Staff Director. Larry E Smith. **202-224-0283**

VETERANS' AFFAIRS. 414 Russell Senate Office Bldg, 20510. **202-224-9126**

Chairman. Alan Cranston (D–FL)

Chief Counsel. Jonathan R Steinberg

Press. Peg Lotito

Ranking Minority Member. Robert T Stafford (R–VT)

Minority Counsel. Garner Shriver. **202-224-9132**

Subcommittees and Chairmen. Compensation and Pension (Talmadge, GA); Health and Readjustment (Cranston, CA); Housing, Insurance, and Cemeteries (Stone, FL)

Select and Special Committees

SELECT COMMITTEE ON ETHICS. 1417 Dirksen Senate Office Bldg, 20510. **202-224-2674**

Chairman. Adlai Stevenson (D–IL)

Staff Director. Kenneth E Gray. **202-224-2981**

Ranking Minority Member. Harrison Schmitt (R–NM)

SELECT COMMITTEE ON INTELLI-GENCE. G-308 Dirksen Senate Office Bldg, 20510. **202-224-1700**

Chairman. Birch Bayh (D–IN)

Staff Director. William G Miller

Ranking Minority Member. Barry Goldwater (R–AZ)

Minority Staff Director. Earl Eisenhower

Press Secretary. Spencer Davis

Subcommittees and Chairmen. Budget Authorization (Hathaway, ME); Collection, Production, and Quality of Intelligence (Stevenson, IL); Intelligence and the Rights of Americans (Bayh, IN); Charters and Guidelines—ad hoc (Huddleston, KY); Investigations—ad hoc (Morgan, NC); Security Classifications—ad hoc (Biden, DE)

SELECT COMMITTEE ON NUTRITION AND HUMAN NEEDS. A-511 Senate Annex, 20510. **202-224-7326**

Chairman. George McGovern (D–SD)

Staff Director. Alan J Stone

Ranking Minority Member. Charles H Percy (R–IL)

Minority Staff Director. 202-224-3921

SELECT COMMITTEE ON SMALL BUSINESS. 424 Russell Senate Office Bldg, 20510. **202-224-5175**

Chairman. Gaylord Nelson (D–WI)

Executive Director. William B Cherkasky. **202-224-8494**

Chief Counsel. Herbert L Spira. **202-224-8490**

Ranking Minority Member. Lowell P Weicker Jr (R–CT)

Minority Staff Director. Robert J Dotchin. **202-224-8498**

Subcommittees and Chairmen. Monopoly and Antitrust (Nelson, WI); Government Regulation and Small Business Advocacy (McIntyre, NH); Economic Development, Marketing, and the Family Farmer (Nunn, GA); Government Procurement (Hathaway, ME); Financing, Investment, and Taxation (Haskell, CO); Future of Small Business (Culver, IA)

SPECIAL COMMITTEE ON AGING. G-225 Dirksen Senate Office Bldg, 20510. **202-224-5364**

Chairman. Frank Church (D–ID)

Staff Director. William E Oriol

Chief Counsel. David A Affeldt

Ranking Minority Member. Pete V Domenici (R–NM)

Minority Staff Director. Letitia Chambers. **202-224-1467**

Important Subcommittees

ADMINISTRATIVE PRACTICE AND PROCEDURE. 162 Russell Senate Office Bldg, 20510. **202-224-5617**

ANTITRUST AND MONOPOLY (JUDI-CIARY). A517 Old Immigration Bldg, 20510. **202-224-5573**

ARMED SERVICES. 224 Russell Senate Office Bldg, 20510. **202-224-2127**

CONSTITUTION. 102B Russell Senate Office Bldg, 20510. **202-224-8191**

HOUSING. 5226 Dirksen Senate Office Bldg, 20510. **202-224-6348**

IMMIGRATION AND NATURALIZA-TION. 2306 Dirksen Senate Office Bldg, 20510. **202-224-2347**

INTERNAL SECURITY. 6B Russell Senate Office Bldg, 20510. **202-224-6241**

PERMANENT SUBCOMMITTEE ON INVESTIGATIONS. 101 Russell Senate Office Bldg, 20510. **202-224-3721.** Henry Jackson (D–WA), chairman

JUVENILE DELINQUENCY. US Senate, 20510. **202-224-2951.** John C Culver (D–IA), chairman

MIGRATORY LABOR. A705 Immigration Bldg, 20510. **202-224-4538**

PATENTS, TRADEMARKS, AND COPYRIGHTS. 349A Russell Senate Office Bldg, 20510. **202-224-2268**

PRIVILEGES AND ELECTIONS. 310 Russell Senate Office Bldg, 20510. **202-224-5647**

House Committees

Standing Committees

AGRICULTURE. 1301 Longworth House Office Bldg, 20515. **202-225-2171**

Chairman. Thomas S Foley (WA)

Majority Staff. 202-225-1867

Minority Staff. 202-225-2342

Press. L T (Tex) Easley. **202-225-2171**

Subcommittees and Chairmen. Conservation and Credit (Jones, TN), **202-225-2171.** Cotton (Bowen, MS), **2171.** Dairy and Poultry (Rose, NC), **2171.** Department Investigations, Oversight, and Research (de la Garza, TX), **2172.** Domestic Marketing, Consumer Relations, and Nutrition (Richmond, NY), **2171.** Family Farms, Rural Development, and Special Studies (Nolan, MN), **2171.** Forests (Weaver, OR), **2171.** Livestock and Grains (Poage, TX), **2171.** Oilseeds and Rice (Mathis, GA), **2171.** Tobacco (Jones, NC), **2171**

APPROPRIATIONS. H-218 The Capitol, 20515. **202-225-2771**

Chairman. George H Mahon (TX)

Minority Staff. 202-225-3481

Subcommittees and Chairmen. Agriculture and Related Agencies (Whitten, MS),

202-225-2638. Defense (Mahon, TX), **2847.** Ditrict of Columbia (Natcher, KY), **5338.** Foreign Operations (Long, MD), **2041.** HUD —Independent Agencies (Boland, MA), **3241.** Interior (Yates, IL), **3081.** Labor— HEW (Flood, PA), **3508.** Legislative (Shipley, IL), **5338.** Military Construction (McKay, UT), **3047.** Public Works (Bevill, AL), **3421.** State, Justice, Commerce, and Judiciary (Slack, WV), **3351.** Transportation (McFall, CA), **2141.** Treasury, Postal Service, and General Government (Steed, OK), **5834**

ARMED SERVICES. 2120 Rayburn House Office Bldg, 20515. **202-225-4151**

Chairman. Melvin Price (IL)

Subcommittees and Chairmen. Intelligence and Military Application of Nuclear Energy (Price, IL), **202-225-4151.** Investigations (Stratton, NY), **4221.** Military Compensation (Nichols, AL), **4151.** Military Installations and Facilities (Nedzi, MI), **4151.** Military Personnel (White, TX), **4151.** Research and Development (Ichord, MO), **4151.** Sea Power and Strategic and Critical Materials (Bennett, FL), **4151**

BANKING, FINANCE, AND URBAN AFFIARS. 2129 Rayburn House Office Bldg, 20515. **202-225-4247**

Chairman. Henry S Reuss (WI)

Minority Staff. 202-225-2258

Subcommittees and Chairmen. Consumer Affairs (Annunzio, IL), **202-225-9181.** Domestic Monetary Policy (Mitchell, MD), **7315.** Economic Stabilization (Moorhead, PA), **7145.** Financial Institutions—Supervision, Regulation, and Insurance (St Germain, RI), **2924.** General Oversight and Renegotiation (Minish, NJ), **2828.** Historic Preservation and Coinage (Fauntroy, DC), **1280.** Housing and Community Development (Ashley, OH), **7054.** International Development, Institutions, and Finance (Gonzalez, TX), **0419.** International Trade, Investment, and Monetary Policy (Neal, NC), **1271.** The City (Reuss, WI), **2495**

BUDGET. 214 House Office Bldg Annex 1, 20515. **202-225-7200**

Chairman. Robert N Giaimo (CT)

DISTRICT OF COLUMBIA. 1310 Longworth House Office Bldg, 20515. **202-225-4457**

Chairman. Charles C Diggs, Jr (MI)

Minority Staff. 202-225-7158

EDUCATION AND LABOR. 2181 Rayburn House Office Bldg, 20515. **202-225-4527**

Chairman. Carl D Perkins (KY)

Chief Clerk. 202-225-6916

Minority Clerk. 202-225-3725

Subcommittees and Chairmen. Compensation, Health, and Safety (Gaydos, PA), **202-225-6876.** Economic Opportunity (Andrews, NC), **1850.** Elementary, Secondary, and Vocational Education (Perkins, KY), **4368.** Employment Opportunities (Hawkins, CA), **1927.** Labor-Management Relations (Thompson, NJ), **5768.** Labor Standards (Dent, PA), **5331.** Postsecondary Education (Ford, MI), **8881.** Select Education (Brademas, IN), **5954**

GOVERNMENT OPERATIONS. 2157 Rayburn House Office Bldg, 20515. **202-225-5051**

Chairman. Jack Brooks (TX)

Minority Clerk. 202-225-5074

Subcommittees and Chairmen. Commerce, Consumer, and Monetary Affairs (Rosenthal, NY), **202-225-4407.** Environment, Energy, and Natural Resources (Ryan, CA), **6427.** Government Activities and Transportation (Burton, CA), **3252.** Government Information and Individual Rights (Preyer, NC), **3741.** Intergovernmental Relations and Human Resources (Fountain, NC), **2548.** Legislation and National Security (Brooks, TX), **5147.** Manpower and Housing (Collins, IL), **6751**

HOUSE ADMINISTRATION. H-326 The Capitol, 20515. **202-225-2061.**

Chairman. Frank Thompson, Jr (NJ)

INTERIOR AND INSULAR AFFAIRS. 1324 Longworth House Office Bldg, 20515. **202-225-2761**

Chairman. Morris K Udall (AZ)

Public Affairs. Robert A Neuman. **202-225-2843.** (h) **202-543-3943**

Subcommittees and Chairmen. Energy and the Environment (Udall, AZ), **202-225-8831.** General Oversight and Alaska Lands (Seiberling, OH), **6013.** Indian Affairs and Public Lands (Roncalio, WY), **1684.** Mines and Mining (Kazen, TX), **1661.** National Parks and Insular Affairs (Burton, CA), **6044.** Special Investigations (Runnels, NM), **2761.** Water and Power Resources (Meeds, WA), **6042**

INTERNATIONAL RELATIONS. 2170 Rayburn House Office Bldg, 20515. **202-225-5021**

Chairman. Clement J Zablocki (WI)

Minority Staff. 202-225-6735

Subcommittees and Chairmen. Africa (Diggs, MI), **202-225-3157.** Asian and Pacific Affairs (Wolff, NY), **3044.** Europe and the Middle East (Hamilton, IN), **3345.** Inter-American Affairs (Yatron, PA), **9404.** International Development (Harrington, MA), **3555.** International Economic Policy and Trade (Bingham, NY), **3246.** International Operations (Fascell, FL), **3424.** International Organizations (Fraser, MN), **5318.** International Security and Scientific Affairs (Zablocki, WI), **4089.** Investigation of Korean-American Relations (Fraser, MN), **7722**

INTERSTATE AND FOREIGN COMMERCE. 2125 Rayburn House Office Bldg, 20515. **202-225-2927**

Chairman. Harley O Staggers (WV)

Minority Counsel 202-225-3641

Subcommittees and Chairmen. Communications (Van Deerlin, CA), **202-225-9304.** Consumer Protection and Finance (Eckhardt, TX), **7790.** Energy and Power (Dingell, MI), **1030.** Health and the Environment (Rogers, FL), **4952.** Oversight and Investigations (Moss, CA), **4441.** Transportation and Commerce (Rooney, PA), **1467**

JUDICIARY. 2137 Rayburn House Office Bldg, 20515. **202-225-3951**

Chairman. Peter W Rodino, Jr (NJ)

Minority Clerk. 202-225-6506

Publications. 202-225-0408

Subcommittees and Chairmen. Administrative Law and Governmental Relations (Danielson, CA), **202-225-5741.** Civil and Constitutional Rights (Edwards, CA), **1680.** Courts, Civil Liberties, and the Administration of Justice (Kastenmeier, WI), **3926.** Crime (Conyers, MI), **1695.** Criminal Justice (Mann, SC), **0406.** Immigration, Citizenship, and International Law (Eilberg, PA), **5727.** Monopolies and Commercial Law (Rodino, NJ), **8088**

MERCHANT MARINE AND FISHERIES. 1334 Longworth House Office Bldg, 20515. **202-225-4047**

Chairman. John M Murphy (NY)

Minority Counsel. 202-225-2650

Subcommittees and Chairmen. Coast Guard and Navigation (Biaggi, NY), **202-225-3728.** Fisheries and Wildlife Conservation and the Environment (Leggett, CA), **7307.** Merchant Marine (Murphy, NY), **6785.** Oceanography (Breaux, LA), **7508.** Panama Canal (Metcalfe, IL), **8186.** Ad Hoc Select Subcommittee on Maritime Education and Training (Studds, MA), **3444**

POST OFFICE AND CIVIL SERVICE.
309 Cannon House Office Bldg, 20515.
202-225-4054

Chairman. Robert N C Nix (PA)

Franking Commission. 202-225-0436

Subcommittees and Chairmen. Census and Population (Lehman, FL), **202-225-6741.** Civil Service (Clay, MO), **9124.** Compensation and Employee Benefits (Spellman, MD), **6831.** Employee Ethics and Utilization (Schroeder, CO), **4025.** Investigations (Nix, PA), **2821.** Postal Operations and Services (Hanley, NY), **6295.** Postal Personnel and Modernization (Wilson, CA), **3718**

PUBLIC WORKS AND TRANSPORTATION. 2165 Rayburn House Office Bldg, 20515. **202-225-4472.**

Chairman. Harold T Johnson (CA)

Subcommittees and Chairmen. Aviation (Anderson, CA), **202-225-4472.** Economic Development (Roe, NJ), **6151.** Investigations and Review (Ginn, GA), **3274.** Public Buildings and Grounds (Mineta, CA), **4472.** Surface Transportation (Howard, NJ), **4472.** Water Resources (Roberts, TX), **4474**

RULES. H-313 The Capitol, 20515.
202-225-9486

Chairman. James J Delaney (NY)

Minority Staff 202-225-6991

SCIENCE AND TECHNOLOGY. 2321 Rayburn House Office Bldg, 20515.
202-225-6371

Chairman. Olin E Teague (TX)

Executive Director. Charles Mosher

Publications Office. 202-225-6275

Subcommittees and Chairmen. Advanced Energy Technologies and Energy Conservation Research, Development, and Demonstration (McCormack, WA), **202-225-9117.** Domestic and International Scientific Planning, Analysis, and Cooperation (Scheuer, NY), **6371.** Fossil and Nuclear Energy Research, Development, and Demonstration (Flowers, AL), **9117.** Science, Research, and Technology (Thornton, AR), **6371.** Space Science and Applications (Fuqua, FL), **6371.** The Environment and the Atmosphere (Brown, CA), **6371.** Transportation, Aviation, and Weather (Milford, TX), **6371**

SMALL BUSINESS. 2361 Rayburn House Office Bldg, 20515. **202-225-5821**

Chairman. Neal Smith (IA)

Subcommittees and Chairmen. Antitrust, Consumers, and Employment (Breckinridge,

KY), **202-225-7797.** Capital, Investment, and Business Opportunities (La Falce, NY), **9321.** Energy, Environment, Safety, and Research (Baldus, WI), **6026.** Minority Enterprise and General Oversight (Addabbo, NY), **9321.** SBA and SBIC Authority and General Small Business Problems (Smith, IA), **5821.** Special Small Business Problems (Russo, IL), **9368**

STANDARDS OF OFFICIAL CONDUCT. 2360 Rayburn House Office Bldg, 20515.
202-225-7103

Chairman. John J Flynt, Jr (GA)

VETERANS' AFFAIRS. 335 Cannon House Office Bldg, 20515. **202-225-3527**

Chairman. Ray Roberts (TX)

Minority Clerk. 202-225-3551

Subcommittees and Chairmen. Cemeteries and Burial Benefits (Carney, OH), **202-225-3527.** Compensation, Pension, and Insurance (Montgomery, MS), **3527.** Education and Training (Teague, TX), **3527.** Housing (Brinkley, GA), **3527.** Medical Facilities and Benefits (Satterfield, VA), **3527**

WAYS AND MEANS. 1102 Longworth House Office Bldg, 20515. **202-225-3625**

Chairman. Al Ullman (OR)

Subcommittees and Chairmen. Health (Rostenkowski, IL), **202-225-7785.** Miscellaneous Revenue Measures (Waggonner, LA), **3625.** Oversight (Gibbons, FL), **2743.** Public Assistance and Unemployment Compensation (Corman, CA), **1025.** Social Security (Burke, MA), **9263.** Trade (Vanik, OH), **3943**

Ad Hoc Committee

ENERGY. 321 Cannon House Office Bldg, 20515. **202-225-5321**

Chairman. Thomas L Ashley (OH)

Select Committees

AGING. 712 House Office Bldg Annex 1, 20515. **202-225-9375**

Chairman. Claude Pepper (FL)

Staff Director. Robert Weiner. **202-225-9694**

Subcommittees and Chairmen. Federal, State, and Community Services (Biaggi, NY), **202-225-4348.** Health and Long-Term Care (Pepper, FL), **3281.** Housing and Consumer Interests (Roybal, CA), **4242.** Retirement Income and Employment (Rooney, PA), **4045**

ASSASSINATIONS. 3331 House Office Bldg Annex 2, 20515. **202-225-4624**

Chairman. Louis Stokes (OH)

Public Information Officer. Burt Chardak. **202-225-4282**

CONGRESSIONAL OPERATIONS. 1628 Longworth House Office Bldg, 20515. **202-225-8267**

Chairman. Jack Brooks (TX)

ETHICS. 3506 House Office Bldg Annex 2, 20515. **202-225-8461**

Chairman. Richardson Preyer (NC)

Press. Paul Stone

NARCOTICS ABUSE AND CONTROL. 3260 House Office Bldg Annex 2, 20515. **202-225-1753**

Chairman. Lester L Wolff (NY)

Chief Counsel. Joseph L Nellis

OUTER CONTINENTAL SHELF— AD HOC. 720 House Office Bldg Annex 1. 20515. **202-225-3426**

Chairman. John M Murphy (NY)

Press. Art Kosatka. **202-225-3371**

Joint Senate-House Committees

CONGRESSIONAL OPERATIONS. 1630 Longworth House Office Bldg, 20515. **202-225-8267**

Vice-Chairman. Representative Jack Brooks (R–TX)

Executive Director. Eugene F Peters

DEFENSE PRODUCTION. A-421 Senate Office Building Annex III, 20510. **202-224-2337**

Chairman. Senator William Proxmire (D–WI)

Vice-Chairman. Representative Parren Mitchell (D–MD)

Professional Staff. Leon S Reed

Press. Lory Conconnon

ECONOMIC. G-133 Dirksen Senate Office Bldg, 20510. **202-224-5171**

Chairman. Representative Richard Bolling (D–MO)

Vice-Chairman. Senator Muriel B Humphrey (D–MN)

Executive Director. John R Stark

Publications. 202-224-5321

Press. Katie MacArthur. **202-224-0369**

PRINTING. S-151 The Capitol, 20510.
202-224-5241

Chairman. Senator Howard W Cannon
(D–NV)

Vice-Chairman. Representative Frank W
Thompson, Jr (D–NJ)

Staff Director. Denver Dickerson

Congressional Record **Index Office.** 507-B
Senate Courts, 120 C St NE, 20510.
202-224-1385

TAXATION. 1015 Longworth House Office
Bldg, 20510. **202-225-3621**

Chairman. Representative Al Ullman
(D–OR)

Vice-Chairman. Senator Russell Long
(D–LA)

Chief of Staff. Bernard M (Bob) Shapiro

Chief Economist. James W Wetzler.
202-225-6801

EXECUTIVE BRANCH

*The general information number for federal
offices is* **202-655-4000**.

The President

THE WHITE HOUSE. 1600 Pennsylvania
Ave NW, Washington, DC 20500. Switchboard: **202-456-1414**. Central reference:
202-456-2579

PRESIDENT. Jimmy Carter. **202-456-2573**

**PERSONAL ASSISTANT/SECRETARY
TO THE PRESIDENT.** Susan Clough.
202-456-2573

**SOCIAL ASSISTANT TO THE PRESI-
DENT.** Maxie Wells. **202-456-2731**

Office of the Press Secretary

**PRESS SECRETARY TO THE PRESI-
DENT.** Joseph L Powell. **202-456-2100**

DEPUTY PRESS SECRETARY. Rex L
Granum. **202-456-2100**

DEPUTY PRESS SECRETARY. Walter W
Wurfel. **202-456-2100**

CHIEF SPEECHWRITER. James M
Fallows. **202-456-6573**

**SPECIAL ASSISTANT TO THE PRESI-
DENT FOR MEDIA AND PUBLIC
AFFAIRS.** Barry Jagoda. **202-456-2222**

ASSISTANT TO JAGODA. Rick Neustadt.
202-456-2222

ASSOCIATE PRESS SECRETARY. Walter
E Duka. **202-456-2100**

ASSOCIATE PRESS SECRETARY.
William Drummond. **202-456-2100**

PHOTOGRAPHIC OFFICE. Billie Shaddix.
202-456-2531

EDITOR, NEWS SUMMARY. Claudia M
Townsend. **202-456-2950**

OFFICE OF MEDIA LIAISON. Patricia Y
Bario. **202-456-6623** (handles inquiries from
out-of-town press)

WHITE HOUSE CORRESPONDENTS.
202-737-2934

Appointments Office

**SPECIAL ASSISTANT TO THE PRESI-
DENT FOR APPOINTMENTS.** Timothy
E Kraft. **202-456-1268**

**DEPUTY APPOINTMENTS
SECRETARY.** Timothy G Smith.
202-456-7070

DIRECTOR OF SCHEDULING. Frances
M Voorde. **202-456-7073**

DIRECTOR OF ADVANCE. Ellis A
Woodward. **202-456-6441**

Assistants to the President

ASSISTANT TO THE PRESIDENT.
Hamilton Jordan. **202-456-6797**

**ASSISTANT TO THE PRESIDENT FOR
NATIONAL SECURITY AFFAIRS.**
Zbigniew Brzezinski. **202-456-1414**

**DEPUTY ASSISTANT FOR NATIONAL
SECURITY AFFAIRS.** David L Aaron.
202-456-1414

**ASSISTANT TO THE PRESIDENT FOR
ENERGY POLICY.** James R Schlesinger.
202-456-6210

**ASSISTANT TO THE PRESIDENT FOR
REORGANIZATION.** Richard Pettigrew.
202-456-2706

**DEPUTY ASSISTANT TO THE PRESI-
DENT.** Landon Butler. **202-456-2861**

DEPUTY ASSISTANT FOR RESEARCH.

Elizabeth A Rainwater. **202-456-6754**

**DEPUTY ASSISTANT FOR POLICY
ANALYSIS.** Mark A Siegel. **202-456-2147**

CHIEF SPEECHWRITER. James M
Fallows. **202-456-6753**

ASSISTANT SPEECHWRITER. Hendrik
Hertzberg. **202-456-7094**

ASSISTANT SPEECHWRITER. Griffin
Smith, Jr. **202-456-2990**

**SPECIAL ASSISTANT TO THE PRESI-
DENT FOR SPECIAL PROJECTS.**
Martha M Mitchell. **202-456-6478**

**SPECIAL ASSISTANT TO THE PRESI-
DENT AND WHITE HOUSE OMBUDS-
MAN.** Joseph W Aragon. **202-456-6697**

**SPECIAL ASSISTANT TO THE PRESI-
DENT FOR BUDGET AND ORGANIZA-
TION.** Richard M Harden. **202-456-6690**

STAFF SECRETARY. Richard G
Hutcheson III. **202-456-7052**

**DIRECTOR OF WHITE HOUSE PROJ-
ECTS.** Gregory S Schneiders. **202-456-2943**

**SCIENCE ADVISER TO THE PRESI-
DENT.** Frank Press. **202-456-7116**

Office of Domestic Affairs and Policy

**ASSISTANT TO THE PRESIDENT FOR
DOMESTIC AFFAIRS AND POLICY.**
Stuart E Eizenstat. **202-456-6515**

**DEPUTY ASSISTANT FOR DOMESTIC
AFFAIRS AND POLICY.** David M
Rubenstein. **202-456-6405**

**DEPUTY DIRECTOR OF DOMESTIC
COUNCIL.** Bertram Carp. **202-456-2562**

Counsel to the President

COUNSEL TO THE PRESIDENT. Robert
J Lipshultz. **202-456-2632**

DEPUTY COUNSEL. Margret A
McKenna. **202-456-6611**

SENIOR ASSOCIATE COUNSEL.
Michael H V Cardozo. **202-456-6246**

SENIOR ASSOCIATE COUNSEL.
Douglas B Huron. **202-456-6297**

ASSOCIATE COUNSEL. Patrick Apodaca. 202-456-2397

Office of Congressional Liaison

ASSISTANT TO THE PRESIDENT FOR CONGRESSIONAL LIAISON. Frank B Moore. 202-456-2230

DEPUTY ASSISTANT FOR CONGRESSIONAL LIAISON. Robert K Russell Jr. 202-456-2230

LEGISLATIVE PROJECTS COORDINATOR. Leslie C Francis. 202-456-7003

ASSOCIATE FOR CONGRESSIONAL LIAISON (SPECIAL PROJECTS). Ronald D Royal. 202-456-7140

DEPUTY IN CHARGE OF CONGRESSIONAL LIAISON (HOUSE). Bill Cable. 202-456-7130

ASSOCIATE FOR CONGRESSIONAL LIAISON (SENATE). Danny C Tate. 202-456-7140

VISITORS' OFFICE COORDINATOR. Nancy A Willing. 202-456-2323

Office of Public Liaison

ASSISTANT TO THE PRESIDENT FOR PUBLIC LIAISON. Margret Costanza. 202-456-6585

DEPUTY ASSISTANT FOR PUBLIC LIAISON. Robert A Nastanovich. 202-456-7172

ASSOCIATE FOR PUBLIC LIAISON. Stephen S Selig III. 202-456-6413

Office of Health Issues

SPECIAL ASSISTANT TO THE PRESIDENT FOR HEALTH ISSUES. Peter G Bourne. 202-456-7120

EXECUTIVE DIRECTOR, PRESIDENT'S COMMISSION ON MENTAL HEALTH. Thomas Bryant, MD. 202-456-7100

ASSOCIATE SPECIAL ASSISTANT FOR DRUG ABUSE POLICY. Lee Dogoloff. 202-456-6594

ASSOCIATE SPECIAL ASSISTANT FOR INTERNATIONAL HEALTH. Jerry Fill. 202-395-4903

Secretary to the Cabinet

SECRETARY TO THE CABINET AND ASSISTANT TO THE PRESIDENT FOR INTERGOVERNMENTAL AFFAIRS. Jack H Watson Jr. 202-456-2335

DEPUTY SECRETARY TO THE CABINET. Jane L Frank. 202-456-6537

ASSISTANT TO THE SECRETARY TO THE CABINET. Cynthia Wilkes. 202-456-2174

DEPUTY ASSISTANT FOR INTERGOVERNMENTAL AFFAIRS. Lawrence A Bailey. 202-456-2310

ASSOCIATE FOR INTERGOVERNMENTAL AFFAIRS. Bruce Kirchenbaum. 202-456-7154

Presidential Personnel Office

SPECIAL ASSISTANT TO THE PRESIDENT FOR PERSONNEL. James B King. 202-456-2995

ASSOCIATE DIRECTOR FOR FINANCIAL, REGULATORY, AND LEGAL ACTIVITIES. Lisabeth K Godley. 202-456-2821

ASSOCIATE DIRECTOR FOR HUMAN SERVICES. Diana Rock. 202-456-7110

Administration

SPECIAL ASSISTANT TO THE PRESIDENT FOR ADMINISTRATION. Hugh A Carter Jr. 202-456-2702

DIRECTOR OF THE WHITE HOUSE MILITARY OFFICE. Warren L Gulley. 202-456-2150

PHYSICIAN TO THE PRESIDENT. Rear Admiral William M Lukash, MD. 202-456-2672

CHIEF EXECUTIVE CLERK. Robert D Linder. 202-456-2594

CHIEF USHER. Rex W Scouten. 202-456-2650

Office of the First Lady

FIRST LADY. Rosalynn Carter

PRESS SECRETARY TO THE FIRST LADY AND EAST WING COORDINATOR. Mary Finch Hoyt. 202-456-2164

PERSONAL ASSISTANT TO THE FIRST LADY. Madeline F MacBean. 202-456-6633

SOCIAL SECRETARY TO THE FIRST LADY. Gretchen Poston. 202-456-7064

APPOINTMENTS SECRETARY TO THE FIRST LADY. Jane S Fenderson. 202-456-2850

SPEECHWRITER TO THE FIRST LADY. Coates Redmon. 202-456-2520

DIRECTOR OF PROJECTS, ISSUES, AND RESEARCH FOR THE FIRST LADY. Kathryn E Cade. 202-456-2207

The Vice-President

Old Executive Office Bldg, 17th St and Pennsylvania Ave, Washington, DC 20501

VICE-PRESIDENT. Walter F Mondale. 202-456-7045

CHIEF OF STAFF. Richard Moe. 202-456-6606

COUNSEL AND DEPUTY OF STAFF. Michael S Berman. 202-456-7034

EXECUTIVE ASSISTANT. James A Johnson. 202-456-7123

ASSISTANT AND PRESS SECRETARY. Albert Eisele. 202-456-6303

DEPUTY PRESS SECRETARY. Maxine I Burns. 202-456-6303

ASSISTANT FOR ISSUES DEVELOPMENT. Gail Harrison. 202-456-6772

ASSISTANT FOR CONGRESSIONAL RELATIONS. William C Smith. 202-224-0636

DEPUTY COUNSEL. Peter N Kyros Jr. 202-456-7034

EXECUTIVE ASSISTANT TO MRS MONDALE. Bess Abell. 202-456-7022

Other Executive Offices

Addresses of the following executive offices are in the White House, Washington, DC 20500 unless otherwise noted.

FEDERAL COUNCIL ON THE AGING
Chairman. Nelson Cruikshank. 202-456-7097 or 202-245-0441

COUNCIL OF ECONOMIC ADVISERS.
Old Executive Office Bldg, 17th St and
Pennsylvania Ave, Washington, DC 20506.
202-395-3000

Chairman. Charles L Schultze. **202-395-5042**

Special Assistant to the Chairman. Peter
Gould. **202-395-5084**

Member. Lyle E Gramley. **202-395-5036**

Member. William Nordhaus. **202-395-5046**

**COUNCIL ON ENVIRONMENTAL
QUALITY.** See filings under The Independent Agencies

COUNCIL ON WAGE AND PRICE STABILITY. New Executive Office Bldg, 726
Jackson Pl NW, Washington, DC 20506

Director. Barry P Bosworth. **202-456-6466**

Assistant Director, Wage and Price Monitoring. Jack Meyer. **202-456-7000**

**Assistant Director, Government Operations
and Research.** Thomas Hopkins.
202-456-6510

Assistant Director, Public Affairs and Congressional Relations. Tom Joyce.
202-456-6757

General Counsel. Peter Lowry. **202-456-2653**

DOMESTIC COUNCIL

**Assistant to the President for Domestic
Affairs.** Stuart E Eizenstat. **202-456-6515**

Deputy Director. Bert Carp. **202-456-2562**

Deputy Assistant. David Rubenstein.
202-456-6405

ENERGY RESOURCES COUNCIL.
Washington, DC 20461

Secretary of Commerce and Chairman.
Juanita M Kreps. **202-377-2112**

Executive Director. John F O'Leary.
202-566-9222

White House Fellow. Raoul H Alcala.
202-566-9358

NATIONAL SECURITY COUNCIL. Old
Executive Office Building, 17th St and
Pennsylvania Ave NW, Washington, DC
20506. **202-395-3000**

Staff Secretary. Michael Hornblow (acting).
202-456-2255

**Associate Press Secretary (Congressional
Liaison).** Jerrold L Schecter. **202-395-3440**

National Security Agency: **202-688-6311**

CENTRAL INTELLIGENCE AGENCY. See
listing under Independent Agencies.

**OFFICE OF MANAGEMENT AND
BUDGET.** Executive Office Bldg, 17th St
and Pennsylvania Ave, Washington, DC
20503

Director. James T Mcintyre, Jr.
202-395-4840

Special Assistant. A D Frazier, Jr.
202-395-6190

General Counsel. William M Nichols.
202-395-4550

**Assistant to Director for Congressional
Relations.** Hubert Harris, Jr (NC).
202-395-4657

Assistant to Director for Public Affairs. Alan
B Wade. **202-395-4747**

OFFICE OF THE SPECIAL REPRESENTATIVE FOR TRADE NEGOTIATIONS. 1800 G St NW, Washington, DC
20506

Special Representative for Trade Negotiations. Robert Strauss. **202-395-3204**

Deputy Special Representative. Alan W
Wolff. **202-395-5116**

General Counsel. Richard R Rivers.
202-395-5116

**OFFICE OF TELECOMMUNICATIONS
POLICY.** 1800 G St NW, Washington, DC
20504

Chief Scientist. Dr William Thaler.
202-395-6161

Assistant Director for Frequency Management. Samuel E Probst (acting).
202-395-5623

Assistant Director for Government Communications. Donald M Jansky.
202-395-4876

Assistant Director for International Communication. William L Fishman.
202-395-5190

Assistant Director for Planning and Policy.
Sidney Goldman. **202-395-3200**

General Counsel. Gregg P Skall (acting).
202-395-5616

Special Assistant for Public Affairs. Walda
W Roseman. **202-395-4990**

Military Assistant to the Director. Colonel
Wayne G Kay. **202-395-3977**

Budget Officer. Daniel L O'Neill.
202-395-5174

Administrative Officer. Eliza S Johnston.
202-395-3606

Department of Agriculture

The Mall, between 12th and 14th Sts SW,
Washington, DC 20250. Listed telephone
number: **202-655-4000.** Secretary's office
locator number: **202-447-5781**

SECRETARY OF AGRICULTURE. Bob
Bergland. **202-447-3631**

DEPUTY SECRETARY OF AGRICULTURE. 202-447-6158

OFFICE OF INSPECTOR GENERAL.
Thomas F McBride. **202-447-8001**

JUDICIAL OFFICER. Donald A Campbell.
202-447-4764

Information Contacts

**DIRECTOR, GOVERNMENTAL AND
PUBLIC AFFAIRS.** James C Webster.
202-447-7977

Executive Assistant. 202-447-3117

**ACTING DEPUTY DIRECTOR FOR
CONGRESSIONAL AFFAIRS.** K Richard
Cook. **202-447-7095**

**ACTING DEPUTY DIRECTOR FOR
INTERGOVERNMENTAL AFFAIRS.**
Maynard C Dolloff. **202-447-6643**

Assistant. James S Wood. **202-447-7615**

Special projects. 202-447-3493

DIRECTOR OF PUBLIC AFFAIRS. Edwin
W Goodpaster. **202-447-5247** or **6311**

DEPUTY DIRECTOR. Hal R Taylor.
202-447-7903

ASSISTANT DIRECTOR. 202-447-4613

ASSISTANT TO THE DIRECTOR. Frank
A Shea. **202-447-3117**

*Current Information and Special
Programs*

DIRECTOR. Stanley D Weston.
202-447-7903

Press Division. Joseph T McDavid, chief.
202-447-4026. (h) **703-273-5523**

Editor, *USDA Farm Paper Letter.* Edward
D Curran. **202-447-5480**

Editor, *Food and Home Notes.* Shirley
Wagener. **202-447-5898**

Minority Media. Rufus Wells. **202-447-3088**

Public Liaison Director. Bob Dugan.
202-447-4894

Distribution. Edgar Poe, Jr. **202-447-7488**

Printing. Paul Wertz. **202-447-5983**

Editorial. Edna Carmichael. **202-447-7175**

RADIO AND TELEVISION DIVISION.
Layne R Beaty, chief. **202-447-5163**

Television. Larry Quinn. **202-447-5746**

Radio. James Johnson. **202-447-7067**

SPECIAL REPORTS DIVISION. Theodore R Crane, chief. **202-447-4335**

Consumer Information. Lillie Vincent. **202-447-5437**

Environmental and Rural Areas Programs. John Crowley. **202-447-2505**

International Information. Larry B Marton. **202-447-4330**

Magazine Contact. Clay Napier. **202-447-3008**

Visual Information

ASSISTANT DIRECTOR, PUBLICATIONS AND VISUAL COMMUNICATIONS. Claude W Gifford. **202-447-8005,** (h) **703-528-8873**

DESIGN DIVISION. David Sutton, chief. **202-447-6641**

Arts and graphics. Ben Murow. **202-447-5370**

Exhibits. George Baka. **202-447-4337**

MOTION PICTURE DIVISION. Chief, V Buddy Renfro. **202-447-6072 or 6073**

PHOTOGRAPHY DIVISION. Byron Schumaker, chief. **202-447-6633**

Picture Editor. Dave Warren. **202-447-6633**

PUBLICATIONS DIVISION. Chief, Nelson Fitton. **202-447-6623**

RADIO SPOT NEWS SERVICE. A continuous offering of spot news by automatic telephone coupler, with one or more short news stories or actualities. Stories are changed at 4:30 pm Mon–Fri except holidays. *Northwest.* **202-448-8359.** *Midwest.* **202-488-8358.** *South.* **202-488-3461.** *West.* **202-488-3462.** *Consumer line.* **202-488-1110.** *Press.* **202-447-2545**

Agricultural Economics

ECONOMIC RESEARCH SERVICE

Director, Information Division. Benjamin Blankenship. **202-447-8038**

Acting Chief, Food and Fiber. James Sayre. **202-447-7305**

Chief, Resource and Development. James Sayre. **202-447-6965**

Chief, Popular Publications. Martin Schubkegel. **202-447-3681**

Printing Officer. Joe Zuessman. **202-447-4640**

Publications. 202-447-7255

FARMER COOPERATIVE SERVICE

Director, Information Division. Gene Ingalsbe. **202-447-2739**

Chief, Editorial Services. Howard Mobley. **202-447-2596**

Chief, Publications and Audiovisuals. Clarence Johnson. **202-447-7275**

STATISTICAL REPORTING SERVICE

Director, Information Staff. Kent Miller. **202-447-5455**

Assistant and Editor, *Agricultural Situation.* Diane Decker. **202-447-2989**

Publications. 202-447-4021

International Affairs and Commodity Programs

AGRICULTURAL STABILIZATION AND CONSERVATION SERVICE

Director, Information Division. M Ray Waggoner. **202-447-5237**

Chief, Broadcast Services Branch. Nelson Robinson. **202-447-7780**

Chief, Commodity Services Branch. Robert Feist. **202-447-6787**

Chief, Field Services Branch. Otis Thompson. **202-447-4094**

FEDERAL CROP INSURANCE CORPORATION

Chief, Review Staff. George Vohs. **02-447-3289**

Director, Marketing Staff. John B O'Connor, Jr. **202-447-4364**

Marketing Staff Specialist. Tom Lodge. **202-447-4006**

FOREIGN AGRICULTURAL SERVICE

Director, Information Division. J Don Looper. **202-447-3448**

Assistant Director. Wallace Lindell. **202-447-7115**

Chief, Publications Division. Kay Patterson. **202-447-5412**

Head, Information Services Staff. Sally Turett. **202-447-7937**

Marketing and Consumer Services

AGRICULTURAL MARKETING SERVICE

Director, Information Division. Stan W Prochaska. **202-447-6766**

Deputy Director. Sebastian Filippone. **202-447-7201**

Chief, Program Services. Eleanor A Ferris. **202-447-7607 or 7587**

Chief, Broadcasts, Visuals, and Publications. Dale E May. **202-447-2399**

ANIMAL AND PLANT HEALTH INSPECTION SERVICE

Director, Information Division. King Lovinger. **202-447-3977**

Chief, Media Services Branch. Charles Herron. **202-447-2731**

Chief, Meat and Poultry Inspection. William B Bloom. **202-447-8293**

Chief, Veterinary Services. Larry Mark. **202-447-6315**

Chief, Plant Protection and Quarantine. Susan Hess. **202-447-6190**

Chief, Broadcast and Visual Media. Kevin Shields (acting). **202-447-2731**

Chief, Publications. Val Weyl. **202-447-2521**

FOOD AND NUTRITION SERVICE. (500 12th St SW, Washington, DC).

Director, Information Division. Philip V Fleming. **202-447-8138**

Deputy Director. Bonnie S Whyte. **202-447-8138**

Chief, Programs Division. Bonnie W Polk. **202-447-8138**

Chief, Media Branch. Charles A Tennyson. **202-447-6659**

FOOD SAFETY AND QUALITY SERVICE

Director, Information Division. Robert W Norton. **202-447-3977**

Deputy Director. Eleanor Ferris. **202-447-7607**

Chief, Commodity Services Staff. Charlene Olson. **202-447-7607**

Chief, Meat and Poultry Inspection. Herbert Gantz. **202-447-8293**

Chief, Broadcast and Visual Media. Kevin Shields. **202-447-2731**

Rural Development

RURAL DEVELOPMENT SERVICE

Executive Assistant to Administrator; Public Information Officer. Bill Hunt. **202-447-7595**

FARMERS HOME ADMINISTRATION

Director, Information Staff. Walter C Bunch. **202-447-4323 or 4523**

Assistant Director. Fred E McGhee. **202-447-6150**

RURAL ELECTRIFICATION ADMINISTRATION

Director, Information Service Division. Wilbur C Jennings. **202-447-5606**

Chief, Current Information. Donald Runyon. **202-447-3564**

Chief, Publication, Special Reports. Luis L Granados Jr. **202-447-5606**

Visual Information Specialist. Richard Houghton. **202-447-3103**

Conservation, Research, and Education

AGRICULTURAL RESEARCH

Director, Information Division. Eugene M Farkas. **202-447-4433**

Assistant Director. 202-447-5787

Chief, Information Services Branch. H G Hass. **202-447-6785**

Chief, Publications Branch. Don K Childers. **301-436-8480**

Publications Inquiries. James C Hill. **301-436-8611**

COOPERATIVE STATE RESEARCH SERVICE

Director of Information. Mason Miller. **202-447-3880**

EXTENSION SERVICE

Director of Information. Ovid Bay. **202-447-6283**

Publications. Jean Brand. **202-447-7186**

Radio and Television. Gary Nugent. **202-447-2805**

FOREST SERVICE

Director of Information. Robert M Lake. **202-447-3760** or **5920**

Deputy Director of Information. Arthur E Merriman. **202-447-3709**

Publications and General Information. 202-447-3957

Current Information. George Castillo. **202-447-6957**

Public Involvement. Charles J Newlon. **202-447-7013**

Audio visual. Glenn A Kovar. **202-447-3789**

NATIONAL AGRICULTURAL LIBRARY

Information Office. Leila P Moran. **301-344-3725**

Lending Division. Patricia Condon. **301-344-3761**

Reference Division. Charles Bebee. **301-344-3836**

SOIL CONSERVATION SERVICE

Director, Information Division. Hubert W Kelley. **202-447-4543**

Assistant Director. Lee B Shields. **202-447-5240**

Chief, Audiovisual Branch. E Joseph Larson. **202-447-7547**

Chief, Conservation News and Reports Branch. Henry C Wyman. **201-447-3875**

Chief, Education and Publications Branch. Walter E Jeske. **201-447-5063**

Department of Commerce

Commerce Building, 14th St between Constitution Ave and E St, Washington, DC 20230. **202-377-2000.** Listed number: **202-783-9200.** Locator number: **301-443-8910** NOAA

SECRETARY OF COMMERCE. Juanita M Kreps. **202-377-2112** (h) Prospect House, 1200 N Nash St, Arlington, VA 22209

UNDER SECRETARY OF COMMERCE. Sidney Harman. **202-377-4625**

Office of Communications Personnel

DIRECTOR OF COMMUNICATIONS. Ernest A Lotito. **202-377-3263.** (h) **703-256-7423**

BROADCAST MEDIA DIVISION. Earl Cox. **202-377-5610.** (h) **703-768-5116**

PRINT MEDIA DIVISION. Richard Hoffmann. **202-377-3142.** (h) **703-979-4181**

NEWSROOM. Anne Wiesner. **202-377-4901.** (h) **703-620-2210**

COMMERCE AMERICA **MAGAZINE.** Richard Balentine. **202-377-3251.** (h) **202-265-2729**

Broadcast Spotmaster Service

Hard News and Economic Report. 202-393-4100

Features and Regional News. 202-393-4102

Commerce News Announcements. 202-393-1847

Important Offices, Bureaus, and Administrations

OFFICE OF ASSISTANT SECRETARY FOR SCIENCE AND TECHNOLOGY. Rm 3867, Main Commerce, 14th St and Constitution Ave, Washington, DC 20230. *Contact.* **202-377-3914**

OFFICE OF THE CHIEF ECONOMIST. Rm 4857, Main Commerce, 14th St and

Constitution Ave, Washington, DC 20230. *Contact.* Adren Cooper, **202-377-2235.** (h) **703-820-9346**

OFFICE OF MINORITY BUSINESS ENTERPRISE. Rm 5087B, Main Commerce, 14th St and Constitution Ave, Washington, DC 20230. *Contact.* Elliott McLean, **202-377-3024.** (h) **301-647-2703**

OFFICE OF TELECOMMUNICATIONS. Rm 271, 1325 G St NW, Washington, DC 20005. *Contact.* Lois Adams, **202-724-3361.** (h) **301-423-2077**

PATENT AND TRADEMARK OFFICE. Rm 31D01, Crystal Plz, 2021 Jefferson Davis Hwy, Arlington, VA 20231. *Contact.* Isaac Fleischmann, **703-557-3428.** (h) **703-534-3647**

BUREAU OF THE CENSUS. Rm 2089, Federal Office Bldg 3, Suitland, MD 20233. *Contact.* Henry Smith, **301-763-7273.** (h) **301-652-5788.** For more detail, *see* Bureau of the Census (p. 000).

BUREAU OF ECONOMIC ANALYSIS. Rm 912, Tower Bldg, 1401 K St NW. Mailing address: US Department of Commerce, 14th St and Constitution Ave, Washington, DC 20230. *Contact.* Ago Ambre, **202-523-0777.** (h) **301-587-9115**

NATIONAL BUREAU OF STANDARDS. Rm A621, Administration Bldg, National Bureau of Standards, Washington, DC 20234. *Contact.* Richard Franzen, **301-921-3181.** (h) **703-768-4181**

DOMESTIC AND INTERNATIONAL BUSINESS ADMINISTRATION. Rm 3804, Main Commerce, 14th St and Constitution Ave, Washington, DC 20230. *Contact.* Robert Amdur, **202-377-3808.** (h) **703-860-1546**

ECONOMIC DEVELOPMENT ADMINISTRATION. Rm 7019, Main Commerce, 14th St and Constitution Ave, Washington, DC 20230. *Contact.* Arch Parsons, **202-377-5113.** (h) **202-483-5322**

MARITIME ADMINISTRATION. Rm 3895, Main Commerce, 14th St and Constitution Ave, Washington, DC 20230. *Contact.* Walter Oates, **202-377-2746.** (h) **301-384-7627**

NATIONAL FIRE PREVENTION AND CONTROL ADMINISTRATION. Rm 600, 2400 M St, NW. Mailing address: US Department of Commerce, 14th St and Constitution Ave, Washington, DC 20230.

Contact. Peg Maloy, **202-634-7663.** (h) **703-360-4230**

NATIONAL OCEANIC AND ATMOS-PHERIC ADMINISTRATION. Rm 221, Washington Science Ctr 5, 6010 Executive Blvd, Rockville, MD 20852. *Contact.* Stanley Eames, **301-443-8243.** (h) **301-460-3245.** See WEATHER for more detail on the NOAA.

NATIONAL TECHNICAL INFORMA-TION SERVICE. Suite 620, Pennsylvania Bldg, 425 13th St NW, Washington, DC 20004. *Contact.* Terrance Lindemann, **202-724-3366.** (h) **202-362-3707**

UNITED STATES TRAVEL SERVICE. Rm 1521, Main Commerce, 14th St and Constitution Ave, Washington, DC 20230. *Contact.* **202-377-4987**

Subject Directory of Information Officers

AERONAUTICAL CHARTING. John Stringer. **301-443-8708**

AGRICULTURE CENSUS. Henry Smith. **301-763-7273**

APPLIANCE LABELING. Madeleine Jacobs. **301-921-2435**

APPLIED TECHNOLOGY. Fred McGehan. **301-921-2816**

ATOMIC, NUCLEAR, AND ISOTOPIC RESEARCH. Joe Crumlish. **301-921-3181**

AUTOMATION TECHNOLOGY. Stan Lichtenstein. **301-921-3181**

BALANCE OF PAYMENTS. Ago Ambre. **202-523-0777**

BASIC STANDARDS, INSTITUTE OF. Joe Crumlish. **301-921-3181**

BROADCAST NEWS. Earl Cox. **202-377-5610**

BUILDING TECHNOLOGY. Fred McGehan. **301-921-2816**

BUSINESS CENSUSES. Henry Smith. **301-763-7273**

BUSINESS DEVELOPMENT LOANS. Arch Parsons. **202-377-5113**

BUSINESS CONDITIONS DIGEST. Ago Ambre. **202-523-0777**

CAPITAL EQUIPMENT. Dan Landa. **202-377-3259**

CENSUSES. Henry Smith. **301-763-7273**

COAL GASIFICATION. Madeleine Jacobs. **301-921-2435**

COASTAL ZONE MANAGEMENT. Joe Jacobson. **202-634-4245**

COMMERCE AMERICA MAGAZINE. Richard Balentine. **202-377-3251**

COMMERCE TECHNICAL ADVISORY BOARD (CTAB). Florence Feinberg. **202-377-5065**

COMMODITY STATISTICS. Dan Landa. **202-377-3259**

COMPUTER SCIENCE AND TECHNOL-OGY. Stan Lichtenstein. **301-921-3181**

CONSTRUCTION AND FOREST PROD-UCTS. Dan Landa. **202-377-3259**

CONSUMER GOODS. Dan Landa. **202-377-3259**

CONSUMER PRODUCTS SAFETY. Fred McGehan. **301-921-2816**

CORPORATE PROFITS. Ago Ambre. **202-523-0777**

DATES OF FIRES. Peg Maloy. **202-634-7663**

DISASTER RESEARCH. Stan Lichtenstein. **301-921-3181**

DOMESTIC COMMERCE, BUREAU OF. Dan Landa. **202-377-3259**

EAST-WEST TRADE. James Rourke. **202-377-2253**

ECONOMIC AFFAIRS. Adren Cooper. **202-377-2235**

ECONOMIC CENSUSES. Henry Smith. **301-763-7273**

ECONOMIC DEVELOPMENT PRO-GRAMS. Barbara Estabrook. **202-377-5113**

EDUCATION AND TRAINING (FIRE). Peg Maloy. **202-634-7663**

EDUCATION STATISTICS. Henry Smith. **301-763-7273**

ENERGY CONSERVATION PRO-GRAMS. Tim Lankton. **202-377-4703**

ENERGY (CONSERVATION). Madeleine Jacobs. **301-921-2435**

ENERGY (EFFICIENCY STANDARDS AND INVENTIONS). Madeleine Jacobs. **301-921-2435**

ENVIRONMENTAL AFFAIRS. Jane Lewis. **202-377-4335**

ENVIRONMENTAL SATELLITES. Bill Brennan. **301-443-8243**

ENVIRONMENT (POLLUTION). Madeleine Jacobs. **301-921-2435**

ENVIRONMENT DATA SERVICES. Roland Paine. **303-443-8243**

EMPLOYMENT AND UNEMPLOY-MENT SURVEYS. Henry Smith. **301-763-7273**

EXPORT AWARDS. Britt Vanden Eykel. **202-377-2253**

EXPORT INFORMATION. James Rourke. **202-377-2253**

EXPORT LICENCES. James Rourke. **202-377-2253**

EXPOSITIONS (INTERNATIONAL). Robert Jackson. **202-377-4987**

FAILURE ANALYSIS. Stan Lichtenstein. **301-921-3181**

FIELD OPERATIONS. Britt Vanden Eykle. **202-377-5088**

FIRE PREVENTION. Peg Maloy. **202-634-7663**

FIRE PROTECTION (see also (1) Research and Data and (2) Education and Training). Fred McGehan. **301-921-2816**

FOREIGN INVESTMENT STATISTICS. Ago Ambre. **202-523-0777**

FOREIGN TRADE ANALYSIS. James Rourke. **202-377-2253**

FOREIGN TRADE STATISTICS. Henry Smith. **301-763-7273**

FREEDOM OF INFORMATION. Carol Wong. **202-377-5659**

GEODETIC SURVEYS. John Stringer. **301-443-8708**

GOVERNMENT FINANCES (STATE AND LOCAL). Henry Smith. **301-763-7273**

GRANTS TO LOCAL GOVERNMENT. Barbara Estabrook. **202-377-5113**

GROSS NATIONAL PRODUCT. Ago Ambre. **202-523-0777**

HEALTH. Madeleine Jacobs. **301-921-2435**

HOUSING AND CONSTRUCTION STATISTICS. Henry Smith. **301-763-7273**

HURRICANE WARNING. Ed Weigel. **301-427-7622**

HYDROLOGY, OFFICE OF. Ed Weigel. **301-427-7622**

IMPORT PROGRAMS. Dan Landa. **202-377-3259**

INCOME, FAMILY. Henry Smith. **301-763-7273**

INCOME, PERSONAL (NATIONAL AND REGIONAL). Ago Ambre. **202-523-0777**

INDUSTRY SURVEYS. Henry Smith. **301-763-7273**

INPUT–OUTPUT ANALYSIS. Ago Ambre. **202-523-0777**

INTERNATIONAL COMMERCE, BUREAU OF. James Rourke. **202-377-2253**

INTERNATIONAL FINANCE, INVESTMENT AND MARKETING. James Rourke. **202-377-2253**

INTERNATIONAL INVESTMENT STATISTICS. Ago Ambre. **202-523-0777**

INVESTMENT SERVICES. James Rourke. **202-377-2253**

LASER INFORMATION. Madeleine Jacobs. **301-921-2435**

LAW ENFORCEMENT STANDARDS. Stan Lichtenstein. **301-921-3181**

LEADING ECONOMIC INDICATORS. Ago Ambre. **202-523-0777**

MANUFACTURING INDUSTRY (BY COMMODITY). Dan Landa. **202-377-3259**

MARINE TECHNOLOGY. Roland Paine. **301-443-8243**

MARITIME TECHNOLOGY. Walter Oates. **202-377-2746**

MATERIALS RESEARCH. Madeleine Jacobs. **301-921-2435**

METEOROLOGICAL CENTER. Ed Weigel. **301-427-7622**

METRIC SYSTEM. Fred McGehan. **301-921-2816**

MINORITY BUSINESS PROGRAMS. Elliott McLean. **202-377-3024**

NATIONAL MARINE FISHERIES. Jerry Hill. **202-634-7281**

NAUTICAL CHARTS. John Stringer. **301-443-8708**

NEWS RELEASES AND SPEECHES. Anne Wiesner. **202-377-4901**

OCCUPATION AND INDUSTRY INFORMATION. Henry Smith. **301-763-7273**

OMBUDSMAN FOR BUSINESS. Dan Landa. **202-277-3259**

OVERSEAS BUSINESS OPPORTUNITIES. James Rourke. **202-377-2253**

PATENTS, GOVERNMENT–OWNED, FOREIGN FILING. Doug Campion. **703-557-4735**

PATENTS AND TRADEMARKS. Isaac Fleischmann. **703-557-3428**

PLANT AND EQUIPMENT EXPENDITURES. Ago Ambre. **202-523-0777**

POLLUTION ABATEMENT AND CONTROL EXPENDITURES. Ago Ambre. **202-523-0777**

POPULATION INFORMATION. Henry Smith. **301-763-7273**

PRODUCT STANDARDS. Howard Forman. **202-377-3221**

PUBLICATIONS: SALES AND DISTRIBUTION. 202-377-4348

PUBLIC WORKS PROJECTS. Barbara Estabrook. **202-377-5113**

RADIATION MEASUREMENTS. Joe Crumlish. **301-921-3181**

REGIONAL PLANNING COMMISSION. Anne Wiesner. **202-377-4901**

RESEARCH (ECONOMIC). Adren Cooper. **202-377-2235**

RESEARCH AND DATA (FIRE). Peg Maloy. **202-634-7663**

RESEARCH (MARITIME). Walter Oates. **202-377-2746**

RESOURCE AND TRADE ASSISTANCE, BUREAU OF. Dan Landa. **202-377-3259**

RETAIL AND WHOLESALE TRADE. Henry Smith. **301-763-7273**

SCIENCE AND TECHNOLOGY. Florence Feinberg. **202-377-5065**

SEA GRANTS. Jim Elliott. **202-634-4034**

SECRETARIAL STATEMENTS. Anne Wiesner. **202-377-4901**

SERVICE INDUSTRIES (STATISTICS). Dan Landa. **202-377-3259**

SHIP OPERATIONS, SHIPBUILDING. Walter Oates. **202-377-2746**

STANDARD REFERENCE MATERIALS. Madeleine Jacobs. **301-921-2435**

TECHNICAL DOCUMENT SALES (ALL GOVERNMENT AGENCIES). 202-724-3382

TECHNICAL HELP TO EXPORTERS. George Kudrovetz. **703-557-4733**

TECHNOLOGY TRANSFER TO DEVELOPING COUNTRIES. Terrance Lindemann. **202-724-3366**

TELECOMMUNICATIONS, OFFICE OF. Lois Adams. **202-724-3361**

TEXTILES. Dan Landa. **202-377-3259**

TIME AND FREQUENCY (STANDARDS). Ralph Desch. **303-499-1000**

TORNADO WARNING. Ed Weigel. **301-427-7622**

TOURISM, INTERNATIONAL AND DOMESTIC. Melinda Carr. **202-377-4987**

TRADE ADJUSTMENT ASSISTANCE. Bernie Jenkins. **202-377-5133**

TRADE FAIRS, TRADE CENTERS, AND TRADE MISSIONS. James Rourke. **202-377-2253**

TRADEMARKS. Isaac Fleischmann. **202-377-3428**

TRADE NEGOTIATIONS. James Rourke. **202-377-2253**

TRADE ZONE BOARD. Dan Landa. **202-377-3259**

TRANSPORTATION EQUIPMENT. Dan Landa. **202-377-3259**

TRAVEL. Melinda Carr. **202-377-4987**

WEATHER SERVICE. Ed Weigel. **301-427-7622**

WEIGHTS AND MEASURES. Fred McGehan. **301-921-2816**

Bureau of the Census

Federal Bldg 3, Suitland, MD 20233. **202-763-7273**

DIRECTOR. Manuel D Plotkin. **301-763-5190**

DEPUTY DIRECTOR. Robert L Hagan. **301-763-5192**

PROGRAM POLICY AND DEVELOP-MENT OFFICE. Theodore G Clemence, chief. **301-763-2758**

CONGRESSIONAL LIAISON. Pennie Harvison. **301-763-5360**

PUBLIC INFORMATION OFFICE. Henry H Smith, chief. **301-763-7273**. Mary Cagle, assistant.

Demographic Fields: Data Users' Contacts

ASSOCIATE DIRECTOR FOR DEMO-GRAPHIC FIELDS. Daniel B Levine. **301-763-5167**
Demographic Surveys Division. Earle J Gerson, chief. **301-763-2777**

Housing Division. Arthur F Young, chief. **301-763-2863**
Population Division. Meyer Zitter, chief. **301-763-7646**
Statistical Methods Division. Charles D Jones, chief. **301-763-2672**
International Statistical Programs Center. J Timothy Sprehe, chief. **301-763-2832**
Office of Demographic Analysis. Robert P Parkinson, acting chief. **301-763-1774**

ASSISTANT DIRECTOR FOR DEMO-GRAPHIC CENSUSES AND CHIEF, DEMOGRAPHIC CENSUS STAFF. David L Kaplan. **301-763-7670**

Demographic Subject Matter Contacts

AGE AND SEX, UNITED STATES. Jennifer Peck. **301-763-5184**

AGE, STATES. Gilbert Felton. **301-763-5072**

ALIENS. Elmore Seraile. **301-763-7571**

AMERICANS OVERSEAS. Nampeo McKenney. **301-763-7890**

ANNEXATION POPULATION COUNTS. Joel Miller. **301-763-5716**

APPORTIONMENT. Robert Speaker. **301-763-5161**

ARMED FORCES. Jennifer Peck. **301-763-5184**

BIRTHS AND BIRTH EXPECTATIONS; FERTILITY STATISTICS. Maurice Moore. **301-763-5303**

CENSUS TRACT POPULATION. Robert Speaker. **301-763-5161**

CITZENSHIP—FOREIGN BORN PER-SONS, COUNTRY OF BIRTH; FOREIGN STOCK PERSONS, MOTHER TONGUE. Elmore Seraile. **301-763-7571**

COMMUTING: JOURNEY TO WORK—MEANS OF TRANSPORTA-TION; PLACE OF WORK. Philip Fulton. **301-763-5226**

CONSUMER PURCHASES AND OWNERSHIP OF DURABLES. Jack McNeil. **301-763-5032**

CRIME VICTIMIZATION SURVEY. Linda Murphy. **301-763-1735**

DECENNIAL CENSUS: CONTENT AND TABULATIONS. Marshall Turner. **301-763-7325**

DECENNIAL CENSUS: GENERAL PLANS. Morris Gorinson. **301-763-2748**

DECENNIAL CENSUS: MINORITY STATISTICS PROGRAM. Clifton Jordon. **301-763-5169**

DISABLED PERSONS. Jack McNeil. **301-763-5032**

EDUCATION; SCHOOL ENROLLMENT. Larry Suter. **301-763-5050**

EMPLOYMENT; UNEMPLOYMENT; LABOR FORCE. Paula Schneider. **301-763-2825**

FAMILIES—SIZE, NUMBER, MARITAL STATUS. Arthur Norton. **301-763-5189**

FARM POPULATION. Robert Speaker. **301-763-5161**

HEALTH SURVEYS. Evan Davey. **301-763-5508**

HOUSING: INFORMATION, DECENNIAL CENSUS. Bill Downs. **301-763-2873**

HOUSING SURVEY, ANNUAL. Elmo Beach. **301-763-2881**

HOUSING VACANCY DATA. Aneda France. **301-763-2880**

RESIDENTIAL FINANCE. Betty Kent. **301-763-2866**

INCOME STATISTICS: CURRENT SURVEYS. Gordon Green. **301-763-5060**

INCOME STATISTICS: DECENNIAL CENSUS. George Patterson. **301-763-5682**

INCOME STATISTICS: REVENUE SHARING. Frank Burns. **301-763-5682**

INCORPORATED AND UNINCORPO-RATED PLACES. Robert Speaker. **301-763-5161**

INDUSTRY AND OCCUPATION STA-TISTICS. John Priebe. **301-763-5144**

INSTITUTIONAL POPULATION. Arthur Norton. 301-763-5189

INTERNATIONAL POPULATION. Samuel Baum. 301-763-2870

LAND AREA. Richard Forstall. 301-763-5161

LONGITUDINAL SURVEYS. Robert Mangold. 301-763-2764

MIGRATION; MOBILITY. Kris Hansen. 301-763-5255

MORTALITY AND/OR DEATH. Martin O'Connell. 301-763-5303

POPULATION: FEDERAL—STATE COOPERATIVE PROGRAM FOR LOCAL ESTIMATES. Linda Braun. 301-763-7722

POPULATION: GENERAL INFORMATION; CENSUS DATA; CHARACTERISTICS; SURVEY. Nellie Harris. 301-763-5002 or 5020

POPULATION BY CONGRESSIONAL DISTRICTS. Donald Starsinic. 301-763-5072

POPULATION COUNT COMPLAINTS. Joel Miller. 301-763-5716

POPULATION ESTIMATES AND PROJECTIONS: COUNTIES AND LOCAL AREAS; REVENUE SHARING. Frederick Cavanaugh. 301-763-7722

POPULATION ESTIMATES RESEARCH. Richard Irwin. 301-763-7883

POPULATION OF INDIVIDUAL STATES; STANDARD METROPOLITAN STATISTICAL AREAS. Marianne Roberts. 301-763-5313

POPULATION OF THE US (NATIONAL). Jennifer Peck. 301-763-5184

PROJECTIONS OF THE POPULATION. Signe Wetrogan. 301-763-5300

POVERTY STATISTICS; LOW INCOME AREAS. Arno Winard. 301-763-5790

PRISONER SURVEYS; NATIONAL PRISONER STATISTICS. Carolyn Thompson. 301-763-1832

RACE AND ETHNIC STATISTICS— BLACK, AMERICAN INDIANS, AND

OTHER RACES. Nampeo McKenney. 301-763-7890

RACE—SPANISH POPULATION. Edward Fernandez. 301-763-5219

RELIGION. Elmore Seraile. 301-763-7571

REVENUE SHARING. Joseph Knott. 301-763-5179

SAMPLING METHODS. Charles Jones. 301-763-2672

SOCIAL STRATIFICATION. Larry Suter. 301-763-5050

SPECIAL CENSUSES. George Hurn. 301-763-5806

STANDARD METROPOLITAN STATISTICAL AREAS—AREA DEFINITION AND TOTAL POPULATION. Richard Forstall. 301-763-5161

SPECIAL SURVEYS. George Gray. 301-763-5507

TRAVEL SURVEYS. John Cannon. 301-763-1798

URBAN/RURAL RESIDENCE. Richard Forstall. 301-763-5161

VETERAN STATUS. Jerry Jennings. 301-763-5050

VOTING AND REGISTRATION. Larry Suter. 301-763-5050

VOTING RIGHTS. Gilbert Felton. 301-763-5072

Economic Fields: Data Users' Contacts

ASSOCIATE DIRECTOR FOR ECONOMIC FIELDS. Shirley Kallek. 301-763-5274

Business Division. John R Wikoff, chief. 301-763-7564

Construction Statistics Division. Jack S Silver, chief. 301-763-7163

Foreign Trade Division. Emanuel A Lipscomb, chief. 301-763-5342

Governments Division. Sherman Landau, chief. 301-763-7366

Industry Division. Milton Eisen, chief. 301-763-5850

ASSISTANT DIRECTOR FOR ECONOMIC AND AGRICULTURE CENSUSES, AND CHIEF, ECONOMIC CENSUS STAFF. Melvin A Hendry. 301-763-7356

Agriculture Division. Orvin L Wilhite, chief. 301-763-5230

Economic Surveys Division. Roger H Bugenhagen, chief. 301-763-7735

Economic Subject Matter Contacts

AGRICULTURE

General Information. Arnold Bollenbacher. 301-763-5170

Census/Industries Surveys. Alan Blum. 301-763-5435

County Business Patterns. Robert Schiedel. 301-763-7642

Crop Statistics. Donald Jahnke. 301-763-1939

Current Programs. David Siskind. 301-763-7165

Enterprise Statistics. John Dodds. 301-763-7086

Environmental Surveys. Wayne McCaughey. 301-763-5616

Exports, Origin of. Wayne McCaughey. 301-763-5616

Farm Economics. Arnold Bollenbacher. 301-763-5170

Foreign Trade Information. Paul Finn. 301-763-5140

Fuels and Electric Energy Consumed. John McNamee. 301-763-5938

Livestock Statistics. Thomas Monroe. 301-763-1974

Special Surveys. Kenneth Norell. 301-763-5914

GOVERNMENTS

Eastern States Government Sector. Howard Sales. 301-763-7783

Western States Government Sector. Ulvey Harris. 301-763-2886

Criminal Justice Statistics. Diana Cull. 301-763-2842

Employment. Alan Stevens. 301-763-5086

Finance. Vancil Kane. 301-763-5847

Governmental Organization. Muriel Miller. 301-763-5308

Industry and Commodities Classification. Walter Neece. 301-763-5449

Revenue Sharing. John Coleman. 301-763-5272

Taxation. Earle Knapp. 301-763-5302

MANUFACTURES AND TRADE

Census/Annual Survey of Manufactures. Arthur Horowitz. **301-763-7666**

Current Programs. James Werking. **301-763-7800**

Mineral Industries. John McNamee. **301-763-5938**

Minority Businesses. Cotty Smith. **301-763-7690**

Puerto Rico: Censuses of Retail Trade, Wholesale Trade, and Selected Services Industries. Alvin Barten. **301-763-5282**

Retail Trade: Census. Bobby Russell. **301-763-7038**

Monthly Retail Trade Report, Accounts Receivable, and Monthly Department Store Sales. Conrad Alexander. **301-763-7128**

Weekly Retail Sales Report, Advance Monthly Retail Sales, and Retail Inventories Survey. Irving True. **301-763-7660**

Selected Services Industries: Census. Dorothy Reynolds. **301-763-7039**

Current Services Reports. Edward Gutbrod. **301-763-7077**

Transportation: Commodity Transportation Survey, Truck Inventory and Use, and Domestic Movement of Foreign Trade Data. Zigmund Decker. **301-763-5430**

Wholesale Trade

Census. John Trimble. **301-763-5281**

Current Wholesale Sales and Inventories, Green Coffee Survey, and Canned Food Survey. Ronald Piencykoski. **301-763-5294**

User Services

AGE SEARCH. Mary Mundell. **301-763-7662**

BUREAU OF THE CENSUS CATALOG. Mary Gordon. **301-763-5574**

CENSUS PROCEDURES, HISTORY OF. Frederick Bohme. **301-763-7337**

CENTRAL CITY PROFILES. Paul Manka. **301-763-2400**

COLLEGE CURRICULUM SUPPORT PROJECT. Paul Zeisset. **301-763-7368**

COMPUTER TAPES; COMPUTER PRO-GRAMS. Larry Carbaugh. **301-763-2400**

DATA USER NEWS, **MONTHLY NEWS-LETTER.** Larry Hartke. **301-763-7454**

DATA USER TRAINING—SEMINARS, WORKSHOPS, TRAINING COURSES,

AND CONFERENCES. Ann D Casey. **301-763-5293**

INDEXES TO 1970 CENSUS SUMMARY TAPES AND TO SELECTED 1970 CENSUS PRINTED REPORTS. Paul Zeisset. **301-763-7368**

MAP ORDERS. Deloris Fentress. **301-763-2400**

MICROFILM. Paul Manka. **301-763-2400**

PUBLIC USE SAMPLES. Paul Zeisset. **301-763-7368**

SPECIAL TABULATIONS. Larry Carbaugh. **301-763-2400**

STATISTICAL COMPENDIA: CON-GRESSIONAL DISTRICT DATA RE-PORTS; *COUNTY AND CITY DATA BOOK;* **HISTORICAL STATISTICS OF THE US.** Helen Teir. **301-763-5475**

STATISTICAL ABSTRACT; POCKET DATA BOOK. William Lerner. **301-763-7024**

SUMMARY TAPE PROCESSING CENTERS. Gary Young. **301-763-7454**

UNPUBLISHED CENSUS TABLES. Paul Manka. **301-763-2400**

Geographic Matters

AREA MEASUREMENT AND CENTERS OF POPULATION. Lawrence Taylor. **301-763-5437**

BOUNDARIES AND ANNEXATIONS. Frances Barnett. **301-763-5437**

1970 CENSUS GEOGRAPHY. Donald Hirschfeld. **301-763-2668**

COMPUTER GRAPHICS AND COM-PUTER MAPPING. Frederick Broome. **301-763-7442**

GEOGRAPHIC STATISTICAL AREAS. Alice Winterfeld. **301-763-7291**

GEOGRAPHIC USES OF EARTH RESOURCES SATELLITE TECH-NOLOGY—US. Alice Winterfeld. **301-763-7291**

GEOGRAPHIC USES OF EARTH RESOURCES SATELLITE TECH-NOLOGY—INTERNATIONAL. Robert Durland. **301-763-5720**

LAW ENFORCEMENT ASSISTANCE PROGRAM—USE OF GBF/DIME SYSTEM. Bruce Strahan. **301-763-7742**

GE-50 SERIES MAPS. Conrad Thoren. **301-763-5035**

REVENUE SHARING GEOGRAPHY. Donald Hirschfeld. **301-763-2668**

URBAN ATLAS. Richard Schweitzer. **301-763-5126**

Publications

LIBRARY. Salme Gorokhoff. **301-763-5040**

PUBLICATIONS, MICROFICHE. Theresa Allen. **301-763-5042**

SUBSCRIBER SERVICES (PUBLICA-TIONS). Dorothy Dunham. **301-763-7472**

Department of Defense

The Pentagon, Washington, DC 20301. **202-545-6700.** Personnel locator numbers: Army and DOD, **202-695-3241.** Air Force, **202-695-4803.** Navy, **202-694-1183**

SECRETARY OF DEFENSE. Harold Brown. Rm 3E880. **202-695-5261**

MILITARY ASSISTANTS. Rear Admiral M S Holcomb and Colonel Elmer T Brooks.

SECRETARY TO THE SECRETARY OF DEFENSE. Thelma Stubbs

Office of the Assistant Secretary of Defense (Public Affairs)

ASSISTANT SECRETARY. Thomas B Ross. **202-697-9312**
Military Advisor. Captain Sidney V Wright, USN. **202-695-1624**
Special Assistant. John A Goldsmith. **202-697-6648**
Military Assistant. Lieutenant Colonel Jerry D Lindauer, USMC. **202-697-9314**

PRINCIPAL DEPUTY ASSISTANT SECRETARY. **202-697-0713**
Military Assistant. Captain Hallie E Robertson, USAF. **202-697-9143**

DEPUTY ASSISTANT SECRETARY. Major General Guy E Hairston, USAF. **202-695-3381**
Assistant. Major Ronald C Lindeke, USAF. **202-695-0769**

DIRECTORATE FOR MANAGEMENT
Director. Robert C Kinkor. 202-697-0792
Administrative Officer. Liz Wheeler.
202-697-0792
Chief, Mail Control and Distribution Branch.
Senior Master Sergeant C R Turner, USAF.
202-697-5007
Staff Assistant, Public Corespondence. Philip
A Farris. 202-697-5737

DIRECTORATE FOR DEFENSE INFOR-MATION
Director. Colonel Thomas D Byrne, USA
(acting). 202-695-9082
Broadcast and Engineering Branch. William
Brown. 202-697-2902
Research and Distribution Branch. John
Sullivan. 202-697-3189
News Division. Lieutenant Colonel Jack T
Munsey, USA (acting). 202-697-5131
Armed Forces News Branch. Lieutenant
Colonel Donald Y Wakefield, USA (acting).
202-697-5131
Defense News Branch. Orval G Willoughby.
202-695-0192
Operations News Branch. James B Freeman.
202-697-5331
Audiovisual Division. Norman T Hatch.
202-697-4162
Acquisitions Branch. Major Peter K Friend,
USA. 202-697-6161
Documentary Branch. Russell W Wagner.
202-695-0168
Production Branch. Donald E Baruch.
202-697-4596
Plans and Programs Division. Colonel
William S Clarke, USAF. 202-697-2873

DIRECTORATE FOR COMMUNITY RELATIONS
Director. Captain Donald J Maynard, USN.
202-695-2113
Special Assistant for Plans and Policy.
Commander John M Rusch, USN.
202-697-9816
Public Service Division. Dr David A Smith.
202-697-4170
Government and Special Events. Commander
Richard E Busby, USN. 202-697-4170
Business and Labor Organizations.
Lieutenant Colonel George Ogles, USAF.
202-695-2036
Aviation Support. Lieutenant Colonel Eugene
F Fudge, USA. 202-697-4170
Civic and Minority Activities. Frances
Conner. 202-695-2733
Veterans' and Youth Organizations. Major
Eric M Solander, USAF. 202-695-6795
Programs Division. Colonel Francis R
Cipolla, USA. 202-697-6005
Speakers Bureau. John R German.
202-695-6108

Conferences and Visitors. Ruth Kirby.
202-695-7676
Tours and Briefings. Captain Douglas
Jocobsen, USAF. 202-697-5976

DIRECTORATE FOR FREEDOM OF INFORMATION AND SECURITY REVIEW
Director. Charles W Hinkle. 202-697-4325
Freedom of Information Specialist. Arthur
E Fajans. 202-697-1180
Programs Management Division. Donald R
Pollock. 202-697-4326
Office of the Secretary of Defense Division.
Robert E Kellogg. 202-695-9556
Army Division. Thompson M Colkitt.
202-697-1182
Navy Division. 202-697-2716
Air Force Division. Clay E Thompson.
202-697-5458

DIRECTORATE FOR INFORMATION FOR THE ARMED FORCES
Director. John C Broger. 202-697-6125
**Special Assistant for Management and
Operations.** Henry Valentino. 202-695-9330
Operations Coordinator. John G Uschold.
202-695-4782
Employer Support of Guard and Reserve.
Captain G K Meriwether, USN.
202-697-6966
Director Audiovisual Activities. Colonel Felix
L Casipit, USA. 202-694-2616
Equipment. Lieutenant Colonel Frank W
Curtis, USAF. 202-694-4913
Facilities. Lieutenant Colonel Willard C
Conley, USA. 202-694-1050
Products. Lieutenant Colonel Fred C Wist,
USA. 202-694-4611
Director, Electronic Media. Robert Cranston.
202-694-4903

AFRTS—Washington. Lieutenant Colonel
Howard Myrick, USA. 202-694-4823
Information Program Development. Kirk
Logie. 202-694-4904
Chief, TV Production Service. George
Gallivan. 202-694-5256
Director, Print and Motion Picture Media.
Colonel Robert Delaney, USA.
202-694-5008
Chief, Armed Forces Information Service.
Lieutenant Colonel Brian T Sheehan, USAF.
202-694-5070
Chief, Joint Interest Media Support Division.
Major John Ford, USAF. 202-694-4914
Chief, Defense Information Guidance. Robert
E Bartlett. 202-694-5024
Chief, Publication and Printing Services.
John P Forbes. 202-694-5000

Federal Voting Assistance. David C Steward.
202-694-4928
Director, Program Analysis and Data Support. Joseph Powers. 202-694-5005

Other Key Department of Defense Officials

DEPUTY SECRETARY OF DEFENSE.
Charles W Duncan, Jr. 202-695-6352

**DIRECTOR OF DEFENSE RESEARCH
AND ENGINEERING.** 202-697-9111.
ASSISTANT SECRETARY (INSTALLA-TIONS AND LOGISTICS). Dale R
Babione. 202-695-5254

**ASSISTANT SECRETARY (INTELLI-GENCE) AND DIRECTOR OF DEFENSE
INTELLIGENCE.** 202-695-0348

ASSISTANT SECRETARY (INTERNA-TIONAL SECURITY AFFAIRS). David
E McGiffert. 202-695-4351

**ASSISTANT TO THE SECRETARY
(LEGISLATIVE AFFAIRS).** Jack L
Stempler. 202-697-6210

Joint Chiefs Of Staff

CHAIRMAN, JOINT CHIEFS OF STAFF.
George S Brown, USAF. 202-697-9121

DIRECTOR, JOINT STAFF. Ray B Sitton,
USAF. 202-697-4084

DIRECTOR J–3 (OPERATIONS). C J Le
Van. 202-697-3702

DIRECTOR J–4 (LOGISTICS). Maurice
F Cassey. 202-697-7000

DIRECTOR J–5 (PLANS AND POLICY).
P J Hannifin. 202-695-5618

JOINT SECRETARIAT. P M Hartington.
202-697-2700

Key Defense Agencies

**DEFENSE ADVANCED RESEARCH
PROJECTS AGENCY.** George H
Heilmeier, director. 202-694-3007

**DEFENSE CIVIL PREPAREDNESS
AGENCY.** Personnel locator number:
202-697-1621
Director. John E Davis. 202-697-4484

Duty Officer (nonduty hours, Sunday, and Holidays). **202-638-3983**
Civil Defense Information. 202-695-9441

DEFENSE COMMUNICATIONS AGENCY
Office of the Director. L M Paschall. **202-692-0018**
Duty Officer (duty hours). **202-692-2006**

DEFENSE INTELLIGENCE AGENCY. Personnel locator numbers: **202-697-7072** (duty hours). **202-697-7072** (nonduty hours)

DEFENSE MAPPING AGENCY
Office of the Director. Shannon D Cramer, Jr. **202-254-4504**
Duty Officer. 202-254-4400

DEFENSE NUCLEAR AGENCY
Office of the Director. Warren D Johnson. **202-325-7004**
Duty Officer. 202-325-7595

Department of the Army

Office of the Secretary of the Army

SECRETARY OF THE ARMY. Clifford L Alexander, Jr. **202-695-3211**

ASSISTANT SECRETARY OF THE ARMY (CIVIL WORKS). 202-697-8986.

ASSISTANT SECRETARY OF THE ARMY (FINANCIAL MANAGEMENT). Hadlai A Hull. **202-695-4291**

ASSISTANT SECRETARY OF THE ARMY (INSTALLATIONS AND LOGISTICS). Edwin Greiner. **202-695-2254**

ASSISTANT SECRETARY OF THE ARMY (MANPOWER AND RESERVE AFFAIRS). Paul D Phillips. **202-697-9253**

ASSISTANT SECRETARY OF THE ARMY (RESEARCH AND DEVELOPMENT). Edward A Miller. **202-695-6153**

CHIEF OF STAFF. Bernard W Rogers. **202-695-2077**

INFORMATION. 202-695-5554

Office of Public Affairs

CHIEF OF PUBLIC AFFAIRS. Major General L Gordon Hill. **202-695-5135.**

PUBLIC INFORMATION INQUIRIES. 202-697-2352.

Duty Officer or Night line. **202-697-4200**; if no answer, call **202-695-0441.**

DEPUTY CHIEF OF PUBLIC AFFAIRS. Robert B Solomon. **202-697-4482.**

EXECUTIVE. Lieutenant Colonel Jack G Cozad. **202-697-4482.**

OFFICE FOR FREEDOM OF INFORMATION. William J Donohue. **202-697-4122.**

PUBLIC INFORMATION DIVISION. Colonel Ralph E Ropp, chief. **202-695-5136.**
News. Lieutenant Colonel Hugh G Waite. **202-697-2351.**
Special Activities and Media Services. Lieutenant Colonel Jerry J Hoopert. **202-697-8193.**
Newspaper Section. 202-695-3696.

Department of the Navy

Office of the Secretary of the Navy

SECRETARY OF THE NAVY. W Graham Clayter, Jr. **202-695-3131.**

ASSISTANT SECRETARY OF THE NAVY (MANPOWER AND RESERVE AFFAIRS). Joseph T McCullen, Jr. **202-697-2179.**

ASSISTANT SECRETARY OF THE NAVY (INSTALLATIONS AND LOGISTICS). 202-692-2202.

ASSISTANT SECRETARY OF THE NAVY (FINANCIAL MANAGEMENT). 202-697-2325.

ASSISTANT SECRETARY OF THE NAVY (RESEARCH AND DEVELOPMENT). 202-695-6315.

Office of Information

CHIEF OF INFORMATION. Rear Admiral D M Cooney. **202-697-7391.**
Executive Assistant. Lieutenant Commander J S Sirmans. **202-697-6724.**
Personal Aide. Lieutenant (Junior Grade) L G Pallas. **202-697-7391.**

DEPUTY CHIEF OF INFORMATION. Captain R L Slawson. **202-697-6724.**

PUBLIC INFORMATION DIVISION. Commander T Coldwell, chief. **202-697-4627.**

News Desk. Lieutenant Commander J S Baker. **202-697-5342.**
Media Services Branch. Lieutenant E A Shackelford. **202-695-0911.**

Office of the Chief of Naval Operations

CHIEF OF NAVAL OPERATIONS. J L Holloway III. **202-695-6007.**

INFORMATION. 202-695-3667.

Marine Corps, US Headquarters

COMMANDANT. Louis H Wilson. **202-694-2500**

ASSISTANT COMMANDANT. S Jaskilka. **202-694-1201**

CHIEF OF STAFF. L E Brown. **202-694-2541**

INFORMATION. 202-694-2344 (from 0800 to 1630 Monday through Friday). **202-694-2645** (from 1630 to 0800 Monday through Friday)

Office of Information

DIRECTOR OF INFORMATION. Brigadier General W R Maloney. **202-694-2958**

DEPUTY DIRECTOR OF INFORMATION Colonel M J Gravel. **202-694-8010**

INFORMATION BRANCH. Major M L Hefti, chief. **202-694-1492**
Information Coordinator. Gunnery Sargeant R N Groscost. **202-694-1492**
Information Officers. Captain J W Schmidt. **202-694-1492.** Captain P C G Coulter. **202-694-4309**

Department of the Air Force

Office of the Secretary of the Air Force

SECRETARY OF THE AIR FORCE. 202-697-7376

ASSISTANT SECRETARY OF THE AIR FORCE (FINANCIAL MANAGEMENT). Everett T Keech. **202-697-2302**

ASSISTANT SECRETARY OF THE AIR FORCE (INSTALLATIONS AND LOGISTICS). 202-697-8147

ASSISTANT SECRETARY OF THE AIR FORCE (RESEARCH AND DEVELOPMENT). John J Martin. 202-697-6361

ASSISTANT SECRETARY OF THE AIR FORCE (MANPOWER AND RESERVE AFFAIRS). 202-695-6383

GENERAL COUNSEL. 202-697-0941

ADMINISTRATIVE ASSISTANT TO THE SECRETARY OF THE AIR FORCE. Thomas W Nelson. 202-695-9492

Office of the Chief of Staff, US Air Force

CHIEF OF STAFF. David C Jones. 202-697-9225

VICE–CHIEF OF STAFF. William V McBride. 202-695-7911

ASSISTANT CHIEF OF STAFF, INTELLIGENCE. Eugene F Tighe, Jr. 202-695-5613

INFORMATION (not directory). 202-695-2246
Duty Officer (Saturday, Sunday, and Nights). 202-697-0135

Office of Information

DIRECTOR. Brigadier General Harry J Dalton, Jr. 202-697-6061

DEPUTY DIRECTOR. Colonel Robert Hermann. 202-697-6061

ASSISTANT DIRECTOR. Colonel Louis W Cantelou, Jr. 202-697-4259
Assistant Director. Herbert L Wurth. 202-695-4602
Special assistant. Major Lawrence McCracken. 202-695-5227
Executive. Captain James E Jasch. 202-695-5227

PUBLIC INFORMATION DIVISION. Colonel William M Taylor, chief. 202-695-5554

OFFICE FOR SECURITY REVIEW. Colonel John J Pelszynski. 202-697-3222

Department of Energy

Washington, DC 20545. 202-252-5000

SECRETARY OF ENERGY. James R Schlesinger. 202-456-6210

DEPUTY SECRETARY OF ENERGY. John F O'Leary

DEPUTY ASSISTANT SECRETARY FOR PUBLIC AFFAIRS. Jim Bishop. 202-395-6806
Director of Editorial Services. Bill Anderson. 202-376-4055.
Communications Services. Ed Stokely. 301-353-3338
Special Projects. Pete Keay. 202-566-7104
Press Services. Alfred Alibrando. 202-566-9549

Federal Energy Regulatory Commission

(Formerly the independent Federal Power Commission, now an independent agency within the Energy Department.) 825 N Capitol St NE, Washington, DC 20426. Listed number: 202-655-4000

CHAIRMAN. Charles B Curtis

COMMISSIONERS. Don S Smith, Georgiana Sheldon, George R Hall, and Matthew Holden

EXECUTIVE DIRECTOR. William G McDonald

OFFICE OF PUBLIC INFORMATION. William L Webb, director. 202-275-4006

Energy Research and Development Administration

20 Massachusetts Ave NW, Washington, DC 20545. 202-376-4000

OFFICE OF PUBLIC AFFAIRS. Robert Newlin, assistant director. 202-353-3335

Federal Energy Administration

13th and Penn Ave NW, Washington, DC 20461. 202-566-9043 Communications. Alfred Rosenthal, director

Department of Health, Education, and Welfare (HEW)

200 Independence Ave SW, Washington, DC 20201. 202-245-7000. Locator number: 202-245-6296. Listed number: 202-655-4000

SECRETARY OF HEW. Joseph A Califano, Jr. 202-245-6306. (h) 3551 Springland Ln, Washington, DC 20008

UNDER SECRETARY OF HEW. Hale Champion. 202-245-7431

EXECUTIVE ASSISTANT TO THE SECRETARY. Ben W Heineman, Jr. 202-245-7163. (h) 4914 30th Pl, Washington, DC 20008. 202-966-0696

ASSISTANT SECRETARY FOR PUBLIC AFFAIRS. Eileen Shanahan. 202-245-1850. (h) 3608 Van Ness St, Washington, DC 20008. 202-362-8471

Other Key Officials

INSPECTOR GENERAL. Thomas Morris. 202-472-3148

DIRECTOR, OFFICE FOR CIVIL RIGHTS. David S Tatel. 202-245-6403

DIRECTOR, OFFICE OF CONSUMER AFFAIRS. Frank E McLaughlin (acting). 202-755-8875

DIRECTOR, OFFICE OF CHILD SUPPORT ENFORCEMENT. James B Cardwell. 202-245-6764

ASSISTANT SECRETARY (EDUCATION). Dr Mary Berry. 202-245-8430

ASSISTANT SECRETARY (LEGISLATION). Richard D Warden. 202-245-7627

ASSISTANT SECRETARY (PLANNING AND EVALUATION). Henry Aaron. 202-245-1858

ASSISTANT SECRETARY (MANAGEMENT AND BUDGET). John D Young. 202-245-6396

ASSISTANT SECRETARY (HUMAN DEVELOPMENT). Arabella Martinez. 202-245-7246

ASSISTANT SECRETARY (HEALTH). Dr Julius B Richmond. 202-245-7694

ADMINISTRATOR, HEALTH CARE FINANCING ADMINISTRATION. Robert A Derzon. 202-245-6726

COMMISSIONER, SOCIAL SECURITY ADMINISTRATION. James B Cardwell. 202-245-6764

Contacts at Key Offices, Administrations, and Institutes

OFFICE OF ASSISTANT SECRETARY FOR EDUCATION. Rm 314G, South Portal Bldg, 200 Independence Ave SW, Washington, DC 20201. **202-245-8248.** *Contact.* Mary Hallisy, (h) **202-554-9487**

OFFICE OF ASSISTANT SECRETARY FOR HEALTH. Rm 731G, South Portal Bldg, 200 Independence Ave SW, Washington, DC 20201. **202-245-6867.** *Contact.* John Blamphin, (h) **301-757-6450**

OFFICE OF ASSISTANT SECRETARY FOR HUMAN DEVELOPMENT SERVICE. Rm 362G, South Portal Bldg, 200 Independence Ave SW, Washington, DC 20201. **202-245-2790.** *Contact.* Norman Subotnik, (h) **301-424-4062**

OFFICE OF CHILD DEVELOPMENT. Rm 4107, Donohoe Bldg, 400 6th St SW, Washington, DC 20201. **202-755-7724.** *Contact.* Hal Eidlin, (h) **301-460-9172**

OFFICE FOR CIVIL RIGHTS. Rm 5410, DHEW North Bldg, 330 Independence Ave SW, Washington, DC 20201. **202-245-6700.** *Contact.* Colleen O'Conner

OFFICE OF CONSUMER AFFAIRS. Rm 624, DHEW, Reporters Bldg, Washington, DC 20201. **202-755-8810.** *Contact.* Howard Seltzer, (h) **301-652-7408**

OFFICE OF EDUCATION. Rm 2097, Federal Office Bldg 6, 400 Maryland Ave SW, Washington, DC 20202. **202-245-6677.** *Contact.* Jack Billings, (h) **301-654-6849**

ALCOHOL, DRUG ABUSE, AND MENTAL HEALTH ADMINISTRATION. Rm 16-95, Parklawn Bldg, 5600 Fishers Ln, Rockville, MD 20857. **301-443-3783.** *Contact.* James C Helsing, (h) **202-338-4826**

CENTER FOR DISEASE CONTROL. 1600 Clifton Rd NE, Atlanta, GA 30333. **404-633-3311.** William H Foege, director. Donald A Berreth, director, Office of Information, Ext 3286, (h) **404-939-3574.** Night line: **404-633-2176** or **8673**

FOOD AND DRUG ADMINISTRATION. 5600 Fishers Ln, Rockville, MD 20857. Donald Kennedy, commissioner. **301-443-2410.** *Contact.* John T Walden, assistant commissioner, **301-443-4177**, (h) **301-567-3148**

Wayne L Pines, deputy assistant commissioner, **301-443-3285.** (h) **202-363-4104**

HEALTH CARE FINANCING ADMINISTRATION. Rm 5032, Mary Switzer Bldg, 330 C St SW, Washington, DC 20201. **202-245-0381.** *Contact.* Patricia Schoeni, (h) **703-960-2078**

HEALTH RESOURCES ADMINISTRATION. Rm 1044, Center Bldg, 3700 East-West Hwy, Hyattsville, MD 20782. **301-436-8988.** *Contact.* Morton Lebow, (h) **301-588-2613**

NATIONAL CENTER ON CHILD ABUSE AND NEGLECT. PO Box 1182, Washington, DC 20017. **202-755-0590.** Joseph Wechsler, acting chief, Clearinghouse Branch. *See also* FEDERAL AGENCY REGIONAL OFFICES for a list of specialists on child abuse throught the country.

NATIONAL INSTITUTE ON DRUG ABUSE. 11400 Rockville Pike, Rockville, MD 20852. **301-443-6245.** Robert L Du Pont, director. *Press contact.* Mary Carol Kelly. **301-443-6245.** Night line. **301-656-1933**

NATIONAL INSTITUTE OF EDUCATION. Rm 719, Brown Bldg, 1200 19th St NW, Washington, DC 20208. **202-254-5800.** *Contact.* Tim McCarthy, (h) **703-354-5856**

NATIONAL INSTITUTES OF HEALTH. Rm 309, Bldg 1, Bethesda, MD 20014. **301-496-4461.** *Contact.* Storm Whaley, (h) **301-652-2989**

SOCIAL SECURITY ADMINISTRATION. Rm 944, Altmeyer Bldg, 6401 Security Blvd, Baltimore, MD 21235. **202-245-1272.** *Contact.* Michael Naver, press officer, (h) **301-747-8241**

FREEDOM OF INFORMATION OFFICE OF ASSISTANT SECRETARY FOR PUBLIC AFFAIRS. Lobby, 1st Floor, South Portal Bldg, 200 Independence Ave SW, Washington, DC 20201. **202-472-7453.** *Contact.* Russ Roberts, (h) **703-524-6451**

Subject Directory of Information Officers

HEALTH

Alcoholism. Alcohol, Drug Abuse, and Mental Health Administration. Harry Bell. **301-444-3306**

Cancer. National Institutes of Health. Paul Van Nevel. **301-496-6641**

Child Mental Health. Alcohol, Drug Abuse, and Mental Health Administration. Ed Long. **301-443-3600**

Coal Mine Safety. Center for Disease Control. Jack Hardesty. **301-443-2140**

Cosmetics. Food and Drug Administration. Emil Corwin. **202-245-1144**

Cost Containment. Health Care Financing Administration. Patricia Schoeni. **202-245-0381**

Crime and Delinquency Studies. Alcohol, Drug Abuse, and Mental Health Administration. Ed Long. **301-443-3600**

Disease Control. Center for Disease Control. Don Berreth. **404-633-3311**, Ext 3286

Drug Abuse. Alcohol, Drug Abuse, and Mental Health Administration. Mary Carol Kelly. **301-443-6245**

Drugs and Drug Labeling. Food and Drug Administration. Edward Nida. **301-443-3285**

Emergency Medical Services. Health Services Administration. Bernie Moore. **301-443-2065**

Epidemic Aid/Disease Outbreaks. Center for Disease Control. Don Berreth. **404-633-3311**, Ext 3286

Early Periodic Screening, Diagnosis, and Treatment (EPSDT). Health Care Financing Administration. Frances Kaplan and John Kittrell. **202-245-0347**

Family Planning. Health Services Administration. Ina Heyman. **301-443-2097**

Food Additives. Food and Drug Administration. Emil Corwin. **202-245-1144**

Health Facilities. Health Resources Administration. Frances Dearman. **301-436-6110**

Health Maintenance Organizations. Health Services Administration. Irv Weinstein. **301-443-2096**

Health Manpower. Health Resources Administration. Frank Sis. **301-436-6448**

Health Planning. Health Resources Administration. Frances Dearman. **301-436-6110**

Health Service Areas. Health Resources Administration. Frances Dearman. **301-436-6110**

Health Services Research. Health Resources Administration. Adrian W. Sybor. **301-443-5440**

Health Statistics. Health Resources Administration. Alice Haywood. **301-436-7019**

Health Surveys. Health Resources Administration. Alice Haywood. **301-436-7019**

Immunization Practices. Center for Disease Control. Don Berreth, **404-633-3311**, Ext

3286. Office of Assistant Secretary for Health. Shirley Barth. **202-472-5663**

Indian Health. Health Services Administration. Robert Isquith and Otto McClarrin. **301-443-2065** and **2096**

International Health Activities. Office of Assistant Secretary for Health. Shirley Barth. **202-472-5663**

Intrauterine Devices (IUDs). Food and Drug Administration. Michael Shaffer. **301-443-3434**

Lead-Based Paint Poisoning. Center for Disease Control. Don Berreth. **404-633-3311, Ext 3286**

Long-Term Care and Alternatives. Health Care Financing Administration. Frances Kaplan and John Kittrell. **202-245-0347**

Maternal and Child Health. Health Services Administration. Ina Heyman. **301-443-2097**

Medicaid. Health Care Financing Administration. Frances Kaplan. **202-245-0347**

Medical Devices. Food and Drug Administration. Michael Shaffer. **301-443-3434**

Medicare. Health Care Financing Administration. Frances Kaplan and John Kittrell. **202-245-0347**

Mental Health. Alcohol, Drug Abuse, and Mental Health Administration. Ed Long. **301-443-3600**

Microwave Ovens. Food and Drug Administration. Michael Shaffer. **301-443-3434**

Minority Mental Health Concerns. Alcohol, Drug Abuse, and Mental Health Administration. Ed Long. **301-443-3600**

Migrant Health. Health Services Administration. Ina Heyman. **301-443-2097**

National Cancer Institute. National Institutes of Health. Paul Van Nevel. **301-496-6641**

National Eye Institute. National Institutes of Health. Julian Morris. **301-496-5248**

National Health Service Corps. Health Services Administration. George Bragaw. **301-443-2065**

National Heart, Lung, and Blood Institute. National Institutes of Health. York Onnen. **301-496-4236**

National Library of Medicine. National Institutes of Health. Robert Mehnert. **301-496-6308**

National Institute of Allergy and Infectious Diseases. National Institutes of Health. Bob Schreiber. **301-496-5717**

National Institute on Aging. National Institutes of Health. Jane Shure. **301-496-5597**

National Institute on Alcohol Abuse and Alcoholism. Alcohol, Drug Abuse, and Mental Health Administration. Harry Bell. **301-443-3306**

National Institute of Arthritis, Metabolism, and Digestive Diseases. National Institutes of Health. Victor Wartofsky. **301-496-3583**

National Institute of Child Health and Human Development. National Institutes of Health. Marc Stern. **301-596-5133**

National Institute of Dental Research. National Institutes of Health. Shelbia Lengel. **301-596-4261**

National Institute on Drug Abuse. Alcohol, Drug, and Mental Health Administration. Mary Carol Kelly. **301-443-6245**

National Institute of Environmental Health Sciences. National Institutes of Health. Elizabeth James. **919-541-3345**

National Institute of General Medical Sciences. National Institutes of Health. Paul Deming. **301-496-7301**

National Institute of Mental Health. Alcohol, Drug Abuse, and Mental Health Administration. Ed Long. **301-443-3600**

National Institute of Neurological and Communicative Disorders and Stroke. National Institutes of Health. Bob Hinkel. **301-496-5751**

Neighborhood Health Centers. Health Services Administration. Ina Heyman. **301-443-2097**

Nursing Homes. Health Care Financing Administration. Patricia Schoeni. **202-245-0381**

Occupational Safety and Health. Center for Disease Control. Jack Hardesty. **301-443-2140**

Pacemakers. Food and Drug Administration. Michael Shaffer. **301-443-3434**

Professional Standards Review. Health Care Financing Administration. Patricia Schoeni and Frances Kaplan. **202-245-0381** and **0347**

Public Health Service. Office of the Assistant Secretary for Health. Shirley Barth. **202-472-5663**

Public Health Service Hospitals and Clinics. Health Services Administration. Pierce Rollins. **301-443-2096**

Quackery. Food and Drug Administration. Wallace Janssen. **301-443-3934**

Rape Studies. Alcohol, Drug Abuse, and Mental Health Administration. Ed Long. **301-443-3600**

Rat Control. Center for Disease Control. Don Berreth. **404-633-3311, Ext 3286**

Regional Medical Programs. Health Re-

sources Administration. Frances Dearman. **301-436-6110**

Rural Health and Appalachian Program. Health Services Administration. George Bragaw. **301-443-2065**

Smoking and Health. Center for Disease Control. Don Berreth. **404-633-3311, Ext 3286**

Television Radiation and X-Rays. Food and Drug Administration. Michael Shaffer. **301-443-3434**

Television Violence. Alcohol, Drug Abuse, and Mental Health Administration. Ed Long. **301-443-3600**

Vaccines. Food and Drug Administration. Edward R Nida. **301-443-3285**

Vitamins and Minerals. Food and Drug Administration. Emil Corwin. **202-245-1144**

EDUCATION

Adult Education. Office of Education. Edith Roth. **202-472-2890**

Alternative Schools. National Institute of Education. Tim McCarthy. **202-755-8811**

Arts and Humanities. Office of Education. Edith Roth. **202-472-2890**

Asian American Affairs. Office of Education. Myron Becker. **202-245-8589**

Audits. Office of Education. Lou Zekiel. **202-245-7923**

Basic Grants (BEOGS). Office of Education. Jeanne Park. **202-245-7915**

Bilingual Education. Office of Education. Jane Glickman. **202-245-8207**

Black American Concerns. Office of Education. Allen Alexander. **202-245-8787**

Black Colleges. Office of Education. Rita Bobowski. **202-245-8487**

Career Education. Office of Education. Jane Glickman. **202-245-8207.** National Institute of Education. Tim McCarthy. **202-254-5800**

Community Education. Office of Education. Jane Glickman. **202-245-8207**

Compensatory Education. Office of Education. Jeanne Park. **202-245-7915**

Comprehensive Employment and Training Act (CETA). Office of Education. Jane Glickman. **202-245-8207**

Consumer Education. Office of Education. Ken Coggeshall. **202-245-7115**

Contracts and Grants. Office of Education. Beverley Blondell. **202-245-8907**

Cooperative Education. Office of Education. Rita Bobowski. **202-245-8487**

Desegregation Programs. Office of Education. Dick Elwell. **202-245-8207**

Developing Institutions. Office of Education. Rita Bobowski. **202-245-8487**

Disadvantaged Persons (Postsecondary). Office of Education. Skee Smith. 202-245-7949

Dropout Prevention. Office of Education. Charlotte Hoffman. 202-245-3381

Drug Education. Office of Education. Charlotte Hoffman. 202-245-3381

Educational Opportunity Centers. Office of Education. Skee Smith. 202-245-7949

Education and Work. National Institute of Education. Tim McCarthy. 202-254-5800

Education Equity. National Institute of Education. Tim McCarthy. 202-254-5800

Education Research and Development. National Institute of Education. Tim McCarthy. 202-254-5800

Education Research Information. National Institute of Education. Tim McCarthy. 202-254-5800

Education Technology. Office of Education. Jane Glickman. 202-245-8207. National Institute of Education. Tim McCarthy. 202-254-5800

Education Testing, Test Bias, and Test Scores. National Institute of Education. Tim McCarthy. 202-254-5800

Elementary and Secondary Education. Office of Education. Jeanne Park. 202-245-7915

Energy. Office of Education. Marie Robinson. 202-245-8557

Environmental Education. Office of Education. Rita Bobowski. 202-245-8487

Emergency School Assistance Act Television Grants. Office of Education. Dick Elwell. 202-245-8207

Ethnic Heritage. Office of Education. Wilma Bailey. 202-245-7964

Federal Interagency Committee on Education (FICE). Office of the Assistant Secretary for Education. Mary Hallisy. 202-245-8248

Financing of Schools. Office of Education. Nyron Becker. 202-245-8589

Follow-Through. Office of Education. Rita Bobowski. 202-245-8487

Fund for the Improvement of Postsecondary Education (FIPSE). Office of the Assistant Secretary for Education. Mary Hallisy. 202-245-8248

Gifted and Talented. Office of Education. Edith Roth. 202-472-2890

Graduate Training. Office of Education. Rita Bobowski. 202-245-8487

Guaranteed Student Loans. Office of Education. Skee Smith. 202-245-7949

Handicapped, Education for the. Office of Education. Jane Hoyt. 202-245-7060

Health and Nutrition. Office of Education. Charlotte Hoffman. 202-245-3381

Higher and Continuing Education. Office of Education. Skee Smith. 202-245-7949

Indian Education. Office of Education. Story Moorefield. 202-245-8787

Institutional Eligibility. Office of Education. Skee Smith. 202-245-7949

International Studies. Office of Education. Wilma Bailey. 202-245-7964

Libraries. Office of Education. Wilma Bailey. 202-245-7964

Metric Education. Office of Education. Beverly Blondell. 202-245-8907

Migrant Education. Office of Education. Norman Greenberg. 202-245-8575

National Direct Student Loan (NDSL). Office of Education. Skee Smith. 202-245-7949

Nonpublic Schools. Office of Education. Wilma Bailey. 202-245-7964

Occupational and Adult Education. Office of Education. Edith Roth. 202-472-2890

Parenthood Education. Office of Education. Allen Alexander. 202-245-8787

Presidential Scholars. Office of Education. Edith Roth. 202-472-2890

Reading and Math Comprehension. National Institute of Education. Tim McCarthy. 202-254-5800

Right to Read. Office of Education. Marie Robinson. 202-245-8557

School Finance. National Institute of Education. Tim McCarthy. 202-254-5800

Sex Education. Office of Education. Charlotte Hoffman. 202-245-3381

Spanish-Speaking Affairs. Office of Education. Allen Alexander. 202-245-8787

State Student Incentive Grants (SSIG). Office of Education. Skee Smith. 202-245-7949

Statistics, Education. Office of Education. Vance Grant. 202-245-8511

Student Financial Assistance. Office of Education. Skee Smith. 202-245-7949

Talent Search. Office of Education. Skee Smith. 202-245-7949

Teenage Parents. Office of Education. Allen Alexander. 202-245-8787

Teacher Corps. Office of Education. Dick Elwell. 202-245-8207

Teacher Training. Office of Education. Charlotte Hoffman. 202-245-3381

Teaching and Learning Skills. National Institute of Education. Tim McCarthy. 202-254-5800

Technical Education. Office of Education. Beverly Blondell. 202-245-8907

Trio Programs. Office of Education. Skee Smith. 202-245-7949

Upward Bound. Office of Education. Skee Smith. 202-245-7949

Veterans' Education. Office of Education. Myron Becker. 202-245-8589

Vietnam Refugees. Office of Education. Myron Becker. 202-245-8589

Vocational Education. Office of Education. Beverly Blondell. 202-245-8907

Women's Issues. Office of Education. Charlotte Hoffman. 202-245-3381

HUMAN DEVELOPMENT

Architectural Barriers. Architectural and Transportation Barriers Compliance Board. Larry Allison. 202-245-1591

Area Agencies on Aging. Administration on Aging. Don Smith. 202-245-0188

Child Abuse and Neglect. Office of Child Development. Hal Eidlin. 202-755-7724

Child Day Care Services. Office of Child Development. Hal Eidlin. 202-755-7724

Child Development Associate Program. Office of Child Development. Hal Eidlin. 202-755-7724

Child Welfare Services. Public Services Administration. Kay Davison. 202-245-0197

Children and Family Resource Program. Office of Child Development. Hal Eidlin. 202-755-7724

Community-Based Services. Public Services Administration. Kay Davison. 202-245-0197

Day Care. Public Services Administration. Kay Davison. 202-245-0197

Developmental Continuity Program. Office of Child Development. Hal Eidlin. 202-755-7724

Developmental Disabilities. Developmental Disabilities Office. Tom Brubeck. 202-245-3379

Education for Parenthood. Office of Child Development. Hal Eidlin. 202-755-7724

Family Planning Services. Public Services Administration. Kay Davison. 202-245-0197

Foster Care and Adoption. Office of Child Development. Hal Eidlin. 202-755-7724

Foster Home Services. Public Services Administration. Kay Davison. 202-245-0197

Half-Way Houses. Public Services Administration. Kay Davison. 202-245-0197

Handicapped Individuals. Office of Handicapped Individuals. Ned Burman. 202-245-6646

Head Start. Office of Child Development. Hal Eidlin. 202-755-7724

Homemaker Services Information and Referral. Public Services Administration. Kay Davison. 202-245-0197

Home Start. Office of Child Development. Hal Eidlin. 202-755-7724

Mental Retardation. President's Committee on Mental Retardation. Marty Bouhan. **202-245-9563**

National Center for Deaf-Blind Youths and Adults. Rehabilitation Services Administration. Dave Touch. **202-245-3477**

National Center on Child Abuse and Neglect. Office of Child Development. Hal Eidlin. **202-755-7724**

Native American Affairs. Office of Native American Programs. Jerry Nordquist. **202-245-2790**

Nutrition for the Elderly. Administration on Aging. Don Smith. **202-245-0188**

Protective Services. Public Services Administration. Kay Davison. **202-245-0197**

Rehabilitation Facilities. Rehabilitation Services Administration. Dave Touch. **202-245-3477**

Rehabilitation Services for Severely Handicapped Individuals. Rehabilitation Services Administration. Dave Touch. **202-245-3477**

Rehabilitation Training. Rehabilitation Services Administration. Dave Touch. **202-245-3477**

Runaway Youth. Office of Youth Development. Jerry Nordquist. **202-245-2790**

Rural Development. Office of Human Development Services. Jerry Nordquist. **202-245-2790**

Social Services. Public Services Administration. Kay Davison. **202-245-0197**

Special Projects and Demonstrations. Rehabilitation Services Administration. Dave Touch. **202-245-3477**

Teenage Counseling. Public Services Administration. Kay Davison. **202-245-0197**

Title XX. Public Services Administration. Kay Davison. **202-245-0197**

Veterans' Program. Office of Human Development Services. Jerry Nordquist. **202-245-2790**

Vocational Rehabilitation Programs. Rehabilitation Services Administration. Dave Touch. **202-245-3477**

Vocational Rehabilitation Social Security Programs. Rehabilitation Services Administration. Dave Touch. **202-245-3477**

Volunteer Program. Office of Human Development Services. Jerry Nordquist. **202-245-2790**

Work Incentive (WIN) Program. Merwin Hans. **202-376-6694**

Youth Participation. Office of Youth Development. Jerry Nordquist. **202-245-2790**

CONSUMER AFFAIRS

Consumer Affairs. Office of Consumer Affairs. Howard Seltzer. **202-755-8810**

Consumer News—**Newsletter.** Office of Consumer Affairs. Marion Ciaccio. **202-755-8830**

"Help"—Radio Series. Office of Consumer Affairs. Julie Dickinson. **202-755-8811**

SOCIAL SECURITY

Aid to Families with Dependent Children (AFDC); Black Lung; Child Support Enforcement; Disability Benefits; Hearings and Appeals; Refugee Program; Retirement Benefits; Supplemental Security Income (SSI); Survivor Benefits. Social Security Administration. Mike Naver. **202-245-1272**

CIVIL RIGHTS

Discrimination—Race, Color, National Origin, Sex, Religion; Physically and Mentally Handicapped; School Desegregation. Office for Civil Rights. Colleen O'Connor. **202-245-6671**

AUDITS, INVESTIGATIONS, AND REVIEWS

Audits; Antifraud, Antiabuse, and Antiwaste Projects; Investigations; Project Integrity; Reviews of Departmental Systems. Office of the Inspector General. Bob Wilson. **202-472-3153**

Department of Housing and Urban Development (HUD)

HUD Bldg, 451 7th St SW, Washington, DC 20410.
202-755-6417. Locator number: **202-724-8595** (records)

SECRETARY OF HUD. Patricia Roberts Harris. **202-755-6417**

UNDER SECRETARY OF HUD. Jay Janis. **202-755-7123**

EXECUTIVE SECRETARY TO THE SECRETARY. Catherine E Burton. **202-755-6417.** (h) 8801 Wandering Trail Dr, Potomac, MD 20854.

Office of Public Affairs

ASSISTANT TO THE SECRETARY FOR PUBLIC AFFAIRS. Arch Parsons. **202-755-6980** (h) 2301 Cathedral Ave, Washington, DC 20008. **202-483-5322**

DEPUTY ASSISTANT. 202-755-6980

ASSOCIATE DEPUTY, PLANS AND POLICIES. Bruce E McCarthy. **202-755-6685**

ASSOCIATE DEPUTY, HEADQUARTERS OPERATIONS. Gerald Huard. **202-755-6980**

ASSOCIATE DEPUTY, FIELD POLICIES AND INFORMATION SERVICES. Fred W Stuart. **202-755-6685**

DIVISIONAL DIRECTORS

Scheduling and Liaison Division **202-755-7398**

News Services Division. Donald Hall. **202-755-5284**

Audiovisual Division. Lawrence Beckerman. **202-755-6073**

Research and Production Division. Rick La Falce. **202-755-6687**

ADMINISTRATIVE OFFICER. Dorothy P Babcock. **202-755-6687**

Other Key Officials

GENERAL COUNSEL. 202-755-7244

ASSISTANT SECRETARY (COMMUNITY PLANNING AND DEVELOPMENT). 202-755-6270

ASSISTANT SECRETARY (HOUSING—FEDERAL HOUSING COMMISSIONER). 202-755-6600

ASSISTANT SECRETARY (FAIR HOUSING AND EQUAL OPPORTUNITY). 202-755-7252

ASSISTANT SECRETARY (ADMINISTRATION). 202-755-6940

PRESIDENT, GOVERNMENT NATIONAL MORTGAGE ASSOCIATION, 202-755-5926

Important HUD Agencies

FEDERAL DISASTER ASSISTANCE ADMINISTRATION. B-133 HUD Bldg, 451 7th St SW, Washington, DC 20410. **202-634-7800**

Administrator. Thomas P Dunne. **202-634-7820**

Director, Office of Preparedness. Jack McGraw. **202-634-7865**

Chief, Emergency Information Staff. Robert Blair. **202-634-6666.** (h) 1661 Strine Dr, McLean, VA 22101. **703-821-3237**

Assistant Director, Public Information. John P Coleman. **202-634-6666.** (h) **703-751-2975**

FEDERAL INSURANCE ADMINISTRA-TION

Administrator. John Robert Hunter, Jr (acting). **202-755-6770**

NEW COMMUNITIES ADMINISTRA-TION. 202-755-7920

Department of the Interior

Interior Bldg, C St between 18th and 19th Sts, Washington, DC 20240. **202-343-1100**

SECRETARY OF THE INTERIOR. Cecil D Andrus. **202-343-6412**

ASSISTANT SECRETARY (INDIAN AFFAIRS). Forrest Gerard. **202-343-5166**

DIRECTOR OF PUBLIC AFFAIRS. David C Carlson. **202-343-6412.** (h) 11913 Bayswater Rd, Gaithersburg, MD 20760. **301-869-6356**

OFFICE OF PUBLIC AFFAIRS. 202-343-6316 or **3171**

Information Officers. Edward P Essertier, Andrew L Newman, Gerald A Waindel, and Charles E Wallace

OFFICE OF TERRITORIAL AFFAIRS. Interior Bldg, Washington, DC 20240. **202-343-4736**

Interior Agencies

BUREAU OF MINES. 2401 E St, Washington, DC 20241. **202-634-1300**

Office of Mineral Information. Bob Swinerton, chief. **202-634-1001**

GEOLOGICAL SURVEY. 12201 Sunrise Valley Dr, Reston, VA 22092. **202-860-7000.**

Information Office. Frank Forrester. **703-860-7444**

MINING ENFORCEMENT AND SAFETY ADMINISTRATION. 4015 Wilson Blvd, Arlington, VA 22203. **703-235-1372.** Also National Mine Health and Safety Academy, PO Box 1166, Beckley, WV 25801. **304-255-0451**

Administrator. Robert E Barrett

Information Office. Dick Neillus. **703-235-1452**

ALASKA POWER ADMINISTRATION. PO Box 50, Juneau, AK 99802. **907-586-7405**

Administrator. Robert J Cross

BONNEVILLE POWER ADMINISTRA-

TION. PO Box 3621, Portland, OR 97208. **503-234-3361**

Administrator. Donald P Hodel

SOUTHEASTERN POWER ADMINISTRATION. Elberton, GA 30634. **404-283-3261**

Administrator. William Jan Fortune

SOUTHWESTERN POWER ADMINISTRATION. PO Drawer 1619, Tulsa, OK 74101. **918-581-7474**

NATIONAL PARK SERVICE. Interior Building, Washington, DC 20240. **202-343-8067**

Director. William J Whalen. **202-343-4621**

Office of Public Affairs. Tom Wilson, Rm 3043. **202-343-6843**

NATIONAL PARK FOUNDATION. Washington, DC 20240. **202-343-6578**

US FISH AND WILDLIFE SERVICE. Interior Bldg, Washington, DC 20240. **202-343-5634**

Director. Lynn Greenwalt

Office of Public Affairs. John Mattoon. **202-343-5634**

BUREAU OF OUTDOOR RECREATION. Interior South Bldg, Washington DC 20240. **202-343-1100**

Director. Chris Delaporte

Office of Communications. Rochelle Fashaw. **202-343-5726**

BUREAU OF RECLAMATION. Interior Bldg, Washington, DC 20240. **202-343-1100**

Commissioner. Keith Higginson,

Information Office. Jim Hart. **202-343-4662**

BUREAU OF LAND MANAGEMENT. Interior Bldg, Washington, DC 20240. **202-343-5101**

Office of Public Affairs. Don Alferri. **202-343-5717**

BUREAU OF INDIAN AFFAIRS. 1951 Constitution Ave NW, Washington, DC 20245. **202-343-2896**

Information Office. Lynn Engles, (Rm 4628, Interior Bldg, Washington, DC 20245). **202-343-7445**

Department of Justice

Main Justice Bldg, Constitution Ave between 9th and 10th Sts, Washington, DC 20530. Switchboard and locator: **202-737-8200**

ATTORNEY GENERAL. Griffin B Bell. **202-739-2001**

DEPUTY ATTORNEY GENERAL. Benjamin R Civiletti. **202-739-2101**

ASSOCIATE ATTORNEY GENERAL. Michael J Egan. **202-739-2107**

SOLICITOR GENERAL. Wade H McCree, Jr. **202-739-2201**

COUNSELOR TO THE ATTORNEY GENERAL. J Michael Kelly. **202-739-3892**

Offices of the Justice Department

OFFICE OF LEGAL COUNSEL. John M Harmon, acting assistant attorney general. **202-739-2041.** Robert L Saloschin, chairman, Freedom of Information Committee. **202-739-2674**

OFFICE OF LEGISLATIVE AFFAIRS. Patricia M Wald, assistant attorney general. **202-739-2141**

OFFICE FOR IMPROVEMENTS IN THE ADMINISTRATION OF JUSTICE. Daniel J Meador, assistant attorney general. **202-739-3824**

OFFICE OF PROFESSIONAL RESPON-SIBILITY. Michael E Shaheen, Jr, counsel. **202-739-5211**

OFFICE OF PRIVACY AND INFORMA-TION APPEALS. Quinlan J Shea, Jr, director. **202-739-4082**

Office of Public Information

DIRECTOR OF PUBLIC INFORMA-TION. Marvin Wall. **202-739-2014.** (h) 127 Grafton St, Chevy Chase, MD 20015. **202-652-6377**

DEPUTY DIRECTOR. Robert J Havel. **202-739-2028.** (h) 9408 Duxford Ct, Potomac, MD 20854. **301-299-6013**

ASSISTANT INFORMATION DIREC-TORS

John V Wilson, Jr. **202-739-2014.** (h) 907 Caddington Ave, Silver Spring, MD 20901. **301-593-3742**

Dean St Dennis. **202-739-2017.** (h) 4924 N 26th St, Arlington, VA 22209

Robert L Stevenson. **202-739-2014.** (h) 6605 Jerry Pl, McLean, VA 22101. **703-356-1949**

Mark T Sheehan. **202-739-2014.** (h) Apt 802S, 429 N St SW, Washington, DC 20024

SECURITY OFFICER. John K Russell. **202-739-2017.** (h) Apt B-1410, 1400 S Joyce St, Arlington, VA 22202. **703-979-1846**

Community Relations Service

Todd Bldg, 550 11th St, Washington, DC 20530

DIRECTOR. Benjamin F Holman. **202-739-4011**

PUBLIC INFORMATION OFFICER. Harvey L Brinson. **202-739-4077.** (h) 12818 Broadmore Rd, Silver Spring, MD 20904. **301-384-9672**

Antitrust Division

Todd Bldg, 550 11th St, Washington, DC 20530

ACTING ASSISTANT ATTORNEY GENERAL. John H Shenefield. **202-739-2401**

ACTING DEPUTY ASSISTANT ATTORNEY GENERAL. Hugh P Morrison, Jr. **202-739-2404**

DIRECTOR, OPERATIONS. William E Swope. **202-739-3543**

DIRECTOR, ECONOMIC POLICY OFFICE. George A Hay. **202-739-2466**

SECTION CHIEFS
Appellate Section. B Barry Grossman. **202-739-2413**
Consumer Affairs Section. Charles R McConachie (acting). **202-739-4173**
Evaluation Section. Neil E Roberts. **202-739-2512**
Foreign Commerce Section. Joel Davidow. **202-739-2464**
General Litigation Section. Gerald A Connell. **202-739-2441**
Public Counsel and Legislative Section. Joseph J Saunders. **202-739-2515**
Regulated Industries Section. Donald Flexner. 202-739-2950
Special Litigation Section. Mark P Leddy. **202-739-2425**
Special Trial Section. John W Clark (acting). **202-739-2471**
Administrative Officer. Frank V Battle. **202-739-2421**

Civil Division

Main Justice Bldg Washington, DC 20530. **202-739-2014**

ASSISTANT ATTORNEY GENERAL. Barbara Allen Babcock. **202-739-3301**

CHIEF, INFORMATION AND PRIVACY SECTION. Jeffrey Axelrad. **202-739-3300**

PRESS OFFICER: 202-739-2007

Civil Rights Division

Todd Bldg, 550 11th St, Washington, DC 20530. *Press.* **202-739-3847**

ASSISTANT ATTORNEY GENERAL. Drew S Days III. **202-739-2151**

DEPUTY ASSISTANT ATTORNEY GENERAL. James P Turner. **202-739-3828**

DEPUTY ASSISTANT ATTORNEY GENERAL. Frank M Dunbaugh. **202-739-3845**

EXECUTIVE OFFICER. Harry Fair. **202-739-3855** (h) 4143 Century Ct, Alexandria, VA 22315

SECTION CHIEFS
Appellate Section. Brian K Landsberg. **202-739-2195**
Criminal Section. William L Gardner. **202-739-4067**
Education Section. Alexander C Ross. **202-739-4092**
Employment Section. David L Rose. **202-739-3831**
Federal Programs Section. Stephen Koplan. **202-739-4734**
Housing Section. Frank E Schwelb. **202-739-4123**
Public Accommodations and Facilities Section. Jesse H Queen. **202-739-4701**
Voting Section. Gerald W Jones. **202-739-2167**

DIRECTOR, OFFICE OF INDIAN RIGHTS. James M Schermerhorn. **202-739-5296**

DIRECTOR, OFFICE OF SPECIAL LITIGATION. Louis M Thrasher. **202-739-5303**

Criminal Division

Main Justice Bldg, Washington, DC20530. **202-737-8200.** *Press.* **202-739-2641**

ASSISTANT ATTORNEY GENERAL. **202-739-2601**

DEPUTY ASSISTANT ATTORNEY GENERAL. John C Keeney. **202-739-2621**

DEPUTY ASSISTANT ATTORNEY GENERAL. Robert L Keuch. **202-739-2333**

DEPUTY ASSISTANT ATTORNEY GENERAL. Russell T Baker, Jr. **202-739-2636**

SPECIAL ASSISTANT. William Brady. **202-739-2825**

EXECUTIVE ASSISTANT. James W Muskett. **202-739-2641**

SECTION CHIEFS
Appellate Section. George Gilinsky. **202-739-2657**
Fraud Section. Mark Richard. **202-739-2648**
General Crimes Section. Alfred Hantman. **202-739-2624**
Government Regulations and Labor Section. Philip Wilens. **202-739-3761**
Internal Security Section. John H Davitt. **202-739-2307**
Legislation and Special Projects Section. Philip White. **202-739-2613**
Narcotic and Dangerous Drug Section. William Lynch. **202-739-3928**
Organized Crime and Racketeering Section. Kurt Muellenberg. **202-739-3516**
Public Integrity Section. Thomas Henderson. **202-739-2676**
Special Litigation Section. George Calhoun. **202-739-3885**

Other Justice Divisions and Boards

LAND AND NATURAL RESOURCES DIVISION. Peter R Taft, assistant attorney general. **202-739-2701**

TAX DIVISION. Myron C Baum, assistant attorney general. **202-739-2901**

EXECUTIVE OFFICE FOR US ATTORNEYS. William B Gray, director. **202-739-2121.** For a complete list of US attorneys, *see* REGIONAL GOVERNMENT OFFICES.

PARDON ATTORNEY. Lawrence M Traylor. **202-739-2894**

BOARD OF IMMIGRATION APPEALS. David L Milhollan, chairman. **202-739-4472**

BOARD OF PAROLE. Maurice H Sigler, chairman. **202-739-2871** or **202-724-3252**

Federal Bureau of Investigation

J Edgar Hoover Bldg, Washington, DC 20535. **202-324-3000.** *See* POLICE for a list of local FBI offices.

DIRECTOR. William Webster. **202-324-3444**

PUBLIC INFORMATION OFFICERS. Inspector Homer A Boynton, chief. **202-324-5352.** Tom Harrington, Tom Coll, and Mike Griffin. **202-324-3691**

ASSOCIATE DIRECTOR. Richard Held. **202-324-3315**

ASSISTANT TO THE DIRECTOR— DEPUTY ASSOCIATE DIRECTOR. John McDermott. **202-324-3333**

ASSISTANT TO THE DIRECTOR— DEPUTY ASSOCIATE DIRECTOR. James B Adams. **202-324-5555**

ASSISTANT DIRECTORS

Identification Division. 202-324-5401
Training Division. Kenneth E Joseph, FBI Academy. **202-324-2726**
Finance and Personnel Division. Richard E Lons. **202-324-3514**
Intelligence Division. Thomas Learitt. **202-324-4880**
Criminal Investigative Division. Donald W Moore. **202-324-4260**
Laboratory Division. Thomas F Kelleher, Jr. **202-324-4410**
Records Management Division. Andrew J Decker, Jr. **202-324-4840**
Special Investigative Division. Herb Monahan (acting). **202-324-5740**
Legal Counsel Division. John A Mintz. **202-324-5018**
Administrative Services Division. Harold Bassett. **202-324-3851**
Office of Planning and Inspection. Lee Colwell. **202-324-2901**

Other Justice Agencies

DRUG ENFORCEMENT ADMINISTRA-TION. 1405 I St, Washington, DC 20537. Locator number: **202-633-1289**
Administrator. Peter B Bensinger. **202-633-1337.** (h) 5936 N 1st St, Arlington, VA 22203
Public Information Officer. Con Dougherty. **202-633-1333.** (h) **301-933-6270**
Director, Office of Public Affairs. Robert H Feldkamp. **202-633-1249**

Acting Assistant Administrator, Office of Enforcement. Donald E Miller. **202-633-1329**
Director, Office of Science and Technology. John W Gunn, Jr. **202-633-1211**
Director, Office of Program Planning and Evaluation. Ed Barnett. **202-633-1132**
Assistant Administrator, Office of Intelli-gence. William G Fink. **202-633-1071**

LAW ENFORCEMENT ASSISTANCE ADMINISTRATION. Indiana Bldg, 633 Indiana Ave, Washington, DC 20530. **202-376-3701**
Administrator. Richard W Velda **202-376-3985.** (h) 2715 S Hayes St, Arling-ton, VA 22202
Public Information Officer. Malcolm Barr, **202-376-3820.** (h) 6023 Lowell Ave, Alexandria, VA 22312

BUREAU OF PRISONS. HOLC Bldg, 320 1st St, Washington, DC 20534. Locator number: **202-737-8200** or **202-655-4000.** All direct phones are 202-724 plus extension.
Director. Norman A Carlson. **202-724-3250** or **202-739-2226**
Public Information Officer. Mike Aun. **202-724-3198.** (h) **202-524-7026**

IMMIGRATION AND NATURALIZA-TION SERVICE. 425 I St, Washington, DC 20536. Locator number: **202-655-4000**
Commissioner. Leonel J Castillo. **202-376-8330.** (h) 2117 E St, Washington, DC
Associate Commissioners
Enforcement. Robert L Stewart. **202-376-8366**
Examinations. Carl J Wack, Jr. **202-376-8363**
Management. Stanley E McKinley. **202-376-8401**
Assistant Commissioners
Adjudications. Solomon Isenstein. **202-376-8425**
Administration. Robert A Kane. **202-376-8421**
Border Patrol. Robin J Clack. **202-376-8380**
Detention and Deportation. William P O'Brien. **202-376-8467**
Information Services. Thomas R Hunt. **202-376-8291**
Inspections. Thomas J Brobson. **202-376-8305**
Investigations. Glenn T Bertness. **202-376-8367**
Naturalization. Andrew Carmichael. **202-376-8455**
Public Information Officer. Vern Jervis. **202-376-8353.** (h) 4119 Holden St, Fairfax, VA 22030. **703-978-4365**

US MARSHALS SERVICE. Safeway Bldg, 521 12th St, Washington, DC 20001. **202-739-2175.** Locator number: **202-655-4000**
Director. William E Hall. **202-739-5345.** (h) 9709 Breckenridge Pl, Gaithersburg, MD 20760
Public Information Officer. Bill Dempsey. **202-739-4183**
Security Officers. William B Waser and Thomas G Milburn. **202-739-2173**

Department of Labor

3rd St, and Constitution Ave NW, Washing-ton, DC 20210. Locator number: **202-523-6666**

SECRETARY OF LABOR. Ray Marshall. **202-523-8271**

APPOINTMENT SECRETARY. Sharon Shay. **202-523-8271**

EXECUTIVE ASSISTANT. Paul Jensen. **202-523-8231**

UNDER SECRETARY OF LABOR. Robert J Brown. **202-523-6151**

Office of Information, Publications, and Reports

DIRECTOR. John W Leslie. **202-523-9711**

ASSISTANT DIRECTOR. Dorothy J Dunkle. **202-523-7343**

DIVISION OF FIELD SERVICES 202-523-7334

DIVISION OF MEDIA AND EDITORIAL SERVICES. Donald S Smyth. **202-523-7316**

PRESS INFORMATION. Beverly Madden. **202-523-7316**

FORUM. 202-523-7323

PHOTOGRAPHIC SERVICES. Harrison Allen. **202-523-9380**

DIVISION OF GRAPHIC SERVICES. Donald Berry, Lionel White, and Richard Mathews. **202-523-7910**

HISTORIAN. Jonathan Grossman. **202-523-6461**

DEPARTMENT PROGRAM INFORMA-TION OFFICERS
Labor-Management Relations. Tom Cosgrove. **202-523-7408**

Employee Benefits and Security. William C Russell (acting). **202-523-8813**

International Labor Affairs. Mac Shields. **202-523-6259**

Employment Standards. Robert Cuccia. **202-523-8743**

Employment and Training Programs. Larry Moen. **202-376-6270**

Occupational Safety and Health. James Foster. **202-523-8148**

Labor Statistics. Henry Lowenstern. **202-523-1327**

PRESS ROOM
Associated Press. **202-523-6238**
United Press International. **202-393-3430**

Other Personnel, Offices, and Programs

DEPUTY UNDER SECRETARY FOR INTERNATIONAL AFFAIRS. Howard Samuel. **202-523-6043**

ASSISTANT SECRETARY (EMPLOYMENT STANDARDS). Donald E Elisburg. **202-523-6191**

ASSISTANT SECRETARY (LABOR-MANAGEMENT RELATIONS). Francis X Burkhardt. **202-523-6045**

ASSISTANT SECRETARY (OCCUPATIONAL SAFETY AND HEALTH ADMINISTRATION). Eula Bingham. **202-523-9361**

OFFICE OF EQUAL EMPLOYMENT OPPORTUNITY. Velma M Strode, director. **202-523-6996**

NATIONAL EQUAL ECONOMIC OPPORTUNITY OFFICER (AFFIRMATIVE ACTION). Robert Neyhart. **202-523-7001**

NATIONAL HISPANIC PROGRAM. Babil Arrieta, coordinator. **202-523-7009**

NATIONAL FEDERAL WOMEN'S PROGRAM. Ruth W Britt, coordinator. **202-523-7026**

BUREAU OF LABOR STATISTICS. Julius Shiskin, commissioner. **202-523-1102**

WOMEN'S BUREAU. Alexis M Herman, director. **202-523-6611**

OFFICE OF FEDERAL CONTRACT COMPLIANCE PROGRAMS. Weldon Rougeau, director. **202-523-9475**

OFFICE OF WORKERS' COMPENSATION PROGRAMS. Everett P Sennings, director. **202-523-7501**

WAGE AND HOUR DIVISION. Xavier Vela, administrator. **202-523-8305**

UNITED STATES EMPLOYMENT SERVICE. William B Lewis, administrator. **202-376-6289**

THE PRESIDENT'S COMMITTEE ON EMPLOYMENT OF THE HANDICAPPED. Harold Russell, chairman. **202-653-5044**

Department of State

2201 C St NW, Washington, DC 20520. Listed number: **202-655-4000**. Locator number: **202-632-9885**. Personal locator: **202-632-3686**. Retirement Division: **202-632-3342** (to reach a former State Department official)

For a list of US ambassadors and consuls abroad, *see* WORLD.

SECRETARY OF STATE. Cyrus Roberts Vance. **202-632-9630**

EXECUTIVE SECRETARY. Peter Tarnoff. **202-632-2540.** (h) 201 Niblick Dr SE, Vienna, VA 22180. **703-938-1492**

DEPUTY SECRETARY. Warren M Christopher. **202-632-9640**

UNDER SECRETARY FOR POLITICAL AFFAIRS. Philip C Habib. **202-632-2471**

UNDER SECRETARY FOR ECONOMIC AFFAIRS. Richard N Cooper. **202-632-3256**

UNDER SECRETARY FOR SECURITY ASSISTANCE, SCIENCE, AND TECHNOLOGY. Lucy Wilson Benson. **202-632-0410**

DEPUTY UNDER SECRETARY FOR MANAGEMENT. Benjamin H Reed. **202-632-1500**

INSPECTOR GENERAL, FOREIGN SERVICE. Robert M Sayre. **202-632-3320**

CONGRESSIONAL RELATIONS. Assistant Secretary Douglas J Bennet, Jr. **202-632-3436**

DIRECTOR, BUREAU OF POLITICO-MILITARY AFFAIRS. Leslie H Gelb. **202-632-9022**

AMBASSADOR-AT-LARGE. Ellsworth Bunker. **202-632-3232**

AMBASSADOR-AT-LARGE. Elliot L Richardson. **202-632-3131**

CHIEF OF PROTOCOL. Evan S Dobelle. **202-632-0866**

Office of Press Relations

SPECIAL ASSISTANT TO THE SECRETARY FOR PRESS RELATIONS AND SPOKESMAN OF THE DEPARTMENT. Hodding Carter III. **202-632-9590**

DIRECTOR, OFFICE OF PRESS RELATIONS. John H Trattner. **202-632-2492**

DEPUTY DIRECTOR. Kenneth L Brown. **202-632-2492**

STAFF ASSISTANT. John Medeiros. **202-632-9590**

Bureau of Public Affairs

ASSISTANT SECRETARY. Hodding Carter III. **202-632-9606**

DEPUTY ASSISTANT SECRETARY. William D Blair Jr. **202-632-0954**

DEPUTY ASSISTANT SECRETARY. William J Dyess. **202-632-1620** (h) 4444 Dexter St, Washington, DC 20007, **202-338-1222**

OFFICE OF PLANS AND MANAGEMENT. Charles W Freeman Jr, director. **202-632-0472**

Deputy Director (Information Systems). Phillip J Metzler. **202-632-2257**

Deputy Director (Plans). Lars H Hydle. **202-632-2376**

Public Opinion Analysis. Bernard Roshco. **202-632-0474**

Speech Review. Edward F Roeder. **202-632-0782**

Budget. Eleanor G Jacobson. **202-632-2174**

Personnel. Frances W Taylor. **202-632-2685**

FREEDOM OF INFORMATION STAFF. Barbara Ennis, director. **202-632-0772**

Freedom of Information Officer. Gerard O Forcier. **202-632-2556**

OFFICE OF THE HISTORIAN. David F Trask, historian. **202-632-1931** or **1937**

OFFICE OF MEDIA SERVICES. Paul E Auerswald, director. **202-632-3656** or **2083**

Editorial Division Chief. Carlton Brower. **202-632-2159 or 1143**

Media Liaison Division Chief. Edward F Roeder. **202-632-8203**

Public Correspondence Division Chief. Susan Haufe. **202-632-0776 or 1394**

OFFICE OF PUBLIC PROGRAMS. James M Montgomery, director. **202-632-1433**

National Capital Division Chief. Ilmar Heinaru. **202-632-1710**

Southern Division Chief. Kenneth Longmyer. **202-632-2234**

Northern Division Chief. Gene R Preston. **202-632-2234**

Western Division Chief. Joan H Colbert. **202-632-2133**

Other Key Bureaus and Offices

BUREAU OF AFRICAN AFFAIRS

Assistant Secretary. William E Schaufele, Jr. **202-632-2530**

Public Affairs Adviser. Robert W Holliday. **202-632-2683**

BUREAU OF EAST ASIAN AND PACIFIC AFFAIRS

Assistant Secretary. Richard Holbrooke. **202-632-9596**

Public Affairs Adviser. John F Cannon. **202-632-2538**

BUREAU OF EUROPEAN AFFAIRS

Assistant Secretary. George S Vest. **202-632-9626**

Public Affairs Adviser. Francis J Seidner. **202-632-0850**

BUREAU OF INTER-AMERICAN AFFAIRS (STATE); BUREAU FOR LATIN AMERICAN (AID)

Assistant Secretary and US Coordinator, Alliance for Progress. Terence A Todman. **202-632-9210**

US Permanent Representative, Permanent Mission of the US of America to the Organization of American States (USOAS). Gale W McGee. **202-632-9376**

BUREAU OF NEAR EASTERN AND SOUTH ASIAN AFFAIRS

Assistant Secretary. Alfred L Atherton, Jr. **202-632-9588**

Public Affairs Adviser. George F Sherman, Jr. **202-632-0448**

BUREAU OF CONSULAR AFFAIRS

Assistant Secretary. Barbara M Watson. **202-632-9576**

BUREAU OF ECONOMIC AND BUSINESS AFFAIRS

Assistant Secretary. Julius L Katz. **202-632-0396**

Special Assistant for Legislative Matters and Public Affairs. Alexander F Watson. **202-632-9310 or 1733**

BUREAU OF INTELLIGENCE AND RESEARCH

Harold H Saunders, director. **202-632-0342**

BUREAU OF INTERNATIONAL ORGANIZATION AFFAIRS

Assistant Secretary. C William Maynes. **202-632-9600**

Public Affairs Adviser. Frederick Blachly. **202-632-0462**

BUREAU OF OCEANS AND INTERNATIONAL ENVIRONMENTAL AND SCIENTIFIC AFFAIRS

Assistant Secretary. Patsy T Mink. **202-632-1554**

LEGAL ADVISER. Herbert J Hansell. **202-632-9598**

PASSPORT OFFICE. Loren Lawrence, director. **202-532-4412**

VISA OFFICE. Julio J Arias, director. **202-632-1978**

Agency for International Development (AID)

320 21st St NW, Washington, DC 20523. Locator number: **202-655-4000**

ADMINISTRATOR. John J Gilligan. **202-632-9620**

DEPUTY ADMINISTRATOR. Robert H Nooter. **202-632-8578**

Office of Public Affairs

DIRECTOR. John W McCulla. **202-632-8628.** (h) **703-821-2236**

DEPUTY DIRECTOR. Christine Camp. **202-632-8632**

DEPUTY DIRECTOR. Griff Ellison. **202-632-8632**

PUBLIC ACTIVITIES AND SERVICES DIVISION. Jim Dunn, chief. **202-632-0674**

Freedom of Information/Congressional and Public Inquiries. Arnold H Dadian. **202-632-1850**

Speakers' Program. Wade Fleetwood. **202-632-3755**

Radio and Television. Michael Marlow. **202-632-8636**

Photo, Film, and Audiovisual. Carl Purcell. **202-632-8194**

PRESS AND PUBLICATIONS DIVISION. Ed Caplan, chief. **202-632-8332**

Senior Press Officer. Gale D Wallace. **202-632-8332**

Press Officer. John Metelsky. **202-632-8332**

Press Officer. Emmett George. **202-632-8332**

Press Officer. Betty Snead. **202-632-8332**

Editor, *Front Lines.* Alexanderina Shuler. **202-632-7978**

US Arms Control and Disarmament Agency

See THE INDEPENDENT AGENCIES.

Department of Transportation

400 7th St SW, Washington, DC 20590. **202-427-4000**

SECRETARY OF TRANSPORTATION. Brock Adams. **202-426-1111**

CONFIDENTIAL SECRETARY. Brenda C Campbell. **202-426-1111**

SPECIAL ASSISTANT. Woodruff M Price. **202-426-4591**

Other Offices and Staffs

DEPUTY SECRETARY. Alan A Butchman. **202-426-2222**

DEPUTY UNDER SECRETARY. Mortimer L Downey. **202-426-9191**

EXECUTIVE SECRETARY. Linda L Smith. **202-426-4277**

Office of Public Affairs

DIRECTOR. David A Jewell. **202-426-4570.** (h) 6122 Breezewood Dr, Greenbelt, MD. **301-474-8361**

DEPUTY DIRECTOR. Bob Holland. **202-426-0434**

ASSISTANT DIRECTOR FOR PUBLIC INFORMATION. Frances Levine. **202-426-4531**

PUBLICATIONS DIVISION. Edward A O'Hara. **202-426-1276**

Visitor/Information Center. Christine D Ware. **202-426-2144**

ASSISTANT DIRECTOR FOR COMMUNICATIONS COORDINATION. Frances L Lewine. **202-426-0434**

SPEECH DIVISION. John D Demeter. **202-426-4321**

Regional Coordinator. Robert M Beasley. **202-426-0398**

Intermodal Coordinator. Lucille R Wendt. **202-426-0434**

ASSISTANT DIRECTOR FOR PUBLIC INFORMATION. Robert S Marx. **202-426-2147**

NEWS DIVISION. William W Bishop. **202-426-4321**

AUDIOVISUAL SERVICES DIVISION. Donald G Marion. **202-426-4333**

BROADCAST SERVICES DIVISION. Patricia J Weber. **202-426-4333**

OFFICE OF THE ASSISTANT SECRETARY FOR ENVIRONMENT, SAFETY, AND CONSUMER AFFAIRS. Martin Convisser, assistant secretary (acting). **202-426-4474**

OFFICE OF THE ASSISTANT SECRETARY FOR POLICY, PLANS, AND INTERNATIONAL AFFAIRS. Chester C Davenport, assistant secretary. **202-426-4544**

OFFICE OF DEEPWATER PORTS

Director. Lonell Johnson (acting). **202-426-4144**

General Counsel. Linda H Kamm. **202-426-4702**

OFFICE OF TRANSPORTATION SYSTEMS ANALYSIS AND INFORMATION. Ira Dye, director. **202-426-4220**

OFFICE OF TRANSPORTATION PLANNING. Arthur L Webster, director. **202-426-4331**

OFFICE OF TRANSPORTATION ECONOMIC ANALYSIS. Richard F Walsh, director. **202-426-4416**

OFFICE OF INTERNATIONAL TRANSPORTATION PROGRAMS. Ray W Bronez, director. **202-426-4368**

OFFICE OF TRANSPORTATION REGULATORY POLICY. Gary M Broemser, director. **202-426-4411**

OFFICE OF EMERGENCY TRANSPORTATION. Clarence G Collins, director (acting). **202-426-4262**

TRANSPORTATION ENERGY POLICY STAFF. Donald J Igo, director. **202-426-0783**

AIR TRANSPORTATION POLICY STAFF. John B Flynn, director. **202-426-4428**

TRANSPORTATION SYSTEMS CENTER. Kendall Sq, Cambridge, MA 02142. Information and after hours. **617-837-2000**

Director. James Constantino. **617-837-2222**

Public Information Officer. Frances J Donoghue. **617-837-2227**

US Coast Guard

400 7th St SW, Washington, DC 20590. **202-426-2158.** Night line (Coast Guard duty officer). **202-426-1830**

COMMANDANT. Admiral Owen W Siler. **202-426-2390**

MARINE SAFETY COUNCIL CHAIRMAN. Rear Admiral G H Patrick Bursley. **202-426-1616**

CHIEF OF STAFF. Rear Admiral R H Scarborough. **202-426-1642**

Office of Public and International Affairs

CHIEF OF PUBLIC AND INTERNATIONAL AFFAIRS. Rear Admiral R H Wood. **202-426-2267**

DEPUTY CHIEF. Captain E L Cope. **202-426-2267**

PUBLIC AFFAIRS DIVISION. Captain R E Larson, chief. **202-426-1587**

Assistant Chief. Commander J C Goldthorpe. **202-426-1587**

Coast Guard Daily News Brief. 202-426-1587

Audiovisual Branch. Chief Warrant Officer J Greco, Jr. **202-426-1855**

Assistant. Keith Tasker. **202-426-1855**

Still Photo Editor. Betty Segedi. **202-755-7792**

Media Relations Branch. Chief Leo Loftus. **202-426-1587**

National Spot News Center. 202-755-9082

Community Relations Branch. Chief James Ward. **202-426-1587**

Freedom of Information Coordinator. Yeoman C T Rogers. **202-426-1587**

Boating Information Branch. Lieutenant (Junior Grade) F Lynch, chief. **202-426-9716**

INTERNATIONAL AFFAIRS DIVISION. Captain Donald C Hintze, chief. **202-426-2280**

ASSISTANT CHIEF. Commander James R Costello. **202-426-2280**

OFFICE OF BOATING SAFETY. Rear Admiral David Lauth, chief. **202-426-1088**

OFFICE OF RESEARCH AND DEVELOPMENT. Rear Admiral J P Stewart, chief. **202-426-1040**

OFFICE OF MERCHANT MARINE SAFETY. Rear Admiral William M Benkert, chief. **202-426-2200**

Federal Aviation Administration (FAA)

800 Independence Ave SW, Washington, DC 20591. **202-426-4000**

ADMINISTRATOR. Langhorne M Bond. **202-426-3111**

DEPUTY ADMINISTRATOR. Quentin S Taylor. **202-426-8111**

Office of Public Affairs

ASSISTANT ADMINISTRATOR. Peter R Clapper (acting). **202-426-3883**

DEPUTY ASSISTANT ADMINISTRATOR. Dennis S Feldman. **202-426-3883**

SPECIAL ASSISTANT. Mary M Alexander. **202-426-3883**

AGENCY HISTORIAN. Nick Komons. **202-755-7234**

ADMINISTRATIVE OFFICER. 202-426-3893

PLANS AND AUDIOVISUALS DIVISION. Sue F Silverman, chief. **202-426-3894**

PUBLIC AND EMPLOYEE COMMUNICATIONS DIVISION. John G Leyden, chief. **202-426-8521**

COMMUNITY AND CONSUMER LIAISON DIVISION. Frederick H Pelzman, chief. **202-426-1960**

Key Personnel

ASSOCIATE ADMINISTRATOR FOR AIR TRAFFIC AND AIRWAY FACILITIES. William M Flener. **202-426-3366**

ASSOCIATE ADMINISTRATOR FOR ENGINEERING AND DEVELOPMENT. J W Cochran. **202-426-8181**

ASSISTANT ADMINISTRATOR FOR AIRPORT PROGRAMS. Joseph A Foster. **202-426-3050**

AIR TRAFFIC SERVICE DIRECTOR. Raymond G Belanger. **202-426-3666**

AIRWAY FACILITIES SERVICE DIRECTOR. Warren C Sharp. **202-426-3555**

FLIGHT STANDARDS SERVICE DIRECTOR. R P Skully. **202-426-8237**

ASSISTANT ADMINISTRATOR, OFFICE OF INTERNATIONAL AVIATION AFFAIRS. Charles O Cary. **202-426-3213**

Federal Highway Administration (FHA)

400 7th St SW, Washington, DC 20590. **202-426-0677**. Personnel locator number: **202-426-0539**

FEDERAL HIGHWAY ADMINISTRATOR. William M Cox. **202-426-0650**

DEPUTY FEDERAL HIGHWAY ADMINISTRATOR. Karl S Bowers. **202-426-0641**

CHIEF COUNSEL. Dowell H Anders. **202-426-0740**

Office of Public Affairs

DIRECTOR. Werner A Siems. **202-426-0648**

PROGRAM ASSISTANT. **202-426-0677**

PUBLIC INFORMATION OFFICERS
Richard Reilly. 202-426-0660
Thomas R Hyland. 202-426-0662
Ruth Ann Patrick. 202-426-0644
William E Johnson. 202-426-0645

EDITOR, *FHWA NEWS.* John Zolyak. **202-426-0677**

ASSOCIATE ADMINISTRATOR FOR PLANNING. John Hassell. **202-426-0585**

ASSOCIATE ADMINISTRATOR FOR RESEARCH AND DEVELOPMENT. G D Love. **202-426-0714**

Director. Office of Environmental Policy. M Lash. **202-426-0351**

Director. Office of Right of Way. D R Levin. **202-426-0342**

ASSOCIATE ADMINISTRATOR FOR ENGINEERING AND TRAFFIC OPERATIONS. H A Lindberg. **202-426-0370**

ASSOCIATE ADMINISTRATOR FOR SAFETY. H L Anderson. **202-755-9347**

Director. Bureau of Motor Carrier Safety. Dr Robert A Kaye. **202-426-1790**

Federal Railroad Administration (FRA)

400 7th St SW, Washington, DC 20590. **202-426-4000**

ADMINISTRATOR. John M Sullivan. **202-426-0710**

DEPUTY ADMINISTRATOR. Robert E Gallamore. **202-426-0857**

PUBLIC AFFAIRS OFFICER. David J Umansky. **202-426-0881**

CONSUMER AFFAIRS OFFICER. Eric Hanson. **202-426-0881**

ASSOCIATE ADMINISTRATOR FOR ADMINISTRATION. Frederick G Bremer. **202-426-0862**

NORTHEAST CORRIDOR PROJECT. Kenneth T Sawyer, director. **202-426-9660**

THE ALASKA RAILROAD. PO Box 7-2111, Anchorage, AK 99510
General Manager. William L Dorcy. **907-265-2411**
Assistant General Manager. Delbert L Allen. **907-265-2611**

National Highway Traffic Safety Administration (NHTSA)

400 7th St SW, Washington, DC 20590. **202-426-1828.**
Locator number: **202-426-4000.**
Recall information: **800-424-9393**
(in District of Columbia, **202-426-0123**)

ADMINISTRATOR. Joan Claybrook. **202-426-1836**

DEPUTY ADMINISTRATOR. Howard Dugoff. **202-426-1614**

OFFICE OF PUBLIC AFFAIRS AND CONSUMER SERVICES. Duayne Trecker, director. **202-426-9550**

Consumer Services. Gilbert Watson. **202-426-0670**

Auto Safety Hotline. **800-424-9393** (in Washington, DC area, **202-426-0123**)

Public Affairs. Bobby A Boaz, chief. **202-426-9550**

ASSOCIATE ADMINISTRATOR FOR MOTOR VEHICLE PROGRAMS. Robert L Carter. **202-426-1810**

ASSOCIATE ADMINISTRATOR FOR TRAFFIC SAFETY PROGRAMS. Fred W Vetter, Jr. **202-426-0837**

OFFICE OF AUTOMOTIVE FUEL ECONOMY. **202-426-0846**

Urban Mass Transportation Administration (UMTA)

400 7th St SW, Washington, DC 20590. **202-426-4043.** Locator number: **202-755-8070**

ADMINISTRATOR. Richard S Page. **202-426-4040**

ASSOCIATE ADMINISTRATOR FOR ADMINISTRATION. William H Boswell. **202-426-4007**

CHIEF COUNSEL. Theodore A Munter (acting). **202-426-4063**

Office of Public Affairs

DIRECTOR. Joseph W Marshall (acting). **202-426-4043**

GENERAL INFORMATION. Diane Enos. **202-426-4043**

PRESS INQUIRIES. Joseph Marshall. **202-426-4043**

Saint Lawrence Seaway Development Corporation (SLSDC)

Rm 814, Bldg 10-A, 800 Independence Ave SW, Washington, DC 20591. **202-426-3574.**
Also PO Box 520, Massena, NY 13662 **315-764-0271**

ADMINISTRATOR. David W Oberlin. **202-426-3574**

DIRECTOR. OFFICE OF COMMUNICATIONS. Dennis E Deuschl (acting). **202-426-3574**

ASSOCIATE ADMINISTRATOR AND RESIDENT MANAGER. William H Kennedy. **315-764-0212**

PUBLIC INFORMATION OFFICER. Madelyn H Pruski. **315-764-0232**

Department of the Treasury

15th St and Pennsylvania Ave NW, Washington, DC 20220. Information: **202-566-2111**. 24-hour telephone: **202-566-2120**

SECRETARY OF THE TREASURY. W Michael Blumenthal. **202-566-2533**

DEPUTY SECRETARY OF THE TREASURY. Robert Carswell. **202-566-2801**

UNDER SECRETARY (MONETARY AFFAIRS). Anthony M Solomon. **202-566-5164**

UNDER SECRETARY. Bette B Anderson. **202-566-5847**

GENERAL COUNSEL. Robert H Mundheim. **202-566-2093**

Office of Public Affairs

ASSISTANT SECRETARY (PUBLIC AFFAIRS). Joseph Laitin. **202-566-5252.** (h) 7204 Exfair Rd, Bethesda, MD. **301-654-0234**
Confidential Assistant. Dorothy L Clark. **202-566-5252**

DEPUTY ASSISTANT SECRETARY. Everard Munsey. **202-566-8191**

PUBLIC AFFAIRS ASSISTANT. Carol W Cira. **202-566-8191**

DIRECTOR OF OPERATIONS AND SPECIAL PROJECTS. Jesse B Brown. **202-566-5158**

PUBLIC INFORMATION OFFICER, NEWS AND QUERIES. Charles Arnold. **202-566-2041**

Key Personnel

ASSISTANT SECRETARY (DOMESTIC FINANCE). Roger C Altman. **202-566-2103**

ASSISTANT SECRETARY (ECONOMIC POLICY). Daniel H Brill. **202-566-2551**

ASSISTANT SECRETARY (INTERNATIONAL AFFAIRS). C Fred Bergsten. **202-566-5363**

ASSISTANT SECRETARY (LEGISLATIVE AFFAIRS). Gene E Godley. **202-566-2037**

ASSISTANT SECRETARY (TAX POLICY). Laurence N Woodworth. **202-566-5561**

TREASURER OF THE UNITED STATES. Azie Taylor Morton. **202-566-2843**

SPECIAL ASSISTANT TO THE SECRETARY (NATIONAL SECURITY). J Foster Collins. **202-566-2631**

CHIEF DEPUTY TO THE UNDER SECRETARY (ENFORCEMENT AND OPERATIONS). Richard J Davis (designate). **202-566-2568**

OFFICE OF REVENUE SHARING
Director. Bernadine Denning. **202-634-5157**
Public Affairs Manager. Priscilla Crane. **202-634-5248**

Bureau of Alcohol, Tobacco and Firearms (ATF)

1200 Pennsylvania Ave NW, Washington, DC 22026. **202-566-7511.** Listed number and information: **202-566-2111**

DIRECTOR. Rex D Davis. **202-566-7511**

DEPUTY DIRECTOR. John G Krogman. **202-566-7511**

ASSISTANT TO THE DIRECTOR (DISCLOSURE). Paul Mosny. **202-566-7118**

ACTING ASSISTANT TO THE DIRECTOR (PUBLIC AFFAIRS). Howard Criswell. **202-566-7135**

SPECIAL ASSISTANT TO THE DIRECTOR (RESEARCH AND DEVELOPMENT). A Atley Peterson. **202-566-7436**

ASSISTANT DIRECTORS
Administration. William Rhodes
Criminal Enforcement. Marvin O Shaw (acting). **202-566-7585**
Inspection. Jarvis Brewer. **202-566-7128**
Regulatory Enforcement. Stephen Higgins. **202-566-7513**

TECHNICAL AND SCIENTIFIC SERVICES. William H Richardson (acting). **202-566-7462**

CHIEF COUNSEL. Marvin Dessler. **202-566-7772**

Comptroller of the Currency

490 L'Enfant Plz E, SW, Washington, DC 20219. **202-447-1810**

COMPTROLLER OF THE CURRENCY. John G Heimann. **202-447-1750**

DIRECTOR OF PUBLIC AFFAIRS. William B Foster. **202-447-1798**

DIRECTOR OF COMMUNICATIONS (FOI). Caryl Austrian. **202-447-1693**

INFORMATION RECEPTIONIST. Marsha White. **202-442-1801**

US Customs Service

1301 Constitution Ave NW, Washington, DC 20229. **202-566-8195.** Locator number: **202-566-2451**

COMMISSIONER. Robert E Chasen. **202-566-2101**

CHIEF COUNSEL. Thaddeus Rojek (acting). **202-566-5476**

Public Affairs Division

SPECIAL ASSISTANT TO THE COMMISSIONER. Richard J McGowan. **202-566-2475**

CONSUMER SERVICES BRANCH. Michael N Ingrisano, chief. **202-566-8050**

INFORMATION SERVICES BRANCH. Charles Warren. **202-566-2202**
Library Section. Patricia Dobrosky. **202-566-5642**
Exhibit Hall and Information Center. **202-566-2822**
Information and Publications Section. **202-566-8195**

Other Divisions

OFFICE OF INVESTIGATIONS. George C Corcoran, Jr, Assistant Commissioner. **202-566-5401**

GENERAL INVESTIGATION DIVISION. David C Muegge, director. **202-566-5104**

FRAUD INVESTIGATIONS DIVISION.
Kenneth E Ryan, director. **202-566-5871**

SPECIAL INVESTIGATIONS DIVISION.
Stanley F Verusio, director. **202-566-5104**

HEADQUARTERS PATROL DIVISION.
Horace W Cavitt, director. **202-566-8137**

Bureau of Engraving and Printing

14th and C Sts SW, Washington, DC 20228.
202-447-0273

DIRECTOR. Seymour Berry (acting).
202-447-1364

SPECIAL PROJECTS COORDINATOR.
Peter H Daly. **202-447-9939**

TOUR INFORMATION. 202-447-9916

Internal Revenue Service (IRS)

1111 Constitution Ave NW, Washington,
DC 20224. **202-566-2111.** Night line:
202-566-2120

COMMISSIONER. Jerome Kurtz.
202-566-4115

ADMINISTRATIVE AIDE. Judith E Dixon.
202-566-4115

ASSISTANT TO THE COMMISSIONER.
Marvin Katz. **202-566-4071**

Public Affairs Division

**ASSISTANT TO THE COMMISSIONER
(PUBLIC AFFAIRS).** A James Golato.
202-566-4743

**DEPUTY ASSISTANT TO THE COM-
MISSIONER (PUBLIC AFFAIRS).** Neil
Patton. **202-566-4743**

**ASSISTANT TO THE DIRECTOR,
PUBLIC AFFAIRS DIVISION (NA-
TIONAL MEDIA LIAISON).** Terence F
Gastelle. **202-566-4953**

PROGRAMS BRANCH. Edgar D York,
chief. **202-566-2136**
Chief, Program Development Section.
Francis M Boches. **202-566-6860**
Chief, Field Coordination Section. Paul K
Cesander. **202-566-6236**

OPERATIONS BRANCH. Leon H Levine,
chief. **202-566-4021**

Assistant Chief. A Wilson Fadely.
202-566-4021
Chief, Media Relations Section. Scott D
Waffle. **202-566-4024**
Chief, Editorial Services Section. Joseph
R Weikel. **202-566-4037**

LIBRARY SERVICES GROUP.
202-566-4920

REFERENCE INFORMATION GROUP.
202-566-4054
For contact during evenings and weekends,
call Public Affairs Duty Officer through
IRS telephone operator at **202-566-2120.**

Other IRS Divisions, Branches and Offices

CORPORATION TAX DIVISION
Director. John W Holt. **202-566-4504**

DISCLOSURE OPERATIONS DIVISION
Director. Howard T Martin. **202-566-4263**

**FREEDOM OF INFORMATION
BRANCH**
Chief. Marcus Farbenblum. **202-566-4441**
Chief, Section I. Victor Rickey. **202-566-3212**
Chief, Section II. Stanley Stein.
202-566-4745

TAX DISCLOSURE BRANCH
Chief. Earl Klema. **202-566-2299**

INTELLIGENCE DIVISION
Director. Thomas J Clancy. **202-566-6723**

INDIVIDUAL TAX DIVISION
Director. Aaron Feibel. **202-566-3767**

TAXPAYERS SERVICE DIVISION
Director. Stanley Goldberg. **202-566-6352**

**OFFICE OF ASSISTANT COMMIS-
SIONER (ADMINISTRATION)**
Assistant Commissioner. Joseph T Davis.
202-566-4731

**OFFICE OF ASSISTANT COMMIS-
SIONER (COMPLIANCE)**
Assistant Commissioner. S B Wolfe.
202-566-4386
Administrative Officer. Mary Galloway.
202-566-6801

**OFFICE OF ASSISTANT COMMIS-
SIONER (EMPLOYEE PLANS AND
EXEMPT ORGANIZATIONS)**

Assistant Commissioner. Alvin D Lurie.
202-566-3171

**OFFICE OF ASSISTANT COMMIS-
SIONER (INSPECTION)**
Assistant Commissioner. Warren A Bates.
202-566-4656

**OFFICE OF ASSISTANT COMMIS-
SIONER (TECHNICAL)**
Assistant Commissioner. John L Withers.
202-566-4735

**OFFICE OF THE ASSOCIATE CHIEF
COUNSEL (TAX LITIGATION).** Dennis
J Fox. **202-566-4241**

Bureau of the Mint

1500 Pennsylvania Ave NW, Washington,
DC 20220. **202-376-0555.** Information:
202-566-5011 (general). **202-376-0555** (personnel)

DIRECTOR. 202-376-0560

DEPUTY DIRECTOR. Frank H
MacDonald. **202-376-0560**

**ASSISTANT TO THE DIRECTOR
(PUBLIC AFFAIRS).** James A Parker.
202-376-0872

Bureau of the Public Debt

15th St and New York Ave NW, Washington, DC 20226. **202-393-6400**

COMMISSIONER. H J Hintgen.
202-376-0256

EDITORIAL ASSISTANT. Earl G Jensen.
202-376-0833

US Secret Service

1800 G St NW, Washington, DC 20223.
202-634-5700. Locator number:
202-634-5744. Information: **202-634-5708**
(general). **202-634-5800** (personnel)

DIRECTOR. H Stuart Knight. **202-634-5700**

**ASSISTANT DIRECTOR (PUBLIC
AFFAIRS).** John W Warner, Jr.
202-634-5708

**ASSISTANT DIRECTOR (PROTECTIVE
RESEARCH).** James T Burke. **202-634-5725**
Communications Division. O T Russell.
202-634-5762

Intelligence Division. James M Mastrovito. 202-634-5731

ASSISTANT DIRECTOR (INVESTIGA-TIONS). Burrill A Peterson. 202-634-5716

ASSISTANT DIRECTOR (PROTECTIVE OPERATIONS). Thomas J Kelley. 202-634-5721

PROTECTIVE DIVISIONS
Presidential. Richard E Keiser, special agent in charge. 202-395-4000
Vice-Presidential. Jimmy C Taylor, special agent in charge. 202-566-5890
Dignitary. Warren W Taylor, special agent in charge. 202-566-8328
Protective Vehicle. Robert T Melchiori, special agent in charge. 202-566-2641
White House. Bobby F Coates, special agent in charge 202-395-4077
Foreign Missions. Don A Edwards, special agent in charge. 202-566-8477

THE INDEPENDENT AGENCIES

Action

806 Connecticut Ave, Washington, DC 20525. 202-254-6886. Locator number: 202-254-6886. WATS: 800-424-8580

DIRECTOR. Sam Brown. 202-254-3120

ASSOCIATE DIRECTOR (DOMESTIC AND ANTIPOVERTY OPERATIONS). John R Lewis. 202-254-7290

ASSOCIATE DIRECTOR (INTERNA-TIONAL OPERATIONS: PEACE CORPS). Carolyn Payton. 202-254-7970

DEPUTY ASSOCIATE DIRECTOR (VISTA AND AEP). Marge Tabankin. 202-254-7376

DEPUTY ASSOCIATE DIRECTOR (OLDER AMERICANS). Helen Kelley. 202-254-7310

FREEDOM OF INFORMATION/ PRIVACY ACT OFFICER. 202-254-8105

OFFICE OF COMMUNICATIONS. George Wakiji, acting assistant director. 202-254-7526
News Bureau Division. Carol Honsa director. 202-254-6480
Public Information Division. 202-254-7526

Advertising Division. Joe Cooper, director. 202-254-7520

Agency for International Development.

See Department of State

Bureau of Alcohol, Tobacco and Firearms.

See Department of the Treasury

Bureau of the Census.

See Department of Commerce

Bureau of Indian Affairs.

See Department of the Interior

Bureau of Mines.

See Department of the Interior

Bureau of Prisons.

See Department of Justice

Center for Disease Control.

See Department of HEW

Central Intelligence Agency (CIA).

Mailing address: Washington, DC 20505. Offices in Langley, VA. Switchboard number: 202-351-1100. Direct line: 202-351-7676. *Employment office.* Ames Bldg, 1820 N Fort Myer Dr, Arlington, VA. 703-351-2028. Congressional inquiry: 202-351-6136

DIRECTOR OF CENTRAL INTELLI-GENCE. Admiral Stansfield Turner. 202-351-6363

PRESS SPOKESMAN. Herbert E Hetu, assistant to the director for public affairs. 202-351-7575. Night line: 202-351-5320

DEPUTY DIRECTOR. E H Knoche. 202-351-6464

LEGISLATIVE COUNSEL. George L Cary. 202-351-6121

Civil Aeronautics Board (CAB)

1825 Connecticut Ave, Washington, DC 20428. Listed number: 202-655-4000. Direct number: 202-673-5260.

MEMBERS. Alfred E Kahn, chairman; Richard J O'Melia, G Joseph Minetti, Lee R West, Elizabeth E Bailey.

BUREAU OF ENFORCEMENT. 202-673-5930.

OFFICE OF THE CONSUMER ADVO-CATE. 202-673-5158. Jack Yohe, director.

OFFICE OF INFORMATION. 202-673-5990. Wallace E Stefany, director.

OFFICE OF COMMUNITY AND CON-GRESSIONAL RELATIONS. 202-673-5191. James L Kolstad, director. (h) 1618 Courtland Rd, Alexandria, VA 22306. 703-765-2584.

CONGRESSIONAL RELATIONS OFFICER. Charles T Donnelly. 202-673-5193.

Consumer Product Safety Commission (CPSC)

1111 18th St, NW, Washington, DC 20207. 202-634-7700

COMMISSIONERS. S John Byington, chairman. 202-634-7740; Barbara Franklin, Lawrence Kushner, R David Pittle.

EXECUTIVE DIRECTOR. Michael Brown. 301-492-6550

DIRECTOR, COMMUNICATIONS. Susan Schiffen. 202-634-7780

DIRECTOR, OFFICE OF THE SECRETARY. Richard Rapps. 202-634-7700

OFFICE OF MEDIA RELATIONS. 202-634-7780
Director. Herbert M Koster. 202-634-7780. (h) 703-360-6364
Writers and Editors. Heidi Halter, Susan Smirnoff Charles, Tom E Davis, Mike Feinstein.
Speakers Bureau. Martha M Doss. 202-634-7780

Council on Environmental Quality (CEQ)

722 Jacksoh Pl NW, Washington, DC 20006. **202-633-7027**

MEMBERS. Charles Warren, chairman; Gus Speth

EXECUTIVE DIRECTOR. Edward L Strohbehn. **202-633-7034**

ACTING GENERAL COUNSEL. Nicholas Yost. **202-633-7032**

PUBLIC INFORMATION OFFICER. Caroline Isber. **202-633-7005**

See also, Other Executive Officers under The President.

Drug Enforcement Administration.

See Department of Justice

Energy Research and Development Administration.

See Department of Energy

Environmental Protection Agency (EPA)

401 M St SW, Washington, DC 20460. Locator number: **202-755-2673**. Listed number: **202-655-4000**

ADMINISTRATOR. Douglas M Costle. **202-755-2700**

DIRECTOR, SCIENCE ADVISORY BOARD. Richard Dowd. **202-755-0263**

OFFICE OF GENERAL COUNSEL. G William Frick. **202-755-2511**

OFFICE OF FEDERAL ACTIVITIES. Rebecca W Hanmer. **202-755-0777**

OFFICE OF LEGISLATION. Charles S Warren. **202-755-2930**

OFFICE OF INTERNATIONAL ACTIVITIES. K Kirke Harper (acting). **202-755-2780**

OFFICE OF PUBLIC AFFAIRS

Administrative Services. Joseph Handy. **202-755-0730**
News Services. Marlin Fitzwater. **202-755-0344**
Media Research Staff. Robin Woods. **202-755-0863**

Program Support. Leighton Price. **202-755-0720**
Information Service. Charles Rogers. **202-755-0715**
Audiovisual Staff. Luke Hester. **202-755-0872**
Design and Graphics Staff. Robert Flanagan. **202-755-0872**
DOCUMERICA. Gifford Hampshire. **202-755-0138**
Publications Management. Charles Pierce. **202-755-0736**
Visitors' Center. Scott Connolly. Lobby, West Tower. **202-755-0713**
Speakers' Coordination. Susan Sladek. **202-755-4188**
Youth Activities. Mattie Montgomery. **202-755-0496**
Field and External Operations. James Bowyer. **202-755-0710**
Regional Operations. Lynda Brownlow. **202-755-0710**

Key EPA Offices

OFFICE OF OCCUPATIONAL SAFETY AND HEALTH. Dr David Shearer (acting). **202-755-4390**

ASSISTANT ADMINISTRATOR FOR ENFORCEMENT. Stanley W Legro. **202-755-2500**

National Enforcement Investigations Center. (Denver, CO) Thomas Gallagher. **303-837-4650**
Deputy Assistant Administrator for General Enforcement. Richard D Wilson. **202-755-2977**
Stationary Source Enforcement Division. Edward Reich. **202-755-2550**
Pesticides and Toxic Substances Enforcement Division. Augustine E Conroy II. **202-755-0970**
Deputy Assistant Administrator for Mobile Source and Noise Enforcement. Norman D Shutler. **202-755-2530**

ASSISTANT ADMINISTRATOR FOR WATER AND HAZARDOUS MATERIALS. Thomas C Joring. **202-755-2800**
Deputy Assistant Administrator for Pesticide Programs. Edwin L Johnson. **202-755-8033**

ASSISTANT ADMINISTRATOR FOR AIR AND WASTE MANAGEMENT. **202-755-2640**
Deputy Assistant Administrator for Radiation Programs. Dr William D Rowe. **202-755-4894**
Deputy Assistant Administrator for Air Quality Planning and Standards. Walter C

Barber, Jr (Research Triangle Park, NC 27711). **919-541-5576**

ASSISTANT ADMINISTRATOR FOR TOXIC SUBSTANCES. 202-755-0310
Office of Toxic Substances. Glenn E Schweitzer. **202-755-8040**

SPECIAL ASSISTANT FOR CONSUMER AFFAIRS. 202-755-0425

Equal Employment Opportunity Commission (EEOC)

2401 E St, Washington, DC 20506. **202-634-6831**

STAFF DIRECTOR. Robert Ross

OFFICE OF PUBLIC AFFAIRS. 202-634-6930. Alred L Sweeney, director; Mary Ann Parmley and Reginald A Welch

Export–Import Bank of the United States

811 Vermont Ave, NW, Washington, DC 20571. **202-566-2111**

PRESIDENT AND CHAIRMAN. John L Moore, Jr

DIRECTORS. R Alex McCullough and Margaret W Kahliff

SENIOR VICE–PRESIDENT, RESEARCH AND COMMUNICATIONS. Donald A Furtado. **202-566-8873**

Farm Credit Administration (FCA)

490 L'Enfant Plz E, SW, Washington, DC 20578. **202-755-2130**

GOVERNOR. Donald E Wilkinson

DIRECTOR, INFORMATION DIVISION, OFFICE OF ADMINISTRATION. Roland W Olson. **202-755-2170**

PRESS CONTACT. Harold K Street. **202-755-2170**

Farmers Home Administration

See Department of Agriculture

Federal Aviation Administration

See Department of Transportation

Federal Bureau of Investigation

See Department of Justice

Federal Communications Commission (FCC)

1919 M St, Washington, DC 20554. Listed number: **202-655-4000**. Locator number: **202-632-6379**

COMMISSIONERS. Charles D Ferris, chairman; Robert E Lee, Benjamin L Hooks, James H Quello, Abbott M Washburn, Joseph R Fogarty, Margita E White

EXECUTIVE DIRECTOR. R D Lichtwardt

CONSUMER ASSISTANCE CHIEF. Belle O'Brien. **202-632-6999**

PUBLIC INFORMATION OFFICER. Samual M Sharkey, Jr. **202-632-7260.** (h) 3900 Watson Pl, Washington, DC 20016

CHIEF ENGINEER. Raymond E Spence, Jr

OFFICE OF OPINIONS AND REVIEW. David W Warren, Jr, chief

BROADCAST BUREAU. Wallace E Johnson, chief

CABLE TELEVISION BUREAU. James R Hobson, chief

COMMON CARRIER BUREAU. Walter R Hinchman, chief

SAFETY AND SPECIAL RADIO SERVICES BUREAU. Charles A Higginbotham, chief

FIELD OPERATIONS BUREAU. C Phyll Horne, chief

ENFORCEMENT DIVISION. Willis E Ours, Jr, chief

VIOLATIONS DIVISION. Abraham Sickle, chief

Federal Deposit Insurance Corporation (FDIC)

550 17th St, Washington, DC 20429. **202-393-8400**

CHAIRMAN. George A LeMaistre

PRESS CONTACT. Sandra P Walls. **202-389-4212**

Federal Disaster Assistance Administration

See Department of HUD

Federal Election Commission (FEC)

1325 K St NW, Washington, DC 20463. **202-523-4089.** Toll-free number: **800-424-9530**

CHAIRMAN. Vernon W Thompson

STAFF DIRECTOR. Orlando B Potter

ASSISTANT STAFF DIRECTOR FOR INFORMATION. David H Fiske, press officer. **202-523-4065.** (h) 5918 Broad Branch Rd NW, Washington, DC 20015. **202-244-0554**

ASSISTANT PRESS OFFICER. Susan Tifft. **202-523-4065**

PUBLIC RECORDS OFFICE. **202-523-4181**

Federal Energy Administration

See Department of Energy

Federal Highway Administration

See Department of Transportation

Federal Home Loan Bank Board (FHLBB)

FHLBB Bldg, 1700 G St NW, Washington, DC 20552. **202-377-6000**

CHAIRMAN. Robert H McKinney

OFFICE OF COMMUNICATIONS. Michael B Scanlon, director (h) 9403 Beauregard Ave, Manassas, VA 22110. **703-361-2675**

Federal Maritime Commission (FMC)

1100 L St, Washington, DC 20573. **202-523-5764**

COMMISSIONERS. Richard J Daschbach, chairman. **202-523-5911;** Clarence Morse, Karl E Bakke, Bob Casey, James V Day

MANAGING DIRECTOR. Arthur Pankopf. **202-523-5800**

GENERAL COUNSEL. Joseph N Ingolia. **202-523-5740**

BUREAU OF ENFORCEMENT. James K Cooper, director. **202-523-5860**

BUREAU OF COMPLIANCE. W Jarrel Smith, Jr, director. **202-523-5810**

PUBLIC INFORMATION OFFICER. C William Cardin. **202-523-5764**

Federal Mediation and Conciliation Service (FMCS)

2100 K St NW, Washington, DC 20427. **202-653-5290**

DIRECTOR. Wayne Horwitz. **202-653-5300**

DIRECTOR OF INFORMATION. Norman Walker. **202-653-5290,** night line: **703-536-9637.** John Rogers. **202-653-5290**

Federal Power Commission

See Federal Energy Regulatory Commission under deptartment of Energy

Federal Reserve System Board of Governors

20th St and Constitution Ave NW, Washington, DC 20551. **202-452-3000**

For complete details, *see* BUSINESS.

Federal Trade Commission (FTC)

Pennsylvania Ave at 6th St NW, Washington, DC 20580. Listed number: **202-655-4000.** Locator number: **202-523-3625.** Information: **202-523-3830.** Recorded announcements about public meetings: **202-523-3806**

COMMISSIONERS. Michael Petschuk, chairman, **202-523-3711.** Paul Rand Dixon, **202-523-3732.** Elizabeth Hanford Dole, **202-523-3525.** Calvin J Collier, **202-523-4503.** David A Clanton, **202-523-3530**

OFFICE OF THE EXECUTIVE DIRECTOR. Margery W Smith. **202-523-3740**

OFFICE OF THE GENERAL COUNSEL. Michael N Sohn. **202-523-3613**

OFFICE OF PUBLIC INFORMATION
Director. Theodore O Cron. **202-523-3830**
Deputy Director. Leonard J McEnnis.
202-523-3830
Administrative Assistant. Mary Ellen
Stemper. **202-523-3830**
Assistant Director for News. Wilbur (Bill)
Weaver. **202-523-3830**
Information Division. John E Bokel, director.
202-523-3564
Freedom of Information and Privacy Act
Branches. **202-523-3582**
Correspondence Branch. **202-523-3567**
Public Reference Branch. **202-523-3600**
Inquiry and Search Branch. **202-523-3001**

Records Division. Dr John D Macoll, direc-
tor. **202-523-3485**
Public Records Section. **202-523-3467**
Nonpublic Records Section. **202-523-3667**

Key FTC Bureaus

**BUREAU OF CONSUMER PROTEC-
TION.** Albert H Kramer, director.
202-523-3727
Assistant Director (Compliance). Eric M
Rubin. **202-524-6915**
Assistant Director (Marketing Practices).
Richard C Foster. **202-523-3355**
Assistant Director (National Advertising).
Wallace S Snyder (acting). **202-724-1499**

BUREAU OF ECONOMICS. Dr Darius W
Gaskins, Jr, director. **202-254-7721**

BUREAU OF COMPETITION. Alfred F
Dougherty, Jr, director. **202-523-3601**
Deputy Director. Daniel C Schwartz.
202-523-3475
Assistant Director (Compliance). Joseph J
Gercke. **202-254-6024**
Assistant Director (Regional Operations). E
Perry Johnson. **202-523-3522**
Assistant Directors (Special Projects). Harry
A Garfield II, **202-523-3644** and Edmund B
Frost, **202-523-3362**

ADMINISTRATIVE LAW JUDGES
Chief Judge. Daniel H Hanscom.
202-724-1511
Assistant Chief Judge. Ernest G Barnes.
202-724-1530

Food and Drug Adminstration

See Department of HEW

Forest Service

See Department of Agriculture

General Accounting Office (GAO)

GAO Bldg, 441 G St NW, Washington, DC
20548. **202-275-2812**

COMPTROLLER GENERAL OF THE US.
Elmer B Staats

INFORMATION OFFICER. Roland
Sawyer. Also Laura Kopelson and Joseph
Rosapepe

**OFFICE OF CONGRESSIONAL RELA-
TIONS.** Martin J Fitzgerald

For details on ordering GAO publications,
see GOVERNMENT DOCUMENTS.

General Services Administration

General Services Bldg, 18th and F St,
Washington, DC 20405. Listed number:
202-655-4000. Locator number:
202-472-1082

ADMINISTRATOR. Jay Solomon.
202-566-1212

**DIRECTOR OF CONGRESSIONAL
AFFAIRS.** Paul E Goulding. **202-566-1250**

DIRECTOR OF PUBLIC AFFAIRS. Rilla
Moran Woods. **202-566-1297**

DIRECTOR OF INFORMATION. Richard
Q Vawter. **202-566-1231**
Media Division. Peter J Hickman, Patricia
Thomasson, and Robert Aaron, public
information specialists
Publications Division. Faith Payne,
writer/editor; Patricia D Bradford, public
information specialist; Roberta Weilgus,
editorial assistant

Important GSA Services

FEDERAL SUPPLY SERVICE. Crystal
Mall, Washington, DC 20406. **202-557-8667**
Commissioner. Robert P Graham.
202-557-8667
Executive Director. LL Mitchell.
202-557-8644

**NATIONAL ARCHIVES AND RECORDS
SERVICE.** 7th St and Pennsylvania Ave,
Washington, DC 20408. **202-523-3134.** Loca-
tor number: **202-472-1082**

Archivist of the US. James B Rhoads.
202-523-3134
Public Information Officer. Benjamin Ruhe.
202-523-3099

PUBLIC BUILDINGS SERVICE.
202-566-1100
Commissioner. James B Shea, Jr.
202-566-0615

Government Printing Office (GPO)

North Capitol and H Sts, Washington, DC
20401. **202-275-2051.** Locator number:
202-275-3648. Calls about orders:
202-783-3238

PUBLIC PRINTER OF THE US. John J
Boyle

**ASSISTANT PUBLIC PRINTER (SUPER-
INTENDENT OF DOCUMENTS).** Carl A
La Barre

**ASSISTANT PUBLIC PRINTER (PLAN-
NING).** Wellington H Lewis

CUSTOMER SERVICE MANAGER.
Robert J McKendry. **202-275-2491**

PRESS INQUIRIES. Office of the Special
Assistant to the Public Printer, Rm 818-C.
202-275-2958. David H Brown, special
assistant. (h) 2272 Dunster Ln, Rockville,
MD 20854. **301-762-2295**

CONGRESSIONAL INFORMATION. W
Scott Sonntag III, chief

CONGRESSIONAL RECORD CLERK.
William M Murphy

See GOVERNMENT DOCUMENTS for
information on ordering GPO publications
and location of bookstores. *See* also
LIBRARIES for a list of GPO's regional
depository libraries.

Immigration and Naturalization Service

See Department of Justice

Internal Revenue Service

See Department of the Treasury

International communication agency

See US Information Agency

Interstate Commerce Commission (ICC)

12th St and Constitution Ave NW, Washington, DC 20423. Locator number: **202-343-1100**. Listed number: **202-655-4000**. Direct number: **202-275-7252**. Energy hotline (toll-free) numbers: **800-424-9312** (except Washington, DC and Florida). **202-275-7301** (Washington). **800-432-4537** (Florida)

COMMISSIONERS. A Daniel O'Neal, Jr, chairman **202-275-7519**; Rupert L Murphy, Charles L Clapp, Virginia Mae Brown, Robert C Gresham, Betty Jo Christian

MANAGING DIRECTOR. Pierce A Quinlan. **202-275-7480**

OFFICE OF INFORMATION AND CONSUMER AFFAIRS: 202-275-7252
Public Information Officer. Douglas P Baldwin
Press Information Officer. Edgar B Hamilton, Jr. (h) 3306 Trafalgar Ct, Springfield, VA 22151. **703-978-6477**

OFFICE OF THE GENERAL COUNSEL. Mark L Evans. **202-275-7312**

OFFICE OF PROCEEDINGS. Robert J Brooks, director. **202-275-7426**

OFFICE OF HEARINGS. Robert C Bamford, chief administrative law judge. **202-275-7408**

OFFICE OF THE SECRETARY. H Gordon Homme, Jr, acting secretary. **202-275-7428**

RAIL SERVICES PLANNING OFFICE. 1900 L St NW, Washington, DC 20036. **202-254-6983**. Alan M Fitzwater, director. **202-254-3281**

PUBLIC TARIFF ROOM. Rm 6217, **202-275-7389**

BUREAU OF INVESTIGATIONS AND ENFORCEMENT. Peter M Shannon, Jr, director. **202-275-7594**

BUREAU OF TRAFFIC. Martin E Foley, director. **202-275-7348**

BUREAU OF OPERATIONS. Joel E Burns, director. **202-275-7849**

BUREAU OF ECONOMICS. Ernest R Olson, director. **202-275-7684**

BUREAU OF ACCOUNTS. John A Grady, director. **202-275-7565**

Law Enforcement Assistance Administration

See Department of Justice

Library of Congress

10 1st St SE, Washington, DC 20540. **202-426-5000**

LIBRARIAN OF CONGRESS. Daniel J Boorstin. **202-426-5205**

INFORMATION OFFICER. Mary C Lethbridge. **202-426-5108**

ADMINISTRATIVE DEPARTMENT. **202-426-5560**. Edmond L Applebaum, director

CONGRESSIONAL RESEARCH SERVICE. 202-426-5775. Gilbert Gude, director

PROCESSING DEPARTMENT. **202-426-5325**. Joseph H Howard, director
Catalog Publication Division. Gloria H Hsia, chief
Cataloging Instruction Office. Edith Scott, chief instructor
Decimal Classification Division. Benjamin A Custer, chief

READER SERVICES DEPARTMENT. **202-426-6562**. F E Croxton, director
Loan Division. Jack McDonald, Jr, chief
Science and Technology Division. Marvin W McFarland, chief
Serial Division. Donald F Wisdom, chief
Stack and Reader Division. Steven J Herman, chief
General Reference and Bibliography Division. Guy A Marco, chief

RESEARCH DEPARTMENT. **202-426-5543**. Alan Fern, director

COPYRIGHT OFFICE. Crystal Mall Annex, Arlington, VA 20559. **202-557-8700**
Register of Copyrights. Barbara A Ringer
Executive Officer. Michael R Pew
Library of Congress researchers will often handle brief inquiries over the phone, locating material and doing quick researches, particularly for journalists, whose telephone contact for this purpose is **202-426-5108**

Mining Enforcement and Safety Administration

See Department of the Interior

National Academies: National Academy of Sciences, National Academy of Engineering, National Research Council, Institute of Medicine

2101 Constitution Ave NW, Washington, DC 20418. **202-393-8100**

PRESIDENT, NATIONAL ACADEMY OF SCIENCES, AND CHAIRMAN, NATIONAL RESEARCH COUNCIL. Philip Handler. **202-389-6231**

PRESIDENT, NATIONAL ACADEMY OF ENGINEERING. Courtland Perkins. **202-389-6868**

PRESIDENT, INSTITUTE OF MEDICINE. David Hamburg. **202-389-6187**

OFFICE OF INFORMATION FOR THE NATIONAL ACADEMIES. 202-389-6518. Howard J Lewis, director

DIRECTOR OF MEDIA RELATIONS. Barbara Jorgenson. **202-389-6511**

EDITOR, NEWS REPORT. Gerald S Schatz. **202-389-6360**

National Aeronautics and Space Administration (NASA)

400 Maryland Ave SW, Washington, DC 20546. **202-755-2320**. Locator number: **202-755-2320** or (after hours) **202-755-3333**. Contact to locate former astronauts: Eugene Marianetti, **202-755-8364**

ADMINISTRATOR. James C Fletcher. **202-755-3918**

DEPUTY ADMINISTRATOR. Alan M Lovelace. **202-755-3886**

GENERAL COUNSEL. S Neil Hosenball. **202-755-3875**

ASSISTANT ADMINISTRATOR (LEGISLATIVE AFFAIRS). Joseph P Allen. **202-755-8344**

ASSISTANT ADMINISTRATOR (INTERNATIONAL AFFAIRS). Arnold W Frutkin. **202-755-3868**

ASSISTANT ADMINISTRATOR (SPE-CIAL PROJECTS). David Williamson, Jr. **202-755-3907**

ASSISTANT ADMINISTRATOR (EN-ERGY PROGRAMS). R D Ginter. **202-755-3127**

ASSOCIATE ADMINISTRATOR (AERONAUTICS AND SPACE TECH-NOLOGY). James J Kramer. **202-755-2393**

ASSOCIATE ADMINISTRATOR (SPACE FLIGHT). John F Yardley. **202-755-2444**

ASSOCIATE ADMINISTRATOR (SPACE SCIENCE). Noel W Hinners. **202-755-3672**

OFFICE OF PUBLIC AFFAIRS
Assistant Administrator. Robert A Newman. **202-755-3828.** (h) **301-652-4387**
Director, Community and Human Relations. Curtis M Graves. **202-755-8414.** (h) **202-584-8182**
Public Affairs Officers Division. William J O'Donnell, director. **202-755-3090.** (h) **703-524-3665**
Office of Applications. Richard McCormack. **202-755-8487.** (h) **703-360-3415**
Offices of Aeronautics and Space Technology. Kenneth Atchison. **202-755-3147.** (h) **301-292-3141**
Energy Programs and Tracking Data Acquisition. Dennis Williams. **202-755-8420.** (h) **202-338-7423**
Office of Industry Affairs and Technology Utilization. Ken Senstad. **202-755-8649.** (h) **301-577-1069**
Office of International Affairs. Kenn Morris. **202-755-3897**
Office of Space Science. Nick Panagakos. **202-755-3680.** (h) **202-554-0510**
Public Information Division. Miles Waggoner, director. **202-755-8341.** (h) **202-488-8251**
News Chief. Donald Zylstra. **202-755-8370.** (h) **301-789-6308**
Feature Editor. Mary Fitzpatrick. **202-755-8370.** (h) **202-543-7880**
Media Services. James Kukowski. **202-755-8366.** (h) **301-762-7354**
Office of Space Flight. David W Garrett. **202-755-3090.** (h) **703-549-4714**
Audiovisual. Les Gaver, chief. **202-755-8366.** (h) **301-384-6125**
Audiovisual Specialist. Margaret Ware. **202-755-8366.** (h) **301-336-7409**
Radio and Television Programs. Joseph Headlee, chief. **202-755-8354.** (h) **703-451-3023**

Educational Programs. Dr Fred B Tuttle, director. **202-755-3518.** (h) **703-780-2332**
Public Services
Director O B Lloyd, Jr. **202-755-8326.** (h) **301-929-3105**
Deputy Director and Chief, Public Inquiries Branch. Ralph E Gibson. **202-755-8364.** (h) **301-530-4234**
Media Development. Alex P Nagy, acting director and acting chief, Exhibits Production and Operations. **202-755-3936.** (h) **301-736-4571**

NASA Facilities

AMES RESEARCH CENTER. Mountain View, CA 94035. **415-965-5111**
Public Affairs Officer. Stanley A Miller. **415-965-5091.** (h) **408-356-6849**
Public Information Officer. Larry D King. **415-965-5091.** (h) **408-738-4166**
Public Information Officer. Peter W Waller. **415-965-5091.** (h) **415-493-9406**
Public Information Specialist. Darlyne Moen. **415-965-5091.** (h) **408-247-9775**
Educational Programs Officer. Garth A Hull. **415-965-5543.** (h) **415-941-3250**

HUGH L DRYDEN FLIGHT RESEARCH CENTER. PO Box 273, Edwards, CA 93523. **805-258-3311**
Public Affairs Officer. Ralph B Jackson. **805-258-8311.** (h) **805-942-5427**
Public Information Specialist. Trudy Tiedemann. **805-258-8311.** (h) **805-948-3595**

GODDARD SPACE FLIGHT CENTER. Greenbelt, MD 20771. **301-982-5042**
Chief, Office of Public Affairs. Edward Mason. **301-982-6255.** (h) **301-643-6240**
Deputy, Office of Public Affairs. James Lynch. **301-982-6255.** (h) **301-424-6284**
Chief, Public Information. Joseph McRoberts. **301-982-5566.** (h) **703-780-1392**
Public Information Officers
John Kley. **301-982-4922.** (h) **301-292-2162**
James Lacy. **301-982-5565.** (h) **703-768-0044**
Donald E Witten. **301-982-4955.** (h) **301-531-6289**
William W Watson. **301-982-4101.** (h) **301-242-8513**
Alfred Shehab. **301-982-4101.** (h) **301-674-7333**
Protocol, Tours, and Special Events. William P O'Leary. **301-982-4101.** (h) **301-HE4-4102**

JET PROPULSION LABORATORY. 4800 Oak Grove Dr, Pasadena, CA 91103. **213-354-3405**
Manager, Public Affairs. Frank J Colella. **213-354-5011.** (h) **213-790-1652**
Manager, Public Information. Frank E Bristow. **213-354-5011.** (h) **213-848-8464**
Senior Information Specialist. Robert J MacMillin. **213-354-5011.** (h) **213-790-7849**
Senior Representative, Public Information. Alan S Wood. **213-354-5011.** (h) **213-355-1814**

LYNDON B JOHNSON SPACE CENTER. Houston, TX 77058. **713-483-4588**
Public Affairs Officer. Harold S Stall. **713-483-3671.** (h) **713-334-5166**
Executive Assistant. Roy A Alford. **713-483-3671.** (h) **713-334-1417**
Administrative Assistant. Charles J Bauer. **713-483-4744.** (h) **713-923-5139**
Chief, Public Information. John E McLeaish. **713-483-5111.** (h) **713-471-3210**
Photographic Documentation. Andrew Patnesky. **713-483-5111.** (h) **713-353-4313**
Public Information Specialists
Charles Redmond. **713-483-5111.** (h) **713-493-3426**
Milton E Reim. **713-483-5111.** (h) **713-944-3795**
Douglas K Ward. **713-483-5111.** (h) **713-488-0715**
Robert T (Terry) White. **713-483-5111.** (h) **713-554-4472**
Janet V Wrather. **713-483-5111**
Louis Parker. **713-483-5111.** (h) **713-481-4372**
Robert V Gordon. **713-483-5111.** (h) **713-333-3511**
John E Riley. **713-483-5111.** (h) **713-471-0624**
Chief, Special Events. J C Waite. **713-483-4241.** (h) **713-333-2442**
Protocol Specialist. Edward S Barker. **713-483-4241.** (h) **713-333-2869**

JOHN F KENNEDY SPACE CENTER. Kennedy Space Center, FL 32899. **305-867-3333**
Chief, Public Affairs. Charles T Hollinshead. **305-867-2201.** (h) **305-784-1138**
Chief, Public Information. Hugh Harris. **305-867-2468.** (h) **305-784-1071**
Public Information Officers
Edward K Harrison. **305-867-2468.** (h) **305-452-0910**
Darleen Hunt. **305-867-2468.** (h) **305-773-3849**

Karl K Kristofferson. **305-867-2468.** (h) **305-267-9302**
Alfred H Lavender. **305-867-2468.** (h) **305-254-3404**
Richard N Young. **305-867-2468.** (h) **305-452-5141**
Visitors Information Branch. Prosper A Fagnant, chief. **305-867-2363.** (h) **305-773-8815**
Visitors Information. Mike Bishop. **305-867-2363.** (h) **305-267-0293.** Gatha F Cottee. **305-867-2363.** (h) **305-254-3424**
Educational Programs. Raymond Corey, chief. **305-867-4444.** (h) **305-831-3561**

KENNEDY SPACE CENTER, WESTERN LAUNCH OPERATIONS DIVISION. PO Box 425, Lompoc, CA 93436. Walter Dundon, public affairs officer. **805-865-3015.** (h) **805-733-1754**

LANGLEY RESEARCH CENTER. Hampton, VA 23665. **804-827-2761**
Public Affairs Officer. Maurice H Parker. **804-827-3966.** (h) **804-851-9635**
Educational Programs Officer. Harold E Mehrens. **804-827-3966.** (h) **804-722-4660**
Public Information Specialist. Karen E Miller. **804-827-3966.** (h) **804-898-4748**

LEWIS RESEARCH CENTER. 21000 Brookpark Rd, Cleveland, OH 44135. **216-433-2200**
Director, Technology Utilization and Public Affairs. Walter T Olson. **216-433-4000,** Ext 300, (h) **216-331-2848**
Public Information Specialist. Marilyn Edwards. **216-433-4000,** Ext 415, (h) **216-845-5658**
Public Information Assistant. Mary Ann Peto. **216-433-4000.** (h) **216-225-2038**

MARSHALL SPACE FLIGHT CENTER. Marshall Space Flight Center, AL 35812. **205-453-2121**
Director of Public Affairs. Joseph M Jones. **205-453-0031.** (h) **205-852-4109** PAO: Guy B Jackson. **205-453-0034.** (h) **205-586-4647**
Public Information Specialists
Edward S Schorsten. **205-453-0036.** (h) **205-837-2585**
Curtis Hunt. **205-453-0034.** (h) **205-852-1763**
Don Worrell. **205-453-0035.** (h) **205-881-0909**
Bill C Mayes. **205-453-0037.** (h) **205-881-9094**

Christine S Duncan. **205-453-0035.** (h) **205-561-3559**
Chief, Public Services and Education Branch. Richard B Pratt. **205-453-0040.** (h) **205-582-4716**
Foreign Information Specialist. Ruth von Saurma. **205-453-0042.** (h) **205-534-5582**

NATIONAL SPACE TECHNOLOGY LABORATORIES. Bay St Louis, MS 39520. **601-688-2125.** Mack R Herring, public affairs officer. **601-688-3341.** (h) **601-452-9516**

WALLOPS FLIGHT CENTER. Wallops Island, VA 23337. **804-824-2201.** Joyce B Milliner, public affairs officer. **804-824-3411,** Ext 579 or 584. (h) **804-665-4703**

National Bureau of Standards

See Department of Commerce

National Center on Child Abuse and Neglect

See Department of HEW

National Endowments

NATIONAL ENDOWMENT FOR THE ARTS. 2401 E St NW, Washington, DC 20506. **202-634-4811**
Chairman. Livingston L Biddle, Jr
Assistant to the Chairman for Public Affairs. Florence Lowe. **202-634-6033**
Director of Administration. Paul P Berman

NATIONAL ENDOWMENT FOR THE HUMANITIES. 806 15th St NW, Washington, DC 20506. **202-724-0291** or **0331**
Chairman. Joseph D Duffey
Public Information Officer. Darrel de Chaby. **202-724-0331**

National Labor Relations Board (NLRB)

1717 Pennsylvania Ave, Washington, DC 20570. Listed number: **202-655-4000**

BOARD MEMBERS. John H Fanning, chairman. **202-254-9266.** Howard Jenkins, Jr, John A Penello, Betty Southard Murphy, John C Truesdale

EXECUTIVE SECRETARY. 202-254-9430

GENERAL COUNSEL. John S Irving. **202-254-9150**

DIVISION OF INFORMATION
Director. Thomas W Miller, Jr. **202-254-9033**
Associate Director. Iliff R McMahan. **202-254-9130**
Public Inquiry Specialist. 202-254-9033

DIVISION OF ADMINISTRATIVE LAW JUDGES. 1229 25th St NW, Washington, DC 20037. Thomas N Kessel, chief judge. **202-254-9570**

National Oceanic and Atmospheric Administration

See Department of Commerce

National Park Service

See Department of the Interior

National Science Foundation (NSF)

1800 G St NW, Washington, DC 20550. Locator number: **202-632-7970.** Listed number: **202-655-4000**

DIRECTOR. Richard C Atkinson. **202-632-4001**

PUBLIC INFORMATION BRANCH. Jack Renirie, head. **202-632-5728**
Deputy. Ralph Kazarian. **202-632-5728**
Public Service Officer. Nathan Kassack. **202-632-5722**

COMMUNICATIONS RESOURCES BRANCH. Bruce R Abell, head. **202-632-7390**

DIRECTORATE FOR MATHEMATICAL AND PHYSICAL SCIENCES, AND ENGINEERING. 202-632-7342
Division of Physics (PHYS). William E Wright, director. **202-632-4320**
Division of Chemistry. Richard C Nicholson, director. **202-632-4262**
Division of Engineering. Charles Polk, director. **202-632-5790**
Division of Materials Research. Ronald E Kagarise, director. **202-632-7412**
Division of Mathematical and Computer Sciences. John R Pasta, director. **202-632-5960**

DIRECTORATE FOR ASTRONOMICAL, ATMOSPHERIC, EARTH, AND OCEAN SCIENCES. John B Slaughter, director. **202-632-7300**

Division of Astronomical Sciences. William E Howard III, director. **202-632-5717**

Division of Atmospheric Sciences. Alan J Grobecker, director. **202-634-4190**

Division of Earth Sciences. Norman D Watkins, director. **202-632-4274**

Division of Ocean Sciences. Mary K Johrde, director. **202-632-5913**

Division of Polar Programs. Edward P Todd, director. **202-632-4024**

DIRECTORATE FOR BIOLOGICAL, BE-HAVIORAL, AND SOCIAL SCIENCES (BBS). Eloise E Clark, director. **202- 632-7867**

Division of Physiology and Cellular and Molecular Biology. Henry C Reeves, director. **202-632-4338**

Division of Environmental Biology. **202-632-4338**

Division of Behavioral and Neural Sciences. Richard T Louttit, director. **202-634-4230**

Division of Social Sciences. Herbert L Costner, director. **202-632-4286**

DIRECTORATE FOR SCIENCE EDUCA-TION. (5225 Wisconsin Ave NW, Washington, DC 20550). F James Rutherford, director. **202-282-7922**

Office of Science and Society. Alexander J Morin, director. **202-282-7770**

Division of Science Education, Development, and Research. Jerome S Daen, director. **202-282-7900**

Division of Science Education Resources Improvement. Walter L Gillespie, director. **202-282-7786**

Division of scientific personnel improvement. Lewis A Gist, director. **202-282-7754**

DIRECTORATE FOR RESEARCH AP-PLICATIONS. Jack T Sanderson, director. **202-632-7424**

Division of Advanced Environmental Research and Technology. Charles C Thiel, director. **202-632-4345**

Division of Advanced Productivity Research and Technology. L Vaughn Blankenship, director. **202-634-6260**

Division of Advanced Energy and Resources Research and Technology. Donald Senich, director. **202-632-5957**

Division of Exploratory Research and Sys-tems Analysis. Joshua Menkes, director. **202-634-7181**

Division of Intergovernmental Science and Public Technology. William Wetmore, director. **202-634-7672**

DIRECTORATE FOR SCIENTIFIC, TECHNOLOGICAL, AND INTERNA-TIONAL AFFAIRS. Harvey Averch, acting assistant director. **202-254-3020**

Division of Policy Research and Analysis. Alden Bean, acting director. **202-632-5990**

Division of Science Resources Studies (2000 L St NW, Washington DC 20550). Charles E Falk, director. **202-634-4634**

Division of Science Information. Lee G Burchinal, director. **202-632-5824**

Division of International Programs. Bodo Bartocha, director. **202-632-5798**

DIRECTORATE FOR ADMINISTRA-TION. Eldon D Taylor, assistant director. **202-632-5710**

Division of Grants and Contracts. George Pilarinos, acting director. **202-632-5772**

National Security Council

See Other Executive Offices under The President

National Transportation Safety Board

800 Independence Ave SW, Washington, DC 20594. **202-426-8787**

CHAIRMAN. Webster B Todd, Jr

MANAGING DIRECTOR. Harry J Zink

OFFICE OF PUBLIC AFFAIRS

Director. Edward E Slattery, Jr. **202-426-8787.** (h) 12200 Autumn Wood Ln, Tantallon, MD 20022. **301-292-1095**

Deputy Director. Arthur B Dunbar, Jr. **202-426-8787.** (h) 9518 Wallingford Dr, Burke, VA 22015. **703-323-5484**

National Weather Service

See Department of Commerce. *See* also WEATHER

Nuclear Regulatory Commission (NRC)

Bethesda, MD. Mailing address: Washington, DC 20555. **301-492-7000**

COMMISSIONERS. Joseph Hendrie, chairman. **202-634-1459.** Victor Gilinsky. **202-634-1461.** Richard T Kennedy. **202-634-1463.** Peter A Bradford. **202-634-1760**

DIRECTOR, OFFICE OF PUBLIC AFFAIRS. Joseph J Fouchard (acting). **301-492-7715**

EXECUTIVE DIRECTOR, OPERATIONS. Lee V Gossick. **301-492-7511**

ASSISTANT EXECUTIVE DIRECTOR, OPERATIONS. William J Dircks. **301-492-7561**

DIRECTOR, OFFICE OF NUCLEAR REACTOR REGULATION. Edson G Case (acting). **301-492-7691**

DIRECTOR, OFFICE OF NUCLEAR REGULATORY RESEARCH. Saul Levine. **301-427-4341**

DIRECTOR, OFFICE OF INSPECTION AND ENFORCEMENT. Ernest Volgenau. **301-492-7397**

DIRECTOR, OFFICE OF NUCLEAR MATERIAL SAFETY AND SAFEGUARDS. Clifford Smith, Jr. **301-427-4063**

DIRECTOR, OFFICE OF STANDARDS DEVELOPMENT. Robert B Minogue. **301-443-6914**

DIRECTOR, OFFICE OF ADMINISTRA-TION. Daniel J Donoghue. **301-492-7335**

EXECUTIVE LEGAL DIRECTOR. Howard K Shaper. **301-492-7308**

Occupational Safety and Health Administration

See Department of Labor

Occupational Safety and Health Review Commission (OSHRC)

1825 K St NW, Washington, DC 20006. **403-634-7960**

CHAIRMAN. Timothy F Cleary

DIRECTOR OF INFORMATION AND PUBLICATIONS. Linda P Dodd. **202-634-7943**

Office of Management and Budget

See Other Executive Offices under The President

Postal Rate Commission (PRC)

2000 L St NW, Washington, DC 20268. Listed number: **202-655-4000**. Direct number: **202-254-3800**

Chairman. Clyde S du Pont

Chief Administrative Officer. David F Harris. **202-254-3800**

Information Officer. Ned Callan

Renegotiation Board

2000 M St NW, Washington, DC 20446. **202-254-8266**

Assistant General Counsel, Secretary, and Public Information Officer. John S Webster. **202-254-7019**

Securities and Exchange Commission (SEC)

500 N Capitol St, Washington, DC 20549. (Public Reference Room: Suite 6101, 1100 L St) Listed number: **202-655-4000**. Information: **202-755-4846**. Investor complaints: **202-523-5516**. Filings by registered companies: **202-523-5506**

OFFICE OF PUBLIC AFFAIRS. Andrew L Rothman, director. **202-376-8093**

OFFICE OF THE EXECUTIVE DIRECTOR. 202-755-8111

DIVISION OF CORPORATE REGULATION. Aaron Levy, director. **202-523-5691**

DIVISION OF CORPORATION FINANCE. Richard H Rowe, director. **202-755-1136**

DIVISION OF ENFORCEMENT. Stanley Sporkin, director. **202-755-1184**

DIVISION OF INVESTMENT MANAGEMENT. Anne P Jones, director. **202-755-1310**

DIVISION OF MARKET REGULATION. Andrew M Klein, director. **202-755-1138**

DIRECTORATE OF ECONOMIC AND

POLICY RESEARCH. J Richard Zecher, director. **202-755-0222**

OFFICE OF ADMINISTRATIVE LAW JUDGES. Warren E Blair, chief judge. **202-523-5657**

OFFICE OF ADMINISTRATIVE SERVICES. Richard J Kanyan, director. **202-755-1323**

OFFICE OF THE CHIEF ACCOUNTANT. A Clarence Sampson, acting chief accountant. **202-755-1180**

OFFICE OF THE COMPTROLLER. Lawrence H Haynes, comptroller. **202-755-1515**

OFFICE OF DATA PROCESSING. Ralph L Bell, director. **202-755-1152**

OFFICE OF THE GENERAL COUNSEL. Harvey L Pitt, general counsel. **202-755-1108**

OFFICE OF OPINIONS AND REVIEW. Bernard Wexler, director. **202-523-5638**

OFFICE OF PERSONNEL. Albert Fontes, director. **202-755-1354**

OFFICE OF REGISTRATIONS AND REPORTS. James C Foster, director. **202-523-5510**

OFFICE OF THE SECRETARY. George A Fitzsimmons, secretary. **202-755-1160**

Small Business Administration (SBA)

1441 L St NW, Washington, DC 20416. **202-653-6600**. Listed number: **202-655-4000**

ADMINISTRATOR. A Vernon Weaver. **202-653-6605**

ASSISTANT ADMINISTRATOR (ADVOCACY AND PUBLIC INFORMATION). Anthony S Stasio. **202-653-6924**

DIRECTOR, OFFICE OF PUBLIC INFORMATION. Paul A Lodato. **202-653-6365**

DIRECTOR, OFFICE OF PUBLIC AFFAIRS. Jean M Nowak. **202-653-6822**

PRIVACY ACT AND FREEDOM OF INFORMATION OFFICER. Nicholas Kalcounos. **202-653-6458**

Smithsonian Institution

900 Jefferson Dr SW, Washington, DC 20560. **202-628-4422**. General information and news: **202-381-5911**

Secretary. S Dillon Ripley. **202-381-5005**

OFFICE OF PUBLIC AFFAIRS. Carl Larsen, director. **202-381-6218**. Night line: **703-821-2529**

Social Security Administration

See Department of HEW

US Arms Control and Disarmament Agency

Department of State Bldg, 320 21st St, Washington, DC 20451. Listed number: **202-655-4000**. Locator number: **202-632-3636**

DIRECTOR. Paul C Warnke. **202-632-9610**

ASSISTANT DIRECTOR, INTERNATIONAL RELATIONS BUREAU. Leon Sloss. **202-632-3612**

ASSISTANT DIRECTOR, MILITARY AND ECONOMIC AFFAIRS BUREAU. Robert M Behr. **202-632-9472**

ASSISTANT DIRECTOR, NUCLEAR WEAPONS AND ADVANCED TECHNOLOGY BUREAU. Thomas D Davies. **202-632-0972**

ASSISTANT DIRECTOR, BUREAU OF INTERNATIONAL SECURITY PROGRAMS. John Newhouse. **202-632-3612**

ASSISTANT DIRECTOR, BUREAU OF WEAPONS EVALUATION AND CONTROL. Barry Blechman. **202-632-9472**

PUBLIC AFFAIRS ADVISER. Thomas A Halsted. **202-632-0392**

DEPUTY PUBLIC AFFAIRS ADVISERS. Adalyn Davis and James M Pope. **202-632-9505**

US Board on Geographic Names

Defense Mapping Agency, Bldg 56, US Naval Observatory, Washington, DC 20305. **202-254-4453**. Richard R Randall, executive secretary

US Civil Service Commission (USCSC)

1900 E St, Washington, DC 20415. Listed number: **202-655-4000**. Direct number: **202-632-6292**

EXECUTIVE DIRECTOR. Raymond Jacobson. **202-632-6111**

OFFICE OF PUBLIC AFFAIRS. Joseph E Oglesby, director. **202-632-4588**
Publications and Communications Division. Edward H Koenig, director. **202-632-5491**

MEDIA SERVICES DIVISION. **202-632-5491**

MEDIA SERVICES, ORGANIZATIONAL AFFAIRS. Johnnie A Moore. **202-632-5491**

US Coast Guard

See Department of Transportation

US Commission on Civil Rights

1121 Vermont Ave NW, Washington, DC 20425. **202-254-6697**. Listed number: **202-655-4000**

STAFF DIRECTOR. John A Buggs. **202-254-8130**

PUBLIC AFFAIRS UNIT. Barbara J Brooks, acting director. **202-254-6697**. Also M E Hartley and L Ward

US Customs Service

See Department of the Treasury

US Fish and Wildlife Service

See Department of the Interior

US Geological Survey

See Department of the Interior

US Information Agency (USIA)

(Name changed to **International Communication Agency***)*

1750 Pennsylvania Ave NW, Washington, DC 20547. Listed number: **202-655-4000**

DIRECTOR. John E Reinhardt. **202-632-4906**

OFFICE OF ASSISTANT DIRECTOR (BROADCASTING). Kenneth R Giddens. **202-235-4180**

OFFICE OF ASSISTANT DIRECTOR (INFORMATION CENTERS). Harold F Schneidman. **202-632-6700**

OFFICE OF ASSISTANT DIRECTOR (MOTION PICTURES AND TELEVISION). Robert S Scott. **202-376-7806**
Media Affairs Officer. Ken Boles. **202-376-7717 or 7714**
Media Liaison Officer. Elaine McDevitt. **202-376-7731**

OFFICE OF ASSISTANT DIRECTOR (PRESS AND PUBLICATIONS). Charles R Beecham. **202-632-4804**

OFFICE OF ASSISTANT DIRECTOR (PUBLIC INFORMATION). Alan Carter. **202-632-4963**

DEPUTY DIRECTOR. Paul J Rappaport. **202-632-5158**
Public Programs Section. H Preston Pitts. **202-632-4960**
Media Relations and Support Section. Erwin van Swol. **202-632-4947**
Access to Information. Donald Mulligan. **202-632-4983**

FOREIGN CORRESPONDENT SUPPORT SERVICES
Foreign Press Center. 202 National Press Building, Washington, DC 20045. **202-382-7701**
Foreign Press Center. 866 2nd Ave, New York, NY 10017. **202-971-5721**

US Marshals Service

See Department of Justice

US Postal Service (USPS)

475 L'Enfant Plz SW, Washington, DC 20250. **202-245-4000**

POSTMASTER GENERAL OF THE US. Benjamin F Bailar

ASSISTANT POSTMASTER GENERAL FOR PUBLIC AND EMPLOYEE COMMUNICATIONS. Walter E Duka. **202- 245-4034**

DIRECTOR, OFFICE OF PUBLIC AND MEDIA RELATIONS. 202-245-5198

GENERAL MANAGER, PRESS RELATIONS. D Jamison Cain. **202-245-4144**

GENERAL MANAGER, BROADCAST RELATIONS. Louis Eberhardt. **202-245-4163**

PROGRAM MANAGER, CUSTOMER COMMUNICATIONS. Van Seagraves. **202-245-4089**

Subject Directory of Press Contacts

Board of Governors, Postmaster General, Government Relations. D Jamison Cain. **202-245-4144**
Administration, Planning, Customer Services, Consumer Advocate, Broadcast Services. Lou Eberhardt. **202-245-4144**
Finance, Rates, Manpower and Cost Control, International Postal Affairs, Memo to Mailers. Van Seagraves. **202-245-4144**
Operations Group, Employee and Labor Relations Group, Management Information Systems. David McLean. **202-245-4168**
Real Estate and Buildings, Research and Development, Philately, Special Projects. Ron Powell. **202-245-4144**
Deputy Postmaster General, Postal Inspection Service, Judicial Officer. Martin Caine. **202-245-4168**

US Secret Service

See Department of the Treasury

Urban Mass Transportation Administration

See Department of Transportation

Veterans Administration (VA)

810 Vermont Ave, Washington, DC 20420. **202-393-4120**

ADMINISTRATOR OF VETERANS' AFFAIRS. Max Cleland

DIRECTOR, INFORMATION SERVICE. Frank R Hood. **202-389-2443**

REGIONAL GOVERNMENT OFFICES

FEDERAL INFORMATION CENTERS

Federal Information Centers (FICs), staffed by the General Services Administration, are located in most important federal buildings. Their primary function is to give out direct phone numbers for federal personnel and agencies in their regions, but in theory they are also equipped to provide a variety of other information on the operations and services of the federal government anywhere in the country. Most of the centers will allow users to browse through their extensive collections of staff phone directories and informational publications. The nearest center is the first place to call when in search of an elusive portion of the bureaucracy —provided that the line is not busy. According to a government publication: "Their purpose is to give the individual citizen the answer to his question or to put him directly in touch with an expert who can. There is no question too complicated, or too simple, for a Federal Information Center. The staff's job is to search until they find someone in the government who can provide an answer."

AKRON, OH. Call Cleveland FIC (toll-free). **375-5638**

ALBANY, NY. Call New York FIC (toll-free). **463-4421**

ALBUQUERQUE, NM, FIC. Federal Bldg, US Courthouse, 500 Gold Ave SW, Albuquerque, NM 87101. **505-766-3091**

ALLENTOWN/BETHLEHEM, PA. Call Philadelphia FIC (toll-free). **821-7785**

ATLANTA, GA, FIC. Federal Bldg, 275 Peachtree St NE, Atlanta, GA 30303. **404-221-6891**

AUSTIN, TX. Call Houston FIC (toll-free). **472-5494**

BALTIMORE, MD, FIC. Federal Bldg, 31 Hopkins Plz, Baltimore, MD 21201. **301-962-4980**

BIRMINGHAM, AL. Call Atlanta FIC (toll-free). **322-8591**

BOSTON, MA, FIC. Government Ctr, John F Kennedy Federal Bldg, Boston, MA 02203. **617-223-7121**

BUFFALO, NY, FIC. Federal Bldg, 111 W Huron St, Buffalo, NY 14202. **716-842-5770**

CHARLOTTE, NC. Call Atlanta FIC (toll-free). **376-3600**

CHATTANOOGA, TN. Call Memphis FIC (toll-free). **265-8231**

CHICAGO, IL, FIC. Everett M Dirksen Bldg, 219 S Dearborn St, Chicago, IL 60604. **312-353-4242**

CLEVELAND, OH, FIC. Federal Bldg, 1240 E 9th St, Cleveland, OH 44199. **216-522-4040**

CINCINNATI, OH, FIC. Federal Bldg, 550 Main St, Cincinnati, OH 45202. **513-684-2801**

COLORADO SPRINGS, CO. Call Denver FIC (toll-free). **471-9491**

COLUMBUS, OH. Call Cincinnati FIC (toll-free). **221-1014**

DALLAS, TX. Call Fort Worth FIC (toll-free). **749-2131**

DAYTON, OH. Call Cincinnati FIC (toll-free). **223-7377**

DENVER, CO, FIC. Federal Bldg, 1961 Stout St, Denver, CO 80294. **303-837-3602**

DES MOINES, IA. Call Omaha FIC (toll-free). **284-4448**

DETROIT, MI, FIC. McNamara Federal Bldg, 477 Michigan Ave, Detroit, MI 48226. **313-226-7016**

FORT LAUDERDALE, FL. Call Miami FIC (toll-free). **522-8531**

FORT WORTH, TX, FIC. Fritz Garland Lanham Federal Bldg, 819 Taylor St, Fort Worth, TX 76102. **817-334-3624**

GARY, IN. Call Indianapolis FIC (toll-free). **883-4110**

HARTFORD, CT. Call New York FIC (toll-free). **527-2617**

HONOLULU, HI, FIC. 300 Ala Moana Blvd (PO Box 50091), Honolulu, HI 96850. **808-546-8620**

HOUSTON, TX, FIC. Federal Bldg, US Courthouse, 515 Rusk Ave, Houston, TX 77002. **713-226-5711**

INDIANAPOLIS, IN, FIC. Federal Bldg, 575 N Pennsylvania, Indianapolis, IN 46204. **317-269-7373**

JACKSONVILLE, FL. Call St Petersburg FIC (toll-free). **354-4756**

KANSAS CITY, MO, FIC. Federal Bldg, 601 E 12th St, Kansas City, MO 64106. **816-374-2466**

LITTLE ROCK, AR. Call Memphis FIC (toll-free). **378-6177**

LOS ANGELES, CA, FIC. Federal Bldg, 300 N Los Angeles St, Los Angeles, CA 90012. **213-688-3800**

LOUISVILLE, KY, FIC. Federal Bldg, 600 Federal Pl, Louisville, KY 40202. **502-582-6261**

MEMPHIS, TN, FIC. Clifford Davis Federal Bldg, 167 N Main St, Memphis, TN 38103. **901-521-3285**

MIAMI, FL, FIC. Federal Bldg, 51 SW 1st Ave, Miami, FL 33130. **305-350-4155**

MILWAUKEE, WI. Call Chicago FIC (toll-free). **271-2273**

MINNEAPOLIS, MN, FIC. Federal Bldg, US Courthouse, 110 S 4th St, Minneapolis, MN 55401. **612-725-2073**

MOBILE, AL. Call New Orleans FIC (toll-free). **438-1421**

NASHVILLE, TN. Call Memphis FIC (toll-free). **242-5056**

NEWARK, NJ, FIC. Federal Bldg, 970 Broad St, Newark, NJ 07102. **201-645-3600**

NEW ORLEANS, LA, FIC. Rm 1210, Federal Bldg, 701 Loyola Ave, New Orleans, LA 70113. **504-589-6696**

NEWPORT NEWS, VA. Call Norfolk FIC (toll-free). **244-0480**

NEW YORK, NY, FIC. Rm 1-114, Federal Bldg, 26 Federal Plz, New York, NY 10007. **212-264-4464**

NORFOLK, VA, FIC. Rm 106, Stanwick Bldg, 3661 E Virginia Beach Blvd, Norfolk, VA 23502. **804-441-6723**

OGDEN, UT. Call Salt Lake City FIC (toll-free). **399-1347**

OKLAHOMA CITY, OK, FIC. US Post Office and Courthouse, 201 NW 3rd St, Oklahoma City, OK 73102. **405-231-4868**

OMAHA, NE, FIC. Federal Bldg, US Post Office and Courthouse, 215 N 17th St, Omaha, NE 68102. **402-221-3353**

ORLANDO, FL. Call St Petersburg FIC (toll-free). **422-1800**

PHILADELPHIA, PA, FIC. William J Green, Jr, Federal Bldg, 600 Arch St, Philadelphia, PA 19106. **215-597-7042**

PHOENIX, AZ, FIC. Federal Bldg, 230 N 1st Ave, Phoenix, AZ 85025. **602-261-3313**

PITTSBURGH, PA, FIC. Rm 119, Federal Bldg, 1000 Liberty Ave, Pittsburgh, PA 15222. **412-644-3456**

PORTLAND, OR, FIC. Federal Bldg, 1220 SW 3rd Ave, Portland, OR 97204. **503-221-2222**

PROVIDENCE, RI. Call Boston FIC (toll-free). **331-5565**

PUEBLO, CO. Call Denver FIC (toll-free). **544-9523**

ROCHESTER, NY. Call Buffalo FIC (toll-free). **546-5075**

SACRAMENTO, CA, FIC. Federal Bldg, US Courthouse, 650 Capitol Mall, Sacramento, CA 95814. **916-440-3344**

ST JOSEPH, MO. Call Kansas City FIC (toll-free). **233-8206**

ST LOUIS, MO, FIC. Federal Bldg, 1520 Market St, St Louis, MO 63103. **314-425-4106**

ST PETERSBURG, FL, FIC. William C Cramer Federal Bldg, 144 1st Ave S, St Petersburg, FL 33701. **813-893-3495**

SALT LAKE CITY, UT, FIC. Federal Bldg, US Post Office and Courthouse, 125 S State St, Salt Lake City, UT 84138. **801-524-5353**

SAN ANTONIO, TX. Call Houston FIC (toll-free). **224-4471**

SAN DIEGO, CA, FIC. Government Information Ctr, Federal Bldg, 880 Front St, San Diego, CA 92188. **714-293-6030**

SAN FRANCISCO, CA, FIC. Federal Bldg, US Courthouse, 450 Golden Gate Ave, San Francisco, CA 94102. **415-556-6600**

SAN JOSE, CA. Call San Francisco FIC (toll-free). **275-7422**

SANTA FE, NM. Call Albuquerque FIC (toll-free). **983-7743**

SCRANTON, PA. Call Philadelphia FIC (toll-free). **346-7081**

SEATTLE, WA, FIC. Federal Bldg, 915 2nd Ave, Seattle, WA 98174. **206-442-0570**

SYRACUSE, NY. Call Buffalo FIC (toll-free). **476-8545**

TACOMA, WA. Call Seattle FIC (toll-free). **383-5230**

TAMPA, FL. Call St Petersburg FIC (toll-free). **229-7911**

TOLEDO, OH. Call Cleveland FIC (toll-free). **241-3223**

TOPEKA, KS. Call Kansas City FIC (toll-free). **232-7229**

TRENTON, NJ. Call Newark FIC (toll-free). **396-4400**

TULSA, OK. Call Oklahoma City FIC (toll-free). **584-4193**

TUCSON, AZ. Call Phoenix FIC (toll-free). **622-1511**

WASHINGTON, DC, FIC. Rm 5716, Regional Office Bldg, 7th and D Sts SW, Washington, DC 20407. **202-755-8660**

WEST PALM BEACH, FL. Call Miami FIC (toll-free). **833-7566**

WICHITA, KS. Call Kansas City FIC (toll-free). **263-6931**

FEDERAL AGENCY REGIONAL OFFICES

This section includes the regional offices of most federal agencies, which are arranged alphabetically by agency name. (Regional offices of the National Weather Service are listed in WEATHER; FBI field offices are in POLICE; Federal Reserve Banks are in BUSINESS; and US District Courts are in THE FEDERAL GOVERNMENT: JUDICIAL BRANCH. Many of the federal agencies have standard regions, as shown below:

REGION I (Northeast). Connecticut, Maine, Massachusetts, New Hampshire, Rhode Island, Vermont

REGION II. New Jersey, New York, Puerto Rico, the Virgin Islands

REGION III (Mid–Atlantic). Delaware, District of Columbia, Maryland, Pennsylvania, Virginia, West Virginia

REGION IV (South). Alabama, Florida, Georgia, Kentucky, Mississippi, North Carolina, South Carolina, Tennessee

REGION V (Great Lakes). Illinois, Indiana, Michigan, Minnesota, Ohio, Wisconsin

REGION VI (South Central). Arkansas, Louisiana, New Mexico, Oklahoma, Texas

REGION VII (Plains). Iowa, Kansas, Missouri, Nebraska

REGION VIII (Rocky Mountains). Colorado, Montana, North Dakota, South Dakota, Utah, Wyoming

REGION IX (West). Arizona, California, Guam, Hawaii, Nevada

REGION X (Northwest). Alaska, Idaho, Oregon, Washington

ACTION Regional Offices and Regional Directors

BOSTON—REGION I. Rm 1420, John W McCormack Federal Bldg, Boston, MA 02109. **617-223-4501.** John Torian

NEW YORK—REGION II. Suite 1611, 16th Floor, 26 Federal Plz, New York, NY 10007.

212-264-5710. Mrs Ronald Jean Johnson (acting)

PHILADELPHIA—REGION III. Suite 600, 320 Walnut St, Philadelphia, PA 19106. 215-597-9972. Jack Facenda (acting)

ATLANTA—REGION IV. Rm 895, 730 Peachtree St, NE, Atlanta, GA 30308. 404-221-3337. Paul R Jones

CHICAGO—REGION V. Rm 322, 3rd Floor, 1 N Wacker Dr, Chicago, IL 60606. 312-353-5107. Michael F Doyle

DALLAS—REGION VI. Suite 1600, Corrigan Tower Bldg, 212 N St Paul St, Dallas, TX 75201. 214-749-1361. H "Zeke" Rodriguez (acting)

KANSAS CITY—REGION VII. Suite 330, II Gateway Ctr, 4th and State Sts, Kansas City, KS 66101. 816-374-4486. John L Campbell

DENVER—REGION VIII. 1845 Sherman St, Denver, CO 80203. 303-837-2671. Jack L Stiegelmeier

SAN FRANCISCO—REGION IX. 5th Floor, 211 Main St, San Francisco, CA 94105. 415-556-1736. Donald L Brown

SEATTLE—REGION X. 1601 2nd Ave, Seattle, WA 98101. 206-442-4520. John Keller

Child Abuse Specialists by Region National Center on Child Abuse and Neglect (HEW)

REGION I. Child Abuse Specialist, John F Kennedy Federal Bldg, Government Ctr, Boston, MA 02203. 617-223-6450. John Tretton

REGION II. Child Protective Services Specialist, 26 Federal Plz, New York, NY 10007. 212-264-4118. Bobbette Stubbs

REGION III. Child Abuse Specialist, 3535 Market St (PO Box 13716), Philadelphia, PA 19101. 215-596-6763. Gary Koch

REGION IV. Child Abuse and Neglect Program Specialists, 50 7th St, NE, Atlanta, GA 30323. 404-881-3019. Carol Osborne and Jerry White

REGION V. Child Abuse Specialist, 29th Floor, 300 S Wacker Dr, Chicago, IL 60606. 312-353-4722. Forrest Lewis

REGION VI. Child Abuse Specialist, Fidelity Union Tower, 1507 Pacific Ave, Dallas, TX 75201. 214-749-2491. Jean Manning

REGION VII. Child Abuse and Neglect Specialist, 3rd Floor, 601 E 12th St, Kansas City, MO 64106. 816-374-5401. Harry McDaniel

REGION VIII. Child Abuse Specialist, Rm 455, Federal Office Bldg, 50 United Nations Plz, San Francisco, CA 94102. 415-556-6187

REGION X. Child Abuse Specialist, HEW MS 622, Arcade Plaza Bldg, 1321 2nd Ave, Seattle, WA 98101. 206-442-0838. Mark Emanuel

Department of Commerce District Offices

ALBUQUERQUE. Suite 1015, 505 Marquette, NW, Albuquerque, NM 87102. 505-766-2386.

ANCHORAGE. Suite 412, Hill Bldg, 632 6th Ave, Anchorage, AK. 907-265-5307.

ATLANTA. 1365 Peachtree St, NE, Atlanta, GA 30309. 404-881-7000.

BALTIMORE. 415 US Customhouse, Gay and Lombard Sts, Baltimore, MD 21202. 301-962-3560.

BIRMINGHAM. Suite 200-201, 908 S 20th St, Birmingham, AL 35205. 205-254-1331.

BOSTON. 10th Floor, 441 Stuart St, Boston, MA 02116. 617-223-2312.

BUFFALO. Rm 910, Federal Bldg, 111 W Huron St, Buffalo, NY 14202. 716-842-3208.

CHARLESTON. 3000 New Federal Office Bldg, 500 Quarrier St, Charleston, WV 25301. 304-343-6181.

CHEYENNE. 6022 O'Mahoney Federal Ctr, 2120 Capitol Ave, Cheyenne, WY 82001. 307-778-2151.

CHICAGO. Rm 1406, Mid-Continental Plaza Bldg, 55 E Monroe St, Chicago, IL 60603. 312-353-4450.

CINCINNATI. 10504 Federal Office Bldg, 550 Main St, Cincinnati, OH 45202. 513-684-2944.

CLEVELAND. Rm 600, 666 Euclid Ave, Cleveland, OH 44114. 216-522-4750.

COLUMBIA. 2611 Forest Dr, Forest Ctr, Columbia, SC 29403. 803-765-5345.

DALLAS. Rm 3E7, 1100 Commerce St, Dallas, TX 75202. 214-749-1515.

DENVER. Rm 161, New Customhouse, 19th and Stout Sts, Denver, CO 80202. 303-837-3246.

DES MOINES. 817 Federal Bldg, 210 Walnut St, Des Moines, IA 50309. 515-284-4222.

DETROIT. 445 Federal Bldg, Detroit, MI 48226. 313-226-3650.

GREENSBORO. 203 Federal Bldg, W Market St (PO Box 1950), Greensboro, NC 27402. 919-275-9111, Ext 345

HARTFORD. Rm 610-B, Federal Office Bldg, 450 Main St, Hartford, CT 06103. 203-244-3530.

HONOLULU. 286 Alexander Young Bldg, 1015 Bishop St, Honolulu, HI 96813. 808-546-8694.

HOUSTON. 201 Fannin, 1017 Federal Office Bldg, Houston, TX 77002. 713-226-4231.

KANSAS CITY. Rm 1840, 601 E 12th St, Kansas City, MO 64106. 816-374-3142.

LOS ANGELES. 11201 Federal Bldg, 11000 Wilshire Blvd, Los Angeles, CA 90024. 213-824-7591.

MEMPHIS. Rm 720, 147 Jefferson Ave, Memphis, TN 38103. 901-534-3214.

MIAMI. Rm 821, City National Bank Bldg, 25 W Flagler St, Miami, FL 33130. 305-350-5267.

MILWAUKEE. 517 E Wisconsin Ave, Milwaukee, WI 53202. 414-291-3473.

MINNEAPOLIS. 218 Federal Bldg, 110 S 4th St, Minneapolis, MN 55401. 612-725-2133.

NEWARK. 4th Floor, Gateway Bldg 1, Newark, NJ 07102. 201-645-6214.

NEW ORLEANS. Rm 432, International Trade Mart, 2 Canal St, New Orleans, LA 70130. 504-527-6546.

NEW YORK. Rm 3718, 26 Federal Plz, New York, NY 10007. 212-264-0634.

PHILADELPHIA. 10112 Federal Bldg, 600 Arch St, Philadelphia, PA 19106. **215-597-2850.**

PHOENIX. Valley Bank Ctr 2950, Phoenix, AZ 85073. **602-261-3285.**

PITTSBURGH. Rm 2002, 1000 Liberty Ave, Pittsburgh, PA 15222. **412-644-2850.**

PORTLAND. Rm 618, 1220 SW 3rd Ave, Portland, OR 97204. **503-221-3001.**

RENO. 2028 Federal Bldg, 300 Booth St, Reno, NV 89502. **702-784-5203.**

RICHMOND. 8010 Federal Bldg, 400 N 8th St, Richmond, VA 23240. **804-782-2246.**

ST LOUIS. 120 S Central Ave, St Louis, MO 63105. **314-622-4243.**

SALT LAKE CITY. 1203 Federal Bldg, 125 S State St, Salt Lake City, UT 84138. **801-524-5116.**

SAN FRANCISCO. Box 36013, Federal Bldg, 450 Golden Gate Ave, San Francisco, CA 94102. **415-556-5860.**

SAN JUAN. Box 4275, Bldg 10, Governmental Ctr, E La Grande, San Juan, PR 00905. **809-723-9489.**

SAVANNAH. 235 US Courthouse and Post Office Bldg, 125-29 Bull St, Savannah, GA 31402. **912-232-4321,** Ext 204.

SEATTLE. 706 Lake Union Bldg, 1700 Westlake Ave N, Seattle, WA 98109. **206-442-5615.**

Community Services Administration Regional Offices

REGION I. John F Kennedy Federal Bldg, Boston, MA 02203. **617-223-4080.**

REGION II. 26 Federal Plz, New York, NY 10007. **212-264-1900.**

REGION III. 3535 Market St, Philadelphia, PA 19104. **215-596-1000.**

REGION IV. 730 Peachtree St, NE, Atlanta, GA 30308. **404-881-3172.**

REGION V. 300 S Wacker Dr, Chicago, IL 60606. **312-353-5562.**

REGION VI. 1200 Main St, Dallas, TX 75202. **214-749-1301.**

REGION VII. 911 Walnut St, Kansas City, MO 64106. **816-374-3761.**

REGION VIII. 1961 Stout St, Denver, CO 80202. **303-837-4767.**

REGION IX. 100 McAllister St, San Francisco, CA 94102. **415-556-5400.**

REGION X. 1321 2nd Ave, Seattle, WA 98101. **206-442-4910.**

Consumer Product Safety Commission Regional Offices

ATLANTA (Alabama, Florida, Georgia, Kentucky, Mississippi, North Carolina, South Carolina, Tennessee). 1330 W Peachtree St, NW, Atlanta, GA 30309. **404-881-2259.**

BOSTON (Connecticut, Maine, Massachusetts, New Hampshire, Rhode Island, Vermont). 100 Summer St, Boston, MA 02110. **617-223-5576.**

CHICAGO (Illinois, Indiana). 230 S Dearborn St, Chicago, IL 60604. **312-353-8260.**

CLEVELAND (Ohio, Michigan). Plaza 9 Bldg, 55 Erieview Plz, Cleveland, OH 44114. **216-522-7160.**

DALLAS (New Mexico, Oklahoma, Texas). 500 S Ervay St, Dallas, TX 75201. **214-749-3871.**

DENVER (Colorado, Montana, North Dakota, South Dakota, Utah, Wyoming). 817 17th St, Denver, CO 80202. **303-837-2904.**

KANSAS CITY (Iowa, Kansas, Missouri, Nebraska). 1125 Grand Ave, Kansas City, MO 64106. **816-374-2034.**

LOS ANGELES (Arizona, lower California). 3660 Wilshire Blvd, Los Angeles, CA 90010. **213-688-7272.**

MINNEAPOLIS (Minnesota, Wisconsin). Federal Bldg, Fort Snelling, Twin Cities, MN 55111. **612-725-3424.**

NEW YORK (New Jersey, New York, Puerto Rico, Virgin Islands). 6 World Trade Ctr, Vesey St, New York, NY 10048. **212-264-1372.**

PHILADELPHIA (Delaware, District of Columbia, Maryland, Pennsylvania, Virginia, West Virginia). 400 Market St, Philadelphia, PA 19106. **215-597-9105.**

SAN FRANCISCO (Hawaii, upper California, Nevada). 100 Pine St, San Francisco, CA 94111. **415-556-1819.**

SEATTLE (Alaska, Idaho, Oregon, Washington). 915 2nd Ave, Seattle, WA 98174. **206-442-5276.**

Drug Enforcement Administration Regional Offices (Justice)

REGION 1. Boston Regional Office, Rm G-64, John F Kennedy Bldg, Boston, MA 02203. **617-223-2170.**

REGION 2. New York Regional Office, 555 W 57th St, New York, NY 10019. **202-264-5151.**

REGION 3. Philadelphia Regional Office, Rm 10224, William J Green Federal Bldg, 600 Arch St, Philadelphia, PA 19106. **215-597-9530.**

REGION 4. Merged with Region 3.

REGION 5. Miami Regional Office, 8400 NW 53rd St, Miami, FL 33166. **305-591-4800.**

REGION 6. Detroit Regional Office, 357 Federal Bldg, 231 W Laayette, Detroit, MI 48226. **313-226-7290.**

REGION 7. Chicago Regional Office, 1800 Dirksen Federal Bldg, 219 S Dearborn St, Chicago, IL 60604. **312-353-7875.**

REGION 8. New Orleans Regional Office, 1001 Howard Ave, New Orleans, LA 70113. **504-589-6841.**

REGION 10. Kansas City Regional Office, Suite 211, US Courthouse, 811 Grand Ave, Kansas City, MO 64106. **816-374-2631**

REGION 11. Dallas Regional Office, Rm 4A5, Earle Cabell Federal Bldg, 1100 Commerce St, Dallas, TX 75202. **214-749-3631**

REGION 12. Denver Regional Office, Rm 336, US Customhouse (PO Box 1860), Denver, CO 80201. **303-837-3951**

REGION 13. Seattle Regional Office, Suite 200, 221 1st Ave W, Seattle, WA 98119. **206-442-5443**

REGION 14. Los Angeles Regional Office, Suite 800, 350 S Figueroa St, Los Angeles, CA 90071. **213-688-2650**

REGION 15. Mexico City Regional Office, DEA/Justice, American Embassy, Apartado Postal 88 Bis, Mexico 1, DF, Mexico. **905-525-9100**, Ext 507

REGION 16. Bangkok Regional Office, DEA/Justice, American Embassy, APO San Francisco, CA 96346. **252-5040**, Ext 422

REGION 17. Paris Regional Office, DEA/Justice, American Embassy, APO New York, NY 09777. **Paris 265-7400**

REGION 18. Caracas Regional Office, DEA/Justice, American Embassy, APO New York, NY 09893. **283-8888**, Ext 80

REGION 19. Ankara Regional Office, DEA/Justice, American Embassy, APO New York, NY 09254. **263616**

REGION 20. Manila Regional Office, DEA/Justice, American Embassy, APO San Francisco, CA 96528. **59-80-11**, Ext 609

Environmental Protection Agency Regional Offices and Regional Administrators

REGION I. Rm 2203, John F Kennedy Federal Bldg, Boston, MA 02203. **617-223-7210.** John A S McGlennon

REGION II. Rm 908, 26 Federal Plz, New York, NY 10007. **212-264-2525.** Gerald M Hansler

REGION III. Curtis Bldg, 6th and Walnut Sts, Philadelphia, PA, 19106. **215-597-9815.** Daniel J Snyder III

REGION IV. 1421 Peachtree St NE, Atlanta, GA 30309. **404-526-5727.** Jack E Ravan

REGION V. 230 S Dearborn St, Chicago, IL 60604. **312-353-5250.** George R Alexander, Jr

REGION VI. Suite 1100, 1600 Patterson St, Dallas, TX 75201. **214-749-1962.** John C White

REGION VII. 1735 Baltimore Ave, Kansas City, MO 64108. **816-374-5493.** Jerome H Svore

REGION VIII. Suite 900, 1860 Lincoln St, Denver, CO 80203. **303-837-3895.** John A Green

REGION IX. 100 California St, San Francisco, CA 94111. **415-556-2320.** Paul De Falco, Jr

REGION X. 1200 6th Ave, Seattle, WA 98101. **206-442-1220.** Clifford V Smith, Jr

Equal Employment Opportunity Commission Regional Offices

REGION II. 26 Federal Plz, New York, NY 10007. **212-264-3640**

REGION III. 127 N 4th St, Philadelphia, PA 19106. **215-597-7784**

REGION IV. 75 Piedmont Ave NE, Atlanta, GA 30303. **404-526-6991**

REGION V. 230 S Dearborn St, Chicago, IL 60604. **312-353-9386**

REGION VI. 1100 Commerce St, Dallas TX 75202. **214-749-1841**

REGION VII. 601 E 12th St, Kansas City, MO 64106. **816-374-2781**

REGION VIII. Denver area handled by Region IX

REGION IX. 300 Montgomery St, San Francisco, CA 94104. **415-556-1775**

REGION X. Seattle area handled by Region IX

Farm Credit System District Offices (Agriculture)

DISTRICT I (Connecticut, Maine, Massachusetts, New Hampshire, New Jersey, New York, Rhode Island, Vermont). Box 141, Springfield, MA 01101. **413-786-7600**

DISTRICT II (Delaware, District of Columbia, Maryland, Pennsylvania, Puerto Rico, Virginia, West Virginia). St. Paul and 24th Sts, Baltimore, MD 21218. **301-235-9100**

DISTRICT III (Florida, Georgia, North Carolina, South Carolina). 1401 Hampton St, Columbia, SC 29201. **803-799-5000**

DISTRICT IV (Indiana, Kentucky, Ohio, Tennessee). Riverview Sq, Louisville, KY 40202. **502-587-9621**

DISTRICT V (Alabama, Louisiana, Mississippi). 860 St Charles Ave, New Orleans, LA 70130. **504-586-8101**

DISTRICT VI (Arkansas, Illinois, Missouri). 1415 Olive St, Louis, MO 63103. **314-342-3380**

DISTRICT VII (Michigan, Minnesota, North Dakota, Wisconsin). 375 Jackson St, St Paul, MN 55101. **612-221-0600**

DISTRICT VIII (Iowa, Nebraska, South Dakota, Wyoming). 206 S 19th St, Omaha, NE 68102. **402-444-3333**

DISTRICT IX (Colorado, Kansas, New Mexico, Oklahoma). 151 N Main St, Wichita KS 67202. **316-264-5371**

DISTRICT X (Texas). 430 Lamar Ave, Houston, TX 77002. **713-227-6111**

DISTRICT XI (Arizona, California, Hawaii, Nevada, Utah). 3636 American River Dr, Sacramento, CA 95825. **916-485-6000**

DISTRICT XII (Alaska, Idaho, Montana, Oregon, Washington). W 705 1st Ave, Spokane, WA 99204. **509-456-7300**

Federal Communications Commission Regional Offices

ANCHORAGE. PO Box 644, US Post Office and Courthouse Bldg, Anchorage, AK 99510. **907-272-1822**

ATLANTA. 1365 Peachtree St NE, Atlanta, GA 30309. **404-881-7381**

BALTIMORE. 31 Hopkins Plz, Baltimore, MD 21201. **301-962-2727**

BOSTON. 1600 Customhouse, Boston, MA 02109. **617-223-6608**

BEAUMONT. 300 Willow St, Beaumont, TX 77701. **713-838-0271**

BUFFALO. 111 W Huron St, Buffalo, NY 14202. **716-842-3216**

CHICAGO. 230 S Dearborn St, Chicago, IL 60604. **312-353-0195**

DALLAS. 1100 Commerce St, Dallas, TX 75242. **214-749-3243**

DENVER. 1405 Curtis St, Denver, CO 80202. **303-837-4053**

DETROIT. Washington Blvd and Lafayette St, Detroit, MI 48226. **313-226-6077**

HONOLULU. PO Box 1021, Honolulu, HI 96808. **808-546-5640**

HOUSTON. 515 Rusk Ave, Houston, TX 77002. **713-226-4307**

KANSAS CITY. 601 E 12th St, Kansas City, MO 64106. **816-374-5527**

LONG BEACH. 3711 Long Beach Blvd, Long Beach, CA 90807. **213-426-7886**

MIAMI. 51 SW 1st Ave, Miami, FL 33130. **305-350-5541**

NEW ORLEANS. 829 F Edward Herbert Federal Bldg, New Orleans, LA 70130. **504-589-2094**

NEW YORK. 201 Varick St, New York, NY 10014. **212-620-3437**

NORFOLK. 870 N Military Hwy, Norfolk, VA 23502. **804-441-4000**

PHILADELPHIA. 601 Market St, Philadelphia, PA 19106. **215-597-4411**

PORTLAND. 1220 SW 3rd Ave, Portland, OR 97204. **503-221-3097**

ST PAUL. 316 N Robert St, St Paul, MN 55101. **612-725-7819**

SAN DIEGO. 1245 7th Ave, San Diego, CA 92101. **714-293-5460**

SAN FRANCISCO. 555 Battery St, San Francisco, CA 94111. **415-556-7700**

SEATTLE. 915 2nd Ave, Seattle, WA 98174. **206-442-7610**

TAMPA. 1000 Ashley Dr, Tampa, FL 33602. **813-228-2605**

WASHINGTON. 1919 M St NW, Washington, DC 20554. **202-632-8834**

Federal Home Loan Bank Board District Offices

DISTRICT I (Connecticut, Maine, Massachusetts, New Hampshire, Rhode Island, Vermont). 1 Federal St, Boston, MA 02110. **617-223-3206**

DISTRICT II (New Jersey, New York, Puerto Rico, Virgin Islands). Floor 103, 1 World Trade Ctr, New York, NY 10048. **212-264-1447**

DISTRICT III (Delaware, Pennsylvania, West Virginia). 11 Stanwix St, Pittsburgh, PA 15222. **412-644-2666**

DISTRICT IV (Alabama, District of Columbia, Florida, Georgia, Maryland, North Carolina, South Carolina, Virginia). 10th Floor, 260 Peachtree St, Atlanta, GA 30303. **404-525-5778**

DISTRICT V (Kentucky, Ohio, Tennessee). 2700 Du Bois Tower, Cincinnati, OH 45202. **513-684-2855**

DISTRICT VI (Indiana, Michigan). 2950 Indiana Tower, Indiana Sq, Indianapolis, IN 46204. **317-269-6559**

DISTRICT VII (Illinois, Wisconsin). 111 E Wacker Dr, Chicago, IL 60601. **312-353-8045**

DISTRICT VIII (Iowa, Minnesota, Missouri, North Dakota, South Dakota). 714 2nd Ave, Des Moines, IA 50309. **515-284-4310**

DISTRICT IX (Arkansas, Louisiana, Mississippi, New Mexico, Texas). 1350 Tower Bldg, Little Rock, AR 72201. **501-378-5374**

DISTRICT X (Colorado, Kansas, Nebraska, Oklahoma). 120 E 6th St, (PO Box 828), Topeka, KS 66601. **913-295-2615**

DISTRICT XI (Arizona, California, Nevada). 600 California St, San Francisco, CA 94108. **415-556-1910**

DISTRICT XII (Alaska, Guam, Hawaii, Idaho, Montana, Oregon, Utah, Washington, Wyoming). 600 Stewart St, Seattle, WA 98101. **206-442-7584**

Federal Maritime Commission Regional Offices

ATLANTIC (Connecticut, Delaware, District of Columbia, Illinois, Indiana, Kentucky, Maine, Maryland, Massachusetts, Michigan, New Hampshire, New Jersey, New York, North Carolina, Ohio, Pennsylvania, Rhode Island, Tennessee, Vermont, Virginia, West Virginia, Wisconsin). 6 World Trade Ctr, New York, NY 10048. **212-264-1430**

PUERTO RICO (Puerto Rico, Virgin Islands). US District Courthouse and Federal Office Bldg, Carlos Chardon St, Hato Rey, PR 00917. **809-753-4198**

GULF (Alabama, Arkansas, Florida, Georgia, Kansas, Louisiana, Mississippi, Missouri, Oklahoma, South Carolina, Texas). 610 South St (PO Box 30550), New Orleans, LA 70190. **504-589-6662.** US Courthouse and Federal Bldg, 125 Bull St, Savannah, GA 31401. **912-232-4321**

PACIFIC (Alaska, Arizona, California, Colorado, Hawaii, Idaho, Iowa, Minnesota, Montana, Nebraska, Nevada, New Mexico, North Dakota, Oregon, South Dakota, Utah, Washington, Wyoming). 525 Market St, San Francisco, CA 94105. **415-556-5272.** US Customshouse Bldg (PO Box 3184, Terminal Island Station), San Pedro, CA 94431. **213-796-2542**

Federal Mediation and Conciliation Service Regional Offices

REGION I (Connecticut, Maine, Massachusetts, New Hampshire, New Jersey (part), New York, Puerto Rico, Rhode Island, Vermont, Virgin Islands). 26 Federal Plz, New York, NY 10007. **212-264-1000**

REGION II (Delaware, District of Columbia, Maryland, New Jersey—(part, Ohio—part, Pennsylvania, Virginia—part, West Virginia) 4th and Chestnut Sts, Philadelphia, PA 19106. **215-597-7676**

REGION III (Alabama, Arkansas, Florida, Georgia, Louisiana, Mississippi, North Carolina, South Carolina, Tennessee, Virginia—part). 1422 W Peachtree St NW, Atlanta, GA 30309. **404-881-2473**

REGION IV (Kentucky—part, Michigan—east of Lake Michigan, Ohio). 815 Superior Ave NE, Cleveland, OH 44114. **216-522-4800**

REGION V (Illinois (part), Indiana—part, Michigan—west of Lake Michigan, Minnesota, North Dakota, South Dakota, Wisconsin). 175 W Jackson St, Chicago, IL 60604. **312-353-7350**

REGION VI (Iowa, Kansas, Missouri, Nebraska, Oklahoma, Texas—part, Illinois—part). Chromalloy Plz, 120 S Central, St Louis, MO 63105. **314-425-3291**

REGION VII (Arizona, California, Guam, Hawaii, Nevada—part, New Mexico, Texas —western, largest part). 50 Francisco St, San Francisco, CA 94133. **415-556-4670**

REGION VIII (Alaska, Colorado, Idaho, Montana, Nevada—northeastern part,

Oregon, Washington, Wyoming). 2615 4th Ave, Seattle, WA 98121. **206-442-5800**

Federal Railroad Administration Transportation Regional Offices and Regional Administration

EASTERN REGION. Rm 1020, Independence Bldg, 434 Walnut St, Philadelphia, PA 19106. **215-597-0750.** Wallace F Holl (acting)

SOUTHERN REGION. Suite 216-B, 1568 Willingham Dr, College Park, GA 30337. **404-526-7801.** Charles R Meyrick (acting)

CENTRAL REGION. Rm 210, 536 S Clark St, Chicago, IL 60605. **312-353-6203.** Albert L Hynes

SOUTHWEST REGION. Rm 11A23, Federal Office Bldg, 819 Taylor St, Fort Worth, TX 76102. **817-334-3601.** Trini Guillen

WESTERN REGION. Suite 630, 2 Embarcadero Ctr, San Francisco, CA 94111. **415-556-6411.** Earl H Anderson (acting)

Federal Trade Commission Regional Offices

ATLANTA. Rm 1000, 1718 Peachtree St, NW, Atlanta, GA 30309. **404-881-4836.**

BOSTON. Rm 1301, 150 Causeway St, Boston, MA 02114. **617-223-6621.**

CHICAGO. Suite 1437, 55 E Monroe St, Chicago, IL 60603. **312-353-4423.**

CLEVELAND. Suite 500, Mall Bldg, 118 St Clair Ave, Cleveland, OH 44114. **216-522-4207.**

DALLAS. Suite 2665, 2001 Bryan St, Dallas, TX 75201. **214-749-3056.**

DENVER. Suite 2900, 1405 Curtis St, Denver, CO 80202. **303-837-2271.**

LOS ANGELES. Rm 13209, 11000 Wilshire Blvd, Los Angeles, CA 90024. **213-824-7575.**

NEW YORK. 22nd Floor, Federal Bldg, 26 Federal Plz, New York, NY 10007. **212-264-1207.**

SAN FRANCISCO. Box 36005, 450 Golden Gate Ave, San Francisco, CA 94102. **415-556-1270.**

SEATTLE. 28th Floor, Federal Bldg, 915 2nd Ave, Seattle, WA 98174. **206-442-4655.**

WASHINGTON. Rm 600-C, Gelman Bldg, 2120 L St, NW, Washington, DC 20017. **202-254-7700.**

General Services Administration Business Service Centers

REGION I. John W McCormack Bldg, Boston, MA 02109. **617-223-2868.**

REGION II. 26 Federal Plz, New York, NY 10007. **212-264-1234.**

REGION III. 7th and D Sts, SW, Washington, DC 20407. **202-472-1804.** 600 Arch St, Philadelphia, PA 19106. **215-597-9613.**

REGION IV. 1776 Peachtree St, NW, Atlanta, GA 30309. **404-881-4661.**

REGION V. 230 S Dearborn St, Chicago, IL 60604. **312-353-5383.**

REGION VI. 1500 E Bannister Rd, Kansas City, MO 64131. **816-926-7203.**

REGION VII. 819 Taylor St, Fort Worth, TX 76102. **817-334-3284.** 515 Rusk St, Houston, TX 77002. **713-226-5787.**

REGION VIII. Bldg 41, Denver Federal Ctr, Denver, CO 80225. **303-234-2216.**

REGION IX. 525 Market St, San Francisco, CA 94105. **415-556-2122.** 300 N Los Angeles St, Los Angeles, CA 90012. **213-688-3210.**

REGION X. 440 Federal Bldg, 915 2nd Ave, Seattle, WA 98174. **206-442-5556.**

Department of Health Education and Welfare Regional Public Information Contacts

REGION I. BOSTON REGIONAL OFFICE (Connecticut, Maine, Massachusetts, New Hampshire, Rhode Island, Vermont). John F Kennedy Federal Office Bldg, Government Ctr, Boston, MA 02203. **617-223-7291.** Frank Bucci. (h) **617-259-9687.**

REGION II. NEW YORK REGIONAL OFFICE (New York, New Jersey, Puerto Rico, Virgin Islands). 26 Federal Plz, New York, NY 10007. **212-264-4483** or **3621.** Robert O'Connell. (h) **201-647-3298.**

REGION III. PHILADELPHIA REGIONAL OFFICE (Delaware, District of Columbia, Maryland, Pennsylvania, Virginia, West Virginia). 3535 Market St (PO Box 13716), Philadelphia, PA 19104. **215-596-6482.** Dave Frankel. (h) **215-638-4736.**

REGION IV. ATLANTA REGIONAL OFFICE (Alabama, Florida, Georgia, Kentucky, Mississippi, North Carolina, South Carolina, Tennessee). Rm 404, 50 7th St, NE, Atlanta, GA 30323. **404-881-4001.** Joseph Juska. (h) **404-351-3551.**

REGION V. CHICAGO REGIONAL OFFICE (Illinois, Indiana, Minnesota, Michigan, Ohio, Wisconsin). 35th Floor, 300 S Wacker Dr, Chicago, IL 60606. **312-353-5164** or **4640.** Lee Feldman. (h) **312-472-5624.**

REGION VI. DALLAS REGIONAL OFFICE (Arkansas, Louisiana, New Mexico, Oklahoma, Texas). 11th Floor, 1200 Main Tower Bldg, Dallas, TX 75202. **214-655-3311.** Hal Coley. (h) **214-882-4826.**

REGION VII. KANSAS CITY REGIONAL OFFICE (Iowa, Kansas, Missouri, Nebraska). 601 E 12th St, Kansas City, MO 64106. **816-374-3436.** Dick Wall. (h) **913-362-3167.**

REGION VIII. DENVER REGIONAL OFFICE (Colorado, Montana, North Dakota, South Dakota, Utah, Wyoming). Federal Office Bldg, 1961 Stout St, Denver, CO 80202. **303-837-2694.** Carl Coleman. (h) **303-979-3152.**

REGION IX. SAN FRANCISCO REGIONAL OFFICE (American Samoa, Arizona, California, Guam, Hawaii, Nevada). 50 Fulton St, San Francisco, CA 94102. **415-556-2246** or **2255.** Robert Fouts. (h) **415-563-8388.**

REGION X. SEATTLE REGIONAL OFFICE (Alaska, Idaho, Oregon, Washington). 1321 2nd Ave, Seattle, WA 98101. **206-442-0486.** Harvey Chester. (h) **206-232-2339.**

Department of Housing and Urban Development Regional Offices and Regional Administrators

REGION I. Rm 800, John F Kennedy Federal Bldg, Boston, MA 02203. **617-223-4066.** Edward T Martin, Jr

REGION II. Rm 3541, 26 Federal Plz, New York, NY 10007. **212-264-8068.** Thomas Appleby

REGION III. Curtis Bldg, 6th and Walnut Sts, Philadelphia, PA 19106. **215-597-2560.** Thomas G Maloney

REGION IV. Rm 211, Pershing Point Plz, 1371 Peachtree St NE, Atlanta, GA 30309. **404-881-4585.** A Russell Marane

REGION V. 300 S Wacker Dr, Chicago, IL 60606. **312-353-5680.** Ronald Gatton

REGION VI. Rm 14C2, Earle Cabell Federal Bldg, US Courthouse, 1100 Commerce St, Dallas, TX 75202. **214-749-7401.** Thomas J Armstrong

REGION VII. Rm 300, Federal Office Bldg, 911 Walnut St, Kansas City, MO 64106. **816-374-2661.** William O Anderson

REGION VIII. Executive Tower, 1405 Curtis St, Denver, CO 80202. **303-837-4513.** Betty Jane Miller

REGION IX. PO Box 36003, 450 Golden Gate Ave, San Francisco, CA 94102. **415-556-4752.** Emma D McFarlin

REGION X. Arcade Plaza Bldg, 1321 2nd Ave, Seattle, WA 98101. **206-442-5414.** George J Roybal

Department of the Interior Regional Offices

ATLANTA. 148 Cain St NE, Atlanta, GA 30303. **404-221-2524**

DENVER. Bldg 67, Denver Federal Ctr, Denver, CO 80225. **303-234-3120**

SEATTLE. 1321 2nd Ave, Seattle, WA 98101. **206-778-8387**

ANCHORAGE. 1675 C St (PO Box 120), Anchorage, AK 99501. **907-265-5278**

Internal Revenue Service (Treasury) Regional and District Public Information Officers

Central Region

REGIONAL OFFICE. Richard L White, PO Box 1699, Cincinnati, OH 45201. **513-684-2841**

CINCINNATI DISTRICT. Joyzell M Friason, PO Box 1818, Cincinnati, OH 45201. **513-684-2424**

CLEVELAND DISTRICT. Rollie E Woods, PO Box 99181, Cleveland, OH 44199. **216-522-7008**

DETROIT DISTRICT. Walter A Dunnigan, PO Box 32501, Detroit, MI 48232. **313-226-7288**

INDIANAPOLIS DISTRICT. Robert B Branson, PO Box 44687, Indianapolis, IN 46244. **317-269-6034**

LOUISVILLE DISTRICT. Robert J Kobel, PO Box 1735, Louisville, KY 40201. **502-582-5376**

PARKERSBURG DISTRICT. Garry Wright, PO Box 1388, Parkersburg, WV 26101. **304-422-8551**

CINCINNATI SERVICE CENTER. Robert E Norris, PO Box 267, Covington, KY 41019. **513-684-1682**

Mid-Atlantic Region

REGIONAL OFFICE. Peter J Jaensch, Internal Revenue Service, 2 Penn Center Plz, Philadelphia, PA 19102. **215-597-2080**

BALTIMORE DISTRICT. David R Estey, PO Box 538, Baltimore, MD 21203. **301-962-3330**

NEWARK DISTRICT. Henry Holmes, PO Box 1261, Newark, NJ 07101. **201-645-3856**

PHILADELPHIA DISTRICT. Charles H Powers, PO Box 12805, Philadelphia, PA 19106. **215-597-4245**

PITTSBURGH DISTRICT. Louis E Romito, PO Box 2488, Pittsburgh, PA 15230. **412-644-5633**

RICHMOND DISTRICT. Raymond S Taylor, PO Box 10107, Richmond, VA 23240. **804-782-2262**

WILMINGTON DISTRICT. Margaret Brenner, PO Box 28, Wilmington, DE 19899. **302-571-6052**

PHILADELPHIA SERVICE CENTER. Richard Arter, PO Box 245, Cornwell Heights, PA 19020. **215-969-2506**

Midwest Region

REGIONAL OFFICE. Diane F Roth, Internal Revenue Service, Room 822, 1 No Wacker Dr, Chicago, Ill 60606. **312-353-1826**

ABERDEEN DISTRICT. Jerald P Ryan, PO Box 370, Aberdeen, SD 57401. **605-225-7215**

CHICAGO DISTRICT. Jeffrey B Raymond, PO Box 1193, Chicago, Il 60690. **312-353-3121**

DES MOINES DISTRICT. David R Evans, PO Box 1337, Des Moines, IA 50305. **515-284-4710**

FARGO DISTRICT. Alexander G Lawrence, PO Box 8, Fargo, ND 58102. **701-237-5771**

MILWAUKEE DISTRICT. Ronald A Fleissner, PO Box 495, Milwaukee, WI 53201. **414-291-3386**

OMAHA DISTRICT. Daniel C Seklecki, PO Box 1052, Omaha, NE 68102. **402-221-3504**

ST LOUIS DISTRICT. Herbert D Freer, PO Box 1548, Central Station, St Louis, MO 63188. **314-425-5661**

ST PAUL DISTRICT. William L Knight, PO Box 3556, St. Paul, MN 55165. **612-725-7435**

SPRINGFIELD DISTRICT. Frank A Bryson, PO Box 1468, Springfield, IL 62704 **217-525-4123**

KANSAS CITY SERVICE CENTER. Mary Ann Ruth, PO Box 5321, Kansas City, MO 64131. **816-926-5784**

North Atlantic Region

REGIONAL OFFICE. John A Demme, PO Box 2815, Church St Station, New York, NY 10007. **212-264-7544**

ALBANY DISTRICT. Donald D Roberts, Jr, Internal Revenue Service, Leo W O'Brien, Federal Office Bldg, Clinton Ave and N Pearl St, Albany, NY 12207. **518-472-2425**

AUGUSTA DISTRICT. Malcolm W Callison, PO Box 787, Augusta, ME 04330. **207-622-6171**

BOSTON DISTRICT. Edward V Callanan, PO Box 9112, John F Kennedy Post Office, Boston, MA 02203. **617-223-6020**

BROOKLYN DISTRICT. Joseph Rosta, PO Box 380, GPO, Brooklyn, NY 11202. **212-330-7257**

BUFFALO DISTRICT. William J Gorman, PO Box 60, Buffalo, NY 14201. **716-842-3627**

BURLINGTON DISTRICT. John J Hassett, Internal Revenue Service, 11 Elmwood Ave, Burlington, VT 05401. **802-862-6351**

HARTFORD DISTRICT. Edward J Rodonis, PO Box 959, Hartford, CT 06101. **203-244-2700**

MANHATTAN DISTRICT. Milton A Waldman, PO Box 3000, New York, NY 10008. **212-264-0609**

PORTSMOUTH DISTRICT. William P Maguire, PO Box 720, Portsmouth, NH 03801. **603-436-7720**

PROVIDENCE DISTRICT. Joseph M Burke, PO Box 6528, Providence, RI 02904. **401-528-5225**

ANDOVER SERVICE CENTER. John S Mannion, PO Box 311, Andover, MA 01810. **617-475-8330**

BROOKHAVEN SERVICE CENTER. William M Caine, PO Box 400, Brookhaven, NY 11719. **516-654-6026**

Southeast Region

REGIONAL OFFICE. Melvin R Mill, PO Box 926, Atlanta, GA 30301. **404-221-6621**

ATLANTA DISTRICT. Giles A Hollingsworth, PO Box 1642, Atlanta, GA 30301. **404-221-4501**

BIRMINGHAM DISTRICT. Denton Lankford, Internal Revenue Service, Rm 1205, 2121 8th Ave N, Birmingham, AL 35203. **205-254-1260**

COLUMBIA DISTRICT. Thomas M Williams, PO Box 407, Columbia, SC 29201. **803-765-5703**

GREENSBORO DISTRICT. B Glenn Jones, PO Box 20541, Greensboro, NC 27420. **919-378-5266**

JACKSON DISTRICT. Roy D Caves, PO Box 370, Jackson, MS 39205. **601-969-4235**

JACKSONVILLE DISTRICT. Holger E Euringer, PO Box 35045, Jacksonville, FL 32202. **904-791-2989**

NASHVILLE DISTRICT. Evelyn M Miller, PO Box 1107, Nashville, TN 37202. **615-749-5788**

ATLANTA SERVICE CENTER. Emory D Paris, PO Box 47421, Doraville, GA 30341. **404-455-2231**

MEMPHIS SERVICE CENTER. J D Smith, PO Box 30309, Airport Mail Facility, Memphis, TN 38130. **910-365-5333**

Southwest Region

REGIONAL OFFICE. Stanley C Jensen, PO Box 5781, Dallas, TX 75222. **214-655-5019**

ALBUQUERQUE DISTRICT. Rosie Armijo, PO Box 1967, Albuquerque, NM 87103. **505-766-2753**

AUSTIN DISTRICT. Charles G Bailey, PO Box 250, Austin, TX 78767. **512-397-5315**

CHEYENNE DISTRICT. Phyllis J Elbrecht, PO Box 1829, Cheyenne, WY 82001. **307-778-2343**

DALLAS DISTRICT. Marlene A Gaysek, Mail Code 410, 1100 Commerce St, Dallas, TX 75242. **214-749-3567**

DENVER DISTRICT. Robert P Morris, Internal Revenue Service, 1050 17th St, Denver, CO 80202. **303-837-3575**

LITTLE ROCK DISTRICT. Maeline D Hornbeck, PO Box 3778, Little Rock, AR 72203. **501-378-5340**

NEW ORLEANS DISTRICT. Donald G Hetzler, PO Box 30309, New Orleans, LA 70190. **504-589-2453**

OKLAHOMA CITY DISTRICT. Robert L Deurbrouck, PO Box 66, Oklahoma City, OK 73101. **405-231-5091**

WICHITA DISTRICT. James T Manuszak, PO Box 400, Wichita, KS 67201. **316-267-6311**

AUSTIN SERVICE CENTER. Douglass R Sefcik, PO Box 934, Austin, TX 78767. **512-397-7626**

Western Region

REGIONAL OFFICE. Francis R Busalacchi, PO Box 889, San Francisco, CA 94101. **415-556-3666**

ANCHORAGE DISTRICT. Virginia H Gray, PO Box 1500, Anchorage, AK 99501. **907-265-4767**

BOISE DISTRICT. Marshall D Rutherford, PO Box 041, 550 W Fort St, Boise, ID 83724. **208-384-1324**

HELENA DISTRICT. John A Rigler, Internal Revenue Service, 2nd Floor W, Federal Bldg, Helena, MT 59601. **406-449-5245**

HONOLULU DISTRICT. Leonard F Lachel, PO Box 2810, Honolulu, HI 96803. **808-546-8929**

LOS ANGELES DISTRICT. Kenneth L Sutton, PO Box 391, Los Angeles, CA 90053. **213-688-4113**

PHOENIX DISTRICT. Vincent E Bond, PO Box 2350, Phoenix, AZ 85002. **602-261-3488**

PORTLAND DISTRICT. Dale G Potts, PO Box 3341, Portland, OR 97208. **503-221-3246**

RENO DISTRICT. Martin Bibb, PO Box 891, Reno, NV 89504. **702-784-5661**

SALT LAKE CITY DISTRICT. Albert A Wallberg, PO Box 2069, Salt Lake City, UT 84110. **801-524-5811**

SAN FRANCISCO DISTRICT. Gregory L Crosby, PO Box 36020, 450 Gloden Gate Ave, San Francisco, CA 94102. **415-556-0551**

SEATTLE DISTRICT. James Aguirre, PO Box 854, Seattle, WA 98111. **206-442-5515**

FRESNO SERVICE CENTER. Robert L Marion, PO Box 12866, Fresno, CA 93779. **209-448-6382**

OGDEN SERVICE CENTER. Douglas R Green, PO Box 9941, Ogden, UT 84409. **801-399-6129**

Interstate Commerce Commission Field Offices

Alabama

BIRMINGHAM. Rm 1616, 2121 Bldg, 2121 8th Ave N, Birmingham, 35203. **205-254-1286**

MOBILE. PO Box 2112, Mobile, 36601. **205-690-2868**

Alaska

ANCHORAGE. PO Box 1532, Rm 268, Federal Bldg Anchorage, 99510. **907-265-5351**

Arkansas

LITTLE ROCK. 2519 Federal Bldg, Little Rock, 72201. **501-378-4361**

California

LOS ANGELES. 7708 Federal Bldg, 300 N Los Angeles St, Los Angeles, 90012. **213-668-4008** or **4009**

SAN FRANCISCO. PO Box 36004, 13001 Federal Bldg, 450 Golden Gate Ave, San Francisco, 94102. **415-556-1392**

Connecticut

HARTFORD. 324 US Post Office, 135 High St, Hartford, 06101. **203-244-2560**

District of Columbia

WASHINGTON. ICC Building, 12th st and Constitution Ave NW, Washington, 20423. **202-343-4671**

Florida

JACKSONVILLE. 288 Federal Bldg, 400 W Bay St (PO Box 35008), Jacksonville, 32202. **904-791-2551** or **2552**

MIAMI. Suite 101, Monterey Bldg, 8401 NW, 53rd Ter, Miami, 33166. **305-350-5551**

Georgia

ATLANTA. Rm 300, 1252 W Peachtree St NW, Atlanta, 30309. **404-526-5371, 5307,** or **5455**

Idaho

BOISE. Box 07, 555 W Fort St, Boise, 83724. **208-342-2711,** Ext 2505

Illinois

CHICAGO. Rm 1086, Everett McKinley Dirksen Bldg, 219 S Dearborn St, Chicago, 60604. **312-353-7275** or **6185**

SPRINGFIELD. 414 Leland Office Bldg, 527 Capital Ave, Springfield, 62701. **217-525-4075**

Indiana

FORT WAYNE. Suite 113, 345 W Wayne St, Fort Wayne, 46802. **219-422-6131**

INDIANAPOLIS. 429 Federal Bldg, E Ohio St, Indianapolis, 46204. **317-269-7701**

Iowa

DES MOINES. 518 Federal Bldg, 210 Walnut St, Des Moines, 50309. **515-284-4416**

Kansas

TOPEKA. 234 Federal Bldg, Topeka, 66603. **913-234-8661,** Ext 401

WICHITA. 501 Petroleum Bldg, 221 Broadway, Wichita, 67202. **316-267-6311,** Ext 608

Kentucky

LEXINGTON. 216 Bakhaus Bldg, 1500 W Main St, Lexington, 40505. **606-233-2511**

LOUISVILLE. 426 US Post Office, 601 W Broadway, Louisville, 40202. **502-582-5167**

Louisianna

NEW ORLEANS. T-9038 Federal Bldg and US Post Office, 701 Loyola Ave, New Orleans, 70113. **504-527-6101** or **6102**

Maine

PORTLAND. PO Box 167, PSS, 305 US Post Office and Courthouse, 76 Pearl St, Portland, 04112. **207-775-3131**

Maryland

BALTIMORE. 814-B Federal Bldg, Charles Ctr, 31 Hopkins Plz, Baltimore, 21201. **301-962-2560**

Massachussets

BOSTON. Rm 501, 150 Causeway St, Boston, 02114. **617-223-2372**

SPRINGFIELD. 338-342 Federal Bldg, 436 Dwight St, Springfield, 01103. **413-781-2420**

Michigan

DETROIT. 1110 David Broderick Tower Bldg, 10 Witherill St, Detroit, 48226. **313-226-4966**

LANSING. 225 Federal Bldg, 325 Allegan St, Lansing, 48933. **517-372-1910,** Ext 568

Minnesota

MINNEAPOLIS. 414 Federal Bldg and US Courthouse, 110 S 4th St, Minneapolis, 55401. **612-725-2326**

Mississippi

JACKSON. Rm 212, 145 E Amite Bldg, Jackson, 39201. **601-948-7821,** Ext 348 or 357

Missouri

KANSAS CITY. 600 Federal Bldg, 911 Walnut St, Kansas City, 64106. **816-374-5561**

ST LOUIS. Rm 1465, 210 N 12th St, St Louis, 63101. **314-425-4103**

Montana

BILLINGS. 222 US Post Office, Billings, 59101. **406-245-6711,** Ext 6261 or 6350

Nebraska

LINCOLN. 285 Federal Bldg and US Courthouse, 100 Centennial Mall, North Lincoln, 68508. **402-471-5088**

OMAHA. Suite 620, Union Pacific Plaza Bldg, 110 N 14th St, Omaha, 68102. **402-221-4644**

Nevada

CARSON CITY. 203 Federal Bldg, 705 N Plaza St, Carson City, 89701. **702-882-2085**

New Hampshire

CONCORD. 424 Federal Bldg, 55 Pleasant St, Concord, 03301. **603-224-1887**

New Mexico

ALBUQUERQUE. 1106 Federal Office Bldg, 517 Gold Ave SW, Albuquerque, 87101. **505-766-2241**

New Jersey

NEWARK. Rm 618, 9 Clinton St, Newark, 07102. **201-645-3550**

TRENTON. 204 Carroll Bldg, 428 E State St, Trenton, 08608. **609-989-2207-8**

New York

ALBANY. 518 New Federal Bldg, Maiden Lane and Broadway, Albany, 12207. **518-472-2273**

BUFFALO. 612 Federal Bldg, 111 W Huron St, Buffalo, 14202. **716-842-2008**

NEW YORK. Rm 1807, 26 Federal Plz, New York, 10007. **212-264-1072**

SYRACUSE. Rm 1259, US Courthouse and Federal Bldg, 100 S Clinton St, Syracuse, 13202. **315-423-5095**

North Carolina

CHARLOTTE. Rm cc-516, Mart Office Bldg, 800 Briar Creek Rd, Charlotte, 28205. **704-372-0711,** Ext 451 or 452

RALEIGH. PO Box 26896, 624 Federal Bldg, 320 New Bern Ave, Raleigh, 27611. **919-755-4650**

North Dakota

FARGO. PO Box 2340, Federal Bldg and US Post Office, 657 2nd Ave N, Fargo, 58102. **701-237-5771,** Ext 5285

Ohio

CINCINNATI. 5514-B Federal Bldg, 550 Main St, Cincinnati, 45202. **513-684-2975** or **2976**

CLEVELAND. 731 Federal Bldg, 1240 E 9th St, Cleveland, 44199. **216-522-4000** or **4001**

COLUMBUS. 220 Federal Bldg and US Courthouse, 85 Marconi Blvd, Columbus, 43215. **614-469-5620**

TOLEDO. 313 Federal Office Bldg, 234 Summit St, Toledo, 43604. **419-259-7486** or **7487**

Oklahoma

OKLAHOMA CITY. 240 Old Post Office and Courthouse, 215 NW 3rd St, Oklahoma City, 73102. **405-231-4496**

Oregon

PORTLAND. 114 Pioneer Courthouse, 555 SW Yamhill St, Portland, 97204. **503-221-3102**

Pennsylvania

HARRISBURG. PO Box 869, 278 Federal Bldg, 228 Walnut St, Harrisburg, 17108. **717-782-4437**

PHILADELPHIA. Rm 3238, Wm J Green, Jr, Federal Bldg, 600 Arch St, Philadelphia, 19106. **215-597-4449** or **4453**

PITTSBURGH. 2111 Federal Bldg, 1000 Liberty Ave, Pittsburgh, 15222. **412-644-2929**

SCRANTON. 314 US Post Office, N Washington Ave and Linden St, Scranton, 18503. **717-347-2020**

Rhode Island

PROVIDENCE. Rm 402, 187 Westminster St, Providence, 02903. **401-528-4306**

South Carolina

COLUMBIA. Rm 302, 1400 Bldg, 1400 Pickens St, Columbia, 29201. **803-765-5586**

South Dakota

PIERRE. 369 Federal Bldg, Pierre, 57501. **605-224-2812**

Tennessee

MEMPHIS. Suite 2006, 100 N Main St, Memphis, 38103. **901-534-3437**

NASHVILLE. Rm A-422, US Federal Bldg, Nashville, 37203. **615-251-5391**

Texas

AMARILLO. 1010 Herring Plz, 317 E 3rd St, Amarillo, 79101. **806-376-2138**

DALLAS. Rm 13C12, 1100 Commerce St, Dallas, 75202. **214-749-3691**

FORT WORTH. 9A27 Fritz Garland Lanham Federal Bldg, 819 Taylor St, Fort Worth, 76102. **817-334-2794**

HOUSTON. 8610 Federal Bldg and US Courthouse, 515 Rusk Ave, Houston, 77002.

713-226-4241. Mailing address: PO Box 61212, Houston, TX 77061

SAN ANTONIO. Rm B-400, 727 E Durango, San Antonio, 78206. **512-229-6120**

Utah

SALT LAKE CITY. 5301 Federal Bldg, 125 S State St, Salt Lake City, 84138. **801-524-5680**

Vermont

MONTPELIER. Rm 303, 87 State St (PO Box 548), Montpelier, 05602. **802-223-6001**

Virginia

RICHMOND. 10-502 Federal Bldg, 400 N 8th St, Richmond, 23240. **804-782-2541**

ROANOKE. 5104 FB Thomas Bldg, 215 Campbell Ave SW, Roanoke, 24011. **703-343-1581**

Washington

SEATTLE. 858 Federal Bldg, 915 2nd Ave, Seattle, 98174. **206-442-5421**

West Virginia

CHARLESTON. 3108 Federal Bldg, 500 Quarrier St, Charleston, 25301. **304-343-6181,** Ext 354 or 355

WHEELING. 416 Old Post Office Bldg, 12th and Chapline Sts, Wheeling, 26003. **304-232-6960**

Wisconsin

MADISON. Rm 202, 139 W Wilson St, Madison 53703. **608-252-5427**

MILWAUKEE. Rm 619, 517 E Wisconsin Ave, Milwaukee, 53202. **414-224-3183**

Wyoming

CASPER. 105 Federal Bldg and Courthouse, 111 S Wolcott, Casper, 82601. **307-265-5550,** Ext 5243

Department of Labor
Regional Information Officers

REGION I. Rm E-308, John F Kennedy Federal Bldg, Boston, MA 02203 . **617-223-6767.** Paul F Neal

REGION II. Rm 3570, 1515 Broadway, New York, NY 10036. **212-399-5477.** Edward I Weintraub

REGION III. Rm 2460, 3535 Market St, Philadelphia, PA 19104. **215-596-1139.** John P Hord

REGION IV. Rm 317, 1371 Peachtree St NE, Atlanta, GA 30309. **404-526-5495.** Frances Ridgway

REGION V. Rm 737, 230 S Dearborn St, Chicago, IL 60606. **312-353-6976.** John D Mellott

REGION VI. Rm 220, 555 Griffin Square Bldg, Griffin and Young Sts, Dallas, TX 75202. **214-749-2308.** Les Gaddie

REGION VII. Rm 2509, Federal Office Bldg, 911 Walnut St, Kansas City, MO 64106. **816-374-5481.** Neal A Johnson

REGION VIII. Rm 14010, Federal Bldg, 1961 Stout St, Denver, CO 80294. **303-837-4235.** Ernest E Sanchez

REGION IX. Rm 10007, Federal Bldg, 450 Golden Gate Ave, San Francisco, CA 94102. **415-556-3423.** Joe B Kirkbride

REGION X. Rm 8001, Federal Office Bldg, 909 1st Ave, Seattle, WA 98174. **206-442-7620.** Jack Strickland

Office of Minority Business Enterprise (Commerce) Regional Headquarters

ATLANTA (Alabama, Florida, Georgia, Kentucky, Mississippi, North Carolina, South Carolina, Tennessee). 1371 Peachtree St NE, Atlanta, GA 30309. **404-881-4091**

CHICAGO (Illinois, Indiana, Iowa, Kansas, Michigan, Minnesota, Missouri, Nebraska, Ohio, Wisconsin). 55 E Monroe St, Chicago, IL 60603. **312-353-5210**

DALLAS (Arkansas, Colorado, Louisiana, Montana, New Mexico, North Dakota, Oklahoma, South Dakota, Texas, Utah, Wyoming). 1412 Main St, Dallas, TX 75202. **214-749-7581**

NEW YORK (Connecticut, Maine, Massachusetts, New Hampshire, New Jersey, New York, Puerto Rico, Rhode Island, Vermont, Virgin Islands). 26 Federal Plz, New York, NY 10007. **212-264-3262**

SAN FRANCISCO (Alaska, Arizona, California, Hawaii, Idaho, Nevada, Oregon, Washington). PO Box 36114, 450 Golden Gate Ave, San Francisco, CA 94102. **415-556-6733**

WASHINGTON, DC (Delaware, District of Columbia, Maryland, Pennsylvania, Virginia, West Virginia). 1730 K St NW, Washington, DC 20006. **202-634-7897**

National Highway Traffic Safety Administration (Transportation) Regional Offices and Regional Administrators

REGION I. Transportation Systems Ctr, 55 Broadway, Cambridge, MA 02142. **617-494-2680.** James F Williamson

REGION II. Suite 204, 222 Mamaroneck Ave, White Plains, NY 10601. **914-761-4250.** Dean Van Gorden

REGION III. Airport Plaza Bldg, 6701 Elkridge Landing Rd, Linthicum, MD 21090. **301-796-5117.** Vincent D Walsh, Sr

REGION IV. Suite 501, 1720 Peachtree Rd NW, Atlanta, GA 30309. **404-881-4571.** Stanley M Keesling

REGION V. Suite 214, Executive Plz, 1010 Dixie Hwy, Chicago Heights, IL 60411. **312-756-1950.** Gordon G Lindquist

REGION VI. Rm 11A26, 819 Taylor St, Fort Worth, TX 76102. **817-334-3653.** E Robert Anderson

REGION VII. PO Box 19515, Kansas City, MO 64141. **816-926-7887.** Everett L McBride

REGION VIII. 330 S Garrison St, Lakewood, CO 80226. **303-234-3253.** R C O'Connell

REGION IX. Suite 610, 2 Embarcadero Ctr, San Francisco, CA 94111. **415-556-6415.** Bradford M Crittenden

REGION X. 3140 Federal Bldg, 915 2nd Ave, Seattle, WA 98174. **206-442-5934.** William L Hall

National Labor Relations Board Regional Offices

REGION I. 99 High St, Boston, MA 02110. **617-223-3300**

REGION II. 26 Federal Plz, New York, NY 10007. **212-264-0300**

REGION III. 111 W Huron St, Buffalo, NY 14202. **716-842-3100**

REGION IV. 600 Arch St, Philadelphia, PA 19106. **215-597-7601**

REGION V. 101 W Lombard St, Baltimore, MD 21201. **301-962-2822**

REGION VI. 601 Grant St, Pittsburgh, PA 15219. **412-644-2977**

REGION VII. 477 Michigan Ave, Detroit, MI 48226. **313-226-3200**

REGION VIII. 1240 E 9th St, Cleveland, OH 44199. **216-522-3715**

REGION IX. 550 Main St, Cincinnati, OH 45202. **513-684-3686**

REGION X. 730 Peachtree St NW, Atlanta, GA 30308. **404-881-4760**

REGION XI. 251 N Main St, Winston-Salem, NC 27101. **919-723-3201**

REGION XII. 500 Zack St (PO Box 3322), Tampa, FL 33602. **813-228-2659**

REGION XIII. 219 S Dearborn St, Chicago, IL 60604. **312-353-7570**

REGION XIV. 210 N 12th Blvd, St Louis, MO 63101. **314-425-4167**

REGION XV. 1001 Howard Ave, New Orleans, LA 70113. **504-589-6361**

REGION XVI. 819 Taylor St, Fort Worth, TX 76102. **817-334-2921**

REGION XVII. 2 Gateway Ctr, 4th and State Sts, Kansas City, KS 66101. **816-374-4518**

REGION XVIII. 110 S 4th St, Minneapolis, MN 55401. **612-725-2611**

REGION XIX. 915 2nd Ave (Box 36047), Seattle, WA 98174. **206-442-4532**

REGION XX. 450 Golden Gate Ave, San Francisco, CA 94102. **415-556-3197**

REGION XXI. 606 S Olive St, Los Angeles, CA 90014. **213-688-5200**

REGION XXII. 970 Broad St, Newark, NJ 07102. **201-645-2100**

REGION XXIII. 500 Dallas Ave, Houston, TX 77002. **713-226-4296**

REGION XXIV. PO Box UU, Federal Bldg, Hato Rey, PR 00919. **809-753-4347**

REGION XXV. 575 N Pennsylvania St, Indianapolis, IN 46204. **317-269-7430**

REGION XXVI. 1407 Union Ave, Memphis, TN 38104. **901-222-2725**

REGION XXVII. 721 19th St, Denver, CO 80202. **303-837-3551**

REGION XXVIII. 6107 N 7th St, Phoenix, AZ 85014. **602-261-3717**

REGION XXIX. 16 Courth St, Brooklyn, NY 11241. **212-596-3535**

REGION XXX. 744 N 4th St, Milwaukee, WI 53203. **414-224-3861**

REGION XXXI. 11000 Wilshire Blvd, Los Angeles, CA 90024. **213-824-7351**

REGION XXXII. 7901 Oak Port St, Oakland, CA 94621. **415-632-9000**

Small Business Administration Field Offices

Region I

BOSTON. 10th Floor, 60 Batterymarch St, Boston, MA 02110. *Public information officer.* **617-223-4495**

HOLYOKE. 4th Floor, 302 High St, Holyoke, MA 01040. **413-536-8770.** *Public information officer.* **413-536-9324**

AUGUSTA. Rm 512, Federal Bldg, 40 Western Ave, Augusta, ME 04330. **207-622-6171.** *Public information officer,* Harvey L Bryant, Ext 227

CONCORD. Rm 213, 55 Pleasant St, Concord, NH 03301. **603-224-4041.** *Public information officer.* **603-224-4041**

HARTFORD. 1 Financial Plz, Hartford, CT 06103. **203-244-3600.** *Public information officer.* **203-244-2411**

MONTPELIER. Rm 231, Federal Bldg, 87 State St, Montpelier, VT 05602. **802-229-0538.** *Public information officer.* **802-832-4422**

PROVIDENCE. 7th Floor, 57 Eddy St, Providence, RI 02903. **401-528-1000.** *Public information officer.* **401-838-4538**

Region II

NEW YORK. Rm 3214, 26 Federal Plz, New York, NY 10007. **212-264-1468.** *Public information officer.* **212-264-4480**

MELVILLE. Rm 205, 425 Broad Hollow Rd, Melville, NY 11746. **516-752-1626.** *Public information officer.* **516-752-1626**

SYRACUSE. Rm 1073, Federal Bldg, 100 S Clinton St, Syracuse, NY 13202. **315-423-5370.** *Public information officer.* **315-423-5111**

BUFFALO. Rm 1311, Federal Bldg, 111 W Huron St, Buffalo, NY 14202. **716-842-3240.** *Public information officer.* **716-442-3311**

ELMIRA. Rm 412, 180 State St, Elmira, NY 14901. **607-733-4686.** *Public information officer.* **607-733-5050**

ALBANY. Rm 921, Twin Towers Bldg, 99 Washington Ave, Albany, NY 12210. **518-472-6300.** *Public information officer.* **518-472-4411**

ROCHESTER. Federal Bldg, 100 State St, Rochester, NY 14614. **716-263-6700.** *Public information officer.* **716-263-5700**

HATO REY. Rm 691, 45 Courthouse and Federal Office Bldg, C Chardon Ave, Hato Rey, PR 00918. **809-763-6363.** *Public information officer.* **809-763-4422**

ST THOMAS. Rm 283, US Federal Office Bldg, Veterans Dr, St Thomas, VI 00801. **809-774-8530.** *Public information officer.* **809-774-8530**

NEWARK. Rm 1635, 970 Broad St, Newark, NJ 07102. **201-645-2434.** *Public information officer.* **201-645-6265**

CAMDEN. 1800 E Davis St, Camden, NJ 08104. **609-757-5183**

Region III

HARRISBURG. 1500 N 2nd St, Harrisburg, PA 17102. **717-782-3840.** *Public information officer.* **717-782-3840**

PHILADELPHIA. 1 Bala Cynwyd Plz, Bala Cynwyd, PA 19004. **215-596-5906-07.** H L

Reinhart, Jr. *public information officer.* **215-597-3311**

PITTSBURGH. Rm 1401, Federal Bldg, 1000 Liberty Ave, Pittsburgh, PA 15222. **412-644-3311.** *Public information officer.* **412-644-2780**

WILKES-BARRE. Penn Pl, 20 N Pennsylvania Ave, Wilkes-Barre, PA 18702. **717-826-6497**

WILMINGTON. Rm 5207, Federal Bldg, 844 King St, Wilmington, DE 19801. **302-571-6294**

BALTIMORE. Rm 630, Oxford Bldg, 8600 La Salle Rd, Towson, MD 21204. **301-962-4392.** *Public information officer.* **301-962-2054**

CLARKSBURG. Rm 301, Lowndes Bldg, 109 N 3rd St, Clarksburg, WV 26301. **304-623-5631.** *Public information officer.* **304-623-3411**

CHARLESTON. Suite 628, Charleston National Plz, Charleston, WV 25301. **304-343-6181**

RICHMOND. Rm 3015, Federal Bldg, 400 N 8th St, Richmond, VA 23240. **804-782-2011.** *Public information officer.* **804-782-2765**

WASHINGTON. Suite 250, 1030 15th St NW, Washington, DC 20417. **202-653-6365**

Region IV

ATLANTA. 1375 Peachtree St NE, Atlanta, GA 30309. **404-881-4943.** *Public information officer.* **404-881-2797.** 6th Floor, 1720 Peachtree St, NW, Atlanta, GA 30309. **404-881-4325.** *Public information officer.* **404-881-2797**

BIRMINGHAM. Rm 202, 908 S 20th St, Birmingham, AL 35205. **205-254-1344.** *Public information officer.* **205-254-1341**

CHARLOTTE. 230 S Tryon St, Charlotte, NC 28202. **704-372-0711.** *Public information officer.* **704-372-7448**

GREENVILLE. Rm 206, 215 S Evans St, Greenville, NC 27834. **919-752-3798.** *Public information officer.* **919-752-2420**

COLUMBIA. Rm 131, 1801 Assembly St, Columbia, SC 29201. **803-765-5376.** *Public information officer.* **803-765-5131**

JACKSON. Suite 690, Providence Capitol Bldg, 200 E Pascagoula St, Jackson, MS 39201. **601-969-4371.** *Public information officer.* **601-969-4384**

BILOXI. 2nd Floor, Gulf National Life Insurance Bldg, 111 Fred Haise Blvd, Biloxi, MS 39530. **601-435-3676.** *Public information officer.* **601-435-3676**

JACKSONVILLE. PO Box 35067, Rm 261, Federal Bldg, 400 W Bay St, Jacksonville, FL 32202. **904-791-3782.** *Public information officer.* **904-791-2011**

LOUISVILLE. Rm 188, New Federal Bldg, 600 Federal Pl, Louisville, KY 40202. **502-582-5971.** *Public Information Officer.* James A Beazley **502-582-5976**

MIAMI. 5th Floor, 2222 Ponce De Leon Blvd, Coral Gables, FL 33134. **305-350-5521.** *Public information officer.* **305-350-5533**

TAMPA. 700 Twiggs St, Tampa, FL 33602. **813-228-2594**

WEST PALM BEACH. Rm 229, Federal Bldg, 701 Clematis St, West Palm Beach, FL 33402. **305-659-7533**

NASHVILLE. Suite 1012, 404 James Robertson Pkwy, Nashville, TN 37219. **615-251-5881.** *Public information officer.* **615-251-5887**

KNOXVILLE. Rm 307, Fidelity Bankers Bldg, 502 S Gay St, Knoxville, TN 37902. **615-637-9300.** *Public information officer.* **615-637-4011**

MEMPHIS. Rm 211, Federal Bldg, 167 N Main St, Memphis, TN 38103. **901-521-3588.** *Public information officer.* **901-521-3588**

Region V

CHICAGO. Rm 838, Federal Bldg, 219 S Dearborn St, Chicago, IL 60604. **312-353-0355.** *Regional public affairs director.* **312-353-0359.** Rm 437, Federal Bldg, 219 S Dearborn St, Chicago, IL 60604. **312-353-4528.** *Illinois public information officer.* **312-353-5057**

SPRINGFIELD. 1 North, Old State Capital Plz, Springfield, IL 62701. **217-525-4416.** *Public relations officer.* **217-525-4200**

CLEVELAND. Rm 317, 1240 E 9th St, Cleveland, OH 44199. **216-522-4180.** *Public information officer.* **216-522-4194**

COLUMBUS. Federal Court Bldg, 5th floor 85 Marconi Blvd, Columbus, OH 43215. **614-469-6860.** *Public information officer.* **614-469-5548**

CINCINNATI. Federal Bldg, 550 Main St, Cincinnati, OH 45202. **513-684-2814.** *Public information officer.* **513-684-2200**

DETROIT. McNamara Bldg, 477 Michigan Ave, Detroit, MI 48226. **313-226-6075.** *Public information officer.* **313-226-6000**

MARQUETTE. Don H Bottum University Center, 540 W Kaye Ave, Marquette, MI 49855. **906-225-1108**

INDIANAPOLIS. Rm 552, New Federal Bldg, 575 N Pennsylvania St, Indianapolis, IN 46204. **317-269-7272.** *Public information officer.* **317-269-7286**

MADISON. Rm 700, 122 W Washington Ave, Madison, WI 43703. **608-252-5261**

MILWAUKEE. Rm 690, Continental Bank Bldg, 735 W Wisconsin Ave, Milwaukee, WI 53233. **414-224-3941.** *Public information officer.* **414-224-0111**

EAU CLAIRE. Rm 89AA, Federal Office Bldg and US Courthouse, 500 S Barstow St, Eau Claire, WI 54701. **715-834-9012.** *Public information officer.* **715-834-4242**

MINNEAPOLIS. Plymouth Bldg, 12 S 6th St, Minneapolis, MN 55402. **612-725-2362.** *Public information officer.* **612-725-2358**

Region VI

DALLAS. Rm 230, Regal Park Office Bldg, 1720 Regal Row, Dallas, TX 75235. **214-749-1840.** *Public information officer.* **214-749-1840.** Rm 300, 1100 Commerce St, Dallas, TX 75670. **214-749-3961.** *Public information officer.* **214-749-1109**

MARSHALL. Federal Bldg G-12, 100 S Washington St, Marshall, TX 75670. **214-935-5257**

HOUSTON. 1 Allen Ctr, 500 Dallas St, Houston, TX 77002. **713-226-4341.** *Public information officer.* **713-226-4945**

LUBBOCK. 1205 Texas Ave, 712 Federal Office Bldg and US Courthouse, Lubbock, TX 79401. **806-762-7011.** *Public information officer.* **806-762-7462**

EL PASO. Suite 300, 4100 Rio Bravo, El Paso, TX 79901. **915-543-7200**

LOWER RIO GRANDE VALLEY. 222 E Van Buren St, Harlingen, TX 78550. **512--423-8934.** *Public information officer.* **512-423-4534**

CORPUS CHRISTI. 3105 Leopard St (PO Box 9253), Corpus Christi, TX 78408. **512-888-3306.** *Public information officer.* **512-888-3306**

SAN ANTONIO. Rm A-513, 727 E Durango, San Antonio, TX 78206. **512-229-6250.** *Public information officer.* **512-730-6270**

ALBUQUERQUE. Patio Plaza Bldg, 5000 Marble Ave NE, Albuquerque, NM 87110. **505-766-3430.** *Public information officer.* **505-766-3588**

LITTLE ROCK. Suite 900, 611 Gaines St, Little Rock, AR 72201. **501-378-5871**

NEW ORLEANS. 17th Floor, Plaza Tower, 1001 Howard Ave, New Orleans, LA 70113. **504-589-2611**

SHREVEPORT. US Post Office and Courthouse Bldg, Fannin St, Shreveport, LA 71101. **318-226-5196**

OKLAHOMA CITY. Suite 670, Federal Bldg, 200 NW 5th St, Oklahoma City, OK 73102. **405-231-4491**

Region VII

KANSAS CITY. 23rd Floor, 911 Walnut St, Kansas City, MO 64106. **816-374-3318.** *Public information officer.* **816-374-7212.** 5th Floor, 1150 Grand Ave, Kansas City, MO 64106. **816-374-5557.** *Public information officer.* **816-374-5558**

ST LOUIS. Suite 2500, Mercantile Tower, 1 Mercantile Ctr, St Louis, MO 63101. **314-425-4191.** *Public information officer.* **314-425-4516**

DES MOINES. Rm 749, New Federal Bldg, 210 Walnut St, Des Moines, IA 50309. **515-284-4422.** *Public information officer.* **515-284-4760**

OMAHA. Empire State Bldg, 19th and Farnam Sts, Omaha, NE 68102. **402-221-4691** *Public information officer.* **402-221-3620**

WICHITA. Main Place Bldg, 110 E Waterman St, Wichita, KS 67202. **316-267-6311.** *Public information officer.* **316-267-6311**

Region VIII

DENVER. 22nd Floor, Executive Tower Bldg, 1405 Curtis St, Denver, CO 80202. **303-837-0111**

CASPER. Rm 4001, Federal Bldg, 100 E B St, Casper, WY 82601. **307-265-5550.** *Public information officer.* **307-265-5266**

FARGO. Rm 218, Federal Bldg, 653 2nd Ave N, Fargo, ND 48102. **701-237-5131**

HELENA. New Federal Bldg, 301 S Park, Helena, MT 59601. **406-449-5381**

SALT LAKE CITY. Rm 2237, Federal Bldg, 125 S State St, Salt Lake City, UT 84138. **801-524-5800**

SIOUX FALLS. Rm 402, National Bank Bldg, 8th and Main Ave, Sioux Falls, SD 57102. **605-336-2980.** *Public information officer.* **605-336-4231**

RAPID CITY. Rm 246, Federal Bldg, 515 9th St, Rapid City, SD 57701. **605-343-5074**

Region IX

SAN FRANCISCO. Box 36044, 450 Golden Gate Ave, San Francisco, CA 94102. **415-556-7487.** *Public information officer.* **415-556-0860.** 211 Main St, San Francisco, CA 94105. **415-556-7490.** *Public information officer.* **415-556-0860**

FRESNO. 1229 N St, Fresno, CA 93271. **209-487-5189**

SACRAMENTO. 2800 Cottage Way, Sacramento, CA 94825. **916-484-4726.** *Public information officer.* **916-484-2000**

LOS ANGELES. 6th Floor, 350 S Figueroa St, Los Angeles, CA 90071. **213-688-2956.** *Public information officer.* **213-688-4568**

SAN DIEGO. Rm 4-S-33, Federal US Bldg, 880 Front St, San Diego, CA 92188. **717-293-5444**

LAS VEGAS. 301 E Stewart, Las Vegas, NV 89101. **702-385-6011.** *Public information officer.* **702-385-6011**

RENO. Rm 308, 50 S Virginia St (PO Box 3216), Reno, NV 89505. **702-784-5268**

HONOLULU. Rm 2213, 300 Ala Moana (PO Box 50207), Honolulu, HI 96850. **808-546-7590.** *Public information officer.* **808-546-8901**

AGANA. Ada Plaza Center Bldg, Agana, Guam 96910. **777-8420**

PHOENIX. 112 N Central Ave, Phoenix, AZ 85004. **602-261-3611.** *Public information officer.* **602-261-4568**

Region X

SEATTLE. 5th Floor, Drexter Horton Bldg, 710 2nd Ave, Seattle, WA 98104. **206-442-1455.** *Public information officer.* **206-442-1530.** Rm 1744, Federal Bldg, 915 Second Ave, Seattle WA 98174. **206-442-5534.** *Public information officer.* **206-442-7791**

PORTLAND. Federal Bldg, 1220 SW 3rd Ave, Portland, OR 97204. **503-221-2682.** *Public information officer.* **503-221-3441**

SPOKANE. Rm 651, Courthouse Bldg, Spokane, WA 99210. **509-456-5310.** *Public information officer.* Kay B Simmons, **509-456-3786**

ANCHORAGE. Suite 200, Anchorage Legal Ctr, 1016 W 6th Ave, Anchorage, AK 99501. **907-265-4356.** *Public information officer.* **907-265-4357**

FAIRBANKS. 501½ 2nd Ave, Fairbanks, AK 99701. **907-452-151**

BOISE. 1005 Main (PO Box 2618), Boise, ID 83701. **208-384-1096.** *Public information officer.* **208-384-1780**

Securities and Exchange Commission Regional Offices

CALIFORNIA. Suite 1710, Tishman Westwood Bldg, 10960 Wilshire Blvd, Los Angeles, 90024. **213-473-4511.** Gerald E Boltz, administrator

CALIFORNIA. Federal Bldg and US Courthouse, PO Box 36042, 450 Golden Gate Ave, San Francisco 94102. **415-556-5264.** Leonard Rossen, associate administrator

COLORADO. Rm 640, 2 Park Central Bldg, 1515 Arapahoe St, Denver 80202. **303-837-2071.** Robert H Davenport administrator

FLORIDA. Suite 1114, Dupont Plaza Ctr, 300 Biscayne Blvd Way, Miami, 33131. **305-350-5765.** William Nortman, associate administrator

GEORGIA. Suite 788, 1375 Peachtree St NE, Atlanta, 30309. **404-881-2524.** Jule B Green, administrator

ILLINOIS. Rm 1204, Everett M Dirkson Bldg, 219 S Dearborn St, Chicago, 60604. **312-353-7390.** William D Goldsberry, administrator

MASSACHUSETTS. 150 Causeway St, Boston, 02114. **617-223-2721.** Floyd H Gilbert, administrator

MICHIGAN. Federal Bldg and US Courthouse, 231 W Lafayette St, Detroit, 48226. **313-226-6070.** Mark A Loush, attorney-in-charge

MISSOURI. Rm 1452, 210 N 12th St, St Louis, 63101. **314-425-5555.** John F Kern, attorney-in-charge

NEW YORK. US Customs Courthouse and Federal Bldg, 26 Federal Plz, New York, 10007. **212-264-1636.** William D Moran administrator

OHIO. 1020 Standard Bldg, 1370 Ontario St, Cleveland, 44113. **216-522-4060.** Orazio Sipari, attorney-in-charge

PENNSYLVANIA. Rm 2204, William J Green, Jr, Federal Bldg, 600 Arch St, Philadelphia, 19106. **215-597-2278.** Thomas H Monahan, assistant administrator

TEXAS. US Courthouse, 10th and Lamar Sts, Fort Worth, 76102. **817-334-3393.** Richard M Hewitt, administrator

TEXAS. Rm 5615, Federal Bldg and Courthouse, 515 Rusk Ave, Houston, 77002. **713-226-4986.** Daniel R Kirshbaum, assistant administrator

UTAH. Federal Reserve Bank, 120 S State St, Salt Lake City, 84111. **801-524-5796.** G Gail Weggeland, attorney-in-charge

VIRGINIA. Ballston Tower 3, 4015 Wilson Blvd, Arlington, 22203. **703-557-8201.** Paul F Leonard, administrator

WASHINGTON. 3040 Federal Bldg, 915 2nd Ave, Seattle, 98174. **206-442-7990.** Jack H Bookey, administrator

Social Security Administration (HEW) Regional Offices

ATLANTA (Alabama, Florida, Georgia, Kentucky, Mississippi, North Carolina,

South Carolina, Tennessee). 50 7th St NE, Atlanta, GA 30323. **404-526-5961**

BOSTON (Connecticut, Maine, Massachusetts, New Hampshire, Rhode Island, Vermont). John F Kennedy Federal Bldg, Boston, MA 02203. **617-223-6810**

CHICAGO (Illinois, Indiana, Minnesota, Wisconsin). 300 S Wacker Dr, Chicago, IL 60606. **312-353-4247**

CLEVELAND (Michigan, Ohio). 14725 Detroit Ave, Cleveland, OH 44107. **216-522-3794**

DALLAS (Arkansas, Louisiana, New Mexico, Oklahoma, Texas). 1114 Commerce St, Dallas, TX 75202. **214-749-3837**

DENVER (Colorado, Montana, North Dakota, South Dakota, Utah, Wyoming). 1961 Stout St, Denver, CO 80202. **303-837-3489**

KANSAS CITY (Iowa, Kansas, Missouri, Nebraska). 601 E 12th St, Kansas City, MO 64106. **816-374-5691**

NEW YORK (New Jersey, New York, Puerto Rico, Virgin Islands). 26 Federal Plz, New York, NY 10007. **212-264-2500**

PHILADELPHIA (Delaware, District of Columbia, Maryland, Pennsylvania, Virginia, West Virginia). 3535 Market St (PO Box 8788), Philadelphia, PA 19101. **215-597-6941**

SAN FRANCISCO (American Samoa, AZ, CA, Guam, HI, NV). 50 Fulton St, San Francisco, CA 94102. **415-556-4910**

SEATTLE (Alaska, Idaho, Oregon, Washington). 1321 2nd Ave, Seattle, WA 98101. **206-442-0417**

Department of Transportation Regional Offices and Secretarial Representatives

REGION I. Transportation Systems Ctr, 55 Broadway, Cambridge, MA 02142. **617-494-2709**. William Schwob (acting)

REGION II. Rm 2339, 26 Federal Plz, New York, NY 10007. **212-264-2672**. W Rea (acting)

REGION III. Suite 1000, 434 Walnut St, Philadelphia, PA 19106. **215-597-9430**. Franz Gimmler (acting)

REGION IV. Suite 515, 1720 Peachtree Rd NW, Atlanta, GA 30309. **404-881-3738**. James Lacy (acting)

REGION V. 17th Floor, 300 S Wacker Dr, Chicago, IL 60606. **312-353-4000**. John Zyrocki (acting)

REGION VI. 9-C-18 Federal Ctr, 1100 Commerce St, Dallas, TX 75242. **214-749-1851**. Henry Newman (acting)

REGION VII. Rm 634, 601 E 12th St, Kansas City, MO 64106. **816-374-5801**. John Kemp (acting)

REGION VIII. Suite 1822, Prudential Plz, 1050 17th St, Denver, CO 80202. **303-837-3242**. Mervyn Martin (acting)

REGION IX. Suite 610, 2 Embarcadero Ctr, San Francisco, CA 94111. **415-556-5961**. Frank Hawley (acting)

REGION X. 3112 Federal Bldg, 915 2nd Ave, Seattle, WA 98174. **206-442-0590**. Glenn Thompson (acting)

United States Civil Service Commission Regional Offices

REGION I. John W McCormack Post Office and Courthouse, Boston, MA 02109. **617-223-2538**

REGION II. 26 Federal Plz, New York, NY 10007. **212-264-0440**

REGION III. 600 Arch St, Philadelphia, PA 19106. **215-597-4543**

REGION IV. 1340 Spring St NW, Atlanta, GA 30309. **404-881-2436**

REGION V. 230 S Dearborn St, Chicago, IL 60604. **312-353-2901**

REGION VI. 1100 Commerce St, Dallas, TX 75242. **214-749-3352**

REGION VII. 1520 Market St, St Louis, MO 63103. **314-425-4252**

REGION VIII. Bldg 20, Denver Federal Ctr, Denver, CO 80225. **303-234-2023**

REGION IX. PO Box 36010, 450 Golden Gate Ave, San Francisco, CA 94102. **415-556-0581**

REGION X. 915 2nd Ave, Seattle, WA 98174. **206-442-7536**

US Coast Guard Districts and Units with Public Affairs Officers

FIRST DISTRICT. 150 Causeway St, Boston, MA 02114. Lieutenant H R Williams. **617-223-3610**

SECOND DISTRICT. 1430 Olive St, St Louis, MO 63103. Lieutenant Gabe Kinney. **314-425-4628**

THIRD DISTRICT. Governors Island, New York, NY 10004. Lieutenant Commander Tom Osborne. **212-264-4996**

FIFTH DISTRICT. Federal Bldg, 431 Crawford St, Portsmouth, VA 23705. Lieutenant John Fishburn. **804-393-9611**

SEVENTH DISTRICT. 51 SW 1st Ave, Miami, FL 33130. Lieutenant Norris Turner. **305-350-5606** or **5641**

EIGHTH DISTRICT. Rm 1122, 500 Camp St, New Orleans, LA 70130. Lieutenant Thomas W Pearson, Jr. **504-589-6198**

NINTH DISTRICT. 1240 E 9th St, Cleveland, OH 44199. Lieutenant Winfrey. **216-522-3950**

ELEVENTH DISTRICT. Union Bank Bldg, 400 Oceangate, Long Beach, CA 90822. Lieutenant Jim Underwood. **213-590-2213**

TWELFTH DISTRICT. 630 Sansome St, San Francisco, CA 94126. George Groskopf. **415-556-9000** or **5831**

THIRTEENTH DISTRICT. Rm 3510, Federal Bldg, 915 2nd Ave, Seattle, WA 98174. Lieutenant Dave Jones. **206-442-5896**

FOURTEENTH DISTRICT. 300 Ala Moana Blvd, Honolulu, HI 96850. Chief Journalist Jim Gilman. **808-546-7595** or **7596**

SEVENTEENTH DISTRICT. PO Box 3-5000, Juneau, AK 99801. Lieutenant (junior grade) Stephen Venckus. **907-586-7281** (if no answer, **7340**)

US COAST GUARD ACADEMY. New London, CT 06320. Lieutenant George Whiting. **203-443-8463**, Ext 280

COAST GUARD INSTITUTE. PO Substation 18, Oklahoma City, OK 73169. PAC James Whalen. **405-686-4263**

US COAST GUARD TRAINING CENTER. Government Island, Alameda, CA 94501. Public Affairs Office. **415-273-7392**

US COAST GUARD TRAINING CENTER. Cape May, NJ 08204. **609-884-8451**

US COAST GUARD TRAINING CENTER. Governors Island, New York, NY 10004. **212-264-3757**

US COAST GUARD RESERVE TRAINING. Yorktown, VA 23490. **804-887-2811**

US COAST GUARD AIRCRAFT REPAIR AND SUPPLY CENTER. Elizabeth City, NC 27909. **919-338-3941**

FLEET HOME TOWN NEWS CENTER. Bldg X-18, Naval Station, Norfolk, VA 23511. Chief Warrant Officer Paul M Short, admin/editorial officer. **804-444-2221** or **4346**

US COAST GUARD YARD. Curtis Bay, Baltimore, MD 21226. **301-789-1600**

Urban Mass Transportation Administration (Transportation) Field Offices and Regional Directors

REGION I. Transportation Systems Ctr, Kendall Sq, 55 Broadway, Cambridge, MA 02142. **617-494-2055.** Peter N Stowell

REGION II. Suite 1811, 26 Federal Plz, New York, NY 10007. **212-264-8162.** Hiram Walker

REGION III. Suite 1010, 434 Walnut St, Philadelphia, PA 19106. **215-597-8098.** Franz K Gimmler

REGION IV. Suite 400, 1720 Peachtree Rd NW, Atlanta, GA 30309. **404-881-3948.** Doug Campion

REGION V. Suite 1740, 300 S Wacker Dr, Chicago, IL 60606. **312-353-0100.** Theodore Weigle

REGION VI. Suite 9A32, 819 Taylor St, Fort Worth, TX 76102. **817-334-3787.** Glen Ford

REGION VII. Rm 303, 6301 Rock Hill Rd, Kansas City, MO 64131. **816-926-5053.** Lee Waddleton

REGION VIII. Suite 1822, Prudential Plz, 1050 17th St, Denver, CO 80202. **303-837-3242.** Lou Mraz

REGION IX. Suite 620, 2 Embarcadero Ctr, San Francisco, CA 94111. **415-556-2884.** Dee Jacobs

REGION X. Suite 3106, Federal Bldg, 915 2nd Ave, Seattle, WA 98174. **206-442-4210.** F William Fort

TRANSPORTATION TEST CENTER. Pueblo, CO 81001. **303-545-5660.** Reagin F Parker, programs director

United States Postal Service Regional Offices

CENTRAL (Illinois, Indiana, Iowa, Kansas —part, Kentucky, Michigan, Minnesota, Missouri, Nebraska, North Dakota, Ohio, South Dakota, Wisconsin). Main Post Office Bldg, 433 W Van Buren St, Chicago, IL 60699. **312-886-2001.** Ed Gold, general manager, communications and public affairs

SOUTHERN (Alabama, Arkansas, Florida, Georgia, Kansas—part, Louisiana, Mississippi, North Carolina, Oklahoma, South Carolina, Tennessee, Texas). Memphis, TN 38166. **901-521-2711.** Mike McManus, general manager, communications and public affairs

EASTERN (Delaware, District of Columbia, Maryland, New Jersey, New York, Pennsylvania, Virginia, West Virginia). 1845 Walnut St, Philadelphia, PA 19101. **215-597-9766.** Bob Hoobing, general manager, communications and public affairs

WESTERN (Alaska, Arizona, California, Colorado, Hawaii, Idaho, Montana, Nevada, New Mexico, Oregon, Pacific Territories, Utah, Washington, Wyoming). San Bruno, CA 94099. **415-876-9200.** George Saunders, general manager, communications and public affairs

NORTHEASTERN (Connecticut, Maine, Massachusetts, New Hampshire, New Jersey, New York, Puerto Rico, Rhode Island, Vermont, Virgin Islands). 33rd St and 8th Ave, New York, NY 10098. **212-971-7881.** Harry Nigro, general manager, communications and public affairs

Veterans Administration Information Service Field Offices and Officers

ATLANTA (Alabama, Florida, Georgia, Puerto Rico, South Carolina, Tennessee). VA Regional Office, 730 Peachtree St SE, Atlanta, GA 30308. **404-881-2266.** Christopher J Scheer

BOSTON (Connecticut, Maine, Massachusetts, New Hampshire, Rhode Island, Vermont). Rm 400, John F Kennedy Federal Bldg, Boston, MA 02203. **617-223-3364** or **3365.** Francis A Hunt

CHICAGO (Illinois, Indiana, Kentucky, Michigan). VA Regional Office, 536 S Clark St (PO Box 8136), Chicago, IL 60680. **312-353-4076.** Verdon L Rogers

DALLAS (Louisiana, Mississippi, Texas). Rm 204, VA Office, 1100 Commerce St, Dallas, TX 75202. **214-749-3850** or **1880.** Jones R Vestal

DENVER (Colorado, New Mexico, Utah, Wyoming). VA Ctr, Denver Federal Ctr, Denver, CO 80225. **303-234-4165** or **4166.** Delbert M Berry

KANSAS CITY (Arkansas, Kansas, Missouri, Oklahoma). Rm 1436, Federal Office Bldg, 601 E 12th St, Kansas City, MO 64106. **816-374-3786.** Leo R Welter

LOS ANGELES (Arizona, southern California, Hawaii). VA Regional Office, Federal Bldg, 11000 Wilshire Blvd, Los Angeles, CA 90024. **213-324-7686, 7687,** or **7564.** Paul W Mills

NEW YORK (New Jersey, New York). VA Regional Office, 252 7th Ave, New York, NY 10001. **212-620-6525.** Newton H Fulbright

PHILADELPHIA (Delaware, Ohio, Pennsylvania). PO Box 8079, VA Center, Philadelphia, PA 19101. **215-438-5246.** Richard W Baker

ST PAUL (Iowa, Minnesota, Nebraska, North Dakota, South Dakota, Wisconsin). Rm 288, Federal Bldg, Fort Snelling, St Paul, MN 55111. **612-725-4380, 4381** or **4383.** Arthur Selikoff

SAN FRANCISCO (Northern California, Nevada). Rm 1610, VA Regional Office, 211 Main St, San Francisco, CA 94105. **415-556-5070.** Theodore M Jorgenson

SEATTLE (Alaska, Idaho, Oregon, Montana, Washington). Rm 1364, VA Regional Office, 915 2nd Ave, Seattle, WA 98174. **206-442-5045.** Karl R Edgerton

WASHINGTON (District of Columbia, Maryland, North Carolina, Virginia, West Virginia). Rm 904, VA Central Office, Washington, DC 20420. **202-389-2828.** Donald R Smith

UNITED STATES ATTORNEYS

See also The Federal Government: Executive Branch, (Department of Justice)

ALABAMA (NORTHERN). 200 Federal Bldg, 1800 5th Ave N, Birmingham, 35203. **205-254-1785.** Wayman G Sherrer

ALABAMA (MIDDLE). 306 US Post Office and Courthouse Bldg, 15 Lee St, Montgomery, 36104. **205-832-7280.** Barry Teague

ALABAMA (SOUTHERN). 311 Federal Bldg, Mobile, 36602. **205-690-2845.** W A Kimbrough, Jr

ALASKA. Rm 175, Federal Bldg, 4th and G Sts, Anchorage, 99510. **907-277-1491.** G Kent Edwards

ARIZONA. 3rd Floor, La Placita Village, Acapulco Bldg, 120 W Broadway, Tucson, 85701. **602-792-6511.** Michael D Hawkins

ARKANSAS (EASTERN). 327 Post Office and Courthouse Bldg, 600 W Capitol, Little Rock, 72203. **501-378-5342.** W H Dillahunty

ARKANSAS (WESTERN). US Post Office and Courthouse Bldg, 6th and Rogers, Fort Smith, 72901. **501-783-5125.** Robert E Johnson

CALIFORNIA (NORTHERN). Rm 16201, Federal Bldg and US Courthouse, 450 Golden Gate Ave, San Francisco, 94102. **415-556-1126.** G William Hunter

CALIFORNIA (EASTERN). 2058 Federal Bldg, 650 Capitol Mall, Sacramento, 95814. **916-440-2331.** D Dwayne Keyes

CALIFORNIA (MIDDLE). Rm 1200, 312 N Spring St, Los Angeles 90012. **213-688-2434.** Robert L Brosio

CALIFORNIA (SOUTHERN). Rm 5-N-19, 940 Front St, San Diego 92189. **717-293-5690.** Terry J Knoepp

CANAL ZONE. Box 2090, Balboa. Dial 9-0 and ask operator for **Balboa 523415.** Frank J Violanti

COLORADO. 323 US Courthouse, 1961 Stout St (PO Box 3615), Denver 80294. **303-837-2081.** Joseph F Dolan

CONNECTICUT. PO Box 1824, New Haven 06508. **203-432-2108.** Rm 250,

Federal Bldg, 450 Main St, Hartford 06103. **203-244-2570.** Peter C Dorsey

DELAWARE. 5001 New Federal Bldg, 844 King St, Wilmington 19801. **302-571-6277.** James W Garvin, Jr

DISTRICT OF COLUMBIA. Rm 3600-E, US Courthouse, 3rd St and Constitution Ave NW, Washington 20001. **202-426-7511.** Earl J Silbert. Superior Court Division, Rm 333, Pension Bldg, 400 F St NW, Washington 20001. **202-426-7511.** Chief, Superior Court Division, Rm 110, Bldg B, 400 F St NW, Washington 20001. **202-426-7212**

FLORIDA (NORTHERN). Rm 310, Post Office and Courthouse Bldg, 100 N Palafox St, Pensacola 32501. **904-434-3251.** Nicholas P Geeker. Staffed branch office, Rm 221, Post Office and Courthouse Bldg, 110 Park Ave, Tallahassee 32301. **904-224-3186**

FLORIDA (MIDDLE). 409 Post Office Bldg, 311 W Monroe St, Jacksonville 32201. **904-791-2682.** John L Briggs. 405 Post Office Bldg, 611 Florida Ave, Tampa 33601. **813-228-2135.** Federal Bldg and US Courthouse, 80 N Hughey Ave, Orlando 32801. **305-420-6341**

FLORIDA (SOUTHERN). 300 Ainsley Bldg, 14 NE 1st Ave, Miami 33132. **305-350-5401.** J V Eskenazi

GEORGIA (NORTHERN). 428 US Courthouse, 56 Forsyth St NW, Atlanta 30303. **404-221-6954.** William L Harper

GEORGIA (MIDDLE). Rm 303, Old Post Office Bldg, Mulberry and 3rd Sts, Macon 31202. **912-745-9211.** Denver L Rampey, Jr

GEORGIA (SOUTHERN). PO Box 8999, Rm 311, US Courthouse, Wright Square, Savannah 31402. **912-232-3145.** William T Moore, Jr

GUAM. Rm 502-A, Pacific Nes Bldg, Agana 96910. **472-6886.** Ralph F Bagley, Jr

HAWAII. Rm C-242, US Courthouse, 300 Ala Moana Blvd, Honolulu 96850. **808-546-7170.** Harold M Fong

IDAHO. Box 037, Rm 693, Federal Bldg, 550 W Fort St, Boise 83724. **208-384-1211.** M Karl Shurtliff

ILLINOIS (NORTHERN). Rm 1500S, Everett McKinley Dirksen Bldg, 219 S

Dearborn St, Chicago 60604. **312-353-5333.** Samuel K Skinner

ILLINOIS (EASTERN). Rm 330, 750 Missouri Ave, E St Louis 62202. **618-274-2361.** Henry A Schwarz

ILLINOIS (SOUTHERN). Rm 312, US Post Office and Federal Bldg, 600 E Monroe St, Springfield 62705. **217-525-4450.** Donald B Mackay, Rm 271, US Post Office and Federal Bldg, 100 N E Monroe St, Peoria 61601. **309-671-7050**

INDIANA (NORTHERN). Rm 220, US Post Office and Courthouse, 1300 S Harrison St, Fort Wayne 46802. **219-422-6131.** John R Wilks. Rm 312, Federal Bldg, 507 State St, Hammond 46325. **219-932-5500**

INDIANA (SOUTHERN). Rm 246, Federal Bldg and US Courthouse, 46 E Ohio St, Indianapolis 46204. **317-269-6333.** James B Young

IOWA (NORTHERN). Rm 327, US Post Office and Courthouse, Sioux City 51102. **712-252-4161,** Ext 227. Evan L Hultman. 236 Federal Bldg, Waterloo 50703. **319-232-6403**

IOWA (SOUTHERN). Iowa Court of Appeals, State Capitol, Des Moines 50319. **515-281-5221.** Allen L Donielson

KANSAS. Rm 218, Federal Bldg, 5th St and Kansas Ave, Topeka 66601. **913-234-8661,** Ext 421. E Edward Johnson. Rm 306, US Courthouse and Post Office Bldg, 401 N Market, Wichita 67202. **316-267-6311,** Ext 481. Rm 148, New Federal Bldg, 812 N 7th St, Kansas City 66101. **816-374-4666**

KENTUCKY (EASTERN). 326 Federal Bldg, Limestone and Barr Sts, Lexington 40507. **606-233-2661.** Patrick H Malloy

KENTUCKY (WESTERN). Rm 211, US Post Office and Courthouse Bldg, 601 W Broadway, Louisville 40202. **502-582-5911.** Albert Jones

LOUISIANA (EASTERN). Hale Boggs Federal Bldg, 500 Camp St, New Orleans 70130. **504-589-2921.** Gerald J Gallinghouse

LOUISIANA (MIDDLE). Rm 130, Federal Bldg and US Courthouse, 707 Florida St, Baton Rouge 70801. **504-387-0181,** Ext 251. Cheney C Joseph, Jr

LOUISIANA (WESTERN). PO Box 33, Rm 3B12, Federal Bldg, 500 Fannin St, Shreveport 71101. **318-226-5277.** Donald E Walter

MAINE. Rm 107, Federal Courthouse, 156 Federal St, Portland 04112. **207-775-3258.** Peter Mills

MARYLAND. 405 US Courthouse, 111 N Calvert St, Baltimore 21202. **301-539-2940.** Jervis S Finney

MASSACHUSETTS. 1107 John W McCormack Post Office and Courthouse, Boston 02109. **617-223-3181.** Edward F Harrington

MICHIGAN (EASTERN). 817 Federal Bldg, 231 W Lafayette, Detroit 48226. **313-226-7715.** Philip M Van Dam. PO Box 26, 204 Federal Bldg, Bay City 48709. **617-895-5712.** 113 Federal Bldg, 600 Church St, Flint 48502. **313-234-5208**

MICHIGAN (WESTERN). 544 Federal Bldg and US Courthouse, 110 Michigan Ave NW, Grand Rapids 49503. **616-456-2404.** James Brady

MINNESOTA. 596 US Courthouse, 110 S 4th St, Minneapolis 55401. **612-332-8961.** Andrew W Danielson. 678 US Courthouse, 316 N Robert St, St Paul 55101. **612-725-7171**

MISSISSIPPI (NORTHERN). Rm 255, Federal Bldg, 911 W Jackson Ave, Oxford 38655. **601-234-3351.** H M Ray

MISSISSIPPI (SOUTHERN). Rm 324, US Post Office and Courthouse, Capitol and West Sts, Jackson 39205. **601-969-4480.** Robert E Hauberg

MISSOURI (EASTERN). Rm 414, US Court and Custom House, 1114 Market St, St Louis 63101. **314-425-5885.** Barry A Short

MISSOURI (WESTERN). 549 US Courthouse, 811 Grand Ave, Kansas City 64106. **816-374-3122.** Bert C Hurn

MONTANA. 26th St and 3rd Ave, N Billings 59101. **406-252-7555.** Robert O'Leary. 173 Federal Bldg, 400 N Main, Butte 59701 . **406-723-6561**

NEBRASKA. Rm 8000, US Post Office and Courthouse Bldg, 215 N 17th St, Omaha 68101. **402-221-4774.** Edward Warin. 530 Federal Bldg, 100 Centennial Mall N, Lincoln 68508. **402-471-5241**

NEVADA. Rm 4-523, 300 Las Vegas Blvd S, Las Vegas 89101. **702-385-6336.** B Mahlon Brown. Rm 5011, 300 Booth St, Reno 89502. **702-784-5439**

NEW HAMPSHIRE. Rm 411, Federal Bldg, 55 Pleasant St, Concord 03301. **603-225-5588.** William H Shaheen

NEW JERSEY. Rm 502, Federal Bldg, 970 Broad St, Newark 07102. **201-645-2289.** Robert Del Tufo. Rm 251G, Post Office Bldg, 402 E State St, Trenton 08607. **609-599-3371.** Rm 330, Post Office Bldg, 401 Market St, Camden 08101. **609-488-5026**

NEW MEXICO. Rm 12020, US Courthouse, 500 Gold Ave SW, Albuquerque 87103. **505-766-3341.** Victor R Ortega

NEW YORK (NORTHERN). Rm 202, Federal Bldg, Clinton Sq, Syracuse 13201. **315-473-6660.** Paul V French, Rm 411, Federal Bldg, Albany 12207. **518-472-5522**

NEW YORK (SOUTHERN). 1 St, Andrews Plz, New York 10007. **212-791-0055.** Robert B Fiske, Jr

NEW YORK (EASTERN). US Courthouse, 225 Cadman Plz E, Brooklyn 11201. **212-330-7596.** David G Trager

NEW YORK (WESTERN). 502 US Courthouse, Buffalo 14202. **716-842-3483.** Richard J Arcara. Branch office, 233 US Courthouse, 100 State St, Rochester 14614. **716-263-6760**

NORTH CAROLINA (EASTERN). 874 Federal Bldg, 310 New Bern Ave, Raleigh 27611. **919-755-4530.** Thomas P McNamara

NORTH CAROLINA (MIDDLE). Rm 326, US Courthouse and Post Office Bldg, 324 W Market St, Greensboro 27402. **919-378-5351.** N Carlton Tilley, Jr

NORTH CAROLINA (WESTERN). Rm 310, Post Office Bldg, Asheville 28802. **704-258-2850,** Ext 655. Harold M Edwards. Rm 251, Federal Bldg, Charlotte 28230. **704-372-0711,** Ext 461

NORTH DAKOTA. 219 Federal Bldg, 655 1st Ave N, Fargo 48102. **701-237-5771,** Ext 5671. James R Britton. 470 US Post Office and Courthouse, 3rd and Rosser Aves, Bismark 58501. **701-255-4011,** Ext 4396

OHIO (NORTHERN). Rm 400, US Courthouse, 215 Superior Ave NE, Cleveland 44114. **216-522-4389.** William D Beyer. 307 US Courthouse, 1704 Spielbusch Ave, Toledo 43624. **419-259-6376.** (Unstaffed) US Courthouse and Federal Office Bldg, W Market and S Main Sts, Akron 44308. **216-292-5716**

OHIO (SOUTHERN). 200 US Courthouse, 85 Marconi Blvd, Columbus 43215. **614-469-5715.** William W Milligan. 722 US Post Office and Courthouse, 5th and Walnut Sts, Cincinnati 45202. **513-684-3711.** PO Box 280, Mid-City Station, Dayton 45402; 802 Federal Bldg and US Courthouse, 200 W 2nd St, Dayton 45402. **513-225-2910**

OKLAHOMA (NORTHERN). Rm 460, US Courthouse, 333 W 4th St, Tulsa 74103. **918-581-7463.** Nathan G Graham

OKLAHOMA (EASTERN). 333 Federal Bldg, 5th and Okmulgee Sts, Muskogee 74401. **918-683-3111.** Julian Fite

OKLAHOMA (WESTERN). Rm 4434, US Courthouse and Federal Office Bldg, Oklahoma City 73102. **405-231-5281.** John E Green

OREGON. 506 US Courthouse, 620 SW Main St, Portland 97205. **503-221-2101.** Sidney I Lezak

PENNSYLVANIA (EASTERN). 3310 US Courthouse, Independence Mall W, 601 Market St, Philadelphia 19106. **215-597-2556**

PENNSYLVANIA (MIDDLE). US Post Office Bldg, Scranton 18501. **717-961-2924.** S John Cottone. Federal Bldg, 3rd and Walnut Sts, Harrisburg 17101. **717-782-4482.** US Post Office Bldg, Lewisburg 17837. **717-524-4415**

PENNSYLVANIA (WESTERN). 633 US Post Office and Courthouse, 7th Ave and Grant St, Pittsburgh 15219. **412-644-3500.** Blair A Griffith

PUERTO RICO. PO Box 3391, 4th Floor, Old Post Office and Courthouse Bldg, Comercio St, San Juan 00904. **809-722-1550.** Julio Morales-Sanchez

RHODE ISLAND. 223 Federal Bldg and Courthouse, Kennedy Plz, Providence 02903. **401-528-4311.** Lincoln C Almond

SOUTH CAROLINA. 151 US Courthouse, Columbia 29201. **803-765-5483.** Thomas E Lydon, Jr. Rm 308, Post Office Bldg, Meeting and Broad Sts, Charleston 29402. **803-723-3462.** Rm 318, Federal Bldg, 300 E Washington St, Greenville 39601. **803-232-5646**

SOUTH DAKOTA. 231 Federal Bldg and US Courthouse, 400 S Phillips Ave, Sioux Falls 57102. **605-336-2980,** Ext 395. William

F Clayton. 321 Courthouse and Federal Bldg, 515 9th St, Rapid City 57701. **605-342-7822**

TENNESSEE (EASTERN). 201 US Post Office and Courthouse Bldg, Knoxville 37902. **615-637-9300,** Ext 4261. John L Bowers, Jr. 359 US Post Office and Courthouse Bldg, Chattanooga 37402. **615-756-4250,** Ext 8211

TENNESSEE (MIDDLE). Rm 879, US Courthouse, 801 Broadway, Nashville 37203. **615-251-5151.** Hal D Hardin

TENNESSEE (WESTERN). 1058 Federal Office Bldg, 167 N Main St, Memphis 38103. **901-534-4231.** Thomas F Turley, Jr

TEXAS (NORTHERN). 310 US Courthouse, 10th and Lamar Sts, Fort Worth 76102. **817-334-3291.** Michael P Carnes. Rm 16G28, US Federal Bldg and Courthouse, 1100 Commerce St, Dallas 75202. **214-749-3491.** Rm C-201, US Federal Bldg and Courthouse, 1205 Texas Ave, Lubbock 79401. **806-738-7351**

TEXAS (SOUTHERN). Courthouse and Federal Bldg, 515 Rusk Ave, Houston 77002. **713-226-4741.** J A (Tony) Canales. Federal Bldg, Matamoras St, Laredo 78040. **512-723-6523.** Post Office Bldg, 1001 Elizabeth St, Brownsville 78520. **512-542-7132.** US Courthouse, 521 Star St, Corpus Christi 78401. **512-884-3454**

TEXAS (EASTERN). PO Box 1049, 221 W Ferguson St, Tyler 75710. **214-597-8146.** Roby Hadden. Rm 248, US Courthouse and Post Office Bldg, corner of Liberty and Willow Sts, Beaumont 77704. **713-838-0271**

TEXAS (WESTERN). Hemisfair Plz, 655 E Durango Blvd, San Antonio 78206. **512-229-5511,** Ext 6500. John E Clark. Rm 353, US Courthouse, 511 San Antonio St, El Paso 79941. **915-543-7550**

UTAH. 200 Post Office and Courthouse Bldg, 350 S Main St, Salt Lake City 84101. **801-524-5685.** Ronald Rencher

VERMONT. Federal Bldg, 151 W St, Rutland 05701. **802-774-1431.** George W F Cook

VIRGINIA (EASTERN). 117 S Washington St, Alexandria 22314. **703-557-9100.** William B Cummings. 3rd Floor, Federal Courthouse Annex, 1102 E Main St, Richmond 23210.

804-782-2186. Rm 409, US Post Office and Courthouse, Granby St, Norfolk 23510. **804-441-6331**

VIRGINIA (WESTERN). 3rd Floor, 210 Franklin Rd SW, Roanoke 24008. **703-982-6253.** Paul R Thomson, Jr

VIRGIN ISLANDS. District Court Bldg Annex, Charlotte Amalie, St Thomas 00801. **809-774-1432.** Julio A Brady. 56 King St, Christiansted, St Croix 00820. **809-773-3920**

WASHINGTON (EASTERN). 841 US Courthouse, 920 Riverside, Spokane 99210. **509-456-3811.** James J Gillespie, 303 Federal Bldg, 3rd and Chestnut, Yakima 98907. **509-575-5836**

WASHINGTON (WESTERN). 1012 US Courthouse, 1010 5th Ave, Seattle 98104. **206-442-7970.** Stan Pitkin. 324 Federal Bldg, 11th and A Sts, Tacoma 98402. **206-593-6316**

WEST VIRGINIA (NORTHERN). Rm 243, Federal Bldg, 1125-1141 Chapline St, Wheeling 26003. **304-232-4026.** Stephen G Jory. Rm 301, Federal Bldg, 401 Davis Ave, Elkins 26241. **304-636-1739**

WEST VIRGINIA (SOUTHERN). PO Box 3234, Charleston 25332. **304-345-2200.** Robert B King. PO Box 1239, Huntington 25714. **304-529-3258**

WISCONSIN (EASTERN). 330 Federal Bldg, 517 E Wisconsin Ave, Milwaukee 53202. **414-291-1700.** Joan Kessler

WISCONSIN (WESTERN). Rm 241, 215 Monona Ave, Madison 53701. **608-252-5158.** David C Mebane

WYOMING. Rm 2139, U C O'Mahoney Federal Ctr, 2120 Capitol Ave, Cheyenne 82001. **307-778-2220,** Ext 2124. Charles E Graves

EASTERN REGION. Federal Bldg, Rm 507, Providence, RI 02901. **401-528-4469.** Ernest R Bengtson

WESTERN REGION. 611 Capitol Federal Bldg, 700 Kansas Ave, Topeka, KS 66603. **913-752-8417.** Edward H Funston

SOUTHERN REGION. Rm 4509, Main Justice Bldg, 10th St and Constitution Ave NW, Washington, DC 20530. **202-739-2131.** Laurence S McWhorter

INTERSTATE AGENCIES AND COMMISSIONS

The following is a list of interstate governmental bodies established by compact between states.

ARKANSAS RIVER COMPACT ADMINISTRATION. PO Box 98, Meeker, CO 81052. **303-336-2422**
Chairman. Frank G Cooley

ATLANTIC STATES MARINE FISHERIES COMMISSION. Suite 703, 1717 Massachusetts Ave NW, Washington DC 20036. **202-387-5330**
Chairman. Theodore B Bampton, Connecticut
Executive Director. Irwin M Alperin, District of Columbia

BEAR RIVER COMMISSION. 22 E Center St, Logan UT 84321. **801-752-3161**

BI-STATE DEVELOPMENT AGENCY. 3869 Park Ave, St. Louis, MO 63101. **314-771-1414**
Director of Public Information. Shirley Browne

CANADIAN RIVER COMMISSION. Box H-4377, Herring Plz, Amarillo, TX 79101. **806-372-9120**

CONNECTICUT RIVER VALLEY FLOOD CONTROL COMMISSION. 28 Mechanic St, Keene, NH 03431. **603-352-4202**
Chairman. John E Cerutti

DELAWARE RIVER BASIN COMMISSION. 25 State Police Dr (PO Box 360), Trenton, NJ 08603. **609-883-9500**
Executive Director. James F Wright

DELAWARE RIVER PORT AUTHORITY. PO Box 1949, Camden, NJ 08101. **609-963-6420, 215-925-8780**
Executive Director. W W Watkin, Jr
Public Information Manager. William A Lynch, (h) **609-299-2539**

DELAWARE VALLEY REGIONAL PLANNING COMMISSION. 3rd Floor, Penn Towers Bldg, 1819 J F Kennedy Blvd, Philadelphia, PA 19103. **215-567-3000**
Executive Director. Walter K Johnson

EDUCATION COMMISSION OF THE STATES. 300 Lincoln Tower Bldg, 1860 Lincoln St, Denver, CO 80295. **303-893-5200**

Executive Director. Warren G Hill

Director of Communications. Sally V Allen

GREAT LAKES COMMISSION. 5104 Institute of Science and Technology Bldg, 2200 Bonisteel Blvd, Ann Arbor, MI 48109. **313-665-9135**

Director of Research. Dr Albert G Ballert

GULF STATES MARINE FISHERIES COMMISSION. PO Box 726, Ocean Springs, MS 39564. **601-875-5912**

Executive Director. Charles H Lyles

INTERSTATE COMMISSION ON THE POTOMAC RIVER BASIN. Suite 814, East-West Towers, 4350 East-West Hwy, Bethesda, MD 20014. **301-652-5758**

Executive Director. Paul W Eastman

Public Information Officer. Kevin Flynn

INTERSTATE MINING COMPACT COMMISSION. PO Box 11751, Iron Works Pike, Lexington, KY 40511. **606-253-1576**

Executive Director. Kenes C Bowling

INTERSTATE OIL COMPACT COMMISSION. 900 NE 23, PO Box 53127, Oklahoma City OK 73105. **405-525-3556**

Executive Director. W Timothy Dowd

Director of Communications. Richard L Hess

INTERSTATE PEST CONTROL COMPACT, NATIONAL ASSOCIATION OF STATE DEPARTMENTS OF AGRICULTURE. 1616 H St NW, Washington, DC 20006. **202-628-1566**

Executive Secretary. William S Cath

INTERSTATE SANITATION COMMISSION. Rm 1620, 10 Columbus Cir, New York NY 10019. **212-582-0380**

Director and Chief Engineer. Thomas R Glenn, Jr

KANSAS CITY AREA TRANSPORTATION AUTHORITY. 1350 E 17th St, Kansas City, MO 64108. **816-471-6600**

Executive Director. Jack Reitzes

LAKE CHAMPLAIN BRIDGE COMMISSION. 12 St Paul St (PO Box 354), Burlington, VT 05401. **802-862-0587**

Secretary-Treasurer. H Clifford Dubie

MISSOURI RIVER BASIN COMMISSION. Suite 403, 10050 Regency Cir, Omaha, NE 68114. **402-221-9351**

MULTISTATE TAX COMMISSION. 1790 30th St, Boulder, CO 80301. **303-447-9645.** Suite 204, 25 W 43rd St, New York, NY 10036. **212-575-1820.** 32 W Washington, Chicago, IL 60602. **312-263-3232**

Executive Director. Eugene F Corrigan. **303-447-9645**

NEW ENGLAND HIGHER EDUCATION COMPACT. 40 Grove St, Wellesley, MA 02181

Executive Secretary and Director. Alan D Ferguson

NEW ENGLAND INTERSTATE WATER POLLUTION CONTROL COMMISSION. 607 Boylston St, Boston, MA 02116. **617-261-3758**

Executive Secretary. Alfred E Peloquin

Public Affairs Director. Robert A McCarthy

NORTHEASTERN FOREST FIRE PROTECTION COMMISSION. 68 Buckley Hwy, Stafford Springs, CT 06076. **203-684-3509**

Executive Secretary-Treasurer. John C Greene, Jr

OHIO RIVER VALLEY WATER SANITATION COMMISSION. 414 Walnut St, Cincinnati, OH 45202. **513-421-1151**

Executive Director. Leo Weaver

Information Specialist. Deborah Decker

PACIFIC MARINE FISHERIES COMMISSION. 528 SW Mill St, Portland OR 97201. **503-229-5840**

Executive Director. John P Harville

PACIFIC NORTHWEST RIVER BASIN COMMISSION. PO Box 908, Vancouver, WA 98660. **206-694-2581**

PORT AUTHORITY OF NEW YORK AND NEW JERSEY. 1 World Trade Ctr, New York, NY 10048. **212-466-7000**

Executive Director. A Gerdes Kuhbach

SOUTHERN GROWTH POLICIES BOARD. PO Box 12293, Research Triangle Park, NC 27709. **919-549-8167**

Executive Director and Secretary. E Blaine Liner

Director of Administration. Sandra Copeland

SOUTHERN INTERSTATE NUCLEAR BOARD. Suite 1230, 1 Exchange Pl, Atlanta, GA 30338. **404-455-8841**

Executive Director. Kenneth J Nemeth

SOUTHERN REGIONAL EDUCATION BOARD. 130 6th St NW, Atlanta, GA 30313. **404-875-9211**

President. Dr Winfred L Godwin

TRI-STATE REGIONAL PLANNING COMMISSION. 1 World Trade Ctr, New York, NY 10048. **212-938-3300**

Executive Director. J Douglas Carroll, Jr. **212-938-3315**

Manager of Public Information. Lyman B Coddington. **212-938-3321.** Night line: **203-226-3473**

Public Information Coordinator. Courtney Bayer. **212-938-3324.** Night line: **201-768-0946**

UPPER COLORADO RIVER COMMISSION. 355 SE 4th East St, Salt Lake City, UT 84111. **801-531-1150**

Executive Director. Ival V Goslin

UPPER MISSISSIPPI RIVER BASIN COMMISSION. Rm 510, Federal Office Bldg, Fort Snelling, Twin Cities, MN 55111. **612-725-4690**

WASHINGTON METROPOLITAN AREA TRANSIT AUTHORITY. 600 5th St NW, Washington, DC 20001. **202-637-1047**

WATERFRONT COMMISSION OF NEW YORK HARBOR. 150 William St, New York, NY 10038. **212-964-3520**

Executive Director. Leonard Newman

Press Contact. Jerome J Klied, deputy executive director

WESTERN INTERSTATE COMMISSION FOR HIGHER EDUCATION. University East Campus, PO Drawer P, Boulder, CO 80302. **303-492-8666**

Executive Director. Dr Robert H Kroepsch

WESTERN INTERSTATE ENERGY BOARD. Suite 2500, 3333 Quebec St, Denver, CO 80207. **303-837-5851**

Interim Director. Fred A Gross, Jr

WESTERN STATES WATER COUNCIL. 220 S 2nd East St, Salt Lake City, UT 84111. **801-521-2800**

Executive Director. Jack A Barnett

STATE GOVERNMENTS

GOVERNORS, PRESS SECRETARIES, AND STAFFS

ALABAMA

Governor. George C Wallace (D). State Capitol, Montgomery, 36104. Main number: **205-832-6011.** *Governor's office.* **205-832-3511**

Executive Secretary. Henry B Steagall II

Legal Advisor. William A Jackson

Press Secretary. Billy Joe Camp

Assistant Press Secretary. Elvin Stanton. **205-832-3517**

ALASKA

Governor. Jay S Hammond (R). State Capitol, Juneau, 99811. *Governor's office.* **907-465-3500**

Executive Assistant. Kent Dawson

Legislative Assistant. Kent Dawson

Press Secretary. Scott Foster. **907-465-3500**

ARIZONA

Governor. Bruce Babbitt (D). State House, Phoenix, 85007. Main number: **602-271-4900.** *Governor's office.* **602-271-4331**

Executive Assistant. Dino DeConcini

Administrative Assistant. Al Rogers

Press Contact. Tom Rippey. **602-271-4331**

ARKANSAS

Governor. David H Pryor (D). State Capitol, Little Rock, 72201. *Governor's office.* **501-371-2345.** Also **501-371-2133** and **2171**

Administrative Assistant (Liaison for State Departments). Bill Gaddy

Special Assistant. Parker Westbrook

Administrative Assistant (Appointments). Ann Pride. **501-371-2133**

Executive Secretary. Steve Clark

Director, Office of Management and Planning. Vance Jones

CALIFORNIA

Governor. Edmund G Brown, Jr (D). State Capitol, Sacramento, 95814. Main number: **916-445-4711.** *Governor's office.* **916-445-2841** or **2843.** *Washington office.* Suite 708, 1101 17th St NW, Washington, DC 20036. **202-223-1742**

Executive Secretary and Chief of Staff. Gray Davis

Special Assistant to the Governor. Mark Lubow

Director of Administration. Rudy Ahumada

Assistant to the governor and legislative secretary. Marc Poche

Director of Public Affairs and Press Secretary. Elisabeth Coleman. **916-445-4571**

COLORADO

Governor. Richard D Lamm (D). State Capitol, Denver, 80203. Main number: **303-892-9911.** *Governor's office.* **303-829-2471**

Executive Assistant. John Lay

Personal Secretary. Shirley Feller

Assistant (Natural Resources). Jim Monaghan

Assistant (Legislation). Wallace Stealey

Assistant (Legislation and Political Liaison). Lee White

Press Secretary. Jack Olsen, Jr. **303-566-4840**

Staff Assistant (Ombudsman). Margie Major

CONNECTICUT

Governor. Ella T Grasso (D). State Capitol, Hartford, 06115. **203-566-4840**

Press Secretary. Larrye de Bear

DELAWARE

Governor. Pierre S du Pont (R). Legislative Hall, Dover, 19901. Main number: **302-678-4000.** *Governor's office.* **302-678-4101.** Also 1800 Pennsylvania Ave, Wilmington, 19806. **302-571-3210**

Press Contact. Fredrick H Stern

Press Secretary. 302-678-4101 or **302-571-3210**

FLORIDA

Governor. Reubin O'D Askew (D). State Capitol, Tallahassee, 32304. Main number: **904-488-1234.** *Governor's office.* **904-488-4441.** *Washington office.* 225 Constitution Ave NE–1, Washington, DC 20002. **202-547-7997**

Senior Executive Assistant. Jim Tait

Executive Assistant. Harvey Cotten

Legal Counsel. Bruce Starling

Press Secretary. Paul Schnitt. **904-488-5152**

GEORGIA

Governor. George Busbee (D). State Capitol, Atlanta, 30334. Main number: **404-656-2000.** *Governor's office.* **404-656-1776**

Executive Counsel. William L Harper

Assistant Executive Counsel. David Trippe

Administrative Assistant. Tom K Perdue

News Secretary. Duane Riner. **904-488-5152**

Executive Secretary. Norman L Underwood

HAWAII

Governor. George R Ariyoshi (D). State Capitol, Honolulu, 96813. Main number: **808-548-2211.** *Governor's office.* **808-548-5420**

Administrative Director. Susumu Ono

Press Secretary. Hobert E Duncan. **808-548-5420**

Private Secretary. Ruby S Kimoto

Assistant. Francis Lum

IDAHO

Governor. John V Evans (D). State Capitol, Boise, 83720. Main number: **208-384-2411.** *Governor's office.* **208-384-2100**

Administrative Assistant (Chargé d'Affaires). Pat Hawley

Press Secretary and Public Relations. Steve Leroy. **208-384-2100**

ILLINOIS

Governor. James R Thompson (R). State Capitol, Springfield, 62706. Main number: **217-782-2000.** *Governor's office.* **217-782-6830**

Deputy to the Governor. James Fletcher. **217-782-6830**

Counsel to the Governor. Gary Starkman. **312-793-2121**

Press Secretary. David R Gilbert. **217-782-7355**

INDIANA

Governor. Otis R Bowen, MD (R). State Capitol, Indianapolis, 46204. Main number: **317-633-4000.** *Governor's office.* **317-633-4567.** *Washington office.* (422 1st St SE, Washington, DC 20003). **202-543-2042**

Executive Assistant (Legislative Affairs). Raymond W Rizzo

Executive Assistant (Media Relations). William J Watt. **317-633-4567**

Executive Assistant (Administration). William C Lloyd

Executive Assistant (Public Safety). James T Smith

Executive Assistant (Urban and Community Relations). William T Ray

IOWA

Governor. Robert D Ray (R). State Capitol, Des Moines, 50319. Main number: **515-281-5011.** *Governor's office.* **515-281-5211**

Executive Assistant. Wythe Willey

Administrative Assistant. Elmer ("Dutch") Vermeer

Administrative Assistant. Jan Van Note

Press Secretary. David Oman. **515-281-5211**

KANSAS

Governor. Robert F Bennett (R). State House, Topeka, 66612. *Governor's office.* **913-296-3232**

Legislative Liaison. Jim Maag

Press Secretary. Leroy Towns. **913-296-4030**

KENTUCKY

Governor. Julian M Carroll (D). State Capitol, Frankfort, 40601. Main number: **502-564-2500.** *Governor's office.* **502-564-2611**

Chief Executive Officer (Internal Affairs). Jack Hall

Chief Executive Officer (External Affairs). Roy Stevens

Press Secretary. John Nichols

General Counsel. Andrew Palmer

Deputy Press Secretary (Communications). Bill Bradford

Deputy Press Secretary (Press Relations). Gary Auxier. **502-564-2611**

LOUISIANA

Governor. Edwin Edwards (D). State Capitol, Baton Rouge, 70804. Main number: **504-389-6321.** *Governor's office.* **504-389-5281**

Executive Secretary. Dan S Borné

Executive Counsel. Camille Gravel

Chief Administrative Aide. Jim Harris

Executive Assistant. Diane McNabb

Executive Aide. Rene Chehardy

MAINE

Governor. James B Longley (Ind). State House, Augusta, 04330. Capitol switchboard: **207-289-1110.** *Governor's office.* **207-289-3531.** *Federal–state coordinator.* **207-289-3138**

Assistant to the Governor. Jim McGregor

Communications Coordinator. Ralph Lowe. **207-289-3531**

MARYLAND

Acting Governor. Blair Lee 3d (D) **Gov** (suspended from office) Marvin Mandel (D). State House, Annapolis, 21404. State capitol information: **301-267-0100.** Governor's office information. **301-269-6200.** *Governor's office.* **301-267-5901.** Also Rm 1513, 301 W Preston St, Baltimore, 21201. **301-383-4950.** District Office Bldg, 9300 Kenilworth Ave, Greenbelt, 20705. **301-474-2500.** *Washington office.* Suite 319, 1730 K St NW, Washington, DC 20006. **202-659-8621**

MASSACHUSETTS

Governor. Michael S Dukakis (D). State House, Boston, 02133. Main number: **617-727-2121.** *Governor's office.* **617-727-3600.** *Washington office.* Suite 307, Hall of States, 444 N Capitol St, Washington, DC 20001. **202-628-1065**

Chief Secretary. David S Liederman

Deputy Chief Secretary. Michael Widmer

Chief Legal Counsel. Daniel A Taylor

Director, Legislative Office. Tony Gallugi

Press Secretary. Alan Raymond. **617-727-2766**

MICHIGAN

Governor. William G Milliken (R). State Capitol, Lansing, 48909. Main number: **517-373-1837.** *Governor's office.* **517-373-3400**

Executive Secretary. George Weeks

Executive Assistant (State Affairs). Robert Berg

Executive Assistant (Political Affairs). Joyce Braithwaite

Press Secretary. Al Sandner. **517-373-3430**

MINNESOTA

Governor. Rudy Perpich (D). State Capitol, St Paul, 55155. Main number: **612-296-6013.** *Governor's office.* **612-296-3391**

Personal Secretary. Lynn Anderson

Executive Secretary. Terry Montgomery

Press Secretary. Bob Aronson. **612-296-3391**

MISSISSIPPI

Governor. Cliff Finch (D). State Capitol, Jackson, 39205. *Governor's office.* **601-354-7575**

Executive Assistant. Herman Glazier

Legislative Assistant. Bob Perry

Press Secretary. Leroy Morganti. **601-354-7080**

MISSOURI

Governor. Joseph P Teasdale (D). State Capitol, Jefferson City, 65101. Main number: **314-751-2151.** *Governor's office.* **314-751-3222**

Communications Assistant. Dale A Amick. **314-751-3222**

MONTANA

Governor. Thomas L Judge (D). State Capitol, Helena, 59601. Main number: **406-449-2511.** *Governor's office.* **406-449-3111.** *Federal–state coordinator* (Suite 720, 1600 Wilson Blvd, Arlington, Va 22209. **703-524-2211**

Executive Assistant. Keith L Colbo

General Counsel. Lawrence M Elison

Press Secretary. John E Linder. **406-449-3111**

NEBRASKA

Governor. J James Exon (D). State Capitol, Lincoln, 68509. Main number: **402-471-2311.** *Governor's office.* **402-471-2244**

Executive Administrative Assistant. Norman A Otto

Administrative Assistant and Legal Counsel. Bill Hoppner

Press Secretary. Bill Hoppner. **402-471-2244**

NEVADA

Governor. Mike O'Callaghan (D). State Capitol, Carson City, 89710. Main number: **702-885-5000.** *Governor's office.* **702-885-5670.** Also PO Box 791, Las Vegas, NV 89101. **702-385-0213**

Executive Administrator. Chris Schaller

Administrative Assistant. John McGroarty

Executive Assistant. Faith Greaves

Administrative Assistant and Press Secretary. Bob Stewart. **702-885-5670**

Special Assistant (Las Vegas). Harriet Trudell

NEW HAMPSHIRE

Governor. Meldrim Thomson, Jr (R). State House, Concord, 03301. Main number: **603-271-1110.** *Governor's office.* **603-271-2121**

Chief of Staff. Peter M Thomson

Deputy Chief of Staff (Public Affairs). John J McDuffee

Public Relations Reference Librarian. Faye Letendre

Press Contact. Joseph Zellner. **603-271-2176**

NEW JERSEY
Governor. Brendon T Byrne (D). State House, Trenton, 08625. Main number: **609-292-2121.** *Governor's office.* **609-292-6000**

Executive Secretary. John J Degnan

Director of Public Information. Ben A Borowsky

Press Secretary. Kathryn A Forsyth. **609-292-8956.** (h) **609-298-7412**

NEW MEXICO
Governor. Jerry Apodaca (D). State Capitol, Santa Fe, 87503. Main number: **505-827-4011.** *Governor's office.* **505-827-2221**

Press Secretary. Richard de Uriarte. **505-827-2221**

NEW YORK
Governor. Hugh L Carey (D). State Capitol, Albany, 12224. Main number: **518-474-2121.** *Governor's office.* **518-474-8390.** Also 1350 Avenue of the Americas, New York, 10019. **212-977-2700.** *Press.* **518-474-8418**

Secretary. Robert Morgado

Counsel. Judah Gribetz

Executive Assistant. Martha A Golden

Press Secretary. James S Vlasto

Deputy Secretary (Analysis and Coordination). Walter T Kicinski

Deputy Secretary. Carol Opton

Budget Director. Philip Toia

NORTH CAROLINA
Governor. James B Hunt, Jr (D). Administration Building, State Capitol, Raleigh, 27611. Main number: **919-829-1110.** *Governor's office.* **919-829-5811**

News Secretary. Gary Pearce. **919-733-5612**

Deputy News Secretary. Stephanie Bass. **919-733-5612**

NORTH DAKOTA
Governor. Arthur A Link (D). State Capitol, Bismarck, 58505. Main number: **701-224-2000.** *Governor's office.* **701-224-2200**

Director of Administration. George W (Woody) Gagnon

Administrative Assistant. Arthur McKinney

Research and Information Assistant Press Secretary. Katherine Satrom. **701-224-2200**

OHIO
Governor. James A Rhodes (R). State House, Columbus, 43215. Main number: **614-466-2000.** *Governor's office.* **614-466-3526**

Executive Assistant. Roy Martin

Executive Assistant (Legal, Legislative). Tom Moyer

Administrative Assistant (Press). Chan Cochran. **614-466-3526**

OKLAHOMA
Governor. David L Boren (D). State Capitol, Oklahoma City, 73105. Main number: **405-521-2011.** *Governor's office.* **405-521-2345**

Executive Assistant. Robert M Morgan

Administrative Assistant. Dave Holliday

Press Secretary. Rob Pyron. **405-521-2795**

OREGON
Governor. Robert W Straub (D). State Capitol, Salem, 97310. Main number: **503-378-3131.** *Governor's office.* **503-378-3111**

Executive Assistant. Keith Burns

Administrative Assistant (Public Relations). Ken Fobes. **503-378-3111**

Legal Counsel. Ed Sullivan

PENNSYLVANIA
Governor. Milton J Shapp (D). State Capitol, Harrisburg, 17120. Main number: **717-787-2121.** *Governor's office.* **717-787-2500**

Executive Assistant. Richard A Doran

Special Assistant and Press Secretary. Edward Mitchell. **717-787-2867**

PUERTO RICO
Governor. Carlos Romero Barceló (NPP). La Fortaleza, San Juan, 00902. Main number: **809-724-2100**

Special Assistant (Press Matters). Antonio Quiñones Calderón. **809-723-2080** or **809-725-1785**

RHODE ISLAND
Governor. J Joseph Garrahy (D). State House, Providence, 02903. Main number: **401-277-2000.** *Governor's office.* **401-277-2397**

Press Secretary. Lorraine Silberthau. **401-277-2383**

SOUTH CAROLINA
Governor. James B Edwards (R). State House, Columbia, 29211. Governor's mailing address: PO Box 11450, Columbia. *Governor's office.* **803-758-3261**

Administrative Assistant. Walter R Pettiss

Executive Assistant (Legislative Liaison). John H La Fitte

Executive Assistant (Legal). Harold E Trask, Jr

Executive Assistant (Public Affairs). Robert G Liming. **803-758-7911**

SOUTH DAKOTA
Governor. Richard F Kneip (D). State Capitol, Pierre, 57501. Main number: **605-224-3011.** *Governor's office.* **605-224-3212.** *Governor's office, unlisted.* **605-224-3723.** *Governor's residence.* **605-224-2324**

Executive Assistant (Chief of Staff, Press, and Scheduling). Daniel B Garry. **605-224-3212.** (h) **605-224-4595**

Administrative Assistant (Office Manager and Extraditions). Dolores M Hall

TENNESSEE
Governor. Ray Blanton (D). State Capitol, Nashville, 37219. Main number: **615-741-3011.** *Governor's office.* **615-741-2001**

Administrative Assistant. O H ("Shorty") Freeland

Legal Counsel. Eddie Sisk

Director of Information. Brooks Parker. **615-741-3763**

TEXAS
Governor. Dolph Briscoe (D). State Capitol, Austin, 78711. Capitol complex information: **512-475-2323.** *Governor's office.* **512-475-4101**

Executive Assistant. Charles D Travis

Press Secretary. Charles D Morris. **512-475-4215**

UTAH
Governor. Scott M Matheson (D). State Capitol, Salt Lake City, 84114. Main number: **801-533-5111.** *Governor's office and press.* **801-533-5231**

Administrative Assistant. Michael A Youngren

VERMONT
Governor. Richard A Snelling (R). State House, Montpelier, 05602. *Capitol complex information:* **802-828-1110.** *Governor's office and press.* **802-828-3333**

Press Secretary. Charles K Butler, Jr

VIRGIN ISLANDS
Governor. Juan Luis. Government House, Charlotte Amalie, St Thomas, 00801.

Main number: **809-774-0001.** *Governor's office.* Ext 202

Executive Assistant. Peter de Zela

Administrative Assistant. Leopold E Benjamin

Press Secretary. Ann Q Stanwood. **809-774-0001**

VIRGINIA

Governor. John N Dalton (R). State Capitol, Richmond, 23219. Main number: **804-786-0000.** *Governor's office and press.* **804-786-2211**

Senior Executive Assistant. Larry Murphy (tentative)

WASHINGTON

Governor. Dixy Lee Ray (D). State Capitol, Olympia, 98504. Main number: **206-753-5000.** *Governor's office and press.* **206-753-6780**

Press Secretary. Duayne Trecker

WEST VIRGINIA

Governor. John D Rockefeller IV (D). State Capitol, Charleston, 25305. Main number: **304-348-3456.** *Governor's office.* **304-348-2000**

Executive Assistant. Don R Richardson

Administrative Assistant. Sandra W Lopinsky

Counsel. M Blane Michael

Special Assistants. Jack Canfield, Jack Pauley, Paul Crabtree, Sally Richardson, and Dr Z Erik Farag (health)

Appointments Secretary. Norwood W Bentley III

Press Secretary. Scott D Widmeyer. **304-348-2015.** (h) **304-346-7442**

WISCONSIN

Governor. Martin J Schreiber (acting). State Capitol, Madison, 53702. Main number: **608-266-2211.** *Governor's office.* **608-266-1212**

Executive Assistant. Joe Thomas

Legal Counsel. Ed Parsons

Press Secretary. H Carl Mueller (acting). **608-266-1212**

WYOMING

Governor. Ed Herschler (D). State Capitol, Cheyenne, 82002. Main number: **307-777-7011.** *Governor's office.* **307-777-7434**

Administrative Assistant. Dick Skinner

Press Secretary. Jerry Mahoney. **307-777-7434**

Administrative Coordinator. Adeline McCabe

State Planning Coordinator. Steve Freudenthal. **307-777-7574**

ATTORNEYS GENERAL

ALABAMA. William J Baxley. State Administration Bldg, Montgomery, 36131. **205-832-6050**

ALASKA. Avrum Gross. Juneau, 99811. **907-465-3600**

ARIZONA. John A La Sota. 159 State House, Phoenix, 85007. **501-371-2007**

ARKANSAS. Bill Clinton. Justice Bldg, Little Rock, 72201. **501-371-2007**

CALIFORNIA. Evelle J Younger. 555 Capitol Mall, Sacramento, 95814. **916-445-9555**

COLORADO. John D MacFarlane. 3rd Floor, 1525 Sherman St, Denver, 80203. **303-892-3611** or **3621**

CONNECTICUT. Carl R Ajello. Capitol Annex, 30 Trinity St, Hartford, 06115. **203-566-2027**

DELAWARE. Richard R Wier, Jr. Department of Justice, Wilmington, 19801. **302-571-2500**

FLORIDA. Robert L Shevin. State Capitol, Tallahassee, 32304. **904-488-2490**

GEORGIA. Arthur K Bolton. 132 State Judicial Bldg, Atlanta, 30334. **404-656-4586**

HAWAII. Ronald Amemiya. State Capitol, Honolulu, 96813. **808-548-4740**

IDAHO. Wayne L Kidwell. State Capitol, Boise, 83701. **208-384-2400**

ILLINOIS. William J Scott. 500 S 2nd St, Springfield, 62701. **217-782-1090**

INDIANA. Theodore L Sendak. 219 State House, Indianapolis, 46204. **317-633-5512**

IOWA. Richard C Turner. State Capitol, Des Mines, 50319. **515-281-5164**

KANSAS. Curt T Schneider. State House, Topeka, 66612. **913-296-2215**

KENTUCKY. Robert Stephens. State Capitol, Frankfort, 40601. **502-564-7600**

LOUISIANA. William J Guste. Jr, State Capitol, Baton Rouge, 70804. **504-389-6761**

MAINE. Joseph Brennan. State House, Augusta, 04330. **207-289-3661**

MARYLAND. Francis B Burch. 1 S Calvert St, Baltimore, 21202. **301-383-3737**

MASSACHUSETTS. Francis X Bellotti. 1 Ashburton Pl, Boston, 02108. **617-727-2200**

MICHIGAN. Frank J Kelley. 525 W Ottawa St, Lansing, 48913. **517-373-1110**

MINNESOTA. Warren R Spannaus. 102 State Capitol, St Paul, 55155. **612-296-6196**

MISSISSIPPI. AF Summer. Carroll Gartin Justice Bldg, Jackson, 39205. **601-354-7130**

MISSOURI. John Ashcroft. PO Box 899, Supreme Court Bldg, Jefferson City, 65101. **314-751-3321**

MONTANA. Michael T Greely. State Capitol, Helena, 59601. **406-449-2026**

NEBRASKA. Paul L Douglas. State Capitol, Lincoln, 68509. **402-471-2682**

NEVADA. Robert List. Supreme Court Bldg, Carson City, 89701. **702-885-4170**

NEW HAMPSHIRE. Warren B Rudman. State House Annex, Concord, 03301. **603-271-3665**

NEW JERSEY. John Degnan. State House Annex, Trenton, 08625. **609-292-4925**

NEW MEXICO. Toney Anaya. Bataan Memorial Bldg, Santa Fe, 87501. **505-988-8851**

NEW YORK. Louis Lefkowitz. State Capitol, Albany, 12224. **518-474-7330**

NORTH CAROLINA. Rufus L Edmisten. PO Box 629, Justice Bldg, Raleigh, 27602. **919-233-3377**

NORTH DAKOTA. Allen I Olson. State Capitol, Bismarck, 58501. **701-224-2210**

OHIO. William J Brown. 30 E Broad St, Columbus, 43215. **614-466-3376**

OKLAHOMA. Larry Derryberry. 112 State Capitol, Oklahoma City, 73105. **405-521-3921**

OREGON. James Redden. 100 State Office Bldg, Salem, 97310. **503-378-6002**

PENNSYLVANIA. (Vacant). Rm 1, Capitol Annex, Harrisburg, 17120. **717-787-3391**

PUERTO RICO. Miguel Giminez-Munoz. Calle Fortaleza 50, San Juan, 00904

RHODE ISLAND. Julius C Michaelson. Providence County Courthouse, Providence, 02903. **401-831-6850**

SOUTH CAROLINA. Daniel R McLeod. Wade Hampton Office Bldg, Columbia, 29211. **803-758-3970**

SOUTH DAKOTA. William Janklow. State Capitol, Pierre, 57501. **605-224-3215**

TENNESSEE. Brooks McLemore. 450 James Robertson Pkwy, Nashville, 37219. **615-741-3491**

TEXAS. John L Hill. Supreme Court Bldg, Austin, 78711. **512-475-4643**

UTAH. Robert Hansen. State Capitol, Salt Lake City, 84114. **801-533-5261**

VERMONT. M Jerome Diamond. Pavilion Office Bldg, Montpelier, 05602. **802-828-3171**

VIRGIN ISLANDS. Edgar D Ross, PO Box 280, Charlotte Amalie, St Thomas, 00801. **809-774-1163**

VIRGINIA. J Marshall Coleman. Supreme Court Library Bldg, Richmond, 23219. **804-786-2071**

WASHINGTON. Slade Gorton. Temple of Justice, Olympia, 98504. **206-753-2550**

WEST VIRGINIA. Chauncey H Browning. Jr, State Capitol, Charleston, 25305. **304-348-2021**

WISCONSIN. Bronson C La Follette. State Capitol, Madison, 53702. **608-266-1221**

WYOMING. V Frank Mendicino. State Capitol, Cheyenne, 82001. **307-777-7384**

SECRETARIES OF STATE

ALABAMA. Agnes Baggett. Montgomery, 36130. **205-832-3570**

ARIZONA. Rose Mofford. 1700 W Washington St, Phoenix, 85007. **602-271-4286**

ARKANSAS. Winston Bryant. 256 State Capitol, Little Rock, 72201. **501-371-1010**

CALIFORNIA. March Fong Eu. Suite 605, 925 L St, Sacramento, 95814. **916-445-6371**

COLORADO. Mary E Buchanan. Department of State, Denver, 80203. **303-892-3301**

CONNECTICUT. Gloria Schaffer. State Capitol, Hartford, 06115. **203-566-4135**

DELAWARE. Glenn C Kenton. Townsend Bldg, Dover, 19901. **302-678-4111**

FLORIDA. Bruce A Smathers. State Capitol, Tallahassee, 32304. **904-488-8472**

GEORGIA. Ben W Fortson, Jr. 214 State Capitol, Atlanta, 30334. **404-656-2881**

IDAHO. Peter T Cenarrusa. Rm 203, State Capitol, Boise, 83720. **208-384-2300**

ILLINOIS. Alan J Dixon. State Capitol, Springfield, 62706. **217-782-2201**

INDIANA. Larry A Conrad. State Capitol, Indianapolis, 46204. **317-633-6531**

IOWA. Melvin D Synhorst. State Capitol, Des Moines, 50319. **515-281-5864**

KANSAS. Elwill M Shanahan. State House, Topeka, 66612. **913-296-2236**

KENTUCKY. Drexell Davis. State Capitol, Frankfort, 40601. **502-564-3490**

LOUISIANA. Paul J Hardy. State Capitol, Baton Rouge, 70804. **504-389-6181**

MAINE. Markham L Gartley. State House, Augusta, 04330. **207-289-3501**

MARYLAND. Fred L Wineland. State House, Annapolis, 21404. **301-267-3421**

MASSACHUSETTS. Paul Guzzi. State House, Boston, 02133. **617-727-2800**

MICHIGAN. Richard H Austin. Treasury Bldg, Lansing, 48918. **517-373-2510**

MINNESOTA. Joan A Growe. 180 State Office Bldg, St Paul, 55155. **612-296-3266**

MISSISSIPPI. Heber Ladner. New Capitol Bldg, Jackson, 39205. **601-354-6541**

MISSOURI. James C Kirkpatrick. State Capitol, Jefferson City, 65101. **314-751-2331**

MONTANA. Frank Murray. State Capitol, Helena, 59601. **406-449-2034**

NEBRASKA. Allen J Beermann. Suite 2300, State Capitol, Lincoln, 68509. **402-471-2554**

NEVADA. William D Swackhamer. State Capitol Complex, Carson City, 89710. **702-885-5203**

NEW HAMPSHIRE. William M Gardner. State House, Concord, 03301. **603-271-3242**

NEW JERSEY. Donald Lan. State House, Trenton, 08625. **609-292-3790**

NEW MEXICO. Ernestine D Evans. Executive Bldg, Santa Fe, 87501. **505-827-2844**

NEW YORK. Mario Cuomo. Department of State, Albany, 12231. **518-474-4750**

NORTH CAROLINA. Thad Eue. State Capitol, Raleigh, 27603. **919-733-3433**

NORTH DAKOTA. Ben Meier. State Capitol, Bismarck, 58501. **701-224-2900**

OHIO. Ted W Brown. 30 E Broad St, Columbus, 43216. **614-466-2530**

OKLAHOMA. Jerome Byrd. State Capitol, Oklahoma City, 73105. **405-521-3911**

OREGON. Norma Paulus. State Capitol, Salem, 97310. **503-378-4400**

PENNSYLVANIA. Barton Fields. 302 North Office Bldg, Harrisburg, 17120. **717-787-7630**

PUERTO RICO. Reinaldo Paniagua. Box 3271, San Juan, 00904.

RHODE ISLAND. Robert F Burns. State House, Providence, 02903. **401-277-2371**

SOUTH CAROLINA. O Frank Thornton. Wade Hampton Office Bldg, Columbia, 29211. **803-758-2744**

SOUTH DAKOTA. Lorna Herseth. State Capitol, Pierre, 57501. **605-224-3537**

TENNESSEE. Gentry Crowell. State Capitol, Nashville, 37219. **615-741-2816**

TEXAS. Mark W White. Jr, State Capitol, Austin, 78711. **512-475-2015**

UTAH. David S Monson. State Capitol, Salt Lake City, 84114. **801-533-5151**

VERMONT. James Guest. 109 State St, Montpelier, 05602. **802-828-2363**

VIRGINIA. Patricia Perkinson. 9th St Office Bldg, Richmond, 23219. **804-786-2441**

WASHINGTON. Bruce Chapman. Legislative Bldg, Olympia, 98504. **206-753-7121**

WEST VIRGINIA. A James Manchin. State Capitol, Charleston, 25305. **304-348-2112**

WISCONSIN. Douglas J La Follette. State Capitol, Madison, 53702. **608-266-5801**

WYOMING. Thyra Thomson. State Capitol, Cheyenne, 82002. **307-777-7378**

PUBLIC UTILITY COMMISSIONS

ALASKA PUBLIC UTILITIES COMMISSION. 338 Denali St, Anchorage, AK 99501. **907-272-1487.** Robert Cacy, executive director

ARIZONA CORPORATION COMMISSION. 2222 W Encanto Blvd, Phoenix, AZ 85009. **602-271-3931.** Donald E Vance, executive secretary

ARKANSAS PUBLIC SERVICE COMMISSION. Justice Bldg, Little Rock, AR 72201. **501-371-1794.** John S Choate, director

CALIFORNIA PUBLIC UTILITIES COMMISSION. 350 McAllister St, San Francisco, CA 94102. **415-557-3914.** Eugene Raleigh, information officer, **213-620-2240.** *Los Angeles office,* Carole Kretzer

COLORADO PUBLIC UTILITIES COMMISSION. 500 State Services Bldg, 1525 Sherman St, Denver, CO 80203. **303-839-3154.** Harry A Galligan, Jr, executive secretary

CONNECTICUT PUBLIC UTILITIES COMMISSION. State Office Bldg, 165 Capitol Ave, Hartford, CT 06115. **203-566-7384.** King Quillen, publicist

DELAWARE PUBLIC SERVICE COMMISSION. 1560 S DuPont Hwy, Dover, DE 19901. **302-678-4247.** Robert J Kennedy III, executive director

DISTRICT OF COLUMBIA PUBLIC SERVICE COMMISSION. 1625 I St NW, Washington, DC 20006. **202-727-3050.** Mary E Brazelton, executive secretary

FLORIDA PUBLIC SERVICE COMMISSION. Fletcher Bldg, Tallahassee, FL 32304. **904-488-7238.** George B Hanna, director

GEORGIA CONSUMERS' UTILITY COUNSEL. Suite 933, 15 Peachtree St NW, Atlanta, GA 30303. **404-656-3982.** Sidney L Moore, counsel

HAWAII PUBLIC UTILITIES COMMISSION. Suite 911, 1164 Bishop St, Honolulu, HI 96813. **808-548-3990.** Melvin S Ishihara, administrative director

IDAHO PUBLIC UTILITIES COMMISSION. Statehouse, Boise, ID 83720. **208-384-3143.** Garth E Andrews, public information coordinator

ILLINOIS COMMERCE COMMISSION. 527 E Capitol Ave, Springfield, IL 62706. **217-782-2024.** Thomas O'Brien, supervisor, consumer protection section

INDIANA PUBLIC SERVICE COMMISSION. 901 State Office Bldg, Indianapolis, IN 46204. **317-633-4630.** Sherry O'Brien, public information officer

IOWA STATE COMMERCE COMMISSION. State Capitol, Des Moines, IA 50319. **515-281-5256.** Dean A Briley, executive secretary

KANSAS STATE CORPORATION COMMISSION. State Office Bldg, Topeka, KS 66612. **913-296-3326.** Steven Carter, Executive secretary

KENTUCKY PUBLIC SERVICE COMMISSION. PO Box 496, Frankfort, KY 40601. **502-564-3940.** Richard D Herman, Jr, secretary

LOUISIANA PUBLIC SERVICE COMMISSION. PO Box 44035, Capitol Station, Baton Rouge, LA 70804. **504-389-5867.** Louis S Quinn, secretary

MAINE PUBLIC UTILITIES COMMISSION. 242 State St, Augusta, ME 04330. **207-289-2448.** Howard M Cunningham, secretary

MARYLAND PUBLIC SERVICE COMMISSION. 904 State Office Bldg, 301 W Preston St, Baltimore, MD 21201. **301-383-2369.** Ronald E Hawkins, assistant executive secretary

MASSACHUSETTS DEPARTMENT OF PUBLIC UTILITIES. Rm 1210, 100 Cambridge St, Boston, MA 02202. **617-727-3500.** Harold J Keohane, chairman

MICHIGAN PUBLIC SERVICE COMMISSION. 6545 Mercantile Way (PO Box 30221), Lansing, MI 48909. **517-373-0777.** Eric Schneidewind, director, policy

MINNESOTA PUBLIC SERVICE COMMISSION. 7th Floor, American Center Bldg, Kellogg and Robert Sts, St Paul, MN 55101. **612-296-6176.** Larry J Anderson

MISSISSIPPI PUBLIC SERVICE COMMISSION. 19th Floor, PO Box 1174, Walter Sillers State Office Bldg, Jackson, MS 39205. **601-354-7474.** Keith Howle, director, utilities

MISSOURI PUBLIC SERVICE COMMISSION. PO Box 360, Jefferson Bldg, Jefferson City, MO 65101. **314-751-2452.** Lawson Phaby, information officer

MONTANA PUBLIC SERVICE COMMISSION. 1227 11th Ave, Helena, MT 59601. **406-449-3007.** Gail E Behan, secretary

NEBRASKA PUBLIC SERVICE COMMISSION. 3rd Floor, 1342 M St, Lincoln, NE 68508. **402-475-2641.** Joyce Durand, contact

NEVADA PUBLIC SERVICE COMMISSION. Kinkead Bldg, 505 E King St, Carson City, NV 89710. **702-885-4180.** William W Proksch, Jr, secretary

NEW HAMPSHIRE PUBLIC UTILITIES COMMISSION. 26 Pleasant St, Concord, NH 03301. **603-271-2452.** Dom S D'Ambruoso, secretary

NEW JERSEY BOARD OF PUBLIC UTILITY COMMISSIONERS. 101 Commerce St, Newark, NJ 07102. **201-648-2013.** Charles Garrity, contact

NEW MEXICO STATE CORPORATION COMMISSION. PO Drawer 1269, Santa Fe, NM 87501. **505-827-2163.** John A Elliott, director, pipeline division

NEW YORK PUBLIC SERVICE COMMISSION. Empire State Plz, Albany, NY 12223. **518-474-7080.** Francis S Rivett, public information officer

NORTH CAROLINA UTILITIES COMMISSION. PO Box 991, Raleigh, NC 27602. **919-829-7328.** Katherine M Peele, chief clerk

NORTH DAKOTA PUBLIC SERVICE COMMISSION. State Capitol Bldg, Bismarck, ND 58501. **701-224-2411.** Janet Satur, secretary

OHIO PUBLIC UTILITIES COMMISSION. 180 E Broad St, Columbus, OH 43215. **614-466-7750.** Steven L Brash, public information officer

OKLAHOMA CORPORATION COMMIS-SION. Jim Thorpe Office Bldg, Oklahoma City, OK 73105. **405-521-2264.** Rex Privett, chairman

OREGON PUBLIC UTILITY COMMIS-SIONER. Labor and Industries Bldg, Salem, OR 97310. **503-378-6604.** Frank Dillow, assistant commissioner

PENNSYLVANIA PUBLIC UTILITY COMMISSION. PO Box 3265, Harrisburg, PA 17120. **717-787-5722** or **6660.** David M Bramson, director, public information

PUERTO RICO PUBLIC SERVICE COM-MISSION. PO Box S-952, San Juan, PR 00902. **809-725-7575.** Enrique Rodriguez, chief information officer

RHODE ISLAND PUBLIC UTILITIES COMMISSION. 100 Orange St, Providence, RI 02903. **401-277-3500.** Bruce A Stevenson, associate administrator for operations

SOUTH CAROLINA PUBLIC SERVICE COMMISSION. PO Box 11649, Columbia, SC 29211. **803-758-3565.** James H Still, director, administrative services

SOUTH DAKOTA PUBLIC UTILITIES COMMISSION. Capitol Bldg, Pierre, SD 57501. **605-224-3203.** Joe Norton, executive secretary and director

TENNESSEE PUBLIC SERVICE COM-MISSION. C1-102 Cordell Hull Bldg, Nashville, TN 37219. **615-741-3939.** Don Bagwell

TEXAS PUBLIC UTILITY COMMIS-SION. PO Box 12577, Capitol Station, Austin, TX 78711. **512-475-7901.** Nancy Ross, contact

TEXAS RAILROAD COMMISSION. Drawer 12967, Capitol Station, Austin, TX 78711. **512-475-3208.** James H Cowden, director, transportation division

UTAH PUBLIC SERVICE COMMIS-SION. 330 E 4th St, Salt Lake City, UT 84111. **801-533-5515.** Ronald E Casper, secretary

VERMONT PUBLIC SERVICE BOARD. State Office Bldg, Montpelier, VT 05602. **802-828-2319.** Richard Saudek, chairman

VIRGINIA STATE CORPORATION COMMISSION. PO Box 1197, Blanton Bldg, Richmond, VA 23209. **804-786-8967.** John F Daffron, public information director

VIRGIN ISLANDS PUBLIC SERVICE COMMISSION. PO Box 40, Charlotte Amalie, St Thomas, VI 00801. **809-774-1219.** Patrick M Rice, executive director

WASHINGTON UTILITIES AND TRANSPORTATION COMMISSION. Highways-Licenses Bldg, Olympia, WA 98504. **206-753-6402.** Tony Cook

WEST VIRGINIA PUBLIC SERVICE COMMISSION. Rm E-217, Capitol Bldg, Charleston, WV 25305. **304-348-2182.** S Grover Smith, Jr, executive secretary

WISCONSIN PUBLIC SERVICE COM-MISSION. 432 Hill Farms State Office Bldg, Madison, WI 53702. **608-266-1241**

WYOMING PUBLIC SERVICE COMMIS-SION. Capitol Hill Bldg, 320 W 25th St, Cheyenne, WY 82002. **307-777-7427.** Alex J Eliopulos, secretary and chief counsel

CITY GOVERNMENTS

The following is a quick-reference list of all US cities having populations of over 29,000 (based on 1970 Census). Many noteworthy cities with smaller populations are also included. Each listing includes population in thousands, mayor or equivalent official's name, and city hall address and telephone number. Additional contact information is listed for selected major cities.

Alabama

ANNISTON (32). Norwood Hodges. PO Box 670, 36201. **205-236-3421**

BESSEMER (33). Ed Porter. 1800 3rd Ave N, 35020. **205-424-4060**

BIRMINGHAM (301). David J Vann. **205-254-2277.** City Hall, 35203. **205-254-2000.** Bill Davis, public information officer, **205-254-2494.** Night line: **205-254-2000**

DECATUR (38). Bill J Dukes. PO Box 488, 35602. **205-355-7410**

DOTHAN (37). James W Grant. III. Box 2128, 36301. **205-794-0361**

FLORENCE (34). William E Batson. PO Box 98, 35630. **205-764-7271**

GADSDEN (54). Stephen A Means. PO Box 267, 35902. **205-543-9870**

HUNTSVILLE (138). Joe W Davis. 308 Fountain Row, 35804. **205-539-9612**

MOBILE (190). Lambert C Mims. PO Box 1827, 36601. **205-438-7011**

MONTGOMERY (133). Emory Folmar. PO Box 1111, 36102. **205-262-4421**

PRICHARD (42). A J Cooper. Jr. PO Box 10427, 36610. **205-457-3381.** Charles W Porter, director, public relations

TUSCALOOSA (66). Ernest Collins. 2201 University Blvd, 35401. **205-349-2010**

Alaska

ANCHORAGE (175). George M Sullivan. Pouch 6-650, 99502. **907-264-4422.** Kelly Gay, public information officer

FAIRBANKS (15). John A Carlson. 410 Cushman St, 99701. **907-452-1881**

JUNEAU (14). William O Overstreet. 155 S Seward St, 99801. **907-586-3300**

Arizona

FLAGSTAFF (26). Robert L Moody. PO Box 1208, 86001. **602-774-5281**

GLENDALE (36). Sterling Ridge. PO Box 1556, 85311. **602-931-5543**

MESA (63). Wayne Pomeroy. PO Box 1466 85201. **602-834-2256**

PHOENIX (582). Margaret Hance, **602-262-6011**, Ext 7111. City Hall, 251 W Washington St, 85003. **602-262-6011**. Patsy Perez, administrative assistant, Ext 7111

SCOTTSDALE (68). William C Jenkins, **602-994-2533**. 3939 Civic Center Plz, 85251. **602-994-2521**. Barbara V Markiewicz, public information officer, **602-994-2335**

TEMPE (63). William J Lo Piano. PO Box 5002, 85281. **602-968-8225**

TUCSON (263). Lewis C Murphy. PO Box 5547, 85703. **602-791-4326**. Bill Kimmey, aide to mayor, **602-791-4201**

YUMA (29). James P. Dayo. 180 1st St, 85364. **602-782-2271**. Edward J Lohnes, administrative assistant, **602-782-3817**

Arkansas

EL DORADO (25). W M Rodman. City Hall, 71730. **501-862-7911**

FAYETTEVILLE (31). Ernest Lancaster. PO Drawer F, 72701. **501-521-7700**

FORT SMITH (63). Jack Freeze. PO Box 1908, 72901. **501-785-2801**

LITTLE ROCK (132). Donald L Mehlburger. 500 W Markham St, 72201. **501-371-4512.**

NORTH LITTLE ROCK (60). Eddie Powell. 3rd and Main, 72114. **501-374-2233**

PINE BLUFF (57). Charles Moore. 200 E 8th, 71601. **501-534-5420**

California

ALAMEDA (71). Chuck Corica. Oak and Santa Clara Sts, 94501. **415-522-4100**

ALHAMBRA (62). Steve Ballreich. 111 S 1st St, 91801. **213-282-5111**

ANAHEIM (167). W J (Bill) Thom, PO Box 3222, 92803. **714-533-5617**. Ken Clements, public information officer, **714-533-5615**

ARCADIA (43). Floretta K Lauber. 240 W Huntington Dr, 91006. **213-446-4471**

BAKERSFIELD (70). Donald M Hart. 1501 Truxton Ave, 93301. **805-861-2751**

BALDWIN PARK (47). Emmit Waldo. 1 Civic Ctr, 91706. **213-338-1181**. Leo P Sopicki, Ext 52

BELLFLOWER (51). Robert Leavell. 9838 E Belmont, 90706. **213-866-9003**

BERKELEY (117). Warren Widener. Civic Center Bldg, 2180 Milvia St, 94704. **415-644-6484**. Jo Ann Lawson, executive assistant

BEVERLY HILLS (33). Donna Ellman. 450 N Crescent Dr, 90210. **213-550-4700**. Fred C Cunningham, assistant to city manager, **213-550-4815**

BUENA PARK (64). James T Jarrell. 6650 Beach Blvd, 90620. **714-521-9900**

BURBANK (89). D Verner Gibson. 275 E Olive Ave, 91502. **213-847-8600**

CARSON (71). John A Marbut. 21919 S Avalon Blvd, 90745. **213-830-7600**

CHULA VISTA (68). Will T Hyde. PO Box 1087, 92012. **714-575-5044**

COMPTON (79). Lionel B Cade. 600 N Alameda, 90224. **213-537-8000**

CONCORD (85). Richard La Pointe. 1950 Parkside Dr, 94519. **415-671-3158**. Olga Byrd, administrative assistant

COSTA MESA (73). Norma Hertzog. PO Box 1200, 92626. **714-556-5327**

COVINA (30). Elaine W Donaldson. 125 E College St, 91723. **213-331-0111**

CULVER CITY (35). Richard M Alexander. PO Box 507, 90230. **213-837-5211**

CYPRESS (31). Donald G Hudson. 5275 Orange Ave, 90630. **714-828-2200**

DALY CITY (67). Anthony A Giammona. 333 90th St, 94015. **415-992-4500**

DOWNEY (88). Richard M Jennings. 8425 2nd St, 90241. **213-861-0361**

EL CAJON (52). Robert L Cornett. 200 E Main St, 92020. **714-440-1776**

EL MONTE (70). Jack T Crippen. 11333 Valley Blvd, 91734. **213-575-2225**

ESCONDIDO (54). Alan B Skuba. 100 Valley Blvd, 92025. **714-741-4631**

FAIRFIELD (44). Bill Jenkins. 1000 Webster St, 94533. **707-425-1031**

FOUNTAIN VALLEY (32). Al Hollinden. 10200 Slater Ave, 92708. **714-963-8321**

FREMONT (101). Gene Rhodes. 39700 Civic Center Dr, 94538. **415-791-4500**

FRESNO (166). Daniel K Whitehurst. 2326 Fresno St, 93721. **209-488-1561**

FULLERTON (86). Robert E Ward. 303 W Commonwealth, 92632. **714-525-7171**

GARDENA (41). Edmond J Russ. 1700 W 162nd St, 90247. **213-327-0220**

GARDEN GROVE (123). J Tilman Williams. 11391 Acacia Pkwy, 92640. **714-638-6623**

GLENDALE (133). Carroll W Parcher. 613 E Broadway, 91205. **213-956-4000**

GLENDORA (31). Joe M Finkbiner. 249 E Foothill Blvd, 91740. **213-335-4071**

HAWTHORNE (53). Guy Hocker. 4460 W 126th St, 90250. **213-676-1181**. Tom Quintana, public information officer

HAYWARD (93). Ilene Weinreb. 22300 Foothill Blvd, 94541. **415-581-2345**

HUNTINGTON BEACH (116). Ronald R Pattinson. PO Box 190, 92648. **714-536-5511**

HUNTINGTON PARK (34). Thomas E Jackson. 6550 Miles Ave, 90255. **213-582-6161**

INGLEWOOD (90). Merle Mergell. 1 Manchester Blvd, 90301. **213-649-7111**

LA HABRA (41). Charles V Stevens. Civic Ctr, 90631. **213-694-1011**

LA MESA (39). Paul W Fordem. 8130 Allison Ave, 92041. **714-463-6611**

LA MIRADA (31). Wayne Grisham. 13700 La Mirada Blvd, 90638. **213-943-0131**

LA PUENTE (31). Allen T Le Fever. 15900 E Main St, 91744. **213-330-4511**

LAKEWOOD (83). Dan Branstine. 5050 Clark Ave, 90714. **213-866-9771**. Mike Stover, public information officer

LIVERMORE (38). Helen Tirsell. 2250 1st St, 94550. **415-447-2100**

LODI (32). Richard L Hughes. 221 W Pine St, 95240. **209-368-0641**

LONG BEACH (359). Thomas J Clark. 333 W Ocean, 90802. **213-590-6801**. Gerrie Schipske, public information officer

LOS ANGELES (2816). Thomas Bradley. City Hall, 90012. **213-485-5175**. Tom Sullivan, press secretary. **213-485-5182**. Brenda Banks, assistant press secretary

LYNWOOD (43). James E Rowe. 11330 Bullis Rd, 90262. **213-537-0800**

MANHATTAN BEACH (35). Stephen Blumberg. 1400 Highland Ave, 90262. **213-545-5621**

MERCED (30). William P Quigley. PO Box 2068, 95340. **209-383-4444**

MODESTO (62). Lee H Davies. PO Box 642, 96353. **209-534-4011**

MONROVIA (30). Robert Bartlett. 415 S Ivy Ave, 91016. **213-359-3231**

MONTEBELLO (43). William O Nighswonger. 1600 Beverly Blvd, 90640. **213-722-4100**

MONTEREY PARK (49). George Ige. 320 W Newmark Ave, 91754. **213-573-1211**

MOUNTAIN VIEW (51). Matthew A Allen. PO Box 10, 94042. **415-967-7211**

NAPA (36). Ralph C Bolin. PO Box 660, 94558. **707-252-7711**

NATIONAL CITY (43). Kile Morgan. 1243 National Ave, 92050. **714-477-1181**

NEWPORT BEACH (49). Milan M Dostal. 3300 Newport Blvd, 92663. **714-640-2110**

NORWALK (92). Cecil Green. 12700 Norwalk Blvd, 90650. **213-868-3254**. Marilyn J Morin, public information officer

NOVATO (31). David Milano. PO Box 578, 94947. **415-897-6111**

OAKLAND (362). Lionel J Wilson. 1421 Washington St, 94612. **415-273-3141**. *Press contact.* Toni Adams

OCEANSIDE (40). Paul G Graham. 706 3rd St, 92054. **714-433-9000**

ONTARIO (64). Paul A Treadway. 225 S Euclid Ave, 91761. **714-986-1151**

ORANGE (77). Robert D Hoyt. 300 E Chapman Ave, 92666. **714-532-0321**

OXNARD (71). Tsujio Kato. 225-305 W 3rd St, 93030. **805-486-2601**

PACIFICA (36). Sidney Lorvan. 170 Santa Maria Ave, 94044. **415-355-4151**

PALM SPRINGS (50). William A Foster. PO Box 1786, 92262. **714-323-8171**

PALO ALTO (56). Stanley R Norton. 250 Hamilton Ave, 94301. **415-329-2311**

PARAMOUNT (35). John A Mies. 16420 Colorado Ave, 90723. **213-634-2123**. Charles D Cameron, community relations officer

PASADENA (113). Robert G White. 100 N Garfield Ave, 91009. **213-577-4000**

PETALUMA (25). Helen Putnam. Post and English Sts, 94951. **707-763-2613**

PICO RIVERA (54). James M Patronite. 6615 Passons Blvd, 90660. **213-692-0401**

PLEASANTON (32). Robert C Philcox. 200 Bernal Ave, 94566. **415-846-3202**

POMONA (87). Charles W Bader. PO Box 660, 91766. **714-620-2311**

RANCHO PALOS VERDES (40). Gunther W Buerk. 30940 Hawthorne Blvd, 90274. **213-378-0383**

REDLANDS (36). Charles G De Mirjyn. PO Box 280, 92373. **714-793-2641**

REDONDO BEACH (56). David K Hayward, **213-372-1171**, Ext 254. City Hall, 415 Diamond St, 90277. **213-372-1171**. *Press contact,* Timothy J Casey, assistant to city manager, Ext 294. (h) **213-375-0178**

REDWOOD CITY (56). Marguerite Leipzig. PO Box 468, 94064. **415-369-6251**

RICHMOND (79). Don Wagerman. 27th St and Barrett Ave, 94804. **415-232-1212**

RIVERSIDE (155). A B Brown. 3900 Main St, 92522. **714-787-7551**

ROSEMEAD (41). Roberta Trujillo. 8838 E Valley Blvd, 91770. **213-288-6671**

SACRAMENTO (254). Philip L Isenberg, **916-449-5400**. 915 I St, 95814. **916-449-5011**. Ms. Luen Fong, secretary, **916-449-5400**

SALINAS (59). Henry K Hibino. 200 Lincoln Ave, 93901. **408-758-7011**

SAN BERNARDINO (104). W R Holcomb, **714-383-5004**. City Hall, 300 N D St, 92418. **714-383-5211**. Night line: **714-383-5266**. Dave Light, Executive assistant, **714-383-5004**

SAN BRUNO (39). Gary J Mondfrans. 567 El Camino Real, 94066. **415-583-3083**

SAN BUENAVENTURA (56). Harriet Kosma. PO Box 99, 93001. **805-648-7881**

SAN DIEGO (697). Pete Wilson, City Hall, 202 C St, 92101. **714-293-6030**. Larry Thomas, press secretary

SAN FRANCISCO (716). George Moscone, City Hall, 400 Van Ness Ave, 94102. **415-558-3456**. Corey Busch, press secretary, **415-558-3755**

SAN GABRIEL (30). Michael Falabrino. PO Box 130, 91778. **213-282-4104**

SAN JOSE (446). Janet Gray Hayes, City Hall, 801 N 1st St, 95110. **408-277-4237**. Barbara Krause, administrative assistant

SAN LEANDRO (69). Jack D Maltester. 835 E 14th St, 94577. **415-577-3000**

SAN MATEO (79). John J Murray, Jr. 330 W 20th Ave, 94403. **415-574-6765**

SAN RAFAEL (39). C Paul Bettini. 1400 5th Ave, 94901. **415-456-1112**

SANTA ANA (157). Vernon S Evans. 20 Civic Center Plz, 92701. **714-834-4973**

SANTA BARBARA (70). David T Shiffman. PO Drawer P-P, 93102. **805-963-0611**

SANTA CLARA (88). William A Gissler. 1500 Warburton Ave, 95050. **408-984-3000**

SANTA CRUZ (32). John G Mahaney. 809 Center St, 95060. **408-426-5000**

SANTA MARIA (33). Elwin E Mussell. 110 E Cook St, 93454. **805-925-0951**

SANTA MONICA (88). Donna O'Brien Swink. 1685 Main St, 90401. **213-393-9975, Ext 200**

SANTA ROSA (50). Gerald M Poznanovich. PO Box 1678, 95403. **707-528-5361**

SEASIDE (36). Oscar C Lawson. 440 Harcourt Ave, 93955. **408-394-8531**

SIMI VALLEY (56). William T Carpenter. 3200 Cochran St, 93065. **805-522-1333**

SOUTH GATE (57). John J Murdock. 8650 California Ave, 90280. **213-567-1331**

SOUTH SAN FRANCISCO (47). Leo Padreddii. PO Box 711, 94080. **415-873-8000**

STOCKTON (108). Arnold I Rue. 425 N El Dorado St, 95202. **209-944-8459**

SUNNYVALE (95). Donald S Logan. 456 W Olive Ave, 94086. **408-736-0531**

THOUSAND OAKS (36). Alex T Fiore. 401 W Hillcrest Dr, 91360. **805-497-8611**

TORRANCE (135). Kenneth M Miller. 3031 Torrance Blvd, 90503. **213-328-5310**

UPLAND (33). George M Gibson. PO Box 460, 91786. **714-982-1352**

VALLEJO (67). Florence E Douglas. 555 Santa Clara St, 94590. **707-553-4377**

VISALIA (35). Reinhold A Peterson. 707 W Acequia St, 93277. **209-734-2011**

WALNUT CREEK (40). James Hazard. 1445 Civic Dr, 94596. **415-935-3300.** Contact Thomas G Dunne

WEST COVINA (68). Nevin Browne. PO Box 1440, 91790. **213-962-8631**

WESTMINSTER (60). Joy L Neugebauer. 8200 Westminster Ave, 92683. **714-898-3311.** Don Anderson, public information officer

WHITTIER (73). Jack A Mele. 13230 Penn St, 90602. **213-698-2551**

Colorado

ARVADA (47). Kenneth Gorrell. 8101 Ralston Rd, 80002. **303-421-2550**

AURORA (75). Fred H Hood. 1470 Emporia St, 80012. **303-750-5000, Ext 299**

BOULDER (67). Ruth Correll. PO Box 791, 80302. **303-441-3131**

COLORADO SPRINGS (135). Lawrence D Ochs. PO Box 1575, 80901. **303-471-6699**

DENVER (515). Williams H McNichols, Jr. City and County Bldg, 80202. **303-623-1133.** Edward Sullivan and Shari Sloan, administrative assistants, **303-292-2721**

ENGLEWOOD (34). James L Taylor. 3400 S Eluti, 80110. **303-761-1140**

FORT COLLINS (43). Arvid R Bloom. PO Box 580, 80522. **303-484-4220**

GRAND JUNCTION (20). Lawrence L Kozisek. PO Box 968, 81501. **303-243-2633**

GREELEY (39). George W Hall. Civic Ctr Complex, 80632. **303-353-6123**

LAKEWOOD (93). Charles Whitlock. 44 Union Blvd, 80228. **303-234-8601**

NORTHGLENN (32). Alvin B Thomas. Suite 313, 10701 Melody Dr, 80233. **303-451-8326.** *Press contact.* Shirley Whitten, (h) **303-287-6451**

PUEBLO (97). Melvin Takaki. 1 City Hall Plz, 81001. **303-545-0561**

WHEAT RIDGE (30). Oliver Phillips. PO Box 610, 80033. **303-421-8480**

Connecticut

BRIDGEPORT (157). John C Mandanici. **203-576-7201.** 45 Lyon Ter B, 06604. **203-576-7575**

BRISTOL (55). Michael Werner. 111 N Main St, 06010. **203-583-1811**

DANBURY (51). Donald Boughton. 155 Deer Hill Ave, 06810. **203-744-7160**

EAST HARTFORD (58). Richard H Blackstone. 740 Main St, 06108. **203-289-2781**

ENFIELD (46). James Baum. 820 Enfield St, 06082. **203-745-0371**

FAIRFIELD (56). John J Sullivan. 610 Old Post Rd, 06430. **203-259-8361**

GREENWICH (60). Ruth L Sims. Greenwich Ave, 06830. **203-622-7000**

GROTON (39). Town mayor: Betty Chapman. 45 Fort Hill Rd, 06340. **203-445-8551.** City mayor: Donald B Sweet. 295 Meridian St, 06340. **203-445-9718**

HAMDEN (49). Lucien A Di Meo. 2372 Whitney Ave, 06518. **203-288-5641**

HARTFORD (158). George A Athanson. City Hall, 550 Main St, 06103. **203-566-6610.** Hyveth Williams, executive assistant

MANCHESTER (48). Stephen Penny. 41 Center St, 06040. **203-649-5281**

MERIDEN (56). Walter Evilia. 142 E Main St, 06450. **203-634-0003**

MIDDLETOWN (37). Anthony S Marino. PO Box 141, 06457. **203-347-4671**

MILFORD (51). Henry A Povinelli. River St, 06460. **203-878-1731**

NEW BRITAIN (83). William J McNamara. 27 W Main St, 06051. **203-224-2491**

NEW HAVEN (130). Frank Logue. City Hall, 06508. **203-562-0151.** Edward J Losgrove, executive assistant for public information

NEW LONDON (32). Margaret Curtin. 181 Captain's Walk, 06320. **203-443-2861**

NORWALK (79). William A Collins. 41 N Main St, 06856. **203-838-7531**

NORWICH (41). Konstant W Morell. City Hall, 06360. **203-889-8408**

SOUTHINGTON (31). Andrew Meade. Main St, 06489. **203-628-5523**

STAMFORD (109). Louis A Clapes. 429 Atlantic St, 06904. **203-358-4153**

STRATFORD (50). William Haberlin. 2725 Main St, 06497. **203-375-5621**

TORRINGTON (32). Hodges Waldron. 140 Main St, 06790. **203-482-8521**

TRUMBULL (31). James A Butler. 5866 Main St, 06611. **203-261-3631**

WALLINGFORD (36). Rocco J Vumbaco. 350 Center St, 06492. **203-265-1555**

WATERBURY (108). Edward D Bergin. 236 Grand St, 06702. **203-756-9494**. Paul O Bessette, administrative assistant, **203-753-2307**

WEST HARTFORD (68). Anne P Streeter. 28 S Main St, 06107. **203-236-3231**

WEST HAVEN (53). Robert A Johnson. 355 Main St, 06516. **203-934-3421**

Delaware

DOVER (17). Charles A Legates. PO Box 475, 19901. **302-674-1000**

WILMINGTON (80). William T McLaughlin. 800 French St, 19801. **302-571-4100**. John S Forte, public information officer, **302-571-4123**

District of Columbia

WASHINGTON (757). Walter E Washington. District Bldg, 20004. **202-628-6000**. Sam Eastman, press secretary

Florida

CLEARWATER (52). Gabriel Cazares. PO Box 4748, 33618. **813-442-6131**

CORAL GABLES (42). James Dunn. 405 Biltmore Way, 33134. **305-442-6400**

DADE COUNTY (1268). Stephen Clark. 73 W Flagler St, Miami, 33133. **305-579-5900**

DAYTONA BEACH (45). Lawrence J Kelly. PO Box 551, 32015. **904-252-6461**

FORT LAUDERDALE (140). E Clay Shaw, Jr. PO Box 14250, 33302. **305-761-2245**

GAINESVILLE (65). Aaron A Green. PO Box 490, 33602. **904-377-1717**, Ext 332

HIALEAH (102). Dale G Bennett. PO Box 40, 33011. **305-885-1531**

HOLLYWOOD (107). David R Keating, **305-921-3321**. PO Box 2207, 33022. **305-921-3000**

JACKSONVILLE (529). Hans G Tanzler, Jr. 220 E Bay St, 32202. **904-633-2500**

KEY WEST (28). Charles McCoy. PO Box 1550, 33040. **305-294-3721**

LAKELAND (42). Curtis I. Walker. City Hall, 33802. **813-682-1141**

MELBOURNE (40). Vernon L Dicks. 900 E Strawbridge Ave, 32901. **305-727-2900**

MIAMI (335). Maurice A Ferre. PO Box 330708, City Hall, 33133. **305-579-6010**. Frank Lobo, administrative assistant, **305-445-4461**. *Washington office.* 1620 I St NW, Washington, DC 20006. **202-293-2949**. Mark Israel, city representative

MIAMI BEACH (87). Leonard Haber. 505 17th St, 33139. **305-673-7373**

NORTH MIAMI (35). Mike Colodny. 776 NE 125th St, 33161. **305-893-6511**

NORTH MIAMI BEACH (31). Walter S Pesetsky. 17011 NE 19th Ave, 33162. **305-947-7581**

ORLANDO (99). Carl T Langford. 400 S Orange Ave, 32801. **305-849-2221**

PANAMA CITY (32). M B Miller. 9 Harrison Ave, 32401. **904-763-6641**

PENSACOLA (60). Warren M Briggs. PO Box 12910, 32521. **904-436-4201**

POMPANO BEACH (38). Betty L Wistedt. PO Box 1300, 33061. **305-942-1100**

ST PETERSBURG (216). Corinne Freeman. PO Box 2842, 33731. **813-893-7171**

SARASOTA (40). Ronald W Norman. 1565 1st St, 33577. **813-365-2200**

TALLAHASSEE (72). James R Ford. City Hall, 32304. **904-599-8100**

TAMPA (278). William F Poe. City Hall, 33607. **813-223-8251**. Peggy Allison, executive secretary

TITUSVILLE (31). Robert Telfer, Jr. 555 S Washington Ave, 32780. **305-269-4400**

WEST PALM BEACH (57). James M Adams. PO Box 3366, 33402. **305-655-6811**

Georgia

ALBANY (73). James H Gray, Sr. PO Box 447, 31702. **912-883-1216**

ATHENS (44). Upshaw Bentley, Jr. City Hall, 30601. **404-548-3116**

ATLANTA (497). Maynard Jackson. City Hall, 30303. **404-658-6000**. Jaci Harrison, office of the mayor, **404-658-6058**

AUGUSTA (60). Lewis Newman. Municipal Bldg, 30902. **404-724-4391**

COLUMBUS (154). Jack P Mickle, Sr. PO Box 1340, 31902. **404-324-7711**

EAST POINT (39). Bruce Bannister. 2777 E Point St, 30344. **404-766-1481**

MACON (122). Buckner Melton. City Hall, 31202. **912-745-9411**

ROME (31). Harold Hunter. PO Box 1433, 30161. **404-291-8222**

SAVANNAH (118). John P Rovsakis. PO Box 1027, City Hall, 31402. **912-233-9321**. Mr A A Mendonsa, city manager

VALDOSTA (32). Gil A Harbin. PO Box 1125, 31601. **912-342-2600**

WARNER ROBINS (33). Foy Evans. PO Box 1488, 31093. **912-923-2631**

Hawaii

HONOLULU (325). Frank F Fasi, City Hall, 96813. **808-523-4385**. James L Loomis, director of information and complaints

Idaho

BOISE (75). Richard R Eardley. PO Box 500, 83702. **208-384-4000**

IDAHO FALLS (36). Thomas Campbell. PO Box 220, 83401. **208-522-3191**

LEWISTON (26). D. C. St. Marie. 1134 F St, 83501. **208-746-3671**

POCATELLO (40). Donna Boe. PO Box 4169, 83201. **208-232-4311**, Ext 230. Charles W Moss, city manager, Ext 230

Illinois

ALTON (40). Paul A Lenz. 101 E 3rd St, 62002. **618-463-3500**

ARLINGTON HEIGHTS (65). James Ryan. 33 S Arlington Heights Rd, 60005. **312-353-2340**

AURORA (74). Jack Hill. 44 E Downer Pl, 60504. **312-892-8811**

BELLEVILLE (42). Charles E Nichols. 101 S Illinois St, 62220. **618-233-6810**

BERWYN (53). Thomas Hett. 6700 W 26th St, 60402. **312-788-2660**

BLOOMINGTON (40). Richard Buchanan. 109 E Olive St, 61701. **309-828-7361**

CALUMET CITY (33). Robert C Stefaniak. 204 Pulaski Rd, 60409. **312-868-2100**

CHAMPAIGN (57). William D Bland. 102 N Neil St, 61820. **217-351-4417**

CHICAGO (3367). Michael A Bilandio. City Hall, 121 N La Salle St, 60411. **312-756-2110.** Bruce Stevens, director of public relations, Ext 247

CHICAGO HEIGHTS (41). Charles L Panici. 1601 Chicago Rd, 60411. **312-756-2110**

CICERO (67). Christy Berkos. 4937 W 25th St, 60650. **312-656-3600**

DANVILLE (43). David S Palmer. 402 N Hazel St, 61832. **217-446-0803**

DECATUR (90). Elmer Walton. 707 E Wood St, 62523. **217-424-2708**

DEKALB (33). Judy King. 200 S 4th , 60115. **815-756-4881**

DES PLAINES (57). Herbert H Volberding. 1412 Miner St, 60018. **312-297-1200**

DOWNERS GROVE (33). Frank W Houck. 801 Burlington Ave, 60515. **312-964-0300**

EAST ST LOUIS (70). William E Mason, Sr. 7 Collinsville Ave, 62201. **618-274-0727**

ELGIN (56). Richard L Verbic. 150 Dexter Ct, 60120. **312-695-6500**

ELMHURST (51). Abner S Ganet. 119 Schiller St, 60126. **312-834-1800.** Robert T Palmer, city manager

EVANSTON (80). James C Lytle. 2100 Ridge Ave, 60204. **312-328-2100**

GALESBURG (36). Robert W Kimble. City Hall, 61401. **309-343-4181**

GRANIT CITY (40). Paul Schuler. 2000 Edison Ave, 62040. **618-877-3216**

HARVEY (35). James A Haines. 15320 Broadway, 60426. **312-339-4200**

HIGHLAND PARK (32). Robert W Buhai. 1707 St Johns Ave, 60035. **312-432-1924**

HOFFMAN ESTATES (32). Virginia M Hayter. 1200 N Gannon Dr, 60172. **312-882-9100**

JOLIET (80). Norman Keck. 150 W Jefferson St, 60435. **815-727-5401**

KANKAKEE (31). Thomas J Ryan, Jr. 385 E Oak St, 60901. **815-933-3344**

LOMBARD (36). Mardyth Pollard. 48 N Park, 60148. **312-627-5000**

MAYWOOD (30). James J Parrilli. 115 S 5th Ave, 60153. **312-344-1200**

MOLINE (46). Lawrence Lorensen. 619 16th St, 61265. **309-797-0735**

MOUNT PROSPECT (46). Carolyn H Krause. 100 S Emerson, 60056. **312-392-6000**

NILES (31). Nicholas B Blase. 7601 Milwaukee Ave, 60648. **312-697-6100**

NORMAL (31). Richard T Godfrey. 124 North St, 61761. **309-454-2449**

NORTH CHICAGO (47). Leo F Kukla. 1850 Lewis Ave, 60064. **312-689-0900**

OAK LAWN (60). Ernest Kolb. 5252 W James St, 60453. **312-636-4400**

OAK PARK (63). President James J McClure, Jr. Village Hall Plaza, 60301. **312-383-6400.** Agnes M Fowles, public information officer, Ext 270

PARK FOREST (31). Mayer Singerman. 200 Forest Blvd, 60466. **312-748-1112**

PARK RIDGE (42). Martin J Butler. 505 Park Pl, 60068. **312-823-1161**

PEKIN (31). William L Waldmeier. City Hall, 61554. **309-346-0826**

PEORIA (127). Richard E Carver. 419 Fulton St, 61602. **309-672-8500**

QUINCY (45). C David Nuessen. 507 Vermont St, 62301. **217-223-6370**

ROCKFORD (147). Robert W McGaw. 425 E State St, 61104. **815-987-5500**

ROCK ISLAND (50). Alan Campbell. 1528 3rd Ave, 61201. **309-788-7463**

SCHAUMBURG (37). Ray Kessell. 101 Schaumburg Ct, 60193. **312-894-4500**

SKOKIE (69). Albert J Smith. 5127 Oakton St, 60076. **312-673-0500**

SPRINGFIELD (92). William C Telford. Municipal Bldg, 62701. **217-789-2000**

URBANA (33). Jeffrey T Markland. 400 S Vine St, 61801. **217-384-2456**

WAUKEGAN (65). Bill Morris. 106 N Utica St, 60085. **312-689-7500**

WHEATON (31). Ralph H Barger. 303 W Wesley, 60187. **312-668-3130**

WILMETTE (32). Warren L Burmeister. 1200 Wilmette Ave, 60091. **312-251-2700**

Indiana

ANDERSON (71). Robert L Rock. PO Box 2100, 46011. **317-646-5716**

BLOOMINGTON (43). Francis X McCloskey. Municipal Bldg, 47401. **812-339-2261**

EAST CHICAGO (47). Robert A Pastrick. 4527 Indianapolis Blvd, 46312. **219-392-8200.** James W Parker, director, public relations, **219-392-8201.**

ELKHART (43). Peter Sarantos. Municipal Bldg, 46514. **219-294-5471**

EVANSVILLE (139). Russell G Lloyd. 302 Civic Ctr Complex, 47708. **812-426-5486**

FORT WAYNE (178). Robert E Armstrong. City-County Bldg, 46802. **219-423-7646.** John F Gray, director, public affairs, **219-423-7296**

GARY (175). Richard G Hatcher. City Hall, 46902. **219-944-1500.** Ivan Silverman, press secretary, **219-944-6509**

HAMMOND (108). Edward Raskosky. 5925 Calumet Ave, 46320. **219-853-6301.**

INDIANAPOLIS (745). William Hudnut. 2501 City-County Bldg, 46204. **317-633-6141** Dennis Rosebrough, press secretary. Night line: **317-633-3371**

KOKOMO (44). Arthur J La Dow. City Bldg, 46901. **317-459-9444**

LAFAYETTE (45). James Riehle. 20 N 6th St, 47901. **317-742-8404**

MARION (40). Anthony Maidenberg. City Hall, 46952. **317-662-9931**

MICHIGAN CITY (39). Joseph R La Rocco. Warren Bldg, 46360. **219-874-3288**

MISHAWAKA (36). Margaret H Prickett. 1st and Church Sts, 46544. **219-259-5274**

MUNCIE (69). Robert G Cunningham. City Hall, 47305. **317-747-4844**

NEW ALBANY (38). Robert L Real. City-County Bldg, 47150. **812-944-3751**

RICHMOND (44). Clifford J Dickman. 50 N 5th St, 47374. **317-966-5561**

SOUTH BEND (126). Peter Nemeth. 227 W Jefferson Blvd, 46601. **219-284-9261**

TERRE HAUTE (70). William J Brighton. 17 Harding Ave, 47807. **812-232-9467**. Vicki Weger, press secretary, **812-232-4132**

Iowa

AMES (40). Etta Lee Fellinger. 5th and Kellogg, 50010. **515-232-6210**

BURLINGTON (32). Tom Diewold. 4th and Washington, 52601. **319-763-2241**

CEDAR FALLS (34). Jon T Crews. 220 Clay St, 50613. **319-268-0141**

CEDAR RAPIDS (111). Donald J Canney. City Hall, 52401. **319-398-5012**

CLINTON (35). Dwain Walters. PO Box 337, 52732. **319-242-7545**

COUNCIL BLUFFS (60). Ronald Cleveland. 209 Pearl St, 51501. **712-328-4616**

DAVENPORT (98). Charles Wright. 226 W 4th St, 52801. **319-326-7711**

DES MOINES (201). Richard E Olson. E 1st and Locust Sts, 50307. **515-283-4944**

DUBUQUE (62). Thomas Tully Jr. 13th and Central, 52001. **319-583-6441**

FORT DODGE (31). Herbert S Conlon. 813 1st Ave S, 50501. **515-576-9551**

IOWA CITY (47). Robert Vevera. 410 E Washington St, 52240. **319-354-1800**

MASON CITY (30). Kenneth E Kew. 19 S Delaware, 50401. **515-423-2614**

OTTUMWA (30). Paul Derby. 105 E 3rd, 52501. **515-682-8551**

SIOUX CITY (86). Donald Lawrenson. PO Box 447, 51102. **712-279-6310**

WATERLOO (76). Leo P Rooff. City Hall, 50705. **319-291-4301**

Kansas

HUTCHINSON (37). Burt Alumbaugh. 125 E Ave B, 67501. **316-663-6151**

KANSAS CITY (168). John E Reardon. Civic Center Plz 66101. **913-371-2000**

LAWRENCE (46). Marjorie Argersinger. PO Box 708, 66044. **913-841-7700**

LEAVENWORTH (25). E Paul Lessig. 5th and Shawnee, 66048. **913-682-9201**

OVERLAND PARK (77). Ben M Sykes 8500 Sante Fe Dr, 66212. **913-381-5252** Christine Chapman, information director

SALINA (38). Keith Duckers. 300 W Ash St, 67401. **913-827-9653**

TOPEKA (125). Bill McCormick. 215 E 7th, 66603. **913-295-4000**

WICHITA (277). Tony Casado 455 N Main, 67202. **316-268-4331**

Kentucky

BOWLING GREEN (36). BL Steen. PO Box 130, 42101. **502-842-4285**

COVINGTON (53). George E Wermeling. City-County Bldg, 41011. **606-292-2265**

LEXINGTON (108). James Amato. Municipal Bldg, 40507. **606-255-5719** or **5631**

LOUISVILLE (361). William Stansbury. City Hall, 40202. **502-587-3371**. Allen Bryan, office of the mayor, **502-589-4320**. *Washington Office.* Noel Klores of Boasberg, Hewes, Klores, Smith and Kass, 1225 19th St NW, Washington, DC 20036. **202-659-3436**

OWENSBORO (50). Jack C Fisher. PO Box 847, 4th and St Ann Sts, 42301. **502-684-7251**

PADUCAH (32). William S Murphy. PO Box 891, 42001. **502-442-7561**

Louisiana

ALEXANDRIA (42). Carroll E Lanier. PO Box 71, 71301. **318-442-8801**

BATON ROUGE (166). W W (Woody) Dumas. PO Box 1471, 70821. **504-389-3001**

BOSSIER CITY (42). Marvin E Anding. 635 Barksdale Blvd, 71010. **318-742-9622**

HOUMA (31). Charles Davidson. City Hall, 70360. **504-868-5050**

LAFAYETTE (69). Kenneth F Bowen. 733 Jefferson St, 70501. **318-233-6611**

LAKE CHARLES (78). William Boyer. PO Box 1178, 70601. **318-436-3331**

MONROE (56). Jack Howard. PO Box 123, 71201. **318-387-3521**. *Press contact.* George W Parsons

NEW IBERIA (30). J Allen Daigre. PO Box 11, 70560. **318-365-2471**

NEW ORLEANS (593). Ernest N Morial. City Hall, 70112. **504-586-4311**. Winston C Lill, public relations director, **504-586-4322**

SHREVEPORT (182). L Calhoun Allen, Jr. PO Box 1109, 71163. **318-226-6250**

Maine

AUGUSTA (22). David N Elvin. 1 Cony St, 04330. **207-623-8540**

BANGOR (33). Arthur Brountas. 73 Harlow St, 04401. **207-947-4341**

BIDDEFORD (20). Lucien A Dutremble. PO Box 586, 04005. **207-284-4881**

LEWISTON (42). Lillian L Caron. Pine St, 04240. **207-784-2951**

PORTLAND (65). Bruce Taliento. 389 Congress St, 04111. **207-775-5451**

SANFORD (16). Norman S Hall. 267 Main St, 04073. **207-324-3312**

WATERVILLE (18). Paul La Verdiere. City Hall, 04901. **207-872-6922**

Maryland

ANNAPOLIS (30). John C Apostol. 166 Duke of Gloucester St, 21401. **301-263-3322**

BALTIMORE (906). William Donald Schaefer. 230 City Hall, 21202. **301-396-3100**. Paul Samuels, press officer, **301-396-4900**. Night line: **301-396-3100**

BOWIE (35). Audrey E Scott. Tulip Grove Dr, 20715. **301-262-6200**

COLLEGE PARK (26). St Clair Reeves. 4500 Knox Rd, 20740. **301-864-8877**

CUMBERLAND (30) F Perry Smith, Jr. City Hall, 21502. **301-722-2000**

HAGERSTOWN (36). Varner L Paddack. City Hall, 21740. **301-731-3200**

ROCKVILLE (42). William E Hanna, Jr. 111 Maryland Ave, 20850. **301-424-8000**

Massachusetts

ARLINGTON (54). Arthur D Saul. 730 Massachusetts Ave, 02174. **617-643-6700**

ATTLEBORO (33). Gerald Keane. 29 Park St, 02703. **617-222-9222**

BEVERLY (38). Peter Fortunaco. 191 Cabot St, 01915. **617-922-3311**

BILLERICA (32). Thomas H Conway, Jr. Concord Rd, 01821. **617-667-1512**

BOSTON (641). Kevin H White. City Hall, 02201. **617-725-4400**. Geraldine Pleshaw, office of the mayor

BRAINTREE (35). Robert Frazier. 1 J F Kennedy Memorial Dr, 02185. **617-843-0570**

BROCKTON (89). David E Crosby. 45 School St, 02401. **617-580-1100**

BROOKLINE (59). Robert Cochrane, Jr. City Hall, 02146. **617-232-9000**

CAMBRIDGE (100). Alfred E Vellucci. 795 Massachusetts Ave, 02139. **617-876-6800**

CHELMSFORD (31). Paul C Hart. 1 North Rd, 01824. **617-256-2441**

CHELSEA (31). Joel M Pressman. City Hall, 02150. **617-884-0407**

CHICOPEE (67). John Moylan. City Hall, 01013. **413-594-4711**. East Weymouth. See Weymouth.

EVERETT (42). George R McCarthy. 484 Broadway, 02149. **617-389-2100**

FALL RIVER (97). Carlton Viveiros. 123 Main St, 02720. **617-765-6011**

FITCHBURG (43). David Gilmartin. 718 Main St, 01420. **617-343-4821**

FRAMINGHAM (64). Peter W Ablondi. Memorial Bldg, 01701. **617-872-4806**

HAVERHILL (46). George Katsaros. 4 Summer St, 01830. **617-373-3818**

HOLYOKE (50). Ernest E Proulx. 536 Dwight St, 01040. **413-536-5571**

LAWRENCE (67). Lawrence Le Febre. 200 Common St, 01840. **617-685-5839**

LEOMINSTER (33). Joseph Moriarity. City Hall, 01453. **617-537-6311**

LEXINGTON (32). Margery Battin. 1625 Massachusetts Ave, 02173. **617-862-0500**

LOWELL (94). Raymond Rourke. City Hall, 01853. **617-454-8821**

LYNN (90). Antonio Marino. City Hall Sq, 01901. **617-598-4000**

MALDEN (56). James S Conway. 200 Pleasant St, 02148. **617-324-6600**

MEDFORD (64). Eugene F Grant. 85 George P Hassett Dr, 02155. **617-396-5500**

MELROSE (33). James E Milano. 562 Main St, 02176. **617-665-0170**

METHUEN (35). Raffi Takesian. 90 Hampshire St, 01844. **617-682-2646**

NATICK (31). Daniel J O'Leary. City Hall, 01760. **617-653-9450**

NEW BEDFORD (102). John A Markey. 133 William St, 02740. **617-999-2931**

NEWTON (91). Theodore D Mann. 1000 Commonwealth Ave, 02159. **617-244-4700**

NORTHAMPTON (30). Harry S Chapman, Jr. 210 Main St, 01060. **413-584-2264**

NORWOOD (31). Joseph Curran. Municipal Bldg, 02062. **617-762-1240**

PEABODY (48). Nicholas Mavroulas. 24 Lowell St, 01960. **617-531-7733**

PITTSFIELD (57). Paul E Brindle III. City Hall, 01201. **413-499-1100**

QUINCY (88). Arthur Tobin. 1305 Hancock St, 02169. **617-773-1380**

REVERE (43). George Coleola. Broadway, 02151. **617-284-3600**

SALEM (41). Jean A Levesque. 93 Washington St, 01970. **617-744-0282**

SOMERVILLE (89). Thomas August. Highland Ave, 02144. **617-625-6600**

SPRINGFIELD (164). Theodore DiMauro. 36 Court St, 01103. **413-736-2711**

TAUNTON (44). Al Amaral. 15 Summer St, 02780. **617-822-0581**

WALTHAM (62). Arthur J Clark. City Hall, 02154. **617-893-4040**

WATERTOWN (39). Thomas J McDermott. 149 Main St, 02072. **617-924-2078**

WESTFIELD (31). Garrett Lynch. 59 Court St, 01085. **413-568-0316**

WEYMOUTH (55). William B Barry, Jr. 75 Middle St, East Weymouth, 02189. **617-335-2000**

WOBURN (37). Thomas Higgins. 10 Common St, 01801. **617-933-0700**

WORCESTER (177). Thomas Early. Main St, 01608. **617-798-8151**

Michigan

ALLEN PARK (41). Frank J Lada. 16850 Southfield, 48101. **313-928-1400**

ANN ARBOR (100). Albert H Wheeler. 100 5th Ave, 48107. **313-994-2700**

BATTLE CREEK (39). Frederick R Brydges. PO Box 1717, 49014. **616-962-5561**

BAY CITY (49). John R Willertz. 301 Washington Ave, 48706. **517-893-7511**

BURTON (33). Richard L Wurtz. 4303 S Center Rd, 48519. **313-743-1500**

DEARBORN (104). John B O'Reilly. 13615 Michigan Ave, 48126. **313-584-1200**

DEARBORN HEIGHTS (80). Frank Swapka. 6045 Fenton, 48127. **313-277-7214**

DETROIT (1511). Coleman A Young. City-County Bldg, 2 Woodward Ave, 48226. **313-224-3400.** Robert L Pisor, press secretary, **313-224-3471.** Don Wilson, director, department of public information, **313-224-3760**

EAST DETROIT (46). Allyn Carl Weinert. 23200 Gratiot Ave, 48021. **313-775-7800**

EAST LANSING (48). George L Griffiths. 410 Abbott Rd, 48823. **517-337-1731**

FARMINGTON HILLS (51). D Keith Deacon. 31555 Eleven Mile Rd, 48024. **313-474-6115**

FERNDALE (31). Robert J Paczkowski. 300 E Nine Mile Rd, 48220. **313-547-6000.**

FLINT (193). James W Rutherford. 1101 S Saginaw, 48502. **313-766-7346**

GARDEN CITY (42). Samuel T Pappas. 6000 Middlebelt Rd, 48135. **313-421-1262**

GRAND RAPIDS (198). Abe L Drasin, **616-456-3166.** 300 Monroe NW, 49503. **616-456-3000**

HIGHLAND PARK (35). Jesse Miller. 30 Gerald Ave, 48203. **313-868-5400.** Lee Craft, director, public information

INKSTER (39). Terrel M Le Cesne. 2121 Inkster Rd, 48141. **313-565-4100**

JACKSON (45). Fred C Janke. 132 W Washington, 49201. **517-788-4000**

KALAMAZOO (86). Francis P Hamilton. 241 W South St, 49006. **616-385-8000**

LANSING (132). Gerald W Graves. 125 W Michigan Ave, 48933. **517-487-1000**

LINCOLN PARK (53). Victor Bonara. 1355 Southfield, 48146. **313-386-1800**

LIVONIA (110). Edward H McNamara. 33001 Five Mile Rd, 48154. **313-421-2000**

MADISON HEIGHTS (39). George W Suarez. 300 W Thirteen Mile Rd, 48071. **313-588-1200**

MENOMINEE (11). Harry F Johnson. City Hall, 49858. **906-863-2656**

MIDLAND (35). Robert D Goodenough. 202 Ashman, 48640. **517-835-7711**

MUSKEGON (45). John E Midendorp. 933 Terrace St, 49443. **616-726-3111**

OAK PARK (37). David H Shepherd. 13600 Oak Park Blvd, 48237. **313-547-1331**

PONTIAC (85). Wallace E Holland. 450 E Widetrack Dr, 48058. **313-857-7611**

PORTAGE (34). Betty Lee C Ongley. 7800 Shaver Rd, 49081. **616-327-4411**

PORT HURON (36). Timothy Lozen. 201 McMorran Blvd, 48060. **313-985-9631**

ROSEVILLE (61). Leonard Haggerty. 29777 Gratiot Ave, 48066. **313-778-2800**

ROYAL OAK (85). Pecky D Lewis, Jr. PO Box 64, 48068. **313-546-1000**

SAGINAW (92). Joe L Stephens. 1315 S Washington Ave, 48601. **517-753-5411**

ST CLAIR SHORES (88). Frank J McPharlin. 27600 Jefferson, 48081. **313-776-7900**

SOUTHFIELD (69). Donald F Fracassi. 26000 Evergreen Rd, 48076. **313-354-9601**

SOUTHGATE (34). William Brainard. 13763 Northline Rd, 48195. **313-283-1300**

STERLING HEIGHTS (61). Anthony Dobry. 40555 Utica Rd, 48078. **313-268-8500**

TAYLOR (70). Donald Zub. 23555 Goddard, 48180. **313-287-6550**

TROY (39). Richard E Doyle. 500 W Big Beaver, 48084. **313-689-4900**

WARREN (179). Ted Bates. 29500 Van Dyke Ave, 48093. **313-573-9500**

WESTLAND (87). Thomas F Taylor. 36601 Ford Rd, 48185. **313-721-6000**

WYANDOTTE (41). William L Cook. 3131 Briddle Ave, 48192. **313-283-3800**

WYOMING (57). Harold Isenga. 1151 28th St SW, 49509. **616-534-7671**

Minnesota

AUSTIN (25). Robert J Enright. 500 4th Ave NE, 55912. **507-437-7671**

BLOOMINGTON (82). Jim Lindau. 2215 W Old Shakopee Rd, 55431. **612-881-5811**

BROOKLYN CENTER (35). Dean Nyquist. 6301 Shingle Creek Pkwy, 55430. **612-425-4542**

COON RAPIDS (31). George White. 1313 Coon Rapids Blvd, 55433. **612-755-2880**

CRYSTAL (31). Peter E Meintsma. 4141 Douglas Drive N, 55422. **612-537-8421**

DULUTH (101). Robert Beaudin. 403 City Hall, 55802. **218-723-3295**

EDINA (49). James Van Valkenburg. 4801 W 50th St, 55424. **612-927-8861**

MANKATO (31). Herbert Mocol. 202 E Jackson St, 56001. **507-625-3161.** Nancy Girouard, public information officer

MINNEAPOLIS (434). Albert Hofstede. 127 City Hall, 55415. **612-348-2100.** Spencer Mack, executive secretary

MINNETONKA (36). Sam Higuchi. 14600 Minnetonka Blvd, 55343. **612-933-2511**

RICHFIELD (47). Loren L Law. 6700 Portland Ave S, 55423. **612-869-7521**

ROCHESTER (54). Alex P Smekta. 200 City Hall, 55901. **507-288-3624**

ROSEVILLE (35). June Demos. 2701 N Lexington Ave, 55113. **612-484-3371**

ST CLOUD (40). Alcuin G Loehr. City Hall, 56301. **612-251-5541**

ST LOUIS PARK (49). Irving M Stern. 5005 Minnetonka Blvd, 55416. **612-920-3000**

ST PAUL (310). George Latimer 347 City Hall, 55102. **612-298-4323.** Peg O'Keefe, media aide

Mississippi

BILOXI (48). Jeremiah J O'Keefe. PO Drawer 429, 39533. **601-432-8633**

GREENVILLE (40). William C Burnley, Jr. PO Box 897, 38701. **601-335-2361**

GULFPORT (41). Jack Barnett. PO Box 1780, 39501. **601-864-1171**

HATTIESBURG (38). A L Gerrard, Jr. PO Box 1898, 39401. **601-584-8831**

JACKSON (154). Dale Danks, Jr. PO Box 17, 39205. **601-969-7500.** Dan Dubose, director, public relations

LAUREL (24). William L Patrick, Jr. PO Box 647, 39440. **601-428-5228**. Sue C Craven, public information officer, **601-649-7622**. (h) **601-426-9900**

MERIDIAN (45). IA Rosenbaum. PO Box 1430, 39301. **601-693-1820**

Missouri

CAPE GIRARDEAU (31). Howard C Tooke. 402 Chesley Dr, 63701. **314-344-1155**

COLUMBIA (59). Leslie T Proctor. PO Box N, 65201. **314-874-7214**

FLORISSANT (66). James J Eagan. 955 Rue St Francois, 63031. **314-921-5700**

INDEPENDENCE (112). Richard A King. 103 N Main, 64050. **816-836-8300**

JEFFERSON CITY (32). Robert L Hyder. 240 E High St, 65101. **314-636-4712**

JOPLIN (39). William O Mauldin. City Hall, 64801. **417-624-0820**

KANSAS CITY (507). Charles B Wheeler, Jr. City Hall, 414 E 12th St, 64106. **816-274-2000**. Dorothy Hauser, executive director Night line: **816-279-9595, 2596,** or **2597**

KIRKWOOD (32). Philip Hallof, Jr. 139 S Kirkwood Rd, 63122. **314-822-8200**

RAYTOWN (34). Willard H Ross. 10000 E 59th St, 64133. **816-737-0550**

ST CHARLES (32). FB Brockgreitens. 11th and Federal Sts, 64501. **314-925-2000**

ST JOSEPH (73). William J Bennett. 11th St and Frederick Ave, 64501. **816-232-5408**

ST LOUIS (622). James Conway. 200 City Hall, 63103. **314-453-3201**. Robert W Duffe, executive assistant

SPRINGFIELD (120). Jim Payne. 830 Boonville, 65802. **417-865-1611**

UNIVERSITY CITY (46). Nathan B Kaufman. 6801 Delmar Blvd, 63130. **314-862-6767**

Montana

BILLINGS (62). William B Fox. PO Box 1178, 59103. **406-248-7511**

GREAT FALLS (60). John C Bulen. PO Box 1609, 59403. **406-727-5881**

HELENA (23). Kathleen Ramey. Civic Ctr, 59601. **406-442-9920**

Nebraska

GRAND ISLAND (31). J F Minor. PO Box 1968, 68801. **308-382-8600**

LINCOLN (150). Helen G Boosalis. 555 S 10th St, 68508. **402-475-5611**

NORTH PLATTE (19). Carl Bieber. PO Box 1329, 69101. **308-534-2610**

OMAHA (347). Al Veys. Omaha-Douglas Civic Ctr, 68102. **402-444-5001**. Terry Forsberg, administrative assistant, **402-444-5004**

Nevada

CARSON CITY (18). Harold J Jacobsen. 813 N Carlson St, 89701. **702-882-5114**

LAS VEGAS (126). William H Briare. City Hall, 89101. **702-386-6011**. *Press Contact.* Pat Cyr, executive aide, Ext 241, Night line: **702-878-7791**

NORTH LAS VEGAS (48). Ray H Daines. 2200 Civic Center Dr., 89030. **702-649-5811**

RENO (73). Bruno Menicucci, **702-785-2001**. PO Box 1900, 89505. **702-785-2000**

SPARKS (24). James C Lillard. 431 Prater Way, 89431. **702-359-2700**

New Hampshire

CONCORD (30). Martin Gross. City Hall, 03301. **603-224-0591**

MANCHESTER (88). Charles R Stanton. 904 Elm St, 03101. **603-625-9573**

NASHUA (56). Dennis J Sullivan. 229 Main St, 03060. **603-883-3711**

New Jersey

ATLANTIC CITY (48). Joseph Lazarow. Tennessee and Bacharach, 08401. **609-344-2121**

BAYONNE (73). Dennis P Collins. 630 Ave C, 07002. **201-823-1000**. Robert S Zywicki, public relations, **201-858-3400**

BELLEVILE (35). Michael V Marotti. 152 Washington Ave, 07109. **201-759-9100**

BERGENFIELD (33). James Lodato. 198 N Washington Ave, 07621. **201-384-3000**

BLOOMFIELD (52). John W Kinder. Municipal Bldg, 07003. **201-743-4400**

BRICK TOWNSHIP (35). John P Kinnevy. 401 Chamber Bridge Rd, 08723. **201-477-3000**

BRIDGEWATER TOWNSHIP (30). Alfred H Griffith. PO Box 6300, 08807. **201-725-6300**

CAMDEN (103). Angelo J Errichetti. 6th and Market Sts, 08101. **609-757-7000**

CHERRY HILL TOWNSHIP (64). John A Rocco. 820 Mercer St, 08002. **609-665-6500**

CLIFTON (82). Frank Sylvester. 1187 Main Ave, 07012. **201-473-2600**

DOVER TOWNSHIP (44). Richard P Strada. PO Box 728, Toms River, 08753. **201-341-1000**

EAST BRUNSWICK TOWNSHIP (34). William F Fox. 1 Jean Walling Civic Ctr, 08816. **201-254-4600**

EAST ORANGE (75). Thomas H Cooke, Jr. 44 City Hall Plz, 07017. **201-266-5100**

EDISON TOWNSHIP (67). Tony Yelencsics. Plainfield and Woodbridge Aves, 08817. **201-287-0900**

ELIZABETH (113). Thomas G Dunn. W Scott Pl, 07201. **201-353-6000**

EWING TOWNSHIP (33). David Evans. 1872 Pennington Rd, Trenton, 08618. **609-883-2900**

FAIRLAWN (38). Louis Raffiani. Fairlawn Ave, 07410. **201-796-1700**

FORT LEE (31). Richard A Nest. 309 Main St, 07024. **201-947-9400**

FRANKLIN TOWNSHIP (30). John J Cullen. 475 De Mott Ln, Somerset, 08873. **201-873-2500**

GARFIELD (31). Frank B Calandriello. Outwater Ln, 07026. **201-478-7040**

GLOUCESTER TOWNSHIP (36). John W Shorter. PO Box 8, Blackwood, 08021. **609-586-3500**

HACKENSACK (36). Frank Zisa. 65 Central Ave, 07602. **201-342-3000**

HAMILTON TOWNSHIP (80). John K Rafferty. 2090 Greenwood Ave, Trenton, 08609. **609-586-3500**. James F Babeu, public information officer, Ext 242

HOBOKEN (45). Steve J Cappiello. 1st and Washington Sts, 07030. **201-792-3000**

IRVINGTON (60). Robert H Miller. Civic Sq, 07111. **201-372-2100**

JERSEY CITY (261). Thomas F X Smith. City Hall, Grove St, 07302. **201-547-5200**. William Tremper and Eugene Scanlon, mayor's press office

KEARNY (38). David C Rowlands. 400 Kearny Ave, 07032. **201-991-2700**

LINDEN (41). John T Gregorio. N Wood Ave, 07036. **201-486-3800**

LONG BRANCH (32). Henry R Cioffi. 344 Broadway, 07740. **201-222-7000**

MIDDLETOWN TOWNSHIP (55). Allan J MacDonald. King's Highway, 07748. **201-671-3100**

MONTCLAIR (44). Grant M Gille. 647 Bloomfield Ave, 07042. **201-744-1400**

NEWARK (382). Kenneth A Gibson. City Hall, 07102. **201-733-3669**. Bernard Moore, communications director. **201-733-3687**

NEW BRUNSWICK (42). Richard J Mulligan. 78 Bayard St, 08903. **201-745-5040**

NORTH BERGEN TOWNSHIP (48). Peter M Mocco. 4233 Kennedy Blvd, 07047. **201-863-8500**. *Press Contact.* Lawrence Blisko, Ext 24

NUTLEY (32). Harry W Chenowth. Public Safety Bldg, 07110. **201-667-2800**

OLD BRIDGE TOWNSHIP (51). Sonja Fineburg. Box 70C, RD 1, 08857. **201-721-5600**

ORANGE (33). Carmine E Capone. 29 N Day St, 07050. **201-266-4025**

PARSIPPANY-TROY HILLS (55). John T Fahy. 1001 Parsippany Blvd, 07054. **201-334-3600**

PASSAIC (55). Robert Hare. 101 Passaic Ave, 07055. **201-471-3300**

PATERSON (145). Lawrence F Kramer. 155 Market St, 07505. **201-684-5800**

PENNSAUKEN TOWNSHIP (36). Angelo B Cardone, Sr, 5605 N Crescent Blvd, 08110. **609-665-1000**. (h) **609-663-0281**

PERTH AMBOY (39). George Otlowski. 260 High St, 08861. **201-826-0290**

PISCATAWAY TOWNSHIP (36). Ted H Light. 455 Hoes Ln, 08854. **201-981-0800**

PLAINFIELD (47). Paul J O'Keefe. 515 Watchung Ave, 07061. **201-753-3310**

SAYREVILLE (33). John E Czernikowski. 167 Main St, 08872. **201-257-3200**

TEANECK TOWNSHIP (42). Eleanor M Kieliszek. Municipal Bldg, 07666. **201-837-1600**

TRENTON (105). Arthur J Holland. 319 E State St, 08608. **609-989-3000**

UNION TOWNSHIP (53). Edward Goodkin. 1976 Morris Ave, 07083. **201-688-2800**

UNION CITY (59). William V Musto. 3715 Palisade Ave, 07087. **201-348-5731**

VINELAND (47). Patrick R Fiorilli. 7th and Wood Sts, 08360. **609-691-3000**

WAYNE TOWNSHIP (49). Walter Jasinski. 475 Valley Rd, 07470. **201-694-1800**

WESTFIELD (34). Alexander S Williams. 425 E Broad St, 07090. **201-232-8000**

WEST NEW YORK (40). Anthony M De Fino. 428 60th St, 07093. **201-861-7000**

WEST ORANGE (44). William F Cuozzi, Jr. 66 Main St, 07052. **201-325-4100**

WILLINGBORO TOWNSHIP (43). Steven E Heath. Salem Rd, 08046. **609-877-2200**

WOODBRIDGE TOWNSHIP (99). John J Cassidy. 1 Main St, 07095. **201-634-4500**

New Mexico

ALBUQUERQUE (244). David Rusk. City Hall, 87103. **505-766-7400**. Public information officer. **505-766-7550**

LAS CRUCES (38). Albert N Johnson. PO Box 760, 88001. **505-526-0280**

ROSWELL (34). Jerry N Smith. PO Drawer 1838, 88201. **505-622-5811**

SANTA FE (41). Sam Pick. PO Box 909, 87501. **505-982-4471**

New York

ALBANY (115). Erastus Corning II. City Hall, 12207. **518-472-8900**. William L Keefe, executive assistant

AUBURN (35). Paul W Lattimore. 24 South St, 13021. **315-252-9531**

BINGHAMTON (64). Alfred J Libous. City Hall, 13901. **607-772-7001**

BUFFALO (463). James D Griffin. 65 Niagara Sq, 14202. **716-856-4200**. (also night line)

ELMIRA (40). John Kennedy. Lake and Church Sts, 14901. **607-733-3742**

FREEPORT (40). William H White. 46 N Ocean Ave, 11520. **516-378-4000**

HEMPSTEAD (39). Dalton R Miller. 99 Nichols Ct, 11551. **516-489-5000**

JAMESTOWN (40). Steven Carlson. Municipal Bldg, 14701. **716-661-2300**

LONG BEACH (33). Harvey Wiesenberg. City Hall, 11561. **516-431-1000**

MOUNT VERNON (73). Thomas E Sharpe. City Hall, 10500. **914-668-2200**

NASSAU COUNTY (1423). County Executive Francis Purcell. Mineola, 11501. **516-535-2663**. Gene Turner, press secretary. **516-535-2280**. (h) **516-485-7085**. Bob Allen, deputy press secretary. (h) **516-546-0122**. Assistant press secretaries: Elaine King, special assistant. **516-223-4232**; Joe Iacona. **516-535-5664**. (h) **516-485-1787**

NEWBURGH (26). George J Shaw, Jr. 93 Broadway, 12550. **914-565-3333**

NEW ROCHELLE (75). Vincent R Rippa. 515 North Ave, 10801. **914-632-2021**

NEW YORK CITY (7868). Edward I Koch. City Hall, 10007. **212-566-5700**. Maureen Connelly, press secretary. **212-566-5090**. *Washington office.* Rm 203, 1825 K St NW, Washington DC 20006. Larry O'Brien

NIAGARA FALLS (86). Michael C O'Laughlin. 745 Main St, 14302. **716-278-8200**

NORTH TONAWANDA (36). William C Wittkowsky. 216 Payne Ave, 14120. **716-694-4340**

POUGHKEEPSIE (32). John T Kennedy. Memorial Sq, 12602. **914-485-4757**

ROCHESTER (296). City Manager Elisha Freedman. City Hall, Church and Fitzhugh Sts, 14614. **716-428-7120**. Tanya Yudelson, public information director. **716-428-7136**. (also night line). Rita Hoffman, public information officer.

ROCKVILLE CENTRE (27). Albert D Wood. College Pl, 11570. **516-766-0300**

ROME (50). William A Valentine. 207 N James St, 13440. **315-336-6000**

SCHENECTADY (78). Frank Duci. City Hall, 12305. **518-382-5005**

SYRACUSE (197). Lee Alexander. City Hall, 13202. **315-473-6605**. Ann Michel, director, office of federal and state aid. **315-473-5690**

TROY (63). Steven K Dworsky. City Hall, 12181. **518-270-4000**

UTICA (92). Steven Pawlinga. 1 Kennedy Pl, 13502. **315-798-3200**

VALLEY STREAM (40). Dominick M Minerva. 123 S Central Ave, 11580. **516-825-4200**

WATERTOWN (31). Karl R Burns. Municipal Bldg, 13601. **315-788-6560**

WHITE PLAINS (50). Alfred Del Vecchio. 255 Main St, 10601. **914-682-4411**

YONKERS (204). Angelo R Martinelli. City Hall, 10701. **914-963-3980**

North Carolina

ASHEVILLE (58). Roy Trantham. PO Box 7148, 28807. **704-255-5475**

BURLINGTON (36). William Durham. PO Box 1358, 27215. **919-227-3603**

CHAPEL HILL (32). James C Wallace. 306 N Columbia St, 27514. **919-929-1111**

CHARLOTTE (241). Ken Harris. 600 E Trade St, 28202. **704-374-2244**

DURHAM (95). Wade L Cavin. PO Box 2251, 27702. **919-682-9191**

FAYETTEVILLE (54). Beth Dail Finch. PO Box 437, 28302. **919-483-6168**

GASTONIA (47). T Jeffers. PO Box 1748, 28052. **704-864-3211**

GREENSBORO (144). E S Melvin. **919-373-2396**. PO Drawer W-2, City Hall. 27402. **919-373-2065**. Night line: **919-373-2222**. Hazel N Burch, secretary

HIGH POINT (63). Roy B Culler, Jr. PO Box 230, 27261. **919-887-2511**

RALEIGH (121). Isabella Cannon. PO Box 590, 27602. **919-755-6920**

ROCKY MOUNT (34). Frederick Turnage. PO Box 1180, 27801. **919-977-2111**

SALISBURY (23). James A Summers. PO Box 479, 28144. **704-633-2311**

WILMINGTON (46). Benjamin B Halterman. PO Box 1810, 28401. **919-762-0832**

WILSON (31). H B Benton. PO Box 10, 27893. **919-727-2071**

WINSTON-SALEM (133). Wayne Corpening. PO Box 2511, 27102. **919-237-2121**

North Dakota

BISMARCK (35). Robert O Heskin. PO Box 1578, 58501. **701-223-4170**

FARGO (53). Richard A Hentges. 201 4th St, 58102. **701-235-4269**

GRAND FORKS (39). Cyril P O'Neill. Box 1518, 58201. **701-775-8103**

Ohio

AKRON (275). John S Ballard. 166 S High St, 44308. **216-375-2345**. Dot W Brandstetter, appointments secretary and press liaison

BARBERTON (33). Lawrence A Maurer. 576 W Park Ave, 44203. **216-753-6611**

BEDFORD HEIGHTS (13). Lucille Reed. 5661 Perkins Rd, 44146. **215-439-1600**

BROOK PARK (31). Angelo Wedo. 6161 Engle Rd, 44142. **216-433-1300**

CANTON (110). Stanley A Cmich. City Hall, 44702. **216-489-3283**. Robert F Fisher, director of public service. **216-456-4989**

CINCINNATI (453). James T Luken. City Hall, 45202. **513-352-3250** (also night line). Florence McGraw, administrative assistant

CLEVELAND (751). Dennis J Kucinich. City Hall, 44114. **216-694-2220**. Ina Keegan, press Secretary

CLEVELAND HEIGHTS (61). Marjorie Wright. 2953 Mayfield Rd, 44118. **216-321-0100**

COLUMBUS (540). Tom Moody. City Hall, 90 W Broad St. **614-461-5671**. Night line: **614-461-8120**. Ralph Bangs, public relations director

CUYAHOGA FALLS (50). Robert J Quirk. 2310 2nd St, 44222. **216-923-9921**

DAYTON (244). James H McGee, 104 W 3rd St, 45402. **513-225-5148**. Night line: **513-299-0183**. Melvin Weinberg, public relations officer, **513-225-5117**

EAST CLEVELAND (40). Mae E Stewart. 14340 Euclid Ave, 44112. **216-681-5020**

ELYRIA (53). Marguerite E Bowman. 328 Broad St, 44035. **216-322-1829** or **9388**

EUCLID (72). Tony J Sustarsic. 585 E 222 St, 44123. **216-731-6000**

FAIRBORN (32). Herb Carlisle. 44 W Hebble Ave, 45324. **513-879-1730**

FINDLAY (36). Donald Renninger. 119 Court Place, 45840. **419-422-1012**

GARFIELD HEIGHTS (41). Raymond A Stachewicz. 5555 Turney Rd, 44125. **216-475-1100**

HAMILTON (68). Frank Witt. 2 High St, 45011. **513-895-7401**

KETTERING (70). Charles F Horn. 3600 Shroyer Rd, 45429. **513-296-2400**. Clerk. **513-296-2416**

LAKEWOOD (70). Robert Lawther. 12650 Detroit Ave, 44107. **216-521-7580**

LANCASTER (33). Edward C Rutherford. 104 E Main St, 43130. **614-653-1201**

LIMA (54). Harry J Moyer. 219 E Market St, 45801. **419-228-5462**

LORAIN (78). Joseph J Zahorec. 200 W Erie Ave, 44052. **216-244-3204**

MANSFIELD (55). Richard A Porter. 30 N Diamond St, 44902. **419-526-2600**

MAPLE HEIGHTS (34). Emil J Lisy, Jr. 5353 Lee Rd, 44137. **216-662-6000**

MARION (39). Don E Quaintance. 685 Delaware Ave, 43302. **614-383-3123**

MASSILLON (33). Mark Ross. City Hall, 44646. **216-833-4625**

MENTOR (37). Gordon Hodgins. 8500 Civic Center Blvd, 44060. **216-255-1100**

MIDDLETOWN (49). Thomas C Blake. City Bldg, 45042. **513-425-7766**

NEWARK (42). Richard E Baker. 40 W Main St, 43055. **614-349-7185**

NORTH OLMSTED (35). Robert Swietyniowski. 5206 Dover Center Rd, 44070. **216-777-8000**

NORWOOD (30). Donald Prues. Montgomery and Elm Aves, 45212. **513-631-2700**

PARMA (100). John Petruska. 6611 Ridge Rd, 44129. **216-886-2323**

SANDUSKY (33). John Mears. 222 Meigs St, 44870. **419-625-6120**

SHAKER HEIGHTS (36). Walter Kelley. 3400 Lee Rd, 44120. **216-752-5000**

SPRINGFIELD (82). Roger L Baker. City Bldg, 45501. **513-325-0511**

STEUBENVILLE (31). William Crabbe. 123 S 3rd St, 43952. **614-282-4441**

TOLEDO (384). Doug DeGood. City Hall, 525 N Erie St, 43614. **419-247-6077**. Night line: **419-247-6000**. Ted Reams, public information and industrial promotion officer. **419-247-6048**

UPPER ARLINGTON (39). Richard H Moore. 3600 Tremont Rd, 43221. **614-457-5080**

WARREN (63). Arthur J Richards. 391 Mahoning NW, 44483. **216-399-3681**

YOUNGSTOWN (140). J Phillip Richley. City Hall, 44503. **216-746-1892**

ZANESVILLE (33). George W Frueh. 401 Market St, 43701. **614-452-5441**

Oklahoma

BARTLESVILLE (30). Keith Carter. PO Box 699, 74003. **918-336-0000**

ENID (44). Paul Crosslin. PO Box 1768, 73701. **405-234-0400**

LAWTON (74). Wayne Gilley. 4th and A Sts, 73501. **405-357-6100**

MIDWEST CITY (48). Marion C Reed. 100 N Midwest Blvd, 73110. **405-732-2281**

MUSKOGEE (37). William R Collins. PO Box 19278 74401. **918-686-6602**

NORMAN (52). W S Morgan. PO Box 370, 73069. **405-321-1600**

OKLAHOMA CITY (366). Patience S Latting. 200 N Walker, 73102. **405-231-2011**

STILLWATER (31). Jon H Patton. PO Box 631, 74074. **405-372-0025**

TULSA (332). Robert J La Fortune. 200 Civic Ctr, 74102. **918-581-5011**

Oregon

CORVALLIS (35). Donald Walker. 501 SW Madison Ave, 97330. **503-757-6900**

EUGENE (96). Gus Keller. 777 Pearl St, 97401. **503-687-5010**

MEDFORD (28). Al Densmore. 411 W 8th St, 97501. **503-776-7455**

PORTLAND (382). Neil Goldschmidt. 1220 SW 5th Ave, 97204. **503-248-3511**. David Kottkamp, press secretary. **503-248-4120**. *Washington office.* 620 I St NW, Washington, DC 20006. **202-293-2355**. Robert Gordon, city representative

SALEM (68). Kent Aldrich. 555 Liberty SE, 97301. **503-588-6161**

Pennsylvania

ALLENTOWN (110). Frank Fischl. City Hall, 435 Hamilton St, 18101. **215-437-7546**

ALTOONA (63). William C Stouffer. 13th Ave and 12th St, 16603. **814-944-7131**.

BETHEL PARK (35). James E Hadsell. 5100 W Library Ave, 15102. **412-831-6800**

BETHLEHEM (73). Paul M Marcincin. 10 E Church St, 18018. **215-865-7100**

Patricia Keshing, public relations

CHESTER (56). John H Nacrelli. 5th and Welsh Sts, 19013. **215-876-8251**

EASTON (30). Henry J Schultz. 650 Ferry St, 18042. **215-253-7141**

ERIE (129). Louis J Tullio. Municipal Bldg, 16501. **814-456-8561**

HARRISBURG (68). Paul Doutrich, Jr. City Hall, 17101. **717-255-3040**

HAZELTON (30). James Paisley. City Hall, 18201. **717-454-6601**

JOHNSTOWN (42). Charles Tomljanovic Main and Market Sts, 15901. **814-539-8761**

LANCASTER (58). Richard M Scott. 120 N Duke St, 17604. **717-397-3501**

MCKEESPORT (38). Thomas J Fullard. 201 Lysle Blvd, 15132. **412-678-0151**

MOUNT LEBANON (40). William H Hartsough. 710 Washington Rd, 15228. **412-343-3400**

NEW CASTLE (39). Francis J Rogan. 230 N Jefferson St, 16101. **412-652-7781**

NORRISTOWN (38). Barney Marberger. E Airy St, 19404. **215-272-8080**

PHILADELPHIA (1949). Frank L Rizzo. City Hall, 19107. **215-686-1776**. Tony Zecca, office of the mayor. **215-686-6213**. Joseph A La Sala, office of the city representative, 1660 Municipal Service Bldg, 19107. **215-686-3640**. *Washington office.* Suite 309, 1140 Connecticut Ave NW, Washington, DC 20006. **202-872-0033**. John Field, Washington representative

PITTSBURGH (520). Richard S Caliguiri, Office of the Mayor, 15219. **412-255-2632** or **2626**. Night line: **412-765-1212**. Dave Welty, public information secretary. **412-255-2632**. (h) **412-561-7355**

READING (88). Joseph P Kuzminski. 8th and Washington Sts, 19601. **215-373-5111**

SCRANTON (104). Eugene J Hickey. Municipal Bldg, 18503. **717-348-4100**

STATE COLLEGE (34). Arnold Addison. 118 S Fraser St, 16801. **814-237-1411**

WILKES-BARRE (59). Walter Lisman. 40 E Market St, 18701. **717-823-5119**

WILLIAMSPORT (38). Daniel P Kirby. 454 Pine St, 17701. **717-326-2831**. *Press contact.* Jean A Sutkins, office of the mayor

YORK (50). Elizabeth Marshall. City Hall, 50 W King St, 17405. **717-843-8841**. *Press contact.* Lynn E Kraft, office of the mayor

Puerto Rico

BAYAMON (148). Ramon L Rivera. Maceo and Degetau Sts, 00619. **809-785-1715**

CAGUAS (163). Miguel Hernandez. City Hall, 00625. **809-743-3400**

PONCE (128). Jose G Tormos Vega. PO Box 1709, 00731. **809-844-6118**

SAN JUAN (453). Hernan Padilla. PO Box 4355, 00905. **809-724-7171**

Rhode Island

CRANSTON (73). James L Taft, Jr. 869 Park Ave, 02910. **401-461-1000**

EAST PROVIDENCE (48). Edward J Doyle. 60 Commercial Way, 02914. **401-434-3311**

NEWPORT (35). Humphrey J Donnelly III. City Hall, 02840. **401-846-7200**

PAWTUCKET (77). Dennis M Lynch. 137 Roosevelt Ave, 02860. **401-728-0500**

PROVIDENCE (179). Vincent Albert Cianci, Jr. 25 Dorrance St, 02903. **401-421-7740**, Ext 233. Kurt Oden, press secretary, Ext 343. Cindy Flowers, assistant press secretary

WARWICK (84). Joseph W Walsh. 3275 Post Rd, 02864. **401-738-2000**

WOONSOCKET (47). Gerard J Bouley. 169 Main St, 02895. **401-762-6400**

South Carolina

CHARLESTON (67). Joseph P Riley, Jr. City Hall, 29401. **803-722-4407**

COLUMBIA (114). John T Campbell. PO Box 147, 29217. **803-765-1041**

GREENVILLE (61). Max M Heller. PO Box 2207, 29602. **803-242-1250**

NORTH CHARLESTON (54). John E Bourne, Jr. PO Box 5817, 29406. **803-554-5700**

ROCK HILL (34). David Lyle. PO Box 11706, 29730. **803-328-6171**

SPARTANBURG (45). Franklin W Allen 480 N Church St PO Box 4689, 29303. **803-585-4361**. Buddy Womick, director, public information

South Dakota

ABERDEEN (26). Preston A Solem. PO Box 1299, 57401. **605-225-4800**

RAPID CITY (44). Arthur P La Croix. 22 Main St, 57701. **605-394-4110**

SIOUX FALLS (72). Rick W Knobe. 224 W 9th St, 57102. **605-339-7200**

Tennessee

CHATTANOOGA (119). Charles A Rose. City Hall, Municipal Bldg, 37402. **615-757-5152**. Evelyn Shankles, office of the mayor

CLARKSVILLE (32). Charles W Crow. City Hall, 37040. **615-645-2306**

JACKSON (40). Robert D Conger. 312 E Main St, 38301. **901-424-3440**

JOHNSON CITY (34). Robert Arnold. Municipal-Safety Bldg, 37601. **615-929-9171**

KINGSPORT (32). R E Bevington. 225 W Center St, 37660. **615-245-5131**

KNOXVILLE (175). Randy Tyree. City Hall, 37902. **615-523-2151**. Robert F Horner Jr, mayor's press secretary. Patricia C Hunnell, information officer

MEMPHIS (624). Wyeth Chandler. 125 N Main St, 38103. **901-528-2800**. Robert A Baird, executive assistant

NASHVILLE (448). Richard H Fulton. Metropolitan Courthouse, 37201. **615-259-5000**. *Press contact.* Joseph Foster, assistant to the mayor. **615-259-6047**. (h) **615-356-4235**

Texas

ABILENE (90). Fred Lee Hughes. PO Box 60, 79604. **915-673-3781**

AMARILLO (127). Jerry Hodge. PO Box 1971, 79186. **806-372-4211**

ARLINGTON (91). S J Stovall. PO Box 280, 76010. **817-275-3271**

AUSTIN (252). Carole McClellan. PO Box 1088, 78767. **512-477-6511**

BAYTOWN (44). Tom Gentry. PO Box 424, 77520. **713-422-8281**

BEAUMONT (116). Ken Ritter. PO Box 3827, 77704. **713-838-6651**

BROWNSVILLE (53). Ruben Edelstein. PO Box 911, 78520. **512-542-4391**

BRYAN (34). Lloyd Joyce. PO Box 1000, 77801. **713-823-0071**

CORPUS CHRISTI (205). Jason Luby. PO Box 9277, 78408. **512-884-3011**

DALLAS (844). Robert Folsom. City Hall, 2014 Main St, 75201. **214-748-9711**

DENTON (40). Elinor Hughes. 215 E McKinney, 76201. **817-382-9601**

EL PASO (322). Ray Salazar. 500 E San Antonio, 79901. **915-543-2900**

FORT WORTH (393). Hugh Parmer. 1000 Throckmorton, 76102. **817-335-7211**

GALVESTON (62). John C Unbehagen. PO Box 779, 77550. **713-766-2103**

GARLAND (81). Charles G Clack. PO Box 401889, 75040. **214-272-2511**

GRAND PRAIRIE (51). Weldon Parkhill. PO Box 11, 75050. **214-263-5221**

HARLINGEN (34). R D Youker. PO Box 2207, 78550. **512-423-4230**

HOUSTON (1233). Jim McConn. City Hall, 77001. **713-222-3011**. Bruce Badd, press secretary. **713-222-3141**

IRVING (97). Marvin Randle. PO Box 3008, 75061. **214-253-2600** or **2493**

KILLEEN (36). Major E Blair. 400 N 2nd St, 76541. **817-634-2191**

LAREDO (69). J C Martin, Jr. City Hall, 78040. **512-723-6326**

LONGVIEW (46). William Y Rice. P O Box 1952, 75601. **214-757-6666**

LUBBOCK (149). Roy Bass. PO Box 2000, 79457. **806-762-6411**

MCALLEN (38). Othal Brand. PO Box 220, 78501. **512-686-6551**

MESQUITE (55). B J Smith. PO Box 137, 75149. **214-288-7711**

MIDLAND (59). Ernest Angelo, Jr. PO Box 1152, 79701. **915-683-4281**

ODESSA (78). Dan B Hemphill. PO Box 4398, 79760. **915-337-7381**

PASADENA (89). John Ray Harrison. 1211 E Southmore, 77506. **713-477-1511**

PLANO (44). Norman Whitsitt. PO Box 358, 75074. **214-424-6531**

PORT ARTHUR (57). Bernis W Sadler. PO Box 1089, 77640. **713-983-3321**

RICHARDSON (49). Raymond D Noah. PO Box 309, 75080. **214-235-8331**

SAN ANGELO (64). Thomas Parrett. PO Box 1751, 76901. **915-658-1381**

SAN ANTONIO (654). Lila Cockrell. PO Box 9066, 78285. **512-225-5661**. Night line: **512-222-2084**. Shirl Thomas, executive assistant

TEMPLE (33). William R Courtney. Municipal Bldg, 76501. **817-778-5561**

TEXARKANA (30). David L Keller. PO Box 1967, 75501. **214-794-3434**

TEXAS CITY (39). Emmett F Lowry. PO Box 2608, 77590. **713-948-3111**

TYLER (58). Bob Nall. PO Box 2039, 75701. **214-597-6651**

VICTORIA (41). C C Carsner, Jr. 105 W Juan Linn St, 77901. **512-573-2401**

WACO (95). M A Smith. PO Box 1370, 76703. **817-756-6161**

WICHITA FALLS (98). J C Boyd, Jr. PO Box 1431, 76307. **817-322-5611**

Utah

BOUNTIFUL (28). Elmer Barlow. 745 S Main St, 84010. **801-295-2301**

OGDEN CITY (69). A Stephen Dirks. Municipal Bldg, 84401. **801-399-8011**

PROVO (53). James E Ferguson. PO Box 799, 84601. **801-375-1822**

SALT LAKE CITY CORP (176). Ted Wilson, 300 City and County Bldg, 84111. **801-328-7704**. *Press contact.* John Hiskey, office of the mayor

Vermont

BURLINGTON (38). Gordon H Paquette. City Hall, 05401. **802-862-9684**

MONTPELIER (9). Frederic Bertrand. Main St, 05602. **802-223-3031**

Virginia

ALEXANDRIA (111). Frank Mann. 125 N Royal St, 22314. **703-750-6000**

CHARLOTTESVILLE (39). Nancy K O'Brien. PO Box 911, 22902. **804-977-4050**

CHESAPEAKE (90). Marian P Whitehurst. PO Box 15225, 23320. **804-547-6462**

DANVILLE (46). Robert H Clarke. Municipal Bldg, 24541. **804-799-5100**

HAMPTON (121). Ann H Kilgore. **800-727-6315,** 22 Lincoln St, 23669. **804-727-6000**

LYNCHBURG (54). Joseph F Freeman, III. PO Box 60, 24505.. **804-847-1443**

NEWPORT NEWS (138). Joseph C Ritchie. 2400 Washington Ave, 23607. **804-247-8411**

NORFOLK (308). Vincent J Thomas. **804-441-2679**. City Hall, 23501. **804-441-2471**. Alexander J Halmai, public relations officer. **804-441-5152**. June Toher, public relations assistant

PETERSBURG (45). H E Fauntleroy, Jr. City Hall, 23803. **804-733-6131**

PORTSMOUTH (111). Richard J Davis. PO Box 820, 23705. **804-393-8746**

RICHMOND (250). Henry L Marsh, III. 900 E Broad St, 23219. **804-780-4711**

ROANOKE (92). Noel Taylor. Municipal Bldg, 24011. **703-981-2000**

SUFFOLK (45). James F Hope. PO Box 1858, 23434. **804-539-2351**

VIRGINIA BEACH (172). Clarence A Holland. Municipal Ctr, 23456. **804-427-4581**. Willa Redding, assistant to the mayor

Washington

BELLEVUE (61). Gary Zimmerman. PO Box 1768, 98009. **206-455-6800**

BELLINGHAM (39). Ken Hertz. 210 Lottie St, 98225. **206-676-6950**

BREMERTON (35). Glenn K Jarstad. 239 4th St, 98310. **206-478-5252**

EVERETT (54). Bill Moore. City Hall, 98201. **206-259-8755**

RICHLAND (28). Tom Logston. PO Box 190, 99352. **509-943-9161**

SEATTLE (531). Charles Royer. City Hall, 98104. **206-625-4000**. Tim Hillard, office of the mayor. **206-625-2485**

SPOKANE (171). Ron Blair. N 221 Wall St, 99201. **509-456-2665**

TACOMA (155). Mike Parker. County-City Bldg, 98402. **206-593-4411**

VANCOUVER (42). Jim Justin. City Manager. 210 E 13th St, 98660. **206-696-8121**

YAKIMA (46). Betty L Edmonson. 129 N 2nd St, 98901. **509-575-6050**

West Virginia

CHARLESTON (72). John G Hutchinson. PO Box 2749, City Hall, 25330. **304-348-8175**. James C Johnson, II, federal-state relations. **304-348-8176**

HUNTINGTON (74). William A Evans. PO Box 1659, 25717. **304-696-5880**

MORGANTOWN (29). Earl L McCartney. 389 Spruce St, 26505. **304-296-4421**

PARKERSBURG (44). Alvin Smith. PO Box 1348, 26101. **304-485-6371**

WHEELING (48). John Fahey. City-County Bldg, 26003. **304-234-3694**

Wisconsin

APPLETON (57). James P Sutherland. PO Box 1857, 54911. **414-739-0481**. James R Grassman, administrative assistant

BELOIT (36). Everett C Haskell. Municipal Ctr, 53511. **608-365-0131**

BROOKFIELD (32). William A Mitchell, Jr. 2000 N Calhoun Rd, 53005. **414-782-9650**

EAU CLAIRE (45). Marie S Evans. 203 S Farwell St, 54701. **715-839-4902**

FOND DU LAC (36). Joseph H Petersen. PO Box 150, 54935. **414-922-2600**

GREEN BAY (88). Michael Monfils. Jefferson St, 54301. **414-497-3600**

JANESVILLE (46). Clyde Miles. 18 N Jackson St, 53545. **608-754-2811**. *Press contact*. Philip L Deaton

KENOSHA (79). Paul Saftig. 625 52nd St, 53140. **414-658-4811**

LA CROSSE (51). Patrick T Zielke. City Hall, 54601. **608-782-5585**

MADISON (173). Paul Soglin. Rm 403, City Hall, 210 Monona Ave, 53709.

608-266-6366. Jim Rowen, administrative assistant. **608-266-4611**. John Urich, city planner

MANITOWOC (33). Anthony V Dufek. 817 Franklin St, 54220. **414-684-3331**

MENOMONEE FALLS (32). Harry B Titus. PO Box 100, 53051. **414-251-7800**

MILWAUKEE (717). Henry W Maier. City Hall, 200 E Wells, 53202. **414-278-2200**. Arthur M Strickland III, press secretary

OSHKOSH (53). George N Singstock. PO Box 1130, 54901. **414-424-0275**

RACINE (95). Stephen F Olsen. 730 Washington Ave, 53403 **414-334-2326**

SHEBOYGAN (48). Richard W Suscha. 828 Center Ave, 53081. **414-459-3317**

SUPERIOR (32). Bruce C Hagen. 1407 Hammond Ave, 54880. **715-394-0200**

WAUKESHA (40). Paul G Vrakas. 201 Delafield St, 53186. **414-547-2201**

WAUSAU (33). John L Kannenberg, 407 Grant St, 54401. **715-845-5279**, Ext 300. (h) **715-845-5058**

WAUWATOSA (59). James A Benz. 7725 W North Ave, 53213. **414-258-3000**

WEST ALLIS (72). Jack F Barlich. 7525 W Greenfield Ave, 53214. **414-476-4340**

Wyoming

CASPER (39). Jack Hopkins. City-County Bldg, 82601. **307-265-5705**

CHEYENNE (41). Don Erickson. City-County Bldg, 82001. **307-635-5621**

COUNTY GOVERNMENTS

The following list of US counties includes the county seat, the zip code, and telephone number of the county courthouse or its executive offices.

Alabama

AUTAUGA. Prattville, 36067. **205-365-2281**

BALDWIN. Bay Minette, 36507. **205-937-9561**

BARBOUR. Clayton, 36016. **205-775-3203**

BIBB. Centreville, 35042. **205-926-3471**

BLOUNT. Oneonta, 35121. **205-274-2125**

BULLOCK. Union Springs, 36089. **205-738-2250**

BUTLER. Greenville, 36037. **205-382-2612**

CALHOUN. Anniston, 36201. **205-236-3421**

CHAMBERS. Lafayette, 36862. **205-864-8833**

CHEROKEE. Centre, 35960. **205-927-3368**

CHILTON. Clanton, 35045. **205-755-1551**

CHOCTAW. Butler, 36905. **205-459-2417**

CLARKE. Grove Hill, 36451. **205-275-3507**

CLAY. Ashland, 36251. **205-354-2198**

CLEBURNE. Heflin, 36264. **205-463-5627**

COFFEE. Elba, 36323. **205-897-2213**

COLBERT. Tuscumbia, 35674. **205-383-4981**

CONECUH. Evergreen, 36401. **205-578-2095**

COOSA. Rockford, 35136. **205-377-4383**

COVINGTON. Andalusia, 36420. **205-222-3613**

CRENSHAW. Luverne, 36049. **205-335-5640**

CULLMAN. Cullman, 35055. **205-734-5832**

DALE. Ozark, 36360. **205-774-6025**

DALLAS. Selma, 36701. **205-872-3461**

DE KALB. Fort Payne, 35967. **205-845-0404**

ELMORE. Wetumpka, 36092. **205-567-4347**

ESCAMBIA. Brewton, 36426. **205-867-5615**

ETOWAH. Gadsden, 35901. **205-546-2821**

FAYETTE. Fayette, 35555. **205-932-4510**

FRANKLIN. Russellville, 35653. **205-332-1210**

GENEVA. Geneva, 36340. **205-684-2276**

GREENE. Eutaw, 35462. **205-372-3349**

HALE. Greensboro, 36744. **205-624-8740**

HENRY. Abbeville, 36310. **205-585-3371**

HOUSTON. Dothan, 36301. **205-794-5441**

JACKSON. Scottsboro, 35768. **205-585-3257**

JEFFERSON. Birmingham, 35203. **205-325-5311**

LAMAR. Vernon, 35592. **205-695-7274**

LAUDERDALE. Florence, 35630. **205-766-5180**

LAWRENCE. Moulton, 35650. **205-974-0262**

LEE. Opelika, 36801. **205-745-4641**

LIMESTONE. Athens, 35611. **205-232-1320**

LOWNDES. Haynesville, 36040.
205-548-2331

MACON. Tuskeegee, 36083. **205-727-5121**

MADISON. Huntsville, 35801. **205-536-5911**

MARENGO. Linden, 36748. **205-295-3631**

MARION. Hamilton, 35570. **205-921-3172**

MARSHALL. Guntersville, 35976.
205-582-3642

MOBILE. Mobile, 36602. **205-438-3481**

MONROE. Monroeville, 36460.
205-743-3778

MONTGOMERY. Montgomery, 36102.
205-269-1261

MORGAN. Decatur, 35601. **205-353-6753**

PERRY. Marion, 36756. **205-683-2491**

PICKENS. Carrollton, 35447. **205-367-8715**

PIKE. Troy, 36081. **205-566-1246**

RANDOLPH. Wedowee, 36278.
205-357-4933

RUSSELL. Phenix City, 36867.
205-298-6426

ST CLAIR. Ashville, 35953. **205-594-5116**

SHELBY. Columbiana, 35051. **205-669-2191**

SUMTER. Livingston, 35470. **205-652-2731**

TALLADEGA. Talladega, 35160.
205-362-4175

TALLAPOOSA. Dadeville, 36853.
205-825-4266

TUSCALOOSA. Tuscaloosa, 35401.
205-345-0444

WALKER. Jasper, 35501. **205-384-5546**

WASHINGTON. Chatom, 36518.
205-847-2203

WILCOX. Camden, 36726. **205-682-4883**

WINSTON. Double Springs, 35553.
205-489-5026

Alaska

BRISTOL BAY. Naknek, 99633.
907-268-4224

FAIRBANKS NORTH STAR. Fairbanks,
99701. **907-452-4761**

ANCHORAGE. Anchorage, 99510.
907-274-2525

GREATER JUNEAN. Juneau, 99801.
907-586-3300

GREATER SITKA. Sitka, 99835.
907-747-3294

HAINES. Haines, 99827. **907-766-2433**

KENAI PENINSULA. Soldotna, 99669.
907-262-4441

KETCHIKAN GATEWAY. Ketchikan,
99901. **907-225-6151**

KODIAK ISLAND. Kodiak, 99615.
907-486-5736

MATANUSKA SUSITNA. Palmer, 99645.
907-745-3246

NORTH SLOPE. Barrow, 99723.
907-852-4865

Arizona

APACHE. St Johns, 85936. **602-337-4364**

COCHISE. Bisbee, 85603. **602-432-2209**

COCONINO. Flagstaff, 86001. **602-774-5011**

GILA. Globe, 85501. **602-425-5763**

GRAHAM. Safford, 85546. **602-428-3250**

GREENLEE. Clifton, 85533. **602-864-2072**

MARICOPA. Phoenix, 85007. **602-262-3011**

MOHAVE. Kingman, 86401. **602-753-2141**

NAVAJO. Holbrook, 86025. **602-524-6632**

PIMA. Tucson, 85701. **602-792-8126**

PINAL. Florence, 85232. **602-868-5801**

SANTA CRUZ. Nogales, 85621.
602-287-3271

YAVAPAI. Prescott, 86301. **602-445-7450**

YUMA. Yuma, 85364. **602-782-4534**

Arkansas

ARKANSAS. Stuttgart, 72160. **501-673-7311**

ASHLEY. Hamburg, 71646. **501-853-5144**

BAXTER. Mountain Home, 72653.
501-425-2755

BENTON. Bentonville, 72712. **501-273-7442**

BOONE. Harrison, 72601. **501-741-6168**

BRADLEY. Warren, 71671. **501-226-3853**

CALHOUN. Hampton, 71744. **501-798-2517**

CARROLL. Berryville, 72616. **501-423-2967**

CHICOT. Lake Village, 71653. **501-265-2208**

CLARK. Arkadelphia, 71923. **501-246-4281**

CLAY. Piggott, 72454. **501-598-2813**

CLEBURNE. Heber Springs, 72543.
501-362-2523

CLEVELAND. Rison, 71665. **501-325-6521**

COLUMBIA. Magnolia, 71753.
501-234-2542

CONWAY. Morrilton, 72110. **501-354-2561**

CRAIGHEAD. Jonesboro, 72401.
501-932-2921

CRAWFORD. Van Buren, 72956.
501-474-1312

CRITTENDEN. Marion, 72364.
501-739-3200

CROSS. Wynne, 72396. **501-238-2461**

DALLAS. Fordyce, 71742. **501-352-3371**

DESHA. Arkansas City, 71630.
501-877-2323

DREW. Monticello, 71655. **501-367-3574**

FAULKNER. Conway, 72032. **501-329-6979**

FRANKLIN. Ozark, 72949. **501-667-3720**

FULTON. Salem, 72576. **501-895-3310**

GARLAND. Hot Springs, 71901.
501-623-3681

GRANT. Sheridan, 72150. **501-942-2631**

GREENE. Paragould, 72450. **501-236-3061**

HEMPSTEAD. Hope, 71801. **501-777-2241**

HOT SPRING. Malvern, 72104. **501-332-2261**

HOWARD. Nashville, 71852. **501-845-3622**

INDEPENDENCE. Batesville, 72501. **501-793-5126**

IZARD. Melbourne, 72556. **501-368-4328**

JACKSON. Newport, 72112. **501-523-2972**

JEFFERSON. Pine Bluff, 71601. **501-534-1391**

JOHNSON. Clarksville, 72830. **501-754-3967**

LAFAYETTE. Lewisville, 71845. **501-921-4633**

LAWRENCE. Walnut Ridge, 72476. **501-886-6121**

LEE. Marianna, 72360. **501-295-2339**

LINCOLN. Star City, 71667. **501-628-4822**

LITTLE RIVER. Ashdown, 71822. **501-898-3362**

LOGAN. Booneville, 72927. **501-675-2951**

LONOKE. Lonoke, 72086. **501-676-2368**

MADISON. Huntsville, 72740. **501-738-6721**

MARION. Yellville, 72687. **501-449-6231**

MILLER. Texarkana, 75501. **501-774-3256**

MISSISSIPPI. Blytheville, 72315. **501-762-2411**

MONROE. Clareddon, 72029. **501-747-3632**

MONTGOMERY. Mount Ida, 71957. **501-867-3521**

NEVADA. Prescott, 71857. **501-887-2710**

NEWTON. Jasper, 72641. **501-446-5125**

OUSCHITA. Camden, 71701. **501-836-2412**

PERRY. Perryville, 72126. **501-889-2562**

PHILLIPS. Helena, 72342. **501-338-7234**

PIKE. Murfeesboro, 71958. **501-285-4311**

POINSETT. Harrisburg, 72432. **501-578-5408**

POLK. Mena, 71953. **501-394-3031**

POPE. Russelville, 72801. **501-968-6046**

PRAIRIE. Des Arc, 72040. **501-256-4434**

PULASKI. Little Rock, 72201. **501-374-4805**

RANDOLPH. Pocahontas, 72455. **501-892-5822**

ST FRANCIS. Forrest City, 72335. **501-633-1185**

SALINE. Benton, 72015. **501-778-2350**

SCOTT. Waldron, 72958. **501-637-2642**

SEARCY. Marshall, 72650. **501-448-3807**

SEBASTIAN. Fort Smith, 72901. **501-783-6139**

SEVIER. De Queen, 71832. **501-584-2425**

SHARP. Hardy, 72542. **501-994-7338**

STONE. Mountain View, 72560. **501-269-3271**

UNION. El Dorado, 71730. **501-863-5244**

VAN BUREN. Clinton, 72031. **501-745-2443**

WASHINGTON. Fayetteville, 72701. **501-521-8400**

WHITE. Searcy, 72143. **501-268-5528**

WOODRUFF. Augusta, 72006. **501-347-2531**

YELL. Danville, 72833. **501-495-2933**

California

ALAMEDA. Oakland, 94612. **415-874-6252**

ALPINE. Markleeville, 96120. **916-694-2281**

AMADOR. Amador City, 95601. **209-223-0840**

BUTTE. Oroville, 95965. **916-534-4224**

CALAVERAS. San Andreas, 95249. **209-754-3241**

COLUSA. Colusa, 95932. **916-458-4516**

CONTRA COSTA. Martinez, 94553. **415-372-4080**

DEL NORTE. Crescent City, 95531. **707-464-3101**

EL DORADO. Placerville, 95667. **916-626-2371**

FRESNO. Fresno, 93721. **209-488-3033**

GLENN. Willows, 95988. **916-934-3834**

HUMBOLDT. Eureka, 95501. **707-445-7520**

IMPERIAL. El Centro, 92243. **714-352-3610**

INYO. Independence, 93526. **714-878-2411**

KERN. Bakersfield, 93301. **805-861-2111**

KINGS. Hanford, 93230. **209-582-3211**

LAKE. Lakeport, 95453. **707-263-5461**

LASSEN. Susanville, 96130. **916-257-3633**

LOS ANGELES. Los Angeles, 90012. **213-974-5101**

MADERA. Madera, 93637. **209-674-4641**

MARIN. San Rafael, 94902. **415-479-1100**

MARIPOSA. Mariposa, 95338. **209-966-2005**

MENDOCINO. Ukiah, 95482. **707-462-4731**

MERCED. Merced, 95340. **209-726-7434**

MODOC. Alturas, 96101. **916-233-2215**

MONO. Bridgeport, 93517. **714-932-7911**

MONTEREY. Salinas, 93901. **408-424-8611**

NAPA. Napa, 94558. **707-253-4421**

NEVADA. Nevada City, 95959. **916-265-2461**

ORANGE. Santa Ana, 92701. **714-834-2200**

PLACER. Auburn, 95603. **916-823-4381**

PLUMAS. Quincy, 95971. **916-283-1060**

RIVERSIDE. Riverside, 92501. **714-787-6151**

SACRAMENTO. Sacramento, 95814. **916-440-5000**

SAN BENITO. Hollister, 95023. **408-637-3786**

SAN BERNARDINO. San Bernardino, 95801. **714-383-1839**

SAN DIEGO. San Diego, 92101. **714-236-3279**

SAN FRANCISCO. San Francisco, 94102. **415-558-6161**

SAN JOAQUIN. Stockton, 95202. **209-944-2611**

SAN LUIS OBISPO. San Luis Obispo, 93401. **805-543-1550**

SAN MATEO. Redwood City, 94063. **415-364-5600**

SANTA BARBARA. Santa Barbara, 93101. **805-966-1611**

SANTA CLARA. San Jose, 95110. **408-299-2323**

SANTA CRUZ. Santa Cruz, 95060. **408-425-0111**

SHASTA. Redding, 96001. **916-246-5557**

SIERRA. Downieville, 95936. **916-289-3271**

SISKIYOU. Yreka, 96097. **916-842-3531**

SOLANO. Fairfield, 94533. **707-422-0010**

SONOMA. Santa Rosa, 95402. **707-527-2241**

STANISLAUS. Modesto, 95352. **209-526-6501**

SUTTER. Yuba City, 95991. **916-673-9125**

TEHAMA. Red Bluff, 96080. **916-527-3350**

TRINITY. Weaverville, 96093. **916-623-2271**

TULAR. Visalia, 93277. **209-732-5511**

TUOLUMNE. Sonora, 95370. **209-532-4574**

VENTURA. Ventura, 93001. **805-648-6131**

YOLO. Woodland, 95695. **916-666-8204**

YUBA. Marysville, 95901. **919-743-1511**

Colorado

ADAMS. Brighton, 80601. **303-659-2120**

ALAMOSA. Alamosa, 81101. **303-589-6681**

ARAPAHOE. Littleton, 80120. **303-794-9211**

ARCHULETA. Pagosa Springs, 81147. **303-968-2536**

BACA. Springfield, 81073. **303-523-4372**

BENT. Las Animas, 81054. **303-456-0172**

BOULDER. Boulder, 80302. **303-441-3500**

CHAFFEE. Salida, 81201. **303-539-4004**

CHEYENNE. Cheyenne Wells, 80810. **303-767-5575**

CLEAR CREEK. Georgetown, 80444. **303-569-2923**

CONEJOS. Conejos, 81129. **303-376-5929**

COSTILLA. San Luis, 81152. **303-672-3301**

CROWLEY. Ordway, 81063. **303-267-4643**

CUSTER. Westcliffe, 81252. **303-783-2441**

DELTA. Delta, 81416. **303-874-9792**

DENVER. Denver, 80203. **303-297-2601**

DOLORES. Dove Creek, 81324. **303-677-2381**

DOUGLAS. Castle Rock, 80104. **303-688-4811**

EAGLE. Eagle, 81631. **303-328-6377**

EL PASO. Colorado Springs, 80902. **303-471-6711**

ELBERT. Kiowa, 80117. **303-621-2080**

FREMONT. Canon City, 81212. **303-275-1511**

GARFIELD. Glenwood Springs, 81601. **303-945-6892**

GILPIN. Central City, 80427. **303-582-5214**

GRAND. Hot Sulphur Springs, 80451. **303-725-3332**

GUNNISON. Gunnison, 81230. **303-641-0070**

HINSDALE. Lake City, 81235. **303-955-2223**

HUERFANO. Walsenburg, 81089. **303-738-2370**

JACKSON. Walden, 80480. **303-723-4334**

JEFFERSON. Golden, 80401. **303-279-6511**

KIOWA. Eads, 81036. **303-438-5421**

KIT CARSON. Burlington, 80407. **303-346-8638**

LA PLATA. Durango, 81301. **303-247-4530**

LAKE. Leadville, 80461. **303-486-0993**

LARIMER. Fort Collins, 80521. **303-221-2100**

LAS ANIMAS. Trinidad, 81082. **303-846-3314**

LINCOLN. Hugo, 80821. **303-743-2444**

LOGAN. Sterling, 80751. **303-522-1544**

MESA. Grand Junction, 81501. **303-243-9200**

MINERAL. Creede, 81130. **303-658-2440**

MOFFAT. Craig, 81625. **303-824-5484**

MONTEZUMA. Cortez, 81321. **303-565-7484**

MONTROSE. Montrose, 81401. **303-249-4373**

MORGAN. Fort Morgan, 80701. **303-867-8202**

OTERO. La Junta, 81050. **303-384-4221**

OURAY. Ouray, 81427. **303-325-2650**

PARK. Fairplay, 80440. **303-836-2246**

PHILLIPS. Holyoke, 80734. **303-854-3131**

PITKIN. Aspen, 81611. **303-925-5232**

PROWERS. Lamar, 81052. **303-336-9001**

PUEBLO. Pueblo, 81003. **303-543-3550**

RIO BLANCO. Meeker, 81641. **303-878-5522**

RIO GRANDE. Del Norte, 81132. **303-657-2580**

ROUTT. Steamboat Springs, 80477. **303-879-1710**

SAGUACHE. Saguache, 81149. **303-655-2512**

SAN JUAN. Silverton, 81433. **303-387-5671**

SAN MIGUEL. Telluride, 81435. **303-728-3954**

SEDGWICK. Julesburg, 80737.
303-474-2485

SUMMIT. Breckenridge, 80424.
303-453-2561

TELLER. Cripple Creek, 80813.
303-689-2404

WASHINGTON. Akron, 80720.
303-345-6565

WELD. Greeley, 80631. 303-353-2212

YUMA. Wray, 80758. 303-332-5796

Connecticut

In 1960 Connecticut abolished its counties as governmental bodies, but they remain in existence as geographical divisions, with a county court in one city of each "county."

FAIRFIELD. County Courthouse, 1061 Main St, Bridgeport, 06430. 203-334-5178

HARTFORD. State Court Bldg, 95 Washington St, Hartford, 06115.
203-566-4130

LITCHFIELD. Litchfield County Courthouse, West St, Litchfield, 06759.
203-567-0844

MIDDLESEX. PO Box 111, De Koven Dr, Middletown, 06457. 203-346-4968

NEW HAVEN. County Courthouse, 235 Church St, New Haven, 06510. 203-789-1937

NEW LONDON. State Courthouse, New London, 06320. 203-887-0410

TOLLAND. State Court House, Brooklyn St, Rockville, 06066. 203-872-3878

WINDHAM. Superior Bldg, Church St, Putnam, 06280. 203-928-5181

Delaware

KENT. Dover, 19901. 302-678-3100

NEW CASTLE. Wilmington, 19801.
302-571-7520

SUSSEX. Georgetown, 19947. 302-856-7701

Florida

ALACHUA. Gainesville, 32601.
904-376-3241

BAKER. Macclenny, 32063. 904-259-3121

BAY. Panama City, 32401. 904-763-2885

BRADFORD. Starke, 32091. 904-964-5512

BREVARD. Titusville, 32780. 305-269-8541

BROWARD. Fort Lauderdale, 33301.
305-765-5121

CALHOUN. Blounstown, 32424.
904-674-8312

CHARLOTTE. Punta Gorda, 33950.
813-639-3111

CITRUS. Inverness, 32650. 904-726-2881

CLAY. Green Cover Springs, 32043.
904-284-9861

COLLIER. Naples, 33940. 813-774-8971

COLUMBIA. Lake City, 32055.
904-752-1264

DADE. Miami, 33132. 305-579-5311

DE SOTO. Arcadia, 33821. 813-494-3766

DIXIE. Cross City, 32628. 904-498-3344

DUVAL. Jacksonville, 32202. 904-633-3700

ESCAMBIA. Pensacola, 32502.
904-434-0326

FLAGLER. Bunnell, 32010. 904-437-3565

FRANKLIN. Apalachicola, 32320.
904-653-8861

GADSDEN. Quincy, 32351. 904-627-7514

GILCHRIST. Trenton, 32693. 904-463-2345

GLADES. Moore Haven, 33471.
813-946-2731

GULF. Port St Joe, 32456. 904-229-6113

HAMILTON. Jasper, 32052. 904-792-1288

HARDEE. Wauchula, 33873. 813-773-6952

HENDRY. La Belle, 33935. 813-675-2341

HERNANDO. Brooksville, 33512.
904-796-3538

HIGHLANDS. Sebring, 33870. 813-385-2581

HILLSBOROUGH. Tampa, 33602.
813-272-5660

HOLMES. Bonifay, 32425. 904-547-2835

INDIAN RIVER. Vero Beach, 32960.
305-567-5146

JACKSON. Marianna, 32446. 904-482-2501

JEFFERSON. Monticello, 32344.
904-997-3596

LAFAYETTE. Mayo, 32066. 904-294-1600

LAKE. Tavares, 32778. 904-343-5152

LEE. Fort Myers, 33902. 813-335-2111

LEON. Tallahassee, 32304. 904-488-4710

LEVY. Bronson, 32621. 904-486-2008

LIBERTY. Bristol, 32321. 904-643-3041

MADISON. Madison, 32340. 904-973-4176

MANATEE. Bradenton, 33505.
813-958-9711

MARION. Ocala, 32670. 904-629-9633

MARTIN. Stuart, 33494. 305-283-6760

MONROE. Key West, 33040. 305-294-4641

NASSAU. Fernandina Beach, 32034.
904-261-3811

OKALOOSA. Crestview, 32536.
904-682-2711

OKEECHOBEE. Okeechobee, 33427.
813-763-4115

ORANGE. Orlando, 32801. 305-420-3122

OSCEOLA. Kissimmee, 32741.
305-420-3122

PALM BEACH. West Palm Beach, 33401.
305-837-2033

PASCO. Dade City, 33525. 813-849-8581

PINELLAS. Clearwater, 33516.
813-446-7161

POLK. Bartow, 33830. 813-533-1161

PUTNAM. Palatka, 32077. 904-328-5181

ST JOHNS. St Augustine, 32084.
904-824-8131

ST LUCIE. Fort Pierce, 33450. 305-461-7752

SANTA ROSA. Milton, 32570.
904-623-3639

SARASOTA. Sarasota, 33577. **813-958-9711**

SEMINOLE. Sanford, 32771. **305-323-4330**

SUMTER. Bushnell, 33513. **904-793-2848**

SUWANNEE. Live Oak, 32060.
904-362-2827

TAYLOR. Perry, 32347. **904-584-3531**

UNION. Lake Butler, 32054. **904-496-3711**

VOLUSIA. De Land, 32720. **904-736-2700**

WAKULLA. Crawfordville, 32327.
904-926-3341

WALTON. De Funiak Springs, 32433.
904-892-3137

WASHINGTON. Chipley, 32428.
904-638-4399

Georgia

APPLING. Baxley, 31513. **912-367-7761**

ATKINSON. Pearson, 31642. **912-422-3343**

BACON. Alma, 31510. **912-632-5214**

BAKER. Newton, 31770. **912-734-5391**

BALDWIN. Milledgeville, 31061.
912-452-1025

BANKS. Homer, 30547. **404-677-2231**

BARROW. Winder, 30680. **404-867-9721**

BARTOW. Cartersville, 30120. **404-382-4766**

BEN HILL. Fitzgerald, 31750. **912-423-2455**

BERRIEN. Nashville, 31639. **912-686-5421**

BIBB. Macon, 31201. **912-785-6891**

BLECKLEY. Cochran, 31014. **912-934-2731**

BRANTLEY. Nahunta, 31553. **912-462-5256**

BROOKS. Quitman, 31643. **912-263-5561**

BRYAN. Pembroke, 31321. **912-653-4912**

BULLOCH. Statesboro, 30458.
912-764-6245

BURKE. Waynesboro, 30830. **404-554-2326**

BUTTS. Jackson, 30233. **404-775-7277**

CALHOUN. Morgan, 31766. **912-849-2715**

CAMDEN. Woodbine, 31569. **912-576-5623**

CANDLER. Metter, 30439. **912-685-2835**

CARROLL. Carrollton, 30117. **404-832-3541**

CATOOSA. Ringgold, 30736. **404-935-2500**

CHARLTON. Folkston, 31537.
912-496-2289

CHATHAM. Savannah, 31401. **912-233-2257**

CHATTAHOOCHEE. Cusseta, 31805.
404-959-3603

CHATTOOGA. Summerville, 30747.
404-857-2594

CHEROKEE. Canton, 30114. **404-479-2461**

CLARKE. Athens, 30601. **404-546-7305**

CLAY. Fort Gaines, 31751. **912-768-2631**

CLAYTON. Jonesboro, 30236. **404-478-9911**

CLINCH. Homerville, 31634. **912-487-2667**

COBB. Marietta, 30060. **404-422-2320**

COFFEE. Douglas, 31533. **912-384-4799**

COLQUITT. Moultrie, 31768. **912-985-6859**

COLUMBIA. Appling, 30802. **404-541-1050**

COOK. Adel, 31620. **912-896-7717**

COWETA. Newnan, 30263. **404-253-2668**

CRAWFORD. Knoxville, 31050.
912-836-3328

CRISP. Cordele, 31015. **912-273-2672**

DADE. Trenton, 30752. **404-657-4625**

DAWSON. Dawsonville, 30534.
404-265-3164

DE KALB. Decatur, 30030. **404-371-2881**

DECATUR. Bainbridge, 31717.
912-246-5703

DODGE. Eastman, 31023. **912-374-4361**

DOOLY. Vienna, 31092. **912-268-4228**

DOUGHERTY. Albany, 31702.
912-436-0514

DOUGLAS. Douglasville, 30134.
404-942-2250

EARLY. Blakely, 31723. **912-723-3033**

ECHOLS. Statenville, 31648. **912-559-5253**

EFFINGHAM. Springfield, 31329.
912-754-3310

ELBERT. Elberton, 30635. **404-283-4702**

EMANUEL. Swainsboro, 30401.
912-237-3881

EVANS. Claxton, 30417. **912-739-3868**

FANNIN. Blue Ridge, 30513. **404-632-2203**

FAYETTE. Fayetteville, 30214.
404-461-6041

FLOYD. Rome, 30161. **404-234-0251**

FORSYTH. Cumming, 30130. **404-887-5923**

FRANKLIN. Carnesville, 30521.
404-384-2483

FULTON. Atlanta, 30303. **404-572-2000**

GILMER. Ellijay, 30540. **404-635-4362**

GLASCOCK. Gibson, 30810. **404-598-2671**

GLYNN. Brunswick, 31520. **912-265-0600**

GORDON. Calhoun, 30701. **404-629-3795**

GRADY. Cairo, 31728. **912-377-2912**

GREENE. Greensboro, 30642. **404-453-7716**

GWINNETT. Lawrenceville, 30245.
404-963-0271

HABERSHAM. Clarkesville, 30523.
404-754-2924

HALL. Gainesville, 30501. **404-536-6681**

HANCOCK. Sparta, 31087. **404-444-6644**

HARALSON. Buchanan, 30113.
404-646-5528

HARRIS. Hamilton, 31811. **404-628-5038**

HART. Hartwell, 30643. **404-376-2531**

HEARD. Franklin, 30217. **404-453-7716**

HENRY. McDonough, 30253. **404-957-9131**

HOUSTON. Warner Robins, 31093. 912-922-7764

IRWIN. Ocilla, 31774. 912-468-5356

JACKSON. Jefferson, 30549. 404-367-8317

JASPER. Monticello, 31064. 404-468-6645

JEFF DAVIS. Hazlehurst, 31539. 912-375-5882

JEFFERSON. Louisville, 30434. 404-625-3332

JENKINS. Millen, 30442. 912-982-2563

JOHNSON. Wrightsville, 31096. 912-864-3484

JONES. Gray, 31032. 912-986-6671

LAMAR. Barnesville, 30204. 404-358-3624

LANIER. Lakeland, 31635. 912-482-3594

LAURENS. Dublin, 31021. 912-272-4755

LEE. Leesburg, 31763. 912-759-6875

LIBERTY. Hinesville, 31313. 912-876-2164

LINCOLN. Lincolnton, 30817. 404-359-4444

LONG. Ludowici, 31316. 912-545-2143

LOWNDES. Valdosta, 31601. 912-242-7053

LUMPKIN. Dahlonega, 30533. 404-864-3742

MCDUFFIE. Thomson, 30824. 404-595-3982

MCINTOSH. Darien, 31305. 912-437-4567

MACON. Oglethorpe, 31068. 912-472-7021

MADISON. Danielsville, 30633. 404-795-2125

MARION. Buena Vista, 31803. 912-649-3841

MERIWETHER. Greenville, 30222. 404-672-4416

MILLER. Colquitt, 31737. 912-758-2731

MITCHELL. Camilla, 31730. 912-336-5102

MONROE. Forsyth, 31029. 912-994-2035

MONTGOMERY. Mount Vernon, 30445. 912-583-4401

MORGAN. Madison, 30650. 404-342-3605

MURRAY. Chatsworth, 30705. 404-695-2413

MUSCOGEE. Columbus, 31902. 404-324-7711

NEWTON. Covington, 30209. 404-786-2686

OCONEE. Watkinsville, 30677. 404-769-5120

OGLETHORPE. Lexington, 30648. 404-743-8247

PAULDING. Dallas, 30132. 404-445-2571

PEACH. Fort Valley, 31030. 912-825-2535

PICKENS. Jasper, 30143. 404-692-2121

PIERCE. Blackshear, 31516. 912-449-6648

PIKE. Zebulon, 30295. 404-567-3406

POLK. Cedartown, 30125. 404-748-1305

PULASKI. Hawkinsville, 31036. 912-783-4154

PUTNAM. Eatonton, 31024. 404-485-4501

QUITMAN. Georgetown, 31754. 912-334-3697

RABUN. Clayton, 30525. 404-782-5271

RANDOLPH. Cuthbert, 31740. 912-732-2671

RICHMOND. Augusta, 30902. 404-724-1831

ROCKDALE. Conyers, 30207. 404-483-8701

SCHLEY. Ellaville, 31806. 912-937-2609

SCREVEN. Sylvania, 30467. 912-564-7535

SEMINOLE. Donalsonville, 31745. 912-524-2878

SPALDING. Griffin, 30223. 404-227-2819

STEPHENS. Toccoa, 30577. 404-886-9491

STEWART. Lumpkin, 31815. 912-838-4394

SUMTER. Americus, 31709. 912-924-3090

TALBOT. Talbotton, 31827. 404-665-3239

TALIAFERRO. Crawfordville, 30631. 404-456-2229

TATTNALL. Reidsville, 30453. 912-557-4335

TAYLOR. Butler, 31006. 912-862-3336

TELFAIR. McRae, 31055. 912-868-6653

TERRELL. Dawson, 31742. 912-995-4476

THOMAS. Thomasville, 31712. 912-226-0516

TIFT. Tifton, 31794. 912-382-5350

TOOMBS. Lyons, 30436. 912-526-3311

TOWNS. Hiawassee, 30546. 404-896-3633

TREUTLEN. Soperton, 30457. 912-529-3664

TROUP. La Grange, 30240. 404-882-1478

TURNER. Ashburn, 31714. 912-567-2041

TWIGGS. Jeffersonville, 31044. 912-945-3629

UNION. Blairsville, 30512. 404-745-2654

UPSON. Thomaston, 30286. 404-647-7012

WALKER. La Fayette, 30728. 404-638-1437

WALTON. Monroe, 30655. 404-267-7531

WARE. Waycross, 31501. 912-283-7265

WARREN. Warrenton, 30828. 404-465-2171

WASHINGTON. Sandersville, 31082. 912-552-2325

WAYNE. Jesup, 31545. 912-427-3789

WEBSTER. Preston, 31824. 912-828-5775

WHEELER. Alamo, 30411. 912-568-3071

WHITE. Cleveland, 30528. 404-865-2235

WHITFIELD. Dalton, 30720. 404-278-8717

WILKINSON. Irwinton, 31042. 912-946-2221

WILCOX. Abbeville, 31001. 912-467-2442

WILKES. Washington, 30673. 404-678-2511

WORTH. Sylvester, 31791. 912-776-3456

Hawaii

HAWAII. Hilo, 96720. 808-961-8222

HONOLULU. Honolulu, 96813. **808-523-4111**

KAUAI. Lihue, 96766. **808-245-4785**

MAUI. Wailuku, 96793. **808-244-7825**

Idaho

ADA. Boise, 83702. **208-343-4605**

ADAMS. Council, 83612. **208-253-4561**

BANNOCK. Pocatello, 83201. **208-232-8231**

BEAR LAKE. Paris, 83261. **208-945-2212**

BENEWAH. St Maries, 83861. **208-245-3212**

BINGHAM. Blackfoot, 83221. **208-785-1670**

BLAINE. Hailey, 83333. **208-788-4280**

BOISE. Idaho City, 83631. **208-392-4411**

BONNER. Sandpoint, 83864. **208-263-6841**

BONNEVILLE. Idaho Falls, 83401. **208-523-1163**

BOUNDARY. Bonners Ferry, 83805. **208-267-2242**

BUTTE. Arco, 83231. **208-527-3021**

CAMAS. Fairfield. **208-764-2242**

CANYON. Caldwell, 83605. **208-454-0442**

CARIBOU. Soda Springs, 83276. **208-547-4324**

CASSIA. Burley, 83318. **208-678-5240**

CLARK. Dubois, 83423. **208-374-5454**

CLEARWATER. Orofino, 83544. **208-476-5596**

CUSTER. Challis, 83226. **208-879-2360**

ELMORE. Mountain Home, 83647. **208-587-3385**

FRANKLIN. Preston, 83236. **208-852-1090**

FREMONT. St Anthony, 83445. **208-624-3148**

GEM. Emmett, 83617. **208-365-4561**

GOODING. Gooding, 83330. **208-934-4841**

IDAHO. Grangeville, 83530. **208-983-2390**

JEFFERSON. Rigby, 83442. **208-745-7756**

JEROME. Jerome, 83338. **208-324-8811**

KOOTENAI. Coeur d'Alene, 83814. **208-664-8291**

LATAH. Moscow, 83843. **208-882-8580**

LEMHI. Salmon, 83467. **208-756-2815**

LEWIS. Nezperce, 83543. **208-937-2661**

LINCOLN. Shoshone, 83352. **208-886-7641**

MADISON. Rexburg, 83440. **208-356-3662**

MINIDOKA. Rupert, 83350. **208-436-9331**

NEZ PERCE. Lewiston, 83501. **208-746-1331**

ONEIDA. Malad City, 83252. **208-766-4116**

OWYHEE. Murphy, 83650. **208-495-2421**

PAYETTE. Payette, 83661. **208-642-4641**

POWER. American Falls, 83211. **208-226-2522**

SHOSHONE. Wallace, 83873. **208-752-1264**

TETON. Driggs, 83422. **208-354-2482**

TWIN FALLS. Twin Falls, 83301. **208-734-3300**

VALLEY. Cascade, 83611. **208-382-4297**

WASHINGTON. Weiser, 83672. **208-549-2092**

Illinois

ADAMS. Quincy, 62301. **217-223-6300**

ALEXANDER. Cairo, 62914. **618-734-0111**

BOND. Greenville, 62246. **618-664-1966**

BOONE. Belvidere, 61008. **815-544-3103**

BROWN. Mount Sterling, 62353. **217-773-3421**

BUREAU. Princeton, 61356. **815-875-2014**

CALHOUN. Hardin, 62047. **618-576-2351**

CARROLL. Mount Carroll, 61053. **815-244-3822**

CASS. Virginia, 62691. **217-452-7217**

CHAMPAIGN. Urbana, 61801. **217-384-3720**

CHRISTIAN. Taylorville, 62568. **217-824-4969**

CLARK. Marshall, 62441. **217-826-8311**

CLAY. Louisville, 62858. **618-665-3626**

CLINTON. Carlyle, 62231. **608-594-2464**

COLES. Charleston, 61920. **217-345-5612**

COOK. Chicago, 60602. **312-443-5500**

CRAWFORD. Robinson, 62454. **618-546-1212**

CUMBERLAND. Toledo, 62468. **217-899-2631**

DE KALB. Sycamore, 60178. **815-395-9161**

DE WITT. Clinton, 61727. **217-935-2119**

DOUGLAS. Tuscola, 61953. **217-253-2411**

DU PAGE. Wheaton, 60187. **312-682-7100**

EDGAR. Paris, 61944. **217-265-4151**

EDWARDS. Albion, 62806. **618-445-2115**

EFFINGHAM. Effingham, 62401. **217-342-6535**

FAYETTE. Vandalia, 62471. **618-283-0394**

FORD. Paxton, 60957. **217-379-2721**

FRANKLIN. Benton, 62812. **618-439-3751**

FULTON. Lewistown, 61542. **309-647-0351**

GALLATIN. Shawneetown, 62984. **618-269-3025**

GREENE. Carrollton, 62016. **217-942-3141**

GRUNDY. Morris, 60450. **815-942-0335**

HAMILTON. McLeansboro, 62859. **618-643-2721**

HANCOCK. Carthage, 62321. **217-357-2115**

HARDIN. Elizabethtown, 62931. **618-287-2251**

HENDERSON. Oquawka, 61469. **309-867-2911**

HENRY. Cambridge, 61238. **309-937-2011**

IROQUOIS. Watseka, 60970. **815-432-4911**

JACKSON. Murphysboro, 62966.
618-684-2151

JASPER. Newton, 62448. **618-783-3124**

JEFFERSON. Mount Vernon, 62864.
618-242-5400

JERSEY. Jerseyville, 62052. **618-498-4052**

JO DAVIESS. Galena, 61036. **815-777-0161**

JOHNSON. Vienna, 62995. **618-658-4391**

KANE. Geneva, 60134. **312-232-2400**

KANKAKEE. Kankakee, 60901.
815-939-4401

KENDALL. Yorkville, 60560. **312-553-7573**

KNOX. Galesburg, 61401. **309-343-3121**

LA SALLE. Ottawa, 61350. **815-433-0043**

LAKE. Waukegan, 60085. **312-689-6336**

LAWRENCE. Lawrenceville, 62439.
618-943-2346

LEE. Dixon, 61021. **815-288-3309**

LIVINGSTON. Pontiac, 61764.
815-844-5166

LOGAN. Lincoln, 62656. **217-732-4148**

MCDONOUGH. Macomb, 61455.
309-833-2474

MCHENRY. Woodstock, 60098.
815-338-2040

MCLEAN. Bloomington, 61701.
309-828-4521

MACON. Decatur, 62525. **217-429-4548**

MACOUPIN. Carlinville, 62626.
217-854-3214

MADISON. Edwardsville, 62025.
618-692-4400

MARION. Salem, 62881. **618-548-3400**

MARSHALL. Lacon, 61540. **309-246-6325**

MASON. Havana, 62644. **309-543-6661**

MASSAC. Metropolis, 62960. **618-524-5213**

MENAI D. Petersburg, 62675. **217-632-2415**

MERCER. Aledo, 61231. **309-582-7021**

MONROE. Waterloo, 62298. **618-939-8681**

MONTGOMERY. Hillsboro, 62049.
217-532-2552

MORGAN. Jacksonville, 62650.
217-245-5304

MOULTRIE. Sullivan, 61951. **217-728-4389**

OGLE. Oregon, 61061. **815-732-2211**

PEORIA. Peoria, 61602. **309-672-6000**

PERRY. Pinckneyville, 62274. **618-357-5116**

PIATT. Monticello, 61856. **217-762-4661**

PIKE. Pittsfield, 62363. **217-285-6812**

POPE. Golconda, 62938. **618-683-4466**

PULASKI. Mound City, 62963.
618-748-9360

PUTNAM. Hennepin, 61327. **815-925-7129**

RANDOLPH. Chester, 62233. **618-826-2510**

RICHLAND. Olney, 62450. **618-392-3111**

ROCK ISLAND. Rock Island, 61201.
309-786-4451

ST CLAIR. Belleville, 62222. **618-234-8205**

SALINE. Harrisburg, 62946. **618-252-6905**

SANGAMON. Springfield, 62706.
217-528-4351

SCHUYLER. Rushville, 62681.
217-322-4734

SCOTT. Winchester, 62694. **217-742-3178**

SHELBY. Shelbyville, 62565. **217-774-4421**

STARK. Toulon, 61483. **309-286-5911**

STEPHENSON. Freeport, 61032.
815-233-7189

TAZEWELL. Pekin, 61554. **309-347-6551**

UNION. Jonesboro, 62952. **618-833-5711**

VERMILLION. Danville, 61832.
217-442-3700

WABASH. Mount Carmel, 62863.
618-262-4561

WARREN. Moumouth, 61462. **309-734-2666**

WASHINGTON. Nashville, 62263.
618-327-8314

WAYNE. Fairfield, 62837. **618-842-5182**

WHITE. Carmi, 62821. **618-382-7211**

WHITESIDE. Morrison, 61270.
815-772-7201

WILL. Joliet, 60434. **815-729-8400**

WILLIAMSON. Marion, 62959.
618-997-1301

WINNEBAGO. Rockford, 61104.
815-987-3000

WOODFORD. Eureka, 61530. **309-467-2822**

Indiana

ADAMS. Decatur, 46733. **219-724-4303**

ALLEN. Fort Wayne, 46802. **219-423-7311**

BARTHOLOMEW. Columbus, 47201.
812-372-8818

BENTON. Fowler, 47944. **317-884-0760**

BLACKFORD. Hartford City, 47348.
317-348-1620

BOONE. Lebanon, 46052. **317-482-2940**

BROWN. Nashville, 47448. **317-988-2788**

CARROLL. Delphi, 46923. **317-546-4485**

CASS. Logansport, 46947. **219-753-2916**

CLARK. Jeffersonville, 47130. **812-283-4451**

CLAY. Brazil, 47834. **812-448-8727**

CLINTON. Frankfort, 46041. **317-654-8529**

CRAWFORD. English, 47118. **812-338-2565**

DAVIESS. Washington, 47501.
812-254-2713

DE KALB. Auburn, 46706. **219-925-0912**

DEARBORN. Lawrenceburg, 47025.
812-537-1040

DECATUR. Greensburg, 47240.
812-662-5705

DELAWARE. Muncie, 47302. **317-288-9929**

DUBOIS. Jasper, 47546. **812-482-6545**

ELKHART. Goshen, 46526. **219-533-3610**

FAYETTE. Connersville, 47331.
317-825-1813

FLOYD. New Albany, 47150. **812-944-3665**

FOUNTAIN. Covington, 47932.
317-793-2192

FRANKLIN. Brookville, 47012.
317-647-4631

FULTON. Rochester, 46975. **219-223-2911**

GIBSON. Princeton, 47670. **812-385-5529**

GRANT. Marion, 46952. **317-668-8121**

GREENE. Bloomfield, 47424. **812-384-8532**

HAMILTON. Noblesville, 46060.
317-773-6110

HANCOCK. Greenfield, 46140.
317-462-4141

HARRISON. Corydon, 47112. **812-738-2935**

HENDRICKS. Danville, 46122.
317-745-2794

HENRY. New Castle, 47362. **317-529-2800**

HOWARD. Kokomo, 46901. **317-452-5441**

HUNTINGTON. Huntington, 46750.
219-356-7618

JACKSON. Brownstown, 47220.
812-358-4242

JASPER. Rensselaer, 47978. **219-866-7421**

JAY. Portland, 47371. **317-726-7575**

JEFFERSON. Madison, 47250.
812-265-5245

JENNINGS. Vernon, 47282. **812-346-2131**

JOHNSON. Franklin, 46131. **317-736-5031**

KNOX. Vincennes, 47591. **812-882-4127**

KOSCIUSKO. Warsaw, 46580.
219-267-5071

LA PORTE. La Porte, 46350. **219-362-7061**

LAGRANGE. Lagrange, 46761.
219-463-3442

LAKE. Crown Point, 46307. **219-663-0760**

LAWRENCE. Bedford, 47421. **812-275-7543**

MADISON. Anderson, 46011. **317-646-9212**

MARION. Indianapolis, 46204.
317-633-3200

MARSHALL. Plymouth, 46563.
219-936-3359

MARTIN. Shoals, 47581. **812-247-3651**

MIAMI. Peru, 46970. **317-472-3994**

MONROE. Bloomington, 47401.
812-336-3424

MONTGOMERY. Crawfordsville, 47933.
317-362-6302

MORGAN. Martinsville, 46151.
317-342-7124

NEWTON. Kentland, 47951. **219-474-5812**

NOBLE. Albion, 46701. **219-636-4670**

OHIO. Rising Sun, 47040. **812-438-2062**

ORANGE. Paoli, 47450. **812-723-2649**

OWEN. Spencer, 47460. **812-829-2325**

PARKE. Rockville, 47872. **812-569-5132**

PERRY. Cannelton, 47520. **812-547-3741**

PIKE. Petersburg, 47567. **812-354-8448**

PORTER. Valparaiso, 46383. **219-462-3841**

POSEY. Mount Vernon, 47620.
812-838-3266

PULASKI. Winamac, 46996. **219-946-3653**

PUTNAM. Greencastle, 46135.
317-653-4019

RANDOLPH. Winchester, 47394.
317-584-7261

RIPLEY. Versailles, 47042. **812-689-6115**

RUSH. Rushville, 46173. **317-932-2086**

ST JOSEPH. South Bend, 46601.
219-284-9011

SCOTT. Scottsburg, 47170. **812-752-4745**

SHELBY. Shelbyville, 46176. **317-398-7448**

SPENCER. Rockport, 47635. **812-649-4376**

STARKE. Knox, 46534. **219-772-3821**

STEUBEN. Angola, 46703. **219-665-3014**

SULLIVAN. Sullivan, 47882. **812-268-4491**

SWITZERLAND. Vevay, 47043.
812-437-3175

TIPPECANOE. Lafayette, 47902.
317-742-1126

TIPTON. Tipton, 46072. **317-675-2795**

UNION. Liberty, 47353. **317-458-5464**

VANDERBURG. Evansville, 47708.
812-426-5160

VERMILLION. Newport, 47966.
317-492-3570

VIGO. Terre Haute, 47808. **812-234-2671**

WABASH. Wabash, 46992. **219-563-5217**

WARREN. Williamsport, 47993.
317-762-3275

WARRICK. Boonville, 47601. **812-897-3590**

WASHINGTON. Salem, 47167.
812-883-5748

WAYNE. Richmond, 47374. **317-966-7541**

WELLS. Bluffton, 46714. **219-824-2320**

WHITE. Monticello, 47960. **219-583-7032**

WHITLEY. Columbia City, 46725.
219-248-8212

Iowa

ADAIR. Greenfield, 51022. **515-743-2546**

ADAMS. Corning, 50841. **515-322-3340**

ALLAMAKEE. Waukon, 52172.
319-568-3522

APPANOOSE. Centerville, 52544.
515-856-6101

AUDUBON. Audubon, 50025. **712-563-2584**

BENTON. Vinton, 52349. **319-472-2365**

BLACK HAWK. Waterloo, 50705. **319-291-2500**

BOONE. Boone, 50036. **515-432-1122**

BREMER. Waverly, 50677. **319-352-1565**

BUCHANAN. Independence, 50644. **319-334-2196**

BUENA VISTA. Storm Lake, 50588. **712-732-5123**

BUTLER. Allison, 50602. **319-267-2487**

CALHOUN. Rockwell City, 50579. **712-297-7741**

CARROLL. Carroll, 51401. **712-792-9802**

CASS. Atlantic, 50022. **712-243-2105**

CEDAR. Tipton, 52772. **319-886-6346**

CERRO GORDO. Mason City, 50401. **515-423-0013**

CHEROKEE. Cherokee, 51012. **712-225-4890**

CHICKASAW. New Hampton, 50659. **515-394-2100**

CLARKE. Osceola, 50213. **515-342-2213**

CLAY. Spencer, 51301. **712-262-1569**

CLAYTON. Elkader, 52043. **319-245-1106**

CLINTON. Clinton, 52732. **319-242-5307**

CRAWFORD. Denison, 51442. **712-263-3045**

DALLAS. Adel, 50003. **515-468-2713**

DAVIS. Bloomfield, 52537. **515-664-2344**

DECATUR. Leon, 50144. **515-446-4382**

DELAWARE. Manchester, 52057. **319-927-4701**

DES MOINES. Burlington, 52601. **319-752-6318**

DICKINSON. Spirit Lake, 51360. **712-336-3356**

DUBUQUE. Dubuque, 52001. **319-583-3511**

EMMET. Estherville, 51334. **712-362-4261**

FAYETTE. West Union, 52175. **319-422-3146**

FLOYD. Charles City, 50616. **515-228-5165**

FRANKLIN. Hampton, 50441. **515-456-3324**

FREMONT. Sidney, 51652. **712-374-2232**

GREENE. Jefferson, 50129. **515-386-2316**

GRUNDY. Grundy Center, 50638. **319-824-3122**

GUTHRIE. Guthrie Center, 50115. **515-747-3415**

HAMILTON. Webster City, 52355. **515-832-1771**

HANCOCK. Garner, 50438. **515-923-3163**

HARDIN. Eldora, 50627. **515-858-3461**

HARRISON. Logan, 51546. **712-644-2401**

HENRY. Mount Pleasant, 52641. **319-385-2552**

HOWARD. Cresco, 52136. **319-547-2880**

HUMBOLDT. Dakota City, 50529. **515-332-1571**

IDA. Ida Grove, 51445. **712-364-2626**

IOWA. Marengo, 52301. **319-642-3041**

JACKSON. Maquoketa, 52158. **319-652-3181**

JASPER. Newton, 50208. **515-792-7016**

JEFFERSON. Fairfield, 52556. **515-472-3454**

JOHNSON. Iowa City, 52240. **319-338-2321**

JONES. Anamosa, 52205. **319-462-4341**

KEOKUK. Sigourney, 52591. **515-622-2210**

KOSSUTH. Algona, 50511. **515-295-2718**

LEE. Fort Madison, 52627. **319-372-6557**

LINN. Cedar Rapids, 52401. **319-398-3421**

LOUISA. Wapello, 52653. **319-523-3771**

LUCAS. Chariton, 50049. **515-774-2018**

LYON. Rock Rapids, 51246. **712-472-2701**

MADISON. Winterset, 50273. **515-462-3914**

MAHASKA. Oskaloosa, 52577. **515-673-7148**

MARION. Knoxville, 50138. **515-842-3815**

MARSHALL. Marshalltown, 50158. **515-752-4285**

MILLS. Glenwood, 51534. **712-427-4880**

MITCHELL. Osage, 50461. **515-732-3104**

MONONA. Onawa, 51040. **712-423-2191**

MONROE. Albia, 52531. **515-932-5212**

MONTGOMERY. Red Oak, 51566. **712-623-5127**

MUSCATINE. Muscatine, 52761. **319-263-5821**

O'BRIEN. Primghar, 51245. **712-757-3045**

OSCEOLA. Sibley, 51249. **712-754-2117**

PAGE. Clarinda, 51632. **712-542-3219**

PALO ALTO. Emmetsburg, 50536. **712-852-2924**

PLYMOUTH. Le Mars, 51031. **712-852-6100**

POCAHONTAS. Pocahontas, 50574. **712-335-4127**

POLK. Des Moines, 50307. **515-284-6074**

POTTAWATTAMIE. Council Bluffs, 51501. **712-328-5700**

POWESHIEK. Montezuma, 50171. **515-623-5723**

RINGGOLD. Mount Ayr, 50854. **515-464-3231**

SAC. Sac City, 50583. **712-662-7789**

SCOTT. Davenport, 52801. **319-326-8611**

SHELBY. Harlan, 51537. **712-755-5543**

SIOUX. Orange City, 51041. **712-737-2216**

STORY. Nevada, 50201. **515-382-6581**

TAMA. Toledo, 52342. **515-484-2740**

TAYLOR. Bedford, 50833. **712-523-2060**

UNION. Creston, 50801. **515-782-7315**

VAN BUREN. Keosauqua, 52565.
319-293-3240

WAPELLO. Ottumwa, 52501. **515-684-4671**

WARREN. Indianola, 50125. **515-961-2860**

WASHINGTON. Washington, 52353.
319-653-3655

WAYNE. Corydon, 50060. **515-872-2242**

WEBSTER. Fort Dodge, 50501.
515-576-2401

WINNEBAGO. Forrest City, 50436.
515-582-3412

WINNESHIEK. Decorah, 52101.
319-382-5085

WOODBURY. Sioux City, 51101.
712-279-6100

WORTH. Northwood, 50459. **515-324-2316**

WRIGHT. Clarion, 50525. **515-532-2771**

Kansas

ALLEN. Iola, 66749. **316-365-2118**

ANDERSON. Garnett, 66032. **913-448-5924**

ATCHISON. Atchison, 66002. **913-367-1653**

BARBER. Medicine Lodge, 67104.
316-886-4212

BARTON. Great Bend, 67530. **316-792-4721**

BOURBON. Fort Scott, 66701.
316-223-1870

BROWN. Hiawatha, 66434. **913-742-2581**

BUTLER. El Dorado, 67042. **316-321-1960**

CHASE. Cottonwood Falls, 66845.
316-273-6423

CHAUTAUQUA. Sedan, 67361.
316-725-3370

CHEROKEE. Columbus, 66725.
316-429-2042

CHEYENNE. St Francis, 67756.
913-332-2351

CLARK. Ashland, 67831. **316-635-2813**

CLAY. Clay Center, 67432. **913-632-2552**

CLOUD. Concordia, 66901. **913-243-4319**

COFFEY. Burlington, 66839. **316-364-2191**

COMANCHE. Coldwater, 67029.
316-582-2361

COWLEY. Winfield, 67156. **316-221-4066**

CRAWFORD. Girard, 66743. **316-724-8217**

DECATUR. Oberlin, 67749. **913-475-2132**

DICKINSON. Abilene, 67410. **913-263-3774**

DONIPHAN. Troy, 66087. **913-985-3513**

DOUGLAS. Lawrence, 66044. **913-843-2494**

EDWARDS. Kinsley, 67547. **316-659-3121**

ELK. Howard, 67349. **316-374-2490**

ELLIS. Hays, 67601. **913-625-6558**

ELLSWORTH. Ellsworth, 67439.
913-472-4161

FINNEY. Garden City, 67846. **316-276-3051**

FORD. Dodge City, 67801. **316-227-3184**

FRANKLIN. Ottawa, 66067. **913-242-1471**

GEARY. Junction City, 66441. **913-238-3912**

GOVE. Gove, 67736. **913-938-2161**

GRAHAM. Hill City, 67642. **913-674-5433**

GRANT. Ulysses, 67880. **316-356-1335**

GRAY. Cimarron, 67835. **316-855-3618**

GREELEY. Tribune, 67879. **316-376-4256**

GREENWOOD. Eureka, 67045.
316-583-7421

HAMILTON. Syracuse, 67878. **316-384-5629**

HARPER. Anthony, 67003. **316-842-5555**

HARVEY. Newton, 67114. **316-283-7232**

HASKELL. Sublette, 67877. **316-668-2231**

HODGEMAN. Jetmore, 67854.
316-357-6421

JACKSON. Hotton, 66436. **913-364-2891**

JEFFERSON. Oskaloosa, 66066.
913-863-2272

JEWELL. Mankato, 66956. **913-378-3121**

JOHNSON. Olathe, 66061. **913-782-5000**

KEARNY. Lakin, 67860. **316-355-6435**

KINGMAN. Kingman, 67068. **316-532-2521**

KIOWA. Greensburg, 67054. **316-723-3021**

LABETTE. Oswego, 67356. **316-795-2138**

LANE. Dighton, 67839. **316-397-5356**

LEAVENWORTH. Leavenworth, 66048.
913-682-2271

LINCOLN. Lincoln, 67455. **913-524-4757**

LINN. Mound City, 66056. **913-795-2668**

LOGAN. Oakley, 67748. **913-672-4244**

LYON. Emporia, 66801. **316-342-3832**

MCPHERSON. McPherson, 67460.
316-241-3656

MARION. Marion, 66861. **316-382-2185**

MARSHALL. Marysville, 66508.
913-562-3721

MEADE. Meade, 67864. **316-873-2581**

MIAMI. Paola, 66071. **913-294-3976**

MITCHELL. Beloit, 67420. **913-738-3652**

MONTGOMERY. Independence, 67301.
316-331-2710

MORRIS. Council Grove, 66846.
316-767-5518

MORTON. Elkhart, 67950. **316-697-2559**

NEMAHA. Seneea, 66538. **913-336-2170**

NEOSHO. Erie, 66733. **316-244-3473**

NESS. Ness City, 67560. **913-798-2401**

NORTON. Norton, 67654. **913-927-2363**

OSAGE. Lyndon, 66451. **913-828-4812**

OSBORNE. Osborne, 67473. **913-346-2431**

OTTAWA. Minneapolis, 67467.
913-392-2279

PAWNEE. Larned, 67550. **316-672-5181**

PHILLIPS. Phillipsburg, 67661.
913-543-5513

POTTAWATOMIE. Westmoreland, 66549.
913-457-3314

PRATT. Pratt, 67124. **316-672-5181**

RAWLINS. Atwood, 67730. **913-626-3351**

RENO. Hutchinson, 67501. **316-662-4411**

REPUBLIC. Belleville, 66935. **913-527-2021**

RICE. Lyons, 67554. **316-257-2232**

RILEY. Manhattan, 66502. **913-776-8831**

ROOKS. Stockton, 67669. **913-425-6391**

RUSH. La Crosse, 67548. **913-222-2731**

RUSSELL. Russell, 67665. **913-483-4641**

SALINE. Salina, 67401. **913-827-1961**

SCOTT. Scott City, 67871. **316-872-2420**

SEDGWICK. Wichita, 67202. **316-268-7166**

SEWARD. Liberal, 67901. **316-624-1826**

SHAWNEE. Topeka, 66603. **913-357-1241**

SHERIDAN. Hoxie, 67740. **913-675-3361**

SHERMAN. Goodland, 67735.
913-889-6125

SMITH. Smith Center, 66967. **913-282-6533**

STAFFORD. St John, 67576. **316-549-3509**

STANTON. Johnson, 67855. **316-492-2140**

STEVENS. Hugoton, 67951. **316-544-2541**

SUMNER. Wellington, 67152. **316-326-3395**

THOMAS. Colby, 67701. **913-462-2561**

TREGO. Wakeeney, 67672. **913-743-2302**

WABAUNSEE. Alma, 66401. **913-765-3414**

WALLACE. Sharon Springs, 67758.
913-852-4282

Kentucky

ADAIR. Columbia, 42728. **502-384-5215**

ALLEN. Scottsville, 42164. **502-237-3706**

ANDERSON. Lawrenceburg, 40342.
502-839-3041

BALLARD. Wickliffe, 42087. **502-335-3531**

BARREN. Glasgow, 42141. **502-651-3783**

BATH. Owingsville, 40360. **606-674-2613**

BELL. Pineville, 40977. **606-337-6143**

BOONE. Burlington, 41005. **606-586-6101**

BOURBON. Paris, 40361. **606-987-2430**

BOYD. Catlettsburg, 41129. **606-739-4134**

BOYLE. Danville, 40422. **606-236-2306**

BRACKEN. Brooksville, 41004.
606-735-2952

BREATHITT. Jackson, 41339.
606-666-5472

BRECKINRIDGE. Hardinsburg, 40143.
502-756-2269

BULLITT. Shepherdsville, 40165.
502-543-2263

BUTLER. Morgantown, 42261.
502-526-3433

CALDWELL. Princeton, 42445.
502-365-6660

CALLOWAY. Murray, 42071. **502-753-3923**

CAMPBELL. Newport, 41071. **606-292-3854**

CARLISLE. Bardwell, 42023. **502-628-3233**

CARROLL. Carrollton, 41008. **502-732-4426**

CARTER. Grayson, 41143. **606-474-5366**

CASEY. Liberty, 42539. **606-787-6471**

CHRISTIAN. Hopkinsville, 42240.
502-886-6665

CLARK. Winchester, 40391. **606-744-3189**

CLAY. Manchester, 40962. **606-598-2544**

CRITTENDEN. Marion, 42064.
502-965-3403

CUMBERLAND. Burkesville, 42717.
502-864-3444

DAVIESS. Owensboro, 42301. **502-684-7285**

EDMONDSON. Brownsville, 42210.
502-597-2624

ELLIOTT. Sandy Hook, 41171.
606-738-6193

ESTILL. Irving, 40336. **606-723-4512**

FAYETTE. Lexington, 40507. **606-255-5631**

FLEMING. Flemingsburg, 41041.
606-845-8461

FLOYD. Prestonsburg, 41653. **606-886-3055**

FRANKLIN. Frankfort, 40601. **502-227-4502**

FULTON. Hickman, 42050. **502-236-2727**

GALLATIN. Warsaw, 41095. **606-567-5411**

GARRARD. Lancaster, 40444. **606-792-3071**

GRANT. Williamstown, 41097.
606-823-5251

GRAVES. Mayfield, 42066. **502-247-1676**

GRAYSON. Leitchfield, 42754.
502-259-3201

GREEN. Greensburg, 42743. **502-932-4024**

GREENUP. Greenup, 41144. **606-792-3071**

HANCOCK. Hawesville, 42348.
502-927-8137

HARDIN. Elizabethtown, 42701.
502-765-2350

HARLAN. Harlan, 40831. **606-573-2600**

HARRISON. Cynthiana, 41031.
606-234-2232

HART. Munfordville, 42765. **502-524-2751**

HENDERSON. Henderson, 42420.
502-826-3971

HENRY. New Castle, 40050. **502-845-2892**

HICKMAN. Clinton, 42031. **502-653-4369**

HOPKINS. Madisonville, 42431. **502-821-3174**

JACKSON. McKee, 40447. **606-287-7800**

JEFFERSON. Louisville, 40202. **502-581-6161**

JESSAMINE. Nicholas, 40356. **606-885-9464**

JOHNSON. Paintsville, 41240. **606-789-4616**

KENTON. Covington, 41011. **606-292-2320**

KNOX. Barbourville, 40906. **606-546-3568**

LARUE. Hodgenville, 42748. **502-358-3120**

LAUREL. London, 40741. **606-864-4640**

LAWRENCE. Louisa, 41230. **606-638-4102**

LEE. Beattyville, 41311. **606-464-8365**

LESLIE. Hyden, 41749. **606-672-2198**

LETCHER. Whitesburg, 41858. **606-633-2432**

LEWIS. Vanceburg, 41179. **606-796-3062**

LINCOLN. Stanford, 40484. **606-365-2534**

LIVINGSTON. Smithland, 42081. **502-928-2162**

LOGAN. Russellville, 42276. **502-726-6061**

LYON. Eddyville, 40203. **502-388-2331**

MCCRACKEN. Paducah, 42001. **502-442-9137**

MCCREARY. Whitley City, 42653. **606-376-2411**

MCLEAN. Calhoun, 42327. **502-273-3082**

MADISON. Richmond, 40475. **606-623-2760**

MAGOFFIN. Salyersville, 41465. **606-349-2216**

MARION. Lebanon, 40033. **502-692-3451**

MARSHALL. Benton, 42025. **502-527-6631**

MARTIN. Inez, 41224. **606-298-3508**

MASON. Maysville, 41056. **606-564-3631**

MEADE. Bradenburg, 40108. **502-422-3967**

MENIFEE. Frenchburg, 40322. **606-768-6811**

MERCER. Harrodsburg, 40330. **606-734-4481**

METCALFE. Edmonton, 42129. **502-432-4821**

MONROE. Tompkinsville, 42167. **502-487-5505**

MONTGOMERY. Mount Sterling, 40353. **606-498-1992**

MORGAN. West Liberty, 41472. **606-743-3949**

MUHLENBERG. Greenville, 42345. **502-338-2520**

NELSON. Bardstown, 40004. **502-348-5941**

NICHOLAS. Carlisle, 40311. **606-289-5591**

OHIO. Hartford, 42347. **502-298-3673**

OLDHAM. La Grange, 40031. **502-222-9311**

OWEN. Owenton, 40359. **502-484-3405**

OWSLEY. Boonieville, 42731. **606-593-5735**

PENDLETON. Falmouth, 41040. **606-654-4321**

PERRY. Harzard, 41701. **606-436-4513**

PIKE. Pikeville, 41501. **606-432-2553**

POWELL. Stanton, 40380. **606-663-4957**

PULASKI. Somerset, 42501. **606-679-5435**

ROBERTSON. Mount Olivet, 41064. **606-724-5212**

ROCKCASTLE. Mount Vernon, 40456. **606-256-2831**

ROWAN. Morehead, 40351. **606-679-5435**

RUSSELL. Jamestown, 42629. **502-343-4277**

SCOTT. Georgetown, 40324. **502-863-0349**

SHELBY. Shelbyville, 40065. **502-845-2134**

SIMPSON. Franklin, 42134. **502-586-5126**

SPENCER. Taylorsville, 40071. **502-477-8121**

TAYLOR. Campbellsville, 42718. **502-465-6677**

TODD. Elkton, 42220. **502-265-2363**

TRIGG. Cadiz, 42211. **502-522-6618**

TRIMBLE. Bedford, 40006. **502-255-7196**

UNION. Morganfield, 42437. **502-389-1081**

WARREN. Bowling Green, 42101. **502-842-9416**

WASHINGTON. Springfield, 40069. **606-336-3636**

WAYNE. Monticello, 42633. **606-348-2221**

WEBSTER. Dixon, 42409. **502-639-2341**

WHITLEY. Williamsburg, 40769. **606-549-1330**

WOLFE. Campton, 41301. **606-668-3515**

WOODFORD. Versailles, 40383. **606-873-2421**

Louisiana

ACADIA. Crowley, 70526. **318-783-0953**

ALLEN. Oberlin, 70655. **318-639-4351**

ASCENSION. Donaldsonville, 70346. **504-473-9866**

ASSUMPTION. Napoleonville, 70390. **504-369-7435**

AVOYELLES. Marksville, 71351. **318-253-9203**

BEAUREGARD. De Ridder, 70634. **318-463-8595**

BIENVILLE. Arcadia, 71001. **318-263-2326**

BOSSIER. Benton, 71006. **318-965-2329**

CADDO. Shreveport, 71101. **318-222-0711**

CALCASIEU. Lake Charles, 70601. **318-433-3661**

CALDWELL. Columbia, 71418. **318-649-2272**

CAMERON. Cameron, 70631. **318-775-5718**

CATAHOULA. Harrisonburg, 71340.
318-744-5497

CLAIBORNE. Homer, 71040. 318-927-2818

CONCORDIA. Vidalia, 71373. 318-336-5953

DESOTO. Mansfield, 71052. 318-872-3110

EAST BATON ROUGE. Baton Rouge,
70801. 504-389-3100

EAST CARROLL. Lake Providence, 71254.
318-559-2399

EAST FELICIANA. Clinton, 70722.
504-683-5145

EVANGELINE. Ville Platte, 70586.
318-363-5651

FRANKLIN. Winnsboro, 71295.
318-335-9429

GRANT. Colfax, 71417. 318-627-3246

IBERIA. New Iberia, 70560. 318-365-8246

IBERVILLE. Plaquemine, 70764.
504-687-6373

JACKSON. Jonesboro, 71251. 318-259-2361

JEFFERSON. Gretna, 70053. 504-367-6611

JEFFERSON DAVIS. Jennings, 70546.
318-824-1160

LA SALLE. Jena, 71342. 318-992-2101

LAFAYETTE. Lafayette, 70501.
318-233-0150

LAFOURCHE. Thibodaux, 70301.
504-446-8427

LINCOLN. Ruston, 71270. 318-255-3663

LIVINGSTON. Livingston, 70754.
504-686-2216

MADISON. Tallulah, 71282. 318-574-3451

MOREHOUSE. Bastrop, 71220.
318-281-4132

NATCHITOCHES. Natchitoches, 71457.
318-352-2714

ORLEANS. New Orleans, 70112.
504-586-4311

OUACHITA. Monroe, 71201. 318-323-5188

PLAQUEMINES. Pointe a la Hache, 70082.
504-333-4343

PINTE COUPEE. New Roads, 70760.
504-638-9556

RAPIDES. Alexandria, 71301. 318-445-3617

RED RIVER. Coushatta, 71019.
318-932-4302

RICHLAND. Rayville, 71269. 318-728-4171

SABINE. Many, 71449. 318-256-2091

ST BERNARD. Chalmette, 70043.
504-271-3434

ST CHARLES. Hahnville, 70057.
504-581-5309

ST HELENA. Greensburg, 70441.
504-222-4549

ST JAMES. Convent, 70723. 504-562-7229

ST JOHN THE BAPTIST. Laplace.
504-497-3431

ST LANDRY. Opelousas, 70570.
318-948-3688

ST MARTIN. St Martinville, 70582.
318-394-3711

ST MARY. Franklin, 70538. 318-828-4100

ST TAMMANY. Covington, 70433.
504-892-5214

TANGIPAHOA. Amite, 70422.
504-748-9710

TENSAS. St Joseph, 71366. 318-766-3921

TERREBONNE. Houma, 70360.
504-868-3000

UNION. Farmerville, 71241. 318-368-3296

VERMILLION. Abbeville, 70510.
318-893-3641

VERNON. Leesville, 71446. 318-239-2378

WASHINGTON. Franklinton, 70438.
504-839-3420

WEBSTER. Minden, 71055. 318-377-3620

WEST BATON ROUGE. Port Allen, 70767.
504-383-4755

WEST CARROLL. Oak Grove, 71263.
318-428-3281

WEST FELICIANA. St Francisville, 70775.
504-635-3794

WINN. Winnfield, 71483. 318-628-5824

Maine

ANDROSCOGGIN. Auburn, 04210.
207-782-6131

AROOSTOOK. Houlton, 04730.
207-532-2216

CUMBERLAND. Portland, 04111.
207-774-4258

FRANKLIN. Farmington, 04938.
207-778-2116

HANCOCK. Ellsworth, 04605. 207-667-9542

KENNEBEC. Augusta, 04330. 207-622-0971

KNOX. Rockland, 04841. 207-594-9379

LINCOLN. Wiscasset, 04578. 207-882-7517

OXFORD. South Paris, 04281. 207-743-8372

PENOBSCOT. Bangor, 04401. 207-942-6334

PISCATAQUIS. Dover-Foxcroft, 04426.
207-564-2161

SAGADAHOC. Bath, 04530. 207-443-9332

SOMERSET. Skowhegan, 04976.
207-474-9861

WALDO. Belfast, 04915. 207-338-1620

WASHINGTON. Machias, 04654.
207-255-6545

YORK. Alfred, 04002. 207-324-5250

Maryland

ALLEGANY. Cumberland, 21502.
301-724-5710

ANNE ARUNDEL. Annapolis, 21401.
301-224-1311

BALTIMORE. Baltimore, 21202.
301-396-3100

BALTIMORE. Towson, 21204.
301-494-3100

CALVERT. Prince Frederick, 20678.
301-535-1600

CAROLINE. Denton, 21629. **301-479-0660**

CARROLL. Westminster, 21157.
301-848-4500

CECIL. Elkton, 21921. **301-398-4100**

CHARLES. La Plata, 20646. **301-934-8141**

DORCHESTER. Cambridge, 21613.
301-228-1700

FREDERICK. Frederick, 21701.
301-663-8300

GARRETT. Oakland, 21550. **301-334-3917**

HARFORD. Bel Air, 21014. **301-838-6000**

HOWARD. Ellicott City, 21043.
301-465-5000

KENT. Chestertown, 21620. **301-778-4600**

MONTGOMERY. Rockville, 20850.
301-279-1211

PRINCE GEORGES. Upper Marlboro,
20870. **301-627-3000**

QUEEN ANNES. Centreville, 21617.
301-758-0322

ST MARYS. Leonardtown, 20650.
301-475-9121

SOMERSET. Princess Anne, 21853.
301-651-0320

TALBOT. Easton, 21601. **301-822-2401**

WASHINGTON. Hagerstown, 21740.
301-733-8660

WICOMICO. Salisbury, 21801.
301-749-5127

WORCESTER. Snow Hill, 21863.
301-632-1194

Massachusetts

BARNSTABLE. Barnstable, 02630.
617-362-2511

BERKSHIRE. Pittsfield, 01201.
413-448-8424

BRISTOL. Taunton, 02780. **617-824-9681**

DUKES. Edgartown, 02539. **617-627-5535**

ESSEX. Salem, 01970. **617-744-2840**

FRANKLIN. Greenfield, 01301.
413-774-4015

HAMPDEN. Springfield, 01101.
413-732-1161

HAMPSHIRE. Northampton, 01060.
413-584-0557

MIDDLESEX. Concord, 01742.
617-494-4000

NANTUCKET. Nantucket, 02554.
617-228-0691

NORFOLK. Dedham, 02026. **617-326-1600**

PLYMOUTH. Plymouth, 02360.
617-746-4313

SUFFOLK. Boston, 02201. **617-742-9250**

WORCESTER. Worcester, 01601.
617-756-2441

Michigan

ALCONA. Harrisville, 48740. **517-724-6807**

ALGER. Munising, 49862. **906-387-2076**

ALLEGAN. Allegan, 49010. **616-673-8471**

ALPENA. Alpena, 49707. **517-356-0015**

ANTRIM. Bellaire, 49615. **616-533-8542**

ARENAC. Standish, 48658. **517-846-4184**

BARAGA. L'Anse, 49946. **906-524-6183**

BARRY. Hastings, 49058. **616-945-3953**

BAY. Bay City, 48706. **517-892-3528**

BENZIE. Beulah, 49617. **616-882-7232**

BERRIEN. St Joseph, 49085. **616-983-7111**

BRANCH. Coldwater, 49036. **517-279-8411**

CALHOUN. Marshall, 49068. **616-781-9811**

CASS. Cassopolis, 49031. **616-445-8621**

CHARLEVOIX. Charlevoix, 49720.
616-547-9272

CHEBOYGAN. Cheboygan, 49721.
616-627-4233

CHIPPEWA. Sault Ste Marie, 49783.
906-632-6821

CLARE. Harrison, 48625. **517-539-7132**

CLINTON. St Johns, 48879. **517-224-6761**

CRAWFORD. Grayling, 49738.
517-348-3581

DELTA. Escanaba, 49829. **906-786-1763**

DICKINSON. Iron Mountain, 49801.
906-744-0988

EATON. Charlotte, 48813. **517-543-0010**

EMMET. Petroskey, 49770. **616-347-2801**

GENESEE. Flint, 48502. **313-766-8770**

GLADWIN. Gladwin, 48624. **517-426-7351**

GOGEBIC. Bessemer, 49911. **906-667-1451**

GRAND TRAVERSE. Traverse City, 49684.
616-947-0330

GRATIOT. Ithaca, 48847. **517-875-3343**

HILLSDALE. Hillsdale, 49242.
517-437-3391

HOUGHTON. Houghton, 49931.
906-482-1150

HURON. Bad Axe, 48413. **517-269-9942**

INGHAM. Mason, 48854. **517-677-9411**

IONIA. Ionia, 48846. **616-527-0300**

IOSCO. Tawas City, 48763. **517-362-3497**

IRON. Crystal Falls, 49920. **906-875-3221**

ISABELLA. Mount Pleasant, 48858.
517-772-0911

JACKSON. Jackson, 49201. **517-787-3800**

KALAMAZOO. Kalamazoo, 49003.
616-383-8700

KALKASKA. Kalkaska, 49646. **616-258-2332**

KENT. Grand Rapids, 49502. **616-774-3512**

KEWEENAW. Eagle River, 49924.
906-337-2229

LAKE. Baldwin, 49304. **616-745-4641**

LAPEER. Lapeer, 48446. **313-664-3842**

LEELANAU. Leland, 49654. **616-256-9824**

LENAWEE. Adrian, 49221. **517-263-8831**

LIVINGSTON. Howell, 48843. **517-546-0500**

LUCE. Newberry, 49868. **906-293-5521**

MACKNIAC. St Ignace, 49781. **906-643-8640**

MACOMB. Mount Clemens, 48043. **313-465-1211**

MANISTEE. Manistee, 49660. **616-723-3331**

MARQUETTE. Marquette, 49855. **906-228-8500**

MASON. Ludington, 49431. **616-843-8202**

MECOSTA. Big Rapids, 49307. **616-796-5835**

MENOMINEE. Menominee, 49858. **906-863-9968**

MIDLAND. Midland, 48640. **517-835-8881**

MISSAUKEE. Lake City, 49651. **616-839-4967**

MONROE. Monroe, 48161. **313-243-6900**

MONTCALM. Stanton, 48888. **517-831-5272**

MONTMORENCY. Atlanta, 49709. **517-785-4794**

MUSKEGON. Muskegon, 49440. **616-724-6231**

NEWAYGO. White Cloud, 49349. **616-689-2821**

OAKLAND. Pontiac, 48053. **313-858-1000**

OCEANA. Hart, 49420. **616-873-4835**

OGEMAW. West Branch, 48661. **517-345-0215**

ONTONAGON. Ontonagon, 49953. **906-884-4255**

OSCEOLA. Reed City, 49677. **616-832-5818**

OSCODA. Mio, 48647. **517-826-5021**

OTSEGO. Gaylord, 49735. **517-732-4686**

OTTAWA. Grand Haven, 49417. **616-842-0080**

PRESQUE ISLE. Rogers City, 49779. **517-734-3288**

ROSCOMMON. Roscommon, 48653. **517-275-5923**

SAGINAW. Saginaw, 48601. **517-793-9100**

ST CLAIR. Port Huron, 48060. **313-985-9631**

ST JOSEPH. Centreville, 49032. **313-467-6361**

SANILAC. Sandusky, 48471. **313-648-3212**

SCHOOLCRAFT. Manistique, 49854. **906-341-5532**

SHIAWASSEE. Corunna, 48817. **517-743-3421**

TUSCOLA. Caro, 48623. **517-673-3118**

VAN BUREN. Paw Paw, 49079. **616-657-5581**

WASHTENAW. Ann Arbor, 48108. **313-994-2424**

WAYNE. Detroit, 48226. **313-224-0903**

WEXFORD. Cadillac, 49601. **616-775-3621**

Minnesota

AITKIN. Aitkin, 56431. **218-927-2102**

ANOKA. Anoka, 55303. **612-421-4760**

BECKER. Detroit Lake, 56501. **218-847-7659**

BELTRAMI. Bemidji, 56601. **218-751-4616**

BENTON. Foley, 56329. **612-968-7013**

BIG STONE. Ortonville, 56278. **612-839-2105**

BLUE EARTH. Mankato, 56001. **507-387-3013**

BROWN. New Ulm, 56073. **507-354-2215**

CARLTON. Carlton, 55718. **218-384-4281**

CARVER. Chaska, 55318. **612-448-3435**

CASS. Walker, 56484. **218-547-3300**

CHIPPEWA. Montevideo, 56265. **612-269-7447**

CHISAGO. Center City, 55012. **612-257-1300**

CLAY. Moorhead, 56560. **218-233-2781**

CLEARWATER. Bagley, 56621. **218-694-4545**

COOK. Grand Marais, 55604. **218-387-2705**

COTTONWOOD. Windom, 56101. **507-831-1905**

CROW WING. Brainerd, 56401. **218-829-1481**

DAKOTA. Hastings, 55033. **612-437-3191**

DODGE. Mantorville, 55955. **507-635-3541**

DOUGLAS. Alexandria, 56308. **612-763-6053**

FARIBAULT. Blue Earth, 56013. **507-526-5145**

FILLMORE. Preston, 55965. **507-765-4701**

FREEBORN. Albert Lea, 56007. **507-373-0628**

GOODHUE. Red Wing, 55066. **612-388-2000**

GRANT. Elbow Lake, 56531. **218-685-4150**

HENNEPIN. Minneapolis, 55415. **612-348-3000**

HOUSTON. Caledonia, 55921. **507-724-3930**

HUBBARD. Park Rapids, 56470. **218-732-3196**

ISANTI. Cambridge, 55008. **612-689-1644**

ITASCA. Grand Rapids, 55744. **218-326-9777**

JACKSON. Jackson, 56143. **507-827-2763**

KANABEC. Mora, 55051. **612-679-1030**

KANDIYOHI. Willmar, 56201. **612-235-2727**

KITTSON. Hallock, 56728. **218-843-4531**

KOOCHICHING. International Falls, 56649

LAC QUI PARLE. Madison, 56256.
612-598-7444

LAKE. Two Harbors, 55616. **218-834-2254**

LAKE OF THE WOODS. Baudette, 56623.
218-634-2836

LE SUEUR. Le Center, 56057. **612-357-2251**

LINCOLN. Ivanhoe, 56142. **507-695-1529**

LYON. Marshall, 56258. **507-532-2631**

MCLEON. Glencoe, 55336. **612-864-5551**

MAHNOMEN. Mahnomen, 56557.
218-935-5163

MARSHALL. Warren, 56762. **218-742-3521**

MARTIN. Fairmont, 56031. **507-238-4421**

MEEKER. Litchfield, 55355. **612-693-2887**

MILLE LACS. Milaca, 56353. **612-983-6282**

MORRISON. Little Falls, 56345.
612-632-9215

MOWER. Austin, 55912. **507-433-2077**

MURRAY. Slayton, 56172. **507-836-6158**

NICOOLETT. St Peter, 56082. **507-931-1800**

NOBLES. Worthington, 56187.
507-376-4151

NORMAN. Ada, 56510. **218-784-2101**

OLMSTED. Rochester, 55901. **507-285-8115**

OTTER TAIL. Fergus Falls, 56537.
218-739-2271

PENNINGTON. Thief River Falls, 56701.
218-681-4011

PINE. Pine City, 55063. **612-629-3615**

PIPESTONE. Pipestone, 56164.
507-825-4494

POLK. Crookston, 56716. **218-281-2554**

POPE. Glenwood, 56334. **612-634-3338**

RAMSEY. St Paul, 55103. **612-298-5591**

RED LAKE. Red Lake Falls, 56750.
218-253-2598

REDWOOD. Redwood Falls, 56283.
507-637-8325

RENVILLE. Olivia, 56277. **612-523-2071**

RICE. Faribault, 55021. **507-334-3961**

ROCK. Luverne, 56156. **507-283-8212**

ROSEAU. Roseau, 56751

ST LOUIS. Duluth, 55802. **218-727-4522**

SCOTT. Shakopee, 55379. **612-445-1578**

SHERBURNE. Elk River, 55330

SIBLEY. Gaylord, 55334. **612-237-2369**

STEARNS. St Cloud, 56301. **612-251-7833**

STEELE. Owatonna, 55060. **507-451-8040**

STEVENS. Morris, 56267. **612-589-4660**

SWIFT. Benson, 56215. **612-842-6271**

TODD. Long Prairie, 56347. **612-732-2727**

TRAVERSE. Wheaton, 56296. **612-563-4242**

WABASHA. Wabasha, 55981. **612-565-3978**

WADENA. Wadena, 56482. **218-631-2425**

WASECA. Waseca, 56093. **507-835-1880**

WASHINGTON. Stillwater, 55082.
612-430-3220

WATONWAN. St James, 56081.
507-375-3541

WILKIN. Breckenridge, 56520.
218-643-4981

WINONA. Winona, 55987. **507-452-3337**

WRIGHT. Buffalo, 55313. **612-682-1671**

YELLOW MEDICINE. Granite Falls,
56241. **612-564-3122**

Mississippi

ADAMS. Natchez, 39120. **601-446-6326**

ALCORN. Crinth. **601-286-6265**

AMITE. Liberty, 39645. **601-657-3661**

ATTALA. Kosciusko, 39090. **601-289-1471**

BENTON. Ashland, 38603. **601-224-8142**

BOLIVAR. Cleveland, 38732. **601-843-2061**

CALHOUN. Pittsboro, 38951. **601-983-2424**

CARROLL. Carrollton, 38917. **601-237-8661**

CHICKASAW. Houston, 38851.
601-456-2513

CHOCTAW. Ackerman, 39735.
601-285-6329

CLAIBORNE. Port Gibson, 39150.
601-437-5841

CLARKE. Quitman, 39355. **601-776-2126**

CLAY. West Point, 39773. **601-494-3123**

COAHOMA. Clarksdale, 38614.
601-627-1141

COPIAH. Hazlehurst, 39083. **601-894-1241**

COVINGTON. Collins, 39428. **601-765-4956**

DE SOTO. Hernando, 38632. **601-368-7028**

FORREST. Hattiesburg, 39401.
601-582-0101

FRANKLIN. Meadville, 39653. **601-384-2330**

GEORGE. Lucedale, 39452. **601-947-7506**

GREENE. Leakesville, 39451. **601-394-5363**

GRENADA. Grenada, 38901. **601-226-1821**

HANCOCK. Bay St Louis, 39520.
601-467-5265

HARRISON. Gulfport, 39501. **601-864-5161**

HINDS. Jackson, 39201. **601-354-3406**

HOLMES. Lexington, 39095. **601-834-2508**

HUMPHREYS. Belzoni, 39038.
601-247-1740

ISSAQUENA. Mayersville, 39113.
601-873-2761

ITAWAMBA. Fulton, 38843. **601-862-3421**

JACKSON. Pascagoula, 39567.
601-769-7900

JASPER. Bay Springs, 39422. **601-764-3368**

JEFFERSON. Fayette, 39069. **601-786-3422**

JEFFERSON DAVIS. Prestiss, 39474.
601-792-4740

JONES. Lauree, 39440. **601-428-0527**

KEMPER. De Kalb, 39328. **601-743-2460**

LAFAYETTE. Oxford, 38655. **601-234-4951**

LAMAR. Purvis, 39475. **601-794-8055**

LAUDERDALE. Meridian, 39301.
601-693-2951

LAWRENCE. Monticello, 39654.
601-587-4791

LEAKE. Carthage, 39051. **601-267-7371**

LEE. Tupelo, 38801. **601-842-2311**

LEFLORE. Greenwood, 38930.
601-453-3528

LINCOLN. Brookhaven, 39601.
601-833-4911

LOWNDES. Columbus, 39701.
601-327-7880

MADISON. Canton, 39046. **601-859-4365**

MARION. Columbia, 39429. **601-736-2691**

MARSHALL. Holly Springs, 38635.
601-252-3434

MONROE. Aberdeen, 39730. **601-369-8143**

MONTGOMERY. Winona, 38967.
601-283-2333

NESHOBA. Philadelphia, 39350.
601-656-4781

NEWTON. Decatur, 39327. **601-635-2367**

NOXUBEE. Macon, 39341. **601-126-4244**

OKTIBBEHA. Starkville, 39759.
601-323-1356

PANOLA. Batesville, 38606. **601-563-3171**

PEARL RIVER. Poplarville, 39470.
601-795-4539

PERRY. New Augusta, 39462. **601-964-3218**

PIKE. Magnolia, 39652. **601-783-2581**

PONTOTOC. Pontotoc, 38863.
601-489-3451

PRENTISS. Booneville, 38829.
601-728-4611

QUITMAN. Marks, 38646. **601-326-8003**

RANKIN. Rankin. **601-825-2217**

SCOTT. Forest, 39074. **601-469-1922**

SHARKEY. Rolling Fork, 39159.
601-873-2755

SIMPSON. Mendenhall, 39114.
601-847-2626

SMITH. Raleigh, 39153. **601-782-4751**

STONE. Wiggins, 39577. **601-928-5246**

SUNFLOWER. Indianola, 38751.
601-887-4703

TALLAHATCHIE. Charleston, 38921.
601-647-8758

TATE. Senatobia, 38668. **601-562-7071**

TIPPAH. Ripley, 38663. **601-837-7374**

TISHOMINGO. Iuka, 38852. **601-423-6126**

TUNICA. Tunica, 38676. **601-363-2451**

UNION. New Albany, 38652. **601-534-4217**

WALTHALL. Tylertown, 39667
601-876-5667

WARREN. Vicksburg, 39180. **601-636-4415**

WASHINGTON. Greenville, 38701.
601-378-2747

WAYNE. Waynesboro, 39367. **601-735-2873**

WEBSTER. Walthall, 39771. **601-258-4131**

WILKINSON. Woodville, 39669.
601-888-4387

WINSTON. Louisville, 39339. **601-773-3581**

YALCBUSHA. Water Valley, 38965.
601-473-3581

YAZOO. Yazoo City, 39194. **601-746-1401**

Missouri

ADAIR. Kirksville, 63501. **816-665-2283**

ANDREW. Savannah, 64485. **816-324-3624**

ATCHISON. Rockport, 64482.
816-744-6214

AUDRAIN. Mexico, 62565. **314-591-4201**

BARRY. Cassville, 65625. **417-847-2561**

BARTON. Lamar, 64759. **417-682-2471**

BATES. Butler, 64730. **816-679-3371**

BENTON. Warsaw, 65355. **816-438-7326**

BOLLINGER. Marble Hill, 63764.
314-238-2126

BOONE. Columbia, 65201. **314-449-3711**

BUCHANAN. St Joseph, 64501.
816-279-3858

BUTLER. Poplar Bluff, 63901. **314-785-2325**

CALDWELL. Kingston, 64650.
816-586-2571

CALLAWAY. Fulton, 65251. **314-642-5139**

CAMDEN. Camdenton, 65020.
314-346-2250

CAPE GIRARDEAU. Jackson, 63755.
314-243-3547

CARROLL. Carrollton, 64633. **816-542-0615**

CARTER. Van Buren, 63965. **314-323-4527**

CASS. Harrisonville, 64701. **816-884-4511**

CEDOR. Stockton, 65785. **417-276-3514**

CHARITON. Keytesville, 65261.
816-288-3273

CHRISTIAN. Ozark, 65721. **417-485-6360**

CLARK. Kahoka, 63445. **816-737-3283**

CLAY. Liberty, 64068. **816-781-4400**

CLINTON. Plattsburg, 64477. **816-539-2943**

COLE. Jefferson City, 65101. **314-636-5022**

COOPER. Boonville, 65233. **816-882-2114**

CRAWFORD. Steelville, 65565.
314-675-2376

DADE. Greenfield, 65661. **417-637-2724**

DALLAS. Buffalo, 65622. **417-345-2632**

DAVIESS. Gallatin, 64640. **816-663-2641**

DE KALB. Maysville, 64469. **816-449-5402**

DENT. Salem, 65560. **314-729-4144**

DOUGLAS. Ava, 65608. **417-683-4174**

DUNKLIN. Kennett, 63857. **314-888-2796**

FRANKLIN. Union, 63084. **314-583-2494**

GASCONADE. Hermann, 65041.
314-486-5427

GENTRY. Albany, 64402. **816-726-3525**

GREENE. Springfield, 65802. **417-869-3581**

GRUNDY. Trenton, 64683. **816-359-6305**

HARRISON. Bethany, 64424. **816-425-6424**

HENRY. Clinton, 64735. **816-885-5301**

HICKORY. Hermitage, 65668. **417-745-6450**

HOLT. Oregon, 64473. **816-446-3303**

HOWARD. Fayette, 65248. **816-348-2284**

HOWELL. West Plains, 65775. **417-256-2591**

IRON. Ironton, 63650. **314-546-2912**

JACKSON. Kansas City, 64106.
816-881-3000

JASPER. Carthage, 64836. **417-358-4449**

JEFFERSON. Hillsboro, 63050.
314-789-3911

JOHNSON. Warrensburg, 64093.
816-747-6161

KNOX. Edika, 63537. **816-397-2184**

LACLEDE. Lebanon, 65536. **417-532-5471**

LAFAYETTE. Lexington, 64067.
816-259-4369

LAWRENCE. Mount Vernon, 65712.
417-466-2638

LEWIS. Monticello, 63457. **314-767-5205**

LINCOLN. Troy, 63379. **314-528-4415**

LINN. Linneus, 64653. **816-895-5417**

LIVINGSTON. Chillicothe, 64601.
816-646-2293

MCDONALD. Pineville, 64856.
417-223-4717

MACON. Macon, 63552. **816-385-2913**

MADISON. Fredericktown, 63645.
314-783-2176

MARIES. Vienna, 65582. **314-422-3388**

MARION. Palmyra, 63461. **314-769-2549**

MERCER. Princeton, 64673. **816-748-3425**

MILLER. Tuscumbia, 65082. **314-369-2317**

MISSISSIPPI. Charleston, 63834.
314-683-6613

MONITEAU. California, 65018.
314-796-4661

MONROE. Paris, 65275. **816-327-5817**

MONTGOMERY. Montgomery City, 63361.
314-569-3357

MORGAN. Versailles, 65084. **314-378-5300**

NEW MADRID. New Madrid, 63869.
314-748-5725

NEWTON. Neosho, 64850. **417-451-0252**

NODAWAY. Maryville, 64468. **816-582-2251**

OREGON. Alton, 65606. **417-778-7475**

OSAGE. Linn, 65051. **314-897-2139**

OZARK. Gainesville, 65655. **417-679-3516**

PEMISCOT. Caruthersville, 63830.
314-333-4203

PERRY. Perryville, 63775. **314-547-4242**

PETTIS. Sedalia, 65301. **816-826-4892**

PHELPS. Rolla, 65401. **314-364-1891**

PIKE. Bowling Green, 63334. **314-324-2412**

PLATTE. Platte City, 64079. **816-431-2421**

POLK. Bolivar, 65613. **417-326-4031**

PULASKI. Waynesville, 65583.
314-774-2241

PUTNAM. Unionville, 63565. **816-947-2674**

RALLS. New London, 63459. **314-985-7111**

RANDOLPH. Huntsville, 65259.
816-277-4717

RAY. Richmond, 64085. **816-776-3184**

REYNOLDS. Centerville, 63633.
314-648-2302

RIPLEY. Doniphan, 63935. **314-996-3215**

ST CHARLES. St Charles, 63301.
314-724-2166

ST CLAIR. Osceola, 64776. **417-646-2315**

ST FRANCOIS. Farmington, 63640.
314-756-3623

STE GENEVIEVE. Ste Genevieve, 63670.
314-883-5133

ST LOUIS. Clayton, 63105. **314-889-2000**

SALINE. Marshall, 65340. **816-886-3331**

SCHUYLER. Lancaster, 63548.
816-457-3842

SCOTLAND. Memphis, 63555.
816-465-7027

SCOTT. Benton, 63736. **314-545-3549**

SHANNON. Eminence, 65466. **314-226-3414**

SHELBY. Shelbyville, 63469. **314-633-2181**

STODDARD. Bloomfield, 63825.
314-568-3339

STONE. Galena, 65656. **417-357-6127**

SULLIVAN. Milan, 63556. **816-265-3786**

TANEY. Forsyth, 65653. **417-546-2241**

TEXAN. Houston, 65483. **417-967-2112**

VERNON. Nevada, 64772. **417-667-3157**

WARREN. Warrenton, 63383. **314-456-3331**

WASHINGTON. Potosi, 63664.
314-438-4901

WAYNE. Greenville, 63944. **314-224-3513**

WEBSTER. Marshfield, 65706.
417-468-2223

WORTH. Grant City, 64456. **816-564-2219**

WRIGHT. Hartville, 65667. **417-741-6661**

Montana

BEAVERHEAD. Dillon, 59725. **406-683-2642**

BIG HORN. Hardin, 59034. **406-665-1506**

BLAINE. Chinock, 59523. **406-357-3240**

BROADWATER. Townsend, 59644. **406-266-3443**

CARBON. Red Lodge, 59068. **406-446-1220**

CARTER. Ekalaka, 59324. **406-775-2131**

CASCADE. Great Falls, 59401. **406-761-6700**

CHOUTEAU. Fort Benton, 59442. **406-622-3631**

CUSTER. Miles City, 59301. **406-232-1347**

DANIELS. Scobey, 59263. **406-487-5561**

DAWSON. Glendive, 59330. **406-365-3058**

DEER LODGE. Anaconda, 59711. **406-563-6541**

FALLON. Baker, 59313. **406-778-2228**

FERGUS. Lewistown, 59457. **406-538-5119**

FLATHEAD. Kalispell, 59901. **406-755-5300**

GALLATIN. Boxeman, 59715. **406-587-7316**

GARFIELD. Jordan, 59337. **406-435-2760**

GLACIER. Cut Bank, 59427. **406-938-2041**

GOLDEN VALLEY. Ryegate, 59074. **406-568-2231**

GRANITE. Philipsburg, 59858. **406-859-3771**

HILL. Havre, 59501. **406-265-7813**

JEFFERSON. Boulder, 59632. **406-225-3332**

JUDITH BASIN. Stanford, 59479. **406-566-2301**

LAKE. Polson, 59860. **406-883-4361**

LEWIS AND CLARK. Helena, 59601. **406-442-6430**

LIBERTY. Chester, 59522. **406-759-5365**

LINCOLN. Libby, 59923. **406-293-5431**

MCCONE. Circle, 59215. **406-485-3505**

MADISON. Virginia City, 59755. **406-843-5311**

MEAGHER. White Sulphur Springs, 59645. **406-547-3612**

MINERAL. Superior, 59872. **406-822-4541**

MISSOULA. Missoula, 59801. **406-543-5128**

MUSSELSHELL. Roundup, 59072. **406-323-1104**

PARK. Livingston, 59047. **406-222-0450**

PETROLEUM. Winnett, 59087. **406-429-4555**

PHILLIPS. Malta, 59538. **406-654-2423**

PONDERA. Conrad, 59425. **406-278-3226**

POWDER RIVER. Broadus, 59317. **406-436-2361**

POWELL. Deer Lodge, 59722. **406-846-2772**

PRAIRIE. Terry, 59349. **406-637-5431**

RAVALLI. Hamilton, 59840. **405-363-1833**

RICHLAND. Sidney, 59270. **406-482-1708**

ROOSEVELT. Wolf Point, 59201. **406-653-1322**

ROSEBUD. Forsyth, 59327. **406-356-7322**

SANDERS. Thompson Falls, 59873. **406-827-3491**

SHERIDAN. Plentywood, 59254. **406-765-1660**

SILVER BOW. Buete, 59701. **406-893-1427**

STILLWATER. Columbus, 59019. **406-322-5328**

SWEET GRASS. Big Timber, 59011. **406-932-2713**

TETON. Choteau, 59422. **406-466-2151**

TOOLE. Shelby, 59474. **406-434-2232**

TREASURE. Hysham, 59038. **406-342-5547**

VALLEY. Glasgow, 59230. **406-228-4713**

WHEATLAND. Harlowton, 59036. **406-632-5621**

WIBAUX. Wibaux, 59353. **406-795-2433**

YELLOWSTONE. Billings, 59101. **406-252-5181**

Nebraska

ADAMS. Hastings, 68901. **402-463-2491**

ANTELOPE. Nelight, 68756. **402-887-4410**

ARTHUR. Arthur, 69121. **308-764-2203**

BANNER. Harrisburg, 69345. **308-436-5265**

BLAINE. Brewster, 68821. **308-547-2222**

BOONE. Albion, 68620. **402-395-2055**

BOX BUTTE. Alliance, 69301. **308-762-3360**

BOYD. Butte, 68722. **402-775-2391**

BROWN. Ainsworth, 69210. **402-387-2705**

BUFFALO. Kearney, 68847. **308-337-5981**

BURT. Tekamah, 68061. **402-374-1955**

BUTLER. David City, 68632. **402-367-3091**

CASS. Plattsmouth, 68048. **402-296-2164**

CEDAR. Hartington, 68739. **402-254-3983**

CHASE. Imperial, 69033. **308-882-5266**

CHERRY. Valentine, 69201. **402-376-2771**

CHEYENNE. Sidney, 69162. **308-254-2141**

CLAY. Clay Center, 68933. **402-762-5235**

COLFAX. Schuyler, 68661. **402-352-3434**

CUMING. West Point, 68788. **402-372-2144**

CUSTER. Broken Bow, 68822. **308-872-5701**

DAKOTA. Dakota City, 68731. **402-987-3471**

DAWES. Chadron, 69337. **308-432-2863**

DAWSON. Lexington, 68850. **308-324-2127**

DEUEL. Chappeli, 69219. **303-874-3308**

DIXON. Ponca, 68770. **402-755-2208**

DODGE. Fremont, 68025. **402-721-3494**

DOUGLAS. Omaha, 68102. **402-444-7025**

DUNCY. Benkelman, 69021. **308-423-2058**

FILLMORE. Geneva, 68361. **402-759-3018**

FRANKLIN. Franklin, 68939. **308-425-3492**

FRONTIER. Stockville, 69042. **308-367-8641**

FURNAS. Beaver City, 68726. **308-268-4145**

GAGE. Beatric, 68310. **402-223-3128**

GARDEN. Oshkosh, 69154. **308-772-3924**

GARFIELD. Burwell, 68823. **308-346-4161**

GOSPER. Elwood, 68937. **308-785-2611**

GRANT. Hyannis, 69350. **308-458-2488**

GREELEY. Greeley Center, 68842.
308-428-4151

HALL. Grand Island, 68801. **308-381-1000**

HAMILTON. Aurora, 68818. **402-694-3443**

HARLAN. Alma, 68920. **308-928-2173**

HAYES. Hayes Center, 69032. **308-286-3413**

HITCHCOCK. Trenton, 69044.
308-334-5646

HOLT. O'Neill, 68763. **308-336-1762**

HOOKER. Mullen, 69152. **308-546-2244**

HOWARD. St Paul, 68873. **308-754-4343**

JEFFERSON. Fairbury, 68352.
402-729-2323

JOHNSON. Tecumseh, 68450. **402-335-3246**

KEARNEY. Minden, 68959. **308-832-1172**

KEITH. Ogallaia, 69153. **308-284-4726**

KEYA PAHA. Springview, 68778.
402-497-3791

KIMBALL. Kimball, 69145. **308-235-4056**

KNOX. Center, 68724. **402-288-4282**

LANCASTER. Lincoln, 68509. **402-475-5611**

LINCOLN. North Platte, 69101.
308-534-4350

LOGAN. Stapleton, 69163. **308-636-2311**

LOUP. Taylor, 68879. **308-942-3135**

MCPHERSON. Tryon, 69167. **308-587-2363**

MADISON. Madison, 68748. **402-454-2726**

MERRICK. Central City, 68826.
308-946-2881

MORRILL. Bridgeport, 69336. **308-262-0860**

NANCE. Fullerton, 68638. **308-536-2331**

NEMAHA. Auburn, 68305. **402-274-4213**

NUCKOLLS. Nelson, 68961. **402-225-4361**

OTOE. Nebraska City, 68410. **402-873-3586**

PAWNEE. Pawnee City, 68420.
402-852-6001

PERKINS. Grant, 69140. **308-352-4643**

PHELPS. Holdrege, 68949. **308-995-4469**

PIERCE. Pierce, 68767. **402-329-4225**

PLATTE. Columbus, 68601. **402-564-0593**

POLK. Osceola, 68651. **402-747-5431**

RED WILLOW. McCook, 69001.
308-345-1552

RICHARDSON. Falls City, 68355.
402-245-2911

ROCK. Bassett, 68714. **402-684-3933**

SALINE. Wilber, 68465. **402-821-3361**

SARPY. Papillion, 68046. **402-339-3225**

SAUNDERS. Wahoo, 68066. **402-443-4335**

SCOTTS BLUFF. Gering, 69341.
308-821-3361

SEWARD. Seward, 68434. **402-643-2883**

SHERIDAN. Rushville, 69360. **308-327-2633**

SHERMAN. Loup City, 68853.
308-745-1513

SIOUX. Harrison, 69346. **308-668-2443**

STANTON. Stanton, 68779. **402-439-2222**

THAYER. Hebron, 68370. **402-768-6693**

THOMAS. Thedford, 69166. **308-645-2261**

THURSTON. Pender, 68047. **402-385-2343**

VALLEY. Ord, 68862. **308-728-3700**

WASHINGTON. Blair, 68008. **402-426-2323**

WAYNE. Wayne, 68787. **402-375-2288**

WEBSTER. Red Cloud, 68970.
402-746-2716

WHEELER. Bartlett, 68622. **308-654-3235**

YORK. York, 68467. **402-362-4039**

Nevada

CHURCHILL. Fallon, 89046. **702-423-6028**

CLARK. Las Vegas, 89114. **702-386-4011**

DOUGLAS. Minden, 89423. **702-782-5176**

ELKO. Elko, 89801. **702-738-5398**

ESMERALDA. Goldfield, 89013.
702-485-6367

EUREKA. Eureka, 89316. **702-237-5262**

HUMBOLDT. Winnemucca, 89445.
702-623-3130

LANDER. Austin, 89310. **702-964-2439**

LINCOLN. Pioche, 89043. **702-962-5390**

LYON. Yerington, 89447. **702-463-2382**

MINERAL. Hawthorne, 89415.
702-945-2446

NYE. Tonopah, 89049. **702-482-3330**

ORMSBY. Carson City, 89701.
702-882-1594

PERSHING. Lovelock, 89419. **702-273-2208**

STOREY. Virginia City, 89440.
702-847-0577

WASHOE. Reno, 89501. **702-785-6180**

WHITE PINE. Ely, 89301. **702-289-2341**

New Hampshire

BELKNAP. Laconia, 03246. **603-524-3570**

CARROLL. Ossipee, 03864. **603-539-2201**

CHESIRE. Keene, 03431. **603-352-0050**

COOS. Lancaster, 03584. **603-752-4100**

GRAFTON. Woodsville, 03785.
603-787-6941

HILLSBOROUGH. Nashua, 03060.
603-424-9951

MERRIMACK. Concord, 03301.
603-228-0331

ROCKINGHAM. Exeter, 03833.
603-778-8573

STRAFFORD. Dover, 03820. **603-742-1458**

SULLIVAN. Newport, 03773. **603-863-2560**

New Jersey

ATLANTIC. Mays Landing, 08330.
609-625-4011

BERGEN. Hackensack, 07602. **201-646-2000**

BURLINGTON. Mount Holly, 08060.
609-267-3300

CAMDEN. Camden, 08101. **609-757-0520**

CAPE MAY. Cape May Court House,
08210. **609-465-7111**

CUMBERLAND. Bridgeton, 08302.
609-451-8000

ESSEX. Newark, 07102. **201-961-7033**

GLOUCESTER. Woodbury, 08096.
609-845-1600

HUDSON. Jersey City, 07302. **201-792-3737**

HUNTERDON. Flemington, 08822.
201-782-6214

MERCER. Trenton, 08625. **609-989-8000**

MIDDLESEX. New Brunswick, 08903.
201-246-6000

MONMOUTH. Freehold, 07728.
201-431-4000

MORRIS. Morristown, 07960. **201-285-6212**

OCEAN. Toms River, 08753. **201-244-2121**

PASSAIC. Paterson, 07505. **201-525-5000**

SALEM. Salem, 08079. **609-935-1661**

SOMERSET. Somerville, 08876.
201-725-4700

SUSSEX. Newton, 07860. **201-383-2224**

UNION. Elizabeth, 07207. **201-353-5000**

WARREN. Belvidere, 07823. **201-775-5361**

New Mexico

BERNALILLO. Albuquerque, 87102.
505-766-4000

CATRON. Reserve, 87830. **505-533-6449**

CHAVES. Roswell, 88201. **505-623-2126**

COLFAC. Raton, 87740. **505-445-2671**

CURRY. Clovis, 88101. **505-763-5591**

DE BACA. Fort Sumner, 88119.
505-355-2601

DONA ANA. Las Cruces, 88001.
505-523-5634

EDDY. Carlsbad, 88220. **505-887-2323**

GRANT. Silver City, 88061. **505-538-3338**

GUADALUPE. Santa Rosa, 88435.
505-472-3791

HARDING. Mosquero, 87733. **505-673-2301**

HIDALGO. Lordsburg, 88045. **505-542-9213**

LEA. Lovington, 88260. **505-396-3921**

LINCOLN. Carrizozo, 88301. **505-648-2313**

LOS ALAMOS. Los Alamos, 87544.
505-662-4122

LUNA. Deming, 88030. **505-546-2734**

MCKINLEY. Gallup, 87301. **505-722-3869**

MORA. Mora, 87732. **505-387-2448**

OTERO. Alamogordo, 88310. **505-437-7427**

QUAY. Tucumcari, 88401. **505-461-0510**

RIO ARRIBA. Tierra Amarilla, 87575.
505-588-7246

ROOSEVELT. Portales, 88130.
505-477-8271

SAN JUAN. Aztec, 87410. **505-334-9464**

SAN MIGUEL. Las Vegas, 87701.
505-425-9331

SANDOVAL. Bernalillo, 87004.
505-867-2209

SANTA FE. Santa Fe, 87501. **505-983-4351**

SIERRA. Truth or Consequences, 87901.
505-894-2840

SOCORRO. Socorro, 87801. **505-835-0589**

TAOS. Taos, 87571. **505-758-4281**

TORRANCE. Estancia, 87016. **505-384-2221**

UNION. Clayton, 88415. **505-314-9491**

VALENCIA. Los Lunas, 87031.
505-865-9681

New York

ALBANY. Albany, 12207. **518-445-7711**

ALLEGANY. Belmont, 14813. **716-268-7612**

BROOME. Binghamton, 13901.
607-772-2100

BRONX. Bronx, 10451. **212-293-8000**

CATTARAUGUS. Little Valley, 14755.
716-938-3141

CAYUGA. Auburn, 13021. **315-253-1211**

CHAUTAUQUA. Mayville, 14757.
716-753-7111

CHEMUNG. Elmira, 14902. **607-737-2912**

CHENANGO. Norwich, 13815.
607-335-4500

CLINTON. Plattsburgh, 12901.
518-563-0530

COLUMBIA. Hudson, 12534. **518-828-1527**

CORTLAND. Cortland, 13045.
607-756-2808

DELAWARE. Delhi, 13753. **607-746-2123**

DUTCHESS. Poughkeepsie, 12602. **914-485-9861**

ERIE. Buffalo, 14202. **716-846-8500**

ESSEX. Elizabethtown, 12932. **518-873-6301**

FRANKLIN. Malone, 12953. **518-483-0600**

FULTON. Johnstown, 12095. **518-762-4128**

GENESEE. Batavia, 14020. **716-343-5424**

GREENE. Catskill, 12414. **518-943-3080**

HAMILTON. Lake Pleasant, 12101. **518-548-7111**

HERKIMER. Herkimer, 13350. **315-866-4010**

JEFFERSON. Watertown, 13601. **315-785-3075**

KINGS. Brooklyn, 11201. **212-630-3131**

LEWIS. Lowville, 13367. **315-376-3560**

LIVINGSTON. Geneseo, 14454. **716-243-2500**

MADISON. Wampsville, 13163. **315-366-2011**

MONROE. Rochester, 14614. **716-428-4500**

MONTGOMERY. Fonda, 12068. **518-853-3431**

NASSAU. Mineola, 11501. **516-535-3131**

NEW YORK. 10007. **212-374-5600**

NIAGARA. Lockport, 14094. **716-434-6148**

ONEIDA. Utica, 13503. **315-798-5800**

ONONDAGA. Syracuse, 13202. **315-425-2222**

ONTARIO. Canandaigua, 14424. **315-394-7070**

ORANGE. Goshen, 10924. **914-294-5151**

ORLEANS. Albion, 14411. **716-589-4511**

OSWEGO. Oswego, 13126. **315-343-9154**

OTSEGO. Cooperstown, 13326. **607-547-9901**

PUTNAM. Carmel, 10512. **914-225-3641**

QUEENS. Jamaica, 11434. **212-520-3137**

RENSSELAER. Troy, 12180. **518-270-5000**

RICHMOND. St George, 10301. **212-727-1086**

ROCKLAND. New City, 10956. **914-638-0500**

SAINT LAWRENCE. Canton, 13617. **315-379-2000**

SARATOGA. Ballston Spa, 12020. **518-885-5381**

SCHENECTADY. Schenectady, 12307. **518-382-3200**

SCHOHARIE. Schoharie, 12157. **518-295-7147**

SCHUYLER. Watkins Glen, 14891. **607-535-2181**

SENECA. Waterloo, 13165. **315-539-9285**

STEUBEN. Bath, 14810. **607-776-7127**

SUFFOLK. Riverhead, 11901. **516-727-4700**

SULLIVAN. Monticello, 12701. **914-794-3000**

TIOGA. Owego, 13827. **607-687-3633**

TOMPKINS. Ithaca, NY 14850. **607-273-2080**

ULSTER. Kingston, 12401. **914-331-9300**

WARREN. Lake George, 12845. **518-792-9951**

WASHINGTON. Fort Edward, 12828. **518-747-4113**

WAYNE. Lyons, 14489. **315-946-9767**

WESTCHESTER. White Plains, 10601. **914-682-2000**

WYOMING. Warsaw, 14569. **716-796-2840**

YATES. Penn Yan, 14527. **315-536-4221**

North Carolina

ALAMANCE. Graham, 27253. **919-228-1312**

ALEXANDER. Taylorsville, 28601. **704-632-9332**

ALLEGHANY. Sparta, 28675. **919-372-4342**

ANSON. Wadesboro, 28170. **704-694-2796**

ASHE. Jefferson, 28640. **919-246-8841**

AVERY. Newland, 28657. **704-733-9366**

BEAUFORT. Washington, 27889. **919-946-2427**

BERTIE. Windsor, 27983. **919-794-2139**

BLADEN. Elizabethtown, 28337. **919-862-2203**

BRUNSWICK. Southport, 28461. **919-457-9551**

BUNCOMBE. Asheville, 2880. **704-255-5000**

BURKE. Morganton, 28655. **704-437-5701**

CABARRUS. Concord, 28025. **704-782-4183**

CALDWELL. Lenoir, 28645. **704-758-8451**

CAMDEN. Camden, 27921. **919-335-4077**

CARTERET. Beaufort, 28516. **919-335-7877**

CASWELL. Yanceyville, 27379. **919-694-4762**

CATAWBA. Newton, 28658. **704-464-7880**

CHATHAM. Pittsboro, 27312. **919-542-4814**

CHEROKEE. Murphy, 28906. **704-837-5527**

CHOWAN. Edenton, 27932. **919-482-2323**

CLAY. Hayesville, 28904. **704-309-6411**

CLEVELAND. Shelby, 28150. **704-482-8311**

COLUMBUS. Whiteville, 28472. **919-642-3860**

CARAVEN. New Bern, 28560. **919-638-1424**

CUMBERLAND. Fayetteville, 28301. **919-483-8131**

CURRITUCK. Currituck, 27929. **919-232-2075**

DARE. Manteo, 27954. **919-473-2950**

DAVIDSON. Lexington, 27292. **704-246-2549**

DAVIE. Mocksville, 27028. **704-634-2631**

DUPLIN. Kenansville, 28349. **919-296-2041**

DURHAM. Durham, 27702. **919-688-3360**

EDGECOMBE. Tarboro, 27886.
919-823-8131

FORSYTH. Winston-Salem, 27101.
919-727-2797

FRANKLIN. Louisburg, 27549.
919-496-5104

GASTON. Gastonia, 28052. **704-865-6411**

GATES. Gatesville, 27938. **919-357-6071**

GRAHAM. Robbinsville, 28771.
704-479-8502

GRANVILLE. Oxford, 27565. **919-683-2649**

GREENE. Snow Hill, 28580. **919-747-3446**

GUILFORD. Greensboro, 27402.
919-373-2000

HALIFAX. Halifax, 27839. **919-583-3641**

HARNETT. Lillington, 27546. **919-893-2091**

HAYWOOD. Waynesville, 28786.
704-456-9812

HENDERSON. Hendersonville, 28739.
704-693-5415

HERTFORD. Winton, 27986. **919-358-3551**

HOKE. Raeford, 28376. **919-875-2034**

HYDE. Swanquarter, 27885. **919-926-4101**

IREDELL. Statesville, 28677. **704-872-9821**

JACKSON. Sylva, 28779. **704-586-4312**

JOHNSTON. Smithfield, 27577.
919-934-5960

JONES. Trenton, 28585. **919-448-5111**

LEE. Sanford, 27330. **919-775-5606**

LENOIR. Kinston, 28501. **919-527-6231**

LINCOLN. Lincolnton, 28092. **704-735-6510**

MCDOWELL. Marion, 28752. **704-652-7121**

MACON. Franklin, 28734. **704-524-6421**

MADISON. Marshall, 28753. **704-649-2521**

MARTIN. Williamston, 27892. **919-792-3345**

MECKLENBURG. Charlotte, 28202.
704-374-2472

MITCHELL. Bakersville, 28705.
704-688-3311

MONTGOMERY. Troy, 27371.
919-576-5011

MOORE. Carthage, 28327. **919-947-5800**

NASH. Nashville, 27856. **919-459-3018**

NEW HANOVER. Wilmington, 28401.
919-762-0901

NORTHAMPTON. Jackson, 27845.
919-534-2501

ONSLOW. Jacksonville, 28540.
919-347-4717

ORANGE. Hillsborough, 27278.
919-732-8181

PAMLICO. Bayboro, 28515. **919-745-3861**

PASQUOTANK. Elizabeth City, 27909.
919-335-0865

PENDER. Burgaw, 28425. **919-259-2636**

PERQUIMANS. Hertford, 27944.
919-426-5660

PERSON. Roxboro, 27573. **919-599-9184**

PITT. Greenville, 27834. **919-752-2934**

POLK. Columbus, 28722. **704-894-3302**

RANDOLPH. Asheboro, 27203.
919-629-2131

RICHMOND. Rockingham, 28379.
919-997-2542

ROBESON. Lumberton, 28358.
919-739-4550

ROCKINGHAM. Wentworth, 27375.
919-349-2922

ROWAN. Salisburg, 28144. **704-636-0361**

RUTHERFORD. Rutherfordton, 28139.
704-687-4205

SAMPSON. Clinton, 28328. **919-592-2659**

SCOTLAND. Laurinburg, 28352.
919-276-3224

STANLY. Albemarle, 28001. **704-983-2181**

STOKES. Danbury, 27016. **919-593-8307**

SURRY. Dobson, 27017. **919-386-8322**

SWAIN. Bryson City, 28713. **704-488-3121**

TRANSYLVANIA. Brevard, 28712.
704-884-2125

TYRRELL. Columbia, 27925. **919-796-5611**

UNION. Monroe, 28110. **704-289-4523**

VANCE. Henderson, 27536. **919-492-2141**

WAKE. Raleigh, 27611. **919-755-6160**

WARREN. Warrenton, 27589. **919-257-3337**

WASHINGTON. Plymouth, 27962.
919-793-2410

WATAUGA. Boone, 28607. **704-264-1300**

WAYNE. Goldsboro, 27530. **919-735-4331**

WILKES. Wilesboro, 28697. **919-667-6193**

WILSON. Wilson, 27893. **919-237-3913**

YADKIN. Yadkinville, 27055. **919-679-8838**

YANCEY. Burnsville, 28714. **704-682-2122**

North Dakota

ADAMS. Hettinger, 58639. **701-567-2460**

BARNES. Valley City, 58072. **701-845-0881**

BENSON. Minnewaukan, 58351.
701-473-5340

BILLINGS. Medora, 58645. **701-623-4491**

BOTTINEAU. Bottineau, 58318.
701-228-2225

BOWMAN. Bowman, 58623. **701-523-5271**

BURKE. Bowbells, 58721. **701-377-2718**

BURLEIGH. Bismarck, 58501. **701-255-1353**

CASS. Fargo, 58102. **701-232-2536**

CAVALIER. Langdon, 58249. **701-256-2229**

DICKEY. Ellendale, 58436. **701-349-3249**

DIVIDE. Crosby, 58730. **701-965-6351**

DUNN. Manning, 58642. **701-573-6655**

EDDY. New Rockford, 58356. **701-947-2454**

EMMONS. Linton, 58552. **701-254-4807**

FOSTER. Carrington, 58421. **701-652-2241**

GOLDEN VALLEY. Beach, 58621.
701-872-4331

GRAND FORKS. Grand Forks, 58201.
701-775-2571

GRANT. Carson, 58529. **701-622-3275**

GRIGGS. Cooperstown, 58425.
701-797-3117

HETTINGER. Mott, 58646. **701-824-2515**

KADDER. Steele, 58482. **701-475-2632**

LA MOURE. La Moure, 58458.
701-883-4295

LOGAN. Napoleon, 58561. **701-754-2425**

MCHENRY. Towner, 58788. **701-537-5724**

MCINTOSH. Ashley, 58413. **701-388-3450**

MCKENZIE. Watford City, 58854.
701-842-3450

MCLEAN. Washburn, 58577. **701-462-3650**

MERCER. Stanton, 58571. **701-745-3292**

MORTON. Mandan, 58554. **701-663-9831**

MOUNTRAIL. Stanley, 58784.
701-628-2145

NELSON. Lakota, 58344. **701-247-2463**

OLIVER. Center, 58530. **701-794-8777**

PEMBINA. Cavalier, 58220. **701-265-4231**

PIERCE. Rugby, 58368. **701-776-5225**

RAMSEY. Devils Lake, 58301. **701-662-2189**

RANSOM. Lisbon, 58054. **701-683-5541**

RENVILLE. Mohall, 58761. **701-756-6301**

RICHLAND. Wahpeton, 58075.
701-642-5632

ROLETTE. Rolla, 58367. **701-477-3481**

SARGENT. Forman, 58032. **701-724-3361**

SHERIDAN. McClusky, 58463.
701-363-2205

SIOUX. Fort Yates, 58538. **701-854-3481**

SLOPE. Amidon, 58620. **701-879-6276**

STARK. Dickinson, 58601. **701-225-3901**

STEELE. Finley, 58230. **701-524-2110**

STUTSMAN. Jamestown, 58401.
701-252-7172

TOWNER. Cando, 58324. **701-968-3414**

TRAIL. Hillsboro, 58045. **701-436-4458**

WALSH. Grafton, 58237. **701-352-2851**

WARD. Minot, 58701. **701-838-5437**

WELLS. Fessenden, 58438. **701-547-3521**

WILLIAMS. Williston, 58801. **701-572-6373**

Ohio

ADAMS. West Union, 45693. **513-544-3286**

ALLEN. Lima, 45802. **419-228-3700**

ASHLAND. Ashland, 44805. **419-289-0000**

ASHTABULA. Jefferson, 44047.
216-576-2040

ATHENS. Athens, 45701. **614-593-6888**

AUGLAIZE. Wapakoneta, 45895.
419-738-3612

BELMONT. St Clairsville, 43950.
614-695-2121

BROWN. Georgetown, 45121. **513-378-3956**

BUTLER. Hamilton, 45012. **513-867-5000**

CARROLL. Carrollton, 44615. **216-627-2250**

CHAMPAIGN. Urbana, 43078.
513-653-4152

CLARK. Springfield, 45501. **513-324-5871**

CLERMONT. Batavia, 45103. **513-732-1220**

CLINTON. Wilmington, 45177.
513-382-2103

COLUMBIANA. Lisbon, 44432.
216-457-2272

COSHOCTON. Coshocton, 43812.
614-622-1753

CRAWFORD. Bucyrus, 44820. **419-562-5876**

CUYAHOGA. Cleveland, 44114.
216-241-2700

DARKE. Greenville, 45331. **513-548-2325**

DEFIANCE. Definace, 43512. **419-782-4761**

DELAWARE. Delaware, 43015.
614-369-8761

ERIE. Sandusky, 44870. **419-626-9440**

FAIRFIELD. Lancaster, 43130.
614-653-0341

FAYETTE. Washington Court House,
43160. **614-335-0720**

FRANKLIN. Columbus, 43215.
614-462-3322

FULTON. Wauseon, 43567. **419-335-5921**

GALLIA. Gallipolis, 45631. **614-446-4612**

GEAUGA. Chardon, 44024. **216-285-2222**

GREENE. Xenia, 45385. **513-372-4461**

GUERNSEY. Cambridge, 43725.
614-432-2139

HAMILTON. Cincinnati, 45202.
513-632-6500

HANCOCK. Findlay, 45840. **419-422-7466**

HARDIN. Kenton, 43326. **419-673-6283**

HARRISON. Cadiz, 43907. **614-942-2301**

HENRY. Napoleon, 43545. **419-592-4876**

HIGHLAND. Hillsboro, 45133.
513-393-3333

HOCKING. Logan, 43138. **614-385-5195**

HOLMES. Millersburg, 44654.
216-674-1896

HURON. Norwalk, 44857. **419-668-3092**

JACKSON. Jackson, 45640. **614-286-3301**

JEFFERSON. Steubenville, 43952.
614-283-4111

KNOX. Mount Vernon, 43050. **614-397-2727**

LAKE. Painesville, 44077. **215-352-6281**

LAWRENCE. Ironton, 45638. **614-532-7980**

LICKING. Newark, 43055. **614-345-0060**

LOGAN. Bellefontaine, 43311. **513-592-0931**

LORAIN. Elyria, 44035. **216-323-5776**

LUCAS. Toledo, 43624. **419-259-8650**

MADISON. London, 43140. **614-852-2972**

MAHONING. Youngstown, 44503.
216-747-2092

MARION. Marion, 43302. **614-382-0637**

MEDINA. Medina, 44256. **216-723-3641**

MEIGS. Pomeroy, 45769. **614-992-2895**

MERCER. Celina, 45822. **419-586-3178**

MIAMI. Troy, 45373. **513-335-8341**

MONROE. Woodsfield, 43793.
614-472-0761

MONTGOMERY. Dayton, 45402.
513-225-4000

MORGAN. McConnelsville, 43756.
614-962-4752

MORROW. Mount Gilead, 43338.
419-946-4027

MUSKINGUM. Zanesville, 43360.
614-452-4577

NOBLE. Caldwell, 43724. **614-732-4044**

OTTAWA. Port Clinton, 43452.
614-732-2523

PAULDIN. Paulding, 45879. **419-399-3786**

PERRY. New Lexingoon, 43764.
614-342-3484

PICKAWAY. Circleville, 43113.
614-474-6094

PIKE. Waverly, 45690. **614-947-4817**

PORTAGE. Ravenna, 44266. **216-296-9911**

PREBLE. Eaton, 45320. **513-456-3020**

PUTNAM. Ottawa, 45875. **419-523-3656**

RICHLAND. Monsfield, 44902.
419-524-4004

ROSS. Chillicothe, 45601. **614-772-5115**

SANDUSKY. Fremont, 43420. **419-332-6411**

SCIOTO. Portsmouth, 45662.
614-354-5664

SENECA. Tiffin, 44883. **419-447-4550**

SHELBY. Sidney, 45365. **513-492-5175**

STARK. Canton, 44702. **216-454-5651**

SUMMIT. Akron, 44308. **216-379-5005**

TRUMBULL. Warren, 44482. **216-399-8811**

TUSCARAWAS. New Philadelphia, 44663.
216-364-8811

UNION. Marysville, 43040. **513-642-2841**

VAN WERT. Van Wert, 45891.
419-238-6159

VINTON. McArthur, 45651. **614-596-4571**

WARREN. Lebanon, 45036. **513-932-4040**

WASHINGTON. Marietta, 45750.
614-373-6623

WAYNE. Wooster, 44691. **216-262-1831**

WILLIAMS. Bryan, 43506. **419-636-2059**

WOOD. Bowling Green, 43402.
419-352-6531

WYANDOT. Upper Sandusky, 43351.
419-294-3436

Oklahoma

ADAIR. Stillwell, 74960. **918-774-7198**

ALFALFA. Cherokee, 73728. **405-596-3158**

ATOKA. Atoka, 74525. **405-889-3565**

BEAVER. Beaver, 73932. **405-625-3141**

BECKHAM. Sayre, 73662. **405-928-3330**

BLAINE. Watonga, 73772. **405-623-5890**

BRYAN. Durant, 74701. **405-924-2202**

CADDO. Anadarko, 73005. **405-247-6609**

CANADIAN. El Reno, 73036. **405-262-5096**

CARTER. Ardmore, 73401. **405-223-8162**

CHEROKEE. Tahlequah, 74464.
918-456-4121

CHOCTAW. Hugo, 74743. **405-326-5331**

CIMARRON. Boise City, 73933.
405-544-2251

CLEVELAND. Norman, 73069.
405-321-6480

COAL. Coalgate, 74538. **405-927-2103**

COMANCHE. Lawton, 73501. **405-353-3717**

COTTON. Walter, 73572. **405-875-3026**

CREEK. Sapulpa, 74066. **918-224-4084**

CUSTER. Arapaho, 73620. **405-323-1221**

DELAWARE. Jay, 74346. **918-253-4520**

DEWEY. Taloga, 73667. **405-328-5361**

ELLIS. Arnett, 73832. **405-885-2311**

GARFIELD. Enid, 73701. **405-237-0225**

GARVIN. Pauls Valley, 73075. **405-238-2685**

GRADY. Chickasha, 73018. **405-224-7388**

GRANT. Medford, 73759. **405-395-2274**

GREER. Mangum, 73554. **405-782-3664**

HARMON. Hollis, 73550. **405-688-3658**

HARPER. Buffalo, 73834. **405-735-2012**

HASKELL. Stigler, 74462. **918-967-2107**

JACKSON. Altus, 73521. **405-482-4070**

JEFFERSON. Waurika, 73573.
405-228-2039

JOHNSTON. Tishomingo, 73460.
405-371-3184

KAY. Newkirk, 74647. **405-362-3272**

KINGFISHER. Kingfisher, 73750.
405-375-3887

KIOWA. Hobart, 73651. **405-726-2484**

LATIMER. Wilburton, 74578. **918-465-2021**

LE FLORE. Poteau, 74953. **918-647-2527**

LINCOLN. Chandler, 74834. **405-258-1309**

LOGAN. Guthrie, 73044. **405-282-0266**

LOVE. Marietta, 73448. **405-276-3059**

MCCLAIN. Purcell, 73080. **405-527-3117**

MCCURTAIN. Idabel, 74745. **405-286-3693**

MCINTOSH. Eufaula, 74432. **918-689-2741**

MAJOR. Fairview, 73737. **405-227-4732**

MARSHALL. Madili, 73446. **405-795-3220**

MAYES. Pryor, 74361. **918-825-2426**

MURRAY. Sulphur, 73086. **405-622-3920**

MUSKOGEE. Muskogee, 74401.
918-682-7781

NOBLE. Perry, 73077. **405-336-2141**

NOWATA. Nowata, 74048. **918-273-0175**

OKFUSKEE. Okemah, 74859. **918-623-1724**

OKLAHOMA. Oklahoma City, 73105.
405-236-2727

OKMULGEE. Okmulgee, 74447.
918-756-3042

OSAGE. Pawhuska, 74056. **918-287-2615**

OTTAWA. Miami, 74354. **918-542-9408**

PAWNEE. Pawnee, 74058. **918-762-2732**

PAYAN. Stillwater, 74074. **405-372-4209**

PITTSBURG. McAlester, 74501.
918-423-6865

PONTOTOC. Ada, 74820. **405-332-1425**

POTTAWATOMIE. Shawnee, 74801.
405-273-4305

PUSHMATAHA. Antlers, 74523.
405-298-2274

ROGER MILLS. Cheyenne, 73628.
405-497-3395

ROGERS. Claremore, 74017. **918-341-0585**

SEMINOLE. Wewoka, 74884. **405-257-2501**

SEQUOYAH. Sallisaw, 74955. **918-775-4516**

STEPHENS. Duncan, 73533. **405-255-0977**

TEXAS. Guymon, 73942. **405-338-3233**

TILLMAN. Frederick, 73542. **405-335-3421**

TULSA. Tulsa, 74103. **918-584-0471**

WAGONER. Wagoner, 74467. **918-485-2216**

WASHINGTON. Bartlesville, 74003.
918-336-0330

WASHITA. Cordell, 73632. **405-832-3548**

WOODS. Alva, 73717. **405-327-0998**

WOODWARD. Woodward, 73801.
405-256-3625

Oregon

BAKER. Baker, 97814. **503-523-3903**

BENTON. Corvallis, 97330. **503-753-2251**

CLACKAMAS. Oregon City, 97045.
503-655-8581

CLATSOP. Astoriz, 97103. **503-325-7441**

COLUMBIA. St Helens, 97051.
503-397-4322

COOS. Coquille, 97423. **503-396-3121**

CROOK. Prineville, 97754. **503-447-6553**

CURRY. Gold Beach, 97444. **503-247-7011**

DESCHUTES. Bend, 97701. **503-382-4000**

DOUGLAS. Roseburg, 97470. **503-672-3311**

GILLIAM. Condon, 97823. **503-384-2311**

GRANT. Canyon City, 97820. **503-575-0198**

HARNEY. Burns, 97720. **503-573-6641**

HOOD RIVER. Hood River, 97301.
503-386-3970

JACKSON. Medford, 97501. **503-776-7211**

JEFFERSON. Madras, 97741. **503-475-2449**

JOSEPHINE. Grants Pass, 97526.
503-476-8881

KLAMATH FALLS. 97601. **503-882-2501**

LAKE. Lakeview, 97630. **503-947-2421**

LANE. Eugene, 97401. **503-687-4207**

LINCOLN. Newport, 97365. **503-265-5341**

LINN. Albany, 97321. **503-926-5569**

MALHEUR. Vale, 97918. **503-473-3123**

MARION. Salem, 97310. **503-588-5212**

MORROW. Heppner, 97836. **503-676-9233**

MULTNOMAH. Portland, 97205.
503-248-3511

POLK. Dallas, 97338. **503-623-8171**

SHERMAN. Moro, 97039. **503-565-3606**

TILLAMOOK. Tillamook, 97141.
503-842-5511

UMATILLA. Pendleton, 97801.
503-276-7111

UNION. La Grande, 97850. **503-963-5214**

WALLOWA. Enterprise, 97828.
503-426-3226

WASCO. The Dalles, 97058. **503-296-4656**

WASHINGTON. Hillsboro, 97123.
503-648-8611

WHEELER. Fossil, 97830. **503-763-2400**

YAMHILL. McMinnville, 97128.
503-472-9371

Pennsylvania

ADAMS. Gettysburg, 17325. **717-334-6781**

ALLEGHENY. Pittsburgh, 15219.
412-355-5303

ARMSTRONG. Kittanning, 16201.
412-542-2741

BEAVER. Beaver, 15009. **412-774-5000**

BEDFORD. Bedford, 15522. **814-623-1173**

BERKS. Reading, 19601. **215-375-6121**

BLAIR. Hollidaysburg, 16648. **814-695-5541**

BRADFORD. Towanda, 18848.
717-265-9137

BUCKS. Doylestown, 18901. **215-348-2911**

BUTLER. Butler, 16001. **412-285-4731**

CAMBRIA. Ebensburg, 15931. **814-472-8960**

CAMERON. Emporium, 15834.
814-483-3349

CARBON. Jim Thorpe, 18229. **717-325-3611**

CENTRE. Bellefonte, 16823. **814-355-5521**

CHESTER. West Chester, 19380.
215-431-6100

CLARION. Clarion, 16214. **814-226-9461**

CLEARFIELD. Clearfield, 16830.
814-765-6546

CLINTON. Lock Haven, 17745.
717-748-7779

COLUMBIA. Bloomsburg, 17815.
717-784-1991

CRAWFORD. Meadville, 16335.
814-336-1151

CUMBERLAND. Carlisle, 17013.
717-249-1133

DAUPHIN. Harrisburg, 17101. **717-234-7001**

DELAWARE. Media, 19063. **215-891-2191**

ELK. Ridgway, 15853. **814-776-1161**

ERIE. Erie, 16501. **814-456-8851**

FAYETTE. Uniontown, 15401. **412-437-4525**

FOREST. Tionesta, 16353. **814-755-3526**

FRANKLIN. Chambersburg, 15723.
717-264-4125

FULTON. McConnellsburg, 17233.
717-485-3691

GREENE. Waynesburg, 15370. **412-627-7525**

HUNTINGDON. Huntingdon, 16652.
814-643-3091

INDIANA. Indiana, 15701. **412-465-2661**

JEFFERSON. Brookville, 15825.
814-849-8031

JUNIATA. Mifflintown, 17059.
717-436-6242

LACKAWANNA. Scranton, 18503.
717-961-6800

LANCASTER. Lancaster, 17602.
717-397-8201

LAWRENCE. New Castle, 16101.
412-658-2541

LEBANON. Lebanon, 17042. **717-273-8867**

LEHIGH. Allentown, 18101. **215-434-9471**

LUZERNE. Wilkes-Barre, 18703.
717-832-6161

LYCOMING. Williamsport, 17701.
717-323-9811

MCKEAN. Smethport, 16749. **814-887-5571**

MERCER. Mercer, 16137. **412-662-3800**

MIFFLIN. Lewistown, 17044. **717-248-8147**

MONROE. Stroudsburg, 18360.
717-424-5100

MONTGOMERY. Norristown, 19404.
215-275-5000

MONTOUR. Danville, 17821. **717-275-1331**

NORTHAMPTON. Easton, 18042.
215-253-4111

NORTHUMBERLAND. Sunbury, 17801.
717-286-7721

PERRY. New Bloomfield, 17068.
717-582-2131

PHILADELPHIA. Philadelphia, 19107.
215-686-1776

PIKE. Milford, 18337. **717-296-7613**

POTTER. Coudersport, 16915.
814-274-8290

SCHUYLKILL. Pottsville, 17901.
717-622-5570

SNYDER. Middleburg, 17842. **717-837-2724**

SOMERSET. Somerset, 15501.
814-445-7991

SULLIVAN. Laporte, 18626. **717-946-7331**

SUSQUEHANNA. Montrose, 18801.
717-278-3878

TIOGA. Wellsboro, 16901. **717-724-1906**

UNION. Lewisburg, 17837. **717-524-4461**

VENANGO. Franklin, 16323. **814-437-6871**

WARREN. Warren, 16365. **814-723-7550**

WASHINGTON. Washington, 15301.
412-225-0100

WAYNE. Honesdale, 18431. **717-253-4241**

WESTMORELAND. Greensburg, 15601.
412-834-2191

WYOMING. Tunkhannock, 18657.
717-836-3200

YORK. York, 17405. **717-848-3301**

South Carolina

ABBEVILLE. Abbeville, 29620.
803-459-5312

AIKEN. Aiken, 29801. **803-648-7833**

ALLENDALE. Allendale, 29810.
803-584-2013

ANDERSON. Anderson, 29621.
803-225-0022

BAMBERG. Bamberg, 29003. **803-245-2549**

BARNWELL. Barnwell, 29812.
803-259-3464

BEAUFORT. Beaufort, 29902. **803-524-7150**

BERKELEY. Moncks Corner, 29461.
803-899-7391

CALHOUN. St Matthews, 29135.
803-874-2435

CHARLESTON. Charleston, 29401.
803-577-7800

CHEROKEE. Gaffney, 29340. **803-489-5224**

CHESTER. Chester, 29706. **803-385-5133**

CHESTERFIELD. Chesterfield, 29709.
803-623-2535

CLARENDON. Manning, 29102.
803-435-2714

COLLETON. Walterboro, 29488.
803-549-5791

DARLINGTON. Darlington, 29532.
803-393-3836

DILLON. Dillon, 29536. **803-774-2391**

DORCHESTER. St George, 29477.
803-563-2331

EDGEFIELD. Edgefield, 29824.
803-637-6661

FAIRFIELD. Winnsboro, 29180.
803-635-4021

FLORENCE. Florence, 29501. **803-665-3036**

GEORGETOWN. Georgetown, 29440.
803-546-4189

GREENVILLE. Greenville, 29601.
803-242-3910

GREENWOOD. Greenwood, 29646.
803-229-6622

HAMPTON. Hampton, 29924. **803-943-3014**

HORRY. Conway, 29526. **803-248-2261**

JASPER. Ridgeland, 29936. **803-726-3173**

KERSHAW. Camden, 29020. **803-432-1191**

LANCASTER. Lancaster, 29720.
803-285-1565

LAURENS. Laurens, 29360. **803-984-5214**

LEE. Bishopville, 29010. **803-484-5341**

LEXINGTON. Lexington, 29072.
803-359-3400

MCCORMICK. McCormick, 29835.
803-465-2195

MARION. Marion, 29571. **803-423-3904**

MARLBORO. Bennettsville, 29512.
803-479-4462

NEWBERRY. Newberry, 29108.
803-276-0681

OCONEE. Walhalla, 29691. **605-638-5835**

ORANGEBURG. Orangeburg, 29115.
803-534-6052

PICKENS. Pickens, 29671. **803-878-4753**

RICHLAND. Columbia, 29201.
803-252-4905

SALUDA. Saluda, 29138. **803-445-3303**

SPARTANBURG. Spartanburg, 29301.
803-585-4811

SUMTER. Sumter, 29150. **803-775-2346**

UNION. Union, 29379. **803-427-3351**

WILLIAMSBURG. Kingstree, 29556.
803-354-9321

YORK. York, 29745. **803-684-6631**

South Dakota

AURORA. Plankinton, 57368. **605-942-5231**

BEADLE. Huron, 57350. **605-352-8436**

BENNETT. Martin, 57551. **605-685-6591**

BON HOMME. Tyndall, 57066.
605-589-3391

BROOKINGS. Brookings, 57006.
605-692-6284

BROWN. Aberdeen, 57401. **605-225-6933**

BRULE. Chamberlain, 57325. **605-734-6521**

BUFFALO. Gannvalley, 57341.
605-293-3217

BUTTE. Belle Fourche, 57717. **605-892-2516**

CAMPBELL. Mound City, 57646.
605-955-3366

CHARLES MIX. Lake Andes, 57356.
605-487-7511

CLARK. Clark, 57225. **605-532-5851**

CLAY. Vermillion, 57069. **605-624-2281**

CODINGTON. Watertown, 57201.
605-886-8497

CORSON. McIntosh, 57641. **605-273-4229**

CUSTER. Custer, 57730. **605-673-4815**

DAVISON. Mitchell, 57301. **505-996-2474**

DAY. Webster, 57274. **605-345-3102**

DEUEL. Clear Lake, 57226. **605-874-2312**

DEWEY. Timber Lake, 57656. **605-865-3672**

DOUGLAS. Armour, 57313. **605-724-2423**

EDMUNDS. Ipswich, 57451. **605-426-3131**

FALL RIVER. Hot Springs, 57747.
605-745-5130

FAULK. Faulkton, 57438. **605-598-4223**

GRANT. Milbank, 57252. **605-432-6711**

GREGORY. Burke, 57523. **605-775-2442**

HAAKON. Philip, 57567. **605-859-2800**

HAMLIN. Hayti, 57241. **605-783-3201**

HAND. Miller, 57362. **605-853-2182**

HANSON. Alexandria, 57311. **605-239-4446**

HARDING. Buffalo, 57720. **605-375-3313**

HUGHES. Pierre, 57501. **605-224-2181**

HUTCHINSON. Olivet, 57052.
605-387-2822

HYDE. Highmore, 57345. **605-852-2512**

JACKSON. Kadoka, 57543. **605-837-2422**

JERAULD. Wessington Springs, 57832.
605-539-4121

JONES. Murdo, 57559. **605-669-2242**

KINGSBURY. De Smet, 57231.
605-854-3832

LAKE. Madison, 57042. **605-256-4876**

LAWRENCE. Deadwood, 57732.
605-578-1941

LINCOLN. Canton, 57013. **605-987-2581**

LYMAN. Kennebec, 57544. **605-869-2247**

MCCOOK. Salem, 57058. **605-425-2791**

MCPHERSON. Leola, 57456. **605-439-3314**

MARSHALL. Britton, 57430. **605-448-2401**

MEADE. Sturgis, 57785. **605-347-2360**

MELLETTE. White River, 57579.
605-259-3291

MINER. Howard, 57349. **605-772-4671**

MINNEHAHA. Sioux Falls, 57102.
605-336-2350

MOODY. Flandreau, 57028. **605-997-3161**

PENNINGTON. Rapid City, 57701.
605-343-1184

PERKINS. Bison, 57620. **605-244-5626**

POTTER. Gettysburg, 57442. **605-765-4461**

ROBERTS. Sisseton, 57262. **605-698-7336**

SANBORN. Woonsocket, 57385.
605-796-4513

SPINK. Redfield, 57469. **605-472-1825**

STANLEY. Fort Pierre, 57532. **605-223-2673**

SULLY. Onida, 57564. **605-258-2541**

TRIPP. Winner, 57580. **605-842-2727**

TURNER. Parker, 57053. **605-297-3115**

UNION. Elk Point, 57025. **605-356-2101**

WALWORTH. Selby, 57472. **605-649-7878**

YANKTON. Yankton, 57078. **605-665-2143**

ZIEBACH. Dupree, 57623. **605-365-3161**

Tennessee

ANDERSON. Clinton, 37716. **615-457-2921**

BEDFORD. Shelbyville, 37160.
615-684-7944

BENTON. Camden, 38320. **901-584-6053**

BEEDSOE. Pikeville, 37367. **615-447-2137**

BLOUNT. Maryville, 37801. **615-982-1302**

BRADLEY. Cleveland, 37311. **615-479-9654**

CAMPBELL. Jacksboro, 37757.
615-562-3827

CANNON. Woodbury, 37190. **615-563-4278**

CARROLL. Huntingdon, 38344.
901-986-5237

CARTER. Elizabethton, 37643. **615-542-2021**

CHEATHAM. Ashland City, 37015.
615-792-4620

CHESTER. Henderson, 38340. **901-989-2233**

CLAIBORNE. Tazewell, 37879.
615-626-5236

CLAY. Celina, 38551. **615-243-2249**

COCKE. Newport, 37821. **615-623-6176**

COFFEE. Manchester, 37355. **615-728-3024**

CROCKETT. Alamo, 38001. **901-696-2424**

CUMBERLAND. Crossville, 38555.
615-484-5654

DAVIDEON. Nashville, 37210.
615-747-4355

DE KALB. Smithville, 37166. **615-597-5177**

DECATUR. Decaturville, 38329.
901-852-3691

DICKSON. Charlotte, 37036. **615-789-4106**

DYER. Dyersburg, 38024. **901-285-1692**

FAYETTE. Somerville, 38068. **901-465-3082**

FENTRESS. Jamestown, 38556.
615-879-8014

FRANKLIN. Winchester, 37398.
615-967-2905

GIBSON. Trenton, 38382. **901-855-9292**

GILES. Pulaski, 38478. **615-363-5300**

GRAINGER. Rutledge, 37861. **615-828-3513**

GREENE. Greeneville, 37743.
615-638-4841

GRUNDY. Altamount, 37301. **615-692-3718**

HAMBLEN. Morristown, 37814.
615-586-1931

HAMILTON. Chattanooga, 37402.
615-757-2496

HANCOCK. Sneedville, 37869.
615-733-2519

HARDEMAN. Bolivar, 38008. **615-658-3541**

HARDIN. Savannah, 38372. **901-925-5078**

HAWKINS. Rogersville, 37857.
615-272-8833

HAYWOOD. Brownsville, 38012.
901-772-1432

HENDERSON. Lexington, 38351.
901-968-2856

HENRY. Paris, 38242. **901-642-5212**

HICKMAN. Centerville, 37033.
615-729-2492

HOUSTON. Erin, 37061. **615-289-3633**

HUMPHREYS. Waverly, 37185.
615-296-2631

JACKSON. Gainesboro, 38562.
615-268-9212

JEFFERSON. Dandridge, 37725.
615- 397-3800

JOHNSON. Mountain City, 37683.
615-727-9633

KNOX. Knoxville, 37902. **615-524-0733**

LAKE. Tiptonville, 38079. **901-253-7582**

LAUDERDALE. Ripley, 38063.
901-635-2561

LAWRENCE. Lawrenceburg, 38464.
615-762-4851

LEWIS. Hohenwald, 38462. **715-796-2200**

LINCOLN. Fayetteville, 37334.
615-433-3045

LOUDON. Loudon, 37774. **615-458-4664**

MCMINN. Athens, 37303. **615-745-3140**

MCNAIRY. Seler, 38375. **901-645-3472**

MACON. Lafayette, 37083. **615-666-2363**

MADISON. Jackson, 38301. **901-427-9441**

MARION. Jasper, 37347. **615-942-2552**

MARSHALL. Lewisburg, 37091.
615-359-1279

MAURY. Columbia, 38401. **615-388-6233**

MEIGS. Decatur, 37322. **615-334-5850**

MONROE. Madisonville, 37354.
615-442-2220

MONTGOMERY. Clarksville, 37040.
615-647-6787

MOORE. Lynchburg, 37352. **615-759-7346**

MORGAN. Warthburg, 37887. **615-346-6288**

OBION. Union City, 38261. **901-885-3831**

OVERTON. Livingston, 38570.
615-823-2631

PERRY. Linden, 37096. **615-589-2216**

PICKETT. Byrdstown, 38549. **615-864-3798**

POLK. Benton, 37307. **615-338-2841**

PUTNAM. Cookeville, 38501. **615-526-2161**

RHEA. Dayton, 37321. **615-775-1881**

ROANE. Kingston, 37763. **615-376-6541**

ROBERTSON. Springfield, 37172. **615-384-2476**

RUTHERFORD. Murfreesboro, 37130. **615-893-6644**

SCOTT. Huntsville, 37756. **615-663-2355**

SEQUATCHIE. Dunlap, 37327. **615-949-2522**

SEVIER. Sevierville, 37862. **615-453-3472**

SHELBY. Memphis, 38103. **901-528-3131**

SMITH. Carthage, 37030. **615-735-2294**

STEWART. Dover, 37058. **615-232-5371**

SULLIVAN. Blountville, 37617. **615-968-1941**

SUMNER. Gallatin, 37066. **615-452-3604**

TIPTON. Covington, 38019. **901-476-2604**

TROUSDALE. Hartsville, 37074. **615-374-2461**

UNICOI. Erwin, 37650. **615-743-9391**

UNION. Maynardville, 37807. **615-992-8043**

VAN BUREN. Spencer, 38585. **615-946-2121**

WARREN. McMinnville, 37110. **615-473-2623**

WASHINGTON. Jonesboro, 37659. **615-753-3722**

WAYNE. Waynesboro, 38485. **615-722-3805**

WEAKLEY. Dresden, 38225. **901-364-2279**

WHITE. Sparta, 38583. **615-836-8028**

WILLIAMSON. Franklin, 37064. **615-794-2559**

WILSON. Lebanon, 37087. **615-444-0314**

Texas

ANDERSON. Palestine, 75801. **214-729-7170**

ANDREWS. Andrews, 79714. **915-523-3630**

ANGELINA. Lufkin, 75901. **713-634-5612**

ARANSAS. Rockport, 78382. **512-729-2152**

ARCHER. Archer City, 76351. **817-574-4615**

ARMSTRONG. Claude, 79019. **806-226-2081**

ATASCOSA. Jourdanton, 78026. **512-769-3093**

AUSTIN. Bellville, 77418. **713-865-3644**

BAILEY. Muleshoe, 79347. **806-272-3077**

BANDERA. Bandera, 78003. **512-796-3332**

BASTROP. Bastrop, 78602. **512-321-2579**

BAYLOR. Seymour, 76380. **817-888-2662**

BEE. Beeville, 78102. **512-358-1394**

BELL. Belton, 76513. **817-939-3521**

BEXAR. San Antonio, 78205. **512-220-2200**

BLANCO. Johnson City, 78363. **512-868-4266**

BORDEN. Gail, 79838. **915-856-4255**

BOSQUE. Meridian, 76665. **817-435-2382**

BOWIE. Boston, 75557. **214-628-2721**

BRAZORIA. Angleton, 77551. **713-849-5711**

BRAZOS. Bryan, 77801. **713-822-7373**

BREWSTER. Alpine, 79830. **915-837-2213**

BRISCOE. Silverton, 79257. **806-823-79257**

BROOKS. Falfurrias, 78355. **512-325-2022**

BROWN. Brownwood, 76801. **915-643-2594**

BURLESON. Caldwell, 77836. **713-567-4326**

BURNET. Burnet, 78611. **512-756-4601**

CALDWELL. Lockhart, 78644. **512-398-2424**

CALHOUN. Port Lavaca, 77979. **512-552-2954**

CALLAHAN. Baird, 79504. **915-854-1217**

CAMERON. Brownsville, 78520. **512-546-2476**

CAMP. Pittsburg, 75686. **214-856-2731**

CARSON. Panhandle, 79068. **806-537-3622**

CASS. Linden, 75563. **214-756-5071**

CASTRO. Dimmitt, 79027. **806-647-4451**

CHAMBERS. Anahuac, 77514. **713-267-3671**

CHEROKEE. Rusk, 75785. **214-783-2350**

CHILDRESS. Childress, 79201. **817-937-2221**

CLAY. Henrietta, 76365. **817-538-4551**

COCHRAN. Morton, 79346. **806-266-5450**

COKE. Robert Lee, 76945. **915-453-2641**

COLEMAN. Coleman, 76834. **915-625-4218**

COLLIN. McKinney, 75069. **214-542-3561**

COLLINGSWORTH. Wellington, 79095. **806-447-2408**

COLORADO. Columbus, 78934. **713-732-2604**

COMAL. New Braunfels, 78130. **512-625-8531**

COMANCHE. Comanche, 76442. **915-356-2466**

CONCHO. Paint Rock, 76866. **915-732-4321**

COOKE. Gainesville, 76240. **817-665-5362**

CORYELL. Gatesville, 76528. **817-865-5911**

COTTLE. Pauucah, 79248. **806-492-3613**

CRANE. Crane, 79731. **915-558-3581**

CROCKETT. Ozona, 76943. **915-392-8022**

CROSBY. Crosbyton, 79322. **806-675-2334**

CULBERSON. Van Horn, 79855. **915-283-2059**

DALLAM. Dalhart, 79022. **806-249-2450**

DALLAS. Dallas, 75201. **214-749-8585**

DAWSON. Lamesa, 79331. **806-872-3778**

DE WITT. Cuero, 77954. **512-275-5312**

DEAF SMITH. Hereford, 79045. **806-364-1746**

DELTA. Cooper, 75432. **214-395-2211**

DENTON. Denton, 76201. **817-382-9729**

DICKENS. Dickens, 79229. **806-623-5532**

DIMMIT. Carrizo Springs, 78834.
512-876-2323

DONLEY. Clarendon, 79226. **806-874-3436**

DUVAL. San Diego, 78384. **512-279-3978**

EASTLAND. Eastland, 76448. **817-629-1583**

ECTOR. Odessa, 79760. **915-332-9601**

EDWARDS. Rocksprings, 78880.
512-683-6590

EL PASO. El Paso, 79901. **915-543-2900**

ELLIS. Waxahachie, 75165. **214-937-1801**

ERATH. Stephenville, 76401. **817-965-3219**

FALLS. Marlin, 76661. **817-883-3182**

FANNIN. Bonham, 75418. **214-583-3711**

FAYETTE. La Grange, 78945. **713-968-3459**

FISHER. Roby, 79543. **915-776-2151**

FLOYD. Floydada, 79235. **806-983-2244**

FOARD. Crowell, 79227. **817-684-3261**

FORT BEND. Richmond, 77469.
713-342-2896

FRANKLIN. Mount Vernon, 75457.
214-537-2342

FREESTONE. Fairfield, 75840.
214-389-2635

FRIO. Pearsall, 78061. **512-334-2154**

GAINES. Seminole, 79360. **915-758-3521**

GALVESTON. Galveston, 77550.
713-762-8621

GARZA. Post, 79356. **806-495-3352**

GILLESPIE. Fredericksburg, 78624.
512-997-2854

GLASSCOCK. Garden City, 79739.
915-354-2382

GOLIAD. Golaid, 77963. **512-645-3294**

GONZALES. Gonzales, 78629.
512-672-2327

GRAY. Pampa, 79065. **806-665-1114**

GRAYSON. Sherman, 75090. **214-892-9623**

GREGG. Longview, 75601. **214-758-6181**

GRIMES. Anderson, 77830. **713-873-2662**

GUADALUPE. Seguin, 78155. **512-379-4188**

HALE. Plainview, 79072. **806-293-2596**

HALL. Memphis, 79245. **806-259-2627**

HAMILTON. Hamilton, 76531.
817-386-3815

HANSFORD. Spearman, 79081.
806-659-2626

HARDEMAN. Quanah, 79252. **817-663-2911**

HARDIN. Kountze, 77625. **713-246-3371**

HARRIS. Houston, 77002. **713-221-5000**

HARRISON. Marshall, 75670. **214-935-7872**

HARTLEY. Channing, 79018. **806-235-3582**

HASKELL. Haskell, 79521. **817-864-2451**

HAYS. San Marcos, 78666. **512-392-2601**

HEMPHILL. Canadian, 79014.
806-323-6212

HENDERSON. Athens, 75751.
214-675-2207

HIDALGO. Edinburg, 78539. **512-383-2751**

HILL. Hillsboro, 76645. **817-582-5372**

HOCKLEY. Levelland, 79336. **806-894-6856**

HOOD. Granbury, 76048. **817-573-1353**

HOPKINS. Sulphur Springs, 75482.
214-885-3929

HOUSTON. Crockett, 75835. **713-544-3263**

HOWARD. Big Spring, 79720. **915-267-8561**

HUDSPETH. Sierra Blanca, 79851.
915-369-2301

HUNT. Greenville, 75401. **214-455-6460**

HUTCHINSON. Stinnett, 79083.
806-878-2801

IROON. Mertzon, 76941. **915-835-2421**

JACK. Jacksboro, 76056. **817-567-2111**

JACKSON. Edna, 77957. **512-782-2352**

JASPER. Jasper, 75951. **713-384-4362**

JEFF DAVIS. Fort Davis, 79734.
915-426-3968

JEFFERSON. Beaumont, 77704.
713-835-8466

JIM HOGG. Hebbronville, 78361.
512-527-4031

JIM WELLS. Alice, 78332. **512-664-9522**

JOHNSON. Cleburne, 76031. **817-645-2292**

JONES. Anson, 79501. **915-823-3741**

KARNES. Karnes City, 78118. **512-780-3732**

KAUFMAN. Kaufman, 75142. **214-932-2821**

KENDALL. Boerne, 78006. **512-249-2541**

KENEDY. Sarita, 78385. **512-294-5224**

KENT. Jayton, 79528. **806-237-3881**

KERR. Kerrville, 78028. **512-257-6181**

KIMBLE. Junction, 76849. **915-446-3353**

KING. Guthrie, 79236. **806-596-2115**

KINNEY. Brackettville, 78832. **512-563-2521**

KLEBERG. Kingsville, 78363. **512-592-2411**

KNOX. Benjamin, 79505. **817-454-2191**

LA SALLE. Cotulla, 78014. **512-879-2117**

LAMAR. Paris, 75460. **214-784-4117**

LAMB. Littlefield, 79339. **806-385-4222**

LAMPASAS. Lampasas, 76550.
512-556-3812

LAVACA. Hallettsville, 77964. **512-798-2301**

LEE. Giddings, 78942. **713-542-3355**

LEON. Centerville, 75833. **214-536-2331**

LIBERTY. Liberty, 77575. **713-336-6122**

LIMESTONE. Groesbeck, 76642.
817-729-3810

LIPSCOMB. Lipscomb, 79056.
806-862-4131

LIVE OAK. George West, 78022.
512-449-1624

LLANO. Llano, 78643. **915-247-5054**

LOVING. Mentone, 79754. **915-377-2362**

LUBBOCK. Lubbock, 79404. **806-763-5351**

LYNN. Tahoka, 79373. **806-998-4750**

MCCULLOCH. Brady, 76825. **915-597-2978**

MCLENNAN. Waco, 76887. **817-756-7171**

MCMULLEN. Tilden, 78072. **512-274-3215**

MADISON. Madisonville, 77864.
713-348-2639

MARION. Jefferson, 75657. **214-665-3971**

MARTIN. Stanton, 79782. **915-756-3412**

MASON. Mason, 76856. **915-347-5263**

MATAGORDA. Bay City, 77414.
713-245-2801

MAVERICK. Eagle Pass, 78852.
512-773-2829

MEDINA. Hondo, 78861. **512-426-2313**

MIDLAND. Midland, 79701. **915-682-9481**

MILAM. Cameron, 76520. **817-697-2932**

MILLS. Goldthwaite, 76844. **915-648-2222**

MITCHELL. Colorado City, 79512.
915-728-2615

MONTAGUE. Montague, 76251.
817-894-2401

MONTGOMERY. Conroe, 77301.
713-756-0571

MOORE. Dumas, 79029. **806-935-5588**

MORRIS. Daingerfield, 75638.
214-645-3691

MOTLEY. Matador, 79244. **806-347-2621**

NACOGDOCHES. Nacogdoches, 75961.
713-564-0496

NAVARRO. Corsicana, 75110. **214-874-5201**

NEWTON. Newton, 75966. **713-379-5691**

NOLAN. Sweetwater, 79556. **915-235-2263**

NUECES. Corpus Christi, 78401.
512-884-8259

OCHILTREE. Perryton, 79070.
806-435-2562

OLDHAM. Vega, 79092. **806-267-2607**

ORANGE. Orange, 77630. **713-883-7740**

PALO PINTO. Palo Pinto, 76072.
817-659-2665

PANOLA. Carthage, 75633. **214-693-3382**

PARKER. Weatherford, 76086. **817-594-7461**

PARMER. Farwell, 79325. **806-481-3691**

PECOS. Fort Stockton, 79735. **915-336-2792**

POLK. Livingston, 77351. **713-327-8113**

POTTER. Amarillo, 79101. **806-372-4231**

PRESIDIO. Marfa, 79843. **915-729-4452**

RAINS. Emory, 75440. **214-473-2555**

RANDALL. Canyon, 79015. **806-655-3251**

REAGAN. Big Lake, 76932. **915-884-2665**

REAL. Leakey, 78873. **512-232-5304**

RED RIVER. Clarksville, 75426.
214-427-2680

REEVES. Pecos, 79772. **915-445-4817**

REFUGIO. Refugio, 78377. **512-526-4434**

ROBERTS. Miami, 79059. **806-868-3721**

ROBERTSON. Franklin, 77856.
713-828-3542

ROCKWALL. Rockwall, 75087.
214-722-5141

RUNNELS. Ballinger, 76821. **915-365-2633**

RUSK. Henderson, 75652. **214-657-5584**

SATINE. Hemphill, 75948. **713-787-3543**

SAN AUGUSTINE. San Augustine, 75972.
713-275-2452

SAN JACINTO. Coldspring, 77331.
713-653-2265

SAN PATRICIO. Sinton, 78387.
512-364-1120

SAN SABA. San Saba, 76877. **915-372-3614**

SCHLEICHER. Eldorado, 76936.
919-853-2833

SCURRY. Snyder, 79549. **915-573-5332**

SHACKELFORD. Albany, 76430.
817-762-2122

SHELBY. Center, 75935. **712-598-3863**

SHERMAN. Stratford, 79084. **806-396-2021**

SMITH. Tyler, 75701. **214-597-6347**

SOMERVELL. Glen Rose, 76043.
817-897-4427

STARR. Rio Grande City, 78582.
512-487-2307

STEPHENS. Breckenridge, 76024.
817-559-3700

STERLING. Sterling City, 76951.
915-378-4941

STONEWALL. Aspermont, 79052.
817-989-2272

SUTTON. Sonora, 76950. **915-387-2950**

SWISHER. Tulia, 79088. **806-995-3294**

TARRANT. Fort Worth, 76102.
817-336-9551

TAYLOR. Abilene, 79601. **915-677-1711**

TERRELL. Sanderson, 79848. **915-345-2421**

TERRY. Brownfield, 79316. **806-637-6421**

THROCKMORTON. Throckmorton, 76083.
817-849-2501

TITUS. Mount Pleasant, 75455.
214-572-3791

TOM GREEN. San Angelo, 76901.
915-655-5542

TRAVIS. Austin, 78767. **512-476-7162**

TRINITY. Groveton, 75845. **713-642-1208**

TYLER. Woodville, 75979. **214-283-2281**

UPSHUR. Gilmer, 75644. **214-843-3118**

UPTON. Rankin, 79778. **915-693-2321**

UVALDE. Uvalde, 78801. **512-278-6614**

VAL VERDE. Del Rio, 78840. **512-775-7262**

VAN ZANDT. Canton, 75103. **214-567-4071**

VICTORIA. Victoria, 77901. **512-575-4558**

WALKER. Huntsville, 77340. **713-295-3811**

WALLER. Hempstead, 77445. **713-295-5787**

WARD. Monahans, 79756. **915-943-4271**

WASHINGTON. Brenhan, 77833.
713-836-8400

WEBB. Laredo, 78040. **512-722-1725**

WHARTON. Wharton, 77488. **713-532-4612**

WHEELER. Wheeler, 79096. **806-826-5544**

WICHITA. Wichita Falls, 76301.
817-322-0721

WILBARGER. Vernon, 76384. **817-552-2652**

WILLACY. Raymondville, 78580.
512-689-3393

WILLIAMSON. Georgetown, 78626.
512-863-3323

WILSON. Floresville, 78114. **512-393-2845**

WINKLER. Kermit, 79745. **915-586-6658**

WISE. Decatur, 76234. **817-627-5743**

WOOD. Quitman, 75783. **214-763-2716**

YOAKUM. Plains, 79355. **806-456-8606**

YOUNG. Graham, 76046. **817-549-2030**

ZAPATA. Zapata, 78076. **512-765-4342**

ZAVALA. Crystal City, 78839. **512-374-3810**

Utah

BEAVER. Beaver, 84713. **801-438-2352**

BOX ELDER. Brigham City, 84302.
801-723-3277

CACHE. Logan, 84321. **801-752-3542**

CARBON. Price, 84501. **801-637-0327**

DAGGETT. Manila, 84046. **801-784-3154**

DAVIS. Farmington, 84025. **801-295-2394**

DUCHESNE. Duchesne, 84021.
801-739-5722

EMERY. Castle Dale, 84513. **801-748-2468**

GARFIELD. Panguitch, 84759. **801-676-2327**

GRAND. Moab, 84532. **801-259-5645**

IRON. Parowan, 84761. **801-586-9974**

JUAB. Nephi, 84648. **801-623-0271**

KANE. Kanab, 84741. **801-644-2458**

MILLARD. Fillmore, 84631. **801-743-6223**

MORGAN. Morgan, 84050. **801-829-3311**

PIUTE. Junction, 84740. **801-577-2840**

RICH. Randolph, 84064. **801-793-2415**

SALT LAKE. Salt Lake City, 84110.
801-328-7541

SAN JUAN. Monticello, 84535.
801-587-2232

SANPETE. Manti, 84642. **801-835-2131**

SEVIER. Richfield, 84701. **801-896-4870**

SUMMIT. Coalville, 84017. **801-336-5951**

TOOELE. Tooele, 84074. **801-882-5550**

UINTAH. Vernal, 84078. **801-789-1622**

UTAH. Provo, 84601. **801-373-5510**

WASATCH. Heber City, 84032.
801-654-0661

WASHINGTON. St George, 84770.
801-673-2468

WAYNE. Loa, 84747. **801-836-2731**

WEBER. Ogden, 84401. **801-399-8401**

Vermont

ADDISON. Middlebury, 05853.
802-388-7741

BENNINGTON. Bennington, 05201.
802-442-8528

CALEDONIA. St Johnsbury, 05819.
802-748-3813

CHITTENDEN. Burlington, 05401.
802-863-3467

ESSEX. Guildhall, 05905. **802-676-3910**

FRANKLIN. St Albans, 05478. **802-524-2739**

GRAND ISLE. North Hero, 05474.
802-372-8350

LAMOILLE. Hyde Park, 05655.
802-888-2207

ORANGE. Chelsea, 05038. **802-685-4610**

ORLEANS. Newport, 05855. **802-334-2711**

RUTLAND. Rutland, 05701. **802-775-4394**

WASHINGTON. Montpelier, 05602.
802-223-2091

WINDHAM. Newfane, 05345. **802-254-4994**

WINDSOR. Woodstock, 05091.
802-457-2121

Virginia

ACCOMACK. Accomac, 23301.
804-787-4289

ALBEMARIE. Charlottesville, 22901.
804-296-5822

ALLEGHANY. Covington, 24426.
703-863-8646

AMELIA. Amelia Court House, 23002.
804-561-3039

AMHERST. Amherst, 24521. **804-946-7206**

APPOMATTOX. Appomattox, 24522.
804-352-5275

ARLINGTON. Arlington, 22210.
703-558-0200

AUGUSTA. Staunton, 24401. **703-885-8931**

BATH. Warm Springs, 24484. **703-839-2361**

BEDFORD. Bedford, 24523. **703-586-0421**

BLAND. Bland, 24315. **703-688-4562**

BOTETOURT. Fincastle, 24090.
703-473-8220

BRUNSWICK. Lawrenceville, 23868.
804-848-3107

BUCHANAN. Grundy, 24614. **703-935-2745**

BUCKINGHAM. Buckingham, 23921.
804-969-4371

CAMPBELL. Rustburg, 24588.
804-332-5161

CAROLINE. Bowling Green, 22427.
804-633-5380

CARROLL. Hillsville, 24343. **703-728-3331**

CHARLES CITY. Charles City, 23030.
804-829-2402

CHARLOTTE. Charlotte Court House,
23923. **804-542-5600**

CHESAPEAKE. Chesapeake, 23320.
804-547-6166

CHESTERFIELD. Chesterfield, 23822.
804-748-1211

CLARKE. Berryville, 22611. **703-955-1309**

CRAIG. New Castle, 24127. **703-864-5010**

CULPEPER. Culpeper, 22701. **703-825-3035**

CUMBERLAND. Cumberland, 23040.
804-492-4442

DICKENSON. Clintwood, 24228.
703-926-4549

DINWIDDIE. Dinwiddie, 23841.
804-469-2611

ESSEX. Tappahannock, 22560.
804-443-4331

FAIRFAX. Fairfax, 22039. **703-691-2321**

FAUQUIER. Warrenton, 22186.
703-347-9550

FLOYD. Floyd, 24091. **703-745-2610**

FLUVANNA. Palmyra, 22963. **804-589-3138**

FRANKLIN. Rocky Mount, 24151.
703-483-1315

FREDERICK. Winchester, 22601.
703-667-3434

GILES. Pearisburg, 24134. **703-921-2525**

GLOUCESTER. Gloucester, 23061.
804-693-2502

GOOCHLAND. Goochland, 23063.
804-556-2501

GRAYSON. Independence, 24348.
703-773-7302

GREENE. Stanardsville, 22973.
804-985-2311

GREENSVILLE. Emporia, 23897.
804-634-2038

HALIFAX. Halifax, 24558. **804-476-2141**

HAMPTON. Hampton, 23369.
703-723-6011

HANOVER. Hanover, 23069. **804-798-6081**

HENRICO. Richmond, 23219. **804-649-1461**

HENRY. Martinsville, 24112. **703-738-3961**

HIGHLAND. Monterey, 24465.
703-468-2260

ISLE OF WIGHT. Isle of Wight, 23397.
804-357-3191

JAMES CITY. Williamsburg, 23185.
804-220-1122

KING AND QUEEN. King and Queen
Court House, 23085. **804-785-7955**

KING GEORGE. King George, 22485.
703-775-3322

KING WILLIAM. King William, 23086.
804-769-2671

LANCASTER. Lancaster, 22503.
804-462-2631

LEE. Jonesville, 24263. **703-346-2691**

LOUDOUN. Leesburg, 22075. **703-777-2660**

LOUISA. Louisa, 23093. **703-967-0401**

LUNENBERG. Lunenberg, 23952.
804-696-2230

MADISON. Madison, 22727. **703-948-4561**

MATHEWS. Mathews, 23109. **804-725-7171**

MECKLENBURG. Boydton, 23917.
804-738-6488

MIDDLESEX. Saluda, 23149. **804-758-3511**

MONTGOMERY. Christiansburg, 24073.
703-382-2661

NELSON. Lovingston, 22949. **804-263-4873**

NEW KENT. New Kent, 23124.
804-966-2764

NEWPORT NEWS. Newsport News, 23607.
804-247-8411

NORTHAMPTON. Eastville, 23347.
804-678-5126

NORTHUMBERLAND. Heathsville, 22473.
804-580-7666

NOTTOWAY. Nottoway, 23955.
804-645-8696

ORANGE. Orange, 22960. **703-672-4574**

PAGE. Luray, 22835. **703-743-4064**

PATRICK. Stuart, 24171. **703-694-7213**

PITTSYLVANIA. Chatham, 24531.
804-432-2041

POWHATAN. Powhatan, 23139.
804-598-3852

PRINCE EDWARD. Farmville, 23901.
804-392-4129

PRINCE GEORGE. Prince George, 23875.
804-732-8818

PRINCE WILLIAM. Manassas, 22110.
703-900-9171

PULASKI. Pulaski, 24301. **703-980-8888**

RAPPAHANNOCK. Washington, 22747.
703-675-3621

RICHMOND. Warsaw, 22572. **804-333-5781**

ROANOKE. Salem, 24153. **703-389-0811**

ROCKBRIDGE. Lexington, 24450.
703-463-4361

ROCKINGHAM. Harrisonburg, 22801.
703-434-5941

RUSSELL. Lebanon, 24266. **703-889-2372**

SCOTT. Gate City, 24251. **703-386-6521**

SHENANDOAH. Woodstock, 22664.
703-459-2195

SMYTH. Marion, 24354. **703-783-3298**

SOUTHAMPTON. Courtland, 23837. **804-653-2465**

SPOTSYLVANIA. Spotsylvania, 22553. **703-582-6371**

STAFFORD. Stafford, 22554. **703-659-4101**

SUFFOLK. Suffolk, 23434. **703-539-2351**

SURRY. Surry, 23883. **804-294-3266**

SUSSEX. Sussex, 23884. **804-246-5521**

TAZEWELL. Tazewell, 24651. **703-988-5552**

VIRGINIA BEACH. Virginia Beach, 73458. **804-427-4242**

WARREN. Front Royal, 22630. **703-635-9973**

WASHINGTON. Abingdon, 24210. **703-628-2983**

WESTMORELAND. Montross, 22520. **804-493-6101**

WISE. Wise, 24293. **703-328-6111**

WYTHE. Wytheville, 24382. **703-228-4991**

YORK. Yorktown, 23490. **804-887-5811**

Washington

ADAMS. Ritzville, 99169. **509-659-0110**

ASOTIN. Asotin, 99402. **502-243-4165**

BENTON. Prosser, 99350. **509-786-2262**

CHELAN. Wenatchee, 98801. **509-663-4803**

CLALLAM. Port Angeles, 98362. **206-452-2102**

CLARK. Vancouver, 98660. **206-699-2000**

COLUMBIA. Dayton, 99328. **509-382-4542**

COWLITZ. Kelso, 98626. **206-577-3020**

DOUGLAS. Waterville, 98858. **509-745-3001**

FERRY. Republic, 99166. **509-775-3705**

FRANKLIN. Pasco, 99301. **509-545-3536**

GARFIELD. Pomeroy, 99347. **509-843-3858**

GRANT. Ephrata, 98823. **509-754-2011**

GRAYS HARBOR. Montesano, 98563. **206-249-3731**

ISLAND. Coupeville, 98239. **206-678-5111**

JEFFERSON. Port Townsend, 98368. **206-385-2016**

KING. Seattle, 98101. **206-344-4100**

KITSAP. Port Orchard, 98366. **206-876-7147**

KITTITAS. Ellensburg, 98926. **509-925-9325**

KLICKITAT. Goldendale, 98620. **509-773-4612**

LEWIS. Chehalis, 98532. **206-748-0026**

LINCOLN. Davenport, 99122. **509-725-1401**

MASON. Shelton, 98584. **206-426-3222**

OKANOGAN. Okanogan, 98840. **509-422-3521**

PACIFIC. South Bend, 98586. **206-875-6107**

PEND OREILLE. Newport, 99156. **509-447-4119**

PIERCE. Tacoma, 98402. **206-593-4000**

SAN JUAN. Friday Harbor, 98250. **206-378-2161**

SKAGIT. Mount Vernon, 98273. **206-336-2196**

SKAMANIA. Stevenson, 98648. **509-427-5141**

SNOHOMISH. Everett, 98201. **206-259-9494**

SPOKANE. Spokane, 99201. **509-456-2265**

STEVENS. Colville, 99114. **509-684-4301**

THURSTON. Olympia, 98501. **206-753-8031**

WAHKIAKUM. Cathlamet, 98612. **206-794-3219**

WALLA WALLA. Walla Walla, 99362. **509-525-6161**

WHATCOM. Bellingham, 98225. **206-676-6700**

WHITMAN. Colfax, 99111. **509-397-4601**

YAKIMA. Yakima, 98901. **509-575-4111**

West Virginia

BARBOUR. Philippi, 26416. **304-457-2232**

BERKELEY. Martinsburg, 25401. **304-263-3511**

BOONE. Madison, 25130. **304-369-3925**

BRAXTON. Sutton, 26601. **304-765-5511**

BROOKE. Wellsburg, 26070. **304-737-3661**

CABELL. Huntington, 25717. **304-525-8071**

CALHOUN. Grantsville, 26147. **304-354-6725**

CLAY. Clay, 25043. **304-587-4259**

DODDRIDGE. West Union, 26456. **304-873-2631**

FAYETTE. Fayetteville, 25840. **304-574-1200**

GILMER. Glenville, 26351. **304-462-7641**

GRANT. Petersburg, 26847. **304-257-6936**

GREENBRIER. Lewisburg, 24901. **304-645-2373**

HAMPSHIRE. Romney, 26757. **304-822-5112**

HANCOCK. New Cumberland, 26047. **304-564-3311**

HARDY. Moorefield, 26836. **304-538-2929**

HARRISON. Clarksburg, 26301. **304-624-7431**

JACKSON. Ripley, 25271. **304-372-2011**

JEFFERSON. Charles Town, 25414. **304-725-2315**

KANAWHA. Charleston, 25301. **304-348-7100**

LEWIS. Weston, 26452. **304-269-3371**

LINCOLN. Hamlin, 25523. **304-824-3336**

LOGAN. Logan, 25601. **304-752-2000**

MCDOWELL. Welch, 24801. **304-436-6216**

MARION. Fairmont, 26554. **304-366-2210**

MARSHALL. Moundsville, 26041. **304-845-8660**

MASON. Point Pleasant, 25550. **304-675-1110**

MERCER. Princeton, 24740. **304-425-9571**

MINERAL. Keyser, 26726. **304-788-0341**

MINGO. Williamson, 25661. **304-235-5060**

MONONGALIA. Morgantown, 26505. **304-292-6351**

MONROE. Union, 24983. **304-772-3096**

MORGAN. Berkeley Springs, 25411. **304-258-2774**

NICHOLAS. Summersville, 26651. **304-872-3630**

OHIO. Wheeling, 26003. **304-234-0211**

PENDLETON. Franklin, 26807. **304-358-2505**

PLEASANTS. St Marys, 26170. **304-688-2815**

POCAHONTAS. Marlinton, 24954. **304-799-4710**

PRESTON. Kingwood, 26537. **304-329-0070**

PUTNAM. Winfield, 25213. **304-755-2824**

RALEIGH. Beckley, 25801. **304-255-0441**

RANDOLPH. Elkins, 26241. **304-636-0543**

RITCHIE. Harrisville, 26362. **304-643-2164**

ROANE. Spencer, 25276. **304-927-2860**

SUMMERS. Hinton, 25951. **304-466-4235**

TAYLOR. Grafton, 26354. **304-265-1401**

TUCKER. Parsons, 26287. **304-478-2414**

TYLER. Middlebourne, 26149. **304-758-2311**

UPSHUR. Buckhannon, 26201 **304-472-1360**

WAYNE. Wayne, 25570. **304-272-5101**

WEBSTER. Webster Springs, 26288. **304-847-2508**

WETZEL. New Martinsville, 26155. **304-455-1390**

WIRT. Elizabeth, 26143. **304-275-4271**

WOOD. Parkersburg, 26105. **304-485-4479**

WYOMING. Pineville, 24874. **304-732-8000**

Wisconsin

ADAMS. Friendship, 53934. **608-339-7811**

ASHLAND. Ashland, 54806. **715-682-2533**

BARRON. Barron, 54812. **715-537-3212**

BAYFIELD. Washburn, 54891. **715-373-5370**

BROWN. Green Bay, 54301. **414-437-3211**

BUFFALO. Alma, 54610. **608-685-4940**

BURNETT. Grantsburg, 54840. **715-463-5344**

CALUMET. Chilton, 53014. **414-849-2361**

CHIPPEWA. Chippewa Falls, 54729. **715-723-4168**

CLARK. Neillsville, 54456. **715-743-3101**

COLUMBIA. Portage, 53901. **608-742-2191**

CRAWFORD. Prairie du Chien, 53821. **608-326-2122**

DANE. Madison, 53701. **608-266-4121**

DODGE. Juneau, 53039. **414-386-4411**

DOOR. Sturgeon Bay, 54235. **414-743-5511**

DOUGLAS. Superior, 54880. **715-395-0341**

DUNN. Menomonie, 54751. **715-232-2429**

EAU CLAIRE. Eau Claire, 54701. **715-834-2991**

FLORENCE. Florence, 54121. **715-528-3201**

FOND DU LAC. Fond du Lac, 54935. **414-921-5600**

FOREST. Crandon, 54520. **715-478-2422**

GRANT. Lancaster, 53813. **608-723-2675**

GREEN. Monroe, 53566. **608-325-4166**

GREEN LAKE. Green Lake, 54941. **414-294-6581**

IOWA. Dodgeville, 53533. **608-935-5445**

IRON. Hurley, 54534. **715-561-3375**

JACKSON. Black River Falls, 54615. **715-284-2221**

JEFFERSON. Jefferson, 53549. **414-674-2500**

JUNEAU. Mauston, 53948. **608-843-3121**

KENOSHA. Kenosha, 53140. **414-657-6111**

KEWAUNEE. Kewaunee, 54216. **414-338-3580**

LA CROSSE. La Crosse, 54601. **608-784-4888**

LAFAYETTE. Darlington, 53530. **608-776-4003**

LANGLADE. Antigo, 54409. **715-623-3305**

LINCOLN. Merrill, 54452. **715-536-7444**

MANITOWOC. Manitowoc, 54220. **414-682-8811**

MARATHON. Wausau, 54401. **715-842-2141**

MARINETTE. Marinette, 54143. **715-735-3371**

MARQUETTE. Montello, 53949. **414-297-2532**

MENOMINEE. Keshena, 54135. **715-799-3311**

MILWAUKEE. Milwaukee, 53202. **414-278-4211**

MONROE. Sparta, 54656. **608-269-4411**

OCONTO. Oconto, 54153. **414-834-5322**

ONEIDA. Rhinelander, 54501. **715-369-2727**

OUTAGAMIE. Appleton, 54911. **414-739-4491**

OZAUKEE. Port Washington, 53074. **414-284-9411**

PEPIN. Durand, 54376. **715-672-8857**

PIERCE. Ellsworth, 54011. **715-273-5272**

POLK. Balsam Lake, 54810. **715-485-3365**

PORTAGE. Stevens Point, 54481. **715-346-2113**

PRICE. Phillips, 54555. **715-339-3325**

RACINE. Racine, 53403. **414-636-3118**

RICHLAND. Richland Center, 53581. **608-647-2747**

ROCK. Janesville, 53545. **608-752-7471**

RUSK. Ladysmith, 54848. **715-532-5555**

ST CROIX. Hudson, 54016. **715-386-5581**

SAUK. Baraboo, 53913. **608-356-5581**

SAWYER. Hayward, 54834. **715-634-4866**

SHAWANO. Shawano, 54166. **715-526-9150**

SHEBOYGAN. Sheboygan, 53081. **414-457-5521**

TAYLOR. Medford, 54451. **715-748-3131**

TREMPEALEAU. Whitehall, 54773. **715-538-4717**

VERNON. Viroqua, 54665. **608-637-3569**

VILAS. Eagle River, 54521. **715-479-4151**

WALWORTH. Elkhorn, 53121. **414-723-4900**

WASHBURN. Shell Lake, 54871. **715-468-7808**

WASHINGTON. West Bend, 53095. **414-334-3491**

WAUKESHA. Waukesha, 53186. **414-544-8227**

WAUPACA. Waupaca, 54981. **715-258-2128**

WAUSHARA. Wautoma, 54982. **414-787-2320**

WINNEBAGO. Oshkosh, 54901. **414-235-2500**

WOOD. Wisconsin Rapids, 54494. **715-423-3000**

Wyoming

ALBANY. Laramie, 82070. **307-742-2150**

BIG HORN. Basin, 82410. **307-568-2357**

CAMPBELL. Gillette, 82716. **307-682-4763**

CARBON. Rawlins, 82301. **307-324-3446**

CONVERSE. Douglas, 82633. **307-358-2244**

CROOK. Sundance, 82729. **307-283-1323**

FREMONT. Lander, 82520. **307-332-2405**

GOSHEN. Torrington, 82240. **307-864-3515**

HOT SPRINGS. Thermopolis, 82443. **307-864-3515**

JOHNSON. Buffalo, 82834. **307-684-7272**

LARAMIE. Cheyenne, 82001. **307-634-3565**

LINCOLN. Kemmerer, 83101. **307-877-6673**

NATRONA. Casper, 82601. **307-265-1904**

NIOBRARA. Lusk, 82225. **307-334-2211**

PARK. Cody, 82414. **307-587-2204**

PLATTE. Wheatland, 82201. **307-322-2315**

SHERIDAN. Sheridan, 82801. **307-674-6822**

SUBLETTE. Pinedale, 82941. **307-367-4372**

SWEETWATER. Green River, 82935. **307-875-2611**

TETON. Jackson, 83001. **307-733-4430**

UINTA. Evanston, 82930. **307-789-3815**

WASHAKIE. Worland, 82401. **307-347-3131**

WESTON. Newcastle, 82701. **307-746-2684**

POLICE AND EMERGENCY AGENCIES

CITY POLICE

ALBANY POLICE DEPARTMENT. Morton Ave and Broad St, Albany, NY 12202. **518-463-4141** (also night line)
Chief. Edward McArdle
Community Relations Officer. Lieutenant John Dale

ANAHEIM POLICE DEPARTMENT. 425 S Harbour Rd, Anaheim, CA 92803. **714-533-5515.** Night line: **714-533-5708**
Chief. Harold A Bastrup
Press Information Officer. Lieutenant R A Zippel. **714-533-5878**

ATLANTA BUREAU OF POLICE SERVICES. 175 Decatur St SE, Atlanta, GA SE 30303. **404-658-6700**
Commissioner. A Reginald Eaves
Public Information Officer. Pam Crayton. **404-658-6777**

BALTIMORE POLICE DEPARTMENT. 601 E Fayette St, Baltimore, MD 21202. **301-396-2525.** Night line. **301-396-2284**
Commissioner. Donald D Pomerleau
Director of Public Information. Dennis S Hill. **301-396-2012**

BIRMINGHAM POLICE DEPARTMENT. City Hall, 710 N 20th St, Birmingham, AL 35203. **205-254-2000**

Chief. James C Parsons
Press Officer. Captain Jack E Le Grand

BOSTON POLICE. 154 Berkeley St, Boston, MA 02116. **617-247-4200**
Commissioner. Joseph M Jordan
Press Officer. Sergeant William Mullane. **617-247-4520** (also night line)

BUFFALO POLICE DEPARTMENT. 74 Franklin St, Buffalo, NY 14202. **716-847-2222**
Commissioner. Thomas Blair. **716-847-2260**
Press Officer. Captain Marianne Bass. **716-842-1360**

CHICAGO POLICE DEPARTMENT. 1121 S State St, Chicago, IL 60605. **312-744-4000**
Superintendent. James Rochford
Public Relations Officer. David Mozee. **312-744-5480**

CINCINNATI POLICE DIVISION. 310 Ezzard Charles Dr, Cincinnati, OH 45214. **513-352-3536**
Chief. Colonel Myron J Leistler
Media Information Officers. William T Ries and Chris Robertson. **513-352-3514**

CLEVELAND POLICE DEPARTMENT. 1300 Ontario, Cleveland, OH 44113. **216-623-5000**
Chief. Lloyd F Garey
Press Officer. None designated. Address inquiries to the chief's office between 7:30 am and 6 pm during the business week. After business hours and on weekends call the police captain designated as operations officer at **216-623-5723**

COLUMBUS DIVISION OF POLICE. City Hall, 90 W Broad, Columbus, OH 43215. **614-462-4545.** Night line: **614-462-4580**
Chief. Earl Burden (120 W Gay St). **614-462-4600**
Director of Public Safety. Bernard Chupka. **614-222-8210**
Public Information Assistants. Mary Helen Van Dyke and J Jeffrey Rennie (120 W Gay St). **614-462-4610**

DALLAS POLICE DEPARTMENT. 106 S Karwood St, Dallas, TX 75201. **214-748-9711.** Night line: **214-742-2431**
Chief. Donald Byrd
Public Relations Officer. Bob Shaw

DAYTON POLICE DEPARTMENT. 335 W 3rd St, Dayton, OH 45402. **513-222-9511** (also night line)
Director. Grover W O'Connor
Press Officer. Joseph P Moore. Ext 210

DENVER POLICE DEPARTMENT. 1257 Champa St, Denver, CO 80203. **303-534-2424**
Chief. Arthur Dill
Press Contact. Arthur Dill. **303-297-2004**

DETROIT POLICE DEPARTMENT. 1300 Beaubin St, Detroit, MI 48226. **313-224-4400**
Chief. William L Hart
Public Information Unit. Lieutenant Fred Williams, commanding officer. **313-224-1200**

HARTFORD POLICE DEPARTMENT. 155 Morgan St, Hartford, CT 06103. **203-527-0112**
Chief. Hugo J Masini
Public Information Advisor. Gordon Damon. Ext 280 (also night line)

HOUSTON POLICE DEPARTMENT. 61 Riesner St, Houston, TX 77002. **713-222-3311**
Chief. Harry Caldwell
Public Information Director. Rick Hartley. **713-222-5348**

INDIANAPOLIS POLICE DEPART-MENT. 50 N Alabama St, Indianapolis, IN 46204. **317-633-3000**
Chief. Eugene Gallagher
Police Information Officer. Ruth Beaver

KANSAS CITY, MO, POLICE DEPART-MENT. 1125 Locust St, Kansas City, MO 64106. **816-842-6525.** Night line: Ext 204 (communications supervisor)
Chief. Marvin L Van Kirk
Media Liaison. Scott Hoober. Ext 451
Public Information Commander. Sergeant James Harmon. Ext 346

LOS ANGELES POLICE DEPARTMENT. City Hall, 200 N Spring St, Los Angeles, CA 90012. **213-485-3586.** Night line: **213-485-3261** (Investigative Headquarters Division will contact a press relations representative)
Chief. Edward M Davis
Press Relations Officer. William D Booth. **213-485-3586**

LOUISVILLE POLICE DEPARTMENT. City Hall, 6th and Jefferson, Louisville, KY 40202. **502-581-3450**
Chief. Colonel John Nevin
Press Contact. Officer Carl Yates. **502-581-3582**

MEMPHIS POLICE DEPARTMENT. 128 Adams St, Memphis, TN 38102. **901-528-2222**
Deputy Director. M S Jones
Public Relations Officer. Lieutenant B J Johnson. **901-528-2370** (also night line)

MIAMI POLICE DEPARTMENT. Miami, FL 33133. **305-579-6111.** Night lines: **305-579-6424** (recording) and **305-579-6404** (report, control, and processing unit). "We also have one of our public information officers on stand-by from 12:00 midnight to 0700 hours on weekends. This officer may

be contacted through a pager by the duty captain or the staff duty officer."
Chief. Garland Watkins
Press Officers. Sergeant Richard Gause, supervisor; Officer Calvin Ross, public information officer; Officer Harry Cunill, public information officer **305-579-6420**

MILWAUKEE POLICE DEPARTMENT. 749 W State St, Milwaukee, WI 53233. **414-273-8660.** Night line, emergency: **414-765-2323**
Chief. Harold A Breiser
Press Officer. Inspector Kenneth Hagopian. **414-273-8660**

MINNEAPOLIS POLICE. 119 City Hall, Minneapolis, MN 55415. **612-348-2861**
Chief. Carl E Johnson
Press Contact. Captain Bruce Lindberg. **612-348-6870**

NASHVILLE METROPOLITAN POLICE DEPARTMENT. Metropolitan Court House, Public Sq, Nashville, TN 37201. **615-259-6321**
Chief. Joe Casey
Press Contact. Joe Casey. **615-259-5321**

NASSAU COUNTY POLICE DEPART-MENT. 1490 Franklin Ave, Mineola, NY 11501. **516-535-4131.** Night line: **516-535-4116**
Commissioner. Daniel P Guido
Public Information Officer. Captain Robert Yaccarino, commanding officer, public information office

NEWARK POLICE DEPARTMENT. 22 Franklin St, Newark, NJ 07102. **201-733-6000** (also night line, emergency).
Chief. Charles Zizzi
Press Contact. Charles Zizzi. **201-733-8058**

NEW ORLEANS POLICE DEPART-MENT. City Hall, 1300 Perdido St, New Orleans, LA 70112. **504-586-5183.** Night line: **504-586-5136**
Superintendent. Clarence B Giarrusso
Press Contacts. Anthony R Buonagura and August C Krinke, deputy information officers. **504-586-5191**

NEW YORK CITY POLICE DEPART-MENT. Police Plz, New York, NY 10038. **212-374-6700** (also night line)
Deputy Commissioner, Public Information. Frank McLoughlin
Press Contact. Police Officer George Kurth

NORFOLK POLICE DEPARTMENT. 811 E City Hall Ave, Norfolk, VA 23510. **804-441-2261.** Night line: **804-441-2281** (Detective Division)

Chief. C D Grant

Public Information Officer. Officer Ron R Rollins. **804-441-2264.** (h) **804-480-1269**

OAKLAND POLICE DEPARTMENT. 455 7th St, Oakland, CA 94607. **415-273-3000.** Night line, emergency: **415-273-3211**

Chief. George T Hart

Press Officer. Sergeant R Nichelini. **415-273-3131**

PHILADELPHIA POLICE DEPART-MENT. 8th and Race Sts, Philadelphia, PA 19106. **215-686-1776.** Night line: **215-231-3131.** Police radio: **215-686-3125.** Detective Bureau, major crimes: **215-686-3346**

Commissioner. Joseph O'Neill. **215-686-3356**

Press Contact. Joseph O'Neill

PHOENIX POLICE DEPARTMENT. 620 W Washington, Phoenix, AZ 85003. **602-262-6151.** Night lines: **602-262-6141** (Detective Bureau) and **602-262-6151** (emergencies).

Chief. Lawrence Wetzel

Public Information Specialist. Michelle Loewel. **602-262-7331**

PITTSBURGH DEPARTMENT OF POLICE. Public Safety Bldg, 100 Grant St, Pittsburgh, PA 15219. **412-225-2800.** Night line: **412-765-1212**

Superintendent. Robert J Coll, Jr

Press Contact. Albert L Mills, assistant superintendent. **412-255-2918**

PORTLAND POLICE BUREAU. 222 SW Pine St, Portland, OR 97204. **503-248-5600.** Night lines: **503-248-5810** or **503-760-6911** (emergency communications center)

Chief. Bruce R Baker

Public Information Officer. Sergeant Roy E Kindrick. **503-248-5610**

PROVIDENCE POLICE DEPARTMENT. 209 Fountain St, Providence, RI 02903. **401-272-3121**

Chief. Robert E Ricci

Public Relations Officer. Major William Paniccia. Ext 288

ROCHESTER POLICE DEPARTMENT. Public Safety Bldg, Civic Center Plz, Plymouth Ave S, Rochester, NY 14614. **716-428-7070**

Chief. Thomas F Hastings. **716-428-7033**

Administrative Assistant. Sergeant Donald Williams. **716-428-6729**

ST LOUIS METROPOLITAN POLICE DEPARTMENT. City Hall, 1206 Market St, St Louis, MO 63103. **314-444-5555**

Chief. Colonel Eugene J Camp

Public Affairs Division. Robert J Barton. **314-444-5668**

SALT LAKE CITY POLICE DEPART-MENT. 450 S 3rd East St, Salt Lake City, UT 84111. **801-328-7222** (also night line)

Chief. E L Willoughby

Press Contact. Max Yospe. (h) **801-277-2009**

SAN ANTONIO POLICE DEPARTMENT. City Hall, Military Plz, San Antonio, TX 78204. **512-225-7484** (also night line)

Chief. E E Peters

Press Contact. E E Peters

SAN BERNARDINO POLICE DEPART-MENT. 453 N Arrowhead Ave, San Bern-ardino, CA 92401. **714-383-5011** (also night line)

Chief. Raymond B Rucker. **714-383-5034**

Press Contact. B Warren Cocke, assistant chief of police. **714-383-5238**

Watch Commander. **714-383-5011**

SAN DIEGO POLICE DEPARTMENT. City Concourse, San Diego, CA 92101. **714-236-6566** (also night line)

Chief. William B Kolender, Sr

Public Information Officer. Bill Robinson. **714-236-6733**

SAN FRANCISCO POLICE DEPART-MENT. 850 Bryant St, San Francisco, CA 94103. **415-553-9111.** Emergency number: **415-553-0123**

Chief. Charles R Gain

Public Relations Officer. Michael O'Toole. **415-553-1551**

SAN JOSE POLICE DEPARTMENT. 201 W Mission, San Jose, CA 95110. **408-277-4212**

Chief. Joseph D McNamara

Press Contact. Sergeant Bob Burroughs, staff inspections. **408-277-5281**

Watch Commander. **408-277-4728**

SEATTLE POLICE DEPARTMENT. 610 3rd Ave, Seattle, WA 98104. **206-625-2044.** Night line: **206-625-2092** ·

Chief. Robert L Hanson

Press Assistant. Gary Flynn. **206-625-2051**

TAMPA POLICE DEPARTMENT. 1710 Tampa St, Tampa, FL 33602. **813-223-8181**

Chief. Charles Otero. **813-223-8687**

Public Information Director. John R Barker. **813-223-8479**

Uniform District I Shift Commander. **813-223-8834**

Uniform District II Shift Commander. **813-223-8705**

TOLEDO POLICE DEPARTMENT. 2927 Monroe St, Toledo, OH 43610. **419-247-6037** (also night line)

Captain. Edward Sobcizak

Press Contact. Edward Sobcizak. **419-247-6465**

WASHINGTON, DC, METROPOLITAN POLICE. Washington, DC 20001. **202-626-2000**

Chief. Maurice J Cullinane

Public Information Officer. Sergeant Charles E Collins, Jr. **202-626-2871**

WINSTON–SALEM POLICE DEPART-MENT. City Hall, Winston–Salem, NC 27101. **919-727-2184** (also night line)

Chief. T A Surratt

Director of Public Relations. Corporal Bob Hammons. **919-727-2409**

STATE POLICE

ALABAMA DEPARTMENT OF PUBLIC SAFETY. 500 Dexter Ave, Montgomery, 36130. **205-832-6448**

Director. Colonel Eldred C Dothard. **205-832-5245**

Safety Education Unit. Captain John G Henderson. **205-832-5043**

Public Information Unit. Lieutenant H Roy Smith. **205-832-5245**

ALASKA DEPARTMENT OF PUBLIC SAFETY. Pouch N, Juneau, 99811. Night lines: **907-465-4300** (Juneau) and **907-337-1515** (Anchorage)

Commissioner. Richard L Burton

Community Services Bureau, Anchorage. Chief Warrant Officer Ed Rhodes. **907-337-1515,** Ext 131

ARIZONA DEPARTMENT OF PUBLIC SAFETY. 2310 N 20th Ave, Phoenix, 85005. **602-262-8011**

Director. V L Hoy

Media Relations Officer. Sergeant Allan S Schmidt. **602-262-8460.** Night line: **602-262-8011**

ARKANSAS STATE POLICE. 1818 W Capitol St, Little Rock, 72202. **501-371-2026.** Night line: **501-371-2151**

Director. Colonel Douglas W Harp

Press Contact. Trooper Jerry Reinold. **501-371-1844**

CALIFORNIA HIGHWAY PATROL. PO Box 898, Sacramento, 95804. **916-445-2211** (also night line)

Commissioner. G B Craig

Public Affairs Officer. Kent R Milton. **916-445-3908**

COLORADO STATE PATROL. 4201 E Arkansas, Denver, 80222. **303-757-9011.** Night line: **303-757-9422**

Chief. Colonel C Wayne Keith

Press Officer. Lieutenant Richard L Downey. **303-757-9428**

CONNECTICUT STATE POLICE DE-PARTMENT. 100 Washington St, Hartford, CT 06101. **203-566-4054** (also night line)

Commissioner. Colonel Edward P Leonard. **203-566-3200**

Public Information Officers. Trooper Harry K Boardsen and Adam F Berluti. **203-566-4054**

DELAWARE STATE POLICE. PO Box 430, Dover, 19901. **302-734-5973.** Night line: **302-734-5973**

Superintendent. Colonel Irvin B Smith, Jr. Ext 10

Public Information Officer. Captain Ray J Bryan. Ext 39

News coordinator (New Castle County). Lieutenant Francis Talmo. **302-571-3036**

FLORIDA HIGHWAY PATROL. Neil Kirkman Bldg, Tallahassee, 32304. **904-488-6517.** Night line: **904-488-8676**

Director. Colonel Eldrige Beach

Press Officer. Major Robert C Collar. **904-488-7134**

Education Coordinator. Captain B J Barnett. **904-488-5370**

GEORGIA DEPARTMENT OF PUBLIC SAFETY. PO Box 1456, Atlanta, 30301. **406-656-6140.** Night line: **406-656-6077**

Commissioner. Colonel J Herman Cofer

Public Information Officer. Bill Wilson.

IDAHO DEPARTMENT OF LAW EN-FORCEMENT. PO Box 34, Boise, 83731. **208-384-3628** (also night line)

Director. Kelly Pearce

INDIANA STATE POLICE. 100 N Senate Ave, Indianapolis, 46204. **219-633-5674.** Night line: **219-633-5271**

Superintendent. John T Shettle

Public Information Director. Lieutenant Richard W Jones

IOWA DEPARTMENT OF PUBLIC SAFETY. Lucas Bldg, Des Moines, 50319. **515-281-5261.** Night line: **515-281-3561** or **515-223-0477**

Commissioner. Charles W Larson

Press Contact. Robert G Holetz, deputy commissioner

KANSAS BUREAU OF INVESTIGATION. 3420 Van Buren, Topeka, 66611. **913-296-3026.** Night line: **913-266-3774**

Director. William L Albott

Press Contacts. William L Albott and Jack H Ford

KANSAS HIGHWAY PATROL. Bldg 2-130, Townsite Plz, 200 E 6th St, Topeka, 66603. **913-296-3801** (also night line)

Colonel Allen C Rush

BUREAU OF KENTUCKY STATE POLICE. Frankfort, 40601. **502-564-4686.** Night line: **502-564-3000**

Commissioner. Kenneth E Brandenburgh

Press Contact. Lieutenant Ernest Bivens. **502-564-4435**

LOUISIANA STATE POLICE. 265 S Foster Drive (PO Box 1791), Baton Rouge, 70821. **504-389-7501.** Night line: **504-389-7501**

Deputy Secretary. Grover W Garrison. **504-389-7585**

Department of Public Safety, Public Informa-tion Unit Supervisor. Lieutenant Norris Deville. **504-389-7336**

MAINE DEPARTMENT OF PUBLIC SAFETY. 36 Hospital St, Augusta, 04333. **207-289-2155.** Night line: **207-289-2155**

Commissioner. Colonel Allan H Weeks. **207-289-3801**

Public Information Officer. Richard A Moore. **207-289-3038**

MARYLAND DEPARTMENT OF PUBLIC SAFETY AND CORRECTIONAL SERVICES. Suite 500, Executive Plz 1, Hunt Valley, 21031. **301-667-1100.** Night line: **301-486-3101**

Superintendent, Maryland State Police. Thomas S Smith

Commissioner, Division of Correction, Public Information Office. Mark A Levine. **301-944-7028,** Ext 33

Public Information Officer. William Clark. **301-486-3101,** Ext 237

MASSACHUSETTS DEPARTMENT OF PUBLIC SAFETY. 1010 Commonwealth Ave, Boston, 02215. **617-566-4500** (also night line)

Commissioner. John F Kehoe, Jr

Public Relations Officers. Captain Harold Reddish and Corporal Paul M Beloff. Ext 272

MICHIGAN STATE POLICE. 714 S Harri-son Rd, East Lansing, 48823. **517-332-2521.** Night line: **517-332-2521**

Director. Colonel Gerald L Hough

Director of Public Affairs. Paul A Hill. **517-373-8349**

MINNESOTA DEPARTMENT OF PUB-LIC SAFETY. State Highway Bldg, St Paul, 55155. **612-296-6652**

Commissioner. Edward G Novak

Director of Safety Information. Howard Owen (318 Transportation Bldg, St Paul, 55155). **612-296-6652**

MISSISSIPPI DEPARTMENT OF PUB-LIC SAFETY. PO Box 958, Jackson, 39205. **601-982-1212** (also night line). Associated Press number: **601-948-5897.** United Press International number: **601-353-2907**

Commissioner of Public Safety. James Finch. **601-982-1212**

Director, public relations bureau. Officer T G Sadler. **601-982-1212**

Public Relations Representative. Shirley Walker. **601-982-1212**

MISSOURI HIGHWAY PATROL. 1510 E Elm St, Jefferson City, 65101. **314-751-3313**

Superintendent. A R Lubker

MONTANA HIGHWAY PATROL BUREAU. 1437 Helena Ave, Helena, 59601. **406-449-3000**

Chief. Colonel Joe R Sol

NEBRASKA STATE PATROL. Box 94907, Lincoln, 68509. **402-477-3951**

Superintendent. Colonel C P Karthauser

NEVADA HIGHWAY PATROL. Depart-ment of Motor Vehicles, 555 Wright Way, Carson City, 89711. **702-885-5300**

Chief. Colonel James L Lambert

NEW HAMPSHIRE STATE POLICE. Department of Safety, Concord, 03301. **603-271-3636** (also night line)
Colonel Harold E Knowlton
Press Contact. Sergeant Mark C Thompson. **603-271-2535.** Night line: **603-271-3636**

NEW JERSEY STATE POLICE. PO Box 7068 W, Trenton, 08625. **609-882-2000** (also night line)
Superintendent. Colonel Clinton L Pagano
Public Information Officer. Lieutenant Gordon R Hector. Ext 209

NEW MEXICO STATE POLICE. PO Box 1628, Santa Fe, 87501. **505-827-5111.** Night line: **505-827-2551**
Chief. Martin E Vigil
Press Contact. Captain Donald W Moberly, commander, personnel and training division. **505-827-5104**

NEW YORK STATE POLICE. State Campus, Albany, 12226. **518-457-6811**
Superintendent. William G Connelie
Supervisor of Public Relations. Kurt Wachenheim. **518-457-2180.** (h) **518-869-8263**

NORTH CAROLINA STATE HIGHWAY PATROL. 512 N Salisbury St (PO Box 27687), Raleigh, 27611. **919-733-7952.** Night line: **919-733-3861** ("Highway Patrol Telecommunication Center or telecommunicator on duty will provide name and number of responsible person to contact.")
Commander. Colonel John T Jenkins
Press Officer. Colonel John T Jenkins. **919-733-7952**

NORTH CAROLINA DIVISION OF MOTOR VEHICLES. 1100 New Bern Ave, Raleigh, 27611. **919-733-2403.** Night line: **919-733-3025** (this number can provide verification of North Carolina license plates)
Commissioner. Elbert L Peters, Jr
Information Officer. Maxine Thomas. **919-733-7322**

NORTH DAKOTA HIGHWAY PATROL. State Capitol, Bismarck, 58505. **701-224-2455**
Superintendent. Ralph M Wood

OHIO HIGHWAY PATROL. Department of Highway Safety, 660 E Main St, Columbus, 43205. **614-466-2990**
Superintendent. Colonel Adam G Reiss

OKLAHOMA DEPARTMENT OF PUBLIC SAFETY. PO Box 11415, Oklahoma City, 73111. **405-424-4011** (also night line)

Chief of Patrol. Colonel Jerry Matheson
Commissioner. W Roger Webb
Press Contact. Lieutenant Kenneth Vanhoy. Ext 291

OREGON STATE POLICE. Public Service Bldg, Salem, 97310. **503-378-3720** (also night line)
Superintendent. Robert R Fisher
Press Contact. Robert R Fisher

PENNSYLVANIA STATE POLICE. PO Box 2771, Harrisburg, 17120. **717-783-5556**
Commissioner. Colonel Paul J Chylak
Public Information Director. James D Cox. (h) **717-652-3547**
Assistant Director. Thomas C Lyon. (h) **717-273-4056**

RHODE ISLAND STATE POLICE. Danielson Pike, PO Box 185, North Scituate, 02857. **401-647-3311** (also night line)
Superintendent. Colonel Walter E Stone
Press Contact. Lieutenant Dennis M Taber

SOUTH CAROLINA STATE HIGHWAY PATROL. Box 191, Columbia, 29202. **803-758-3315.** Night line: **803-758-2815**
Director of Law Enforcement. Colonel W J Seaborn
Director of Public Relations. Jim Walker. **803-758-2101**

SOUTH DAKOTA HIGHWAY PATROL. Department of Public Safety, 118 W Capitol, Pierre, 57501. **605-224-3105**
Director. Colonel Dennis Eisnach

TENNESSEE DEPARTMENT OF SAFETY. Nashville, 37219. **615-741-2101.** Night line: **615-444-5639**
Commissioner. Joel Plummer
Press Contact. Jim Henderson. **615-741-2491**

TEXAS DEPARTMENT OF PUBLIC SAFETY. Box 4087, Austin, 78773. **512-452-0331** (also night line)
Director. Colonel Wilson E (Pat) Speir
Public Information Officer. William F Carter
Assistant Public Information Officers. James Robinson and Richard Grimmett

VERMONT STATE POLICE. Department of Public Safety, State Office Bldg, Montpelier, 05602. **802-828-2104**
Major. Glenn E Davis

UTAH STATE DEPARTMENT OF PUBLIC SAFETY. 317 State Office Bldg, Salt Lake City, 84114. **801-533-4900.** Night line:

801-533-5306 (Utah Highway Patrol radio room)
Commissioner. Larry E Lunnen
Press Contact. Robert F Parenti. **801-533-4900**

VIRGINIA DEPARTMENT OF STATE POLICE. PO Box 27472, Richmond, 23261. **804-272-1431** (also night line)
Superintendent. Colonel D M Slane
Information Director. Charles L Vaughan. Ext 269

WASHINGTON STATE PATROL. General Administration Bldg, Olympia, 98504. **206-753-6540.** Night line: **206-753-6856**
Chief. Robert W Landon. **206-754-6545**
Administrative Assistant and Information Officer. Lieutenant Mike Feldhausen. **206-753-6562**

WEST VIRGINIA DEPARTMENT OF PUBLIC SAFETY. 725 Jefferson Rd, South Charleston, 25309. **304-348-2351.** Night line: **304-348-2361**
Superintendent. General Harley F Mooney, Jr
Press Contact. Sergeant Gary D Hill. **304-348-2366**

WISCONSIN STATE PATROL. PO Box 7912, Madison, 53707. **608-266-3212** (also night line)
Colonel Lew V Versnik
Office of Public Information. George Bechtel. **608-266-7744**

WYOMING HIGHWAY PATROL. PO Box 1708, Cheyenne, 82001. **307-777-7301.** Night line: **307-777-7244**
Director. Colonel Stan Warne
Public Information Officer. Keith Rounds. **307-777-7267**

FBI FIELD DIVISIONS

In the following list of the 59 principal FBI offices, persons named are special-agents-in-charge unless otherwise noted.

ALBANY. 502 US Post Office and Courthouse, Albany, NY 12207. **518-465-7551.** Ervin L Recer

ALBUQUERQUE. 4303 Federal Office Bldg, Albuquerque, NM 87101. **505-247-1555.** Forrest S Putman, Jr

ALEXANDRIA. Rm 500, 300 N Lee St, Alexandria, VA 22314. **703-683-2680.** Robert G Kunkel

ANCHORAGE. Rm 238, Federal Bldg, Anchorage, AK 99510. **907-272-6414.** Mount C Dulinsky, Jr

ATLANTA. 275 Peachtree St NE, Atlanta, GA 30303. **404-521-3900.** James J Dunn, Jr

BALTIMORE. 7142 Ambassador Rd, Baltimore, MD 21207. **301-265-8080.** George T Quinn

BIRMINGHAM. Rm 1400, 2121 Bldg, Birmingham, AL 35203. **205-252-7705.** Leroy R Kirkpatrick

BOSTON. John F Kennedy Federal Office Bldg, Boston, MA 02203. **617-742-5533.** Richard F Bates

BUFFALO. Rm 1400, 111 W Huron St, Buffalo, NY 14202. **716-856-7800.** Walter A Weiner

BUTTE. 115 US Courthouse and Federal Bldg, Butte, MT 59701. **406-792-2304.** Thomas P Druken

CHARLOTTE. 1120 Jefferson Standard Life Bldg, Charlotte, NC 28202. **704-372-5485.** Edgar N Best

CHICAGO. Rm 905, Everett McKinley Dirksen Bldg, Chicago, IL 60604. **312-431-1333.** William F Beane

CINCINNATI. 415 US Post Office and Courthouse Bldg, Cincinnati, OH 45202. **513-421-4310.** Thomas W Kitchens, Jr

CLEVELAND. 3005 Federal Office Bldg, Cleveland, OH 44199. **216-522-1400.** Charles R McKinnon

COLUMBIA. PO Box 137, Columbia, SC 29201. **803-252-1911.** Joseph J Loefiler

DALLAS. Rm 200, 1810 Commerce St, Dallas, TX 75201. **214-741-1851.** Theodore L Gunderson

DENVER. Rm 18218, Federal Office Bldg, Denver, CO 80202. **303-629-7171.** Theodore P Rosack

DETROIT. PO Box 2118, Detroit, MI 48231. **313-965-2323.** Robert E Kent

EL PASO. 202 US Courthouse Bldg, El Paso, TX 79901. **915-533-7451.** George R Steel

HONOLULU. Rm 605, Bishop Trust Bldg, Honolulu, HI 96813. **808-521-1411.** Charles J Devic

HOUSTON. 6015 Federal Bldg and US Courthouse, Houston, TX 77002. **713-224-1511.** Robert Russ Franck

INDIANAPOLIS. 575 Pennsylvania St, Indianapolis, IN 46202. **317-639-3301.** Franklin O Lowie

JACKSON. 800 Unifirst Federal Savings and Loan Bldg, Jackson, MS 39205. **601- 948-5000.** Homer R Hauer

JACKSONVILLE. 414 US Courthouse and Post Office Bldg, Jacksonville, FL 32202. **904-355-1401.** Arthur F Nehrbass

KANSAS CITY. Rm 300, US Courthouse, Kansas City, MO 64106. **816-221-6100.** Bill D Williams

KNOXVILLE. RM 8008 1111 Northshore Dr, Knoxville, TN 37919. **615-588-8571.** Harold C Swanson

LAS VEGAS. Rm 2-011, Federal Office Bldg, Las Vegas, NV 89101. **702-385-1231.** Jack Keith, Jr.

LITTLE ROCK. 215 US Post Office Bldg, Little Rock, AR 72201. **501-372-7211.** John T Kelly

LOS ANGELES. 11000 Wilshire Blvd, Los Angeles, CA 90024. **213-272-6161.** Robert E Gebhardt, assistant director. Robert H Matheson, Jr, SAC—Administrative Division. Elmer F Linberg, SAC—Intelligence Division. Robert J McCarthy, SAC—Criminal Division

LOUISVILLE. Rm 502, Federal Bldg, Louisville, KY 40202. **502-583-3941.** Stanley S Czarnecki

MEMPHIS. 841 Clifford Davis Federal Bldg, Memphis, TN 38103. **901-525-7373.** Joseph H Trimbach

MIAMI. 3801 Biscayne Blvd, Miami, FL 33137. **305-573-3333.** Julius Lee Mattson

MILWAUKEE. Rm 700, Federal Bldg and US Court House, Milwaukee, WI 53202. **414-276-4684.** J Gerard Hogan

MINNEAPOLIS. 392 Federal Bldg, Minneapolis, MN 55401. **612-583-3941.** John E Otto

MOBILE. 520 Federal Bldg, Mobile, AL 36602. **205-438-3674.** C Edwin Enright

NEWARK. Gateway I, PO Box 1158, Newark, NJ 07101. **201-622-5613.** Louis A Giovanetti

NEW HAVEN. 770 Chapel Bldg, New Haven, CT 06510. **203-777-6311.** Thomas R Dugan

NEW ORLEANS. 701 Loyota Ave, New Orleans, LA 70113. **504-522-4671.** J T Sylvester, Jr.

NEW YORK. 201 E 69th St, New York, NY 10021. **212-535-7700.** J Wallace La Prade, assistant director. Herbert A Grubert, SAC—Administrative Division. Edward F Foley, SAC—Criminal Division. Alfred E Smith, SAC—Counterintelligence: Soviet Division. John J Schwartz, SAC—Counterintelligence: Sino-Satellite Division. Thomas J Emery, SAC—Organized Crime Division. Robert K Besley, SAC—New Rochelle Metro Resident Agency

NORFOLK. Rm 300, 870 Military Hwy, Norfolk, VA 23502. **804-461-2121.** Herbert D Clough, Jr

OKLAHOMA CITY. 50 Penn Pl NW, 50th at Pennsylvania, Oklahoma City, OK 73118. **405-842-7471.** Kenneth W Whittaker

OMAHA. 1010 Federal Office Bldg, Omaha, NE 68102. **402-348-1210.** Edward J Krupinsky

PHILADELPHIA. 8th Floor, Federal Office Bldg, 600 Arch St, Philadelphia, PA 19106. **215-629-0800.** Neil J Welch

PHOENIX. 2721 N Central Ave, Phoenix, AZ 85004. **602-279-5511.** Leon M Gaskill

PITTSBURGH. 1300 Federal Office Bldg, Pittsburgh, PA 15222. **412-471-2000.** Vincent E Ruehl

PORTLAND. Crown Plaza Bldg, Portland, OR 97201. **503-224-4181.** John G Devine

QUANTICO. FBI Academy, Quantico, VA 22135. **703-640-6131.** William A Meincke

RICHMOND. PO Box 12325, Richmond, VA 23241. **804-644-2631.** Charles E Price

SACRAMENTO. Federal Bldg, 2800 Cottage Way, Sacramento, CA 95825. **916-481-9110.** Richard E White

ST LOUIS. 2704 Federal Bldg, St Louis, MO 63103. **314-241-5357.** Harlan C Phillips

SALT LAKE CITY. 3203 Federal Bldg, Salt Lake City, UT 84138. **801-355-7521.** Clark F Brown

SAN ANTONIO. 432 Post Office Bldg, San Antonio, TX 78296. **512-225-6741.** Joseph E O'Connell

SAN DIEGO. Suite 6S-31, Federal Office Bldg, 880 Front St, San Diego, CA 92188. **714-231-1122.** Ronald L Maley

SAN FRANCISCO. 450 Golden Gate Ave, San Francisco, CA 94102. **415-552-2155.** Charles R McKinnon

SAN JUAN. Rm 526, US Court House and Federal Bldg, Hato Rey, San Juan, PR 00918. **809-765-6000.** John J Hinchcliffe

SAVANNAH. 5401 Paulsen St, Savannah, GA 31405. **912-354-9911.** Garry Owen Watt

SEATTLE. 915 2nd Ave, Seattle, WA 98174. **206-622-0460.** John M Reed

SPRINGFIELD. 535 W Jefferson St, Springfield, IL 62702. **217-522-9675.** Victor R Schaefer

TAMPA. Rm 610, Federal Office Bldg, Tampa, FL 33602. **813-228-7661.** Philip A McNiff

WASHINGTON. Washington Field Office, Washington, DC 20535. **202-252-7770.** Nick F Stames. (See Quantico, VA for FBI Academy)

ORGANIZED CRIME AND RACKETEERING STRIKE FORCES

In the following list of the US Justice Department's Strike Forces, names given are those of attorneys working on the strike forces. In most instances the first name is that of the attorney-in-charge.

ATLANTA. (Miami Strike Force). PO Box 834, Atlanta, GA 30301. **404-242-4274.** William L McCulley

BOSTON. 1905 John W McCormack Federal Bldg, Boston, MA 02109. **617-223-3390.** Gerald E McDowell, George F Kelly, Martin D Boudreau, Nancy Ely, Richard D Gregorie, Stephen Jigger, Jeremiah T O'Sullivan, John R Tarrant

BROOKLYN. Rm 327-A, Federal Bldg, Brooklyn, NY 11201. **212-656-7461.** Thomas

P Puccio, Fred F Barlow, Jr, Stanley E Greenidge, Donald McCaffrey, David Ritchie, Alan Sleppin

BUFFALO. Suite 921, Genesee Bldg, 1 W Genesee St, Buffalo, NY 14202. **716-842-3285.** Robert C Stewart, Lloyd G Parry, Richard Endler, Jeffrey Fisher, Dennis P O'Keefe, Gregory A Baldwin

CHICAGO. Rm 1552, 219 S Dearborn St, Chicago, IL 60604. **312-353-5267.** Peter F Vaira, James D Henderson, Jeffrey Johnson, J Kenneth Lowrie, Stephen H Pugh, Robert Rose, Gary Shapiro, James P Walsh, Gregory H Ward, Charles C Wehner

CLEVELAND. Suite 450, Investment Bldg, 601 Rockwell Ave, Cleveland, OH 44114. **216-293-3765.** Douglas Roller, Stephen Olah, Kenneth A Bravo, Robert Delgrosso, David S Felman, Michael B Michelson, Rebekah Poston

DETROIT. Rm 940, Federal Bldg, Detroit, MI 48226. **313-226-7252.** Geoffrey A Anderson, C Stanley Hunterton, Marsha Katz, John L Newcomer, Robert C Power, Arnold G Shulman, Richard Zuckerman

HARTFORD (Boston Strike Force). c/o US Attorney, Federal Bldg, Hartford, CT 06103. **203-244-2679.** Peter R Casey III

KANSAS CITY. Suite 717, 906 Grand Ave, Kansas City, MO 64106. **816-374-2771.** David Helfrey, Edward D Holmes, William A Keefer, William E Zleit, Michael Defeo

LOS ANGELES. Rm 2307, Federal Bldg, 300 N Los Angeles St, Los Angeles, CA 90012. **213-798-5808.** Michael A Defeo, Terry R Lord, Kevin F O'Malley, Ronald W Rose, Robert S Thaller, Michael White

MIAMI. 111 NW 5th St, Miami, FL 33128. **305-350-4258.** Atlee W Wampler III, Gary L Betz, John F Evans, Edward A Hanna, Jay Moskowitz, S Michael Levin, Leonard Sands, Martin L Steinberg

NEWARK. Rm 635, Federal Bldg, 970 Broad St, Newark, NJ 07101. **201-645-2155.** William W Robertson, James M Deichert, Carl Lo Presti, Charles A Matison, V Grady O'Malley, Thomas L Weisenbeck

PHOENIX. Rm 5000, Federal Bldg, 230 1st Ave, Phoenix, AZ 85025. **602-261-3011**

PHILADELPHIA. Suite 900-PNB, Plaza Bldg, 5th and Market Sts, Philadelphia, PA 19106. **215-597-2790.** Joel M Friedman,

Edward Levitt, Robert E Madden, Donald F Manno, John D McCullough, Louis R Pichini, Albert Wicks, Ronald G Cole

PROVIDENCE (Boston Strike Force). PO Box 996, Postal Annex Bldg, Providence, RI 02901. **401-838-4546** or **4547.** Edwin J Gale

ROCHESTER (Buffalo Strike Force). Rm 318, New Federal Bldg, 100 State St, Rochester, NY 14614. **716-473-6712.** Gregory A Baldwin

SAN FRANCISCO. Box 36132, 450 Golden Gate Ave, San Francisco, CA 94102. **415-556-0750.** Thomas E Kotoske, Gerard J Hinckley, Robert J Breakstone, John C Emerson, Edmund C Lyons, Michael L Sterret

TAMPA (Miami Strike Force). Rm 711, 700 Twiggs St, Tampa, FL 33602. **813-826-2704.** Milton J Carp, L Eades Hogue

WASHINGTON (Strike Force 18). Box 571, Ben Franklin Station, Washinton, DC 20044. **202-739-3608.** John M Dowd, Paul R Corradini, William Kramer, Craig Starr, Edward C Weiner.

NATIONAL GUARD

NATIONAL GUARD BUREAU, OFFICE OF PUBLIC AFFAIRS. Washington, DC 20310. **202-695-0421**

Public Affairs Officer. Colonel Andrew G Wolf, Jr, USA

Deputy Public Affairs Officer. Lieutenant Colonel Robert G Steeves, USAF

ALABAMA. 1720 Federal Drive (PO Box 1311), Montgomery, 36102. **205-272-6953**

Adjutant General. Major General Henry B Gray III

Public Affairs Officer. Captain Norman W Arnold. Ext 207

ALASKA. 610 Mackay Bldg, 338 Denali St, Anchorage, 99501. **907-276-3656**

Adjutant General. Major General Conrad F Necrason

Public Affairs Officer. William M Mack. Ext 219

ARIZONA. 5636 E McDowell Rd, Phoenix, 85008. **602-244-9411**

Adjutant General. John G Smith, Jr

Public Affairs Officer. Lieutenant Colonel Jay Brashear. **602-271-8475**

ARKANSAS. PO Box 678, Fort McAlister, North Little Rock, 72115. **501-753-1151,** Ext 21

Adjutant General. Thomas C Armstrong

Public Affairs Officer. Lieutenant Cissy Coleman. **501-758-4053,** Ext 231

CALIFORNIA. PO Box 214405, Sacramento, 95821. **916-920-6605.** Night line: **916-920-6597.**

Adjutant General. Frank J Schober, Jr

Public Affairs Officer. Major Mike Teilmann. **916-920-6584**

COLORADO. 300 Logan St, Denver, 80203. **303-733-2431**

Adjutant General. William D Weller

Public Affairs Officer. Lieutenant Colonel Paul A Parsons

CONNECTICUT. 360 Broad St, Hartford, 06115. **203-566-4120** or **4121**

Adjutant General. John F Freund

Public Affairs Officer. **203-566-5266**

DELAWARE. 1401 Newport Gap Pike, Wilmington, 19804. **302-322-2261,** Ext 341

Adjutant General. Francis A Ianni

Public Affairs Officer. Major James P Adams

DISTRICT OF COLUMBIA. National Guard Armory, 2001 E Capitol St, Washington, 20003. **202-544-4600,** Ext 200

Adjutant General. Brigadier General W W Bridges

Commanding General. Major General C C Bryant

Public Affairs Officer. Lieutenant Colonel Richard A Cheney

FLORIDA. State Arsenal, St Augustine, 32084. **904-829-2231**

Adjutant General. Major General Kennedy C Bullard

Public Affairs Officer. Colonel Frank Persons. **904-829-2231**

GEORGIA. Department of Defense, Military Division. PO Box 17965, Atlanta, 30316. **404-656-1700**

Adjutant General. Billy M Jones

Public Affairs Officer. Colonel Douglas Embry. **404-656-6182**

HAWAII. Fort Ruger, Honolulu, 96816. **808-734-2195**

Adjutant General. Major General Valentine A Siefermann

Public Affairs Officer. Gail Warok. **808-732-1711**

IDAHO. PO Box 45, Boise, 83707. **208-385-5242**

Adjutant General. James S Brooks

Public Affairs Officer. Kent J Jewell. **208-385-5267**

ILLINOIS. Rm 200, Armory Office Bldg, Springfield, 62706. **217-782-7221**

Adjutant General. Brigadier General John R Phipps (acting)

Public Affairs Officer. Lieutenant Colonel Carl O Johnson, Jr. **217-782-7337**

INDIANA. Military Department of Indiana, PO Drawer AO, Indianapolis, 46241. **317-247-3274**

Adjutant General. Alfred F Ahner

Public Affairs Officer. First Lieutenant Michael Goss. **317-247-3278,** (h) **317-839-3192**

IOWA. PO Box 616, Des Moines, 50303. **515-278-9211**

Adjutant General. Joseph G May

Public Affairs Officer. Major Robert W Anderson

KANSAS. 535 Kansas Ave, Topeka, 66603. **913-233-7560**

Adjutant General. Edward R Fry

Public Affairs Officer. Captain Krull. **913-296-2203**

KENTUCKY. Boone National Guard Ctr, Frankfort, 40601. **502-564-7800.** Night line: **502-564-7815.**

Adjutant General. Richard L Frymire, Jr

Public Affairs Officer. First Lieutenant Tom Little. Ext 335.

LOUISIANA. Headquarters Bldg, Jackson Barracks, New Orleans, 70146. **504-271-6262**

Adjutant General. Major General O J Daigle, Jr

Public Affairs Officer. Captain Gary Borne. **504-271-6262** or **504-737-0105**

MAINE. Camp Keyes, Augusta, 04333. **207-622-9331,** Ext 24, 25, or 26

Adjutant General. Major General Paul R Day

Public Affairs Officer. Captain Richard A Moore. Ext 24

MARYLAND. 5th Regiment Armory, Baltimore, 21201. **301-728-3388**

Adjutant General. Edwin Warfield III

Public Affairs Officer. Colonel Bernard Feingold. Ext 240

MASSACHUSETTS. 905 Commonwealth Ave, Boston, 02215. **617-782-7842** or **5656**

Adjutant General. Vahan Vartanian

Public Affairs Officer. Captain Chip Hoar. **617-782-7842**

MICHIGAN. 2500 S Washington Ave, Lansing, 48913. **517-373-0354**

Adjutant General. John A Johnston

Public Affairs Officer. Captain Tim Everett. **517-373-0372**

MINNESOTA. Veterans Service Bldg, St Paul, 55155. **612-296-4666**

Adjutant General. Major General James G Sieben

Public Affairs Officer. First Lieutenant John Plaster. **612-296-4684**

MISSISSIPPI. PO Box 5027, Fondren Station, Jackson, 39216. **601-354-7511**

Adjutant General. Glenn D Walker

Public Affairs Officer. Major James L Jones. **601-354-7505**

MISSOURI. 1717 Industrial Dr, Jefferson City, 65101. **314-751-2321**

Adjutant General. Robert E Buechler

Public Affairs Officer. John G Warren

MONTANA. PO Box 4789, Helena, 59601. **406-449-3692**

Adjutant General. John J Womack

Public Affairs Officer. Lieutenant Colonel James Maness. **406-449-3437**

NEBRASKA. 1300 Military Rd, Lincoln, 68508. **402-432-7641,** Ext 210

Adjutant General. Edward C Binder

Public Affairs Officer. Major Leonard Krenk

NEVADA. 2525 S Carson St, Carson City, 89701. **702-885-4140**

Adjutant General. Major General Floyd L Edsall

Public Affairs Officer. Colonel William F Engel. **702-885-7434**

Public Affairs Supervisor. First Sergeant Frank C Simpson. **702-885-4140.** (h) **702-882-1879**

NEW HAMPSHIRE. State Military Reservation, Airport Rd, Concord, 03301. **603-228-1135**

Adjutant General. John Blatsos

Public Affairs Officer. Lieutenant Colonel Grant, ANG, and Colonel Parker, ARNG. **603-271-2331**

NEW JERSEY. PO Box 979, Trenton, 08625. **609-292-3887** and **3888**
Adjutant General. Wilfred C Menard, Jr
Public Affairs Officer. First Lieutenant Jim Dufford. **609-292-3995**

NEW MEXICO. PO Box 4277, Santa Fe, 87502. **505-982-3841**, Ext 200
Adjutant General. Franklin E Miles
Public Affairs Officer. Captain Henry G Boxberger. **505-983-0550**

NEW YORK. Public Security Bldg, State Campus, Albany, 12226. **518-457-6966**
Adjutant General. Vito J Castellano
Public Affairs Officer. Lieutenant Colonel Raymond S Joyce. **518-457-6990**

NORTH CAROLINA. PO Drawer 26268, Raleigh, 27611. **919-733-3770**
Adjutant General. William E Ingram
Public Affairs Officer. Lieutenant Colonel Joseph M Parker

NORTH DAKOTA. PO Box 1817, Bismarck, 58505. **701-224-2132**
Adjutant General. C Emerson Murry
Public Affairs Officer. Major Vernon F Fetch. **701-224-2137**

OHIO. PO Box 660, Worthington, 43085. **614-889-7000**
Adjutant General. Major General James C Clem
Public Affairs Officer. Captain Don J Vaquera

OKLAHOMA. 3501 Military Cir NE, Oklahoma City, 73111. **405-427-8371**
Adjutant General. John Coffey, Jr
Public Affairs Officer. Major William Francis

OREGON. 2150 Fairgrounds Rd NE, Salem, 97303. **503-378-3981**
Adjutant General. Richard A Miller
Public Affairs Officer. Lieutenant Colonel John Mewha. **503-378-3917** or **3939**

PENNSYLVANIA. RD 2, Annville, 17003. **717-787-7200**
Adjutant General. Major General Nicholas P Kafkalas
Public Affairs Officer. Captain Clinton L Tennill, Jr. **717-787-8620**

PUERTO RICO. PO Box 3786, San Juan, 00904. **809-723-3131**
Adjutant General. Orlando Llenza
Public Affairs Officer. 809-723-4066

RHODE ISLAND. 1051 N Main St, Providence, 02904. **401-227-2100**
Adjutant General. Major General Leonard Holland
Public Affairs Officer. Lieutenant Colonel Nicholas Annicelli, Jr

SOUTH CAROLINA. 1225 Bluff Rd, Columbia, 29201. **803-758-2796**
Adjutant General. Robert L McCrady
Public Affairs Officer. Lieutenant Colonel William T Hedgepath, Jr. **803-799-2896**

SOUTH DAKOTA. PO Box 2150, Rapid City, 57709. **605-394-2211**
Adjutant General. Duane L Corning
Public Affairs Officer. Major Joseph T Murphy. **605-394-2503**

TENNESSEE. National Guard Armory, Sidco Dr, Nashville, 37204. **615-741-5166**
Adjutant General. Carl D Wallace
Public Affairs Officer. Captain Don Smith. **615-741-5266**

TEXAS. Box 5218, Austin, 78763. **512-475-5006**
Adjutant General. Thomas S Bishop
Public Affairs Officer. Captain Terry Denson. **512-475-5059**

UTAH. PO Box 8000, Salt Lake City, 84108. **801-533-5474**
Adjutant General. Maurice L Watts
Public Affairs Officer. Warrant Officer Wallace Devey

VERMONT. Bldg 1, Camp Johnson, Winooski, 05404. **802-655-0270**
Adjutant General. Reginald M Cram
Public Affairs Officer. Captain Mike Gately

VIRGINIA. 401 E Main St, Richmond, 23219. **804-786-2401**
Adjutant General. William J McCaddin
Public Affairs Officer. Major Gray. **804-786-2407**

VIRGIN ISLANDS. PO Box 3240, Christiansted, St Croix, 00820. **809-773-5200**
Adjutant General. Joe E Burke
Public Affairs Officer. Captain Du Pree Heard. **809-773-6036**

WASHINGTON. Camp Murray, Tacoma, 98430. **206-552-3833**
Adjutant General. Major General Howard S McGee
Public Affairs Officer. Captain Rick Read. **206-552-3896**

WEST VIRGINIA. 1703 Coonskin Dr, Charleston, 25311. **304-348-5300**
Adjutant General. Robert L Childers
Public Affairs Officer. Captain Ramon P Lopez

WISCONSIN. PO Box 8111, Madison, 53708. **608-241-6300**
Adjutant General. Brigadier General Hugh M Simson
Public Affairs Officer. Donald S Erickson. **608-244-5631**

WYOMING. 5500 Bishop Blvd (PO Box 1709), Cheyenne, 82001. **307-777-7221**
Adjutant General. Major General James L Spence
Public Affairs Officer. Captain John Cornelison

AMERICAN NATIONAL RED CROSS

National Headquarters: 17th and D Sts NW, Washington, DC 20006. **202-737-8300.** Press contact. Robert Walhay, chief, news, magazines and photo sections, **202-857-3512.** *See also* Special Interests. The National Headquarters Public Affairs Office is covered on a 24-hour basis, and Mr Walhay is available by beeper at any hour. He suggests that, in the event of a crisis somewhere in the country involving the Red Cross, contact with authorities at the scene can be made most quickly by calling him first.

The following is a list of chapters, with office and home numbers for making direct contact with public relations persons in the major local divisions of the Red Cross.

Northeastern US

Appalachian Division

ROANOKE VALLEY CHAPTER. 352 Church Ave SW, Roanoke, VA 24016. **703-982-2491.** John F Kain, director, public relations. (h) **703-989-4639**

HUNTINGTON-CABELL COUNTY CHAPTER. 724 10 Ave (PO Box 605), Huntington, WV 25701. **304-522-0328.** Joyce Snider, director, public relations

Caribbean Division

PUERTO RICO CHAPTER. PO Box 1067, San Juan, PR 00902. **809-722-0420.** Onysa Vazquez, director, public relations

Central New York Division

SYRACUSE AND ONONDAGA COUNTY CHAPTER. 636 S Warren St, Syracuse, NY 13202. **315-476-9071**. Betty K Sherman, director, community relations. (h) **315-673-1441**

BROOME COUNTY CHAPTER. 93 Chestnut St, Binghamton, NY 13905. Merry Harris, public relations coordinator

Central Pennsylvania Division

HARRISBURG AREA CHAPTER. 230 State St, Harrisburg, PA 17101. **717-234-3101**. Trude N Hursen, director, public relations. (h). **717-766-0365**

LANCASTER COUNTY CHAPTER. 430 W Orange St, Lancaster, PA 17603. **717-299-5561**. Bob Foiles, manager

Chesapeake Division

BALTIMORE REGIONAL CHAPTER. 2701 N Charles St, Baltimore, MD 21218. **301-467-9905**, Ext 240. Patricia Owens, director, community relations. (h) **301-377-0785**

Cincinnati Division

CINCINNATI AREA CHAPTER. 720 Sycamore St, Cincinnati, OH 45202. **513-721-2665**. Ray Carmichael, director, public relations

Columbus Division

COLUMBUS AREA CHAPTER. 995 E Broad St (PO Box 6959), Columbus, OH 43205. **614-253-7981**. Bertha J Dell, director, public relations. (h) **614-965-3698**

Connecticut Division

GREATER HARTFORD CHAPTER. 209 Farmington Ave, Farmington, CT 06032. **203-677-4531**. Gail H (Barry) Barents, director, public relations. (h) **203-667-1717**

SOUTH CENTRAL CONNECTICUT CHAPTER. 703 Whitney Ave, New Haven, CT 96511. **203-787-6721**. Anne C Foster, director, public relations and fund raising

SOUTHEASTERN FAIRFIELD COUNTY CHAPTER. 2400 Main St (PO Box 6340), Bridgeport, CT 06606. **203-576-1010**. Philip G Flaker, director, public relations

Eastern New York Division

ALBANY AREA CHAPTER. PO Box 8668, Hackett Blvd at Clara Barton Dr, Albany, NY 12208. **518-462-7461**, Ext 65. Richard Danzig, director, public relations

SCHENECTADY COUNTY CHAPTER. 8 S Church St, Schenectady, NY 12305. **518-393-3606**. Alice M Swanson, director, public relations

First Colonies Division

TIDEWATER CHAPTER. 414 W Bute St (PO Box 1836), Norfolk, VA 23501. **804-625-6791**. Jeanette K Maygarden, director, public relations. (h) **804-464-4895**

Harriman-Metropolitan Division

AMERICAN RED CROSS IN GREATER NEW YORK. 150 Amsterdam Ave, New York, NY 10023. **212-787-1000**, Ext 391. Harry M Cohn, director, public relations. (h) **914-939-5955**

NASSAU COUNTY CHAPTER. 264 Old Country Road, Mineola, NY 11501. **516-747-3500**. Mrs Borgne Keith, director, public information. (h) **516-431-4384**

WESTCHESTER COUNTY CHAPTER. 106 N Broadway, White Plains, NY 10603. **914-949-6500**, Ext 33. Judy Meyer, director, development

ESSEX CHAPTER. 106 Washington St, East Orange, NJ 01017. **201-676-1616**. William D Davis, director, public relations

TRENTON AREA CHAPTER. 399 W State St, Trenton, NJ 08618. **609-394-1161**. Joseph S Ancker, director, chapter development

Mid-Atlantic Division

SOUTHEASTERN PENNSYLVANIA CHAPTER. 23rd and Chestnut Sts, Philadelphia, Pa 19103. **215-561-8200**. David Butcher, director, public relations. (h) **215-336-0998**

CHESTER-WALLINGFORD CHAPTER. 930 Avenue of States, Chester, PA 19103. **215-874-1484**. Margaret E Pepper, coordinator, community relations

WYOMING VALLEY CHAPTER. 156 S Franklin St, Wilkes-Barre, PA 18701. **717-823-7161**. Sally L Metzger, director, public information. (h) **717-822-9365**

DELAWARE CHAPTER. 910 Gilpin Ave, Wilmington, DE 19806. **302-655-3341**. Bette McNear, part-time public relations director

CAMDEN COUNTY CHAPTER. Box 228, 312 Cooper St, Camden, NJ 08101. **609-365-7100**. Camy Trinidad, director, public relations

National Capital Division

DISTRICT OF COLUMBIA CHAPTER. 2025 E St NW, Washington, DC 20006. **202-857-3750**. Peter J (Pete) Barreca, director, public relations. (h) **202-223-3331**

ARLINGTON COUNTY CHAPTER. 4333 Arlington Blvd, Arlington, VA 22203. **703-527-3010**. Muriel Sullivan, director, public relations

FAIRFAX COUNTY CHAPTER. 4117 Chain Bridge Rd, Fairfax, VA 22030. **703-591-8091**. Virginia H Foster, director, public relations

MONTGOMERY COUNTY CHAPTER. 2020 East-West Hwy, Silver Spring, MD 20910. **301-588-2515**. Lynda T Tupling, director, public relations

PRINCE GEORGES COUNTY CHAPTER. 6206 Belcrest Rd, Hyattsville, MD 20782. **301-559-8500**. Deborah Ziska, director, public relations and development. (h) **301-630-4625**

New England Division

GREATER BOSTON CHAPTER. 99 Brookline Ave, Boston, MA 02115. **617-262-1234**. Donald L Consolmagno, director, public affairs. (h) **617-756-2178**

BERKSHIRE COUNTY CHAPTER. 63 Wendell Ave, Pittsfield, MA 01201. **413-422-1506**

NEW BEDFORD CHAPTER. 52 Ash St, New Bedford, MA 02740. **617-996-8286**. Margaret Sweet, director, public relations. (h) **617-992-0342**

PIONEER VALLEY CHAPTER. 275 Maple St, Springfield, MA 01105. **413-737-4306**

New York-Pennsylvania Western Division

GREATER BUFFALO REGIONAL CHAPTER. 786 Delaware Ave, Buffalo, NY

14209. **716-886-7500.** Janet B Hughes, director, public relations. (h) **716-882-7550**

ERIE CHAPTER. PO Box 1880, Perry Station, 150 W 6th St, Erie, PA 16507. **814-452-6411.** Thomas Coatoam, director, public relations. (h) **814-739-2952**

Northeast Ohio Division

GREATER CLEVELAND CHAPTER. 1227 Prospect Ave, Cleveland, OH 44115. **216-781-1800.** Frank Stipkala, director, public relations. (h) **216-381-5016**

CANTON CHAPTER. 618 2nd St NW, Canton, OH 44703. **216-453-0146**

MAHONING CHAPTER. 266 W Wood St, Youngstown, OH 44502. **216-744-0161.** Brenda Davanzo, director, public relations

SUMMIT COUNTY CHAPTER. 501 W Market St, Akron, OH 44303. **216-535-6131.** Rosemary Cozart, director, public relations

TRUMBULL COUNTY CHAPTER. 661 Mahoning Ave NW (PO Box 1266), Warren, OH 44482. **216-392-2551.** Mrs Gene A Brown, director, public information

Northwest Ohio Division

GREATER TOLEDO AREA CHAPTER. 2275 Collingwood Blvd, Toledo, OH 43620. **419-248-2221,** Ext 241. Teresa M Arnold, director, public relations. (h) **419-382-0642**

Pittsburgh Division

PITTSBURGH-ALLEGHENY COUNTY CHAPTER. PO Box 1769, 200 4th Ave, Pittsburgh, PA 15230. **412-263-3142.** Barry Kukovich, director, public relations. (h) **412-856-9406**

Rochester Regional Division

ROCHESTER-MONROE COUNTY CHAPTER. 50 Prince St, Rochester, NY 14607. **716-275-9800.** Carol O'Connor, public relations director. (h) **716-394-0097**

Virginia–Capital Division

RICHMOND CHAPTER. 409 E Main St, Richmond, VA 23219. **804-643-7451,** Ext 23. Marian G Mahon, director, public relations. (h) **804-321-7684**

Western Ohio Division

DAYTON AREA CHAPTER. 370 W 1st St, Dayton, OH 45402. **513-222-6711,** Ext 58. Midge Battin, director, public relations. (h) **513-434-8894**

Southern US

Alabama Division

BIRMINGHAM AREA CHAPTER. 2316 4th Ave, N Birmingham, AL 35203. **205-322-5661.** Cynthia Clemmer, acting director, public relations

MONTGOMERY AREA CHAPTER. 364 S Ripley St (PO Box 6136), Montgomery, AL 36104. **205-263-5741.** Lexie Pound, director, public relations. (h) **205-362-5741**

Arkansas Division

PULASKI COUNTY CHAPTER. 401 S Monroe, Little Rock, AR 72205. **501-666-0351.** Karen Miller, director, public information. (h) **501-376-6761**

Carolinas Division

ASHEVILLE AREA CHAPTER. 518 Kenilworth Rd, Asheville, NC 28805. **704-254-9603.** Morris White, representative, public relations

GREATER CAROLINAS CHAPTER. 2425 Park Rd (PO Box 3507), Charlotte, NC 28203. **704-376-1661,** Ext 239. Jane R Lesser, director, public relations. (h) **704-523-8760**

CAROLINA LOW-COUNTRY CHAPTER. 144 Wentworth St, Charleston, SC 29401. **803-577-7830.** Dick Anderson, director, public relations

Georgia Division

METROPOLITAN ATLANTA CHAPTER. 1925 Monroe Dr NE, Atlanta, GA 30324. **404-874-1601.** Marianne Barnett, director, public relations. (h) **404-475-5781**

Gulf States Division

MOBILE COUNTY CHAPTER. Corner Dauphin and Broad Sts, Mobile, AL 36602. **205-438-2571.** Mailing address: PO Box 1764, Mobile, AL 36601. David Little, division representative. (h) **205-342-7532.**

Susan Rehm, assistant public relations designee. (h) **205-343-1319**

Kentucky Division

LOUISVILLE AREA CHAPTER. PO Box 1675, 510 E Chestnut St, Louisville, KY 40201. **502-589-4450.** Lewis Bondurant, director, public relations. (h) **502-451-4425**

Louisiana Division

NEW ORLEANS CHAPTER. 1523 St Charles Ave, New Orleans, LA 70130. **504-586-8191.** Betty Hugh, director, public relations. (h) **504-891-7265**

BATON ROUGE CHAPTER. 1165 S Foster Dr, Baton Rouge, LA 70806. **504-926-2747.** Linda Hawks, director, volunteer and information services. (h) **504-383-4382**

Mississippi Division

CENTRAL MISSISSIPPI CHAPTER. PO Box 4523, Fondren Station, Jackson, MS 39216. **601-353-5442.** Tom Egan, director, public relations. (h) **601-355-4464**

South Florida Division

DADE COUNTY CHAPTER. PO Box 370968, Buena Vista Station, 5020 Biscayne Blvd, Miami, FL 33137. **305-576-4600.** Anibal Irastorza, assistant manager. (h) **305-264-8354**

SOUTH PINELLAS COUNTY CHAPTER. 818 4th St N, St Petersburg, FL 33701. **813-898-3111.** Georgiana Anderson, director, public relations

Suwannee Division

JACKSONVILLE AREA CHAPTER. 2525 Riverside Ave, Jacksonville, FL 32204. **904-358-8091,** Ext 14. Mailing address: PO Box 40809, Jacksonville, FL 32203. Phyllis Cherault, director, public relations. (h) **904-725-7960**

CENTRAL FLORIDA CHAPTER. 2401 E Central Boulevard (PO Box 6726), Orlando, FL 32803. **305-894-4141.** William W Wohlfarth, Jr, director, public affairs and financial development. (h) **305-894-1463**

DAYTONA BEACH AREA CHAPTER. 341 White St, Daytona Beach, FL 32014. **904-255-5555.** Georgeanne Watercutter, director, public relations. (h) **904-736-3720**

Tennessee Division

NASHVILLE–DAVIDSON COUNTY CHAPTER. 321 22nd Ave N, Nashville, TN 37203. **615-327-1931.** Owen Meredith, director, public relations. (h) **615-298-3104**

MEMPHIS AREA CHAPTER. 1400 Central Ave, Memphis, TN 38104. **901-726-1690.** Betty Black, director, public relations. (h) **901-692-1334**

KNOX COUNTY CHAPTER. 507 W Cumberland Ave, Knoxville, TN 37901. **615-524-3031.** Alice Lewis, director, public relations

Midwestern US

Bistate Division

ST LOUIS BISTATE CHAPTER. 4050 Lindell Blvd, St Louis, MO 63108. **314-658-2056.** Mel Muskopf, director, public relations. (h) **314-631-6867**

Capital Area Division

CENTEX CHAPTER. 2218 Pershing Dr, Austin, TX 78723. **512-928-4271.** Diane Wheeler, director, public relations. (h) **512-452-2339**

Cornhusker Division

LANCASTER COUNTY CHAPTER. 1701 E St (PO Box 83267), Lincoln, NE 68501. **402-432-5581.** Patricia Nefzger, director, public relations. (h) **402-432-5061**

Eastern Oklahoma Division

TULSA AREA CHAPTER. 3345 S Harvard, Tulsa, OK 74135. **918-743-9741.** Mailing address: PO Box 45726, Tulsa, OK 74145. Linda J Daxon, public relations director. (h) **918-584-4010**

Heart of America Division

GREATER KANSAS CITY CHAPTER. 3521 Broadway, Kansas City, MO 64111. **816-756-2365.** Robert E Jones, director, public relations. (h) **816-921-6577**

Heart of Illinois Division

CENTRAL ILLINOIS CHAPTER. 1224 N Berkeley Ave, Peoria, IL 61603.

309-674-7171. Mildred L Nunes, director, public relations. (h) **309-682-1137**

Heartland Division

DOUGLAS-SARPY COUNTY CHAPTER. 432 S 39th St, Omaha, NE 68131. **402-341-2723.** Lynn Agee, director, public relations. **402-455-7114**

Illinois Division

MID-AMERICA CHAPTER. 43 E Ohio St, Chicago, IL 60611. **312-440-2020.** Robert E Kilbride, director, public relations. (h) **312-561-6128**

Indiana Division

ALLEN-WELLS CHAPTER. PO Box 5025, Fort Wayne, IN 46805. **219-483-3158.** Cheryl Ann Kunberger, director, public relations. (h) **219-432-8216**

INDIANAPOLIS AREA CHAPTER. 441 E 10th St, Indianapolis, IN 46202. **317-634-1441.** Florine Rogers, director, public relations. (h) **317-846-3348**

Iowa Division

CENTRAL IOWA CHAPTER. 2116 Grand Ave, Des Moines, IO 50312. **515-243-7681.** R Pat O'Brien, manager. (h) **515-964-2545**

Midway Kansas Division

MIDWAY KANSAS CHAPTER. 321 N Topeka, Wichita, KS 67202. **316-265-6601.** Colleen Wooley, director, public relations. (h) **316-683-8120**

Minnesota-Wisconsin Division

ST PAUL AREA CHAPTER. 100 S Robert St, St Paul, MN 55107. **612-291-6701.** John De Haven, director, public relations. (h) **612-559-3663**

Northeast Texas Division

DALLAS COUNTY CHAPTER. 2300 McKinney Ave, Dallas, TX 75201. **214-741-4421.** Wanda Dulaney, director, public relations. (h) **214-522-1194**

CADDO PARISH CHAPTER. 3833 Southern Ave, Shreveport, LA 71106. **318-865-5114.** Lillian Campisi, director, public relations. (h) **318-865-7265**

Northwest Division

MINNEAPOLIS AREA CHAPTER. 11 Dehl Pl, Minneapolis, MN 55403. **612-871-7676,** Ext 44. Gary San Souce, director, public relations. (h) **612-377-1445**

Pere Marquette Division

GREATER MILWAUKEE CHAPTER. 2600 W Wisconsin Ave, Milwaukee, WI 53233. **414-342-8680.** Rosemary Murphy, director, public relations. (h) **414-873-6997**

Texas Gulf Coast Division

HOUSTON-HARRIS COUNTY CHAPTER. 2006 Smith St, Houston, TX 77002. **713-659-8300.** Mailing address: PO Box 397, Houston, TX 77001. Reinette Cottingham, director, public relations. (h) **713-721-1966**

BEXAR COUNTY CHAPTER. 90 Brees Blvd, San Antonio, TX 78209. **512-826-8611.** Bob Graham, director, public relations

West Texas Division

TARRANT COUNTY CHAPTER. PO Box 12406, 6640 Camp Bowie, Fort Worth, TX 76116. **817-732-4491.** Randy Weddle, director, public relations. (h) **817-292-9408**

Western Michigan Division

KENT COUNTY CHAPTER. 1050 Fuller Ave NE, Grand Rapids, MI 49503. **616-456-8661.** Gloria M Simon, director, public relations. (h) **616-241-0349**

Western Oklahoma Division

OKLAHOMA COUNTY CHAPTER. 323 NW 10th St, Oklahoma City, OK 73103. **405-232-7121.** Henry Dickason, director, public relations. (h) **405-672-4729**

Wisconsin Capital Division

DANE COUNTY CHAPTER. 1202 Ann St (PO Box 603), Madison, WI 53701. **608-255-0021.** Doris Green, director, public relations. (h) **608-241-5191**

Wolverine Division

SOUTHEASTERN MICHIGAN CHAPTER. 100 Mack Ave (PO Box 351), Detroit, MI 48232. **313-833-4440.** Ronald Kelly, director, public relations. (h) **313-293-1056**

Western US

Arizona Division

MARICOPA COUNTY CHAPTER. 1510 E Flower, Phoenix, AZ 85014. **602-264-9481.** Chuck Smith, director, public relations. (h) **602-839-4198**

Cascades Division

OREGON TRAIL CHAPTER. 4200 SW Corbett Ave (PO Box 70), Portland, OR 97207. **503-243-5205.** Ms Marty Yoder, director, public relations. (h) **503-288-8972**

Golden Spike Division

SALT LAKE AREA CHAPTER. 555 Foothill Dr, Salt Lake City, UT 84113. **801-582-3431,** Ext 41. Patricia A Jones, public relations designee. (h) **801-582-3431**

Inland Empire Division

INLAND EMPIRE CHAPTER. W 1203 Riverside Ave, Spokane, WA 99201. **508-747-7124.** Mary Craig, director, public relations. (h) **509-838-3400**

Northern California-Western Nevada Division

GOLDEN GATE CHAPTER. 1625 Van Ness Ave, San Francisco, CA 94109. **415-776-1500.** Robert Vainowski, director, public relations. (h) **415-593-1553**

MARIN COUNTY CHAPTER. 712 5th Ave, San Rafael, CA 94901. Charlotte Riznik, director, public relations

OAKLAND-SOUTH ALAMEDA COUNTY CHAPTER. 2111 E 14th St (PO Box 1257), Oakland, CA 94604. **415-533-2321,** Ext 22. Jacklyn McCarty, director, public relations. (h) **415-654-0384**

SACRAMENTO AREA CHAPTER. 1300 G St (PO Box 1046), Sacramento, CA 95805. **916-452-6541.** Art Dreyer, director, public relations

Pacific Division

HAWAII STATE CHAPTER. PO Box 3948, Honolulu, HI 96812. **808-734-2101.** James J Kline, director, public affairs and financial development. (h) **808-734-7663**

Pacific Northwest Division

SEATTLE-KING COUNTY CHAPTER. 2515 S Holgate St (PO Box 24286), Seattle, WA 98124. **206-323-2345.** Mary Karabaich, director, public relations. (h) **206-763-2447**

Pacific Southwest Division

SAN DIEGO COUNTY CHAPTER. 3650 5th Ave, San Diego, CA 92103. **714-291-2620.** Walter Manion, director, community relations. (h) **714-284-4578**

Roadrunner Division

BERNALILLO COUNTY CHAPTER. 5006 Copper NE (PO Box 8706), Albuquerque, NM 87108. **505-265-8514.** Jim Wilkerson, public relations chairman. (h) **505-821-9872**

Rocky Mountain Division

MILE HIGH CHAPTER. 170 Steele St, Denver, CO 80206. **303-399-0550.** Arthur J Smith, director, public relations. (h) **303-794-7742**

PIKES PEAK CHAPTER. 1600 N Cascade Ave, Colorado Springs, CO 80907. **303-632-3563.** Mrs N Leslie Cook, director, public relations

Southern California Division

LOS ANGELES COUNTY CHAPTER. 1200 S Vermont Ave, Los Angeles, CA 90006. **213-384-5261.** James Kalivas, director, public relations. (h) **213-349-4668**

PASADENA CHAPTER. 420 Madeline Dr (PO Box 399), Pasadena, CA 91102. **213-799-0841.** Nancy K Williams, director, public relations

GREATER LONG BEACH CHAPTER. 3150 E 29th St, Long Beach, CA 90806. **213-595-6341.** Kristin L Nelson, director, public relations. (h) **213-439-7412**

Wrangler Division

CASCADES COUNTY CHAPTER. Civil Ctr (PO Box 2406), Great Falls, MT 59403.

406-452-6486 or **6488.** Katherine J Watson, volunteer director, public relations. (h) **406-453-3465**

UNITED STATES CIVIL DEFENSE COUNCIL STATE REPRESENTATIVES

Region I

CONNECTICUT. City Hall, 155 Deerhill Ave, Danbury, 06810. **203-784-5254.** Peter P Winter

MAINE. Church St, Presque Isle, 04769. **207-444-5156.** Joseph A Gagnon

MASSACHUSETTS. Box 83A, Route 6, Plymouth, 02360. **617-759-7450.** Robert C Rohlmann

NEW HAMPSHIRE. 36 Arlington St, Nashua, 02360. **603-882-5789.** George Papadoulos

NEW JERSEY. Community Ctr, Audon, 08106. **609-547-1581.** Frank Hull

NEW YORK. Box 127, Yaphank, 11980. **516-473-3808.** Major Norman Kelly

PUERTO RICO. PO Box 239, Utado, 00761. Longinos M Valez

RHODE ISLAND. 25 Winthrop Rd, East Greenwich, 02818. **401-884-2048.** A J Nocera

VERMONT. Box 876, White River Junction, 05001. **603-795-4516.** Robert W Mornacy

VIRGIN ISLANDS. PO Box 834, Charlotte Amalie, St Thomas. **809-714-8503.** Edmond A Penn

Region II

DELAWARE. 1213 Walnut St, Wilmington, 19801. **302-366-0885.** Harlan Justice

MARYLAND. Courthouse, La Plata, 20646. **301-934-9371.** Harris S Matthews

PENNSYLVANIA. 900 E King St, Lancaster, 17602. **717-393-4532.** Paul L Leese

VIRGINIA. Apt 606, 408 Dundaff St, Norfolk, 23507. **804-632-0872.** William G Frey

WEST VIRGINIA. Box 1748, Charleston, 15300. **304-744-5232.** Colonel R H Gray

Region III

ALABAMA. Box 566, Scottsboro, 35768. **205-574-3482.** J Rodney Gentle

FLORIDA. City Hall, Tallahassee, 32304. **904-877-5448.** Mrs B Y Atkinson

GEORGIA. Courthouse, Ashburn, 31714. **912-567-3511.** Deral Dukes

KENTUCKY. PO Box 337, Sheperdsville, 40165. **502-543-4583.** Charles Long

MISSISSIPPI. PO Box 895, Natchez, 39120. **601-445-4049.** J B White

NORTH CAROLINA. Box 125, Konansville, 28349. **919-296-0901.** Hiram Brinson

SOUTH CAROLINA. PO Box 543, Anderson, 29622. **803-225-2212.** Robert B King

TENNESSEE. Floor 7M, Metropolitan Courthouse, Nashville, 37201. **615-228-2395.** Hilary H Linaner

Region IV

ILLINOIS. 2205 Sunset Dr, Tremont, 61544. Clarence Burke

INDIANA. 1230 S Wabash Dr, Kokomo, 46901. **317-457-5166.** Paul Whilhoite

MICHIGAN. 26000 Evergreen Rd, Southfield, 48075. **313-356-5429.** Colonel Arthur C Becker

MINNESOTA. Regional Law Enforcement Ctr, Mankato, 56001. **507-388-1852.** Robert C Shaw

OHIO. 84 Shadybrook Dr, Cincinnati, 45216. **513-385-8827.** Liore Maccarone

WISCONSIN. 8814 Libson Ave, Milwaukee, 53222. **414-462-5392.** Daniel J Gracz

Region V

ARKANSAS. PO Box 550, Star City, 71667. **561-628-4548.** Bill Hundley

LOUISIANA. PO Box 1293, Lafayette, 70501. **318-984-9384.** Colonel Oliver B Fowler

NEW MEXICO. PO Box 1293, Albuquerque, 87103. **505-296-5608.** George W Dunham

OKLAHOMA. 4600 N Eastern St, Oklahoma City, 73111. Clyde Mitchell

TEXAS. City Hall, Pasadena, 77501. **713-991-3891.** Mrs Robert Fife

Region VI

COLORADO. Courthouse, Pueblo, 81003. **303-948-3891.** Betty Jo Hopper

IOWA. Courthouse, Iowa City, 53340. Wayne D Walters

KANSAS. PO Box 329, Salina, 67402. **913-827-8681.** Don Rectenwald

MISSOURI. PO Box N, Columbia, 65201. **314-474-2725.** George Hughes

MONTANA. PO Box 66, Glasgow, 59230. **406-228-8434.** Terry Mercer

NEBRASKA. Box 369, Chadron, 69337. **308-432-2819.** Robert Zeman

NORTH DAKOTA. Ward County Courthouse, Minot, 58261. **701-838-1234.** Harold Carnahan

SOUTH DAKOTA. Box 667, Mitchell, 57301. **605-996-9279.** Jerry Diamond

UTAH. Box 236, Magna, 84004. **801-250-2251.** Roy Smith

WYOMING. 318 W 19th St, Cheyenne, 82001. **307-652-1847.** Jim Fowler

Region VII

ARIZONA. PO Box 348, Globe, 85501. **602-425-4745.** Carmen C Corso

CALIFORNIA. 435 E 13th St, Merced, 95340. James L Hurn

HAWAII. 650 S King St, Honolulu, 96813. **808-395-1406.** John Bohn

NEVADA. PO Box 11130, Reno, 89510. **702-358-2197.** Robert B Hay

Region VIII

ALASKA. 625 C St, Anchorage, 99501. **907-277-3000.** Colonel Bruce Staser

IDAHO. 8th and Bannoc, Boise, 83702. **208-375-7387.** Charles Snider

OREGON. 2106 S Kane Rd, Oregon City, 97045. Richard K Bass

WASHINGTON. 3125 First W, Kelso, 98626. Lu Ann Pedersen

BUSINESS

THE MOST NEWSWORTHY AMERICAN BUSINESSES

This list of most important American businesses, from the standpoint of journalists, is somewhat subjective, and for this reason it differs, for better or worse, from other such lists. The top 300 firms in each of the categories of assets, sales, market value, and net profits, as ranked by *Forbes Magazine*, are here; so are most of the *Fortune* 500; and so are all firms with more than 30,000 employees. But added to this list are firms whose size alone might not qualify them, but which are nevertheless consistent newsmakers, as well as firms that because of their nature are particularly important socially or journalistically, and firms that because of their activities might be expected to be the subject of intense journalistic interest. A company name consisting of a given name (or initials) and a surname is alphabetized by the first letter of the surname.

ABBOTT LABORATORIES. Abbott Park, (North Chicago, IL 60064. **312-688-6100.** William D Pratt, vice-president, public affairs, **312-688-3931**

ACCO (American Chain and Cable Company, Inc). 929 Connecticut Ave (PO Box 430), Bridgeport, CT 06602. **203-335-2511.** Joseph H Maloney, president and chief executive officer. Robert B Morgan, publications services manager

ACF INDUSTRIES INC. 750 3rd Ave, New York, NY 10017. **212-986-8600.** Curtis L Anders, director, communications.

ACME MARKETS INC. 124 N 15th St, Philadelphia, PA. 19101. **215-568-3000.** George L Beiswinger, vice-president, communication

ADDRESSOGRAPH-MULTIGRAPH CORPORATION. 20600 Chagrin Blvd, Cleveland, OH 44122. **216-283-3000.** Night line: **216-248-1599.** Alan G Easton, vicepresident, communications, **216-283-3473.** James H McConnell, director, product information, **216-283-3432**

ADMIRAL CORP. *See* Rockwell International Corporation

AETNA LIFE AND CASULATY CO. 151 Farmington Ave, Hartford, CT 06156. **203-273-0123.** Paul B Cullen, assistant vice-president, public relations and advertising, **203-273-3346.** H Cranston Lawton, director, corporate communication services, **203-273-3157.** Thomas J Collins, director, public relations services, **203-273-7141.** Thomas F Rooney, manager, editorial and news media services

AGWAY, INC. 333 Butternut Dr, Dewitt, NY 13214. Mailing adddress: PO Box 4933, Syracuse, NY 13221. **315-477-7061.** Arthur J Fogerty, director, public relations

H F AHMANSON & CO. 3731 Wilshire Blvd, Los Angeles, CA 90010. **213-487-4277.** Gayle Morris, vice-president and manager, investor relations

AIR PRODUCTS AND CHEMICALS, INC. Trexlertown, PA 18087. Mailing address: PO Box 538, Allentown, PA 18105. **215-395-4911.** Dayton E Pryer, director, public relations and advertising

AIRCO INDUSTRIAL GASES (Air Reduction Co.) 575 Mountain Ave, Murray Hill, NJ 07974. **201-464-8100.** Pete Finlay, director, communications, Ext 332

AKZONA INCORPORATED. 1 Pack Sq, Asheville, NC 28802. **704-253-6851** (also night line). Claude Ramsey, chairman and president. Alan Englander, director, investor relations, **212-730-5380.** Brian Smith, director, corporate communications, **704-253-6851**

ALASKA INTERSTATE CO. PO Box 6554, Houston, TX 77005. **713-621-8710.** *Press contact.* Willard Hanzlik

ALBERTSONS INC. 1623 Washington St, Boise, ID 83726. **208-344-7441.** *Press contact.* Robert D Bolinder, vice-chairman

ALCAN ALUMINUM CORP. 100 Erieview Plz, Cleveland, OH 44114. **216-523-6800.** *Press Contact.* R Terry Olbrysh, **216-523-6915**

ALCO STANDARD CORPORATION. PO Box 834, Valley Forge, PA 19482. **215-666-0760.** Ray B Mundt, president. Myron S Gelbach, Jr, vice-president. Tinkham Veale II, chairman, **216-464-8452.** Larry L Leedy, corporate relations and planning administrator, **216-464-8452**

ALLEGHENY POWER SYSTEMS. 320 Park Ave, New York, NY 10022. **202-752-2121.** Joe Bannon, public relations director

ALLIED CHEMICAL. Morris Township, NJ 07960. **201-455-2000.** *Press contact.* Harvey W Greisman, **201-455-5686**

ALLIS-CHALMERS CORPORATION. 1205 S 70th St, Milwaukee, WI 53201. **414-475-2000.** Quentin J O'Sullivan, manager, news bureau, **414-475-2457**

ALUMINUM COMPANY OF AMERICA. 1501 Alcoa Bldg, Pittsburgh, PA, 15219. **412-553-4545.** William H Shepard, vicepresident, public relations and advertising, (h) **412-741-5106.** Gordon C Meek, manager, corporate news, **412-553-4466.** (h) **412-835-4708.** Timothy M Wilkinson, supervisor, corporate news, **412-553-3655.** (h) **412-242-2007.** Laurence S Sewell, Jr, manager, public relations, **412-553-2861.** (h) **412-921-6314.** Richard R Schalk, manager, New York City public relations, **212-972-5350.** (h) **914-779-9654.** Jack E Nettles, manager, corporate communications, **412-553-4458,** (h) **412-531-0146**

AMERADA HESS CORP. 1185 Avenue of the Americas, New York, NY 10036. **212-997-8500**

AMERICAN AIRLINES. 633 3rd Ave, New York, NY 10017. **212-557-1234.** Albert V Casey, chairman and president. David C Frailey, vice-president, public relations, **212-557-6286.** Night line: A public relations staffer is on call nights, weekends, and holidays through the operator at **212-476-4321**

Subject matter and regional contacts

Public Relations Staff. Joe Moran, News and editorial, **212-557-6290.** Al Becker, field services, **212-557-6292.** David Lobb, marketing, **212-557-6308.** Larry Strain, operations, **212-557-6304.** Joe Scott, Caribbean, **212-557-6305.** Bill Dreslin, freight, **212-557-6294.** Carolyn Bowers, passenger services, **212-557-6320**

Regional Public Relations Staff. Tom Lyons, Boston, MA, **617-569-1652.** Walt Boyd, Detroit, MI, **313-965-5511.** John Raymond, Dallas-Fort Worth, TX, **214-574-2312.** Bill Hipple, Los Angeles, CA, **213-937-6662.** Dick Tyler, San Francisco, CA, **415-877-6426**

AMERICAN BAKERIES. 10 Riverside Plz, Chicago, IL 60606. **312-454-7400.** *Press contact.* Raymond J Lahvic, vice-president

AMERICAN BEEF PACKERS INC. 7000 W Center Rd, Omaha, NE 68106. **402-391-4700.** *Press contact.* Michael Sheehan

AMERICAN BRANDS. 245 Park Ave, New York, NY 10017. **212-557-7000.** *Press contact.* Richard H Stinnette

AMERICAN BROADCASTING COMPANIES. 1330 Avenue of the Americas, New York, NY 10019. **212-581-7777.** Ellis O Moore, vice-president, public relations for ABC, Inc, **212-581-7717.** For further details, *see* BROADCASTING NETWORKS.

AMERICAN CAN COMPANY. American Ln, Greenwich, CT 06830. **203-552-2000.** John F McGoldrick, director, corporate communications. Henning Nielsen, director, public information, **203-552-2223.** Night line: **914-761-5998.** Brian Martin, public relations representative, **203-552-2230**

AMERICAN CHAIN AND CABLE. See ACCO

AMERICAN CYANAMID CO. Berdan Ave, Wayne, NJ 07470. **201-831-1234.** New York tie-line: **212-586-5850.** Joseph Calitri, director, public affairs. James Ryan, manager, press relations. Helen Ostrowski, coordinator, press relations

AMERICAN DISTRICT TELEGRAPH COMPANY. 1 World Trade Ctr, New York, NY 10048. **212-558-1100.** *Press contact.* Edward L Hansen

AMERICAN ELECTRIC POWER CO INC. 2 Broadway, New York, NY 10004. **212-422-4800.** Harold R Johnson, vice-president, public affairs

AMERICAN EXPRESS. American Express Plz, New York, NY 10004. **212-480-2000.** C Ramon Greenwood, vice-president, public affairs

AMERICAN GENERAL INSURANCE CO. 2727 Allen Pkwy, Houston, TX 77019. **713-522-1111.** C M (Bud) Schauerte, director, public relations

AMERICAN HOIST. 63 S Robert St, St Paul, MN 55107. **612-228-4321.** J P Heihn, director, public relations

AMERICAN HOME PRODUCTS. 685 3rd Ave, New York, NY 10017. **212-986-1000.** *Press contact.* Kenneth R Baumbusch, advertising

AMERICAN HOSPITAL SUPPLY CORPORATION. 2020 Ridge Ave, Evanston, IL 60201. **312-866-7200.** Night line: **312-273-5847.** Karl D Bays, chairman of the board. Jerry Parrott, new manager. Steven Polcyn, manager, corporate communications

AMERICAN INTERNATIONAL GROUP. 102 Maiden Ln, New York, NY 10005. **212-791-7000.** Barbara A Bauer, director, corporate communications

AMERICAN MOTORS CORPORATION. American Ctr, 27777 Franklin Rd, Southfield, MI 48034. **313-827-1000.** John R Pichurski, press relations manager, **313-827-2844.** Frank S Hedge, vice-president, public relations, **313-827-2840.** Gene Swaim, director, public relations, **313-827-2850.** Lloyd Northard, assistant director, research, television, and radio, **313-827-2848**

AMERICAN NATURAL RESOURCES COMPANY (American Natural Gas). 1 Woodward, Detroit, MI 48226. **313-965-8300.** Arthur R Seder, Jr, chairman. William M Hutchins, manager, media relations, **313-965-1634.** (h) **313-646-7042**

AMERICAN PETROFINA INC. 50 Rockefeller Plz, New York, NY 10020. **212-586-8510.** Also PO Box 2159, Dallas, TX 75221. **214-750-2400.** R I Galland, chairman

and chief executive officer. J W Cahill, public relations director, **214-750-2900**

AMERICAN SAVINGS AND LOAN ASSN. *See* First Charter Financial Corp

AMERICAN STANDARD INC. 40 W 40th St, New York, NY 10018. **212-484-5100.** Jeanne Golly, director, investor and public relations

AMERICAN STERILIZER CO INC. 2222 W Grandview Blvd, Erie, PA 16509. **814-452-3100.** *Press contact.* Frank De Fazio, vice-president

AMERICAN TELEPHONE & TELE-GRAPH. 195 Broadway, New York, New York 10007. **212-393-9800.** Edward M Block, vice-president, public relations. David M Bicofsky, press relations supervisor, **212-393-4335.** John H Connolly, director, public relations, **212-393-8223**

AMF INC. 777 Westchester Ave, White Plains, NY 10604. **914-694-9000.** Eldon E Fox, vice-president, public affairs

AMFAC, INC. 700 Bishop St, Honolulu, HI 96801. **808-546-8111.** Dale M Walwark, director, public relations, **808-395-4034**

AMP, INC. Eisenhower Blvd, Harrisburg, PA 17105. **717-564-0101**

AMSTAR CORP. 1251 Avenue of the Americas, New York, NY 10020. **212-489-9000.** *Press contact.* Raymond C Guth, vice-president

AMSTED INDUSTRIES. 3700 Prudential Plz, Chicago, IL 60601. **312-645-1700.** Goff Smith, president. Hugh R Tassey, director, public affairs and advertising, **312-645-1717.** Thomas R Karow, supervisor, public affairs and advertising, **312-645-1719**

AMTEL INC. 40 Westminster St, Providence, RI 02903. **401-331-2400.** L G Crumpler, vice-president, public relations

AMTRAK (National Rail Passenger Corporation). 955 L'Enfant Plz, SW, Washington, DC 20024. **202-484-7220.** Night line: **202-484-2725.** Edwin E Edel, vice-president, public affairs. Brian Duff, director, news services. *Press spokespersons.* Joseph Vranich, Sue Stevens, and Jim Bryant

News bureau contacts

Western Region News Bureau. Art Lloyd. **415-556-4009**

Central Region News Bureau. Bob Casey. **312-443-4861**

Northeast Corridor News Bureau. Lois Morasco. **215-597-9957**

ANACONDA CO. 1271 Avenue of the Americas, New York, NY 10020. **212-397-3800.** Harry L Storey, vice-president, public relations Jeannette E Paladino, assistant director, public relations

ANCHOR HOCKING CORP. 109 N Broad St, Lancaster, OH 43130. **614-687-2212.** C J Arnsbarger, vice-president and public affairs director

ANDERSON, CLAYTON & CO. PO Box 2538, Houston, TX 77001. **713-651-0641.** Night line: **713-651-1698.** T J Barlow, chairman and chief executive officer. Steward P Smith, vice-president, public relations. Robert H Gersky, director, investor relations

ANHEUSER BUSCH INC. 721 Pestalozzi St, St Louis, MO 63118. **314-577-0577.** Ronald S Humiston, manager, external affairs

ARA SERVICES. Independence Sq W, Philadelphia, PA 19106. **215-574-5000.** William S Fishman, chairman and chief executive officer. Harry Belinger, director, community relations, **215-574-5525.** (h) **215-877-3525.** David D Dayton, vice-president, financial communications, **215-574-5465.** Larry Murray, director, financial communications, **215-574-5469.** Bert Wilson, manager, financial communications, **215-574-5493**

Public Restaurants. Ligita Dienhart (Hancock Bldg, Chicago, IL), **312-787-2454**

ARCHER-DANIELS MIDLAND. 4666 Faires Pkwy, Decatur, IL 62525. **217-424-5200.** *Press contact.* Richard Burket, vice-president and assistant to president

ARLEN REALTY AND DEVELOPMENT CO. 888 7th Ave, New York, NY 10019. **212-333-2100.** *Press contact.* Arthur G Cohen

ARMOUR & CO. See Greyhound Corporation

ARMSTRONG CORK COMPANY. Lancaster, PA 17604. **717-397-0611.** James H Binns, president and chief executive officer. Robert K Marker, manager, press services and product information, Ext 2274. C Eugene Moore, manager, corporate and financial information, Ext 2101

ARVIN INDUSTRIES. 1531 13th St, Columbus, IN 47201. **812-372-7271.** Fred Meyer, vice-president, public relations

ASARCO INC. 120 Broadway, New York, NY 10005. **212-732-9500.** William K Murray, director, public relations and advertising

ASHLAND OIL INC. PO Box 391, Ashland, Ky 41101. **606-329-3333.** (also night line) Orin E Atkins, chairman and chief executive officer. Robert E Yancey, president. William R Seaton, vice-chairman. *Press contacts.* Frank P Justice, **606-329-4523**; Donn B Rooks, **606-329-3262**; Robert J Thomas, **606-329-4125**

ASSOCIATED DRY GOODS. 417 5th Ave, New York, NY 10016. **212-679-8700.** *Press contact.* Peter W Brengel, vice-president and treasurer

AT&T. *See* American Telephone & Telegraph

ATCHISON, TOPEKA & SANTA FE RAILWAY. 80 E Jackson Blvd, Chicago, IL 60604. **312-427-4900.** (also night line). John S Reed, chairman, Santa Fe Industries. Bill Burk, vice-president, public relations. Robert E Gehrt, assistant to vice-president, public relations. John W Tilsch, special representative, public relations

Regional press contacts. G L Sweet, Topeka, KS; W B Cox, Los Angeles, CA; G T Grader, Dallas, TX

ATLANTIC RICHFIELD CO. 515 S Flower St, Los Angeles, CA 90071. **213-486-3511.** Anthony Hatch, manager, media relations, **213-486-2740.** Raymond E Parr, manager, news services, **213-486-3380**

Regional press contacts. Michael Webb, Anchorage, AK, **907-277-5637.** J Q Beck, Dallas, TX, **214-651-4947.** J J Ackler, Denver, CO, **303-573-3595.** Manuel Jimenez, Los Angeles, CA, **213-486-2652.** R Paul Hassler, Philadelphia, PA, **215-557-2859.** Dean Baxter, Houston, TX, **713-965-6011**

ATO INC. 4420 Sherwin Rd, Willoughby, OH 44094. **216-946-9000**

AVCO CORP. 1275 King St, Greenwich, CT 06830. **203-552-1800** Robert E Nichols, director, public relations, **415-622-5322.** Adri G Boudewyn, associate director, public relations, **415-622-5321.** Stephen L Johnson, senior public information officer, **415-622-2645.** Raymond V Toman, public information manager, **415-622-2775**

AVNET INC. 765 5th Ave, New York, NY 10021. **212-644-1050**

BANK OF NEW YORK. 48 Wall St, New York, NY 10015. **212-530-1784.** Kenneth Bacon, vice-president, public relations

BANKERS LIFE. 711 High St, Des Moines, IA 50309. **515-244-3131.** Walter J Walsh, director, public relations, **515-247-5098**

BANKERS TRUST COMPANY. 16 Wall St, New York, NY 10005. **212-775-2500.** 280 Park Ave, New York, NY 10017. **212-775-2500.** Alfred Brittain III, chairman of the board. Thomas A Parisi, vice-president, **212-692-5576**

BAUSCH AND LOMB INC. 635 Paul St, Rochester, NY 14602. **716-338-6000.** Ronald J Eisen, director, public relations

BAXTER TRAVENAL LABORATORIES. 1 Baxter Pkwy, Deerfield, IL 60015. **312-945-2000.** Lincoln R Dowell, director, public affairs. *Press contact.* William B Graham

BEATRICE FOODS CO. 120 S LaSalle St, Chicago, IL 60603. **312-782-3820.** Wallace N Rasmussen, chairman and chief executive officer. Neil R Gazel, assistant vice-president, director, public relations, **312-782-3822.** Robert I Seger, assistant public relations director, **312-782-3820**

BECTON DICKINSON AND CO. Stanley and Cornelia Sts, Rutherford, NJ 07070. **201-460-2000.** Wesley J Howe, president and chief executive officer, **201-460-2834.** Harold W Smith, Jr, director, public relations, **201-460-3324.** Marvin L Krasnansky, director, corporate communications, **201-460-3321.** James R Tobin, director, public affairs, **201-460-3326**

BELCO PETROLEUM. 1 Dag Hammarskjold Plz, New York, NY 10017. **212-644-2200**

BEMIS CO. 800 Northstar Ctr, Minneapolis, MN 55402. **312-340-6000.** Lisa Locken, director, corporate communications

BENEFICIAL CORP. 1300 Market St, Wilmington, DE 19899. **302-658-5171.** Charles W Bower, senior vice-president

BETHLEHEM STEEL CORP. 701 E 3rd St, Bethlehem, PA 18016. **215-694-2424.** Marshall D Post, manager, news media division (Martin Tower, 18016), **215-694-5896.** Leonard B Williams, news

media representative (Suite 800, 1000 16th St NW, Washington, DC 20036), **202-393-4720**

BLUE BELL INC. 335 Church St, Greensboro, NC 27401. **919-373-3400.** Tom R Collins, manager, corporate communications. **373-4340**

BOEING CO. 7755 E Marginal Way, Seattle, WA 98124. **206-655-2121.** Stanley M Little, Jr, vice-president
   News contacts
Corporate Activities. Peter Bush, corporate director, public relations, **206-655-6123**
Jet transport. Harold Carr, news bureau chief, **206-237-1710**
Military and aerospace. Bill Jury, aerospace public relations director, **206-775-0530**

BOISE CASCADE CORP. 114 S 10th St, Boise, ID 83701. **208-383-9000.** Robert B Hayes, director, corporate communications

BORDEN, INC. 180 E Broad St, Columbus, OH 43215. **614-225-4000.** Maurice O'Reilly, public affairs director

BORG-WARNER CORPORATION. 200 S Michigan Ave, Chicago, IL 60604. **312-322-8500.** James F Beré, chairman and chief executive officer, **312-322-8510.** Douglas Mueller, director, public relations and advertising, **312-322-8670.** (h) **312-769-2843.** Terry Wilson, manager, public and investor relations, **312-322-8672.** Robert F Kelly, account executive, Carl Byoir & Associates, Inc, **312-322-8676.** (h) **312-848-7468**

   Product information contacts
Air Conditioning and Refrigeration (York, PA). Charles S Smith, **717-846-7890,** Ext 3256. (h) **717-246-1570**
Chemicals and Plastics (Parkersburg, W V). William J Moran, **304-485-1771,** Ext 2266. (h) **614-989-2821**
Energy Equipment (California and Oklahoma divisions). James J Kehoe, **213-627-6421.** (h) **213-793-7925**
Transportation Equipment (Troy, MI). Raymond W Zielinski, director, marketing communications, **313-649-2252.** (h) **313-646-4149**

BOSTON EDISON. 800 Boylston St, Boston, MA 02199. **617-424-2000.** James Lydon, vice-president and director, corporate relations. *Press contact.* Charles G Newton, Jr

BRANIFF AIRWAYS, INC. Braniff Ave Bldg, Dallas, TX 75235. **214-358-8577.** Jere Cox, vice-president, public relations

BRIGGS AND STRATTON. 3300 N 124th St, Milwaukee, WI 53201. **414-461-1212.** John Trost, vice-president, industrial relations

BRISTOL-MYERS CO. 345 Park Ave, New York, NY 10022. **212-644-2100.** Harry Levine, vice-president, corporate communications

BROCKWAY GLASS. McCullough St, Brockway, PA 15824. **814-261-6426.** Don Hughes, director, corporate communications

BROWN GROUP INC. 8400 Maryland Ave, St Louis, MO 63105. **314-997-7500.** *Press contact.* James Taylor, vice-president

BRUNSWICK CORPORATION. 1 Brunswick Plz, Skokie, IL 60076. **312-982-6000.** Philip Webster, director, corporate communications

BUCYRUS-ERIE. 1100 Milwaukee Ave, Milwaukee, WI 53172. **414-768-4000.** Harold Row, director, public relations and advertising

BURLINGTON INDUSTRIES INC. 3330 W Frindly Ave, Greensboro, NC 27420. **919-379-2000.** J K Hanson, corporate director, public relations and advertising

BURLINGTON NORTHERN. 176 E 5th St, St Paul, MN 55101. **612-298-3307.** P A Briggs, news director

BURROUGHS CORP. Burroughs Pl, Detroit, MI 48232. **313-972-7254.** Daniel P Lutzeier, director, public affairs

CABOT CORP. 125 High St, Boston, MA 02110. **617-423-6000.** Priscilla R Duncan, manager, investment relations

CAMERON IRON WORKS, INC. Silber and Katy Fwy (PO Box 1212), Houston, TX 77001. **713-683-2211.** M A Wright, chairman and president. Nixon Quintrelle, account executive, Glenn, Bozell, & Jacobs, public relations, **713-224-2761.** Jerry Stark, oil tool division, and Mike McNabb, ball valve division, **713-224-2761** (Glenn, Bozell, & Jacobs)

CAMPBELL SOUP COMPANY. Campbell Pl, Camden, NJ 08101. **609-964-4000.** Harold A Shaub, president and chief executive officer. Graham Sudbury, director, information services, **609-964-4000.** (h) **215-545-5272.** Scott Rombach, manager, information services, **609-964-4000.** (h) **609-654-6984**

CAMPBELL TAGGART INC. 6211 Lemmon Ave, Dallas, TX 75221. **214-358-9211.** Harold Flankard, vice-president, human resources

CANNON MILLS COMPANY. Main St (PO Box 107), Kannapolis, NC 28081. **704-933-1221.** Night line: **704-786-1344.** Harold Hornada, chairman and president. *Press contact.* Edward L Rankin Jr, vice-president

CAPITAL CITIES BROADCASTING. 485 Madison Ave, New York, NY 10022. **212-421-9595.** Andrew E Jackson, vice-president, community relations

CAPITAL HOLDING CORP. 1111 Commonwealth Bldg, Louisville, KY 40201. **502-584-8157.** *Press contact.* Roy Lind

CARBORUNDUM CO. Carborundum Ctr, Niagara Falls, NY 14302. **716-278-2000.** Robert H Quayle, Jr, vice-president, marketing. Marjorie Mitchell, manager, public relations, **716-278-2706**

CARNATION CO. 5045 Wilshire Blvd, Los Angeles, CA 90053. **213-931-1911.** George Wilkins, manager, communications

CAROLINA POWER AND LIGHT. 336 Fayetteville St, Raleigh, NC 27602. **919-828-8211.** J R Riley, vice-president, public affairs

CARPENTER TECHNOLOGY CORPORATION. 101 W Bern St, Reading, PA 19603. **215-372-4511.** *Press contact.* John Tyrrell

CARRIER CORPORATION. Carrier Tower, Syracuse, NY 13221. **315-424-4747.** Night line: **315-432-6000.** Melvin C Holm, board chairman and chief executive officer, **315-424-4848.** Curtis B Barnard, director, corporate communications, **315-424-4857.** Jerry D Hickey, manager, news bureau, **315-424-4747**

CARTER HAWLEY HALE STORES. 550 S Flower St, Los Angeles, CA 90071. **213-620-0150.** E Harcan Smith, investor relations

CASTLE & COOKE INC. 130 Merchant St, Honolulu, HI 96813. **808-548-6611.** Mailing address: PO Box 2990, Financial Plz of the Pacific, Honolulu, HI 96802. Emil A Schneider, director of public relations. **808-548-2985.** *West Coast office.* 50 California St, San Francisco, CA 94111. **415-986-3000.** N John Douglas, director, public and investor relations

CATERPILLAR TRACTOR CO. 100 NE Adams St, Peoria, IL 61629. **309-675-5100.** Byron De Haan, manager, public affairs

CBS INC. 51 W 52nd St, New York, NY 10019. **212-975-4321.** Leonard Spinrad, vice-president, corporate information, **212-975-3895.** *See* BROADCASTING NETWORKS for further details.

CELANESE CORP. 1211 Avenue of the Americas, New York, NY 10036. **212-764-8780.** Dorothy Gregg, corporate vice-president, communications

CENTRAL HUDSON GAS & ELECTRIC CORPORATION. 284 South Ave, Poughkeepsie, NY 12602. **914-452-2000.** H Clifton Wilson, president. James E Russell, news director. Peter R Burdash, manager, information services

CENTRAL & SOUTH WEST CORP. 300 Delaware Ave, Wilmington, DE 19899. **302-655-1526**

CENTRAL SOYA COMPANY INC. 1300 Fort Wayne National Bank Bldg, Fort Wayne, IN 46802. **219-422-8541.** Ronald H Greenfield, manager, public relations

CERTAINTEED PRODUCTS. 750 E Swedesford Rd, Valley Forge, PA 19482. **215-687-5000.** Dorothy C Wackerman, director, public relations. Donald E Meads, chairman and chief executive officer

CESSNA AIRCRAFT CO. PO Box 1521, Wichita, KS 67201. **316-685-9111.** Russell W Meyer Jr, chairman and chief executive officer. Dean Humphrey, director, public relations, (h) **316-788-2780**

CF INDUSTRIES. Salem Lake Dr, Long Grove, IL 60047. **312-438-9500.** Kenneth C Hochstetler, director, public relations, (h) **312-438-4924**

CHAMPION INTERNATIONAL. 1 Landmark Sq, Stamford, CT 06921. **203-357-8500.** A C Sigler, president and chief executive officer. J L Pokorny, director, public relations, **203-357-9320.** Night line: **203-268-7026.** Larry Miller, manager, press relations, **203-357-8611.** Night line: **203-372-2625**

CHARTER CO. 208 Laura St, Jacksonville, FL 32202. **904-358-4111.** Park L Beeler, corporate communications

CHARTER NEW YORK CORP. 1 Wall St, New York, NY 10005. **212-487-6338**

CHASE MANHATTAN BANK. 1 Chase Manhattan Plz, New York, NY 10015. **212-552-2222.** David Rockefeller, chairman. *Spokesman.* Fraser P Seitel, vice-president, **212-552-4503.** Night line: **201-886-1924.** Sharon Schlein, public relations, **212-552-4407.** *Public relations officers.* Allison Kellog, **212-552-4505**; Steve Rautenberg, **212-552-4507**

CHEMETRON CORPORATION. 111 E Wacker Dr, Chicago, IL 60601. **312-565-5000.** John P Gallagher, principal official, **312-565-5042.** Neil J Devroy, public relations manager, **312-565-5090.** Night line: **312-541-1865.** Public relations supervisors: Joanne Tremulis, **312-565-5094**; Don Gruening, **312-565-5092**

CHEMICAL BANK. 20 Pine St, New York, NY 10015. **212-770-1234.** William J C Carlin, vice-president and director, public relations, **212-770-2591.** Susan Weeks, assistant manager, public relations, **212-770-3620.** Mary Whalen, assistant manager, press relations, **212-770-3620**

CHESEBOROUGH-POND'S. 33 Benedict Pl, Greenwich, CT 06830. **203-661-2000.** Howard E Casler, vice-president, public affairs

CHESSIE SYSTEM (Chesapeake and Ohio, and Baltimore and Ohio, railroads). Terminal Tower, Cleveland, OH 44101. **216-623-2400.** Or B & O Bldg, Baltimore, MD 21201. **301-237-3821.** Mays T Watkins, chairman and president. Howard Skidmore, vice-president, public relations. Milt Dolinger, assistant vice-president, public relations, **216-623-2400.** Public relations managers: Willis Cook, Baltimore, MD, **301-237-3821**; Tom Johnson, Huntington, W V, **304-522-5491**

CHICAGO BRIDGE & IRON CO. 800 Jorie Blvd, Oak Brook, IL 60521. **312-654-7000.** G Graham Harper, director, public relations and advertising, **312-654-2000**

CHROMALLOY AMERICAN CORP. 120 S Central Ave, St Louis, MO 63105. **314-721-6777.** Stephanie Lipnick, advertising and public relations

CHRYSLER CORPORATION. PO Box 1919, Detroit, MI 48288. **313-956-5252**
Press contacts
Automotive Manufacturing and Assembly Plants. Jerry Moore. **313-956-4427**
Automotive sales. Moon Mullins, **313-956-5342**; Frank Wylie,

313-956-5392. *Chrysler-Plymouth.* Tony Weiss, **313-956-5344.** *Dodge.* John McCandless, **313-956-5346.** *Trucks and recreational vehicles.* Lee Sechler, **313-956-5348.** *Service and parts.* Rosemarie Kitchin, **313-956-5349**
Chrysler Canada. Walt McCall, **313-965-7580,** Ext 3634; Bob Young, **313-965-7580,** Ext 3685
Corporate activities. Marty Whitmyer, **313-965-2894**; Bob Heath, **313-956-2894**; Tom Houston, **313-956-2995**; Bill Stempien, **313-956-4988**
International. Joe Ris. **313-956-2937**
Engineering and Styling. Tom Jakobowski and Howard Hendricks. **313-956-4207**
Labor and Personnel. John Montgomery. **313-956-3257**
Los Angeles. Joe Tetherow. **213-655-8650**
Marine Group. Doug Talbot, **313-497-3430**; Hal Koch (Los Angeles), **213-466-4451**
New York. Bob Neale. **212-697-7500**
Nonautomotive. Bob Heath. **313-956-2894**
Radio and television. Britt Temby. **313-956-2894**
Washington, DC. Dick Muller. **202-296-3500**

CINCINNATI BELL, INC. 307 E 4th St, Cincinnati, OH 45202. **513-397-9900.** Charles L Shawver, news supervisor, **513-397-4527**

CINCINNATI MILACRON. 4701 Marburg, Cincinnati, OH 45209. **513-841-8100.** John Reading, director, public relations

CIT FINANCIAL CORP. 650 Madison Ave, New York, NY 10022. **212-572-6500.** Lawrence R Tavcar, director, public relations, **212-572-6302.** Medwin Seriff, manager, communications services, **212-572-6308.** William P Fox, vice-president, Carl Byoir & Associates, Inc public relations counsel, **212-572-6385** or **212-986-6100**

CITICORP. CITIBANK, NA. 399 Park Ave, New York, NY 10022. **212-559-1000.** Walter B Wriston, chief executive. Lamson B Smith, vice-president, press information. **212-599-4285**

CITIES SERVICE CO. 100 W 7th St, Tulsa, OK 74102. **918-586-2211.** Robert E Spann, manager, corporate communications

CITY INVESTING CO. 767 5th Ave, New York, NY 10022. **212-759-5300.** Thomas McDonnell, director, public relations

CITY STORES CO. 500 5th Ave, New York, NY 10036. **212-730-0700.** *Press contact.* Irving Zipin, vice-president

CLARK EQUIPMENT. Circle Dr, Buchanan, MI 49107. **616-697-8000.** B E Phillips, president and chief executive officer. Louis J Behre, director, public relations, **616-697-8929**

CLARK OIL & REFINING CORP. 8530 W National Ave, Milwaukee, WI 53227. **414-321-5100.** Mary Moudry, manager, corporate communications. W J LaBadie, administrative vice-president

CLEVELAND ELECTRIC ILLUMINATING. 55 Public Sq, Cleveland, OH 44101. **216-623-1350.** Arthur M Merims, manager, public information

THE CLOROX COMPANY. PO Box 24305, Oakland, CA 94623. **415-271-7000.** F A Reicker, manager, corporate relations, **415-271-7291**

CLUETT, PEABODY & CO, INC. 510 5th Ave, New York, NY 10036. **212-697-6100.** Night line: **212-697-6103.** Henry H Henley, Jr, president. *Press contact.* Cochran B Supplee, vice-president

THE COCA-COLA COMPANY. PO Drawer 1734, Atlanta, GA 30301. **404-897-2121.** William Pruett, vice-president and manager, public relations. Anthony J Tortorici, manager, corporate services, and assistant manager public relations department. Eric Churchward, manager, international public relations. William Bass, manager, public relations services

COLLINS AND AIKMAN. 210 Madison Ave, New York, NY 10016. **212-953-4100.** John T Sharkey, vice-president, corporate affairs, **212-953-4142.** *Charlotte office.* 701 McCullough Dr, Charlotte, NC 28215. **704-596-8500.** J D Michael O'Hara, director, public relations

COLT INDUSTRIES INC. 430 Park Ave, New York, NY 10022. **212-980-3500.** John F Campbell, vice-president, public relations

COLUMBIA GAS SYSTEM INC. 20 Montchanin Rd, Wilmington, DE 19807. **302-429-5000.** R Bruce Quayle, director, public relations, **302-429-5261**
Columbia Gas System Service Corp. Clarence F Mantooth, manager, news services, **302-429-5443**

COLUMBIA PICTURES. 711 5th Ave, New York, NY 10022. **212-751-4400.** Jean Vagnini, director, corporate public relations

COMBUSTION ENGINEERING. 900 Long Ridge Rd, Stamford, CT 06902. **203-329-8771.** Dean C Miller, director, public information, Ext 418

COMMONWEALTH EDISON COMPANY. PO Box 767, Chicago, IL 60690. **312-294-4321.** (also night line). Thomas G Ayers, chairman and president. Bill Harrah, general news coordinator, **312-294-3000.** Jerry Stanbrough, nuclear news coordinator, **312-294-3000**

COMMUNICATIONS SATELLITE CORPORATION. 950 L'Enfant Plz SW, Washington, DC 20024. **202-554-6000.** Joseph V Charyk, president. Judith S Elnicki, manager, media relations, **202-554-6100**
COMSAT General Corporation (wholly owned subsidiary), Hale Montgomery, director, business promotion. **202-554-6379**

CONAGRA INC. 200 Kiewit Plz, Omaha, NE 68131. **402-346-8004.** Warren McCoy, vice-president, public relations

CONE MILLS. Maple and 4th Sts, Greensboro, NC 27405. **919-379-6220.** W O Leonard, vice-president, public relations
Congoleum Industries. 195 Belgrove Dr, Kearny, NJ 07032. **201-991-1000**

CONNECTICUT GENERAL LIFE INSURANCE COMPANY. Hartford, CT 06152. **203-243-8811.** Robert D Kilpatrick, president and chief executive officer. Richard G Claeys, director, public relations, Ext 7808, (h) **203-653-7534.** James M Mason, Jr, community relations, Ext 7060

CONNECTICUT MUTUAL LIFE INSURANCE COMPANY. 140 Garden St, Hartford, CT 06115. **203-549-4111.** George S Wachtel, associate director, communications

CONRAIL. see Consolidated Rail Corporation

CONSOLIDATED EDISON. Rm 1635, 4 Irving Pl, New York, NY 10003. **212-460-4600.** *Press contacts.* Charles D Lohrfink, assistant to the vice-president, (h) **914-428-8140.** Ward M Rockey, assistant to the vice-president

CONSOLIDATED FREIGHTWAYS, INC. 601 California St, San Francisco, CA 94108. **415-397-4161.** W J Grant, director, corporate communications

Consolidated Freightways Corporation of Delaware (trucking subsidiary). 175 Linfield Dr, Menlo Park, CA 94025. **415-326-1700.** R E Kershner, director, public relations
Freightliner Corp (manufacturing subsidiary). 4747 N Channel Ave, Portland, OR 97217. **503-283-8000.** C L Luebbert, vice-president, personnel and public affairs

CONSOLIDATED NATURAL GAS. 4 Gateway Ctr, Pittsburgh, PA 15222. **412-391-7801.** John Conti, manager, public relations

CONSOLIDATED RAIL CORPORATION (Conrail). Suite 1040, 6 Penn Ctr, Philadelphia, PA 19104. **215-594-1000.** Night line (24 hours a day for press information): **215-594-3121.** Conrail information: **215-594-2663.** Edward G Jordan, chairman and chief executive officer, **215-594-3693.** Donald J Martin, vice-president, public affairs and advertising, **215-594-3112.** Mark B Sullivan, senior director, information services, **215-594-3114.** Thomas E Hoppin, director, press information services, **215-594-3121.** Howard A Gilbert, director, press relations operations. *Other contacts.* Cecil G Muldoon and Joseph K Harvey, senior press representatives; Gary J Fulton, press representative. *New York City.* Robert Von Wagoner. **212-340-2879**

CONSUMERS POWER COMPANY. 212 W Michigan Ave, Jackson, MI 49201. **517-788-0550.** A H Aymond, chairman of the board and chief executive officer, **517-788-0600.** Robert J Fitzpatrick, vice-president, public relations, **517-788-0630.** Michael G Koschik, general supervisor, public information, **517-788-0333.** Night line: **517-784-4656**

THE CONTINENTAL CORPORATION. 80 Maiden Ln, New York, NY 10038. **212-374-2300.** John B Ricker, Jr, chairman and president. Bruce R Abrams, vice-president and director, corporate communications. William S Cooper, Jr, assistant vice-president, public relations services, **212-374-3290.** William J Killen, public relations manager

CONTINENTAL GRAIN CO. 277 Park Ave, New York, NY 10017. **212-826-5100.** Marvin P Hammer, manager, public relations and advertising, **212-826-5578**

CONTINENTAL ILLINOIS NATIONAL BANK AND TRUST CO. 231 S LaSalle, Chicago, IL 60693. **312-828-7770.** John V Egan, Jr, vice-president and director, corporate communications. Daniel T Derrington, senior press relations associate, **312-828-7780**

CONTINENTAL OIL CO. High Ridge Park, Stamford, CT 06904. **203-359-3500.** E J Mulligan, vice-president, public relations. David Moffit, director, news services, (h) **914-769-3195.** John Lord, assistant director, news services, (h) **212-873-0449**

CONTINENTAL TELEPHONE CORP. PO Box 401, Merrifield, VA 22116. **703-661-2100.** Burton Green, director, information, **703-661-2240**

CONTINENTAL TELEPHONE INTERNATIONAL CORPORATION. 56 Perimeter Ctr E, Atlanta, GA 30346. **404-393-2323.** Gary E Lasher, president. *Press contact.* Pat Franks

CONTINENTAL TRAILWAYS. *See* Trailways.

CONTROL DATA CORP. 8100 34th Ave (PO Box O), Minneapolis, MN 55440. **612-853-8100.** W C Norris, chairman and chief executive officer. J J Bowe, vice-president, corporate relations, **612-853-3877.** *Public relations.* Donna B Burke, **612-853-4094.** Duane B Andrews, **612-853-3326.** Kent R Nichols, **612-853-4682**

COOPER INDUSTRIES. 2410 First City Bank, Houston, TX 77002. **713-654-4451.** Russell Burgett, director, community and public relations

ADOLPH COORS CO. East of Town, Golden, CO 80401. **303-278-1332.** Bob Russo, public relations

CORNING GLASS WORKS. Corning, NY 14830. **607-974-9000.** *Press contacts.* Eugene F Saunders and James A Burt, **607-974-8318**

CPC INTERNATIONAL INC. International Plz, Englewood Cliffs, NJ 07632. **201-894-4000.** William Cody, vice-president, public affairs. *Press contact.* Maureen E Kane

CRANE CO. 300 Park Ave, New York, NY 10022. **212-752-3600.** Albert E Scherm, Jr, director, advertising and public relations, **212-980-7285.** Catherine Rohan, public relations manager, **212-980-7287**

CROCKER NATIONAL BANK. 1 Montgomery St, San Francisco, CA 94138. **415-983-0456.** Ward B Stevenson, senior vice-president, public affairs, and marketing, **415-983-7189.** Thomas F Pelandini, vice-president, public affairs, **415-983-2461**

CROWN CENTRAL PETROLEUM. 1 N Charles St (PO Box 1168), Baltimore, MD 21203. **301-539-7400.** Henry A Rosenberg, chairman of the board and chief executive officer. *Press contact.* William R Synder, vice-president, administration

CROWN CORK & SEAL. 9300 Ashton Rd, Philadelphia, PA 19136. **215-698-5100.** Francis Lederer, community relations director

CROWN ZELLERBACH CORP. 1 Bush St, San Francisco, CA 94119. **415-823-5000.** C R Dahl, president. Donald L Winks, director, corporate communications, **415-825-5524.** Carol Ann Eckert, supervisor, information bureau, **415-823-5426**

Branch office contacts. Jeff Clausen, Portland, OR **503-221-7000.** Delos Knight, Baton Rouge, LA, **504-387-6267**

CUMMINS ENGINE CO INC. 1000 Fifth St, Columbus, IN 47201. **812-372-7211.** Randall Tucker, director, public relations, **812-379-6532.** Joe Holwager, manager, financial public relations

CURTISS-WRIGHT CORPORATION. 1 Passaic St, Wood-Ridge, NJ 07075. **201-777-2900.** T Roland Berner, chairman and president. *Press contact.* Donald H Slocum, executive director

CUTLER HAMMER. 4201 N 27th St, Milwaukee, WI 53216. **414-442-7800.** James S Trudgeon, manager, public relations

CYCLOPS. 650 Washington Rd, Pittsburgh, PA 15228. **412-343-4000.** Hubert W Delano, assistant vice-president, public relations

CYPRUS MINES. 555 S Flower St, Los Angeles, CA 90071. **213-489-3700.** Alma Ryan, director, corporate communications

DAIRYLEA COOPERATIVE. 1 Blue Hill Plz, Pearl River, NY 10965. **914-627-3280.** Bruce Snow, manager, public relations

DAN RIVER, INC. *See* River, Dan

DANA CORP. Box 1000, Toledo, OH 43697. **419-535-4500.** Frank Voss, vice-president, corporate relations

DANA WORLD TRADE CORP. 4100 Bennett Rd, Toledo, OH 43601. **419-479-8241**

DANIEL INTERNATIONAL CORP. Daniel Bldg, Greenville, SC 29602. **803-298-2500.** Buck Mickel, chairman and president. C R Canup, director, public relations, **803-298-4220**

DART INDUSTRIES INC. PO Box 3157, Terminal Annex, Los Angeles, CA 90051. **213-658-2000.** Justin Dart, Chief executive officer. Thomas P Mullaney, chief operating officer. *Press contact.* Richard K Moore, **213-658-2115.** (h) **213-473-1346**

DAYCO CORP. 333 W 1st St, Dayton, OH 45402. **513-226-7000** (also night line). Thomas Ryan, vice-president, corporate communications, **513-226-5929.** Steve Beard, public relations manager, **513-226-5927.** Frank Drury, investor relations manager, **513-226-5926.** Steve Meador, public relations coordinator, **513-226-5926**

DAYTON HUDSON CORP. 777 Nicollet Mall, Minneapolis, MN 55402. **612-370-6948.** D K Ewing, director, corporate communications. T E Langenfeld, manager, corporate relations

DEERE & COMPANY. John Deere Rd, Moline, IL 61265. **309-792-8000.** Tim H Henney, director, communication activities, **309-792-4837.** Ray Brune, director, press relations

DEL MONTE CORP. 1 Market Plz, San Francisco, CA 94119. **415-442-4000.** M P Roudnev, vice-president, public affairs

DELTA AIRLINES, INC. Atlantic Airport, Atlantic, GA 30320. **404-762-2531.** Frank Rox, vice-president, public affairs. For further details, *see* Airlines.

DENNY'S, INC. 14256 Firestone Blvd, La Mirada, CA 90637. **714-521-4152.** Verne H Winchell, president, chief executive officer, and chairman of the board. David Crawley, corporate public relations representative, **213-651-3015.** (h) **213-876-6898.** Thomas R Pflimlin, marketing director, food and promotional news releases, **714-521-4152**

DENTSPLY INTERNATIONAL. York, PA 17404. **717-845-7511.** *Press contact.* Alan J Davis

THE DETROIT EDISON CO. 2000 2nd Ave, Detroit, MI 48226. **313-237-8000.** John U Harkness, supervisor, press information, **313-237-8808.** Press representatives: Margaret L Furlong, **313-237-8807;** Frederick J Sullivan, **313-237-8809**

DIAMOND SHAMROCK CORP. 1100 Superior, Cleveland, OH 44114. **216-694-9000**

DIGITAL EQUIPMENT CORPORATION. 146 Main St, Maynard, MA 01754. **617-897-5111.** Kenneth H Olsen, president. Richard O Berube, public relations manager. Peter D Connell, corporate information

DILLON COMPANIES. 2700 E 4th St, Hutchinson, KS 67501. **316-665-5511**

WALT DISNEY PRODUCTIONS. 500 S Buena Vista, Burbank, CA 91505. **213-849-3411**

DOME MINES LTD (Canadian). Suite 600, 365 Bay St, Toronto, Ont, Canada M5H 2V9. **416-364-3453**

R R DONNELLEY AND SONS. 2223 Martin Luther King Dr, Chicago, IL 60616. **312-431-8000**

DOVER CORP. 277 Park Ave, New York, NY 10017. **212-826-7160**

DOW CHEMICAL COMPANY. 2030 Dow Ctr, Midland, MI 48640. **517-636-1000.** Night line: **517-635-6816.** Zoltan Merszei, president. *Press contact.* Mark Batterson, **517-636-2406.**

Dow Chemical USA. Mike Carroll, manager, public relations, **517-636-1513**

Divisional press contacts. Roland Carson, Louisiana Division, Plaquemine, LA. James Case, Texas Division, Freeport, TX. Twila Coffey, Dowell Division, Houston, TX. William Falk, Western Division, Walnut Creek, CA

DOW JONES & COMPANY, INC. 22 Cortland St, New York, NY 10007. **212-285-5000.** Warren H Phillips, president and chief executive officer. David Kemp, manager of public relations, **212-285-5466.** Night line: **212-580-1449.** *Other press contacts.* Ann Green, **212-285-5467;** Mark Thorn, **212-285-5468**

DRESSER INDUSTRIES INC. 3000 Republic National Bank, Dallas, TX 75221. **214-745-8000.** T W Campbell, director, public affairs

DUKE POWER CO. 422 S Church St, Charlotte, NC 28201. **704-373-4100.** Richard R Pierce, assistant vice-president, corporate communications

DUN & BRADSTREET COMPANIES, INC. 299 Park Ave, New York, NY 10017. **212-593-6800.** Night line: **914-472-5756.** Harrington Drake, chairman, **212-593-6914.** Robert S Diamond, senior vice-president, corporate communications, **212-593-6858.** John M Williams, manager, corporate communications, **212-593-6925**

E I DU PONT DE NEMOURS & CO.
1007 Market St, Wilmington, DE 19898.
302-774-1000. Thomas W Stephenson,
director, public affairs department,
302-774-4855

DUQUESNE LIGHT COMPANY. 435 6th
Ave, Pittsburgh, PA 15219. **412-471-4300,**
Ext 6281 or 6273. John M Arthur, chairman
of the board and chief executive officer.
William S Morris, manager, public informa-
tion department, Ext 6279. W G Ott, Ext
6281, (h) **412-242-7167.** Also Frank M
Skledar, **412-471-4300,** Ext 6779; Richard
M Dwyer, Ext 6273; Ken Scherer, Ext 6269
or **412-391-4805**

EAGLE-PICHER INDUSTRIES. PO Box
779, 580 Bldg, Cincinnati, OH 45202.
513-721-7010. *Press contact.* Ron Nall

EASTERN AIRLINES. International Airport, Miami, Fl 33148. **305-873-2211.** Robert
Christian, vice-president, public relations

EASTERN GAS & FUEL ASSOCIATES.
1 Beacon St, Boston, MA 02108.
617-742-9200. John D'Addieco, assistant
vice-president, public relations

EASTMAN KODAK CO. 343 State St,
Rochester, NY 14650. **716-325-2000.** Henry
J Kaska, manager, news services, corporate
information department, **716-724-4642.**
Robert W Edwards, director, corporate
information department, **716-724-4888.**
David J Metz, assistant director, corporate
information department, **716-724-4581**

EATON CORPORATION. 100 Erieview
Plz, Cleveland, OH 44114. **216-523-5000.**
Richard S Stoddart, vice-president, com-
munications, **216-523-5193.** G Richard
Mullen, director, corporate communications,
216-523-5270

ECONOMICS LABORATORY, INC.
370 Wabasha St, St Paul, MN 55102,
612-224-4678. John Thielke, vice-president,
public affairs

EL PASO NATURAL GAS. Tex and
Stanton Sts, El Paso, TX 79978.
915-543-2600. (Subsidiary of El Paso Company, PO Box 2185, Houston, TX 77001)
713-524-3911. John McFall, director, public
relations, **713-524-3911.** (h) **713-273-1275**

EMERSON ELECTRIC. 8100 Florissant
Ave, St Louis, MO 63136. **315-553-2000.**
Press contact. Howard Johnson

EMHART CORP. 426 Colt Hwy, Farmington, CT 06032. **203-677-4631.** T M Ford,
chairman and chief executive officer. John
Budd, vice-president, public relations, (h)
203-873-1175. Kathleen Deniega, assistant

**ENGELHARD MINERALS AND CHEMI-
CALS CORP.** 1221 Avenue of the Americas,
New York, NY 10020. **201-665-7000.** Lester
G Shapiro, manager, public affairs,
201-321-5673

ENVIROTECH CORPORATION. 3000
Sand Hill Rd, Menlo Park, CA 94025.
415-854-2000. R L Chambers, chairman and
chief executive officer. James W Murphy,
vice-president, corporate communications

EQUIBANK NA. Oliver Plz, Pittsburgh, PA
15222. **412-288-5000.** Lawrence R Werner,
vice-president, communications department,
412-288-5204. Jack L Sholl, manager, communications, **412-288-5329.** Patricia L
Quolke, manager, employee communications, **412-288-5207**

EQUIFAX INC. 1600 Peachtree Rd NW,
Atlanta, GA 30309. **404-875-8321.** Night
line: **404-875-1958.** W Lee Burge, chairman
and president. Hal Arnold, director, public
relations, (h) **404-451-4997**

EQUIMARK CORP. 445 Smithfield St,
Pittsburgh, PA 15222. **412-288-5000.** L R
Werner, vice-president, communications

**THE EQUITABLE LIFE ASSURANCE
SOCIETY OF THE UNITED STATES.**
1285 Avenue of the Americas, New York,
NY 10019. **212-554-3795.** Wallace C Fulton,
vice-president, communications department,
212-554-3627. Raymond A Boyce, assistant
vice-president, corporate communications
division, **212-554-3795.** Public relations
directors: Andrew R Baer, **212-554-1796;**
Agnes Bogart, **212-554-2321.** John T
McDonald, executive director, publications,
212-554-2874

ESMARK. 55 E Monroe St, Chicago, IL
60603. **312-431-3600.** Robert Palenchar,
vice-president, public relations

ETHYL CORP. 330 S 4th St (PO Box 2189),
Richmond, VA 23217. **804-644-6081.** Night
line: **804-643-2629.** *Press contacts.* A
Prescott Rowe, director, corporate communications, (h) **804-285-2626;** Ray
Kozakewicz, (h) **804-285-1236;** Rob Buford,
(h) **804-288-3783**

EX-CELL-O CORP. 2855 Coolidge, Troy,
MI 48084. **313-649-1000.** Carl Westberg,
manager, press relations

EXXON CORPORATION. 1251 Avenue
of the Americas, New York, NY 10020.
212-398-3000. James A Morakis, manager,
press services. William D Smith, press
advisor. Elaine F Townsend, press adviser
(radio and television)

FAIRMOUNT FOODS. 333 W Loop N,
Houston, TX 77024. **713-683-8383.** Sabra
Gill, manager, public relations (h)
713-622-7008

FARMERS GROUP INC. 4680 E Wilshire
Blvd, Los Angeles, CA 90005. **213-931-1961**

FARMLAND INDUSTRIES INC. 3315 N
Oak Trafficway, Kansas City, MO 64116.
816-459-6000. Robert Beasely, vice-president, public relations

THE FEDERAL COMPANY. 2900 Sterick
Bldg, PO Box 3623, Memphis, TN 38103.
901-525-7382. Lewis K McKee, president.
Press contacts. R Lee Taylor II, vice-president, and W F Bailey

FEDERAL-MOGUL. PO Box 1966, Detroit,
MI 48235. **313-354-7700.** David Snyder,
director, corporate public relations

**FEDERAL NATIONAL MORTGAGE
ASSOCIATION.** 1133 15th St NW,
Washington, DC 20005. **202-293-6000.**
Oakley Hunter, chairman of the board and
president. Gordon Nelson, vice-president,
corporate relations. Charles Barry, director,
public affairs, **202-293-6057.** Beth Van
Houten, public information officer

FEDERAL PAPER BOARD. 75 Chestnut
Ridge, Montvale, NJ 07645. **201-391-1176.**
Quentin Kennedy, vice-president, corporate
information

**FEDERATED DEPARTMENT STORES
INC.** 222 W 7th St, Cincinnati, OH 45202.
513-852-3000. *Press contact.* William Best,
Jr, **513-852-3700**

FERRO CORPORATION. 1 Erieview Plz,
Cleveland, OH 44114. **216-641-8580.** *Press
contact.* Stanley Blackburn

FIELDCREST MILLS. Stadium Dr, Eden,
NC 27288. **919-623-2123.** Camille Perkins,
public relations department

FIRESTONE TIRE & RUBBER COMPANY. 1200 Firestone Pkwy, Akron, OH 44317. **216-379-7000.** *Press contact.* Bernard W Frazier

FIRST BANK SYSTEM. 1400 First National Bank, Minneapolis, MN 55402. **612-370-5100.** J Ron Pratt, vice-president, corporate relations

FIRST CHARTER FINANCIAL CORP (parent of American Savings and Loan Association). 9465 Wilshire Blvd, Beverly Hills, CA 90212. **213-273-3300.** S Mark Taper, chairman and chief executive officer. *Press contact.* Gilmore Thompson. Ext 233 or 234

FIRST CHICAGO CORPORATION. 1 First National Plz, Chicago, IL 60670. **312-732-4000.** A Robert Abboud, chairman. Nick Poulos, vice-president, press and public relations, **312-732-2496.** William Colwell, vice-president, public relations, **312-732-6202.** William Baldwin, assistant vice-president, press and public relations, **312-732-6208**

FIRST INTERNATIONAL BANC-SHARES. 1201 Elm St, Dallas, TX 75270. **214-744-7100.** Robert E Tripp, vice-president, public relations. Robert H Stewart, chief executive officer

FIRST NATIONAL BANK OF BOSTON. 100 Federal St, Boston, MA 02110. **617-434-2200.** Kenneth R Rossano, senior vice-president, **617-434-2270.** Gardner C Norcross, public information officer, **617-434-3638.** (h) **617-653-7492.** Arthur M Jones, vice-president, public relations

FIRST NATIONAL BANK, DALLAS. PO Box 6031, Dallas, TX 75222. **214-746-4996.** Robert E Tripp, vice-president, advertising and public relations

FIRST PENNSYLVANIA BANK NA. Centre Sq, 15th and Market Sts, Philadelphia, PA 19101. **215-786-5000.** John R Bunting, chairman and chief executive officer, **215-786-8500.** Nancy Foltz, public relations officer and press relations manager, **215-786-8333.** (h) **215-735-6407.** Patricia Schweiker, press relations assistant, **215-786-8333**

FISHER FOODS, INC. 5300 Richmond St, Cleveland, OH 44146. **216-292-7000.** Sam Giammo, manager, public relations

FISHER SCIENTIFIC. 711 Forbes Ave, Pittsburgh, PA 15219. **412-562-8300.** Carolyn Noah, public relations manager

FLEETWOOD ENTERPRISES. 3125 Myers St, Riverside, CA 92503. **714-785-3500.** *Press contact.* Booke & Co, 2811 Wilshire Blvd Santa Monica, CA 90403. **213-829-4601**

FLEMING CO INC. 2 Townsite Plz, Topeka, KS 66601. **913-233-2800**

THE FLINTKOTE COMPANY. 1351 Washington Blvd, Washington Plz, Stamford, CT 06902. **203-324-9300.** James D Moran, chairman of the board and chief executive officer. W Robert Ingram, corporate director, public relations and advertising. Night line: **914-769-4128**

FLORIDA POWER & LIGHT. PO Box 013100, Miami, FL 33101. **305-552-3894.** J H Francis, Jr, director, corporate public relations

FLUOR CORPORATION. 2500 S Atlantic Blvd, Los Angeles, CA 90040. **213-262-6111.** Paul Etter, vice-president, public relations, Ext 1212. Fred Fajardo, director, investor relations, Ext 1213. Night line: **213-833-6327**

FMC CORP. 200 E Randolph Dr, Chicago, IL 60601. **312-861-6000.** Also 1105 Coleman Ave, San Jose, CA 95110. **408-289-0110.** *Contact.* Fred Rosewater, **408-289-2882**

FOOD FAIR STORES. 3175 JFK Blvd, Philadelphia, PA 19104. **215-382-9500.** Bernard Lipskin, director, communications

FORD MOTOR COMPANY. World Headquarters, The American Rd, Dearborn, MI 48121. **313-322-3000.** Henry Ford II, chairman of the board. Jerry L Sloan, corporate news department manager, **313-322-9600** (also news department night line)

Public Relations Staff (Detroit News Media)

Executive. Walter T Murphy, executive director, **313-322-2010.** (h) **313-646-4639.** William J Goodell, director, corporate information and services office, **313-322-9605.** (h) **313-642-8974.** Richard W Anthony, director, international public relations office, **313-322-4466.** (h) **313-665-3523.** Richard W Judy, manager, diversified products public relations, **313-322-9545.** (h) **313-647-2662**

Corporate News Department. **313-322-9600.** Jerry L Sloan, manager, (h) **313-647-7289.**

J William Harris, (h) **313-761-2660;** Carolyn D Burke, (h) **313-255-7954;** Peter R Kollins, (h) **313-474-8067;** Mary Sharon Vrobel, **313-274-2218;** James J Williams, (h) **313-354-1671**

Film and Electronic Communications Department. **313-322-8570.** Johna Pepper, manager, (h) **313-855-2064.** Frank G Benesh, (h) **313-476-7823**

International Communications Services. John G Miller, manager, **313-322-5845.** (h) **313-642-6918**

Research and Analysis. L Raymond Windecker, manager, **313-323-3754.** (h) **313-464-8293**

Ford Tractor Operations. 2500 E Maple Rd, Troy, MI 48084. **313-643-2764.** Marc Parsons, public relations manager, (h) **313-649-2585.** Richard W Dewey, public relations manager, western hemisphere, (h) **313-646-9775**

Ford Aerospace and Communications Corporation. Ford Rd, Newport Beach, CA 92663. Donald E Flamm, director, public affairs, **714-759-5996.** (h) **714-673-4361.** James A Allen, eastern public relations manager (Union Meeting Rd, Blue Bell, PA 19422). **215-646-9100.** (h) **215-688-3009**

Ford Motor Credit Company. Thomas E Foote, public relations manager, **313-594-1096.** (h) **313-642-7096**

Special Projects. Stanley J Drall, manager, **313-323-3754.** (h) **313-535-3419**

Detroit Downtown Development Corporation. Suite 3600, 100 Renaissance Ctr, Detroit, MI 48243. **313-594-1000.** John F Mayhew, consultant, (h) **313-769-0233.** John Coxeter, (h) **313-624-0815**

Public Relations Staff (North American)

Executive. Robert W Hefty, director, public relations office, Ford North American Automotive Operations, **313-337-8011.** (h) **313-271-0947.** William T Peacock, Jr, director, public information office, **313-322-3860.** (h) **313-646-3917.** John E Sattler, director, public relations services office, **313-322-9340.** (h) **313-642-4392**

Technical and Product Information Department. Research and Engineering Center, Bldg 3, 20000 Rotunda Dr, Dearborn, MI 48121. Michael W R Davis, manager, **313-322-8975.** (h) **313-647-6237.** William E Pauli, assistant manager, **313-322-8800.** (h) **313-349-5145.** Paul M Preuss, assistant manager, **313-322-1300.** (h) **313-349-3937.** Dewood A Haines, **313-322-8800.** (h) **313-962-8189.** Charlotte W Slater, **313-322-8800.** (h) **313-689-6816.** Charles M Gumushian, **313-322-1300.** (h) **313-681-4741.**

Cara L Kazanowski, **313-322-1300.** (h) **313-561-1135.** Edward J Sawtell, **313-322-1300.** (h) **313-643-7225**

Divisional Public Relations. Earl L Miller, manager, **313-322-1185.** (h) **313-562-3075**

Ford Division. 17101 Rotunda Dr, Dearborn, MI 48121. Owen W Bombard, public relations manager, **313-337-7900.** (h) **313-476-1130.** Walter L Thomson, **313-322-0365.** (h) **313-261-4885**

Lincoln-Mercury Division. 3000 Schaefer Rd, Dearborn, MI 48121. Edward S Gorman, public relations manager, **313-323-4766.** (h) **313-836-3648.** James R Olson, **313-322-2250.** (h) **313-483-1676**

Ford Parts and Service Division. 29500 Plymouth Rd, Livonia, MI 48151. George E Trainor, public relations manager, **313-525-2035.** (h) **313-563-8151.** Thomas P Rhoades, **313-525-2008.** (h) **313-889-0755**

Truck and Recreation Products Operations. Research and Engineering Center, Bldg 1, 20000 Rotunda Dr, Dearborn, MI 48121. Eugene E Koch, public relations manager, **313-594-1700.** (h) **313-642-9687**

Ford of Canada. The Canadian Rd, Oakville, Ont, Canada. **416-845-2511.** John D Waddell, vice-president, public affairs, (h) **416-844-2513.** Catherine R Charlton, public affairs programs manager, (h) **416-486-0258.** Anthony J Fredo, public relations manager, **416-639-5213**

FOREMOST MCKESSON INC. Crocker Plz, 1 Post St, San Francisco, CA 94104. **415-983-8417.** James Cohune, director, public relations, (h) **415-284-9737**

FORT HOWARD PAPER. 1919 S Broadway, Green Bay, WI 54305. **414-435-8821**

FOSTER WHEELER ENERGY CORPORATION (major subsidiary of Foster Wheeler Corp). 110 S Orange Ave, Livingston, NJ 07039. **201-533-1100.** Frank A Lee, president and chief executive officer, **201-533-3402.** Edward F Vitolo, director, advertising and public relations, **201-533-2200.** (h) **201-766-4880.** John Decker, publications manager, **201-533-2688.** Richard G Strippel, publications supervisor, **201-533-2679**

FOXBORO. 38 Neponset Ave, Foxboro, MA 02035. **617-543-2711.** *Press contact.* John Fuller, **617-543-2711**

FRANKLIN MINT CORPORATION. Franklin Ctr, PA 19091. **215-459-6900.** Charles L Andes, chairman and chief executive officer, **215-459-6116.** David C Schreiber, manager, news services,

215-459-7270 or **6529.** Night line: **215-566-7575.** Norman L Braun, director, communications (in charge of all public relations activities) **215-459-6118**

FREEPORT MINERALS. 200 Park Ave, New York, NY 10017. **212-578-9200.** E C K Read, assistant vice-president and director, public relations, **212-578-9297.** *New Orleans office.* Franklin C Bacon, manager, public relations, **504-529-4393**

FRUEHAUF CORP. 10900 Harper Ave, Detroit, MI 48232. **313-267-1150.** J E Olson, director, advertising and public relations

FUQUA INDUSTRIES. 3800 First National Tower, Atlanta, GA 30303. **404-658-9000.** J B Fuqua, chairman of the board and chief executive officer. *Press spokesman.* L P Klamon, senior vice-president. Pamela A Evans, manager, corporate communications

GAF CORPORATION. 140 W 51st St, New York, NY 10020. **212-582-7600.** Dr Jesse Werner, chairman and chief executive officer. Philip B Dalton, president and chief operating officer. R G Button, manager, public relations services, Ext. 8531, (h) **212-490-2884**

GAMBLE SKOGMO, INC. 5100 Gamble Dr, Minneapolis, MN 55416. **612-374-6586.** Don Dreblow, corporate vice-president

GANNETT CO, INC. Lincoln Tower, Rochester, NY 14604. **716-546-8600.** Allen H Neuharth, president and chief executive officer. Tom Curley, director, information. Night line: **716-244-4003**

GARDNER-DENVER COMPANY. Gardner Expy, Quincy, IL 62301. **217-222-5400.** Don Kipley, vice-president, Industrial Machinery Division. *Press contact.* Dave Montgomery. Toni Johnston, editor, *Gardner-Denver News,* personnel assistant

GATX. 120 S Riverside Plz, Chicago, IL 60606. **312-621-6200.** Don Pazdur, director, advertising and public relations, **312-621-6488**

GENERAL CABLE. 500 W Putnam Ave, Greenwich, CT 06830. **203-661-0100.** Patricia J Ludorf, manager, corporate communications, Ext 282 or 283

GENERAL CIGAR CO INC. 605 3rd Ave, New York, NY 10016. **212-687-7575**

GENERAL DYNAMICS CORP. Pierre LaClede Ctr, St Louis MO 63105.

314-862-2440. D S Lewis, chairman, president and chief executive officer. Frank S Johnson, Jr, director, public affairs and advertising. R E Forbes, manager, news and information

Regional and divisional news contacts. A A Spivak, director, news and information, Washington, DC. F J Bettinger, director, news and information, West (San Diego, CA). S J Wornom, Jr, director, news and information, Northeast (electric boat division, Groton, CT). Robert B Ford, manager, news and information, Stromberg-Carlson Corp (Rochester, NY). D J Luchsinger, manager, news and information, Pomona (CA) division. Rob W Mack, manager, news and information, Fort Worth (TX) division. Alex E H Piranian, senior staff assistant, Quincy (MA) shipbuilding division

GENERAL ELECTRIC CO. 3135 Easton Tpke, Gairfield, CT 06431. **203-373-2036.** Evelyn Reynolds, administrator, corporate press relations, **203-373-2039.** A J Tortorella, manager, news bureau programs, **212-750-3461.** James R Squires, corporate public relations, Washington representative (Suite 721, 777 14th St NW, Washington, DC 20005). **202-637-4420**

GENERAL FOODS CORPORATION. 250 North St, White Plains, NY 10625. **914-683-2500.** John F Manfredi, director, public relations, **914-683-2415.** Richard A Aszling, vice-president, public relations and public affairs, **914-683-2445**

GENERAL HOST CORPORATION. 22 Gate House Rd, Stamford, CT 06902. **203-357-9900.** Louis Guzzetti, vice-president

GENERAL INSTRUMENT. 225 Allwood Rd, Clifton, NJ 07012. **201-779-3088.** Lynn Russell, director, corporate communications

GENERAL MILLS INC. PO Box 1113, Minneapolis, MN 55440. **612-540-2311.** A Louis Champlin, director, public relations, **612-540-2460.** Glen Gath, assistant director, publicity

GENERAL MOTORS CORPORATION. 3044 W Grand Blvd, Detroit, MI 48202. **313-556-5000.** Thomas A Murphy, chairman and chief executive officer

Corporate Public Relations (Detroit). General Motors Bldg, 3044 W Grand Blvd, Detroit, MI 48202. **313-556-2030.** Clifford D Merriott, director, news relations, **313-556-2027.** (h) **313-646-4651.** Philip F Workman, manager, news relations, **313-556-2028.** (h) **313-626-2004.** Chris J

Edmonds, manager, general publicity, procurement, and production control logistics staff, **313-556-2034.** (h) **313-626-6473**

Research laboratories and proving grounds. William M Adams. **313-575-1265.** (h) **313-544-9192**

Manufacturing staff, information handbook, executive pictures and biographies. David C Andersen. **313-556-2184.** (h) **313-641-8649**

Marketing staff (including sales and advertising), (including vehicle service and recalls), and feature pictures. Colleen Belli. **313-556-2030.** (h) **313-774-3182**

Industrial relations and personnel administration and development staffs. James W Crellin. **313-556-2030.** (h) **313-294-2169**

Environmental activites staff (including vehicle emissions and fuel economy). Jack R Harned. **313-556-2030.** (h) **313-647-6407**

Environmental activities staff (including automotive safety, vehicle noise control, and plant and environmental engineering) and plant energy management programs. Donald Postman. **313-556-2030.** (h) **313-851-6838**

Design and engineering staffs. Joseph H Karshner. **313-575-1265.** (h) **313-543-9697**

Radio and television activities, financial staff, and transportation systems division. James C Smidebush. **313-556-2034.** (h) **313-641-7061**

Corporate Public Relations (New York).

General Motors Bldg, 767 5th Ave, New York, NY 10022. **212-486-2306.** Paul E Svoboda, director, New York office, **212-486-2300.** (h) **201-652-1538.** Harry A Turton, assistant director, New York office, **212-486-2306.** (h) **203-255-6385.** William B Winters, manager, media relations, **212-486-2304.** (h) **212-879-6411.** Robert E Kulungian, manager, financial relations, **212-486-2325.** (h) **516-484-4169.** Ann E Corwell, media coordinator, **212-486-2302.** (h) **212-752-3734**

Corporate Public Relations (Washington, DC).

Suite 804, 1660 L St NW, Washington, DC 20036. **202-237-5012.** Frank R Faraone, manager, Washington office, **202-537-5012.** (h) **202-966-6107.** Fred J Archibald, manager, community relations, **202-537-5015.** (h) **202-338-3974.** Clarence H Hunter, **202-537-5040.** (h) **301-977-1247**

Regional Public Relations Offices

Atlanta (Southern Region): Alabama, Florida, Georgia, Mississippi, North Carolina, South Carolina, Tennessee, Virginia Suite 2700, 5730 Glenridge Dr, Atlanta, GA 30328. **404-252-2234.** G E (Ed) Freer, regional manager, (h) **404-394-2846.** Floyd

M (Mike) McCurdy III, regional representative, (h) **404-475-3942**

Boston (New England Region): Connecticut, Maine, Massachusetts, New Hampshire, Rhode Island, Vermont Suite 507, 1 Gateway Ctr, Newton, MA 02158. **617-965-3220.** Paul J Wetzel, regional manager, (h) **617-826-5265**

Buffalo (New York Region): New York except Southeastern Area, Pennsylvania except Philadelphia Area Suite 3320, Marine Midland Center Bldg, Buffalo, NY 14202. **716-854-6368.** Jerome P Bishop, regional manager, (h) **716-688-6273.** Mark Cocroft, assistant, (h) **716-691-4562**

Chicago (Northern Central Region): Northern Illinois, Iowa, Minnesota, North Dakota, South Dakota, Wisconsin Rm 1010, 500 N Michigan Ave, Chicago, IL 60611. **312-337-4601.** J Bruce McCristal, regional manager, (h) **312-381-4586.** Ronald F Updyke, assistant

Cleveland (Northern Ohio Region): Northern Ohio 1846 Illuminating Bldg, 55 Public Sq, Cleveland, OH 44113. **216-621-6022.** Richard E Wilmot, regional manager, (h) **216-871-1939.** Ron L Beeber, assistant, (h) **216-734-7752**

Dallas (Southwestern Region): Arkansas, Louisiana, New Mexico, Oklahoma, Texas 3008 Southland Ctr, Dallas, TX 75201. **214-688-5695.** Robert W Hartnagel, regional manager, (h) **214-233-8090**

Dayton (Southern Ohio Region): Southern Ohio, West Virginia except Martinsburg Area 2410 Winters Bank Tower, Dayton, OH 45402. **513-445-5020.** Myron A (Ron) Hartwig, regional manager, (h) **513-433-5563**

Flint (Northern Michigan Region): Michigan except Southeastern Area 1626 Mott Foundation Bldg, Flint, MI 48502. **313-766-1802.** Duane E Poole, regional manager, (h) **313-732-2953.** Sharon J Baisel, regional representative, (h) **313-625-2683**

Hackensack (Eastern Region): Delaware, New Jersey, Southeastern New York, Philadelphia, Maryland, Martinsburg, West Virginia Area 1 University Plz, Hackensack, NJ 07601. **201-342-3211.** John J Hartnett, Jr, regional manager, (h) **201-327-1923.** Peter J Peterson, assistant, (h) **201-334-1325**

Indianapolis (Central Region): Indiana, Kentucky 710 Chamber of Commerce Bldg, Indianapolis, IN 46204. **317-269-5022.** August R (Gus) Buenz, regional manager, (h) **317-255-9103**

Kansas City (Midwestern Region): Colorado, Southern Illinois, Kansas, Missouri, Nebraska, Wyoming 2730 Commerce Tower, Kansas City, MO 64105. **913-281-6777.**

James F Hughes, regional manager, (h) **816-561-4550.** Kurt T Antonius, regional representative

Los Angeles (Western Region): Arizona, Southern California, Southern Nevada, Utah Suite 311, 1800 Avenue of the Stars, Los Angeles, CA 90067. **213-277-2511.** C Carlton Brechler, regional manager, (h) **213-659-5475.** Thomas R Stumpo, assistant, (h) **213-996-3539**

San Francisco (Northwestern Region): Alaska, Northern California, Idaho, Montana, Northern Nevada, Oregon, Washington Suite 2207, 1 Embarcadero Ctr, San Francisco, CA 94111. **415-981-1617.** R Stanley Maddox, regional manager, (h) **415-349-3348**

Southfield (Southeastern Michigan Region): Southeastern Michigan and Canadian Operations 311 Travelers Tower, Southfield, MI 48076. **313-424-2867.** Kenneth A Cameron, regional manager, (h) **313-649-5896.** Thomas R Klipstine, regional representative, (h) **313-649-0547**

Divisional Public Relations

AC Spark Plug Division. 1300 N Dort Hwy, Glint, MI 48556. John R Wilson, Jr, general manager. John V Dinan, Jr, public relations, **313-766-4830.** (h) **313-694-7314**

Buick Motor Division. 902 E Hamilton Ave, Flint, MI 48550. David C Collier, general manager. Gerald H Rideout, public relations, **313-766-5845.** (h) **313-767-6040**

Cadillac Motor Car Division. 2860 Clark Ave, Detroit, MI 48232. Edward C Kennard, general manager. William J Knight, public relations, **313-554-5066.** (h) **313-626-0338**

Central Foundry Division. PO Box 1629, Saginaw, MI 48605. Thomas R Wiltse, general manager. Fred C Hammer, public relations, **517-776-3212.** (h) **517-792-6238**

Chevrolet Motor Division. 3044 W Grand Blvd, Detroit, MI 48202. Robert D Lund, general manager. James L Tolley, public relations, **313-556-6045.** (h) **313-626-4139**

Delco Air Conditioning Division. PO Box 824, Dayton, OH 45401. Leonard P Roberts, general manager. David L Drury, public relations, **513-445-5076.** (h) **513-433-4120**

Delco Electronics Division. 700 E Firmin St, Kokomo, IN 46901. Donald J Atwood, general manager. William B Draper, public relations, **317-459-2453.** (h) **317-453-5511**

Delco Moraine Division. 1420 Wisconsin Blvd, Dayton, OH 45401. John D Debbink, general manager. Rodney L Andrew, public relations, **513-445-4237.** (h) **513-434-2165**

Delco Products Division. PO Box 1042, Dayton, OH 45401. W Blair Thompson, general manager. Michael V Tierney, public relations, **513-445-7456.** (h) **513-433-9465**

Delco-Remy Division. 2401 Columbus Ave, Anderson IN 46011. Edward P Czapor, general manager. Charles F (Chuck) Hardy, public relations, **317-646-3367.** (h) **317-642-0571**

Detroit Diesel Allison Division. 13400 W Outer Dr, Detroit, MI 48228. James E Knott, general manager. James V Lecoco, public relations, **313-424-4960.** (h) **313-642-2986**

Diesel Equipment Division. 2100 Burlingame Ave SW, Grand Rapids, MI. 49501. Carson O Donley, general manager. Peter H Iversen, public relations, **616-247-5068.** (h) **616-243-2197**

Electric-Motive Division. 9301 55th St, La Grange, IL 60525. Peter K Hoglund, general manager. Robert D Innes, public relations, **312-485-7000.** (h) **312-354-2624**

Fisher Body Division. 30001 Van Dyke Ave, Warren, MI 48090. Paul D Pender, general manager. Norman E May, public relations, **313-575-5213.** (h) **313-652-7120**

Frigidaire Division. 300 Taylor St, Dayton, OH 45442. Emmett B Lewis, general manager. Rex W Smith, public relations, **513-445-9076.** (h) **513-885-5054**

GM Assembly Division. 3007 Van Dyke Ave, Warren, MI 48090. Charles Katko, general manager. Andrew V O'Keefe, public relaions, **313-575-7528.** (h) **313-646-6535**

GM Transportation Systems Division. General Motors Technical Center, Warren, MI 48090. **313-575-1652.** Frederick W Walker Jr, general manager

GMC Truck and Coach Division. 660 South Blvd, East Pontiac, MI 48053. Robert W Truxell, general manager. Frank E Cronin, public relations, **313-857-2911.** (h) **313-732-2989**

Guide Division. 2915 Pendleton Ave, Anderson, IN. 46011. Carl W Dobos, general manager. William R (Russ) Merritt, public relations, **317-646-4244.** (h) **317-642-2372**

Harrison Radiator Division. Lockport, NY 14094. Glenn W Wiegand, general manager. H Eugene Brown, public relations, **716-439-2133.** (h) **716-735-7070**

Hydramatic Division. Ypsilanti, MI 48197. George W Griffith, general manager. John T Lynch, public relations, **313-485-5100.** (h) **313-455-1752**

Inland Division. PO Box 1224, Dayton, OH 45401. Thomas O Mathues, general manager. Erwin W Stines, public relations, **513-445-3536.** (h) **513-275-6162**

New Departure-Hyatt Bearings Division. Hayes Ave, Sandusky, OH 44870. Philip B

Zeigler, general manager. Patricia H Montgomery, public relations, **419-626-2120.** (h) **419-433-6745**

Oldsmobile Division. 920 Townsend St, Lansing, MI 48921. Robert J Cook, general manager. F W ("Fritz") Bennetts, public relations, **517-373-4430.** (h) **517-332-5448**

Packard Electric Division. PO Box 431, Warren, OH 44482. James R Rinehart, general manager. Mary Jane Taylor, public relations, **216-373-2364.** (h) **216-856-3606**

Pontiac Motor Division. 1 Pontiac Plz, Pontiac, MI 48053. Alex C Mair, general manager. Stanley T Richards, public relations, **313-857-1567.** (h) **313-851-7117**

Rochester Products Division. 1000 Lexington Ave, Rochester, NY 14603. Thomas E Hustead, general manager. William P Blackmon, public relations, **716-254-5050.** (h) **716-381-6523**

Saginaw Steering Gear Division. 3900 Holand Rd, Saginaw, MI 48605. Ellis M Ivey, Jr, general manager. William K Mitchell, public relations, **517-776-4005.** (h) **517-792-3292**

Terex Division. Hudson, OH 44236. George M Perry, general manager. Rollin N Rothacker, public relations, **216-655-5253.** (h) **216-688-5978**

Service Parts Operations and Divisions

Service Parts Operation. 3044 W Grand Blvd, Detroit, MI 48202. Michael C Meehan, executive in charge. Harold C L Jackson, Jr, public relations, **313-556-3664.** (h) **313-335-0660**

AC-Delco Division. 400 Renaissance Ctr, Detroit, MI 48243. William C Lee, general manager. W L Vande Water, public relations, **313-567-5030.** (h) **313-651-6743**

General Motors Parts Division. 6060 W Bristol Rd, Flint, MI 48554. Lewis G Kalush, general manager. Robert F Amesbury, public relations, **313-635-5663.** (h) **313-659-4094**

Finance and Insurance Units

General Motors Acceptance Corporation. 767 5th Ave, New York, NY 10022. S Kreis Smith, president. Van Buren Thorne, Jr, public relations, **212-486-3844.** (h) **516-627-7315**

Motors Holding Division. 3044 W Grand Blvd, Detroit, MI 48202. **313-556-3020.** William Harvey III, general manager

Motors Insurance Corporation. 767 5th Ave, New York, NY 10022. **212-486-3600.** Frank A Mingle, president

Canadian Unit: General Motors of Canada Limited.

William St E, Oshawa, Ont L1G1K7. Donald H McPherson, president and general man-

ager. James R Hamilton, public relations, **416-644-6185.** (h) **416-576-1936**

Ste Catharines, Ont, activities. **416-685-2011**

Ste Therese, Que, activities. Paulette Charbonneau, public relations. **514-435-6131**

Scarborough, Ont, activities. **416-750-2500**

Windsor, Ont, activities. Transmission plant: **519-256-8281.** Trim plant: **519-948-7611**

Diesel Division (London, Ont). **519-451-3600.** A Grant Warner, general manager

Diesel Coach (St Laurent, Que). **514-344-4161**

General Motors Institute. 1700 W 3rd Ave, Flint, MI 48502. Dr William B Cottingham, president. Lawrence C Swanson, public relations, **313-766-9445.** (h) **313-659-5915**

GENERAL PUBLIC UTILITIES CORP. 260 Cherry Hill Rd, Parsippany, NJ 07054. **201-263-4900.** Jack Dunn, director, public affairs

GENERAL REFRACTORIES COMPANY. 50 Monument Rd, Bala Cynwyd, PA 19004. **215-667-7900.** J G Solari, chairman. J E Moran, president. *Press contact.* G R Rittenhouse, vice-president and secretary

GENERAL REINSURANCE. 600 Steamboat Rd, Greenwich, CT 06830. **203-622-4000**

GENERAL SIGNAL CORP. High Ridge Park, Stamford, CT 06904. **703-357-8800**

GENERAL TELEPHONE AND ELECTRONICS. 1 Stamford Forum, Stamford, CT 06904. **203-357-2157.** George W Griffin, Jr, vice-president, public affairs. John B Lawrence, Jr, manager, public information, **203-357-2923.** Thomas E McCarthy, director, public information, **203-357-2935**

GENERAL TIRE AND RUBBER. 1 General St, Akron, OH 44309. **216-798-3000.** Jack Marshall, director, public relations

GENESCO INC. 111 7th Ave N, Nashville, TN 37202. **615-367-7693.** Night line: **615-367-7900.** John L Hanigan, principal official, **615-367-6307.** Mike Brandon, director, public relations and communications, **615-367-6371.** John Pennington, director, graphic communications. Joan Sinclair, manager, employee communications and community relations. Les Nelson, manager, corporate information services.

GENUINE PARTS CO. 299 Piedmont Ave NE, Atlanta, GA 30312. **404-659-2450.** *Press contact.* Earl Dolive

GEORGIA PACIFIC CORP. 900 SW 5th Ave, Portland, OR 97204. **503-222-5561.** H J Ellicott, director, corporate communications

GERBER PRODUCTS. 445 State St, Fremont, MI 49412. **616-928-2000.** John Whitlock, director, public relations, **616-928-2227**

GETTY OIL. 3810 Wilshire Blvd, Los Angeles, CA 90010. **213-381-7151.** Henry C Londean, Jr, corporate public relations manager

Regional contacts. Muriel G Havens, 660 Madison Ave, New York, NY 10021. **212-832-7800.** Michelle Beale, 1 Allen Ctr, 500 Dallas St, Houston, TX 77001. **713-658-9361.** Charles E Smith, 1437 S Boulder, Tulsa, OK 74102. **918-584-2311**

GILLETTE CO. Prudential Tower Bldg, Boston, MA 02199. **617-421-7000.** Stuart M Saunders, manager, corporate news bureau, **617-421-7741**

GOLD KIST INC. 3348 Perimeter Center Pkwy, Atlanta, GA 30346. **404-393-5090.** Jean C Rice, vice-president, public relations and advertising

B F GOODRICH CO. 500 S Main St, Akron, OH 44318. **216-379-2000.** W Thomas Duke, director, community relations, **216-379-3410**

THE GOODYEAR TIRE AND RUBBER CO. 1144 E Market St, Akron, OH 44316. **216-794-2121.** Charles J Pilliod, Jr, board chairman and chief executive. W B de Mezn, director, public information, **216-794-2490.** Night line: **216-688-2177.** William L Newkirk, director, public relations, **216-794-2170.** Robert H Lane, vice-president, public relations, **216-794-2244**

Regional contacts. Robert B Masson, Los Angeles, **213-583-3083.** William R Fair, Washington, DC, **202-638-4054.** J Robert Rowley, Houston, **713-658-0195.** Peter Thurber Earle, New York, **212-582-3934.** John P Perduyn, Chicago, **312-782-7326**

GOULD INC. 10 Gould Ctr, Rolling Meadows, IL 60008. **312-640-4000.** Delbert O Fuller, vice-president, communications. Marion G Durk, vice-president, public relations, **312-640-4116**

W R GRACE AND CO. 1114 Avenue of the Americas, New York, NY 10036. **212-764-5555.** J Peter Grace, president and chief executive officer. Dick Moore, vice-president, corporate communications division, **212-764-6010.** (h) **201-746-5164.** Tony Navarro, vice-president, corporate administration group, **212-764-6012.** (h) **212-794-1846.** Fred Bona, manager, press relations, **212-764-6022.** (h) **201-335-6868** or **3987.** Yanis Bibelnieks, divisional press relations manager, **212-764-6024.** (h) **212-789-6033**

GREAT ATLANTIC AND PACIFIC TEA COMPANY. 2 Paragon Dr, Montvale, NJ 07645. **201-573-9700.** Daniel M Doherty, public relations counsel, **201-573-9744**

GREAT NORTHERN NEKOOSA COR-PORATION. 75 Prospect St, Stamford, CT 06901. **203-359-4000.** Night line: **914-359-1911.** Samuel A Casey, chairman, Ext 303. Davis Crippen, manager, corporate communications, Ext 354.

Great Northern Paper Division. Millinocket, ME. *Press contact.* Paul McCann, **207-723-5131,** Ext 228

Nekoosa Papers Subsidiary. Port Edwards, WI. *Press contact.* Don Krohn, **715-887-5061**

GREAT WESTERN FINANCIAL CORP. 8484 Wilshire Blvd, Beverly Hills, CA 90211. **213-658-6000.** Ralph Rivet, director, office of information

GREAT WESTERN UNITED. 716 Metrobank Bldg, Denver, CO 80202. **303-893-4300**

GREEN GIANT CO. Hazeltine Gates, Chaska, MN 55318. **612-448-2828.** A B Fiskett, director, public relations.

GREYHOUND CORPORATION. Greyhound Tower, Phoenix, AZ 85077. **602-248-4000.** Dorothy Lorant, vice-president, public relations and advertising. Donald L Behnke, director, publications, **602-248-5714**

Armour & Co. Edward W Spear, director, public relations, **602-248-5715**

GRUMMAN CORPORATION. 1111 Stewart Ave, Bethpage, NY 11714. **516-575-0574.** John C Bierwirth, chairman of the board and chief executive officer. Joseph G Gavin, Jr, president and chief operating officer

Press contacts. W B Jones, vice-president, public affairs, **516-575-6622.** (h) **516-757-0230.** Stephen G Kerekes, manager, New York press and financial relations,

516-575-2464. (h) **516-751-8942.** Peter Costiglio, assistant manager, New York press relations, **516-575-7521.** (h) **212-534-2774.** V E Pesqueira, manager, Washington press and investor relations, **703-525-2800.** (h) **301-948-0405**

Grumman Aerospace Corporation (the major subsidiary of Grumman Corporation). S Oyster Bay Rd, Bethpage, NY 11714. **516-575-0574.** George M Skurla, chairman of the board and president

Press contacts. Brian P Masterson, director, public affairs, **516-575-7747.** (h) **516-589-3893.** Robert P Harwood, manager, media relations, **516-575-5287.** (h) **516-427-9154**

Grumman Energy Systems (the division of Grumman Corporation that produces solar and wind energy systems). 4175 Veterans Memorial Highway, Ronkonkoma, NY 11779. **516-575-0574.** Ronald B Peterson, director. Joseph Dawson, manager, public affairs, **516-575-7291.** (h) **516-689-9597**

GULF AND WESTERN INDUSTRIES, INC. 1 Gulf and Western Pl, New York, NY 10023. **212-333-6000.** Fred Phillus, director, public relations, **212-333-4707**

GULF OIL CORPORATION. 435 7th Ave, Pittsburgh, PA 15230. **412-263-5000.** Thomas D Walker, manager, public information, **412-263-5938.** William R Cox, public relations director. Sheryll S Zippay, supervisor, research information. Jon L Allen, public relations director (1290 Avenue of the Americas, NY 10019), **212-397-1323.** James I Gatten, Philadelphia news representative (Suite 626, 3 Parkway, Philadelphia, PA 19102), **215-564-3970**

HALLIBURTON CO. 1015 Bois d'Arc, Duncan, OK 73533. **405-251-3760.** *Press contact.* Stan Houston

JOHN HANCOCK MUTUAL LIFE IN-SURANCE CO. John Hancock Pl (PO Box 111), Boston, MA 02117. **617-421-6000.** John S Feeley, director, public information, **617-421-2771.** Charles C McGillicuddy, director, financial communications, **617-421-6468**

HANDY AND HARMAN. 850 3rd Ave New York, NY 10022. **212-752-3400**

HANES CORP. 2000 W 1st St, Winston-Salem, NC 27103. **919-744-3711.** Perry G Harmon, director, community services

HANNA MINING. 100 Erieview Plz, Cleveland, OH 44121. **216-523-3111.** Fred Walker, director, public relations, **216-368-4924**

HARNISCHFEGER CORPORATION. 13400 Bishops Ln, Brookfield, WI 53005. Mailing address: PO Box 554, Milwaukee, WI 53201. **414-671-4400.** Henry Harnischfeger, president and chairman of the board. Richard W Schulze, director, public relations, Ext 352. Night line: **414-671-4400.** Charlene Ryder, manager, communications

HARRIS CALORIFIC. 5501 Cass Ave, Cleveland, OH 44102. **216-961-5700**

HARRIS TRUST AND SAVINGS BANK. 111 W Monroe St, Chicago, IL 60690. **312-461-2121.** Charles M Bliss, president and chief executive officer, **312-461-7528.** Barbara B McNear, vice-president, public relations. Brace Pattou, manager, press relations, **312-461-6624.** (h) **312-337-7961**

HARSCO. 350 Poplar Church Rd, Camp Hill, PA 17011. **717-233-8771.** Robert Haynos, public affairs

HART SCHAFFNER AND MARX. 36 S Franklin St, Chicago, IL 60606. **312-372-6300.** Robert Connors, director, public relations

Divisions. Hart Schaffner and Marx Clothes (Chicago, IL), M Wile and Company, Inc (Buffalo, NY), Jaymar-Ruby, Inc (Michigan City, IN), Hickey-Freeman Co, Inc (Rochester, NY), Gleneagles, Inc (Baltimore), Blue Jeans Corporation (Whiteville, NC), and Retail Stores Division (Chicago)

H J HEINZ. 1062 Progress St, Pittsburgh, PA 15230. **412-237-5757, 5464,** or **5465.** Thomas McIntosh, director, corporate public relations

WALTER E HELLER INTERNATIONAL CORPORATION. 105 W Adams St, Chicago, IL 60603. **312-346-2300.** Franklin A Cole, chairman and chief executive officer. *Press contact.* Lawrence R Foerster, Sr, treasurer. Harvey S Lederman, vice-president, marketing and public relations

HERCULES INC. 910 Market St, Wilmington, DE 19899. **302-575-5000.** *Press contact.* Richard B Douglas, **302-575-6915**

HERSHEY FOODS CORPORATION. 19 E Chocolate Ave, Hershey, PA 17033. **717-534-4200.** William E Dearden, vice-chairman and chief executive officer. K L Bowers, director, public relations, **717-534-4390.** J A Edris, manager, public information, **717-534-4392**

HEWLETT-PACKARD CO. 1501 Page Mill Rd, Palo Alto, CA 94304. **415-493-1501.** William R Hewlett, chief executive officer. John A Young, president. J Peter Nelson, press relations, Ext 4220. David Kirby, public relations director. Night line: **415-493-1501**

HILTON HOTELS CORP. 720 S Michigan Ave, Chicago, IL 60605. **312-341-1770**

HOBART CORPORATION. World Headquarters Blvd, Troy, OH 45374. **513-335-7171.** David B Meeker, president and chief executive officer, Ext 2100. John B Biggs, Jr, director, public affairs, Ext 2130

HOERNER WALDORF. 2250 Wabash Ave, St Paul, MN 55114. **612-645-0131.** M L Knoll, Jr, vice-president, public affairs

HOLIDAY INNS INC. 3742 Lamar Ave, Memphis, TN 38118. **901-362-4001.** Darrell Luery, vice-president, corporate public relations. Robert R Boepple, media relations manager (3754 Lamar Ave), **901-362-4491.** Leslie Nelson, media relations

HONEYWELL INC. Honeywell Plz, Minneapolis, MN 55408. **612-870-5200.** Edson W Spencer, president and chief executive officer. Stuart G Baird, manager, corporate public relations, **612-870-2700.** Night line: **612-474-6086**

Divisional press contacts

Residential Division. Roger Hammer. **612-870-6605**

Commercial Division. Ed O'Brien. **612-887-4032**

Aerospace and Defense Group. Larry Eiler. **612-378-4444**

Honeywell Information Systems. Joanne Full. **617-890-3246;** Ron Mueller, **617-890-3246;** Jerry Kalman, **602-993-4922**

Process Control Division. Ed Watson. **215-643-2261**

Microswitch. Francis Kafka. **815-232-5731**

H P HOOD. 500 Rutherford Ave, Boston, MA 02019. **617-242-0600**

HOOVER BALL AND BEARING. 135 E Bennett St, Saline, MI 48176. **313-429-2552.** John F Daly, chairman, president, and chief executive officer. Charles H Keller, corporate director, public relations

GEORGE A HORMEL & CO. 501 5th Ave NE, Austin, MN 55912. **507-437-5611.** *Press Contact.* C D Nyberg, secretary

HOSPITAL TRUST AND FUND (RHODE ISLAND). 1 Hospital Trust Plz, Providence, RI 02903. **401-278-8000.** Henry S Woodbridge, Jr, president, **401-278-8410.** *Press contact.* Alice Macintosh, vice-president, **401-278-8156.** Hospital Trust Corp. Joseph M Barrett, public relations administrative assistant, **401-278-8152**

HOUSEHOLD FINANCE. Prudential Plz, Chicago, IL 60601. **312-944-7174.** James McCormick, vice-president and director, public relations

HOUSTON LIGHTING AND POWER. 611 Walker Ave, Houston, TX 77001. **713-228-9211.** J D Parsons, manager, public relations. *Press contact.* Patricia Amerman

HOUSTON NATURAL GAS CORPORATION. 1200 Travis, PO Box 1188, Houston, TX 77001. **713-654-6161.** Robert R Herring, chairman of the board and chief executive officer, **713-654-6423.** Dave Keith, vice-president, corporate communications, **713-654-6498.** Night line: **713-654-6444.** Richard Tuttle, corporate communications manager, **713-654-6509**

HOUSTON OIL AND MINERAL. 242 Main Bldg, Houston, TX 77002. **713-222-2431**

HOWARD JOHNSON CO (Ground Round Restaurants and Red Coach Grills). 222 Forbes Rd, Braintree, MA 02184. **617-848-2350.** Evelyn G Sullivan, manager, public relations

HUGHES AIRCRAFT COMPANY. Culver City, CA 90230. **213-391-0711.** E J Beam, director, public relations, **213-670-1515,** Ext 6577

HUGHES TOOL. 5425 Polk St, Houston, TX 77001. **713-926-3101.** *Press Contact.* Travis Parish, assistant to the president

HUYCK INC. Highway 1 N, Wake Forest, NC 27587. **919-556-2071.** J P Riedy, vice-president, corporate relations

HYATT CORP. 1338 Bayshore Hwy, Burlingame, CA 94010. **415-342-0200.** Donna Barron, director, public relations

HYGRADE FOOD PRODUCTS COMPANY. 11801 Mack Ave, Detroit, MI 48214. **313-355-1100**

HYSTER. 700 NE Multonomah St, Portland, OR 97209. **503-228-5011.** George Green, vice-president, press relations

IBM. *See* International Business Machines

IC INDUSTRIES. 1 Illinois Ctr, Chicago, IL 60601. **312-565-3000.** William B Johnson, chairman and chief executive officer, **312-565-3001.** Granger F Kenly, vice-president, corporate relations, **312-565-3070.** Night line: **312-256-4054.** Harry A Grove, director, advertising, **312-565-3074.** Frank J Allston, director, financial communications, **312-565-3072**

ILLINOIS POWER CO. 500 S 27th St, Decatur, IL 62525. **217-424-6600.** *Press contact.* Johnson Kanapy

IMPERIAL CORPORATION OF AMERICA. 2320 5th Ave, San Diego, CA 92112. **714-232-2011.** *Press contact.* Pat Harden, **714-236-1222**

INA. *See* Insurance Company of North America Corporation

INCO LIMITED (formerly the International Nickel Co Inc). 1 New York Plz, New York, NY 10004. **212-742-4221.** John H Page, president, **212-742-4822.** Eugene P Glisky, public relations manager, **212-742-4221.** J M Williamson, product publicity manager, **212-742-4513**

INDIAN HEAD INC. 1211 Avenue of the Americas, New York, NY 10036. **212-764-3100.** M F Smith, president and chief executive officer. *Press contact.* Stuart Pearlman, **212-764-3195.** Night line: **212-764-3195.** Corinne L Wilson, manager, editorial services, **212-764-3193**

INDUSTRIAL NATIONAL CORPORATION, INDUSTRIAL NATIONAL BANK OF RHODE ISLAND. 55 Kennedy Plz, Providence, RI 02903. **401-278-5800.** John J Cummings, Jr, president. Georgina Macdonald, director, corporate communications, **401-278-5879.** Bruce P Crooks, public affairs officer, **401-278-6241**

INGERSOL-RAND CO. 200 Chestnut Ridge Rd, Woodcliff Lake, NJ 07675. **201-573-3426.** Wynn Moseley, director, public relations

INLAND STEEL CO. 30 W Monroe St, Chicago, IL 60603. **312-346-0300.** Night line: **312-346-0313.** F G Jaicks, chairman. Sam H Saran, director, corporate communications, (h) **312-362-6061.** Donald R Shiras, manager, public information, corporate communications, (h) **219-938-2378**

INMONT CORP. 1133 Avenue of the Americas, New York, NY 10036. **212-765-1100.** William Perdue, investment relations

INSILCO. 1000 Research Pkwy, Meriden, CT 06540. **203-634-2000.** Craig Bossi, director, corporate communications

INSURANCE COMPANY OF NORTH AMERICA CORPORATION. (INA Corp). 1600 Arch St, Philadelphia, PA 19101. **215-241-4000.** Stephen R Lawrence, associate director, public relations, **215-241-4384.** James M Beattie, manager, editorial services, **215-241-4625**

INTERCO INC. 10 Broadway, St Louis, MO 63102. **314-231-1100.** Ed Grace, corporate information officer

INTERLAKE, INC. 2015 Spring Rd, Oak Brook, IL 60521. **312-986-6600.** H H Henderson, marketing and public affairs, **312-986-6639**

INTERNATIONAL BUSINESS MACHINES. Old Orchard Rd, Armonk, NY 10504. **914-765-1900.** Charles G Francis, director, communications programs, **914-765-6406.** Bruce S Odom, communications programs administrator

Divisional contacts

Data Processing Division. Bert Reisman, director, communications. Thomas E Mattausch, information representative, news bureau

Office Products Division. Fred J Steinberg, information manager

INTERNATIONAL FLAVORS AND FRAGRANCES. 521 W 57th St, New York, NY 10019. **212-765-5500.** Van Vechten Sayre, director, public relations

INTERNATIONAL HARVESTER. 401 N Michigan Ave, Chicago, IL 60611. **312-527-2000.** Harry W Conner, corporate director, public relations, **312-670-2284**

Product group press contacts. John Davies, agricultural equipment, **312-670-3816.** William Greenhill, components, **312-670-2577.** John Dierbeck, trucks, **312-670-2519.** Lee Tashjian, construction equipment, **312-884-3530.** Payne Johnson, solar gas turbines (PO Box 80966, San Diego, CA 92138), **714-238-5888**

Regional public relations offices and contacts. W Norman Buckingham, 1 Penn Plz, New York, NY 10001. **212-947-5155.** John Isbell, PO Box 3176, Atlanta, GA 30302. **404-763-4609.** Bill Mason, PO Box 23884, Oakland, CA 94623. **415-577-8590**

INTERNATIONAL MINERALS AND METALS. 46th floor, 919 3rd Ave, New York, NY 10022. **212-486-8686**

THE INTERNATIONAL NICKEL CO INC. *See* INCO Limited.

INTERNATIONAL PAPER. 200 E 42nd St, New York, NY 10017. **212-490-6000.** Philip Farin, manager, communications. Fred Clay, manager, public relations

INTERNATIONAL SYSTEMS AND CONTROL. 2727 Allen Pkwy, Houston, TX 77001. **713-526-5461.** *Press contact.* Larry Lau

INTERNATIONAL TELEPHONE & TELEGRAPH. 320 Park Ave, New York, NY 10022. **212-752-6000.** David H Kiernan, director, public relations. William Bennington, director, public information. Thomas J Freeman, manager, news services. *Washington office.* 1707 L St NW, Washington, DC 20036. Bernard A Goodrich, director, news services, **202-296-6000**

INTERSTATE BRANDS CORPORATION. 12 E Armour Blvd (PO Box 1627), Kansas City, MO 64141. **816-561-6600.** Ellen B Hoffman, director, public and consumer communications

INTERTEL, INC. 6 Vine Brook Park, Burlington, MA 01803. **617-273-0950.** H Richard Cossaboon, Jr, vice-president, marketing

IOWA BEEF PROCESSORS. Hwy 77, Dakota City, NE 68731. **402-494-2061.** Cornelius Bodine, vice-president, public relations

IOWA POWER AND LIGHT. 666 Grand Ave, Des Moines, IO 50303. **515-281-2900.** *Press contact.* Eugene E Young

IRVING TRUST CO. 1 Wall St, New York, NY 10015. **212-487-3794.** *Press contact.* Don E Phelps

ITE IMPERIAL CORP. 1900 Hamilton St, Philadelphia, PA 19130. **215-561-1500**

IT&T. *See* International Telephone & Telegraph

IU INTERNATIONAL CORP. 1500 Walnut St, Philadelphia, PA 19102. **215-985-6600.** E K Sheldon, manager, public relations, **215-985-6477.** L F Lamb, manager, information service, **215-985-6896**

JEWEL COMPANIES INC. 5725 E River Rd, Chicago, IL 60631. **312-693-6000.** Donald S Perkins, chairman of the board and chief executive officer. Robert D Jones, vice-president, public affairs

JONATHAN LOGAN INC. 1411 Broadway, New York, NY 10018. **212-695-4440.** *Press contact.* David Keery

JOHN HANCOCK— *See* Hancock, John

JOHNS-MANVILLE CORP. Ken-Caryl Ranch, Denver, CO 80217. **303-979-1000.** Neal Amarino, manager, national media relations. Gerald Murray, manager, regional media relations

JOHNSON CONTROLS. 507 E Michigan St, Milwaukee, WI 53201. **414-276-9200**

JOHNSON & JOHNSON. 501 George St, New Brunswick, NJ 08903. **201-524-0400.** Lawrence Foster, corporate vice-president, public relations, **201-524-6055.** F Robert Kniffin, associate public relations director, **201-524-6558**

JOY MANUFACTURING. 537 Smithfield St, Pittsburgh, PA 15222. **412-562-4500**

KAISER ALUMINUM & CHEMICAL CORPORATION. 300 Lakeside Dr, Oakland, CA 94643. **415-271-3353.** Gary Simpson, manager, corporate public relations. Ron Rhody, vice-president, public relations and public affairs

KAYSER-ROTH. 640 5th Ave, New York, NY 10019. **212-757-9600.** David Ruth, corporate information officer

KELLOGG CO. 235 Porter St, Battle Creek, MI 49016. **616-962-5151.** J E Lonning, chairman and chief executive officer. Harry W Boesch, manager, public relations, **616-966-2820.** Night line: **616-721-3439.** R Jenkins, manager, corporate communications, **616-966-2822**

KELLWOOD COMPANY PO Box 14374, St Louis, MO 63178. **314-576-3100.** Susan Switzer, corporate relations

KENNECOTT COPPER CORPORATION. 161 E 42nd St, New York, NY 10017. **212-687-5800.** Night line: **212-687-5806.** Frank R Milliken, president and chief executive officer. Edwin E Dowell, director, public relations, (h) **203-226-3847.** Night line: **212-687-5822.** Joseph W Shenton, director, investor relations, (h) **201-273-2321**

Divisional contacts

Chino Mines Division. Hurley, NMe 88043. **505-537-3381.** R R Leveille, general manager. W P Visick, director, public relations, (h) **505-388-4416**

Nevada Mines Division. McGill, NV 89318.

702-235-7741. Dean D Kerr, general manager. R F Alkire, director, public relations, (h) **702-289-3936**

Ray Mines Division. Hayden, AZ 85235. **602-356-7811.** K H Matheson, Jr, general manager. J H Maize, director, public relations, (h) **602-363-5486**

Utah Copper Division. PO Box 11299, Salt Lake City, UT 84147. **801-322-1533.** R N Pratt, general manager. K E Kefauver, director, public relations, (h) **801-532-7144**

Kennecott Refining Corporation. PO Box 3407, Baltimore, MD 21226. **301-789-1000.** M B O'Shaughnessy, refinery manager

KERR-MCGEE CORPORATION. Kerr-McGee Ctr, Oklahoma City, OK 73102. **405-236-1313.** Patrick Petree, director, public relations

KEWANEE OIL. 40 Morris Ave, Bryn Mawr, PA 19010. **215-525-5050.** Hedy Margolies, director, public relations

WALTER KIDDE AND COMPANY, INC. 9 Brighton Rd, Clifton, NJ 07015. **201-777-6500.** Harvey Ekenstierna, director, public relations

KIMBERLY CLARK. Lake St, Neehah, WI 54956. **414-729-1212**

K MART CORPORATION (formerly S S Kresge). 3100 W Big Beaver, Troy, MI 48084. **313-643-1000.** Ann C Wolff, director, publicity

KNIGHT-RIDDER NEWSPAPERS. 1 Herald Plz, Miami, FL 33101. **305-350-2671.** Don Becker, director, corporate relations, (h) **305-822-9860**

KOEHRING CO. 200 Executive Dr, Brookfield, WI 53005. **414-784-5800.** Martin Jaeger, director, corporate communications

KOPPERS CO INC. Koppers Bldg, Pittsburgh, PA 15219. **412-391-3300.** F L Byrom, chairman of the board, R J O'Gara, manager, public relations

KRAFT, INC. Kraft Ct, Glenview, IL 60025. **312-998-2000.** Margaret P MacKimm, vice-president and director, public relations, **312-998-2462.** Night line: **312-998-2000.** Gerald J Sweda, communications manager, **312-998-2871**

S S KRESGE. *See* K mart Corporation

THE KROGER COMPANY. 1014 Vine St, Cincinnati, OH 45201. **513-381-8000.** Manly

Molpus, vice-president, public affairs. Audrey J McCafferty, manager, public information

LAND O' LAKES INC. 614 McKinley Pl NE, Minneapolis, MN 55413. **612-331-6330.** Ralph Hofstad, president, Ext 200. *Press contact.* William Turner, Ext 407. Ken Tvedten, director, publications. Roger Dunnette, communications specialist

Agri-Services. *Press contact.* Rich Burton (Fort Dodge, IA). **515-576-7313**

LEAR SIEGLER INC. 3171 S Bundy Dr, Santa Monica, CA 90406. **213-391-7211.** William O'Hern, vice-president, public relations and advertising. Jack E Cressman, corporate manager, public relations

LEVI STRAUSS & CO. 2 Embarcadero Ctr, San Francisco, CA 94106. **415-391-6200.** Bud Johns, director, corporate communications

LIBBEY-OWENS-FORD COMPANY. 811 Madison Ave, Toledo, OH 43695. **419-247-3731.** Melvin Barger, director, corporate communications

LIGGETT GROUP. 4100 Roxboro Rd, Durham, NC 27702. **919-471-7511.** *Press contact.* Daniel E Provost III

ELI LILLY & CO. 307 E McCarty St, Indianapolis, IN 46206. **317-261-3570.** Russell L Durbin, manager, media and press relations

LINCOLN NATIONAL BANK. 116 E Berry St, Fort Wayne, IN 46802. **219-423-6111.** William Leming, marketing manager

THOMAS J LIPTON INC. 800 Sylvan Ave, Englewood, NJ 07632. **617-935-3000** or **201-567-8000**

LITTON INDUSTRIES INC. 360 N Crescent Dr, Beverly Hills, CA 90210. **213-273-7860.** Claude V Meconis, corporate director, public relations and advertising. *Washington office.* Suite 8206, 490 L'Enfant Plz ESW, Washington, DC 20024. Robert S Knapp, manager, public relations

LOCKHEED CORPORATION. 2555 N Hollywood Way, Burbank, CA 91520. **213-847-6121.** William Perreault, vice-president, public relations. Grover D Nobles, Jr, director, corporate news bureau, **213-847-6515**

LOEWS CORPORATION. 666 5th Ave, New York, NY 10019. **212-586-4400.** Preston Robert Tisch, president and chief executive officer. Philip Miles, vice-president, advertising and public relations. Night line: **212-586-4274**

LONE STAR INDUSTRIES INC. 1 Greenwich Plz, Greenwich, CT 06830. **203-661-3100.** Theodore Price, director, corporate relations

LONG ISLAND LIGHTING. 250 Old Country Rd, Mineola, NY 11501. **516-228-2890.** Charles R Pierce, chief executive officer. June N Bruce, manager, media information department. LILCO representatives. Jan Hickman and Eugene Hosansky, **516-228-2308** (also night line)

M LOWENSTEIN AND SONS. 1430 Broadway, New York, NY 10018. **212-560-5000.** Steven Radding, vice-president and director, communications

THE LTV CORPORATION. PO Box 5003, Dallas, TX 75222. **214-742-9555.** John W Johnson, vice-president, public relations

LUBRIZOL CORP. 29400 Lakeland Bldg, Wicklesse, OH 44092. **216-943-4200.** M J O'Connor, manager, community relations

LUCKY STORES INC. 6300 Clark Ave, Dublin, CA 94558. **415-828-1000.** James Stell, president. Wayne Fisher, chairman. Theodore Brunner, vice-president. Ivan Owen, senior vice-president. Don Ritchey, executive vice-president

LUDLOW CORPORATION. 145 Rosemary St, Needham Hts, MA 02194. **617-444-4900.** Night line: **617-444-4917.** A B Mason, president. G D Lewis, director of advertising

Divisional contacts

Crown Industries (cast vinyl and latex products). 2100 Commerce Dr, Industrial Park, Fremont, OH 43420. **419-332-5531.** *Contact.* W L Burdorf, vice-president

Forest Products (furniture). 1010 Cherokee Dr, Morristown, TN 37814. **615-586-7460.** *Contact.* N H Fowler, president

Ludlow Carpet Cushion. 145 Rosemary St, Needham Hts, MA 02194. **617-444-4900.** *Contact.* R T Bush, vice-president

Ludlow Carpets, Walter Carpets. 14641 E Don Julian Rd, City of Industry, CA 91749. **213-968-1464.** *Contact.* D H Kuhn, president

Ludlow Packaging (flexible packaging materials). 111 Mosher St, Holyoke, MA 01040. **413-538-9000.** *Contact.* F G McDermott, vice-president

Ludlow Specialty Papers. Cummings St, Ware, MA 01082. **413-967-6204.** *Contact.* W C King, vice-president

Ludlow Textiles. 145 Rosemary St, Needham Hts, MA 02194. **617-444-4900.** *Contact.* J E Williams, vice-president

LYKES FINANCIAL CORPORATIONS. 100 Paydras St, New Orleans, LA 70130. **504-523-6611.** Thomas Bartle, corporate communications director

MACK TRUCKS INC. 2100 Mack Blvd (PO Box M), Allentown, PA 18105. **215-439-3011.** Alfred W Pelletier, president and chief executive officer. *Press contact.* Richard M Buttenheim, director, corporate communications, **215-439-3591**

MACY'S NEW YORK (R H Macy & Co Inc.). 151 W 34th St, New York, NY 10001. **212-695-4400.** Thomas K Raney, vice-president, sales and promotion, Ext 2233 or 3370. *Press contacts.* Hillary Garrison and Judy Cohen, Ext 3740.

MANUFACTURERS HANOVER TRUST COMPANY. 350 Park Ave, New York, NY 10022. **212-350-3300.** *Press contact.* James R Hambelton, vice-president, **212-350-6766.** Robert J Messner, deputy director, information, **212-350-4452**

MAPCO INC. 1437 S Boulder Ave, Tulsa, OK 74119. **918-584-4471.** Robert Thomas, investor relations

MARATHON OIL COMPANY. 539 S Main St, Findlay, OH 45840. **419-422-2121.** Harold D Hoopman, president and chief executive officer. Michael B Russo, manager, press and publications. William P Ryder, manager, media relations department

MARCOR INC. See Montgomery Ward and Co, Inc.

MARINE MIDLAND BANKS, INC. Marine Midland Bank, 1 Marine Midland Ctr, Buffalo, NY 14240. **716-843-2424.** Edward W Duffy, chairman of the board and chief executive officer. Arthur B Ziegler, executive vice-president, public affairs, **716-843-4187.** (h) **716-662-4019.** Charles J O'Connor, vice-president, public affairs, **716-843-5875.** (h) **716-839-1167.** James A Catalano, vice-president, public affairs, **212-797-6556.** (h) **516-921-0627.** William L Martin, assistant vice-president, public affairs, internal communications, **716-843-4197**

Regional contacts

Western Region. Susan C Buerk, public relations officer. **716-843-2681**

Central Region. 360 S Warren St, Syracuse, NY 13201. James C Lamanna, Jr, director of communications. **315-622-3327**

Southern Region. 150 Lake St, Elmira, NY 14902. Susan A Geise, public relations officer. **607-629-2124**

Capital Region. 125 Wolf Rd, Albany, NY 12205. Mary L Casey, vice-president, public affairs. **518-453-5000**

Rochester Region. 1 Marine Midland Plz, Rochester, NY 14639. Peg McKinley, marketing officer. **716-229-3649**

MARRIOTT HOTELS, INC. 5161 River Rd, Washington, DC 20016. **301-986-5000.** Paul Lazzaro, vice-president, public relations

MARSH & MCLENNAN COMPANIES. 1221 Avenue of the Americas, New York, NY 10020. **212-997-5000.** Kenneth A Klein, manager, corporate communications, **212-997-5752.** Dong Kingman, Jr, assistant manager, corporate communications, **212-997-5754**

MARTIN MARIETTA CORP. 6801 Rockledge Dr, Bethesda, MD 20034. **301-897-6000.** William Harwood, director, public relations

MASCO CORP. 21001 Van Born Rd, Taylor, MI 48180. **313-274-7400.** John Nichols, corporate information officer

MASSACHUSETTS MUTUAL LIFE INSURANCE. 1295 State St, Springfield, MA 01101. **413-788-8411.** Nathan S Garrison, Jr, director, communications. Richard W Kipperman, associate director, public relations

MAY DEPARTMENT STORES. 611 Olive St, St Louis, MO 63101. **314-436-3300.** David E Babcock, chairman of the board and chief executive officer. Frank J Reilly, vice-president and treasurer. Harry Wilson, chairman, general public relations. William Grafstrom, manager, corporate information. *Press contact.* Harry Wilson, of Fleishman Hillard, 1 Memorial Dr, St Louis, MO 63102, **314-231-1733**

OSCAR MAYER & CO INC. 910 Mayer Ave, Madison, WI 53704. **608-241-3311.** P Goff Beach, chairman of the board and chief executive officer. James P Aehl, external communications manager, (h) **608-244-5864.** Harry G Backer, vice-president, corporate relations, (h) **608-244-6575**

MCA INC. (Universal Pictures and Television). 100 Universal City Plz, Universal City, CA 91608. **213-985-4321**. *Contact.* Frank Wright

MCA Inc. 445 Park Ave, New York, NY 10022. **212-759-7500**

J RAY McDERMOTT AND CO. 1010 Common St, New Orleans, LA 07160. **504-587-4411**. Paul Stafford, director, public relations

McDONALD'S CORPORATION. McDonald's Plz, Oak Brook, IL 60521. **312-887-3200**. Ray A Kroc, senior chairman of the board. Fred L Turner, chairman of the board and chief executive officer. Edward H Schmitt, president and chief administrative officer. Richard J Boylan, senior executive vice-president and chief financial officer. Doug Timberlake, corporate communications manager, **312-887-3678**

McDONNELL DOUGLAS CORP. Lambert Airport, St Louis, MO 63166. **314-232-0232**. Richard J Davis, corporate vice-president, external relations, **314-232-5565**. (h) **314-994-1423**. *Washington, DC, office.* Frank Tomlinson, **202-466-4558**. (h) **703-893-7394**. Gerald J Meyer, director, external relations, **314-232-5913**. (h) **314-821-1185**. Raymond A Deffry, director, news services, **314-232-5911**. (h) **314-727-0435**. John Bickers, director, advertising and external relations administration, **314-232-5823**. (h) **314-822-2528**

Company and divisional contacts

McDonnell Aircraft Company.. John J (Jack) McGrath, director, external relations, **314-232-4121**. (h) **314-921-0340**

Douglas Aircraft Company. Long Beach, CA 90846. Ray Towne, director, external relations, **213-593-3648**. (h) **213-433-1244**. Jack Cooke, deputy director, **213-593-4710**. (h) **213-429-7218**. Harry Calkins, manager, editorial services, **213-593-8443**. (h) **714-523-5131**. Elayne Bendel, senior representative, external relations, **213-593-2492**. (h) **213-373-8226**

McDonnell Douglas Astronautics Company. Huntington Beach, CA 92647. Walt Cleveland, director, external relations, **714-896-1301**. (h) **714-846-9501**. Don Hanson, manager, press relations (also corporate information contact for McDonnell Douglas West Coast activities not listed above), **714-896-1301**. (h) **213-966-3162**

Tulsa Division. Jess Hightower. **918-836-1616**. (h) **918-939-7417**

McGRAW EDISON. 333 W River Rd, Elgin, IL 60120. **312-888-6861**. James Houy, director, corporate communications

McGRAW-HILL, INC. 1221 Avenue of the Americas, New York, NY 10020. **212-997-1221**. Harold W. McGraw, Jr, chairman and president. George Finnegan, vice-president, public affairs, **212-997-6277**. (h) **203-762-9760**. Peter Haas, director, public relations, **212-997-2825**. (h) **212-799-1247**

Divisional press contacts

McGraw-Hill Book Company. Victor de Keyserling, director, public information and publicity, **212-997-2486**. (h) **212-392-1233**

McGraw-Hill Information Systems Company. Bernard Merems, director, public affairs, **212-997-3851**. (h) **516-487-0157**

McGraw-Hill Publications Company (magazines, newletters, publications services). Ruth Sherman, director, public relations, **212-997-6107**. (h) **212-759-5819**

Standard & Poor's Corporation. Don Moser, director, public relations, **212-924-6400**. (h) **914-735-7206**

McLOUTH STEEL. 300 S Liverois Ave, Detroit, MI 48217. **313-843-3000**. William Murphy, vice-president, public relations

MEAD CORPORATION. 118 W 1st St, Dayton, OH 45463. **513-222-9561**. *Press contact.* W J Ahlfeld, vice-president

MELLON BANK NA. Mellon Sq, Pittsburgh, PA 15230. **412-232-4100**. Hud Englehart, public relations manager, **412-232-5383**

MELVILLE CORPORATION (formerly Melville Shoe Corporation). 3000 Westchester Ave, Harrison, NY 10528. **914-253-8000**. Michael Federman, director, public relations

MERCK & CO (parent of Merck, Sharp & Dohme). PO Box 2000, Rahway, NJ 07065. **201-574-4000**. Glem L Hallquist, manager, health information services. John Fletcher, vice-president, public affairs, **201-574-5256**

MERRILL LYNCH & CO, INC. 1 Liberty Plz, 165 Broadway, New York, NY 10006. **212-766-1212**. John Kelley, manager, corporate public relations

METROPOLITAN LIFE INSURANCE CO. 1 Madison Ave, New York, NY 10010. **212-578-2211**. John Harvey, vice-president, corporate communications, **212-578-6658**. Sheila Millen, public relations, **212-578-2642**

MIDDLE SOUTH SERVICES INC. PO Box 61000, New Orleans, LA 70161. **504-529-5262**. Scott B Walker, director, communications

MINNESOTA MINING AND MANUFAC-TURING. 3-M Ctr, St Paul, MN 55101. **612-733-1110**. John Verstraete, vice-president, public relations

MISSOURI PACIFIC RAILROAD. 210 N 13th St, St Louis, MO 63103. **314-662-0123**

MOBIL OIL CORP. 150 E 42nd St, New York, NY 10017. **212-883-4242**. Herbert Schmertz, vice-president, public affairs. Paul A Laudicina, senior staff associate, public relations department, **212-883-2757**

MOHASCO CORPORATION. 57 Lyon St, Amsterdam, NY 12010. **518-841-2111**. Stanley I Landgraf, president. *Press contact.* Rex R Maltbie

MONFORT OF COLORADO. PO Box G, Greeley, CO 80631. **303-353-2311**. Gene Meakins, vice-president, public relations

MONSANTO CO. 800 N Lindbergh Blvd, St Louis, MO 63166. **314-694-1000**. J E McKee, director, corporate public relations. J Kenneth Clark, news bureau, **314-694-2883**

MONTGOMERY WARD & CO, INC. 1 Montgomery Ward Plz, Chicago, IL 60671. **312-467-2000**. Kenneth R Dorre, corporate news director, **312-467-2427**. John R Bell, field public relations coordinator, **312-467-8979**

MOODY'S INVESTORS SERVICE, INC. 99 Church St, New York, NY 10007. **212-267-8800**. *Press contacts.* Municipals: Jackson Phillips, executive vice-president; Freda Ackerman, vice-president. Corporate: Bob Burke, senior vice-president. Public relations: Eve Kram

Branch offices

Atlanta. 1031 Lenox Towers, Atlanta, GA 30301. **404-237-0629**

Boston. 75 Federal St, Boston, MA 02110. **617-426-3617**

Chicago. 222 S Riverside Plz, Chicago, IL 60606. **312-648-0520**

Cincinnati. 120 E 4th St, Cincinnati, OH 45202. **513-381-1271**

Cleveland. Suite 426, 14600 Detroit Ave, Cleveland, OH 44107. **216-228-1094**

Cranford. 118 North Ave W, Cranford, NJ 07016. **201-276-9050**

Dallas. Suite 706, Expressway Tower, 6116 North Central Expy, Dallas TX 75206. **214-369-8738**

Detroit (Southfield). 21711 W 10 Mile Rd, Somerset Bldg, Detroit, MI 48075. **313-355-1150**

Houston. Suite 309, 1770 St James Pl, Houston, TX 77056. **713-626-1939**

Kansas City. Penntower Office Ctr, 3100 Broadway, Kansas City, MO 64111. **816-561-2776**

Los Angeles. 611 W 6th St, Los Angeles, CA 90017. **213-624-8724**

Miami. 2200 NE 174th St, Miami, FL 33160. **305-945-5335**

Milwaukee. Rm 1717, 111 E Wisconsin Ave, Milwaukee, WI 53202. **414-276-0119**

Minneapolis. 7900 Xerxes Ave S, Minneapolis, MN 55431. **612-835-5135**

Philadelphia. 2038 Suburban Station Bldg, Penn Center Plz, Philadelphia, PA 19103. **215-563-7333**

Pittsburgh. Suite 639, Manor Oak 2, 1910 Cochran Rd, Pittsburgh, PA 15220. **412-563-7177**

Richmond. 203 Meadowbrook Professional Bldg, 4222 Bonniebank Rd, Richmond, VA 23234. **804-271-0197**

San Francisco. Suite 3040, 1 California St, San Francisco, CA 94111. **415-397-6136**

Seattle. Rm 816, 1402 3rd Ave, Seattle, WA 98101. **206-624-2536**

Washington. 801 Washington Bldg, Washington, DC 20005. **202-783-7858**

West Hartford. 81 S Main St, West Hartford, CT 06107. **203-232-8415**

J P MORGAN & CO INCORPORATED (and Morgan Guaranty Trust Company of New York). 23 Wall St, New York, NY 10015. **212-483-2323**. Ellmore C Patterson, chairman of the board and chief executive officer. *Press contact.* John M Morris, vice-president, **212-483-2882** or **2866**. (h) **914-834-2502**. James R Brugger, senior vice-president, **212-483-2866**. Bruce L Roberts, vice-president, **212-483-2870**. Russell W Everett, assistant vice-president, **212-483-2880**. *Brussels office.* Stanislaw Ciechanowski, vice-president, **(02)511-65-10**

MORTON-NORWICH PRODUCTS, INC. 110 N Wacker Dr, Chicago, IL 60606. **312-621-5200**. John W Simmons, chairman, president and chief executive officer. Carson B Trenor, director, communications, **312-621-5420**

MOTOROLA INC. 9401 W Girard Ave, Schaumburg, IL 60131. **312-625-6000**. Toni Dewey, corporate director, public relations

MURPHY OIL CORP. 200 Jefferson Ave, El Dorado, AR 71730. **501-862-6411**. Ben S Smith, vice-president, nonfinancial information, **501-862-4278**. George E Breazeal, controller, financial information

WALLACE MURRAY CORP. 299 Park Ave, New York, NY 10017. **212-486-6400**. Charles V Myers, president and chief executive officer. Joseph A Abbott, vice-president, corporate communications

MUTUAL OF NEW YORK. 1740 Broadway, New York, NY 10019. **212-586-4000**. John Kelly, vice-president, public relations

NATIONAL RAIL PASSENGER CORPORATION. *See* AMTRAK

NABISCO. East Hanover, NJ 07936. **201-884-0500**. W Glenn Craig, director, public relations

NALCO CHEMICAL CO. 2901 Butterfield Rd, Oakbrook, IL 60521. **312-887-7500**. Don Weber, manager, corporate communications

NASHUA CORPORATION. 44 Franklin St, Nashua, NH 03060. **603-880-2323**. John Cameron, director, public relations

NATIONAL BANK OF DETROIT. 611 Woodward Ave, Detroit, MI 48232. **313-965-6000**. James E Glynn, director, public relations

NATIONAL BROADCASTING COMPANY. 30 Rockefeller Plz, New York, NY 10020. **212-664-4444**. (For more information, see BROADCASTING NETWORKS.)

NATIONAL DISTILLERS AND CHEMICAL. 99 Park Ave, New York, NY 10016. **212-949-5000**. C Ernest Nauen, vice-president, corporate relations, **212-949-5058**

NATIONAL FUEL GAS CO. 30 Rockefeller Plz, New York, NY 10020. **212-541-7533**. William H Campbell, director, public information

NATIONAL LED INDUSTRIES see NL Industries, Inc.

NATIONAL SEMICONDUCTOR CORPORATION. 2900 Semiconductor Dr, Santa Clara, CA 95051. **408-737-5000**. Charles E Sporck, president and chief executive operating officer. Roy Twitty, public relations manager, **408-737-5287**. Charles Signor, marketing services director, **408-737-5140**. *European press contact.* Chris Soter (Germany), **08141/1371**

NATIONAL SERVICE INDUSTRIES. 1180 Peachtree NE, Atlanta, GA 30309. **404-892-2400**. Erwin Zaban, president. Garland Fritts, vice-president, management services

NATIONAL STANDARD INSURANCE CO. 2727 Allen Pkwy, Houston, TX 77019. **713-522-1111**

NATIONAL STEEL CORPORATION. Grant Bldg, Pittsburgh, PA 15219. **412-471-5600**. W S Schwoebel, investor relations. Robert M Rine, special public relations representative (Weirton, WV 26062). **304-723-8449**. Arthur H Warmuskerken, director, public relations, Great Lake division (Ecorse, MI 48229). **313-843-8000**

NEW ENGLAND MUTUAL LIFE INSURANCE. 501 Boylston St, Boston, MA 02117. **617-266-3700**. Abram T Collier, chairman and chief executive officer. David V Lustig, manager, public relations, **617-266-3726**. Night line: **617-227-7037**. Bronwyn Smith, manager, public relations, **617-266-3700**

NEWMONT OIL CO. 300 Park Ave, New York, NY 10007. **212-754-4800**. Jack Ross, director, public relations

NEW YORK LIFE INSURANCE CO. 51 Madison Ave, New York, NY 10010. **212-576-7000**. Nathan Kelne, vice-president, public relations and advertising, **212-576-5069**. William C Shepherd, Midwest public relations director (Suite 1430, 1 IBM Plz, Chicago, IL 60611). **312-467-1070**

THE NEW YORK TIMES COMPANY. 229 W 43rd St, New York, NY 10036. **212-556-1234**. W Barry McCarthy, director, corporate communications

NEWSWEEK. *see* Washington Post Company

NIAGARA MOHAWK POWER CORP. 300 Erie Blvd W Syracuse, NY 13202. **315-474-1511.** Robert H Wells, director, communications planning. O Mark De Michele, vice-president, public relations. J Edward Kaish, assistant to vice-president, public relations. *Albany Office.* 126 State St, Albany, NY 12207. Robert O O'Brien, director, public relations, **518-449-8000.** *Buffalo office.* 535 Washington St, Buffalo, NY 14203, E Alfred Osborne, director, public relations, **716-856-2424**

A C NIELSON & CO. Nielsen Plz, Northbrook, IL 60062. **312-498-6300**

NL INDUSTRIES, INC. 1230 Avenue of the Americas, New York, NY 10020. **212-399-9400.** Night line: **212-399-9370** or **201-273-8558.** Ray C Adam, chairman of the board, president, and chief executive officer, **212-399-9405.** R W Unwin, Jr, director, public affairs and corporate communications, **212-399-9370.** John N Magee, contact, **212-399-9371**

NLT CORP. National Life Center, Nashville, TN 37250. **615-749-1443.** William M Holder, investor relations, **615-749-1404**

NORELCO. see North American Phillips

NORFOLK AND WESTERN RAILWAY CO. 8 N Jefferson St, Roanoke, VA 24042. **703-981-4400.** John P Fishwick, president and chief executive officer, **703-981-4300.** *Press contacts.* Lewis M Phelps, director, public relations and advertising, **703-981-4941.** (h) **703-982-1686;** William A Martin, manager, news service, **703-981-4359.** (h) **703-342-3942**

NORRIS INDUSTRIES. 5215 S Boyle St, Los Angeles, CA 90058. **213-588-7111**

NORTH AMERICAN PHILIPS. 100 E 42nd St, New York, NY 10017. **212-697-3600.** Pieter C Vink, chairman and president. Albert Ruttner, director, public relations

NORTHEAST UTILITIES SERVICE CO. PO Box 270, Hartford, CT 06101. **203-666-6911.** William J Keveney, manager, system news services. (h) **203-248-0708**

NORTHERN NATURAL GAS. 2223 Dodge St, Omaha, NE 68102. **402-348-4000.** John Harding, vice-president, public relations, **402-348-4539**

NORTHERN STATES POWER COMPANY. 414 Nicollet Mall, Minneapolis, MN 55401. **612-330-5500.** Donald W McCarthy, president and chief executive officer. Beth Willis, supervisor, media services, **612-330-6368.** (h) **612-473-6845.** Night line ("Hotline"; has a recorded message with name of person to contact): **612-330-6199.** Communications representatives: Steve London, nuclear power and transmission lines, **612-330-6925.** Gary Urban, electric and gas rates, **612-330-6585.** Wayne Kaplan, system operation, **612-330-6670**

NSP-Wisconsin Company. Eau Claire, WI. Robert J Metzgar, administrator, public information, **715-839-2474**

NORTHROP CORP. 1800 Century Park, Los Angeles, CA. **214-553-6262.** William Schoneberger, director, corporate communications

NORTHWEST AIRLINES (Northwest Orient). St Paul International Airport, St Paul, MN 55111. **612-726-2111.** Roy Erickson, vice-president, public relations

NORTHWESTERN MUTUAL LIFE INSURANCE CO. 720 E Wisconsin Ave, Milwaukee, WI 53202. **414-276-3320.** Robert O Carboni, vice-president, communications, **414-271-1444**

NORTHWESTERN STEEL AND WIRE CO. 121 Wallace St, Sterling IL 61081. **815-625-2500.** *Press contact.* W Martin Dillon

NORTON COMPANY. 1 New Bond St, Worcester, MA 01606. **617-853-1000.** Robert Cushman, president and chief executive officer. Alfred J Cotton, Jr, public relations director and public affairs officer. (h) **617-754-4584**

NORTON SIMON INC. 277 Park Ave, New York, NY 10017. **212-832-1000.** Robert Amen, vice-president, public relations

NVF COMPANY. Yorklyn Rd, PO Box 68, Yorklyn, DE 19736. **302-239-5281.** Victor Posner, chief executive, **305-866-7771.** *Press contact.* Leo Murphy, **216-448-4011**

OCCIDENTAL PETROLEUM. 10889 Wilshire Blvd, Los Angeles, CA 90024. **213-879-1700.** Dr Armand Hammer, chairman and chief executive officer. Carl W Blumay, director, public relations. Bruce McWilliams, assistant director, public relations. Sheri Hirst, manager, publications

OGDEN CORP. 277 Park Ave, New York, NY 10017. **212-754-4000**

OHIO EDISON CO. 47 N Main St, Akron, OH 44308. **216-762-9661.** Frank Derry, manager, communications services

OIL SHALE CO. *See* Tosco Corporation

OLIN CORP. 120 Long Ridge Rd, Stamford, CT 06904. **203-356-2000.** James F Towey, chairman and chief executive officer. Henry Hunter, vice-president, public relations and communications. Jack R Ryan, director, public relations. *New York office.* 460 Park Ave, New York, NY 10022. **212-486-7200.** Eugene Boyo, manager, public relations

OSCAR MAYER *See* Mayer, Oscar

OTIS ELEVATOR CO. 1 Farm Springs, Farmington, CT 06032. **203-677-6000.** Herbert M Doherty, director, communications, Ext 6264. Peter Thompson, manager, public relations, Ext 6265

OWENS-CORNING FIBERGLAS CORP. Fiberglas Tower, Toledo, OH 43659. **419-248-8000.** *Press contact.* Stanley E Collins, **419-248-8050**

OWENS-ILLINOIS. 405 Madison Ave, Toledo, OH 43666. **419-247-1917.** Jack K Paquette, vice-president, corporate relations. Sam P Allen, director, public and employee information

PACIFIC GAS & ELECTRIC CO. 77 Beale St, San Francisco, CA 94106. **415-781-4211.** James McCollum, vice-president, public relations. Lawrence R McDonnell, manager, public information. Don J Baxter, news director. Frederick R Draeger, supervisor, public information, Ext 1495

PACIFIC LIGHTING CORPORATION. 810 S Flower St, Los Angeles, CA 90017. **213-689-3556.** Stephen H Baer, manager, public and employee information. Rich Nemec, supervisor, news bureau, **213-689-2171.** Stephen M Gray, public relations specialist, energy supply projects, **213-689-2413**

PACIFIC POWER AND LIGHT COMPANY. 920 SW 6th Ave, Portland, OR 97204. **503-243-1122.** Don C Frisbee, chairman and president, **503-243-4700.** Edward Prince, news bureau manager, **503-243-4761.** James H Ferguson, assistant vice-president, investor/financial media relations, **503-243-4543**

PACIFIC TELEPHONE AND TELE-GRAPH. 140 New Montgomery St, San Francisco, CA 94105. **415-421-9000.** Gerald Foster, vice-president, public relations. Lawrence R Benefield, public relations manager

PAN AMERICAN WORLD AIRWAYS. 200 Park Ave, New York, NY 10017. **212-973-7700.** Brad Dressler, staff vice-president, public relations, **212-973-4190**

PANHANDLE EASTERN PIPE LINE COMPANY. 3000 Bissonnet Ave, Houston, TX 77005. **713-664-3401.** Richard L O'Shields, president and chief executive officer. Stanford A Wallace, vice-president, public relations, (h) **713-464-2387.** J Fred Ebdon, manager, public relations, (h) **713-774-9140.** Tony Turbeville, manager, media relations, (h) **713-529-1797.** Bob Van Leuvan, manager, publications, (h) **713-497-4554.** Dan Mullis, editorial director, (h) **713-466-4207.** G L Johnson, manager, audiovisual, (h) **713-497-1702**

PARKER HANNIFIN CORPORATION. 17325 Euclid Ave, Cleveland, OH 44112. **216-531-3000.** Patrick S Parker, chairman of the board and chief executive officer, Ext 2200. Rena C Brenner, director, corporate communications, Ext 2750, (h) **216-249-7014**
Group contacts
Seal Group. Dave Knoepp. **213-837-5101**
Automotive Aftermarket Group. Art Maresz. **212-498-4000**

PATHMARK DIVISION, SUPER-MARKETS GENERAL CORP. 301 Blair Rd, Woodbridge, NJ 07095. **201-499-3000.** Bernard Paroly, president, Pathmark. Robert E Wunderle, vice-president, public affairs, **201-499-3299.** Night line: **201-232-2731**

PEABODY INTERNATIONAL CORPO-RATION. Landmark Sq, Stamford, CT 06901. **203-348-0000.** Nedd McArthur, vice-president, communications and marketing services

PEAVEY COMPANY. 730 2nd Ave S, Minneapolis, MN 55415. **612-370-7500.** Tom Hammill, director, public affairs, **612-370-7612**

J C PENNEY CO, INC. 1301 Avenue of the Americas, New York, NY 10019. **212-957-4321.** C T Stewart, senior vice-president, director, public relations

PENNSYLVANIA POWER & LIGHT CO. 2 N 9th St, Allentown, PA 18101.

215-821-5151. Jack K Busby, chief executive officer and chairman of the board, **215-821-5218.** Richard H Lichtenwalner, vice-president, information services, **215-821-5630.** Tom Ruddell, director, information services, **215-821-5429**
Information editors
Consumer Information. Michael P Kislow, **215-821-5311**
Financial Information. H James Marsh, **215-821-5241**
Public Information. Paul F Schock, **215-821-5532**

PENNWALT CORP. 3 Parkway, Philadelphia, PA 19102. **215-587-7000.** William P Drake, chairman and chief executive officer, **215-587-7202.** Kathleen G Putnam, director, public relations, **215-587-7286.** *Press contact.* Amy De Marco, public relations supervisor, **215-587-7347**

PENNZOIL UNITED INC. PO Box 2967, Pennzoil Pl, Houston, TX 77001. **713-236-7878.** Vincent Guarino, director, public relations

PEOPLES GAS COMPANY. 122 S Michigan Ave, Chicago, IL 60603. **312-431-4000.** Robert Wilson, vice-president, corporate communications

PEPSICO INC. Anderson Hill Rd, Purchase, NY 10577. **914-253-2000.** Al Goetz, Jr, director, corporate communications. Michael T Berger, director, public relations field operations, **914-253-3298**

PERKIN ELMER CORPORATION. Main St, Norwalk, CT 06852. **203-762-1000.** Charles Dayton, director, corporate communications, **203-762-6971**

PET INCORPORATED. 400 S Fourth St, St Louis, MO 63166. **314-621-5400.** Lila Spencer, director, public relations, Ext 423

PFIZER, INC. 235 E 42nd St, New York, NY 10017. **212-573-2255.** Edward Littlejohn, vice-president, public affairs, **213-573-3209**

PHELPS DODGE INDUSTRIES. 300 Park Ave, New York, NY 10022. **212-751-3200.** Cynthia Brown, manager, advertising and public relations

PHILADELPHIA ELECTRIC CO. 2301 Market St, Philadelphia, PA 19101. **215-841-4000.** Clifford Brenner, vice-president, corporate communications, **215-841-4100**

PHILIP MORRIS INC. 100 Park Ave, New York, NY 10017. **212-679-1800.** Frank Saunders, director, corporate relations and communications

PHILLIPS PETROLEUM CO. Bartlesville, OK 74004. **918-661-6600.** Philip R Caudill, media relations coordinator, **918-661-4982.** "If after regular business hours, or on weekends or holidays, reporter should call Phillips' switchboard (**918-661-6600**) and ask to be connected with the residence of Mr Caudill or other appropriate person."

PHILLIPS VAN HEUSEN CORP. 1290 Avenue of the Americas, New York, NY 10019. **212-541-5200.** Lawrence Phillips, corporate information officer

PILLSBURY CO. 608 2nd Ave S, Minneapolis, MN 55402. **612-330-4966.** Forler Massnick, vice-president, corporate relations. Louis Gelfand, director, public relations

PITNEY BOWES. Walnut and Pacific Sts, Stamford, CT 06904. **203-356-5000.** Fred T Allen, chairman and president. Ralph H Major, Jr, manager, public relations, **203-356-5090.** (h) **203-966-4209.** Maureen Gorman, editor, information services, **203-356-5089.** Robert Strickland, manager, editorial services, **203-356-5086**

PITTSTON CO. 1 Pickwick Plz, Greenwich, CT 06830. **203-622-0900.** Hugh E Flaherty, director, public affairs

POLAROID CORPORATION. 549 Technology Sq, Cambridge, MA 02139. **617-864-6000.** Donald Dery, director, communications

POTLATCH FORESTS INC. 1 Maritime Plz, San Francisco, CA 94119. **415-981-5980.** Richard Nordholm, vice-president, public affairs

PPG INDUSTRIES, INC. 1 Gateway Ctr, Pittsburgh, PA 15222. **412-434-3131.** Howard H Babcock, director, public relations, **412-434-2491.** (h) **412-367-3514.** Arthur J Marino, Jr, manager, public relations, **412-434-3011.** (h) **412-243-3711.** Raymond G Fleckenstein, manager, community relations, **412-434-3012.** (h) **412-366-0152.** John S Ruch, manager, eastern regional public relations (600 3rd Ave, New York, NY 10016). **212-682-1205.** (h) **201-584-4574**

PROCTOR AND GAMBLE. 301 E 6th St (PO Box 599), Cincinnati, OH 45201. **513-562-1100**

Press contacts

Corporate Affairs. W F (Bill) Dobson, **513-562-2496.** (h) **513-531-4798.** R M (Bob) Norrish, **513-562-2462.** (h) **513-321-4823.** S L (Sydney) Friel, **513-562-2595.** (h) **513-871-6078**

Coffee/Paper/Food/Industrial Products. R P (Ron) Lustik, **513-562-2393.** (h) **513-351-7226.** J S (Jack) Rue, **513-562-2883.** (h) **513-871-3472**

Packaged Soap/Detergents/Bar Soaps and Household Cleaning Products/Toilet Goods Products. L V (Vate) Powell, **513-562-4845.** (h) **513-281-7424.** R B (Bob) Stewart, **513-562-3812.** (h) **513-351-6542**

THE PRUDENTIAL INSURANCE COMPANY OF AMERICA. 763 Broad St, Newark, NJ 07101. **201-336-1234.** Philip R Warth, director, public relations, **201-336-2863**

PUBLIC SERVICE CO. 1000 E Main St, Plainfield, IN 46168. **317-839-6511.** Barton Grabow, vice-president, public relations, **317-839-9611**

PUBLIC SERVICE ELECTRIC AND GAS. 80 Park Pl, Newark, NJ 07101. **201-622-7000.** W A Maginn, vice-president, investor relations

PULLMAN INCORPORATED. 200 S Michigan Ave, Chicago, IL 60604. **312-322-7070.** Neil F Gabbert, manager, public relations. Richard D Johnson, assistant vice-president, corporate communications, **312-322-7159**

PUREX CORP. 5101 Clark Ave, Lakewood, CA 90712. **213-634-3300.** *Press contact.* Burston-Marsteller, **213-386-8776**

QUAKER OATS CO. Merchandise Mart Pl, Chicago, IL 60654. **312-222-6881.** John A Rourke, director, public relations, (h) **312-446-6754**

QUESTOR CORPORATION. 1801 Spielbusch, Toledo, OH 43691. **419-248-1515.** P M Grieve, president. Patricia M Durdel, public relations assistant

RALSTON PURINA CO. 835 S 8th St, St Louis, MO 63199. **314-982-3219.** George Kyd, director, public relations

RAPID-AMERICAN CORP. 1290 Avenue of the Americas, New York, NY 10019. **212-581-6700**

RATH PACKING CO. Sycamore and Elm Sts, Waterloo, IA 50704. **319-235-8900.** John Stevens, director, public relations

RAYBESTOS-MANHATTAN, INC. 100 Oakview Dr, Trumbull, CT 06611. **203-371-0101.** William S Simpson, chairman of the board and chief executive officer, Ext 201. Bruce Bagger, director, corporate communications, Ext 314

RAYTHEON COMPANY. 141 Spring St, Lexington, MA 02173. **617-862-6600.** Thomas L Phillips, chairman and chief executive officer. A Newell Garden, corporate public relations manager, Ext 414. (h) **617-332-0920.** Richard P Axten, vice-president, public and financial relations, Ext 820. (h) **617-235-7028**

Group contacts

Commercial Group. Robert P Suarez, publicity manager, Ext 413. (h) **617-664-5083**

Government Group and Technical Information. John E Severance, public relations manager, Ext 415. (h) **617-688-7148.** H Davis Bushnell, publicity manager, Ext 412. (h) **617-263-4763**

RCA CORPORATION. 30 Rockefeller Plz, New York, NY 10020. **212-598-5900.** Henry J Bechtold, staff vice-president, news and information, **212-598-4755.** Howard C Enders, manager, product news, **212-598-4522**

RCA Government Systems. Nicholas F Pensiero, director, public affairs (Moorestown, NJ 08057). **609-234-1234.** (h) **609-779-6971**

REICHHOLD CHEMICALS, INC. 525 N Broadway, White Plains, NY 10603. **914-682-5700.** Peter J Fass, president. Robert F Lynch, advertising manager, **914-682-5785.** Night line. **203-637-0809**

RELIANCE ELECTRIC CO. 29325 Chagrin Blvd, Cleveland, OH 44122. **216-266-7000.** G C McDonough, vice-president, investor relations. R B Ainsworth, Jr, **216-266-5834**

REPUBLIC NATIONAL BANK OF DALLAS. Pacific at Ervay (PO Box 5961), Dallas, TX 75222. **214-653-5000.** James W Keay, chairman of the board and chief executive officer, **214-653-5239.** Charles H Pistor, Jr, president, **214-653-5259.** James L Hemmingson, vice-president and director of public relations, **214-653-5742.** (h) **214-351-3633.** James R Bowman, administrative officer, public relations division, **214-653-5556**

REPUBLIC STEEL CORP. 25 W Prospect Ave, Cleveland, OH 44101. **216-574-7100.** H W Hopwood, vice-president, public relations

RESERVE OIL AND GAS COMPANY. 550 S Flower St, Los Angeles, CA 90071. **213-626-4108.** Paul D Meadows, president and chief executive officer, **303-861-7800.** John R Ulf, director, corporate communications, **213-626-4108.** Night line: **213-887-0698**

REVERE COPPER AND BRASS. 605 3rd Ave, New York, NY 10016. **212-578-1575**

REVLON INC. 767 5th Ave, New York, NY 10022. **212-758-5000.** Joseph Liebman, senior vice-president, public relations

REXNORD INC. PO Box 2022, Milwaukee, WI 53201. **414-643-3000.** W C Messinger, chairman. R V Krikarian, president. John A Bartels, director, public affairs, **414-784-5000.** David Shanks, director, corporate relations and advertising, **414-784-5000.** Herbert H Kister, director, public relations, **414-784-5000**

R J REYNOLDS INDUSTRIES INC. 405 N Main St, Winston-Salem, NC 27102. **919-748-7517.** Frank Slover, financial communications manager, **919-748-2861.** Ron Sustana, director, public relations. **919-748-7517.** *Press contacts.* David Fishel, tobacco company, **919-748-2491.** Dan Stepanek, foods, **919-748-2044.** Richard Drasen, energy, **919-748-2051.** Phillip Fleming, packaging, **919-748-2862**

REYNOLDS METALS CO. 6603 Broad St, Richmond, VA 23261. **804-281-2000.** Joseph F Awad, general director, public relations, **804-281-2171.** David M Clinger, director, information, **804-281-2965.** D Brickford Rider, director, community relations

RHODE ISLAND HOSPITAL TRUST/ *See* Hospital Trust and Fund

RICHARDSON-MERREL INC. 10 Westport Rd, Wilton, CT 06897. **203-762-2222.** J G McIntyre, investor relations

DAN RIVER, INC. PO Box 6126, Station B, Greenville, SC 29606. **803-242-5950.** M A Cross, vice-president, public and industrial relations

RIVIANA FOODS INC. 277 Allen Pkwy (PO Box 2636), Houston, TX 77001. **713-529-3251.** W H Lane, president. J J Halbach, vice-president, corporate relations and services

ROADWAY EXPRESS. 1077 Gorge Blvd, Akron, OH 44309. **216-434-1641.** *Press contact.* John Tormey

H H ROBERTSON COMPANY. 2 Gateway Ctr, Pittsburgh, PA 15222. **412-281-3200.** *Press contact.* John W Viehman, vice-president, finance

ROCKWELL INTERNATIONAL CORPORATION. 800 Grant St, Pittsburgh, PA 15219. **412-565-2000.** Sam Petok, staff vice-president, public relations, **412-565-7166.** Jay A Clark, manager, media relations, **412-565-7467**

Group contacts

Admiral Group. 1701 E Woodfield Rd, Schaumburg, IL 60194. H C Clapp, manager, advertising and public relations, **312-884-2888**

Collins Radio Group. Robert R Knott, manager, news bureau (1200 N Alma Rd, Richardson, TX 75080). **214-690-5160**

ROHM AND HAAS COMPANY. Independence Mall W, Philadelphia, PA 19105. **215-592-3000.** Vincent L Gregory, Jr, president. John M Reed, manager, public relations, **215-592-3248.** John F McKeogh, director, communications, **215-592-2740**

ROPER CORPORATION. 1905 W Court St, Kankakee, IL 60901. **815-937-6000.** C M Hoover, chairman of the board and chief executive officer. J C Gibson, president and chief operating officer. *Contact for corporate information.* R E Cook, vice-president, administration, and secretary-treasurer

SAFECO CORP. Safeco Plz, Seattle, WA 98185. **206-545-5000.** Gordon Sweany, chairman and chief executive officer, **206-545-5555.** Gordon Hamilton, media relations, **206-545-5705.** Night line: **206-364-3102.** Mark Cooper, vice-president, public relations, **206-545-5708.** Pat Hillis, public relations representative news writer, **206-545-5771**

SAFEWAY STORES. 201 4th St, Oakland, CA 94604. **415-891-3000.** Calvin P Pond, vice-president, corporate public affairs, **415-891-3265.** Felicia Del Campo, public relations section manager, **415-891-3267**

SAGA CORPORATION. 1 Saga Ln, Menlo Park, CA 94025. **415-854-5150.** Night line: **415-854-3856.** William F Scandling, president. Joseph S Shakes, director, corporate relations, **415-329-7811**

ST JOE MINERAL CORP. 250 Park Ave, New York, NY 10019. **212-953-5000.** Robert Pelkham, director, corporate communications

ST PAUL COMPANIES INC. 385 Washington St, St Paul, MN 55102. **612-221-7911.** David McDonnell, manager, public relations

ST REGIS PAPER CO. 150 E 42nd St, New York, NY 10017. **212-697-4400.** Ronald E Martin, employee communications

SAN DIEGO GAS AND ELECTRIC. PO Box 1831, San Diego, CA 92112. **714-232-4252.** Albert C Welti, Jr, news bureau director. Denis Richter, vice-president, public relations

SANTE FE INDUSTRIES. 224 S Michigan, Chicago, IL 60604. **312-426-4900.** William Burk, vice-president, public relations

SAVANNAH FOODS AND INDUSTRIES INC. 2–8 Bryant St, Savannah, GA 31402. **912-234-1261.** *Press contact.* Walter Scott

SAXON INDUSTRIES. 450 7th Ave, New York, NY 10001. **212-736-3663.** Charles Morris, vice-president, corporate relations

SCHERING-PLOUGH. Galloping Hill Rd, Kenilworth, NJ 07033. **201-931-2000.** Robert Garofalo, director, public relations

JOSEPH SCHLITZ BREWING CO. 235 W Galena St, Milwaukee, WI 53201. **414-224-5000.** James Ritchie, director, public relations

SCHLUMBURGER LIMITED. 277 Park Ave, New York, NY 10017. **212-350-9400.** Jean Riboud, chairman and president. S T McCormick, manager, public relations, **212-350-9503**

SCM CORP. 299 Park Ave, New York, NY 10017. **212-752-2700.** H J Katz, director, public relations

SCOTT PAPER CO. Scott Plz, Philadelphia, PA 19113. **215-521-5000.** William E Fulwider, manager, public and financial information, (h) **215-647-7358.** William F Mahoney, director, corporate communications, (h) **215-388-7201.** Harold P Mueller, Jr, manager, public affairs/operations, (h) **215-LO6-2517**

SCOVILL MANUFACTURING. 99 Mill St, Waterbury, CT 60702. **203-757-6061.** Paul Beetz, director, corporate relations

SEABOARD ALLIED MILLING CO. 200 Boylston St, Newton, MA 02617. **617-332-8492.** *Press contact.* Harry Bresky

SEABOARD COAST LINE INDUSTRIES, INC. 500 Water St, Jacksonville, FL 32202. **904-353-2011.** Prime F Osborn, president and chief executive officer, Ext 203. Donald T Martin, vice-president, public relations and advertising, Ext 483. Night line: **904-353-7589.** Raymond L Bullard, assistant vice-president, public relations and advertising, Ext 485. S Owen Pride, public relations representative, Ext 484. E Leo Koester, assistant vice-president, public relations and advertising (Louisville, KY), **502-587-5321**

SEAFIRST CORPORATION (Seattle First National Bank). PO Box 3586, Seattle, WA 98124. **206-583-3131.** Esther M Murphy, assistant vice-president, corporate communications, **206-583-3200.** Night line: **206-784-3545.** Mitchell Day, assistant vice-president, investor relations, **206-583-3421**

G D SEARLE AND CO. Searle Pkwy (PO Box 1045), Skokie, IL 60076. **312-982-7000.** Donald Rumsfeld, president and chief executive officer. Stephen J Kaye, director, public relations, **312-982-7421**

SEARS, ROEBUCK & CO. Sears Tower, Chicago, IL 60684. **312-875-8300.** W F McCurdy, vice-president, public relations, **312-875-5703.** Ernest L Arms, national news director, **312-875-8371.** Donald A Deutsch, national public relations director, **312-875-8300**

Regional press contacts

Midwest Territory. John D Austin, director, press relations, (Skokie, IL 60076). **312-967-3215.** Rembrandt C Hiller, Jr, director, public relations, **312-967-3213**

Northwest Region. William G Casterline, director, public relations (Seattle, WA 98184). **206-344-4808**

Central Pacific Coast Area. Philo K Holland, Jr (Hayward, CA 94545), **415-783-6000**

Pacific Coast Territory. David D Hurford, director, public relations, **213-576-4703.** Nat B Read, Jr, director, communications, (Alhambra, CA 91802). **213-576-4182.** Also Walter H Rees

Southwestern Territory. C William Rule, Jr, director, public relations (Dallas, TX 75295). **214-565-4703**

Southern Territory. Donald H Gareis, director, public relations (Atlanta, GA 30395). **404-885-3710**

Eastern Territory. Francis E Pettit, Jr, director, public relations (St Davids, PA 19087). **215-293-2100**

SEATTLE FIRST NATIONAL BANK *See* Seafirst Corporation

SECURITY PACIFIC NATIONAL BANK. 333 S Hope St, Los Angeles, CA 90071. 213-613-6211. Toll-free number in California: **800-252-0308.** Piers R De Neyrac, public information officer, **213-613-6838.** J Thomas Chapman, public affairs officer, **213-613-6841.** Barbara Karbe, public information specialist, **415-445-4556**

SEVEN-ELEVEN. Third Avenue Bldg, 711 3rd Ave, New York, NY 10016. **212- 682-3934**

SHELL OIL CO. 1 Shell Plz, Houston, TX 77002. **713-241-6161.** H E Walker, vice-president, public affairs. J H Walter, manager, public affairs-operating, **713-241-4528.** M H Boeger, manager, corporate public affairs, **713-241-3881.** J Boyajian, manager, public affairs-editorial services, **713-241-3690**

SHELLER-GLOBE. 1505 Jefferson Ave (PO Box 962), Toledo, OH 43697. **419-255-8840.** Ed Talty, vice-president, public affairs. Bob Snell, director, public relations

SHERWIN-WILLIAMS COMPANY. 101 Prospect Ave NW, Cleveland, OH 44115. **216-566-2000.** Thomas C Hassey, director, corporate identification

SIGNAL COMPANIES, INC. 9665 Wilshire Blvd, Beverly Hills, CA 90212. 213-278-7400. Forrest N Shumway, president and chief executive officer. John W Bold, manager, public relations, Exts 263 and 264

SIGNODE CORPORATION. 3600 W Lake Ave, Glenview, IL 60025. **312-724-6100.** J Thomas Schanck, president and chief executive officer. *Additional contact.* Hugh Bunten

SIMMONS CO. Jones Bridge Rd (PO Box 49000), Atlanta, GA 30362. **404-449-5000**

SIMON NORTON INC. *See* Norton Simon Inc.

THE SINGER COMPANY. 30 Rockefeller Plz, New York, NY 10020. **212-581-4800.** Night line: **212-581-7362.** Joseph B Flavin, chairman and chief executive officer. Richard J Kosmicki, director, public affairs, Ext 231. Carrie Thomas, assistant manager, media relations, Ext 237

A O SMITH CORP. 3533 N 27th St, Milwaukee, WI 53201. **414-447-4438.** Jack Birchill, director, public relations

SMITH KINE AND FRENCH. 1500 Spring Garden St, Philadelphia, PA 19101. **215-854-5154.** Peter Sena, director, corporate communication

SOUTHERN CALIFORNIA EDISON CO. 2244 Walnut Grove Ave, Rosemead, CA 91770. **213-572-1212.** John D Wyatt, supervisor, energy communications, 213-572-2249

THE SOUTHERN COMPANY. PO Box 720071, 64 Perimeter Ctr E, Atlanta, GA 30346. **404-393-0650.** Night line: **404-393-0658.** Alvin W Vogtle, Jr, president. Gale Klappa, manager, news and corporate information

SOUTHERN PACIFIC CO. 1 Market St, San Francisco, CA 94105. **415-362-1212.** James Shea, vice-president, public relations

SOUTHERN RAILWAY CO. 920 15th St NW, Washington, DC 20013. **202-628-4460.** W F Geeslin, assistant vice-president, public relations. Charles Morgret, manager, public relations

SOUTHLAND CORP. 2828 N Haskell Ave, Dallas, TX 75221. **214-828-7011.** Allen Liles, director, public relations

SOUTHWEST FOREST INDUSTRIES. 3443 N Central, Phoenix, AZ 85012. **602-279-5381.** E J Wren, vice-president, public affairs

SPENCER FOODS. 71 N Box 12228, Spencer, IA 51302. **712-262-4250.** *Press contact.* Dan Mueller, vice-president

SPERRY-RAND. 1290 Avenue of the Americas, New York, NY 10019. **212-956-2121.** J Peter Hynex, director, public information. P J Durocher, director, public relations and advertising

SPRING MILLS, INC. PO Box 70, Fort Mill, SC 29715. **803-547-2901.** H W Close, chairman of the board. Marshall Doswell, vice-president, corporate communications. Bob E Slough, director, community relations. Bob Thompson, director, public relations, (h) **803-366-1667**

SQUIBB CO. 40 W 57th St, New York, NY 10019. **212-489-2000.** Norman Ritter, vice-president, public relations. Sean D Ryan, manager, public affairs

S S KRESGE *See* K mart

STANDARD BRANDS INC. 625 Madison Ave, New York, NY 10022. **212-759-4400.**

Roy Fishman, vice-president, public relations

STANDARD OIL CO OF CALIFORNIA. 225 Bush St, San Francisco, CA 94104. **415-894-7700.** Dale Basye, public relations counsel, news service. **415-349-7035**

STANDARD OIL CO (INDIANA). 200 E Randolph, Chicago, IL 60601. **312-856-6111.** Carl F Meyerdirk, director, corporate media relations, **312-856-5566.** (h) **312-871-7027.** William C Adams, consultant, media relations (Suite 503, 1000 16th St NW, Washington, DC 20036). **202-638-1196**

STANDARD OIL CO OF NEW JERSEY. Name changed to Exxon Corp

STANDARD OIL CO OF OHIO. 101 Prospect Ave NW, Cleveland, OH 44115. **216-575-4141.** Charles E Spahr, chief executive officer. Richard Nash, manager, investor relations

STANLEY WORKS. 195 Lake St, New Britain, CT 06050. **203-225-5111.** Managers of public information: Edward C Benfield and William J Shanahan. Murray E Fisher, manager, communication and training

STATE FARM INSURANCE COMPANIES. 1 State Farm Plz, Bloomington, IL 61701. **309-662-2311.** David Phillips, vice-president, public relations, **309-662-2063**
Information contacts
Auto Insurance Information. Robert Sasser. **309-662-2625**
Fire Insurance Information. David Hurst. **309-662-2845**
Life and Health Insurance Information. Vicki Hopper. **309-662-2449**
State Farm provides to the news media, without charge, a detailed and continuously updated "No-Fault Press Reference Manual," a series of publications called "Insurance Backgrounder," and a publication entitled "So You're Thinking about Doing a Story on...."

STAUFFER CHEMICAL COMPANY. Westport, CT 06880. **203-222-3000.** Ed Bloch, manager, public relations

STERLING DRUG, INC. 90 Park Ave, New York, NY 10016. **212-972-4141.** *Press contact.* William J Brooks, **212-972-2316**

J P STEVENS AND CO. 1185 Avenue of the Americas, New York, NY 10036. **212-575-2000.** J R Franklin, director, corporate public relations

STOKELY-VAN CAMP, INC. 941 Meridian St, Indianapolis, IN 46206. **317-631-2551.** *Press contact.* K Marvin Eberts, Jr

THE STOP AND SHOP COMPANIES, INC. PO Box 369, Boston, MA 02101. **617-463-7000.** Avram J Goldberg, president. William J McCarthy, director, media relations, **617-463-4345.** (h) **617-662-8196.** Jill A Gabbe, assistant to media relations director, **617-463-4346**

STUDEBAKER-WORTHINGTON INC. 885 2nd Ave, New York, NY 10017. **212-371-2720.** Scott Taylor, director, public relations, **212-350-8173**

SUCREST CORPORATION. 120 Wall St, New York, NY 10005. **212-344-4920.** Allerton D Marshall, vice-president, secretary, and treasurer. Linda R Henderson, director, corporate relations

SUN COMPANY INC (formerly Sun Oil Co, "Sunoco"). 100 Matsonford Rd, Radnor, PA 19087. **215-293-6000.** James H Moran, manager, external communications. W E Hanson, director, public relations. *Offshore oil exploration.* W F Oxford, Jr, senior public relations representative and petroleum engineer (PO Box 2880, Dallas, TX 75221), **214-744-4411**

SUNDSTRAND CORP. 4751 Harrison, Rockford, IL 61101. **815-226-6200.** Robert E Carlson, director of corporate communications, **815-226-6245**

SUPERIOR OIL. First National City Bank, Houston, TX 77001. **713-751-4111.** *Press contact.* Alan Durham, vice-president

SUPERMARKETS GENERAL CORP. *See* Pathmark Division

SUPER VALU STORES INC. 101 Jefferson Ave, Hopkins, MN 55343. **612-932-4444.** Jack J Crocker, chairman and chief executive officer. Robert R Hosokawa, vice-president, communications

SWIFT INDUSTRIES. 1 Chicago Ave, Elizabeth, PA 15037. **412-892-0700**

SYBRON CORP. 1100 Midtown Tower, Rochester, NY 14604. **716-546-4040.** B H Dumbleton, director, communications

TALLEY INDUSTRIES INC. 3500 N Greenfield Rd, Mesa, AZ 85201. **602-832-3830**

TAMPA ELECTRIC. PO Box 111, Tampa, FL 33601. **813-879-4111.** Gerald L Dawson, director, public affairs

TANDY CORPORATION. 2727 W 7th St, Fort Worth, TX **817-335-2551.** Rachel Barber, director, public relations

TEACHERS INSURANCE AND ANNUITY ASSOCIATION. 730 3rd Ave, New York, NY 10017. **212-490-9000.** William C Greenough, chairman and chief executive officer, Ext 2114. William T Slater, vice-president, Ext 2283. Claire M Sheahan, corporate communications specialist, Ext 2287

TEKTRONIX, INC. 14150 SW Karl Braun, Beaverton, OR 97005. **503-664-0161.** Earl Wantland, president. Susan Stone, manager, corporate communications

TELEDYNE INC. 1901 Avenue of the Stars, Los Angeles, CA 90067. **213-277-3311.** Berkley Baker, assistant to the president, public relations. Henry E Singleton, chief executive officer

TENNECO INC. 1010 Milan, Houston, TX 77001. **713-757-2131.** George O Jackson, director, public relations

TESORO PETROLEUM CORP. 8700 Tesoro Dr, San Antonio, TX 78286. **512-828-8484**

TEXACO, INC. 2000 Westchester Ave, White Plains, NY 10650. **914-253-4000.** Edgar Williams, media relations manager, Ext 3177. (h) **914-279-9026.** James F Robertson, assistant manager, media relations, Ext 3175. (h) **914-769-0168**

TEXAS EASTERN TRANSMISSION. PO Box 2521, Houston, TX 77001. **713-224-7961.** Fred Wichlep, director, public relations

TEXASGULF INC. High Ridge Park, Stamford, CT 06904. **203-358-5000.** Charles F Fogarty, chairman of the board and chief executive officer, **203-358-5227.** William D Askin, director, corporate public relations, **203-358-5028.** Night line: **203-323-5720.** Dr Gino P Giusti, vice-president, employee relations and administration, **203-358-5232**

Regional contacts. Devon Smith, Toronto, Ont, Canada. **416-869-1200.** Bob Upton, Raleigh, NC. **919-782-7070.** Clint White, Newgulf, TX. **713-657-4481**

TEXAS GULF SULPHUR *See* Texasgulf Inc.

TEXAS INSTRUMENTS. PO Box 5474, Dallas, TX 75222. **214-238-2011.** Richard M Perdue, director, corporate public relations, **214-238-3481**

TEXAS UTILITIES. 2001 Bryan Tower, Dallas, TX 75201. **214-653-4600.** James Ghiotto, director, public relations

TEXTRON INC. 40 Westminster St, Providence, RI 02903. **401-421-2800.** Robert Eisenhauer, vice-president, corporate relations

THIOKOL CORPORATION. Newportville Rd, Bristol, PA 19007. **215-946-9150.** Thomas Zack, director, corporate communications

THREE-M *See* Minnesota Mining and Manufacturing

TICOR (formerly The TI Corp). 6300 Wilshire Blvd, Los Angeles, CA 90048. **213-852-6300.** Rocco C Siciliano, chairman of the board and chief executive officer, **213-852-6301.** Craig Parsons, director, corporate public relations, **213-852-6340.** Night line: **213-826-1225.** James R Galbraith, vice-president, corporate communications, **213-852-6311**

TIME INC. Time & Life Bldg, Rockefeller Ctr, New York, NY 10020. **212-586-1212.** Donald M Wilson, vice-president, corporate and public affairs, **212-556-4151.** Louis J Slovinsky, manager, press relations, **212-556-3911**

TIMES MIRROR CO. 202 W 1st Ave, Los Angeles, CA 90053. **213-486-3700.** Paul Bertness, corporate public relations

TIMKEN CO. 1835 Dueber Ave SW, Canton, OH 44706. **216-453-4511.** Donald E Eagon, Jr, public relations manager, Ext 3126

TOLEDO EDISON. 300 Madison Ave, Toledo, OH 43652. **419-259-5000.** John R Dyer, assistant vice-president, public relations, **419-259-5157**

TOSCO CORPORATION (and Oil Shale Co.). 10100 Santa Monica Blvd, Los Angeles, CA 90067. **213-552-7000.** John H Powers, public relations manager, **213-552-7341**

Divisional contacts

Lion Oil Company, Avon Refinery. Martinez, CA. W E Redding. **415-228-1220**

Lion Oil Company. El Dorado, AR. Lindell Forbes. **501-863-3111**

TRAILWAYS (or Continental Trailways). 1500 Jackson, Dallas, TX 75201. **214-655-7895.** Fred G Currey, chairman of the board, **214-655-7800.** David Dunnigan, director, public relations, **214-655-7895.** Night line: **214-948-8908**

TRANE COMPANY. 3600 Pammel Creek Rd, La Crosse, WI 54601. **608-782-8000.** Thomas Hancock, chairman and chief executive officer. William G Roth, deputy chairman. Richard J Campbell, president and chief operating officer

Divisional contacts

Commercial Air Conditioning Division. Dennis R Bridges, manager, advertising and public relations

Consumer Products Division. Donald F Spriduso, manager, advertising

TRANSAMERICA CORPORATION. 600 Montgomery St, San Francisco, CA 94111. **415-983-4000.** Robert H Warren, director, corporate relations, **415-983-4087**

TRANS UNION CORP. 90 Half Day Rd, Lincolnshire, IL 60015. **312-295-4233.** J W Van Gorkom, president, **312-295-4350.** Joseph J Graves, Jr, director, corporate communications, **312-295-4233**

TRANS WORLD AIRLINES. 605 3rd Ave, New York, NY 10016. **212-557-3000.** Don Rosendale, vice-president, corporate communications

TRAVELERS INSURANCE COMPANIES (subsidiary of Travelers Corp.). 1 Tower Sq, Hartford, CT 06115. **203-277-0111.** Andrew Letendre, second vice-president, public relations and advertising, **203-277-4079**

TRW INC. 23555 Euclid Ave, Cleveland, OH 44117. **216-383-2121.** Stephen Bowen, director, public relations and advertising

TWENTIETH CENTURY FOX. 10201 W Pico Blvd, Los Angeles, CA 90035. **213-277-2211.** Jonas Rosenfield, Jr, vice-president, publicity. Mike Hunter, publicity manager, New York, **212-397-8500**

UNION BANCORP INC. (Union Bank). 445 S Figueroa St, Los Angeles, CA 90071. **213-687-6877.** John Reese, vice-president and director, advertising and public relations, **213-687-6473.** Night line: **714-968-2202**

UNION CAMP CORP. 1600 Valley Rd, Wayne, NJ 04740. **201-628-9000.** Thomas Freston, director, public relations

UNION CARBIDE CORPORATION. 270 Park Ave, New York, NY 10017.

212-551-2345. Marshall C Lewis, director, corporate communications, **212-551-2203.** Ralph A Leviton, assistant director, corporate communications, **212-551-2633**

UNION ELECTRIC COMPANY. PO Box 87, St Louis, MO 63166. **314-621-3222.** James Beisman, public relations. Herman Leibovich, assistant manager, public information

UNION OIL COMPANY OF CALIFORNIA. Union Oil Ctr, Los Angeles, CA 90017. **213-486-7600.** John H Robinson, manager, public relations

UNION PACIFIC CORPORATION. 345 Park Ave, New York, NY 10022. **212-826-8200.** Harvey S Turner, director, public relations

UNION PACIFIC RAILROAD (subsidiary of Union Pacific Corporation). 1416 Dodge St, Omaha, NE 68179. **402-281-5822.** John C Kenefick, president. Edwin C Schafer, general director, public relations, **402-271-3258.** (h) **402-346-9219.** Barry B Combs, director, **402-271-3476.** (h) **402-393-3295**

Regional contacts

Salt Lake City. 10 S Main, 84101. Clarence R Rockwell, director, public relations, **801-363-1544.** (h) **801-295-8140.** Wes D Soulier, assistant director, public relations, **801-363-1544.** (h) **801-581-0808**

Portland, OR. 720 Pittock Block, 921 SW Washington, 97205. George J Skorney, director, public relations, **503-288-8221.** (h) **503-235-2741.** Ray E Troyer, assistant director, **503-288-8221.** (h) **503-285-4398**

Los Angeles, CA. 5500 Ferguson Dr, 90022. John Forbes, director, **213-722-1200,** Ext 441. (h) **213-249-0934.** Allan Krief, assistant director, **213-685-4350.** Ext. 573. (h) **213-795-1282**

UNIROYAL INC. 2130 Avenue of the Americas, New York, NY 10020. **212-489-4000.** James Hill, director, corporate communications

UNITED AIRLINES. Box 66100, O'Hare International Airport, Chicago, IL 60666. **312-952-4000.** Jim Kennedy, director, public relations

UNITED BRANDS. 30 Rockefeller Plz, New York, NY 10020. **212-397-4000.** Ready access and night line: **212-397-4300.** Seymour Millstein, president and chief executive officer. Elkins Oliphant II, director, information, **212-397-4124.** Dennis A Sullivan, manager, media relations, **212-397-4127**

UNITED CALIFORNIA BANK. 707 Wilshire Blvd, Los Angeles, CA 90017. **213-614-4111.** Norman Barker, Jr, chairman and chief executive officer, **213-614-5001.** Robert W Campbell, manager, news and editoral services, **213-614-3655.** Night line: **213-377-4143.** Ralph A Cohen, assistant news bureau manager, **213-614-3656**

UNITED ILLUMINATING. 80 Temple St, New Haven, CT 06506. **203-777-7981.** Anne G Spinney, vice-president, communications

UNITED MERCHANTS AND MANUFACTURERS INC. 1407 Broadway, New York, NY 10018. **212-564-6000.** *Press contact.* Michael Morano

UNITED REFINING COMPANY. Bradley St, Warren, PA 16365. **814-723-1500**

UNITED STATES FIDELTY AND GUARANTY. Calvert and Redwood, Baltimore, MD 21203. **301-547-3000.** Roger Metelson, director, advertising and publicity, **301-547-3750**

UNITED STATES GYPSUM COMPANY. 101 S Wacker Dr, Chicago, IL 60606. **312-321-4000.** Graham J Morgan, chairman. Edward W Duffy, president, **312-321-4014.** *Press contact.* James J McLaughlin, vice-president, corporate marketing services. Night line: **312-824-3607.** D E Tiskus and S M Fitzgerald, public relations co-ordinators, **312-321-4000**

US INDUSTRIES INC. 250 Park Ave, New York, NY 10017. **212-697-4141.** I John Billera, chief executive officer. Doug Barnes, director, corporate communications, **203-259-4064**

US STEEL CORPORATION. Rm 5544, 600 Grant St, Pittsburgh, PA 14230. **412-433-6906.** Earl Mallick, vice-president, public affairs. Milton J Wurzbach, director, public affairs staff

US TOBACCO CO. 100 W Putnam Ave, Greenwich, CT 06830. **203-661-1100**

UNITED TECHNOLOGIES CORPORATION. United Technologies Bldg, Hartford, CT 06101. **203-728-7000.** Raymond D'Argenio, senior vice-president, communications. Francies L Murphy, vice-president, public relations and advertising, Ext 410. Francis J Giusti, corporate director, communications. Phillip Norton, manager, media relations

UNITED TELECOMMUNICATIONS, INC. 2330 Johnson Dr, Shawnee Mission, KS 66205. Mailing address: PO Box 11315, Kansas City, MO 64112. **913-384-7400.** Paul H Henson, chairman. J F McCarthy, vice-president, corporate communications, **913-384-7314.** (h) **816-333-8190.** D G Forsythe, director, publications and information, **913-384-7343**

UPJOHN CO. 7000 Portage Rd, Kalamazoo MI 49001. **616-323-4000.** Charles T Mangee, vice-president, public relations. Harry J Tomlinson, **616-324-4337**

VARIAN ASSOCIATES. 611 Hansen Way, Palo Alto, CA 94303. **415-493-4000.** Jon Wilcox, director, corporate communications

VF CORP. 1047 N Park Rd, Reading, PA 19610. **215-378-1151.** *Press contact.* Lori Tarnoski

VIRGINIA ELECTRIC AND POWER CO. 700 E Franklin St, Richmond, VA 23261. **804-771-3000.** Thomas R Fulghum, manager, public relations, **804-771-3629.** Michael J Molloy, director, public relations, **804-771-3195**

VOLKSWAGEN OF AMERICA, INC. Englewood Cliffs, NJ 07632. **201-894-5000.** J Stuart Perkins, president. Baron K Bates, director, public relations, **201-894-6310.** (h) **914-359-7027.** Philip A Hutchinson, Jr, government relations manager, **202-484-6096.** (h) **301-261-5243**

Divisional and regional contacts. Herbert W Williamson, VW Division public relations manager, **201-894-6306.** (h) **201-461-3043.** Andy Schupack, West Coast public relations, **213-390-8011.** (h) **213-399-3560.** Fred Heyler, Porsche-Audi public relations manager, **201-894-6304.** (h) **201-728-9454**

Volkswagen Manufacturing Corporation of America, Inc. Warren, MI 48089. **313-759-0900.** James W McLernon, president. Thomas F McDonald, public relations manager, (h) **313-645-0265.** Chester B Bahn, public relations manager, Westmoreland assembly plant, **412-696-6000.** (h) **412-439-1951**

VULCAN MATERIALS COMPANY. 1 Metroplex, Birmingham, AL 35209. **205-877-3000.** L Daniel Morris, Jr, **205-877-3206**

WALGREEN COMPANY. 200 Wilmot Rd, Deerfield, IL 60015. **312-948-5000.** David Carlson, manager, corporate information

WALLACE MURRAY *See* Murray, Wallace.

JIM WALTER CORP. 1500 N Dale Mabry, Tampa, FL 33607. **813-871-4811.** John Cassato, Jr, vice-president, public relations

WARD FOODS. 2 Pennsylvania Plz, New York, NY 10001. **212-594-5400**

WARNACO INC. 350 Lafayette St, Bridgeport, CT 06602. **203-579-8038.** John Maloney, director, public relations, (h) **203-374-3208**

WARNER-LAMBERT. 201 Tabor Rd, Morris Plains, NJ 07950. **201-540-2000.** Ron Zier, director, corporate relations. William A Logan, manager, professional relations

WASHINGTON GAS LIGHT CO. 1100 H St, NW, Washington, DC 20080. **703-750-4440.** John M Raymond, Jr, director, communications

WASHINGTON POST COMPANY (also publishes *Newsweek*). 1150 15th St NW, Washington, DC 20071. **202-223-6000.** Katharine Graham, chairman of the board and president. *Press contact for the Washington Post.* John M Dower, vice-president, communications, **202-223-5110**

WEAN UNITED. 948 Fort Duquesne Blvd, Pittsburgh, PA 15222. **412-261-6300.** *Press contact.* R J Wean III, vice-president

WELLS FARGO AND COMPANY (Wells Fargo Bank NA). 420 Montgomery St, San Francisco, CA 94104. **415-396-3606.** George F Caulfield, vice-president, public relations, **415-396-2507**
Wells Fargo Bank. Lona Jupiter, vice-president, public relations, **415-396-3983.** Peter Braddock, assistant vice-president, press bureau, **415-396-3710**

WEST POINT PEPPERELL INC. 4th St, West Point, GA 21833. **404-645-1111**

WESTERN BANCORPORATION. 707 Wilshire Blvd, Los Angeles, CA 90017. Mailing address: PO Box 54068, Los Angeles, CA 90054. **213-614-3001.** Ralph J Voss, chairman of the board and chief executive officer, **213-614-3004.** Arthur J Montgomery, assistant vice-president, **213-614-3016**

WESTERN UNION CORPORATION. 1 Lake St, Upper Saddle River, NJ 07458. **201-825-5000.** New York City tie-line: **212-371-3520.** Helen Horwitz, public relations manager

WESTINGHOUSE ELECTRIC CORPORATION. Westinghouse Bldg, Gateway Ctr,

Pittsburgh, PA 15222. **412-255-3500.** Robert E Kirby, chairman. Charles Carroll, director, public relations, **412-255-3370.** Ronald Hart, director, executive communications, **412-255-3373**

Regional contacts. Hal Daubert, Washington, DC. **202-833-5054.** Robert Henderson, New York, **212-692-5110**

WESTMORELAND COAL COMPANY. 123 S Broad St, Philadelphia, PA 19109. **215-545-0510.** Stephen Anderson, director, communications

WESTVACO CORPORATION. 299 Park Ave, New York, NY 10017. **212-688-5000.** Public relations managers: Harris W Le Few and Norman E Spell, Jr

WEYERHAUSER COMPANY. Tacoma, WA 98401. **206-924-2345.** William D Ruckelshaus, senior vice-president, law and corporate affairs. Bernard L Orell, vice-president, public affairs. *Washington, DC, office.* Keith Hundley, **202-293-7222**

Press contacts.

Corporate Information and Media Relations. Tom Ambrose, **206-924-3921.** (h) **206-839-1873.** Monty Dennison, **206-924-3922.** (h) **206-927-0953.** Helen Upperman, **206-924-3920.** (h) **206-272-5490**

Forest Recreation Information. Norman E Nelson, Jr, **206-924-3912**

Product Publicity. John F Ketter, Fiber, packaging, news business, **206-924-3471.** C W Masterman, wood products, **206-924-2963.** George Sherwood, paper, **215-825-1110**

WHEELABRATOR-FRYE INC. Liberty Ln, Hampton, NH 03842. **603-926-5911.** Steve Snulman, vice-president, corporate development

WHIRLPOOL CORPORATION. Administrative Ctr, Benton Harbor, MI 49022. **616-926-5000.** John H Platts, chairman of the board and chief executive officer, **616-926-3312.** Andrew J Takacs, director, government and public affairs, **616-926-3219.** Stephen R Sizer, manager, public relations, **616-926-3225**

WHITE CONSOLIDATED INDUSTRIES INC. 11770 Borea Rd, Cleveland, OH 44111. **216-252-3700**

WHITE MOTOR CORP. 35129 Curtis Blvd, Eastlake, OH, 44094. **216-951-2221.** Craig Thompson, vice-president, public relations, **216-951-4144.** (h) **216-751-0396**

WHITTAKER CORPORATION. 10880 Wilshire Blvd, Los Angeles, CA 90024. **213-475-9411.** Robert Murray, director, corporate communications

WICKES CORP. 110 West A St, San Diego, CA 92101. **714-238-0304.** Thomas Kennedy, corporate communications

WILLIAMETTE INDUSTRIES. Foot of North Portsmouth, Portland, OR 97203. **503-227-5581.** William Paxson, director, public relations, **503-926-7771**

WILLIAMS BROTHERS OVERSEAS COMPANIES. 320 Boston, Tulsa, OK 74103. **918-588-2000.** Ben Boddie, vice-president, corporate communications

WINN-DIXIE STORES INC. 5050 Edgewood Ct, Jacksonville, FL 32203. **904-783-1800.** Glen Woodward, vice-president, public relations

WITCO CHEMICAL CORPORATION. 277 Park Ave, New York, NY 10017. **212-644-6480.** Burt Dermer, manager, public relations

F W WOOLWORTH CO. 233 Broadway, New York, NY 10007. **212-227-1000.** E F Gibbons, president and chief executive officer. H P Smith, vice-president, public affairs. Night line: **203-661-7856.** Public relations counsel: Ernest Downing of Carl Byoir & Associates, Inc, **212-986-6100**

WM WRIGLEY JR COMPANY. 410 N Michigan Ave, Chicago, IL 60611. **312-644-2121.** David Sloane, assistant vice-president, communications

XEROX CORPORATION. Stamford, CT 06904. **203-329-8711.** Fred Isley, manager, public relations. Thomas C Abbott, manager, public relations operations. Thomas D Anglim, manager, international communications, **203-329-8711**

New York City. Alfred R Zipser, manager, press relations, **212-397-7399.** Robert N Stahl, manager, Broadcast relations, **212-397-7402**

Rochester, NY. John C Rasor, manager, news media relations. Earl Dobert, manager, editorial and information services, Information Systems Group, **716-423-5078.** Robert L Stearns, manager, product information and special events, **716-423-4265.** O K (Sam) Houston, manager, trade publication programs, **716-423-3535**

Western operations (El Segundo, CA). Sandy A Lanzarotta, manager, communications; Donald Ramsay, manager, public relations, Western operations, **213-679-4511**

Center for Training and Development. Harriette R Behringer, manager, public/community relations, Leesburg, VA **703-777-8000**

YELLOW FREIGHT SYSTEM, INC. 10990 Roe Ave, Shawnee Mission, KS 66207. **913-383-3000.** Donald L McMorris, president. Stephen P Murphy, vice-president, secretary. W H Glenn, director, investor relations. Jim Felkner, editor, corporate publications

ZENITH RADIO CORPORATION. 1000 Milwaukee Ave, Glenview, IL 60025. **312-391-7000.** William Nail, director, public relations, **312-391-8181**

STOCK AND COMMODITY EXCHANGES

AMERICAN STOCK EXCHANGE. 86 Trinity Pl, New York, NY 10006. **212-938-6000.** Night line: **212-938-2356.** Robert J Birnbaum, president. Paul Kolton, chairman of the board, **212-938-2401.** John J Sheehan, vice-president, press relations, **212-938-2350.** The number two national securities exchange

BOSTON STOCK EXCHANGE. 53 State St, Boston, MA 02109. **617-723-9500.** James E Dowd, president. Jane E Koloski, director, public relations

CHICAGO BOARD OF TRADE. 141 W Jackson Blvd, Chicago, IL 60604. **312-435-3500.** Robert K Wilmouth, president, **312-435-3603.** Edward M Lee, director, public relations, **312-435-3621.** Night line: **312-427-0964.** John Hundley, assistant manager, public relations, **312-435-3627**

The Chicago Board of Trade is the world's oldest and largest commodity futures market. Futures contracts traded include wheat, corn, oats, soybeans, soybean oil and meal, iced broiler chickens, plywood, gold, silver, long-term US Treasury bonds, 90-day commercial paper loans, and Government National Mortgage Association certificates ("Ginnie Maes"). The Chicago Board of Trade itself does not trade futures but provides facilities for its 1402 members to do so.

CHICAGO BOARD OPTIONS EXCHANGE. 141 W Jackson Blvd, Chicago, IL 60604. **312-431-5600.** *Press contact.* Joe Marconi, **312-431-5719** ˙

CHICAGO MERCANTILE EXCHANGE. 444 W Jackson Blvd, Chicago, IL 60606. **312-648-1000**

CINCINNATI STOCK EXCHANGE. 205 Dixie Terminal Bldg, Cincinnati, OH 45202. **513-621-1410.** D Rosemary Goodrich, executive secretary

INTERMOUNTAIN STOCK EXCHANGE. 39 Exchange Pl, Salt Lake City, UT 84111. **801-363-2531**

MIDAMERICA COMMODITY EXCHANGE. 175 W Jackson Blvd, Chicago, IL 60604. **312-939-0606.** David H Morgan, president, Beatrice B Briggs, director, marketing and public relations

MidAmerica is a commodity exchange that offers trading in futures contracts in grain, livestock, and metals. MidAmerica specializes in "mini" contracts, one-half to one-fifth the size of comparable contracts traded on other exchanges. The exchange has 1205 members, the second largest membership in the nation, and its annual trading volume ranks MidAmerica as the fourth most active of the nation's 10 commodity exchanges.

MIDWEST STOCK EXCHANGE, INC. 120 S LaSalle St, Chicago, IL 60603. **312-368-2222.** Michael E Tobin, president. Patricia Resseguie, public relations coordinator, **312-368-2573**

MONTREAL STOCK EXCHANGE. Stock Exchange Tower, 800 Victoria Sq, Montreal, Que, Canada H4Z 1A9. **514-871-2432**

NEW ORLEANS BOARD OF TRADE. 316 Board of Trade Pl, New Orleans, LA 70130. **504-525-3271**

NEW YORK COTTON EXCHANGE. 4 World Trade Ctr, SE Plaza Bldg, New York, NY 10048. **212-938-2650**

NEW YORK MERCANTILE EXCHANGE. 4 World Trade Ctr, New York, NY 10048. **212-938-2222.** Jacob Stern, chairman, **212-422-6718.** Richard B Levine, president, **212-938-2233.** Richard Elfenbein, public relations consultant, **212-532-3550.** (h) **201-484-4714.** Allen E Abrahams, PhD, vice-president, research and education; background information on economic aspects of commodity futures trading. Offers futures trading in the following commodities: Maine round white potatoes, platinum, palladium, US silver coins, gold, imported frozen and fresh boneless beef, international currency

NEW YORK PRODUCE EXCHANGE. 2 Broadway, New York, NY 10004. **212-269-3400**

NEW YORK STOCK EXCHANGE. 11 Wall St, New York, NY 10005. 212-623-3000. Philip J Keuper, vice-president, communications, 212-623-2080. Charles D Storer, director, media communications, 212-623-2076. The nations's major national securities exchange

OMAHA GRAIN EXCHANGE. 534 Grain Exchange Bldg, Omaha, NE 68102. 402-341-6733

PACIFIC STOCK EXCHANGE, INC. 618 S Spring St, Los Angeles, CA 90014. 213-489-4800. G Robert Ackerman, president, Ext 217. *San Francisco Office* (301 Pine St, San Francisco, CA 94104). 415-392-6533 or 415-393-4044. Howard Stubblefield, vice-president, marketing

PHILADELPHIA STOCK EXCHANGE, INC. 17th St and Stock Exchange Pl, Philadelphia, PA 19103. 215-563-4700. Elkins Wetherill, president. Karen Wickman, director, public relations. Marketplace for equity and options trading. Subsidiary: Stock Clearing Corporation of Philadelphia

SPOKANE STOCK EXCHANGE. 225 Peyton Bldg, Spokane, WA 99201. 509-624-4632

TORONTO STOCK EXCHANGE. 234 Bay St, Toronto, ON, Canada M5J 1R1. 416-363-6121

VANCOUVER STOCK EXCHANGE. 536 Howe St, Vancouver, BC, Canada V6C 2E1. 604-685-0331

THE FED

FEDERAL RESERVE SYSTEM: BOARD OF GOVERNORS. Federal Reserve Bldg, Constitution Ave between 20th and 21st Sts, Washington, DC 20551. 202-452-3000

Chairman. G William Miller

Governors. Stephen S Gardner, Henry C Wallach, Philip E Coldwell, Philip C Jackson, Jr, J Charles Partee, David M Lilly, Arthur F Burns

Staff Director for Monetary Policy. Stephen H Axilrod

Staff Director for Federal Reserve Bank Activities. William H Wallace

Staff Director for Management. John M Denkler

General Counsel. John D Hawke, Jr

Secretary. Theodore E Allison

Public Information Officers. Joseph R Coyne, 202-452-3204. Frank O'Brien, Jr, 202-452-3215

Division of Research and Statistics. James L Kichline, director

Division of International Finance. Edwin M Truman, director

Division of Banking Supervision and Regulation. John E Ryan, director

Division of Consumer Affairs. Janet O'Hart, director

Division of Federal Reserve Bank Operations. James R Kodlinski, director

Division of Federal Reserve Bank Examinations and Budgets.

Division of Administrative Services. Walter W Kreimann, director

Division of Data Processing. Charles L Hampton, director

Division of Personnel. David L Shannon, director

Controller. John Kakalec

Federal Reserve Banks and Branches

(Federal Reserve Banks are shown in capital letters; their respective branches follow.) For each branch listed, the person named is the vice-president in charge of the branch.

BOSTON. 30 Pearl St, Boston, MA 02106. 617-426-7100
President. Frank E Morris
First Vice-President. James A McIntosh

NEW YORK. 33 Liberty St, New York, NY 10045. 212-791-5000
President. Paul A Volcker
First Vice-President. Thomas M Timlen

Buffalo. 160 Delaware Ave, Buffalo, NY 14240. 716-849-5000. John T Keane

PHILADELPHIA. 925 Chestnut St, Philadelphia, PA 19105. 215-574-6000
President. David P Eastburn
First Vice-President. Richard L Smoot

CLEVELAND. 1455 E 6th St, Cleveland, OH 44101. 216-293-9800
President. Willis J Winn
First Vice-President. Walter H MacDonald

Cincinnati. 150 E 4th St, Cincinnati, OH 45201. 513-774-0011. Robert E Showalter

Pittsburgh. 717 Grant St, Pittsburgh, PA 15230. 412-723-7800. Robert D Duggan

RICHMOND. 100 N 9th St, Richmond, VA 23261. 804-649-3611

President. Robert P Black
First Vice-President. George C Rankin

Baltimore. 114 E Lexington St, Baltimore, MD 21203. 301-539-6552. Jimmie R Monhollon

Charlotte. 401 S Tryon St, Charlotte, NC 28230. 704-373-0200. Stuart P Fishburne

ATLANTA. 104 Marietta St NW, Atlanta, GA 30303. 404-231-8500
President. Monroe Kimbrel
First Vice-President. Kyle K Fossum

Birmingham. 1801 5th Ave N, Birmingham, AL 35202. 205-228-9141. Hiram J Honea

Jacksonville. 515 Julia St, Jacksonville, MS 32203. 904-947-4110. Edward C Rainey

Miami. 3770 SW 8th St, Coral Gables, FL 33134. 305-445-6281. W M Davis

Nashville. 301 8th Ave N, Nashville, TN 37203. 615-854-9006. Jeffrey J Wells

New Orleans. 525 St Charles Ave, New Orleans, LA 70161. 504-680-8011. George C Guynn

CHICAGO. 230 S LaSalle St, Chicago, IL 60690. 312-380-2320
President. Robert P Mayo
First Vice-President. Daniel M Doyle

Detroit. 160 Fort St W, Detroit, MI 48231. 313-961-6880. William C Conrad

ST LOUIS. 411 Locust St, St Louis, MO 63166. 314-421-1700
President. Lawrence K Roos
First Vice-President. Donald W Moriarty

Little Rock. 325 W Capitol Ave, Little Rock, AR 72203. 501-372-5451. John F Breen

Louisville. 410 S 5th St, Louisville, KY 40201. 502-587-7351. Donald L Henry

Memphis. 200 N Main St, Memphis, TN 38101. 901-523-7171. L Terry Britt

MINNEAPOLIS. 250 Marquette Ave, Minneapolis, MN 55480. 612-783-2345
President. Mark H Willes
First Vice-President. Clement A Van Nice

Helena. 400 N Park Ave, Helena, MT 59601. 406-585-5361. John D Johnson

KANSAS CITY. 925 Grand Ave, Kansas City, MO 64198. **816-881-2000**
President. Roger Guffey
First Vice-President. Henry R Czerwinski

Denver. 1020 16th St, Denver, CO 80217. **303-292-4020.** Wayne W Martin

Oklahoma City. 226 NW 3rd St, Oklahoma City, OK 73125. **405-235-1721.** William G Evans

Omaha. 102 S 17th St, Omaha, NE 68102. **402-341-3610.** Robert D Hamilton

DALLAS. 400 S Akard St, Dallas, TX 75222. **214-651-6111**

President. Ernest T Baughman
First Vice-President. Robert H Boykin

El Paso. 301 E Main St, El Paso, TX 79999. **915-544-4730.** Frederic W Reed

Houston. 1701 San Jacinto St, Houston, TX 77001. **713-659-4433.** J Z Rowe

San Antonio. 126 E Nueva St, San Antonio, TX 78295. **512-224-2141.** Carl H Moore

SAN FRANCISCO. 400 Sansome St, San Francisco, CA 94120. **415-450-2000**

President. John J Balles
First Vice-President. John B Williams

Los Angeles. 409 W Olympic Blvd, Los Angeles, CA 90051. **213-799-6312.** Richard C Dunn

Portland. 915 SW Stark St, Portland, OR 97208. **503-421-7584.** Angelo S Carella

Salt Lake City. 120 S State St, Salt Lake City, UT 84110. **801-588-0611.** A Grant Holman

Seattle. 1015 2nd Ave, Seattle, WA 98124. **206-399-1376.** James J Curran

CONSUMERS

FEDERAL AGENCY CONSUMER OFFICES AND CONTACTS

AGRICULTURE, DEPARTMENT OF. Special Assistant to the Secretary for Consumer affairs, Washington, DC 20250. **202-447-3165.** Nancy H Steorts

CIVIL AERONAUTICS BOARD. Director, Office of the Consumer Advocate, Washington, DC 20428. **202-382-6376.** Jack Yohe

COMMERCE, DEPARTMENT OF. Director, Office of the Ombudsman for Business, Washington, DC 20230. **202-967-4054.** John P Kearney

COMPTROLLER OF THE CURRENCY (Treasury). Consumer Affairs Division, Washington, DC 20219. **202-447-1600.** Thomas Taylor

CONSUMER PRODUCT SAFETY COMMISSION. Bureau of Information and Education, 501 Westbard Ave, Bethesda, MD 20207. **301-496-7621.** William White

DEFENSE, DEPARTMENT OF. Director, Personnel Services (Military Personnel Policy), Office of Assistant Secretary of Defense, Rm 2B-279, Pentagon, Washington, DC 20301. **202-697-9271.** Colonel Frank J Wasko, Jr

ENVIRONMENTAL PROTECTION AGENCY. Administrator, Environmental Protection Agency, 401 M St SW, Washington, DC 20460. **202-755-2700.** Russell Train

FEDERAL AVIATION ADMINISTRATION. Chief, Community and Consumer Liaison Division, Department of Transportation, Washington, DC 20591. **202-426-1960.** Frederick H Pelzman

FEDERAL COMMUNICATIONS COMMISSION. Consumer Liaison Officer, 1919 M St NW, Washington, DC 20554. **202-632-7213.** Alexander Korn

FEDERAL DEPOSIT INSURANCE CORPORATION. Office of Bank Customer Affairs, 550-17th St NW, Washington, DC 20429. **202-393-8400**

FEDERAL ENERGY ADMINISTRATION. Director, Office of Consumer Affairs/Special Impact, Rm 4310, Federal Bldg, 12th St and Pennsylvania Ave NW, Washington, DC 20461. **202-961-6055.** Hazel Rollins

FEDERAL HOME LOAN BANK BOARD. Office of Housing and Urban Affairs, 320 1st St NW, Washington, DC 20552. **202-376-3262.** Robert S Warwick

FEDERAL POWER COMMISSION. Director, Public Information, 825 N Capitol St, Washington, DC 20426. **202-275-4006.** William L Webb

FEDERAL RESERVE SYSTEM. Office of Saver and Consumer Affairs, Washington, DC 20551. **202-452-3401.** Frederic Solomon

FEDERAL TRADE COMMISSION. The Secretary, 6th St and Pennsylvania Ave NW,

Washington, DC 20580. Attention: Correspondence. **202-962-0378**

FOOD AND DRUG ADMINISTRATION. Director, Consumer Inquiries Office, 5600 Fishers Ln. Rockville, MD 20856. **301-443-3170.** Dr Ruth Beeler White

GENERAL SERVICES ADMINISTRATION. Administrator, 18th and F St NW, Washington, DC 20405. **202-343-6161.** Jack Eckerd

GOVERNMENT PRINTING OFFICE. Superintendent of Documents. Attention: Customer Information Branch, Service Section, Washington, DC 20402. **202-275-3050**

HEALTH, EDUCATION, AND WELFARE, DEPARTMENT OF (Administration on Aging). Director, National Clearinghouse on Aging, Administration on Aging, Washington, DC 20201. **202-245-0669.** Dr Clark Tibbitts

HEALTH, EDUCATION, AND WELFARE, DEPARTMENT OF (Office of Education). Commissioner's Correspondence Staff, Rm 4044, Federal Office Bldg 6, Washington, DC 20201

HEALTH, EDUCATION, AND WELFARE, DEPARTMENT OF (Social and Rehabilitation Service). Rm 3116, HEW South Bldg, Washington, DC 20201. Paul Howard

HEALTH, EDUCATION, AND WELFARE, DEPARTMENT OF (Social Security Administration). Office of External Affairs, Rm 100, Altmeyer Bldg, Baltimore, MD 21235. **301-594-2302.** Sarah M Juni

HOUSING AND URBAN DEVELOPMENT, DEPARTMENT OF. Special Assistant to the Secretary, Washington, DC 20410. **202-755-7976.** Wilbur Jones

INTERIOR, DEPARTMENT OF. Departmental Consumer Liaison, Rm 5134, Washington, DC 20240. **202-343-6007.** Lena P Beauregard

INTERSTATE COMMERCE COMMISSION. Consumer Affairs Office, Washington, DC 20423. **202-373-4141.** Warner L Baylor

JUSTICE, DEPARTMENT OF. Consumer Affairs Section, Antitrust Division, Rm 7601, Main Justice, Washington, DC 20530. **202-739-4174**

LABOR, DEPARTMENT OF. Consumer Representative Office of Information, Washington, DC 20210. **202-524-7316**

NATIONAL HIGHWAY TRAFFIC SAFETY ADMINISTRATION. Chief, Consumer Affairs, NHTSA, Washington, DC 20590. **202-426-0670.** Gilbert L Watson

PUBLIC HEALTH SERVICE. Rm 17B08, Parklawn Bldg, 5600 Fishers Ln, Rockville, MD 20852. **301-443-6656.** Martin Frankel

RAIL SERVICES PLANNING OFFICE. Public Counsel, 1900 L St NW, Washington, DC 20036. **202-254-3900.** A Grey Staples

SECURITIES AND EXCHANGE COMMISSION. Director, Office of Public Information, Washington, DC 20549. **202-755-4846.** S James Rosenfeld

SMALL BUSINESS ADMINISTRATION. Administrator, 1441 L St NW, Rm 1008, Washington, DC 20416. **202-382-5181.** Thomas S Kleppe

STATE, DEPARTMENT OF. Claims Officer, Office of Special Consular Services, Washington, DC 20520. **202-632-3651**

TRANSPORTATION, DEPARTMENT OF. Director, Office of Consumer Affairs, Washington, DC 20590. **202-426-4518.** Antonina P Uccello

TREASURY, DEPARTMENT OF. Special Assistant to the Secretary for Consumer Affairs, Rm 1454, Main Treasury, Washington, DC 20220. Dave Le Feve

US POSTAL SERVICE. Consumer Advocate, Washington, DC 20260. **202-245-4550.** Thomas W Chadwick

STATE AND LOCAL CONSUMER OFFICES

ALABAMA

Governor's Office of Consumer Protection. 138 Adams Ave, Montgomery, 36103. **205-832-5936. 800-392-5658.** Annie Laurie Gunter, director

Consumer Services Coordinator, Office of Attorney General. 669 S Lawrence St, Montgomery, 36107. **205-832-6820.** J Thomas Brassell

ALASKA

Assistant Attorney General, Consumer Protection Section, Office of Attorney General. Suite 105, 360 K St, Anchorage, 99501. **907-279-0428.** Connie J Sipe, **907-274-9033**

ARIZONA

Chief Counsel, Economic Protection Division, Department of Law. 159 State Capitol Bldg, Phoenix, 85007. **602-271-5763.** Anthony B Ching

Pima County. Consumer Protection Division, Pima County Attorney's Office, 9th Floor, 111 W Congress, Tucson, 85701. **602-792-8668.** Robert C Brauchli, director

Phoenix. Consumer Affairs Operation, Mayor's Citizens Assistance Office, 251 W Washington, Phoenix, 85002. **602-262-7777.** Lillian Hoyos, director

Tucson. Supervising Attorney, Consumer Affairs and Human Relations, Public Affairs Division, Tucson City Attorney's Office, Suite 2027 2302 E Speedway, (PO Box 27210), Tucson, 85726. **602-791-4886.** Ronald M Detrick

ARKANSAS

Consumer Counsel, Consumer Protection Division, Office of Attorney General. Justice Bldg, Little Rock, 72201. **501-371-2341. 800-482-8982.** Nathan M Norton, Jr

Deputy Commissioner/Chief Counsel, Consumer Service Division, Department of Insurance. University Tower Bldg, 12th and University, 400-18, Little Rock, 72204. **501-371-1325.** Bill Woodyard

CALIFORNIA

Department of Consumer Affairs. 1020 N St, Sacramento, 95814. **916-445-1254.**

800-952-2880 (auto repair complaints only). Taketsugu Takei, director. *Branch offices.* Rm 8020, 107 Broadway, Los Angeles, 90012. **213-620-2003.** Rm 2100, 30 Van Ness Ave, San Francisco, 94102. **415-557-2046**

Deputy Attorney General, Environment/Consumer Protection Section, Office of Attorney General. 350 McAllister St, San Francisco, 94102. **800-952-5225** (consumer complaints in California) **916-952-5225** (consumer complaints from out of state). E Clement Shute

Consumer Affairs Division, Department of Insurance. 600 S Commonwealth Ave, Los Angeles, 90005. **213-620-4639** (insurance only). *Branch office.* 1407 Market St, San Francisco, 94103. **415-557-3646**

Alameda County. Deputy District Attorney for Consumer Protection, Almeda County Office of District Attorney, Rm 207, 125 12th St, Oakland, 94607. **415-874-5656.** Frederic M Hanelt

Fresno County. Consumer Fraud Division, District Attorney's Office, 1100 Van Ness Ave Courthouse, Fresno, 93721. **209-488-3135.** Brinton Bowles, assistant district attorney

Los Angeles County. Consumer and Environment Protection Division, District Attorney's Office, 540 Hall of Records, 320 W Temple, Los Angeles, 90012. **213-974-3974.** Gill Garcetti, director

Los Angeles County. Department of Consumer Affairs, 500 W Temple St, Los Angeles, 90012. **213-974-2417.** Shirley Goldinger, director, **213-974-9750.** Len Cassel, public information officer, **213-974-9757**

Marin County. District Attorney, Consumer Fraud Division, Rm 155, Hall of Justice, Civic Ctr, San Rafeal, 94903. **415-479-1100**

Monterey County. Department of Consumer Affairs, 1220 Natividad Rd, Salinas, 93901. **408-758-3859.** Paul Angelucci, director, weights, measures, and consumer affairs

Orange County. Office of Consumer Affairs, 511 N Sycamore St, Santa Ana, 92701. **714-834-6100.** M S Shimanoff, director

San Diego County. Consumer Fraud Division, District Attorney's Office, 220 W Broadway, San Diego, 92101. **714-236-2382.** M James Lorenz, director

Long Beach Division of Consumer Affairs. 333 W Ocean Blvd, Long Beach, 90802. **213-590-6375.** Charlotte Pownell, director

COLORADO

Attorney General's Consumer Section. 3rd Floor, 1525 Sherman St, Denver, 80203. **303-892-3611.** Tucker K Trautman, first assistant attorney general

CONNECTICUT

Department of Consumer Protection. State Office Bldg, Hartford, 06115. **203-566-2294. 800-842-2649.** Mary M Heslin, commissioner

Consumer Counsel, Office of Consumer Counsel, Connecticut Public Utility Commission. State Office Bldg, 165 Capitol Ave, Hartford, 06115. **203-566-7287.** David Silverstone

Middletown. Office of Consumer Protection, City Hall, Middletown, 06457. **203-347-4671.** Guy J Tommasi, director

DELAWARE

Consumer Affairs Division, Department of Community Affairs and Economic Development. 6th Floor, 200 W 9th St, Wilmington, 19801. **302-571-3250.** Frances M West, director

DISTRICT OF COLUMBIA

Director, District of Columbia Office of Consumer Protection. 1407 L St NW, Washington, 20005. **202-629-2617** or **5944**

FLORIDA

Department of Legal Affairs. State Capitol, Tallahassee, 32304. **904-488-4481.** Clarence Holmes, consumer counsel, Consumer Protection and Fair Trade Practices Bureau

Bureau of Consumer Research and Education, Department of Insurance. LL-25, State Capitol, Tallahassee, 32304. **904-488-6084** (insurance only). David N Lakin, chief

Department of Consumer Affairs, Public Service Commission. Fletcher Bldg, Tallahassee, 32304. **904-488-7238. 800-342-3552** (utility complaints only). George B Hanna, director

Broward County. Office of Consumer Affairs, Rm 202, 200 SE 6th St, Fort Lauderdale, 33301. **305-765-5307.** Harry M Appel, director

Dade County. Consumer Protection Division, Metropolitan Dade County, 16th Floor, 140 W Flagler St, Miami, 33130. **305-579-4222.** John C Mays, director

Dade County. Consumer Advocate, Office of County Manager, 16th Floor, 140 W Flagler St, Miami, 33130. **305-579-4222.** Walter T Dartland

Hillsboro County. Hillsboro County Department of Consumer Affairs, 4th Floor, 3725 W Grace St, Tampa, 33607. **813-272-6750.** Sam Uccello, director

Palm Beach County. Department of Consumer Affairs, 301 N Olive Ave, West Palm Beach, 33401. **305-837-2670.** Alice C Skaggs, director

St Petersburg. Director, Division of Consumer Affairs, 175 5th St N, St Petersburg, 33701. **813-893-7395.** William M Bateman Jr

GEORGIA

Governor's Office of Consumer Affairs. Suite 400, 225 Peachtree St NE, Atlanta, 30303. **404-656-3790. 800-282-4900.** Dr Tim C Ryles, administrator

Consumers' Utility Counsel of Georgia. 15 Peachtree St, Atlanta, 30303. **404-656-3982.** Wheeler Bryan

Atlanta. Office of Consumer Affairs, City Hall-Memorial Dr Annex, 121 Memorial Dr, SW, Atlanta, 30303. **404-658-6704.** Muriel Mitchell Smith, director

HAWAII

Director of Consumer Protection, Office of Governor. 602 Kamamalu Bldg, 250 S King St, (PO Box 3767), Honolulu, 96811. **808-548-2560** (administration). **808-584-2540** (complaints). Walter T Yamashiro

IDAHO

Deputy Attorney General, Consumer Protection Division, Office of Attorney General. Rm 225, State Capitol, Boise, 83720. **208-384-2400.** Rudy Barchas

ILLINOIS

Consumer Advocate's Office, Office of Governor. Rm 2010, State of Illinois Bldg, 160 N LaSalle Street, Chicago, 60601. **312-793-2755. 312-793-2754.** Gerald J Rafferty, administrative assistant

Assistant Attorney and Chief Consumer Protection and Franchise Division, Office of Attorney General. 500 S 2nd S, Springfield, 62706. **217-782-1090.** Tim J Bonansinga

Cook County. Consumer Complaint Division, Office of State's Attorney. Suite 303, Civic Ctr, Randolph at Clark, Chicago, 60602. **312-443-8425.** John P Brundage, supervisor

Chicago. Commissioner, Department of Consumer Sales, Weights, and Measures, City Hall, 121 N LaSalle Street, Chicago, 60602. **312-744-4092.** Jane M Byrne

Park Forest. Commission Liaison Officer, Consumer Protection Commission, Village Hall, 200 Forest Blvd, Park Forest, 60466. **312-748-1112.** Norman M Dublin

INDIANA

Director, Consumer Protection Division, Office of Attorney General. 215 State House, Indianapolis, IN 46204. **317-633-6496** or **6276. 800-382-5516.** David A Miller, assistant attorney general

Office of Public Counselor. 807 State Office Bldg, Indianapolis, 46204. **317-633-4659**

(utilities only). Frank J Biddinger, public counselor

Gary. Office of Consumer Affairs, City of Gary, Annex E, 1100 Massachusetts, Gary, 46402. **219-883-8532, 8533,** or **8534.** Brian Nelson, director

IOWA

Consumer Protection Division, Office of Attorney General. 1209 E Ct, Executive Hills W, Des Moines, 50319. **515-281-5926.** Julian B Garrett, assistant attorney general in charge

KANSAS

Consumer Protection Division, Office of Attorney General. State Capitol, Topeka, 66612. **913-262-3751.** William Griffin, assistant attorney general and chief

Kansas City. Department of Consumer Affairs, Rm 350, Municipal Office Bldg, 1 Civic Plz, 701 N 7th St, Kansas City, 66101. **913-371-2000,** Ext 230 or 231. Joe L Wilhm, director

Topeka. Assistant City Attorney, Consumer Protection Division, City Attorney's Office, 215 E 7th St, Topeka, 66603. **913-295-3883.** Douglas S Wright

KENTUCKY

Assistant Deputy Attorney General, Consumer Protection Division, Office of Attorney General. Rm 34, State Capitol, Frankfort, 40601. **502-564-6607. 800-372-2960.** Robert V Bullock

Jefferson County. Consumer Protection Department, Rm 401, 208 S 5th St, Louisville, 40202. **502-581-6280.** David R Vandeventer, director

Louisville. Department of Consumer Affairs, 701 W Jefferson St, Louisville, 40204. **502-587-3595.** Minx M Auerbach, director

LOUISIANA

Office of Consumer Protection, Department of Urban and Community Affairs. 1885 Wooddale Blvd, 1218 (PO Box 44091, Capitol Station), Baton Rouge, 70804. **504-389-7483. 800-272-9868.** Charles W Tapp, assistant secretary

East Baton Rouge Parish. Consumer Protection Ctr, 1779 Government St, Baton Rouge, 70802. **504-344-8506.** Elliott P Smart, acting director

Monroe. Office of Consumer Affairs, City Plz, Monroe City Hall, Monroe, 71201. **504-387-3521.** John L Russell, administrative assistant

New Orleans. Mayor's Office of Consumer Affairs, City Hall-1W12, New Orleans, 70112. **504-586-4441.** Nell Weekly, director

MAINE

Bureau of Consumer Protection/Consumer Credit. 51 Chapel St, Augusta, 04330. **207-289-3731** (credit, truth-in-lending, collection agencies). John E Quinn, superintendent

MARYLAND

Office of Attorney General, Chief Consumer Protection Division. 131 E Redwood St, Baltimore, 21202. **301-383-5344.** John N Ruth

People's Counsel, Public Service Commission. 301 W Preston St, Baltimore, 21201. **301-383-2375.** John K Keane, Jr

Anne Arundel County. Board of Consumer Affairs, Rm 403, Arundel Ctr, Annapolis, 21404. **301-224-7300.** Nancy Eilers, coordinator

Baltimore County. Assistant State's Attorney and Chief, Consumer Fraud Division, State's Attorney's Office, 316 Equitable Bldg, Baltimore, 21202. **301-396-4997.** Gerald Glass

Montgomery County. Office of Consumer Affairs, 24 Maryland Ave, Rockville, 20850. **301-340-1010.** Barbara B Gregg, executive director

Prince Georges County. Consumer Protection Commission, Rm 1142, County Administration Bldg, Upper Marlboro, 20870. **301-952-4700.** Albert R Wynn, executive director

MASSACHUSETTS

Consumer Complaint Division, Executive Office of Consumer Affairs. John W McCormack Bldg, 1 Ashburton Pl, Boston, 02108. **617-727-8000.** Barbara J Newman, director Lola Dickerman, secretary

Consumer Protection Division, Department of Attorney General. John W McCormack State Office Bldg, 1 Ashburton Pl, Boston, 02108. **617-727-7591.** Paula W Gold, chief

Boston. Boston Consumers' Council, Rm 401, City Hall, Boston, 02201. **617-725-3320.** Richard A Borten, director

Lowell. Consumer Advisory Council, City Hall, Lowell, 01852. **617-454-8821.** Donald P Pizzano, chairman

MICHIGAN

Michigan Consumers Council. 414 Hollister Bldg, Lansing, 48933. **517-373-0947.** Linda Joy, executive director

Wayne County. Consumer Protection Agency, 601 Lafayette Bldg, 144 W Lafayette, Detroit, 48226. **313-224-2150.** F Clifton Lind, director, **313-224-2157**

Detroit. City Consumer Affairs Department, 10801 Curtis, Detroit, 48221. **313-224-3508. 313-342-6500.** Esther K Shapiro, director

MINNESOTA

Minneapolis. Consumer Services Division, Department of Licenses and Consumer Services, 101A City Hall, 3rd Ave and 4th St, Minneapolis, 55415. **612-348-2080.** John A Bergquist, director

MISSISSIPPI

Consumer Protection Division, Department of Agriculture and Commerce. High and President Sts (PO Box 1609), Jackson, 39205. **601-354-6566.** Bruce Bryant

MISSOURI

Missouri Consumer Information Center, Department of Consumer Affairs, Regulation and Licensing. PO Box 1157, Jefferson City, 65101. **314-751-4996.** David E Duelling, director

Kansas City. Consumer Affairs Specialist, Action Ctr, City Hall, Kansas City, 64106. **816-274-2222.** Tom Hogan

MONTANA

Consumer Affairs Division, Department of Business Regulation. 805 N Main St, Helena, 59601. **406-449-3163.** Dick M Disney, administrator

Montana Consumer Counsel. 330 Fuller Ave, Helena, 59601. **406-449-2771. 406-449-2772** (utility and transportation matters only). Geoffrey Brazier

NEBRASKA

Consumer Consultant, Nebraska Department of Agriculture. PO Box 94947, 301 Centennial Mall S, Lincoln, 68609. **402-471-2341.** Linda Bortis

Douglas County. Consumer Fraud Division, County Attorney's Office, Rm 909, Omaha-Douglas Civic Ctr, 18th and Farnam Sts, Omaha, 68102. **402-444-7625.** Arthur S Raznick, director

NEVADA

Consumer Affairs Division, Department of Commerce. Suite 304, 2501 E Sahara Ave, Las Vegas, 89104. **702-385-0344. 800-992-0900.** Rex W Lundberg, commissioner

Division of Consumer Relations, Public Service Commission.. Kinkead Bldg, 505 E King St, Carson City, 89710. **702-885-4180.** R B Clark, director.

Washoe County. Investigator-in-Charge, Consumer Protection Division, District Attorney's Office, PO Box 11130, Reno, 89510. **702-785-5652.** Shirley Katt

NEW JERSEY

Department of Public Advocate. PO Box 141, Trenton, 08625. **609-292-7087. 800-792-8600** (state agency action only). Stanley Van Ness, public advocate, division of administration

Assistant Commissioner, Consumer Services, Department of Insurance. 201 E State St, Trenton, 08625. **609-292-5364.** Dr Eleanor J Lewis

NEW MEXICO

Consumer and Economic Crimes Division, Office of Attorney General. PO Drawer 1508, Santa Fe, 87501. **505-988-8851.** Robert N Hilgendorf, director

Bernalillo County. Office of Consumer Affairs, Second Judicial District Attorney's Office, 403, Copper NW, Albuquerque, 87102. **505-766-4340.** Elton L Boyd, director

NEW YORK

Consumer Protection Board. Rm 1000, 99 Washington Ave, Albany, 12210. **518-474-8583.** Rosemary Pooler, chairman and executive director. *Branch office.* Rm 8225, 82nd Floor, 2 World Trade Ctr, New York, 10047. **212-488-5666**

Assistant Attorney General in Charge, Consumer Frauds and Protection Bureau, Office of Attorney General. 2 World Trade Ctr, New York, 10047. **212-488-7530.** Barnett Levy

Assistant Attorney General, Consumer Frauds and Protection Bureau, Office of Attorney General. State Capitol, Albany, 12224. **518-474-8686.** Frank S Pantalone

Consumer Complaint Bureau, State Insurance Department. 2 World Trade Ctr, New York, 10047. **212-488-4005** (insurance only). Nathan Silver, chief

Erie County. Consumer Protection Committee, Office of Erie County Executive, 95 Franklin Rd, Buffalo 14202. **716-846-6690.** Elizabeth Bowen, chairwoman

Monroe County. Consumer Affairs Council, Rm 410C, County Office Bldg, Rochester, 14614. **716-381-1833.** Patricia Haydanek, chairwoman

Nassau County. Office of Consumer Affairs, 160 Old Country Rd, Mineola, 11501. **516-535-3282.** James E Picken, commissioner. Ina Alcabes, public information specialist, **516-535-3860**

Oneida County. Consumer Advocate, County Office Bldg, 800 Park Ave, Utica, 13501. **315-798-5601.** Virginia Gallagher

Onondaga County. Office of Consumer Affairs, County Civic Ctr, 421 Montgomery St, Syracuse, 13202. **315-477-7911.** Erik Dressler, director

Suffolk County. Department of Consumer Affairs, Suffolk County Ctr, Veterans Highway, Hauppauge, 11787. **516-979-3100.** James J Lack, commissioner

New York City. Department of Consumer Affairs, 80 Lafayette St, New York, 10013. **212-566-5456.** Bruce C Ratner, commissioner

Schenectady. Bureau of Consumer Protection, Rm 206, City Hall, Jay St, Schenectady, 12305. **518-382-5061 or 5062.** D A Massaroni, director

Syracuse. Director, Consumer Affairs Office, Rm 419, City Hall, 233 E Washington St, Syracuse, 13202. **315-473-3240.** Jeanne L Schultheis, director

NORTH CAROLINA

Special Deputy Attorney General and Director, Consumer Protection Division, Office of Attorney General. PO Box 629, Justice Bldg, Raleigh, 27602. **919-733-7741.** John R B Matthis

NORTH DAKOTA

Assistant Attorney General and Counsel, Consumer Fraud Division, Office of Attorney General. State Capitol, Bismarck, 58501. **701-224-2210.** Dale V Sandstrom

OHIO

Cincinnati. Consumer Protection Division, City Solicitor's Office, Rm 236, City Hall, Cincinnati, 45202. **513-352-3971.** Noel M Morgan, chief

Cleveland. Office of Consumer Affairs, Rm 119, City Hall, 601 Lakeside Ave, Cleveland, 44114. **216-694-3200.** Luke Owens, director

Columbus. Program Administrator, Consumer Affairs, Department of Community Services, 720 E Broad St, Columbus, 43215. **614-222-7397.** Dorothy S Teater

Dayton. Consumer Advocate, Consumer Services Division, 7 E 4th St, Dayton, 45402. **513-225-5048.** Ronald C Roat

Toledo. Consumer Protection Agency, Suite 1120, 420 Madison Ave, Toledo, 43604. **419-247-6191.** Thomas E Fought, chief

OKLAHOMA

Department of Consumer Affairs. Rm 460, Jim Thorpe Bldg, Oklahoma City, 73105. **405-521-3653.** Patrick C Ryan, administrator

OREGON

Consumer Protection Division, Office of Attorney General. 500 Pacific Bldg, 520 SW Yamhill, Portland, 97204. **503-229-5522.** Ross L Laybourn, chief counsel

Consumer Services Division, Department of Commerce. Salem, 97310. **503-378-4320.** Caroline Wilkins, administrator

PENNSYLVANIA

Bureau of Consumer Protection, Office of Attorney General. 301 Market St, Harrisburg, 17101. **717-787-9714.** Joel Weisburg, deputy attorney general and director

Bureau of Consumer Protection, Department of Justice. 342–44 N Broad St, Philadelphia, 19102. **215-238-6475.** John E Kelly, deputy attorney general

Allegheny County. Bureau of Consumer Affairs, 3rd Floor, Jones Law Annex, 4th and Ross Sts, Pittsburgh, 15219. **412-355-5402.** Rick Chess, director

Bucks County. Department of Consumer Protection, Courthouse Annex, Broad and Union Sts, Doylestown, 18901. **215-348-2911,** Ext, 496. Peggy H Adams, director, (h) **215-795-2149**

Montgomery County. County Consumer Affairs, County Courthouse, Norristown, 19404. **215-275-5000,** Ext 228. Betty B Linker, director

Westmoreland County. Bureau of Consumer Affairs, 3rd Floor, Box Q, 102 W Otterman St, Greenburg, 15601. **412-836-6170.** Bruce C Tobin, director

Philadelphia. Mayor's Office of Consumer Services, Rm 143, City Hall, Philadelphia, 19107. **215-686-2798.** Thomas McIntosh, director

Pittsburgh. Office of Consumer Advocate, City-County Bldg, Pittsburgh, 15219. **412-281-3900,** Ext 538. Kathryn Katsafanas, consumer advocate

PUERTO RICO

Department of Consumer Affairs. Minillas Governmental Ctr, Torre Norte Bldg, De Diego Ave, Stop 22 (PO Box 13934), Santurce, 00908. **809-726-6090 or 8190.** Federico Hernandez Denton, secretary

RHODE ISLAND

Rhode Island Consumer's Council. 365 Broadway, Providence, 02902. **401-277-2764.** Edwin P Palumbo, executive director

SOUTH CAROLINA

Department of Consumer Affairs. Five Points Bldg, 2221 Devine St (PO Box 5757), Columbia, 29250. **803-758-2040.** **800-922-1594.** Irvin D Parker, administrator

SOUTH DAKOTA

Department of Commerce and Consumer Affairs. State Capitol, Pierre, 57501. **605-224-3177.** John Culberson, deputy secretary

TENNESSEE

Office of Attorney General and Reporter. 450 James Robertson Pkwy, Nashville, 37219.

615-741-1671. William C Koch, Jr, deputy attorney general

TEXAS

Office of Attorney General. PO Box 12548, Capitol Station, Austin, 78711. **512-475-3288.** Philip K Maxwell, assistant attorney general and chief, consumer protection division

Travis County. Consumer Affairs Office, 624 Pleasant Valley Rd, Austin, 78702. **512-474-6554.** Rory M O'Malley, consumer coordinator

Dallas. Department of Consumer Affairs, Rm 108, City Hall, Dallas, 75201. **214-744-1133.** Charles H Vincent, director

San Antonio. Office of Consumer Services, Department of Human Resources, Bldg 249, 600 Hemisfair Way, San Antonio, 78205. **512-226-4301.** Richard J Brown, director

UTAH

Division of Consumer Affairs, Utah Trade Commission, Department of Business Regulation. 330 E 4th S, Salt Lake City, 84111. **801-533-6441.** Eueda McCoy Stevenson, executive secretary

VERMONT

Consumer Protection Division, Office of Attorney General. 109 State St, Montpelier, 05602. **802-828-3385 or 3171.** John J Easton, Jr, assistant attorney general in charge

VIRGINIA

Office of Consumer Affairs, Department of Agriculture and Commerce. 825 E Broad St, Richmond, 23219. **804-786-2042. 800-552-9963** (regarding state agencies). Roy L Farmer, administrator of consumer affairs

Arlington County. Office of Consumer Affairs, 2049 15th St, North Arlington, 22201. **703-558-2142.** Charles E Hammond, executive director

Fairfax County. Department of Consumer Affairs, Suite 402, Erlich Bldg, 4031 University Dr, Fairfax, 22030. **703-691-3214.** Ronald B Mallard, acting director

Prince William County. Office of Consumer Affairs, Garfield Administration Bldg, 15920 Cardinal Dr, Woodbridge, 22191. **703-221-4156.** Peter Drymalski, director

Alexandria. Office of Consumer Affairs, 405 Cameron St, Alexandria, 22314. **703-750-6675 or 6697.** Wendy Alfsen-Cleveland, consumer affairs coordinator

Newport News. Office of Consumer Affairs, City Hall, 2400 Washington Ave, Newport News, 23607. **804-247-8616 or 8618.** James F Topping, Sealer of Weights and Measures

Norfolk. Division of Consumer Protection, Rm 804, City Hall Bldg, Norfolk, 23501. **804-441-2821.** Martin D Greenwell, chief

Virginia Beach. Division of Consumer Protection, Municipal Ctr, Virginia Beach, 23456. **804-427-4421.** J N McClanan, consumer protection officer

VIRGIN ISLANDS (US)
Consumer Services Administration, Office of the Governor. Golden Rock Shopping Ctr, Christiansted, St Croix, 00820. **809-773-2226.** Dr Dorene Carter, director

WASHINGTON
Consumer Protection and Antitrust Division, Office of Attorney General. 1366 Dexter

Horton Bldg, 710 2nd Ave, Seattle, 98104. **206-464-7744. 800-552-0700.** Thomas L Boeder, assistant attorney and chief

Seattle. Department of Licenses and Consumer Affairs, Rm 102, Municipal Bldg, 600 4th Ave, Seattle, 98104. **206-625-2536.** Audrey L Olson, director

WEST VIRGINIA
Consumer Protection Division, Office of Attorney General. State Capitol, Charleston, 25305. **304-348-8986.** James S Arnold, director

Charleston. Consumer Protection Depart-

ment, PO Box 2749, Charleston, 25330. **304-348-8172** or **8173.** Jane Theiling, director

WISCONSIN
Office of Consumer Protection, Wisconsin Department of Justice. State Capitol, Madison, 53702. **608-266-7340.** Barbara Anderson, consumer affairs coordinator

WYOMING
Office of Attorney General. Capitol Bldg, Cheyenne, 82002. **307-777-7384.** Art Hanscum, special assistant attorney general

LABOR

NATIONAL AND INTERNATIONAL LABOR FEDERATIONS

AMERICAN FEDERATION OF LABOR AND CONGRESS OF INDUSTRIAL ORGANIZATIONS (AFL-CIO). 815 16th St NW, Washington, DC 20006. **202-637-5000.** George Meany, president. Lane Kirkland, secretary-treasurer. Albert J Zack, director, department of public relations. **202-637-5010.** Night line: **202-484-8282.** Consists of 50 state federations, 749 local central bodies, 109 affiliated national and international unions, and 62,000 local unions

INTERNATIONAL LABOR PRESS ASSOCIATION, AFL-CIO. 815 16th St NW, Washington, DC 20006. **202-637-5068** or **202-347-5564.** Allen Y Zack, secretary-treasurer

ILPA is a member organization for newsletters, magazines, and newspapers published by AFL-CIO organizations and by the Canadian Labour Congress (CLC). There are over 500 member publications with a combined per-issue circulation in excess of 20 million. The basic objective of this association is to increase the effectiveness of the labor press in the US and Canada as a communications medium between union leaders and union members, and as an instrument of support for the goals of the AFL-CIO and the CLC.

NATIONAL FEDERATION OF INDE-PENDENT UNIONS. 821 Cafritz Bldg, 1625 I St NW, Washington, DC 20006. **202-659-1490.** Roger M Rettig, national president. *Press contacts.* Roger M Rettig

and Doris L Fuller, administrative assistant. Night line: **202-244-1248.** A clearinghouse for information and education on independent unions

LABOR UNIONS

Items are arranged alphabetically by the type of employment.

ASSOCIATED ACTORS AND ARTISTES OF AMERICA (AAAA). 1500 Broadway, New York, NY 10036. **212-869-0358.** Frederick O'Neal, international president. *Press contact:* Dick Moore, of Dick Moore & Associates, Inc. **212-265-0610**

The "Four A's" is the international parent body of the entertainment unions, and a member of the AFL-CIO, with which the nine entertainment unions are affiliated. Their names and addresses follow.

Actors' Equity Association. 1500 Broadway, New York, NY 10036. **212-869-8530.** Donald Grody, executive secretary. Theodore Bikel, president. Legitimate theatre union

American Federation of Television and Radio Artists. 1350 Avenue of the Americas, New York, NY 10019. **212-265-7700.** See separate listing.

American Guild of Musical Artists. 1841 Broadway, New York, NY 10023. **212-CO5-3687.** De Lloyd Tibbs, executive secretary. Cornell MacNeil, president

American Guild of Variety Artists. 1540 Broadway, New York, NY 10036. **212-765-0800.** Penny Singleton, executive president

Asociacion Puertorriqueña de Artistas y Tecnicos del Espectacula. Oficina 404, Ponce de Leon 804, Santurce, PR 00907. **809-722-4154.** Orlando Lopez, secretary general

Hebrew Actors Union. 31 E 7th St, New York, NY 10003. **212-674-1923.** Leon Liebgold, president

Italian Actors Union. 1674 Broadway, New York, NY 10019. **212-582-6170.** Sal Carollo, executive secretary

Screen Actors Guild. 7750 Sunset Blvd, Hollywood, CA 90046. **213-876-3030.** Chester L Migden, executive secretary. Kathleen Nolan, president

Screen Extras Guild. 3629 Cahuenga Blvd W, Hollywood, CA 90029. **213-461-9301.** H O'Neil Shanks, executive secretary. Murray Pollack, president

AIR LINE PILOTS ASSOCIATION. 1625 Massachusetts Ave NW, Washington, DC 20036. **202-797-4000.** Captain J J O'Donnell, president, **202-797-4010.** Paul Reneau, communications, **202-797-4174**

INTERNATIONAL UNION OF ALUMINUM WORKERS. 818 Olive St, St Louis, MO 63101. **314-621-7292.** Vernon E Kelley, president

AUTHORS' GUILD. *See* SPECIAL INTERESTS.

AMERICAN GUILD OF AUTHORS AND COMPOSERS. 6430 W Sunset Blvd, Los Angeles, CA 90028. **213-462-1108**

UNITED AUTOMOBILE, AEROSPACE, AND AGRICULTURAL IMPLEMENT WORKERS OF AMERICA—UAW International Union. 8000 E Jefferson, Detroit, MI 48214. **313-926-5000.** Douglas Fraser, president, **313-926-5202.** Don Stillman, director, UAW public relations and publications department, **313-926-5297.** Jerry Dale, assistant, public relations, **313-926-5291.** (h) **313-559-3814**

BAKERY AND CONFECTIONERY WORKERS' INTERNATIONAL UNION OF AMERICA. Suite 900, 1828 L St NW, Washington, DC 20036. **202-466-2500.** Daniel E Conway, international president. Albert K Herling, director, public relations, (h) **301-474-4621**

INTERNATIONAL UNION OF BRICKLAYERS AND ALLIED CRAFTSMEN. 815 15th St NW, Washington, DC 20005. **202-783-3788.** Thomas F Murphy, president

INTERNATIONAL BROTHERHOOD OF BOILERMAKERS. 8th St and State Ave, Kansas City, KS 66101. **913-371-2640.** Harold J Buoy, president. *Washington office.* 400 1st St NW, Washington, DC 20001. **202-638-5768**

UNITED BROTHERHOOD OF CARPENTERS AND JOINERS OF AMERICA. 101 Constitution Ave NW, Washington, DC 20001. **202-546-6206.** R E Livingston, editor. Roger A Sheldon, associate editor. *Other contact.* Al Silverman, 1125 17th St NW, Washington, DC 20036

UNITED CEMENT, LIME, AND GYPSUM WORKERS INTERNATIONAL UNION, AFL-CIO, CLC. 7830 W Lawrence Ave, Chicago, IL 60656. **312-457-1177.** Thomas F Miechur, international president. Richard A Northrip, international secretary-treasurer. Patricia H Strandt, *Voice* managing editor. Night line: **312-478-1968.**

INTERNATIONAL CHEMICAL WORKERS UNION. 1655 W Market St, Akron, OH 44313. **216-867-2444.** Frank D Martino, president. Bob Kasen, director, communications

AMALGAMATED CLOTHING AND TEXTILE WORKERS UNION. 15 Union Sq, New York, NY 10003. **212-255-7800.** Burt Beck, director, public relations. Night line: **914-357-3005**

COMMUNICATIONS WORKERS OF AMERICA. 1925 K St NW, Washington, DC 20006. **202-785-6700.** Glenn E Watts, president, **202-785-6710.** Lee M White, administrative assistant, public information, **202-785-6740** (also night line)

INTERNATIONAL UNION OF ELECTRICAL, RADIO, AND MACHINE WORKERS, AFL-CIO, CLC. 1126 16th St NW, Washington, DC 20036. **202-296-1200.** Night line: **202-296-1208.** David J Fitzmaurice, president. Jerry Borstel, director, public relations and publications, Ext 287, or **202-882-8662**

UNITED ELECTRICAL, RADIO, AND MACHINE WORKERS OF AMERICA (UE). 11 East 51st St, New York, NY 10022. **212-753-1960.** Albert J Fitzgerald, international president. *Press contact.* James Lerner. The collective bargaining representative for 165,000 workers in the electrical manufacturing industry (GE, Westinghouse, Sylvania, etc.) in the US and Canada

INTERNATIONAL BROTHERHOOD OF ELECTRICAL WORKERS. 1125 15th St NW, Washington, DC 20005. **202-833-7000.** Charles H Pillard, president. *Press contact.* R W McAlwee

UNITED FARM WORKERS OF AMERICA, AFL-CIO. La Paz, Keene, CA 93531. **805-822-5571.** Cesar E Chavez, president. Marc Grossman, press secretary to the president

NATIONAL FEDERATION OF FEDERAL EMPLOYEES. 1016 16th St NW, Washington, DC. **202-862-4400.** James M Peirce, president. Frank Taylor, director, publications and public relations. "The nation's oldest and largest independent federal employee union"

INTERNATIONAL ASSOCIATION OF FIRE FIGHTERS. 1750 New York Ave NW, Washington, DC 20006. **202-872-8484.** William H McClennan, president

UNITED GARMENT WORKERS OF AMERICA. 200 Park Ave S, New York, NY 10003. **212-677-0573, 0574,** or **0575.** Howard D Collins, Sr, president. Catherine C Peters, editor

INTERNATIONAL LADIES GARMENT WORKERS' UNION. 1710 Broadway, New York, NY 10019. **212-265-7000.** Sol C Chaikin, president, **212-265-7000.** Michael Pollack, editor

AMERICAN FEDERATION OF GOVERNMENT EMPLOYEES, AFL-CIO. 1325 Massachusetts Ave NW, Washington, DC 20005. **202-737-8700.** Night line: **202-737-8708.** Kenneth T Blaylock, president. Greg Kenefick, director, public relations, (h) **301-593-4297.** Dick Calistri, assistant director

AFGE is the largest union representing federal employees (bargains for more than 700,000, both white collar and blue collar). It has very active publications and news release programs.

NATIONAL ASSOCIATION OF GOVERNMENT EMPLOYEES. 2139 Wisconsin Ave NW, Washington, DC 20007. **202-965-4411.** Kenneth T Lyons, president. Daniel C Boyle, national representative, and William G Norton, national secretary. Night line: **413-594-6830.** *Boston office.* 285 Dorchester Ave, Boston, MA 02127. **617-268-5002.** *Other contacts.* Alan Whitney (Washington); Bill Norton (Boston). Provides representation for employees in every segment of public employment

GRAPHIC ARTS INTERNATIONAL UNION. 1900 L St NW, Washington, DC 20036. **202-872-7900.** Kenneth J Brown, president, **202-872-7910.** William Moody, information director, **202-872-7952.** The trade union in the printing industry, combining the merged crafts of lithography (offset), photoengraving (1964), and bookbinding (1972)

INTERNATIONAL UNION OF HOTEL AND RESTAURANT EMPLOYEES AND BARTENDERS, AFL-CIO. 120 E 4th St, Cincinnati, OH 45202. **513-621-0300.** Edward T Hanley, president

ALLIED INDUSTRIAL WORKERS INTERNATIONAL UNION, AFL-CIO. 3520 W Oklahoma Ave, Milwaukee, WI 53215. **414-645-9500.** Dominick D'Ambrosio, international president. Kenneth Germanson, spokesperson, (h) **414-483-1754**

INTERNATIONAL ASSOCIATION OF BRIDGE, STRUCTURAL, AND ORNAMENTAL IRON WORKERS. 1750 New York Ave NW, Washington, DC 20006. **202-872-1566.** John H Lyons, president, Ext 200. William M Lawbaugh, editor, Ext 272. Night line: **301-946-1237**

LABORERS' INTERNATIONAL UNION, AFL-CIO. 905 16th St NW, Washington, DC 20006. **202-737-8320.** Angelo Fosco

NATIONAL ASSOCIATION OF LETTER CARRIERS, AFL-CIO. 100 Indiana Ave NW, Washington, DC 20001. **202-393-4695.** J Joseph Vacca, president. Gerald Cullinan, assistant to president

BROTHERHOOD OF LOCOMOTIVE ENGINEERS. Engineers Bldg, 1365 Onatrio Ave, Cleveland, OH 44144. **216-241-2630.** John F Sytsma, president. L S Loomis, first vice-president

INTERNATIONAL LONGSHOREMEN'S ASSOCIATION, AFL-CIO. Suite 1530, 17 Battery Pl, New York, NY 10004. **212-425-1200.** Night line: **212-425-1206.** Thomas W Gleason, president. Larry G Molloy, public relations counsel

INTERNATIONAL LONGSHOREMEN'S AND WAREHOUSEMEN'S UNION. 1188 Franklin St, San Francisco, CA 94109. **415-775-0533.** Harry R Bridges, president emeritus. James R Herman, president. Daniel S Beagle, editor and information director

INTERNATIONAL ASSOCIATION OF MACHINISTS AND AEROSPACE WORKERS, AFL-CIO. 1300 Connecticut Ave NW, Washington, DC 20036. **202-857-5200.** William W Winpisinger, president, **202-857-5180.** Robert J Kalaski, director, public relations, **202-857-5220.** (h) **301-460-8097**

BROTHERHOOD OF MAINTENANCE OF WAY EMPLOYEES. 12050 Woodward Ave, Detroit, MI 48203. **313-868-0492.** H C Crotty, president, **313-868-0489.** R J Williamson, associate editor and director, public relations, **313-868-0492**

NATIONAL MARITIME UNION OF AMERICA, AFL-CIO. 346 W 17th St, New York, NY 10011. **212-924-3900.** Shannon J Wall, president, Ext 730, 731, or 732. Samuel Thompson, director, publications, Ext 725 or 726. Night line: **212-978-4904.** The labor union representing unlicensed seamen

AMALGAMATED MEAT CUTTERS AND BUTCHERS OF AMERICA. 2800 N Sheridan Rd, Chicago, IL 60657. **312-248-8700.** Harry R Poole, president

UNITED MINE WORKERS OF AMERICA. 900 15th St NW, Washington, DC 20005. **202-638-0530.** Arnold Miller, president

AMERICAN FEDERATION OF MUSICIANS, AFL-CIO, CLC. 1500 Broadway, New York, NY 10036. **212-869-1330.** Hal C Davis, president. *Press contact.* Dick Moore, of Dick Moore & Associates, director, public relations, **212-265-0610**

THE NEWSPAPER GUILD. 1125 15th St NW, Washington, DC 20005. **202-296-2990.** Charles A Perlik, Jr, president, (h) **703-560-6192.** David J Eisen, research and information director, (h) **703-241-2565**

Local guilds and officers

Akron (Local 7). William Sclight, president, 63 Kenilworth Dr, Akron, OH 44313

Albany (Local 34). John Funiciello, president, 890 3rd St, Albany, NY 12206. **518-482-9218**

Bakersfield (Local 202). Andrew Milinich, president, PO Box 1652, Bakersfield, CA 93302

Battle Creek (Local 148). 72 Allison Dr, Battle Creek, MI 49017

Bay City (Local 96). Ann Gager, president, Box 715, Bay City, MI 48706

Boston (Local 32). Kevin Kelly, president, 38 Main St, Saugus, MA 01906. **617-289-8495**

Brockton (Local 27). Donald Waterman, president, 60 Main St, Brockton, MA 02403

Buffalo (Local 26). Richard J Roth, president, 290 Franklin St, Buffalo, NY 14202. **716-856-2828**

Canadian Wire Service (Local 213). Rick Welbourn, treasurer, Apt 6, 57 Leacrest Rd, Toronto, Ont, Canada, M4G 1E5

Central California (Local 92). Gene Turner, president, Rm 426, 1107 9th St, Sacramento, CA 95814. **916-446-4885**

Chattanooga (Local 164). Richard Kopper, president, 117 E 10th St, Chattanooga, TN 37402

Chicago (Local 71). Michael Kaeser, president, 2800 N Lake Shore Dr, Chicago, IL 60657. **312-642-3032**

Cincinnati (Local 9). Ben Schilmeister, president, 1200 Times Star Tower, 8th and Broadway, Cincinnait, OH 45202. **513-381-5358**

Cleveland (Local 1). Mary T Englert, president, Rm 1201, 815 Superior Ave, Cleveland, OH 44114. **216-621-6792**

Columbus (Local 13). Raymond C Volt, president, Rm 117, 137 E State St, Columbus, OH 43215. **614-221-7075**

Denver (Local 74). Richard E Wanek, adminsitrative secretary, Rm 521, Empire Bldg, 430 16th St, Denver, CO 80202. **303-629-1132**

Detroit (Local 22). Lou Mleczko, president, 2012 Book Bldg, Detroit, MI 48226. **313-963-4254**

Erie (Local 187). Bill Buchanan, president, Rm 211, 12 E 10th St, Erie, PA 16501. **814-456-4646**

Eugene (Local 194). Mike Thoele, president, PO Box 1431, Eugene, OR 97401

Gary (Local 14). Forbes Scott, president, 8626 Oak Ave, Gary, IN 46403

Great Falls (Local 81). Stuart S White, president, PO Box 2712, Great Falls, MT 59403

Greensboro (Local 80). Darwin Honeycuff, president, 110 S Mendenhall St, Greensboro, NC 27403

Hampton Roads (Local 219). Mike Smith, president, c/o *Norfolk Virginian-Pilot,* 150 W Brambleton Ave, Norfolk, VA 23501

Harrisburg (Local 16). Donald C Sarvey, president, 3301 Ridgeway Rd, Harrisburg, PA 17109

Hawaii (Local 117). Stanley Souza, president, 451 Atkinson Dr, Honolulu, HI 96814. **808-949-4161,** Ext 20

Hazleton (Local 216). William Crooks, president, 14 West 1st St, Hazleton, PA 18201. **717-455-3636**

Hudson County (Local 42). Peter J Wevurski, president, 7117 Park Ave, North Bergen, NJ 07047. **201-861-5751**

Indianapolis (Local 70). Dennis J Hoffman, president, 502 Fletcher Ave, Indianapolis, IN 46203. **317-635-7076**

Kenosha (Local 159). Norbert Bybee, president, 1629 Maple St, Racine, WI 50404

Kingston (Local 180). Charles J Tiano, president, Uptown PO Box 805, Kingston, NY 12403

Knoxville (Local 76). Sam Venable, president, 9013 Carlton Cir, Route 5, Concord, TN 37720

Lansing (Local 24). Michael Hughes, president, PO Box 20024, Lansing MI 48911

Lehigh Valley (Local 49). Sally L Schaffer, president, Box 1422, Allentown, PA 18105. **215-820-6561**

Lexington (Local 229). Steve Anderson, president, PO Box 449, Lexington, KY 40585. **606-266-5365**

Los Angeles (Local 69). Linda L Zink, president, Suite 337, 1543 W Olympic Blvd, Los Angeles, CA 90015. **213-386-2068**

Lynn (Local 55). William S Kettinger, president, *Daily Evening Item,* 38 Exchange St, Lynn, MA 01901. **617-233-8334**

Madison (Local 64). Diane Woodstock, president, 620 W Wilson St, Madison, WI 53703. **608-255-6041**

Manchester (Local 167). John F Barker, president, Box 108J, RD 1, Manchester, NH 03104

Memphis (Local 91). Brown Alan Flynn, president, 401 S Reese, Memphis, TN 38111

Mountaineer (Local 231). John Carlock, president, PO Box 359, Morgantown, WV 26505

New York (Local 3). Thomas P Murphy, president, 133 W 44th St, New York, NY 10035. **212-582-0530**

Northern Ontario (Local 232). Ronald Gibbons, president, PO Box 454, Sudbury, Ont, Canada, P3E 4P7

Ottawa (Local 205). Katie FitzRandolph, president, CLC Bldg, 2841 Riverside Dr, Ottawa, Ont, Canada K1V 8N4. **613-731-7849**

Pacific Northwest (Local 82). Shirley Caldwell, president, 903 Tower Bldg, Seattle, WA 98101. **206-623-7761**

Pawtucket (Local 185). David Chmielewski, president, Box 595, Pawtucket, RI 02860

Peoria (Local 86). Richard Schneider, president, PO Box 1061, Peoria, IL 61601

Greater Philadelphia (Local 10). Richard Aregood, president, Rm 1016, 401 N Broad St, Philadelphia, PA 19108. **215-928-0118**

Pittsburgh (Local 61). Edward Bell, president, Apt 104, 190 Sycamore Dr, Pittsburgh, PA 15235. **412-795-1384**

Portland (Local 128). Elwood B Bigelow, president, PO Box 576, Peaarl St Station, Portland, ME 04112

Providence (Local 41). Lee Dykas, president, 96 Fountain St, Providence, RI 02903. **401-421-9466**

Pueblo (Local 174). Phil Ruegg, president, PO Box 1040, Puebleo, CO 81002

Puerto Rico (Local 225). Angel Baez, president, Calle 25 NE 347, Puerto Nuevo, PR 00920. **809-781-8500**

Rochester (Local 17). Paul Warren, president, PO Box 3194, Rochester, NY 14614

Rockford (Local 5). Ben Rubendall, president, 4574 Tenby Ct, Loves Park, IL 61111

St Louis (Local 47). Robert C Hermann, president, Rm 707A, 710 N 12th Blvd, St Louis, MO 63101. **314-241-7046**

Salem (Local 105). PO Box 522, Salem, MA 01970. **617-745-9142**

San Antonio (Local 25). Bruce Beal, president, 779 W Mayfield, San Antonio, TX 78211. **512-927-5901**

San Diego (Local 95). Gerald L Schultz president, Suite E-220, 123 Camino de la Reina, San Diego, CA 92108. **714-299-4083**

San Francisco-Oakland (Local 52). 433 Natoma St (PO Box 42490), San Francisco, CA 94142. **415-421-6833**

San Jose (Local 98). William Ernst, president, 1280 N 4th St, San Jose, CA 95112. **408-294-0761**

Saskatoon (Local 234). James Duggleby, president, 1014 Eastlake Ave, Saskatoon, Sask, Canada S7N 0B7. **306-664-2920** or **306-652-9200**

Scranton (Local 177). Chris Vanston, secretary, 205 Ridge St, Clarks Summit, PA **717-342-9151.** (h) **717-586-8956**

Sheboygan (Local 179). Milt Freimuth, president, 1409 Humboldt, Sheboygan, WI 53082

Sioux City (Local 123). Harvey Sanford, president, 1916 Douglas, Sioux City, IA 51104

Terre Haute (Local 46). Tom C Reck, president, Rm 205, 22 S 8th St, Terre Haute, IN 47801. **812-232-4216**

Toledo (Local 43). Sidney Goldberg, president, 537½ Huron St, Toledo, OH 43604. **419-241-3419**

Toronto (Local 87). John Lowe, president, Suite 29, King Edward Hotel, 37 King St E, Toronto, Ont, Canada M5C 1E9. **416-362-2571**

Twin Cities (Local 2). Jack Coffmans, president, Rm 406, 512 Nicollet Mall Bldg, Minneapolis, MN 55402. **612-339-7031**

Utica (Local 129). Francis Crumb, president, 5 White St, Clark Mills, NY 13321. **315-853-6827**

Vancouver-New Westminister (Local 115). Ed McGurin, acting president, Rm 10, 1557 W Broadway, Vancouver, B C, Canada V6J 1W6. **604-738-2829**

Victoria (Local 223). Bridget Petersen, president, 11-2750 Quadra St, Victoria, BC Canada V8T 4E5. **604-382-7211.** (c/o *Victoria Press*)

Washington-Baltimore (Local 35). Thomas Grubisich, president, Rm 210, 3408 Wisconsin Ave NW, Washington, DC 20016. **202-362-4300**

Wilkes-Barre (Local 120). Paul Golias, president, 111 Charles St, Ashley, PA 18706

Winnipeg (Local 233). Steve Riley, president, PO Box 1383, Smith St and Graham Ave Station, Winnipeg, Man, Canada R3C 2Z1

Wire Service Guild (Local 222). 133 W 44th St, New York, NY 10036. **212-869-9290**

Woonsocket (Local 182). Frank S Visgatis, president, 20 Crescent St, Whitinsville, MA 01580

Yakima (Local 227). Jack Richards, president, PO Box 365, Yakima, WA 98901

York (Local 218). Donald W Grable, president, 441 Madison Ave, York, PA 17404

Youngstown (Local 11). Larry Quinn, president, PO Box 1135, Youngstown, OH 44501

OIL, CHEMICAL, AND ATOMIC WORKERS INTERNATIONAL UNION. 1636 Champa St (PO Box 2812), Denver, CO 80201. **303-893-0811.** A F Grospiron, president. Jerry Archuleta, publicity director. A labor union representing approximately 200,000 workers in oil, chemical, and atomic allied industries

INTERNATIONAL UNION OF OPERATING ENGINEERS, AFL-CIO. 1125 17th St NW, Washington, DC 20036. **202-347-8560.** J C Turner, general president

INTERNATIONAL BROTHERHOOD OF PAINTERS AND ALLIED TRADES. 1750 New York Ave, NW, Washington, DC 20006. **202-872-1444.** General secretary-treasurer, Robert Petersdorf, Ext. 204. Journal editor, Rodney Wolford, Ext. 280

UNITED PAPERWORKERS INTERNATIONAL UNION. 163-03 Horace Harding Exp, Flushing NY 11365. **212-762-6000.** Joseph P Tonelli, president. Richard A Estep, director, technical services. Has a membership of about 300,000 in the US and Canada, with about 3000 contracts in the pulp, paper, and converting industries

OPERATIVE PLASTERERS' AND CEMENT MASONS' INTERNATIONAL ASSOCIATION OF THE UNITED STATES AND CANADA. 6th Floor, 1125 17th St NW, Washington, DC 20036. **202-393-6569.** Joseph T Power, general president. John J Hauck, general secretary-treasurer. Melvin H Roots, executive vice president

UNITED ASSOCIATION OF PLUMBING AND PIPE FITTING INDUSTRY EMPLOYEES. 901 Massachusetts Ave NW, Washington, DC 20001. **202-628-5823.** Martin J Ward, president

INTERNATIONAL CONFERENCE OF POLICE ASSOCIATIONS. 1239 Pennsylvania Ave SE, Washington, DC 20003. **202-544-2700.** Edward J Kiernan, president, Robert D Gordon, secretary-treasurer

AMERICAN POSTAL WORKERS UNION, AFL-CIO. 817 14th St NW, Washington, DC 20005. **202-638-2304.** Emmet Andrews, general president

INTERNATIONAL PRINTING AND GRAPHIC COMMUNICATIONS UNION, AFL-CIO. 1730 Rhode Island Ave NW, Washington, DC 20036. **202-293-2185.** Sol Fishko, president

BROTHERHOOD OF RAILWAY, AIRLINE, AND STEAMSHIP CLERKS, FREIGHT HANDLERS, EXPRESS AND STATION EMPLOYEES. 6300 River Rd, Rosemont, IL 60018. **312-692-7711.** Fred J Kroll, international president. Diane S Curry, director, publications. *Other contact.* Henry C Fleisher, of Maurer, Fleisher, Zon and Anderson (1120 Connecticut Ave, Washington, DC 20036), **202-331-8070**

BROTHERHOOD OF RAILWAY CARMEN OF THE US AND CANADA. 4929 Main, Kansas City, MO 64112. **816-561-1112.** O W Jacobson, general president. C W Hauck, editor and manager, **816-561-8449.** Night line: **913-888-1463**

RETAIL CLERKS INTERNATIONAL UNION, AFL-CIO. 1775 K St NW, Washington, DC 20006. **202-223-3111.** William H Wynn, international president. Jay H Foreman and Walt Davis, assistants to president. Night line. **202-223-3113**

RETAIL, WHOLESALE, AND DEPARTMENT STORE UNION, AFL-CIO. 101 W 31st St, New York, NY 10001. **212-947-9303.** Alvin E Heaps, president. Tor Cedervall, editor. Lenore Miller, assistant to president

UNITED RUBBER, CORK, LINOLEUM, AND PLASTIC WORKERS OF AMERICA, AFL-CIO, CLC. 87 S High St, Akron, OH 44308. **216-376-6181.** Night line: **216-376-0228.** Peter Bommarito, international president. Curt Brown, director, public relations

SERVICE EMPLOYEES INTERNATIONAL UNION, AFL-CIO. Suite 200, 2020 K St NW, Washington, DC 20006. **202-452-8750.** George Hardy, international president. Dave Stack, director, publications. Formerly (1968) Building Service Employees International Union

AMERICAN FEDERATION OF STATE, COUNTY, AND MUNICIPAL EMPLOYEES, AFL-CIO. 1625 L St NW

Washington, DC 20036. **202-452-4800.** Jerry Wurf, president, **202-452-4900.** Donovan McClure, public affairs director, **202-452-4913.** Consists of 750,000 members who work for state and local governments

UNITED STEELWORKERS OF AMERICA. 5 Gateway Ctr, Pittsburgh, PA 15222. **412-562-2400.** Lloyd McBride, president. Raymond W Pasnick, director, public relations, **412-562-2666**

AMERICAN FEDERATION OF TEACHERS. 11 Dupont Cir NW Washington, DC 20036. **202-767-4400.** Albert Shanker, president. Peter Laarman, director, public relations, **202-797-4458**

AFT is a nationwide union of classroom teachers, affiliated with the AFL-CIO. It has over 475,000 members in over 2200 locals in the US and overseas.

INTERNATIONAL BROTHERHOOD OF TEAMSTERS. 25 Louisiana Ave NW, Washington, DC 20001. **202-624-6800.** Frank E Fitzsimmons, general president. Allen Biggs, director, public relations, **202-624-6911**

TELECOMMUNICATIONS INTERNATIONAL UNION. 3055 Dixwell Ave, Hamden, CT 06518. **203-288-2445.** John W Shaughnessy, Jr, treasurer-president. Robert Leventhal, administrative assistant to president. A labor union representing primarily Bell System workers in Connecticut, New York, Pennsylvania, Delaware, Maryland, and Illinois

AMERICAN FEDERATION OF TV AND RADIO ARTISTS, AFL-CIO. 1350 Avenue of the Americas, New York, NY 10019. **212-265-7700.** Sanford I (Bud) Wolff, national executive secretary. *Spokesperson.* Dick Moore, **212-265-0610**

UNITED TEXTILE WORKERS OF AMERICA, AFL-CIO. 420 Common St, Lawrence, MA 01842. **617-686-2901.** Francis Schaufenbil, president

INTERNATIONAL ALLIANCE OF THEATRICAL STAGE EMPOLYEES AND MOVING PICTURE OPERATORS. 1515 Broadway, New York, NY 10036. **212-730-1770.** Walter F Diehl, president. Rene L Ash, publicity director

TOBACCO WORKERS INTERNATIONAL UNION. Suite 616, 1522 K St NW, Washington, DC 20005. **202-659-1366.** Homer Cole, secretary-treasurer

AMALGAMATED TRANSIT UNION. 5025 Wisconsin Ave NW, Washington, DC 20016. **202-537-1645.** Dan V Maroney, international president

UNITED TRANSPORTATION UNION. 14600 Detroit Ave, Cleveland, OH 44107. **216-228-9400.** Al H Chesser, president. Lou Corsi, director, public relations. J R Snyder (400 1st St NW, Washington, DC 20001), national legislative director, **202-783-3939.** A railway labor union representing 250,000 workers in operating crafts and bus companies

INTERNATIONAL TYPOGRAPHICAL UNION. 301 S Union Blvd (PO Box 157), Colorado Springs, CO 80901. **303-636-2341.** A Sandy Bevis, president. Horst A Reschke, director, public relations bureau. An international labor organization servicing approximately 575 local unions

UTILITY WORKERS UNION OF AMERICA, AFL-CIO. 815 16th St NW, Washington, DC 20006. **202-347-8105.** Harold T Rigley, president, **202-685-8703.** Represents employees of gas, electricty, and water utilities

INTERNATIONAL WOODWORKERS OF AMERICA, AFL-CIO. CLC. 1622 N Lombard St, Portland, OR 97217. **503-285-5281.** Robert Gerwig, international secretary-treasurer. Richard Spohn, acting editor. Keith Johnson, president. Membership employed in all aspects of the wood industry (logging, boommen, sawmills, plywood production, etc)

EDUCATION

EDUCATION ORGANIZATIONS

AMERICAN ASSOCIATION OF SCHOOL ADMINISTRATORS. 1801 W Moore St, Arlington, VA 22209. **703-528-0700.** Paul B Salmon, executor

director, Ext 213. William E Henry, associate director, Ext 208 or 209. Marian Strange, managing editor, Ext 209 or 208. Sharon Ford, publications assistant, Ext 208 or 209. AASA claims 20,000 members nationwide and has been operating since 1865. It

provides governmental relations, annual convention, management training institute, research materials, and publications for school administrators, on the university level and below. Membership is open to others on an associate basis.

THE AMERICAN COLLEGE TESTING PROGRAM (ACT). 2201 N Dodge St (PO Box 168), Iowa City, IO 52240. **319-356-3711.** Oluf M Davidsen, president. Bob Elliott, coordinator, information services, **319-356-3740.** A nonprofit, national organization that provides a variety of educational services and programs used each year by about eight million students and more than 25,000 educational institutions

AMERICAN COUNCIL ON EDUCATION. 1 Dupont Cir, Washington, DC 20036. **202-833-4700.** Jack W Peltason, president, **202-833-4710.** Frank Skinner, information officer, **202-833-4766** (office hours: 8:45 am to 4:45 pm), (h) **202-362-9430**

AMERICAN SCHOOLS ASSOCIATION. 24 N Wabash Ave, Chicago 60602. **312-236-6646.** Carl M Dye, president. Gerald B Flora, secretary. A nonprofit corporation that works in educational consulting, counseling, and scholarship administration

ASSOCIATION OF AMERICAN COLLEGES. 1818 R St NW, Washington, DC 20009. **202-387-3760.** Dr Frederic W Ness, president

Founded in 1915, the association has 800 members and a staff of 10. It promotes higher education through research and publications.

COLLEGE BOARD. 888 7th Ave, New York, NY 10019. **212-582-6210.** S P Marland, Jr, president. Carol P Halstead, director, public information

The board provides its institutional members with information and services in regard to admissions testing, career counseling, financial aid, and some special areas. It has a membership of about 2400 colleges and universities, secondary schools, school systems, and education associations.

COUNCIL FOR ADVANCEMENT AND SUPPORT OF EDUCATION. Suite 600, 1 Dupont Cir, Washington, DC 20036. **202-659-3820.** Alice L Beeman, president CASE is the professional association for advancement officers at 1900 colleges, universities, and independent secondary schools. The 8000 individual members work in the areas of information services, fund raising, alumni affairs, government relations, publications, and periodicals, and in the management of these areas. Over 2000 members list public information as their primary function

COUNCIL FOR BASIC EDUCATION. 725 15th St NW, Washington, DC 20005. **202-347-4171.** A Graham Down, executive director. George Weber, associate director The council, organized in 1956, consists of a group of administrators, teachers, and other persons providing an information service and numerous studies on education. It is financed through royalties, corporate and private donations, and membership and subscription dues.

THE COUNCIL OF THE GREAT CITY SCHOOLS. 5th Floor, 1707 H St NW, Washington, DC 20006. **202-298-8707.** Samuel B Husk, executive vice-president. Milton Bims, senior associate. Gail G Fullington, staff associate. Carolyn J Pittman, executive assistant, **202-387-0151.** Milton Bims, senior associate, program development. Kristi R Hanson, legislative specialist

Founded in 1961, the Council has 28 members and a staff of 17, and is organized to deal with problems of school systems in large urban centers. It provides information on legislation and lobbying activities, as well as on desegregation, funding, teacher preparation, data processing, and instructional materials in schools.

EDUCATION COMMISSION OF THE STATES. Suite 300, 1860 Lincoln, Denver, CO 80295. **303-893-5200.** Dr Warren G Hill, executive director, Ext 200. Sally V Allen, director, communications, Ext 369.

The commission, which has about 180 staff members working on 18 projects in education and related fields, is funded primarily through federal grants. It promotes cooperation among state educational and political leaders for the improvement of education. In addition, it "provides information on state-related activities [and] also serves as a liaison between the states and the federal government."

EDUCATIONAL RECORDS BUREAU. Suite 150, 2 Sunlife Executive Park, 100 Worcester Rd, Wellesley Hills, MA 02181. **617-235-8920.** R Bruce McGill, president. Provides testing services to member schools, of which there are about 840

EDUCATIONAL TESTING SERVICE. Princeton, NJ 08540. **609-921-9000.** John P Smith, director, news office. Provides the major testing service offered to universities, colleges, and public schools

Midwestern regional offices and directors
Evanston. 960 Grove St, Evanston, IL 60201. **312-869-7700.** Jayjia Hsia

Austin. Suite 100, 3724 Jefferson, Austin, TX 78731. **512-452-8817.** Donald E Hood

Western regional offices and directors
Berkeley. 1947 Center St, Berkeley, CA 94704. **415-849-0950.** Herman Smith

Los Angeles. Rm 216, 2200 Merton Ave, Los Angeles, CA 90041. **213-254-5236.** J Richard Harsh

Northeastern regional offices and directors
New England. 2 Sun Life Executive Park, 100 Worcester Rd, Wellesley Hills, MA 02181. **617-235-8860.** George Elford

Mid-Atlantic. Rosedale Rd, Princeton, NJ 08540. **609-921-9000.** J Robert Cleary

Southern regional offices and directors
Washington. Suite 210, 1 Dupont Cir, Washington, DC 20036. **202-296-5930.** David M Nolan

Atlanta. Suite 1040, 3445 Peachtree Rd NE, Atlanta, GA 30326. **404-262-7634.** Scarvia Anderson

Puerto Rico. Suite 1115, Banco Popular, 209 Munoz Rivera Ave, Hato Rey, PR 00918. **809-763-3636.** Ennio Belen-Trujillo

NATIONAL ASSESSMENT OF EDUCATIONAL PROGRESS. Suite 700, 1860 Lincoln St, Denver, CO 80295. **303-861-4917.** Dr Roy H Forbes, director. Helen K Masterson, director, public information, (h) **303-233-1934.** A project of the Education Commission of the States; studies educational methods and results

NATIONAL ASSOCIATION OF COLLEGE ADMISSIONS COUNSELORS. Suite 500, 9933 Lawler Ave, Skokie, IL 60076. **312-676-0500.** Robert P Hanrahan, executive director. Jan Hamilton, director, communications. Jill Formeister, administrative assistant. A professional organization that "aims to improve relations between high school counselors and college admissions officers"

NATIONAL ASSOCIATION OF STATE BOARDS OF EDUCATION (NASBE). 526 Hall of the States, 444 N Capitol St NW, Washington, DC 20001. **202-624-5845.** Dr Wesley Apker, executive secretary. Clare Desmond, associate editor

The organization, with members from 48 states, gathers and disseminates information useful to state school board members. NASBE has a monthly publication and holds four conferences a year.

NATIONAL CATHOLIC EDUCATIONAL ASSOCIATION. Suite 350, 1 Dupont Cir, Washington, DC 20036. **202-293-5954.** The Reverend John F Meyers, president, Ext 30. Carl Balcerak, director, communications, Ext 58. Rhoda Goldstein, membership director and data bank, statistics, and research on Catholic education

The association offers a number of publications and seminars for training Catholic educators. Membership is open to both individuals and institutions

NATIONAL EDUCATION ASSOCIATION OF THE UNITED STATES. 1201 16th St NW, Washington, DC 20036. **202-833-4484.** John Ryor, president, **202-833-4303.** Susan Lowell, director, or Phil King, manager, **202-833-4484** (also night line). *New York office.* Rm 302, 1270 Avenue of the Americas, New York, NY 10020. Linley Stafford, **212-481-2360**

The National Education Association claims to be the largest professional organization in the nation. Its purposes are "to elevate the character and advance the interests of the profession of teaching and to promote the cause of education"

NATIONAL HOME STUDY COUNCIL. 1601 18th St NW, Washington, DC 20009. **202-234-5100.** William A Fowler, executive director

The council is the nationally recognized accrediting agency for correspondence courses and schools, having accredited about 70 schools in 23 states. It also provides information about home study

NATIONAL INTERFRATERNITY CONFERENCE. 3901 W 86th St, Indianapolis, IN 46268. **317-297-1112.** Jack L Anson, executive director. A federation of national and international college general and social fraternities; its purposes are to promote the general well-being of these fraternities, to gather information and data, to engage in research, and to conduct workshops

NATIONAL PARENT-TEACHER ASSOCIATION. *See Special Interests*

NATIONAL SCHOOL BOARDS ASSOCIATION. 1055 Thomas Jefferson St NW, Washington, DC 20007. **202-337-7666.** Philip A Smith, director, information. A federation of 50 state school board associations that provides information on topics relating to policies and administration of public school systems

NATIONAL SCIENCE TEACHERS ASSOCIATION. 1742 Connecticut Ave NW, Washington, DC 20009. **202-265-4150.** Robert L Silber, executive director. Eleanor Snyder, editor, *NSTA News Bulletin*

The association is an organization of about 40,000 science teachers from elementary through college level. It offers a number of publications and services, including teaching aids, an employment registry, and summer school sessions

SOCIETY FOR THE ADVANCEMENT OF EDUCATION. 1860 Broadway, New York, NY 10023. **212-265-6680.** Robert S Rothenberg, secretary

The society is composed of educators and school administrators. Its chief activity is publication of a number of pamphlets and booklets on educational issues, including *Intellect*

MAJOR COLLEGES AND UNIVERSITIES

ABILENE CHRISTIAN UNIVERSITY. Abilene, TX 79601. **915-677-1911.** Night line: **915-677-6681.** Irvin D Hiler, director, communication services, Ext 577 or 578. Milton B Fletcher, vice-president, public relations and development, Ext 561. Jennifer A Mullins, information director, Ext 575 or 576, (h) **915-672-6658**

ADAMS STATE COLLEGE. Alamosa, CO 81102. **303-589-7011.** James V Biundo, director, public affairs, **303-589-7121**

UNIVERSITY OF AKRON. Akron, OH 44325. **216-375-7111.** Mary K O'Neil, director, university news service, **216-375-7230**

ALABAMA A & M UNIVERSITY. Normal, AL 35762. **205-859-7011.** *Contact.* Arthur A Burks. **205-859-7458.** Linda Ammons, publications and news specialist, **205-859-7404**

ALABAMA STATE UNIVERSITY. Montgomery, AL 36101. **205-262-3581.** John F Knight, director, public relations

UNIVERSITY OF ALABAMA. University, AL 35486. **205-348-6010.** David Mathews, president, **205-348-5100.** Bob Inman, director, university relations, **205-348-5765.** Lawrence C Falk, director, information services, **205-348-5320**

UNIVERSITY OF ALABAMA IN BIRMINGHAM. Birmingham, AL 35294.

205-934-4204. James Bosarge, news bureau editor, office of public affairs

UNIVERSITY OF ALASKA. Fairbanks, AK 99701. **907-479-7272.** Robert J Hilliard, director, university relations and development. Gerald E Bowkett, director, information services, **907-479-7273**

ALBION COLLEGE. Albion, MI 49224. **517-629-6725.** Steve Drake, director, college relations. Jean Taylor, director, media relations. A private, 4-year, liberal arts college for men and women that offers special preparatory courses in premedicine, predentistry, prelaw, and professional management

ALBRIGHT COLLEGE. Reading, PA 19603. **215-921-2381.** Night line: **215-921-0422.** Dr Morley J Mays, interim president. Harrie G Burdan, director, public information, (h) **215-374-6481**

ALCORN STATE UNIVERSITY. Lorman, MS 39096. **601-877-3711.** Ralph L Payne, Sr, director, public relations

ALLEGHENY COLLEGE. Meadville, PA 16335. **814-724-3100.** Dr Lawrence L Pelletier, president, **814-724-5380.** Robert S Wycoff, director, public relations, **814-724-2369.** Beth Giese, assistant director, **814-724-2369**

AMERICAN UNIVERSITY. Washington, DC 20016. **202-686-2100.** Cynthia K Moran, director, public information

AMHERST COLLEGE. Amherst, MA 01002. **413-542-2000.** *Contact.* Douglas C Wilson. **413-542-2321**

ANTIOCH COLLEGE. Yellow Springs, OH 45387. **513-767-7346.** Roger Nelson, director, public relations

APPALACHIAN STATE UNIVERSITY. Boone, NC 28608. **704-262-2000.** Lee Adams, director, public affairs, **704-262-2090.** Tom Corbitt, director, news bureau, **704-262-2090**

ARIZONA STATE UNIVERSITY. Tempe, AZ 85281. **602-965-9011.** *Contact.* Troy F Crowder

UNIVERSITY OF ARIZONA. Tucson, AZ 85721. **602-884-0111.** Harry Marshall, director, news bureau, **602-884-1877**

ARIZONA WESTERN COLLEGE. Yuma, AZ 85364. **602-726-1000.** H Stephen Carlson, director, public information services

ARKANSAS STATE UNIVERSITY. State University, AR 72467. **501-972-3056.** Andy Morris, director, public relations

ARKANSAS TECH UNIVERSITY. Russellville, AR 72801. **501-968-0389.** Gerald E Edgar, director, news bureau, **501-968-0284**

UNIVERSITY OF ARKANSAS. Fayetteville, AR 72701. **501-575-2000.** William W Hughes, director, information, **501-575-5501**

UNIVERSITY OF ARKANSAS AT LITTLE ROCK. Little Rock, AR 72204. **501-569-3262.** Jerol Garrison, director, information

ASHLAND COLLEGE. Ashland, OH 44805. **419-289-4142.** Dr Arthur L Schultz, president, **419-289-5038.** Dr Donald B Swegan, vice-president, student and resource development, **419-289-4157.** Chuck Mistovich, director, communication services, **419-289-4135.** Thomas L Seddon, director, college relations, **419-289-5017.** A nonprofit, 4-year, career-oriented, liberal arts institution with nearly 1700 students

ASSUMPTION COLLEGE. Worcester, MA 01609. **617-752-5615.** Maureen Ryan Kelleher, director, public relations

ATLANTA UNIVERSITY. Atlanta, GA 30314. **404-681-0251.** Dr Cleveland L Dennard, president. *Contact.* Lise C White. A nonsectarian institution, offering graduate and professional courses in the School of Business Administration, the School of Education, the School of Library Service, the School of Social Work, and the School of Arts and Sciences

AUBURN UNIVERSITY. Auburn, AL 36830. **205-826-4075.** Trudy Cargile, editor, news bureau

AURORA COLLEGE. Aurora, IL 60507. **312-892-6431.** Scott B Palmer, director, public information and publications

BALL STATE UNIVERSITY. Muncie, IN 47306. **317-289-1241.** Marie Fraser, director, public information services, **317-285-4134.** (h) **317-288-3486**

UNIVERSITY OF BALTIMORE. Baltimore, MD 21201. **301-727-6350.** J C Shay, director, public information

BARNARD COLLEGE. New York, NY 10027. **212-280-2001.** Sallie Y Slate, director, public relations, **212-280-2037**

BAYLOR UNIVERSITY. Waco, TX 76703. **817-755-1011.** Chris Hansen, public relations, **817-755-1961**

BEAVER COLLEGE. Glenside, PA 19038. **215-884-3500.** Caroline Bartlett, director, public information

BEMIDJI STATE UNIVERSITY. Bemidji, MN 56601. **218-755-2000.** Jim Klatt, director, information services, **218-755-2041**

BENEDICTINE COLLEGE. Atchison, KS 66002. **913-367-5340.** Roger Swafford, director, public relations

BENTLEY COLLEGE. Waltham, MA 02154. **617-891-2000.** G Allen Peckham, director, public relations

BETHANY COLLEGE. Bethany, WV 26032. **304-829-7000.** Ruth L Westlake, director, public information and publications

BIRMINGHAM-SOUTHERN COLLEGE. Birmingham, AL 35204. **205-328-5250.** James Bennett, director, public affairs

BLOOMSBURG STATE COLLEGE. Bloomsburg, PA 17815. **717-389-2115.** Kenneth Hoffman, special advisor for public relations

BOSTON COLLEGE. Chestnut Hill, MA 02167. **617-969-0100.** J Donald Monah, SJ, president. Edward D Miller, director, public relations. Vic Schlitzer, press relations assistant

BOSTON STATE COLLEGE. Boston, MA 02115. **617-731-3300.** Joseph A Vaccaro, director, information services

BOSTON UNIVERSITY. Boston, MA 02215. **617-353-2000.** Wesley J Christenson, director, public affairs, **617-353-2240.** Frederick G Lehman, director, development, **617-353-2362**

BOWLING GREEN STATE UNIVERSITY. Bowling Green, OH 43403. **419-372-2531.** Clifton P Boutelle, director, news and photography service, **419-372-2616**

BRADLEY UNIVERSITY. Peoria, IL 61625. **309-676-7611.** *Contact.* L Victor Atchison

BRANDEIS UNIVERSITY. Waltham, MA 02154. **617-647-2222.** Amram M Ducovny, director, public affairs

UNIVERSITY OF BRIDGEPORT. Bridgeport, CT 06602. **203-576-4000.** John J Cox, vice-president, university relations, **203-576-4500.** Arthur Greenfield II, director, public relations, **203-576-4525**

BRIGHAM YOUNG UNIVERSITY. Provo, UT 84602. **801-374-1211.** Edwin J Butterworth, director, public communications

BROWN UNIVERSITY. Providence, RI 02912. **401-863-1000.** Howard R Swearer, president. Martha Matzke, director, news bureau, **401-863-2477**

BRYN MAWR COLLEGE. Bryn Mawr, PA 19010. **215-525-1000.** Ellen Reisner, acting director, public information

BUTLER UNIVERSITY. Indianapolis, IN 46208. **317-283-8000.** Chris Theofanis, director, public relations

CALIFORNIA INSTITUTE OF TECHNOLOGY. Pasadena, CA 91125. **213-795-6811.** James B Black, director, public relations

CALIFORNIA POLYTECHNIC STATE UNIVERSITY, SAN LUIS OBISPO. San Luis Obispo, CA 93407. **805-546-0111.** Dr Robert E Kennedy, president. Lachlan P MacDonald, director, public affairs, **805-546-2246** or **805-543-5404.** Donald L McCaleb, public information officer, **805-546-2576** or **805-543-8585**

CALIFORNIA STATE COLLEGE OF PENNSYLVANIA. California, PA 15419. **412-938-4000.** Robert T Wood, director, news bureau, **412-938-4418.** Dan R Kraft, director, college relations, **412-938-4195**

CALIFORNIA STATE POLYTECHNIC UNIVERSITY, POMONA. Pomona, CA 91768. **714-598-4726.** Nancy A Throp, director, information services, **714-598-4733**

CALIFORNIA STATE UNIVERSITY, FRESNO. Fresno, CA 93740. **209-487-2795.** Jim Miller, director, public information

CALIFORNIA STATE UNIVERSITY, FULLERTON. Fullerton, CA 92634. **714-870-2011.** Jerry J Keating, director, public affairs, **714-870-2414.** Judy M Mandel, associate director, public affairs, **714-870-2414**

CALIFORNIA STATE UNIVERSITY, LOS ANGELES. Los Angeles, CA 90032. **213-224-3271**

CALIFORNIA STATE UNIVERSITY, SACRAMENTO. Sacramento, CA 95819. **916-454-6011.** Chuck McFadden, director, university relations, **916-454-6156**

UNIVERSITY OF CALIFORNIA, BERKELEY. Berkeley, CA 94720. **415-642-6000.** Ray Colvig, public information officer, **415-642-3734.** (h) **415-524-8687.** Richard P Hafner, Jr, public affairs officer, **415-642-3965.** John Zane, publications manager, **415-642-0702**

UNIVERSITY OF CALIFORNIA, IRVINE. Irvine, CA 92717. **714-833-6922.** Dr Daniel G Aldrich, Jr, chancellor, **714-833-5111.** Helen Johnson, public information officer, **714-833-6922**

UNIVERSITY OF CALIFORNIA, DAVIS. Davis, CA 95616. **916-752-1930.** Robert C Bynum, public information officer

UNIVERSITY OF CALIFORNIA, LOS ANGELES. Los Angeles, CA 90024. Chandler Harris, director, public information, **213-825-2585.** Nancy Naylor, director, communications, UCLA Alumni Association, **213-825-9125.** Al Hicks, public information officer, Center for the Health Sciences, **213-825-6519.** Public information representatives: Thomas Tugend, physical sciences, **213-825-2520** James Ward, radio and television, **213-825-2585**

UNIVERSITY OF CALIFORNIA, SAN FRANCISCO. San Francisco, CA 94143. **415-666-4392.** Sue Clark, director, university relations

UNIVERSITY OF CALIFORNIA, SAN DIEGO. La Jolla, CA 92093. **714-452-3120.** Paul W West, director, public information. Paul Lowenberg, national news coordinator. *Branch offices*
Scripps Institution of Oceanography. Nelson Fuller, public affairs director, **714-452-3624**
School of Medicine. Winifred Cox, public affairs director, **714-452-3714**
University Hospital. Pat Jacoby, public information director, **714-294-6163**

UNIVERSITY OF CALIFORNIA, SANTA BARBARA. Santa Barbara, CA 93106. **805-961-2311.** Robert A Huttenback, chancellor, **805-961-2231.** George Obern, manager, public information, **805-961-3071**

UNIVERSITY OF CALIFORNIA, SANTA CRUZ. Santa Cruz, CA 95064. **408-429-2602.** Tom O'Leary, public information officer

UNIVERSITY OF CALIFORNIA, SYSTEM-WIDE OFFICE. Berkeley, CA 94720. **415-642-2325.** Sarah R Molla, public information officer

CARNEGIE-MELLON UNIVERSITY. Pittsburgh, PA 15213. **412-578-2900.** Kenneth P Service, director, public relations, (h) **412-831-9864**

CARROLL COLLEGE. Waukesha, WI 53186. **414-547-1211.** Genevieve G Caspari, director, public relations

CASE WESTERN RESERVE UNIVERSITY. Cleveland, OH 44106. **216-368-2000.** Arthur Ellis, director, public information, **216-368-4440.** (h) **321-6422.** James Castagnera, director, university communications, **216-368-2156.** Margaret Marshall, director, medical school information, **216-368-2500.** (h) **216-991-4407**

CENTENARY COLLEGE FOR WOMEN. Hackettstown, NJ 07840. **201-852-1400.** *Contact.* Charles H Dick

CENTRAL MICHIGAN UNIVERSITY. Mount Pleasant, MI 48859. **517-774-3151.** Russell L Herron, director, information services, **517-774-3197**

CENTRAL MISSOURI STATE UNIVERSITY. Warrensburg, MO 64093. **816-429-4111.** Carl B Foster, director, public relations, **816-429-4640**

CENTRAL WASHINGTON UNIVERSITY. Ellensburg, WA 98926. **509-963-3111.** Bill Lipsky, director, information, **509-963-1491**

CHAMPLAIN COLLEGE. Burlington, VT 05401. **802-658-0800.** Stephen L Harris, director, communications and publications

COLLEGE OF CHARLESTON. Charleston, SC 29401. **803-722-0181.** Daniel C Coleman, public information specialist

CHEYNEY STATE COLLEGE. Cheyney, PA 19319. **215-399-6880.** Claire Walsh, information specialist

CHICAGO STATE UNIVERSITY. Chicago, IL 60628. **312-995-2000.** Dr Martha Bass, director, university relations

UNIVERSITY OF CHICAGO. Chicago, IL 60637. **312-753-1234.** DJR Bruckner, vice-president, public affairs, **312-753-4401.** Hoke Norris, assistant vice-president, public affairs, and director, public information, **312-753-4485**

UNIVERSITY OF CINCINNATI. Cincinnati, OH 45221. **513-475-8000.** Al Kuettner, director, information, **513-475-3344.** Joyce G Endejann, public information officer, medical center, **513-872-5676**

THE CITADEL. Charleston, SC 29409. **803-577-6900.** Major Richard R Clarke, director, public relations

CITY UNIVERSITY OF NEW YORK. New York, NY 10021. **212-794-5555.** John Anderson, assistant to director, university relations. Directors of public relations: Israel E Levine, City College; Samuel I Rovener, Mt Sinai School of Medicine; Flora Rheta Schreiber, John Jay College of Criminal Justice

CLAREMONT MEN'S COLLEGE. Claremont, CA 91711. **714-626-8511.** Martha Tpschereau, director, public relations

CLARION STATE COLLEGE. Clarion, PA 16214. **814-226-6000.** William A Proudfit, director, information services

CLARK UNIVERSITY. Worcester, MA 01610. **617-793-7711**

CLEMSON UNIVERSITY. Clemson, SC 29631. **803-656-3311.** Melvin Long, director, public relations, **803-656-2061**

CLEVELAND STATE UNIVERSITY. Cleveland, OH 44115. **216-687-2000.** Thomas Hallet, coordinator, information services, **216-687-2290**

COLGATE UNIVERSITY. Hamilton, NY 13346. **315-824-1000,** Ext 417. Paul J Hennessy, director, office of public communications

COLORADO COLLEGE. Colorado Springs, CO 80903. **303-473-2233.** Ann B Sanger, director, news bureau

COLORADO SCHOOL OF MINES. Golden, CO 80401. **303-279-0300.** Guy T McBride, Jr, president. Charles S Morris, director, public relations. Leanne M Gibson, coordinator, public information, and director, sports information, (h) **303-279-8166.** A mineral engineering school offering degrees in chemistry, chemical and petroleum refining, geology, geophysics, mathematics, metallurgy, mining, mineral economics, petroleum, and physics

COLORADO STATE UNIVERSITY. Fort Collins, CO 80523. **303-491-5313.** James Bennett, assistant to president and director, university communications

UNIVERSITY OF COLORADO. Boulder, CO 80309. **303-492-0111.** Donald K Lee, director, information services, **303-492-6431**

COLUMBIA UNIVERSITY. New York, NY 10027. **212-280-1754.** Frederick H Knubel, director, office of public information, **212-280-5573**

COLUMBUS COLLEGE. Columbus, GA 31907. **404-568-2011.** Marie Bergin Goff, director, public information

COMMUNITY COLLEGE OF PHILA-DELPHIA. Philadelphia, PA 19107. **215-972-7000.** Lawrence Jacksina, public relations assistant, **215-972-7038.** Edward M Williams, assistant to president, **215-972-7037**

CONCORDIA COLLEGE. Moorhead, MN 56560. **218-299-3146.** David M Benson, director, college relations

CONNECTICUT COLLEGE. New London, CT 06320. **203-442-1285.** Margaret Thomson, director, news office

UNIVERSITY OF CONNECTICUT. Storrs, CT 06268. **203-486-3543.** Walter S McGowan, Jr, director, office of public information, **203-486-3530**

CORNELL UNIVERSITY. Ithaca, NY 14853. **607-256-1000.** Richard M Ramin, vice president, public affairs, **607-256-5142.** Kelvin J Arden, director, university publications, **607-256-4945**

CREIGHTON UNIVERSITY. Omaha, NE 68178. **402-449-2700.** Michael A Byrne, director, public relations and information, **402-449-2738**

DALLAS BAPTIST COLLEGE. Dallas, TX 75211. **214-331-8311.** Jim Willis, director, public information

DARTMOUTH COLLEGE. Hanover, NH 03755. **603-646-1110.** Robert B Graham, Jr, director, news services

DAVIDSON COLLEGE. Davidson, NC 28036. **704-892-2000.** Martha B Roberts, director, communications

UNIVERSITY OF DAYTON. Dayton, OH 45469. **513-229-2911.** Mark F Pomerleau, director, information services

UNIVERSITY OF DELAWARE. Newark, DE 19711. **302-738-2000.** Harry L Connor, director, office of information services, **302-738-2874**

DENISON UNIVERSITY. Granville, OH 43023. **614-587-0810.** Robert E Kinney, director, news services and publications

UNIVERSITY OF DENVER. Denver, CO 80208. **303-753-1964.** Dr Mort Stern, executive director, public affairs, **303-753-3584**

DE PAUL UNIVERSITY. Chicago, IL 60604. **312-321-8000.** Jeanne M Barry, director, public relations, **312-321-7656.** Allan Kipp, director, publicity, **312-321-7659**

DE PAUW UNIVERSITY. Greencastle, IN 46135. **317-653-9721.** J Patrick Aikman, director, public relations

THE DETROIT INSTITUTE OF TECH-NOLOGY. Detroit, MI 48031. **313-962-0830.** Dr Hugh Thompson, president. Dr John Miller, executive vice-president. Fred Shadrick, vice-president, institutional advancement. Doris De Deckere, director, public relations, (h) **313-882-6932.** The Detroit Institute of Technology has three colleges: Engineering, Business Administration, and Arts and Sciences, and offers special associate degree programs in criminal justice, banking, secretarial sciences, accounting, general business, management, marketing, manufacturing, computer electronics, construction surveying, and occupational safety and health

UNIVERSITY OF DETROIT. Detroit, MI 48221. **313-927-1250.** Eleanor Luedtke, director, public relations

DRAKE UNIVERSITY. Des Moines, IA 50311. **515-271-2011.** Dr Wilbur C Miller, president, **515-271-2191.** Frank De Fazio, director, university relations, **515-271-2169.** (h) **515-262-1192.** Joseph Brisben, associate director, public information and university relations, **515-271-3119.** (h) **515-277-0630.** Denny Rehder, associate director, publications and university relations, **515-271-2833.** (h) **515-277-4354.** A major private university having an enrollment of approximately 6200 and located in a residential/urban area of Des Moines, IA; major university divisions are as follows: colleges of business administration, education, fine arts, liberal arts, and pharmacy; continuing education; and schools of journalism, law, and graduate studies

DREXEL UNIVERSITY. Philadelphia, PA 19104. **215-895-2600.** William P Davis, III, vice-president, university relations

DUKE UNIVERSITY. Durham, NC 27706. **919-684-8111.** William L Green, Jr, director, public relations, **919-684-3973.** Donald M

Seaver, director, news service, **919-684-2823.** Joe H Sigler, director, public relations, medical center, **919-684-3384**

DUQUESNE UNIVERSITY. Pittsburgh, PA 15219. **412-434-6000.** The Reverend Henry J McAnulty, CSSp, president, **412-434-6060.** Regis J Ebner, assistant vice-president, communications, **412-434-6049.** Michael L McGrael, director, public relations, **412-434-6050** or **6051.** Mary R Kukovich, assistant director, public relations, **412-434-6050** or **6051.** A private, coeducational institution

EASTERN ILLINOIS UNIVERSITY. Charleston, IL 61920. **217-581-3820.** Harry Read, director, information and publications

EASTERN KENTUCKY UNIVERSITY. Richmond, KY 40475. **606-622-0111.** Donald R Feltner, vice president, public affairs, **606-622-3116.** John E Winnecke, director, public information, **606-622-2301**

EASTERN MICHIGAN UNIVERSITY. Ypsilanti, MI 48197. **313-487-4401.** John C Fountain, director, information services

EASTERN NEW MEXICO UNIVERSITY. Portales, New Mexico 88130. **505-562-2131.** Winston Cox, director, information services (h) **505-356-6868**

EASTERN OKLAHOMA STATE COL-LEGE. Wilburton, OK 74578. **918-465-2361.** Jim D Sullivan, director, public information

EASTERN OREGON STATE COLLEGE. La Grande, OR 97850. **503-963-2171.** Mark Claesgens, director, college information

EASTERN WASHINGTON UNIVERSITY. Cheney, WA 99004. **509-359-2230.** Phillip L Briggs, director, university news bureau

EAST STROUDSBURG STATE COL-LEGE. East Stroudsburg, PA 18301. **717-424-3532.** Charles O Baughman, director, public relations and publications

EAST TENNESSEE STATE UNIVER-SITY. Johnson City, TN 37601. **615-929-4112.** Dr Arthur H De Rosier, Jr, president, **615-929-4211.** Fred W Middleton, director, public relations, **615-928-4317**

EAST TEXAS STATE UNIVERSITY. Commerce, TX 75428. **214-886-8477.** Jack B Gray, Jr, assistant to president and director, communication services

ELIZABETH SETON COLLEGE. Yonkers, NY 10701. **914-969-4000.** Mary McGilvray, director, public relations

EMORY UNIVERSITY. Atlanta, GA 30322. **404-329-6123.** John Rozier, director, information services, **404-329-6216**

FAIRFIELD UNIVERSITY. Fairfield, CT 06430. **203-255-5411.** The Reverend Thomas R Fitzgerald, SJ, president. George E Diffley, vice-president, development and public relations. James A Fessler, director, public relations

FAIRLEIGH DICKINSON UNIVERSITY. Rutherford, NJ 07070. **201-933-5000.** Dr Earle W Clifford, vice-president, university resources and public affairs

FEDERAL CITY COLLEGE. Washington, DC 20005. **202-727-2818.** Paul Mathless, director, public affairs

FLORIDA A & M UNIVERSITY. Tallahassee, FL 32307. **904-599-3491.** Robert L Allen, director, university relations

FLORIDA ATLANTIC UNIVERSITY. Boca Raton, FL 33431. **305-395-5100,** Ext 2466. Dr Glenwood L Creech, president. Adelaide R Snyder, director, university relations. Sallee Arnoff, news bureau chief. Heather Langan, news writer. Marette Jackson, director, publications. An upper-division and graduate state university main campus, located in Boca Raton and having centers in Fort Lauderdale and West Palm Beach

FLORIDA STATE UNIVERSITY. Tallahassee, FL 32306. **904-644-4030.** Michael J Beaudoin, director, information services

FLORIDA TECHNOLOGICAL UNIVERSITY. Orlando, FL 32816. **305-275-9101.** C Barth Engert, director, office of public information, **305-275-2504.** (h) **305-671-8875.** William A (Bill) Daum, head, news bureau, **305-275-2504.** One of nine universities in the state university system of Florida; offers over 90 bachelor-level and 16 master-level programs in six colleges

UNIVERSITY OF FLORIDA. Gainesville, FL 32604. **904-392-3261.** Hugh Cunningham, director, university information, **904-392-1311**

FORDHAM UNIVERSITY. New York, NY 10023. **212-956-3712.** Robert M Brown, director, university relations

FRANKLIN AND MARSHALL COLLEGE. Lancaster, PA 17604. **717-291-3981.** Bruce G Holran, director, public relations

FRANKLIN UNIVERSITY. Columbus, OH 43215. **614-224-6237.** Robert Wilson, director, public relations

GENERAL MOTORS INSTITUTE. Flint, MI 48502. **313-766-9452.** Lawrence C Swanson, administrative assistant to president

GEORGETOWN UNIVERSITY. Washington, DC 20057. **202-625-0100.** Michael A Byrnes, director, public relations, **202-625-4151**

GEORGE WASHINGTON UNIVERSITY. Washington, DC 20052. **202-447-0877.** Joy Aschenbach, manager, news service, **202-676-6460**

GEORGIA INSTITUTE OF TECHNOLOGY. Atlanta, GA 30332. **404-894-5070.** John P Culver, director, public relations, **404-894-2454**

GEORGIA STATE UNIVERSITY. Atlanta, GA 30303. **404-658-2000.** Deanna S Strickland, director, public information, **404-928-3571**

UNIVERSITY OF GEORGIA. Athens, GA 30605. **404-542-3030.** R Barry Wood, director, public relations, **404-542-3354.** Larry Dendy, assistant director, public relations for information. Robert D Wilson, assistant director, public relations for publications

GOLDEN GATE UNIVERSITY. San Francisco, CA 94105. **415-391-7800.** Dr Otto W Butz, president. Jay P Goyette, director, public relations, (h) **415-587-7927.** A private university that specializes in upper-division and graduate professional education through the doctoral level in management, public administration, and law

GOSHEN COLLEGE. Goshen, IN 46526. **219-533-3616.** Janice Martin, director, news services. Judith M Davis, director, communications

GRINNELL COLLEGE. Grinnell, IA 50112. **515-236-6181.** Gordon E Brown, director, communication

HAHNEMANN MEDICAL COLLEGE AND HOSPITAL. Philadelphia, PA 19102. **215-448-7000.** William Likoff, MD, acting president and chief executive officer. Marjorie R Carmosin, director, public relations, **215-448-8284.** Night line: **215-448-7000.** A 500-bed general hospital that grants the degrees of Associate in Science, Bachelor of Science, Master of Science, Doctor of Philosophy, Doctor of

Psychology, and Doctor of Medicine, and has a college of allied health professions, a graduate school, and a medical college

HAMPSHIRE COLLEGE. Amherst, MA 01002. **413-549-4600.** Peter Gluckler, director, public relations

UNIVERSITY OF HARTFORD. West Hartford, CT 06117. **203-243-4351.** Edwin Matesky, director, public information

HARVARD UNIVERSITY. Cambridge, MA 02138. **617-495-1585.** Deane Lord, director, information. Jean R Phinney, director, public information office, business school, **617-495-6158**

HAVERFORD COLLEGE. Haverford, PA 19041. **215-649-9600.** Mary Ann Meyers, director, public relations

UNIVERSITY OF HAWAII. Honolulu, HI 96822. **808-948-8111.** Frederick Y Smith, director, university relations, **808-948-7522**

HOBART AND WILLIAM SMITH COLLEGES. Geneva, NY 14456. **315-789-5500.** Thom Lamond, director, news bureau. Gordon Brown, director, department of information services

HOFSTRA UNIVERSITY. Hempstead, NY 11550. **516-560-3513** or **3514.** Harold A Klein, director, university relations

UNIVERSITY OF HOUSTON. Houston, TX 77004. **713-749-4147.** Farris F Block, director, information and publications

HOWARD UNIVERSITY. Washington, DC 20059. **202-636-6100.** Paul R Hathaway, director, university relations and publications, **202-636-6000**

HUNTINGDON COLLEGE. Montgomery, AL 36106. **205-263-1611.** W Ron Crocker, director, public relations and alumni affairs

IDAHO STATE UNIVERSITY. Pocatello, ID 83209. **208-236-3620.** Stan Martin, assistant director, publicity, publications, and services

UNIVERSITY OF IDAHO. Moscow, ID 83843. **208-885-6163.** Carolyn S Cron, director, university relations. Barbara B Petura, news bureau manager, **208-885-6291.** William M Stellmon, head agricultural editor, **208-885-6436**

ILLINOIS COLLEGE. Jacksonville, IL 62650. **217-245-7126.** Mark J Schwartz, director, public relations and alumni affairs

ILLINOIS INSTITUTE OF TECHNOL-OGY. Chicago, IL 60616. 312-567-3000. Lawrence D Stuart, university relations director, 312-567-3107

UNIVERSITY OF ILLINOIS—CHICAGO. Chicago, IL 60680. 312-996-8535. David Landman, university director, public information, 312-996-5148. Marilyn Pierce, director, public information, 312-996-3456

UNIVERSITY OF ILLINOIS—MEDICAL CENTER. Chicago, IL 60680. 312-996-7000. Jack Righeimer, director, public information, 312-996-7680

UNIVERSITY OF ILLINOIS—URBANA —CHAMPAIGN. Urbana, IL 61801. 217-333-1000. Frederick Mohn, acting director, public information, 217-333-1085

INDIANA STATE UNIVERSITY, TERRE HAUTE. Terre Haute, IN 47809. 812-232-6311. Dr Donald J Roberts, vice-president, development and public affairs. Joseph E Kish, director, information services. Ms Marian P Groscop, director, news services. David L Piker, electronic media specialist

INDIANA UNIVERSITY. Bloomington, IN 47401. 812-332-0211. James L Green, director, news bureau

INDIANA UNIVERSITY—PURDUE UNI-VERSITY AT FORT WAYNE. Fort Wayne, IN 46805. 219-482-5121. Carl W Vandagrift, director, university relations, 219-482-5721

INDIANA UNIVERSITY—PURDUE UNI-VERSITY AT INDIANAPOLIS. Indianapolis, IN 46202. 317-264-8710. Dr Glenn W Irwin, vice-president, Indiana University (Indianapolis), 317-264-4417. Kenneth A Beckley, director, university relations, 317-264-2134. Noel H Duerden, director, publications and information services, 317-264-2101

INDIANA UNIVERSITY OF PENNSYL-VANIA. Indiana, PA 15701. 412-357-2233. Randy L Jesick, director, public information

IOWA STATE UNIVERSITY. Ames, IA 50011. 515-294-4777. Carl Hamilton, vice-president, information and development. Robert P Hogan, editor, news service

UNIVERSITY OF IOWA. Iowa City, IA 52242. 319-353-2121. Thomas L Tobin, director, public information and university relations, 319-353-5691

ITHACA COLLEGE. Ithaca, NY 14850. 607-274-3201. Marjory Spraycar, director, public information. Walter Borton, director, college relations

JACKSON STATE UNIVERSITY. Jackson, MS 39217. 601-968-2121. Obra V Hackett, director, public information

JACKSONVILLE STATE UNIVERSITY. Jacksonville, AL 36265. 205-435-9820. Jack Hopper, director, public relations, and assistant to president

THOMAS JEFFERSON UNIVERSITY. Philadelphia, PA 19107. 215-829-6300. Lewis W Bluemle, Jr, president. George W Belk III, director, public relations. Founded in 1824 and the largest private health-oriented university in the nation; Jefferson Medical College has educated more physicians than any other medical school in the US, and enjoys a national reputation as a leading medical center

THE JOHNS HOPKINS UNIVERSITY. Baltimore, MD 21218. 301-338-8000. Robert Hewes, assistant vice-president, university affairs, 301-338-7160. Mrs B J Norris, director, public affairs, Johns Hopkins medical institutions, 301-955-6680

JUNIATA COLLEGE. Huntingdon, PA 16654. 814-643-4310. Charles R Pollock, director, public relations, Ext 17

KALAMAZOO COLLEGE. Kalamazoo, MI 49007. 616-383-8497. Marilyn Hinkle, director, public relations

KANSAS STATE UNIVERSITY. Manhattan, KS 66506. 913-532-6011. Dr B L Flinchbaugh, assistant to president for public affairs, information, and development, 913-532-6325

UNIVERSITY OF KANSAS. Lawrence, KS 66045. 913-864-2700. James R Collier, director, university relations, 913-864-4115

KENT STATE UNIVERSITY. Kent, OH 44242. 216-672-2210. Dr Brage Golding, president. Anthony J May, director, communications, 216-672-2726. Night line: 216-688-9424. James T Lawless IV, manager, media relations, 216-672-2727. Night line: 216-678-2320. Jacob Urchek, director, university relations, 216-672-2200

KENTUCKY STATE UNIVERSITY. Frankfort, KY 40601. 502-564-6260. Baxter Melton, director, public information

UNIVERSITY OF KENTUCKY. Lexington, KY 40506. 606-258-9000. Dr Raymond R Hornback, vice-president, university relations. B L Vonderheide, director, university information services. David A Holt, director, news bureau. Pete Manchikes, director, radio, television, and films. Shirley Boyd, director, medical center public information and services

KIRKSVILLE COLLEGE OF OSTEO-PATHIC MEDICINE. Kirksville, MO 63501. 816-626-2121. Arthur M Dye, Jr, director, development, 816-626-2395

LAFAYETTE COLLEGE. Easton, PA 18042. 215-253-6281. Tom Murray White, director, public information and community relations

LAMAR UNIVERSITY. Beaumont, TX 77710. 713-838-7611. Russ L De Villier, director, public information

LARAMIE COUNTY COMMUNITY COL-LEGE. Cheyenne, WY 82001. 307-634-5853. Dr Harlan L Heglar, president. Rosalind Routt, director, public information

LA SALLE COLLEGE. Philadelphia, PA 19141. 215-951-1080. Robert S Lyons, Jr, news bureau director

LAWRENCE INSTITUTE OF TECHNOL-OGY. Southfield, MI 48075. 313-356-0200. Bruce J Annett, Jr, director, public and alumni relations

LEHIGH UNIVERSITY. Bethlehem, PA 18015. 215-691-7000. Samuel I Connor, director, office of public information (Alumni Bldg 27)

LEMOYNE—OWEN COLLEGE. Memphis, TN 38126. 901-774-9090. George E Hardin, director, public information

LEWIS AND CLARK COLLEGE. Portland, OR 97219. 503-244-6161. Charles Charnquist, director, public information. Robert C Brendel, information officer. Gregory Gerber, assistant information officer and photographer

LINCOLN UNIVERSITY. Jefferson City, MO 65101. 314-751-4009. L R Hughes, university relations director. Robert C Brendel, university information officer

LINCOLN UNIVERSITY. Lincoln University, PA 19352. 215-932-8300. Earl D Winderman, vice-president, development

LIVINGSTON UNIVERSITY. Livingston, AL 35470. **205-652-9661.** Steve F Martin, public information director

LOCK HAVEN STATE COLLEGE. Lock Haven, PA 17745. **717-748-5351.** Robert M Coltrane, Jr, director, information services

LONG ISLAND UNIVERSITY. University Ctr, Greenvale, NY 11548. **516-299-0200.** Dr Albert Bush–Brown, chancellor, **516-229-2501.** *Press contact.* William W Love, assistant to chancellor, **516-299-2529**

Center contacts

Brooklyn Center. Robert E Gesslein, coordinator, public relations, **212-834-6090**

C W Post Center. West Sheffield, director, communications, **516-299-2332**

Southampton Center. Eleanor Feleppa, director, public relations, **516-283-4000, Ext 268**

LOUISIANA STATE UNIVERSITY IN BATON ROUGE. Baton Rouge, LA 70893. **504-388-3202.** Oscar G Richard, director, information services, **504-388-4461.** Nick Kalivoda, department of media services, **504-388-4461**

LOUISIANA TECH UNIVERSITY. Ruston, LA 71270. **318-257-0211.** *Contact.* William L Pippin, Jr

UNIVERSITY OF LOUISVILLE. Louisville, KY 40208. **502-588-5555.** James E McGovern, director, public relations, **502-588-6171**

LOYOLA COLLEGE OF MARYLAND. Baltimore, MD 21210. **301-323-1010.** Frances M Minakowski, public relations director

LOYOLA UNIVERSITY. Chicago, IL 60611. **312-670-2860.** Alvo E Albini, director, public relations

LOYOLA UNIVERSITY. New Orleans, LA 70118. **504-865-2284.** Eugene R Katsanis, director, public relations and publications

LUTHER COLLEGE. Decorah, IA 52101. **319-387-2000.** Christine Cihlar, director, public information, **319-387-1865.** Jeff Iseminger, news bureau manager, **319-387-1865**

LYNCHBURG COLLEGE. Lynchburg, VA 24501. **804-845-9071.** Dorothy M Ferguson, director, news bureau, Ext 241

JAMES MADISON UNIVERSITY. Harrisonburg, VA 22801. **703-433-6154.** Dr

Ronald E Carrier, president, **703-433-6241.** Rich Murray, public information director. Fred Hilton, assistant to vice-president for university relations, **703-433-6162.** (h) **703-433-1591**

UNIVERSITY OF MAINE AT ORONO. Orono, ME 04473. **207-581-7336.** Leonard Harlow, director, public information. George E Wildey, information specialist, radio and television, **207-581-7369.** Marion Hamilton, acting director, **207-581-7376**

UNIVERSITY OF MAINE AT PORTLAND—GORHAM. Portland, ME 04103. **207-773-2981.** Roger V Snow, Jr, director, publications and public information

MANHATTAN COLLEGE. Bronx, NY 10471. **212-548-1400.** Brother J Stephen Sullivan, FSC, president. Thomas M Gray, director, college relations. Dorothy Bracken, public information officer

MANSFIELD STATE COLLEGE. Mansfield, PA 16933. **717-662-4000.** Dr Donald C Darnton, interim president, **717-662-4046.** John A Holley, director, public relations, **717-662-4293.** (h) **717-662-7525**

MARQUETTE UNIVERSITY. Milwaukee, WI 53233. **414-224-7448.** William N Robersen, director, public relations, **414-224-7514.** David J Foran, associate director, **414-224-7444.** James L Sankovitz, vice-president, university relations, **414-224-7430**

UNIVERSITY OF MARYLAND, BALTIMORE CAMPUS. Baltimore, MD 21201. **301-528-7820.** Louise M White, director, university relations

UNIVERSITY OF MARYLAND, COLLEGE PARK CAMPUS. College Park, MD 20742. **301-454-3322.** Patrick J Hunt, director, university relations

MARYMOUNT COLLEGE. Tarrytown, NY 10591. **914-631-3200.** Robert Shepherd, director, public information

MASSACHUSETTS INSTITUTE OF TECHNOLOGY. Cambridge, MA 02139. **617-253-2701.** Robert M Byers, director, MIT news office, (h) **617-834-6317**

UNIVERSITY OF MASSACHUSETTS—AMHERST. Amherst, MA 01002. **413-545-2212.** Daniel Melley, director, public affairs

UNIVERSITY OF MASSACHUSETTS—BOSTON. Harbor Campus, Boston, MA 02125. **617-287-1900.** James W Ryan, director, public information. Campus is site of new President John F Kennedy Memorial Library

MEDICAL COLLEGE OF VIRGINIA. Richmond, VA 23298. **804-770-5211.** William T Van Pelt, director, medical information, **804-770-7457**

COLLEGE OF MEDICINE AND DENTISTRY OF NEW JERSEY. Newark, NJ 07103. **201-877-4300.** Stanley S Gergen, Jr, MD, president, **201-456-4400.** Martin Z Post, director, external relations, **201-456-5000.** Andrew E Beresky, manager, public information, **201-456-5003.** Public information officers; Carol Pilla, **201-456-5001;** Ron Reisman, **201-456-5002.** *Foundation.* **201-456-4830.** Malachy M Glynn, executive director. The College of Medicine and Dentistry of New Jersey (CMDNJ) is the state's only medical education institution

MEMPHIS STATE UNIVERSITY. Memphis, TN 38152. **901-454-2843.** Sam Lancaster, director, media relations. Debbie Warrington, assistant director

MERCER UNIVERSITY. Macon, GA 31207. **404-745-6811.** B J Trawick, director, news services and publications

METROPOLITAN STATE UNIVERSITY. St Paul, MN 55101. **612-296-3875.** Reatha Clark King, president

MIAMI—DADE COMMUNITY COLLEGE. Miami, FL 33176. **305-596-1223.** Betty Garnet, director, information services

MIAMI UNIVERSITY. Oxford, OH 45056. **513-529-2161.** Robert T Howard, director, office of public information, **513-529-4428**

UNIVERSITY OF MIAMI. Coral Gables, FL 33124. **305-284-4111**

MICHIGAN STATE UNIVERSITY. East Lansing, MI 48824. **517-355-1855.** Dale J Arnold, director, information services, **517-355-2262**

MICHIGAN TECHNOLOGICAL UNIVERSITY. Houghton, MI 49931. **906-487-1885**

UNIVERSITY OF MICHIGAN. Ann Arbor, MI 48109. **313-764-1817.** Joel S Berger, director .nformation services, **313-764-7260.** (h) **313-994-1594.** Louis Graff, director, health sciences relations, **313-764-2220.** (h) **313-971-6918.** Roger Sutton, radio and television information officer, **313-764-7260.** (h) **313-994-5196**

UNIVERSITY OF MICHIGAN—DEARBORN. Dearborn, MI 48128. **313-271-2300.** Richard G Reynolds, director, university relations, Ext 343, (h) **313-525-4278**

UNIVERSITY OF MICHIGAN—FLINT. Flint, MI 48502. **313-767-1863.** Richard P McElroy, assistant to chancellor for university relations, **313-762-3350.** (h) **313-629-4438**

MIDDLEBURY COLLEGE. Middlebury, VT 05753. **802-388-6033.** Kenneth Nourse, director, public affairs

MIDDLE TENNESSEE STATE UNIVERSITY. Murfreesboro, TN 37130. **615-898-2300.** Dorothy Harrison, director, news bureau

MILLERSVILLE STATE COLLEGE. Millersville, PA 17551. **717-872-5411.** Carole L Slotter, director, public relations

MILLIKIN UNIVERSITY. Decatur, IL 62522. **217-424-6200.** Dr J Roger Miller, president. Reggie Syrcle, public information director, **217-424-6350**

UNIVERSITY OF MINNESOTA, DULUTH. Duluth, MN 55812. **218-726-8000.** Julian B Hoshall, director, campus relations

UNIVERSITY OF MINNESOTA. Minneapolis, MN 55455. **612-373-7510.** Elizabeth Petrangelo, news director. *Health sciences contact.* Robert Lee, **612-373-5830**

MISSISSIPPI STATE UNIVERSITY. Mississippi State, MS 39762. **601-325-5872.** Bob V Moulder, public information director

MISSISSIPPI UNIVERSITY FOR WOMEN. Columbus, MS 39701. **601-328-7885.** Gerald E Weaver, director, public information

UNIVERSITY OF MISSISSIPPI. University, MS 38677. **601-232-7211.** Ed Meek, director, public relations

MISSISSIPPI VALLEY STATE UNIVERSITY. Itta Bena, MS 38941. **601-254-9041.**

Mrs M E Fingal, director, development. Larry E Edmond, public relations director

UNIVERSITY OF MISSOURI— COLUMBIA. Columbia, MO 65201. **314-882-6211.** Robert E Kren, director, office of public information, (h) **314-445-4562**

UNIVERSITY OF MISSOURI —KANSAS CITY. Kansas City, MO 64110. **816-276-1000.** William Steinhardt, director, office of public information

UNIVERSITY OF MISSOURI—ROLLA. Rolla, MO 65401. **314-341-4111.** W Dudley Cress, director, public information, **314-341- 4259**

UNIVERSITY OF MISSOURI—ST LOUIS. St Louis, MO 63121. **314-453-0111.** Blair K Farrell, director, university relations, **314-453-5776**

WILLIAM MITCHELL COLLEGE OF LAW. St Paul, MN 55105. **612-227-9171.** Jerry Bjelde, director, development

MONMOUTH COLLEGE. West Long Branch, NJ 07764. **201-222-6600.** Dr Richard J Stonesifer, president. *Contact.* Jane C Schoener

MONTANA STATE UNIVERSITY. Bozeman, MT 59715. **406-994-0211.** Ken Nicholson, director, publications and news services, **406-994-2724**

MOORHEAD STATE UNIVERSITY. Moorhead, MN 56560. **218-236-2555.** Dr G K Haukebo, vice-president, public affairs

MORAVIAN COLLEGE. Bethleham, PA 18018. **215-865-0741.** Richard K Brunner, director, communications

MOUNT HOLYOKE COLLEGE. South Hadley, MA 01075. **413-538-2000.** Irma L Rabbino, director, public information,. **413-538-2222.** A liberal arts college for women, founded in 1837; the oldest continuing institution of higher education for women in the country

UNIVERSITY OF NEBRASKA. Lincoln, NE 68588. **402-472-7211.** Dr Richard L Fleming, director, university information, **402-472-2167**

UNIVERSITY OF NEBRASKA AT OMAHA. Omaha, NE 68101. **402-554-2200.** Dr Delbert D Weber, chancellor, **402-554-2311.** Charles Hein, director, university relations, **402-554-2358.** (h)

402-397-4140. Ellen Ellick, news bureau manager, **402-554-2358.** Tim Fitzgerald, radio and television information, **402-554-2358.** A state-supported, urban institution serving 15,000 graduate and undergraduate students

NEBRASKA WESLEYAN UNIVERSITY. Lincoln NE 68504. **402-466-2371.** Dr John W White, Jr, president, Ext 217. Darrel E Seng, director, publicity, Ext 319

UNIVERSITY OF NEVADA, LAS VEGAS. Las Vegas, NV 89154. **702-739-3011.** Mark Hughes, director, public information services

UNIVERSITY OF NEVADA, RENO. Reno, NV 89557. **702-784-1110.** Edward A Olsen, director, information and news service, **702-784-6739**

NEWBERRY COLLEGE. Newberry, SC 29108. **803-276-5010.** Gordon C Henry, director, public relations, Ext 240

NEW ENGLAND COLLEGE. Henniker, NH 03242. **603-428-2211.** J Kenneth Cummiskey, president, **603-428-2222.** Phyllis Johnston, director, public information, **603-428-2343.** A fully accredited, 4-year, independent, liberal arts institution

NEW ENGLAND SCHOOL OF LAW. Boston, MA 02116. **617-267-9655.** Carol H Healy, public relations director

NEW HAMPSHIRE COLLEGE. Manchester, NH 03104. **603-668-2211.** Benjamin Donatelli, director, development

UNIVERSITY OF NEW HAMPSHIRE. Durham, NH 03824. **603-862-1460.** Peter H Hollister, general information. *Media contacts.* Jake Chapline and Gene Franceware

NEW JERSEY INSTITUTE OF TECHNOLOGY. Newark, NJ 07102. **201-645-5195.** *Contact.* Thomas Reilly

UNIVERSITY OF NEW MEXICO. Albuquerque, NM 87131. **505-277-5813.** Jess E Price, director, public information office

COLLEGE OF NEW ROCHELLE. New Rochelle, NY 10801. **914-632-5300.** Sister Dorothy Ann Kelly, OSV, president, Ext 212. Mary G Farrell, director, public information, Ext 272

NEW YORK INSTITUTE OF TECHNOLOGY. Old Westbury, NY 11568. **516-686-7516.** Christine A Capone, director, public relations, **516-686-7647**

STATE UNIVERSITY OF NEW YORK CENTRAL ADMINISTRATION. Albany, NY 12210. **518-474-4050.** Public relations officers: Harry E Charlton, **518-474-4056.** Hugh J Tuohey, Jr, **518-474-4055**

STATE UNIVERSITY OF NEW YORK AT ALBANY. Albany, NY 12222. **518-457-3300.** Lewis P Welch, vice-president, university affairs, **518-457-4390.** Philip C Johnson, director, community relations, **518-457-4643.** Robert H Rice, Jr, director, news bureau, **518-457-4901**

STATE UNIVERSITY OF NEW YORK AGRICULTURAL AND TECHNICAL COLLEGE AT ALFRED. Alfred, NY 14802. **607-871-6228.** Robert W Grogan, assistant to president for public relations, (h) **607-698-2781**

STATE UNIVERSITY OF NEW YORK AT BINGHAMTON. Binghamton, NY 13901. **607-798-2000.** Clifford D Clark, president. Roberta Scheer, director, university relations, **607-798-2174.** Bebe Landry, news director, **607-798-2174**

STATE UNIVERSITY OF NEW YORK AT BUFFALO. Amherst, NY 14260. **716-831-9000.** James R De Santis, director, public affairs. John T Thurston, director, university news bureau

STATE UNIVERSITY OF NEW YORK AT CORTLAND. Cortland, NY 13045. **607-753-2518.** Norbert W Haley, director, public relations

STATE UNIVERSITY OF NEW YORK DOWNSTATE MEDICAL CENTER. Brooklyn, NY 11203. **212-270-1176.** Ms M Barrie Jacobs, assistant to president and director, public affairs

STATE UNIVERSITY OF NEW YORK AT PLATTSBURGH. Plattsburgh, NY 12901. **518-564-2090.** Don Garrant, assistant to president

STATE UNIVERSITY OF NEW YORK AT POTSDAM. Potsdam, NY 13676. **315-268-3650.** John Oliphant, coordinator, news services, **315-268-3651**

STATE UNIVERSITY OF NEW YORK AT STONY BROOK. Stony Brook, NY 11794. **516-246-3580.** David Woods, director, university relations. Alexis White, news director

NEW YORK UNIVERSITY. Washington Sq, New York, NY 10003. **212-598-1212.** William F Payne, senior vice-president,

external affairs. Herbert Kadison, director, public relations, medical center

NIAGARA UNIVERSITY. Niagara University, NY 14109. **716-285-1212.** The Reverend Lewis F Bennett, CM, director, public relations. Thomas A Hohensee, news bureau and sports publicity director

NORFOLK STATE COLLEGE. Norfolk, VA 23504. **804-623-8600.** Jacob E Simms, assistant vice-president, college relations, **804-623-8373**

NORTH CAROLINA AGRICULTURAL AND TECHNICAL STATE UNIVERSITY. Greensboro, NC 27411. **919-379-7500.** Richard E Moore, director, information services

NORTH CAROLINA STATE UNIVERSITY AT RALEIGH. Raleigh, NC 27607. **919-737-2846.** Hardy D Berry, director, information services

UNIVERSITY OF NORTH CAROLINA AT CHAPEL HILL. Chapel Hill, NC 27514. **919-933-2091.** Wesley Lefler, director, news bureau

UNIVERSITY OF NORTH CAROLINA AT CHARLOTTE. Charlotte, NC 28223. **704-597-2271.** Kenneth Sanford, director, information

UNIVERSITY OF NORTH CAROLINA AT GREENSBORO. Greensboro, NC 27412. **919-379-5371.** Wilson Davis, director, news bureau. Steve Gilliam, assistant director

UNIVERSITY OF NORTH CAROLINA AT WILMINGTON. Wilmington, NC 28401. **919-791-4330.** Gwen Culbreth, director, information services

NORTH DAKOTA STATE UNIVERSITY. Fargo, ND 58102. **701-237-8011.** Jerry Richardson, director, communications

UNIVERSITY OF NORTH DAKOTA. Grand Forks, ND 58202. **701-777-2011.** Richard Larson, news service coordinator, **701-777-2731.** Dave Vorland, director, university relations. James Penwarden, assistant director

UNIVERSITY OF NORTH FLORIDA. Jacksonville, FL 32216. **904-646-2450.** Dr Thomas G Carpenter, president, **904-646-2500.** Dr George W Corrick, vice-president, university relations. Henry A Newman, Jr, director, public relations, **904-646-2450**

NORTH TEXAS STATE UNIVERSITY. Denton, TX 76203. **817-788-2108.** Janice K Odom, director, public information

NORTHEAST MISSOURI STATE UNIVERSITY. Kirksville, MO 63501. **816-665-5121.** Maggie Jarrett, staff assistant, public relations

NORTHEASTERN UNIVERSITY. Boston, MA 02115. **617-437-2000.** Donald G Porter, director, development, **617-437-2108.** Christopher S Mosher, director, public information, **617-437-2192**

NORTHEASTERN ILLINOIS UNIVERSITY. Chicago, IL 60625. **312-583-4050** Gerald Cannon, director, university relations

NORTHEASTERN OKLAHOMA STATE UNIVERSITY. Tahlequah, OK 74464. **918-456-5511.** Dr Kenneth L Collins, assistant to president for media and public relations

NORTHERN ARIZONA UNIVERSITY. Flagstaff, AZ 86011. **602-523-2282.** *Contact.* William G Hort

UNIVERSITY OF NORTHERN COLORADO. Greeley, CO 80639. **303-351-1890.** Eric Lundberg, director, news service, **303-351-2331**

NORTHERN ILLINOIS UNIVERSITY. DeKalb, IL 60115. **815-753-1000.** Donald Peterson, director, office of information, **815-753-1681.** Robert L Woggon, associate director, **815-753-0278**

UNIVERSITY OF NORTHERN IOWA. Cedar Falls, IA 50613. **319-273-2311.** Donald A Kelly, director, office of public information services, **319-273-2761**

NORTHERN KENTUCKY UNIVERSITY. Highland Heights, KY 41076. **606-292-5100.** Robert Knauf, director, public relations and community affairs, **606-292-5129**

NORTHERN MICHIGAN UNIVERSITY. Marquette, MI 49855. **906-227-1000.** Dr John X Jamrich, president, **906-227-2242.** Paul N Suomi, news bureau chief, **906-227-2720.** (h) **906-226-6867.** Matthew J Surrell, vice-president, university affairs, **906-227-2720.** (h) **906-226-6260**

NORTHWEST CHRISTIAN COLLEGE. Eugene, OR 97401. **503-343-1641.** Clifton L Peightal, director, public relations

NORTHWESTERN UNIVERSITY. Evanston, IL 60201. **312-492-5000.** Jack O'Dowd, director, university relations. Ben Harrison, manager, press relations

NORTHWESTERN MICHIGAN COLLEGE. Traverse City, MI 49684. **616-946-5650.** Kathleen E Guy, college relations coordinator

COLLEGE OF NOTRE DAME—MARYLAND. Baltimore, MD 21210. **301-435-0100.** Melady P Klausmeier, public relations director

UNIVERSITY OF NOTRE DAME. Notre Dame, IN 46556. **219-283-6011.** Richard W Conklin, director, information services

OAKLAND UNIVERSITY. Rochester, MI 48063. **313-377-2100.** *Contact.* William W Connellan

OAKWOOD COLLEGE. Huntsville, AL 35806. **205-837-1630.** R T McDonald, director, development. K E Forde, director, public relations and publications. J E Roache, director, recruitment and alumni affairs. Jan Ross, director, placement and cooperative education. C B Tivy, director, institutional relations

OBERLIN COLLEGE. Oberlin, OH 44074. **216-775-8121.** James G Lubetkin, director, college information, **216-775-8474**

OGLETHORPE UNIVERSITY. Atlanta, GA 30319. **404-261-1441.** Dr Manning M Pattillo, Jr, president. William Mark Wolpin, director, public information, (h) **404-875-4640**

OHIO NORTHERN UNIVERSITY. Ada, OH 45810. **419-634-9921.** Karen Winget, director, communications services

OHIO STATE UNIVERSITY. Columbus, OH 43210. **614-422-6446.** William V Merriman, director, communications. Michael J Lombardi, coordinator, broadcast news. Edwin M Crawford, vice-president, public affairs

OHIO UNIVERSITY. Athens, OH 45701. **614-594-5511.** Peggy Sheridan Blac, director, public information, **614-594-6043**

OHIO WESLEYAN UNIVERSITY. Delaware, OH 43015. **614-369-4431.** David E Tull, director, news and information

OKLAHOMA CITY UNIVERSITY. Oklahoma City, OK 73106. **405-521-5000.**

Dr Dolphus Whitten, Jr, president, **405-521-5032.** *Press contact.* David Graham, director, public relations, **405-521-5348.** A 2900-student liberal arts school offering undergraduate degrees in 44 major fields and seven graduate degree programs

OKLAHOMA STATE UNIVERSITY. Stillwater, OK 74074. **405-624-5000.** Ralph L Hamilton, director, public information, **405-624-6260.** Robert McCulloh, general public information officer, **405-624-6260**

UNIVERSITY OF OKLAHOMA. Norman, OK 70319. **405-325-2446.** Mike Treps, director, media information, **405-237-4115.** Dr Koy Floyd, vice-president, university relations and development, health science center, **405-271-4843**

OLD DOMINION UNIVERSITY. Norfolk, VA 23508. **804-489-6000.** Dr Alfred B Rollins, Jr, president. John Battenfield IV, director, public relations, **804-489-6693.** Jill C Nolte, director, information services, **804-489-6638.** A state-supported, urban university, founded in 1930; has an enrollment of 14,000 students and offers 69 bachelor's degree programs, 33 master's degree programs, and doctoral degree programs in engineering, oceanography, and industrial/organizational psychology

OREGON STATE UNIVERSITY. Corvallis, OR 97331. **503-754-0123.** Samuel H Bailey, director, information, **503-754-4611.** Wallace E Johnson, news editor, **503-754-4611**

UNIVERSITY OF OREGON. Eugene, OR 97403. **503-686-3111.** Robert K Bruce, Jr, director, news bureau, **503-686-3134.** Muriel K Jackson, director, university relations, **503-686-3021**

PACE UNIVERSITY. New York, NY 10038. K L Ekirch, assistant vice-president, **914-769-3200.** *New York City campus.* **212-285-3000.** *White Plains campus.* **914-682-7000.** *Pleasantville campus.* **914-769-3200** *Briarcliff campus.* **914-941-6400**

PACIFIC OAKS COLLEGE. Pasadena, CA 91105. **213-795-9161.** Charlotte Huser, director, public information

UNIVERSITY OF THE PACIFIC. Stockton, CA 95211. **209-946-2011.** Doyle Minden, director, public relations, **209-946-2311**

PACIFIC UNIVERSITY. Forest Grove, OR 97116. **503-357-6151.** Charlotte Filer, public information officer

PENNSYLVANIA STATE UNIVERSITY. University Park, PA 16802. **814-865-4700.** Arthur V Ciervo, director, public information and relations, **814-865-7517**

UNIVERSITY OF PENNSYLVANIA. Philadelphia, PA 19174. **215-243-5337.** William G Owen, vice president, development and university relations

PHILADELPHIA COLLEGE OF TEXTILES AND SCIENCE. Philadelphia, PA 19144. **215-843-9700.** Alan Nichols, director, information services

UNIVERSITY OF PITTSBURGH. Pittsburgh, PA 15260. **412-624-4141.** Bernard J Kobosky, vice-chancellor, public affairs, **412-624-4240.** Mary Ann Aug, director, news and publications, **412-624-4238**

POLYTECHNIC INSTITUTE OF NEW YORK. Brooklyn, NY 11201. **212-643-8033**

POMONA COLLEGE. Claremont, CA 91711. **714-626-8511.** David Alexander, president, Ext 2201. W Robert Finegan, director, public relations, Ext 2498 or 3298. An independent, coeducational liberal arts college founded in 1887, and the founding member of the Claremont Colleges cluster

PORTLAND STATE UNIVERSITY. Portland, OR 97207. **503-229-4421.** David Fiskum, director, information services, **503-229-3711**

UNIVERSITY OF PORTLAND. Portland, OR 97203. **503-283-7911.** Barbara Miller, director, public information, **503-283-7202**

PRINCETON THEOLOGICAL SEMINARY. Princeton, NJ 08540. **609-921-8300.** Cara Davis Smith, public relations assistant

PRINCETON UNIVERSITY. Princeton, NJ 08540. **609-452-3000.** William W Weathersby, vice-president, public affairs, **609-452-6428.** George B Eager, director, communications, **609-452-3606**

PROVIDENCE COLLEGE. Providence, RI 02918. **401-865-1000.** Joseph McAleer, public information officer, **401-865-2413**

UNIVERSITY OF PUGET SOUND. Tacoma, WA 98416. **206-756-3100.** Joan Lynott, director, public relations, **206-756-3148**

PURDUE UNIVERSITY. West Lafayette, IN 47907. **317-749-8111.** Douglas W Spangler, director, office of public information, **317-749-2062.** Charles J Leslie, senior editor, office of public information, **317-749-2062**

RADCLIFFE COLLEGE. Cambridge, MA 02138. **617-495-8000.** *Contact.* Hope W Wigglesworth

UNIVERSITY OF REDLANDS. Redlands, CA 92373. **714-793-2121**

REED COLLEGE. Portland, OR 97202. **503-771-1112.** Marge Floren, director, information services

RENSSELEAR POLYTECHNIC INSTITUTE. Troy, NY 12181. **518-270-6000.** George M Low, president, **518-270-6211.** Bruce Hutchison, director, university news office, **518-270-6531.** Night line: **518-270-6000.** A technological university emphasizing engineering and science; the School of Engineering claims the largest undergraduate enrollment in engineering (2650) of any independent university in the country

RHODE ISLAND COLLEGE. Providence, RI 02908. **401-831-6600.** Laurence J Sasso, director, news bureau

UNIVERSITY OF RHODE ISLAND. Kingston, RI 02881. **401-792-1000.** Stan Bernstein, director, news and information services, **401-792-2014.** Charles Hooker, director, photography, radio, and television, **401-792-5885**

RICE UNIVERSITY. Houston, TX 77001. **713-527-8101.** David H Rodwell, director, information services

UNIVERSITY OF RICHMOND. Richmond, VA 23173. **804-285-6281.** H Gerald Quigg, vice-president, university relations. Randolph H Walker, director, public information, **804-285-6473**

RIDER COLLEGE. Lawrenceville, NJ 08648. **609-896-0800.** Walter L Wahlen, director, college relations

ROANOKE COLLEGE. Salem, VA 24153. **703-389-2351.** Charles W Boswell, director, public information

ROCHESTER INSTITUTE OF TECHNOLOGY. Rochester, NY 14623. **716-464-2411.** Dr D Robert Frisina, vice-president, public affairs, **716-464-6403**

UNIVERSITY OF ROCHESTER. Rochester, NY 14627. **716-275-2121.** Judith Ellen Brown, director, public relations, **716-275-4124**

ROCKEFELLER UNIVERSITY. New York, NY 10021. **212-360-1000.** Fulvio Bardossi, director, public information, **212-360-1261.** Eugene H Kone, public information associate, **212-360-1262.** Judy Schwartz, public information officer, **212- 360-1420**

ROCKY MOUNTAIN COLLEGE. Billings, MT 59102. **406-245-6151.** Judy S Hensel, periodicals editor, information services, **406-243-2522**

ROOSEVELT UNIVERSITY. Chicago, IL 60605. **312-341-3620.** *Contact.* Robert Dameron, **312-341-3657**

RUTGERS, THE STATE UNIVERSITY OF NEW JERSEY. New Brunswick, NJ 18903. **201-932-1766.** Jose Ann Steinbock, assistant vice-president, public information, **201-932-7315.** Joseph A O'Rourke, director, Rutgers news service, **201-932-7084.** Public information officers: Joseph Deitch, Newark campus, **201-648-5262.** Sally Schwartz, Camden campus, **609-757-6026**

SAINT AMBROSE COLLEGE. Davenport, IA 52803. **319-324-1681.** Beverly Ginsberg, director, public relations

SAINT BONAVENTURE UNIVERSITY. Saint Bonaventure, NY 14778. **716-375-2000.** Thomas P McElroy, director, public relations

ST CLOUD STATE UNIVERSITY. St Cloud, MN 56301. **612-225-3151.** Dr Charles J Graham, president, **612-255-2122.** Dr Howard Ray Rowland, director, information services, **612-255-3151.** (h) **612-363-4476.** Sharon Deane Lesikar, news editor, **612-255-3151.** A coeducational, comprehensive public university

SAINT JOHN'S UNIVERSITY. Collegeville, MN 56321. **612-363-2594.** Lee A Hanley, director, communications

SAINT JOSEPH'S COLLEGE. Philadelphia, PA 19131. **215-879-7300.** Mary Lou Finlayson, director, public relations

ST LAWRENCE UNIVERSITY. Canton, NY 13617. **315-379-5011.** Thurlow O Cannon, director, public relations, **622-5585**

SAINT LOUIS UNIVERSITY. St Louis, MO 63156. **314-535-3300**

SAINT MARY'S COLLEGE. Winona, MN 55987. **507-452-4430.** Brother Raymond Long, FSC, public relations director

SALISBURY STATE COLLEGE. Salisbury, MD 21801. **301-546-3261.** L Wayne Fox, director, public relations

SAMFORD UNIVERSITY. Birmingham, AL 35209. **205-870-2011.** William A Nunnelley, director, information services, **205-870-2921**

SAN DIEGO STATE UNIVERSITY. San Diego, CA 92182. **714-286-5200.** Gordon F Lee, director, public affairs

UNIVERSITY OF SAN DIEGO. San Diego, CA 92110. **714-291-6480.** Sara S Finn, director, public relations

UNIVERSITY OF SAN FRANCISCO. San Francisco, CA 94117. **415-666-0600.** Ronald R Brill, director, public affairs, **415-666-6107**

SAN JOSE STATE UNIVERSITY. San Jose, CA 95192. **408-277-2255.** John McLain, news bureau manager

UNIVERSITY OF SANTA CLARA. Santa Clara, CA 95053. **408-984-4242.** Peggy Major, news director, **408-984-4545**

UNIVERSITY OF SCRANTON. Scranton, PA 18510. **717-961-7400.** Paul B Kerrigan, director, news bureau, **717-961-7662**

SEATTLE UNIVERSITY. Seattle, WA 98122. **206-626-6200.** William J Sullivan, SJ, president, **206-626-6575.** George Behan, public relations director, **206-626-5656.** Public relations office will provide media contacts book on request, listing members of the university faculty and staff with expertise in various specialty areas

SETON HALL UNIVERSITY. South Orange, NJ 07079. **201-762-9000.** Gene J Collins, director, public relations

SHIPPENSBURG STATE COLLEGE. Shippensburg, PA 17257. **717-532-9121.** Gary L Willhide, director, public relations and publications

SIMMONS COLLEGE. Boston, MA 02115. **617-738-2000.** Margaret A Loeb, director, public information, **617-738-2124**

SMITH COLLEGE. Northampton, MA 01060. **413-584-2700.** Ann E Shanahan, news director

UNIVERSITY OF THE SOUTH. Sewanee, TN 37375. **615-598-5931.** Latham W Davis, director, public relations. Gale Link, director, information services

UNIVERSITY OF SOUTH CAROLINA. Columbia, SC 29208. **803-777-0411.** James B Holderman, president, **803-777-3101.** Lynne Mahaffey, acting director, information services, **803-777-8161.** Clifford L Gray, assistant director, information services, **803-777-8161**

SOUTH DAKOTA STATE UNIVERSITY. Brookings, SD 57007. **605-688-4111.** *Contact.* C F Cecil

UNIVERSITY OF SOUTH DAKOTA. Vermillion, SD 57069. **605-677-5331.** Lars Larmon, editor, information services

UNIVERSITY OF SOUTH FLORIDA. Tampa, FL 33620. **813-974-2011.** James J Bruss, director, information services, **813-974-2181**

SOUTHEAST MISSOURI UNIVERSITY. Cape Girardeau, MO 63701. **314-651-2000.** Dr Charles Wiles, director, public services, **314-651-2509.** Wayne A Norton, director, news services, **314-651-2256.** (h) **314- 335-7143**

SOUTHEASTERN MASSACHUSETTS UNIVERSITY. North Dartmouth, MA 02747. **617-997-9321.** James S Wiley, director, public relations

UNIVERSITY OF SOUTHERN CALIFORNIA. Los Angeles, CA 90007. **213-741-2311.** Charles M Weisenberg, director, news bureau, **213-741-2215**

SOUTHERN ILLINOIS UNIVERSITY AT CARBONDALE. Carbondale, IL 62901. **618-453-3368.** George Mace, vice-president, university relations. Peter B Brown, director, university news services, **618-453-2276**

SOUTHERN ILLINOIS UNIVERSITY AT EDWARDSVILLE. Edwardsville, IL 62026. **618-692-3600.** Sam L Smith, university news services

SOUTHERN METHODIST UNIVERSITY. Dallas, TX 75275. **214-692-2666.** Joe Sherman, director, information services, **214-692-2658.** Herb Reed, director, communications, School of Business Administration. Gerald McGee, director, office of university publications, **214-692-2659**

UNIVERSITY OF SOUTHERN MISSISSIPPI. Hattiesburg, MS 39401.

601-266-7101. Powell G Ogletree, director, alumni affairs

SOUTHWEST MISSOURI STATE UNIVERSITY. Springfield, MO 65802. **417-836-5000.** Don Payton, information and publications director

SOUTHWEST TEXAS STATE UNIVERSITY. San Marcos, TX 78666. **512-245-2180.** Mrs Pat Murdock, director, news and information service

SOUTHWESTERN AT MEMPHIS. Memphis, TN 38112. **901-274-1800.** Denis E Meadows, director, news services

SPRINGFIELD COLLEGE. Springfield, MA 01109. **413-787-2100.** Kenneth Wildes, director, public relations, **413-787-2060,** (h) **413-782-9110**

STANFORD UNIVERSITY. Stanford, CA 94305. **415-497-2862.** Robert M Rosenzweig, vice-president, public affairs. Spyros G Andreopoulos, information officer, School of Medicine, **415-497-6911.** Herbert Blanchette, director of public information, School of Business, **415-497-3157**

STATE UNIVERSITY OF *See* the key word (Alabama, California, etc) in name

SUFFOLK UNIVERSITY. Boston, MA 02114. **617-723-4700.** Louis B Connelly, director, public relations

SWARTHMORE COLLEGE. Swarthmore, PA 19081. **215-544-7900.** Ruth Malone, assistant director, information services

SWEET BRIAR COLLEGE. Sweet Briar, VA 24595. **804-381-5100.** Dr Harold B Whiteman, Jr, president. Janet K Lowrey, director, office of public information and publications, **804-381-5422**

SYRACUSE UNIVERSITY. Syracuse, NY 13210. **315-423-3784.** Richard Wilson, director, news bureau

UNIVERSITY OF TAMPA. Tampa, FL 33606. **813-253-8861.** Tully Vaughn, executive director, development and public affairs

TEMPLE UNIVERSITY. Philadelphia, PA 19122. **215-787-7000**

Contacts

Main Campus. Emilie Mulholland, director, news bureau, **215-787-7476**
Health Sciences Center. Alvin Hornstein, public relations director, **215-221-4839**

Center City. Mary Jane Creamer, public relations director, **215-787-1515**

TENNESSEE STATE UNIVERSITY. Nashville, TN 37203. **615-320-3131.** Mabel Crooks Boddie, director, public relations. **615-320-3688.** James A Washington, media specialist, **615-380-3688**

UNIVERSITY OF TENNESSEE— CENTRAL ADMINISTRATION. Knoxville, TN 37916. **615-974-0111.** Neal O'Steen, acting director, public relations, **615-974-2125.** Bob Gilbert, director, television news, **615-974-2125.** Tom Ballard, manager, information services, Public Service Institute, **615-974-6621**

UNIVERSITY OF TENNESSEE AT CHATTANOOGA,. Chattanooga, TN 37401. **615-755-4363.** William Walker, director, information services

UNIVERSITY OF TENNESSEE AT KNOXVILLE. Knoxville, TN 37916. **615-974-2225.** David H Lauver, director, public relations. John M Clark, Jr, managing director, news services. Jane C Pope, publications editor

UNIVERSITY OF TENNESSEE AT MARTIN. Martin, TN 38238. **901-587-7111.** John H Leeper, news bureau editor, **901-587-7142**

UNIVERSITY OF TENNESSEE AT NASHVILLE. Nashville, TN 37203. **615-251-1111.** Dan B Coleman, director, information services

TEXAS A & I UNIVERSITY. Kingsville TX 78363. **512-595-2111.** William W Holmes, Jr, university information and news services director, **512-595-3901**

TEXAS A & M UNIVERSITY. College Station, TX 77840. **713-845-3211.** Jim Lindsey, director, university news service, **713-845-4641.** Lane B Stephenson, associate director, **713-845-4641**

TEXAS CHRISTIAN UNIVERSITY. Fort Worth, TX 76129. **817-926-2461.** Dr J M Moudy, chancellor, Ext 214. Dr H Lawrence Wilsey, executive vice-chancellor. James L Lehman, director, public relations, Ext 212. Betty D Knox, news service director, Ext 210. Harrell Moten, publications director, Ext 211. John Ohendalski, special editorial projects, Ext 224. An independent institution, founded in 1873 and, since its founding, related to the Christian Church and coeducational.

TEXAS EASTERN UNIVERSITY. Tyler, TX 75701. **214-566-1471.** J Archie Whitfield, director, public information office

TEXAS SOUTHERN UNIVERSITY. Houston, TX 77004. **713-528-0611.** Travis Taylor, coordinator, information services, office of university relations

TEXAS TECH UNIVERSITY. Lubbock, TX 79409. **806-742-2136.** Jane H Brandenberger, director, university news and publications

UNIVERSITY OF TEXAS AT AUSTIN. Austin, TX 78712. **512-471-3151.** Amy Jo Long, director, news and information service

UNIVERSITY OF TEXAS AT DALLAS. Richardson, TX 75080. **214-690-2111.** Millicent Green, director, news and information services, **214-690-2293**

UNIVERSITY OF TEXAS AT EL PASO. El Paso, TX 79968. **915-747-5000.** Dale Walker, director, news and information service, Ext 5526

UNIVERSITY OF TEXAS AT SAN ANTONIO. San Antonio, TX 78285. **512-691-4550.** Janice M Smith, director, news and information office

THE UNIVERSITY OF TEXAS SYSTEM. Austin, TX 78701. **512-471-3434.** Robert L Hardesty, vice-president, administration, **512-471-1820**

UNIVERSITY OF TOLEDO. Toledo, OH 43606. **419-537-2675.** Fred P Mollenkopf, director, public information

TRINITY COLLEGE. Hartford, CT 06106. **203-527-3151.** James K Blake, director, news and public relations

TUFTS UNIVERSITY. Medford, MA 02155. **617-628-5000,** Ext 405. *Contact.* Harry B Zane

TULANE UNIVERSITY. New Orleans, LA 70118. **504-865-5714.** Crozet J Duplantier, director, university relations

UNIVERSITY OF TULSA. Tulsa, OK 74104. **918-939-6351.** Mike Roberts, news bureau manager

TUSKEGEE INSTITUTE. Tuskegee Institute, AL 36088. **205-727-8335.** Cathy Thompson, director, public information

UNION COLLEGE AND UNIVERSITY. Schenectady, NY 12308. **518-370-6131.** Jack L Maranville, director, public relations

UNITED STATES AIR FORCE ACADEMY. US Air Force Academy, CO 80840. **303-472-2640.** *Contact.* Ruth Whitaker

UNITED STATES COAST GUARD ACADEMY. New London, CT 06320. **203-443-8463,** Ext 280

UNITED STATES MILITARY ACADEMY. West Point, NY 10996. **914-938-3808.** Lieutenant Colonel Jere K Forbus, public affairs officer

UNITED STATES NAVAL ACADEMY. Annapolis, MD 21402. **301-267-2291.** Commander J H Barrett, USN, public affairs officer. Del Malkie, assistant public affairs officer, media, **301-267-2291**

UNITED THEOLOGICAL SEMINARY OF TWIN CITIES. New Brighton, MN 55112. **612-633-4311.** Dr Dayton D Hultgren, president

UNIVERSITY OF. *See* the key word (Bridgeport, Pennsylvania, etc) in name

UTAH STATE UNIVERSITY. Logan, UT 84322. **801-752-4100.** J R Allred, director, information services

UNIVERSITY OF UTAH. Salt Lake City, UT 84112. **801-581-7200.** Elizabeth Haglund, director, public relations

VALDOSTA STATE COLLEGE. Valdosta, GA 31601. Dr S Walter Martin, president, **912-247-3226.** *Press contact.* Jean L Holland, head of information services, **912-247-3312.** (h) **912-242-6351.** A multipurpose 4-year unit of the university system of Georgia, with a student population of approximately 5000 and a faculty of about 250 in schools or divisions of Arts and Sciences, Fine Arts, Nursing, Aerospace Studies, Business Administration, Education, and Graduate Studies

VALPARAISO UNIVERSITY. Valparaiso, IN 46283. **219-464-5110.** Richard Koenig, vice-president, public affairs

VANDERBILT UNIVERSITY. Nashville, TN 38240. **615-322-7311.** Jan Belcher, director, news bureau, **615-322-2706**

VASSAR COLLEGE. Poughkeepsie, NY 12601. **914-452-7000.** Herbert C Johnson, Jr, director, communications

UNIVERSITY OF VERMONT. Burlington, VT 05401. **802-656-3131.** William A Carey, director, public relations

VILLANOVA UNIVERSITY. Villanova, PA 19085. **215-527-2100.** Eugene J Ruane, director, public relations

VINCENNES UNIVERSITY. Vincennes, IN 47591. **812-882-3350.** Barbara De Boer, director, public relations, Ext 359

VIRGINIA COMMONWEALTH UNIVERSITY. Richmond, VA 23284. **804-770-6557.** William T Van Pelt, manager, information services and Medical College of Virginia campus information, **804-770-7457.** Toni Radler, academic campus information, **804-770-7375.** Ida Shackelford, feature specialist, **804-770-2352**

VIRGINIA MILITARY INSTITUTE. Lexington, VA 24450. **703-463-6201.** Major James L Adams, public information officer, **703-463-6207**

VIRGINIA POLYTECHNIC INSTITUTE AND STATE UNIVERSITY. Blacksburg, VA 24061. **703-951-6000.** Joe Bryant, news director, information services

VIRGINIA STATE COLLEGE. Petersburg, VA 23803. **804-520-6612.** Dollie C Youkeles, director, public information

UNIVERSITY OF VIRGINIA. Charlottesville, VA 22903. **804-924-7116.** Helaine Patterson, director, university information services. Martin S Ochs, director, medical center information, **804-924-5679**

WABASH COLLEGE. Crawfordsville, IN 47933. **317-362-1400.** Wendy Tucker, director, publications and news

WAGNER COLLEGE. Staten Island, NY 10301. **212-390-3000.** Louis De Luca, director, development and public relations, **212-390-3121.** Russell Johnson, director, public information and publications, **212-390-3224**

WASHINGTON AND LEE UNIVERSITY. Lexington, VA 24450. **703-463-9111.** Robert S Keefe, director, news office. Douglass W Dewing, assistant director

MARY WASHINGTON COLLEGE. Fredericksburg, VA 22401. **702-373-7250,** Ext 270. Barbara B Powell, director, information services, office of information services

WASHINGTON STATE UNIVERSITY. Pullman, WA 99163. **509-335-4527.** Richard B Fry, manager, news bureau, **509-335-3581**

WASHINGTON UNIVERSITY. St Louis, MO 63130. **314-863-0100.** Donald P Anderson, director, public relations

UNIVERSITY OF WASHINGTON. Seattle, WA 98115. **206-543-2580.** Louis L Quigley, assistant vice-president, communications. Fred Cordova, manager, news services

WAYNE STATE UNIVERSITY. Detroit, MI 48202. **313-577-2424.** Paul J Pentecost, director, information services, **313-577-2150**

WELLESLEY COLLEGE. Wellesley, MA 02181. **617-235-0320.** *Contact.* Alla O'Brien

WESLEYAN UNIVERSITY. Middletown, CT 06457. **203-347-9411.** Robert L Kirkpatrick, Jr, vice-president, university relations

WEST CHESTER STATE COLLEGE. West Chester, PA 19380. **215-436-2815**

WESTERN CAROLINA UNIVERSITY. Cullowhee, NC 28723. **704-293-7211.** A Douglas Reed, director, public information, **704-293-7122**

WESTERN ILLINOIS UNIVERSITY. Macomb, IL 61455. **309-298-1993.** John T Fairman, director, university news services

WESTERN KENTUCKY UNIVERSITY. Bowling Green, KY 42101. **502-745-0111.** Donald Armstrong, public relations director

WESTERN MARYLAND COLLEGE. Westminster, MD 21157. **301-848-7000**

WESTERN MICHIGAN UNIVERSITY. Kalamazoo, MI 49008. **616-383-1600.** Martin R (Joe) Gagie, associate director, information services, **616-383-0981**

WESTERN WASHINGTON UNIVERSITY. Bellingham, WA 98225. **206-676-3000.** Paul J Olscamp, president, **206-676-3480.** James A Schwartz, director, public information, **206-676-3350**

WESTMINSTER COLLEGE. Fulton, MO 65251. **314-642-3361.** Dr J Harvey Saunders, president. Jill Ann Bock, public information officer

WEST VIRGINIA INSTITUTE OF TECHNOLOGY. Montgomery, WV 25136. **304-442-3145** or **3071.** Samuel H Stanley, director, public information

WEST VIRGINIA UNIVERSITY. Morgantown, WV 26505. **304-293-0111.** Harry Ernst, director, university relations. Dick Toren, associate director, medical center. Tom Jamrose, radio and television, **304-293-6366**

WHEATON COLLEGE. Norton, MA 02766. **617-285-7722.** Priscilla D Wescott, director, public affairs

WHITTIER COLLEGE. Whittier, CA 90608. **213-693-0771.** *Contact.* Daphne Lorne

WICHITA STATE UNIVERSITY. Wichita, KS 67208. **316-689-3456.** Max A Schaible, director, information and public events, **316-689-3051.** Kitty Adams, editor, news bureau, **316-689-3045**

WIDENER COLLEGE. Chester, PA 19013. **215-876-5551.** Pam Sheridan, director, public relations, Nancy Hesford, assistant director

COLLEGE OF WILLIAM AND MARY. Williamsburg, VA 23185. **804-229-3000.** Barbara Ball, director, news office. James C Rees IV, news officer

WILLAMETTE UNIVERSITY. Salem, OR 97301. **503-370-6300.** Robert C Woodle, director, information services, **503-370-6231**

WILLIAMS COLLEGE. Williamstown, MA 01267. **413-597-2151.** R Cragin Lewis, director, public information

WINSTON-SALEM STATE UNIVERSITY. Winston-Salem, NC 27104. **919-761-2118.** Charisse C Fountain, director, public relations

UNIVERSITY OF WISCONSIN—EAU CLAIR. Eau Claire, WI 54701. **715-836-0123.** G Willard King, director, university relations

UNIVERSITY OF WISCONSIN—GREEN BAY. Green Bay, WI 54302. **414-465-2121.** Betty D Brown, director, news services and publications, **414-465-2214**

UNIVERSITY OF WISCONSIN—LA CROSSE. La Crosse, WI 54601. **608-785-8490.** Christine Koukola, coordinator, information services

UNIVERSITY OF WISCONSIN—MADISON. Madison, WI 53706. **608-262-9946** or **3571.** Arthur O Hove, director, office of information services

UNIVERSITY OF WISCONSIN—MILWAUKEE. Milwaukee, WI 53201. **414-963-1122.** William C Lorentz, director, news services, **414-963-4452**

UNIVERSITY OF WISCONSIN—OSHKOSH,. Oshkosh, WI 54901. **414-424-1234.** Allan Ekvall, news bureau, **414-424-1398.** Harvey Moss, radio and television relations, **414-424-1397**

UNIVERSITY OF WISCONSIN—PARKSIDE. Kenosha, WI 53140. **414-553-2121.** Walter Shirer, director, public information and publications, **414-553-2233**

UNIVERSITY OF WISCONSIN—STOUT. Menomonie, WI 54751. **715-232-2165.** John K Enger, coordinator, news services, and associate director, university relations

UNIVERSITY OF WISCONSIN—SUPERIOR. Superior, WI 54880. **715-392-4665.** Richard E Morrison, director, university relations

WITTENBERG UNIVERSITY. Springfield, OH 45501. **513-327-6231.** Donald R Perkins, director, public information, **513-327-6114**

WOODS HOLE OCEANOGRAPHIC INSTITUTION. Woods Hole, MA 02543. **617-548-1400.** Vicky Cullen, publications and information coordinator

COLLEGE OF WOOSTER. Wooster, OH 44691. **216-264-1234.** George T Richard, director, news services

WORCESTER POLYTECHNIC INSTITUTE. Worcester, MA 01609. **617-753-1411.** Roger N Perry, Jr, director, public relations

WRIGHT STATE UNIVERSITY. Dayton, OH 45435. **513-873-3333.** Donald F Hagerty, director, news and information service, **513-873-3232.** Larry Kinneer, associate director, **513-873-3232**

UNIVERSITY OF WYOMING. Laramie, WY 82071. **307-766-1121.** Vern E Shelton, assistant to the president for information, **307-766-2105.** Karl G Harper, assistant director, division of communications services, **307-766-5153**

XAVIER UNIVERSITY. Cincinnati, OH 45207. **513-745-3000.** Charles J Carey, director, public information, **513-745-3331**

YALE UNIVERSITY. New Haven, CT 06520. **203-436-4771.** Stanley Flink, director, public information

YESHIVA UNIVERSITY. New York, NY 10033. **212-568-8400.** Sam Hartstein, director, public relations. William Mishkin, director, public information, Albert Einstein College of Medicine, **212-430-2000**

YOUNGSTOWN STATE UNIVERSITY. Youngstown, OH 44555. **216-747-1851.** Philip A Snyder, director, university relations

SELECTED MAJOR PUBLIC SCHOOLS

Alabama

BIRMINGHAM PUBLIC SCHOOLS. PO Drawer 10007, Birmingham, 35202. **205-252-1800,** Ext 385. Despina Vodantis, communications specialist

HUNTSVILLE CITY SCHOOLS. PO Box 1256, Huntsville, 35807. **205-539-2111.** Mariola D Jernigan, public information officer

JEFFERSON COUNTY BOARD OF EDUCATION. A-400 Courthouse Bldg, Birmingham, 35203. **205-325-5244.** Inez Morgan Calhoun, director, public information

MOBILE COUNTY PUBLIC SCHOOLS. PO Box 1327, Mobile, 36601. **205-438-6011,** Ext 333. Dixie W Wooten, supervisor, public information

MONTGOMERY PUBLIC SCHOOLS. PO Box 1991, Montgomery, 36103. **205-269-9111.** Helen Goggans, supervisor, special services

Alaska

ANCHORAGE SCHOOL DISTRICT. 4600 DeBarr Rd, Anchorage, 99504. **907-333-9561.** William K Blessington, public information officer

Arizona

GLENDALE UNION HIGH SCHOOL DISTRICT. 7650 N 43rd Ave, Glendale, 85301. **602-934-3411,** Ext 216. Margaret T Beebe, director, communications

PHOENIX UNION HIGH SCHOOL SYSTEM. 2526 W Osborn Rd, Phoenix, 85017. **602-257-3005.** John W Hubley, administrative assistant, public information

TUSCON UNIFIED SCHOOL DISTRICT 1. 1010 E 10th St, Tucson, 85719. **602-791-5247.** Tom C Thompson, communications consultant

Arkansas

LITTLE ROCK SCHOOL DISTRICT. W Markham and Izard Sts, Little Rock, 72203. **501-374-3361.** Ruth S Steele, director, communications

California

BEVERLY HILLS UNIFIED SCHOOL DISTRICT. 255 S Lasky Dr, Beverly Hills, 90212. **213-277-5900.** Kenneth J Gelms, supervisor, information

FRESNO UNIFIED SCHOOL DISTRICT. Education Ctr, Tulare and M Sts, Fresno, 93721. **209-441-3546.** Virginia Dow, public information officer

GLENDALE UNIFIED/COMMUNITY COLLEGE DISTRICTS. 223 N Jackson St, Glendale, 91206. **213-241-3111,** Ext 241. Victor J Pallos, public information officer

LOS ANGELES COUNTY SUPERINTENDENT OF SCHOOLS OFFICE. 9300 E Imperial Hwy, Downey, 90242. **213-922-6369.** Ann H Barkelew, public information officer

LOS ANGELES UNIFIED SCHOOL DISTRICT. PO Box 3307, Los Angeles, 90051. **213-625-6766.** Eva Stern Hain, director, public information unit

MONTEREY PENINSULA UNIFIED SCHOOL DISTRICT. PO Box 1031, 700 Pacific St, Monterey, 93940. **408-649-7413.** Peggy Johnsen, public information

OAKLAND UNIFIED SCHOOL DISTRICT. 1025 2nd Ave, Oakland, 94606. **415-836-2622.** Marjorie Henders, publications and public information director

ORANGE UNIFIED SCHOOL DISTRICT. 370 N Glassell, Orange, 92666. **714-997-6141.** Shirley Goodman, coordinator, public information

PARAMOUNT UNIFIED SCHOOL DISTRICT. 15110 California Ave, Paramount, 90723. **213-630-3131,** Ext 237. Molly McGee, loop media specialist

RIVERSIDE UNIFIED SCHOOL DISTRICT. 3380 14th St, Riverside, 92501. **714-781-2409.** Bill Garbett, information specialist

SAN DIEGO CITY SCHOOLS. Education Ctr, 4100 Normal St, San Diego, 92103. **714-293-8414,** Ext 381. Bob Regan, information services director

SAN FRANCISCO UNIFIED SCHOOL DISTRICT. 135 Van Ness Ave, San Francisco, 94102. **415-565-9000.** Raymond E Kohtz, supervisor, public information

SANTA ROSA CITY SCHOOLS. PO Box 940, Santa Rosa, 95402. **707-528-5456.** Paul N Mullane, coordinator, communications

STOCKTON UNIFIED SCHOOL DISTRICT. 701 N Madison St, Stockton, 95202. **209-463-8845.** Kenneth W Caves, director, employee relations

Colorado

CHEYENNE MOUNTAIN SCHOOLS. 1118 W Cheyenne Rd, Colorado Springs, 80906. **303-473-5240.** Tom B McCord, assistant to superintendent

DENVER PUBLIC SCHOOLS. 900 Grant St, Denver, 80203. **303-837-1000,** Ext 2386. John H Rankin, supervisor, community information

Connecticut

GREENWICH PUBLIC SCHOOLS. Havemeyer Bldg, Greenwich Ave, Greenwich, 06830. **203-869-9400.** Louisa H Stone, communications aide

HAMDEN PUBLIC SCHOOLS. 1450 Whitney Ave, Hamden, 06517. **203-288-8743.** Gertrude L Bollier, public information officer

WESTPORT PUBLIC SCHOOLS. Jesup Rd, Westport, 06880. **203-227-8451.** Joyce Losen, coordinator, communications

Delaware

NEWARK SCHOOL DISTRICT. 83 E Main St, Newark, 19711. **302-731-2110.** Philip A Toman, director, information services

WILMINGTON PUBLIC SCHOOLS. 1400 Washington St, Wilmington, 19801. **302-429-7193.** John T Holton, public information officer

District of Columbia

WASHINGTON, DC, PUBLIC SCHOOLS.
1643 Primrose Rd NW, Washington, 20012.
202-724-4044. Theora G ("Bunny") Webb,
acting director, publications, office of communications

Florida

ALACHUA COUNTY SCHOOL DISTRICT. 1817 E University Ave, Gainesville,
32601. **904-373-5192.** Norma Jean Hill,
communications officer

BROWARD COUNTY SCHOOL BOARD.
1320 SW 4th St, Fort Lauderdale, 33312.
305-765-6170. Mary ("Sallee") Brown, resource specialist—wage and salary

DADE COUNTY PUBLIC SCHOOLS. Rm
203, 1410 NE 2nd Ave, Miami, 33132.
305-350-3871. Georgia M Slack, information
specialist

DUVAL COUNTY SCHOOL BOARD.
1325 San Marco Blvd, Jacksonville, 32207.
904-633-5719. Robert H Gregory, director,
information services

HILLSBOROUGH COUNTY SCHOOLS.
PO Box 3408, Tampa, 33601. **813-223-2311.**
Paul E Dinnis, public information officer

HOLLYWOOD HILLS HIGH SCHOOL.
5400 Stirling Rd, Hollywood, 33021.
305-981-4522. Frank Charles Campana,
principal

**ORANGE COUNTY PUBLIC SCHOOL
SYSTEM.** PO Box 271, Orlando, 32802.
305-849-6450, Ext 237. Miriam Sussman,
public information specialist

Georgia

ATLANTA PUBLIC SCHOOLS. 224
Central Ave SW, Atlanta, 30303.
404-659-3066. Jane Esther Foley, public
information coordinator

CLARKE COUNTY SCHOOL DISTRICT.
PO Box 1708, 500 College Ave, Athens,
30601. **404-546-7721.** Joseph T Taylor,
director, federal programs

**RICHMOND COUNTY BOARD OF
EDUCATION.** 2083 Heckle St, Augusta,
30904. **404-736-8452.** Catherine Ice Osteen,
administrative assistant, public relations and
information services

Hawaii

THE KAMEHAMEHA SCHOOLS.
Kapalama Heights, Honolulu, 96817.
808-842-8317. Lesley K Agard, publications
and public relations assistant

LEEWARD SCHOOL DISTRICT. 94-366
Pupupani St, Waipahu, 96797. **808-671-1721.**
Liberato C Viduya, Jr, superintendent

**OUR REDEEMER LUTHERAN
SCHOOLS.** 1404 University Ave, Honolulu,
96822. **808-949-5302.** Willis W Bredehoft,
principal

PUNAHOU SCHOOL. 1601 Punahou St,
Honolulu, 96822. **808-944-5722.** Lee Ann H
Bowman, publications director

WINDWARD OAHU SCHOOL DISTRICT. 45-955 Kamehameha Hwy,
Kaneohe, 96744. **808-247-6051.** Kengo
Takata, superintendent

Idaho

BOISE SCHOOLS. 1207 Fort St, Boise,
83702. **208-336-1370.** Helen J Williams,
public information consultant

IDAHO FALLS SCHOOL DISTRICT 91.
690 John Adams Pkwy, Idaho Falls, 83401.
208-522-7490, Ext 309. Marya D Martin,
public information officer

**LEWISTON INDEPENDENT SCHOOL
DISTRICT 1.** 12th and Linden, Lewiston,
83501. **208-746-2337.** Sylvia J Lyman, public
information officer

Illinois

**BLOOM TOWNSHIP HIGH SCHOOL
DISTRICT 206.** Chicago Heights, 60411.
312-755-1122. Joanne B McCallum, director,
information

**COOK COUNTY EDUCATION 21
SERVICE REGION.** 33 W Grand, Chicago,
60601. **312-443-7625.** Morton H Kaplan,
director, public information

PEORIA PUBLIC SCHOOLS. 3202 N
Wisconsin Ave, Peoria, 61603. **309-672-6745.**
Douglas E Wells, Jr, director, school-community relations

QUINCY PUBLIC SCHOOLS. 1444 Maine
St, Quincy, 62301. **217-223-8700.** Robert E
Meyer, assistant superintendent

**RICH TOWNSHIP HIGH SCHOOLS,
DISTRICT 227.** 300 Sauk Tri, Park Forest,
60466. **312-748-5800.** Robert A Borich,
communications specialist

**WHEATON COMMUNITY SCHOOL
DISTRICT 200.** 130 W Park Ave, Wheaton,
60187. **312-653-0200.** John Baran, director,
informational services

Indiana

**FORT WAYNE COMMUNITY
SCHOOLS.** 1230 S Clinton St, Fort Wayne,
46802. **219-422-3575.** H Norman Ballinger,
director, information services

**FORT WAYNE SOUTH SIDE HIGH
SCHOOL.** 3601 S Calhoun St, Fort Wayne,
46807. **219-744-2221.** Jack E Weicker, principal

**FRANKLIN TOWNSHIP COMMUNITY
SCHOOL CORP.** 6141 S Franklin Rd,
Indianapolis, 46259. **317-862-2411.** Elisabeth
Good, administrative assistant to superintendent

INDIANAPOLIS PUBLIC SCHOOLS. 120
E Walnut St, Indianapolis, 46204.
317-266-4530. Nancy Louise Brown, public
information assistant

**MONROE COUNTY COMMUNITY
SCHOOL CORP.** 315 North Dr, Bloomington, 47401. **812-339-3481,** Ext 40. David A
Staver, administrative assistant to superintendent

Iowa

**CEDAR RAPIDS GRANT WOOD AREA
EDUCATION AGENCY.** 4401 6th St SW,
Cedar Rapids, 52401. **319-366-7601.** Kay E
Graber, community relations supervisor

**COUNCIL BLUFFS COMMUNITY
SCHOOLS.** 207 Scott St, Council Bluffs,
51501. **712-328-6450.** Deborah Johnson,
administrative assistant

DES MOINES INDEPENDANT COMMUNITY SCHOOL DISTRICT. 1800
Grand Ave, Des Moines, 50307.
515-284-7887. Robert D Baldwin, director,
school-community relations

**WEST DES MOINES COMMUNITY
SCHOOL DISTRICT.** 1101 5th St, West
Des Moines, 60265. **515-274-4836.** Mary C
Oldenburg, information services director

Kansas

KANSAS CITY PUBLIC SCHOOLS, UNIFIED SCHOOL DISTRICT 500. 625 Minnesota Ave, Kansas City, 66101. **913-621-3073.** Glen H Dewerff, director, public information

TOPEKA PUBLIC SCHOOLS. 415 W 8th St, Topeka, 66603. **913-233-0313,** Ext 110. Barbara Kudlacek, director, public information services

WICHITA PUBLIC SCHOOLS. 428 S Broadway, Wichita, 67202. **316-268-7851.** Carroll Macke, director, communications

Kentucky

DAVIESS COUNTY SCHOOLS. Owensboro, 42301. **502-685-3161.** Joe H Overby, public information officer

NEWPORT CITY SCHOOLS. 80 and Washington, Newport, 41071. **606-491-1125.** Robert E Gearhart, director, public relations

Louisiana

CALCASIEU PARISH SCHOOL BOARD. 1732 Kirkman St, Lake Charles, 70601. **318-433-6321,** Ext 14 or 15. Gloria P Ambrose, supervisor, community relations

EAST BATON ROUGE PARISH SCHOOLS. PO Box 2950, Baton Rouge, 70821. **504-926-2790.** Patricia B McCoy, director, communications

ORLEANS PARISH SCHOOLS. 4100 Touro St, New Orleans, 70122. **504-288-6561,** Ext 344. Albertine (Tina) G Perrin, assistant director, public information

Maryland

ALLEGANY COUNTY BOARD OF EDUCATION. PO Box 1608, Cumberland, 21502. **301-777-5836.** Gerald H Murphy, administrative assistant, staff and community relations

BALTIMORE COUNTY BOARD OF EDUCATION. 6901 N Charles St, Towson, 21204. **301-494-4117.** Philip R Stoer, information specialist

FREDERICK COUNTY BOARD OF EDUCATION. 115 E Church St, Frederick, 21701. **301-662-9200,** Ext 226. T Meade Felton, assistant to superintendent for community and staff relations

HOWARD COUNTY PUBLIC SCHOOLS. 8045 Route 32, Columbia, 21044. **301-531-5744.** Paul Fisher Rhetts, public information officer

MONTGOMERY COUNTY PUBLIC SCHOOLS. 850 Hungerford Dr, Rockville, 20850. **301-279-3391.** James E Lashley, assistant director, department of information

Massachusetts

BOSTON PUBLIC SCHOOLS. School Headquarters, 26 Court St, Boston, 02108. *Public Information center.* **617-726-6555.** *Press contact school system.* Fred Foie, **617-726-6531.** *Public information officer, department of implementation.* **617-726-6592** (handles questions regarding desegregation court orders and similar problems)

BROCKTON SCHOOLS. 470 Forest Ave, Brockton, 02401. **617-588-7800,** Ext 474. Harry C Allen, administrator, community education

SPRINGFIELD PUBLIC SCHOOLS. 195 State St, Springfield, 01103. **413-733-2132.** Cornelius K Hannigan, director, school-community relations

WORCESTER PUBLIC SCHOOLS. 20 Irving St, Worcester, 01609. **617-798-2521,** Ext 31. Charles S Kolak, executive assistant, staff and public information

Michigan

DEARBORN PUBLIC SCHOOLS. 4824 Lois, Dearborn, 48126. **313-582-6277,** Ext 261. Jerome E Sherman, information officer

DETROIT PUBLIC SCHOOLS. 5057 Woodward Ave, Detroit, 48202. **313-494-1746.** Ronald Owens, media coordinator

EAST LANSING PUBLIC SCHOOLS. 509 Burcham Dr, East Lansing, 48823. **517-337-1781.** Jane McKinney, director, public information

FLINT SCHOOL DISTRICT. 923 E Kearsley St, Flint, 48502. **313-762-1229,** Ext 508. Robert W Donovan, director, public information and communications

JACKSON PUBLIC SCHOOLS. 1400 W Monroe St, Jackson, 49202. **517-782-8231.** Rick Burnham, coordinator, public information

KALAMAZOO PUBLIC SCHOOLS. 1220 Howard St, Kalamazoo, 49008. **616-385-0561.** Dorothy J Rothrock, coordinator, information services

LANSING SCHOOL DISTRICT. 519 W Kalamazoo St, Lansing, 48933. **517-374-4021.** John D Marrs, director, information services

Minnesota

MINNEAPOLIS PUBLIC SCHOOLS. 807 NE Broadway, Minneapolis, 55413. **612-348-6138.** Floyd J Amundson, consultant, school-community relations

MINNEAPOLIS PUBLIC SCHOOLS (NORTH AREA). 1203 University Ave NE, Minneapolis, 55413. **612-336-5731.** Anne R Desmond, school-community relations coordinator

Mississippi

LE FLORE COUNTY SCHOOL DISTRICT. PO Box 544, Greenwood, 38930. **601-453-3513.** David Lamar Powe

NORTH PANOLA CONSOLIDATED SCHOOL DISTRICT. PO Box 334, Sardis, 38666. **601-487-2305.** Hosea A Grisham, superintendent

Missouri

JEFFERSON CITY PUBLIC SCHOOLS. 315 E Dunklin, Jefferson City, 65101. **314-635-4121.** James B Anderson, director, school-community relations

KANSAS CITY PUBLIC SCHOOLS. 1211 McGee, Kansas City, 64106. **816-221-8034.** Earl A Fleer, director, information

KIRKWOOD SCHOOL DISTRICT R-7. 1110 S Glenwood Ln, Kirkwood, 63122. **314-966-5700,** Ext 225. Nancy P Guyton, director, office of public information

LADUE SCHOOL DISTRICT. 9703 Conway Rd, St Louis, 63124. **314-994-7080.** Elizabeth Schwartz, director, public relations

RIVERVIEW SCHOOL DISTRICT. 1370 N Cumberland, St Louis, 63137. **314-869-2505.** Paul C Koenig, director, information

ST LOUIS COUNTY SPECIAL SCHOOL DISTRICT. 12110 Clayton Rd, Town and Country, 63131. **314-567-3700.** Herbert A Hemmann, administrative assistant, personnel and public relations

SPRINGFIELD SCHOOL DISTRICT R-12. 940 N Jefferson, Springfield, 65802. **417-862-9211.** Richard Grosenbaugh, administrative assistant, public information

Montana

MISSOULA SCHOOL DISTRICT I. 215 S 6th West, Missoula, 59801. **406-728-4000.** Tomme Lu Worden, information officer

Nebraska

LINCOLN PUBLIC SCHOOLS. PO Box 82889, Lincoln, 68510. **402-473-0212.** Margaret M Holman, staff assistant, publications and information

RALSTON PUBLIC SCHOOLS. 8545 Park Dr, Omaha, 68127. **402-331-4700.** Marlin Nelson, public relations consultant

Nevada

CLARK COUNTY SCHOOL DISTRICT. 2832 E Flamingo Rd, Las Vegas, 89121. Charles A Fleming, information services coordinator

WASHOE COUNTY SCHOOL DISTRICT. 425 E 9th St, Reno, 89520. **702-322-7041.** Rose M Bullis, director, school-community relations

New Hampshire

KEENE UNIFIED SCHOOL DISTRICT. 34 West St, Keene, 03431. **603-357-0101.** Phyllis T Peck, public information coordinator

New Jersey

CHERRY HILL PUBLIC SCHOOLS. 1155 Marlkress Rd, Cherry Hill, 08003. **609-424-1020.** Jane P Braunstein, coordinator, information services

ELIZABETH PUBLIC SCHOOLS. Board of Education, 500 N Broad St, Elizabeth, 07207. **201-353-2200,** Ext 221. Rocco J Colelli, assistant superintendent

GLASSBORO PUBLIC SCHOOLS. Administrative Offices, Annex A, N Delsea Dr, Glassboro, 08028. **609-881-2290.** Andrus A Loigu, coordinator, community relations

MONTCLAIR PUBLIC SCHOOLS. 22 Valley Rd, Montclair, 07042. **201-783-4000.** Linda E Nelson, public information officer

NEWARK BOARD OF EDUCATION. 2 Cedar St, Newark, 07102. **201-733-6700.** Alonzo W Kittrels, acting executive superintendent, **201-733-7333.** Gloria D Bryant, public information officer, **201-733-7333**

OCEAN COUNTY VOCATIONAL—TECHNICAL SCHOOL. 350 Chambersbridge, Bricktown, 08723. **201-920-0050.** Frederick W Felice, principal

WILLINGBORO TOWNSHIP PUBLIC SCHOOLS. Rm 34, Garden Plaza Bldg, Willingboro, 08046. Stephen M Scharff, coordinator, community information,. **609-871-9000,** Ext 327

New Mexico

ROSWELL INDEPENDENT SCHOOL DISTRICT. PO Box 1437, Roswell, 88201. **505-622-8942.** H Fred Pomeroy, superintendent

New York

ALBANY CITY SCHOOL DISTRICT. Academy Park, Elm St, Albany, 12207. **518-472-6498.** W C Carpenter, coordinator, publications

BINGHAMTON SCHOOL DISTRICT. 98 Oak St, Binghamton, 13904. **607-723-5411.** Richard P McLean, superintendent

BRONX DISTRICT 11 BOARD OF EDUCATION. 1250 Arnow Ave, Bronx, 10469. **212-920-1410.** T J Sellers, director, education information service and public relations

BUFFALO BOARD OF EDUCATION. 713 City Hall, Buffalo, 14202. **716-842-4646.** James J Foley, director, school-community relations

THE LOYOLA SCHOOL. 980 Park Ave, New York, 10028. **212-288-6200.** John W Kelly, SJ, director, public relations

NEW YORK CITY PUBLIC SCHOOLS. 110 Livingston St, Brooklyn, 11201.

212-596-4190. Jerome G Kovalcik, assistant superintendent

ROCHESTER CITY SCHOOL DISTRICT. 410 Alexander St, Rochester, 14607. **716-325-4560,** Ext 475. Eleanor Peck, communications assistant

North Carolina

CHARLOTTE—MECKLENBURG SCHOOLS. PO Box 149, Charlotte, 28230. **704-332-5114.** Ann C Brandt, assistant, public information and publications

DURHAM COUNTY SCHOOLS. 102 E Seminary Ave, Durham, 27702. **919-683-2591.** Cynthia L Gardiner, public information coordinator

WILKES COUNTY BOARD OF EDUCATION. 201 W Main St, Wilkesboro, 28697. **919-667-1121,** Ext 32. Charles B Parker, director, public information and publications

Ohio

COLUMBUS PUBLIC SCHOOLS. 270 E State St, Columbus, 43215. Beverly Gifford Bowen, director, public information

DAYTON BOARD OF EDUCATION. 348 W 1st St, Dayton, 45402. **513-461-3850,** Ext 223. Susan M Kurczewski, public information officer

DEER PARK COMMUNITY SCHOOLS. 8351 Plainfield Rd, Cincinnati, 45236. **513-891-4200.** Dianne Schobel, public relations

FOREST HILLS SCHOOL DISTRICT. 7600 Forest Rd, Cincinnati, 45230. **513-231-3600.** Kenneth J Furrier, director, community services

LUCAS COUNTY SCHOOLS. 3350 Collingwood St, Toledo, 43610. **419-241-3248.** Dr James A Robarge, education consultant for public relations

MONTGOMERY COUNTY PUBLIC SCHOOLS. 3rd and St Marys St, Dayton, 45402. **513-225-4598.** Larry L Oatman, public information director

SHAKER HEIGHTS CITY SCHOOLS. 15600 Parkland Dr, Shaker Heights, 44120. **216-921-1400.** Joseph V Szwaja, director, school-community relations

Oklahoma

OKLAHOMA CITY PUBLIC SCHOOLS. 900 N Klein, Oklahoma City, 73106. **405-236-2661.** Susan Penney, public relations coordinator

TULSA UNION PUBLIC SCHOOLS. 9134 E 46th St, Tulsa, 74145. **918-664-9400.** Frances Powell, director, public relations

Oregon

LANE INTERMEDIATE EDUCATION DISTRICT. 1200 Hwy 99N, Eugene, 97402. **503-689-6500.** David J Butler, coordinator, school-community relations

PORTLAND PUBLIC SCHOOLS. 631 NE Clackamas St, Portland, 97232. **503-234-3392,** Ext 329. John N Nellor, director, public information department

Pennsylvania

BETHLEHEM AREA SCHOOL DISTRICT. 535 Main St, Bethlehem, 18018. **215-694-8502.** Elizabeth B Nowicki, public information specialist

CHELTENHAM TOWNSHIP SCHOOL DISTRICT. Ashbourne Rd and Washington Ln, Elkins Park, 19117. **215-886-9500,** Ext 128. Helen Stein, director, school-community relations

DERRY TOWNSHIP SCHOOL DISTRICT. Homestead Rd, Hershey, 17033. **717-534-2501.** John A Sider, public relations coordinator

KEYSTONE CENTRAL SCHOOL DISTRICT. 95 W 4th St, Lock Haven, 17745. **717-748-7764**

MOUNT LEBANON SCHOOL DISTRICT. 31 Moffett St, Pittsburgh, 15243. **412-344-8400,** Ext 133. Virginia R Phillips, community information specialist

NORTH ALLEGHENY SCHOOL DISTRICT. 200 Hillvue Lane, Pittsburgh, 15237. **412-366-2100,** Ext 45. Judi Buren, coordinator, public relations and publications

NORTH PENN SCHOOL DISTRICT. 400 Penn St, Lansdale, 19446. **216-368-0400.** Kenneth L Weir, coordinator, school-community relations

SCHOOL DISTRICT OF PHILADELPHIA. 21st and Parkway, Philadelphia, 19103. **215-299-7850.** J William Jones, director, informational services

TREDYFFRIN—EASTOWN SCHOOL DISTRICT. Education Services Ctr, 1st and Bridge Sts, Berwyn, 19312. **215-644-6600.** George F Garwood, superintendent

UPPER DARBY SCHOOL DISTRICT. Lansdowne Ave and School Ln, Upper Darby, 19084. **215-622-7000.** Joseph P Batory, director, communications

Rhode Island

RHODE ISLAND DEPARTMENT OF EDUCATION. 199 Promenade St, Providence, 02908. **401-277-2031.** Lorraine C Webber, special assistant to commissioner

South Carolina

CHARLESTON COUNTY PUBLIC SCHOOLS. PO Box 2218, Charleston, 29403. **803-723-5721.** Maxine Faulkner, director, information services

GREENVILLE COUNTY SCHOOL DISTRICT. 301 Camperdown Way, (PO Box 2848) Greenville, 29602. **803-242-6450.** Samuel L Zimmerman, director, school-community relations

SPARTANBURG COUNTY SCHOOL DISTRICT 7. PO Box 970, Spartanburg, 29304. **803-585-2231.** Carolyn F Halstead, administrative assistant

South Dakota

RAPID CITY PUBLIC SCHOOLS. 809 South St, Rapid City, 57701. **605-342-4020.** Reiff Raymond, assistant superintendent

Tennessee

HAMILTON COUNTY DEPARTMENT OF EDUCATION. 317 Oak St, Chattanooga, 37412. **615-757-2450.** Paul M Starnes, director, public information

NASHVILLE-DAVIDSON COUNTY METROPOLITAN PUBLIC SCHOOLS. 2601 Bransford Ave, Nashville, 37204. **615-259-5263.** Eugene T Carothers, director, public information and publications

SHELBY COUNTY SCHOOLS. 160 S Hollywood, Memphis 38112. **901-458-7561.** Katherine B Stanton, director, public relations

Texas

ABILENE INDEPENDENT SCHOOL DISTRICT. PO Box 981, Abilene, 79604. **915-677-1444.** James C Boyett, coordinator, information services

CORPUS CHRISTI INDEPENDENT SCHOOL DISTRICT. PO Drawer 110, Corpus Christi, 78403. **512-888-7911,** Ext 205. Terry Orr, coordinator, information

DALLAS INDEPENDENT SCHOOL DISTRICT. 3700 Ross Ave, Dallas, 75204. **214-824-1620.** Robert L Johnston, assistant director, communications

EDGEWOOD SCHOOLS. 5358 W Commerce, San Antonio, 78237. **512-435-9961.** Patricia Longoria, community information officer

EL PASO PUBLIC SCHOOLS. PO Box 20100, El Paso, 79998. **915-779-4019.** Ross W Synder, public information consultant

FORT WORTH INDEPENDENT SCHOOL DISTRICT. 3210 W Lancaster, Fort Worth, 76107. **817-336-4951.** Joe R Sherrod, coordinator, communications

SPRING BRANCH INDEPENDENT SCHOOL DISTRICT. 955 Campbell Rd, Houston, 77024. **713-464-1511.** Mary Kay Coleman, coordinator, information services

WHITE SETTLEMENT PUBLIC SCHOOLS. PO Box 7187, White Settlement, 76108. **817-246-3671.** S Schoolar, director, public information

Utah

PROVO CITY SCHOOLS. 280 W 940 North, Provo, 84601. **801-373-6301.** Vern Brimley, director

SALT LAKE CITY SCHOOL DISTRICT. 440 E 100 South, Salt Lake City, 84111. **801-322-1471.** Janice Keller, editor

Vermont

RUTLAND SOUTHWEST SUPERVISORY UNION SCHOOL DISTRICT. 2 Depot St (PO Box A), Poultney, 05764. **802-287-5286.** Philip J Dahlinger, superintendent

Virginia

ALEXANDRIA CITY SCHOOLS. 418 S Washington St, Alexandria, 22313. **703-750-6433.** Dennis Leone, information officer

CHESTERFIELD COUNTY PUBLIC SCHOOLS AND CHESTERFIELD COUNTY SCHOOL BOARD. Chesterfield, 23831. **804-748-1433.** Page Lee Candler, public information officer

FAIRFAX COUNTY PUBLIC SCHOOLS. 10700 Page Ave, Fairfax, 22030. **703-691-2291.** W A McGinnis, coordinator, school-community relations

NORFOLK PUBLIC SCHOOLS. 800 E City Hall Ave, Norfolk, 23510. **804-441-2237.** Gilbert A McLeod, administrative assistant, informational services

RICHMOND PUBLIC SCHOOLS. 301 N 9th St, Richmond, 23219. **804-780-4696.** Robert P Hilldrup, director, public information

ROANOKE CITY PUBLIC SCHOOLS. PO Box 13145, Roanoke, 24031. **703-981-2381.** John W Lambert, coordinator, public information and communications

CLOVER PARK SCHOOL DISTRICT. 10020 Gravelly Lake Dr SW, Tacoma, 98499. **206-552-5625.** Martin Jakes Church and Cecil A Sharpe, public information officers

Washington

OLYMPIA PUBLIC SCHOOLS. 1113 E Legion Way, Olympia, 98506. **206-753-8918.** Robert A Sethre, director, information services

SEATTLE PUBLIC SCHOOLS. 815 4th Ave N, Seattle, 98109. **206-587-5130.** Clarence Hein, public information officer

VANCOUVER SCHOOL DISTRICT. 605 N Devine Rd, Vancouver, 98661. **206-696-7278.** Harold R (Hal) Millen, public information officer

West Virginia

KANAWHA COUNTY SCHOOLS. 200 Elizabeth St, Charleston, 25311. **304-348-7766.** Michael G Bell, director, public relations

Wisconsin

GREEN BAY AREA PUBLIC SCHOOLS. PO Box 1387, Green Bay, 54305. **414-432-0351.** Ann F Weizenegger, director, public information

MADISON PUBLIC SCHOOLS. 545 W Dayton St, Madison, 53703. **608-257-9561.** Linda Haskin, public information

MILWAUKEE PUBLIC SCHOOLS. PO Drawer 10K, Milwaukee, 53201. **414-475-8274.** Robert K Tesch, acting head, division of relationships

Wyoming

LARAMIE COUNTY SCHOOL DISTRICT 1. 2810 House, Cheyenne, 82001. **303-632-0591.** Jennie L Hadden, public information secretary

RELIGION

ADVENT CHRISTIAN. PO Box 23152, Charlotte, NC 28212. **704-545-6161.** The Reverend Adrian B Shepard, executive vice-president

AFRICAN ORTHODOX CHURCH. 122 W 129th St, New York, NY 10027. **212-662-0894.** The Reverend William R Miller, primate most

ALBANIAN ORTHODOX DIOCESE OF AMERICA. 54 Borroughs St, Jamaica Plains, MA 02130. **617-524-0477.** Bishop Mark Lipa, president grace

AMERICAN BAPTIST ASSOCIATION. 4605 N Line Ave, Texarkana, TX 75501. **214-792-2783.** Dr I K Cross, president

CHURCH OF OUR LORD JESUS CHRIST OF THE APOSTOLIC FAITH, INC. 2081 7th Ave, New York, NY 10027. **212-866-1700.** Bishop W L Bonner, senior apostle

CHURCH OF THE BRETHREN. 1451 Dundee Ave, Elgin, IL 60120. **312-742-5100.** Ira B Peters, moderator

CHURCH OF THE LUTHERAN BRETHREN. Box 655, Fergus Falls, MN 56537. **218-736-5666.** The Reverend Everald H Strom, president

CHURCH OF THE LUTHERAN CONFESSION. Markesan, WI 53946. **414-398-2778.** The Reverend Egbert Albrecht, president

CONSERVATIVE BAPTIST ASSOCIATION OF AMERICA. Box 66, Geneva Rd, Wheaton, IL 60187. **312-653-5350.** Dr Lee W Toms, president

THE EPISCOPAL CHURCH. 815 2nd Ave, New York, NY. **212-867-8400.** The Reverend John M Allin, presiding bishop

FREE METHODIST CHURCH OF NORTH AMERICA. 901 College Ave, Winona Lake, IN 46590. **219-267-3870.** George L Ford, director, information, **219-267-7656**

FREE WILL BAPTISTS, NATIONAL ASSOCIATION. 1134 Murfreesboro Rd, Nashville, TN 37202. **615-361-1010.** The Reverend Rufus Coffey, executive secretary

FRIENDS UNITED MEETING. 1520-B Race St, Philadelphia, PA 19102. **215-567-1965.** Stephen Angell, Jr, presiding clerk

FUNDAMENTAL METHODIST CHURCH, INC. 1034 N Broadway, Springfield, MO 65802. **417-678-3692.** The Reverend Fred Cunningham, general superintendent

EVANGELICAL METHODIST CHURCH. 3036 N Meridian, Wichita, KS 67204. **316-838-4237.** The Reverend Ronald D Driggers, secretary-treasurer

THE FIRE BAPTIZED HOLINESS CHURCH. 600 College Ave, Independence, KS 67301. **316-331-3049.** Clarence W Smith, general superintendent

THE GOSPEL MISSION CORPS. Box 175, Hightstown, NJ 08520. **609-448-4596.** Pastor Robert S Turton III, superintendent

GREEK ORTHODOX ARCHDIOSCESE OF NORTH AND SOUTH AMERICA. 8-10 E 79th St, New York, NY 10021. **212-628-2500.** Archbishop Iakovos, primate. Terry Kokas, director, public affairs, (h) **212-988-5014**

INDEPENDENT ASSEMBLIES OF GOD. 3840 5th Ave, San Diego, CA 92103. **714-295-1028.** The Reverend AW Rasmussen, secretary international

INTERNATIONAL CHURCH OF THE FOURSQUARE GOSPEL. Angelus Temple, 1100 Glendale Blvd, Los Angeles, CA 90026. **213-484-1100.** Dr Rolf K McPherson, president

ISRAELITE HOUSE OF DAVID. PO Box 1067, Benton Harbor, MI 49002. **616-926-6695.** Mabel Blackburn, pillar

JEHOVAH'S WITNESSES. 134 Columbia Hts, Brooklyn, NY 11201. **212-625-1240.** Nathan H Knorr, president

THE LIBERAL CATHOLIC CHURCH. Krotona 62, Ojai, CA **805-646-5936.** The Right Reverend Gerritt Munnik, regionary bishop

LUTHERAN CHURCH IN AMERICA. 231 Madison Ave, New York, NY 10016. **212-481-9600.** The Reverend Robert J Marshall, president

MENNONITE CHURCH. 528 E Madison St, Lombard, IL 60148. **312-620-7802.** Ivan Kauffman, general secretary

PROTESTANT REFORMED CHURCHES IN AMERICA. 16516 S Park Ave, South Holland, IL 60473. The Reverend M Joostens, stated clerk, **616-457-4444**

REFORMED BAPTISTS. 4704 Timberhill Dr, Nashville, TN 37211. **615-832-6451** or **9135.** Pastor Jon Zens, correspondent

REFORMED CHURCH IN AMERICA. 475 Riverside Dr, New York, NY 10027. **212-870-3071.** The Reverend Arie R Brouwer, general secretary

REFORMED EPISCOPAL CHURCH. 560 Fountain St, Havre de Grace, MD 21078. **310-939-3210.** The Reverend Theophilus J Herter, president and presiding bishop

THE ROMAN CATHOLIC CHURCH. 1312 Massachusetts Ave NW, Washington, DC 20005. **202-659-6600.** Archbishop Joseph L Bernadin, president

ROMANIAN ORTHODOX CHURCH IN AMERICA. 19959 Riopelle, Detroit, MI 48203. **313-893-7191.** Victoriam Ursache, most reverend archbishop

RUSSIAN ORTHODOX CHURCH IN AMERICA. 15 E 97th St, New York, NY 10029. **212-289-1915.** His Grace Ireney, vicar bishop

THE SALVATION ARMY. 120-30 W 14th St, New York, NY 10011. **212-620-4900.** Paul S Kaiser, national commander. *Press contact.* Ralph Chamberlain, director, national information service. **212-255-5057**

THE SCHWENKFELDER CHURCH. Palm, PA, 18070. **215-679-7175.** Vincent W Nyce, moderator

SECOND CUMBERLAND PRESBYTERIAN CHURCH. 7747 S Cornell Ave, Chicago, IL 60649. **312-374-4236.** The Reverend Virgil T Rice, moderator

SEVENTH DAY ADVENTISTS GENERAL CONFERENCE. 6840 Eastern Ave NW, Washington, DC 20012. **202-723-0800.** Robert H Pierson, president M Carol Hetzell, director, communication

UNITED CHRISTIAN CHURCH. RD 1, Lebanon County, PA 17042. **717-867-2611.** Elder Harry C Heagy, president

UNITED CHURCH OF CHRIST. 297 Park Ave S, New York, NY 10010. **212-475-2121.** The Reverend Avery D Post, president

THE UNITED FREE WILL BAPTIST CHURCH. Kinston College, 1000 University Pl, Kinston, NC 28501. **919-527-0120.** The Reverend O L Williams, vice-moderator

THE UNITED METHODIST CHURCH. Board of Church and Society. 100 Maryland Ave NE, Washington, DC 20002. **202-488-5633**

UNITED PENTECOSTAL CHURCH INTERNATIONAL. 8855 Dunn Rd, Hazlewood, MD 63042. **314-837-7300.** Nathanial A Urshan, general superintendent

UNITED PRESBYTERIAN CHURCH IN THE UNITED STATES OF AMERICA. 475 Riverside Dr, New York, NY 10027. **212-870-2515.** William P Thompson, stated clerk of the General Assembly, **212-870-2005.** Frank H Heinze, director, communications, **212-870-2551.** (h) **215-646-1738.** Vic Jameson, press officer, **212-870-2807.** (h) **609-452-2134**

SCIENCE AND TECHNOLOGY

Selected major firms, laboratories, institutes, and organizations concerned with science or technology are listed below.

THE ACADEMY OF NATURAL SCIENCES OF PHILADELPHIA. 19th and the Parkway, Philadelphia, PA 19103.

215-299-1000. Dr Thomas Peter Bennett, president. *Press contacts.* Mike Quinn, publicist, **215-299-1012;** Elizabeth Allen, director, public affairs, **215-299-1010**

AMERICAN ASSOCIATION FOR THE ADVANCEMENT OF SCIENCE. 1515 Massachusetts Ave NW, Washington, DC 20005. **202-467-4400.** William D Carey, executive officer, **202-467-4470.** Carol L Rogers, public information officer, **202-467-5441.** (h) **202-966-6904.** Nancy C Joyce, assistant to public information officer, **202-467-5441**

The largest general scientific organization, dating from 1848, AAAS has some 124,000 individual members and 290 affiliated science groups. The association's purposes are to "give a more systematic direction to scientific research in our country," to obtain better facilities for scientists, and to promote scientific freedom.

It has a staff of about 150 persons and 21 sections representing scientific disciplines. AAAS generally promotes cooperation among scientists by means of publications, including *Science*, standards, seminars, and awards.

AMERICAN ASSOCIATION OF AUTOMOTIVE MEDICINE. PO Box 222, Martin Grove, IL 60053. **312-751-6581**

AMERICAN ASSOCIATION OF VARIABLE STAR OBSERVERS (AAVSO). 187 Concord Ave, Cambridge, MA 02138. **617-354-0484**

AEROSPACE RESEARCH LABORATORIES. Polytechnic Institute of Brooklyn, Route 110, Farmingdale, NY 11735. **516-694-5500**

AGRICULTURAL ENVIRONMENTAL QUALITY INSTITUTE. Agricultural Research Service, US Department of Agriculture, Beltsville Agricultural Research Ctr, Beltsville, MD 20705. **301-344-3030**

AIR FORCE ROCKET PROPULSION LABORATORY (AFRPL). Edwards Air Force Base, CA 93523. **714-553-2982**

ALCOHOL AND DRUG PROBLEMS ASSOCIATION OF NORTH AMERICA. 1101 15th St NW, Washington, DC 20005. **202-452-0990**

AMERICAN ANTHROPOLOGICAL ASSOCIATION. 1703 New Hampshire Ave NW, Washington, DC 20009. **202-232-8800.** Edward J Lehman, executive director. Don Zies, assistant to executive director

AMERICAN ASTRONOMICAL SOCIETY. 211 FitzRandolph Rd, Princeton, NJ 08540. **609-452-3819.** H M Gurin, executive officer. *Press contact.* Dr Kenneth L Franklin (American Museum-Hayden Planetarium, 81st St at Central Park W, New York, NY 10024), **212-873-1300,** Ext 307. A scientific professional organization seeking the "encouragement and advancement of astronomy and closely related branches of science"

AMERICAN BIO-SYNTHETICS CORPORATION. 710 W National Ave, Milwaukee, WI 53204. **414-384-7017**

AMERICAN CHEMICAL SOCIETY. 1155 16th St NW, Washington, DC 20036. **202-872-4600.** Dr Herman Bloch, board chairman, retired, (h) **312-874-8340.** Dorothy Smith, managing editor, ACS news service, **202-872-4450.** Night line: **202-338-0682**

A congressionally chartered organization, ACS has more than 110,000 members, making it one of the largest scientific groups in the US. It publishes primary journals containing research, as well as other publications, and conducts a program of educational activities.

AMERICAN CONGRESS ON SURVEYING AND MAPPING. 210 Little Falls St, Falls Church, VA 22046. **703-241-2446**

AMERICAN COUNCIL OF INDEPENDENT LABORATORIES, INC. 1725 K St NW, Washington, DC 20006. **202-659-3766**

AMERICAN FOUNDRYMEN'S SOCIETY (AFS). Golf and Wolf Rds, Des Plaines, IL 60016. **312-824-0181**

AMERICAN GENETIC ASSOCIATION. 1028 Connecticut Ave NW, Washington, DC 20036. **202-659-9296**

AMERICAN GEOGRAPHICAL SOCIETY. Broadway at 156th St, New York, NY 10032. **212-234-8100.** Dr Sarah K Myers, director

The Society, founded in 1852, sponsors research projects, holds symposia and lectures, and publishes scientific and popular books, periodicals—*Geographical Review* (quarterly), *Focus* (bimonthly), and *Current Geographical Publications*, a monthly bibliography—and maps. It also maintains the largest private geographical library and map collection in the Western Hemisphere. The society has 10,000 members and subscribers in 120 countries.

AMERICAN GEOLOGICAL INSTITUTE. 5205 Leesburg Pike, Falls Church, VA 22041. **703-379-2480**

AMERICAN HEALTH FOUNDATION. 1370 Avenue of the Americas, New York, NY 10019. **212-489-8700**

AMERICAN INSTITUTE OF BIOLOGICAL SCIENCES. 1401 Wilson Blvd, Arlington, VA 22209. **703-527-6776.** Dr Richard Trumbull, executive director. Walter Peter, managing editor, *Bioscience*

The American Institute of Biological Sciences is a trade organization promoting research and education in the biological sciences. It publishes *BioScience* and *Education Review*

AMERICAN INSTITUTE OF CHEMICAL ENGINEERS (AIChE). United Engineering Ctr, 345 E 47th St, New York, NY 10017. **212-644-8025.** Dr F J Van Antwerpen, executive director, **212-644-8015.** Michael T Denson, assistant secretary and public relations manager, **212-644-7660**

Founded in 1908, AIChE is the chemical engineer's professional society. It has 39,000 members in industry, education, government, and private research.

AMERICAN INSTITUTE OF CROP ECOLOGY. 809 Dale Dr, Silver Spring, MD 20910. **301-589-4185**

AMERICAN INSTITUTE OF MINING, METALLURGICAL, AND PETROLEUM ENGINEERS, INC. United Engineering Ctr, 345 E 47th St, New York, NY 10017. **212-644-7500**

AMERICAN INSTITUTE OF NUTRITION. 9650 Rockville Pike, Bethesda, MD 20014. **301-530-7050**

AMERICAN INSTITUTE OF PHYSICS. 335 E 45th St, New York, NY 10017. **212-685-1940**

AMERICAN INSTITUTE OF STEEL CONSTRUCTION, INC. 1221 Avenue of the Americas, New York, NY 10020. **212-764-0440**

AMERICAN MATHEMATICAL SOCIETY. PO Box 6248, Providence, RI 02940. **401-272-9500**

AMERICAN METEOROLOGICAL SOCIETY. 45 Beacon St, Boston, MA 02108. **617-227-2425.** Dr Kenneth C Spengler, executive director

AMERICAN MUSEUM OF NATURAL HISTORY. Central Park W at 79th St, New York, NY 10024. **212-873-1300.** Thomas D Nicholson, director. Robert G Goelet, president

AMERICAN PETROLEUM INSTITUTE. 2101 L St NW, Washington, DC 20037. **202-457-7266**

AMERICAN PHYSICAL SOCIETY. 335 E 45th St, New York, NY 10017. **212-685-2014**

AMERICAN PHYTOPATHOLOGICAL SOCIETY. c/o Raymond Tarleton, executive vice-president, 3340 Pilot Knob Rd, St Paul, MN 55121. **612-454-7250**

AMERICAN RAILWAY CAR INSTITUTE. 11 E 44th St, New York, NY 10017. **212-867-6577**

AMERICAN ROAD BUILDERS ASSOCIATION. 525 School St SW, Washington, DC 20024. **202-737-5440**

AMERICAN SOCIETY OF AGRICULTURAL ENGINEERS. PO Box 401, St Joseph, MI 49085. **616-429-0300.** J L Butt, executive vice-president. Roger Castenson, public relations manager

A nonprofit engineering society, ASAE concentrates its efforts on service to agriculture. The society and its 8000 members develop standards, facilitate the transfer of research information, and work cooperatively with private, governmental, and academic organizations to improve agricultural efficiency and productivity while conserving soil and water resources.

AMERICAN SOCIETY OF AGRONOMY. 677 S Segoe Rd, Madison, WI 53711. **608-274-1212**

AMERICAN SOCIETY OF CIVIL ENGINEERS. United Engineering Ctr, 345 E 47th St, New York, NY 10017. **212-752-6800**

AMERICAN SOCIETY FOR CYBERNETICS. Suite 914, 1025 Connecticut Ave NW, Washington, DC 20036. **202-293-5467**

This is a professional organization fostering "projects in theoretical, technical, and applied cybernetics by means of multidisciplinary conferences and research programs." It publishes a quarterly journal, a quarterly newsletter, and conference proceedings, and holds an annual symposium.

AMERICAN SOCIETY FOR ENGINEERING EDUCATION. Suite 400, 1 Dupont Cir NW, Washington, DC 20036. **202-293-7080**

AMERICAN SOCIETY OF LUBRICATION ENGINEERS. 838 Bussee Hwy, Park Ridge, IL 60068. **312-825-5536**

AMERICAN SOCIETY FOR METALS. Metals Park, OH 44073. **216-338-5151.** Allan Ray Putnam, managing director. George A Mentzer, director, communications. Lori L Naiman, public relations coordinator. A worldwide organization of 40,000 members in 60 countries, the function of which is "to advance and communicate knowledge in materials technology"

AMERICAN SOCIETY FOR QUALITY CONTROL, INC. 161 W Wisconsin Ave, Milwaukee, WI 53203. **414-272-8575**

AMERICAN SOCIETY OF SAFETY ENGINEERS. 850 Busse Hwy, Park Ridge, IL 60668. **312-692-4121.** Wayne C Christensen, secretary and managing director

AMERICAN SOCIETY FOR TESTING AND MATERIALS. 1916 Race St, Philadelphia, PA 19103. **215-299-5478.** *See also* SPECIAL INTERESTS.

AMERICAN STATISTICAL ASSOCIATION. 806 15th St NW-640, Washington, DC 20005. **202-393-3253**

AMERICAN WELDING SOCIETY. 2501 NW 7th St, Miami, FL 33125. **305-642-7090.** J Edward Dato, executive director. Fred W Kirby, public relations manager

AMES LABORATORY. Iowa State University of Science and Technology, Ames, IA 50010. **515-294-3836**

APPLIED PHYSICS LABORATORY. Johns Hopkins Rd, Laurel, MD 20810. **301-589-7700**

APPLIED RESEARCH LABORATORIES. University of Texas, 10,000 FM Rd 1325 (PO Box 8029), Austin, TX 78712. **512-836-1351**

ARCTIC INSTITUTE OF NORTH AMERICA. University Library Tower, 2920 24th Ave NW, Calgary, Alta, T2N 1N4, Canada. **403-284-3387**

ARGONNE NATIONAL LABORATORY. 9700 S Cass Ave, Argonne, IL 60439. **312-739-7711**

ARLYN RESEARCH INSTITUTE, INC. 329 Cedarview Dr (PO Box 600), Claremont, CA 91711. **714-593-5483**

ARMAMENT DEVELOPMENT AND TEST CENTER. Eglin Air Force Base, FL 32542. **904-882-3212**

THE ASPHALT INSTITUTE. Asphalt Institute Bldg, University of Maryland, College Park, MD 20740. **301-927-0422**

ASSOCIATION OF ASPHALT PAVING TECHNOLOGISTS. Rm 155, Experimental Engineering Bldg, University of Minnesota, Minneapolis, MN 55455. **612-373-2518**

ASSOCIATION OF INFORMATION AND DISSEMINATION CENTERS. PO Box 8105, Athens, GA 30603. **404-542-3106.** J Ron Smith, president, **215-568-4016.** Greg H Payne, newsletter editor, **502-582-4111**

ASSOCIATION OF SCIENCE-TECHNOLOGY CENTERS (ASTC). Rm 811, 2100 Pennsylvania Ave NW, Washington, DC 20037. **202-452-0655.** Sponsored by 50 American and 14 foreign museums; acts as a clearinghouse for science museum information

ASSOCIATION OF SCIENTIFIC INFORMATION DISSEMINATION CENTERS. *See* Association of Information and Dissemination Centers

AUTOMOTIVE SAFETY LABORATORY. Biomechanics Research Ctr, Wayne State University, 5050 Anthony Wayne Dr, Detroit, MI 48202. **313-577-3835**

AVCO-EVERETT RESEARCH LABORATORY. Avco Corporation, 2385 Revere Beach Pkwy, Everett, MA 02149. **617-389-3000,** Ext 617

BALCONES RESEARCH CENTER. University of Texas, Box 189, Route 4, Austin, TX 78757. **512-836-0440**

BARTLESVILLE ENERGY RESEARCH CENTER. US Department of Energy, PO Box 1398, Bartlesville, OK 74003. **918-336-2400**

BATTELLE MEMORIAL INSTITUTE. Columbus Laboratories, 505 King Ave, Columbus, OH 43201. **614-424-4160.** James R Hunkler, coordinator, corporate communications

BELFOUR STULEN, INC. 13919 W Bay Shore Dr, Traverse City, MI 49684. **616-947-4500**

BELL TELEPHONE LABORATORIES, INC. Mountain Ave, Murray Hill, NJ 07974. **201-852-2854**

LAWRENCE BERKELEY LABORATORY. University of California, Berkeley, CA 94720. **415-843-2740,** Ext 5885

BETZ LABORATORIES, INC. Somerton Rd, Trevose, PA 19047. **215-355-3300.** *Contact.* C F Meiers, Jr

BIOSCIENCES INFORMATION SERVICE (BIOSIS). 2100 Arch St, Philadelphia, PA 19103. **215-568-4016**

FRANK P BRACKETT OBSERVATORY. Pomona College, Claremont, CA 91711. **714-626-8511,** Ext 2945 or 2946

BRIGHAM YOUNG UNIVERSITY HIGH PRESSURE DATA CENTER. 5093 Harold B Lee Library, Brigham Young University, Provo, UT 84601. **801-374-1211,** Ext 4442

BROOKHAVEN NATIONAL LABORATORY. Upton, NY 11973. **516-345-2902**

BROOKS INSTITUTE. 2190 Alston Rd, Santa Barbara, CA 93108. **805-969-2291**

CALSPAN CORPORATION. 445 Genesee St (Box 235), Buffalo, NY 14221. **616-632-7500**

CAMBRIDGE RESEARCH LABORATORIES. L G Hanscom Field, Bedford, MA 01730. **617-274-6100,** Ext 3006

CARNEGIE INSTITUTION OF WASHINGTON. 1530 P St NW, Washington, DC 20005. **202-387-6400**

CARNEGIE-MELLON INSTITUTE OF RESEARCH. Carnegie-Mellon University, 4400 5th Ave, Pittsburgh, PA 15213. **412-578-3251**

CENTER OF ALCOHOL STUDIES. Smithers Hall, Rutgers-The State University, New Brunswick, NJ 08903. **201-932-2190.** John A Carpenter, PhD, director

CENTER FOR CONCERNED ENGINEERING. 1224 Dupont Circle Bldg, Washington, DC 20036. **202-833-3320**

CENTER FOR MIGRATION STUDIES OF NEW YORK, INC. 209 Flagg Pl, Staten Island, NY 10304. **212-351-8800.** Lydio F Tomasi, executive director

CENTER FOR NATURAL AREAS. US Smithsonian Institution, 1525 New Hampshire Ave NW, Washington, DC 20036. **202-265-0066**

CENTER FOR REMOTE SENSING INFORMATION AND ANALYSIS. Environmental Research Institute of Michigan, PO Box 8618, Ann Arbor, MI 48107. **313-994-1200,** Ext 290

CENTER FOR REMOTE SENSING RESEARCH. Rm 129, Mulford Hall, University of California, Berkeley, CA 94720. **415-642-1351**

CENTER FOR RESEARCH, INC. Engineering Science Division, University of Kansas, 2291 Irving Hill Rd, Lawrence, KS 66045. **913-864-3441.** B G Barr, executive director, **913-864-4774**

CENTER FOR SCIENCE IN THE PUBLIC INTEREST. 1755 S St NW, Washington, DC 20009. **202-332-9110.** Dr Michael Jacobson, executive director

An activist group that focuses on nutrition and health issues, CSPI seeks to influence government policies and public opinion through taking legal actions, working with officials, and producing publications. The center has a staff of about 12 persons and is supported by donations, grants, and the sale of its own literature.

CENTER FOR SHORT-LIVED PHENOMENA, INC. 129 Mount Auburn St, Cambridge, MA 02138. **617-492-3310.** Richard Golob, director. *see* SPECIAL INTERESTS

CENTER FOR URBAN ENVIRONMENTAL STUDIES. Polytechnic Institute of New York, 333 Jay St, Brooklyn, NY 11201. **212-643-2124.** Professor Paul R DeCicco, director

CHEMICAL DATA CENTER. 3620 N High St, Columbus, OH 43214. **614-261-7101.** Night line: **614-885-2755.** K E Jackson, president

CHEMICAL PROPULSION INFORMATION AGENCY (CPIA). Applied Physics Laboratory, Johns Hopkins University, Johns Hopkins Rd, Laurel, MD 20810. **301-953-7100,** Ext 7800

CHEMICAL SEARCH SERVICE. 116 W Woodland Dr, Round Lake Beach, IL 60073. **312-546-3898**

CHEMICAL SPECIALTIES MANUFACTURERS ASSOCIATION, INC. Suite 1120, 1001 Connecticut Ave NW, Washington, DC 20036. **202-872-8110**

CHEMICAL TRANSPORTATION EMERGENCY CENTER (CHEMTREC). Manufacturing Chemists Association, 1825 Connecticut Ave NW, Washington, DC 20009. *Contact.* Thomas J Gilroy, **202-483-6126.** (h) **703-241-1233**

THE CHEMISTS' CLUB. 52 E 41st St, New York, NY 10017. **212-532-7649.** Sam F Teague, president. Arthur R Kravaler, public relations chairman, **212-732-9820**

THE CHLORINE INSTITUTE. 342 Madison Ave, New York, NY 10017. **212-682-4324**

COLORADO SCHOOL OF MINES RESEARCH INSTITUTE. PO Box 112, Golden, CO 80401. **303-279-2581**

THE COMBUSTION INSTITUTE. 986 Union Trust Bldg, Pittsburgh, PA 15219. **412-391-1366**

COMPRESSED GAS ASSOCIATION, INC. 500 5th Ave, New York, NY 10036. **212-354-1130**

CONTROLLED FUSION ATOMIC DATA CENTER. Oak Ridge National Laboratory, PO Box X, Oak Ridge, TN 37830. **615-483-8611,** Ext 3-0141. C F Barnett (Bldg 6003), director. *Contact.* Sherry Hawthorne (Bldg 6003)

COUNCIL OF ENGINEERS AND SCIENTISTS WEST. 727 W 7th, Los Angeles, CA. **213-624-9317**

EDWIN COX ASSOCIATES AND COMMONWEALTH LABORATORY, INC. Chemists' Bldg, 2209 E Broad St, Richmond, VA 23223. **703-648-8358**

CRANBROOK INSTITUTE OF SCIENCE. 500 Lone Pine Rd, Bloomfield Hills, MI 48013. **313-645-3210** or **3260.** Robert N Bowen, director

CYCLOTRON LABORATORY. Michigan State University, East Lansing, MI 48824. **517-355-9671.** H G Blosser, director

DENVER RESEARCH INSTITUTE. University of Denver, Denver, CO 80210. **303-753-2271**

HARRY DIAMOND LABORATORIES. Scientific and Technical Information Office, Harry Diamond Laboratories, 2800 Powder Mill Rd, Adelphi, MD 20783. **202-394-1010.** John P Carrier, chief

DOD NUCLEAR INFORMATION AND ANALYSIS CENTER (DASIAC). General Electric TEMPO, 816 State St, Santa Barbara, CA 93102. **805-965-0551,** Ext 253

DRUG-ABUSE RESEARCH INSTRUMENT INVENTORY (DARII). Social Systems Analysts, 2 Calvin Rd, Watertown, MA 02172. **617-924-1611**

DRY LANDS RESEARCH INSTITUTE. University of California, Riverside, CA 92521. **714-787-4554**

DUDLEY OBSERVATORY. Plaza 7, 1202 Troy-Schenectady Rd, Latham, NY 12110. **518-783-6399**

ELECTRIC VEHICLE COUNCIL. 90 Park Ave, New York, NY 10016. **212-573-8784**

EMBRY-RIDDLE AERONAUTICAL UNIVERSITY. Daytona Beach Regional Airport, Daytona Beach, FL 32014. **904-252-5561**

EMERGENCY CARE RESEARCH INSTITUTE. 5200 Butler Pike, Plymouth Meeting, PA 19462. **215-825-6000.** Joel J Nobel, MD, director

ENERGY RESEARCH CENTER. US Department of Energy, 4800 Forbes Ave, Pittsburgh, PA 15213. **412-892-2400.** Irving Wender, director, Ext 395. Carol E Steele, public information officer, Ext 187

ENGINEERING INDEX, INC. United Engineering Ctr, 345 E 47th St, New York, NY 10017. **212-644-7600.** John E Creps, Jr, executive director, **212-644-7618.** John H Veyette, Jr, manager, marketing division, **212-644-7615.** A not-for-profit organization that publishes an engineering data base of abstracts and indexes

ENGINEERS' COUNCIL FOR PROFESSIONAL DEVELOPMENT, INC. United Engineering Ctr, 345 E 47th St, New York, NY 10017. **212-644-7684**

ENVIRONMENTAL RESEARCH INSTITUTE OF MICHIGAN. PO Box 8618, Ann Arbor, MI 48107. **313-994-1200.** Dr W M Brown, president

EROS DATA CENTER, EARTH RESOURCES OBSERVATION SYSTEM (EROS). US Geological Survey, Sioux Falls, SD 57198. **605-594-6511**

FARM AND INDUSTRIAL EQUIPMENT INSTITUTE. 410 N Michigan Ave, Chicago, IL 60611. **312-321-1470**

FLAMMABILITY INSTITUTE. University of Detroit, 4001 W McNichols Rd, Detroit, MI 48221. **313-342-1000,** Ext 315

FLAMMABILITY RESEARCH CENTER. College of Engineering, 2020 Merrill Engineering Bldg, University of Utah, Salt Lake City, UT 84112. **801-581-8431**

EDSEL B FORD INSTITUTE FOR MEDICAL RESEARCH . Henry Ford Hospital, 2799 W Grand Blvd, Detroit, MI 48202. **313-876-1214**

FORUM FOR THE ADVANCEMENT OF STUDENTS IN SCIENCE AND TECHNOLOGY (FASST). 2030 M St NW-402, Washington, DC 20036. **202-466-3860.** Alan

Ladwig, president, **202-466-3860.** Night line: **202-244-4290**

A national membership organization, FASST seeks to increase student understanding of science and technology issues by providing the technical student with information on what will be accepted in the form of public policy, and the social science and humanities student with a background on available technical options. It publishes a quarterly tabloid (*FASST News*) and a membership newsletter (*FASST Tracks*), and provides news service for editors of campus and educational publications. It also sponsors conferences and workshops.

JAMES FRANCK INSTITUTE. University of Chicago, 5640 Ellis Ave, Chicago, IL 60637. **312-753-8216**

THE FRANKLIN INSTITUTE. Benjamin Franklin Pkwy at 20th St, Philadelphia, PA 19103. **215-448-1000.** Dr Bowen C Dees, president. Jane Grinspan, director, public affairs

THE FRANKLIN INSTITUTE RESEARCH LABORATORIES. 20th and Race Sts, Philadelphia, PA 19103. **215-448-1227**

GAS PROCESSORS ASSOCIATION. 1812 1st Pl and 15 E 5th St, Tulsa, OK 74103. **918-582-5112**

GENERAL TELEPHONE AND ELECTRONICS LABORATORIES, INC. 208-20 Willets Point Blvd, Bayside, NY 11360. **212-225-5000**

GEOPHYSICAL AND POLAR RESEARCH CENTER. Department of Geology and Geophysics, University of Wisconsin, 1215 W Dayton St, Madison, WI 53706. **608-262-1921**

GULF COAST RESEARCH LABORATORY. East Beach, Ocean Springs, MS 39564. **601-875-2244, 2245** or **2246.** Dr Harold D Howse, director, Ext 210. Catherine Campbell, public information officer, Ext 273 or 254

HALE OBSERVATORIES. 813 Santa Barbara St, Pasadena, CA 91101. **213-577-1122.** Operated jointly by Carnegie Institution of Washington and California Institute of Technology, and consisting of Mount Wilson Observatory, Mount Wilson CA; Palomar Observatory, Palomar Mountain, CA; Big Bear Solar Observatory, Big Bear, CA; Las Campanas Observatory, La Serena, Chile. *Executive contact.* F P

Woodson, **213-577-1122.** *Press contact.* News Bureau, California Institute of Technology, **213-795-6811,** Ext 2326

W W HANSEN LABORATORIES OF PHYSICS. Stanford University, Stanford, CA 94305. **415-497-0279.** Attention: Heffner Library

HARVARD RADIO ASTRONOMY STATION. Fort Davis, TX 79734. **915-426-3201**

HARVARD-SMITHSONIAN CENTER FOR ASTROPHYSICS. 60 Garden St, Cambridge, MA 02138. **617-495-7461.** George B Field, director. James Cornell, public affairs officer

HAWAII INSTITUTE OF GEOPHYSICS. University of Hawaii, 2525 Correa Rd, Honolulu, HI 96822. **808-948-8760**

HIGH ENERGY PHYSICS LABORATORY. Stanford University, Stanford, CA 94305. **415-327-7800,** Ext 201

HIGHWAY SAFETY RESEARCH INSTITUTE. University of Michigan, 2901 Baxter Rd, Ann Arbor, MI 48109. **313-764-2171**

HUMAN SCIENCES RESEARCH, INC. Westgate Research Park, 7710 Old Springhouse Rd, McLean, VA 22101. **703-893-5200**

HUXLEY INSTITUTE FOR BIOSOCIAL RESEARCH. 1114 1st Ave, New York, NY 10021. **212-759-9554**

IIT RESEARCH INSTITUTE. 10 W 35th St, Chicago, IL 60616. **312-567-4000.** Paula C Norton, public relations coordinator, **312-567-4009**

ILLINOIS INSTITUTE FOR ENVIRONMENTAL QUALITY. 309 W Washington St, Chicago, IL 60606. **312-793-3870**

ILLUMINATING ENGINEERING RESEARCH INSTITUTE. United Engineering Ctr, 345 E 47th St, New York, NY 10017. **212-644-7919**

INDUSTRIAL DEVELOPMENT RESEARCH COUNCIL. Peachtree Air Terminal, 1954 Airport Rd, Atlanta, GA 30341. **404-458-6026**

INDUSTRIAL HEALTH FOUNDATION, INC. 5231 Centre Ave, Pittsburgh, PA 15232. **412-687-2100**

INSTITUTE FOR APPLIED TECHNOL-OGY. National Bureau of Standards, US Department of Commerce, Washington, DC 20234. **301-921-2907**

INSTITUTE OF ARCTIC AND ALPINE RESEARCH. University of Colorado, Boulder, CO 80309. **303-492-6387**

INSTITUTE OF ATMOSPHERIC PHYSICS. University of Arizona, Tucson, AZ 85721. **602-884-1211.** Dr Louis J Battan, director

INSTITUTE FOR BEHAVIORAL RE-SEARCH. 2429 Linden Ln, Silver Spring, MD 20910. **202-585-3915.** H McIlvaine Parsons, executive director

INSTITUTE OF CHILD BEHAVIOR RE-SEARCH. 4758 Edgeware Rd, San Diego, CA 92116. **714-281-7165**

INSTITUTE OF ELECTRICAL AND ELECTRONICS ENGINEERS. United Engineering Ctr, 345 E 47th St, New York, NY 10017. **212-752-6800**

INSTITUTE OF ENVIRONMENTAL MEDICINE. New York University Medical Ctr, 550 1st Ave, New York, NY 10016. **212-679-3200**

INSTITUTE OF ENVIRONMENTAL SCI-ENCES. 940 E Northwest Hwy, Mount Prospect, IL 60056. **312-255-1561.** Betty L Peterson, executive director, Night line: **312-259-9369.** Janet Ehmann, associate editor. A professional society of engineers, scientists, and educators dedicated to re-searching, simulating and testing the en-vironments of earth and space and to teaching about them.

INSTITUTE FOR ENVIRONMENTAL STUDIES. University of Wisconsin, 1225 W Dayton St, Madison, WI 53706. **608-262-5957**

INSTITUTE OF GAS TECHNOLOGY. 3424 S State St, Chicago, IL 60610. **312-567-3847**

INSTITUTE OF MAKERS OF EXPLO-SIVES. 420 Lexington Ave, New York, NY 10017. **212-689-3237**

INSTITUTE OF MARINE SCIENCES. University of North Carolina, Box 809, Morehead City, NC 28557. **919-726-6841.** Dr A F Chestnut, director

INSTITUTE OF MINERAL RESEARCH. Michigan Technological University, Hough-ton, MI 49931. **906-487-2600.** Dr W L Freyberger, director

INSTITUTE FOR PHYSICAL SCIENCE AND TECHNOLOGY. University of Mary-land, College Park, MD 20742. **301-454-2636.** Dr J Silverman, director

INSTITUTE OF POLAR STUDIES. Ohio State University, 125 S Oval Mall, Co-lumbus, OH 43210. **614-422-6531.** Dr David H Elliot, director (h) **614-268-2344.** *Contact.* Peter J Anderson, (h) **614-436-2654**

INSTITUTE FOR RESEARCH IN VI-SION. Ohio State University, 1314 Kinnear Rd, Columbus, OH 43212. **614-293-6265**

INSTITUTE FOR SCIENTIFIC INFOR-MATION. 325 Chestnut St, Philadelphia, PA 19106. **215-923-3300.** *European office.* 132 High St, Uxbridge, Middlesex, UK. Indexes and abstracts worldwide scientific and technical literature, including physical, chemical, mathematical, engineering, nuclear, agricultural, biological, pharmaco-logical, medical, behavioral, social, and educational sciences

INSTITUTE OF SCRAP IRON AND STEEL. 1627 K St NW, Washington, DC 20006. **202-466-4050.** Dr Herschel Cutler, executive director. James E Fowler, director, public relations

INSTITUTE OF TEXTILE TECHNOL-OGY. Box 391, Route 250 W, Charlottes-ville, VA 22902. **804-296-5511**

INSTITUTE OF TRANSPORTATION ENGINEERS. Suite 905, 1815 Fort Myer Dr, Arlington, VA 22209. **703-527-5277**

INTERNATIONAL BRIDGE, TUNNEL, AND TURNPIKE ASSOCIATION. Suite 307, 1225 Connecticut Ave NW, Washing-ton, DC 20036. **202-659-4620**

INTERNATIONAL FOOD INFORMA-TION SERVICE. Institute of Food Technol-ogists, Suite 2120, 221 N LaSalle St, Chicago, IL 60601. **312-782-8424.** Calvert L Willey, executive director

INTERNATIONAL OIL SCOUTS ASSOCIATION. PO Box 2121, Austin, TX 78767. **512-472-3357**

INTERNATIONAL PETROLEUM IN-STITUTE. 9 E 53rd St, New York, NY 10022. **212-355-1090.** Mailing address: PO Box 337, Grand Central Station, New York, NY 10017

INTERNATIONAL POPULATION AND URBAN RESEARCH PROGRAM. Univer-sity of California, 2234 Piedmont Ave, Berkeley, CA 94720. **415-642-5796**

JET PROPULSION LABORATORY. California Institute of Technology, 4800 Oak Grove Dr, Pasadena, CA 91103. **213- 354-4200**

JOHNSTON LABORATORIES, INC. 3 Industry Ln, Cockeysville, MD 21030. **301-666-9500**

JOINT INDUSTRIAL COUNCIL. 7901 Westpark Dr, McLean, VA 22101. **703- 893-2900**

JOINT INSTITUTE FOR LABORATORY ASTROPHYSICS INFORMATION ANALYSIS CENTER. University of Col-orado, Boulder, CO 80309. **303-447-1000,** Ext 3649, or **303-492-7801**

CHARLES F KETTERING FOUNDA-TION RESEARCH LABORATORY. 150 E South College St, Yellow Springs, OH 45387. **513-767-7271**

KLINE GEOLOGY LABORATORY. 210 Whitney Ave, New Haven, CT 06520. **203-436-1188**

LABORATORY FOR ATMOSPHERIC AND SPACE PHYSICS. University of Colorado, Boulder, CO 80309. **303-492-7677**

LABORATORY OF SUBSURFACE GE-OLOGY. Department of Geology and Mineralogy, 1006 C C Little Bldg, University of Michigan, Ann Arbor, MI 48109. **313-764-2434**

LADD OBSERVATORY. Brown University, Providence, RI 02912. **401-863-2110** or **401-521-5680**

LANGLEY RESEARCH CENTER. Langley Station, Hampton, VA 23365. **703-827-2788**

LARAMIE ENERGY RESEARCH CENTER. PO Box 3395, University Station, Laramie WY 82071. **307-742-2117**

LAW ENFORCEMENT SCIENCE AND TECHNOLOGY CENTER. IIT Research Institute, 10 W 35th St, Chicago, IL 60616 **312-567-4000**

LAW ENGINEERING TESTING CO. 2600 Century Pkwy NE, Atlanta, GA 30345. **404-325-3933.** A J Glenn III, president

LAWRENCE BERKELEY LABORATORY. University of California, Berkeley, CA 94720. **415-843-2740**

LEWIS RESEARCH CENTER OF THE NATIONAL AERONAUTICS AND SPACE ADMINISTRATION. 21000 Brookpark Rd, Cleveland, OH 44135. **216-433-4000.** Paul T Bohn, public information officer

LINDHEIMER ASTRONOMICAL RESEARCH CENTER. Northwestern University, Evanston, IL 60201. **312-492-7651**

ARTHUR D LITTLE, INC. 25 Acorn Park, Cambridge, MA 02140. **617-864-5770.** Alma Triner, vice-president, public relations, Ext 2542

LAWRENCE LIVERMORE LABORATORY. University of California, Livermore, CA 94550. **415-447-1100**

LIVESTOCK INSECTS LABORATORY. Agricultural Research Service, US Department of Agriculture, PO Box 232, Kerrville, TX 78028. **512-257-3566**

LOS ALAMOS SCIENTIFIC LABORATORY. PO Box 1663, Los Alamos, NM 87545. **505-667-6101.** Harold M Agnew, director, **505-667-5101.** William J Richmond, assistant public information officer

LOWELL OBSERVATORY. Flagstaff, AZ 86001. **602-774-3358**

MANLABS, INC. 21 Erie St, Cambridge, MA 02139. **617-491-2900**

MARSHALL LABORATORY. E I du Pont de Nemours and Co, Inc, 3500 Grays Ferry Ave, Philadelphia, PA 19146. **215-465-3000,** Ext 635

MCGILL SUB-ARCTIC RESEARCH STATION. McGill University, PO Box 790, Schefferville, Que. GOG 2TO, Canada. **418-585-3784**

MELLON INSTITUTE. 4400 5th Ave, Pittsburgh, PA 15213. **412-621-1100**

MENTAL RESEARCH INSTITUTE. 555 Middlefield Rd, Palo Alto, CA 94301. **415-321-3055.** Jules Riskin, MD, director. Luis E Fernandez, deputy director, Night line: **415-327-8686.** A social science research and training organization in the fields of family interaction, communications, and human behavior generally

MIDWEST RESEARCH INSTITUTE. 425 Volker Blvd, Kansas City, MO 64110. **816-753-7600.** John McKelvey, president. J L Schefter, communications manager

MINERAL RESOURCES RESEARCH CENTER. University of Minnesota, Minneapolis, MN 55455. **612-373-3341**

MOBILE HOME MANUFACTURERS ASSOCIATION. PO Box 201, 14650 Lee Rd, Chantilly, VA 22021. **703-968-6970**

MOREHEAD PLANETARIUM. PO Box 1227, University of North Carolina, Chapel Hill, NC 27514. **919-933-1237.** A F Jenzano, director

MOTOR AND EQUIPMENT MANUFACTURERS ASSOCIATION. PO Box 439, Teaneck, NJ 07666. **201-836-9500**

MOTOR VEHICLE RESEARCH OF NEW HAMPSHIRE. Route 152, Newmarket, NH 03857. **603-659-3830**

MOUNT WASHINGTON OBSERVATORY. Revolutionary Rd, Concord, MA 01742. **617-369-5365.** *Chief observer.* Gorham, NH 03581. **603-466-0001**

NATIONAL ACADEMY OF ENGINEERING. *See* THE FEDERAL GOVERNMENT: The Independent Agencies

NATIONAL ACADEMY OF SCIENCES. *See* THE FEDERAL GOVERNMENT: The Independent Agencies

NATIONAL AGRICULTURAL CHEMICALS ASSOCIATION. 1155 15th St NW, Washington, DC 20005. **202-296-1585**

NATIONAL ASSOCIATION OF BIOLOGY TEACHERS. 11250 Roger Bacon Dr, Reston, VA 22090. **703-471-1134**

NATIONAL ASSOCIATION OF CORROSION ENGINEERS. 1440 S Creek, Houston, TX 77084. **713-492-0535**

NATIONAL AUTOMOTIVE PARTS ASSOCIATION. 10400 W Higgins Rd, Rosemont, IL 60018. **312-298-5151**

NATIONAL BUREAU OF STANDARDS. *See* THE FEDERAL GOVERNMENT: Department of Commerce

NATIONAL CENTER FOR ATMOSPHERIC RESEARCH. Astrogeophysics Bldg, University of Colorado, 900 24th St (PO Box 1558), Boulder, CO 80302. **303-444-1550**

NATIONAL CENTER FOR RESOURCE RECOVERY. Suite 800, 1211 Connecticut Ave NW, Washington, DC 20036. **202-223-6154**

NATIONAL CONSTRUCTORS ASSOCIATION. Suite 1000, 1101 15th St NW, Washington, DC 20005. **202-466-8880**

NATIONAL COUNCIL ON RADIATION PROTECTION AND MEASUREMENTS. 7910 Woodmont Ave, Bethesda, MD 20014. **301-657-2652**

NATIONAL ENDOWMENTS. *See* THE FEDERAL GOVERNMENT: The Independent Agencies

NATIONAL FOUNDATION FOR JEWISH GENETIC DISEASES. 608 5th Ave, New York, NY 10020. **212-541-6340**

NATIONAL FOUNDATIONS. *See* THE FEDERAL GOVERNMENT: The Independent Agencies

NATIONAL INSTITUTE FOR OCCUPATIONAL SAFETY AND HEALTH. US Department of Health, Education, and Welfare, Post Office and Courthouse Building, 5th and Walnut Sts, Cincinnati, OH 45202. **513-684-2141**

NATIONAL FOUNDATIONS. *See* THE FEDERAL GOVERNMENT: The Independent Agencies

NATIONAL INSTITUTES OF HEALTH. Division of Research Grants, Public Health Service (PHS), US Department of Health, Education, and Welfare, 5333 Westbard Ave, Bethesda, MD 20014. *Office of Grants Inquires* (Rm 448). **301-496-7441.** *Research Documentation Section* (Rm 3A03). **301-496-7543**

NATIONAL LEGAL CENTER FOR BIOETHICS. 2200 Windham Ln, Silver Spring, MD 20902. **301-649-4421** or **703-759-3658.** Mailing address: Box 24021, Washington, DC 20024. Night line. **703-759-3607.** Paul H Andreini, executive director and president, **703-759-3658.** Seeks to affect public policy in area of biomedical ethics, through litigation, education, research, and the dissemination of information.

NATIONAL LP-GAS ASSOCIATION. 79 W Monroe St, Chicago, IL 60603. **312-372-5484**

NATIONAL OIL JOBBERS COUNCIL. 1750 New York Ave NE 230, Washington, DC 20006. **202-331-1078**

NATIONAL PAINT AND COATINGS ASSOCIATION. 1500 Rhode Island Ave NW, Washington, DC 20005. **202-462-6272**

NATIONAL PEST CONTROL ASSOCIA-TION. Suite 1100, 8150 Leesburg Pike, Vienna, VA 22180. **703-790-8300**

NATIONAL RADIO ASTRONOMY OB-SERVATORY. Edgemont Rd, Charlottesville, VA 22901. **804-296-0211.** Mailing address: PO Box 2, Green Bank, WV 24944. **304-456-2011.** Wally Oret, public information officer

NATIONAL REACTOR TESTING STA-TION. PO Box 1845, Idaho Falls, ID 83401. **208-526-4447**

NATIONAL SCIENCE TEACHERS ASSOCIATION. 1742 Connecticut Ave NW, Washington, DC 20036. **202-265-4150**

NATURAL SCIENCE FOR YOUTH FOUNDATION. 763 Silvermine Rd, New Canaan, CT 06840. **203-966-5643**

NATIONAL SOCIETY OF PROFES-SIONAL ENGINEERS. 2029 K St NW, Washington, DC 20006. **202-331-7020.** Paul H Robbins, executive director. John Cox, director, public relations. Promotes the social, professional, ethical, and economic considerations of engineering as a profession and provides programs in public relations, employment practices, ethical considerations, career guidance, and governmental liaison

NATIONAL STRIPPER WELL ASSOCIA-TION. 5902 S 68th East Ave, Tulsa, OK 74145. **918-627-7880**

NEW YORK ACADEMY OF SCIENCES. 2 E 63rd St, New York, NY 10021. **212-838-0230**

NORTHEAST WEATHER SERVICE. 131A Great Rd, Bedford, MA 01730. **617-275-8860**

NUCLEAR PHYSICS LABORATORY. University of Colorado, Boulder, CO 80309. **303-492-7483**

NUTRITION FOUNDATION, INC. 489 5th Ave, New York, NY 10017. **212-687-4830**

NUTRITION INSTITUTE OF AMERICA (NIA). 200 W 86th St, New York, NY 10024. **212-595-7507**

OAK RIDGE NATIONAL LABORATORY. Oak Ridge, TN 17830. **615-483-8611**

OCEAN LIVING INSTITUTE. Box 470, Kearny, NJ 07032. **201-471-6503.** Adam Starchild, director. Conducts oceanography research and education

OHIO ACADEMY OF SCIENCE. 445 King Ave, Columbus, OH 43201. **614-424-6045.** Lynn Edward Elfner, executive officer

PACIFIC SCIENTIFIC INFORMATION CENTER. Bernice P Bishop Museum, 1355 Kalihi St (PO Box 6037), Honolulu, HI 96818. **808-847-3511**

POLYMER INSTITUTE. Chemical Engineering Department, University of Detroit, 4001 W McNichols Rd, Detroit, MI 48221. **313-927-1270**

POLYMER RESEARCH INSTITUTE. University of Massachusetts, Amherst, MA 01002. **413-545-2727**

POPULATION REFERENCE BUREAU, INC. 1755 Massachusetts Ave NW, Washington, DC 20036. **202-232-2288**

POPULATION RESEARCH CENTER. University of Texas, 200 E 26$\frac{1}{2}$ St, Austin, TX 78705. **512-471-5514**

POPULATION RESEARCH LABORA-TORY. Department of Sociology, University of Southern California, Rm 245, 3716 S Hope St, University Park, Los Angeles, CA 90007. **213-741-2950.** Professor Maurice D Van Arsdol, Jr, director

PRATT INSTITUTE. 215 Ryerson St, Brooklyn, NY 11205. **212-622-2200,** Ext 276

PRIMATE INFORMATION CENTER. Regional Primate Research Center, University of Washington, Seattle, WA 98195. **206-543-4376**

PRINCETON UNIVERSITY OBSERVA-TORY. Peyton Hall, Princeton, NJ 08540. **609-452-3800**

PRINCETON UNIVERSITY OFFICE OF POPULATION RESEARCH. 21 Prospect Ave, Princeton, NJ 08540. **609-452-4870**

PROJECT RFD (RESPECT FOR DRUGS). College of Pharmaceutical Sciences, Columbia University, 115 W 68th St, New York, NY 10023. **212-787-0600,** Ext 33

RADAR METEOROLOGICAL LABORA-TORY. School of Marine and Atmospheric Sciences, University of Miami, Rm 501, Merrick Bldg, (PO Box 8003), Coral Gables, FL 33124. **305-284-3881**

RADIATION CHEMISTRY DATA CENTER. Radiation Laboratory, University of Notre Dame, Notre Dame, IN 46556. **219-283-6527** or **6528**

RAILWAY SYSTEMS AND MANAGE-MENT ASSOCIATION (RSMA). PO Box 330, Ocean City, NJ 08226. **609-398-3956.** Grant C Vietsch, president

REDSTONE SCIENTIFIC INFORMA-TION CENTER. US Army Missile Command, Redstone Arsenal, AL 35809. **205-876-5195**

RELIABILITY ANALYSIS CENTER. IIT Research Institute, Bldg 3, Rome Air Development Ctr, Griffiss Air Force Base, NY 13441. **315-330-4151**

RENSSELAER POLYTECHNIC IN-STITUTE. Troy, NY 12181. **518-270-6200.** George M Low, president, **518-270-6211.** Bruce Hutchison, director, university news office, **518-270-6531**

RESEARCH AND DEVELOPMENT IN-STITUTE OF THE UNITED STATES (RADIUS). Rm 310, Thompson Bldg (PO Box 7220), Tulsa, OK 74105. **918-587-2333**

RESEARCH TRIANGLE INSTITUTE. PO Box 12194, Research Triangle Park, NC 27709. **919-541-6000**

RUBBER MANUFACTURERS ASSOCIA-TION, INC. 1901 Pennsylvania Ave NW, Washington, DC 20006. **202-785-2602**

SADTLER RESEARCH LABORATORIES, INC. 3316 Spring Garden St, Philadelphia, PA 19104. **215-382-7800.** Richard H Shaps, president

SAFETY AND FIRE PROTECTION COMMITTEE. Manufacturing Chemists Association, 1825 Connecticut Ave NW, Washington, DC 20009. **202-483-6126**

ST ANTHONY FALLS HYDRAULIC LABORATORY. University of Minnesota, Mississippi River at 3d Ave SE, Minneapolis, MN 55414. **612-373-2782**

SALT LAKE CITY METALLURGY RE-SEARCH CENTER. Bureau of Mines, US Department of the Interior, 1600 E 1st South St, Salt Lake City, UT 84112. **801-524-5350**

SCIENCE SCREEN REPORT, INC. 201 W 52nd St, New York, NY 10019. **212-586-3057**

SCIENCE SERVICE. 1719 N St NW, Washington, DC 20036. **202-785-2255**

SCIENTISTS' INSTITUTE FOR PUBLIC INFORMATION. 355 Lexington Ave, New York, NY 10017. **212-661-9110.** *Contact.* Fred Jerome. Barry Commoner, chairman.

Alan McGowan, president. An organization devoted to encouraging and helping the press and lay public to gain a better understanding of scientific developments and issues that have great bearing on current social questions.

SCRIPPS FOUNDATION FOR RE-SEARCH IN POPULATION PROBLEMS. 218 Harrison Hall, Miami University, Oxford, OH 45056. **513-529-2812**

SHOCK AND VIBRATION INFORMA-TION CENTER. US Naval Research Laboratory, 4555 Overlook Ave SW-8404, Washington, DC 20375. **202-767-2220**

SOCIETY OF MANUFACTURING EN-GINEERS. 20501 Ford Rd, Dearborn, MI 48128. **313-271-1500**

SOIL CONSERVATION SOCIETY OF AMERICA. 7515 NE Ankeny Rd, Ankeny, IO 50021. **515-289-2331**

SOIL AND MATERIALS RESEARCH LABORATORIES. Engineering Research Institute, Iowa State University of Science and Technology, Ames, IA 50010. **515-294-7689.** (soils and concrete). **515-294-7439** (asphalt)

SMITHSONIAN INSTITUTION. *See* THE FEDERAL GOVERNMENT: The Independent Agencies.

SMITHSONIAN SCIENCE INFORMA-TION EXCHANGE. *See* INFORMATION AND RESEARCH SERVICES.

SNELL MEMORIAL FOUNDATION, INC. c/o Dr George G Snively, 761 Laurel Dr, Sacramento, CA 95825. **916-453-3615** or **916-487-4832**

SOCIETY OF AUTOMOTIVE EN-GINEERS. 400 Commonwealth Dr, Warrendale, PA 15096. **412-776-4841.** Joseph Gilbert, general manager and secretary

A professional society of engineers in ground, flight, and space vehicles, SAE has 27,000 members, 52 local groups, and a staff of 135 persons. It publishes an extensive compilation of technical papers and sets standards; local groups hold monthly meetings to discuss technical problems.

SOCIETY OF MANUFACTURING EN-GINEERS. 20501 Ford Rd (PO Box 930), Dearborn, MI 48128. **313-271-1500.** R William Taylor, executive vice-president and general manager. Thomas C Akas, manager, public relations. A worldwide technical

society "dedicated to disseminating the latest advances in manufacturing technology through the continuing education of manufacturing engineers and managers"

SOCIETY OF MOTION PICTURE AND TELEVISION ENGINEERS, INC. 862 Scarsdale Ave, Scarsdale, NY 10583. **914-472-6606.** Denis A Courtney, executive director, Ext 440. Jeffrey Friedman, advertising manager, Ext 444. Lynne Robinson, conference programs secretary, Ext 441. Holds two yearly conferences, publishes the monthly *SMPTE Journal* and additional special publications, and coordinates international and American motion picture and television engineering standards

SOCIETY OF PLASTICS ENGINEERS. 656 W Putnam Ave, Greenwich, CT 06830. **203-661-4770.** Robert D Forger, executive director. Roger P Fox, manager, promotion

SOCIETY OF THE PLASTICS IN-DUSTRY, INC. 355 Lexington Ave, New York, NY 10017. **212-573-9400**

SOCIETY FOR THE STUDY OF SOCIAL PROBLEMS, COMMITTEE ON DRINK-ING BEHAVIOR. Department of Sociology, Eastern Washington State College, Cheney, WA 99004. **509-359-2335**

SOLID AND HAZARDOUS WASTE RE-SEARCH LABORATORY. Environmental Protection Agency, 26 W St Clair St, Cincinnati, OH 45268. **513-684-7861**

SOLID WASTE RECYCLING INFORMA-TION SERVICE. National Association of Recycling Industries, Inc, 330 Madison Ave, New York, NY 10017. **212-867-7330.** John R McBride, director, public-community relations

SOUTHERN RESEARCH INSTITUTE. 2000 9th Ave S, Birmingham, AL 35205. **205-323-6592**

SOUTHWEST RESEARCH INSTITUTE. 8500 Culebra Rd (PO Drawer 28510), San Antonio, TX 78228. **512-684-2000**

STANFORD LINEAR ACCELERATOR CENTER. Stanford University, 2575 Sand Hill Rd, Menlo Park, CA 94025. *Public Information Office.* **415-854 300,** Ext 2204. *Library.* Ext 2411. Mailing address: Stanford University, PO Box 4349, Stanford, CA 94305

STATISTICAL RESEARCH LABORA-TORY. 106 Rackham Bldg, University of Michigan, Ann Arbor, MI 48104. **313-764-4413**

STEVENS INSTITUTE OF TECHNOL-OGY. Davidson Laboratory, Castle Point Station, 711 Hudson St, Hoboken, NJ 07030. **201-792-2700**

STEWARD OBSERVATORY. University of Arizona, Tucson, AZ 85721. **602-884-2288**

SUICIDE PREVENTION CENTER AND INSTITUTE FOR STUDIES OF SELF-DESTRUCTIVE BEHAVIORS. 1041 S Menlo Ave, Los Angeles, CA 90006. **213-381-5111**

TECHNICAL ASSOCIATION OF THE PULP AND PAPER INDUSTRY. 1 Dunwoody Park, Atlanta, GA 30338. **404-394-6130**

TECHNICAL INFORMATION SERVICES. Institute of Gas Technology, 3424 S State St, Chicago, IL . **312-567-3847**

TEXAS PETROLEUM RESEARCH COM-MITTEE. W T Doherty Petroleum Bldg, Texas A & M University, College Station, TX 77843. **713-846-9614**

TEXAS TRANSPORTATION IN-STITUTE. Texas A & M University, College Station, TX 77843. **713-845-1711**

TEXTILE RESEARCH INSTITUTE. 601 Prospect Ave (PO Box 625), Princeton, NJ 08540. **609-924-3150**

THERMOPHYSICAL PROPERTIES RE-SEARCH CENTER. Purdue University, 2595 Yeager Rd, West Lafayette, IN 47906. **317-463-1581**

THRESHOLD-AN INTERNATIONAL CENTER FOR ENVIRONMENTAL RE-NEWAL. Suite 402, 2030 M St NW, Washington, DC 20036. **202-265-0020.** John P Milton, chairman, (h) **202-333-2488.** Peter H Freeman, president. "Dedicated to the exploration and development of environmental alternatives at local neighborhood, urban, national, and international levels. Research, education, planning, technical assistance, direct consulting, and demonstration projects"

TRACE LEVEL RESEARCH INSTITUTE. Purdue University, West Lafayette, IN 47907. **317-494-8537**

TRANSPORTATION RESEARCH CENTER. Engineering Experiment Station, Ohio State University, 2070 Neil Ave, Columbus, OH 43210. **614-422-2871**

UNISIST WORLD SCIENCE INFORMA-TION SYSTEM. 7, Place de Fontenoy, 75700 Paris, France. Telephone: **566-5757**

UNITED STATES TESTING COMPANY, INC. 1415 Park Ave, Hoboken, NJ 07030. **201-792-2400.** Herbert M Block, president. *Press contact.* Ailan F Maxwell

UNIVERSITY CITY SCIENCE CENTER. 3624 Science Ctr, Philadelphia, PA 19104. **215-387-2255**

UNIVERSITY OF DAYTON RESEARCH INSTITUTE. 300 College Park, Dayton, OH 45409. **513-229-3711**

UNIVERSITY OF NOTRE DAME RADIA-TION LABORATORY. Notre Dame, IN 46556. **219-283-7502.** Robert H Schuler, director

UNIVERSITY SCIENCE CENTER. 5100 Centre Ave, Pittsburgh, PA 15232. **412-687-4700**

WARNER AND SWASEY OBSERVA-TORY. Taylor and Brunswick Rd, East Cleveland, OH 44112. **216-451-5624**

WATER RESOURCES RESEARCH IN-STITUTE. 205 Samford Hall, Auburn University, Auburn, AL 36830. **205-826-5075**

WEST VIRGINIA COAL MINING IN-STITUTE. 213 White Hall, Morgantown, WV 26506. **304-293-3011**

WESTERN RESEARCH APPLICATION CENTER. University of Southern California,

Los Angeles, CA 90007. **213-741-6132.** The repository of NASA's computerized index of nearly one million engineering and scientific documents

WILLOW RUN LABORATORIES. In-stitute of Science and Technology, Univer-sity of Michigan, PO Box 618, Ann Arbor, MI 48107. **313-483-0500**

WORLD DATA CENTER. National Academy of Sciences, 2101 Constitution Ave NW, Washington, DC 20418. **202-389-6478**

YERKES RESEARCH AND DEVELOP-MENT LABORATORY. Station B, River Rd, Tonawanda, Buffalo, NY 14207. **716-876-4420,** Ext 207

SPECIAL INTERESTS

ACADEMY OF COUNTRY MUSIC. Suite 200, 1777 N Vine St, Hollywood, CA 90028. **213-462-2351** (also night line). Cliffie Stone, president, **213-462-6933.** Fran Boyd, execu-tive secretary. An organization that promotes country music and sponsors an annual awards show

ACADEMY OF MOTION PICTURE ARTS AND SCIENCES. 8949 Wilshire Blvd, Beverly Hills, CA 90211. **213-278-8990.** James M Roberts, executive director. Martin M Cooper, public relations counsel, **213-385-5271.** *Margaret Herrick Library reference service.* **213-278-4313** (Mon, Tue, Thurs, and Fri only)
The Academy, a professional honorary organization with 3900 members, describes itself as "the most effective ambassador of the medium" of motion pictures. In addition to sponsoring the Oscar awards, the academy publishes a quarterly *Players Directory* and maintains a library and the National Film Information Service. The Margaret Herrick Library has files of some 40,000 films, and its reference service is available to press and public at no charge. A film library also has a collection of 2000 films for serious re-searchers. The film information service provides by mail, at a nomial charge, film documentation and assistance in locating hard-to-find 16-mm and 35-mm motion picture prints and still photographs.

ACOUSTICAL SOCIETY OF AMERICA. 335 E 45th St, New York, NY 10017. **212-661-9404.** *Press contact.* BH Goodfriend

ACTION FOR CHILD TRANSPORTA-TION SAFETY. 400 Central Park W, 15P, New York, NY 10025. **212-866-8208** or **9527.** Annemarie Shelness, executive director. Gisela Moriarty, president. "The only na-tional, nonprofit citizens group devoted exclusively to the protection of children in motor vehicles"

ACTION NOW. 300 Independence Ave SW Washington, DC 20003. **202-546-5611**

ACTION ON SMOKING AND HEALTH. 2000 H St NW (PO Box 19556), Washington, DC 20006. **202-224-9321**

ACUPUNCTURE AND CHINA HERBS INFORMATION CENTER. 36 Broadway E, New York, NY 10002. **212-966-4333**

ACUPUNCTURE MEDICAL CENTER. 426 E 89th St, New York, NY 10021. **212-534-6800**

ACUPUNCTURE SERVICE CENTER. 1011 N Broadway, Los Angeles, CA 90012. **213-222-5090**

AEROSPACE INDUSTRIES ASSOCIA-TION. 1725 De Sales St NW, Washington,

DC 20036. **202-347-2315.** Karl G Harr, Jr, president. Julian Levine, vice-president, public affairs
This is the national trade association repre-senting manufacturers of aircraft, missles, and spacecraft. It provides technical services to members, lobbies for the trade, and acts as industry spokesman, as well as issuing an annual directory.

AFRICAN-AMERICAN INSTITUTE. 833 United Nations Plz, New York, NY 10017. **212-949-5666**

AIR POLLUTION CONTROL ASSOCIA-TION. 4400 5th Ave, Pittsburgh, PA 15213. **412-621-1090.** Mailing address: PO Box 2861, Pittsburgh, PA 15230. Dr. Lewis H Rogers, executive vice-president. Daniel R Stearn, public information officer
APCA describes itself as a group that is "technical in nature...with the capacity to discuss the air pollution problem from a standpoint that is scientific, not political." The membership comprises engineers, scien-tists, state and local air quality officials, and businesses in the pollution control field. The association sees its role as providing a forum for these various constituencies and promulgating information "founded on fact, not conjecture." It carries on an active publications program.

293

AIR TRAFFIC CONTROL ASSOCIA-TION. 525 School St SW-409, Washington, DC 20024. **202-554-9135**

AIR TRANSPORT ASSOCIATION OF AMERICA. 1709 New York Ave, Washington, DC 20006. **202-872-4000.** Paul R Ignatius, president and chief executive officer, **202-872-4168.** Daniel Z Henkin, vice-president, public relations, **202-872-4172.** Night line: **301-588-2405.** William E Jackman, assistant vice-president, public relations, **202-872-4174** ATA is a trade and service association of scheduled airlines in the US. Member airlines pool their knowledge to promote improvements in handling passenger and cargo traffic, to carry on research, and to influence legislation affecting airlines.

AIRCRAFT OWNERS AND PILOTS ASSOCIATION. Washington, DC 20014. **202-654-0500.** John L Baker, president. Charles Spence, vice-president, public relations. A service organization representing the interests of more than 205,000 pilots and aircraft owners; the influential voice of the small plane owner and pilot

AIRPORT OPERATORS COUNCIL IN-TERNATIONAL. 1700 K Street NW, Washington, DC 20006. **202-296-3270.** J Donald Reilly, executive vice-president. Adele C Schwartz, vice president, public relations. Night line: **301-431-2799.** A non-profit trade association serving the owners and operators of major public airports by promoting policies for financing, constructing, managing, operating, and developing airports

ALCOHOL AND DRUG PROBLEMS ASSOCIATION OF NORTH AMERICA. 1101 15th St NW, Washington, DC 20005. **202-452-0990**

ALCOHOLICS ANONYMOUS, WORLD SERVICES INC. PO Box 459, Grand Central Station, New York, NY 10016. **212-686-1100.** Robert Pearson, general manager. The national service organization for 17,000 loosely confederated local groups that service about one million persons worldwide, using techniques of anonymity, religious faith, and group interaction to help individuals solve their drinking problems

ALL-AMERICAN CONFERENCE. 1028 Connecticut Ave NW, Washington, DC 20036. **202-296-6196**

ALLERGY FOUNDATION OF AMERICA. 801 2nd Ave, New York, NY 10017.

212-867-8875. Harry E Willsey, executive vice-president. One of the major voluntary health agencies; pushes for more qualified allergists and seeks to alert the public to the fact that 35 million Americans are allergic to something

ALTERNATIVE SOURCES OF ENERGY, INC. Route 2, Milaca, MN 56353. **612-983-6892.** Donald L Marier, director and editor. Abby S Marier, promotion manager, program development. A non-profit, tax-exempt organization interested in the dissemination of new ideas dealing with "appropriate technology," alternative energy, and energy conservation

AMERICAN ACADEMY OF ARTS AND SCIENCES. 165 Allandale St, Jamaica Plain Station, Boston, MA 02130. **617-522-2400.** John Voss, executive officer, **617-522-0733.** An honor society that sponsors interdisciplinary projects and research on topics in the public interest, holds seminars and conferences, and awards prizes

AMERICAN ACADEMY OF FACIAL PLASTIC SURGERY INC. 2800 N Lake Shore, Chicago, IL. **312-750-3500**

AMERICAN ACADEMY AND IN-STITUTE OF ARTS AND LETTERS. 633 W 155 Street, New York, NY 10032. **212-286-1480.** Margaret M Mills, executive director. Lydia Kaim, assistant to executive director The "highest honor society in the creative arts," this congressionally chartered organization has only 250 members, elected for distinction in art, literature, and music. The academy gives out awards, including the National Book Awards.

AMERICAN ACADEMY OF PEDIATRICS. 1801 Hinman Ave, Evanston, IL 60204. **312-869-4255.** Robert G Frazier, MD, executive director. Ed Kittrell, chief, department of communications and information. Night line: **312-446-8007.** *Department of Government Liaison.* 1800 N Kent St, Arlington, VA 22209. **703-525-9560.** The medical organization for pediatricians; provides continuing education for doctors and has as its goal "the attainment by all children of the Americas of their full potential for physical, emotional, and social health"

AMERICAN ACCOUNTING ASSOCIA-TION. 653 S Orange Ave, Sarasota, FL 33577. **813-958-2711.** Paul Gerhardt, administrative secretary

This is a professional organization, representing accountants, students, and teachers. Its goals include advancing "a widespread knowledge of accounting among...the public generally." The association publishes a directory.

AMERICAN AGRICULTURE MOVE-MENT. National headquarters: Springfield, CO 81073. **303-523-6223.** The organization that sponsored a farmers' strike in 1978; seeks full parity for farm prices.

AMERICAN ARBITRATION ASSOCIA-TION. 140 W 51st St, New York, NY 10020. **212-977-2000.** Robert Meade, contact
Regional Offices and Directors
Boston. 294 Washington St, Boston, MA 02108. **617-542-1071.** Richard M Reilly
Charlotte. Suite 205, 3235 Eastway Dr (PO Box 12591), Charlotte, NC 28205. **704-568-5420.** John A Ramsey
Chicago. Suite 1025, 180 N LaSalle St, Chicago, IL 60601. **312-346-2282.** Charles H Bridge, Jr
Cincinnati. Suite 2308, Carew Tower, 441 Vine St, Cincinnati, OH 45202. **513-241-8434.** Philip S Thompson
Cleveland. Rm 930, 215 Euclid Ave, Cleveland, OH 44114. **216-241-4741.** Earle C Brown
Dallas. Suite 1115, Praetorian Bldg, 1607 Main St, Dallas, TX 75201. **214-748-4979.** Helmut C Wolff
Detroit. Suite 1234, City National Bank Bldg, 645 Griswold St, Detroit, MI 48226. **313-964-2525.** Harry R Payne II
Hartford. 37 Lewis St, Hartford, CT 06103. **203-278-5000.** J Robert Haskell
Garden City. 585 Stewart Ave, Garden City, NY 11530. **516-222-1660.** Ellen Maltz-Brown
Los Angeles. 2333 Beverly Blvd, Los Angeles, CA 90057. **213-413-1414.** Tom Stevens
Miami. 2451 Brickell Ave, Miami, FL 33129. **305-854-1616** or **1617.** Joseph Fiorillo
Minneapolis. Suite 1001, Foshay Tower, 821 Marquette Ave, Minneapolis, MN 55402. **612-335-6545.** Patricia Levin
New Brunswick. 96 Bayard St, New Brunswick, NJ 08901. **201-247-6080.** Patrick R Westerkamp
Philadelphia. 12th Floor, 1520 Locust St, Philadelphia, PA 19102. **215-732-5260.** Arthur R Mehr
Phoenix. Suite 669, Security Ctr, 222 N Central Ave, Phoenix, AZ 85004. **602-252-7357.** Paul A Newnham
Pittsburgh. 2 Gateway Ctr, Pittsburgh, PA 15222. **412-261-3617.** John F Schano

San Diego. Suite 950, San Diego Trust and Savings Bank Bldg, 530 Broadway, San Diego, CA 92101. **714-239-3051.** John E Scrivner

San Francisco. Suite 800, 690 Market St, San Francisco, CA 94104. **415-981-3901.** William B Allender

Seattle. Rm 330, Central Bldg, 810 3rd Ave, Seattle, WA 98104. **206-622-6435.** Neal M Blacker

Syracuse. 731 James St, Syracuse, NY 13203. **315-472-5483.** Deborah Ann Brown

Washington. Suite 509, 1730 Rhode Island Ave NW, Washington, DC 20036. **202-296-8510.** Garylee Cox

The AAA is a public service, nonprofit association of organizations,—labor unions, civic groups, and so on—that favor the use of voluntary, disinterested arbitration under the auspices of the AAA. The association is often recognized in labor, government, and private contracts as the body designated to establish standards and to provide lists of impartial, trained arbitrators who frequently serve without compensation.

AMERICAN ARCHIVES ASSOCIATION. 449 Washington Bldg, 14th St and New York Ave NW, Washington, DC 20005. **202-737-6090**

THE AMERICAN ASSEMBLY. Columbia University, New York, NY 10027. **212-280-3456.** Clifford C Nelson, president, **212-280-3457.** David H Mortimer, vice-president

"Financed by contributions from individuals, foundations, labor unions, and corporations interested in promoting vigorous and informed consideration of major public questions," the assembly sponsors conferences on major issues and distributes reports. The 1977 conferences included "The Ethics of Corporate Conduct" and "The Future of the Performing Arts." In 1976, conference subjects included nuclear power, manpower goals, and capital needs of the US.

AMERICAN ASSOCIATION OF ACUPUNCTURE PATIENTS. 6th Floor, 384 5th Ave, New York, NY 10017. **212-279-3640**

AMERICAN ASSOCIATION FOR THE ADVANCEMENT OF SCIENCE. Office of Opportunities in Science, 1776 Massachusetts Ave NW, Washington, DC 20036. **202-467-4496.** *See also* **SCIENCE AND TECHNOLOGY**

AMERICAN ASSOCIATION OF ADVERTISING AGENCIES. 1730 M St NW, Washington, DC 20036. **202-331-7345**

AMERICAN ASSOCIATION FOR AFFIRMATIVE ACTION. 210 Administration Bldg, Ball State University, Muncie, IN 47306. **317-285-5162.** *Press contact.* Stephen A Faustina, president, **408-277-2710.** Betty Newcomb, second vice-president, **317-285-5162.** Promotes equal opportunity programs in employment and education

AMERICAN ASSOCIATION OF DENTAL VICTIMS. 3320 E 7th St, Long Beach, CA 90804

AMERICAN ASSOCIATION OF MUSEUMS. Suite 200, 2233 Wisconsin Ave NW, Washington, DC 20007. **202-338-5300**

AMERICAN ASSOCIATION OF POISON CONTROL CENTERS. PO Box C-5371, Seattle, WA 98105. **206-634-5072.** Robert G Scherz, MD, president (311 S L St, Tacoma, WA 98405). **206-272-1281.** W O Robertson, MD, secretary-treasurer, **206-634-5072.** An organization of 350-400 physicians, pharmacists, nurses, and others who are concerned with the management of poison information and poison care centers throughout the US

AMERICAN ASSOCIATION OF POLITICAL CONSULTANTS. 1101 N Calvert St, Baltimore, MD 21202. **301-539-8555.** Phyllis B Brotman, president. Night line: **301-363-0530**

The association provides a vehicle for the exchange of information, ideas, and resources among persons involved in political study and activity. It serves as the US arm of the International Association of Political Consultants.

AMERICAN ASSOCIATION OF PORT AUTHORITIES. 1612 K St NW, Washington, DC 20008. **202-331-1263.** Richard L Schultz, executive vice-president. Donald D Allen, director, public information. Represents port authorities in the Western Hemisphere and serves as an information exchange between officials who run ports

AMERICAN ASSOCIATION OF RETIRED PERSONS (AND NATIONAL RETIRED TEACHERS ASSOCIATION). 1909 K St NW, Washington, DC 20049. **202-872-4700.** Cyril F Brickfield, executive director, **202-872-4880.** Lloyd Wright, director, public relations, **202-872-4780**

Staff Information Specialists and Services

Appropriations, Housing, Mandatory Retirement and Age Discrimination, Administration on Aging, Transportation. John B Martin. **202-872-8432**

Consumer Issues, Age Discrimination and Mandatory Retirement, Problems of Older Women, Regulatory Agencies, Transportation. Faye L Mench. **202-872-4833**

Drugs, Auto Insurance and No-Fault, Probate Reform, Tax Relief. William G Rehrey. **202-872-4932**

General Legislative Policy—Federal. Peter W Hughes. **202-872-4826**

General Legislative Policy—State. Harmon Burns, Jr. **202-872-4830**

Economic and Energy Legislation. Thomas C Borzilleri. **202-872-4718**

Energy Legislation, Health Insurance, Medicare and Medicaid, Pension Reform, Social Security, Tax Relief. James M Hacking. **202-872-4824**

Health Insurance, Medicare and Medicaid, Nursing Homes. Thomas Elwood. **202-872-4828**

Library and Reference Services. Mary Powers. **202-872-4844**

Research Department. Frederick J Ferris. **202-872-4841**

Regional Offices

Boston, MA, **617-426-1185**
New York City, **212-758-1411**
Washington, DC, **202-872-4820**
Atlanta, GA, **404-352-3232**
Des Plaines, IL, **312-298-2852**
Kansas City, MO, **816-842-3959**
Dallas, TX, **214-369-9206**
Salt Lake City, UT, **801-328-0691** or **0692**
Long Beach, CA, **213-432-5781**

This is the major organization representing retired persons. It claims nearly 3000 chapters and 11 million members and is probably also the largest organization of older Americans. The group has a very active public relations office, which issues a useful *Directory of Staff Specialists and Media Services*, as well as a variety of other publications.

AMERICAN ASSOCIATION OF UNIVERSITY PROFESSORS. Suite 500, 1 Dupont Cir, Washington, DC 20036. **202-466-8050.** Peter O Steiner, president. James G Trulove, director, communications

Regional Press Contacts

Northeastern. Martin Lapidus, 155 E 44th St, New York, NY 10017. **212-986-9096**

Western. Richard H Peairs, Suite 1406, 582 Market St, San Francisco, CA 94104. **415-989-5430**

AAUP represents the academic freedom, tenure, legal, and collective bargaining rights of teachers and research scholars in higher education. It has a membership of 75,000.

AMERICAN ASSOCIATION OF UNI-VERSITY WOMEN. 2401 Virginia Ave NW, Washington, DC 20037. **202-785-7707.** Helen B Wolfe, general director, **202-785-7788.** Marjorie Bell Chambers, president. Mary Boyette, staff associate, public information, **202-785-7731.** According to the association:

"We are an organization of 190,000 women college grads whose number one priority is to ratify the Equal Rights Amendment. We also are fighting for equality in education and employment."

AMERICAN ATHEIST CENTER. PO Box 2117, Austin, TX 78768. **512-458-1244.** Madalyn Murray O'Hair, director

AMERICAN AUTOMOBILE ASSOCIA-TION. 8111 Gatehouse Rd, Falls Church, VA 22042. **703-AAA-6000.** JB Creal, president, **703-AAA-6111.** John H Jennrich, public information manager, **703-AAA-6333** The federation of motor clubs is a nonprofit but tax-paying organization whose revenues are used to serve its members—who it says represent 12 percent of the adult population. It provides road and travel services, works on safety programs, and lobbies for the interests of the motoring public.

AMERICAN BANKERS ASSOCIATION. 1120 Connecticut Ave NW, Washington, DC 20036. **202-467-4000.** W Liddon McPeters, president, **202-467-4213.** Richard P Pratt, director, public relations, **202-467-4273.** Night line: **301-654-3034.** Valeen N McNeill, secretary, public relations

This influential association, which represents 93 percent of the banks in the US, has its own staff of 300. Functions include lobbying, research, and, through its American Institute of Banking, providing educational services to bankers.

AMERICAN BAR ASSOCIATION. 1155 E 60th St, Chicago, IL 60687. **312-947-4000.** Bert H Early, Esq, executive director, **312-947-4040.** *Press spokesman.* The current president, whose term runs from August to August

American Bar Association Departments and Offices

Communications and Public Relations. 77 S Wacker Dr, Chicago, IL 60606. **312-621-9230**

Executive Office. 312-947-4027

Finance. 312-947-4133

Fund for Public Education. 312-947-4142

Judicial Service Activities. 312-947-3836

Meetings. 312-947-4090

Operation and Planning. 312-947-3926

Personnel. 312-947-3806

Professional Education. 312-947-3952

Professional Services Activities. 312-947-3848

Public Service Activities. 312-947-3936

Purchasing and Office Service. 312-947-3815

Government Relations Office. 1800 M St, Washington, DC 20036. **202-331-2200**

Although the ABA's membership of 220,000 attorneys represents only about half of the lawyers in the US, the organization performs many semigovernmental functions on behalf of the profession. It accredits law schools, establishes codes of ethics, and plays an important role in the discipline of lawyers and even in the formulation of legislation.

Virtually every state has adopted the ABA's Code of Professional Responsibility, giving the organization's standards the force of law. In addition, 43 states and the federal government have adopted the Code of Judicial Conduct, seven canons governing judicial behavior. The ABA's Center for Professional Discipline maintains a brief file and case index, as well as a computer data bank monitoring disbarments and other disciplinary actions against lawyers, in its role as an information clearinghouse for bar admission and bar disciplinary agencies.

The ABA has a staff of 475 and conducts a variety of publications programs. It is independent of the many local and state bar associations.

Commissions include the Commission on the Mentally Disabled, which is trying to mobilize legal services for mental patients; the Commission on Correctional Facilities and Services, which is "the umbrella group managing the organized bar effort to improve the nation's correctional system"; the Commission on Standards of Judicial Administration, which is trying to recommend a better structuring of the nation's courts; and the Commission on Medical Professional Liability.

One of the ABA's on-going special projects is its "Standards Relating to the Administration of Justice," a 17-volume "ideal" system representing the legal profession's view on how to handle everything from arrests to final appeals. The Criminal Justice Section is working with the 50 states to encourage implementation.

AMERICAN BIKEWAYS FOUNDATION. Suite 119, 1800 Old Meadow Rd, McLean, VA 22101. **703-821-8700.** Roy Morris, president. GR Sykes, director, **703-931-1921.** Encourages the development of bikeways, hostels and inns, and bicycle touring

AMERICAN BOARDS OF CLINICAL HYPNOSIS. c/o Professor M Erik Wright, Department of Psychology, University of Kansas, Lawrence, KS 66054. **913-864-4131.** M Erik Wright, president and coordinator This is a consortium of three other boards: the Board of Medical Hypnosis, the American Board of Psychological Hypnosis, and the American Board of Dental Hypnosis. It gives certifying examinations, establishes a roster of qualified expert hypnotists and tries to foster high levels of competence in the application of hypnosis to medicine.

AMERICAN BUSINESS WOMEN'S ASSOCIATION. 9100 Ward Pkwy, Kansas City, MO 64114. **816-361-6621.** Ruth Bufton, executive director. Sharon K Tiley, public relations coordinator

This organization, founded in 1949 by a man, seeks to promote "the professional, educational, cultural, and social advancement of business women," who number 88,000 in ABWA ranks. The association publishes *Women in Business.*

AMERICAN BUREAU OF SHIPPING. 45 Broad St, New York, NY 10004. **212-785-9800.** Robert T Young, president. William N Johnston, chairman. George Haber, senior writer, **212-785-9755.** A nongovernmental, international ship classification society, whose design, construction, and safety standards for merchant vessels are accepted by as many as 67 nations

AMERICAN CAMPING ASSOCIATION. Bradford Woods, Martinsville, IN 46151. **317-342-8456**

AMERICAN CANCER SOCIETY INC. 777 3rd Ave, New York, NY 10017. **212-371-2900.** Lane W Adams, executive vice-president. Joseph Clark, director of news. Night line: **212-595-4490.** Irving I Rimer, vice-president, public information, **212-371-2900.** (h) **215-945-4262.** *Local press contacts.* The national office can provide the number of the local office or a list of the local offices.

This is probably the nation's largest voluntary national health organization. It supports education and research and provides special services to cancer patients

AMERICAN CHIROPRACTIC ASSOCIA-TION. 2200 Grand Ave, Des Moines, IA 50312. **515-243-1121.** Dr Louis O Gearhart, executive director. *Press contact.* Dr Richard Schafer

AMERICAN CIVIL LIBERTIES UNION.
22 E 40 St, New York, NY 10016.
212-725-1222. Night line: **212-725-0349.**
Aryeh Neier, executive director. Trudi
Schultz, public information director

Regional Offices

Washington. 410 1st St SE, Washington, DC
20003. **202-544-1681**

Southern. 52 Fairlie St NW, Atlanta, GA
30303. **404-523-2721**

Mountain States. 1741 High St, Denver, CO
80218. **303-321-5901**

The ACLU is, in a sense, the nation's biggest
public interest law firm, with over 5000
volunteer lawyers taking cases, through one
of 400 local chapters or 49 state and regional
affiliates, on priorities established by the
275,000 members. It is also the principal
spokesman for the position of absolute civil
liberties

**AMERICAN COLLEGE OF NURSE-
MIDWIVES.** 1000 Vermont Ave NW,
Washington, DC 20005. **202-628-4642**

**AMERICAN COLLEGE OF OBSTETRI-
CIANS AND GYNECOLOGISTS.** Suite
2700, 1 E Wacker Dr, Chicago, IL 60601.
312-222-1600. Warren H Pearse, MD, executive director. Robert R Mander, administrator, communications division. *Branch office.*
400 N Capitol St, Washington, DC 20001.
202-638-4860. A professional association of
physicians and nurses specializing in ob-
stetrics and gynecology; carries on an active
publications program for both professional
and lay people

AMERICAN COLLEGE OF SURGEONS.
55 E Erie, Chicago, IL 60611. **312-644-4050.**
C Rollins Hanlon, MD, FACS, director. Sue
Giffin, media relations director. Night line:
312-871-0565. A scientific and educational
association of 40,000 surgeons organized to
"raise the standards of surgical practice and
improve the care of the surgical patient"

AMERICAN COMMITTEE ON AFRICA.
305 E 46th St, New York, NY 10017.
212-838-5030. George M Houser, executive
director. Paul Irish, associate director

This lobbying and political action group is
devoted to influencing US government and
corporate policies toward African nations,
particularly South Africa. It is associated
with the Africa Fund, an educational and
humanitarian organization

**AMERICAN COMMITTEE ON EAST-
WEST ACCORD** (Formerly American
Commission on US-Soviet Relations). 300
Maryland Ave NE, Washington, DC 20002.

202-546-1700. Carl Marcy and Jeanne Matti-
son, codirectors

AMERICAN CONCRETE INSTITUTE.
PO Box 4754, Redford Station, Detroit,
MI 48219. **313-532-2600**

**THE AMERICAN CONSERVATIVE UN-
ION.** 422 1st St SE, Washington, DC 20003.
202-546-6555. Congressman Philip M Crane,
chairman. Ms Fran Griffin, media director.
Night line: **202-332-4554**

The American Conservative Union, a national organization of some 80,000 political
conservatives, engages in political activity,
lobbying, and legislative research. It also
issues newsletters and annually rates US
congressmen and senators. Its 42 state
affiliates rate state legislators and campaign
for conservative candidates

**AMERICAN CORRECTIONAL ASSOCIA-
TION.** Suite L208, 4321 Hartwick Rd,
College Park, MD 20740. **301-864-1070.**
William D Leeke, president, **803-758-6444.**
Anthony P Travisono, executive director

Formerly known as the American Prison
Association, the ACA has adopted the
euphemism of the times. Its 10,000 professional members are guards, wardens, and
other prison, or "corrections," workers

**AMERICAN COUNCIL OF LIFE IN-
SURANCE.** 1850 K St, Washington, DC
20006. **202-872-8750.** Blake T Newton,
president. *New York office.* 277 Park Ave,
New York, NY 10017. Robert Waldron,
manager, press relations. **212-922-3000**

The council represents the life insurance
business in legislative and regulatory
matters, and before the public. It maintains
statistical and research facilities to record the
performance of the business, and measures
public attitudes about life insurance

AMERICAN DAIRY ASSOCIATION.
6300 N River Rd, Rosemont, IL 60018.
312-696-1860. *Press contact.* John F
Brookman, director, communications

**AMERICAN DEFENSE PREPAREDNESS
ASSOCIATION.** National Headquarters:
Union Trust Bldg, 15th and H Sts, Washing-
ton, DC 20005. **202-347-7250**

AMERICAN DENTAL ASSOCIATION.
211 E Chicago Ave, Chicago, IL 60611.
312-440-2500. Dr C Gordon Watson,
312-440-2567. Mr Lou Joseph, manager,
media relations, **312-440-2806.** (h)
312-296-5192

This is the professional organization for

dentists; it establishes ethics, conducts
research, and polices the profession. Coun-
cils include Dental Education, Health,
Dental Care Programs, Insurance, Judicial
Procedures (discipline of dentists), and
Legislation

**THE AMERICAN DIETETIC ASSOCIA-
TION.** 430 N Michigan, Chicago, IL
60611. **312-822-0330.** Norine D Condon,
RD, assistant executive director, communications, and director, annual meeting. Edith
Wasserman, coordinator, public relations.
A professional organization of hospital,
school, military, institutional, and research
dietiticians and nutritionists seeking "to
improve the nutrition of human beings,
advance the science of dietetics and nutrition, and promote education in these areas "

**AMERICAN ECONOMIC ASSOCIA-
TION.** 1313 21st Ave S, Nashville, TN
37212. **615-322-2595.** C Elton Hinshaw,
secretary. Mary L Winer, administrative
director. Encourages economic research and
publishes economics journals, as well as a
directory of members

**AMERICAN ENTERPRISE INSTITUTE
FOR PUBLIC POLICY RESEARCH.**
1150 17th St NW, Washington, DC 20036.
202-296-5616. William J Baroody, president.
Press contact. Heather M David, Ext 206 or
202-466-8225. Night line: **202-338-3470**

The institute seeks to place scholarly studies
on public issues into the mainstream of
political debate, principally by sponsoring
research and forums, for which it encourages
press coverage. Areas of emphasis include
government regulation, social security and
retirement, health, law, advertising, economics, foreign policy, defense, and energy

**AMERICAN FARM BUREAU FEDERA-
TION.** 225 Toohy Ave, Park Ridge, IL
60068. **312-696-2020.** Allan Grant, president.
J Patrick Batts, director, information.
Washington, DC office. John F Lewis,
director, media relations, **202-638-6315.**
Night line: **815-455-0595** (Batts' home) or
202-638-6315 (John F Lewis)

This federation of the farm bureaus in the
US, 49 on the state and 2818 on the county
level, is the largest and most active farm
organization, with two million members and
a willingness to speak out on issues that
concern farmers. Many of the local organizations also provide technical and other
services to members

THE AMERICAN FEDERATION OF ARTS. 41 E 65th St, New York, NY 10021. **212-988-7700.** Wilder Green, director. Sally J Kuhn, director, public information. A nonprofit, cultural service organization that originates, assembles, and circulates film programs and art exhibitions nationally and internationally

THE AMERICAN FILM INSTITUTE. John F Kennedy Center for the Performing Arts, Washington, DC 20566. **202-833-9300.** Night line: **202-833-9302** or **9305.** George Stevens, Jr, director. Gary H Arlen, public information, (h) **301-229-4388.** *Branch office.* Chris Chesser, AFI Center for Advanced Film Studies, 501 Doheny Rd, Beverly Hills, CA 90210. **213-278-8777.** In charge of film preservation and archives at the Library of Congress; seeks also to preserve and enhance the art of film through educational programs, catalogues, and other activities

AMERICAN FOREIGN SERVICE ASSOCIATION. 2101 E St NW, Washington, DC 20037. **202-338-4045.** Allen B Moreland, executive director

AMERICAN FOREST INSTITUTE. 1619 Massachusetts Ave NW, Washington, DC 20036. **202-667-7807.** George C Cheek, executive vice-president. James W Plumb, vice president, communications. Marvin Katz, director, public information. Ronald Bruner, coordinator, public information (media tours)

Regional Offices and Contacts

Western. John E Benneth, 9711 SW Corbett St, Portland, OR 97219. **503-246-0900.** Harvey H Sachs, Suite 601, 6255 Sunset Blvd, Hollywood, CA 90028. **213-462-7278**

North Central. Gilbert W Zieman, Suite 104, 500 W Central Rd, Mount Prospect, IL 60056. **312-398-6607**

New England. Lester A De Coster, 96 Harlow St, Bangor, ME 04401. **207-947-3544**

Mid-Atlantic. Edward J Stana, 35 Pinkney St, Annapolis, MD 21401. **301-263-3528**

Southern Forest Institute. James M Montgomery, executive vice-president, Suite 380, 3395 Northeast Expy, Atlanta, GA 30341. **404-451-7106**

The institute is an education and information organization supported by the forest products industry. Among its primary goals is the development of "public understanding and support for the conservation of the forest resource," that is. "harvesting trees, converting them to useful products, and regenerating new forests for the future."

AMERICAN FOUNDATION FOR THE BLIND. 15 W 16th St, New York, NY 10011. **212-924-0420.** Loyal Eugene Apple, executive director. Patricia S Smith, director, public information. *Washington office.* 1660 L St NW, Washington, DC 20036. **202-467-5996.** *Other regional offices.* Chicago, **312-321-1880**; Atlanta, **404-525-2303**; Denver, **303-861-9355**; San Francisco, **415-392-4845**

The foundation serves as an information clearinghouse on blindness, with an active publications program. It also conducts research, provides referrals, and sells aids and appliances for blind people at cost. Under contract to the Library of Congress, the AFB records and manufactures talking books.

AMERICAN FREEDOM FROM HUNGER FOUNDATION. Suite 719, 1625 I St NW, Washington, DC 20006. **202-254-3487.** Gerald E Connolly, executive director. Promotes public education on domestic and international hunger to build support for a policy to fight hunger

AMERICAN FRIENDS SERVICE COMMITTEE. 1501 Cherry St, Philadelphia, PA 19102. **215-241-7000.** Louis W Schneider, executive secretary, **215-241-7030.** Paul Brink (Swarthmore, PA), information director, **215-241-7060.** Night line: **215-544-2038.** Carries on charitable, social, philanthropic, and relief work in the US and in several other countries on behalf of the Quakers in America

AMERICAN GAS ASSOCIATION. 1515 Wilson Blvd, Arlington, VA 22209. **703-524-2000.** George H Lawrence, president. The national trade association representing the natural gas transmission and distribution companies; it conducts research, planning, public relations, and lobbying

AMERICAN GI FORUM AND LADIES AUXILIARY. 806 15th St NW, Washington, DC 20005. **202-737-0004**

AMERICAN HEALTH CARE ASSOCIATION (formerly American Nursing Home Association). 1200 15th St NW, Washington, DC 20005. **202-833-2050.** Dr Thomas G Bell, executive vice-president. Michael R Codel, director, public affairs

The association represents the nursing home industry; members include 7000 nursing homes and allied long-term care health facilities, with a federation of 50 state associations. It publishes a brochure, "Think-ing about a Nursing Home?" plus fact books, releases, and so on.

AMERICAN HEART ASSOCIATION. 7320 Greenville Ave, Dallas, TX 75231. **214-750-5300.** William W Moore, executive vice-president, **214-750-5335.** Al Salerno, chief, public relations. **214-750-5397.** Night line: **214-361-9678.** A voluntary health agency

AMERICAN HISTORICAL ASSOCIATION. 400 A St SE, Washington, DC 20003. **202-544-2422**

AMERICAN HOSPITAL ASSOCIATION. 840 N Lakeshore Dr, Chicago, IL 60611. **312-645-9413.** J Alexander McMahon, president, **312-645-9561.** *Press contacts.* Dwight Geduldig, public affairs director, or Dennis Cline, national news manager, **312-645-9413.** Night line: **312-234-5731.** Represents the hospital industry before business, labor, the public, and government; also carries out an extensive program of educational seminars.

AMERICAN HOTEL & MOTEL ASSOCIATION. 888 7th Ave, New York, NY 10019. **212-265-4506.** Robert L Richards, executive vice-president. Albert E Kudrle, director, public relations. *Press contact for principal branch offices.* Educational Institute of AH&MA, 1407 S Harrison Rd, East Lansing, MI 48823. **517-353-5500.** A federation of state and regional lodging associations representing the industry as lobbiest, spokesman, and provider of membership services; publishes the *Hotel & Motel Red Book*

AMERICAN IMPORTED AUTOMOBILE DEALERS ASSOCIATION. 1220 19th St NW, Washington, DC 20036. **202-659-2561**

AMERICAN INDIAN CENTER. Public Relations Office, 1714 W Division St, Chicago, IL 60622. **312-276-7700**

AMERICAN INDIAN LAW CENTER. University of New Mexico School of Law, 1117 Stanford NE, Albuquerque, NM 87131. **505-277-4844.** Philip S Deloria, director. Primarily concerned with providing legal education and training for Indian tribes and organizations throughout the country

AMERICAN INDIAN MOVEMENT. PO Box 190, St Paul, MN 55440. **612-488-7267.** The leading militant Indian political organization

AMERICAN INSTITUTE OF AERONAUTICS AND ASTRONAUTICS. 1290 Avenue of the Americas, New York, NY 10019. **212-581-4300.** James J Harford, executive secretary. *West Coast office.* Suite 800, 9841 Airport Blvd, Los Angeles, CA 90045. Gene Pettler. The largest and oldest American technical society devoted to science and engineering in the fields of astronautics and aeronautics

AMERICAN INSTITUTE OF ARCHITECTS. 1735 New York Ave NW, Washington, DC 20006. **202-785-7300.** William L Slayton, Hon. AIA, executive vice-president, **202-785-7310.** Muriel Campaglia, administrator, public relations department, **202-785-7260.** A professional society representing 26,000 registered architects; has an active publications program

AMERICAN INSTITUTE OF CERTIFIED PUBLIC ACCOUNTANTS. 1211 Avenue of the Americas, New York, NY 10036. **212-575-6200**

AMERICAN INSTITUTE OF PLANNERS. 1776 Massachusetts Ave NW, Washington, DC 20036. **202-872-0611**

AMERICAN INSURANCE ASSOCIATION. 85 John St, New York, NY 10038. **212-433-4400.** T Lawrence Jones, president, **212-433-5696.** Ronald A Krauss, vice-president, communications, **212-433-5665.** Night line: **201-334-7847.** *Property claims services office.* 700 New Brunswick Ave, Rahway, NJ 07065. **201-388-5700.** Walter Swift, vice-president

Regional Offices and Contacts

Mid-Atlantic. 1025 Connecticut Ave NW, Washington, DC 20036. **202-293-3010.** Federal: Leslie Cheek III; Regional: Grover E Czech

Midwest. 230 W Monroe St, Chicago, IL 60606. **312-372-8123.** William S Gibson

New England. 1 State St, Boston, MA 02109. **617-227-4172.** Richard J Underwood

Southwest. Suite 817, Carillon Tower W, 13601 Preston Rd, Dallas, TX 75420. **214-233-9733.** Ronald H Cobb

West. 465 California St, San Francisco, CA 94104. **415-362-2170.** W Victor Slevin

This is a trade association for companies writing all forms of property casualty insurance. It carries on lobbying and public relations activities in such areas as auto insurance and workmen's compensation reform, highway safety, and fire prevention programs

AMERICAN-ISRAELI CULTURAL FOUNDATION. 4 E 54th St, New York, NY 10022. **212-751-2700**

AMERICAN JUDICATURE SOCIETY. Suite 1606, 200 W Monroe St, Chicago, IL 60606. **312-236-0634.** George H Williams, executive director. Mayo H Stiegler, director, communications

The society is concerned with promoting needed change for a more effective administration of justice. It publishes a newsletter and *Judicature*, a monthly magazine. Through education and research it works to improve judicial selection and removal, court structure, financing, and management

AMERICAN LAND DEVELOPMENT ASSOCIATION. Suite 604, 1000 16th St, NW, Washington, DC 20036. **202-659-4582.** Gary A Terry, executive vice-president. George G Potts, director, public affairs. Night line: **703-548-7656.** Represents real estate development companies specializing in recreation, resort, and new community projects

AMERICAN LEGION. 700 N Pennsylvania (PO Box 1055), Indianapolis, IN 46206. **317-635-8411.** Night line: **317-635-1109.** William F Hauck, national adjutant (Washington), **202-393-4811.** James C Watkins, director, national public relations (Washington), **202-393-4811.** *Washington office.* 1608 K St NW, Washington, DC 20006. **202-393-4811.** A fraternal, social, and service organization representing veterans who were in the armed services during war eras, including the Vietnam and Korean wars

AMERICAN LIBRARY ASSOCIATION. 50 E Huron, Chicago, IL 60611. **312-944-6780.** Robert Wedgeworth, executive director. Peggy Barber, director, public information office. Night line: **312-944-6796.** *Washington office.* Suite 101, 110 Maryland Ave NE, Washington, DC 20002, Eileen Cooke. **202-547-4440.** Night line: **202-546-1004** The ALA, the oldest and largest library association in the world, represents librarians and libraries before government, establishes standards, and seeks to improve services. It "maintains a vigorous intellectual freedom program which includes the Freedom to Read Foundation, the Intellectual Freedom Committee, and the Office for Intellectual Freedom." The association has an active publications program of its own, concentrating on tools for the profession

AMERICAN LUNG ASSOCIATION. 1740 Broadway, New York, NY 10019. **212-245-8000.** Charles A Kiesewetter, managing director. Helen J Jones, director, public relations. A voluntary health agency

AMERICAN MANAGEMENT ASSOCIATIONS. 135 W 50th St, New York, NY 10020. **212-586-8100.** Night line: **212-586-7143.** James L Hayes, president and chief executive officer, Ext 101. Joseph P Keyes, vice-president, public relations, Ext 310. Robert M Newton, director, public relations, Ext 309. Al Ilch, manager, program/product publicity. Linda Segal, manager, publishing/product publicity. According to the association:

"American Management Associations is a not-for-profit, educational membership organization devoted to the advancement of the principles, policies, practices, and purposes of modern management. It provides programs, products, and services to the managerial process."

AMERICAN MEAT INSTITUTE. 1600 Wilson Blvd, Arlington, VA 22209. **703-841-1030.** Mailing address: PO Box 3556, Washington, DC 20007. Richard Lyng, president. Judith Winslow, assistant public relations director, (h) **703-525-7260** (also night line). The national trade association of the meat packing and processing industry

AMERICAN MEDICAL ASSOCIATION. 535 N Dearborn St, Chicago, IL 60610. **312-751-6600.** Frank Campion, public relations director

The AMA is, in effect, a semigovernmental organization, whose Principles of Medical Ethics are the standards governing the conduct of physicians. The AMA's Judicial Council, which interprets these guidelines, is often referred to as Medicine's Supreme Court. The AMA also participates in the accreditation of hospitals, medical schools, and schools that train allied health personnel. The group documents the continuing education of doctors, which is an integral part of membership in a local professional society, as well as recertification and licensure.

The AMA also represents and lobbies for the medical profession, publishes journals, and otherwise disseminates scientific information. It serves as a clearinghouse of information on quackery and fraudulent remedies, providing such information to the profession, government, and the public

AMERICAN MEDICAL RECORD ASSOCIATION. 875 N Michigan, Chicago, IL 60611. **312-787-2672**

AMERICAN MENSA LIMITED. 1701 W 3rd St, Brooklyn, NY 11223. **212-376-1925.** Margot Seitelman, executive director. *Public relations agency.* Alice Fixx, 1270 Avenue of the Americas, New York, NY 10020, **212-265-1041.** An association whose qualification for membership is a score on an intelligence test higher than that of 98 percent of the general population

AMERICAN MINING CONGRESS. 1100 Ring Bldg, Washington, DC 20036. **202-331-8900.** J Allen Overton, Jr, president. Jim Murphy, director, communications activities. Night line: **202-331-8078**

This is a trade association whose 550 member companies represent the mining of most of the country's metals, coal, and industrial and agricultural minerals, as well as related industries and financial institutions. It serves as a clearinghouse of information for the industry, provides technical services to members, and carries out lobbying

AMERICAN MUSEUM OF NATURAL HISTORY. 79th St and Central Park W, New York, NY 10024. **212-873-1300.** Robert G Goelet, president. Thomas D Nicholson, director. Ann Metcalfe, manager, office of public affairs. Conducts basic research in systematic zoology, anthropology, and animal behavior, publishes scientific and popular material, and carries out educational and museum functions

AMERICAN NATIONAL CATTLEMEN'S ASSOCIATION. *See* National Cattlemen's Association

AMERICAN NATIONAL RED CROSS. 17th and D Sts NW, Washington, DC 20006. **202-737-8300.** George M Elsey, president, **202-857-3454.** Robert Walhay, chief, news, magazines, and photograph sections, **202-857-3512.** For further contact information, *see* **POLICE AND EMERGENCY AGENCIES**

The Red Cross claims over 36 million members. It is a private, voluntary organization but operates under a congressional charter and is recognized by international treaties. Primarily it serves disaster victims of all kinds, but it also sponsors many blood donor and volunteer programs. It functions cooperatively with Red Cross organizations in other countries

AMERICAN NUCLEAR ENERGY COUNCIL. 1750 K St NW, Washington-300, DC 20006. **202-296-4520**

AMERICAN NUCLEAR SOCIETY. 244 E Ogden Ave, Hinsdale, IL 60521. **312-325-1991.** Octave Du Temple, executive director. Vincent Boyer (Philadelphia Electric), **215-841-4501.** Ed Ronne, manager, public information services. **312-325-1991.** (h) **312-832-6378**

The society is a nonprofit scientific, engineering, and public affairs organization with 12,000 individuals and 230 organizations as members, all of them concerned with some aspect of nuclear energy, and most of them generally pro on the issue. The society has an active public relations effort and issues a 48-page booklet known as "The Communicators," classified by geographic region and subject expertise, listing authorities on various aspects of nuclear power. The people in the directory, the society says, "are willing to talk (in person or via telephone) to critics, consumers, commentators, reporters, civic groups," and so on

AMERICAN NURSES' ASSOCIATION. 2420 Pershing Rd, Kansas City, MO 64108. **816-474-5720.** Myrtle K Aydelotte, executive director. William Kuehn, director, communications. The national professional association of registered nurses

AMERICAN NURSING HOME ASSOCIATION. Name changed to American Health Care Association

AMERICAN OPTOMETRIC ASSOCIATION. 7000 Chippewa St, St Louis, MO 63119. **314-832-5770.** Richard W Averill, executive director. The professional association of optometrists

AMERICAN OSTEOPATHIC ASSOCIATION. 212 E Ohio St, Chicago, IL 60611. **312-944-2713.** Edward P Crowell, DO, executive director. Nancy Bernstein or Robert Klobnak, public relations department, Ext 120 or 119. *Washington office.* 1611 N Kent St, Arlington, VA 22209. **703-527-2412.** John Perrin, director. The professional organization of the nation's 16,000 doctors of osteopathy (DO as opposed to MD)

AMERICAN PAPER INSTITUTE. 260 Madison Ave, New York, NY 10016. **212-889-6200**

AMERICAN PEDIATRIC SOCIETY. 333 Cedar St, New Haven, CT 06510. **203-436-0316**

AMERICAN PERSONNEL AND GUIDANCE ASSOCIATION. 1607 New Hampshire Ave NW, Washington, DC 20009. **202-483-4633**

AMERICAN PETROLEUM INSTITUTE. 2101 L St NW, Washington, DC 20037. **202-457-7000.** Frank N Ikard, president, **202-457-7300.** Charles Di Bona, executive vice-president, **202-457-7310.** Harry H Hardy, director, public relations, **202-457-7020.** Robert O'Rourke, deputy director, **202-457-7022.** Earl A Ross, manager, print media, **202-457-7028.** Night line: **301-384-0769.** *Dallas, TX office.* Roy Carlson, director, department of production, **214-685-6254** or **4429**

The institute is the major organization representing the oil industry, including refiners, producers, and distributors of petroleum and petroleum products. It sets standards, conducts extensive research, publishes manuals, and represents the industry before the public and the government.

AMERICAN PETROLEUM INSTITUTE COMMISSION ON PUBLIC AFFAIRS. 200 E Randolph, Chicago, IL 60601. **312-565-1160**

AMERICAN PHYSIOLOGICAL SOCIETY. 9650 Rockville Pike, Bethesda, MD 20014. **301-530-7164**

AMERICAN PSYCHIATRIC ASSOCIATION. 1700 18th St NW, Washington, DC 20009. **202-232-7878.** Melvin Sabshin, MD, medical director. Robert L Robinson, director, public affairs. Ron McMillen, assistant director, public affairs. Night line: **202-232-7879.** The professional society representing 26,000 psychiatrists; conducts education, lobbies, and publishes journals and a directory

AMERICAN PSYCHOLOGICAL ASSOCIATION. 1200 17th St NW, Washington, DC 20036. **202-833-7600.** Dr Charles A Kiesler, executive officer. Mona Marie Olean, public information officer, **202-833-7883.** Night line: **202-966-1294**

The major psychology organization in the US, the association includes among its 45,000 members a majority of qualified psychologists. It publishes journals and provides public information services

AMERICAN PUBLIC GAS ASSOCIATION. 2600 Virginia Ave NW, Washington, DC 20037. **202-338-0044**

AMERICAN PUBLIC HEALTH ASSOCIATION. 1015 18th St NW, Washington, DC 20036. **202-467-5000.** William McBeath, MD, **202-467-5050.** Kathryn Foxhall, information officer, **202-467-5013**

This is the major organization representing professionals, including doctors, nurses, social workers and administrators, in the public health field. It issues publications, establishes standards, and accredits schools in the public health field

AMERICAN PUBLIC POWER ASSOCIATION. 2600 Virginia Ave NW, Washington, DC 20037. **202-333-9200.** Alex Radin, executive director. The national trade association representing municipally owned electric utility companies, public utility districts, state- and county-owned electric systems, and rural cooperatives; publishes a newsletter and *Public Power,* a bi-monthly magazine

AMERICAN RETAIL FEDERATION. 1616 H St NW, Washington, DC 20006. **202-783-7971.** *Press contact.* Loyd Hackler, president. A trade association composed of 50 state and 31 national retail associations, as well as major retail corporations; lobbies on behalf of the industry

AMERICAN SECURITY COUNCIL. Boston, VA 22713. **703-825-1776.** John M Fisher, president

AMERICAN SECURITY COUNCIL EDUCATION FOUNDATION. Boston, VA 22713. **703-825-1776.** John M Fisher, president

AMERICAN SOCIETY OF ALLIED HEALTH PROFESSIONS. 1 Dupont Cir NW, Washington, DC 20036. **202-293-3422**

AMERICAN SOCIETY OF ANESTHESIOLOGISTS. 515 Busse Hwy, Park Ridge, IL 60068. **312-825-5586**

AMERICAN SOCIETY OF ASSOCIATION EXECUTIVES. 1101 16th St NW, Washington, DC 20036. **202-659-3333.** *Press contact.* James P Low, president. John C Vickerman, director of public affairs, special communications.

This is the voluntary-membership society for more than 7000 executives who manage leading business, professional, educational, technical, and industrial associations. It is

claimed that this membership, in turn, represents an underlying constituency estimated at more than 26 million persons and firms belonging to national, regional, state, and local associations

AMERICAN SOCIETY OF CIVIL ENGINEERS. United Engineering Society, 345 E 47th St, New York, NY 10017. **212-752-6800**

AMERICAN SOCIETY OF COMPOSERS, AUTHORS, AND PUBLISHERS (ASCAP). 1 Lincoln Plz, New York, NY 10006. **212-595-3050.** Stanley Adams, president

Regional Contacts

Western. John Mahan, 6430 Sunset Blvd, Hollywood, CA

Southern. Ed Shea, 2 Music Sq W, Nashville, TN

The society is the preeminent professional association representing those involved in writing and publishing musical compositions

AMERICAN SOCIETY OF CONTEMPORARY MEDICINE AND SURGERY. 6 N Michigan, Chicago, IL 60602. **312-236-4673**

AMERICAN SOCIETY OF HEATING, REFRIGERATION, AND AIR CONDITIONING ENGINEERS (ASHRAE). United Engineering Ctr, 345 E 47th St, New York, NY 10017. **212-644-7939**

AMERICAN SOCIETY FOR INFORMATION SCIENCE. 1155 16th St NW-215, Washington, DC 20036. **202-659-3644.** *Press contact.* Robert McAfee, Jr, assistant managing director

AMERICAN SOCIETY OF INVENTORS (ASI). Engineers Club of Philadelphia, 1317 Spruce, Philadelphia, PA 19107. **213-885-2050.** Albert Fonda, president, **215-687-3311.** John Beck, public relations director, **215-822-3648.** William Evans, executive director and general management. **215-885-2050**

This is the professional organization representing engineers, inventors, scientists, and others interested in helping the inventor. It publishes minutes of monthly meetings, as well as periodic articles of interest.

AMERICAN SOCIETY OF MECHANICAL ENGINEERS. United Engineering Ctr, 345 E 47th St, New York, NY 10017. **212-752-6800**

AMERICAN SOCIETY OF PLASTIC AND RECONSTRUCTIVE SURGEONS. Suite 607, 29 E Madison, Chicago, IL 60602. **312-741-0593**

AMERICAN SOCIETY FOR THE PREVENTION OF CRUELTY TO ANIMALS. 441 E 92nd St, New York, NY 10028. **212-876-7700.** Duncan G Wright, executive director. Carolyn Thompson, staff assistant. Promotes the welfare of animals, campaigns for legislation on their behalf, provides care for them, and in some cases enforces laws protecting them

AMERICAN SOCIETY FOR TESTING AND MATERIALS. 1916 Race St, Philadelphia, PA 19103. **215-299-5400.** William T Cavanaugh, managing director, **215-299-5500.** Henry H Hamilton, public relations director, **215-299-5478**

A nonprofit corporation, ASTM is unsubsidized by either industry or government. It provides voluntary consensus standards for materials, products, systems, and services in fields as diverse as steel and surgical implants. Its active publications program includes the 48-volume, annual *Book of ASTM Standards* and a directory of testing laboratories

AMERICAN SOCIETY OF TRAVEL AGENTS, INC. (ASTA). 711 5th Ave, New York, NY 10022. **212-486-0700.** James A Miller, president and chairman of the board (elected). Richard P Ramaglia, executive vice-president. Donald R Reynolds, director, advertising and public relations. Lynne Peck Rutan, manager, consumer press relations. Marc Rouner, manager, trade press relations

The largest professional travel trade association in the world, ASTA represents all elements of the travel industry. It is "dedicated to the promotion and advancement of the travel agency industry and the safeguarding of the traveling public against fraud, misrepresentation, and other unethical practices"

AMERICAN TEMPERANCE SOCIETY. 6840 Eastern Ave NW, Washington, DC 20012. **202-723-0800,** Ext 501. Dr Ernest HJ Steed, executive director

The society encourages "better living without alcohol, tobacco, or drugs," fights for the "human rights of abstainers," and provides preventive programs and educational services. It issues a directory of local chapters

**AMERICAN TEXTILE MANUFAC-
TURERS INSTITUTE, INC.** Wachovia
Ctr, 400 S Tryon St, Charlotte, NC 28285.
704-334-4734. W Ray Shockley (1150 17th
St NW, Washington, DC 20036), executive
vice-president, **202-833-9420.** Robert W
Armstrong, director, public relations,
704-334-4734. Night line:
704-366-8845

Branch Office Press Contacts

Washington. Ronald L Floor. Suite 1101,
1150 17th St NW, Washington, DC 20036.
202-833-9420. Night line: **703-998-5146**

New York. Donald J Rettig. 1133 Avenue
of the Americas, New York, NY 10036.
212-575-1740. Night line: **201-836-3008**

The institute is the national trade association
for the man-made cotton, wool, and silk
segments of the textile industry. Its functions
include lobbying, research, technical
services, and education. It conducts an active
public relations effort, and issues a 12-page
"Directory of Textile News/Information
Contacts."

AMERICAN THEATRE ASSOCIATION.
1029 Vermont Ave NW, Washington, DC
20005. **202-737-5606.** Jack S Morrison,
executive director. Austin H Henry,
administrative director. *Press contact.* Lynne
Winsten, director, publications. The national
professional association representing the
noncommercial theatre field, with a membership including individuals, theatre companies, and theatrical associations

**AMERICAN TRUCKING ASSOCIA-
TIONS, INC.** 1616 P St NW, Washington,
DC 20036. **202-797-5000.** Bennett C
Whitlock, president, **202-797-5216.** Rupert
Welch, manager, news service department,
202-797-5237. Night line: **202-322-3956.** The
national federation of the state associations
of the trucking industry; issues a directory
listing local associations, as well as national
councils and conferences of the ATA

**AMERICAN TUNABOAT ASSOCIA-
TION.** 1 Tuna Ln, San Diego, CA 92101.
202-785-2130

**AMERICAN VETERINARY MEDICAL
ASSOCIATION.** 930 N Meacham Rd,
Schaumburg, IL 60196

**AMERICAN WATER WORKS ASSOCIA-
TION.** 6666 W Quincy Ave, Denver, CO
80235. **303-794-7711.** Eric F Johnson, executive director. Robert M Spangler, director,
public information

The association is a nonprofit scientific and
educational group whose 27,000 members

are mostly the managers, engineers, and
other employees of water utilities. It is
involved primarily with the drinking water
concerns of society, not with wastewater.

AMERICAN YOUTH HOSTELS, INC.
National Headquarters, Delaplane, VA
22025. **703-592-3271.** William Gilmore,
public relations director

This organization "sponsors inexpensive,
educational and recreational outdoor travel
opportunities, primarily by bicycle or foot
along scenic trails and byways." It sponsors
ski, bicycle, and canoe trips, in addition to
foreign travel, and is affiliated with the
International Youth Hostel Federation.

**AMERICANS FOR CONSTITUTIONAL
ACTION.** Suite 1000, 955 L'Enfant Plz N,
SW, Washington, DC 20024. **202-484-5525.**
Charlene Baker Craycraft, chairperson.
Night line: **301-292-2314.** Edward J Carroll,
treasurer

This nationwide political action committee
is "dedicated to electing and re-electing
Senators and Congressmen who vote to
uphold the spirit and principles of the
Constitution." The conservative counterpart
of Americans for Democratic Action, the
ACA issues regular ratings of the voting
records of congressmen.

**AMERICANS FOR DEMOCRATIC
ACTION.** Suite 850, 1411 K St NW, Wash-
ington, DC 20005. **202-638-6447.** Senator
George McGovern (Rm 4241, Dirksen Bldg,
Washington, DC 20510), president,
202-224-2321. Leon Shull, executive director.
Page S Gardner, press manager,
202-638-6447 or **6206.** Night line:
202-244-7817 (Leon Shull) or **202-543-2682**
(Page Gardner)

The ADA carries on "political, legislative,
and educational work with liberal leanings."
The best known organization of liberals,
particularly liberal Democrats, ADA has
many local chapters and is an influential
force on the left-hand wing of the party. One
of its best known projects, the ADA Voting
Record, is a rating of congressmen on the
basis of how they comply with the ADA's
enunciation of liberal principles.

**AMERICANS FOR ENERGY INDEPEND-
ENCE.** 1250 Connecticut Ave NW-502,
Washington, DC 20036. **202-466-2105.** Dr
Elihu Bergman, executive director. Sherry
J Saunders, director, communications

Chapter Contacts

Southern California Chapter. Laurel Parker.
213-572-1212

Colorado Chapter. Kermit Dacus.
303-455-2200

Western Pennsylvania Chapter. James W
Smith. **412-562-2557**

Austin, TX, Chapter. John B Gordon.
512-471-7792

Houston, TX, Chapter. Norman Pilgrim.
713-977-7059

Tennessee Chapter. Thomas E Douglass.
615-483-8611, Ext 37847

This nonprofit, public interest coalition is
made up of business, labor, academic,
consumer, conservation, and community
leaders who share the following conviction:
An ample and reliable supply of energy is
essential for a healthy American society. To
meet this goal AFEI is committed to a policy
of conserving energy and eliminating energy
waste while increasing energy production in
this country to meet our future needs.

**AMERICANS UNITED FOR SEPARA-
TION OF CHURCH AND STATE.** 8120
Fenton, Silver Spring, MD 20910.
301-589-3107

**AMNESTY ACTION/INFORMATION
CENTER.** 5899 W Pico Blvd, Los Angeles,
CA 90019. **213-937-0284.** Mary Clarke,
coordinator. Provides assistance to Vietnam
War resisters and information about the
need for amnesty

AMNESTY INTERNATIONAL, USA.
Rm 405, 2112 Broadway (PO Box 1020),
New York, NY 10023. **212-787-8906.**
David Hawk, executive director. Larry Cox,
press officer

Regional Offices and Contacts

Washington. Ginger McRae, 6 E St SE,
Washington, DC 20003. **202-544-0200**

San Francisco. Janet Johnston, 3618 Sacramento, San Francisco, CA 94118.
415-536-3733

Los Angeles. Andrea Fishman, Rm 211, 633
Shatto Pl, Los Angeles, CA 90005.
213-388-1237

Boston. Josh Rubenstein, Apt 8, 881
Massachusetts Ave, Cambridge, MA 02139.
617-492-8781

London. International Secretariat, 10
Southampton St, London, WC2E 7HF,
England. Telephone: **01-836-7788**

Amnesty is a worldwide, non-partisan
organization working for the release of
prisoners of conscience (whom it defines as
"nonviolent political prisoners"), the abolition of torture and capital punishment, and
the guarantee of fast and speedy trials for all
prisoners. Its assessments of the status of
these issues in various countries are widely
respected for their fairness.

ANTI-COMMUNIST LEAGUE. Box 365, Park Ridge, IL 60068. NL

ANTIDEFAMATION LEAGUE OF BNAI-BRITH. 315 Lexington Ave, New York, NY 10016. **212-689-7400.** Benjamin R Epstein, national director. Lynne Ianniello, executive manager. David Sureck, director, communications

A national human relations organization founded in 1913 "to end the defamation of Jews and to secure equal treatment for all citizens," the league has 26 field offices and national headquarters active in the areas of civil rights, the improvement of interracial and interreligious relationships, and foreign affairs, particularly those involving Israel, Soviet Jewry, and similar interests. Bnai-Brith is a Jewish fraternal organization.

ANTI-VIVISECTION SOCIETY. 100 E Ohio, Chicago, IL **312-787-4486**

APPALACHIAN MOUNTAIN CLUB. 5 Joy St, Boston, MA 02108. **617-523-0636.** Andrew L Nichols, president, **617-227-5020.** Thomas S Deans, executive director, **617-523-0636.** An educational, conservation, and recreational outdoor organization of approximately 23,000 members, mostly in the Northeast—New England, New York, New Jersey, and Pennsylvania

AQUARIAN RESEARCH FOUNDATION. 5620 Morton St, Philadelphia, PA 19144. **215-849-3237** . Art Rosenblum, director. An organization "into all the things which can contribute to a new age in which humanity will be human"

ARCHAEOLOGICAL INSTITUTE. 260 W Broadway, New York, NY 10013. **212-925-7170**

ART INFORMATION CENTER, INC. 189 Lexington Ave, New York, NY 10016. **212-725-0335.** Betty Chamberlain, director

The center provides free services to artists by appointment to help them find New York City outlets for their work and places to learn special skills and disciplines; to dealers, to help locate new talent; and to the public, to help locate the work of living artists. "Anyone may phone or write the center to find out where a living artist is showing or has shown since 1959"; return postage must accompany written inquiries.

ARTHRITIS FOUNDATION. 221 Park Ave S, New York, NY 10003. **212-677-5790.** Keith G Jones, executive director. Freelon M (Nat) Fowler, public information director

ASIAN-AMERICAN DRUG ABUSE PRO-GRAM. 5318 S Crenshaw Blvd, Los Angeles, CA 213-293-6284. Tommy Chung, executive director. Ron Wakabayasai, administrative assistant. Provides drug abuse treatment and prevention services, with particular interest in serving Asian-American and Pacific Island populations

ASSOCIATED BUILDERS AND CON-TRACTORS, INC. 444 N Capitol St NW, Washington, DC 20001. **202-347-8681.** Lawrence Hogan, executive vice-president. Scott Robertson, director, communications. Night line: **301-248-9443**

This trade association represents builders who favor the nonunion—or, in their terminology, merit—shop. It is an active public relations and lobbying force on the federal level and, through 56 regional or state chapters, on the local level as well.

ASSOCIATED CREDIT BUREAUS, INC. 6767 Southwest Fwy, Houston, TX 77074. **713-774-8701.** John L Spafford, president. D Barry Connelly, vice president, public affairs and public relations. Night line: **713-469-1426.** *Public relations counsel.* Marvin B Kaplan, of Rives, Dyke/Y & R, Inc, PO Box 27359, Houston, TX 77027. **713-783-7640.** Night line: **713-665-2747**

This is a trade association of credit bureaus and collection service offices. It does not own any bureaus or collection agencies. "ACB engages in the usual activities that one associates with trade associations, namely, education, establishing guidelines for ethical conduct, establishing and upgrading professional standards, public affairs, public relations, etc."

ASSOCIATED GENERAL CONTRAC-TORS. 1957 E St NW, Washington, DC 20006. **202-393-2040.** James M Sprouse, executive vice-president. Dick Haas, director, information.

This organization is the leading spokesman of the construction industry, particularly highway, building, heavy industrial, and utilities contractors, with 8300 general contractor members and 114 local chapters throughout the country. It offers to make available information specialists in areas including environment, highways, jobsite crime, labor law, labor relations (open shop and union), land use, mass transit, occupational safety, manpower and training, international contracting, and taxes.

ASSOCIATION ON AMERICAN INDIAN AFFAIRS. 432 Park Ave S, New York, NY

10016. **212-689-8720** . William Byler, executive director. Steven Unger, editor

Founded in 1923, the association is a private, nonprofit, national citizens' organization. It provides technical and legal assistance to American Indian tribes and communities at their request and carries on an active publications program.

ASSOCIATION OF AMERICAN RAILROADS. American Railroads Bldg, 1920 L St NW, Washington, DC 20036. **202-293-4196.** William H Dempsey, president, **202-293-4012.** Lawrence H Kaufman, manager, media relations, **202-293-5016.** Night line: **301-530-5983**

This trade association of the American railroad industry represents all major railroads (those that gross over $10 million yearly) and some short line roads. Its primary functions are exchanging information among members, providing technical services to members, researching and testing, and speaking on behalf of members. It also lobbies and conducts an active publications program, including a directory of all major railroads.

THE ASSOCIATION OF AMERICAN UNIVERSITY PRESSES. Rm 1102, 1 Park Ave, New York, NY 10016. **212-889-6040.** Weldon A Kefauver, president, **614-422-6930.** John B Putnam, executive director. *Press contact.* Weldon A Kefauver, director, Ohio State University Press, 2070 Neil Ave, Columbus, OH 43210. An association of 74 scholarly publishers

ASSOCIATION OF BANK HOLDING COMPANIES. 730 15th St NW, Washington, DC 20005. **202-393-1158.** Donald L Rogers, president

This voluntary trade association consists of companies regulated by the Federal Reserve Board pursuant to the Bank Holding Company Act of 1956. A bank holding company is a corporation that controls one or more banks; collectively, these companies hold more than $1 of every $2 in commercial bank deposits in the US.

ASSOCIATION FOR COMPUTING MACHINERY. 1133 Avenue of the Americas, New York, NY 10036. **212-265-6300.** Sidney Weinstein, executive director. James M Adams, Jr, director, operations. An educational and scientific society for computing professionals in all fields of computer science and its application; publishes journals and directories and provides services to members and the public

ASSOCIATION OF FEDERAL INVESTI-GATORS. 815 15th St NW, Washington, DC 20005. **202-347-5500.** Louis T Williams, executive secretary.

This professional organization of investigators in any of the federal and military agencies seeks benefits for its members and the upgrading of professionalism and standards of conduct. It issues a directory of members.

ASSOCIATION OF FORMER INTELLI-GENCE OFFICERS. Suite 303A, 6723 Whittier Ave, McLean, VA 22101. **703-790-0320.** General Richard G Stilwell, USA retired, president. John J Coakley, executive director, (h) **703-978-8985**

ASSOCIATION FOR FRIENDSHIP AND CULTURAL RELATIONS USA-USSR. Name changed to Society for Cultural Relations USA/USSR

ASSOCIATION OF NATIONAL ADVERTISERS. 1725 K St NW, Washington, DC 20006. **202-785-1525**

ASSOCIATION OF OIL PIPE LINES. 1725 K St NW, Washington, DC 20006. **202-331-8288**

ASSOCIATION OF RESEARCH LIBRARIES. 1527 New Hampshire Ave NW, Washington, DC 20036. **202-232-2466.** John G Lorenz, executive director.

A national professional organization representing the major university, public, private, and governmental research libraries that seeks to "further research by providing scholars and students [with] the research materials needed in their work." It publishes *Academic Library Statistics*, an annual

ASSOCIATION OF RETIRED INTELLI-GENCE OFFICERS. Name changed to Association of Former Intelligence Officers

ASSOCIATION OF STATE LIBRARY AGENCIES. c/o American Library Association, 50 E Huron St, Chicago, IL 60611. **312-944-6780**

ASSOCIATION FOR THE STUDY OF MAN-ENVIRONMENT RELATIONS. PO Box 57, Orangeburg, NY 10962. **914-359-1050** or **212-948-2410.** Aristide H Esser, MD, president, **914-634-0221.** Has as its stated objective "the furtherance of the understanding of the role of the environment in human biological, psychological, and social functioning, as well as the influence of individual and societal forces and institutions on the environment"

ASSOCIATION FOR UNION DEMOC-RACY INC. 215 Park Ave S, New York, NY 10003. **212-533-0880.** H W Benson, executive director. "Aim: To promote principles and practices of internal union democracy in the American labor movement"; publishes *Union Democracy Review*

ASSOCIATION OF THE US ARMY. 1529 18th St NW, Washington, DC 20036. **202-483-1800**

ASSOCIATION FOR VOLUNTARY STERILIZATION, INC. Suite 2300, 708 3rd Ave, New York, NY 10017. **212-986-3880.** Ira Lubell, MD, executive director. Betty Gonzales, RN, director, information and education. Merrie Spaeth, deputy director, national affairs. Night line: **202-227-0451.** Encourages male and female voluntary sterilization for contraception, and seeks to make sterilization widely available; has an active publications program promoting the concept of voluntary sterilization

ASSOCIATION FOR WOMEN IN SCI-ENCE. Suite 1122, 1346 Connecticut Ave NW, Washington, DC 20036. **202-833-1998**

ATLANTIC COUNCIL OF THE US. 1616 H St NW, Washington, DC 20006. **202-347-9353.** Dr Francis O Wilcox, director general

"A bipartisan, nonprofit, voluntary organization of individuals with experience in public and private affairs, academia and the media, government, finance, commerce, [and] labor," the council makes recommendations to elected and appointed officials on intergovernmental relations. "Its aim is to promote better understanding and mutually advantageous ties between Western Europe, North America, and Japan."

ATLANTIC TREATY ASSOCIATION. American Office, 1616 H St NW, Washington, DC 20006. **202-347-0353**

ATOMIC INDUSTRIAL FORUM, INC. 7101 Wisconsin Ave, Washington, DC 20014. **301-654-9260.** Carl Walske, president, Ext 201. Carl Goldstein, assistant vice-president, Ext 234. Night line: **301-983-1097**

Regional Contacts

Washington. Scott Peters, media services manager. **202-833-9234.** (h) **301-983-1074**

New York. Eugene Gantzhorn, media services manager. **212-725-8300.** (h) **212-348-6622.** Myra Shaughnessy, media representative. **212-725-8300.** (h) **212-591-2323**

The forum, a voluntary membership corporation established to serve the nuclear industry as "a medium for open discussion," has a pro-peaceful-nuclear-power emphasis. Its members include utilities, manufacturers, financial institutions, government agencies, universities, and research laboratories. It has active public relations and publications programs, maintains a speakers' bureau, and carries out numerous other media activities.

ATTORNEYS CONGRESSIONAL CAMPAIGN TRUST. 1155 15th St NW, Washington, DC 20005. **202-785-1243**

THE AUTHORS GUILD, INC. 234 W 44th St, New York, NY 10036. **212-398-0838.** Peter Heggie, executive secretary. The national society of professional authors

AUTHORS LEAGUE OF AMERICA. 234 W 44th St, New York, NY 10036. **212-736-4811**

BANK ADMINISTRATION INSTITUTE. 303 S Northwest Hwy, Park Ridge, IL 60068. **312-775-5344**

BANK MARKETING ASSOCIATION. 309 W Washington St, Chicago, IL 60606. **312-782-1442.** Raymond Cheseldine, executive vice-president, Ext 30. William J Murphy, director, communications department, Ext 61. Night line: **312-253-8120.** Susan Feldman, associate director, communications department, **312-782-1442**, Ext 64. A national trade association of banks and bank employees that is "dedicated to delivering innovative services to all segments of the banking industry"

BENEVOLENT AND PROTECTIVE ORDER OF ELKS OF THE USA. 2750 Lakeview Ave, Chicago, IL 60614. **312-477-2750.** Stanley F Kocur, grand secretary. Robert Sconce, public relations and assistant to grand secretary. A patriotic and charitable fraternal organization

BIG BROTHERS OF AMERICA. 220 Suburban Station Bldg, Philadelphia, PA 19103. **215-567-2748.** Lewis P Reade, executive vice-president. Caroline Meline, information services coordinator, (h) **215-438-5854.**

The national voluntary organization provides services to its 360 member agencies throughout the country and also "keeps abreast of current national trends and issues affecting boys and girls from single-parent homes." The principal emphasis is on boys from fatherless homes.

BICYCLE MANUFACTURING ASSOCIATION OF AMERICA. 1101 15th St NW, Washington, DC 20005. **202-452-1166.** James J Hayes, executive director. Philip J Burke, director, information. A domestic trade association of bicycle manufacturers

BIRTHRIGHT. 62 Hunter St, Woodbury, NJ 08096. **609-848-1818.** Denise Cocciolone, national director. *Press contact.* Cora Benson (27 S Lake St, Glassboro, NJ 08028). **609-881-0724.** Emergency number "for interagency use": **609-845-4441**

The group provides counseling and housing for women with problem pregnancies in an effort to persuade them to give birth to the babies. Many of the local organizations maintain hotline-type telephone numbers to counsel pregnant women.

BLACK PANTHER PARTY. 8507 E 14th St, Oakland, CA 94621. **415-638-0195**

BLUE CROSS ASSOCIATION. 840 N Lake Shore Dr, Chicago, IL 60611. **312-329-6000.** Walter J McNerney, president. The national organization representing Blue Cross plans throughout the country; provides services to local plans, as well as educational services, and seeks to promote public acceptance of Blue Cross prepaid medical insurance. *See also* National Association of Blue Shield Plans.

BOY SCOUTS OF AMERICA. North Brunswick, NJ 08902. **201-249-6000.** Harvey C Price, chief scout executive. Russell L Bufkins, director, public relations. Night line: **609-924-6143**

BOYS' CLUBS OF AMERICA. 771 1st Ave, New York, NY 10017. **212-684-4400.** William R Bricker, national director. Joan R Licursi, director, communication services

Regional Offices

Northeast. 771 1st Ave, New York, NY 10017. **212-557-8588**

Southern. 2205 Peachtree Center Office Tower, 230 Peachtree St NW, Atlanta, GA 30303. **404-523-5104**

Midwest. Suite 744, 20 N Wacker Dr, Chicago, IL 60606. **312-332-1252**

West Central. 511 Expressway Towers, 6116 N Central Exwy, Dallas, TX 75206. **214-691-3421**

Pacific. Rm 401, 10850 Riverside Dr, North Hollywood, CA 91602. **213-980-4460**

This national voluntary organization with 1077 affiliates provides recreational, educational, and counseling services to youth, with an emphasis on those from economically deprived neighborhoods.

BRAND NAMES FOUNDATION. 477 Madison Ave, New York, NY 10022. **212-753-4131.** H B Kerr, vice-president, communications

BROADCAST PIONEERS LIBRARY. 1771 N St NW, Washington, DC 20036. **202-223-0088**

THE BROOKINGS INSTITUTION. 1775 Massachusetts Ave NW, Washington, DC 20036. **202-797-6000.** Bruce K MacLaury, president, **202-797-6200.** James D Farrell, information editor, **202-797-6220.** Policy-oriented research and publications in economics, government, foreign relations, and defense

BUSINESS COUNCIL. 888 17th St NW, Washington, DC 20006. **202-298-7650**

BUSINESS-INDUSTRY POLITICAL ACTION COMMITTEE. 1747 Pennsylvania Ave NW, Washington, DC 20006. **202-833-1880.** Joseph J Fanelli, president. Bernadette A Budde, director, political education. An unaffiliated political action committee representing business communities in congressional elections; also engages in political education activities aimed at improving the understanding by business of the electoral process

BUSINESSMEN FOR THE PUBLIC INTEREST INC. 109 N Dearborn, Chicago, IL 60602. **312-641-5570**

CAMP FIRE GIRLS, INC. 4601 Madison Ave, Kansas City, MO 64112. **816-756-1950.** Dr Hester Turner, director. Shirley Montague, public relations director. Night line: **816-333-9742.** A national youth group for girls and boys up to age 21; staffed by volunteers and professionals working in group, day, and resident camping programs

CANDLELIGHTERS. 123 C St SE, Washington, DC 20003. **202-544-1696.** Grace Powers Monaco, national liaison chairperson. An international organization of self-help groups of parents whose children have or have had cancer

CARE. 660 1st Ave, New York, NY 10016. **212-686-3110.** Frank Goffio, executive director. Alexander Klein, director, public information. *Press contact.* E M Ewing, Ext 312 or 315. Night line: **212-924-2163**

Regional Offices

Atlanta, GA **404-237-9501**
Boston, MA **617-266-7565**
Chicago, IL **312-782-5581**
Columbus, OH **614-224-5176**
Coral Gables, FL **305-442-9842**

Dallas, TX **214-748-1313**
Detroit, MI **313-963-4610**
Kansas City, MO **816-931-2626**
Los Angeles, CA **213-385-5408**
Milwaukee, WI **414-271-8438**
New York, NY **212-686-3110**
Philadelphia, PA **215-925-1214**
Pittsburgh, PA **412-471-7685**
San Francisco, CA **415-781-1585**
Seattle, WA **206-682-5500**
Washington, DC (Rm 1014, 1028 Connecticut Ave NW, 20036). **202-296-5696**

Foreign offices. See WORLD.

CARE is an international aid and development agency operating in 37 developing countries in Asia, Africa, Latin America, and the Middle East. It sponsors agricultural expansion, food relief, and various self-help programs. MEDICO, the medical arm of CARE, works to upgrade health care.

CARNEGIE CORPORATION. 437 Madison Ave, New York, NY 10022. **212-371-3200.** Alan Pifer, president. Ms Avery Russell, director, publications. A philanthropic foundation

CARNEGIE ENDOWMENT FOR INTERNATIONAL PEACE. 11 Dupont Cir NW, Washington, DC 20036. **202-797-6400.** *Press contact.* Diane Bandahmane

CATHOLIC RELIEF SERVICES. 1011 1st Ave, New York, NY 10022. **212-838-4700.** Bishop Edwin B Broderick, executive director. James C O'Neill, press officer, Ext 44. Night line: **914-967-2877.** The official overseas relief and development agency of American Catholics, operated under the National Conference of Catholic Bishops

CATHOLIC WAR VETERANS, USA, INC. 2 Massachusetts Ave NW, Washington, DC 20001. **202-737-9600** . Henry W Woyach, national commander. William J Gill, national editor. Francis X McBarron, office administrator. Linda Torreyson, executive secretary. A national organization of persons of the Roman Catholic faith who served in the armed forces during wartime

CCCO/AN AGENCY FOR MILITARY AND DRAFT COUNSELING. 2016 Walnut St, Philadelphia, PA 19103. **215-568-7971.** *Press contact.* Robert A Seeley or any staff member (specify program area). *CCCO-Western Region.* 1251 2nd Ave, San Francisco, CA 94102. **415-566-0500**

Formerly known as the Central Committee for Conscientious Objectors, the organization functions today to counsel persons having problems with the military. It seeks to advise young people about military life and also works on amnesty.

CENTER FOR AUTO SAFETY. 1223 Dupont Circle Bldg, Washington, DC 20036. **202-659-1126.** Clarence M Ditlow III, executive director. *General contact.* Margaret Daigle, office manager. A nonprofit research organization working in the fields of vehicle safety, highway safety, and mobile homes; formerly one of the Ralph Nader groups

CENTER FOR MULTINATIONAL STUDIES. Suite 908, 1625 I St NW, Washington, DC 20006. **202-331-1978.** Ronald L Danielian, director. A research organization supported by several American-based companies interested in international trade and investment; publishes research on the effects of multinational corporations on production, employment, trade, economic growth, and international finance and development

CENTER FOR NATIONAL SECURITY STUDIES. 122 Maryland Ave NE, Washington, DC 20002. **202-544-5380.** Robert Borosage, director. John Marks, director, project on CIA. Morton Halperin, director, Project on National Security and Civil Liberties (listed separately). A nonprofit research organization sponsored by the Fund for Peace; conducts research and publishes information on issues of national security

CENTER FOR NATURAL AREAS. 1525 New Hampshire Ave NW, Washington, DC 20036. **202-265-0066.** John B Noble, Esq, vice-president. William C Reed (PO Box 98, South Gardiner, ME 04359). *Press contact.* **207-582-2706.** A nonprofit environmental research corporation, formerly within the Smithsonian Institution

CENTER FOR NEW SCHOOLS. 59 E Van Buren, Chicago, IL 60605. **312-435-3838**

CENTER FOR SHORT-LIVED PHENOMENA, INC. 129 Mount Auburn St, Cambridge, MA 02138. **617-492-3310.** Richard Golob, director

CSLP is a private, nonprofit, scientific and educational organization, formerly part of the Smithsonian Institution, serving as an international clearinghouse for environmental information on natural and man-induced events. It provides the media with both up-to-date bulletins on major environmental events and in-depth background information that attempts to put these events into meaningful perspective. The center will undertake information searches and related projects for the media under contract. In addition, it provides a "Science Alert" service whereby bulletins of major scientific

events are automatically delivered via Telex and TWX. The center concentrates on "the unexpected, the unusual, the extraordinary natural and man-caused events occurring daily on planet Earth." These include things as diverse as oil spills and rodent infestations, red tides and tidal waves, meteor falls and fireballs

CENTER FOR THE STUDY OF DEMOCRATIC INSTITUTIONS. Box 4068, Santa Barbara, CA 93103. **805-969-3281**

CENTER FOR WAR/PEACE STUDIES. 218 E 18th St, New York, NY 10003. **212-475-0850.** Richard Hudson, executive director

CENTER FOR WOMEN IN MEDICINE. 3300 Henry Ave, Philadelphia, PA 19129. **215-842-7108**

CENTRAL PREMONITIONS REGISTRY. PO Box 482, Times Square Station, New York, NY 10036. N L

CHAMBER OF COMMERCE OF THE US. 1615 H St NW, Washington, DC 20006. **202-659-6000.** Richard Lesher, president, **202-659-6207.** Arch N Booth, executive vice-president. Charles R Armentrout, manager, news department, **202-659-6231.** Night line: **703-533-1592.** Robert Adams, manager, broadcast department, **202-659-6238.** John Kochevar, manager, public affairs department, **202-659-6152**

The US chamber is the national federation of local chambers of commerce and industry and trade associations. More than any other organization, it is the voice of American business. Its 4000 constituent chambers of commerce serve a similar function locally. The chamber has an active publications program, including weekly and biweekly reports on the federal government, and a monthly publication, *Nation's Business*, as well as numerous research reports and brochures on national issues, trends, labor relations, and other topics relating to its goal to strengthen and improve the free enterprise system

CHANGE FOR CHILDREN. c/o Old Wives Tales, 532 Valencia St, San Francisco, CA 94110. **415-626-3311**

CHILD ABUSE PREVENTION EFFORT (CAPE). Box 12662, Philadelphia, PA 19129. **215-831-8877** (also night line). Lee Maggio, president. A nonprofit, volunteer organization to aid troubled parents to cope with problems of child abuse; publishes a

monthly newsletter and conducts anonymous parent workshops and counseling

CHILD WELFARE LEAGUE OF AMERICA, INC. 67 Irving Pl, New York, NY 10003. **212-254-7410.** Joseph H Reid, executive director, Ext 503 or 504. Maxine Phillips, director, public information. Night line: **212-242-2482.** *Washington office.* CWLA Center for Government Affairs, Suite 310, Dupont Circle Bldg, 1346 Connecticut Ave NW, Washington, DC 20036. William L Pierce, director, **202-833-2850**

This federation of groups is concerned with issues involving the care of children, such as adoption, foster parentage, treatment of juvenile offenders, and day care. It conducts research, provides consultation and information, and has an active publications program

CHILDREN'S DEFENSE FUND OF THE WASHINGTON RESEARCH PROJECT, INC. 1520 New Hampshire Ave NW, Washington, DC 20036. **202-483-1470.** Marion Wright Edelman, director. *Branch office.* Rims Barber Children's Defense Fund, PO Box 1684, Jackson, MS 38205. **601-355-7495**

This advocacy group, seeking to help parents and concerned citizens secure support and services for their children, works with policy makers to design and enforce programs aiding children. It is affiliated with the Washington Research Project, Inc. "Through research, public education, litigation, community organizing, and monitoring federal policies and programs, it addresses policies and practices resulting in the neglect or mistreatment of millions of children "

THE CHILDREN'S FOUNDATION. 1028 Connecticut Ave NW, Washington, DC 20036. **202-296-4450.** Barbara Bode, president, (h) **202-462-0792.** *Contacts.* Oleta G Fitzgerald (88 Walton St NW, Atlanta, GA 30303), **404-522-2232,** Carlos R Romero (509 Camino de los Marquez, Santa Fe, NM 87501), **505-983-8710.** A national antihunger advocacy organization monitoring all federal food assistance programs for children and their families

CHILDRENS TELEVISION WORKSHOP. 1 Lincoln Plz, New York, NY 10023. **212-595-3456**

CHINA INSTITUTE IN AMERICA, INC. 125 E 65th St, New York, NY 10021. **212-744-8181.** F Richard Hsu, president. Gloria Seavers, executive assistant to president. Night line: **212-639-4309.** Amy McEwen (gallery programs), assistant director, China House Gallery. **212-744-8181**

China Institute is a national, nonprofit, nonpolitical, nonpartisan organization formed in 1926 to improve understanding between the American and Chinese peoples and to serve the Chinese ethnic minority in the US. Chartered by the Board of Regents of the University of New York and the State of New York, the institute operates the School of Chinese Studies, the China House Gallery, and the Center for Community Study and Service

CHRISTIAN ANTI-COMMUNISM CRUSADE. 124 E 1st St, Long Beach, CA 90801. **213-437-0941.** Dr Fred Schwarz, president. The Reverend James D Colbert, first vice-president and chairman. *Branch office.* Christian Anti-Communism Crusade, 5160 E 65th St, Indianapolis, IN 46220. **317-849-9722**

This educational organization is "devoted to the battle against Communism and [to] the propagation of the Christian faith." It sponsors antisubversive seminars and provides "documented, up-to-date information concerning communist doctrines, programs, and objectives "

CHURCH LEAGUE OF AMERICA. 422 N Prospect St, Wheaton, IL 60187. **312-653-6100.** Major Edgar C Bundy, executive secretary

The tax-exempt league, founded in 1937, bills itself as "the largest private research organization and information center on the operations of the Communist Party and the New Left movement." The league took up where the old House Un-American Activities Committee (later the House Internal Security Committee) left off; it maintains extensive files on individuals and organizations—right and left, it says—and has an extensive publications program, offering monographs with titles such as "Abusing the Girl Scouts" and "Young Women's Christian Association: Tarnished Angel "

CIRCUMNAVIGATORS CLUB. 24 E 39th St, New York, NY 10016. **212-686-1227**

CITIZENS FOR BETTER CARE, INC. 960 E Jefferson, Detroit, MI 48207. **313-568-0513.** Susan Rourke, executive director. Emergency Number: **313-867-3229.** A consumer organization concerned with improving the quality of care in nursing homes, homes for the aged, and other after-care facilities

CITIZENS FOR A BETTER ENVIRON-MENT. Suite 2610, 59 E Van Buren, Chicago, IL 60605. **312-939-1530.** David Dinsmore Comey, executive director,

312-939-1984. Vicki Grayland, newsletter editor, **312-939-1530.** *Milwaukee, WI, branch.* Marty Wojcik or Bill Forcade, **414-271-7475.** *Madison, WI, branch.* Phyllis Walters, **608-281-2804.** A nonprofit environmental organization concerned with air pollution, water pollution, toxic substances, and energy policy

CITIZENS FOR CLEAN AIR, INC. 25 Broad St, New York, NY 10004. **212-943-2400.** Brian T Ketcham, vice-president and chief engineer. Stan Pinkwas, publications director. Night line: **212-260-1399.** A public interest organization providing technical resources on matters relating to air pollution, public transit, transportation planning, and energy and land use

CITIZENS COMMITTEE FOR THE RIGHT TO KEEP AND BEAR ARMS. Suite 151, 1601 114th SE, Bellevue, WA 98004. **206-454-4911.** Alan M Gottlieb, chairman. Tom M Siebel, executive director. *Contact.* John M Snyder, Suite 205 (600 Pennsylvania Ave SE, Washington, DC 20003). **202-543-3363.** A nonprofit political organization supporting the right to keep and bear arms; campaigns against gun control laws

CITIZENS COMMUNICATIONS CENTER. 1914 Sunderland Pl NW, Washington, DC 20036. **202-296-4238.** Nolan A Bowie, executive director. Camdy Miles, librarian, director, information

This public interest law firm represents citizens' groups in regulatory and court proceedings involving various broadcasting, common carrier, and cable television matters. Also, upon request it informs groups and individuals of their rights to participate in these processes. According to the center, it "provides general regulation education to develop consumer sophistication and leverage in media decision-making. As a nonprofit organization, Citizens charges no fee to clients but expects reimbursement for out-of-pocket expenses, ie, travel, postage, telephone, duplication costs "

CITIZENS AGAINST NOISE. PO Box 59170, Chicago, IL 60659. **312-274-0980.** Theodore Berland, president. The major national organization concerned with the issue of noise, at all levels, as an environmental hazard

CLEAN WATER ACTION PROJECT. PO Box 19312, Washington, DC 20036. **202-331-1568.** David Zwick, director. Sophie Ann Aoki, managing director. A national nonprofit citizens' lobby for strong water pollution controls and safe drinking water

regulations; researches public policy and works with citizens on local water problems

CLEARINGHOUSE INTERNATIONAL OF THE WOMEN'S FORUM. 16 N Wabash Ave, Chicago, IL 60602. **312-236-5589**

CLERGY CONSULTATION SERVICE. 3100 W 8th St, Los Angeles, CA 90005. **213-380-9450**

CLERGY & LAITY CONCERNED. 3rd Floor, 198 Broadway, New York, NY 10038. **212-964-6730.** Rick Boardman, director. Becky Cantwell, editor, *CALC Report.* A "religiously based national network of people working together on issues of peace and justice," through social action and education; present areas of concern include international human rights, antimilitarism, politics of food, and reconstruction and reconciliation in Indochina

COAL EXPORTERS ASSOCIATION OF THE UNITED STATES, INC. 1130 17th St NW, Washington, DC 20036. **202-628-4322**

COALITION FOR CHILDREN AND YOUTH. 1910 K St NW, Washington, DC 20006. **202-785-4180**

COALITION FOR A DEMOCRATIC MAJORITY. 1721 De Sales St NW, Washington, DC 20036. Ben J Wattenberg, chairman, **202-296-5616.** Joshua Muravchik, executive director, **202-785-9001.** (h) **301-649-4686.** "A national organization of Democrats seeking to represent, within party councils and to the general public, the views of Democrats who believe in encouraging rapid economic growth, defending human rights around the world, and ensuring a strong national defense"

COALITION AGAINST THE SST. c/o Friends of the Earth, 620 C St SE, Washington, DC 20003. **202-543-4312**

COLLEGE OF AMERICAN PATHOLO-GISTS. 7400 N Skokie Blvd, Skokie, IL 60076. **312-677-3500.** Howard E Cartwright, executive director. Walter J Biel, director, communications. The national professional association of physicians who specialize in pathology (the study of the origin, nature, and course of diseases); provides professional services, inspects laboratories, and fosters education and research

COMMISSION FOR THE ADVANCE-MENT OF PUBLIC INTEREST ORGANI-ZATIONS. Suite 1013, 1875 Connecticut Ave NW, Washington, DC 20009.

202-462-0505. Samuel S Epstein, chairperson. Marlene Halverson, administrative assistant. An organization that seeks ways to enlarge the "constituency and capability of the public interest movement"

COMMISSION ON POLITICAL EDUCATION (American Federation of Teachers). 11 Dupont Cir NW, Washington, DC 20036. **202-797-4400.** *See also* LABOR

COMMISSION ON PROFESSIONAL AND HOSPITAL ACTIVITIES (CPHA). 1968 Green Rd, Ann Arbor, MI 48105. **313-769-6511.** Vergil N Slee, MD, president, Ext 212. Arnold H Spellman, director, project development, Ext 218

This research and education center, sponsored by various medical organizations, is "dedicated to the improvement of hospital and medical care." The heart of its activities, which support a staff of 400, is the Professional Activity Study, an ongoing project that provides computerized data on the discharges of 17,000,000 patients from 2200 hospitals

COMMITTEE ON ATLANTIC STUDIES. 1616 H St NW, Washington, DC 20006. **202-347-9353.** Charles R Foster, chief executive. *Press contact.* Martha Finley. Night line: **202-488-3361.** A forum organization sponsoring a continuing dialogue between American and European academics

COMMITTEE FOR DEFENSE OF SOVIET POLITICAL PRISONERS. 875 West End Ave, New York, NY 10025. **212-850-1315**

COMMITTEE FOR ECONOMIC DEVELOPMENT. 477 Madison Ave, New York, NY 10022. **212-688-2063.** Robert C Holland, president, **202-296-5860.** Claudia Feurey, associate director, information, **212-688-2063.** *Washington, DC office.* 1700 K St NW, 20006. **202-296-5860**

The committee is a privately funded forum organization that "attempts to combine some of the best corporate talent in the United States with leading academic experts and specialists for the purpose of examining important national and international issues." It issues studies and recommendations. Current and recent projects have been concerned with inflation, nuclear energy, productivity in state and local government, unemployment, and energy policy

COMMITTEE FOR FAIR DIVORCE AND ALIMONY LAWS. Name changed to National Committee for Fair Divorce and Alimony Laws

COMMITTEE FOR A FREE CHINA. 1735 De Sales St NW-500, Washington, DC 20036. **202-783-9447**

COMMITTEE FOR FREEDOM OF CHOICE IN CANCER THERAPY. Suite 408, 146 Main St, Los Altos, CA 94022. **415-948-9475.** The major pro-laetrile campaign organization

COMMITTEE FOR NATIONAL HEALTH INSURANCE. 821 15th St NW, Washington, DC 20005. **202-737-1177.** Emergency number: **301-530-1975.** Max W Fine, executive director, **202-737-1907.** A public interest organization providing information on national health insurance and campaigning for it

COMMITTEE ON NOISE AS A PUBLIC HEALTH HAZARD. Box 461 Mayo, University of Minnesota, Minneapolis, MN 55455. **612-373-4565**

COMMITTEE ON POLITICAL EDUCATION (AFL-CIO). 815 16th St NW, Washington, DC 20036. **202-293-5000.** *See also* LABOR

COMMITTEE ON THE PRESENT DANGER. Suite 1108, 1028 Connecticut Ave NW, Washington, DC 20036. **202-296-8654.** Charles Tyroler II, director. *Press contact.* Paul S Green, assistant to director, (h) **301-530-7273.** A nonprofit, nonpartisan, educational organization "devoted to the peace, security, and liberty of the nation," and particularly concerned by what it views as the deteriorating US position in the arms race

COMMITTEE FOR PRISONER HUMANITY AND JUSTICE. 1414 4th St, San Rafeal, CA 94901. **415-454-5700.** The committee stated on October 17, 1977, that all projects had been terminated

COMMITTEE FOR PUBLIC JUSTICE, INC. 10th Floor, 22 E 40th St, New York, NY 10016. **212-686-1245.** Dorothy J Samuels, executive director. Carol R Shaffer, assistant. Night line: **212-674-3803.** A nonprofit civil liberties organization whose primary work is educational and which, through newsletters, books, forums, and conferences, serves the purpose of a "watchdog" committee

COMMITTEE FOR THE SCIENTIFIC INVESTIGATION OF CLAIMS OF THE PARANORMAL. 923 Kensington Ave, Buffalo, NY 14215. **716-837-0306.** Paul Kurtz, chairman. A national committee

promoting critical scientific study of the paranormal; publishes a magazine, *The Zetetic*

COMMITTEE ON UNIFORM CRIME RECORDS. 11 Firstfield Rd, Gaithersburg, MD 20760. **301-948-0922.** *See:* International Association of Chiefs of Police in this chapter

COMMON CAUSE. 2030 M St NW, Washington, DC 20036. **202-833-1200.** David Cohen, president. Eileen Steinhauser, director, public information. A national citizens lobby, with active chapters in every state, that is working to make state and national government "more open, accessible, and accountable to citizens and to eliminate the influence of money on our system"

COMMUNICATIONS SATELLITE. PO Box 115, Clarksburg, MD 20734. **202-428-4531**

COMMUNIST PARTY USA. 7th Floor, 235 W 23rd St, New York, NY 10011. **212-989-4994.** Henry Winston, national chairman. Gus Hall, general secretary. Betty Smith, media representative, Ext 259. "A political party of the working class, dedicated to the interests of all working people and oppressed peoples. Its aim is a socialist society"

COMPUTER AND COMMUNICATIONS INDUSTRY ASSOCIATION. Suite 512, 1500 Wilson Blvd, Arlington, VA 22209. **703-524-1360.** A G W Biddle, president. Stephanie Biddle, communications director. Barbara Grochowski, librarian. A trade association representing manufacturers of computer and communications equipment

CONGRESS OF RACIAL EQUALITY (CORE). 200 W 135th St, New York, NY 10030. **212-281-9650**

CONSERVATION FOUNDATION. 1717 Massachusetts Ave NW, Washington, DC 20036. **202-797-4300.** William K Reilly, president, **202-797-4327.** J Clarence Davies III, executive vice-president, **202-797-4340.** *Press contact.* Jerry Kline, director, communications, **202-797-4355**

This nonprofit research and communications organization, founded in 1948, undertakes nationwide programs to encourage wise management of the earth's resources. It publishes the results of research in the areas of land use and urban growth, coastal resources management, public lands management, energy conservation, water quality, business and the environment, and toxic substances

THE CONSERVATIVE CAUCUS, INC.
National Headquarters: 7777 Leesburg Pike, Falls Church, VA 22043. **703-893-6371.** Howard Phillips, national director, **703-893-2777.** The Honorable Louis W Jenkins, secretary, Citizens Cabinet, **504-389-5657.** A group, chaired by Meldrim Thomson, Jr, the governor of New Hampshire, that campaigns for conservative causes, including right to life (antiabortion), reduced interference by government in personal life, end of forced busing, and establishment of a ceiling on income taxes

CONSTITUTIONAL RIGHTS FOUNDATION. Suite 402, 6310 San Vicente Blvd, Los Angeles, CA 90048. **213-930-1510.** Vivian Monroe, executive director. *Press contact.* Doris Bloch. Todd Clark, education director. A private, nonprofit organization devoted to improving education about law and government; designs programs for use in classrooms to reduce apathy among youth toward government

CONSUMER ACTION FOR IMPROVED FOOD AND DRUGS. 1625 I St NW, Washington, DC 20006. **202-872-8660**

CONSUMER FEDERATION OF AMERICA. Suite 901, 1012 14th St NW, Washington, DC 20012. **202-737-3732.** Kathleen F O'Reilly, executive director. Kathleen Sheekey, director, information. A federation of 225 consumer groups with, it says, an underlying constituency of 30 million consumers; lobbies on behalf of consumer interests

CONSUMERS UNION OF UNITED STATES, INC. 256 Washington St, Mount Vernon, NY 10550. **914-664-6400.** Rhoda H Karpatkin, executive director. Ira J Furman, director, communications, Exts 295 to 300, (h) **201-797-1261**

Regional Offices and Contacts

Washington. 1714 Massachusetts Ave NW, 20036. **202-785-1906.** Mark Silbergeld

West Coast. 1535 Mission St, San Francisco, CA 94103. **415-441-4771.** Harry M Snyder

This independent product-testing and consumer education organization is best known as the publisher of *Consumer Reports*, a 1.8 million circulation magazine with no advertising. The union also functions "to initiate and to cooperate with individual and group efforts to create and maintain decent living standards"

COOPERATIVE LEAGUE OF THE USA. 1828 L St NW, Washington, DC 20036. **202-872-0500**

CORPORATE ACCOUNTABILITY RESEARCH GROUP. 1832 M St NW, Washington, DC 20036. **202-833-3931**

CORPORATE INFORMATION CENTER. *See* Interfaith Center on Corporate Responsibility

CO$T, INC (COMMITTEE OF SINGLE TAXPAYERS). 1628 21st St NW, Washington, DC 20009. **202-387-2678.** Patty Cavin, executive director. Night line: **202-232-5504.** Mae Rapport, executive secretary, **202-387-2678.** *Press contact.* Robert Keith Gray, president and founder, or Patty Cavin This national organization of taxpayers fights tax discrimination against single taxpayers

COUNCIL OF THE AMERICAS. 680 Park Ave, New York, NY 10021. **212-628-3200.** Henry R Geyelon, president. *Washington office.* Suite 680, 1700 Pennsylvania Ave NW, 20006. **202-298-9016.** Otto J Reich, director, Washington operations. A nonprofit business association whose 220 major member companies account for about 90% of US investment in Latin America

COUNCIL OF BETTER BUSINESS BUREAUS, INC. 1150 17th St NW, Washington, DC 20036. **202-467-5200.** William H Tankersley, president, **202-467-5210.** Sydney Eiges, vice-president, public relations, **202-467-5338.** The national federation of local Better Business Bureaus (BBBs), organizations that seek to resolve consumer complaints against businesses through mediation or voluntary means; maintains information on fraudulent operations and issues periodical lists of charitable organizations that meet BBB standards

COUNCIL ON ENERGY INDEPENDENCE. PO Box J, Chicago, IL 60690. Daniel W Kane, president, **312-269-3932.** Night line: **312-248-1965.** A nonprofit Chicago-based organization researching alternative energy sources and their utilization in the US

THE COUNCIL FOR EXCEPTIONAL CHILDREN. 1920 Association Dr, Reston, VA 22091. **703-620-3660.** William C Geer, executive director, Ext 210. Nanda Ward Haynes, director, public relations, Ext 252. *CEC Center on Technical Assistance, Training, and Information on the Exceptional Person.* **800-336-3728** or **703-620-3660.** Don Erikson. This educational resource and information group is composed of some 70,000 teachers, parents, and others concerned with "exceptional children"— a

category that includes all types of handicapped and gifted. The council maintains active publications and public relations programs

COUNCIL FOR FINANCIAL AID TO EDUCATION. 680 5th Ave, New York, NY 10019. **212-541-4050**

COUNCIL ON FOREIGN RELATIONS. 58 E 68th St, New York, NY 10021. **212-734-0400.** Night line: **212-734-2954.** Winston Lord, president. *Press contact.* Kempton Dunn, director, special projects. *Washington office.* **202-797-6460.** A prestigious nonprofit, educational organization that publishes a quarterly journal, *Foreign Affairs*, and other publications, conducts research, and holds symposia on international issues, primarily those involving economics, politics, and military strategy

COUNCIL FOR A LIVABLE WORLD. Suite 500, 100 Maryland Ave, NW, Washington, DC 20002. **202-543-4100.** Stephen M Thomas, national director. A lobbying organization "concentrating its efforts on the US Senate," and claiming to be "instrumental in stalemating biological weapons"

COUNCIL OF STATE CHAMBERS OF COMMERCE. 1028 Connecticut Ave NW, Washington, DC 20036. **202-296-2630**

COUNCIL OF STATE GOVERNMENTS. PO Box 11910, Lexington, KY 40578. *Press contact.* Herbert L Wiltsee, executive director, **606-252-2291.** and Ralph W Derickson. Paul Albright, director, publications, (h) **606-277-9690**

Regional offices and contacts

Eastern. 18th Floor, 1500 Broadway, New York, NY 10036. **212-221-3630.** Alan Sokolow or Mike Irish

Midwestern. 203 N Wabash Ave, Chicago, IL 60601. **312-236-4011.** Jim Bowhay or Virginia Thrall

Southern. 3384 Peachtree Rd NE, Atlanta, GA 30326. **404-266-1271.** Bill Osborne or Ray Dunn

Western. 5th Floor, 165 Post St, San Francisco, CA 94108. **415-986-3760.** Jerry Norris

Washington. Hall of the States, 444 N Capitol St, Washington, DC 20001. **202-624-5450.** Susan Munroe or Ray Marvin

This joint agency of state governments, created, supported and directed by the states, carries on an active publications program, including *The Book of the States*, the major reference almanac on state government, and *State Government News*, a monthly newsletter on state government developments. "The council is an excellent source for information on state government programs, operations, procedures, and developments"

THE COUSTEAU SOCIETY. 777 3rd Ave, New York, NY 10017. **212-826-2940.** Jacques Cousteau, president. An organization recently formed by Cousteau to raise funds to support his oceanographic research and to campaign against pollution of the seas

CUBAN NATIONAL PLANNING COUNCIL. PO Box 650667, Miami, FL 33165. **305-266-3866.** The Reverend Mario Vizcaino, executive director

CUBA RESOURCE CENTER. Box 206, Cathedral Station, New York, NY 10025. **212-222-4566.** Barbara Durr and Elice Higginbotham, co-coordinators. A resource organization doing educational work on the Cuban revolution; sponsors delegations of US church persons for study tours of Cuba and publishes a quarterly magazine

CYSTIC FIBROSIS FOUNDATION. 3379 Peachtree Road NE, Atlanta, GA 30326. **404-262-1100.** Henry Lione, executive director. Ann S Watson, public relations director. R A Burcaw, associate national director. A national voluntary health agency

DATA PROCESSING MANAGEMENT ASSOCIATION. 505 Busse Hwy, Park Ridge, IL 60068. **312-825-8124.** Edward J Palmer, executive director. S P Coha, member and chapter services coordinator. An organization of data processing managers and supervisors that numbers, among its objectives, "increasing...public awareness of the impact of information processing and the computer on society and stressing members' responsibility to employers and society"

DAUGHTERS OF THE AMERICAN REV-OLUTION, NATIONAL SOCIETY. 1776 D Street NW, Washington, DC 20006. **202-628-4980.** Mrs George U Baylies, president general. *Press contact.* Mrs E Neil Patton, chairman, public relations committee. A philanthropic and patriotic society, composed of female lineal descendants of Revolutionary War patriots, that promotes Americanism and is conservative in its oft-voiced positions

DEMOCRATIC FORUM. 1621 Connecticut Ave NW, Washington, DC 20009. **202-332-0603**

DIGNITY. Suite F, 3719 6th Ave, San Diego, CA 92103. **714-295-4424.** Walter Kay, president. Carla Kaesbauer, secretary. A group of Roman Catholic men and women, working within the church for the acceptance of gay people, both laity and clergy

DIRECTORS GUILD OF AMERICA, INC. 7950 Sunset Blvd, Hollywood, CA 90046. **213-656-1220.** Robert Aldrich, president. Joseph C Youngerman, national executive secretary. George Thomas, public relations, **213-395-0428.** *Hollywood office* (same address), Don L Parker, executive secretary. *New York office.* 110 W 57th St, New York, NY 10019. Ernest D Ricca, executive secretary. *Chicago office.* 40 E Oak St, Chicago, IL 60611. E Shields Dierkes, executive secretary

DISABILITY RIGHTS CENTER. 1346 Connecticut Ave NW 1124, Washington, DC 20036. **202-223-3304.** Deborah Kaplan, director

This public interest organization, loosely associated with Ralph Nader, is "committed to protecting and enforcing the legal rights of disabled citizens." It seeks to have federal laws requiring federal affirmative action enforced on behalf of disabled people, and campaigns on other issues affecting the handicapped

DISCOVER AMERICA TRAVEL ORGANIZATION, INC. 1100 Connecticut Ave NW, Washington, DC 20036. **202-293-1433**

DISEASE DETECTION INFORMATION BUREAU. 3553 W Peterson, Chicago, IL 60659. **312-267-7184**

DISTILLED SPIRITS COUNCIL OF THE UNITED STATES (DISCUS). 425 13th St NW, Washington, DC 20004. **202-628-3544.** Malcolm E Harris, president. Paul F Gavaghan, vice-president, research and public information. Duncan H Cameron, assistant director, research and public information. Night line: **703-360-3914.** Represents producers of distilled spirits on matters of common concern, and serves as a source of information on drinking statistics, laws, alcohol abuse problems, social customs, and historical background

DRUG ABUSE COUNCIL. 1828 L St NW, Washington, DC 20036. **202-785-5200.**

Thomas E Bryant, MD, president. Jack Skuce, consultant

The council is a foundation-funded, private organization whose functions are research and public-policy analysis in the drug abuse area. It seeks to present "nonpartisan, objective information and analysis," and to this purpose issues a detailed, 79-page directory of press contacts among state and federal government agencies and private organizations in the subject area. Entitled "Reporter's Guide: Drugs, Drug Abuse Issues, Resources," the directory also contains much useful background information, a drug glossary, and so on

ECOLOGY FORUM. *See* Environment Information Center, Inc

EDISON ELECTRIC INSTITUTE. 90 Park Ave, New York, NY 10003. **212-573-8700.** Night line: **800-223-7560** or **212-573-8833.** (New York State). W Donham Crawford, president. Paul A Wagner III, manager, public relations, **212-573-8825.** *Washington office.* Mike Segel, **202-862-3837.** The principal national trade association of investor-owned electric utilities; serves as national industry spokesman

EDUCATIONAL FILM LIBRARY ASSOCIATION. 43 W 61 St, New York, NY 10023. **212-246-4533.** Nadine Covert, executive director. Judith Trojan, editorial coordinator. Jane Rayleigh, American Film Festival coordinator

The educational Film Library Association serves as a national clearinghouse for information about 16-mm films and other non-print media, including their production, distribution, and use in education, the arts, science, industry, and religion. It sponsors the annual American Film Festival and publishes a quarterly magazine, *Sightlines,* as well as books and filmographies in the field

ELECTRIC POWER RESEARCH IN-STITUTE. 3412 Hillview Ave (PO Box 10412), Palo Alto, CA 94303. **415-493-4800.** Dr Chauncey Starr, president. Robert Sandberg, director, communications. Barry Sulpor, news bureau manager. Ray Schuster, assistant director, communications. *Washington office.* 1750 New York Ave NW, Washington, DC 20006. **202-872-9222.** *Press contacts.* Ben Strange or Bob Loftness. An institute sponsored by the US electric utilities to fund and manage research to improve the production and delivery of electric power

ENVIRONMENTAL ACTION COALITION. Suite 1130, 156 5th Ave, New York, NY 10010. **212-929-8481.** Seymour Josephson, executive director. *Contact.* Barbara Munlin, director, community outreach, **212-595-9354**

The coalition concentrates on environmental problems affecting New York City and other urban areas, with special emphasis on solid waste disposal. Its role is principally informational and educational, working closely with schools, but it also encourages volunteer citizen action and serves as a technical consultant to "concerned community groups and individuals"

ENVIRONMENTAL ACTION, INC. Suite 731, 1346 Conneticut Ave NW, Washington, DC 20036. **202-833-1845.** Peter Harnik, coordinator. *Press contact.* Dennis Bass

This is a major lobbying organization on environmental issues, with major emphasis on water pollution, toxic substances, energy conservation, transportation, solid waste, utility rate reform and deposit legislation. Associated with it is the following organization:

Environmental Action Foundation. **202-659-9682.** Richard Munson, director. *Electric utilities contact.* Claudia Comins. *Solid waste and materials conservation contact.* Kay Pilcher. An organization for public interest research and education

ENVIRONMENTAL DEFENSE FUND. 475 Park Ave S, New York, NY 10016. **212-686-4191.** Arlie Schardt, executive director, **212-593-2185.** Juanita Alvarez, editor, *EDF Letter,* **202-833-1484**

Program Area Chairmen

Energy. Dr Ernst R Habicht, Jr, **212-686-4191**

Eastern water and land resources. James T B Tripp, **212-686-4191**

Western water and land resources. Thomas Graff, **415-548-8906.** Dr Mohamed T El-Ashry, **303-831-7559**

Toxic Chemicals. Dr Robert H Harris or Dr Joseph H Highland, **202-833-1484**

Pesticides. Dr Charles F Wurster (chairman, Scientists' Advisory Committee), State University of New York at Stony Brook. **516-246-4002**

Regional offices. 1525 18th St NW, Washington, DC, **202-833-1484** 475 Park Avenue S, New York, NY 10016, **212-686-4191** 1657 Pennsylvania St, Denver, CO 80203, **303-831-7559** 2728 Durant Ave, Berkeley, CA 94704, **415-548-8906** 701 Canyon Rd, Logan, UT 84321, **801-753-3985**

This organization, which won the lawsuit that banned DDT, is composed of scientists, lawyers, economists, and supporters, working largely through the courts as a sort of law firm whose client is the environment. It also performs educational and research functions

THE ENVIRONMENTAL FUND. 1302 18th St NW, Washington, DC 20036. **202-293-2548.** Justin Blackwelder, president. Night line: **202-337-8989.** *Press contact.* Sharon Lynn. Carries on research in world population

ENVIRONMENT INFORMATION CENTER, INC. 292 Madison Ave, New York, NY 10017. **212-949-9494.** James G Kollegger, president. **212-949-9480.** Karen Ziegler, special projects director, **212-949-9479**

The center describes itself as an independent research and publishing organization specializing in energy and environmental information. "We maintain computerized data bases monitoring documents, laws and regulations, organizations and people, and miscellaneous sources such as conferences, books, and films"

ENVIRONMENTAL LAW INSTITUTE. 1346 Connecticut Ave NW-614, Washington, DC 20036. **202-452-9600**

ENVIRONMENTAL RESEARCH. PO Box 156, Moose, WY 83012. **307-733-3387**

ENVIRONMENTALISTS FOR FULL EMPLOYMENT. Rm 300, 1785 Massachusetts Ave NW, Washington, DC 20036. **202-265-2250.** Richard Grossman, coordinator. An educational organization concerned about the issue of environment vs economy; says it seeks "to counter the mythology that we need to sacrifice the environment in order to create jobs, and vice versa"

EPILEPSY FOUNDATION OF AMERICA. Suite 406, 1828 L St NW, Washington, DC 20036. **202-293-2930.** Jack McAllister, executive director. Peter Van Haverbeke, public information director, (h) **301-434-7686**

Regional Office Contacts

Atlanta. Duane Ostrom. **404-996-6726**

Los Angeles. Charles Stevenson. **213-880-4590**

This is a national voluntary health agency.

ESALEN INSTITUTE. Big Sur, CA 93920. **408-667-2335.** Janet Lederman and Julian Schierman, directors. An educational organization that sponsors seminars and workshops

on many subjects with the common themes of expanding human awareness, exploring consciousness and behavior, and encouraging the development of creative potential

EUTHANASIA EDUCATIONAL COUNCIL, INC. 250 W 57th St, New York, NY 10019. **212-246-6962** (Local). **800-223-7516** (toll-free). Ann-Jane Levinson, executive director. An educational organization concentrating on the issues of death and dying, and advocating the right of the terminally ill to forego life-sustaining measures if they serve only to prolong suffering

THE EXPLORERS CLUB. 46 E 70 St, New York, NY 10021. **212-628-8383.** Marie E Roy, executive secretary. A prestigious professional organization of explorers and scientists

FAIR CAMPAIGN PRACTICES COMMITTEE. 328 Pennsylvania Ave SE, Washington, DC 20036. **202-544-5656**

FAMILY SERVICE ASSOCIATION OF AMERICA. 44 E 23rd St, New York, NY 10010. **212-674-6100.** W Keith Daugherty, general director.

This federation represents some 300 local private agencies that provide counseling and social work services to the family as a unit. It serves as "the national standard-setting and accrediting organization for a network of family-serving agencies." The association provides resource materials on the family, has an active publications program, and maintains "a resource bank of specialized consultants within the FSAA network"

FARM LABOR RESEARCH COMMITTEE. Suite 520, 2000 L St NW, Washington, DC 20036. **202-296-0078.** Betsy Houston, research director. A national committee researching farm labor relations, particularly labor legislation

FARM AND LAND INSTITUTE (of the National Association of Realtors). 430 N Michigan Ave, Chicago, IL 60611. **312-440-8040.** Cy Kuetler, president. *Press spokesman.* John Amos, executive vice-president, **312-362-0856** (also emergency line). A national organization of realtors and associates involved in the sale, management, appraisal, exchange, or development of urban or rural land

THE FASHION GROUP. 117 W 9th, Los Angeles, CA 90015. **213-489-2920**

FEDERAL EXCISE TAX COUNCIL. 1211 Connecticut Ave NW, Washington, DC 20036. **202-628-5923**

FEDERALLY EMPLOYED WOMEN, INC. National Press Bldg 485, Washington, DC 20045. **202-638-4404.** Mae Walterhouse, president. Daisy B Fields, executive director and newsletter editor. A national organization concerned with eliminating sex discrimination in the federal government

FEDERATION OF AMERICAN HOSPITALS. 1101 17th St NW, Washington, DC 20036. **202-833-3070**

THE FOOD AND DRUG LAW INSTITUTE. 818 Connecticut Ave NW, Washington, DC 20006. **202-833-1601.** Gary L Yingling, president. A nonprofit educational association whose activities include conferences on foods, drugs, and related topics; publications on food and drug laws; and sponsorship of food and drug law courses at universities

FOOD MARKETING INSTITUTE. 1750 K St NW, Washington, DC 20006. **202-452-8444.** Robert O Anders, president. Victor R Hirch, director, public information, (h) **301-654-0856** (also night line). Katherine M Boyle, manager, press services, **202-452-8444.** *Branch office.* 303 E Ohio St, Chicago, IL 60611. Leonard Sassenrath, manager broadcast media, **312-467-7150.**

This supermarket industry organization, founded in 1977, is well funded, and represents the largest food store chains, as well as cooperative and voluntary food wholesalers. The Chicago office concentrates on education and research; the Washington office, on lobbying and public affairs

FORD FOUNDATION. 320 E 43rd St, New York, NY 10017. **212-573-4700.** McGeorge Bundy, president. *Press contacts.* Richard Magat, **212-573-4830** Robert Tolles, **212-573-4810**

FORMER MEMBERS OF CONGRESS. 121 2nd St NE, Washington, DC 20002. **202-543-1666.** The Honorable Horace R Kornegay, president, **202-457-4830.** The Honorable Jed Johnson, Jr, executive director, **202-543-1666.** A group that is just what its name says; publishes an annual directory

THE FORTUNE SOCIETY. 29 E 22nd St, New York, NY 10010. **212-677-4600.** David Rothenberg, executive director. A prison reform organization, composed of ex-prisoners working for reform of the criminal justice system, particularly of the prisons; has an active public information program

FOUNDATION FOR RESEARCH ON THE NATURE OF MAN. Box 6847, College Station, Durham, NC 27708. **919-688-8241.** Executive director, J B Rhine. *Press contact.* K Ramakrishna Rao. Parapsychological organization

FRATERNAL ORDER OF POLICE, GRAND LODGE. 3136 W Pasadena Ave, Flint, MI 48504. **313-732-6330.** R Pat Stark, national president, **313-732-6330** or **317-633-7950.** Night line: **317-787-6532**

This influential organization, with 750 lodges and some 80,000 full-time officers on the rolls, is not only fraternal in nature but also campaigns for the social, economic, and professional advancement of police officers. Local lodges, which frequently are not listed in phone books, can be reached through the grand lodge when the need arises

FREE INFORMATION BUREAU. 1795 Lexington Ave, New York, NY 10029. **212-876-3688**

FREEDOM HOUSE. 20 W 40 St, New York, NY 10018. **212-730-7744.** John Richardson, Jr (Washington, DC), president. Leonard R Sussman, executive director, **212-730-7744.** Night line: **212-988-5137**

This educational, public affairs organization espouses the goal of uniting Americans of diverse viewpoints for the maintenance of our society's basic freedoms. "We diffuse appeals of the extremes of right and left, and work toward a broadening American consensus." It also conducts the Comparative Survey of Freedom, assessing the level of political and civil rights in every nation and territory

FREEDOM LEADERSHIP FOUNDATION, INC. Suite 600, 1413 K St NW, Washington, DC 20005. **202-347-8016.** Neil A Salonen, president. Michael C Smith, secretary general. Gerard F Willis, editor, *The Rising Tide.* George Fernsler, research director. William D Gertz, program coordinator. A nationwide, nonprofit, educational organization "working to develop the standards of leadership necessary to advance the cause of freedom in the struggle against Communism"

FREEDOM TO READ FOUNDATION. 50 E Huron St, Chicago, IL 60611. **312-944-6780.** Judith Krug, executive director. An organization sponsored by the American Library Association "to support the right of libraries to include in their collections and make available any work which they may legally acquire"; provides financial and legal assistance to libraries and fights repressive legislation

FREEDOMS FOUNDATION AT VALLEY FORGE. Valley Forge, PA 19481. **215-933-8825.** Night line: **215-933-8827.** Robert W Miller, president. Christina M Dotti, assistant director, public relations. A public affairs and educational organization supporting a belief in God and the Constitution

FRIENDS OF THE EARTH. 620 C St SE, Washington, DC 20003. **202-543-4312.** Also 124 Spear St, San Francisco, CA 94105, **415-495-4770.** David R Brower (California office), president, **415-495-4770.** Jeffrey W Knight (Washington office), legislative director, **202-543-4312.** Night line: **301-229-8165.** A public interest and environmental lobbying organization active in Washington and in state capitals, with 25,000 members and sister organizations in 14 nations; has an active publications program

FRIENDS PEACE COMMITTEE OF THE PHILADELPHIA YEARLY MEETING OF FRIENDS. 1515 Cherry St, Philadelphia, PA 19102. **215-241-7230.** *Press contact.* Bruce Birchard, coordinator, evenings: **609-829-6143.** Marilyn Roper, clark of the committee. A peace education and organizing organization, whose current concerns include conversion of military bases to peacetime uses, abuses of military recruitment, peace in the Middle East, and nonviolent ways of parenting and teaching young children

FUND FOR AN OPEN SOCIETY. 9803 Roosevelt Blvd, Philadelphia, PA 19114. **215-677-7901.** *Press contact.* Morris Milgrave, president, evenings to 10 pm: **215-332-7669.** Gabriele Gutkind, executive assistant. Mike Mayer, Washington representative, **301-585-4396.** A nonprofit mortgage company aiding integration in housing through modest-interest incentive mortgages

THE FUND FOR PEACE. 1995 Broadway, New York, NY 10023. **212-580-8635.** Joel I Brooke, president. James F Tierney, executive director

The Fund for Peace is the administrative headquarters for five research and education projects. One of them, the Institute for the Study of World Politics, is located at the New York address. The following projects operate out of offices located in Washington, DC

The Center for Defense Information. 122 Maryland Ave NE. **202-543-0400.** Rear Admiral Gene R La Rocque, USN (retired), director. Brigadier General B K Gorwitz, USA (retired), deputy director. Provides "independent, objective, and reliable analyses of US defense policies and military spending to journalists, scholars, government officials, and the general public"

The Center For International Policy. 120 Maryland Ave NE. **202-544-4666.** Donald L Ranard, director. William Goodfellow and Susan Weber, associates. Analyzes US foreign policy, with special emphasis on the Third World and human rights in countries receiving US aid

The Center For National Security Studies. 122 Maryland Ave NE. **202-544-5380.** Robert Borosage, director. Studies national security institutions and "alerts the public and the press to the growing use of 'national security' to mask illegal or improper government activities"

"In The Public Interest" Media Service. 110 Maryland Ave NE. **202-544-2262.** Sue Karant, director. Robert Maslow, producer. Provides public affairs commentaries

All Fund for Peace activities have active publications programs, and officials are eager to cooperate with the press

FUTURE FARMERS OF AMERICA. Box 15160, Alexandria, VA 22309. **703-360-3600.** H N Hunsicker, national advisor. A Daniel (Dan) Reuwee, director, information. A national organization for students enrolled in high school vocational agriculture programs; encourages students to develop leadership abilities and provides programs and awards as incentives to careers in agriculture

THE GALLUP POLL (American Institute of Public Opinion). 53 Bank St, Princeton, NJ 08340. **609-924-9600.** Night line: **609-466-1216.** *Press contact.* Dr George Gallup, chairman of the board, or George Gallup Jr, president. The nation's largest public opinion polling and research organization

GAMBLERS ANONYMOUS. PO Box 17173, Los Angeles, CA 90017. **213-386-8789.** James Z, principal official, **213-665-6837.** *Press contact.* Ray, **213-737-3737.** Business office for Gamblers Anonymous, an organization analogous to Alcoholics Anonymous

GENERAL FEDERATION OF WOMEN'S CLUBS. 1734 N St NW, Washington, DC 20036. **202-347-3168.** Mrs Harry Wagner, Jr,

president. *Press contact.* Mildred C Ahlgren. An international federation of women's clubs; the largest volunteer organization of women in the world, claiming 10,000,000 members

GERMAN MARSHALL FUND OF THE UNITED STATES. 11 Dupont Cir NW, Washington, DC 20036. **202-797-6430**

GIRL SCOUTS OF THE USA. 830 3rd Ave, New York, NY 10022. **212-751-6900.** Night line, after 4:30 pm: **212-751-6915.** Frances R Hesselbein, national executive director. Richard G Knox, director, public relations, (h) **212-826-6366**

GIRLS CLUBS OF AMERICA. 133 E 62nd St, New York, NY 10021. **212-832-7756.** Edith Phelps, executive director. Kit Mahon, director, communications. A federation of 250 member clubs providing educational environments for girls; "a priority of the national and local organizations is to assess and speak for girls' needs in today's society"

GLOBAL PERSPECTIVES IN EDUCATION, INC. 218 E 18th St, New York, NY 10003. **212-475-0850.** Larry E Condon, executive vice-president, **212-228-2470.** Andrea B Karls, program associate, **212-228-2470**

This national education organization works "to develop ideas and materials that will assist American schools in producing citizens who are capable of coping with a rapidly changing, interdependent world." It develops instructional materials for grades kindergarten to twelve, and encourages training and support programs for teachers

GOODWILL INDUSTRIES OF AMERICA, INC. 9200 Wisconsin Ave, Washington, DC 20014. **202-530-6500.** Dean Phillips, president and chief executive officer. Matthew Warren, director, public relations, Ext 58. An organization that helps handicapped persons through a variety of programs, principally its employment of such persons at branches throughout the country to recondition donated merchandise for resale

GRAY PANTHERS. 3700 Chestnut St, Philadelphia, PA 19104. **215-382-6644.** Maggie Kuhn, national convener, **215-238-0276.** Edith Giese, office coordinator

Regional Office Contacts

New York. Janet Jamar. **212-866-1854**
Chicago. Alice Adler. **312-251-8951**
California. Billie Heller. **213-271-8087**

GREAT LAKES OWNERS ASSOCIATION. 2000 K St NW, Washington, DC 20006. **202-296-3456.** Shipowners organization

GROCERY MANUFACTURERS OF AMERICA, INC. 1425 K St NW, Washington, DC **202-638-6100.** George W Koch, president. Daniel M Larson, manager, information services

This trade association representing the leading manufacturers of food and nonfood products sold in retail grocery outlets issues a directory with a section on "who to call about what," with detailed calssifications by subject matter listing responsible staff persons in each area. (One of the few conceivable subject areas not mentioned is inflation.)

Here is a selection of the contacts: additives and food safety, R W Harkins; antitrust, S A Brown; consumer complaints, D M Larson; corporate disclosure of confidential information, A Strahota; price controls, A Strahota; legislative and statutory issues, S A Brown (federal), A Strahota and M Milone (state); recalls, R W Harkins and M A Burnette

GROUP AGAINST SMOKERS' POLLUTION. PO Box 632, College Park, MD 20740. **301-474-0967**

JOHN SIMON GUGGENHEIM MEMORIAL FOUNDATION. 90 Park Ave, New York, NY 10016. **212-687-4470**

HAIGHT ASHBURY FREE MEDICAL CLINIC. 1696 Haight, San Francisco, CA 94117. **415-864-6090.** David E Smith, medical director. Rick Seymour, administrator. Diane Blazus, social services coordinator for the medical section

This free clinic specializing in drug detoxification, as well as general medical and women's health concerns, is one of the leaders in dealing with drug problems on a community basis. It sponsors a training and education program and a "rock medicine program," which provides medical services at mass concerts

LOUIS HARRIS & ASSOCIATES, INC./THE HARRIS SURVEY. 630 5th Ave, New York, NY 10020. **212-975-1649.** Sally Reed, director, information services. *West Coast office.* Suite 3381, 707 Wilshire Blvd, Los Angeles, CA 90017. **213-620-1428.** *Contact.* Joseph Farrell, executive vice-president

This is a major opinion research organization, with both private client and public service functions. Says a spokesperson, "we are happy to answer questions and requests for Harris data by mail or phone from the press, business, and the general public. Reasonable quantities of our materials are supplied free of charge to persons making these requests"

HEALTH INSURANCE ASSOCIATION OF AMERICA. 1750 K St NW, Washington, DC 20036. **202-331-1336**

HEALTH INSURANCE INSTITUTE. 277 Park Ave, New York, NY 10017. **212-922-3000**

(PUBLIC CITIZENS') HEALTH RESEARCH GROUP. Suite 708, 2000 P St NW, Washington, DC 20036. **202-872-0320.** Dr Sidney M Wolfe, director. A public interest research organization working on issues of health care delivery, food and drug safety, occupational health, and consumer product safety

HIGH SCHOOL STUDENT INFORMATION CENTER. 1010 Wisconsin Ave NW, Washington, DC 20007. **202-338-6316**

HOMOPHILE EFFORT FOR LEGAL PROTECTION. PO Box 3007, Hollywood, CA 90028. **213-463-3146**

HUMAN RIGHTS FOR WOMEN, INC. 1128 National Press Bldg, Washington, DC 20045. **202-737-1059**

HUNGARIAN FREEDOM FIGHTERS FEDERATION USA. PO Box 214, Union Station, Union City, NJ 07081. **201-567-8156**

IMPROVED BENEVOLENT PROTECTIVE ORDER OF ELKS. 1522 N 16th St, Philadelphia PA 19121. **215-232-0150**

INDEPENDENT BANKERS ASSOCIATION OF AMERICA. Sauk Centre, MN 56378. **612-352-6546.** Howard Bell, executive director. Bill McDonald, associate director. *Washington office.* Suite 203, Alpa Bldg, 1625 Massachusetts Ave NW, 20036. **202-265-1921.** Glenn Swanson, manager. A trade association representing 7350 banks in 41 states east of the Rockies, "the only national spokesman for the community-oriented, locally owned commercial bank (state and national)"; conducts research, education, and lobbying

INDEPENDENT PETROLEUM ASSOCIATION OF AMERICA. 1101 16th St NW, Washington, DC 20036. **202-466-2240.** Lloyd N Unsell, executive

vice-president. David Cullen, director, communications. Night line: **703-860-5615.** Nelson Smith, staff writer, **202-466-8240.** A national nonprofit organization representing 5000 independent producers of domestic crude oil and natural gas, "dedicated to the advancement of an aggressive, competitive domestic petroleum industry"

INDIAN RIGHTS ASSOCIATION. 1505 Race St, Philadelphia, PA 19102. **215-563-8349.** Bette Crouse Mele (988 Kingston Rd, Princeton, NJ), president, **609-924-9223.** *Press contact.* Dr Theodore B Hetzel, 146 Crosslands, Kennet Sq, PA 19348, **215-388-1996.** A public affairs and educational organization that seeks to serve as a liaison between Indians, Indian organizations, and government agencies concerned with Indian affairs

THE INSTITUTE FOR ADVANCED STUDY OF HUMAN SEXUALITY. 1523 Franklin St, San Francisco, CA 94109. **415-928-1133.** Night line: **415-334-2997.** *Press contacts.* Ted McIlvenna, president and Lewis Durham, dean of students

The institute has a graduate school founded in 1976 and qualified under California law to offer programs leading to master's and doctoral degrees in the field of human sexuality. It claims to be the only school of its kind in the world

INSTITUTE FOR DEFENSE ANALYSES. 400 Army-Navy Dr, Arlington, VA 22202. **703-558-1000**

THE INSTITUTE OF ECOLOGY. 608 N Park St, Madison, WI 53706. **608-262-7945**

INSTITUTE FOR THE FUTURE. 2750 Sand Hill Rd, Menlo Park, CA 94025. **415-854-6322.** Roy Amara, president. An independent, nonprofit research organization doing long-range planning in the societal and technological areas

INSTITUTE OF THE IRON WORKING INDUSTRY. 1750 New York Ave NW, Washington, DC 20006. **202-833-3998.** John J McMahon, executive director. A nonprofit corporation, funded jointly by labor and management in the iron industry, "to further the best interests of the industry of fabricating and erecting structural steel on bridges and buildings"

INSTITUTE FOR PARAPSYCHOLOGY. 402 N Buchanan Blvd, Durham, NC 27701. **919-688-8241.** Dr K Ramakrishna K Rao, director. The national "scientific educational

research" organization in the field of parapsychology

INSTITUTE OF POLITICS OF THE JOHN F KENNEDY SCHOOL OF GOVERNMENT AT HARVARD UNIVERSITY. 78 Mount Auburn St, Cambridge, MA 02138. **617-495-5792.** Jonathan Moore, director. Endowed by a grant to Harvard University from the Kennedy Library Corporation, and designed "to promote constructive relationships between the university and the world of public affairs"

INSTITUTE FOR RESPONSIVE EDUCATION. 704 Commonwealth Ave, Boston, MA 02215. **617-355-3309**

INSURANCE CRIME PREVENTION INSTITUTE. 15 Franklin St, Westport, CT 06880. **203-226-6347.** Thomas O'Connor, director, public relations. *New York office.* 84 William St, New York, NY 10038. **212-269-6054**

INSURANCE INFORMATION INSTITUTE (III). 110 William St, New York, NY 10038. **212-233-7650.** Mr J Carroll Bateman, president. Charles C Clarke, executive vice-president. Alfred G Haggerty, vice-president, media relations. Gary Schneider, director, press relations. Samuel Schiff, assistant director, press relations. Edward O'Hare, director, broadcast services. Gary L Pietras, assistant director, broadcast services

Field Offices

Austin. Suite 501, 1011 Congress Ave, Austin, TX 78701. **512-476-7025**

Atlanta. Suite 238, 3070 Presidential Dr, Atlanta, GA 30340. **404-451-8451**

Boston. Suite 305, 27 School St, Boston, MA 02108. **617-227-8877**

Chicago. 175 W Jackson Blvd, Chicago, IL 60604. **312-922-5584**

Dallas. 1777 Fidelity Union Tower, 1507 Pacific, Dallas, TX 75201. **214-741-5195**

San Francisco. 400 Montgomery St, San Francisco, CA 94104. **415-392-3185**

Seattle. 1218 3rd Ave, Seattle WA 98101. **206-624-3330**

Washington. 626 National Press Bldg, 14th and F Sts, Washington, DC 20045. **202-347-3929**

A nonprofit public relations and educational organization serving more than 160 property and casualty insurance companies, "III is a public relations representative for all lines of insurance except life and health." *See also* American Insurance Association

INSURANCE SERVICES OFFICE. 160 Water St, New York, NY 10038. **212-487-5000.** The rating service for the property and casualty insurance industry

INTERFAITH CENTER ON CORPORATE RESPONSIBILITY. (Corporate Information Center). Rm 566, 475 Riverside Drive, New York, NY 10027. **212-870-2293.** Timothy H Smith, director. "Frequently the person answering the phone can provide information or name of contact if the subject for discussion is mentioned."

The center is an ecumenical coalition of 14 Protestant denominations and 150 Roman Catholic orders. "Since all members are shareholders in US corporations, there is an attempt to monitor the activities of those corporations with respect to social responsibility." The center is concerned with the military, ecology, racism, sexism, multinationals, investment in South Africa, and so on

INTERINDUSTRY EMISSION CONTROL PROGRAM. Ford Motor Co, American Rd, Dearborn, MI 48121. **313-322-4888**

INTERNATIONAL AIR TRANSPORT ASSOCIATION (IATA). PO Box 550, International Aviation Sq, 1000 Sherbrooke St W, Montreal, Que, Canada H3A 2R4. **514-844-6311.** Knut Hammarskjold, director general. DB Pengelly, director, information services (Western Hemisphere). Public relations department night line: **514-844-9695.** The world organization of scheduled airlines; Its members carry most of the world's scheduled international and domestic traffic under the flags of over 80 nations

INTERNATIONAL ASSOCIATION OF CHIEFS OF POLICE, INC. 11 Firstfield Rd, Gaithersburg, MD 20760. **301-948-0922.** Glen D King, executive director. Howard C Shook (Middletown Township Police Chief, Levittown, PA), president. The leading association representing and speaking for the law enforcement profession

INTERNATIONAL ASSOCIATION OF CONVENTION AND VISITOR BUREAUS. 702 Bloomington Rd, Champaign, IL 61820. **217-359-8881.** Cindy Clark, office manager

The association publishes an annual directory listing the schedules for forthcoming conventions throughout the country, but it regards the publication as a secret document for distribution only to its members and other convention bureaus. The association also warns that it is "not an office for

information on future convention information. While we have such information, it is not readily available, and persons should not contact us for it." The information is, however, in the directory

INTERNATIONAL ASSOCIATION OF CORONERS, AND MEDICAL EXAMINERS. 2121 Adelbert Rd, Cleveland, OH 44160. **216-721-5610.** S R Gerber, MD, executive secretary-treasurer. A professional organization representing coroners and medical examiners, offices and individuals, in the US and Canada

INTERNATIONAL ASSOCIATION FOR DENTAL RESEARCH. Suite 1636, 211 E Chicago Ave, Chicago, IL 60611. **312-337-1645.** Daniel B Green, DDS, executive director. A professional association of dentists that says its principal objective is "the advancement of dental research and dental health on an international level"

INTERNATIONAL ASSOCIATION OF FISH AND WILDLIFE AGENCIES. 1412 16th St NW, Washington, DC 20036. **202-232-1652**

INTERNATIONAL ASSOCIATION OF LIONS CLUBS. 400 22nd St, Oak Brook, IL 60521. **312-986-1700.** W L Wilson, executive administrator. Frank Brueske, manager, public relations and communications division. William M Collins, manager, public relations department

INTERNATIONAL CENTER FOR RESEARCH ON WOMEN. Suite 403, 2000 P St NW, Washington, DC 20036. **202-466-3544.** *Contact.* Anh Huong Tu

INTERNATIONAL CHILDBIRTH EDUCATION ASSOCIATION, INC. PO Box 20852, Milwaukee, WI 53220. **716-244-7215.** Jamie E Bolane (1 San Gabriel Dr, Rochester, NY 14610), president

This interdisciplinary educational organization represents groups and individuals—parents and professionals—advocating "family-centered maternity care." This is a program that prepares the family for birth, provides for the presence of fathers during birth, and advocates freedom of choice for parents about the type of birth and maternity care

INTERNATIONAL CITY MANAGEMENT ASSOCIATION. 1140 Connecticut Ave NW, Washington, DC 20036. **202-293-2200.** Mark E Keane, executive director. Elizabeth K Kellar, director, communications

The association, the principal organization representing executives in municipal government, including city and county managers, appointed administrators, and other chief executives in local government, provides extensive educational programs, training, research, and data-exchange services and other services for management. It has an active publications program, including national, municipal, and county directories, and also provides member benefits

INTERNATIONAL COMMITTEE AGAINST RACISM. Mailing address: 41 Union Sq W, New York, NY 10003. **212-989-5499.** GPO Box 904, Brooklyn, NY 11202. Finley C Campbell, Tobias L Schwartz, and Catherine Weiser, cochairpersons. Carol Deak, administrative coordinator. A public interest organization opposing racism "in all its economic, social, institutional, and cultural forms"

INTERNATIONAL CONFERENCE OF POLICE ASSOCIATIONS. 1239 Pennsylvania Ave SE, Washington, DC 20003. **202-541-2700.** Edward J Kiernan, president

INTERNATIONAL CONSUMER CREDIT ASSOCIATION. 375 Jackson Ave, St Louis, MO 63130. **314-727-4045.** William Henry Blake, executive vice-president. James A Ambrose, secretary-treasurer. A trade association representing all types of businesses offering consumer credit services; members number 40,000 firms

INTERNATIONAL COUNCIL OF SHOPPING CENTERS. 11th Floor, 665 5th Ave, New York, NY 10022. **212-421-8181**

INTERNATIONAL ECONOMIC POLICY ASSOCIATION. Suite 908, 1625 I St NW, Washington, DC 20006. **202-331-1974.** Timothy W Stanley, president. *Press contact.* Ronald L Danielan, **202-331-1054.**

This tax-exempt research organization offers, to its members, analyses of domestic and foreign government policies affecting international trade and investments. It advocates policies and practices by business concerns that will "keep American trade and investments abroad in a state of good health and repute." The association has an affiliated Center for Multinational Studies

INTERNATIONAL EXECUTIVES ASSOCIATION, INC. Rm 1207, 1 World Trade Ctr, New York, NY 10048. **212-432-1860.** R L Roper, executive director. A membership Association for individuals and companies engaged in manufacturing for export and for organizations serving such companies

INTERNATIONAL FEDERATION OF BUSINESS AND PROFESSIONAL WOMEN'S CLUBS. 2012 Massachusetts Ave NW, Washington, DC 20036. **202-293-1100**

INTERNATIONAL HALFWAY HOUSE ASSOCIATION. Suite 101, 2525 Victory Pkwy, Cincinnati, OH 45206. **513-221-3252.** *Press contact.* E B Henderson III, president, or J Bryan Riley, first vice-president, **617-261-1864.** Norm Chamberlain, immediate past president, **206-722-2436.** Warren Kass, PhD, chairman of Treatment Council and Research Council, **314-652-6004.** An international organization serving as "a unifying force in providing community-based residential treatment alternatives for those with social disabilities," meaning both prisoners and patients

INTERNATIONAL REAL ESTATE FEDERATION (American chapter). 430 N Michigan Ave, Chicago, IL 60611. **312-440-8000.** Executive director, **312-440-8013.** H Jackson Pontius, secretary. Lloyd Kuehn, public relations representative, **312-440-8000.** An international organization of realtors, affiliated with the National Association of Realtors, that "encourages private ownership of real property and understanding of property rights and obligations"

INTERNATIONAL RESCUE COMMITTEE, INC. 386 Park Ave S, New York, NY 10016. **212-679-0010.** Charles Sternberg, executive director, Alton Kastner, deputy director. Provides relief and resettlement assistance for refugees escaping to the free world from political, racial, and religious persecution in totalitarian countries, and aids uprooted war victims

INTERNATIONAL SOCIAL SERVICES OF AMERICA. 345 E 46th St, New York, NY 10017. **212-254-1700**

INTERRACIAL COUNCIL FOR BUSINESS OPPORTUNITY (ICBO). Suite 300, 470 Park Ave S, New York, NY 10016. **212-889-0880.** Malcolm L Corrin, president and chief executive officer.

The council provides management training, consultant aid, and funding assistance to minority members wishing to start or expand a business. It is supported by hundreds of major US businesses and is the private sector's answer to affirmative action. According to the council, "minorities make up 17 percent of the population…minority-owned businesses account for a meager 0.7 percent of the GNP. It is the function of ICBO to help correct this inequity"

INTERSTATE ASSOCIATION OF COMMISSIONS ON THE STATUS OF WOMEN. 1 Dupont Cir 831, Washington, DC 20036. **202-833-4692.** Dr Emily Taylor, president

INTERSTATE NATURAL GAS ASSOCIATION OF AMERICA. 1600 L St NW, Washington, DC 20036. **202-293-5770.** L D Tharp, Jr, news director

INVESTMENT COMPANY INSTITUTE. 1775 K St NW, Washington, DC 20006. **202-293-7700.** *Press contacts.* Reg Green and Harry Guinivan

(AMERICAN) IRON AND STEEL INSTITUTE. 1000 16th St NW, Washington, DC 20036. **202-452-7100.** Night line: **202-452-7164.** Frederick C Langenberg, president, **202-452-7146.** Jeffrey T Wood, director, news and information services, **202-452-7115**

This trade association represents the iron and steel industry in the Western Hemisphere, with activities including public relations, education, research, and technological and statistical services for the industry. It conducts an active publications program, including an annual statistical report

JEWISH DEFENSE LEAGUE. Suite 1003, 76 Madison Ave, New York, NY 10016. **212-686-3041.** *Training headquarters.* 227 W 29th St, New York, NY. 10001 **212-224-8964.** *Press contact.* Bonnie Pechter, national director

JEWISH FAMILY SERVICE OF NEW YORK. 33 W 60 St, New York, NY 10023. **212-586-2900.** Sanford N Sherman, principal official, **212-586-2900.** Esther Davidson, director, community relations. Provides counseling help to families and individuals

JEWISH INFORMATION BUREAU. 250 W 57th St, New York, NY 10019. **212-582-5318**

JEWISH LABOR COMMITTEE. Atran Center for Jewish Culture, 25 E 78th St, New York, NY 10021. **212-535-3700.** Jacob Sheinkman, president. Emanuel Muravchik, executive director. Seeks to combat antisemitism and racial and religious intolerance; cooperates with organized labor and other groups in dealing with human rights issues; sponsors education and cultural programs related to the values and concerns of the Jewish labor movement

JEWISH WAR VETERANS. 1712 New Hampshire Ave NW, Washington, DC 20009. **202-265-6280**

JOBS FOR OLDER WOMEN ACTION PROJECT. 3102 Telegraph Ave, Berkeley, CA 94705. **415-849-0332.** Dorothy Gardner, principal official. A national organization to help older women find suitable employment

THE JOHN BIRCH SOCIETY. 395 Concord Ave, Belmont, MA 02178. **617-489-0600.** Robert Welch, founder. John F McManus, public relations director. *California office.* 2627 Mission St, San Marino, CA 91108. Charles Armour, district governor. A right-wing, anti-Communist public affairs and educational organization

JOINT CENTER FOR POLITICAL SCIENCE. 1426 H St NW, Washington, DC 20005. **202-638-4477.** Eddie N Williams, president. *Press contact.* Oliver W Cromwell. A nonpartisan, nonprofit organization that provides research, training, information, and technical assistance to black and other minority group elected officials

JOINT COMMISSION ON ACCREDITATION OF HOSPITALS. 875 N Michigan Ave, Chicago, IL 60611. **312-642-6061.** Dr John E Affeldt, president. Max Russell, assistant director, public and professional relations, Ext 397. Night line: **312-642-6064.** (h) **312-642-0656**

The organization represents a variety of medical societies. It serves principally to accredit mental and medical hospitals, (mostly those involving MDs, but also some DOs) as well as long-term nursing homes and other facilities. Although participation in its program is voluntary, most legitimate facilities, particularly medical hospitals, seek to obtain and maintain accreditation from the joint commission. The commission serves as a standard setter in the industry, and, through its Quality Resource Center, provides educational programs to persons concerned with the quality of medical care and services

JOINT WASHINGTON OFFICE FOR SOCIAL CONCERN. Rm 106, 100 Maryland Ave NE, Washington, DC 20002. **202-547-0254**

JOSEPH AND ROSE KENNEDY INSTITUTE FOR THE STUDY OF HUMAN REPRODUCTION AND BIOETHICS. Georgetown University, Washington, DC 20057. **202-625-2371**

KNIGHTS OF COLUMBUS. 1 Columbus Plz, New Haven, CT 06507. **203-772-2130.** Virgil C Dechant, supreme knight. Elmer Von Feldt, director, public information. A fraternal organization providing social and other services to its 1.25 million members, who are Catholic men

KU KLUX KLAN. PO Box 248, Lodi, OH 44254. **216-948-2924.** Dale Reusch, imperial wizard. An extremist organization that advocates white supremacy; most chapters are underground. *See also* United Klans

LAW ENFORCEMENT INTELLIGENCE UNITS. PO Box 1859, Sacramento, CA 95809

LAWYERS' COMMITTEE FOR CIVIL RIGHTS UNDER LAW. 733 15th St NW, Washington, DC 20005. **202-628-6700.** Robert A Murphy, director. A public interest organization that provides legal representation to minority members and poor people who are discriminated against in the areas of employment, education, voting rights, revenue sharing, and municipal services

LEADERSHIP CONFERENCE ON CIVIL RIGHTS. 2027 Massachusetts Ave NW, Washington, DC 20036. **202-667-1780**

LEAGUE OF ARAB STATES. 747 3rd Ave, New York, NY 10017. **212-838-8700**

LEAGUE OF FAMILIES. *See* National League of Families.

LEAGUE OF WOMEN VOTERS OF THE US. 1730 M St NW, Washington, DC 20036. **202-296-1770.** Ruth C Clusen, principal official. Elizabeth J Dribben, public relations director (h), **703-525-1516.** Night lines, **202-296-1773** (office). **703-525-1516** (Ms Dribben's home).

A national organization with leagues in each of the 50 states and local organizations in most communities, the league began in the 1920s as a daughter of the womens suffrage movement. Over the years, it came to fill a great need in American society: the compilation of objective information and campaign positions on candidates for elected office, from the level of dog catcher to that of President. In many communities, the league's voter guides are the only source of nonpartisan information on the candidates, particularly those for comparatively minor posts. The league also serves to monitor government and educate the public to good citizenship. It lobbies for good government at all levels in virtually every US congressional district.

In recent years, the league has expanded its efforts to include, in addition to good government and women's issues (The Equal Rights Amendment), a number of issue-oriented projects and lobbying efforts, such as those involving human resources, environmental quality, land use, and international relations.

At all levels, it provides useful services to the press, particularly by keeping it informed about legislation. It has an active publications program

LEUKEMIA SOCIETY OF AMERICA, INC. 211 E 43 St, New York, NY 10017. **212-573-8484.** Meade P Brown, executive director. Florence Phillips, director, publicity. A national voluntary health agency

LIBERTY LOBBY. 300 Independence Ave SE, Washington, DC 20003. **202-546-5611.** Colonel Curtis B Dall, chairman. Robert M Bartell, executive program coordinator

This conservative, public interest lobbying organization says it was formed as a counterweight to minority interest pressure groups, "for the purpose of speaking for the majority." It publishes a tabloid-style newspaper with headlines such as "Harassed Taxpayer Dies," "Quota Hiring Planned for Addicts, Deviates," and "Carter's Cocaine Connection"

LICENSED BEVERAGE INDUSTRY ASSOCIATION. Suite 601, 1025 Vermont Ave NW, Washington, DC 20005. **202-737-9118**

LULAC NATIONAL EDUCATIONAL SERVICE CENTERS, INC. Suite 716, 400 1st St NW, Washington, DC 20001. **202-347-1652.** Narciso Cano, national director. *Press contact.* Jackie Boras, assistant for public affairs and information. An educational counseling outreach program assisting low income and disadvantaged Hispanics in gaining admission to college and finding sources of financial aid

MACHINERY AND ALLIED PRODUCTS INSTITUTE. 1200 18th St NW, Wasington, DC 20036. **202-331-8430.** Charles W Stewart, president

The institute, a trade and research association representing the manufacturers of machinery and other capital goods, serves as national spokesman for the industry. It includes the Council for Technological Advancement and has an active publications program in both technical and economic areas of concern to its members, as well as more general areas such as "Public Inspection of IRS Private Rulings"

MARCH OF DIMES. Box 2000, White Plains, NY 10602. **914-428-1700**

MATERNITY CENTER ASSOCIATION. 48 E 92nd St, New York, NY 10028. **212-369-7300.** Ruth Watson Lubic, general director. Martin Kelly, director, public information. Maintains a childbearing center for low-risk patients, offers health education and information service for expectant parents, supports nurse-midwifery education, sponsors institutes on parent education, and publishes literature on childbearing and maternity care

MAYO CLINIC. 200 1st St SW, Rochester, MN 55901. **507-282-2511.** David E Swanson, communications

MENTAL HEALTH LAW PROJECT. 1220 19th St NW, Washington, DC 20036. **200-467-5730**

MENTAL RESEARCH INSTITUTE. 555 Middlefield Rd, Palo Alto, CA 94301. **415-321-3055.** Jules Riskin, MD, director. Luis E Fernandez, PhD, program administrator. Night line: **415-327-8686.** A social science research organization in the fields of family interaction, communications, and human behavior generally; conducts training programs

MEXICAN-AMERICAN LEGAL DEFENSE AND EDUCATIONAL FUND. Suite 716, 1028 Connecticut Ave NW, Washington, DC 20036. **202-659-5166.** Roseanne Markham, administrative assistant

MIGRANT LEGAL ACTION PROGRAM, INC. Suite 600, 806 15th St NW, Washington, DC 20005. **202-347-5100.** Raphael O Gomez, executive director. Burt Fretz, director, legislation

This specialized legal services center was established in 1970 to provide legal representation for migrant and seasonal farmworkers who cannot afford counsel. It is funded by the Legal Services Corporation, an independepemdent entity created by Congress

MOTION PICTURE ASSOCIATION OF AMERICA. 522 5th Ave, New York, NY 10036. **212-867-1200**

MOTOR VEHICLE MANUFACTURERS ASSOCIATION. 320 New Center Bldg, Detroit, MI 48202. **313-872-4311.** V J Adduci, president and chief executive officer. Louis H Bridenstine, director, communications. *Washington office.* Suite 300, 1909 K St NW, Washington DC 20006.

202-872-9339. Louis V Priebe, manager, Washington public relations. Night line. **202-872-9349**

This is the trade and educational association for US auto, truck, and bus manufacturers. "MVMA member companies make 99 percent of all domestically produced vehicles." The association speaks on behalf of the industry, lobbies, provides technical information and statistics, and answers press queries

MULTIPLE ASSOCIATION MANAGEMENT INSTITUTE. 410 N Michigan, Chicago, IL 60611. **312-644-9030**

MUSCULAR DYSTROPHY ASSOCIATION. 810 7th Ave, New York, NY 10019. **212-586-0808.** Robert Ross, executive director. Horst S Petzall, director, public health education. A national voluntary health agency

NAACP LEGAL DEFENSE AND EDUCATIONAL FUND, INC. 10 Columbus Cir, New York, NY 10019. **212-586-8397.** Jack Greenberg, director-counsel. Norman Bloomfield, public relations

Regional Offices and Contacts

Washington. 733 15th St NW, Washington, DC 20005. **202-638-3278.** Barry Goldstein or Elaine Jones

West Coast. 12 Geary St, San Francisco, CA 94102. **415-788-8736.** Lowell Johnston

The fund is the legal arm of the civil rights movement, and although founded by the NAACP it is a separate organization. It "represents civil rights groups as well as individual citizens who have bona fide civil rights claims" and finances court actions for equality in schools, jobs, voting, housing, municipal services, land use, and so on. The fund runs an organized litigation campaign for prison reform and the abolition of capital punishment, and also carries out educational activities. *See also* National Association for the Advancement of Colored People

THE NADER BUREAUCRACY. Since the establishment of the Center for Study of Responsive Law in 1969, the Ralph Nader umbrella has come to include a variety of organizations with varying degrees of association with the consumer advocate. Many of these organizations are classified in more detail elsewhere in the appropriate sections. Nader can be reached through the Center for Study of Responsive Law.

Public Citizen and Nader-Related Groups

Center for Study of Responsive Law. PO Box 19367, Washington, DC 20036. **202-833-3400.** Ruth Fort, administrator

Congress Watch. 133 C St SE, Washington, DC 20003. **202-546-4936.** Mark Green, director

Corporate Accountability Research Group. 1346 Connecticut Ave NW, Washington, DC 20036. **202-833-3931**

Critical Mass Journal. 133 C St SE, Washington, DC 20003. **202-546-4936.** Richard Pollock, director

Health Research Group. 2000 P St NW, Washington, DC 20036. **202-872-0320.** Dr Sidney Wolfe, director

Housing Research Group. PO Box 19367, Washington, DC 20036. **202-833-3400**

Freedom of Information Act Clearinghouse. 2000 P St NW, Washington, DC 20036. **202-785-3704.** Diane Cohn, director

Litigation Group. 2000 P St NW, Washington, DC 20036. **202-785-3704.** Alan Morrison, director

Public Interest Research Group. 1346 Connecticut Ave NW-419A, Washington, DC 20036. **202-833-3934.** Marty Rogol, director

Resident Utility Consumer Action Group. 1346 Connecticut Ave NW-419A, Washington, DC 20036. **202-833-3934.** Marty Rogol, director

Tax Reform Research Group. 133 C St SE, Washington, DC 20036. **202-544-1710.** Robert Brandon, director

Visitors Center. 1200 15th St NW, Washington, DC 20005. **202-659-9053.** Mike Horrocks, director

Spin-off Nader Groups

Aviation Consumer Action Project. PO Box 19029, Washington, DC 20036. **202-223-4498.** Mimi Cutler

Capitol Hill News Service. 968 National Press Bldg, Washington, DC 20045. **202-638-1096**

Center for Auto Safety. 1346 Connecticut Ave NW-1223, Washington, DC 20036. **202-659-1126.** Clarence Ditlow, director

Clean Water Action Project. PO Box 19312, Washington, DC 20036. **202-311-1568.** David Zwick, director

Disability Rights Center. Suite 1124, 1346 Connecticut Ave NW, Washington, DC 20036. **202-223-3304.** Deborah Kaplan, director

Gray Panthers. 3700 Chestnut St, Philadelphia, PA 19104. **215-382-6644.** Maggie Kuhn, national convenor

Pension Rights Center. Suite 1019, 1346 Connecticut Ave NW, Washington, DC 20036. **202-296-2778.** Karen W Ferguson, director

Professional Drivers Council. Suite 612, 2000 P St NW, Washington, DC 20036.

202-785-3707. John Sikorski, director

NARCOTICS EDUCATION, INC. PO Box 4390, 6830 Laurel St NW, Washington, DC 20012. **202-723-4774.** Ernest H J Steed, executive director. F Soper, editor of *Listen.* Night line: **301-439-4590.** A nonprofit corporation "formed to foster and conduct an education program for the prevention of addiction, through films, publications, forums, and lectures"

NATIONAL ABORTION RIGHTS ACTION LEAGUE. 706 7th St SE, Washington, DC 20003. **202-546-7800.** Emergency line: **301-656-9709.** Karen Mulhanger, executive director. Sylvia Rowe, public relations director. A national lobbying and membership organization "dedicated to maintaining safe, legal abortions"

NATIONAL ACADEMY OF TELEVISION ARTS AND SCIENCES. 110 W 57th St, New York, NY 10019. **212-765-2450**

NATIONAL ALCOHOLIC BEVERAGE CONTROL ASSOCIATION. 5454 Wisconsin Ave NW, Washington, DC 20015. **202-652-3366**

THE NATIONAL ALLIANCE OF BUSINESSMEN. Suite 558, 1730 K St NW, Washington, DC 20006. **202-254-7161.** Robert H Charles, president and chief executive officer, **202-254-7125.** Fred R Wentzel, vice president, operations planning and communications, **202-254-7161.** Frank B Tennant, Jr, director, Public Relations. Joseph D Wolfe, director, Communications. Donald L Dunnington, director, publications

Selected National Headquarters Staff

Corrections Liaison. Ron Burkhart and Stan Lay

Jobs for Veterans. Jerry Wing

Field Support Operations. I Joseph Crowley

Youth Motivation. Barbara A Hudson

Youth Employment. Rose Wheeler

Youth Career Guidance Institutes. Ellen Boyers

Veterans Benefits. Irving Peltz

"The Alliance works to bring chronically unemployed and underemployed people into the nation's economic mainstream." It is a tax-exempt partnership organization of business, labor, government, and education that works to secure jobs and job training for disadvantaged adults, Vietnam-era veterans, needy youth, and ex-offenders. The national headquarters is staffed by executives of corporations, government agencies, and unions on loan to the alliance. Through numerous regional and metropolitan area offices, its functions are both practical and educational

NATIONAL ALLIANCE FOR SAFER CITIES. 165 E 56th St, New York, NY 10022. **212-751-4000.** Harry Fleischman, executive director

The goals of this public affairs and educational coalition of 65 national organizations are to strengthen the criminal justice system and to increase citizen participation in reducing crime. It supports crime watch and similar programs, and seeks to "counteract repressive concepts and activities, whether by extremists of the right or left, and to prevent the expropriation by them of issues of crime and violence for repressive or similar ulterior aims"

NATIONAL ALLIANCE OF SENIOR CITIZENS. PO Box 40031, Washington, DC 20016. **703-524-2350.** *Director.* C C Clinkscales III, **202-347-4936.** *Press contact.* Jerald Aubrey, **202-347-4936.** (h) **202-333-5412** (also night line)

THE NATIONAL ANTIVIVISECTION SOCIETY. 100 E Ohio St, Chicago, IL 60611. **312-787-4486.** C E Richard, managing director. A national animal welfare organization; its specific activity is campaigning against the use of live animals in research and product testing

NATIONAL ASSOCIATION OF ACCOUNTANTS. 919 3rd Ave, New York, NY 10022. **212-754-9700.** W M Young, Jr, executive director, **212-754-9707.** Robert F Nolan, manager, publicity and promotion.

The membership comprises accounting and financial management, ranging from accountants beginning their careers to top corporate executives in business and government, as well as educators. The association carries out a broad educational program in advanced techniques and procedures in the field of management accounting, including a monthly technical journal, a continuing research program, and self-study courses

NATIONAL ASSOCIATION FOR THE ADVANCEMENT OF COLORED PEOPLE. 1790 Broadway, New York, NY 10019. **212-245-2100.** Night line: **212-245-2101.** Benjamin L Hooks, executive director. Denton L Watson, director, public relations, **212-245-2100,** Ext 298. Night line: **914-699-5610.** *Washington office.* Clarence Mitchell, **202-638-2269**

Counsels

General. Nathaniel Jones

Labor. Herbert Hill

Education. Althea Simmons

The association is the nation's largest civil rights organization. With half a million

members and 1700 local chapters it is the mainstream antidiscrimination public affairs group. *See also* NAACP Legal Defense and Educational Fund, Inc

NATIONAL ASSOCIATION OF ARAB AMERICANS. 1825 Connecticut Ave NW-211, Washington, DC 20009. **202-797-7757.** Joseph D Baroody, president, **202-466-8225.** John P Richardson, director, public affairs, **202-797-7757.** A membership organization made up of Americans of Arab heritage; "organized to articulate the members' views on American Middle East policy, to encourage Arab Americans to become involved in the political process, and to assist members of the community in domestic issues of concern"

NATIONAL ASSOCIATION OF BLUE SHIELD PLANS. 211 E Chicago Ave, Chicago, IL 60611. **312-440-5500.** William E Ryan, president, **312-440-5673.** James C Shaffer, director, public relations, **312-440-5667.** A nonprofit administrative organization of Blue Shield plans throughout the country; publishes a directory of public relations persons at local plans. *See also* Blue Cross Association

NATIONAL ASSOCIATION OF BLACK MANUFACTURERS. 1625 I St NW, Washington, DC 20006. **202-785-5133**

NATIONAL ASSOCIATION OF COMMISSIONS FOR WOMEN. Rm 1003, 926 J St, Sacramento, CA 95814. **916-445-3173.** Anita Miller, chairperson. Margaret Fjeldsted, public information coordinator. The national federation of official government commissions and equivalent agencies on the status of women; "major effort is to further legal, social, political, and economic, and education opportunities for women and eliminate sex discrimination"

NATIONAL ASSOCIATION FOR COMMUNITY DEVELOPMENT. 1424 16th St NW, Washington, DC 20036. **202-667-9137**

NATIONAL ASSOCIATION OF CONCERNED VETERANS. 1900 L St NW-314, Washington, DC 20021. **202-785-2155**

NATIONAL ASSOCIATION OF COUNTIES. 1735 New York Ave NW, Washington, DC 20006. **202-785-9577.** Bernard F Hillenbrand, executive director. Beth Denniston, public affairs director

This professional organization represents counties and county officials; its functions are educational, public affairs. It conducts research and information services for county

officials and has a broad publications program

NATIONAL ASSOCIATION OF COUNTY AGRICULTURAL AGENTS. 506 County Administration Bldg, Atlanta, GA 30303 NL

THE NATIONAL ASSOCIATION FOR CREATIVE CHILDREN AND ADULTS. 8080 Springvalley Dr, Cincinnati, OH 45236. **513-631-1777.** Ann Fabe Isaacs, chief executive officer. A nonprofit organization "dedicated to helping us become the best we can be through understanding and applying the research on creativity"

NATIONAL ASSOCIATION OF THE DEAF. 814 Thayer Ave, Silver Spring, MD 20910. **201-587-1788.** Frederick C Schreiber, executive secretary. An educational, public affairs, and lobbying group serving the deaf; acts as an information clearinghouse and referral center for deaf people and other inquirers

NATIONAL ASSOCIATION OF ELECTRIC COMPANIES. Suite 1010, 1140 Connecticut Ave, Washington, DC 20036. **202-223-3460.** David R Toll, president

This trade association represents investor-owned electric utilities. "The association," according to NAEC librarian Mary K Dzurinko, "has no press spokesman or contact," which is perhaps the subject of no great surprise

NATIONAL ASSOCIATION OF FIRE INVESTIGATORS. 53 W Jackson Blvd, Chicago, IL 60604. **312-939-6050.** John Kennedy, president. *Press contact.* Pat Cesak. A national trade organization representing fire investigators and explosion experts

NATIONAL ASSOCIATION OF HOME BUILDERS. 15th and M Sts NW, Washington, DC 20005. **202-454-0432.** Dave Stahl, executive vice-president, **202-452-0401.** Kerry M McMahon, director, communications. Ken Geremia, director, public relations, **202-452-0270.** Betty Christy, director, media liaison, **202-452-0263.** Jay Shackford, editorial director, **202-452-0263**

This trade association for single and multi-family home builders, manufacturers, and suppliers of building materials has 639 local and state affiliates with 85,000 members. It is affiliated with the National Council of the Housing Industry, composed of major national manufacturers, which concentrates on creating "a favorable legislative and economic climate for home building." *See also* National Council of the Housing Industry

NATIONAL ASSOCIATION FOR IRISH FREEDOM. Rm 422, 799 Broadway, New York, NY 10003. **212-254-1757**

NATIONAL ASSOCIATION OF MANU-FACTURERS. 1766 F St NW, Washington, DC 20006. **202-331-3700.** Heath Larry, president, **202-331-3865.** James N Sites, senior vice-president and director, communications

Branch Office Contacts

Great Lakes. 801 Northland Towers W, Southfield, MI 48075. **313-569-2050.** Nelson W Morrow

Mid-Atlantic. 1719 Route 10, Parsippany, NJ 07054. **201-539-4100.** Thomas W Estler

Midwest. 222 S Prospect Ave, Park Ridge, IL 60068. **312-698-3838.** John L Birkinbine, Jr

New England. 2 Militia Dr, Lexington, MA 02173. **617-862-2314.** Richard B Norment

South. Suite 201, 1421 Peachtree St NE, Atlanta, GA 30309. **404-892-0530.** Michael T Swinehart

Southwest. Suite 243, 8320 Gulf Fwy, Houston, TX 77017. **713-641-2074.** Richard D Allen

West. 601 N Vermont Ave, Los Angeles, CA 90004. **213-665-5971.** Patrick L Godfrey

Northwest. 711 Ct A, Tacoma WA 98402. **206-272-5125.** Robert E Wethern

This national trade organization of manufacturers works for legislation and regulations "conducive to good business climate." Its 13,000 member companies represent every state, and it is the nation's most influential industrial association

NATIONAL ASSOCIATION OF MEDI-CAL EXAMINERS. 1402 S Grand Blvd, St Louis, MO 63104. **314-664-9800**

NATIONAL ASSOCIATION FOR MEN-TAL HEALTH. 1800 N Kent St, Roslyn, VA 22209

NATIONAL ASSOCIATION OF MINOR-ITY CONTRACTORS. 1750 K St, Washington, DC 20006

NATIONAL ASSOCIATION OF MOTOR BUS OWNERS. 1025 Connecticut Ave, Washington, DC 20036. **202-239-5890.** Charles Well, president. William C Barnich III, director, government affairs. A national trade organization representing bus owners

NATIONAL ASSOCIATION FOR PUERTO RICAN CIVIL RIGHTS. 175 E 116th St, New York, NY 10029. **212-348-3973.** Emergency number: **212-796-2555.** Robert Munoz, national president. Antonio Riva, director, operations. A national organization representing itself as the spokesman for Puerto Rican civil rights issues

NATIONAL ASSOCIATION OF RAILROAD PASSENGERS. 417 New Jersey Ave SE, Washington, DC 20003. **202-546-1550.** Ross Capon, executive director. Thomas G Crikelair, assistant director. A national consumer lobby working to improve and expand rail passenger services

NATIONAL ASSOCIATION OF REAL ESTATE BROKERS. 1025 Vermont Ave NW, Washington, DC 20005. **202-638-1280**

NATIONAL ASSOCIATION OF REAL ESTATE INVESTMENT TRUSTS, INC. 1101 17th St NW, Washington, DC 20036. **202-785-8717.** John B Nicholson, executive vice-president. Ronald D Utt, director, research. Walter G Laessig, general counsel. A national trade organization representing the real estate industry, particularly investment trusts, in Washington, DC, through research, conferences, and publications

NATIONAL ASSOCIATION OF REAL-TORS (NAR). 430 N Michigan Ave, Chicago, IL 60611. **312-440-8000.** H Jackson Pontius, executive vice-president, **312-440-8001.** Lloyd P Kuehn, staff vice-president, public relations, **312-440-8100.** Nancy J Blumenstein, manager, **312-440-8102**

The organization describes itself as "the nation's largest trade and professional association," representing 500,000 members through 1683 local boards of realtors and 50 state associations. Through its code of ethics, the NAR serves a semiofficial role as the standard setter and de facto licensing agency of the industry. Only members of the association may use the NAR's registered trademark, "Realtor," and thus the great majority of real estate brokers are members. The organization has nine affiliated groups, including the American Institute of Real Estate Appraisers, Farm and Land Institute, American Society of Real Estate Counselors, Institute of Real Estate Management, and American Chapter of the International Real Estate Federation

NATIONAL ASSOCIATION OF RECY-CLING INDUSTRIES, INC. 330 Madison Ave, New York, NY **212-867-7330.** M J Mighdoll, executive vice-president and chief executive officer. John R McBride, director, public and community relations

NATIONAL ASSOCIATION OF REGU-LATORY UTILITY COMMISSIONERS. PO Box 684, Washington, DC 20044. **202-628-7324.** Paul Rodgers, general counsel and administrative director

NATIONAL ASSOCIATION FOR RE-TARDED CITIZENS. (formerly the National Association for Retarded Children). 2709 Ave E East, Arlington, TX 76011. **817-261-4961.** Dr Philip Roos, executive director of national office, **817-261-2961,** Ext 30 or 31. *Press contact.* Public information department, **817-261-4967,** Ext 42. The major national voluntary organization and leading spokesman for mentally retarded persons; performs a national advocacy and educational role and also runs the NARC Research and Demonstration Institute

NATIONAL ASSOCIATION OF SECURI-TIES DEALERS, INC. 1735 K St NW, Washington, DC 20006. **202-833-7200**

NATIONAL ASSOCIATION OF SMALL BUSINESS INVESTMENT COMPANIES. 512 Washington, Bldg, 1435 G St NW, Washington, DC 20005. **202-638-3411**

NATIONAL ASSOCIATION OF SOCIAL WORKERS. Suite 600, 1425 H St NW, Washington, DC 20005. **202-628-6800.** Chauncey A Alexander, executive director. Sheila B Healey, public relations coordinator. A professional organization; conducts lobbying on issues of concern to members and attempts to set standards for the profession

NATIONAL ASSOCIATION OF STATE DEPARTMENTS OF AGRICULTURE. 1616 H St NW, Washington, DC 20006. **202-628-1566**

NATIONAL ASSOCIATION OF STATE DIRECTORS FOR DISASTER. 300 Indiana Ave NW, Washington, DC 20001. **202-629-5151**

NATIONAL AUDUBON SOCIETY. 950 3rd Ave, New York, NY 10022. **212-832-3200.** Dr Elvis J Stahr, president. Robert Boardman, public information director. A prestigious conservation organization that runs wildlife refuges and nature centers, supports citizen action to protect the environment, and provides a variety of educational materials and publications

NATIONAL AUTOMOBILE DEALERS ASSOCIATION. 8400 Westpark Dr, McLean, VA 22101. **703-821-7000.** Frank E McCarthy, executive vice-president, **703-721-7100.** Jack C Neal, director, public relations, **703-821-7120.** Patty Vandergrift, press relations, **703-821-7120.** A national trade association representing franchised new car and truck dealers

NATIONAL BAR ASSOCIATION. c/o Elmer Jackson, Jr, 1314 N 5th St, Kansas City, KS 66101. **413-281-4583**

NATIONAL BUSINESS EDUCATION ASSOCIATION. PO Box 17402, Dulles International Airport, Washington, DC 20041. **202-860-0213**

NATIONAL BUSINESS LEAGUE. 4324 Georgia Ave NW, Washington, DC 20011. **202-726-6200**

NATIONAL CANNERS ASSOCIATION. 1133 20th St NW, Washington, DC 20036. **202-331-5900.** Charles J Carey, president. Roger E Coleman, vice-president, public communications, **202-331-5935.** A trade association whose members represent 85 to 90 percent of the US production of canned foods; maintains research laboratory facilities

NATIONAL CATTLEMEN'S ASSOCIATION. PO Box 569, Denver, CO 80201. **303-861-1904.** George S Spencer, executive vice-president and chief operating officer. C W McMillan, (425 13th St NW, Washington, DC 20004), vice-president, government affairs, **202-347-0228.** Don Magdanz, senior vice-president, association affairs, (Suite 441, 7000 W Center Rd, Omaha, NE 68106), **402-392-1878**

The association is the national spokesman for all segments of the beef cattle industry, including breeders, producers, and feeders. It also provides trade services and lobbies for the industry

NATIONAL CENTER FOR PRODUCTIVITY AND QUALITY OF WORKING LIFE. Rm 3002, 2000 M St NW, Washington, DC 20036. **202-254-9890.** George H Kuper, executive director. Lloyd B Gibson, media relations director, (h) **202-797-8747.** A national organization to "improve productivity in all sectors of economy. Established under public law"

NATIONAL CIVIL SERVICE LEAGUE. 917 15th St NW, Washington, DC 20005. **202-737-5850.** Daniel G Prive, executive director. A national service organization composed of individuals and corporations "interested in improving government at all levels through an efficient personnel system based on merit"

NATIONAL COAL ASSOCIATION. 1130 17th St NW, Washington, DC 20036. **202-628-4322.** Carl E Bagge, president. Rex Chaney, vice-president, public relations. Herb Foster, vice-president, press relations. Night line: **703-256-0233.** (Chaney) **301-422-3442** (Foster). The trade association for the bituminous (soft) coal industry, handling government relations, public relations, statistics, and general information

NATIONAL COALITION FOR MARINE CONSERVATION, INC. PO Box 23298 Savannah, GA 31403. **912-234-8062.** Frank E Carlton, MD, president. "The only national organization devoted exclusively to the preservation of our ocean environment and to the legislative concerns of the marine angler"

THE NATIONAL COMMITTEE FOR FAIR DIVORCE AND ALIMONY LAWS. 370 Lexington Ave, New York, NY 10036. **212-575-1234.** George Dunbar, president. Sidney Siller, Esq, general counsel, **212-683-1043.** A citizens' group campaigning for legislative changes to make divorce, alimony, and custody laws apply equally to men and women

NATIONAL COMMITTEE FOR A HUMAN LIFE AMENDMENT, INC. 1707 L St NW 400, Washington, DC 20036. **202-785-8061.** William J Cox, executive director. Lobbies against legalized abortions

NATIONAL COMMITTEE TO REOPEN THE ROSENBERG CASE. 250 W 57th St, New York, NY **212-265-0918**

NATIONAL CONFERENCE OF CATHOLIC BISHOPS. 1312 Massachusetts Ave NW, Washington, DC 20005. **202-659-6600.** *Press contact.* William Ryan, **202-659-6700**

NATIONAL CONFERENCE ON SOVIET JEWRY. Suite 1075, 11 W 42nd St, New York, NY 10036. **212-345-1510.** Jerry Goodman, executive director. Jonathan Schenker, public relations. A coalition of national Jewish organizations and local Jewish community councils and federations in 300 communities to "coordinate religious, educational, [and] charitable activities on behalf of Soviet Jews"

NATIONAL CONFERENCE OF STATE LEGISLATURES. 444 N Capitol St NW, Washington, DC 20001. **202-624-5400**

NATIONAL CONGRESS OF AMERICAN INDIANS. 1430 K St NW, Washington, DC 20005. **202-347-9520.** Charles Trimble, executive director. Cal Noel, communications coordinator. A national organization of Indian tribes outside the regular purview of the US government, and not under the political or legal jurisdiction of the states in which they are located; membership includes tribes and individuals, both Indian and non-Indian

NATIONAL CONSUMER CENTER FOR LEGAL SERVICES. Suite 303, 1302 18th St NW, Washington, DC 20036. **202-833-9165**

NATIONAL CONSUMER INFORMATION CENTER. 3005 Georgia Ave NW, Washington, DC 20001. **202-723-8090**

NATIONAL CONSUMERS LEAGUE. Suite 522, 1028 Connecticut Ave NW, Washington, DC 20036. **202-797-7600.** Mary Gardiner Jones, president. Sandra L Willet, executive director. April Moore, editor, *National Consumers League Bulletin.* Anne Harrison Clark, legislative director (information on consumer issues in Congress)

The League is a lobbying group fighting against child labor, unfair labor laws for women, inhumane working conditions, and abuses in the marketplace. It is the nations's oldest consumer group, founded in 1899

NATIONAL COORDINATING COUNCIL ON DRUG EDUCATION. Suite 301, 1601 Connecticut Ave NW, Washington, DC 20009. **202-332-1512.** Diana Berek, executive director. Diane Striar, editor, *National Drug Reporter,* **202-332-8894.** A private, nonprofit drug education consortium of organizations making a "coordinated effort to find rational approaches to drug abuse prevention"

NATIONAL CORPORATION FOR HOUSING PARTNERSHIPS. 1133 15th St NW, Washington, DC 20005. **202-857-5700.** George W DeFranceaux, chairman of the board. Edwin L Stoll, director, corporate affairs, **202-857-5848**

The corporation is a private organization entering into partnerships with builders, developers, and nonprofit or community organizations at local levels for the construction of multifamily rental or single-family sale houses. It is the largest private producer of low and moderate income housing

NATIONAL COUNCIL OF ADOPTIVE PARENTS. PO Box 543, Teaneck, NJ 07666

THE NATIONAL COUNCIL ON THE AGING, INC. 1828 L St NW, Washington, DC 20036. **202-223-6250.** Jack Ossofsky, executive director. *Press coordinator, media resource center.* Michael Edgley

Regional Offices and Contacts

Southeast. Suite 1220, Rhodes-Haverty Bldg, 134 Peachtree St NW, Atlanta, GA 30303. **404-524-1206.** Talmadge Fowler

Northeast. Lincoln Bldg, 60 E 42nd St, New York, NY 10017. **212-687-6115.** Mrs Vivian Hunter

Western. Rm 417, 1182 Market St, San Francisco, CA 94102. **415-864-4460.** Bernard Finkelstein

West Coast media office. 7461 Beverly Blvd, Los Angeles, CA 90036. **213-939-3145.** Helyne Landres and Nadine Kearns

This nonprofit organization provides "leadership and guidance in the development of services for older persons in hundreds of communities...." It monitors legislation on the aging, conducts research, and provides training and technical assistance to professionals and organizations offering services for the aging. It also administers research and demonstration projects on contract, provides material assistance to local agencies, and is a leading advocate for the concerns of older Americans

NATIONAL COUNCIL ON ALCOHOLISM, INC. 733 3rd Ave, New York, NY 10019. **212-986-4433.** George C Dimas, executive director. Walter J Murphy, managing director, public information and fund raising Ext 504. A national voluntary health agency concerned with the prevention and treatment of alcoholism and with creating public awareness of alcoholism as a treatable disease; has an active publications program

NATIONAL COUNCIL OF CHURCHES OF CHRIST IN THE USA. 475 Riverside Dr (corner of 120th), New York, NY Dr Claire Randall, general secretary. J Warren Day, executive director, news and information services **212-870-2227.** Pam Richard, director, newspaper services. Roy Lloyd, director, broadcast news services. Faith Pomponio, director, special services (magazines and guest placement).

The council is a cooperative agency of 31 Protestant and Orthodox denominations, whose combined membership totals over 40 million in the US. It works in the areas of social justice, overseas ministries, communications, stewardship, theology, ecumenical relations, national and international issues,

family life and human sexuality, and education

NATIONAL COUNCIL TO CONTROL HANDGUNS. Suite 607, 810 18th St NW, Washington, DC 20006. **202-638-4723.** Nelson T Shields, chairman. Charles J Orasin, executive director. A national public interest lobby seeking federal handgun control legislation

NATIONAL COUNCIL ON CRIME AND DELINQUENCY. Continental Plz, 411 Hackensack Ave, Hackensack, NJ 07601. **201-488-0400.** Milton G Rector, president. Frederick Ward, executive vice-president

This public affairs organization is concerned about reducing crime, and improving criminal justice, with particular emphasis on the proper treatment of youthful offenders and victimless crime offenders. It provides educational, training, and other services to organizations and government agencies, including conducting programs and research activities for local governments. In addition, the council acts as an information clearinghouse, with an extensive library in the field, handling inquiries from press and the public, and maintains an automated information center

NATIONAL COUNCIL OF THE HOUSING INDUSTRY. National Housing Ctr, 15th and M Sts NW, Washington, DC 20005. David Stahl, executive vice-president **202-452-0401.** Kerry Michael McMahon, director, communications **202-452-0432.** An organization within the National Association of Home Builders, composed of manufacturers and suppliers of services to home builders. *See also* National Association of Home Builders

NATIONAL COUNCIL ON HUNGER AND MALNUTRITION. 1000 Wisconsin Ave NW, Washington, DC 20007. **202-338-5515**

NATIONAL COUNCIL OF JEWISH WOMEN. 15 E 26th St, New York, NY 10010. **212-532-1740.** Esther R Landa, national president. Jeanne Edelsan, director public relations. A community service, social action, education, and Israeli support organization

NATIONAL COUNCIL OF ORGANIZATIONS FOR CHILDREN AND YOUTH (formerly the Coalition for Children and Youth). Suite 800, 1910 K St NW, Washington, DC 20006. **202-785-4180.** Margaret J Jones, principal officer. *Press contact.* Laura Tracy, editor. Peggy D Pizzo, public policy

intern program director, **202-466-4840.** Dana Tracy, membership campaign director, **202-466-4848**

The council is a nonprofit coalition of national state and local groups and of individuals serving the needs of youth. It is supported by foundation grants and membership dues

NATIONAL COUNCIL ON PUBLIC POLLS. 1990 M Street NW, Washington, DC 20036. **262-223-4315.** Albert H Cantril, president. Burns W Roper, vice-president. Frederick P Currier, secretary-treasurer

NATIONAL COUNCIL ON RADIATION PROTECTION AND MEASUREMENTS. Suite 1016, 7910 Woodmont Ave, Washington, DC 20014. **301-657-2652.** W Roger Ney, executive director. James A Spahn, staff assistant. A nonprofit corporation, chartered by Congress and composed of nationally known scientists, working on a volunteer basis on radiation problems in the US

NATIONAL COUNCIL FOR A RESPONSIBLE FIREARMS POLICY. 1028 Connecticut Ave NW, Washington, DC 20036. **202-785-3772.** David J Steinberg, executive director

NATIONAL COUNCIL OF SENIOR CITIZENS. 1511 K St NW, Washington, DC 20005. **202-783-6850.** John G Blair, director, information services, (h) **707-354-4133**

NATIONAL COUNCIL FOR URBAN ECONOMIC DEVELOPMENT. 1730 K St NW, Washington, DC 20006. **202-223-4735.** James E Peterson, executive director. Barbara Ifshin, communications director. A membership organization "committed to the economic revitalization of our nation's cities"

NATIONAL COUNCIL OF WOMEN OF THE UNITED STATES, INC. 345 E 46th St, New York, NY 10017. **212-697-1278.** Hope Skillman Schary, president

This national membership organization of women has observer status at the United Nations and is affiliated with the International Council of Women. "Since 1888 the National Council of Women of the United States has been at the forefront of problems affecting the status of women and social issues faced by women everywhere in the world"

NATIONAL DISTRICT ATTORNEYS ASSOCIATIONS. 211 E Chicago Ave 1515, Chicago, IL 60611. **312-944-2577**

THE NATIONAL EASTER SEAL SOCIETY FOR CRIPPLED CHILDREN AND ADULTS. 2023 W Ogden Ave, Chicago, IL 60612. **312-243-8400.** Donald W Ullman, acting executive director. Keith Roberts, director, public relations. Howard McCartney, deputy director, public relations. A voluntary health agency; Easter Seal says it is the oldest and largest such agency providing direct services to the physically handicapped

NATIONAL EMERGENCY CIVIL LIBER-TIES COMMITTEE. 25 E 26th St, New York, NY 10021. **212-683-8120.** Edith Tiger, director. A public interest legal organization that pursues what it regards as important test cases on constitutional issues

NATIONAL FAMILY PLANNING COUNCIL. Suite 414, 7060 Hollywood Blvd, Los Angeles, CA 90028. **213-461-4951**

NATIONAL FEDERATION OF BUSI-NESS AND PROFESSIONAL WOMEN'S CLUBS, INC. 2012 Massachusetts Ave NW, Washington, DC 20036. **202-293-1100.** Mrs Piilani Desha, president, **809-935-9932** or **202-293-1100.** Louise Wheeler, editor and public information. Dr Tena Cummings, executive director

This national nonprofit, nonpartisan, non-sectarian, member-supported organization for the research and expansion of educational opportunites for working women in the United States has 170,000 members from 3800 clubs in 53 state federations. It is "open to all women actively engaged in business or the professions or women enrolled in a college or university"

NATIONAL FEDERATION OF CITIZENS BAND RADIO OPERATORS. 1721 De Sales St NW, Washington, DC 20036. **202-785-3311.** Joseph M Durso, president. Margaret E Boschen, executive director and director, public relations. A national membership organization representing operators of citizens band radios; publishes a newsletter for members

NATIONAL FEDERATION OF INDE-PENDENT BUSINESS. 150 W 20th Ave, San Mateo, CA 94403. **415-341-7441.** Wilson S Johnson, president. *Press contacts.* Richard J Farana, communications manager, and Sue Guyette. *Washington office.* (Suite 3206, 490 L'Enfant Plz E, SW, Washington, DC 20024). **202-554-9000.** *Press contacts.* Lee J Stillwell, associate manager, communications, and Nancy Huheey

A national organization representing small and independent business, the federation has

an active public relations program, lobbies on the national and local level, and provides education and services for its 523,549 members. It also has an active publications program

NATIONAL FIRE PROTECTION ASSOCIATION (NFPA). 470 Atlantic Ave, Boston, MA 02210. **617-482-8755.** Charles S Morgan, president, Ext 110. Richard D Peacock, assistant vice-president, public affairs, Ext 144. *Press relations.* Paul R Sawin, media relations specialist, Ext. 143, and Herbert N Colcord, assistant manager, editorial projects, Ext 135. Robert B Smith (Suite 570 S, 1800 M St NW, Washington, DC 20036), Washington representative. **202-466-3650**

An international, nonprofit, and voluntary organization that says its "sole function is to advance, by science and education, the protection of lives and property from fire," NFPA acts as an international clearinghouse for fire safety information and maintains the world's largest library of fire prevention and fire-related information. It develops and publishes fire prevention, fire protection, and fire suppression codes and standards widely adopted as the bases of laws at every level, from local to national (OSHA standards, for instance)

NATIONAL FOREIGN TRADE COUN-CIL, INC. 10 Rockefeller Plz, New York, NY 10020. **212-581-6420.** Robert M Norris, president. William Baldwin, vice-president and secretary, **203-966-0227**

This nonprofit organization of US businesses active in international trade conducts research and presents expert testimony to government. "The council serves as a constructive, influential force in the mutual formulation of multi-industry points of view for the development of sound international economic, trade, and investment policies"

NATIONAL FOUNDATION FOR CON-SUMER CREDIT, INC. Rm 510, 1819 H St NW, Washington, DC 20006. **202-223-2040.** Robert E Gibson, president. *Press contacts.* Joan W Femister and Mary Quinn

The foundation is a nonprofit, educational and research organization composed of American business, social, and other groups "united to foster a better understanding of consumer credit through education and counseling programs and research." It operates 200 counseling centers throughout the country on money management

NATIONAL FOUNDATION FOR GIFTED CHILDREN. 395 Diamond Hill Rd, Warwick, RI 02886. **401-737-7481**

THE NATIONAL FOUNDATION— MARCH OF DIMES. 1275 Mamaroneck Ave, White Plains, NY 10605. **914-428-7100.** "After working hours, the answering service for **428-7100** refers calls to appropriate spokespeople." Joseph F Nee, president. Arthur A Gallway, vice president, public relations. *Press contact.* Dick McCutcher, editor.

A voluntary health organization, founded in 1938 by President Franklin D Roosevelt, the foundation has some 1600 local chapters and supports nationwide programs of research, medical service, and education. Its purpose is the prevention of birth defects, the nation's most serious child health problem

NATIONAL 4-H COUNCIL. 150 N Wacker Dr, Chicago, IL 60606. **312-782-5021.** Norman C Mindrum, principal official. Diana Williams, associate, educational programs and information service. Raymond D Crabbs, director, educational programs and information services. *Washington office.* 7100 Connecticut Ave, Washington, DC 20015. **301-656-9000.** Margo H Tyler, manager, information services

The council is a national agricultural membership organization "designed to help youth establish goals and become productive, competent citizens." It has 5.8 million boys and girls, 9 to 19 years old, as registered members in the 128,563 locally organized clubs guided by volunteer 4-H leaders

NATIONAL GEOGRAPHIC SOCIETY. 17th and M Sts NW, Washington, DC 20036. **202-296-7500.** Paul Sampson, chief, news service, **202-857-7000.** Publishes *National Geographic*

NATIONAL GOVERNOR'S ASSOCIA-TION (formerly Conference). Suite 202, 444 N Capitol St NW, Washington, DC 20001. **202-624-5300.** Stephen B Farber, director, **202-624-5320.** Sylvia V Hewitt, director, public affairs, **202-624-5330.** An organization representing the governors of the states, and acting as liaison between them and the federal government; membership is dominated by Democrats, who hold a majority of the governships in the US

NATIONAL GRAIN AND FEED ASSOCIATION. 725 15th St NW, Washington, DC 20005. **202-783-2024.** Alvin E Oliver, executive vice-president. Paul A Nelson, director, information services. A trade and service association representing grain and feed producers

NATIONAL GRAIN TRADE COUNCIL. 725 15th St NW, Washington, DC 20005.

202-783-8945. William F Brooks, president and general counsel. A national federation of grain exchanges and a national trade association of grain merchandisers, distributors, exporters, and warehousemen

NATIONAL GRANGE. 1616 H St NW, Washington, DC 20006. **202-628-3507** (also night line). John W Scott, master. Judy Massabny, director, information. Robert M Frederick, director, legislative activities. A professional and fraternal organization, with more than 500,000 members in 5500 local granges and 37 state groups, representing American farmers; takes stands on legislative issues affecting farmers and rural areas

NATIONAL HEALTH COUNCIL. 1740 Broadway, New York, NY 10019. **212-582-6040.** Night line: **212-582-6377.** Edward H Van Ness, executive vice-president. Anne R Warner, director, communications, (h) **201-568-9085.** *Washington office.* Suite 205, 919 18th St NW, Washington, DC 20006. Barney Sellers, **202-785-3919**

The council is an organization claiming to represent over 80 national voluntary, professional, and governmental agencies and other groups concerned with health improvement. "Supported by its members, NHC provides a mechanism through which the member agencies work together, and with others, in the common cause of health protection and improvement"

NATIONAL HEALTH FEDERATION. 212 W Foothill Blvd, Monrovia, CA 91016. **213-357-2181.** Charles I Crecelius, president. Clinton R Miller, executive vice-president.

A public affairs, lobbying, and educational group, the federation describes itself as a "health rights organization," advocating freedom of choice in matters of personal health. It advocates respect for "nonmedical healing professions," organic farming, and the health food industry, and also promotes laetrile and other cancer "cures"

NATIONAL HOUSING CONFERENCE, INC. Suite 221, 1126 16th St NW, Washington, DC 20036. **202-223-4844.** Gene R Schaefer, executive director.

The conference describes itself as "the oldest and most broad-based national organization working to encourage the necessary private and public efforts to deal with the problems of inadequate housing and deterioration of our cities." Membership includes representatives of labor, industry, and government

NATIONAL INFORMATION CENTER ON VOLUNTEERISM. PO Box 4179, Boulder, CO 80306. **303-447-0492**

NATIONAL INSTITUTE OF ARTS AND LETTERS. *See* American Academy and Institute of Arts and Letters

NATIONAL INTERAGENCY COUNCIL ON SMOKING AND HEALTH. 419 Park Ave S, New York, NY 10016. **212-532-6035**

NATIONAL INTERRELIGIOUS SERVICE BOARD FOR CONSCIENTIOUS OBJECTORS. Suite 550, Washington, Bldg, 15th St and New York Ave NW, Washington, DC 20005. **202-393-4868.** Warren W Hoover, executive director. A referral and advisory organization for persons who object to war, conscription, and the military system; also serves as one of the major sources of amnesty information

NATIONAL INTERVENORS. 1757 S St NW, Washington, DC 20009. **202-543-1642.** A public interest organization that campaigns against nuclear power plants

NATIONAL INVESTIGATIONS COMMITTEE ON AERIAL PHENOMENA, INC (NICAP). Suite 23, 3535 University Blvd, West Kensington, MD 20795. **301-949-1267.** John L Acuff, chairman and president, **301-949-1666** or **1267**

The committee has as its purpose to investigate, and to report on, aerial phenomena of unknown origin. Investigations center upon unidentified flying objects (UFOs)

NATIONAL INVESTOR RELATIONS INSTITUTE. 1629 K St NW, Washington, DC 20006. **202-223-4725.** *Press contact.* Laurence F Farrell, executive director

NATIONAL JAIL ASSOCIATION. Department of Corrections, PO Box 12, Lorton VA 22079. **703-629-3971.** Ext 310

NATIONAL JUVENILE LAW CENTER. 3701 Lindell Blvd, St Louis, MO 63108. **314-533-8868.** Paul Piersma, director. Jeanette Ganousis, Patricia Connell, David Howard, and Harry Swanger, staff attorneys. *Press contact.* Jeanette Ganousis, **314-773-8309.** A public interest organization providing expertise to legal services and defender programs in the areas of juvenile and family law

NATIONAL LANDLORDS' ASSOCIATION, INC. 605 W 179th St, New York, NY. **212-568-5355**

NATIONAL LAWYERS GUILD. Suite 1705, 853 Broadway, New York, NY 10003. **212-260-1360.** William Goodman, president, **313-965-0050.** Franklin Siegel, national

office staff, **212-260-1360.** A bar association that serves as a radical alternative to the American Bar Association

NATIONAL LEAGUE OF FAMILIES OF AMERICAN PRISONERS AND MISSING IN ACTION IN SOUTHEAST ASIA (often referred to as League of Families). 1608 K St NW, Washington, DC 20006. **202-628-6811.** Carol Bates, executive director

The league is the major national organization campaigning for the return of all American prisoners and MIA's unaccounted for in the Vietnam War. Membership consists of families of the victims and sympathizers

NATIONAL MANPOWER INSTITUTE. Suite 301, 1211 Connecticut Ave NW, Washington, DC 20036. **202-466-2450.** Stephanie Cole, information specialist, **202-466-4420.** Richard A Ungerer, director, information exchange service

NATIONAL MARITIME COUNCIL. PO Box 7345, Washington, DC 20044. **202-377-3325.** Lewis C Paine, Jr, executive secretary. *Press contact.* Carolyn C Tieger. "A nonprofit organization comprised of labor, management, and government leaders, working together to provide US exporters and importers with [the] finest and most dependable US flag service possible"

NATIONAL MEDICAL ASSOCIATION. 1720 Massachusetts Ave NW, Washington, DC 20036. **202-659-9623**

NATIONAL MULTIPLE SCLEROSIS SOCIETY. 205 E 42nd St, New York, NY 10017. **212-986-3240.** Sylvia Lawry, executive director. George H Weiler, Jr, national public relations director, (h) **201-444-1589.** A national voluntary health agency

NATIONAL MUNICIPAL LEAGUE. 47 E 68th St, New York, NY 10021. **212-535-5700.** A nonprofit, nonpartisan educational association of individuals and organizations "dedicated to the proposition that informed, competent citizens, participating fully in public affairs in their home communities, are the key to good local, state, and national government"

NATIONAL ORGANIZATION FOR NON-PARENTS. 3 N Liberty St, Baltimore, MD 21201. **301-752-7456.** Carole Goldman, executive director. Works, through the media and educational programs on the national and local levels, "to gain acceptance for child-free living, to encourage responsible decisions about parenthood, and to alleviate proparenthood pressures in our society"

NATIONAL ORGANIZATION FOR THE REFORM OF MARIJUANA LAWS (NORML). 2317 M St NW, Washington, DC 20037. **202-223-3170.** *Press contact.* R Keith Stroup, Esq, national director. Peter H Meyers, chief counsel. The principal organization campaigning for the legalization of marijuana

NATIONAL ORGANIZATION FOR WOMEN (NOW). Suite 1001, 425 13th St NW-1001, Washington, DC 20004. **202-347-2279.** Eleanor Cutri Smeal, president. Martha Buck, vice-president, executive. Arlie Scott, vice-president, action. Sandra Reeves Roth, secretary. Eve Norman, treasurer. The public interest and lobbying organization that is the spearhead of the women's liberation movement; has 700 chapters in all 50 states

NOW Women's Study Center. 8271 Melrose Ave 109 Los Angeles, CA, **213-655-3331**

NATIONAL PARAPLEGIA FOUNDATION. 333 N Michigan Ave, Chicago, IL 60601. **312-436-4779.** Ann Ford, associate director. James Smittkamp, director, development. Night line: **312-321-1629.** *Research division.* **305-735-9050.** A national voluntary health agency

NATIONAL PARENTS AND TEACHERS ASSOCIATION. 700 N Rush, Chicago, IL 60611. **312-787-0977.** Night line: **312-787-0979.** Becky Schergens, executive director, Ext 62. Sandra Fink, director, public information, Ext. 58.

The national organization representing 30,574 local PTA's and PTO's in elementary and secondary public schools throughout the country, the association has a total national membership of 6.4 million. "National PTA is dedicated to improving the quality of life for children and young people, in the areas of education and health "

NATIONAL PARKS AND CONSERVATION ASSOCIATION. 1701 18th St NW, Washington, DC 20009. **202-265-2717.** Anthony Wayne Smith, president and general counsel. Rita Molyneau, administrative assistant for communications, (h) **202-543-7025.** Eugenia Connaly, editor, *National Parks & Conservation* magazine. Joan Moody, assistant editor and staff writer

The association is a private, nonprofit public service organization. Its interests and activities relate primarily to protection of the units of the National Park System but extend also to other conservation issues

NATIONAL PEOPLE'S ACTION. 1123 W Washington Blvd, Chicago, IL 60607. **312-243-3038** (also night line). Gale Cincotta, chairperson. Shel Trapp, staff. A coalition of neighborhood organizations throughout the country, "working to make neighborhoods first on the agenda of domestic policy on the local, state and national level"

NATIONAL POLICE OFFICERS ASSOCIATION OF AMERICA, INC. 14600 S Tamiami Tri, Venice, FL 33595. **813-426-1111.** *Press contact.* Richard V Beliles, legal counsel and public relations director, **502-589-4710.**

This is a membership organization of law enforcement officers throughout the US, in all ranks and from all agencies. Local chapters are formed by members; they hold police conferences and training seminars. Award banquets are held biennially. The association publishes *Enforcement Journal*, a quarterly magazine

NATIONAL STATES RIGHTS PARTY. PO Box 1211, Marietta, GA 30061. **404-427-0283.** An extremist right-wing political party

NATIONAL RECREATION AND PARK ASSOCIATION. 1601 N Kent St, Arlington, VA 22209. **703-525-0606.** John H Davis, executive director. Patricia Warden, director, communications and information. Barry Tindall, director, public affairs

This independent, nonprofit, public interest organization represents citizen and professional leadership in the parks, recreation, and leisure field in the US and Canada. It provides services to all facets of this field

NATIONAL RESOURCE CENTER FOR CONSUMERS OF LEGAL SERVICES. 1302 18th St NW, Washington, DC 20036. **202-659-8814.** Sandra De Ment, executive director. Davida Maron, executive editor

A research and education organization monitoring and assessing developments in the delivery of legal services, the center operates a clearinghouse on legal services and materials. Membership includes consumers and providers, and groups and representatives in the legal services delivery field

NATIONAL RESOURCES DEFENSE COUNCIL, INC. 122 E 42nd St, New York, NY 10017. **212-949-0049.** John H Adams, executive director. Carol Hine or Marc Reisner, public information. Each staff attorney is responsible for press and public

relations on his or her particular cases and projects. Richard Ayres, Washington, DC, representative, **202-737-5000.** Roger Beers, Palo Alto, CA, representative, **415-327-1080.** An environmental organization specializing in public interest litigation

NATIONAL RETAIL MERCHANTS ASSOCIATION. 100 W 31st St, New York, NY 10001. **212-244-8780.** James R Williams, president. Jan Aaron, public relations director, Ext 49. An educational and research organization representing 30,000 firms that retail consumer goods, including chain and department stores as well as small stores; dedicated to "helping its members operate more productively"

NATIONAL RIFLE ASSOCIATION. 1600 Rhode Island Ave NW, Washington, DC 20036. **202-783-6506.** Harlon B Carter, executive vice-president, Ext 201. Lee Jorgensen, director, public affairs, Ext 223. Night line: **703-938-5419.** Brink Chipman, communications manager. Ellie Shaffer, information services manager. Ho Thi Kim Sa, film librarian. An organization of gun enthusiasts, with a powerful lobby opposing any form of gun control and supporting the constitutional right to bear arms

NATIONAL RIGHT TO LIFE COMMITTEE, INC. 529 14th St NW-341, Washington, DC 20045. **202-638-4396.** Mildred F Jefferson, MD, president, **617-261-8882.** Judie Brown, director of public relations, **202-638-4396.** Night line: **703-494-8531.** Thea Rossi Barron, Esq, legislative counsel, **202-638-4396.** A national lobby group, with 1400 chapters nationwide, against legalized abortion

NATIONAL RIGHT TO WORK COMMITTEE. 8316 Arlington Blvd, Fairfax, VA 22038. **703-573-8550.** Reed Larson, president. Carter Clews, public relations director. Night line: **703-820-1443.** A nonprofit, nonpartisan, single-purpose citizens' organization, that combats compulsory unionism

National Right to Work Committee. Legal Defense Foundation. Suite 610, 8316 Arlington Blvd, Fairfax, VA 22038. **703-573-7010**

NATIONAL RURAL ELECTRIC COOPERATIVE ASSOCIATION. 2000 Florida Ave NW, Washington, DC 20009. **202-265-7400.** Robert D Partridge, general manager. Robert Nelson, director public relations. The national service organization representing 1000 rural electric systems that bring electric power to over 25 million rural customers in 46 states

NATIONAL SAFETY COUNCIL. 444 N Michigan Ave, Chicago, IL 60611. **312-527-4800.** Vincent L Tofany, president. Bill Hawkins, director, public information, Night line: **312-893-5738**

A public service organization chartered by Congress, but operating as a nongovernmental organization, the council has as its functions research and educational, as well as technical, service, often performed under contract for firms and governments. It has an active publications program and public relations effort

NATIONAL SANITATION FOUNDATION. Box 1468, 3475 Plymouth Rd, Ann Arbor, MI 48106. **313-769-8010.** Robert M Brown, president. Night line: **313-663-3396.** *Information releases.* Will Connelly, public relations counsel, **313-475-2700.** Ed Stockton, executive vice-president, **313-971-5345**

This independent, nonprofit environmental organization of scientists, engineers, technicains, educators, and analysts works for better environmental quality. According to the foundation, "it develops standards for plastics, food equipment, pool equipment, wastewater treatment, and other environment products. [It also] tests and evaluates, and publishes listings of conforming products"

NATIONAL SECURITY TRADERS ASSOCIATION. 55 Broad St, New York, NY 10004. **212-344-5544.** Morton N Weiss, president

Founded in 1934, the association has over 4500 members in 31 affiliates across the country. It is dedicated to maintaining and enhancing the standards and operations of the over-the-counter (OTC) securities markets. *See also* **OTC Information Bureau**

NATIONAL SEX FORUM. 1523 Franklin St, San Francisco, CA 94109. **415-928-1133.** *Contacts.* Ted McIlvenna and Phyllis Lyon, codirectors, and Wardell Pomeroy. Night line: **415-334-2997.** (McIlvenna). **415-824-2790.** (Lyon)

The forum provides courses in sex education for adults, training for professionals in the area of human sexuality, sex therapy and counseling, and consultant services, and develops materials such as films and videotapes for use in sex education and therapy. It also is associated with a sexology graduate school. The forum is "a service of Exodus Trust, a nonprofit California trust "

NATIONAL SHERIFFS' ASSOCIATION. Suite 320, 1250 Connecticut Ave, Washington, DC 20036. **202-872-0422** (also night line). Ferris E Lucas, executive director. Truman H Walrod, director, public affairs. A national professional association of sheriffs; provides services and information to—and about—the criminal justice professional, with emphasis on the office of sheriff

NATIONAL STUDENT ASSOCIATION. 2115 S St NW, Washington, DC 20008. **202-387-5100**

NATIONAL SOCIALIST WHITE PEOPLE'S PARTY (NSWPP) (formerly the American Nazi party; the North American affiliate of the World Union of National Socialists). 2507 N Franklin Rd, Arlington, VA 22201. **703-524-2175.** Mailing address: Box 5505, Arlington, VA 22205. Matt Koehl, commander. Harold Mantius or Martin Kerr, public relations. Cedric N Syrdahl (2442 S Central, Chicago, IL 60650, or Box 5864, Chicago, IL 60680), **312-863-8700**

This militant, white supremacist political party is based "on the teachings and beliefs of Adolf Hitler." Although it claims to conduct only political activities of a strictly legal nature, NSWPP says that it is "the intention of the party to seize complete political power of the North American continent, using legal, nonviolent means "

NATIONAL SOCIETY FOR MEDICAL RESEARCH. Suite 1100, 1000 Vermont Ave NW, Washington, DC 20005. **202-347-9565.** Thurman S Grafton, D V M, executive director. Bettie W Payne, director, public relations. A nonprofit organization whose primary objective is to assure continued progress in the US biomedical research field by protecting the scientific investigator's right to use laboratory animals "whenever such use is justified"

NATIONAL SOLID WASTES MANAGEMENT ASSOCIATION. Suite 930, 1120 Connecticut Ave NW, Washington, DC 20036. **202-659-4613.** Eugene J Wingerter, executive director. Richard L Hanneman, director, public affairs. A membership organization representing the private solid waste management industry; includes 2000 member industries involved in waste management activities, including garbage and refuse collection, sanitary landfill, recycling, and chemical waste treatment and disposal

NATIONAL TAX EQUALITY ASSOCIATION (NTEA). Suite 615, 1000 Connecticut Ave Bldg, Washington, DC 20036.

202-296-5424. Garner M Lester, chairman of the board, **601-372-6211.** Ray M Stroupe, president, **202-296-5424.** David R Pilvelait, director, research, **202-296-5424.** Works through the legislative process to bring about the taxation of the income of cooperatives and mutual financial institutions on the same basis as the income of conventional businesses and commercial banks

NATIONAL TAXPAYERS UNION. 325 Pennsylvania Ave SE. **202-546-2085.** William Bonner, executive director. Steve Chapman, associate director. Research and lobbying organization seeking to eliminate wasteful government spending, reduce government regulation, and lower taxes

NATIONAL TENANTS ORGANIZATION. 340 W 121st St, New York, NY 10027

NATIONAL TRUST FOR HISTORIC PRESERVATION. 740 Jackson Pl NW, Washington, DC 20006. **202-638-5200.** James Biddle, president. Fletcher Cox, Jr, director, media services division. Night line: **202-254-3306**

Regional Contacts

Midwest. 312-341-1930. Mary C Means

Western. 415-543-0325. John Frisbee

New England. 617-227-8054. Kathryn Welch

Southwest and Plains. 405-232-3179. Cynthia Emrick

Southern. 803-722-4151

This is the national historic preservation information clearinghouse—a private, nonprofit organization chartered by Congress to help in the preservation of sites, buildings, structures, and other historically significant objects

NATIONAL URBAN COALITION. 1201 Connecticut Ave NW, Washington, DC 20036. **202-331-2400.** M Carl Holman, president, **202-331-2445.** Evelyn M Levine, communications coordinator, **202-331-2435**

A nonmembership organization with local affiliates and cooperating organizations in major cities, the coalition was formed in response to the urban civil disorders of the 1960s. It is composed of leaders in education, business, politics, labor, and religion who, through public affairs activities and educational programs, seek to alleviate the conditions that gave birth to civil disturbances. Major areas of interest are housing and neighborhood revitalization, community-based crime prevention, youth employment, and urban education

NATIONAL URBAN LEAGUE. 500 E 62nd St, New York, NY 10021. **212-644-6500.** Vernon E Jordan, Jr, executive director. James D Williams, communications. **212-644-6600 or 6601**

The league is an interracial, community service organization that works to secure equal opportunities for black and other minority Americans. It has 109 affiliates, mostly in cities with large, multiracial populations, that provide "services to members of the minority communities and act as an advocate for the voiceless." It has an active publications program, including a directory of local affiliates

NATIONAL WELFARE RIGHTS ORGANIZATION. 11411 S Central Ave, Los Angeles, CA 90059. **202-347-7727**

NATIONAL WILDLIFE FEDERATION. 1412 16th St NW, Washington, DC 20036. **202-797-6800.** Thomas L Kimball, executive vice-president. Charles Roberts, information division director.

The principal area of emphasis of this major conservation organization is education. It has active legal and lobbying divisions, as well as environmental action and resources defense operations. The federation issues wildlife conservation stamps and carries on an active publication program, particularly of educational materials; it issues an annual conservation directory

NATIONAL WOMEN'S CHRISTIAN TEMPERANCE UNION. 1730 Chicago Ave, Evanston, IL 60201. Office hours: 9 am to 4:30 pm CST. **312-864-1396.** Edith K Stanley, president, Ext 24. Mrs Harry E Caylor, public relations counsel, (1308 Pima Ln, Mount Prospect, IL 60056), **312-827-6004.** Night line: **312-328-1252**

The union is one of the organizations responsible for Prohibition. It now describes itself as "an organization concerned with all phases of 'home protection'," which is defined as "character development, purity standards, example in the home, [and] discipline"

NATIONAL WOMEN'S HEALTH COALITION. 222 E 35th St, New York, NY 10016. **212-684-0217 or 212-685-0975**

NATIONAL WOMEN'S POLITICAL CAUCUS. 1411 K St NW-1110, Washington, DC 20005. **202-347-4456.** Jane Pierson McMichael, executive director. Sharon Flynn, associate director (ERA information). A political action organization campaigning for the election and appointment of women to office, and for the Equal Rights Amendment to the US Constitution

THE NATIVE AMERICAN RIGHTS FUND. 1506 Broadway, Boulder, CO 80302. **303-447-8760.** John E Echohawk, executive director, (h) **303-447-1204.** Lorraine Edmo, technical writer.

Other Primary Offices and Contacts

Maine. 173 Main St (PO Box 392), Calais, 04619. **207-454-2113.** Thomas N Tureen

District of Columbia. 1712 N St NW, Washington 20036. **202-785-4166.** Susan Shown Harjo, legislative liaison, (h) **202-966-2653**

Massachusetts. Rm 551, 10 Post Office Sq, Boston, 02109. **617-426-8558.** Barry Margolin, (h) **617-287-0191**

This national public interest law firm specializes in the field of Indian law—the protection of American Indian rights and resources

NEW DIRECTIONS. Suite 405, 2021 L St NW, Washington, DC 20036. **202-452-1050.** Russell W Peterson, president. Jim Cubie, nuclear proliferation and energy. Terry Garcia, international finance, global fairness, and human rights. Joyce Wood, arms sales and SALT talks. A citizens' lobby that considers itself analogous to Common Cause, except that New Directions is concerned with international issues

NEW YORK CITY PROGRAM FOR SUDDEN INFANT DEATH. 520 1st Ave, New York, NY 10016. **212-686-8854**

NO GREATER LOVE. 1750 New York Ave NW, Washington, DC 20006. **202-785-4665.** Night line: **202-547-5411.** Carmella La Spada, chairman of the board. *Press contact.* Nick Mathwich. A public interest organization providing care to children whose fathers were killed or are missing in the Vietnam War, to veterans hospitalized in Veterans Administration hospitals, and to elderly citizens without families

OAK RIDGE ASSOCIATED UNIVERSITIES. PO Box 117, Oak Ridge, TN 37830. **615-483-8411.** *Press contact.* Vance B Whitfield

ODYSSEY INSTITUTE, INC. 24 W 12th St, New York, NY 10011. **212-741-9570** (also night line). Dr Judianne Densen-Gerber, president, **212-369-3351.** Tery Zimmerman, director, public information, **212-741-9570.** A private social welfare agency, affiliated with Odyssey House, particularly concerned with problems of youth and drug abuse; provides treatment and services and performs public advocacy functions on behalf of children

OFFICE OF COMMUNICATION MANAGEMENT AND DEVELOPMENT (American Psychological Association). 1200 17th St NW, Washington, DC 20036. **202-296-7310**

OPERATION PUSH (People United to Save Humanity). 930 E 50th St, Chicago, IL 60615. **312-373-3366.** The Reverend Jesse L Jackson, president. *Branch office.* Los Angeles

OPPORTUNITIES INDUSTRIALIZATION CENTERS OF AMERICA, INC. 100 W Coulter St, Philadelphia, PA 19144. **215-849-3010.** Elton Jolly, national executive director. Alan Zuckerman, director, office of planning and development

This organization and its 200 affiliates provide employment and training for the unemployed and underemployed, using self-help approaches. In addition, OIC focuses on educational and community revitalization programs

OVERSEAS DEVELOPMENT COUNCIL. 1717 Massachusetts Ave NW, Washington, DC 20036. **202-234-8701.** *See* WORLD for more detail.

OVER-THE-COUNTER INFORMATION BUREAU. 120 Broadway, New York, NY 10005. **212-964-5940.** *Contacts.* Ellen Gartner and Richard Ellis

Sponsored by the National Security Traders Association, the OTC Information Bureau is a nationwide group of 4500 professional traders and market makers who specialize in OTC securities. It describes itself as "the voice of the OTC market, dedicated to providing the investing public with informational and educational material about the OTC market and OTC securities. Members of the Bureau are OTC-traded corporations"

OXFAM-AMERICA. 302 Columbus Ave, Boston, MA 02116. Joe Short, director, **617-247-3304.** An independent development organization funded through contributions from individuals or organizations; supports projects most likely to improve the social and economic positions of poor cultures and is active in disaster relief

PACIFIC TECHNICAL INFORMATION SERVICE. 1155 W Arbor Vitae, Inglewood, CA 90301. **213-776-3410**

PARENTS WITHOUT PARTNERS, INC. Suite 1000, 7910 Woodmont Ave, Washington, DC 20014. **301-654-8850.** Virginia L Martin, executive director. *Contacts.* Ms Martin or Ann Parks, information center.

An educational organization which, through self-help programs and seminars, seeks to give support and advice to single parents, including those widowed, divorced, separated, or unmarried

PEOPLE-TO-PEOPLE COMMITTEE FOR THE HANDICAPPED. 1028 Connecticut Ave NW, Washington, DC 20036. **202-785-0755**

PEOPLES BICENTENNIAL COMMISSION. 1346 Connecticut Ave NW, Washington, DC 20036. **202-833-9122**

PHARMACEUTICAL MANUFACTURERS ASSOCIATION. 1155 15th St NW, Washington, DC 20005. **202-296-2440.** C Joseph Stetler, president. Richard B Hamilton, media relations manager, (h) **703-790-8645.** William C Cray, vice-president, public relations. James B Russo, assistant vice-president, public relations. The trade association of the major drug manufacturers

PLACE NAME SURVEY OF THE UNITED STATES (sponsored by the American Name Society). East Texas State University, Commerce, TX 75428. **214-468-5136.** Fred Tarpley, director. Night line: **214-886-6498.** Coordinates the work of state survey directors in the US by recording origins and other information about geographic place names

PLANNED PARENTHOOD FEDERATION OF AMERICA, INC. 810 7th Ave, New York, NY 10019. **212-541-7800.** Henrietta Marshall, chairman of the board. Robin Elliott, director, information and education, **212-541-7813.** Night line: **212-866-3032**

A nationwide voluntary organization, the federation provides family planning, abortion, and sex education to more than one million persons annually. The headquarters office can serve as a resource service to the press on birth control, contraception, and family planning; abortion, including information on services and the medical aspects of all methods; sex education; and population growth. It has a directory of local affiliates and chapters

PLANNED PARENTHOOD WORLD POPULATION/LOS ANGELES. 3100 W 8th St, Los Angeles, CA 90005. **213-380-9300.** Night line: **213-380-9450.** Dr Hugh Anwyl, executive director. Mary Jean Storrs, coordinator, public relations. Linda A Wilson, coordinator, information and education, **213-380-9300.** Diana Sayler, health educator and public affairs specialist, **213-380-9300.**

The organization offers complete family planning services, including educational and medical programs for contraceptives; pregnancy testing and counseling; abortion; gynecological services; sterilization counseling; and medical procedures. It operates a speakers' bureau and special juvenile diversion counseling program for sexual problems

PLAYBOY FOUNDATION. 919 N Michigan Ave, Chicago, IL 60611. **312-751-8000**

POLICE FOUNDATION. 1909 K St NW, Washington, DC 20006. **202-833-1460.** Patrick V Murphy, president. Thomas V Brady, director, communications. An independent, nonprofit organization established by the Ford Foundation in 1970 and dedicated to supporting innovation and improvement in law enforcement

THE POPULATION COUNCIL. 1 Dag Hammarskjold Plz, New York, NY 10017. **212-644-1300.** George Zeidenstein, president. Susan Robbins, head, publications and information office. The council describes itself thus:

"The Population Council is an organization established in 1952 for scientific training and study in the field of population. It endeavors to advance knowledge in the broad field of population by fostering research, training, and technical consultation and assistance in the social and biomedical sciences "

POPULATION CRISIS COMMITTEE. 1120 19th St NW, Washington, DC 20036. **202-659-1833.** Dr Phyllis Piotrow, executive director. Cathy Carton, information assistant. Janet Stanley, librarian. *New York office.* Suite 808, 30 W 54th St, New York, NY 10019

This public service organization promotes the establishment of population control programs and policies around the world. It works with policy makers in Washington, DC, to increase US support for population control assistance overseas

THE POTOMAC INSTITUTE, INC. 1501 18th St NW, Washington, DC 20036. **202-332-5566.** Harold C Fleming, president. Arthur J Levin, executive vice-president. Night lines: **202-965-3513.** (Fleming). **301-268-3461.** (Levin) Herbert M Franklin, land use, housing, and exclusionary zoning, **202-457-6894.** James O Gibson, central city affairs and neighborhood revitalization, **202-332-5566**

The institute is an independent, nonprofit organization engaged in the analysis of public policies affecting lower income groups

and racial minorities. It provides advisory and research services to government and private agencies

PROD, THE PROFESSIONAL DRIVERS COUNCIL. Box 69, Washington, DC 20044. **202-785-3707.** Robert Windrew, research director

The council, a nationwide reform organization associated loosely with Ralph Nader, is trying to clean up the Teamsters Union. A secondary goal is to improve workers' safety and health conditions in the trucking industry

PROFIT SHARING COUNCIL OF AMERICA. Suite 722, 20 N Wacker Dr, Chicago, IL 60606. **312-372-3411.** L L O'Connor, president. Walter Holan, vice-president. A nonprofit membership organization representing 1400 companies subscribing to the view that profit sharing is an important means of fortifying the American system of free enterprise

PROJECT CONCERN. 3802 Houston St (PO Box 81123), San Diego, CA 92138. **714-299-1353.** C R (Bob) Cronk, executive director. Judy Thoele, director, public relations. Night line: **714-272-4986**

Project Concern is a nonprofit, nonsectarian charitable organization providing primary care, preventive medical assistance, public health education, dental assistance, nutrition training, and the training of paramedics from the population of each host country where it serves. It operates 40 clinics and hospitals in five developing nations and rural America

PROJECT ON NATIONAL SECURITY AND CIVIL LIBERTIES. 122 Maryland Ave NE, Washington, DC 20002. **202-544-5380.** Morton H Halperin, director. Christick Marwick, editor

The project, sponsored jointly by the ACLU Foundation and the Center for National Security Studies, is designed to challenge abuses of intelligence agencies. It encourages use of the Freedom of Information Act, coordinates litigation, and exposes information about the policies of national security bureaucracies, using the act to reveal improperly classified information. "Deals with the full range of ways in which official claims of national security have been used to override basic civil liberties"

PROJECT ON THE STATUS AND EDUCATION OF WOMEN. 1818 R St NW, Washington, DC 20009. **202-387-1300**

THE PROPRIETARY ASSOCIATION.
1700 Pennsylvania Ave NW, Washington, DC 20006. **202-393-1700.** James D Cope, president. Lou M Thompson, Jr, director, public affairs. Bonnie D Lewis, public affairs associate

The association represents firms that manufacture and distribute over-the-counter medicines, in accordance with the federal food and drug laws, which are intended for self-care. "Members are dedicated to making available to the public quality products which are both effective and safe for use as directed "

PUBLIC CITIZEN VISITORS CENTER.
1200 15th St NW, Washington, DC 20005. **202-659-9053.** Mike Horrocks, staff assistant to Ralph Nader, director. The center describes itself thus:

"The Public Citizens Visitors Center is a "clearinghouse" for the Nader network. We also provide tours of the US Capitol and general DC information for all visitors "

PUBLIC INTEREST RESEARCH GROUP. 1346 Connecticut Ave NW-419A. **202-833-3934.** Martin H Rogol, director. Ralph Nader's research group, with special emphasis on the areas of energy, conservation, nuclear power and alternatives, utility reform, banking, and corporate accountability

PUBLIC SERVICE RESEARCH COUNCIL. Suite 430, 8320 Old Courthouse Rd, Vienna, VA 22180. **703-790-0700**

THE RAND CORPORATION. 1700 Main St, Santa Monica, CA 90406. **213-393-0411.** Dr Donald B Rice, president. Paul R Weeks, director, public information, (h) **213-884-9819.** Ann M Shoben, deputy director, public information, (h) **213-794-5189.** Judith A Smith, public information assistant, (h) **213-393-5855**

Rand is a private, nonprofit institution engaged in research and analysis, primarily of public policy issues, in problems of national security and domestic affairs. Of its contracts and grants, 95 percent are with agencies of the US government

A PHILIP RANDOLPH INSTITUTE. 260 Park Ave S, New York, NY 10010. **212-533-8000.** Bayard Rustin, president. Stuart Elliott, research director. A public affairs organization conducting voter education and registration, and get-out-the-vote drives in 35 states, particularly in black communities; also trying to build support for a labor movement among blacks

REACT INTERNATIONAL, INC. 111 E Wacker Dr, Chicago, IL 60601. **312-644-7620.** Henry B Kreev, executive director. Gerald H Reese, managing director. Hank Brandt, membership services. A national volunteer organization providing emergency citizens band radio communications; includes volunteer communication teams in local neighborhoods

RELIGIOUS COALITION FOR ABORTION RIGHTS. 100 Maryland Ave NE, Washington, DC 20002. **202-543-7032.** Pat Gavett, national director. Davida Perry, public relations director. Night line: **202-686-9482.** A coalition of national religious organizations (13 denominations), concerned that all women have the right to choose legal abortion, in keeping with the First Amendment guarantee of the separation of church and state

RELIGIOUS RIGHT TO LIFE COMMITTEE. National Press Bldg, 529 14th St NW, Washington, DC 20045. **202-638-4396**

RESOURCES FOR THE FUTURE. 1755 Massachusetts Ave NW, Washington, DC 20036. **202-462-4400.** Charles Hitch, president. Herbert Morton, public affairs officer. Kent A Price, information officer. A foundation-supported social science research and education organization; performs and publishes primarily economics and policy research on questions of natural resources, energy, and environmental quality

RETAIL INFORMATION BUREAU. 60 E 9th St, New York, NY 10003. **212-673-0115**

THE RIPON SOCIETY. Suite 666, 800 18th St NW, Washington, DC 20003. **202-347-6477.** Glenn S Gerstell, president, **212-422-2660.** Dick Behn, editor, *Ripon Forum,* **617-242-4928.** Sandra L Thompson, managing director, **202-347-6477.** Steven D Livengood, assistant to president, **202-347-6477.** An organization of liberal Republicans who seek "to broaden [the] base of [the] Republican party with new and innovative ideas"

RUSSELL SAGE FOUNDATION. 230 Park Ave, New York, NY 10017. **212-949-8990.** Aaron Wildavsky, president. *Media contact.* John Applegath, director for publications and public information, **212-949-8984**

Founded in 1907 by Olivia Sage for the "improvement of social and living conditions in the United States," the foundation conducts and supports social research on public policy issues. Program areas include culture,

citizenship, institutions, and policy analysis. The foundation encourages "a high level of exchange and communication between academic social scientists and members of the journalism and law professions "

SALVATION ARMY. 120 W 14th St, New York, NY 10011. **212-620-4929.** Commissioner Bramwell Tripp, territorial commander. Brigadier Paul D Seiler, development secretary, **212-620-4547.** A religious organization providing social services, particularly to the destitute

SANE. 318 Massachusetts Ave NE, Washington, DC 20002. **202-546-4868.** Seymour Melman, cochairman of the board, **212-280-2936.** David Cortwright, executive director, **202-546-4868**

This peace organization began as an opponent of nuclear proliferation and the arms race as far back as the 1950s. It has since expanded to become one of the major advocates of reduced military spending and economic conversion

SAVE THE CHILDREN FEDERATION. 48 Wilton Rd, Westport, CT 06880. **203-226-7271.** David L Guyer, president. Harold Littledale, coordinator, public information, Ext 213

An "international, nonprofit, nonsectarian, nongovernmental organization dedicated to helping disadvantaged children, their families and their communities in the US and overseas," the federation arranges financial sponsorship of needy children, particularly overseas. It has no relation to Save Our Children

SAVE OUR CHILDREN. Miami Beach, FL 33140. **305-538-0421.** Anita Bryant's anti-gay-rights-campaign organization; no relation to Save the Children Foundation

SCIENTISTS COMMITTEE FOR OCCUPATIONAL HEALTH. 5C Barrett Dr, Kendall Park, NJ 08824

SCIENTISTS' INSTITUTE FOR PUBLIC INFORMATION. 355 Lexington Ave, New York, NY 10017. **212-661-9110.** Fred Jerome, public information director. *See also* SCIENCE AND TECHNOLOGY

SECURITIES INDUSTRY ASSOCIATION. 19th Floor, 20 Broad St, New York, NY 10005. **212-425-2700**

SIERRA CLUB. 530 Bush St, San Francisco, CA 94108. **415-981-8634.** Mike McCloskey, executive director, Ext 476. Jim Belsey, public relations consultant, Ext 523

Although in the vanguard of most environmentalist issues, the Sierra Club is generally respected, even by opponents, as a responsible spokesman for its issues. In addition to advocacy and other environmental action, the club sponsors programs of exploration, field trips, and educational projects. It's 180,000 members are organized in regional chapters and groups throughout the country

SMALL TOWNS INSTITUTE. PO Box 517, Ellensburg, WA 98926. Anne Smith Denman, codirector, **509-963-3221** (mornings). A nonprofit organization that publishes a monthly news journal, *Small Town,* as an educational and information service for its members, who are concerned with the problems involved in maintaining the quality of life in small towns and rural areas

SOCIAL ADVOCATES FOR YOUTH. 655 Castro St, 5, Mountain View, CA 94041. **415-965-4166.** Debra Manchester, executive director. *Contact.* Jack Harrington, **415-928-3222.** Runs crisis intervention, alcohol education and legal counseling programs for youth, with the emphasis on providing "alternatives to the juvenile justice system through community diversion and deliquency prevention"

SOCIAL REGISTER ASSOCIATION. 381 Park Ave, New York, NY 10016

SOCIETY OF CERTIFIED CONSUMER CREDIT EXECUTIVES. 7405 University Dr, St Louis, MO 63130. **314-727-4045.** Mary Alice Minney, associate administrator. A professional society devoted to education and research on behalf of the consumer credit industry

SOCIETY FOR CULTURAL RELATIONS USA-USSR. 1154 N Western Ave, Los Angeles, CA 90029. **213-469-7525**

SOCIETY OF FORMER SPECIAL AGENTS OF THE FBI. 2754 Graybar Bldg, 420 Lexington Ave, New York, NY 10017. **212-687-6222.** Frances M Keough, executive secretary. A fraternal organization

SOCIETY FOR INDIVIDUAL LIBERTY. Box 1147, Warminister, PA 18974. **215-672-4133.** David Walter, **215-672-3892,** and Don Ernsberger, **215-675-6830,** codirectors. A libertarian educational and service organization "dedicated to the principles of individualism, rationality, and the promotion of personal and social freedom, [with] 5,000 members working in 200 clubs throughout the country"

SOCIETY OF MOTION PICTURE AND TELEVISION ENGINEERS. 862 Scarsdale Ave, Scarsdale, NY 10583

SOCIETY OF THE PLASTICS INDUSTRY. 355 Lexington Ave, New York, NY 10017. **212-931-1230**

SOCIETY OF REAL ESTATE APPRAISERS. 7 S Dearborn, Chicago, IL 60605. **312-346-7422.** James V Morgan, director. Bonnie O'Brien, director, public relations. Bob Morin (901 Watergate Bldg, 2600 Virginia Ave NW, Washington, DC 20037) public affairs director, **202-298-8497** This independent organization of professional real estate appraisers and analysts maintains contact with 26 federal agencies that use the services of real estate appraisers. It "acts as an intermediary when an individual member has problems with an agency"

SOLAR ENERGY INDUSTRIES ASSOCIATION. Suite 632, 1001 Connecticut Ave NW, Washington, DC 20036. **202-293-1000.** John Blake III, executive director. Susan Drieband, director, communications, **202-293-1001.** Night line: **301-585-6581.**

The association represents manufacturers and contractors, interested students, and companies involved in research in the solar energy field. It publishes a directory of manufacturers, *Solar Industry Index.* Like the industry, the association is only a few years old

SOLAR ENERGY RESEARCH AND EDUCATION FOUNDATION. **202-293-2982** or **215-942-3123.** Randy Dyer, executive director. Don L Kirkpatrick, technical director

SONGWRITERS RESOURCES AND SERVICES. 6381 Hollywood Blvd, Hollywood, CA 90028. **213-463-7178.** Helen King, president. A nonprofit membership organization of 1200 songwriters that has as its principal function the registration of songs; also provides member services

SOURCE, INC. PO Box 21066, Washington, DC 20009. **202-387-1145**

SOUTHERN CHRISTIAN LEADERSHIP CONFERENCE NATIONAL (SCLC NATIONAL). 334 Auburn Ave NE, Atlanta, GA 30303. **404-522-1420.** Tyrone Brooks, national communications director. Night line: **404-755-4956.** The leading southern-based civil rights organization

SOUTHERN REGIONAL COUNCIL. 75 Marietta St NW, Atlanta, GA 30303.

404-522-8764. Steve Suitts, executive director. A public interest group, chartered in 1944, campaigning for equal opportunity and justice for all people in the Southern region; special concerns are the black minority and the poor of all races

SPACE RESEARCH INSTITUTE. Norwich University, Northfield, VT 05663. **802-485-5011**

SPECIAL LIBRARIES ASSOCIATION. 235 Park Ave S, New York, NY 10003. **212-777-8136**

STANFORD RESEARCH INSTITUTE CENTER FOR OCCUPATIONAL SAFETY AND HEALTH. 1611 N Kent St, Arlington, VA 22209. **703-524-2053**

STOCK TRANSFER ASSOCIATION. 16th Floor, Chase Manhattan Bank, 1 New York Plz, New York, NY 10015. **212-676-3816**

STOCKHOLDERS OF AMERICA, INC. 1825 Connecticut Ave NW Washington, DC 20009. **202-783-3430**

SUBURBAN ACTION INSTITUTE. 257 Park Ave S, New York, NY 10010. **212-777-9119.** Paul Davidoff, executive director. George Dryfoos, information director This nonprofit institute for research and action in the suburbs advocates housing opportunities for minority or lower income persons. It researches exclusionary zoning and has successfully litigated against such practices

TASK FORCE AGAINST NUCLEAR POLLUTION. Box 1817, Washington, DC 20013. **202-547-6661.** *Press contact.* Franklin L Gage, principal offical. *Branch office contact.* Dr John W Gofman (Box 11207, San Francisco CA 94101), **415-664-1933.** A lobbying group that tries to pressure Congress to ban nuclear power, promote solar power, and mandate increased energy efficiency

TAX ANALYSTS AND ADVOCATES. 2369 N Taylor St, Arlington, VA 22207. **703-522-1800.** Thomas F Field, executive director. James S Byrne, editor, *Tax Notes* This public interest law firm and media information service publishes a weekly news magazine, *Tax Notes.* It assists journalists "working on tax stories by means of a program of individualized counseling and research, including compilation of data, legal and economic analysis, and maintenance of the group's roster of volunteer consultants, which contains the names of almost 500 tax professionals "

TAX COUNCIL. 1120 Connecticut Ave NW, Washington, DC 20036. **202-331-8352**

TAX FOUNDATION, INC. 50 Rockefeller Plz, New York, NY 10020. **212-582-0880** (also night line). Robert C Brown, executive vice-president. Elsie M Watters, director, research. C L Harriss, consultant. *Contacts.* Robert C Brown, Elsie M Watters, and C Lowell Harriss, New York; Maynard H Waterfield and Edward A Sprague, Washington, DC, **202-296-8830.**

The foundation is a publicly supported, nonprofit organization founded in 1937 to engage in nonpartisan research and public education on the fiscal and management aspects of government. Its purpose is to aid in the development of more efficient and economical government

TAX REFORM RESEARCH GROUP. 133 C St SE, Washington, DC 20003. **202-544-1710.** Robert M Brandon, director. *Contacts.* Timothy Ward or Robert McIntyre, (staff attorney): Diane Fuchs, state and local tax reform

The group is a Nader organization working for reform of both the federal income tax and local property taxes. It accumulates data, publishes studies and articles on tax reform, presents expert testimony before legislative and executive bodies, and helps to organize and work with citizens groups to build pressure for tax reform on the local level. The group publishes a monthly newspaper, *People & Taxes*

TAXATION WITH REPRESENTATION. 2369 N Taylor St., Arlington, VA 22207. **703-527-6877.** Thomas F Field, executive director. *Press contact.* Thomas J Reese, legislative director, (h). **202-529-1252.** A public interest taxpayers' lobby that works for reform of the federal tax system; publishes a tax reform voting scale that rates each member of Congress on his or her support for tax reform. *See also* Tax Analysts and Advocates

THE TOBACCO INSTITUTE. 1776 K St NW, Washington, DC **202-457-4800.** Horace R Kornegay, principal executive officer, **202-457-4830.** William Kloepfer, Jr, senior vice-president, **202-457-4861.** A trade association representing the major cigarette manufacturers that aims to "foster public understanding of the smoking and health controversy, and public knowledge of the historic role of tobacco and its place in the national economy"

TRANSPORTATION ASSOCIATION OF AMERICA. 1100 17th St NW, Washington, DC 20036. **202-296-2470**

TRAVELERS AID ASSOCIATION OF AMERICA. Suite 600, 701 Lee St, Des Plaines, IL 60016. **312-298-9390.** *See also* TRAVELERS AID SOCIETIES

TWENTIETH CENTURY FUND. 41 E 70th St, New York, NY 10021. **212-535-4441.** M J Rossant, director. Alfred Salvatore, public information officer

This nonprofit research foundation conducts studies of economic, political, and social institutions and issues. Its research is policy-oriented and is aimed at a general, rather than an academic, audience

ULI—THE URBAN LAND INSTITUTE. 1200 18th St NW, Washington, DC 20036. **202-338-6800**

UNDERWRITERS LABORATORIES, INC. 207 E Ohio St, Chicago, IL 60611. **312--642-6969.** Baron Whitaker, president. *Press contact.* Robert Van Brundt

A not-for-profit organization, UL maintains testing laboratories and inspection centers in 200 cities in the US and abroad. It runs a variety of product safety tests and issues standards on numerous products and materials. It also issues widely distributed annual directories of products that have met recognized safety requirements; over 18,000 manufacturers currently have their products listed by UL. Offices and testing stations are located in Chicago, IL Northbrook, IL; Melville, NY; Santa Clara, CA; and Tampa FL

UNITED CEREBRAL PALSY ASSOCIA-TIONS, INC. 66 E 34th St, New York, NY 10016. **212-481-6300.** Earl H Cunerd, executive director, **212-481-6316.** Sara W Kelley, public relations director, **212-481-6344.** Night line: **201-391-8190.** A national voluntary health agency

UNITED DAIRY INDUSTRY ASSOCIA-TION. 6300 N River Rd, Rosemont, IL 60018. **312-696-1860.** John W Sliter, executive vice-president, Ext 200. John F Brookman, director, committee, **312-696-1880.**

A trade association representing the dairy farmers in 40 states, dedicated to "promotion of dairy products on a nonbrand basis to increase the income of the investing members of UDIA—the total promotion effort includes advertising, research, sales promotion, communications, and marketing"

UNITED FRESH FRUIT AND VEGE-TABLE ASSOCIATION. 1019 19th St NW, Washington, DC 20036. **202-293-9210.** Bernard J Imming, president. Roger J Stroh, vice-president, public affairs. Richard A

Galloway, vice president, administration. John D Nelson, Jr, vice-president, member and consumer services

This trade association represents all of the fresh fruit and vegetable industry, including growers, shippers, wholesalers, terminal market operators, retailers, and packagers. It serves as advocate for the industry and as "a focusing point through which joint action can be taken on any problem of general interest to the industry"

UNITED JEWISH APPEAL. 1290 Avenue of the Americas, New York, NY 10019. **212-757-1500.**

UNITED KLANS OF AMERICA. Box 2369, Tuscaloosa, AL 35401. Robert Shelton, Imperial Wizard, (h) **205-339-1930.** *See also* Ku Klux Klan

UNITED NATIONS ASSOCIATION OF THE USA (UNA-USA). 300 E 42nd St, New York, NY 10017. **212-697-3232.** Robert M Ratner, president. Beth Rosenthal, public information service. *Contacts.* Ellie King, inquiries related to the UNA, its publications, and its activities; Beth Rosenthal, inquiries related to the United Nations and its related programs and agencies; and Patti Miller, inquiries related to National United Nations Day observance. *Washington (Capitol Hill) office.* Roger J Cochetti, inquiries related to the United Nations and multilateral affairs in Congress and the executive branch, **202-547-6645**

This independent, nonprofit, nonpartisan organization provides "factual information on the UN and UN issues through information, research, education, and community action programs." It seeks to stimulate American public opinion in support of constructive US policies in the United Nations

UNITED NATIONS INFORMATION CENTER. 2101 L St NW, Washington, DC 20037. **202-296-5370.** *See also* World.

UNITED NEGRO COLLEGE FUND. 500 E 62nd St, New York, NY 10021. **212-644-9600.** Christopher F Edley, executive director, **212-644-9607.** Joseph A Mehan, director, communication, **212-644-9616.** Night line: **203-322-8175.** A nonprofit fund-raising organization for the support of predominantly black, private member colleges

UNITED SERVICE ORGANIZATIONS (USO). 237 E 52nd St, New York, NY 10022. **212-751-3020**

UNITED STATES BREWERS ASSOCIA-TION, INC. 1750 K St NW, Washington, DC 20006. **202-466-2400.** Henry B King, president. Chester E Gardner, vice-president, communications, **202-466-2400** or **3835.** (h) **703-273-8346.** John Rost, public relations counsel. Catherine Marshall, writer-editor

A nonprofit trade organization of brewers and companies supplying the brewing industry, the USBA, founded in 1862, claims to be the oldest trade association in the US, representing the producers of more than 90 percent of all beer in the US. It has field representatives in 49 states

US CB RADIO ASSOCIATION. 682 Prospect Ave, Hartford, CT 06105. **203-736-6035.** *Press contact.* John Henderson

US COMMITTEE FOR UNICEF. 331 E 38th St, New York, NY 10016. **212-686-5522.** C Lloyd Bailey, executive director. Robert Brennan, director, communications. Johanna Grant, public relations coordinator. Night line: **212-686-5528.** A service organization that informs Americans about the United Nations Children's Fund and solicits contributions for it

US CONFERENCE OF MAYORS/NA-TIONAL LEAGUE OF CITIES. 1620 I St NW, Washington, DC 20006. **202-293-7330.** John J Gunther, executive director. Rose Bratton, research and information center

This organization representing most US cities and mayors seeks to help Congress and the executive branch formulate national municipal policy. It provides technical and research services for members and acts as spokesman for the city. It has an active publications program, including a directory of mayors

US INDEPENDENT TELEPHONE ASSOCIATION. 1801 K St NW-1201, Washington, DC 20006. **202-872-1200.** George E Pickett, executive vice-president. Gorman D McMullen, director, public relations. The trade association for independent (non-Bell-system) telephone companies

THE UNITED STATES TRADEMARK ASSOCIATION. 6 E 45th St, New York, NY 10017. **212-986-5880.** Dorothy Fey, executive director. Joan Stein, information assistant (trademark status, generic words). Mary McGrane, communications assistant (speakers' bureau). An organization representing major trademark owners and others concerned, particularly about the proper use of trade names; publishes *Trademark Reporter*, a legal publication

US WATER RESOURCES COUNCIL. Suite 800, 2120 L St NW, Washington, DC 20037. **202-254-6453.** Leo M Eisel, director, **202-254-6303.** Wanda M Phelan, public information officer, **202-254-6453.** A federal agency that encourages the conservation, development, and utilization of water and related land resources on a comprehensive and coordinated basis by federal, state, and local government and by private enterprise

THE UNITED STATES JAYCEES. PO Box 7, Tulsa, OK 74102. **918-584-2481.** Al Simensen, executive vice-president. *Press contact.* Sam Seever, executive director, public relations. Bill Babb, public relations manager. Steve Coury, editor, *Future Magazine.* A service organization of young men aged 17 to 36

UNITED WAY OF AMERICA. 801 N Fairfax St, Alexandria, VA 22314. **703-836-7100.** Night line: **703-836-7101.** William Aramony, national executive. Sandra Butler Harner, vice-president, communications. Alan Rubin, director, public information

United Way of America is the coordinating body for the 2300 United Way and United Fund agencies throughout the US and Canada. The local United Ways are the largest private funding sources for voluntary human services in their communities, raising a total of over $1 billion annually

UNIVERSAL DETECTIVE ASSOCIA-TION. Box 8180, Universal City, CA 91608. **213-848-5513.** William T Patterson, director. "An international fraternal membership organization dedicated to law and order"

UNIVERSAL SERIALS AND BOOK EX-CHANGE, INC. 3335 V St NE, Washington, DC 20018. **202-529-2555.** Alice Dulany Ball, executive director, (h). **202-362-6047.** Elaine A Kurtz, associate executive director, **202-529-2555.** Alice Norton, public relations consultant, **203-438-4064.** A Clearinghouse for the redistribution of publications to libraries (a nonprofit membership corporation)

URBAN ALLIANCE. *See*: National Council for Urban Economic Development

URBAN INSTITUTE. 2100 M St NW, Washington, DC 20036. **202-223-1950**

VARIETY CLUBS INTERNATIONAL. Suite 23-C, Tower 58, 58 W 58th St, New York, NY 10019. **212-751-8600**

VETERANS OF FOREIGN WARS OF THE UNITED STATES. Broadway at 34th

St, Kansas City, MO 64111. **816-756-3390.** Dr John Wasylik, Commander-in-Chief (Commander-in-chief changes each August during the national convention). John L Smith, director, public relations, Ext 150. Night line: **816-561-1692.** Thorne (Tip) Marlow, public affairs director. *Washington office.* 200 Maryland Ave, Washington, DC 20002. **202-543-2239.** A social, fraternal, and service organization for veterans who served overseas

VIETNAM VETERANS CENTER. 1910 K St NW, Washington, DC 20008. **202-785-1158**

VIETNAM VETERANS AGAINST THE WAR. PO Box 20184, Chicago, IL 60620. **312-651-1583**

This national veterans' organization seeks total amnesty for all war resisters, a single type of discharge for all veterans, and a "livable GI bill". Far from disappearing after the end of the war, VVAW has grown increasingly radical and militant

VOLUNTEERS OF AMERICA. 525 Rhode Island Ave NE, Washington, DC 20002. **202-529-1961**

VOTER EDUCATION PROJECT. 52 Fairlie St NW, Atlanta, GA 30303. **404-522-7495.** WATS line for press: **800-241-0730.** Valencia Y Peters, director, communications

IZAAK WALTON LEAGUE OF AMERICA. 1800 N Kent St, Arlington, VA 22209. **703-527-1818**

WAR REGISTERS LEAGUE. 339 Lafayette St, New York, NY 10012. **212-228-0450.** Norma Becker, chairperson

Regional offices

WRL/West. 1380 Howard St, San Francisco, CA 94103. **415-626-6976**

WRL/Southeast. 108 Purefoy Rd, Chapel Hill, NC 27514. **919-967-7244**

A pacifist organization advocating radical social change through nonviolent means, the league is also active in the areas of disarmament, human rights, economics, nuclear weapons, and nuclear power

WAR TAX RESISTANCE INTERNA-TIONAL. 3rd Floor, 330 Lafayette St, New York, NY 10012. **212-477-2970.** Mailing address: Box 226, Glen Oaks PO, New York, NY 11004. Henry A Felison, Jr, executive director. Sallie Marx, chairperson, **212-929-4833.** Night line: **212-347-8172.** Organizes American nationals in the US and around the world to refuse to pay federal taxes used for the military

WASHINGTON BUSINESS GROUP ON HEALTH. 605 Pennsylvania Ave SE, Washington, DC 20003. **202-547-6700.** Willis B Goldbeck, director

WASHINGTON CENTER FOR THE STUDY OF SERVICES. Suite 201, 1910 K St NW, Washington, DC 20006. **202-785-2380.** Robert M Krughoff, president. Gillian Rudd, vice-president. Evaluates consumer services in the Washington metropolitan area and publishes results in a quarterly magazine and other publications

WASHINGTON INTERNATIONAL CENTER. 1630 Crescent Pl NW, Washington, DC 20009. **202-332-1025.** James A Coughlin, executive director. John G Blair, editor, *International Exchange News.* Provides orientation for foreign visitors to the US under government or private agency sponsorship

WATER POLLUTION CONTROL FEDERATION. 2626 Pennsylvania Ave NW, Washington, DC 20037. **202-337-2500.** Robert A Cahnam, executive secretary. Philip A Ridgely, manager, advertising and public relations. A trade association representing engineers, manufacturers, government officials, and others interested in water pollution control systems

WATER RESOURCES CONGRESS. 955 L'Enfant Plz-1101, Washington, DC 20024. **202-488-0688**

THE WILDERNESS SOCIETY. 1901 Pennsylvania Ave NW, Washington, DC 20006. **202-293-2732.** Celia M Hunter, executive director. Roger Scholl, deputy director. Clif Merritt 4260 E Evans Ave, Denver, CO. 80222, Colorado office **303-758-2266.** A national, nonprofit conservation organization whose primary function is the safeguarding and preservation of the American wilderness

WOMEN IN COMMUNITY SERVICE, INC. 1730 Rhode Island Ave NW, Washington, DC 20036. **202-293-1343.** Mary A Hallaren, executive director. Florence Selden, community relations

This national coalition of volunteers from various faiths, races, and ethnic groups seeks "to motivate young people at the bottom of the economic ladder to achieve more satisfying lives." It recruits and screens applicants for the Job Corps. The coalition has 200 local units throughout the US

WOMEN'S CAMPAIGN FUND. 122 Maryland Ave NE, Washington, DC 20002. **202-547-0444.** Anne Zill, chairperson, **202-546-3732.** Carol Randles, director, **202-547-0444.** A nonprofit, national organization "working for the election of progressive women to public office through provision of cash contributions and professional campaign services"

WOMEN'S EQUITY ACTION LEAGUE (WEAL). Suite 822, 805 15th St NW, Washington, DC 20005. **202-638-4560.** Eileen P Thornton, (78 Alberta Ave, Trenton, NJ 08619) national president. **609-292-2470.** (h) **609-586-2741.** Joan King, editor and communications director, **202-638-4560.** Night line: **301-589-4571**

This public affairs organization lobbies and campaigns for women's rights and legislative issues, including the Equal Rights Amendment, Social Security reform, education, career development, equal pay and credit, health, insurance, and enforcement of federal regulatory powers. In addition, WEAL maintains a "Talent Bank Roster" of members qualified for high appointive office

WOMEN'S INTERNATIONAL LEAGUE FOR PEACE AND FREEDOM (WILPF). US Section: 1213 Race St, Philadelphia, PA 19107. **215-563-7110.** Naomi Marcus, national president. Dorothy R Steffens, executive director, **215-789-1439** or **215-569-1289.** Rae Cohn, publicity committee chairperson, **215-742-3834.** An international peace organization whose goal is to unite women in all countries who are opposed to every kind of war, exploitation, and oppression; advocates universal disarmament

WOMEN'S LEGAL DEFENSE FUND. 1010 Vermont Ave, NW, Washington, DC 20005. **202-638-1123.** *Contact.* Theresa H. Bentz

THE WOMEN'S LOBBY. Suite 312, 201 Massachusetts Ave, Washington, DC 20002. **202-547-0444.** *Contacts.* Carol Burris, Kristina Kiehl. A lobbying group concentrating on important women's rights legislation

WOMEN'S RIGHTS PROJECT— CENTER FOR LAW AND SOCIAL POLICY. 1751 N St NW, Washington, DC 20036. **202-872-0670.** *Press contacts.* Marcia Greenberger, director, Ms Schiffer, and Ms Kohn. A nonprofit, public interest law firm supported by grants from private foundations; fights sex discrimination by providing lawyers for cases involving women's issues

WORKERS DEFENSE LEAGUE AND FUND FOR HUMAN RIGHTS. 84 5th Ave., New York, NY 10011. **212-691-7660.** Rowland Watts, president, Workers Defense League, and secretary-treasurer, Fund for Human Rights. Alice D Wolfson, secretary/director, William E Hafer, director, employee protection program. Thomas W R Catlow, director, veterans' assistance program

This public affairs organization says it defends the legal rights of persons who have difficulty obtaining adequate representation because of economic level, nationality, religion, age, sex, or minority status. It places special emphasis on job-related or veterans' problems

WORLD FUTURE SOCIETY. 4916 St Elmo Ave, Bethesda, Washington, DC 20014. **301-656-8274.** *Contact.* Sally Cornish

WORLD INSTITUTE COUNCIL. 777 United Nations Plz, New York, NY 10017. **212-661-0884.** Julius Stulman, president. A research and development institute to assist government and educational organizations toward innovative ideas for the solution of human problems; supports research in "human ecology"

WORLD JEWISH CONGRESS. 15 E 84th St, New York, NY 10028. **212-879-4500**

WORLD WITHOUT WAR COUNCIL. 175 5th Ave, New York, NY **212-674-2085.** Robert Pickus, president **415-845-1992**

YOUNG AMERICANS FOR FREEDOM. Box 1002, Route 1, Woodland Rd, Sterling, VA 22170. **703-450-5162**

YOUNG MEN'S CHRISTIAN ASSOCIATIONS OF THE USA, NATIONAL COUNCIL. 291 Broadway, New York, NY 10007. **212-374-2000.** Dr Robert W Harlan, national executive director, **212-374-2172.** Joe A Pisarro, executive director, office of communications, **212-374-2163.** The national representative organization for the 1834 YMCAs in the US

YOUNG MEN'S AND YOUNG WOMEN'S HEBREW ASSOCIATIONS. 1395 Lexington Ave, New York, NY 10028. **212-427-6000**

YOUNG REPUBLICANS NATIONAL FEDERATION. 310 1st St SE, Washington, DC 20003. **202-484-6680**

YOUNG WOMEN'S CHRISTIAN ASSOCIATION OF THE USA, NATIONAL BOARD. 600 Lexington Ave, New York, NY 10022. **212-753-4700.** Sara-Alyce P Wright, executive director. Kit Kolchin, public relations. A national service organization representing local YWCAs throughout the country

ZERO POPULATION GROWTH, INC.
1346 Connecticut Ave NW, Washington, DC 20036. **202-785-0100.** Roy Morgan, executive director. Sandy Schline, public information

specialist, (h) **301-530-9275.** Peters Willson, political representative, (h) **202-265-6523**

This national public affairs and educational organization advocates stabilizing the populations in the US and the world at present levels, reducing the consumption of resources, and establishing sound growth policies. Its programs include advocating a

US population policy, lobbying for the availability of family planning services, revising the US immigration policy, promoting the right to abortion, lobbying for increased funding for contraceptive research, promoting ways of dealing with the problem of teenage pregnancy, and training teachers in population dynamics

POLITICS

MAJOR PARTIES

For minor party contact information, *see* SPECIAL INTERESTS.

Democratic National Committee

1625 Massachusetts Ave NW, Washington, DC 20036. **202-797-5900** (all DNC personnel). Press night line: **202-797-7466**

Press Office

Press Secretary. Charlotte Scot
Deputy Press Secretary. Debra McGhee
Director, Radio and Television. Flawn Williams
Assistant. John Meehan

Chairperson's Division

Chairman. Kenneth M Curtis
Vice-Chairman. Carmela La Cayo
Vice-Chairman. Coleman Young
Deputy Chairman. Ben Brown
Secretary. Dorothy Bush

Executive Director's Division

Executive Director (in charge of program and policy management). Paul D Curtis

Finance Division

Treasurer. Joel McCleary
Assistant Treasurer. Le Grand Mellon
Finance Director. Hope Boonshaft
Deputy Treasurer (political action committees). Gerald K McFadden
Deputy Treasurer (small donors). Tricia Segall

Special Events Director. Marlys Soderberg
Assistant. Nick Kostopolus

Administrative Division

Administrator. J D Nelson
Comptroller. Patricia Whiteaker
Comptroller's Administrative Assistant (in charge of Federal Elections Commission report). Marie D Kelly
Legal Counsel. Michael J Grealy
Legal Counsel's Administrative Assistant. Susan Mondale

Campaign Services Division

Director. Mary Schecklehoff
Director of Special Events. James E (Chip) Carter III (duties include speaking engagements)
Director of Speakers' Bureau. Shirley Bitting
Research. Mary (Buff) Hunter

Political Coordination Division

Director. Charlotte Wilmer
Director of Nationalities Division. Andrew Valuchek

Field Operations Division

(Responsible for development of an overall plan of action for communications between Washington and Democratic party leaders throughout the country)
Director. David Dunn
Executive Director of the Association of State Democratic Chairpersons. Beegie Truesdale
Director of Young Democrats. George (Nick) Nicholson
Mid-Atlantic Regional Coordinator (District

of Columbia, Maryland, New Jersey, Pennsylvania, Virginia, West Virginia). Joyce Clements
Deep South Regional Coordinator (Alabama, Florida, Georgia, Mississippi). Ralph E Hamilton
Central South Regional Coordinator (Kentucky, North Carolina, South Carolina, Tennessee). Cher Brooks
Southwestern Regional Coordinator (Arkansas, Louisiana, New Mexico, Oklahoma, Texas). Harriet Peppel
Northeastern Regional Coordinator (Connecticut, Maine, Massachusetts, New Hampshire, New York, Rhode Island, Vermont). Paul Sheehan
North Central Regional Coordinator (Illinois, Indiana, Michigan, Minnesota). Tim Davis
Far-Western Regional Coordinator (California, Alaska, Hawaii, Idaho, Nevada, Oregon, Washington). Kevin Smith
States not listed above fall under the nearest region

Republican National Committee

310 1st SE, Washington, DC 20003. **202-484-6500**
Chairman. Senator Bill Brock. **202-484-6700**
Press Secretary. Pete Teeley. **202-484-6550**
Communications Staff. Barbara Chiasson Gleason, **202-484-6690.** Bill Hart, **202-484-6685.** Etta Fielek, **202-484-6687.** Edwin B Greene, Jr, **202-484-6545.** William H Kling, **204-484-6725.** Jack Bonner, **202-484-6573.** Susan Eddington, **202-484-6546**

Divisions and Chiefs

Accounting. Jay Banning. **202-484-6755**
Administration. Sarah Brady. **202-484-6750**
Advisory Council. Roger Semerad

Black Campaign Support. Robert Wright.
202-484-6520

Campaign Division. Charlie Black.
202-484-6693

Campaign Materials. Onis Johnson.
202-484-6553

CoChairperson. Mary Crisp. 202-484-6735

College Republicans. Kelly Sinclair.
202-484-6527

Comptroller. Arlene Triplett. 202-484-6560

Computer Services. Murray Dickman.
202-484-6753

Conventions. Jo Good. 202-484-6630

Counselor. Ben Cotten. 202-484-6704

Engineer. Roy Rusk. 202-484-6511

Executive Assistant. Ed Cowling.
202-484-6706

Facilities. George Lewis. 202-484-6534

Field Operations. Ladonna Younglund.
202-484-6710

Finance. Ted Welch. 202-484-6730

Governor's Association. Ralph Griffith.
202-484-6620

Graphic Services. Otto Wolff. 202-484-6786

Library. Adrienne Kosciusko. 202-484-6626

Local Elections. Joe Gaylord. 202-484-6660

National Black Council. Elizabeth Pillow.
202-484-6664

National Federation of Republican Women.
Pat Hutar. 202-484-6670

National Republican Heritage Group. Jay
Niemczyk. 202-484-6760

Personnel. Doug Winn. 202-484-6508

Phone Banks. Polly James. 202-484-6577

Political Action Committee. Charles
MacManus. 202-484-6730

Print Shop and Mail. Ervin Cook.
202-484-6590

Reception Desk. Ruth Miller. 202-484-6718

Research. Michael Baroody. 202-484-6614

Republican National Hispanic Concerns.
Ileana Fresen. 202-484-6569

Security. James Caudill. 202-484-6719

Senior Citizens. Phil Guarino. 202-484-6543

Speakers' Bureau. A B Hermann.
202-484-6697

Special Projects. Bill Russo. 202-484-6585

Supply Room. Onis Johnson. 202-484-6553

Sustaining Program. Leah Geraghty.
202-484-6643

Telephone Services. Frances Howle.
202-484-6555

Young Republicans. Jim Byrnes.
202-484-6680

Alphabetic Staff Roster

Adams, Richard. Field operations.
202-484-6710

Agnew, Ann C. Research. 202-484-6652

Alford, Valerie. Computer service.
202-484-6594

Allen, Donald K. Administration.
202-484-6518

Alley, Carolyn. Chairman's office.
202-484-6700

Anderson, Deborah A. Word processing.
202-484-6656

Anderson, Katherine M. Comptroller.
202-484-6560

Asbell, Fred T. Special projects.
202-484-6585

Augustin, Jacques. Facilities. 202-484-6515

Bach, Paul H. Phone banks. 202-484-6577

Bailey, Charles. Field force. 202-484-6710

Bailey, Kenneth. Local elections.

Black, Charles. Campaign division.
202-484-6693

Banning, Jay C. Accounting. 202-484-6755

Baroody, Michael E. Research. 202-484-6614

Bass, Sandy B. Phone banks. 202-484-6577

Bathanazas, Joyce M. Telephone and telegraph. 202-484-6500

Bathanazas, Sylvania. Computer services.

Bell, Edward W. Security. 202-484-6718

Beringer, Barry. Research.

Berry, Phyllis. Black campaign support.
202-484-6520

Blanco, Mary F. Computer services.
202-484-6594

Boanton, Paul F. Sustaining. 202-484-6643

Bolten, John. Research.

Bolten, Nancy. Sustaining. 202-484-6643

Bonner, Jack. Communications.
202-484-6573

Boyce, Mary. Word processing.
202-484-6656

Brady, Sarah K. General administration.
202-484-6750

Brock, William E. Chairman's office.
202-484-6700

Brooks, Claudia. Phone banks. 202-484-6577

Brown, Sandra. Women's federation.
202-484-6670

Browning, Carolyn. Chairman's office.
202-484-6700

Bulow, Katherine. Chairman's office.
202-484-6700

Burke, Elizabeth. Graphics services.
202-484-6786

Burke, Kevin. Print shop. 202-484-6590

Burke, Patricia. Finance. 202-484-6730

Burroughs, Harry. Computer services.
202-484-6594

Buzinski, Robert J. Field force. 202-484-6710

Byers, Buckley B. Finance. 202-484-6730

Byrnes, Jim. Young Republicans.

Cain, Jean. Phone banks. 202-484-6577

Cannady, Ruth. Word processing.
202-484-6656

Carabaia, Anthony. Phone banks.
202-484-6577

Carle, Robin. Local elections. 202-484-6600

Carmichael, Barbara. Cochairman's office.
202-484-6735

Carney, Jeb. Special projects. 202-484-6585

Carney, Vinnie Lainson. Chairman's office.
202-484-6747

Carpenter, Birch. Phone banks. 202-484-6577

Carroll, Joan. Heritage. 202-484-6760

Carroll, Patrick. Phone banks. 202-484-6577

Caudill, James. Security. 202-484-6718

Charnock, Ronald. Computer services.
202-484-6753

Chiasson, Barbara. Communications.
202-484-6550

Clark, Barbara. Retrieval. 202-484-6652

Collins, Lynn. Finance. 202-484-6720

Connolly, John C. Communications.
202-484-6545

Conradsen, Anne. Finance. 202-484-6730

Cook, Ervin. Print shop. 202-484-6590

Cornwell, Kevin. Precinct analysis.
202-484-6594

Cotten, Ben. Chairman's office.
202-484-6704

Cowling, Ed. Chairman's office.
202-484-6706

Crisp, Mary. Cochairman's office.
202-484-6785

Crosby, Scott. Phone banks. 202-484-6577

Crunkleton, Penelope. Conventions.
202-484-6630

Cudlip, Chick. Chairman's office.
202-484-6613

Curseen, Michael. Facilities. 202-484-6515

Cusani, Carole. Special projects.

Dalisera, Diane. Sustaining. 202-484-6643

Davenport, Joan M. Speakers' bureau.
202-484-6697

Davis, John. Sustaining. 202-484-6643

Dean, Prentice. Computer services.
202-484-6594

Deforest, Jane A. Chairman's office.
202-484-6704

Demarest, David F. Local election.
202-484-6660

Dickey, Lelia S. Phone banks.

Dickman, Murray G. Computer services.
202-484-6753

Divall, Linda A. Local election. 202-484-6660

Dixon, Diana. Sustaining. 202-484-6643

Dole, Robin C. General administration.
202-484-6750

Dority, Dora A. Printing.

Doubrava, Richard J. Phone banks.
202-484-6577

Durfee, Norman. Sustaining. 202-484-6643

Dusch, Eileen L. Computer services.
202-484-6753

Dyer, William M Sr. Facilities. 202-484-6719

Eddington, Susan. Communication.
202-484-6546

Edwards, Lee A. Special projects.
202-484-6585

Ellis, Julian E. Facilities. 202-484-6719

Emery, Margaret L. Computer services.
202-484-6594

Fahey, Cynthia M. Research. 202-484-6614

Feldman, Joel P. Phone banks. 202-484-6577

Fernstrom, Maxene. Field force.
202-484-6710

Fielek, Etta. Communications. 202-484-6687

Fleig, Anne G. Retrieval. 202-484-6652

Fleishell, William. Art and copy.
202-484-6635

Fleurival, Marie G. Facilities. 202-484-6515

Foley, James. Phone banks. 202-484-6577

Fonrose, Michael. Facilities. 202-484-6515

Forward, Gail H. Conventions and meetings.
202-484-6630

Foster, Mary. Women's federation.
202-484-6670

Francies, Margaret E. Facilities.
202-484-6534

Fresen, Ileana. Hispanic assembly.
202-484-6569

Friday, Julia A. Computer services.
202-484-6594

Froberg, David. Phone banks. 202-484-6577

Galloway, George. Local elections.
202-484-6660

Garland, Teresa. NFRW. 202-484-6670

Garrett, Denise A. Cochairman's office.
202-484-6567

Gaylord, Joseph. Local elections.
202-484-6660

Gaylord, Molly. Special projects.
202-484-6585

Geraghty, Leah M. Sustaining. 202-484-6643

Gildemeister, Thomas R. Local elections.
202-484-6660

Gleason, Barbara C. Communications.
202-484-6690

Good, Josephine L. Conventions and meetings. 202-484-6630

Goodman, Pat. Advisory council.
202-484-6726

Gormley, Joseph. Phone banks.

Gray, William M. Chairman's office.
202-484-6700

Greene, Edwin B Jr. Communications.
202-484-6545

Griffith, Ralph E. Governor's associates.
202-484-6620

Grigor, Jane A. Local elections.
202-484-6660

Guarino, Philip A. Senior citizens.
202-484-6543

Guarino, Sarah. Senior citizens.
202-484-6543

Halbak, Constance C. Phone banks.
202-484-6577

Hall, Eric M. Print shop. 202-484-6590

Hall, Patricia. Phone banks. 202-484-6577

Hart, Bill. Communications. 202-484-6685

Hartman, Shirley. Women's federation.
202-484-6670

Hawkins, Jean B. Cochairman's office.
202-484-6602

Hermann, Albert B. Speakers' bureau.
202-484-6697

Hess, Elizabeth W. Retrieval. 202-484-6652

Heth, Marcus. Computer services.
202-484-6594

Hinds, Keith. Phone banks. 202-484-6577

Hogan, Catherine. Cochairman's office.
202-484-6566

Horowitz, Alan. Computer services.
202-484-6594

Hotman, Donna L. Computer services.
202-484-6594

Howard, Susanne. Cochairman's office.
202-484-6568

Howle, Frances G. Telephone and telegraph.
202-484-6500

Hueter, Kirstin Joan. Chairman's office.
202-484-6747

Hukari, Harvey H. Field force. 202-484-6710

Hutar, Patricia. Women's federation.
202-484-6670

Irby, Jacqueline S. Field force. 202-484-6710

Jackson, Cynthia. Computer services.
202-484-6594

Jackson, Gwen. Computer services.
202-484-6594

James, Cynthia. Computer services.
202-484-6594

James, Polly. Phone banks. 202-484-6577

Janoff, Barbara. Cochairman's office.
202-484-6565

Johnson, Onis. Campaign materials.
202-484-6553

Johnson, Tricia. Field force. 202-484-6710

Joiner, Kenneth. Precinct analysis.
202-484-6753

Jura, Danny. Research. 202-484-6650

Jurlega, Elena. Heritage. 202-484-6760

Keeney, Karen. Sustaining. 202-484-6643

Kennedy, Jacqueline. Computer services.
202-484-6594

Khauss, Mary. Field force. 202-484-6710

Kling, William. Communications.
202-484-6725

Klinge, Kenneth. Political. 202-484-6710

Khauss, Mary. Field force. 202-484-6710

Kosoiusko, Adrienne. Research. 202-484-6652

Kowlor, Phil. Research. 202-484-6753

Kramb, John. Computer services.
202-484-6594

Krawiecki, Robert. Phone banks.
202-484-6577

Leanard, Cliff. Young republicans.
202-484-6680

Lee, Douglas. Women's federation.
202-484-6670

Lee, William. Field force. 202-484-6710

Lewis, George. Facilities. 202-484-6534

Lune, Deborah A. Art and copy.
202-484-6635

Mack, Barbara. Chairman's office.
202-484-6674

Malone, Junius. Print shop. 202-484-6590

Manuel, Eleanor. Accounting. 202-484-6757

Martin, Joseph. Phone banks. 202-484-6577

Masters, Mark. Phone banks. 202-484-6577

McBride, Richard. Field force. 202-484-6710

McCabe, Mike. Information retrieval.
202-484-6654

McCaffrey, Barbara. Political Action Committees. 202-484-6730

McCarley, Diane. Sustaining. 202-484-6643

McCloskey, Ellen. Finance. 202-48´-6730

McCulley, Elizabeth. Phone banks.
202-484-6577

McDaniel, Charlotte. Phone banks.
202-484-6577

McDonough, Mamie. Chairman's office.
202-484-6747

McManus, Charles. Finance.
202-484-6720

McNeill, John. Black campaign support. 202-484-6520

Middleton, Maurice. Print shop. 202-484-6590

Milledge, Dorothea. Computer services

Miller, Patricia. Local elections. 202-484-6660

Miller, Ruth. Reception desk

Mills, Jasper. Facilities. 202-484-6718

Monroe, Charles. Print shop. 202-484-6590

Montoya, Demetrio. Local elections. 202-484-6660

Moorhead, Jay U. Local elections. 202-484-6660

Moorhead, Randall. Local elections. 202-484-6660

Morales, Marisel. Phone banks. 202-484-6577

Morris, Bradley. Phone banks. 202-484-6577

Morse, Leigh. Sustaining. 202-484-6643

Murphy, David. Computer services. 202-484-6594

Myers, Judy. Research. 202-484-6614

Nelson, Gilbert. Phone banks. 202-484-6577

Newell, Nikki. College republicans. 202-484-6527

Niemczyk, Jay. Heritage. 202-484-6760

Nimmer, Ann. Phone banks. 202-484-6577

Nogrady, Susan. Advisory council. 202-484-6726

Nystrom, Jacqueline. Campaign division. 202-484-6693

O'Dwyer, Mary. Major contributions. 202-484-6740

O'Leary, Maureen. Phone banks. 202-484-6577

Patterson, Kathy. Governor's associates. 202-484-6620

Peden, Ned. Political. 202-484-6693

Pendelson, George. Phone banks. 202-484-6577

Perkins, Robert. Finance. 202-484-6730

Phelps, Harold III. Phone banks. 202-484-6577

Pillow, Elizabeth. National Black council. 202-484-6664

Pilvelait, Hazel. Finance. 202-484-6730

Poff, Craig. Retrieval. 202-484-6652

Powell, Camilla S. Special projects. 202-484-6585

Price, Joy. Local election. 202-484-6660

Ray, Alexander C. Field force. 202-484-6710

Raye, Bruce. Mail processing. 202-484-6643

Reel, Anton E. Campaign division. 202-484-6628

Richmond, Steven. Computer services. 202-484-6594

Riddler, Elizabeth W. Chairman's office. 202-484-6700

Ridgeway, Adrian. Field force. 202-484-6710

Robertson, Bernice. NFRW. 202-484-6670

Roth, Tad. Research. 202-484-6652

Royster, Robert. Facilities. 202-484-6515

Rusk, Royce L. Engineer. 202-484-6511

Russo, Paul. Campaign. 202-484-6556

Russo, William. Special projects. 202-484-6585

Ryan, Chip. Local elections. 202-484-6660

Sacharanski, John. Research. 202-484-6653

Santiago, Esther. Heritage. 202-484-6569

Savit, Nancy. Advisory council. 202-484-6726

Sawyer, Michael. Information retrieval. 202-484-6650

Scamhorn, Quinn. Phone banks. 202-484-6577

Schnabl, Linda S. Local elections. 202-484-6660

Schneider, Laurie. Computer services. 202-484-6594

Schrote, Rachel D. Chairman's office. 202-484-6674

Scott, Frances. Communications. 202-484-6703

Semerad, Roger. Advisory council. 202-484-6726

Shea, Donald. Campaign. 202-484-6584

Skinker, Marj. Cochairman's office. 202-484-6566

Slack, Evelyn. Accounting. 202-484-6756

Smith, Edwin J. Senior citizens. 202-484-6543

Smith, Debbie J. Chairman's office. 202-484-6700

Smith, Philip S. Sustaining. 202-484-6643

Smutko, Joan S. Phone banks. 202-484-6577

Snead, Staci. Computer services. 202-484-6594

Stevens, John Jr. Field force. 202-484-6710

Stewart, Paul. Computer services. 202-484-6594

Stone, Roger. Young republicans. 202-484-6680

Taylor, Edward B. Phone banks. 202-484-6577

Teely, Peter E. Communications. 202-484-6550

Thawley, Nancy B. Finance. 202-484-6730

Thawley, Virginia. Phone banks. 202-484-6577

Thaxton, Richard R. Governor's associates. 202-484-6620

Tinsley, Mary. Campaign. 202-484-6693

Tinsley, Sarah. Special projects. 202-484-6560

Tompkins, Arnold. Research. 202-484-6652

Triplett, Arlene A. Comptroller. 202-484-6560

Turgeon, Mary E. Special projects. 202-484-6586

Turnette, Norman. Field force. 202-484-6710

Van Rest, Judy. Research. 202-484-6614

Vasiliou, Rosalie A. Research. 202-484-6650

Virta, Kay. Information retrieval. 202-484-6650

Walker, Jean. Phone banks. 202-484-6577

Watkins, Blanche D. Computer service. 202-484-6594

Weigel, Jane E. Phone banks. 202-484-6577

Welch, Ted. Finance. 202-484-6730

Whitfield, Dennis. Field force. 202-484-6710

Whitney, Margaret. Sustaining. 202-484-6643

Williams, Sally. Sustaining. 202-484-6643

Wilson, James E. Research. 202-484-6652

Winn, Douglas. Personnel director. 202-484-6508

Wirgau, Mark M. Local elections. 202-484-6660

Wolff, Otto. Graphic services. 202-484-6786

Woodley, Rissa. Cochairman. 202-484-6512

Woytassek, Janet. Computer services. 202-484-6594

Wright, Robert. Black campaign support. 202-484-6520

Younglund, Ladonna F. Field force. 202-484-6710

MAJOR PUBLIC POLLSTERS

AMERICAN INSTITUTE FOR PUBLIC OPINION. 53 Bank St, Princeton, NJ 08540. **609-924-9600.** George H Gallup. *See also* SPECIAL INTERESTS

BECKER RESEARCH CORPORATION. 120 Boylston St, Boston, MA 02116. **617-482-9079.** John F Becker

BUREAU OF SOCIAL SCIENCE RESEARCH, INC. 1990 M St NW, Washington, DC 20036. **202-223-4300.** Robert T Bower

CAMBRIDGE SURVEY RESEARCH. 10 Moulton St, Cambridge, MA 02138. **617-661-3212.** Patrick Caddell

ELECTION AND SURVEY UNIT, CBS NEWS. 524 W 57th St, New York, NY 10019. Warren Mitofsky, director

ELECTIONS RESEARCH CENTER. 1619 Massachusetts Ave NW, Washington, DC 20036. **202-387-6066.** Richard M Scammon

FIELD RESEARCH CORPORATION. 234 Front St, San Francisco, CA 94111. **415-392-5763.** Mervin D Field

GALLUP. *See* American Institute for Public Opinion

GMA RESEARCH CORPORATION. Suite 265, 5331 SW Macadam Ave, Portland, OR 97201. **503-248-9531.** Richard D Grant. *Bellevue Office.* Suite 110, Bellfield Office Park, 1621 114th SE, Bellevue, WA 98004

LOUIS HARRIS. 630 5th Ave, New York, NY 10020. **212-975-1600.** *See* SPECIAL INTERESTS for more detail

HART RESEARCH. 1529 O St NW, Washington, DC 20005. **202-234-5570.** Peter Hart

MARKET OPINION RESEARCH. Suite 601, 28 W Adams, Detroit, MI 48226. **313-963-2414.** Frederick P Currier

NBC NEWS POLL. 30 Rockefeller Plz, New York, NY 10020. **212-664-4452.** Sheldon Gawiser

A C NIELSEN COMPANY. *See* BUSINESS *and* INFORMATION AND RESEARCH SERVICES

OPINION RESEARCH CORPORATION. N Harrison St, Princeton, NJ 08540. **609-924-5900.** Harry O'Neill

RESPONSE ANALYSIS CORPORATION. Route 206, Research Park, Princeton, NJ 08540. **609-921-3333.** Reuben Cohen

THE ROPER ORGANIZATION. 1 Park Ave, New York, NY 10016. **212-679-3523.** Burns W Roper. *See also* BUSINESS

JOE B WILLIAMS RESEARCH. PO Box 170, Elmwood NE 68349. **402-994-5395.** Joe B Williams

YANKELOVICH, SKELLY, AND WHITE. 575 Madison Ave, New York, NY 10022. **212-752-7500.** Daniel Yankelovich

PEOPLE

THE MOST NEWSWORTHY AMERICANS

The following list of the most newsworthy Americans is based on a computer search of the data base of The Information Bank, performed by arrangement with *Names and Numbers*. The Information Bank, a subsidiary of the New York Times Company, abstracts and indexes some 62 newspapers and magazines.

The publications indexed for the purpose of this list included *Advertising Age, American Banker, American Scholar, Amsterdam News, Astronautics, Atlanta Constitution, Atlantic Monthly, Atlas, Automotive News, Barron's, Black Scholar, Black World, Bulletin of Atomic Scientists, Business Week, Chicago Defender, Chicago Tribune, Christian Science Monitor, Commentary, Commonweal, Consumer Reports, Current Biography, Ebony, Economist of London, Editor and Publisher, Far Eastern Economic Review, Financial Times, Forbes, Foreign Affairs, Foreign Policy, Fortune, Harper's, Industrial Research, Harvard Business Review, Houston Chronicle, Jet, Journal of Commerce, Latin America, Latin American Economic Review, Life, London Observer, London Sunday Times, Look, Los Angeles Times, McCall's, Manchester Guardian, Manhattan Tribune, Miami Herald, Middle East, Le Monde, Nation, National Journal, National Observer, National Review, New Republic, Newsday, Newsweek, New York, New Yorker, New York Review of Books, New York Times, Pittsburgh Courier, Psychology Today,*

Ramparts, Reader's Digest, San Francisco Chronicle, Saturday Review, Science, Scientific American, Sport, Sports Illustrated, Time, Times of London, Tuesday, US News and World Report, Variety, Village Voice, Vogue, Wall Street Journal, Washington Monthly, Washington Post, Womens Wear Daily.

The Information Bank computer search produced a list of 3990 persons mentioned most often in the abstracts of these publications. The following list of 1200 living persons was obtained from the longer basic list by sifting out certain classes of persons cited by the computer. Many persons were of such intense local interest that they were indexed frequently enough to be included in the list of 3990; most of these have been excluded except when evaluation showed the person to be of national interest or importance. Foreigners were also excluded, unless they are domiciled in the US or are active in American affairs. Journalists cited on the basis of their bylines were excluded, although journalists who were frequently the subjects of news stories were included if they were indexed often enough.

The final list presents a comprehensive survey of who the people are that make the news in America. It is not a *Who's Who* kind of list, based on essentially arbitrary standards of status and position. Rather, it is a list that ranges from murderers and mobsters to statesmen and presidents, but also manages to be grounded in statistical validity.

It is not simply a list of persons mentioned most frequently in the publications that were

indexed. Those included are persons of significance and substance on whom significant and substantive articles have been written often enough for them to make the top 1200. In general, the articles abstracted by The Information Bank are of this type (for further details on The Information Bank, including contact information, *see* INFORMATION AND RESEARCH SERVICES). The result is a sort of built-in —and beneficial—bias in favor of serious and important newsmakers, and a bias against people of little hard news value. Thus John Wayne and Jane Fonda, though in the lower range of citations, both make the list —not so much because they are movie stars, but because of their activity in behalf of conservative and liberal causes, respectively. Similarly, Farah Fawcett-Majors does not make the list because there was probably little material on her that would merit abstracting. This does not mean that all entertainment figures are excluded simply because they are not active in other fields. Those who are of such intense public interest that many serious, in-depth or biographical articles have been written about them also make the list—and as a result the list includes all of the biggest names.

Also added to the list of 1200 living persons, for reference purposes, are the names of a couple of hundred newsmakers who have died recently (or who, although long dead, are still frequently cited), with the years of their births and deaths when known.

Wherever possible, contact information for the living persons on the list includes affiliations and direct-line office and home phone numbers and addresses. When this information is not available, the listing includes names and phone numbers of attorneys, agents, and others who can put journalists into direct contact with the person of interest.

Contact information for the US senators and congressmen included in this list is brief. Full details on them will be found in the alphabetic lists of congressmen in THE FEDERAL GOVERNMENT.

AARON, HENRY (baseball player). c/o Milwaukee Brewers, County Stadium, Milwaukee, WI 53246. **414-933-9000**

ABDUL-JABBAR, KAREEM (basketball player). c/o Los Angeles Lakers, Los Angeles, CA. **213-674-6000**

ABEL, I E (labor leader). Commonwealth Bldg, Pittsburgh, PA 15222. **412-562-2400.** (h) 3216 Apache Rd, Pittsburgh, PA 15241

ABELSON, PHILIP H (DR) (physical chemist; editor). *Science Magazine,* 1515 Massachusetts Ave NW, Washington, DC 20005. **202-467-4353.** (h) 4244 50th St NW, Washington, DC 20016. **202-362-0436**

ABERNATHY, RALPH DAVID (THE REVEREND) (civil rights leader). Southern Christian Leadership Conference, 334 Auburn Ave NE, Atlanta, GA 30310. **404-522-1420**

ABOUREZK, JAMES G (US SENATOR). Congress, Washington, DC 20510. **202-224-5842**

ABRAM, MORRIS B (civic leader) (Field Foundation, United Negro College Fund). 345 Park Ave, New York, NY 10022. **212-644-9600.** (h) 165 E 72nd St, New York, NY 10021

ABRAMS, CREIGHTON W JR (1914–74)

ABZUG, BELLA S (Mrs Martin Abzug) (feminist; former congresswoman). 76 Beaver St, New York, NY 10022. **212-422-1414.** (h) 37 Bank St, New York, NY 20515

ACHESON, DEAN GOODERHAM (1893–1971)

ADAMS, BROCK (government official). Secretary, US Transportation Department, Washington, DC 20005. **202-426-4000**

ADELMAN, MORRIS A (economist; professor). Massachusetts Institute of Technol-ogy, Cambridge, MA 02139. **617-253-1000.** (h) 83 Neihoiden Rd, Waben, MA 02168. **617-332-1857**

AGEE, PHILIP B F (CIA critic; author) **Attorney.** Melvin Wulf, 565 5th Ave, New York, NY 10022. **212-697-5918**

Publisher. Simon and Schuster, 630 5th Ave, New York, NY 10020. **212-245-6400**

AGNEW, SPIRO THEODORE (former Vice-President). c/o Scott Meredith, 845 3rd Ave, New York, NY 10022. **212-245-5500.** (h) Towson, MD 21212

ALBEE, EDWARD (playwright). c/o Jack Hutto, William Morris Agency, 1350 Avenue of the Americas, New York, NY 10019. **212-586-5100.** (h) 967 5th Ave, New York, NY 10021

ALBERT, CARL (former congressman; attorney). McAlester, OK 74501. **918-423-7710**

ALDRIN, EDWIN E JR (BUZZ) (COLONEL) (astronaut). Aerospace Research Pilots School, Edwards Air Force Base, CA 93523. **805-277-1110**

ALEXANDER, CLIFFORD L JR (government official). Secretary, US Department of the Army, 1229 19th St NW, Washington, DC 20036. **202-452-7482.** (h) 512 A St SE, Washington, DC 20003. **202-544-8223**

ALEXANDER, DONALD C (former IRS commissioner). 17th Floor, 299 Park Ave, New York, NY 10017. **212-688-0400.** (h) 425 E 58th St, New York, NY 10022. **212-826-2193**

ALEXANDER, LEE F (MAYOR). Syracuse, NY 13202. **315-473-6605.** (h) 314 Summit Ave, Syracuse, NY 13207. **315-479-8660**

ALI, MUHAMMED (CASSIUS CLAY) (boxer). Deer Lake Training Camp, Deerfield, PA 17972. **717-366-1710**

Manager. Jeremiah Shabazz

Trainer. Angelo Dundee, 1700 Washington Ave, Miami Beach, FL. **305-673-4448**

Promoter. Don King, 32 E 69th St, New York, NY. **212-794-2900**

ALIOTO, JOSEPH L (attorney; former mayor of San Francisco). Law office number: **415-434-2100.** (h) 34 Presidio Ter, San Francisco, CA 94102

ALLBRITTON, JOE L (attorney; executive; civic leader). Houston Citizens Bank Bldg, 1100 Milan, Houston, TX 77002. **713-652-5021.** (h) **713-522-8589**

ALLEN, DICK (baseball player). c/o Philadelphia Phillies, Veterans Stadium, Broad St and Pattison Ave, Philadelphia, PA 19148. **215-463-6000.** (h) Bedminster, PA. **215-795-2538**

ALLEN, GEORGE (football coach). Los Angeles Rams, 10271 West Pico Blvd, Los Angeles, CA 90064. **213-277-4700**

ALLEN, JAMES B (?-1978)

ALLEN, JAMES EDWARD JR (1911–71)

ALLEN, WOODY (actor, author). c/o Mike Hutner, United Artists Corp, 729 7th Ave, New York, NY 10022. **212-245-6000.** (h) 930 5th Ave, New York, NY 10021

ALSOP, STEWART (?–1974)

ALTMAN, ROBERT (producer; director). Lion's Gate Films, Los Angeles, CA 90024. **213-475-4987.** (h) Malibu, CA

AMBRO, JEROME A (US REPRESENTATIVE). Congress, Washington, DC 20515. **202-225-3865**

AMBROSE, MYLES J (attorney; politician; diplomat). 1750 New York Ave, Washington, DC. **202-833-1112.** Also 1 State Street Plz, New York, NY 10004. (h) 5506 Uppingham St, Chevy Chase, MD

AMES, AMYAS (civic leader). c/o New York Philharmonic Orchestra, 1865 Broadway, New York, NY. **212-580-8700.** (h) Moore's Hill Rd, Cold Spring Harbor, NY 11724. **516-692-7461**

ANDERSON, JACK (columnist). 1401 16th St NW, Washington, DC 20036. **202-483-1442.** (h) 7300 Burdette Ct, Bethesda, MD 20034. **202-483-1142**

ANDERSON, JOHN B (US REPRESENTATIVE). Congress, Washington, DC 20515. **202-225-5676**

ANDERSON, ROBERT O (businessman). Atlantic Richfield, 515 S Flower St, Los Angeles, CA 90071. **213-486-2537.** (h) PO Box 1000, Roswell, NM 88201. **505-622-3140**

ANDERSON, WENDELL R (US SENATOR) (former governor of Minnesota). Congress, Washington, DC 20510. **202-224-5641**

ANDRUS, CECIL D (government official; former governor of Idaho). Secretary, US Department of the Interior, Washington, DC. **202-343-7351.** (h) McLean, VA 22101

ANNENBERG, WALTER H (publisher; former ambassador). Triangle Publications, 250 King of Prussia Rd, Radnor, PA 19088. **215-688-7400.** (h) Llanfair Rd, Wynnewood, PA 19096

ARMSTRONG, ANNE (Mrs Tobin Armstrong) (former ambassador). Member, board of directors, General Motors, Detroit, MI 48202. **313-556-5000.** (h) Armstrong Ranch, Armstrong, TX 78338. Toll station call; dial 0 and ask local operator for Armstrong Ranch

ARMSTRONG, LOUIS (1900–71)

ARMSTRONG, NEIL A (former astronaut). College of Engineering, University of Cincinnati, Cincinnati, OH 45221. **513-475-2435 or 6405**

ASH, ROY L (civic leader; former government official). Chairman of the board and chief executive officer, Addressograph-Multigraph Corp, Cleveland, OH 44122. **216-283-3000.** (h) 655 Funchal Rd, Los Angeles, CA 90024. **213-552-1203**

ASHBROOK, JOHN M (US REPRESENTATIVE). Congress, Washington, DC 20515. **202-225-6431**

ASHE, ARTHUR (tennis player). Arthur Ashe and Friends, 19th St, Washington, DC. **202-296-2146.** (h) 888 17th St NW, Washington, DC 20006

ASHLEY, THOMAS L (US REPRESENTATIVE). Congress, Washington, DC 20515. **202-225-4146**

ASIMOV, ISAAC (author). Apt 33A, 10 W 66th St, New York, NY 10023. **212-362-1564**

ASKEW, REUBIN (GOVERNOR). The Capitol, Tallahassee, FL 32304. **904-488-1234.** *Secretary's office.* **904-488-4661.** (h) Governor's Mansion, Tallahassee, FL 32303

ASPIN, LES (US REPRESENTATIVE). Congress, Washington, DC 20515. **202-225-3031**

ASPINALL, WAYNE N (former congressman). *Office.* **303-464-5938.** (h) 150 Aspinall Dr, Palisade, CO 81526. **303-464-7818**

ATHERTON, ALFRED L JR (government official). Assistant Secretary, US State Department, Washington, DC 20037. **202-632-9588.** (h) 2703 Woodley Rd NW, Washington, DC 20008. **202-332-7133**

AUDEN, WYSTAN HUGH (1907–73)

AVON, EARL OF (ANTHONY EDEN) (1897–1977)

AXELSON, KENNETH S (businessman). Peat, Marwich, and Mitchell Co, Accountants, 1301 Avenue of the Americas, New York, NY 10019. **212-758-9700.** (h) 425 E 58th St, New York, NY 10023. **212-752-9713**

BAEZ, JOAN (singer). c/o Chandos Productions (attention: Ruth A Valpey), PO Box 1026, Menlo Park, CA 94025. **415-328-0266**

BAGLEY, WILLIAM T (government official). Chairman, Commodity Futures Trading Commission, Washington, DC 20581. **202-254-6970**

BAILAR, BENJAMIN F (government official). Postmaster General, US Postal Service, 475 L'Enfant Plz W, SW, Washington, DC 20260. **202-245-4000**

BAILEY, F LEE (attorney). 1 Center Plz, Boston, MA 02108. **617-723-1980**

BAILEY, JOHN M (1904–75)

BAILEY, PEARL (entertainer). c/o William Morris Agency, 1350 Avenue of the Americas, New York, NY 10019. **212-586-5100**

BAKER, HOWARD H JR (US SENATOR). Congress, Washington, DC 20510. **202-224-4944**

BALANCHINE, GEORGE (choreographer). c/o New York City Ballet, NY State Theatre, Lincoln Center, New York, NY 10023. **212-877-4700**

BALL, GEORGE W (attorney; banker). 1 William St, New York, NY 10004. **212-269-3700.** (h) 860 United Nations Plz, New York, NY 10017

BANKS, DENNIS J (Indian activist) c/o American Indian Movement, PO Box 190, Minneapolis, MN 55440. **612-488-7267** **Attorney.** William Kunstler, 853 Broadway, New York, NY 10003. **212-674-3303**

BARAKA, IMAMU AMIRI (LEROI JONES) (author) **Publisher.** Howard University Press, 2935 Upton St NW, Washington, DC 20001. **202-686-6696**

BARKER, BERNARD L (convicted Watergate burglar). 5229 NW 4th St, Miami, FL 33126. **305-443-1495**

BARNUM, JOHN W (government official). Under Secretary, US Transportation Department, 400 7th St NW, Washington, DC 20590. **202-426-4000.** (h) 5175 Tilden St NW, 20016. **202-244-2530**

BARTLETT, DEWEY F (US SENATOR). Congress, Washington, DC 20510. **202-224-4721**

BATTEN, WILLIAM M (businessman). President, New York Stock Exchange, 11 Wall St, New York, NY 10005. **212-623-3000.** (h) Heather Ln, Mill Neck, NY 11765

BAUMAN, ROBERT E (US REPRESENTATIVE). Congress, Washington, DC 20515. **202-225-5311**

BAYH, BIRCH (US SENATOR). Congress, Washington, DC 20510. **202-224-5623**

BAZELON, DAVID L (CHIEF JUDGE). US Court of Appeals for the District of Columbia, Washington, DC 20001. **202-426-7118.** (h) 2700 Virginia Ave NW, Washington, DC 20037

BEALL, GEORGE (attorney; former US attorney). Baker and McKenzie, Suite 2800, Prudential Bldg, Chicago, IL 60601. **312-565-0025.** (h) 400 E Randolph St, Chicago, IL 60601. **312-565-0289**

BEAME, ABRAHAM D (former mayor of New York). Chairman, Advisory Commission on Intergovernmental Relations, 726 Jackson Pl, Washington, DC 20575. **202-382-4953**

BEAN, ALAN L (CAPTAIN) (astronaut). Johnson Space Ctr, NASA, Houston, TX 77058. **713-483-2321.** (h) 3601 Allen Pkwy-85, Houston, TX 77019. **713-526-4321**

BEETHOVEN, LUDWIG VAN (1770–1827)

BEGICH, NICK (1932–73)

BELL, ALPHONZO (Former congressman). c/o Ryder-Stillwell Agency, 5900 Wilshire Blvd, Los Angeles, CA 90036. **213-937-5500**

BELL, DANIEL (professor). Harvard University, Cambridge, MA 02138. **617-495-3843.** (h) 65 Francis Ave, Cambridge, MA 02138. **617-547-8524**

BELL, GRIFFIN B (government official). Attorney General, US Justice Department, Washington, DC 20530. **202-739-2001**

BELLMON, HENRY L (US SENATOR). Congress, Washington, DC 20510. **202-224-5754**

BELLOW, SAUL (author; professor). University of Chicago, Chicago, IL 60637. **312-753-3852**

BEN-GURION, DAVID (1896-1973)

BEN-VENISTE, RICHARD (attorney). 1801 K St NW, Washington, DC 20006. **202-833-3700.** (h) **202-965-2323**

BENNETT, JACK FRANKLIN (businessman). Senior vice-president, Exxon, 1251 Avenue of the Americas, New York, NY 10021. **212-398-2000.** (h) 141 Taconic Rd, Greenwich, CT 06830. **203-869-8931**

BENNETT, WALLACE F (former senator). 875 Donner Way, Salt Lake City, UT 84108. **803-583-4502**

BENTLEY, HELEN DELICH (government official). (h) 408 Chapelwood La, Lutherville, MD 21093. **301-252-2517**

BENTSEN, LLOYD M JR (US SENATOR). Congress, Washington, DC 20510. **202-224-5922**

BERGER, RAOUL (attorney; professor). Harvard Law School, Cambridge, MA 02138. **617-495-3670.** (h) 140 Jennie Dugan Rd, Concord, MA 01742. **617-369-3210**

BERGER, STEPHEN (civil libertarian). Executive director, American Civil Liberties Union, 22 E 40th St, New York, NY 10016. **212-725-1222**

BERGLAND, BOB (government official). Secretary, US Department of Agriculture, Washington, DC 20250. **202-447-3631**

BERLE, PETER A A (attorney; author). 45 Rockefeller Plz, New York, NY 10020. (h) 530 E 86th St, New York, NY 10028. **212-737-4996**

BERNARDIN, JOSEPH L (ARCHBISHOP). 29 E 8th St, Cincinnati, OH 45202. **513-721-1532**

BERNSTEIN, CARL (former *Washington Post* reporter). c/o David Obst, 105 E 64th St, New York, NY 10021. **212-249-4417** or **212-572-2462**

BERNSTEIN, LEONARD (conductor; pianist; composer). c/o New York Philharmonic Orchestra, Broadway at 65th St, New York, NY 10023. **212-580-8700.** *Secretary's office.* **212-245-0656.** (h) 205 W 57th St, New York, NY 10019

BERRA, YOGI (baseball coach). New York Mets, Shea Stadium, Flushing, NY 11368. **212-672-2000.** (h) 61 Sutherland Rd, Montclair, NH 07042

BERRIGAN, DANIEL J (THE REVEREND) (social activist). Woodstock Jesuit Community, 220 W 98th St, New York, NY 10025. **212-662-6358**

BERRIGAN, ELIZABETH MCALISTER (MRS PHILIP BERRIGAN)(social activist). Woodstock Jesuit Community, 220 W 98th St, New York, NY 10025. **212-662-6358**

BERRIGAN, PHILIP F (social activist). Jonah House, 1933 Park Ave, Baltimore, MD 21217. **301-669-6265.** Also c/o Jack Lewis. **607-256-4214**

BERRY, CHARLES A (DR)(physician; university administrator). 1100 Holcombe Blvd (PO Box 20036), Houston, TX 77025. (h) 10814 Riverview Dr, Houston, TX 77042. **713-783-6151**

BIAGGI, MARIO (US REPRESENTATIVE). Congress, Washington, DC 20515. **202-225-2464**

BICKEL, ALEXANDER M (1924-74)

BIDEN, JOSEPH R JR (US SENATOR). Congress, Washington, DC. **202-224-5042**

BIENSTOCK, HERBERT L (government official). (Regional Commissioner, Labor Statistics). Bureau of Labor Statistics, 1515 Broadway, New York, NY 10036. **212-399-5401.** (h) 53-12 Oceania St, Bayside, NY 11364

BILANDIC, MICHAEL (MAYOR). Office of Mayor, Chicago, IL. **312-744-4000**

BING, RUDOLF (SIR) (author). c/o Columbia Artists Management, Inc, 165 W 57th St, New York, NY 10019. **212-397-6900.** (h) 5000 Independence Ave, Bronx, NY 10471

BINGHAM, JONATHAN B (US REPRESENTATIVE). Congress, Washington, DC 20515. **202-225-4411**

BLACK, HUGO LAFAYETTE (1886-1971)

BLACK, SHIRLEY TEMPLE (Mrs Charles Black) (former US State Department official; former child star). Washington, DC 20510. **202-632-0866**

BLACKMUN, HARRY A (JUSTICE). Associate Justice, US Supreme Court, Washington, DC 20543. **202-393-1640**

BLACKWELL, ROBERT J (government official). Assistant Secretary, US Department of Commerce, Washington, DC 20510. **202-377-2112**

BLAKE, EUGENE CARSON (THE REVEREND DR) (charity official). President, Bread for the World, 207 E 16th St, New York, NY 10003. **212-260-7000.** (h) 204 Davenport Dr, Stamford, CT 06902. **203-357-7605**

BLANTON, RAY (GOVENOR) Executive Chambers, State Capitol, Nashville, TN 37219. **615-741-2001.** (h) Executive Residence, Curtiswood Ln, Nashville, TN 37204. **615-383-5401**

BLASS, BILL (designer). Tappan Co, Box 606, Mansfield, OH 44901. **419-529-4411.** (h) 550 7th Ave New York, NY 10018. **212-221-6660**

BLATCHFORD, JOSEPH H (professor). Whittier College, Whittier, CA 90607. **213-693-0771.** (h) Norton Ave, Los Angeles, CA 90020

BLOUNT, WINTON MALCOLM (businessman). Blount, Inc, Box 949, 4520 Executive Park, Montgomery, AL 36116. **205-272-8000.** (h) Box 43, Route 10, Vaughn Rd, Montgomery, AL 36111. **205-272-7920**

BLOUSTEIN, EDWARD J (DR) (educator). President, Rutgers, The State University of New Jersey, New Brunswick, NJ 08903. **201-932-7454.** (h) 1245 River Rd, Piscataway, NJ 08854

BLUE, VIDA (baseball player). c/o Oakland A's, Oakland-Alameda County Coliseum, Oakland, CA 94621. **415-762-3100**

BLUMENTHAL, W MICHAEL (government official). Secretary, US Treasury Department, Washington, DC 20220. **203-393-6400**

BOGGS, HALE (1914-72)

BOLDT, GEORGE H (SENIOR JUDGE). US District Court, Federal Bldg, Tacoma, WA 98401. **206-593-6526.** (h) Apt 402, 110 Country Club Dr SW, Tacoma, WA 98498. **206-582-1271**

BOLL, HEINRICH (author). c/o Joan Daves, 515 Madison Ave, New York, NY 10022. **212-759-6250**

BOLLES, DON (1933-76)

BOLLING, RICHARD (US REPRE-SENTATIVE). Congress, Washington, DC 20510. **202-225-4535**

BOND, JULIAN (state senator). State Capitol, Atlanta, GA 30334. **404-656-2000**. *Office.* 361 Westview Dr WS, Atlanta, GA 30310. **404-758-9101**

BOORSTIN, DANIEL J (historian). Librarian of Congress, Library of Congress, Washington, DC 20540. **202-426-5000**. (h) 3541 Ordway St NW, Washington, DC 20016. **202-966-1853**

BORK, ROBERT H (professor). Yale Law School, New Haven, CT 06520. **203-436-2211**

BORMAN, FRANK (COLONEL)(airlines executive; former astrounaut). Eastern Airlines, Inc, International Airport, Miami, FL 33148. **305-873-2211**

BOUDIN, LEONARD B (attorney). 30 42nd St, New York, NY 10017. **212-697-8640**

BOULEZ, PIERRE (composer; conductor). c/o New York Philharmonic Orchestra, Broadway at 65th St, New York, NY 10023. **212-580-8700**. (h) Postfach 22 Baden-Baden, Federal Republic of Germany

BOWIE, ROBERT R (professor). Harvard University, Cambridge, MA 02138. **617-495-1000**

BOWKER, ALBERT H (DR) (educator). Chancellor, University of California, 260 California Hall, Berkeley, CA 94720. **415-642-7464**

BOYER, ERNEST L (government official; educator). Commissioner, Office of Education, US Department of Health, Education, and Welfare, Washington, DC 20202. **202-245-8795**. (h) 40 Marion Ave, Albany, NY 12203

BOYLE, WA (TONY) (former United Mine Workers president)
Attorney. A Charles Peruto, NE Corner 8th and Locust Sts, Philadelphia, PA 19106. **215-925-5800**

BRADEMAS, JOHN (US REPRESENTA-TIVE). Congress, Washington, DC 20515. **202-225-3915**

BRADLEE, BENJAMIN C (journalist; editor). *Washington Post*, 1150 15th St NW, Washington, DC 20071. **202-223-6000**. (h) 1712 21st St NW, Washington, DC 20609

BRADLEY, BILL (basketball player). c/o New York Knickerbockers, 4 Pennsylvania Plz, New York, NY 10001. **212-563-8056**
Publisher. Quadrangle, 15 Columbus Cir, New York, NY 10019. **212-541-7118**.
Attorney Lawrence Fleisher, 15 Columbus Cir, New York, NY 10019

BRADLEY, THOMAS (MAYOR). Office of Mayor, Los Angeles, CA 90012. **213-485-3311**

BRANDO, MARLON (actor). c/o Screen Actors Guild, 7950 W Sunset Blvd, Hollywood, CA 90046. **213-876-3030**. (h) Hawley Rd, Mundelein, IL 60060

BRANDT, WILLY (professor). Southern Illinois University, Carbondale, IL 62901. **618-453-2121**. (h) University House, Southern Illinois University, Carbondale, IL 62901

BRAY, CHARLES W III (government official). Director, US Information Agency, Washington, DC 20201. **202-724-9042**

BREITEL, CHARLES D (CHIEF JUDGE). US Courthouse 74 Trinity Pl, New York, NY 10006. **212-269-4676**. (h) 146 Central Park W, New York, NY 10023. **212-724-8103**

BREMER, ARTHUR HERMAN (convicted attempted assassin). Maryland State Penetentiary, 951 Forrest St, Baltimore, MD 21202. **301-837-2135**

BRENNAN, PETER J (former Secretary of Labor). President, New York Building and Construction Trades Council, 211 E 43rd St, New York, NY 10012. **212-682-7184**

BRENNAN, WILLIAM JOSEPH JR (JUDGE). Associate Justice, US Supreme Court, Washington, DC 20543. **202-393-3466**

BREWSTER, KINGMAN JR (educator; former Yale president). c/o Yale University, New Haven, CT 06511. **203-432-4180**

BRIDGES, HARRY (labor leader). President emeritus, International Longshoremen's Union, 1188 Franklin St, San Francisco, CA 94109. **415-775-0533**. (h) 1188 Franklin St, San Francisco, CA 94109

BRIMMER, ANDREW F (DR)(consultant). Andrew F Brimmer and Co, Inc, Economic and Financial Consultants, 1201 Connecticut Ave NW, Washington, DC. **202-466-3474**

BRINEGAR, CLAUDE S (former Secretary of Transportation). Vice-president, Union Oil Co of California, 461 Boylston, Los Angeles, CA 90017. **213-486-7600**

BRISCOE, DOLPH (GOVERNOR). The Capitol, Austin, TX 78711. **512-475-4101**

BROCK, WILLIAM E III (political leader). Chairman, Republican National Committee, Washington, DC 20001. **202-484-6500**

BRONFMAN, EDGAR M (businessman). 375 Park Ave, New York, NY 10022. **212-572-7000**

BROOKE, EDWARD W (US SENATOR). Congress, Washington, DC 20510. **202-224-2742**

BROOKS, JACK B (US REPRESENTA-TIVE). Congress, Washington, DC 20515. **202-225-6565**

BROWN, CLARENCE J (US REPRE-SENTATIVE). Congress, Washington, DC 20515. **202-225-4324**

BROWN, EDMUND G JR (GOVERNOR). Governor's Office, State Capitol, Sacramento, CA 95814. **916-445-2841**

BROWN, GEORGE S (GENERAL). c/o Joint Chiefs of Staff, Pentagon, Washington, DC 20301. **202-545-6700**

BROWN, H RAP (civil rights) activist
Attorney. William Kunstler, 853 Broadway, New York, NY 10003. **212-674-3303**

BROWN, HAROLD (government official). Secretary, US Department of Defense, Washington, DC 20301. **202-695-5261**. (h) 415 S Hill Ave, Pasadena, CA 91106. **213-795-4856**

BROWN, L DEAN (civic leader). President, Middle East Institute, 1761 N St NW, Washington, DC 20036. **202-785-1141**. (h) 3030 Cambridge Pl, Washington, DC 20007. **202-965-4765**

BROYHILL, JOEL T (former congressman). Chambers of Commerce Bldg, 4600 N Fairfax Dr, Arlington, VA 22203. **703-524-1129**. (h) 4845 Old Dominion Dr, Arlington, VA 22207

BRUCE, DAVID K E (diplomat). (h) 1405 34th St NW, Washington, DC 20007

BRUSTEIN, ROBERT (educator). Dean, School of Drama, Yale University, New Haven, CT 06520. **203-436-1566**. (h) 10 S Ronan Ter, New Haven, CT 06511. **203-777-0650**

BRYANT, ANITA (entertainer; social activist). Save Our Children, Miami, FL 33140. **305-531-1759.** (h) 4682 N Bay Rd, Miami Beach, FL 33140. **305-531-1759**

BRYDGES, EARL W (1905–75)

BRZEZINSKI, ZBIGNIEW (DR) (government official). Assistant to the President for National Security Affairs, National Security Council, Washington, DC 20506. **202-395-3000.** (h) 40 Brayton St, Englewood, NJ 07631

BUCHANAN, PATRICK J (columnist). St Louis Globe-Democrat, 1750 Pennsylvania Ave, Washington, DC 20006. **202-393-7130.** (h) 5052 Loughboro Rd NW, Washington, DC 20016

BUCHEN, PHILIP W (attorney). Dewey, Ballentine, Bushby, Palmer, and Wood, 1800 M St NW, Washington, DC 20036. **202-872-1171.** (h) 800 25th St NW Washington, DC 20037. **202-333-5830**

BUCHWALD, ART (columinst). (Suite 1311), 1750 Pennsylvania Ave NW, Washington, DC 20006. **202-393-6680**

BUCKLEY, JAMES L (former senator). 140 Broadway, New York, NY 10005. **212-943-0300**

BUCKLEY, WILLIAM F JR (author; commentator; editor). *National Review*, 150 E 35th St, New York, NY 10016. **212-679-7330**

BUGLIOSI, VINCENT T (attorney; Manson case prosecutor) 9171 Wilshire Blvd, Beverly Hills, CA 90210. **213-274-8878**

BUMPERS, DALE L (US SENATOR). Congress, Washington, DC 20510. **202-224-4843**

BUNDY, MCGEORGE (philanthropist). President, Ford Fondation, 320 E 43rd St, New York, NY 10017. **212-573-4700**

BUNKER, ELLSWORTH (diplomat). US Department of State, Washington, DC 20520. **202-632-3232.** (h) Dummerston, VT. **802-254-2236**

BUNTING, JOHN R JR (banker). President, First Pennsylvania Bank, 1500 Market St, Centre Sq, Philadelphia, PA 19101. **215-786-5000.** (h) 909 Meetinghouse Rd, Jenkintown, PA 19046

BURCH, DEAN (attorney; former FCC chairman). (h) 9311 Persimmon Tree Rd, Potomac, MD. **301-983-1294**

BURCH, FRANCIS B (government official). State Attorney General, 1 S Calvert Bldg, Baltimore, MD 21202. **301-383-3720.** (h) 207 Chancery Rd, Baltimore, MD 21218. **301-366-2323**

BURDICK, QUENTIN N (US SENATOR). Congress, Washington, DC 20510. **202-224-2551**

BURGER, WARREN E (JUDGE). Chief Justice, US Supreme Court, Washington, DC 20543. **202-393-1640**

BURKE, JAMES A (US representative). Congress, Washington, DC 20515. **202-225-3215**

BURKE, MICHAEL A c/o Madison Square Garden, New York, NY 10001. **212-563-8000.** (h) 52 Gramercy Park, New York, NY 10010

BURNS, ARTHUR F (former CHAIRMAN, Federal Reserve System). Board of Governors, Federal Reserve, Washington, DC. (h) Watergate E, 2510 Virginia Ave, Washington, DC 20037

BURNS, JAMES MACGREGOR (educator; professor). Williams College, Williamstown, MA 01267. **413-597-3131.** (h) High Mowing Bee Hill, Williamstown, MA 01267. *Kitchen telephone.* **413-458-6807**

BURTON, PHILLIP (US REPRESENTATIVE). Congress, Washington, DC 20515. **202-225-4965**

BURTON, RICHARD (actor). c/o John Springer Associates, Inc, 667 Madison Ave, New York, NY. **212-421-6700**

BUSBEE, GEORGE (GOVERNOR). State Capitol, Atlanta, GA 30334. **404-656-1776.** (h) W Pacces Ferry Rd NW, Atlanta, GA 30334. **404-261-1776**

BUSCH, JOSEPH P JR (1926–75)

BUSH, GEORGE (political leader; former chairman, Republican National Committee; former CIA director). (h) 5838 Indian Tri, Houston, TX 77057. **713-652-6743**

BUSKIN, MARTIN (?–1976)

BUTLER, M CALDWELL (US REPRESENTATIVE). Congress, Washington, DC 20515. **202-225-5431**

BUTTERFIELD, ALEXANDER P (former FAA administrator; revealer of Watergate tapes). Executive vice-president, Interna-

tional Air Service Co, 1710 Gilbreth Rd, Burlingame, CA 94010. **415-877-3600.** (h) 3 Brent Ct, Menlo Park, CA 94025. **415-854-7349**

BUTZ, EARL LAUER (former Secretary of Agriculture). 312 Jefferson Dr, West Lafayette, IN 47906. **317-743-1097**

BUZHARDT, J FRED JR (attorney). 2101 L St NW, Washington, DC 20037. **202-785-9700**

BYRD, HARRY FLOOD JR (US SENATOR). Congress, Washington, DC 20510. **202-224-4024**

BYRD, ROBERT C (US SENATOR). Congress, Washington, DC 20510. **202-224-3954**

BYRNE, BRENDAN T (GOVERNOR). State House, Trenton, NJ 08625. **609-292-6000.** (h) Morven, Princeton, NJ 08540. **609-924-3980**

BYRNE, WILLIAM MATTHEW JR (JUDGE). US District Court, Federal Bldg, Los Angeles, CA 90012. **213-264-4464**

CAHILL, WILLIAM T (former New Jersey governor). PO Box 1447, Camden, NJ 08101. **609-963-6650.** (h) 202 Browning Rd, Collingdale, NJ 08108. **609-858-0457**

CALIFANO, JOSEPH A JR (government official). Secretary, US Department of Health, Education, and Welfare, Washington, DC 20201. **202-245-7000**

CALLAWAY, HOWARD H (former Secretary of the Army). (h) Crested Butte, CO 81224. **303-349-6611**

CALLENDER, EUGENE S (DR). (civic leader;)(former president, New York Urban Coalition). **212-399-0200.** 1270 Avenue of the Americas, New York, NY 10020. (h) Apt 16P, 40 W 135th St, New York, NY 10030

CALLEY, WILLIAM L JR (convicted in My Lai case). c/o American Program Bureau, 850 Boylston St, Brookline, MA 02167. **617-731-0500**

CANNON, HOWARD W (US SENATOR). Congress, Washington, DC 20510. **202-224-6244**

CAREY, BERNARD (prosecutor). State's Attorney of Cook County, 500 Daley Ctr, Chicago, IL 60602. **312-443-5440.** *Press contact.* David M Cuprisin, director, public information, **312-443-8916**

CAREY, HUGH L (GOVERNOR). State Capitol, Albany, NY 12224. **518-474-8390.** (h) Mountain Spring Rd, Farmington, CT 06032. **203-677-9658**

CARLSON, EDWARD E (businessman). Chairman and chief executive officer, UAL, Inc, PO Box 66919, Chicago, IL 60666. **312-952-4000.** (h) 990 Lake Shore Dr, Chicago, IL 60666

CARLUCCI, FRANK C (ambassador to Portugal). American Embassy, Lisbon, APO New York, NY 09678. (h) 18 Rua Sacramento a Lapa, Lisbon, Portugal. Telephone: **570-152**

CARR, GERALD P (COLONEL). (former astronaut). c/o Bovay Engineers, Inc, PO Box 8098, Houston, TX 77004. **713-529-4921**

CARROLL, JOHN T (ADMIRAL). US Navy, Washingtohn, DC 20376. **202-545-6700**

CARSON, JOHNNY (entertainer). c/o NBC, 3000 W Alameda Ave, Burbank, CA 91505. **213-845-7000**

CARSWELL, G HARROLD (attorney). PO Box 3833, Tallahassee, FL 32303. (h) 833 Lake Ridge Dr, Tallahassee, FL 32301. **904-997-4027**

CARTER, AMY (daughter of President). The White House, Washington, DC. **202-456-1414**

CARTER, JIMMY (PRESIDENT). The White House, Washington, DC 20500. **202-456-6210.** (h) Woodland Dr, Plains, GA 31780. *See also* THE FEDERAL GOVERNMENT

CARTER, OLIVER J (1911-76)

CARTER, ROBERT L (JUDGE). US Courthouse, New York, NY 10007. **212-791-0959.** (h) Central Park W, New York, NY 10023

CARTER, ROSALYNN (Mrs Jimmy Carter) (wife of President) The White House, Washington, DC 20500. **202-456-1414.** *See also* THE FEDERAL GOVERNMENT

CARTER, RUBIN ("HURRICANE"). Trenton State Prison, Trenton, NJ 08625. **609-292-9700**

CARY, FRANK T (businessman). IBM Corp, Armonk, NY 10504. **914-765-1900.** (h) 6 Haskell Ln, Darien, CT 06820. **203-655-3283**

CASE, CLIFFORD P (US SENATOR). Congress, Washington, DC 20510. **202-224-3224**

CASEY, WILLIAM J (former chairman, Export-Import Bank). (h) 2501 Massachusetts Ave, Washington, DC 20008. **202-323-2528**

CAVETT, DICK (entertainer). c/o Daphne Productions, 1790 Broadway, New York, NY 10019. **212-765-2820**
Agent. Sam Cohn, ICM, 8899 Beverly Blvd, Los Angeles, CA 90048. **213-550-4000**

CELLER, EMANUEL (former congressman). 425 Park Ave, New York, NY 10022. **212-371-5400.** (h) 9 Prospect Park W, Brooklyn, NY 11215. **212-636-1515**

CERNAN, EUGENE A (CAPTAIN) (former astronaut). c/o Coral Petroleum, Inc, Suite 600, 908 Towne Country Blvd, Houston, TX 77024. **713-467-0741**

CHAFEE, JOHN H (US SENATOR). Congress, Washington, DC 20510. **202-224-2921**

CHALK, O ROY (businessman). 714 5th Ave, New York, NY 10019. **212-757-3600.** (h) 100 Fort Worth Ave, Palm Beach, FL 33480

CHAMBERLAIN, WILT (basketball player). c/o International Volleyball Association, 1901 Avenue of the Stars, Los Angeles, CA 90067. **213-553-3005.** Also Wilt Chamberlain Productions: Seymour S Goldberg, 16633 Ventura Blvd, Encino, CA 91316. **213-981-2020**

CHANCELLOR, JOHN (journalist). c/o NBC, 30 Rockefeller Plz, New York, NY 10020. **212-664-4444**

CHAPIN, DWIGHT L (Watergate case; Nixon's appointments secretary; editor). *Success Unlimited Magazine*, Chicago, IL 60690. **312-973-7650.** (h) 620 Ridge, Winnetka, IL 60093

CHAPIN, ROY D JR (businessman). American Motors Corp 14250 Plymouth Rd, Detroit, MI 48232. **313-493-2000**

CHAPIN, SCHUYLER G (impressario and arts administrator). (h) 901 Lexington Ave, New York, NY 10021. **212-737-1761**

CHAPMAN, LEONARD F JR (former commissioner, Immigration and Naturalization Service). 425 I St NW, Washington, DC 20536. (h) 311 Vassar Rd, Alexandria, VA 22314. **703-751-2745**

CHAVEZ, CESAR (labor leader). President, United Farm Workers, AFL-CIO, PO Box 62, Keene, CA 93531. **805-822-5571**

CHEKHOV, ANTON PAVLOVICH (1860–1904)

CHESIMARD, JOANNE (political activist). Yardville Youth Correctional Ctr, Yardville, NJ 08620. **609-298-6300**

CHILES, LAWTON (US SENATOR). Congress, Washington, DC 20510. **202-224-5274**

CHISHOLM, SHIRLEY (US REPRESENTATIVE). Congress, Washington, DC 20515. **202-225-6231**

CHOMSKY, NOAM (professor). Massachusetts Institue of Technology, Massachusetts Ave, Cambridge, MA 02139. **617-253-1000.** (h) 15 Suzanne Rd, Lexington, MA 02713. **617-862-6160**

CHOTINER, MURRAY M (1909–74)

CHOU EN-LAI (1898-1976)

CHURCH, FRANK (US SENATOR). Congress, Washington, DC 20510. **202-224-6142**

CHURCHILL, WINSTON LEONARD SPENCER (SIR) (1874-1965)

CLARK, DICK (US SENATOR). Congress, Washington, DC 20510. **202-224-3254**

CLARK, KENNETH B (DR) (psychologist; civil rights leader). Clarks, Phipps, Clark, and Harris Corp, Inc, 60 E 86th St, New York, NY 10028. **212-794-0250.** (h) 17 Pinecrest Dr, Hastings-on-Hudson, New York 10076

CLARK, MARK (?-1969)

CLARK, RAMSEY (attorney; author). 37 W 12th St, New York, NY 10011. **212-989-6613**

CLAUSEN, AW (banker). Bank of America, PO Box 37000, San Francisco, CA 94317. (h) **415-622-3456**

CLAY, WILLIAM L (US REPRESENTATIVE). Congress, Washington, DC 20515. **202-225-2406**

CLAYTON, HUGH (attorney). PO Box 157, Clayton Bldg, New Albany, MS 48652. **601-543-4101.** (h) 258 Reeves St, New Albany, MS 48652

CLEAVER, ELDRIDGE (author; political activist)
Lecture Agent. Harry Walker, Inc, 350 5th Ave, New York, NY 10001. **212-563-0700**
Publisher. Word Books, 4800 W Waco Dr, Waco, TX 76703. **817-772-7650**

CLEMENTE, ROBERTO (?-1974)

CLEMENTS, WILLIAM P JR (former deputy Secretary of Defense). Sedco Corp, 1901 N Akard, Dallas, TX 75201. **214-748-9281.** (h) Terrell, TX 75160

CLIFFORD, CLARK M (attorney). 815 Connecticut Ave, Washington, DC 20006. **202-298-8686.** (h) 9421 Rockville Pike, Bethesda, MD 20014. **202-530-6181 or 6193**

CODD, MICHAEL J (former police commissioner). c/o New York City Police Department, New York, NY 10002. **212-374-5410**

COFFIN, WILLIAM SLOANE JR (THE REVEREND)(antiwar activist). Senior Minister, Riverside Church, Riverside Dr and 122nd St, New York, NY 10027. **212-749-7000**

COHEN, ALEXANDER H (television and theatre producer). Shubert Theatre, 225 W 44th St, New York, NY 10036. **212-757-1200.** (h) 25 W 54th St, New York, NY 10036

COHEN, WILLIAM S (US REPRESENTATIVE). Congress, Washington, DC 20515. **202-225-6306**

COHN, ROY M (attorney). 39 E 68th St, New York, NY 10021. **212-472-1400**

COLBY, WILLIAM E (former CIA director; attorney). Colby, Miller and Hanes, 1625 I St NW, Washington, DC 20006. **202-857-0571.** (h) 5317 Briley Pl NW, Washington, DC 20016. **200-320-4646**

COLE, EDWARD N (automobile businessman). 10 W Long Lake Rd, Bloomfield Hills, MI 48013. Also 495 W Clyde Rd, Hilly Milford, MI 48042. **313-887-4273**

COLEMAN, JAMES S (DR)(sociologist; desegregation expert). University of Chicago, Chicago, IL 60637. **312-753-2363**

COLEMAN, WILLIAM T JR (former Secretary of Transportation; attorney). 1800 M St NW, Washington, DC 20036. **202-457-5325**

COLES, ROBERT (DR)(research psychiatrist). Harvard University, Cambridge, MA 02178. **617-495-1000**

COLLINS, MICHAEL (MAJOR GENERAL, USAF)(former astronaut; museum director). National Air and Space Museum, Smithsonian Institution, Independence Ave at 7th St SW, Washington, DC 20560. **212-381-5766**

COLSON, CHARLES W (attorney). *Office.* **804-790-0118.** (h) 1350 Ballantrae Ln, McLean, VA 22101

COMMAGER, HENRY STEELE (Professor; historian). (h) 405 S Pleasant St, Amherst, MA 01002. **413-253-3114**

COMMONER, BARRY (professor; ecologist). Washington University Center for Biology Natural Systems, St Louis, MO 63160. **314-863-0100.** (h) 25 Crestwood Dr, Clayton, MO 63105. **314-863-6768**

CONABLE, BARBER B JR (US REPRESENTATIVE). Congress, Washington, DC 20515. **202-225-3615**

CONFUCIUS (551-479? BC)

CONNALLY, JOHN BOWDEN JR (attorney; former governor of Texas). First National City Bank, Houston, TX 77002. **713-658-6011**

CONNOR, JOHN T (businessman). PO Box 3000R, Morristown, NJ 07960. **201-455-4234.** (h)Blue Mill Rd, New Vernon, NJ 07976. **201-377-7075**

CONNORS, JIMMY (tennis player). c/o Mrs Gloria Connors (mother), Gerald Ln, Belleville, IL 60507. **618-398-3313.** Business address: Beverly Hills Tennis Association, 340 N Maple Dr, Beverly Hills, CA 90210
Manager. Stan Kanter, Warner Brothers, 4000 Warner Brothers Blvd, Burbank, CA 91522. **213-843-6000**
Agent. William Morris Agency, 1350 Avenue of the Americas, New York, NY 10019. **212-246-5100.** *Contact.* Peter Kelley

CONRAD, CHARLES JR (Captain)(former astronaut). 75 Mead Ln, Englewood, CO 80110. **303-761-5705**

CONTE, SILVIO O (US REPRESENTATIVE). Congress, Washington, DC 20515. **202-225-5335**

CONWAY, WILLIAM (CARDINAL) (1913–77)

CONYERS, JOHN JR (US REPRESENTATIVE). Congress, Washington, DC 20515. **202-225-5126**

COOK, DONALD C (utility businessman). American Electric Power Service Corp, 2 Broadway, New York, NY 10004. **212-422-4800.** (h) 988 5th Ave, New York, NY 10021

COOK, G BRADFORD (businessman). First National Pl, Chicago, IL. **312-786-5711**

COOKE, TERENCE J (CARDINAL). 1011 1st Ave, New York, NY 10022. **212-371-6100.** (h) 452 Madison Ave, New York, NY 10022

COOPER, JOHN SHERMAN (ambassador). 2900 N St NW, Washington, DC 20007. (h) 503 N Main St, Somerset, KY 42501

COOPER, RICHARD N Under Secretary, (government official). (h) 239 Everit St, New Haven, CT 06511. **203-624-6853**

COOPER, THEODORE (DR)(educator). Provost and dean, Cornell University Medical College, New York, NY 10021. **212-472-6493**

COPPOLA, FRANCIS FORD (film writer; producer; director). American Zoetrope Corp, 529 Pacific, San Francisco, CA 94133. **415-421-0151**

CORMAN, JAMES C (REPRESENTATIVE). Congress, Washington, DC 20515. **202-225-5811**

CORNFELD, BERNARD (financier; founder of defunct Investors Overseas Service). (h) 1100 Carolyn Way, Beverly Hills, CA 90210. **213-274-8696.** (h) 1 W Halkin St, London, England. Telephone: **235-2866.** Attorney: Phyllis Gangel, 502 Park Ave, New York, NY 10022. **212-754-1284**

CORNING, ERASTUS II (MAYOR). City Hall, Albany, NY 12207. **518-472-8900.** (h) 1165 Lake Ave, Albany, NY 12209. **518-465-8627**

CORONA, JUAN V (convicted mass murderer of migrant workers). Vacaville State Prison, Vacaville, CA 95688. **202-448-6841**

COSELL, HOWARD (sportscaster). c/o ABC-TV, 1330 Avenue of the Americas, New York, NY 10019. **212-581-7777**

COSTELLO, TIMOTHY W (DR)(educator). President, Adelphi University, Garden City, NY 11530. **516-294-8700.** (h) 75 Landis Ave, Staten Island, NY 10305

COTTON, NORRIS (former senator). (h) 15 Kimball St, Lebanon, NH 03766

COUSINS, NORMAN (author; editor). Saturday Review, 1290 Avenue of the Americas, New York, NY 10019. **212-246-9700.** (h) Silvermine Rd, New Canaan, CT 06840. **203-966-3591**

COWARD, NOEL (SIR)(1900-73)

COX, ARCHIBALD (Professor). Harvard Law School, Cambridge, MA 02138. **617-495-3133.** (h) Glezen Ln, Wayland, MA 01778. **617-358-2346**

COX, EDWARD FINCH (husband of Tricia Nixon Cox; attorney). Law office: Cravath, Swaine, and Moore, 1 Chase Manhattan Plaza, New York, NY 10003. **212-422-3000.** (h) Adams Tower, 351 E 84th St, New York, NY 10028

COX, TRICIA NIXON (Mrs Edward Finch Cox)(daughter of former President). (h) Adams Tower, 351 E 84th St, New York, NY 10028

CRANE, PHILIP M (REPRESENTATIVE). Congress, Washington, DC 20515. **202-225-3711**

CRANSTON, ALAN (US SENATOR). Congress, Washington, DC 20510. **202-224-3553**

CRONKITE, WALTER (radio-television news correspondent). c/o CBS News, 524 W 57th St, New York, NY 10019. **212-975-3627**

CROSBY, BING (1904-77)

CROSLAND, ANTHONY (1918-77)

CROSSMAN, RICHARD (?-1974)

CULVER, JOHN C (US SENATOR). Congress, Washington, DC 20510. **202-224-3744**

CURTIS, CARL T (US SENATOR). Congress, Washington, DC 20510. **202-224-4224**

CURTIS, KENNETH M (former governor of Maine). 1 Canal Plz, Portland, ME 04104. **207-775-2361.** (h) South Portland, ME 04106. **207-799-3338**

CUSHMAN, ROBERT E JR (GENERAL). c/o Commandant, US Marine Corps, Washington, DC 20380. **202-545-6700**

DALEY, RICHARD J (1902-76)

DANIEL, MARGARET TRUMAN (Mrs Clifton Daniel)(daughter of former President; author). c/o *The New York Times,* New York, NY 10023. **212-556-1234.** (h) Union City, NJ 07087

DANIELSON, GEORGE E (US REPRESENTATIVE). Congress, Washington, DC 20515. **202-225-5464**

DANZANSKY, JOSEPH B (businessman; attorney). Giant Foods, Inc, Box 1804, Washington, DC 20013. **202-857-4000**

DASH, SAMUEL (Attorney). Georgetown University Law Ctr, Washington, DC 20001. **202-624-8222.** (h) Newlands St, Chevy Chase, MD 20015. **301-656-4346**

DAVID, EDWARD E JR (DR). Exxon, 16717 Royalton, Strongsville, OH 44136. **216-238-5956**

DAVIS, ANGELA Y (political activist). c/o Random House, 201 E 50th St, New York, NY 10022. **212-751-2600**

DAVIS, CHESTER C (? to 1975)

DAVIS, EDWARD M (police chief). Los Angeles Police Dept, Los Angeles, CA 90070. **213-485-2121**

DAVIS, NATHANIEL (AMBASSADOR). c/o US State Department, Washington, DC 20520. **202-632-3320**

DAVIS, RENNIE (social activist; Chicago Seven defendant). President, Birth of a New Nation, Inc, 905 S Gilpin, Denver, CO 80209. **303-399-1106**

DAVIS, SAMMY JR (entertainer). c/o Syni Corp, 2029 Century Park E, Los Angeles, CA 90067. **213-553-6895.** Also International Fan Club, PO Box 510, Beverly Hills, CA 90213. *Contact.* Ann Slider. **213-277-5955**

DEAN, JOHN W III (former White House counsel). c/o David Obst, 105 E 64th St, New York, NY 10021. **212-249-4417** or **212-572-2462.** Also Pocket Books (c/o Mary Hall), 1230 Avenue of the Americas, New York, NY 10020. **212-345-6400**

DE BUTTS, JOHN D (businessman). Chairman, American Telephone and Telegraph

Co, 195 Broadway, New York, NY 10007. **212-393-1000.** (h) 200 E 66th St, New York, NY 10021. **212-421-2277**

DE FREEZE, DONALD D (?-1974)

DE KORTE, RICHARD W (?-1975)

DE GAULLE, CHARLES (1890-1970)

DELANEY, JAMES JOSEPH (US REPRESENTATIVE). Congress, Washington, DC 20515. **202-225-3965**

DELLINGER, DAVID T (editor; author; printer). 339 Lafayette St, New York, NY 10012

DELLUMS, RONALD V (US REPRESENTATIVE). Congress, Washington, DC 20515. **202-225-2661**

DENENBERG, HERBERT S (consumerist; columnist). *Philadelphia Evening Bulletin,* Philadelphia, PA 19101. **215-662-7550.** Also WCAU-TV and Radio, Philadelphia, PA 19131. **215-839-7000.** (h) PO Box 146, Wynnewood, PA 19096. **215-525-3000**

DENNIS, DAVID W (former congressman; attorney). 707 S A St, Richmond, IN 47374. **317-962-2567** (h) 610 W Main St, Richmond, IN 47374. **317-962-2995**

DENT, FREDERICK B (businessman; government official). (h) 19 Montgomery Dr, Spartanburg, SC 29302. **803-585-4992**

DENT, HARRY S (Nixon campaign strategist). 485 L'Enfant Plz West, SW, Washington, DC 20010. **202-554-1100**

DENT, JOHN H (US REPRESENTATIVE). Congress, Washington, DC 20515. **202-225-5631**

DEVINE, SAMUEL L (US REPRESENTATIVE). Congress, Washington, DC 20515. **202-225-5355**

DIGGS, CHARLES C JR (US REPRESENTATIVE). Congress, Washington, DC 20515. **202-225-2261**

DINGELI, JOHN D (US REPRESENTATIVE). Congress, Washington, DC 20515. **202-225-4071**

DIRKSEN, EVERETT MCKINLEY (1896–1969)

DJILAS, MILOVAN (Yugoslavian author). c/o Harcourt Brace Jovanovich, Inc, 757 3rd Ave, New York, NY 10017. **212-754-3100**

DOAR, JOHN (attorney). 30 Rockefeller Plz, New York, NY 10020. **212-489-4213.** (h) 9 E 63rd St, New York, NY 10021. **212-752-4773**

DODD, THOMAS J (1907–71)

DOLE, ROBERT J (US SENATOR). Congress, Washington, DC 20510. **202-225-6521**

DOMENICI, PETE V (US SENATOR). Congress, Washington, DC 20510. **202-224-6621**

DOMINICK, PETER H (former ambassador). (h) 550 E Quincy St, Englewood, CA 80110. **303-771-8136**

DONALDSON, WILLIAM H (educator). Dean, School of Organization and Management, Yale University, New Haven, CT 06520. **203-436-4711.** (h) 33 Hillhouse Ave, New Haven, CT 06520. **203-436-4461**

DORSEY, BOB R (businessman). Chief executive officer, Gulf Oil Co, PO Box 1166, Pittsburgh, PA 15230. **412-263-5000**

DOUGLAS, WILLIAM O (JUDGE)(former US Supreme Court justice). c/o US Supreme Court, Washington, DC 20543. **202-252-3000**

DOWNEY, THOMAS J (US REPRESENTATIVE). Congress, Washington, DC 20515. **202-225-3335**

DRINAN, ROBERT F (US REPRESENTATIVE). Congress, Washington, DC 20515. **202-225-5931**

DRUCKER, PETER F (professor). New York University, Washington Sq, New York, NY 10003. **212-598-1212.** (h) 636 Wellesley Dr, Claremont, CA 91711. **714-621-1488**

DUBOS, RENE (DR)(bacteriologist). Rockefeller University, 1230 York Ave, New York, NY 10021. **212-360-1000.** (h) Garrison, NY 10524

DUBRIDGE, LEE A (DR)(physicist). President emeritus, California Institute of Technology, Pasadena, CA 91125. **213-795-6811.** (h) 5309 Cantante, Laguna Hills, CA 92653. **714-830-7689**

DUFFEY, JOSEPH D (government official). Chairman, National Endowment for the Humanities, 806 15th St NW, Washington, DC 20005. **202-382-7465**

DUKAKIS, MICHAEL S (GOVERNOR). State Capitol, Boston, MA 02133.

617-727-3600. *Press contact.* Michael J Widmer, director, communications, **617-727-6391**

DULLES, JOHN FOSTER (1888-1959)

DUNGAN, RALPH A (government official; former chancellor of higher education, New Jersey State). US member, Inter-American Development Bank, 808 17th St NW, Washington, DC 20577. **202-634-8044.** (h) 5000 38th St NW, Washington, DC 20016. **202-244-0054**

DUNHAM, RICHARD L (government official; former chairman, Federal Power Commission). (h) Box 2, Malden Bridge, NY 12115. **518-766-2737**

DUNLOP, JOHN T (former Secretary of Labor; Economics professor). 236 Baker Library, Harvard University, Boston, MA 02163. **617-495-1000.** (h) 509 Pleasant St, Belmont, MA 02178. **617-484-2958**

DU PONT, PIERRE S IV (GOVERNOR). Legislative Hall, Dover, DE 19901. **302-678-4101.** (h) Governor's House, Dover, DE 19901. **302-678-4477**

DUPONT, ROBERT L (DR). (government official) National Institute on Drug Abuse, 11400 Rockville Pike, Rockville, MD 20852. **301-443-4577**

DURKIN, JOHN A (US SENATOR). Congress, Washington, DC 20510. **202-224-3324**

DUVALIER, FRANCOIS (1907-71)

DYLAN, BOB (ROBERT ALLEN ZIMMERMAN)(singer). PO Box 264, Cooper Station, New York, NY 10003. **212-691-6820.** (h) Marina del Ray, CA. *Personal contact.* Naomi Saltzman, PO Box 264, Cooper Station, New York, NY 10003. **212-691-6820**

Manager. Jerry Weintraub, Management Three Ltd, 1345 Avenue of the Americas, New York, NY 10019. **212-752-1563**

EAGLETON, THOMAS F (US SENATOR). Congress, Washington, DC 20510. **202-224-5721**

EASTLAND, JAMES O (US SENATOR). Congress, Washington, DC 20510. **202-224-5054**

EBERLE, WILLIAM D (businessman). Pilot House at Lewis Wharf, Boston, MA 02110. **617-227-7977.** (h) 85 Club Rd, Riverside, CT 06878

ECKHARDT, BOB C (US REPRESENTATIVE). Congress, Washington, DC 20515. **202-225-4901**

ECKSTEIN, OTTO (professor; economist). Department of Economics, Harvard University, Cambridge, MA 02138. **617-495-3356.** Also President, Data Resources, Inc, 29 Hartwell Ave, Lexington, MA 02173. **617-861-0165.** (h) 24 Barberry Rd, Lexington, MA 02173. **617-861-8784**

EDELIN, KENNETH (DR)(proabortion activist). Suite 201, 720 Harrison Ave, Boston, MA 02118. **617-266-7515** **Attorney.** William P Monans, Jr, Boston, MA. **617-523-3716**

EDWARDS, CHARLES C (DR) (physician). US Department of Health, Education, and Welfare, Washington, DC 20101. **202-245-6296.** (h) 4803 Newport St, Washington, DC 20016

EDWARDS, DON (US REPRESENTATIVE). Congress, Washington, DC 20515. **202-225-3072**

EDWARDS, EDWIN W (GOVERNOR). State Capitol, Baton Rouge, LA 70804. (h) Governor's Mansion, Baton Rouge, LA 70804. **504-389-5281**

EGEBERG, ROGER C (DR)(physician). Health Care Finance Administration, Rm 737, East Bldg, Baltimore, MD 21235. **301-594-9020**

EHRLICHMAN, JOHN D (former White House aide). PO Box H-7994, Swift Tri Prison Camp, Safford, AZ 85546. **602-428-6600**

EILBERG, JOSHUA (US REPRESENTATIVE). Congress, Washington, DC 20515. **202-225-8251**

EILTS, HERMANN F (ambassador to Egypt). c/o US State Department, Washington, DC 20520. **202-632-3320**

EINSTEIN, ALBERT (DR) (1879-1955)

EISENHOWER, DAVID (Dwight D Eisenhower II). c/o David Obst, 105 E 64th St, New York, NY 10021. **212-249-4417** or **212-572-2462.** (h) Capistrano Beach, CA 92624. (h) 500 E 77th St, New York, NY 10021

EISENHOWER, DWIGHT DAVID (GENERAL OF THE ARMY) (1890-1969)

EISENHOWER, JOHN S D (former ambassador; historian). office: Valley Forge, PA 19481

Publisher. Doubleday, 245 Park Ave, New York, NY 10017. **212-453-4561**

EISENHOWER, JULIE NIXON (Mrs David Eisenhower)(daughter of former President). (h) Capistrano Beach, CA 92624. (h) 500 E 77th St, New York, NY 10021

EISENHOWER, MAMIE DOUD (Mrs Dwight David Eisenhower)(widow of former President). (h) Gettysburg, PA 19481

EIZENSTAT, STUART (government official)(Assistant to the President for Domestic Affairs and Policy). The White House, Washington, DC 20500. **202-456-6515**

ELAZAR, DAVID (?-1976)

ELLENDER, ALLEN J (1890-1972)

ELLINGHAUS, WILLIAM M (businessman). Vice-chairman, American Telephone and Telegraph Co, 195 Broadway, New York, NY 10007. **202-393-2258**

ELLINGTON, DUKE (EDWARD KENNEDY ELLINGTON) (1899-1974)

ELLSBURG, DANIEL (DR). 3 Aladdin Ter, San Francisco, CA 94133

Attorney. Leonard Boudin, 30 E 42nd St, New York, NY 10017. **212-697-8640**

ENDERS, THOMAS O (ambassador to Canada). Embassy of the USA, Ottawa, Ont, Canada K1P 5T1. **613-238-5335**

ENGLISH, JOSEPH T (DR)(psychiatrist). St Vincent's Hospital and Medical Center, 203 W 12th St, New York, NY 10011. (h) 7 Valley Rd, Bronxville, NY 10708. **914-793-1230**

ENGMAN, LEWIS A (government official; former chairman, Federal Trade Commission). Warner, Norcross, and Judd, Suite 300, 1150 Connecticut Ave NW, Washington, DC 20036. **202-758-1950.** (h) 1163 Daleview Dr, McLean, VA 22101

ERVIN, SAM J JR (former senator). PO Box 69, Morganton, NC 28655. **704-437-5532.** (h) Morganton, NC 28655. **704-437-0543**

ERVING, JULIUS ("Dr J")(basketball player). c/o Philadelphia 76ers, 301 City Line Ave, Bala-Cynwyd, PA 19004. **215-MO7-9700.** (h) Upper Brookville, NY

Agent. Irwin Weiner, Suite 1700, 370 Lexington Ave, New York, NY 10017. **212-689-0445**

ETZIONI, AMITAI. (professor). Director, Center for Policy Research, 475 Riverside Dr, New York, NY 10027. **202-870-2011** or **2071**

EVANS, DANIEL J (educator). President, The Evergreen State College, Olympia, WA 98505. **206-866-6100**

EVERS, CHARLES (Mayor). City Hall, Fayette, MS 39069. **601-786-3682**

EVERT, CHRIS (tennis player). c/o James Evert (father), 1628 7th Pl NE, Fort Lauderdale, FL 33304. **602-252-3735.** Also Women's Tennis Association, 1604 Union St, San Francisco, CA 94123. **415-673-2018**

FAIRBANK, JOHN K (professor). Harvard University, 1737 Cambridge St, Cambridge, MA 02138. **617-495-1000.** (h) 41 Winthrop St, Cambridge, MA 02138. **617-876-1224**

FAISAL IBN ABDEL AZIZ AL SAUD (KING) (1905?-75)

FALK, RICHARD A (professor). Princeton University, Princeton, NJ 08540. **609-452-3000.** (h) 168 Prospect Ave, Princeton, NJ 08540. **609-924-5070**

FANNIN, PAUL J (former senator). (h) 5990 Orange Blossom Ln, Phoenix, AZ 85018

FARENTHOLD, FRANCES T (Mrs George F Farenthold)("Sissy")(educator; women's rights activist). President, Wells College, Aurora, NY 13026. **315-364-3011.** (h) Taylor House, Aurora, NY 13026. **315-364-7426**

FASCELL, DANTE B (US REPRESENTATIVE). Congress, Washington, DC 20515. **202-225-4506**

FAULKNER, BRIAN (1921-77)

FAUNTROY, WALTER E (US REPRESENTATIVE). Congress, Washington, DC 20515. **202-225-8050**

FELKER, CLAY S (publisher). *Esquire* magazine, 488 Madison Ave, New York, NY 10022. **212-644-5699.** (h) 322 E 57th St, New York, NY 10024. **212-759-4565**

FENWICK, MILLICENT H (US REPRESENTATIVE). Congress, Washington, DC 20515. **202-225-7300**

FINCH, ROBERT HUTCHINSON (government official; attorney). Fleming, Anderson, McClung and Finch, Suite 704, 301 E Colorado Blvd, Pasadena, CA 91101. **213-684-0920.** (h) 1106 Las Riendas, Pasadena, CA 91107. **213-681-0054**

FINDLEY, PAUL (US REPRESENTATIVE). Congress, Washington, DC 20515. **202-225-5271**

FINLEY, CHARLES O (baseball team owner). c/o Oakland Athletics, Oakland Alameda County Coliseum, Oakland, CA 94621. **415-762-3100**

FISCHER, BOBBY (chess player). c/o Management Three, Ltd, 1345 Avenue of the Americas, New York, NY 10019. **212-752-1563**

FISH, HAMILTON JR (US REPRESENTATIVE). Congress, Washington, DC 20515. **202-225-5441**

FISHER, JOSEPH L (US REPRESENTATIVE). Congress, Washington, DC 20515. **202-225-5136**

FITZGERALD, A ERNEST (Pentagon cost analyst). The Pentagon (Air Force), Washington, DC 20330. **202-697-7832.** (h) 625 Emerson St NW, Washington, DC 20011. **202-726-1753**

FITZGERALD, F SCOTT (FRANCIS SCOTT KEY FITZGERALD) (1896-1940)

FITZSIMMONS, FRANK E (union leader). President, International Brotherhood of Teamsters, 25 Louisiana Ave NW, Washington, DC 20001. **202-624-6800**

FLAHERTY, PETER F (government official; former mayor of Pittsburgh). Deputy Attorney General, US Department of Justice, Washington, DC 20530. **202-737-8200**

FLEMMING, ARTHUR S (government official). Chairman, US Commission on Civil Rights, Washington, DC 20425. **202-254-6697.** (h) 123 Queen St, Alexandria, VA. **703-548-6812**

FLETCHER, JAMES C (consultant). National Aeronautics and Space Administration, Washington, DC 20546. **202-775-3418.** (h) 7721 Falstaff Rd, McLean, VA 22101. **703-821-2817**

FLORIO, JAMES J (US REPRESENTATIVE). Congress, Washington, DC 20515. **202-225-6501**

FLOWERS, WALTER (US REPRESENTATIVE). Congress, Washington, DC 20515. **202-225-2665**

FLYNT, JOHN J JR (US REPRESENTATIVE). Congress, Washington, DC 20515. **202-225-4501**

FOLEY, THOMAS S (US REPRESENTATIVE). Congress, Washington, DC 20515. **202-225-2006**

FONDA, HENRY (actor). c/o John Springer Associates, 1901 Avenue of the Stars, Los Angeles, CA 90067. **213-277-3744**

FONDA, JANE (Mrs Tom Hayden)(actress). 152 Wadsworth St, Santa Monica, CA 90405. **213-392-3942**

FONG, HIRAM L (former Senator). 195 S King St, Honolulu, HI 96817. **808-548-5143.** (h) 1102 Alewa Dr, Honolulu, HI 96817. **808-595-4518**

FORD, BETTY (Mrs Gerald Rudolph Ford)(wife of former President). (h) Rancho Mirage, CA 92270. **714-324-1763.** (h) Grand Rapids, MI 48502

FORD, GERALD RUDOLPH JR (former President). (h) Rancho Mirage, CA 92270. **714-324-1763.** (h) Grand Rapids, MI 48502
Secretary. Dorothy Downton
Aide. Robert Barrett

FORD, HENRY II (industrialist). CEO, Ford Motor Co, Dearborn, MI 48121. **313-322-3000.** (h) Grosse Pointe Farms, MI 48236

FORD, SUSAN (photographer; daughter of former President). (h) 2277 N Via Miraleste Dr, Palm Springs, CA 92262. **714-323-1909**

FORD, WENDELL H (US SENATOR). Congress, Washington, DC 20510. **202-224-4343**

FOREMAN, GEORGE (boxer). (h) Hayward, CA
Manager. Dick Sadler, PO Box 735, Hayward, CA 94541. **415-538-5458**

FORSYTHE, EDWIN B (US REPRESENTATIVE). Congress, Washington, DC 20515. **202-225-4765**

FORTAS, ABE (former US Supreme Court justice). 1200 29th St NW, Washington, DC 20007. **202-337-5700**

FOSTER, MARCUS A (?-1973)

FOUNTAIN, L H (US REPRESENTATIVE). Congress, Washington, DC 20515. **202-225-4531**

FOWLER, HENRY H (businessman). Goldman, Sachs & Co, 55 Broad St, New York, NY 10004. **212-676-8000.** (h) E 66th St, New York, NY 10021. **212-753-4321**

FRANCO, FRANCISCO (1892-1975)

FRANKEL, MARVIN E (JUDGE). US District Court, Foley Sq, New York, NY 10007. **212-791-0903**

FRANKLIN, BENJAMIN (1706-90)

FRASER, DONALD M (US REPRESENTATIVE). Congress, Washington, DC 20515. **202-225-4755**

FRAZIER, JOE (boxer). Cloverlay, Inc Western Savings Fund Bldg, Broad and Chestnut Sts, Philadelphia, PA 19107. **215-732-2213**

FREUD, SIGMUND (1856-1939)

FRIEDAN, BETTY (feminist; author). Apt 40K, 1 Lincoln Plz, New York, NY 10023. **212-799-4060**

FRIEDHEIM, JERRY W (association manager). General Manager, American Newspaper Publishers Association, 11600 Sunrise Rd, Reston, VA 22091. **703-620-9500**

FRIEDMAN, MILTON (professor; economist). Hoover Institution, Stanford, CA 94305. **415-497-0580.** (h) 1750 Taylor St, San Francisco, CA 94133. **415-928-0690**

FRIENDLY, FRED W (professor; broadcasting). Graduate School of Journalism, Columbia University, New York, NY 10027. **212-280-1754.** (h) Riverdale, NY 10471

FROEHLKE, ROBERT F (government official). Director, Copps Corp, 2828 Wayne St, Stevens Point, WI 54481. **715-344-5900.** (h) 1200 S Marie Ave, Stevens Point, WI 54481

FROMME, LYNETTE ALICE ("Squeeky")(Manson cultist). Federal Reformatory for Women, Alderson, WV 24910. **304-445-2901**

FULBRIGHT, JAMES WILLIAM (former senator; attorney). 815 Connecticut Ave, Washington, DC 20006. **202-331-5756.** (h) **202-234-8383.** (h) Fayetteville, AZ 72701

FULD, STANLEY H (chairman; attorney, communications). 425 Park Ave, New York, NY 10022. **212-759-8400.** (h) 30 Park Ave, New York, NY 10016. **212-684-7448**

FULLER, R BUCKMINSTER (geodesic designer). University City Science Ctr, 3500 Market St, Philadelphia, PA 19104. **215-387-2255**

FURNESS, BETTY (Mrs Betty Furness Midgeley). (consumerist). c/o NBC News, 30 Rockefeller Plz, New York, NY 10020. **212-247-8300**

GALBRAITH, JOHN KENNETH (professor; economist; author). (h) 30 Francis Ave, Cambridge, MA 02138. **617-491-7242**

GALLO, JOSEPH (?–1972)

GALLUP, GEORGE H (DR) (pollster). American Institute of Public Opinion, 53 Bank St, Princeton, NJ 08340. **609-924-9600.** (h) Princeton, NJ. **609-466-1216**

GAMBINO, CARLO (1902–76)

GANDHI, MOHANDAS KARAMCHAND (1869–1948)

GARDNER, JOHN W (DR) (founder of Common Cause; author; consultant). Carnegie Corporation of New York, 437 Madison Ave, New York, NY 10022. **212-371-3200.** Also 2030 M St NW, Washington, DC 20036. (h) Route 108, MD. **301-997-1315**

GARDNER, RICHARD N (ambassador to Italy). c/o US State Department, Washington, DC 20520. **202-632-3320.** (h) 1150 5th Ave, New York, NY 10028

GARMENT, LEONARD (former US representative to Human Rights Commission; attorney). 20 Broad St, New York, NY 10005. **212-422-6767**

GARRIOTT, OWEN K (DR) (astronaut). Assistant director, Space and Life Sciences Directorate, Johnson Space Ctr, Houston, TX 77058. **713-483-0123.** (h) **713-333-3576**

GARRISON, JIM (attorney). 710 Carondelet St, New Orleans, LA 70130. **504-588-9014.** (h) 4600 Owens Blvd, New Orleans, LA 70119

GARRY, CHARLES R (attorney). 1256 Market St, San Francisco, CA 94102. **415-864-3131.** (h) 482 Wellington Ave, Daly City, CA 94014. **415-587-5390**

GENEEN, HAROLD S (communications businessman). President, International Telephone and Telegraph, 320 Park Ave, New York, NY 10022. **212-752-6000**

GERSTENBERG, RICHARD C (automobile businessman). Director, General Motors Corp, Detroit, MI 48224. **313-556-5000.** (h) 80 Cranbrook Rd, Bloomfield Hills, MI 48013

GESELL, GERHARD A (JUDGE). US Courthouse, Washington, DC 20001. **202-426-7451.** (h) 3304 N St, Washington, DC 20007. **202-337-2491**

GETTY, J PAUL (1892–1976)

GIAIMO, ROBERT N (US REPRESENTATIVE). Congress, Washington, DC 20515. **202-225-3661**

GIANCANA, SAM (?–1975)

GIBBONS, SAM M (US REPRESENTATIVE). Congress, Washington, DC 20515. **202-225-3376**

GIBSON, EDWARD G (DR) (space scientist). Johnson Space Ctr, Houston, TX 77058. **714-483-4190**

GIBSON, KENNETH A (MAYOR). City Hall, Broad St, Newark, NJ 07102. **201-733-3669**

GIBSON, PAUL JR (businessman). American Airlines, 633 3rd Ave, New York, NY 10017. **212-557-4575.** (h) 175-40 Grand Central Pkwy, Jamaica, NY 11432. **212-658-6332**

GILLIGAN, JOHN J (administrator). Woodrow Wilson International Center—Scholars, Smithsonian Institution, Washington, DC 20560. **202-381-5911.** (h) Suite 1120, 88 E Broad St, Columbus, OH 43215

GILMORE, GARY MARK (?–1977)

GINSBERG, ALLEN (poet). c/o *City Lights*, 261 Columbus Ave, San Francisco, CA 94133. **415-362-8193.** (h) 490 Park Ave, Paterson, NJ 07504. **201-523-6606**

GINSBURG, MITCHELL I (educator). Dean, Columbia University School of Social Work, New York, NY 10025. **212-280-5189.** (h) 372 Central Park W, New York, NY 10025. **212-865-4965**

GLASSER, IRA (civil libertarian). Executive director, New York Civil Liberties Union,

84 5th Ave, New York, NY 10011. **212-924-7800.** (h) 290 9th Ave, New York, NY. **212-989-3791**

GLEASON, THOMAS W (attorney). 17 Battery Pl, New York, NY 10001. **212-425-3240**

GLENN, JOHN H (former astronaut; US SENATOR). Congress, Washington, DC 20510. **202-224-3353**

GLOVER, CLIFFORD (businessman). Batson Cook Co, Box 151, West Point, GA 31833. **404-643-2101.** (h) 103 Hillcrest Rd, West Point, GA 31833. **404-643-7671**

GODWIN, MILLS E JR (Former governor of Virginia). (h) Cedar Point, Crittenden, VA 23342. **804-238-2888**

GOLDBERG, ARTHUR J (attorney; ambassador-at-large). 1101 17th St NW, Washington, DC 20036. **202-862-5080.** c/o US State Department, Washington, DC 20520. **202-632-3320**

GOLDBERG, JACK R (?–1974)

GOLDMARK, PETER C JR (1906–77)

GOLDSTEIN, JONATHAN L (former US attorney). Hellring, Linderman, Goldstein, and Segal, 1180 Raymond Blvd, Newark, NJ 07102. **201-621-9020**

GOLDWATER, BARRY MORRIS (US SENATOR). Congress, Washington, DC 20510. **202-224-2235**

GOLDWATER, BARRY MORRIS JR (US REPRESENTATIVE). Congress, Washington, DC 20515. **202-225-4461**

GONZALEZ, HENRY B (US REPRESENTATIVE). Congress, Washington, DC 20515. **202-225-3236**

GOODELL, CHARLES E (attorney; former senator; author). (h) 2 Elm Rock Rd, Bronxville, NY 10708. **914-961-2404**

GOODMAN, JULIAN (broadcaster; businessman). c/o NBC, 30 Rockefeller Plz, New York, NY 10020. **212-664-4444**

GOODMAN, ROY M (state senator). Senate, New York State Suite 2400, 270 Broadway, New York, NY 10007. **212-964-1539.** (h) 1035 5th Ave, New York, NY 10028

GORE, ALBERT (coal company businessman; former senator). Island Creek Coal,

1501 Euclid Ave, Cleveland, OH. **216-241-3215.** (h) Carthage, TN 37030. **615-735-1676**

GRAHAM, BILLY (THE REVEREND) (WILLIAM FRANKLIN GRAHAM) (evangelist). 1300 Harmon Pl, Minneapolis, MN 55403. **612-338-0500.** (h) Montreat, NC 28757

GRAHAM, KATHARINE M (publisher). The Washington Post Co, 1150 15th St NW, Washington, DC 20071. **202-223-6000.** (h) 2920 R St NW, Washington, DC 20007

GRAHAM, MARTHA (dancer; choreographer). c/o Columbia Artists Management, Inc, 165 W 57th St, New York, NY 10019. **212-397-6900**

GRANT, ULYSSES SIMPSON (1822–85)

GRASSO, ELLA T (GOVERNOR). State Capitol, Hartford, CT 06115. **203-566-4840**

GRAVEL, MIKE (US SENATOR). Congress, Washington, DC 20510. **202-224-6665**

GRAY, L PATRICK III (government official; former FBI director). Sindlay Way, Stonington, CT 06378. **203-535-1685**

GRAYSON, C JACKSON JR (businessman). Chairman, American Productivity Ctr, Suite 100, 333 West Loop North, Houston, TX 77024. **713-688-2036.** (h) 4 Post Oak Cir, Houston, TX 77024

GREELEY, ANDREW M (THE REVEREND). (columnist). "Perspective," *Chicago Tribune*, 820 N Michigan, Chicago, IL 60611. **312-222-3232.** (*Chicago Tribune*). (h) 1012 E 47th St, Chicago, IL 60653

GREEN, EDITH A (former congresswoman). Christian Church, 8031 Sacajawea Way, Wilsonville, OR 97070

GREEN, JUNE L (JUDGE). US Courthouse, Washington, DC 20001. **201-426-7136.** (h) 261 Joyce Ln, Arnold, MD 21012. (h) 550 N St SW, Washington, DC 20024

GREEN, MARSHALL (ambassador to Australia). Coordinator of Population Affairs, US State Department, OES/CP, Rm 7815, Washington, DC 20520. **202-263-3472.** (h) 5063 Millwood Ln NW, Washington, DC 20016

GREENSPAN, ALAN (economist). New York University, New York, NY 10011. **212-598-1212.** (h) 1 New York Plz, New York, NY 10004. **212-943-9515**

GREGORY, DICK (comedian). c/o Stein & Day, 122 E 42nd St, New York, NY 10017. **212-753-7285.** (h) Long Pond Rd, Manomet, MA 02345. **617-224-6706**

GRIFFIN, ROBERT P (US SENATOR). Congress, Washington, DC 20510. **202-224-6221**

GRIFFITHS, MARTHA W (former congresswoman; attorney). 77940 McFadden Rd, Romeo, MI 48065

GRISWOLD, ERWIN N (attorney). 1100 Connecticut Ave NW, Washington, DC 20036. **202-452-5880.** (h) 36 Kenmore Dr, Belmont, MA 02178. **617-484-0190.** (h) 3900 Watson Pl NW, Washington, DC. **202-337-3296**

GROSS, H R (former congressman). (h) Waterloo, IA 50704

GROSSI, ANTHONY J (?-1976)

GROVER, JAMES R JR (former congressman; attorney). 1801 Argyle Sq, Babylon, NY 11702. **516-669-1028.** (h) 180 Woodsome Rd, Babylon, NY 11702. **516-669-6891**

GUEVARA, ERNESTO CHE (?-1967)

GURFEIN, MURRAY I (JUDGE). US Courthouse, 1 Federal Plz, New York, NY 10007. **212-791-0911.** (h) 530 Park Ave, New York, NY 10021

GURNEY, EDWARD J (former senator; attorney). (h) 800 Greentree Dr, Winter Park, FL 32789. **305-647-8013**

HAACK, ROBERT W (businessman). Chairman of the board, Lockheed Aircraft, 2555 N Hollywood, Burbank, CA 91503. **213-847-6121**

HABIB, PHILIP C (government official). Under Secretary for East Asian and Pacific Affairs, US State Department, Washington, DC 20510. **202-632-9596**

HAIG, ALEXANDER M JR (GENERAL). Saceur SHAPE APO New York, NY 09055. Telephone: **06-5-4113**

HALABY, NAJEEB E (attorney; financier). President, Halaby International Corp, 640 5th Ave, New York, NY 10019. **212-757-7325.** (h) PO Box 894, Alpine, NJ 07620. **201-768-7530**

HALDEMAN, H R (Watergate convict). Federal Correctional Institution, Lampoc, CA 93436. **805-735-2771.** (h) Newport Beach, CA 92660

HALEY, ALEX (author). Kinte Foundation, National Press Bldg, Washington, DC 20004. **202-638-0348.** (h) PO Box 2907, San Francisco, CA 94126
Agent. Paul R Reynolds, 12 E 41st St, New York, NY 10017. **212-689-8711**

HALL, DAVID (former governor of Oklahoma; professor). University of Tulsa School of Law, Tulsa, OK 74104. **918-939-6351**

HALLECK, CHARLES W (JUDGE). Superior Court, Washington, DC 20409. **202-727-1010.** (h) 14211 Turkey Foot Rd, Gaithersburg, MD 20760. **301-748-0782**

HALPERIN, MORTON H (DR) (former National Security Council aide; wiretapping suit). 122 Maryland Ave NE, Washington, DC 20002. **202-544-5380.** (h) 8215 Stone Tri, Bethesda, MD 20014. **201-469-7818**

HALPERN, SEYMOUR (former congressman). Sydney S Baron and Co, 540 Madison Ave, New York, NY. **212-751-7100.** (h) 166-05 Highland Ave, Jamaica, NY 11432

HALSTON (R HALSTON FROWICK) (designer). 550 7th Ave, New York, NY. Also 33 E 68th St, New York, NY 10021. **212-354-6340**

HAMMER, ARMAND (DR) (oil businessman). Knoedler and Co, 595 Madison Ave, New York, NY 10022. **212-794-0550.** Also 10431 Wyton Dr, Los Angeles, CA 90024. **213-938-8967.** (h) PO Box 107, Colts Neck, NJ 07722

HAMPTON, FRED (?-1969)

HAMPTON, ROBERT E (government official). Chairman, Civil Rights Comission, Washington, DC 20415. **202-254-6697.** (h) 10 Savannah Ct, Bethesda, MD 20034. **301-365-1403**

HANDLER, PHILIP E (DR) (administrator). Atomic Energy Commission Fellowship Program, George Washington University, 2101 Constitution Ave, Washington, DC 20418. **202-676-6000.** (h) 2700 Virginia Ave, Washington, DC 20037

HANKS, NANCY (government official). Chairman, National Endowment for the Arts, 806 15th St NW, Washington, DC 20506. **202-655-4000.** (h) 1236 30th St NW, Washington, DC 20007

HANLEY, JAMES M (US REPRESENTATIVE). Congress, Washington, DC 20515. **202-225-3701**

HANSEN, CLIFFORD P (US SENATOR). Congress, Washington, DC 20510. **202-224-3424**

HARDIN, CLIFFORD MORRIS (DR) (businessman). Ralston-Purina Co, Checkerboard Sq, St Louis, MO 66318. (h) 10 Roan Ln, St Louis, MO 63124. **314-993-1130**

HARDING, WARREN GAMALIEL (1865-1923)

HARLAN, JOHN MARSHALL (1899-1971)

HARLOW, BRYCE N (businessman). Procter and Gamble Co, 1801 K St NW, Washington, DC 20006. **202-833-9500.** (h) 3744 30th Rd N, Arlington, VA 22207. **703-524-1346**

HARRIMAN, W AVERELL (former ambassador-at-large; former governor of New York). (h) 3038 N St, Washington, DC 20007. **202-338-8330**

HARRINGTON, MICHAEL (author; editor). *Democratic Left*, 31 Union Sq, New York, NY 10003

HARRINGTON, MICHAEL J (US REPRESENTATIVE). Congress, Washington, DC 20515. **202-225-8020**

HARRIS, EMILY (Mrs William Harris) (Symbionese Liberation Army). California Institute for Women, Frontera, CA 91720. **714-597-1771**
Attorney. Leonard Weinglass 2025 Avon, Los Angeles, CA 90026. **213-660-9000**

HARRIS, FRED R (former senator; attorney; author)
Publisher. W W Norton Co, 500 5th Avenue, New York, NY 10022. **212-354-5500**

HARRIS, HERBERT E (US REPRESENTATIVE). Congress, Washington, DC 20515. **202-225-4376**

HARRIS, LOUIS (public opinion analyst; columnist). Louis Harris and Associates, 630 5th Ave, New York, NY 10020. **212-975-1600**

HARRIS, PATRICIA ROBERTS (attorney; educator; government official). Secretary, US Department of Housing and Urban Development, 600 New Hampshire Ave NW, Washington, DC 20037. **202-965-9400.** (h) 1742 Holly St NW, Washington, DC 20012

HARRIS, WILLIAM (Symbionese Liberation Army). California State Institute for Men, Chino, CA 91720. **714-597-1821**

HART, GARY W (US SENATOR). Congress, Washington, DC 20510. **202-224-5852**

HART, GEORGE L JR (JUDGE). US Courthouse, Washington, DC 20544. **202-655-4000**

HART, PHILIP A (US SENATOR (?–1976))

HARTKE, VANCE (former senator). (h) 6500 Kerns Ct, Falls Church, VA 22044. **703-534-0788**. (h) Suite 340, Watergate 600, Washington, DC 20037. **202-333-5050**

HASKELL, FLOYD K (US SENATOR). Congress, Washington, DC 20510. **202-224-5941**

HATCHER, RICHARD G (MAYOR). City Hall, 401 Broadway, Gary, IN 46402. **219-944-6501**. (h) **219-949-8160**

HATFIELD, MARK O (US SENATOR). Congress, Washington, DC 20510. **202-224-3753**

HATHAWAY, STANLEY K (government official; attorney; former Secretary of the Interior). Suites A and B, 3001 Henderson Dr, Cheyenne, WY 82001. **307-634-7723**. (h) **307-638-3839**

HATHAWAY, WILLIAM D (US SENATOR). Congress, Washington, DC 20510. **202-224-2523**

HAUSER, RITA E (Mrs Gustave M Hauser) (attorney). Stroock and Stroock and Lavan, 61 Broadway, New York, NY 10016. **212-425-5200**. (h) 700 Park Ave, New York, NY 10021. **212-744-8770**

HAWKINS, AUGUSTUS F (US REPRESENTATIVE). Congress, Washington, DC 20515. **202-225-2201**

HAYAKAWA, S I (US SENATOR). Congress, Washington, DC 20510. **202-224-3841**

HAYDEN, TOM (political activist; author). 152 Wadsworth St, Santa Monica, CA 90405. **213-392-3942**
Publisher. Holt, Rinehart and Winston, 383 Madison Ave, New York, NY 10017. **212-688-9100**

HAYES, HELEN (Mrs Charles MacArthur) (actress). (h) Nyack, NY 10960. **914-947-3000**
Agent. Lucy Croll, 390 W End Ave, New York, NY 10024. **212-877-0627**

HAYNSWORTH, CLEMENT F JR (CHIEF JUDGE). US District Court, Federal Bldg, Greenville, SC 29603. **803-235-8949**. (h) 111 Boxwood Ln, Greenville, SC 29601. **803-232-9534**

HAYS, WAYNE L (former congressman). Director, Citizens National Bank, PO Box 95, St Clairsville, OH 43950. **614-695-3291**

HEARST, PATRICIA (newspaper heiress; kidnap victim). (h) Hillsborough, CA 94010. Contact through Randolph Hearst.

HEARST, RANDOLPH APPERSON (publisher). 110 5th St, San Francisco, CA 94103. **415-777-2424**. (h) Hillsborough, CA 94010

HECKSCHER, AUGUST (author; journalist). *The American Scholar*, 159 E 94th St, New York, NY 10021. **212-371-5614**

HEFNER, HUGH (magazine publisher). President, Playboy Enterprises, Inc, 919 N Michigan Ave, Chicago, IL 60611. **312-751-8000**. (h) 1340 N State Pkwy, Chicago, IL 60610

HEILBRONER, ROBERT L (professor). New School for Social Research, 66 W 12th St, New York, NY 10011. **212-741-5717**. (h) 830 Park Ave, New York, NY. **212-794-8602**

HEINEMANN, GUSTAV (?–1976)

HEINZ, H JOHN III (US SENATOR). Congress, Washington, DC 20510. **202-224-6324**

HELLER, WALTER W (professor; former chairman, Council of Economic Advisers). Department of Economics, University of Minnesota, Minneapolis, MN 55455. **612-373-2851**. (h) 2203 Folwell St, St Paul, MN 55108. **612-645-2258**

HELLMAN, LILLIAN (playwright). (h) 630 Park Ave, New York, NY 10021

HELMS, JESSE A (US SENATOR). Congress, Washington, DC 20510. **202-224-6342**

HELMS, RICHARD M (former CIA director; former ambassador). International consultant, Safee Co, Suite 402, 1627 K St NW, Washington, DC 20006. **202-466-4226**

HELPERN, MILTON (1902–77)

HELSTOSKI, HENRY (former congressman; illegal immigration charges). (h): 84 Cottage Pl, East Rutherford, NJ 07073. **201-939-9090**

HEMINGWAY, ERNEST (1899–1961)

HENDERSON, ORAN K (COLONEL) (involved in My Lai case). Director, Pennsylvania State Council of Civil Defense, Harrisburg, PA 17120. **717-787-8150** (24 hours); John J Comey, public information officer

HEPBURN, KATHARINE (actress). (h) PO Box 17154, West Hartford, CT 06117
Agent. William Morris Agency, 1350 Avenue of the Americas, New York, NY 10021. **212-586-5100**

HERRINGER, FRANK C (transportation businessman). San Francisco Bay Area Rapid Transit, 800 Madison St, Oakland, CA 94607. **415-465-4100**. (h) 4175 Canyon Rd, Lafayette, CA 94549

HERTZBERG, ARTHUR (RABBI) (president, American Jewish Congress). 147 Tenafly Rd, Englewood, NY 07631. **201-567-1300**. (h) 83 Glenwood Rd, Englewood, NY 07631. **201-568-3259**

HERZOG, CHAIM (ambassador). Permanent Mission of Israel, 800 2nd Ave, New York, NY 10017. **212-697-5500**

HESBURGH, THEODORE M (THE REVEREND) (educator). President, Notre Dame University, Corby Hall, Notre Dame, IN 46556. **219-283-6011**

HESTER, JAMES M (DR) (educator). Rector, United Nations University, 29th Floor, Toho Seimei Bldg, 15-1 Shibuya, Tokyo 150, Japan. Telephone: **499-2811**. (h) 47 Aobadai, Tokyo, Japan

HICKEL, WALTER JOSEPH (businessman; former government official). (Travelers Inns, Hotel Captain Cook, shopping centers). Suite 607, 510 L St, Anchorage, AK 99501. **907-276-7400**. (h) 1905 Loussac Dr, Anchorage, AK 99503. **907-277-6704**

HICKS, LOUISE DAY (Boston councilwoman; former congresswoman). 493 Broadway, South Boston, MA. **617-269-6085**. (h) 1780 Columbia Rd, South Boston, MA 02127. **617-268-1780**

HILL, JOHN L (government official). State Attorney General, Supreme Court Bldg, Austin, TX 78711. **512-475-4643**

HILLS, CARLA ANDERSON (former Secretary of Housing and Urban Development). (h) 3125 Chain Bridge Rd, Washington, DC 20016. **202-966-5958**

HILLS, RODERICK M (attorney). Chairman of the board and chief executive officer, Peabody Coal Co, 301 N Memorial Dr, St Louis, MO 63102. **314-342-3540**

HISS, ALGER (espionage case)
Attorney. Helen L Buttenwieser, 575 Madison Ave, New York, NY 10022. **212-826-1619**

HITLER, ADOLF (1889–1945)

HOADLEY, WALTER E (economist; financial businessman). World Headquarters Bank of America Ctr, San Francisco, CA 94137. **415-622-6093**. (h) 999 Green St, San Francisco, CA 94133. **415-474-6494**

HO CHI MINH (1890–1969)

HOFFA, JAMES R (1913–75?) (labor leader: Teamsters Union). (h) 16154 Robson St, Detroit, MI 48235. *Contact.* James P Hoffa (son), Guardian Bldg, Detroit, MI. **313-962-4167**

HOFFMAN, ABBIE (author; Yippie)
Attorney. Gerald Lefcourt, 299 Broadway, New York, NY 10007. **212-349-7755**

HOFFMAN, JULIUS J (JUDGE). Illinois District Court, 219 Dearborn St, Chicago, IL 60604. **312-435-5364**. (h) 179 E Lake Shore Dr, Chicago, IL 60604

HOGAN, FRANK S (?-1974)

HOGAN, LAWRENCE J (former congressman). Suite 307, John Hanson Bldg, 7610 Pennsylvania Ave, Forestville, MD 20028. **301-420-4600**. (h) 8400 Hillview Rd, Landover, MD 20786

HOLBROOKE, RICHARD (government official). Assistant Secretary of State, US State Department, Washington, DC 20520. **202-632-9596**. (h) 2101 Connecticut Ave, Washington, DC 20008

HOLLINGS, ERNEST F (US SENATOR). Congress, Washington, DC 20510. **202-224-6121**

HOLT, MARJORIE S (US REPRESENTATIVE). CONGRESS, Washington, DC 20515. **202-225-8090**

HOLSTZMAN, ELIZABETH (US REPRESENTATIVE). Congress, Washington, DC 20515. **202-225-6616**

HOOK, SIDNEY (professor: author). Hoover Institute, Stanford, CA 94305. **415-497-2300**

HOOVER, HERBERT CLARK SR (1874–1964)

HOOVER, J EDGAR (1895–1972)

HOPE, BOB (comedian). Bob Hope Enterprises: 10,000 Riverside Dr, North Hollywood, CA 91602. **213-980-0905**; or 3808 Riverside Dr, Burbank, CA 91505. **213-841-2020**. (h) 10346 Moorpark St., North Hollywood, CA 91602

HOSMER, CRAIG (former congressman). Institute for Congress, 1750 K St NW 300, Washington, DC 20006. **202-797-6460**. (h) 5024 Van Ness St NW, Washington, DC 20016. **202-966-5449**

HOWARD, JAMES J (US REPRESENTATIVE). Congress, Washington, DC 20515. **202-225-4671**

HOWE, IRVING (professor; author; historian; critic). Department of English, Hunter College, New York, NY 10021. **212-570-5118**. (h) **212-362-6700**

HRUSKA, ROMAN L (former senator). (h) 2139 S 38th St Omaha, NE 68111. **402-345-1133**

HUDDLESTON, WALTER D (US SENATOR). Congress, Washington, DC 20510. **202-224-2541**

HUGHES, HAROLD E (former senator). International Christian Leadership Foundation, 5215 58th Ave, East Riverdale, VA 23666. **703-525-2378**. (h) 813 Carrie Ct, McLean, VA 22101. **703-525-2378**

HUGHES, HOWARD R (1905–76)

HUGHES, JOHN H (?-1972)

HUGHES, RICHARD J (JUDGE). Chief Justice, New Jersey Supreme Court, Trenton, NJ 08608. **609-292-4837**

HUGHES, WILLIAM J (US REPRESENTATIVE). Congress, Washington, DC 20515. **202-225-6572**

HUMPHREY, HUBERT HORATIO (?-1978)

HUNT, E HOWARD JR (author; former Nixon aide) (h) 1245 NE 85th St, Miami, FL 33138
Lecture Agent. American Program Bureau, 850 Boylston St, Chestnut Hill, MA 02167. **617-731-0500**
Literary Agent. Scott Meredith, 845 3rd Ave, New York, NY 10021. **212-245-5500**

HUROK, SOL (1888–1974)

IACOCCA, LEE A (businessman). Ford Motor Co, American Rd, Dearborn MI 48121. **313-323-3000**. (h) 571 Edgemere Ct, Bloomfield Hills, MI 48013

IAKOVOS (ARCHBISHOP). Greek Orthodox Archdiocese of North and South America, 8-10 E 79th St, New York, NY 10021. **212-628-2500**

IBSEN, HENRIK (1828–1906)

ICHORD, RICHARD H (US REPRESENTATIVE). Congress, Washington, DC 20515. **202-225-5155**

IKARD, FRANK N (association businessman). American Petroleum Institute, 1801 K St NW, Washington, DC 20006. **202-457-7000**. (h) The Shoreham W, 2700 Calvert St NW, Washington, DC 20008

IKLE, FRED CHARLES (government official). Director, US Arms Control and Disarmament Agency, Department of State Bldg, 320 21st St, Washington, DC 20451. **202-632-3597**. (h) Bethesda, MD. **301-229-1677**

INNIS, ROY C (civil rights leader); (national director of CORE). 200 W 135th St, New York, NY 10030. **212-368-8104**. (h) 800 Riverside Dr, New York, NY 10032

INOUYE, DANIEL K (US SENATOR). Congress, Washington, DC. 20510. **202-224-3934**

IRVING CLIFFORD (h) San Miguel Allende, Apartade 225, Mexico. Telephone: **21553**
Agent. Julian Bach, 3 E 48th St, New York, NY 10017. **212-753-2605**

IRWIN, JAMES B (LIEUTENANT COLONEL) (former astronaut; foundation businessman). High Flight Foundation, 5010 Edison Ave, Colorado Springs, CO 80915. **303-574-1200**. (h) Skyway Blvd, Colorado Springs, CO 80901

IRWIN, JOHN N II (attorney). 30 Rockefeller Plz, New York, NY 10020. **212-541-4000**. (h) 888 Park Ave, New York, NY 10021. **212-228-1851**

JACKSON, GEORGE L (?-1971)

JACKSON, HENRY M (US SENATOR). Congress, Washington, DC 20510. **202-224-3441**

JACKSON, JESSE L (THE REVEREND) (civil rights leader). Operation PUSH, 7941 S Halsted St, Chicago, IL 60621. **312-373-3366**

JACKSON, JONATHAN P (?–1970)

JACKSON, MAYNARD H (MAYOR). City Hall, Atlanta, GA 30303. **404-658-6100.** Ray Patterson, director, communications, **404-658-6115.** (h) **404-763-3635**

JACOBS, ANDREW JR (US REPRE-SENTATIVE). Congress, Washington, DC 20515. **202-225-4011**

JANEWAY, ELIOT (economist). Director, Janeway Publishing and Research Corp, 15 E 80th St, New York, NY 10021. **212-249-8833**

JAVITS, JACOB K (US SENATOR). Congress, Washington, DC 20510. **202-224-6542**

JAWORSKI, LEON (government official). Chief counsel, House of Representatives, Ethics Committee, Washington, DC 20515. **202-225-8461.** (h) 3665 Ella Lee Ln, Houston, TX 77027. **713-651-5151**

JEFFERSON, THOMAS (1743-1826)

JENNER, ALBERT E JR (attorney). National Lawyers Commission for Civil Rights under Law, 1 IBM Plz, Chicago, IL 60611. **312-222-9350.** (h) 119 Tudor Pl, Kenilworth, IL 60043. **312-251-4077**

JOHNSON, ANDREW (1808-75)

JOHNSON, DONALD E (educator). Worcester Polytechnic Institute, Worcester, MA 01609. **617-753-1411.** (h) 16 Lowell Ave, Holden, MA 01520. **617-829-4736**

JOHNSON, FRANK M JR (JUDGE). US District Court, Federal Bldg, Montgomery, AL 36105. **205-832-7521.** (h) 118 N Haardt Dr, Montgomery, AL 36105

JOHNSON, J BENNETT JR. (US SENA-TOR). Congress, Washington, DC 20510. **202-224-5824**

JOHNSON, LADY BIRD (Mrs Lyndon Baines Johnson)(widow of former President). National Historic Site, Johnson City, TX 78636. **512-868-7128.** (h) LBJ Ranch, Stonewall, TX 78671

JOHNSON, LYNDON BAINES (1908-73)

JOHNSON, NICHOLAS (lecturer; writer; broadcasting). c/o National Citizens Commission for Broadcasting, 1028 Connecticut Ave NW, Washington, DC 20036. **202-466-8407.** (h) PO Box 19101, Washington, DC 20036

JOHNSON, PHILIP C (architect: Museum of Modern Art). 375 Park Ave, New York, NY 10022. **212-751-7740.** (h) 842 Ponus Ridge Rd, New Canaan, CT 06840. **203-966-0565.** (h) 242 E 52nd St, New York, NY. **212-753-4246**

JOHNSON, U ALEXIS (ambassador: chief negotiator, SALT talks). c/o US State Department, Washington, DC 20520. **202-632-3220**

JONES, WILLIAM B (JUDGE). US Courthouse, Washington, DC 20001. **202-655-4000.** (h) 5516 Grove St, Chevy Chase, MD 20015

JORDAN, BARBARA C (US REPRE-SENTATIVE). Congress, Washington, DC 20515. **202-225-3816**

JORDAN, HAMILTON (presidential aide). The White House, Washington, DC 20500. **202-456-6797**

JORDAN, VERNON E JR (civil rights leader). National Urban League, 500 E 62nd St, New York, NY 10021. **212-644-6500.** (h) 14 Barnaby Ln, Hartsdale, NY 10607. **914-428-7649**

JOYCE, JAMES (1882-1941)

JUDD, ORRIN G (?-1976)

JUMBLAT, KAMAL (1917-77)

KAHANE, MEIR (RABBI)(formerly with Jewish Defense League). Box 15117, Jerusalem, Israel. Telephone: **526-127**

KAHN, ALFRED E (civic leader). Chairman, Civil Aeronautics Board, 1825 Connecticut Ave NW, Washington, DC 20428. **202-673-5164.** (h) 910 Independence Ave SE, Washington, DC 20003. **202-543-7107**

KAHN, HERMAN (archivist). National Archives Advisory Council, Washington, DC 20408. **202-655-4000.** Also Yale University, New Haven, CT 06520. **203-436-8330.** (h) 596 Prospect St, New Haven, CT 06511

KALMBACH, HERBERT W (attorney; former attorney to Nixon). 1056 Santiago Dr, Newport Beach, CA 92660. (h) **714-642-1618**

KASTENMEIER, ROBERT W (US REP-RESENTATIVE). Congress, Washington, DC 20515. **202-225-2906**

KATZENBACH, NICHOLAS DEB (attorney). IBM Corp, Old Orchard Rd, Armonk, NY 10504. **914-765-1900.** (h) 5225 Sycamore Ave, Riverdale, NY 10471. **212-796-5501**

KAUFMAN, FRANK A (JUDGE). US Courthouse, Baltimore, MD 21202. **301-962-2600.** (h) 7 Clovelly, Pikesville, MD 21208. **301-486-4294**

KAUFMAN, HENRY (DR)(economist). 90 Broad St, New York, NY 10004. **212-422-3500**

KAUFMAN, IRVING R (CHIEF JUDGE). US Courthouse, Foley Sq, New York, NY 10007. **212-791-0103.** (h) 1185 Park Ave, New York, NY 10028. **212-427-9888**

KAUPER, THOMAS E (educator; formerly with the US Department of Justice). University of Michigan Law School, Ann Arbor, MI 48104. **313-764-9341.** (h) 1125 Fair Oaks, Ann Arbor, MI 48104

KAZIN, ALFRED (professor). Center for Advanced Study, Stanford, CA 94305

KELLEY, CLARENCE M (government official; former FBI director). c/o FBI, Washington, DC 20535. **202-324-3000.** Instructor, University of Alabama at Birmingham, Birmingham, AL 35294. **205-934-4204.** Also c/o Police Foundation, 1909 K St NW, Washington, DC 20006. **202-833-1460**

KEMP, JACK F (US REPRESENTATIVE). Congress, Washington, DC 20515. **202-225-5265**

KENDALL, DONALD M (businessman). Chief executive officer, Pepsi Co, Inc, Anderson Hill Rd, Purchase, NY 10577. **914-253-2000.** (h) Prochuk Rd, Greenwich, CT 06830. **203-661-7040**

KENNAN, GEORGE F (educator; former ambassador). Institute for Advanced Study, Princeton, NJ 08540

KENNEDY, CAROLINE (daughter of former President; free-lance photographer). c/o *Rolling Stone* magazine, 78 E 56th St, New York, NY 10021. **212-486-9560.** Also c/o New York *Daily News*, E 42nd St, New York, NY. **212-682-1234**

KENNEDY, DAVID M (former Secretary of Treasury; civic leader). US Mission to NATO, 1110 Brussels, Belgium

KENNEDY, EDWARD M (US SENATOR). Congress, Washington, DC 20510. **202-224-4543**

KENNEDY, ETHEL (Mrs Robert Francis Kennedy)(widow of former senator). *Kennedy office.* **212-949-4600.** (h) Hickory Hill Mansion, McLean, VA 22101

KENNEDY, JACQUELINE (Mrs John F Kennedy). *See* Jacqueline Onassis

KENNEDY, JOAN (Mrs Edward M Kennedy)(wife of Senator Edward M Kennedy). (h) 636 Chain Bridge Rd, McLean, VA 22101; (h) Squaw Island, Hyannisport, MA 02647

KENNEDY, JOHN FITZGERALD (1917-63)

KENNEDY, JOHN FITZGERALD JR (son of former President)(See mother, Jacqueline Onassis)

KENNEDY, ROBERT FRANCIS (1925-68)

KENNEDY, ROSE (Mrs Joseph Patrick Kennedy, Sr)(Mother of John, Robert, and Edward Kennedy). Kennedy office. **212-949-4600.** (h) Palm Beach, FL 33480

KENNY, JOHN V (1893-1975)

KERNER, OTTO (1908-76)

KERR, CLARK (DR)(astronaut). Johnson Space Ctr, NASA, 2101 NASA Rd, Houston, TX 77058. **713-483-0123.** (h) 713-333-3930

KEYNES, JOHN MAYNARD (1883-1946)

KEYSERLING, LEON H (DR)(economist; former chairman, Council of Economic Advisers). President, Conference on Economic Progress, Washington, DC 20510. **203-363-6222.** (h) 2610 Upton St, Washington, DC 20008. **202-363-6222**

KHAALIS, HAMAAS ABDUL (Islamic terrorist). District of Columbia Jail, Washington, DC 20004. **202-544-7000**

KHEEL, THEODORE W (attorney; labor law). 280 Park Ave, New York, NY 10017. **212-949-8320.** (h) 407 W 246th St, Bronx, NY 10471. **212-548-3320**

KHRUSHCHEV, NIKITA SERGEYEVICH (1894-1971)

KIBBEE, ROBERT J (educator). Chancellor, City University of New York, E 80th St,

New York, NY 10021. **212-794-5317.** (h) 169 E 79th St, New York, NY 10021. **212-731-1320**

KIERNAN, EDWARD J (civic leader). President, International Conference of Police Associations, 1239 Pennsylvania Ave SE, Washington, DC 20003. **202-541-2700**

KING, BILLIE JEAN (Mrs Larry King) (tennis player). Womensports Foundation, Suite 266, 1660 S Amphlet Blvd, San Mateo, CA 94402. **415-574-4622**

KING, CORETTA SCOTT (Mrs Martin Luther King, Jr)(civil rights leader). 234 Sunset Ave NW, Atlanta, GA 30314. **404-534-1956**

KING, DON (boxing promoter). 32 E 69th St, New York, NY 10021. **212-794-2900** **Personal publicist.** Irving Rudd

KING, MARTIN LUTHER JR (1929-68)

KIRK, CLAUDE R JR (former governor of Florida). 2937 Broadway, Riviera Beach, FL 33404. **305-842-2479.** (h) 561 N Lake Tri, West Palm Beach, FL, **305-842-1165**

KIRK, NORMAN E (1923-74)

KIRKLAND, LANE (civic leader). Secretary-treasurer, AFL-CIO, 815 16th St NW, Washington, DC 20006. **202-637-5000.** (h) 5709 26th St NW, Washington, DC 20015

KIRKPATRICK, MILES W (attorney). 1140 Connecticut Ave NW, Washington, DC 20036. **202-872-5150.** Also 123 S Broad St, Philadelphia, PA. **215-491-9311.** (h) 40 Hillside Rd, Philadelphia, PA 19087

KISSINGER, HENRY A (DR)(former Secretary of State). Suite 500, 1800 K St NW, Washington, DC 20006. **202-872-0300**

KISSINGER, NANCY MAGINNES (Mrs Henry A Kissinger)(wife of former Secretary of State).

KLASSEN, ELMER T (former Postmaster-General). (h) 7224 Arrowood Rd, Bethesda, MD 20034

KLEIN, HERBERT G (former Nixon press official; businessman). Vice-president, Metromedia, Inc, 5746 Sunset Blvd, Los Angeles, CA 90028. **213-462-7111**

KLEIN, LAWRENCE R (professor). University of Pennsylvania, Philadelphia, PA 19104. **215-243-5000.** (h) 1317 Medford Rd, Wynnewood, PA 19096. **215-649-4947**

KLEINDIENST, RICHARD G (attorney; former Attorney General). Colonial Mortgage Corp of the District of Columbia, 1101 17th St NW, Washington, DC 20036. **202-296-0510.** (h) 8464 Portland Pl, McLean, VA 22101

KLEPPE, THOMAS S (former Secretary of the Interior). (h) 9609 Hillridge Dr, Kensington, MD 20795

KNAPP, WHITMAN (JUDGE)(Knapp Commission). US District Court, Foley Sq, New York, NY 10007. **212-791-0103.** (h) 79 W 12th St, New York, NY 10011

KNAUER, VIRGINIA H (Mrs)(consumer advocate). US Department of Health, Education, and Welfare, Washington, DC 20201. **202-245-6158.** (h) Morelton, 9601 Milnor St, Philadelphia, PA 19114

KOCH, EDWARD I (MAYOR). City Hall, New York, NY 10007 **Press Secretary.** Maureen Connelly. **212-566-5090**

KOPECHNE, MARY JO (?-1969)

KORFF, BARUCH (RABBI)(former head, Nixon Justice Fund; founder, United States Citizens' Congress). 1221 Connecticut Ave NW, Washington, DC 20036. **202-347-6597**

KOSTELANETZ, ANDRE (orchestra conducter). c/o NY Philharmonic, New York, NY. **212-787-3700.** (h) 11th Floor, 1995 Broadway, New York, NY 10023

KRAUSE, ALLISON (?-1970)

KREPS, JUANITA M (government official). Secretary, US Department of Commerce, Washington, DC 20230. **202-377-2000.** (h) 1407 W Pettigrew St, Durham, NC 27705. **919-286-3701**

KROGH, EGIL JR (disbarred attorney; businessman). Swensen's Ice Cream Co, 333 Pine St, San Francisco, CA 94104. **415-989-8466**

KROL, JOHN JOSEPH (CARDINAL). 222 N 17th St, Philadelphia, PA 19103. **215-587-3800.** (h) 5700 City Ave, Philadelphia, PA 19131. **215-473-3972**

KUHN, BOWIE (commissioner of baseball). Office of the Commissioner, 75 Rockefeller Plz, New York, NY 10019. **212-586-7400.** (h) 320 N Murray Ave, Ridgewood, NJ 07450

KUNSTLER, WILLIAM M (attorney). Center for Constitutional Rights, 853 Broadway, New York, NY 10003. **212-674-3303.** (h) 13 Gay St, New York, NY 10014. **212-924-5661**

LACEY, FREDERICK B (JUDGE). US District Court, Newark, NJ 07102. **201-645-3730.** (h) **201-645-6042**

LAIRD, MELVIN ROBERT (former Secretary of Defense). c/o *Reader's Digest,* Suite 212, 1730 Rhode Island Ave NW, Washington, DC 20036. **202-223-1642.** (h) PO Box 279, Marshfield, WI 54449

LAMM, RICHARD D (GOVERNOR). 136 State Capitol, Denver, CO 80203. **303-839-2471.** (h) 400 E 8th Ave, Denver, CO 80203. **303-837-8350**

LANCE, THOMAS BERTRAM (banker; former director, Office of Management and Budget). (h) Atlanta, GA. **404-231-1870.** Office: PO Box 637, Calhoun, GA 30701. **404-629-1226** (Jule Miller, Secretary)

LANDRIEU, MAURICE ("Moon")(MAYOR). City Hall, New Orleans, LA 71025. **504-586-9141.** (h) 4301 S Prieur St, New Orleans, LA 70125

LANGDON, JERVIS JR (businessman). President, Penn Central Transportation, 6 Penn Center Plz, Philadelphia, PA 19104. **215-594-1000.** (h) Querry Farms, Elmira, NY 14902. **607-732-0221**

LAQUEUR, WALTER (Professor). Georgetown University, Washington, DC 20006. **202-625-0100.** Also Ctr for Strategic and International Studies, 1800 K St NW, Washington, DC 20006

LAXALT, PAUL (US SENATOR). Congress, Washington, DC 20510. **202-224-3542**

LEARY, TIMOTHY L (former LSD advocate; turned state's evidence)
Publisher. Grove Press, 55 E 11th St, New York, NY 10012. **212-677-2400**

LEFANTE, JOSEPH A (US REPRESENTATIVE). Congress, Washington, DC 20515. **202-225-2765**

LEFKOWITZ, LOUIS J (government official). State Attorney General, the Capitol, Albany, NY 12201. **518-474-8390.** (h) 575 Park Ave, New York, NY 10021

LEGGETT, ROBERT L (US REPRESENTATIVE). Congress, Washington, DC 20515. **202-225-5716**

LEKACHMAN, ROBERT (professor; economist). City University of New York 10012. **212-794-5317.** (h) 600 W 115th St, New York, NY 10014. **212-864-5037**

LENIN, VLADIMIR (VLADIMIR ILYICH ULYANOV) (1870-1924)

LENNON, JOHN (musician). c/o Capitol Records, 1370 Avenue of the Americas, New York, NY 10019. **212-757-7470.** (h) 1 W 72nd St, New York, NY 10023

LENT, NORMAN F (US REPRESENTATIVE). Congress, Washington, DC 20515. **202-225-7896**

LEONARD, JERRIS (attorney). Leonard, Cohen and Gettings, 1700 Pennsylvania Ave NW, Washington, DC 20006. **202-872-1095.** (h) 5109 Manning Pl NW, Washington, DC 20016. **212-966-1434**

LEONTIEF, WASSILY W (economist; professor). Department of Economics, New York University, 518 Tisch Hall, Washington Sq, NY 10003. **212-598-2181.** (h) Lake West, Buron, VT 05871

LETELIER, ORLANDO (?-1976)

LEVI, EDWARD H (former Attorney General; former president, University of Chicago; professor). University of Chicago, 1116 E 59th St, Chicago, IL 60637. **312-753-2456.** Also Stanford University (1977-78), Stanford, CA 94305. **415-497-2300**

LEVINE, JAMES (conductor). c/o Metropolitan Opera, Lincoln Center Plz, New York, NY 10023. **212-799-3100**
Agent: Columbia Artists Management, Inc. **212-397-6900**

LEVINE, LOUIS L (economist). 1309 L St NW, Washington, DC 20005. (h) 6429 31st St NW, Washington, DC 20015. **212-966-7363**

LEVITT, ARTHUR (government official). State Comptroller, State Office Building, Albany, NY 12207. **518-474-8390.** (h) 203 N 72nd St, New York, NY 10031

LEWIS, ARTHUR D (businessman). President, American Bus Association, 1025 Connecticut Ave NW, Washington, DC 20036. **202-293-5890.** (h) 631 West Rd, New Canaan, CT 06840

LEWIS, JORDON (government official). Director, National Bureau of Standards, Technical Incentives Program, Gaithersburg,

MD 20234. **301-921-1000.** (h) 3707 33rd Pl NW, Washington, DC 20008. **202-966-1734**

LIDDY, G GORDON (former Nixon aide). (h) 9310 Ivanhoe Rd, Oxon Hill, MD 20010. **301-567-3607**

LINCOLN, ABRAHAM (1809-65)

LINCOLN, GEORGE ARTHUR (1907-75)

LINDBERGH, CHARLES AUGUSTUS (1902-74)

LINDSAY, JOHN VLIET (former mayor of New York; former congressman; author). (h) 1 W 67th St, New York, NY 10043

LINOWITZ, SOL M (attorney). Coudert Bros, 1 Farragut Sq S, Washington, DC 20006. **202-783-3010.** (h) 2325 Wyoming Ave NW, Washington, DC 20008. **202-483-9086**

LIN PIAO (1908-?71)

LIPPMANN, WALTER (1889-1974)

LITTLE, JOANNE (North Carolina jail rape case). North Carolina Corrections Center for Women, 1034 Bragg St, Raleigh, NC 27610. **919-828-4366**

LODGE, HENRY CABOT (former senator; author; lecturer). (h) 275 Hale St, Beverly, MA 01915

LOEB, WILLIAM (publisher). . *Manchester Union-Leader,* Manchester, NH 03105. **603-668-4321**

LOGUE, EDWARD J (educator). Yale Law School, New Haven, CT 06520. **203-436-8330.** (h) 80 Pierrepont St, Brooklyn Hts, NY 11201. **212-237-0561**

LOMBARDI, VINCENT T (1913-70)

LONG, CLARENCE D (US REPRESENTATIVE). Congress, Washington, DC 20515. **202-225-3061**

LONG, RUSSELL B (US SENATOR). Congress, Washington, DC 20510. **202-224-4623**

LONGLEY, JAMES B (GOVERNOR). State House, Augusta, ME 04333. **207-289-3531.** (h) The Blaine House, Augusta, ME 04333. **207-289-2121**

LORD, MILES W (JUDGE). US Courthouse, Minneapolis, MN 55401. **612-348-3155.** (h) Box 960, Route 7, Excelsior, MN 55331. **612-474-9557**

LOVE, JOHN A (businessman). Ideal Basic Industries, Ideal Plz, Denver, CO 80201. **303-623-5661.** (h) 100 Lafayette, Denver, CO 80213. **303-744-6873**

LOWERY, ROBERT O (government official). Commissioner, Bureau of Fire Investigation, 110 Church St, New York, NY 10017. **212-566-3488**

LUCE, CHARLES F (utilities businessman). Consolidated Edison Co of New York, 4 Irving Pl, New York, NY 10003. **212-460-4600.** (h) 18 Ridge Rd, Bronxville, NY 10708. **914-793-2111**

LUCE, CLARE BOOTHE (Mrs Henry Robinson Luce)(playwright; former congresswoman; former ambassador). (h) 4559 Kahala Ave, Honolulu, HI 96816

LUCEY, PATRICK J (ambassador to Mexico; former governor of Wisconsin). American Embassy, PO Box 1471, Laredo, TX 78040. **905-553-3333**

LYNN, JAMES T (former official, Office of Management and Budget). (h) 6736 Newbold Dr, Bethesda, MD 20034

MACARTHUR, DOUGLAS (GENERAL OF THE ARMY) (1880-1964)

MACDONALD, TORBERT H (1917-76)

MACGREGOR, CLARK (businessman). Vice-president, United Technologies Corp, 1125 15th St NW, Washington, DC 20005. **202-785-7400.** (h) 2834 Foxhall Rd NW, Washington, DC 20007. **202-966-8252**

MACLAINE, SHIRLEY (actress). c/o Chasin-Park-Citron Agency, 9255 W Sunset Blvd, Los Angeles, CA 90069. **213-273-7190.** (h) Conway, MA 01341

MACOMBER, WILLIAM B JR (ambassador to Turkey). c/o US State Department, Washington, DC 20520. **202-632-3320**

MACPHAIL, LELAND S President, (businessman). American League of Baseball, 280 Park Ave, New York, NY 10017. **212-682-7000**

MADDOX, LESTER G (former governor of Georgia). (h) Mount Paran Rd, Atlanta, GA 30338. **404-261-0718**

MAGNUSON, WARREN G (US SENATOR). Congress, Washington, DC 20510. **202-224-2621**

MAGRUDER, JEB S (former White House aide; author). (h) c/o *Young Life*, 720 W Monument St, PO Box 520, Colorado Springs, CO 80901. **303-473-5368**

MAGUIRE, ANDREW (US REPRESENTATIVE). Congress, Washington, DC 20515. **202-225-4465**

MAHEU, ROBERT A (former aid to Howard Hughes). Leisure Industries, PO Box 11068, Las Vegas, NV 89101. **702-739-8411**

MAIER, HENRY W (MAYOR). City Hall, Milwaukee, WI 53202. **414-278-2200.** (h) 1129 N Jackson St, Milwaukee, WI 53202

MAILER, NORMAN (author). c/o Molly Malone Cook, PO Box 338, Provincetown, MA 02657

Agent. Scott Meredith, 845 3rd Ave, New York, NY 10022. **212-245-5500**

MALCOLM X (1925-65)

MALEK, FREDERIC V (motel businessman). Marriot Corp, 5161 River Rd, Washington, DC 20016. **201-986-5101.** (h) 6709 Lupine Ln, McLean, VA 22101

MANDEL, MARVIN (Suspended Governor; convicted influence peddler). *Contact.* Frank A DeFilippo, former press secretary, Cross Keys Rd, Baltimore, MD, 21210. **301-323-4490**

MANN, JAMES R (US REPRESENTATIVE). Congress, Washington, DC 20515. **202-225-6030**

MANSFIELD, MIKE (MICHAEL J) (former senate majority leader; ambassador to Japan). c/o US State Department, Washington, DC 20520. **202-632-3320**

MANSON, CHARLES M (cult leader; convicted mass murderer). Folsom State Prison, Folsom, CA 95630. **916-985-2561**

MAO TSE-TUNG (1893-1976)

MARAZITI, JOSEPH J (former US congressman; attorney). Maraziti, Maraziti, and Cerra, 117 Cornelia St, Boonton, NJ 07005. **201-334-2728**

MARCHETTI, VICTOR L (former CIA agent). 265 Lafayette St, New York, NY 10013. **212-925-4164**

MARDIAN, ROBERT C (attorney). 2323 N Central Ave, Phoenix, AZ 22101. **602-253-3989**

MARLAND, SIDNEY P JR (educator). National Advisory Council on Career Education, 425 13th St NW, Washington, DC 20010. **212-874-7127.** (h) 20 W 64th St, New York, NY. **212-874-7127.** (h) Bigelow Rd, Hampton, CT 06247

MARSHAK, ROBERT E (DR) (physicist; educator). President, City College of New York. **212-794-5317.** (h) 101 Central Park W, New York, NY 10023

MARSHALL, RAY (government official). Secretary, US Department of Labor, Washington, DC 20210. **202-523-8271** (h) Falls Church, VA 22046

MARSHALL, THURGOOD (JUDGE). Associate Justice, US Supreme Court, Washington, DC 20543. **202-393-1640**

MARTIN, GRAHAM A (former ambassador to Vietnam). c/o Retirement Division, PER/ES/RET, Rm 1251, New State, Washington, DC 20520. **202-632-2242.** (h) 907 N Stratford Rd, Winston-Salem, NC 27104. **919-723-5028**

MARTIN, PRESTON (businessman). Chairman PMI Mortgage Insurance, 555 California St, San Francisco, CA 94104. **415-788-7878.** (h) 399 Atherton Ave, Atherton, CA 94025. **415-854-3383**

MARTIN, WILLIAM McCHESNEY JR (banker; goverment official). 800 17th St NW, Washington, DC 20006. **202-624-2530.** (h) 2861 Woodland Dr NW, Washington, DC 20008. **202-234-2323**

MARTINEZ, EUGENIO R (convicted Watergate burglar). (h) Miami, FL

Attorney. Daniel E Schultz, Suite 510, 1990 M St NW, Washington, DC 20036. **202-223-4007**

MARX, GROUCHO (Julius) (1891-1977)

MARX, KARL (1818-83)

MATHEWS, F DAVID (DR) (former Secretary of Health, Education, and Welfare). President, University of Alabama, University, AL 35486. **205-348-5100**

MATHIAS, CHARLES McC JR (US SENATOR). Congress, Washington, DC 20510. **202-224-4654**

MATISSE, HENRI (1869-1954)

MATSUNAGA, SPARK M (US SENATOR). Congress, Washington, DC 20510. **202-224-6361**

MAYER, JEAN (scientist). Tufts University, Ballou Hall, Medford, MA 02155. **617-628-5000.** (h) 161 Packard Ave, Somerville, MA 02143. **617-666-5508**

MAYS, WILLIE (retired baseball player). c/o New York Mets, Shea Stadium, Flushing, NY 11368. **212-672-3000**

McCARTHY, EUGENE J (educator; former senator). New School for Social Research, 65 5th Ave, New York, NY 10021. **212-741-5600.** (h) 3053 Q St NW, Washington, DC 20007. **202-333-1864**

McCLAIN, JAMES D (?-1970)

McCLELLAN, JOHN L (US SENATOR). Congress, Washington, DC 20510. **202-224-2353**

McCLORY, ROBERT (US REPRESENTATIVE). Congress, Washington, DC 20515. **202-225-5221**

McCLOSKEY, PAUL N JR (US REPRESENTATIVE). Congress, Washington, DC 20515. **202-225-5411**

McCLOSKEY, ROBERT J (ambassador to The Netherlands). c/o Department of State, Washington, DC 20520. **202-632-3320**

McCLOY, JOHN J (attorney). Milbank, Tweed, Hope, Hadley, and McCloy, 1 Chase Manhattan Plz, New York, NY 10005. **212-422-2660**

McCOLOUGH, C PETER (businessman). Xerox Corp, Stamford, CT 06904. **203-329-8911**

McCORD, JAMES W JR (convicted Watergate burglar)
Attorney. William A Mann, 4700 Authority Pl, Camp Springs, MD 20031. **301-423-4422**

McCORMACK, JOHN W (former congressman). (h) 111 Perkins St, Jamaica Plains, Boston, MA 02130

McCRACKEN, PAUL W (professor). Graduate School of Business Administration, Edmund Ezra Day University Ann Arbor, MI 48101. **313-761-7567.** (h) 2564 Hawthorne Rd, Ann Arbor, MI 48104. **313-761-7567**

McFALL, JOHN J (US REPRESENTATIVE). Congress, Washington DC 20515. **202-225-2511**

McGEE, GALE W (ambassador to Organization of American States). US State Department, Rm 6494, Washington, DC 20520. **202-632-9376.** (h) 60 Morningside Dr, New York, NY 10027

McGILL, WILLIAM J (DR), (educator). President, Columbia University, New York, NY 10027. **212-280-1754**

McGOVERN, GEORGE S (US SENATOR). Congress, Washington, DC 20510. **202-224-2321**

McINTYRE, THOMAS J (US SENATOR). Congress, Washington, DC 20510. **202-224-2841**

McKAY, ROBERT B (civic leader). Director, Aspen Institute for Humanistic Studies, 717 5th Ave, New York, NY 10034. (h) 29 Washington Sq W, New York, NY 10021. **212-475-3076**

McKINNEY, STEWART B (US REPRESENTATIVE). Congress, Washington, DC 20515. **202-225-5541**

McLAREN, RICHARD W (JUDGE). (?-1977).

McNAIR, ROBERT E (attorney; former governor of South Carollina). PO Box 11895, Columbia, SC 29211. **803-799-9900.** (h) Lake Morray, Columbia, SC 29201. **803-781-4215**

McNAMARA, ROBERT S (banker). President, World Bank, 1818 H St NW, Washington, DC 20006. **202-393-6360.** (h) 2412 Tracy Pl, Washington, DC 20008

MEAD, MARGARET (DR) (anthropologist). Columbia University, New York, NY 10027, **212-280-5025.** Also, The American Museum of Natural History, 15 W 77th St, New York, NY 10024. **212-873-4225.** (h) 211 Central Park W, New York, NY 10024. **212-799-2845**

MEANS, RUSSELL C (Indian rights leader). American Indian Movement, Virginia St, St Paul, MN 55071. **612-488-7267**
Attorney. William Kunstler, 853 Broadway, New York, NY 10003. **212-674-3303.**

MEANY, GEORGE (labor leader). President, AFL-CIO, 815 16th St NW, Washington, DC 20006. **202-637-5213.** (h) 7535 Cayuga Ave, Bethesda, MD 20234

MEHTA, ZUBIN (musician; conductor). c/o Los Angeles Philharmonic Music Ctr, Los Angeles, CA 90012. **213-972-7211**

MELCHER, JOHN (US SENATOR). Congress, Washington, DC 20510. **202-224-2644**

MENUHIN, YEHUDI (violinist). c/o Columbia Artists Management, Inc, 165 W 57th St, New York, NY 10019. **212-397-6900**

MERHIGE, ROBERT R JR (JUDGE). Federal Court Bldg, Richmond, VA 23219. **804-643-7171.** (h) 5 Kanawha Rd, Richmond, VA 23219. **804-282-6358**

MERRICK, DAVID (theatrical producer). 246 W 44th St, New York, NY 10036. **212-563-7520**

METCALF, LEE (1911-1978)

METCLAFE, RALPH H (US REPRESENTATIVE). Congress, Washington, DC 20515. **202-225-4372**

METZENBAUM, HOWARD M (US SENATOR). Congress, Washington, DC 20510. **202-224-2315**

MEYNER, ROBERT B (attorney). Suite 2500, Gateway 1, Newark, NJ 07102. **201-624-2800.** (h) 372 Lincoln St, Phillipsburg, NJ 08865. **201-859-5189**

MICHEL, ROBERT H (US REPRESENTATIVE). Congress, Washington, DC 20510. **202-225-6201**

MICHENER, JAMES A (author). (h) Pipersville, PA 18947. *Secretary's office.* **215-847-5944**

MIDDENDORF, J WILLIAM II (government official). Office of the Secretary of the Navy, Washington, DC 20350. **202-546-6700**

MIKVA, ABNER J (US REPRESENTATIVE). Congress, Washington, DC 20515. **202-225-4835**

MILLER, ARNOLD R (labor leader). President, United Mine Workers of America, 900 15th St NW, Washington, DC 20005. **202-683-0530**

MILLER, ARTHUR (playwright). c/o IFA, Inc, 1301 6th Ave, New York, NY 10019. **212-490-5700**

MILLER, HERBERT J JR (attorney, former federal affairs counselor). Suite 1000, 1150 Connecticut Ave, NW, Washington, DC 20036. **202-467-5700.** (h) **301-620-4615**

MILLER, JOHNNY (golfer). 10880 Wilshire Blvd, Los Angeles, CA 10024. (h) Silverado Country Club, Napa, CA 94558. **707-255-2970**

MILLIKEN, WILLIAM G (GOVERNOR). State Capitol Bldg, Lansing, MI 48909. **517-373-3400.** (h) 6103 Peninsula Dr, Traverse City, MI 49684

MILLS, WILBUR D (former congressman). (h) 1600 S Eads, Arlington, VA 22202. **703-920-8669**

MINDSZENTY, JOZSEF (CARDINAL). (1892-1975)

MINISH, JOSEPH G (US REPRESENTA-TIVE). Congress, Washington, DC 20515. **202-225-5035**

MINK, PATSY (government official). Assistant Secretary for Oceans and International Environmental and Scientific Affairs, US State Department, Washington, DC 20520. **202-632-1554.** (h) Honolulu, HI. **808-671-0793.** (h) 611 6th Pl SW, Washington, DC 20024. **202-554-4919**

MINNELLI, LIZA (entertainer). c/o Rudin and Perlstein, 9601 Wilshire Blvd, Beverly Hills, CA 90210. **213-278-6060**

MITCHELL, CLARENCE M JR (government official). Director, Washington Bureau, National Association for the Advancement of Colored People, Suite 410, Woodward, Bldg, 733 15th St NW, Washington, DC 20005. **202-638-2269.** *Baltimore law office.* **301-523-6275.** (h) 1324 Druid Hill Ave, Baltimore, MD 21217. **301-523-5083**

MITCHELL, GEORGE W (economist). Federal Reserve Board, Washington, DC 20511. **202-452-3000.** (h) 84 Rittenhouse NE, Washington, DC 20500. **202-723-5455**

MITCHELL, HENRY H (1938-72)

MITCHELL, JOHN NEWTON (former Attorney General). Maxwell Air Force Base Prison, Montgomery, AL 36113. **205-293-2784**

MITCHELL, MARTHA (Mrs John Newton Mitchell) (1918-76)

MITCHELL, PARREN J (US REPRE-SENTATIVE). Congress, Washington, DC 20515. **202-225-4751**

MOLIERE (JEAN BAPTISTE POQUELIN) (1622-73)

MONDALE, WALTER F (Vice-President). Old Executive Office Bldg, Washington, DC. **202-456-6606.** (h) 3421 Lowell St NW, Washington, DC 20016

MONROE, MARILYN (1926-62)

MONTGOMERY, G V (US REPRE-SENTATIVE). Congress, Washington, DC 20515. **202-225-5031**

MONTOYA, JOSEPH M (businessman; former senator). Joseph Montoya Enterprises, 11 E San Francisco, Santa Fe, NM 87501. **505-983-5346.** (h) 209 Callecita Pl, Santa Fe, NM 87501. **505-982-4793**

MOON, SUN MYUNG *See* Sun Myung Moon

MOORE, ARCH A JR (former governor of West Virginia). (h) 507 Jefferson Ave, Glen Dale, WV 26038. **304-845-2609**

MOORE, GEOFFREY H (DR)(economist). National Bureau of Economic Research, Inc, 261 Madison Ave, New York, NY 10016. **212-682-3190.** (h) 1171 Valley Rd, New Canaan, CT 06840. **203-966-2103**

MOORE, GEORGE C (?-1973)

MOORE, PAUL JR (BISHOP). Christ Church Cathedral, 1047 Amsterdam Ave, New York, NY 10025. **212-678-6955**

MOORE, SARA JANE (attempted assassin). Women's Federal Prison, PO Box W, Alderson, WV 24910. **304-445-2901**

MOORE, WILLIAM H (former railroad businessman; retired president of Penn Central). (h) 11012 Stanmore Dr, Potomac, MD 20854. **201-299-8998**

MOORER, THOMAS H (ADMIRAL) (former chairman, Joint Chiefs of Staff). c/o The Pentagon, Washington, DC 20301. **202-697-9121.** (h) 402 Barbour St, Enfaula, AL 36027

MOORHEAD, WILLIAM S (US REPRE-SENTATIVE). Congress, Washington, DC 20515. **202-225-2301**

MORGAN, THOMAS E (DR)(former congressman; Hugh Scott associate). *Fredericktown, PA office.* **412-377-2288.** (h) Fredericktown, PA 15333. **412-377-3144**

MORGENTHAU, HANS J (Professor). New School for Social Research, 66 W 12th St, New York, NY 10011. **212-741-5600.** (h)

19 E 80th St, New York, NY 10021. **212-734-5204**

MORGENTHAU, ROBERT M (attorney; former New York district attorney). (h) 200 E 15th St, New York, NY 10003. **212-228-4676**

MORSE, ROBERT A (1928-73)

MORSE, WAYNE (1900-74)

MORTON, ROGERS C B (former congressman; former Secretary of the Interior; former Secretary of Commerce). (h) RD 1, Easton, MD 21601. **301-822-6353**

MOSBACHER, EMIL JR (businessman). Dollar Savings Bank, 515 Madison Ave, New York, NY 10022. **212-584-6000.** (h) Nipowin Island, Mend Point, Greenwich, CT 06830. **203-661-8116**

MOSCONE, GEORGE R (MAYOR). San Francisco City Hall, San Francisco, CA 94102. **415-558-6161**

MOSES, ROBERT (public official; park developer). Randall's Island, PO Box 35, Triboro Station, New York, NY 10035. **212-876-9700**

MOSS, FRANK E (former senator). 1848 S Wasatch Dr, Salt Lake City, UT 84108. **801-487-5144**

MOSS, JOHN E (US REPRESENTA-TIVE). Congress, Washington, DC 20515. **202-225-7163**

MOTT, STEWART R (political activist). Stewart R Mott and Associates, 515 Madison Ave, New York, NY 10022. **212-421-2155**

MOYNIHAN, DANIEL PATRICK (US SENATOR). Congress, Washington, DC 20510. **202-224-4451**

MUHAMMAD ALI *See* Ali, Muhammed

MUHAMMAD, ELIJAH (1897-1975)

MURPHY, JOHN M (US REPRESENTA-TIVE). Congress, Washington, DC 20515. **202-225-3406**

MURPHY, PATRICK V (civic leader). Police Foundation, 1909 K St NW, Washington, DC 20006. **212-833-1460**

MURPHY, THOMAS A (businessman). Chief executive officer, General Motors, Inc, Detroit, MI 48013. **313-556-5000.** (h) 3044 W Grand Blvd, Detroit, MI 48202

MURTAGH, JOHN M (1911-76)

MUSKIE, EDMUND S (US SENATOR). Congress, Washington, DC 20510. **202-224-5344**

MYERSON, BESS (consumer advocate). New York *Daily News*, 220 E 42nd St, New York, NY 10017. **212-682-1234.** (h) 25 Sutton Pl S, New York, NY 10022

NABOKOV, VLADIMIR (1899-1977)

NADER, RALPH (consumer advocate; attorney; author). PO Box 19367, Washington, DC 20034. **202-234-1978**

NAMATH, JOE (former football player). c/o Los Angeles Rams, 10271 W Pico Blvd, Los Angeles, CA 90064. **213-277-4700.** Or, c/o International Famous Agency, 1301 Avenue of the Americas, New York, NY 10019. **212-556-5600**

NASSER, GAMAL ABDEL (1918-70)

NASSIKAS, JOHN N (attorney; former chairman, Federal Power Commission; member, National Petroleum Council). 21 Dupont Cir NW, Washington, DC 20036. **212-785-0200.** (h) 1131 Litton Ln, McLean, VA 22101. **703-356-6582**

NATCHER, WILLIAM H (US REPRESENTATIVE). Congress, Washington, DC 20515. **202-225-3501**

NEDZI, LUCIEN N (US REPRESENTATIVE). Congress, Washington, DC 20515. **202-225-6276**

NEEDHAM, JAMES J (professor). Graduate Division of the College of Business Administration, St John's University, 20 Broad St, New York, NY 10005. (h) 29 Sturgis Rd, Bronxville, NY 10708. **914-337-6764**

NELSON, GAYLORD A (US SENATOR). Congress, Washington, DC 20510. **202-224-5323**

NESSEN, RON (former Ford press secretary). Board of Trustees, John F Kennedy Center for the Performing Arts, Washington, DC 20566. **202-872-0466.** (h) 4321 Woodberry St, University Park, MD 20782

NEWMAN, PAUL (actor). c/o Rogers and Cowan, Inc, 9665 Wilshire Blvd, Beverly Hills, CA 90210. **213-275-4581**

NEWTON, HUEY P (political activist). President, Black Panther party, 8501 E 14th St, Oakland, CA 94621. **415-638-0195**

NICHOLSON, JACK (actor; producer). c/o Sandy Bresler and Associates, 190 N Cannon Dr, Beverly Hills, CA 90210. **213-278-5200**

NICKLAUS, JACK (golfer). 321 Northlake Blvd, Hwy 1, North Palm Beach, FL 33408. **305-626-3900.** (h) 11397 Old Harbour Rd, North Palm Beach, FL 33048

NIXON, JULIE. *See* Julie Nixon Eisenhower.

NIXON, PATRICIA (Mrs Richard Milhous Nixon) (wife of former President). Home: Casa Pacifica, San Clemente, CA 92672. **714-492-0011**

NIXON, RICHARD MILHOUS (former President). (h) Casa Pacifica, San Clemente, CA 92672. **714-492-0011.** Frequents Estrella Country Club, San Clemente, CA 92672. **714-492-6128**
Agent. Irving Lazar, 465 Madison Ave, New York, NY 10022. **212-355-1177**

NIXON, TRICIA. *See* Tricia Nixon Cox.

NOEL, CLEO A JR (?–1973)

NOEL, PHILIP W (former governor of Rhode Island). 1015 Hospital Trust Bldg, Providence, RI 02889. **401-274-1144.** (h) 21 Kirby Ave, Warwick, RI 02889. **401-738-4544**

NORTON, ELEANOR HOLMES (civic leader). Chairman, Equal Employment Opportunity Commission, Washington, DC 20506. **202-634-7040.** (h) 3817 13th St NW, Washington, DC. **202-829-7005**

NORTON, KEN (boxer). c/o Murray Goodman, 232 Madison Ave, 10016. **212-686-4231.** (h) Los Angeles, CA

NUNN, SAM (US SENATOR). Congress, Washington, DC 20510. **202-224-3541**

NUREYEV, RUDOLF (ballet dancer). *Contact.* Lillian Lidman, c/o Nederlander, 1564 Broadway, New York, NY 10036. **212-765-3906**

O'BRIEN, LAWRENCE F (former National Democratic chairman). Commissioner, National Basketball Association, 645 5th Ave, New York, NY 10026. **212-594-3000.** Also 860 United Nations Plz, New York, NY 10017. **212-486-0995**

O'NEILL, EUGENE (1888–1953)

O'NEILL, THOMAS P JR ("TIP") (Speaker of the House). US Congress, Washington, DC 20515. **202-225-5111**

OATES, JOYCE CAROL (author; professor). Department of English, University of Windsor, Windsor, Ont, Canada. **519-253-4232**

OBEY, DAVID R (US REPRESENTATIVE). Congress, Washington, DC 20515. **202-225-3365**

OGILVIE, RICHARD B (attorney; former governor of Illinois). 1 First National Plz, Chicago, IL 60670. **312-786-7500.** (h) 1500 N Lake Shore Dr, Chicago, IL 60610

OKUN, ARTHUR M (DR) (economist). Senior Fellow, Brookings Institution, 1775 Massachusetts Ave, Washington, DC 20036. **202-797-6000.** (h) 2809 Ellicott St NW, Washington, DC 20008. **202-363-2016**

ONASSIS, ARISTOTLE SOCRATES (1906–75)

ONASSIS, JACQUELINE BOUVIER (Mrs Aristotle Onassis; former Mrs John F Kennedy) (widow of former President). Kennedy office. **212-949-4600.** (h) Hyannisport, MA 02647. (h) 1040 5th Ave, New York, NY 10028

ONO, YOKO (Mrs John Lennon) (wife of musician). (h) 1 W 72nd St, New York, NY 10023

ORMANDY, EUGENE (conductor). c/o Philadelphia Orchestra Association, 1420 Locust St, Philadelphia, PA 19102. **215-893-1900**

OSWALD, LEE HARVEY (1939–63)

OTTINGER, RICHARD L (US REPRESENTATIVE). Congress, Washington, DC 20515. **202-225-6506**

OZAWA, SEIJI (conductor). c/o Boston Symphony Orchestra, Boston, MA 62101. **617-266-1492.** Also Columbia Artists Management, Inc, 165 W 57th St, New York, NY 10019. **212-397-6900**

PACKWOOD, ROBERT W (Bob) (SENATOR). Congress, Washington, DC 20510. **202-224-5244**

PALEY, WILLIAM S (broadcaster). Chairman of the board, CBS, Inc, 51 W 52nd St, New York, NY 10019. **212-975-4321.** (h) Kiluna Farm, Manhasset, NY 11030

PALMER, ARNOLD (golfer). Arnold Palmer Aviation, R D, Latrobe, PA 15650. **412-537-7751.** (h) Box 52, Youngstown, PA 15696.

PAPP, JOSEPH (producer). 425 Lafayette St, New York, NY 10003. **212-677-1750**

PARK, TONG SUN (accused Korean CIA influence peddler). c/o South Korean Embassy, 2320 Massachusetts Ave NW, Washington, DC 20008. **202-483-7383**

PARKINSON, KENNETH W (attorney; civic leader). 1828 L St NW, Washington, DC 20036. **202-457-1600.** (h) 5417 Duvall Dr, Westmoreland Hills, MD 20016. **301-229-8494**

PARSKY, GERALD L (formerly with Treasury Department). (h) 2911 45th St NW, Washington, DC. **202-686-1917**

PASSER, HAROLD C (economist; former bank president). Eastman Savings and Loan, 343 State St, Rochester, NY 14650. **716-724-4994.** (h) 133 Imperial Cir, Rochester, NY 14617. **716-342-8762**

PASTORE, JOHN O (former senator). Turkshead Bldg, Providence, RI. **401-351-1635.** (h) 91 Mountain Laurel Dr, Cranston, RI 02920

PATERSON, BASIL A (politician) (former member Democratic National Committee). 1625 Massachusetts Ave NW, Washington, DC 20036. **202-797-5900.** (h) 888 7th Ave, New York, NY 10021. **212-541-6900**

PATMAN, WRIGHT (1893–1976)

PATTERSON, ELLMORE C (banker). Chairman of Executive Committee, Morgan Guaranty, 23 Wall St, New York, NY 10015. **212-483-2323.** (h) Hook Rd, Bedford Village, NY 10506. **914-234-7818**

PAULING, LINUS C (DR) (chemist; Nobel Prizewinner). Linus Pauling Institute of Science and Medicine, 2700 Sand Hill Rd, Menlo Park, CA 94025. **415-854-0843.** (h) Salmon Creek, Big Sur, CA 93920

PEARSON, JAMES B (US SENATOR). Congress, Washington, DC 20510. **202-224-4774**

PECHMAN, JOSEPH A (DR) (economist). Brookings Institution, 1775 Massachusetts Ave NW, Washington, DC 20006. **202-797-6050.** (h) 7112 Wilson Ln, Bethesda, MD 20034. **201-299-3497**

PELÉ (EDSON ARANTES DO NASCIMENTO) (soccer player). c/o Warner Communications, Inc, 75 Rockefeller Plz, New York, NY 10019. **212-484-6031**

PELL, CLAIBORNE (US SENATOR). Congress, Washington, DC 20510. **202-224-4642**

PEPPER, CLAUDE (US REPRESENTATIVE). Congress, Washington, DC 20515. **202-225-3931**

PERCY, CHARLES H (US SENATOR). Congress, Washington, DC 20510. **202-224-2152**

PERKINS, CARL D (US REPRESENTATIVE). Congress, Washington, DC 20515. **202-225-4935**

PERON, JUAN DOMINGO (1895–1974)

PEROT, H ROSS (philanthropist; businessman). Electronic Data Systems Inc, 7171 Forest Ln, Dallas, TX 75230. **214-661-6000**

PETERSEN, HENRY E (former Justice Department official). 916 Daleview Dr, Silver Spring, MD 20901

PETERSON, PETER G (businessman). Chairman of the board, Lehman Brothers, Inc, 2 S William St, New York, NY 10004. **212-269-3700**

PETERSON, RUSSELL (environmentalist). Council on Environmental Quality, 722 Jackson Pl, Washington, DC 20006. **202-633-7027.** (h) 1413 36th St NW, Washington, DC 20007

PETTY, RICHARD (race car driver). Petty Enterprises, Randleman, NC 27317. **919-498-3745.** (h) Box 621, Route 3, Randleman, NC 27317

PHAM DANG LAM (?–1975)

PICASSO, PABLO (1881–1973)

PIKE, OTIS G (US REPRESENTATIVE). Congress, Washington, DC 20515. **202-225-3826**

PINTER, HAROLD (British playwright). c/o David Fromkin, 950 3rd Ave, New York, NY 10022. **212-838-6333**

PLAYER, GARY (golfer). c/o International Management, Inc, 767 5th Ave, New York, NY 10022. **212-832-4990.** *Contact.* Mike Halstead

PLIMPTON, GEORGE (author; editor). 541 E 72nd St, New York, NY 10021. **212-861-0016**

POAGE, W R (US REPRESENTATIVE). Congress, Washington, DC 20515. **202-225-6105**

PODHORETZ, NORMAN (editor; writer). *Commentary*, 165 E 56th St, New York, NY 10022. **212-751-4000.** (h) 924 W End Ave, New York, NY 10025

POMPIDOU, GEORGES (1911–74)

POOLE, JAMES (businessman). Chairman and chief executive officer, Marquette Company, 2200 First American Ctr, Nashville, TN 37238. **615-259-4000.** (h) 4487 Post Pl, Nashville, TN 37205

PORTER, WILLIAM J (ambassador to Saudi Arabia). c/o US State Department, Washington, DC 20520

POTTINGER, J STANLEY (attorney; former Assistant Attorney General; civil rights leader). Troy, Malin, and Pottinger, Suite 700, 2033 M St NW, Washington, DC 20036. **202-466-4560.** Also president, Pottinger and Company, 2033 M St NW, Washington, DC 20036. **202-466-4044.** (h) 6009 Corbin Rd, Bethesda, MD 20016. **301-229-1324**

POUND, EZRA (1885–1972)

POWELL, ADAM CLAYTON JR (1908–72)

POWELL, JODY (presidential press secretary). The White House, Washington, DC 20500. **202-456-2100.** (h) Foxhall Rd, Washington, DC 20007 or 20016

POWELL, LEWIS F JR (JUDGE). Associate Justice, US Supreme Court, Washington, DC 20543. **202-393-1640**

POWERS, BERTRAM A (labor leader). International Typographical Union, 817 Broadway, New York, NY 10003. **212-533-2000**

PRATT, JOHN H (JUDGE). US District Court, Washington, DC 20001. **202-393-1640.** (h) 4119 Rosemary St, Chevy Chase, MD 20015

PREUS, JACOB A (THE REVEREND DR). President, Lutheran Church, Missouri Synod, 500 N Broadway, St Louis, MO 63102. **314-231-6969.** (h) 400 Mansion House Ctr, St Louis, MO 63102. **314-436-7489**

PRICE, MELVIN (US REPRESENTA-
TIVE). Congress, Washington, DC 20515.
202-225-5611

PRINCE, HAROLD (producer). 1270
Avenue of the Americas, New York, NY
10020. **212-399-0960**

PROXMIRE, WILLIAM (US SENATOR).
Congress, Washington, DC 20510.
202-225-5653

PRYOR, DAVID H (GOVERNOR). Office
of the Governor, Rm 250, State Capitol,
Little Rock, AR 72201. **501-371-2345**

QUIE, ALBERT H (US REPRESENTA-
TIVE). Congress, Washington, DC 20515.
202-225-2271

QUINLAN, KAREN ANNE (comatose
patient). Morris View Nursing Home (Fred
Swanson, administrator), Morris Township,
NJ 07960. **201-285-6501**
Parents. Joseph and Julia Quinlan, Morris-
town, NJ 07960
Attorney. Paul Armstrong, (h) 801 Lindsey
Dr, Morristown, NJ 07960. **201-540-1465**

QUINN, SALLY (journalist). c/o *Washington Post*, 1150 15th St NW, Washington, DC
20071. **202-223-6000**. (h) 1712 21st St NW,
Washington, DC 20009. **202-667-0170**

QUINN, TOM (government official). California Air Resources Board, Sacramento,
CA 95812. **916-322-5840**. *Contact.* Bill Sessa,
public information director. **916-322-2990**

RABE, DAVID (playwright). c/o Ellen
Heuwald, 905 W End Ave, New York, NY
10025. **212-663-1582**

RACKLEY, ALEX (?–1969)

RAILSBACK, THOMAS F (US REPRE-
SENTATIVE). Congress, Washington, DC
20515. **202-225-5905**

RAMPTON, CALVIN L (former governor
of Utah). State Capitol Bldg, Salt Lake City,
UT 84114. **801-533-5321**. (h) 1270 Fairfax
Rd, Salt Lake City, UT 84103. **801-521-3200**

RANDOLPH, JENNINGS (US SENA-
TOR). Congress, Washington, DC 20510.
202-224-6472

RANGEL, CHARLES B (US REPRE-
SENTATIVE). Congress, Washington, DC
20515. **202-225-4365**

RATHER, DAN (broadcast journalist). c/o
CBS News, 524 W 57th St, New York, NY
10019. **212-765-4321**

RAUH, JOSEPH L JR (attorney; labor
leader). 1001 Connecticut Ave, Washington,
DC 20036. **202-331-1795**. (h) 3625 Appleton
St, Washington, DC 20008. **202-363-7993**

RAVITCH, RICHARD (businessman). HRH
Equity Corp, 909 3rd Ave, New York, NY
10022. **212-753-0790**. (h) 1021 Park Ave,
New York, NY 10028. **212-427-1579**

RAY, DIXY LEE (GOVERNOR). State
Capitol, Olympia, WA 98504. **206-753-6780**.
(h) 600 3rd Ave, Fox Island, WA 98333

RAY, ELIZABETH (Wayne Hayes's former
mistress)
Agent. John Cushman Associates, 25 W 43rd
St, New York, NY. **212-685-2052**
Publisher. Dell, 1 Dag Hammerskjold Plz,
New York, NY 10017. **212-832-7300**
Personal Manager. Mark Korman Manage-
ment, 200 W 57th St, New York, NY 10019.
212-586-6363

RAY, JAMES EARL (convicted assassin).
Brushy Mountain State Prison, Petros, TN
37845. **615-324-4011**

RAY, ROBERT D (GOVERNOR). State
Capitol Bldg, Des Moines, IA 50307.
515-281-5211. (h) 2900 Grand Ave, Des
Moines, IA 50312

REAGAN, RONALD WILSON (former
governor of California; former actor). 10960
Wilshire Blvd, Los Angeles, CA 90024.
213-479-8231

REBOZO, CHARLES G (Nixon friend;
businessman). 95 W McIntire St, Key
Biscayne, FL 33149. **305-361-9100**

REDFORD, ROBERT (actor). c/o Pickwick, 545 Madison Ave, New York, NY
10022. **212-759-5202**. Owns Sundance Ski
Resort, Provo, UT 84601. **801-225-4100**

REDLICH, NORMAN L (educator). Dean,
New York University School of Law,
Washington Sq, New York, NY 10003.
212-598-2526. (h) 29 Washington Sq, New
York, NY 10011. **212-234-5691**

REES, ALBERT (economist). Princeton
University, Princeton, NJ 08540.
609-452-4040. (h) 32 Turner Ct, Princeton,
NJ 08540. **609-924-6105**

REGAN, DONALD T (businessman). Chief
executive officer, Merrill, Lynch, Pierce,
Fenner, and Smith, 1 Liberty Plz, 165
Broadway, New York, NY 10006.
212-766-1212. (h) Van Bueren Rd, New
Vernon, NJ 07960

REHNQUIST, WILLIAM H (JUDGE).
Associate Justice, US Supreme Court,
Washington, DC 20543. **202-393-1640**

REISCHAUER, EDWIN OLDFATHER
(professor). Harvard University, 1737 Cambridge St, Cambridge, MA 02138.
617-495-3220. (h) 863 Concord Ave,
Belmont, MA 02178. **617-484-7730**

**REMBRANDT, HARMENSZOON VAN
RIJN** (1606–69)

RESOR, STANLEY R (ambassador to
Austria). US MBFR Delegation, Ober-
steinergasse 11, 1190 Vienna, Austria. Also
c/o US State Department, Washington, DC
20520. (h) 809 Weed St, New Canaan, CT
06840. **203-966-9889**

REUSS, HENRY S (US REPRESENTA-
TIVE). Congress, Washington, DC 20515.
202-225-3571

REUTHER, WALTER P (1907–70)

RHODES, JAMES A (GOVERNOR). State
House, Columbus, OH 43215. **614-466-3555**.
(h) 358 N Parkview, Bexley, OH 43209.
614-252-1121

RHODES, JOHN J (US REPRESENTA-
TIVE). Congress, Washington, DC 20515.
202-225-0600

RIBICOFF, ABRAHAM A (US SENA-
TOR). Congress, Washington, DC 20510.
202-224-2823

RICCARDO, JOHN J (automobile businessman). Chrysler Corp, 12000 Lynn Townsend
Dr, Highland Park, MI 48288. **313-956-5741**

RICHARDSON, ELLIOT L (ambassador:
Law of the Sea Conference). US State
Department, Washington, DC 20520.
202-967-3521

RICHEY, CHARLES R (JUDGE). US
District Court, Constitution Ave and John
Marshall Pl NW, Washington, DC 20001.
202-426-7688. (h) 10800 Lockland Rd,
Potomac, MD 20854

RICHMOND, FREDERICK W (US REP-
RESENTATIVE). Congress, Washington,
DC 20515. **202-225-5936**

RICKOVER, HYMAN G (ADMIRAL). US
Energy Research and Development
Administration, Washington, DC 20010.
202-973-3414

RIEGLE, DONALD W JR (US SENATOR). Congress, Washington, DC 20510. **202-224-4822**

RIFKIND, SIMON H (attorney). 345 Park Ave, New York, NY 10022. **212-644-8602.** (h) 936 3rd Ave, New York, NY 10021. **212-628-4134**

RIKLIS, MESHULAM (businessman). Rapid American Corp, 711 5th Ave, New York, NY 10022. **212-752-0100.** (h) 5 E 80th St, New York, NY 10021. **212-249-7872**

RINALDO, MATTHEW J (US REPRESENTATIVE). Congress, Washington, DC 20515. **202-225-5361**

RIVERS, LUCIUS MENDEL (1905–70).

RIVLIN, ALICE M (DR) (economist). Congressional Budget Office, US Congress, Washington, DC 20515. **202-225-2037.** Also 2842 Chesterfield Pl NW, Washington, DC 20008. **202-362-6947**

RIZZO, FRANK L (MAYOR). City Hall, Philadelphia, PA 19107. **215-686-1776.** (h) 8919 Crefeld St, Philadelphia, PA 19118

ROBBINS, JEROME (choreographer). c/o New York City Ballet, New York State Theatre, Lincoln Ctr, New York, NY 10023. **212-877-4700.** (h) 117 E 81st St, New York, NY 10028. **212-874-0504**

ROBERTSON, JAMES D (anatomist). (h) 132 Oak Dr, Durham, NC 27707. **919-489-4318**

ROBESON, PAUL SR (1898–1976)

ROBINSON, FRANK (baseball player). c/o California Angels, 2000 St College Blvd, Anaheim, CA 92805. **714-634-2000**

ROBINSON, JACKIE ROOSEVELT (1919–72)

ROCHE, JOHN P (educator; columnist). Fletchor School, Tufts University, Medford, MA 02155. **617-628-5000.** (h) 15 Bay State Rd, Weston, MA 02193. **617-893-1969**

ROCKEFELLER, DAVID (attorney; banker). 1 Chase Manhattan Bank, New York, NY 10015. **202-552-2222**

ROCKEFELLER, JOHN D III (businessman). 30 Rockefeller Plz, New York, NY 10020. **212-247-3700**

ROCKEFELLER, JOHN DAVISON IV (GOVERNOR). State Capitol, Charlestown, WV. **304-348-2000**

ROCKEFELLER, LAURANCE S (businessman). Chairman, Rockefeller Brothers Fund, Room 5600, 30 Rockefeller Plz, New York, NY 10021. **212-247-3700.** *Press contact.* George Taylor

ROCKEFELLER, MARGARETTA ("HAPPY") (Mrs Nelson Aldrich Rockefeller) (wife of former Vice-President). (h) Pocantico Hills, North Tarrytown, NY 10591

ROCKEFELLER, NELSON ALDRICH ("ROCKY"). (former Vice-President; former governor of New York). 30 Rockefeller Plz, New York, NY 10020. **212-247-3700.** (h) Pocantico Hills, North Tarrytown, NY 10591

RODINO, PETER W JR (US REPRESENTATIVE). Congress, Washington, DC 20515. **202-225-3436**

ROE, ROBERT A (US REPRESENTATIVE). Congress, Washington, DC 20515. **202-225-5751**

ROGERS, PAUL G (US REPRESENTATIVE). Congress, Washington, DC 20515. **202-225-3001**

ROGERS, WILLIAM PIERCE (attorney). 200 Park Ave, New York, NY 10017. **202-972-7000.** (h) 7007 Glenbrook Rd, Bethesda, MD 20014

ROHATYN, FELIX G (foundation official). Chairman, 1 Rockefeller Foundation, 111 W 50th St, New York, NY 10020. **212-869-8500.** (h) 1125 Park Ave, New York, NY. **202-722-6574**

ROMNEY, GEORGE W (former governor of Michigan; former Secretary of Housing and Urban Development). 12 E 87th St, New York, NY 10028. **212-427-2408.** (h) E Valley Rd, Bloomfield Hills, MI 48013

RONAN, WILLIAM J (professor; public official). New York University, New York, NY 10016. **212-598-1212.** Also chairman, Port Authority, New York and New Jersey, 1 World Trade Ctr, New York, NY 10048. **212-564-8484.** 30 Rockefeller Plz, 5600, New York, NY 10022. (h) 2 Sutton Place S, New York, NY 10022

ROONEY, JOHN J (former congressman). (h) 217 Congress St, Brooklyn, NY 11201. **212-624-5243**

ROOSA, ROBERT V (banker; businessman). Brown Brothers, Harriman and Co, 59 Wall St, New York, NY 10005. **212-483-5318.** (h) 30 Woodlands Rd, Harrison, NY 10528. **914-967-7646**

ROOSEVELT, ELEANOR (Mrs Franklin Delano Roosevelt) (1884–1962)

ROOSEVELT, FRANKLIN DELANO (1882–1945)

ROOSEVELT, THEODORE (1858–1919)

ROSE, ALEX (1898–1976)

ROSELLI, JOHN (?–1976)

ROSENBERG, ETHEL (Mrs Julius Rosenberg) (1921–53)

ROSENBERG, JULIUS (1918–53)

ROSENTHAL, BENJAMIN S (US REPRESENTATIVE). Congress, Washington, DC 20515. **202-225-2601**

ROSTOW, EUGENE V (educator; attorney; economist). Yale Law School, Hartford, CT 06511. **203-436-4771.** (h) 208 S Roman St, New Haven, CT 06511. **201-776-3906**

ROSTOW, WALT W (professor; author). (h) 1 Wildwind Point, Austin, TX 78746. **512-327-0436**

ROTH, PHILIP (author). c/o Random House, Inc, 201 E 50th St, New York, NY 10022. **212-751-2600.** (h) Cornwall Bridge, CT 06754

ROTH, WILLIAM V JR (US SENATOR). Congress, Washington, DC 20510. **202-225-3215**

ROTHKO, MARK (1903–70)

ROYSTER, VERMONT (educator). (h) Chapel Hill, NC 27514. **919-942-1128**

ROZELLE, PETE (sports executive). Commissioner, National Football League, 410 Park Ave, New York, NY 10016. **202-758-1500**

RUBIN, JERRY C (political activist: Yippies). c/o M Evans and Co, Inc (publisher), 216 E 49th St, New York, NY 10017. **212-688-2810**

RUBINSTEIN, ARTHUR (pianist). 22 Square de l'Avenue Foch, Paris 16 Leme, France

Agent. ICM, 40 W 57th St, New York, NY 10019. **212-556-5600**

RUCKELSHAUS, WILLIAM D (attorney; former government official). Weyerhauser Co, 2525 S 36th St, Federal Way, Tacoma, WA 98401. **206-924-2345.** Also PO Box 2700, Jacksonville, FL 32202

RUDEL, JULIUS (conductor). c/o New York City Opera, New York State Theatre, Lincoln Center Plz, New York, NY 10023. **212-877-4700**

Agent. Edgar Vincent Associates, 156 E 52nd St, New York, NY 10022. **212-752-3020**

RUMSFELD, DONALD H (former Secretary of Defense). President, G D Searle and Co, Skokie, IL 60076. **312-982-7100.** (h) 1373 Ashland Ln, Wilmette, IL 60091

RUSH, KENNETH (former ambassador). 3147 O Street NW, Washington, DC 20007. **202-333-8215**

RUSK, DEAN (educator; former Secretary of State). (h) 1 Lafayette Sq, 620 Hill St, Athens, GA 30601. **404-549-6471**

RUSSELL, RICHARD B (1897–1971)

RUSSO, ANTHONY J JR (Pentagon papers case). 168 Broadway, New York, NY 10038. **212-730-0166**

Attorney. Leonard Boudin, 30 E 42nd St, New York, NY 10017. **212-697-8640**

RUSTIN, BAYARD (civil rights activist). 260 Park Ave S, New York, NY 10010. **212-533-8000**

RUTH, GEORGE HERMAN ("BABE") (1895–1948)

RYAN, WILLIAM FITTS (?–1972)

SADLOWSKI, ED (labor leader). President, Chicago-Gary District, United Steelworkers of America, 205 W Wacker Dr, Chicago, IL 60606. **312-782-3126.** *United Steelworkers headquarters in Pittsburgh.* **412-562-2400**

ST GERMAIN, FERNAND J (US REPRE-SENTATIVE). Congress, Washington, DC 20515. **202-225-4911**

SALANT, RICHARD S (broadcasting administrator). President, CBS News, 524 W 57th St, New York, NY 10019. **212-975-2988**

SALINGER, PIERRE E (writer). (h) 9101 Hazen Dr, Beverly Hills, CA 90211. c/o *L'Express*, Paris, France, Telephone, **33-1-256-45-00.** (h) 9101 Hazen Dr, Beverly Hills, CA 90211

Agent. Sterling Lord, 660 Madison Ave, New York, NY 10021. **212-751-2533**

SALMON, THOMAS P (former governor of Vermont). 24 Atkinson St, Bellows Falls, VT 05101. **802-463-4554**

SAMUELS, HOWARD J (former Under Secretary of Commerce; Off-Track Betting Corp official). 355 Lexington Ave, New York, NY 10017. **212-661-9431**

SAMUELS, NATHANIEL (businessman). 40 Wall St, New York, NY 10005. **212-797-2070.** (h) 775 Park Ave, New York, NY 10021. **212-879-8521**

SAMUELSON, PAUL A (professor; economist). Massachusetts Institute of Technology, Cambridge, MA 02134. **617-253-3368.** (h) 75 Clairemont Rd, Belmont, MA 02178. **617-484-6497**

SANDMAN, CHARLES W JR (former congressman). 62 Yacht Ave, Cape May, NJ 08204. (h) Crescent Dr, Erma Park Rd, Cape May, NJ 08204. **609-886-1960**

SANFORD, TERRY (educator; attorney). President, Duke University, Durham, NC 27706. **919-684-2424.** (h) 1508 Pinecrest Rd, Durham, NC 27705. **919-489-2767**

SAPIR, PINHAS (1907–75)

SARBANES, PAUL S (US SENATOR). Congress, Washington, DC 20510. **202-224-4524**

SARGENT, FRANCIS W (former state official). 16 Arlington St, Boston, MA 02116. **617-247-0006**

SARNOFF, ROBERT W (corporate businessman). 30 Rockefeller Plz, New York, NY 10020

SATO, EISAKU (?–1975)

SAUL, RALPH S (investment businessman). INA Corp, 1600 Arch St, Philadelphia, PA 19101. **212-241-4000.** (h) 549 Avonwood Rd, Haverford, PA 19041. **212-LA5-7078**

SAWHILL, JOHN C (government official). State University, New York System, Albany, NY. **518-457-3300**

SAXBE, WILLIAM B (former ambassador). (h) Route 2, Mechanicsburg, OH 43044. **614-834-3456**

SAYPOL, IRVING H (JUSTICE) (1905–77)

SCALI, JOHN A (former ambassador). (h) Waldorf Astoria Towers, Park Ave, New York, NY 10022. **212-355-3100**

SCAMMON, RICHARD M (political scientist; elections research). 1619 Massachusetts Ave NW, Washington, DC 20036. **202-387-0044.** (h) 5508 Greystone St, Chevy Chase, MD 20015. **301-654-5541**

SCHEUER, JAMES H (US REPRE-SENTATIVE). Congressman, Washington, DC 20515. **202-225-5471**

SCHEUER, SANDRA LEE (?–1970)

SCHINDLER, ALEXANDER M (RABBI). President, Union of American Hebrew Congregations, 838 5th Ave, New York, NY 10021. **212-249-0100.** (h) 6 River Ln, Westport, CT 06880. **203-227-0232**

SCHLESINGER, ARTHUR M JR (professor; author). 33 W 42nd St, New York, NY 10036. **212-790-4261**

SCHLESINGER, JAMES R (government official). Secretary, US Energy Department, Washington, DC 20545. **202-456-6210.** (h) 3601 N 26th St, Arlington, VA 22207

SCHMIDT, ALEXANDER M (former commissioner, Food and Drug Administration). Vice-chancellor of Health Services, University of Illinois Medical Ctr, 414 AOB, PO Box 6998, Chicago, IL 60680. **312-996-6400**

SCHMITT, HARRISON H (US SENA-TOR). Congress, Washington, DC 20510. **202-224-5521**

SCHORR, DANIEL (radio-television commentator). 3113 Woodley Rd NW, Washington, DC 20008. **202-483-7150**

SCHROEDER, PATRICIA (US REPRE-SENTATIVE). Congress, Washington, DC 20515. **202-225-4431**

SCHROEDER, WILLIAM K (?–1970)

SCHULTZE, CHARLES (government official). Chairman, Council of Economic Advisors, Washington, DC 20506. **202-395-5042.** (h) 5826 Nevada Ave NW, Washington, DC 20015. **202-966-5667**

SCHWEIKER, RICHARD S (US SENA-TOR). Congress, Washington, DC 20510. **202-224-4254**

SCOTT, HUGH D (former senator). 2011 I St NW, Washington, DC 20006. **202-452-8833.** (h) 3014 Woodland Dr NW, Washington, DC 20008

SCOTT, ROBERT W (former governor of North Carolina). Federal cochairman, Appalachian Regional Commission, 1666 Connecticut Ave NW, Washington, DC 20009. **202-673-7856.** (h) Route 1, Haw River, NC 27258. **919-578-2929**

SCOTT, WILLIAM L (US SENATOR). Congress, Washington, DC 20510. **202-224-2023**

SCOWCROFT, BRENT (LIEUTENANT GENERAL). (former national security adviser). c/o The White House, Washington, DC 20500. **202-456-1414**

SCRANTON, WILLIAM W (former governor of Pennsylvania; former ambassador to the United Nations). (h) Box 116, Dalton, PA 18414. **717-563-1121**

SCREVANE, PAUL R (businessman). Chairman, New York City Off-Track Betting Corp, 1501 Broadway, New York, NY 10036. **212-221-5101.** (h) 52-35 241st St, Douglaston, NY 11326

SCRIBNER, HARVEY B (educator; former chancellor of New York City schools). Professor, School of Education, Hills South, University of Massachusetts, Amherst, MA 01033. **413-545-2764**

SEABORG, GLENN T (educator). Lawrence Berkeley Laboratory, University of California, Berkeley, CA 94720. **415-843-2740,** Ext 5661, or **415-642-3272.** (h) 1154 Glen Rd, Lafayette, CA 94549. **415-283-3418**

SEALE, BOBBY G (founder, Black Panthers). Los Angeles, CA. Exact whereabouts unknown

SEAMANS, ROBERT C JR (former administrator, US Energy Research and Development Administration). Henry R Luce Professor of Environment and Public Policy, Massachusetts Institute of Technology, 50 Memorial Dr, Cambridge, MA 02139. **617-253-7160.** (h) 190 Brattle St, Cambridge, MA 02138. **617-661-9404**

SEARS, JOHN P III (attorney). (h) 718 Falstaff Ct, McLean, VA 22101. **703-356-0561**

SEAVER, TOM (baseball player). Cincinnati Reds Baseball Club, Cincinnati, OH. (h) 10 Golf Club Rd, Greenwich, CT 06830

SEAWELL, WILLIAM T (airline businessman). Pan Am World Airways, 200 Park Ave, New York, NY 10017. **212-973-7700.** (h) 425 E 58th St, New York, NY 10022. **212-759-8372**

SEGAL, ERICH (educator; author). c/o Lazarow, Rm 1106, 119 W 57th St, New York, NY 10019. **212-586-5930**

SEGAL, MARTIN E (economist). Chairman, Martin E Segal Consultants, 730 5th Ave, New York, NY 10019. **212-586-5600**

SEIBERLING, JOHN F (US REPRESENTATIVE). Congress, Washington, DC 20515. **202-225-5231**

SEIDMAN, L WILLIAM (businessman). Senior vice-president, Phelps Dodge Corporation, 300 Park Ave, New York, NY. **212-751-3200.** (h) 1694 31st St NW, Washington, DC 20007. **202-333-5786.** (h) 8 E 67th St, New York, NY. **212-734-4438**

SERPICO, FRANK (former policeman). c/o Ramsey Clark, 37 W 12th St, New York, NY 10011. **212-989-6613**

SEVAREID, ERIC (retired broadcaster). c/o CBS News, 2020 M St NW, Washington, DC 20036. **202-457-4321**

SEYMOUR, WHITNEY NORTH JR (attorney; government official). 1 Battery Park, New York, NY 10004. **212-483-9000.** (h) 290 W 4th St, New York, NY 10014

SHAFER, RAYMOND P (former governor of Pennsylvania; attorney). Meadville, PA 16335. **814-724-4540.** (h) 485 Chestnut St, Meadville, PA 16335. **814-335-1984**

SHAKESPEARE, FRANK J JR (broadcaster). President, RKO General, Inc, 1440 Broadway, New York, NY 10018. **212-764-7163.** (h) Cliff Rd, Greenwich, CT 06803. **203-869-4078**

SHAKESPEARE, WILLIAM (1564–1616)

SHANKER, ALBERT (labor leader). President, American Federation of Teachers, 11 Dupont Cir, Washington, DC 20036. **202-797-4900**

SHAPIRO, IRVING S (businessman). Chairman and chief executive officer, E I du Pont de Nemours and Co, Inc, 9000 Du Pont Bldg, Wilmington, DE 19898. **302-774-1000**

SHAPP, MILTON J (GOVERNOR). State Capitol, Harrisburg, PA 17102. **717-787-2500** or **800-932-0784.** (h) 626 S Bowman Ave, Merion, PA 19066

SHASKIN, JULIUS (government official). Commissioner, Bureau of Labor Statistics, Department of Labor, Washington, DC 20512. **202-655-4000.** (h) 4978 Sentinel Dr, Bethesda, MD 20016. **301-229-6732**

SHAW, CLAY L (1914–74)

SHAW, GEORGE BERNARD (1856–1950)

SHEPARD, ALAN B JR (REAR ADMIRAL) (former astronaut). Suite 200, 3344 Chevy Chase St, Houston, TX 77019. Also c/o NASA, Washington, DC 20546. **202-755-2320**

SHINN, RICHARD R (businessman). Metropolitan Life Insurance Co, 1 Madison Ave, New York, NY 10010. **212-578-2211.** (h) 31 Lindsay Dr, Greenwich, CT 06830. **203-661-1634**

SHOCKLEY, WILLIAM B (professor; physicist; Nobel winner). Stanford Electronics Laboratories, McCullough 202, Stanford University, Stanford, CA 94305. **415-497-4675.** (h) 797 Esplanada Way, Stanford, CA 94305. **415-328-0648**

SHRIVER, SARGENT (attorney). 120 Broadway, New York, NY 10005. **212-964-6500.** (h) Timberlawn Edson Ln, Rockville, MD 20852

SHULA, DON (football coach). Miami Dolphins, 16400-D NW 32nd Ave, Miami, FL 33054. **305-625-1561.** (h) 16220 W Prestwick Pl, Miami Lakes, FL 33014

SHULTZ, GEORGE PRATT (businessman). Bechtel Corp, 50 Beale St, San Francisco, CA 94105. **415-768-1234.** (h) 776 Dolores, Stanford, CA 94305. **415-321-2655**

SIKES, ROBERT L F (US REPRESENTATIVE). Congress, Washington, DC 20515. **202-225-4136**

SILBERMAN, LAURENCE H (former ambassador). (h) 6 Kittery Ct, Bethesda, MD 20034. **301-365-4573**

SILBERT, EARL J (US attorney). US Attorney's Office, US Courthouse, Washington, DC 20001. **202-426-7511.** (h) 6617 31st St NW, Washington, DC 20015. **202-966-5387**

SILLS, BEVERLY (Mrs Peter Greenough). (opera singer). c/o Management Ludwig Lustig, 111 W 57th St, New York, NY 10019. **212-586-3976**

SIMON, NEIL (playwright). c/o Irving ("Swifty") Lazar, 211 S Beverly Dr, Beverly Hills, CA 90212. **213-275-6153**

SIMON, NORTON (art collector; industrialist). Norton Simon Museum, 411 W Colorado Blvd, Los Angeles, CA 90041. **213-449-6840**

SIMON, PAUL (US REPRESENTATIVE). Congress, Washington, DC 20515. **202-225-5201**

SIMON, WILLIAM E (former Secretary of the Treasury). Booz-Allen and Hamilton Co, 245 Park Ave, New York, NY. **212-697-1900.** (h) Morristown, NJ

SIMPSON, O J (ORENTHAL) (football player). Buffalo Bills, Richard Park, Buffalo, NY 14240. **716-648-1800.** (h) 360 N Rockingham, Los Angeles, CA 90049

SIMPSON, RICHARD O (former chairman, Consumer Product Safety Commission). Richard O Simpson Associates, Inc, Suite 935, Washington Bldg, Washington, DC 20005. **202-737-6815**

SINATRA, FRANK (entertainer). c/o Solters and Roskin, Inc, 9255 Sunset Blvd, Los Angeles, CA 90069, **213-278-5692,** or W 45th St, New York, NY 10036, **212-867-8500.** (h) 1041 N Formosa Ave, Hollywood, CA 90046

SIRHAN, SIRHAN BISHARA (convicted assassin). Soledad State Prison, Soledad, CA 93960. **408-678-2616**

Attorney. Godfrey Isaac, 9454 Wilshire Blvd, Beverly Hills, CA 90212. **213-878-0455**

SIRICA, JOHN J (JUDGE). US Courthouse, Washington, DC 20001. **202-426-7226**

SISCO, JOSEPH J (educator). President, American University, Washington, DC 20016. **202-686-2121.** (h) 3300 Nebraska Ave NW, Washington, DC 20016

SISK, B F (US REPRESENTATIVE). Congress, Washington, DC 20515. **202-225-6131**

SIZEMORE, BARBARA A (former superintendent of schools, Washington, DC) visiting associate professor. University of Pittsburgh, Pittsburgh, PA 15260. (h) 6 Bayard Rd-459, Pittsburgh, PA 15213. **412-681-6818** or **412-624-5915, 5916,** or **5917**

SKELTON, GEORGE (JUDGE). US Court of Claims, 717 Madison Pl NW, Washington, DC 20005. **202-382-1984.** (h) Salado, TX 76571. (h) 2500 Virginia Ave NW, Washington, DC 20037

SLAYTON, DONALD K (astronaut). Manned Spacecraft Ctr, NASA, Houston, TX 77058. **713-483-01234.** (h) Box 637, Friendswood, TX 77546. **713-482-7900**

SLOAN, HUGH W JR (Nixon campaign treasurer; businessman). St Regis Paper Co, 150 E 42nd St, New York, NY 10017. **212-697-4400.** (h) 73 Drakes Corner Rd, Princeton, NJ 08540. **609-921-2580**

SMITH, C ARNHOLT (financier). **Attorney.** Thomas Sheridan, Suite 400, 2404 Wilshire Blvd, Los Angeles, CA 90057. **213-380-3330**

SMITH, DON (attorney). 13 N 7th St (PO Box 43), Fort Smith, AR 72901. **501-782-1001.** (h) 4700 Free Ferry Rd, Fort Smith, AR 72901. **501-452-2762**

SMITH, GERALD C (attorney). 1666 K St NW, Washington, DC 20005. **202-872-6000.** (h) 2425 Tracy Pl NW, Washington, DC 20008. **202-667-2064** or **8095**

SMITH, HENRY P III (former congressman). 1717 H St, Washington, DC 20440. (h) 3126 Ordway St NW, Washington, DC 20008. **202-363-2652**

SMITH, JOHN LEWIS JR (JUDGE). US District Court, Washington, DC 20001. **202-426-7226.** (h) 2700 Virginia Ave, Washington, DC 20037. **202-333-0339**

SMITH, MARGARET CHASE (former senator). c/o Freedom House, 20 W 40th St, New York, NY 10018. **212-730-7744.** (h) Norridgewock Ave, Skowhagan, ME 04976. **207-474-9660**

SMITH, MARY LOUISE (civic leader; former chairperson, Republican National Committee). Republican Central Committee, 1540 High St, Des Moines, IA 50309. **515-282-8105.** (h) 654 59th St, Des Moines, IA 50312

SMITH, PRESTON E (former governor of Texas). (h) 4089 Club House Rd, Loropoc, CA 93436. **805-733-2267**

SMITH, STAN (tennis player). Suite 1200, 888 17th St NW, Washington, DC 20006. (h) 706 Schooner Ct, Hilton Head, SC 29948. **803-671-3599**

SOLARZ, STEPHEN J (US REPRESENTATIVE). Congress, Washington, DC 20515. **202-225-2361**

SOLTI, GEORG (SIR) (conductor). c/o Chicago Symphony Orchestra, 220 S Michigan Ave, Chicago, IL 60604. **312-435-8111**

SOLZHENITSYN, ALEKSANDR I (author). c/o Harper and Row Publishers,

Inc, 10 E 53rd St, New York, NY 10022. **212-593-7000**

SOMMER, A A JR (government official; attorney). 1100 Connecticut Ave NW, Washington, DC. **202-452-5938.** (h) 10512 Gainsborough Rd, Potomac, MD 20854. **202-299-2881**

SONDHEIM, STEPHEN J (composer; lyricist). 246 E 49th St, New York, NY 10017

SONNENFELDT, HELMUT (former US State Department official). (h) 4105 Thornapple St, Chevy Chase, MD 20015. **301-656-6731**

SORENSEN, THEODORE C (attorney; former special counsel to President). 345 Park Ave, New York, NY 10022. **212-644-8790**

SPARKMAN, JOHN J (US SENATOR). US Congress, Washington, DC 20510. **202-224-4124**

SPEER, EDGAR B (businessman). US Steel, 600 Grant St, Pittsburgh, PA 15230. **412-433-1101.** (h) Edgewood Rd, Pittsburgh, PA 15215. **412-782-0582**

SPELLMAN, GLADYS N (US REPRESENTATIVE). Congress, Washington, DC 20515. **202-225-4131**

SPENO, EDWARD J (?–1971)

SPITZ, MARK (swimmer). c/o William Morris Agency, 151 El Camino, Beverly Hills, CA 90212. **213-274-7451.** (h) Marina Del Rey, CA 90291

SPOCK, BENJAMIN (DR) (physician; educator). Box N, Rogers, AR 72756. **501-636-6044**

SPONG, WILLIAM B JR (attorney; educator). Dean, Marshall-Wythe School of Law, College of William and Mary, Williamsburg, VA 23185. **804-253-4509.** (h) 111 Montague Cir, Williamsburg, VA 23185

SPORKIN, STANLEY (government official). Director of Enforcement, Securities and Exchange Commission, Washington, DC 20549. **202-755-1184.** (h) 8816 Brierly Rd, Chevy Chase, MD 20015. **301-951-0164**

STAATS, ELMER B (government official). Comptroller General, General Accounting Office, 441 G St, Washington, DC 20548. **202-275-2812.** (h) 5011 Overlook Rd NW, Washington, DC 20016. **202-966-8137**

STAFFORD, GEORGE M (government official). Chairman, Interstate Commerce Commission, 12th St and Constitution Ave NW, Washington, DC 20423. **202-343-5241.** (h) 5704 Newington Rd, Washington, DC 20016. **301-320-4568**

STAFFORD, ROBERT T (US SENATOR). Congress, Washington, DC 20510. **202-224-5141**

STAFFORD, THOMAS P (MAJOR GENERAL) (astronaut). Manned Spacecraft Center, NASA, Houston, TX 77058. **713-483-0123**

STAGGERS, HARLEY O (US REPRESENTATIVE). Congress, Washington, DC 20515. **202-225-4331**

STALIN, JOSEPH VISSARIONOVICH (SZUGASHVILI) (1879-1953)

STANS, MAURICE H (former Nixon finance committee chairman). (h) 5114 N 40th St, Phoenix, AZ 85018
Attorney. Walter J Bonner, 900 17th St NW, Washington, DC 20006. **202-659-4660.**

STANTON, FRANK M (DR) (former CBS president). Interpublic Group of Companies, Inc, 10 E 56th St, New York, NY 10022. **212-399-8000.** (h) 10 E 56th St, New York, NY 10022. **212-752-4445**

STARK, FORTNEY H (US REPRESENTATIVE). Congress, Washington, DC 20515. **202-225-5065**

STEELE, ROBERT H (former congressman). President, Norwich Savings Association, Norwich, CT 06360. **203-889-2621.** (h) Forest View Dr, Vernon, CT 06066

STEIGER, WILLIAM A (US REPRESENTATIVE). Congress, Washington, DC 20515. **202-225-2476**

STEIN, HERBERT (professor; economist). University of Virginia, Charlottesville, VA 22901. **804-924-0311.** (h) 1704 Yorktown Dr, Charlottesville, VA 22901. **804-977-5460**

STEINBRENNER, GEORGE M III (businessman). Chief executive, American Shipbuilding Co, Suite 911, Bond Court Bldg, 1300 East 9th St, Cleveland, OH 44114. **216-621-3155.** (h) Salem Dr, Bay Village, OH 44140. **216-232-8966**

STEINEM, GLORIA (writer; feminist). c/o *Ms Magazine*, 370 Lexington Ave, New York, NY 10017. **212-725-2666**

STENNIS, JOHN C (US SENATOR). Congress, Washington, DC 20510. **202-224-6253**

STEPHENSON, HUGH (DR) (professor of surgery). University of Missouri School of Medicine, 807 Stadium Rd, Columbia, MO 85201. **314-822-7155.** (h) 5 Danforth Cir, Columbia, MO 65201. **314-442-3834**

STERN, HERBERT J (JUDGE). US District Court, Federal Sq, Newark, NJ 07101. **201-645-6340**

STERN, ISAAC (violinist). *Contact.* Sheldon Gold, c/o ICM, 40 W 57th St, New York, NY 10019. **212-556-5600**

STEVENS, JOHN PAUL (JUSTICE). Associate Justice, US Supreme Court, 1 1st St NE, Washington, DC 20543. **202-393-1640**

STEVENS, ROGER L (producer). Chairman, John F Kennedy Ctr for Performing Arts, Washington, DC 20566. **202-872-0466.** (h) 1686 34th St NW, Washington, DC 20007. **202-337-2332**

STEVENS, THEODORE F (US SENATOR). Congress, Washington, DC 20510. **202-224-3004**

STEVENSON, ADLAI EWING III (US SENATOR). Congress, Washington, DC 20510. **202-224-2854**

STEVER, H GUYFORD (DR) (Scientist). National Science Foundation, Washington, DC 20550. **202-632-5710.** (h) 1528 33rd St NW, Washington, DC 20007. **202-338-5537**

STEWART, POTTER (JUDGE). Associate Justice, US Supreme Court, 1 1st St NE, Washington, DC 20543. **202-252-3116.** (h) 5136 Palisade Ln, Washington, DC 20016. **202-362-0211**

STOESSEL, WALTER J JR (ambassador). c/o US State Department, Washington, DC 20520. **202-632-3320**

STOKES, CARL B (former mayor of Cleveland). c/o WNBC-TV, 30 Rockefeller Plz, New York, NY 10020. **212-664-4444.** (h) 1175 York Ave, New York, NY 10021. **212-753-1955**

STOKES, LOUIS (US REPRESENTATIVE). Congress, Washington, DC 20515. **202-225-7032**

STOKOWSKI, LEOPOLD (1882-1977)

STONE, I F (journalist). 4420 29th St NW, Washington, DC 20008. **202-966-1218**

STONE, RICHARD (Dick) (US SENATOR). Congress, Washington, DC 20510. **202-224-3041**

STONE, W CLEMENT (businessman; campaign financer). 222 W Adams St, Chicago, IL 60606. **312-332-7644.** Also Wacker Dr, Chicago, IL 60606. **312-565-1100**

STRACHAN, GORDON C (former aide to H R Haldeman; attorney). Kearns Bldg, Salt Lake City, UT 84222. **801-535-8383.** (h) Holladay, UT 84117. **801-278-9515**

STRATTON, SAMUEL S (US REPRESENTATIVE). Congress, Washington, DC 20515. **202-225-5076**

STRAUSS, PAUL (conductor). 26 Broadway, New York, NY 10004. **212-943-8722.** (h) 315 Riverside Dr, New York, NY 10025. **212-865-9067**

STRAUSS, ROBERT S (ambassador; former Democratic National Committee chairman). Special Representative for Trade Negotiations, Executive Office of the President, Suite 719, 1800 G St NW, Washington, DC 20506. **202-395-3204**

STRAVINSKY, IGOR (1882-1971)

STREISAND, BARBRA (singer). c/o ICM, 8899 Beverly Blvd, Los Angeles, CA 90048. **213-550-4000**

STURGIS, FRANK (convicted Watergate burglar). (h) Miami, FL
Attorney. Henry B Rothblatt, 232 W End Ave, New York, NY. **212-787-7001**

SUGARMAN, JULE M (government official). US Department of Health, Education, and Welfare, Washington, DC 20204. **202-245-6296**

SULLIVAN, LEON H (THE REVEREND). Opportunities Industrialization Centers, Inc, Broad and Thompson Sts, Philadelphia, PA 19122. **215-236-5400**

SULLIVAN, WILLIAM H (ambassador to Iran). c/o US State Department, Washington, DC 20520. **202-632-3320**

SULZBERGER, ARTHUR OCHS (publisher). *The New York Times*, 229 W 43rd St, New York, NY 10036. **212-556-1234**

SUN MYUNG MOON (THE REVEREND). c/o Unification Church, 4 W 43rd St, New York, NY 10036. **212-730-5782.** (h) Irvington, NY 10533. *Press contact.* Susan Reinbold. **212-730-5710.** Night line: **212-947-1187**

SWIDLER, JOSEPH C (attorney). 815 Connecticut Ave NW, Washington, DC 20016. **202-298-8020.** (h) 5405 Potomac Ave NW, Washington, DC 20016. **202-966-6067**

SYMINGTON, STUART (former senator). Suite 400, 1700 K St NW, Washington, DC 20006. **202-785-5300.** (h) 7730 Carondelet, St Louis, MO 63105

TAFT, ROBERT A JR (former senator). **216-381-2838.** (h) 4300 Drake Rd, Cincinnati, OH 45243. **216-321-2842**

TALMADGE, HERMAN E (US SENATOR). Congress, Washington, DC 20510. **202-224-3643**

TAYLOR, ELIZABETH (Mrs John Warner)(actress). c/o John Springer Associates, Inc, 667 Madison Ave, New York, NY 10021. **212-421-6720**

TAYLOR, MAXWELL D (GENERAL, retired). (h) 2500 Massachusetts Ave NW, Washington, DC 20008. **202-483-5050**

TEAGUE, OLIN E (US REPRESENTATIVE). Congress, Washington, DC 20510. **202-225-2002**

TELLER, EDWARD (DR)(physicist). Hoover Institution, Stanford, CA 94305. **415-497-0601**

THALER, SEYMOUR R (1919-76)

THANT, U (1909-74)

THOMAS, MICHAEL TILSON (conductor). c/o Buffalo Philharmonic Orchestra, 26 Richmond Ave, Buffalo, NY 14222. **716-885-0331**

THOMPSON, FRANK JR (US REPRESENTATIVE). Congress, Washington, DC 20515. **202-225-3765**

THOMPSON, JAMES R (GOVERNOR). State Capitol, Springfield, IL 62706. **217-782-6830.** (h) 208 S LaSalle-1988, Chicago, IL 60604

THOMSON, MELDRIM, JR (GOVERNOR). State House, Concord, NH 03301. **603-271-2121**

THORNBURGH, RICHARD L (government official). Assistant Attorney General, Department of Justice, Washington, DC 20530. **202-737-8200.** (h) 3915 Fulton St NW, Washington, DC 20007

THROWER, RANDOLPH W (attorney; government official). Suite 3100, First National Bank Tower, Atlanta, GA 30303. **404-658-8700.** (h) 2240 Woodward Way NW, Atlanta, GA 30305. **404-355-1244**

THURMOND, STROM (SENATOR). Congress, Washington, DC 20510. **202-224-3643**

TILLINGHAST, CHARLES C JR Vicechairman, White, Weld and Co, Inc, 1 Liberty Plz, New York, NY 10006. **212-285-7944.** (h) 56 Oakledge Rd, Bronxville, NY 10016. **914-337-6941**

TIMM, ROBERT D (politician). (h) Box 444, Harrington, WA 99134

TIMMONS, WILLIAM E (businessman). Timmons & Co, Inc, Washington, DC **202-331-1760.** (h) 9501 Newbold Pl, Bethesda, MD 20034. **301-469-6584**

TKACH, WALTER R (MAJOR GENERAL). Command Surgeon, Air Force Systems Command, Andrews Air Force Base, Washington, DC 20335. **202-545-6700**

TOBIN, JAMES (professor). Yale University, New Haven, CT 06520. **203-436-2330.** (h) 117 Alden Ave, New Haven, CT 06515. **203-389-2540**

TONG SUN PARK. *See* Park Tong Sun

TOON, MALCOLM (AMBASSADOR). US State Department, Washington, DC 20521. **202-632-9884**

TOWER, JOHN G (US SENATOR). Congress, Washington, DC 20510. **202-224-2934**

TOWNSEND, LYNN A (businessman). Chrysler Corporation, Bloomfield Hills, MI 48013. **313-626-1880**

TRAIN, RUSSELL E (government official; former EPA administrator). Washington, DC 20034. **202-755-2700.** (h) 1803 Kalorama Sq, Washington, DC 20008. **202-965-9351**

TREVINO, LEE (golf). Lee Trevino Enterprises, PO Drawer 12727, El Paso, TX 79912. **505-589-3466.** (h) Santa Teresa Country Club, Santa Teresa, NM 88063

TRUMAN, HARRY S (1884-1972)

TRUMAN, MARGARET See Margaret Truman Daniel

TUCHMAN, BARBARA W (author). c/o Russell and Volkening, 551 5th Ave, New York, NY 10017. **212-682-5340.** (h) Cos Cob, CT 06807. **203-869-5048**

TUNNEY, JOHN V (former senator). Manatt, Phelps, Rothenberg, Manley, and Tunney, 1888 Century Park E, Los Angeles, CA 90067. **213-556-1500.** (h) 2047 Desford Dr, Beverly Hills, CA 90210

TURNER, GLENN W (promoter: "pyramid" schemes). Box 52, Route 1, Maitland, FL 32751. **305-834-2883.** (h) Orlando, FL. *Press contact.* Edward G Rector, 7 Winding Ridge Rd, Casselberry, FL 32707. **305-834-2883**

TURNER, STANSFIELD (ADMIRAL)(government official). Director, Central Intelligence Agency, Washington, DC 20505. **202-351-1100**

TYDINGS, JOSEPH D (attorney; politician). 1120 Connecticut Ave, Washington, DC 20036. **202-857-4000.** (h) Oakington, Havre de Grace, MD 21078

TYLER, HAROLD R (government official). (h) Indian Hill Rd, Bedford, NY 10506

UDALL, MORRIS K (US REPRESENTATIVE). Congress, Washington, DC 20515. **202-225-4065**

UDALL, STEWART L (former Secretary of the Interior). 1775 Pennsylvania Ave NW, Washington, DC 20006. **202-467-6370**

ULBRICHT, WALTER (1893-1973)

ULLMAN, AL (US REPRESENTATIVE). Congress, Washington, DC 20515. **202-225-5711**

ULLMANN, LIV (actress). c/o Paul Kohner, 9169 Sunset Blvd, Los Angeles, CA 90069. **213-550-1060**

UNRUH, JESSE M (government official). Rm 110, 915 Capitol Mall, Sacramento, CA 95814. **916-445-5316.** Mailing address: PO Box 1919, Sacramento, CA 95809. *Los Angeles office.* 107 S Broadway, Los Angeles, CA **213-620-4467.** (h) 402 S Curson Ave, Los Angeles, CA 90031

UPDIKE, JOHN (author). c/o Knopf Publishers, 201 E 50th St, New York, NY 10022. **212-751-2600**

USERY, W J JR (former Secretary of Labor). (h) 2400 Virginia Ave, Washington, DC 20037. **202-833-8057**

VALENTI, JACK (producer). Motion Picture Association of America, 1600 I St NW, Washington, DC 20006. **202-293-1966**

VANCE, CYRUS R (government official). Secretary, US State Department, Washington, DC 20520. **202-632-9630**

VANDER VEEN, RICHARD F (former congressman; attorney). Varnum, Riddering, Wierengo and Christenson, 1150 Gladstone SE, Grand Rapids, MI 49506. **616-243-9396**

VANIK, CHARLES A (US REPRESENTATIVE). Congress, Washington, DC 20515. **202-225-6331**

VANOCUR, SANDER (television journalist). c/o ABC News, 1124 Connecticut Ave NW, Washington, DC 20036. **202-393-7700**

VENDLER, HELEN (professor). Boston University, Boston, MA 02215. **617-353-2506.** (h) 16A Still St, Brookline, MA 02146. **617-566-4657**

VENEMAN, JOHN G (businessman). Braun and Co, 1725 K St NW, Washington, DC 20006. **202-785-1850.** (h) 2709 O St NW, Washington, DC 20007. **202-337-2372**

VERDI, GIUSEPPE (1813-1901)

VESCO, ROBERT L (fugitive, businessman). Guana Caste Farm, Costa Rica. Attorney's telephone, **Costa Rica 01-506-217-618**

VIDAL, GORE (author). (h) 21 Via Di Torre Argentina, Rome, Italy

VOLCKER, PAUL A (banker). President, Federal Reserve Bank of New York, 33 Liberty St, New York, NY 10045. **212-791-5000.** (h) 151 E 79th St, New York, NY 10021. **212-249-6995**

VOLPE, JOHN A (former ambassador; former governor; former Secretary of Transportation). 15 Tudor Rd, Nahant, MA 01908

VONNEGUT, KURT JR (author). c/o Donald C Farber, 800 3rd Ave, New York, NY 10022. **212-688-7008**

WAGGONNER, JOE D JR (US REPRESENTATIVE). Congress, Washington, DC 20515. **202-225-2777**

WAGNER, RICHARD (1813-83)

WAGNER, ROBERT F (attorney; former ambassador; former mayor of New York City). 425 Park Ave, New York, NY 10022. **212-371-5900**

WALD, GEORGE P (professor; scientist). Harvard University, Cambridge, MA 02138. **617-495-2311.** (h) 21 Lakeview Ave, Cambridge, MA 02138. **617-868-7748**

WALDIE, JEROME R (former congressman). G St, Antioch, CA 94509. **415-757-4545.** (h) 304-B 9th St, Antioch, CA 94509

WALINSKY, ADAM (CIA critic; attorney; author), 1345 Avenue of the Americas, New York, NY 10019. **212-765-6000**

WALKER, CHARLS E (former Under Secretary). Charls E Walker Associates, Inc, 1730 Pennsylvania Ave NW, Washington, DC 20006. **202-393-4760**

WALKER, DANIEL (former governor; attorney). Law office, Oak Brook, IL 60521. **312-920-1105.** (h) 1152 Norman Ln, Deerfield, IL 60015

WALLACE, CORNELIA (formerly Mrs George Corley Wallace)(former wife of Alabama governor).
Attorney. Ira De Ment, 555 S Perry, Montgomery, AL 36104. **205-834-8900** or **5300.** (h) 1916 S Hull St, Montgomery, AL 36104. **205-265-3029**

WALLACE, GEORGE CORLEY (GOVERNOR). State Capitol Bldg, Montgomery, AL 36105. **205-832-3511**

WALLACE, MIKE (television journalist). c/o CBS News, 524 W 57th St, New York, NY 10019. **212-975-4321.** (h) 133 E 74th St, New York, NY 10021

WALLICH, HENRY C (economist). Federal Reserve Board, Washington, DC 20551. **202-452-3211**

WALSH, ALBERT A (banker). 63 Wall St, New York, NY 10005. **212-248-2800**

WALSH, LAWRENCE E (attorney). 44th Floor, 1 Chase Manhattan Plz, New York, NY 10005. **212-764-3067.** (h) 320 E 72nd St, New York, NY 10021. **212-288-8070**

WALTERS, BARBARA (television anchorwoman). c/o ABC Television, 1330 Avenue of the Americas, New York, NY 10019. **212-581-7777**

WALTERS, JOHNNIE M (attorney; former government official). Suite 1060, 1730 Pennsylvania Ave NW, Washington, DC 20006. **202-393-7400.** (h) 1327 Oberon Way, McLean, VA 22101. **703-356-2809**

WALTERS, VERNON A (GENERAL). Former official, Central Intelligence Agency, Washington, DC. **202-697-7076.** (h) 2295 S Ocean Blvd, Palm Beach, FL 33480

WALTON, BILL (basketball player). Portland Trailblazers, Portland, OR 97223. **503-234-9291**

WARHOL, ANDY (artist). Andy Warhol Enterprises, 860 Broadway, New York, NY 10003. **212-475-5550.** *Contacts.* Fred Hughes and Vincent Tremont; also Bob Colaciello, *Interview Magazine*

WARNER, JOHN W (ADMIRAL)(former Secretary of the Navy). (h) Atoka Farm, PO Box 1320, Middleburg, VA 22117. **703-687-6369**

WARNER, RAWLEIGH JR (businessman). Chairman of the board, Mobil Corp, 150 E 42nd St, New York, NY 10017. **212-883-4242**

WARNKE, PAUL C (government official). Director, US Arms Control and Disarmament Agency, Washington, DC 20510. **202-298-8686.** (h) 5037 Garfield St NW, 20016. **202-966-0397**

WARREN, EARL (1891-1974)

WARREN, GERALD L (former deputy press secretary to Nixon; newspaper editor). *San Diego Union*, PO Box 191, San Diego, CA 92112. **714-299-3131.** (h) 306 San Fernando, San Diego, CA 92106

WASHINGTON, GEORGE (1732-99)

WASHINGTON, WALTER E (MAYOR). District Bldg, Washington, DC 20004. **202-628-6000.** (h) 408 T St NW, Washington, DC 20001

WAYNE, JOHN (MARION MICHAEL MORRISON). Suite 400, 9570 Wilshire Blvd, Beverly Hills, CA 90212. **213-278-9870.** (h) Newport Beach, CA 92662

WEBER, ARNOLD R (educator). Dean, Carnegie-Mellon University, Pittsburgh, PA 15213. **412-621-2600**

WEICKER, LOWELL P JR (US SENATOR). Congress, Washington, DC 20510. **202-224-4041**

WEIDENBAUM, MURRAY L (professor). Director, Center for the Study of American Business, Washington University, St Louis, MO 63130. **314-889-5662.** (h) 1531 Heirloom Ct, Creve Coeur, MO 63141. **314-434-0710**

WEINBERGER, CASPAR W (former Secretary of Health, Education, and Welfare). Bechtel Corp, 50 Beale St, San Francisco, CA 94105. **415-768-1234**

WEINGLASS, LEONARD I (attorney). 2025 Avon, Los Angeles, CA 90026. **213-660-9000**

WEINSTEIN, JACK B (JUDGE). US District Court, Brooklyn, NY 11201. **212-330-7443.** (h) 64 Station Rd, Great Neck, NY 11023

WEISL, EDWIN L JR (attorney). 771 Park Ave, New York, NY 10021. **212-861-0212**

WEISS, CORA (peace activist). c/o Friends Shipment, Rm 10G, 777 United Nations Plz, New York, NY 10017. **212-490-3910**

WERBLIN, DAVID A (civic leader). New Jersey Sports and Exposition Authority (c/o Barbara Rudd), East Rutherford, NJ 07073. **201-935-8500.** (h) 860 United Nations Plz, New York, NY 10017. President, Madison Square Garden, 2 Pennsylvania Plz, New York, NY 10001. **212-563-8100**

WESTMORELAND, WILLIAM CHILDS (GENERAL). (h) 107½ Tradd St, Charleston, SC 29401. **803-577-3156**

WESTWOOD, JEAN (politician; former Republican National Committee chairwoman). 5302 N 79th Pl, Scottsdale, AZ 85253. **602-994-8244**

WEXLER, JACQUELINE GRENNAN (Mrs Paul J Wexler)(educator). President, Hunter College, New York, NY 10021. **212-570-5118**

WEYAND, FREDERICK C (GENERAL retired). (h) 1661 Laukahi, Honolulu, HI 96821. **808-373-3701.** *Office.* **808-525-8144**

WHALEN, CHARLES W JR (US REPRESENTATIVE). Congress, Washington, DC 20515. **202-225-6465**

WHEELER, EARLE G (GENERAL). (1908-75)

WHITE, BYRON RAYMOND (JUDGE). Associate Justice, US Supreme Court, Washington, DC 20543. **202-393-1640**

WHITE, KEVIN H (MAYOR). City Hall, Boston, MA 02201. **617-725-4000.** George K Regan, Jr, press secretary, **617-725-3357.** (h) 158 Mt Vernon St, Boston, MA 02108

WHITE, THEODORE H (author). 168 E 64th St, New York, NY 10021. **212-838-7255**

WHITEHEAD, CLAY T (educator). Center for International Studies, Massachusetts Institute of Technology, Cambridge, MA 02139. **617-253-3141.** (h) 1250 28th St NW, Washington, DC 20007

WHITMAN, MARINA VON NEUMANN (DR)(economist). University of Pittsburgh, Pittsburgh, PA 15260. **412-624-5710.** (h) 5440 Aylesboro Ave, Pittsburgh, PA 15217. **412-681-6774**

WHITTEN, JAMIE L (US REPRESENTATIVE). Congress, Washington, DC 20515. **202-225-4306**

WIDNALL, WILLIAM B (civic leader; former congressman). Chairman, National Commission on Electronics Funds Transfer. (h) 214 W Saddle River Rd, Saddle River, NJ 07458. **201-327-9093**

WIESEL, ELIE (author). c/o Georges Borchardt Agency, 145 E 52nd St, New York, NY 10022. **212-753-5785**

WIESNER, JEROME B (DR)(educator). President. Massachusetts Institute of Technology, Cambridge, MA 02139. **617-253-4665.** (h) 61 Shattuck Rd, Watertown, MA 02172. **617-926-1924**

WIGGINS, CHARLES E (US REPRESENTATIVE). Congress, Washington, DC 20515. **202-224-4111**

WILEY, GEORGE A (1931-73)

WILEY, RICHARD E (former chairman, Federal Communications Commission). (h) 3818 N Woodrow St, Arlington, VA 22207. **703-536-4448**

WILKINS, ROY (civil rights leader). (h) 147-15 Village Rd, Jamaica, NY 11435. **212-380-0187**

WILLE, FRANK (former chairman, Federal Deposit Insurance Corp). (h) 4733 Berkeley Ter, Washington, DC 20007. **202-338-4848**

WILLIAMS, DICK (editor). Board of Editors, *Smithsonian Magazine*, 900 Jefferson Dr, Washington, DC 20560. **202-381-6195.** (h) Route 2, Unadilla, NY 13849. **607-369-7497**

WILLIAMS, EDWARD BENNETT (attorney). Democratic National Committee, Hill Bldg, Washington, DC 20006. **202-797-5900.** (h) 8901 Durham Dr, Potomac, MD 20854

WILLIAMS, HARRISON A JR (US SENATOR). Congress, Washington, DC 20510. **202-224-4744**

WILLIAMS, HOSEA L (THE REVEREND)(civil rights leader). Southern Christian Leadership Conference, 334 Auburn Ave NE, Atlanta, GA 30303. **404-522-1420**

WILLIAMS, JOHN J (former senator). (h) Millsboro, DE 19966. **302-934-7876**

WILLIAMS, TENNESSEE (playwright). c/o International Famous Agency, 1301 Avenue of the Americas, New York, NY 10019. **212-556-5600**

WILSON, BOB (US REPRESENTATIVE). Congress, Washington, DC 20515. **202-225-3201**

WILSON, DAVID (JUDGE). 125 S State St, Salt Lake City, UT 84138. **801-535-7541.** (h) 1283 E South Temple, Salt Lake City, UT 84102. **801-355-6093**

WILSON, JOHN J (attorney). 1050 17th St NW, Washington, DC 20036. (h) 3900 Watson Pl NW, Washington, DC 20016. **202-333-0024**

WILSON, MALCOLM (former governor of New York). Bar Bldg, White Plains, NY 12601. **914-948-4700.** (h) 24 Windsor Rd, Scarsdale, NY 10583. **914-472-2334**

WILSON, WILL R JR (?-1974)

WILSON, WOODROW (1856-1924)

WOLFF, LESTER L (US REPRESENTATIVE). Congress, Washington, DC 20510. **202-225-5956**

WOLFSON, LOUIS (producer). 316 N Miami Ave, Miami, FL 33128. (h) 5050 N Bay Rd, Miami Beach, FL 33140. **305-865-2605**

WOOD, ARTHUR M (businessman). Sears Tower, Chicago, IL 60684. **312-875-2500**

WOOD, DAVID A (pathologist). (h) 54 Commonwealth Ave, San Francisco, CA 94118. **415-751-4889**

WOODCOCK, LEONARD (labor leader). c/o United Auto Workers, 8000 E Jefferson St, Detroit, MI 48214. **313-822-1744.** Presently chief envoy to Red China, c/o Department of State, Washington, DC 20521. **202-632-3320**

WOODS, ROSE MARY (Nixon's personal secretary). 716 Jackson Pl NW, Washington, DC 20006. (h) 2500 Virginia Ave, Washington, DC 20037

WORDEN, ALFRED M (former astronaut). c/o NASA, Washington, DC 20546. **202-755-2320.** (h) PO Box 2701, Palm Beach, FL 33480

WRIGHT, CHARLES ALAN (professor; attorney; author). (h) 5304 Western Hills Dr, Austin, TX 78731. **512-453-4855**

WRIGHT, J SKELLY (JUDGE). US Courthouse, Washington, DC 20001. **203-426-7372.** (h) 5317 Blackistone Rd, Washington, DC 20016

WRIGHT, JAMES C JR (US REPRE-SENTATIVE). Congress, Washington, DC 20515. **202-225-5071**

WRISTON, WALTER B (banker). First National City Bank, 399 Park Ave, New York, NY 10022. **212-559-1000.** (h) 870 United Nations Plz, New York, NY 10017

WURF, JERRY (labor leader). American Federation of State, County, and Municipal Employees, 1625 L St NW, Washington, DC 20036. **202-452-4800.** (h) 3846 Cathedral Ave NW, Washington, DC 20016. **202-338-5450**

WYDLER, JOHN W (US REPRESENTA-TIVE). Congress, Washington, DC 20515. **202-225-5516**

WYMAN, LOUIS C (former senator). (h) 121 Shaw St, Manchester, NH 03104. **603-627-3930**

YABLONSKI, JOSEPH A (1910-69)

YABLONSKI, JOSEPH A JR (attorney). Yablonski, Both, and Edelman, 1150 Connecticut Ave NW, Washington, DC 20036. **202-833-9060**

YARBOROUGH, RALPH W (attorney). 721 Brown Bldg, W 8th St and Colorado, Austin, TX 78701. **512-478-2573.** (h) 2527 Jarratt Ave, Austin, TX 78703. **512-476-4253**

YELDELL, JOSEPH P (general assistant to the mayor). Office of Mayor, District of Columbia, Washington, DC 20004.

202-638-0107. (h) 1729 Verbena St, Washington, DC 20012

YORTY, SAMUEL W (attorney; former mayor of Los Angeles). 3435 Wilshire Blvd, Los Angeles, CA 90010. **213-380-3131.** (h) Studio City, CA

YOST, CHARLES WOODRUFF (diplomat). c/o US State Department, 2801 New Mexico Ave, Washington, DC 20007. **202-333-6791**

YOUNG, ANDREW (ambassador to the United Nations). US Mission to the United Nations, 799 United Nations Plz, New York, NY 10017. **212-826-4524**

YOUNG, COLEMAN A (MAYOR). City Hall, 2 Woodward Ave, Detroit, MI 48226. **212-224-3400.** (h) Manogian Mansion, 9246 Dwight St, Detroit, MI 48201

YOUNG, MILTON R (US SENATOR). Congress, Washington, DC 20510. **202-224-2043**

YOUNG, WHITNEY M JR (1921-71)

YOUNGER, EVELLE J (government official). State Attorney General, 3580 Wilshire Blvd, Los Angeles, CA 90010. **213-736-2304**

YUNICH, DAVID L (director; consultant). WR Grace and Co, 1114 Avenue of the Americas, New York, NY 10036. **212-764-4437.** (h) 5 Birches Cooper Rd, Scarsdale, NY 10583

ZABLOCKI, CLEMENT J (US REPRE-SENTATIVE). Congress, Washington, DC 20515. **202-225-4577**

ZARB, FRANK G (former FEA administrator). c/o Federal Energy Administration, Washington, DC 20461. **202-566-6061**

ZAFERETTI, LEO C (US REPRESENTA-TIVE). Congress, Washington, DC 20515. **202-225-4572**

ZIEGLER, RONALD L (former Nixon press secretary). Syska and Hennessy, 1720 I St NW, Washington, DC 20006. **202-296-8940,** or 110 W 50th St, New York, NY 10020. **212-489-9200.** (h) 2008 Fort Dr, Alexandria, VA 22307

ZUMWALT, ELMO R JR (ADMIRAL, retired). President, American Medical Buildings, 515 W Wells St, Milwaukee, WI 53203. **414-276-2277.** (h) 4043 N 41st St, Arlington, VA 22207

CLUBS

ALGONQUIN CLUB. 217 Commonwealth Ave, Boston, MA 02116. **617-266-2400**

AMERICAN YACHT CLUB. Milton Point, Rye, NY 10580. **914-967-4800**

APAWAMIS CLUB. Rye, NY 10580. **914-967-2100**

ARMY AND NAVY CLUB. 1627 I St, Washington, DC 20006. **202-628-8400**

ARTS CLUB. 109 E Ontario, Chicago, IL 60611. **312-787-3997**

BOGEY CLUB, INC. 9266 Clayton Rd, St Louis, MO 63124. **314-993-0161**

BOHEMIAN CLUB. 624 Taylor, San Francisco, CA 94102. **415-885-2440**

BROOK, THE. 111 E 54th St, New York, NY 10022. **212-753-7020**

BUFFALO CLUB. 388 Delaware Ave, Buffalo, NY 14202. **716-886-6400**

CHEVY CHASE CLUB. Chevy Chase, MD 20015. **301-652-4100**

CHICAGO CLUB. 81 Van Buren, Chicago, IL 60605. **312-427-1825**

CHILTON CLUB. 287 Dartmouth, Boston, MA 02116. **617-266-4860**

CHURCH CLUB. 35 E 72 St, New York, NY 10021. **212-988-5452**

CITY MID-DAY CLUB. 140 Broadway, New York, NY 10005. **212-422-5465**

CITY TAVERN CLUB. 3206 M St, Washington, DC 20007. **202-337-8770**

COLONY CLUB. 564 Park Ave, New York, NY 10021. **212-838-4200**

CONTEMPORARY CLUB OF CHICAGO, INC. 120 Bellevue Pl, Chicago, IL 60611. **312-944-1330**

COSMOPOLITAN CLUB. 122 E 66 St, New York, NY 10021. **212-734-5950**

COSMOS CLUB. 2121 Massachusetts Ave, Washington, DC 20008. **202-387-7783**

CREEK, THE. Locust Valley, NY 11560. **516-676-1405**

DUQUESNE CLUB. 325 6th Ave, Pittsburgh, PA 15222. **412-391-1500**

EASTERN YACHT CLUB. Foster St, Marblehead, MA 01945. **617-631-1400**

GROLIER CLUB. 47 E 60 St, New York, NY 10022. **212-838-6690**

HARVARD CLUB. 374 Commonwealth Ave, Boston, MA 02215. **617-536-1260**

HARVARD CLUB. 27 W 44 St, New York, NY 10036. **212-682-4600**

HARVARD CLUB. 1223 Locust St, Philadelphia, PA 10107. **215-735-7619**

KNICKERBOCKER CLUB. 807 5th Ave, New York, NY 10021. **212-838-6700**

METROPOLITAN CLUB. 1 E 60 St, New York, NY 10022. **212-838-7400**

METROPOLITAN CLUB. 1700 H St, Washington, DC 20026. **202-628-7500**

MORRISTOWN CLUB. 27 Elm, Morristown, NJ 07960. **201-539-0116**

NATIONAL ARTS CLUB. 15 Gramercy Park, New York, NY 10003. **212-475-3424**

NEWPORT READING ROOM. 29 Bellevue Ave, Newport, RI 02840. **401-846-0480**

NEW YORK YACHT CLUB. 37 W 44 St, New York, NY 10036. **212-682-0002**

NOONDAY CLUB. 515 Olive, St Louis, MO 63101. **314-231-8452**

PACIFIC UNION CLUB. 1000 California, San Francisco, CA 94108. **415-775-1233**

PHILADELPHIA CLUB. 1301 Walnut, Philadelphia, PA 19107. **215-735-5924**

PITTSBURGH CLUB. Box 1978, Pittsburgh, PA 15230. **412-281-4680**

PRINCETON CLUB. 15 W 43 St, New York, NY 10036. **212-682-6400**

PRINCETON CLUB OF PHILADELPHIA. 1223 Locust St, Philadelphia, PA 19107. **215-735-7619**

QUEEN CITY CLUB. 331 E 4th St, Cincinnati, OH 45214. **513-621-2708**

RACQUET CLUB. 1365 N Dearborn Pkwy, Chicago, IL 60610. **312-787-3200**

RACQUET CLUB. 215 S 16 St, Philadelphia, PA 19102. **215-735-1425**

RACQUET CLUB. 476 N Kings Highway Blvd, St Louis, MO 63108. **314-361-2100**

RACQUET AND TENNIS CLUB. 370 Park Ave, New York, NY 10022. **212-753-9700**

RADNOR HUNT. RD 2, Providence Rd, Malvern, PA 19355. **215-644-9918**

RITTENHOUSE CLUB. 1811 Walnut, Philadelphia, PA 19103. **215-563-1771**

RIVER CLUB. 447 E 52 St, New York, NY 10022. **212-751-0100**

ST ANTHONY CLUB. 16 E 64 St, New York, NY 10021. **212-832-9180**

ST ANTHONY CLUB. 32 S 22nd St, Philadelphia, PA 19103. **215-567-8686**

ST BOTOLPH CLUB. 199 Commonwealth Ave, Boston, MA 02116. **617-536-7570**

TAVERN CLUB. 4 Boylston Pl, Boston, Ma 02116. **617-338-9682**

TAVERN CLUB. 3522 Prospect Ave, Cleveland, OH 44115. **216-431-3220**

TENNIS AND RACQUET CLUB. 939 Boylston, Boston, MA 02115. **617-536-4630**

TOWN AND COUNTRY CLUB. 218 Stockton, San Francisco, CA 94108. **415-362-4951**

TWENTIETH CENTURY CLUB. 4201 Bigelow Blvd, Pittsburgh, PA 15213. **412-621-2353**

UNION CLUB. 8 Park, Boston, MA 02108. **617-227-0589**

UNION CLUB. 1211 Euclid Ave, Cleveland, OH 44115. **216-621-4230**

UNION CLUB. 101 E 69 St, New York, NY 10021. **212-734-5400**

UNION LEAGUE. 140 S Broad, Philadelphia, PA 19102. **215-563-6500**

UNION LEAGUE CLUB. 65 W Jackson Blvd, Chicago, IL 60604. **312-427-7800**

UNION LEAGUE CLUB. 38 E 37 St, New York, NY 10016. **212-685-3800**

UNIVERSITY CLUB. Mercantile Safe Deposit and Trust Bldg, 2 Hopkins Pl, Baltimore, MD 21202. **301-837-0366**

UNIVERSITY CLUB. 426 Stuart, Boston, MA 02116. **617-266-5600**

UNIVERSITY CLUB. 546 Delaware Ave, Buffalo, NY 14202. **716-884-8100**

UNIVERSITY CLUB. 401 E 4th St, Cincinnati, OH 45202. **513-721-2600**

UNIVERSITY CLUB. 3813 Euclid Ave, Cleveland, OH 44115. **216-431-0091**

UNIVERSITY CLUB. 1 W 54 St, New York, NY 10019. **212-257-2100**

UNIVERSITY CLUB. 1034 S Brentwood Blvd, St Louis, MO 63117. **314-725-2222**

UNIVERSITY CLUB. 800 Powell, San Francisco, CA 94108. **415-781-0900**

WILMINGTON CLUB. 1103 Market, Wilmington, DE 19801. **302-658-4287**

YALE CLUB. 50 Vanderbilt Ave, New York, NY 10017. **212-661-2070**

YALE CLUB. 1223 Locust, Philadelphia, PA 19107. **215-735-7619**

YORK CLUB. 4 E 62 St, New York, NY 10021. **212-838-6800**

RECREATION, ARTS, AND ENTERTAINMENT

MAJOR STUDIOS AND PRODUCERS

ALFRED HITCHCOCK PRODUCTIONS.
100 Universal City Plaza, Universal City, CA
91608. **213-985-4321**

ALLIED ARTISTS. 9440 Santa Monica
Blvd, Beverly Hills, CA 90201. **213-657-8270**

**ALLIED ARTISTS PICTURE CORPORA-
TION.** 15 Columbus Cir, New York, NY
10023. **212-541-9200**

**AMERICAN INTERNATIONAL PRO-
DUCTIONS.** 9033 Wilshire Blvd, Beverly
Hills, CA 90211. **213-278-8118.** Milt Moritz,
publicity

**ANIMATION FILMAKERS CORPORA-
TION.** 554 S San Vicente Blvd, Los Angeles,
CA 90048. **213-653-4384.** Night line:
213-465-5038. Richard N Brown, president.
Press contact. Margaret Kerry, executive
vice-president

**ARTIST MANAGEMENT ASSOCIA-
TION.** 200 W 57th St, New York, NY 10019.
212-757-2157

**AVCO EMBASSY PICTURES CORPO-
RATION.** 6601 Romaine St, Hollywood, CA
90038. **213-949-8954**

CASCADE PICTURES OF CALIFORNIA.
6616 Eleanor Ave, Hollywood, CA 90039.
213-463-2121. William Sterling, publicity

CINEMA-VIDEO STUDIO. Sepulueda
Blvd, Bel Air, CA 90620. **213-477-3958**

DICK CLARK PRODUCTIONS. 9125
Sunset Blvd, Los Angeles, CA 90069.
213-278-0311. Don Rogers, publicity

COLUMBIA PICTURES. 1 Columbia Plz,
Burbank, CA 91505. **213-843-6000.** Robert
Cort, vice president, general promotions

COLUMBIA PICTURES CORP. 711 5th
Ave, New York, NY 10022. **212-751-4400.**
John Lee, New York Publicity manager

COMPASS PRODUCTIONS. 1801 Avenue
of the Stars, Los Angeles, CA 90067.
213-553-6205. John Strauss publicity

TROY CORY SHOW. 1224 N Vine St, Los
Angeles, CA 90068. **213-462-1099** or **9043**

DE PATIE-FRELENG ENTERPRISES.
6859 Hayvenhurst, Van Nuys, CA 91406.
213-988-3890. G A Conte, publicity

DINO DE LAURENTIS CORPORATION.
202 N Canon Dr Beverly Hills, CA 90210.
212-550-8700. Gordon R Armstrong, director, advertising and publicity

WALT DISNEY. 500 S Buena Vista,
Burbank, CA 91503. **213-845-3141.** Tom
Jones, publicity

RALPH EDWARDS PRODUCTIONS.
1717 N Highland Ave, Los Angeles, CA
90028. **213-462-2212.** Charles Pomerantz,
publicity

EVE SCREEN GEMS. 3701 W Oak St,
Burbank, CA 91505. **213-843-3221.** William
Barnett, creative director

FILMATION ASSOCIATES. 18107 Sherman Way, Reseda, CA 91335. **213-345-7414**

FILMWAYS, INC. 1800 Century Park E,
Los Angeles, CA 90067. **213-552-1133**

**FIRST ARTISTS PRODUCTIONS COM-
PANY, LTD.** Burbank Studios, 4000 Warner
Blvd, Burbank, CA 91522. **213-843-6000**

FOUR STAR INTERNATIONAL, INC. 400
S Beverly Dr, Beverly Hills, CA 90212.
213-277-7444. Joseph Doyle, publicity

SAMUEL GOLDWYN. 1041 N Formosa,
Los Angeles, CA 90046. **213-469-6151.** Alice
Callaway, public relations, **213-461-6764**

GOODSON-TODMAN PRODUCTIONS.
6430 Sunset Blvd, Hollywood, CA 90028.
213-461-4781

MERV GRIFFIN PRODUCTIONS. 1541
Vine St, Hollywood, CA 90028.
213-461-4701. Larry Strawther, publicity

HANNA-BARBERA PRODUCTIONS.
3400 Cahuenga Blvd W, Los Angeles, CA
90068. **213-851-5000.** John Michaeli, publicity

HEMISPHERE PICTURES, INC. 445 Park
Ave, New York, NY 10022. **212-759-8707.**
Lee Willis, publicity

HOLLYWOOD VIDEO CENTER. 1541 N
Vine, Hollywood, CA 90028. **213-466-2141.**
Randy Luenebunk, controller and public
relations

ROSS HUNTER PRODUCTIONS. Goldwyn Studios, 1041 N Formosa, Los Angeles,
CA 90046. **213-650-2435**

HORIZON PICTURES, INC. 711 5th Ave,
New York, NY 10022. **212-421-6810.** Arthur
Canton, publicity, **212-541-4505**

KTTV STUDIOS. 5746 Sunset Blvd,
Hollywood, CA 90028. **213-462-7111.** Janet
Fede, publicity director

WALTER LANTZ PRODUCTIONS. 861
Seward St, Los Angeles, CA 90038.
213-496-2907

LION'S GATE FILMS. 1334 Westwood
Blvd, Los Angeles, CA 90024. **213-475-4987.**
Robert Altman, producer/director, president

MCA-TV, INC. 100 Universal City Plz,
Universal City, CA 91608. **213-985-4321**

METROTAPE WEST. 5746 Sunset Blvd,
Los Angeles, CA 90028. **213-462-7111**

MGM STUDIOS. 10202 W Washington,
Blvd, Culver City, CA 90230. **213-836-3000.**
Richard Kahn, vice-president, advertising,
publicity, and exploration

PARAMOUNT. 5451 Marathon St,
Hollywood, CA 90038. **213-463-0100.** Dick
Winters, public relations

PARAMOUNT PICTURES. 1 Gulf and
Western Plz, New York, NY 10023.
212-333-6400

**PARAMOUNT PICTURES CORPORA-
TION.** Gulf and Western Plz, New York,
NY 10023. **212-333-7062.** Laurence Mark,
executive director, publicity

Q-M PRODUCTIONS. 8560 Sunset Blvd,
Los Angeles, CA 90069. **213-659-4080**

SCREEN GEMS-EMI MUSIC. Suite 200,
7033 Sunset Blvd, Hollywood, CA 90028.
213-469-8371. Lester Sill, president. Danny
Davis, vice-president and director, national
exploitation

TIME-LIFE FILMS. Time-Life Bldg, New York, NY 10020. **212-566-1212.** Dorothy Dunbar, multimedia publicity

20TH CENTURY-FOX. 10201 W Pico, Los Angeles, CA 90035. **213-277-2211.** Jet Fore, studio publicity manager

UNITED ARTISTS. Roberts Ave, Los Angeles, CA 90046. **213-657-7000.** Buddy Young, publicity director

UNITED ARTISTS CORPORATION. 729 7th Ave, New York, NY 10019. **212-575-3000.** Mike Hutner, worldwide publicity director

UNIVERSAL. 100 Universal City Plz, Universal City, CA 91608. **213-985-4321.** Buddy Young, publicity director. Ben Halpern, television-press department, public relations

UPA PICTURES. 4440 Lakeside, Burbank, CA 91505. **213-842-7171.** Dorothy Schechter, public relations

VINE STREET STAGE/VIDEO MUSIC HALL. 1224 N Vine St, Los Angeles, CA 90038. **213-462-9043.** N Faulkinbury, president. *Press contact.* J White, **213-462-1099**

ANDY WARHOL ENTERPRISES. 860 Broadway, New York, NY 10003. **212-475-5500.** Paul Morrissey

WARNER BROTHERS, INC. 75 Rockefeller Plz, New York, NY 10020. **212-484-8000**

WARNER BROTHERS INC. 4000 Warner Blvd, Burbank, CA 91522. **213-843-6000.** Andrew M Fogelson, publicity and advertising

LEADING AGENTS AND AGENCIES

The following list presents, alphabetically, a nationwide cross section of the best known agents and agencies. It includes talent agents, literary agents, personal managers, celebrities' press agents, theatrical agents, and others who make their living acting as someone's surrogate.

ABRAMS-RUBALOFF AND ASSOCIATES. 10 E 53rd St, New York, NY 10022. **212-758-3636**

ACKERMAN SCIENCE FICTION AGENCY. 2495 Glendower Ave, Hollywood, CA 90027. **213-666-6326**

ROSE ADAIR. 250 W 57th St, New York, NY 10021. **212-582-1957**

BRET ADAMS LTD. 36 E 61st St, New York, NY 10021. **212-752-7864**

ADAMS, RAY, AND ROSENBERG. 9220 Sunset Blvd, Los Angeles, CA 90069. **213-278-3000**

CEIL ADLER AGENCY, INC. 15 W 55th St, New York, NY 10019. **212-757-2535**

AGENCY FOR PERFORMING ARTS. 120 W 57th St, New York, NY 10019. **212-581-8800**

WILLARD ALEXANDER, INC. 660 Madison Ave, New York, NY 10021. **212-751-7070**

ALL TAME ANIMALS AGENCY. 37 W 57th St, New York, NY 10019. **212-752-5885.** *Contact.* Doug Gruber, director

MARIA ALMONTE. 160 W 57th St, New York, NY 10036. **212-224-7481**

AMERICAN ARTIST MANAGEMENT. 303 W 42nd St, New York, NY 10036. **212-265-0430**

AMERICAN INTERNATIONAL TALENT AGENCY. 166 W 125 St, New York, NY 10027. **212-663-4626**

AMERICAN PLAY CO, INC. 52 Vanderbilt Ave, New York, NY 10017. **212-697-9763.** Sheldon Abenol, president

AM-RUS LITERARY AGENCY. 25 W 43rd St, New York, NY 10036. **212-279-8846.** *Contact.* Leah Siegel. Represents the USSR Copyright Agency (VAAP)

BEVERLY ANDERSON AGENCY. 1472 Broadway, New York, NY 10036. **212-279-5553**

ANIMAL TALENT SCOUTS. 331 W 18th St, New York, NY 10011. **212-243-2700.** Patricia Poleskie, director

ARCARA, BAUMAN, AND HILLER. 850 7th Ave, New York, NY 10019. **212-757-0098**

STEVE ARNOLD ENTERPRISES, INC. 300 E 40th St, New York, NY 10018. **212-896-3188**

ASSOCIATED BOOKING. 445 Park Ave, New York, NY 10022. **212-421-5200**

RICHARD ASTOR AGENCY. 119 W 57th St, New York, NY 10019. **212-581-1970**

ATI. 888 7th Ave, New York, NY 10019. **212-977-2300**

AUTHOR AID ASSOCIATES. 340 E 52nd St, New York, NY 10022. **212-758-4213.** Arthur Orrmont, president and author's consultant

AUTHORS AND PUBLISHERS SERVICE. 146-7 29 Ave, Flushing, NY 11354. **212-461-9408.** Karen Simansky, codirector

JULIAN BACH LITERARY AGENCY. 3 E 48th St, New York, NY 10017. **212-753-2605**

THE BALKIN AGENCY. 403 W 115th St, New York, NY 10025. **212-850-5131**

BALSIGER LITERARY SERVICE. PO Box 1820, Park City, UT 84060. **714-642-1596, 801-649-9498**

BARBIZON MODEL AGENCY. 5530 Wisconsin Ave, Washington, DC 20015. **301-656-5996.** Mrs P Hanes, director

RICHARD BAUMAN AGENCY. 1650 Broadway, New York, NY 10019. **212-757-0098**

BILL BERGER ASSOCIATES, INC. 535 E 72nd St, New York, NY 10021. **212-249-2771** or **3887**

LOLA BISHOP. Rm 1204, 650 Broadway, New York, NY 10019. **212-245-4775**

NINA BLANCHARD AGENCY—ARTIST MANAGER. 1717 N Highland Ave -901, Los Angeles, CA 90028. **213-462-7274**

LURTON BLASSIGAME. 60 E 42nd St, New York, NY 10017. **212-687-7491**

BONNIE KID AGENCY . 250 W 57th St, New York, NY 10019. **212-246-0223**

GEORGE BORCHARDT, INC. 136 E 57th St, New York, NY 10022. **212-753-5785**

BRANDT AND BRANDT. 101 Park Ave, New York, NY 10017. **212-683-5890**

THE HELEN BRANN AGENCY. 14 Sutton Pl, New York, NY 10022. **212-751-0137**

BREBNER AGENCIES, INC. 1615 Polk St, San Francisco, CA 94109. **415-775-1802**

SANDY BRESLER AND ASSOCIATES. 190 N Cannon Dr, Beverly Hills, CA 90210. **213-278-3200**

CURTIS BROWN, LTD. 575 Madison Ave, New York, NY 10022. **212-755-4200**

JAMES BROWN ASSOCIATES, INC. 22 E 60th St, New York, NY 10022. **212-355-4182**

BERNARD MAX-ROTH BURKE. 48 W 48th St, New York, NY 10036. **212-757-4540**

BERTHA CASE. 42 W 53rd St, New York, NY 10019. **212-581-6280**

CENTRAL CASTING CORPORATION. 200 W 54th St, New York, NY 10019. **212-582-4933**

THE CEREGHETTI AGENCY. 1564 Broadway, New York, NY 10036. **212-765-5260**

CHASIN-PARK-CITRON AGENCY. 9255 Sunset Blvd, Los Angeles, CA 90069. **213-273-7190**

CHATEAU THEATRICAL ANIMALS. 608 W 48th St, New York, NY 10036. **212-246-0520**

CIRCLE ARTISTS. 501 Madison Ave, New York, NY 10022. **212-757-4668**

COLEMAN-ROSENBERG AGENCY. 667 Madison Ave, New York, NY 10021. **212-838-0734**

COLUMBIA ARTISTS MANAGEMENT. 165 W 57th St, New York, NY 10019. **212-397-6900**

CHARLES W CONAWAY. 345 E 56th St, New York, NY 10022. **212-758-6491**

BILL COOPER ASSOCIATES. 16 E 52nd St, New York, NY 10022. **212-758-6491**

CREATIVE MANAGEMENT ASSOCIA-TION, INC. 40 W 57th St, New York, NY 10019. **212-586-0440**

LIL CUMBER. 6515 Sunset Blvd, Los Angeles, CA 90028. **213-469-1919**

WILLIAM D CUNNINGHAM AND ASSOCIATES. 5900 Wilshire Blvd, Los Angeles, CA 90036. **213-462-7274**

JOHN CUSHMAN ASSOCIATES, INC. 25 W 43rd St, New York, NY 10036. **212-685-2052**

JANE DEACY AGENCY. 119 E 54th St, New York, NY 10022. **212-752-4865**

DIAMOND ARTISTS. 119 W 57th St, New York, NY 10019. **212-247-3025**

DICKENS-HELD. 9911 W Pico Blvd, -970, Los Angeles, CA 90035. **213-937-8500**

DONADIO AND ASSOCIATES. 111 W 57th St, New York, NY 10019. **212-757-5076**

STEPHEN DRAPER AGENCY. 37 W 57th St, New York, NY 10019. **212-421-5780**

THE FAITH AGENCY. Suite 411, 280 S Beverly Dr, Beverly Hills, CA 90212. **213-274-0776**

LESLIE FARGO AGENCY. 811 Fisher Bldg, Detroit, MI 48202. **313-871-4445.** Leslie Fargo Ginn, owner

FLAIRE ENTERPRISES. 8693 Wilshire Blvd, Beverly Hills, CA 90211. **213-659-6721**

FORD MODEL AGENCY. 344 E 59th St, New York, NY 10022. **212-688-8538**

RUTH FOREMAN. 1603 NE 123rd St, North Miami, FL 33181. **305-891-1830**

DAVID FRANKLIN. 950 3rd Ave, New York, NY 10022. **212-838-6333**

SAMUEL FRENCH, INC. 25 W 45th St, New York, NY 10036. **212-582-4700**

THE MARTIN GAGE GROUP. 1650 Broadway, New York, NY 10019. **212-541-5250**

ROBERT W GEWALD. 58 W 58th St, New York, NY 10019. **212-753-0450**

GOLDMARK COMMUNICATIONS. Stamford, CT 06904. **203-327-7270**

MURRAY GOODMAN. 232 Madison Ave, New York, NY 10016. **212-686-4231**

CAROLYN HANSEN FASHION COL-LEGE AND AGENCY. 1516 6th Ave, Seattle, WA 98101. **206-622-4992**

FRED HARRIS. 119 W 57th St, New York, NY 10017. **212-247-3025**

HARTIG-AMBROSE-NANI, LTD. 527 Madison Ave, New York, NY 10022. **212-759-9163**

HELEN HARVEY ASSOCIATES. 110 W 57th St, New York, NY 10019. **212-581-5610**

HENDERSON-HOGAN AGENCY, INC. 200 W 57th St, New York, NY 10019. **212-765-5190**

HESSELTINE-BAKER AND DICKENS, LTD. Suite 970, 9911 W Pico Blvd, Los Angeles, CA 90035. **213-556-3521**

ICM. 8899 Beverly Blvd, Los Angeles, CA 90048. **213-550-4000.** Also 40 W 57th St, New York, NY 10019. **212-556-5600**

INTERNATIONAL CREATIVE MANAGE-MENT. 1301 Avenue of the Americas, New York, NY 10019. **212-556-5600**

KNOX BURGER ASSOCIATES, LTD. 39½ Washington, Sq, New York, NY 10012. **212-533-2360**

LA BELLE AGENCY. Studio III, El Paseo, Santa Barbara, CA 93102. **805-965-4575**

IRVING PAUL (SWIFTY) LAZAR. 211 S Beverly Dr, Beverly Hills, CA 90212. **213-275-6153**

LAZAROW. 119 W 57th St, New York, NY 10019. **212-586-5930**

ELLIOTT MADDOX ENTERPRISES. 250 W 57th St, New York, NY 10022. **212-757-1605**

MAHONEY AND COMPANY. 9720 Wilshire Blvd, Beverly Hills, CA 90212. **213-276-7145**

MANAGEMENT LUDWIG LUSTIG. 111 W 57th St, New York, NY 10019. **212-586-3976**

MAXWELL ALEY ASSOCIATES. 145 E 35th St, New York, NY 10016. **212-679-5377** or **5378**

MCINTOSH, MCKEE, AND DODDS, INC. 22 E 40th St, New York, NY 10016. **212-679-4490**

WILLIAM MORRIS AGENCY. 151 El Camino Dr, Beverly Hills, CA 90212. **213-274-9451.** Also 1350 Avenue of the Americas, New York, NY 10019. **212-586-5100**

NATIONAL TALENT ASSOCIATES. 280 Park Ave, Rutherford, NJ 07070. **201-935-0330**

ELLEN NEUWALD, INC. 905 W End Ave, New York, NY 10025. **212-663-1586**

HAROLD OBER ASSOCIATES, INC. 40 E 49th St, New York, NY 10017. **212-759-8600**

O'BRYAN'S TALENT WEST, INC. 17915 Ventura Blvd-200, Encino, CA 91316. **213-653-0450**

DAVID OBST. c/o Random House Inc., 201 E 50th St, New York, NY 10022. **212-572-2462.** (h) 105 E 64th St, New York, NY 10021. **212-249-4417**

PLAYBOY MODELS. 919 N Michigan Ave, Chicago, IL 60605. **312-664-9024**

MARIAN POLAN TALENT AGENCY. 721 E Las Olas Blvd, Fort Lauderdale, FL 33301. **305-462-0820**

ROGERS AND COWAN, INC. 9665 Wilshire Blvd, Beverly Hills, CA 90212. **213-275-4581**

RYDEN-FRAZER AGENCY. Suite 344, 11901 S Bascom Ave, Campbell, CA 95008. **408-371-1973**

NORMAN SCHUCART ENTERPRISES. 1417 Green Bay Rd, Highland Park, IL 60035. **312-433-1113**

W F SPORTS ENTERPRISES. 370 Lexington Ave, New York, NY 10017. **212-689-0455**

JOHN SPRINGER ASSOCIATES. 1901 Avenue of the Stars, Los Angeles, CA 90067. **213-277-3744.** *Contact.* Ray Stricklyn

THE STERLING LORD AGENCY, INC. 660 Madison Ave, New York, NY 10021. **212-751-2533**

ANN WRIGHT ASSOCIATES, LTD. 8422 Melrose Pl, Los Angeles, CA 90069. **213-655-5040**

MAJOR ENTERTAINMENT FACILITIES

Facilities were chosen on the basis of seating capacity in each of the 50 largest metropolitan areas.

See also, SPORTS.

ALBANY CIVIC AUDITORIUM. PO Box 6172, Albany, NY 12206. **518-462-1297**

ANAHEIM CONVENTION CENTER. 800 W Katella, Anaheim, CA 92802. **714-533-5617**

ATLANTIC CIVIC CENTER. 395 Piedmont Ave NE, Atlanta, GA 30308. **404-523-6275**

BALTIMORE CIVIC CENTER. 201 W Baltimore St, Baltimore, MD 21201. **301-837-0903**

BIRMINGHAM-JEFFERSON CIVIC CENTER. 1 Civic Center Plz, Birmingham, AL 34203. **205-328-9453.** Donald A Brown, director, communications, **205-328-8160**

BOSTON CENTER FOR THE ARTS, INC. 539 Tremont St, Boston, MA 02116. **617-426-5000**

BUFFALO MEMORIAL AUDITORIUM. Main at Terrace, Buffalo, NY 14202. **716-856-4200.** Night line: **716-856-7056**

CHICAGO INTERNATIONAL AMPHITHEATRE COMPANY. 4300 S Halstead St, Chicago, IL 60609. **312-791-5580**

(CHICAGO) MCCORMICK PLACE AND ARIE CROWN THEATRE. McCormick Pl on the Lake, Chicago, IL 60616. **312-791-6000**

CINCINNATI MUSIC HALL. 1234 Elm St, Cincinnati, OH 45210. **513-241-3086**

(CLEVELAND) HANNA THEATRE. 2067 E 14th St, Cleveland, OH 44115. **216-621-5000**

(COLUMBUS) MERSHON AUDITORIUM. Ohio State University, 30 W 15th Ave, Columbus, OH 43210. **614-422-5785**

DALLAS CONVENTION CENTER. 717 S Akard, Dallas, TX 75202. **214-658-7056**

DAYTON CONVENTION AND EXHIBITION CENTER. 22 Dave Hall Plz, Dayton, OH 54502. **513-225-5555.**

(DENVER) CENTER OF PERFORMING ARTS. Loretto Heights College, 3001 S Federal Blvd, Denver, CO 80236. **303-922-4102**

(DETROIT) FORD AUDITORIUM. 20 Auditorium Dr, Detroit, MI 48226. **313-224-1055**

HARTFORD CIVIC CENTER. 1 Civic Center Plz, Hartford, CT 06013. **203-566-6588**

HOUSTON CIVIC CENTER. 615 Louisiana (PO Box 61469), Houston, TX 77208. **713-222-3561**

(INDIANAPOLIS) CLOWES MEMORIAL HALL. 4600 Sunset Ave, Indianapolis, IN 46209. **317-924-6321**

(KANSAS CITY) MUNICIPAL AUDITORIUM. 1311 Wyandotte St, Kansas City, MO 64105. **816-421-8000**

(LOS ANGELES) INNER CITY CULTURAL CENTER. 1308 S New Hampshire Ave, Los Angeles, CA 90006. **213-387-1161**

(LOUISVILLE) CONVENTION CENTER. 525 W Walnut, Louisville, KY 40202. **502-587-3061**

(MEMPHIS) ELLIS AUDITORIUM. Memphis, TN 38104. **901-523-2982**

(MIAMI) DADE COUNTY AUDITORIUM. 2901 W Flager St, Miami, FL 33135. **305-547-5414**

(MILWAUKEE) EMIL BLATZ TEMPLE OF MUSIC. Washington Park, 4420 W Vliet St, Milwaukee, WI 53209. **414-278-4389**

MINNEAPOLIS AUDITORIUM AND CONVENTION CENTER. 1403 Stevens Ave S, Minneapolis, MN 55403. **612-870-4436**

(NASHVILLE) TENNESSEE BOTANICAL GARDEN AND FINE ARTS CENTER—CHEEKWOOD. Cheek Rd, Cheekwood, TN 37205. **615-352-5310**

(NEWARK) SYMPHONY HALL. 1020 Broad St, Newark, NJ 07102. **201-643-4554** or **4550**

(NEW ORLEANS) MUNICIPAL AUDITORIUM. 1201 St Peter St, New Orleans, LA 70016. **504-525-8441**

(NEW YORK) LINCOLN CENTER FOR THE PERFORMING ARTS. 1865 Broadway, New York, NY 10023. **212-765-5100**

(NEW YORK) MADISON SQUARE GARDEN. 30th and 7th Ave (4 Pennsylvania Plz), New York, NY 10001. **212-564-4400**

NORFOLK SCOPE. Scope Plz, Norfolk, VA 23502. **703-441-2764**

(OKLAHOMA CITY) CIVIC CENTER MUSIC HALL. 201 Dewey St, Oklahoma City, OK 73102. **415-525-5411**

THE PHILADELPHIA SPECTRUM. Broad and Pattison Sts, Philadelphia, PA 19148. **215-389-9000.** Larry Rubin, public relations, **215-336-3600**

PHOENIX CIVIC PLAZA. 225 E Adams St, Phoenix, AZ 85004. **602-262-6225**

(PITTSBURGH) HEINZ HALL FOR THE PERFORMING ARTS. Penn Ave and 6th St, Pittsburgh, PA 15222. **412-281-8185**

(PORTLAND) MEMORIAL COLISEUM CENTER. 1401 N Wheeler, Portland, OR 97208. **503-235-6225**

PROVIDENCE CIVIC CENTER. La Salle Sq, Providence, RI 02903. **401-331-0700**

ROCHESTER COMMUNITY WAR MEMORIAL. 100 Exchange St, Rochester, NY 14614. **716-232-6170**

SACRAMENTO BALLET. 3839 H St, Sacramento, CA 95816. **916-452-1436**

(ST LOUIS) THE CHECKERDOME. 5700 Oakland St, St Louis, MO 63110. **314-644-0900**

THE SALT PALACE. 100 SW Temple, Salt Lake City, UT 84101. **801-521-6060**

(SAN ANTONIO) LA VILLITA. 416 Villita St, San Antonio, TX 78205. **512-227-0521**

(SAN BERNARDINO) SYMPHONY ORCHESTRA. Box 2312, Uptown Station, San Bernardino, CA 92406. **714-884-0288**

SAN DIEGO COMMUNITY CONCOURSE. 202 C St, San Diego, CA 92101. **714-236-6500**

SAN FRANCISCO WAR MEMORIAL OPERA HOUSE. Van Ness and Grove Sts, San Francisco, CA **415-621-6600**

SEATTLE CENTER. 305 Harrison St, Seattle, WA 98109. **206-625-4231**

(TAMPA) CURTIS HIXON CONVENTION HALL. 4600 Sunset Ave, Indianapolis, IN 46208. **317-926-3471**

TOLEDO MASONIC AUDITORIUM. 4645 Heather Downs Blvd, Toledo, OH 43614. **419-893-9453**

(WASHINGTON, DC) JOHN F KENNEDY CENTER FOR THE PERFORMING ARTS. 2700 F St NW, Washington, DC 20566. General information: **202-254-3600.** Ticket reservations: **202-857-0900.** Out-of-state: **800-424-8504.** Roger L Stevens, chairman. Martin Feinstein, executive director, performing arts. Facilities include 1142-seat Eisenhower

Theatre, 2753-seat Concert Hall, and 2318-seat Opera House

(WINSTON-SALEM) M B BENTON, JR, CONVENTION AND CIVIC CENTER. PO Box 68, Winston-Salem, NC 27101. **919-727-2976**

TOURIST INFORMATION BY STATES

ALABAMA

Bureau of Publicity and Information. State Highway Bldg, Montgomery, 36130. **205-832-5510** or **800-633-5761**

Greater Birmingham Convention and Visitors' Bureau. Suite 940, First Alabama Bank Bldg, Birmingham, 35203. **205-252-9825**

Travel and Convention Department, Mobile Area Chamber of Commerce. PO Box 2187, Mobile, 36601. **205-433-6951**

ALASKA

Alaska Division of Tourism, Department of Economic Development. Pouch E, Juneau, 99811. **907-465-2010**

AMERICAN SAMOA

Director of the Office of Tourism, Government of American Samoa. Pago Pago, 96799

ARIZONA

Arizona Office of Tourism. Rm 501, 1700 W Washington St, Phoenix, 85007. **602-271-3618**

Tourist Development Department, Phoenix Metropolitan Chamber of Commerce. 805 N 2nd St, Phoenix, 85004. **602-254-5521**

Phoenix and Valley of the Sun Convention and Visitors' Bureau. Suite 200H, 2701 E Camelback, Tucson, 85016. **602-792-1212**

ARKANSAS

Arkansas Department of Parks and Tourism. 149 State Capitol Bldg, Little Rock, 72201. **501-371-1511**

Hot Springs Convention Bureau. PO Box 1500, Hot Springs, 71901. **501-321-1703**

Little Rock Chamber of Commerce. 1 Spring Bldg, Little Rock, 72201. **501-374-4871**

CALIFORNIA

The Redwood Empire Association. 476 Post St, San Francisco, 94102. **415-421-6554**

Southern California Visitors' Council. 705 W 7th St, Los Angeles, 90017. **213-628-3101**

Anaheim Visitor and Convention Bureau. 800 W Katella Ave, Anaheim, 92802. **714-533-5536**

Long Beach Convention and News Bureau. 300 E Ocean Blvd, Long Beach, 90802. **213-436-3636**

Greater Los Angeles Visitors' and Convention Bureau. Level B, 505 S Flower St, Los Angeles, 90071. **213-488-9100**

Convention and Tourist Bureau, Chamber of Commerce. 1939 Harrison St, Oakland, 94612. **415-451-7800**

Palm Springs Convention and Visitors' Bureau. Suite 101, Municipal Airport Terminal, Palm Springs, 92262. **714-327-8411**

Sacramento Convention and Visitors' Bureau. 1100 14th St, Sacramento, 95814. **916-449-5291**

Convention and Visitors' Bureau. Suite 824, 1200 3rd Ave, San Diego, 92101. **714-232-3101**

San Francisco Convention and Visitors' Bureau. Suite 260, 1390 Market St, San Francisco, 94102. **415-626-5500**

COLORADO

Travel Marketing Section, Colorado Division of Commerce and Development. 500 State Centennial Bldg, 1313 Sherman St, 80203. **303-892-3045** or **800-525-3083**

Denver and Colorado Convention and Visitors' Bureau. 225 W Colfax Ave, Denver, 80202. **303-892-1112**

American Indian Travel Commission. Department NL, 10403 W Colfax Ave, Lakewood, 80215. **303-234-1707**

CONNECTICUT

Tourism Promotion Service, Connecticut Department of Commerce. 210 Washington St, Hartford, 06106. **203-566-3977**

Hartford Convention and Visitors' Bureau. 1 Civic Center Plz, Hartford, 06103. **203-728-6789**

DELAWARE

Delaware State Visitors' Service, Division of Economic Development. 630 State College Rd, Dover, 19901. **302-678-4254**

DISTRICT OF COLUMBIA

Washington Area Convention and Visitors' Bureau. 1129 20th St NW, Washington, 20036. **202-857-5500**

Public Citizen Visitors' Center. 1200 15th St NW, Washington, 20005. **202-659-9053**

FLORIDA

Division of Tourism, Florida Department of Commerce. 107 W Gaines St, Tallahassee, 32304. **904-487-1462**

Convention and Tourism, Daytona Beach Area Chamber of Commerce. City Island, PO

Box 2775, Daytona Beach, 32015.
904-255-0981

Jacksonville Convention and Visitors' Bureau.
133 W Monroe St, Jacksonville, 32202.
904-353-9736

Miami Metro Department of Publicity and Tourism. 499 Biscayne Blvd, Miami, 33132.
305-579-6327

Miami Beach Tourist Development Authority.
555 17th St, Miami Beach, 33139.
305-673-7083

Convention and Visitors' Bureau, Orlando Area Chamber of Commerce. PO Box 1913, Orlando, 32802. **305-425-5563** or
305-423-5527

Tourism Department, Greater Tampa Chamber of Commerce. PO Box 420, Tampa, 33601. **813-228-7777**

GEORGIA

TOURIST/COMMUNICATIONS DIVISION, BUREAU OF INDUSTRY AND TRADE. PO Box 1776, Atlanta, 30301.
404-656-3553

DEPARTMENT OF PUBLIC INFORMATION, ATLANTA CHAMBER OF COMMERCE. PO Box 1740, Atlanta, 30301.
404-521-0845

SAVANNAH CHAMBER OF COMMERCE. PO Box 530, Savannah, 31402.
912-233-3067

GUAM

Guam Visitors' Bureau. PO Box 3520, Agana, 96910

HAWAII

Hawaii Visitors' Bureau. PO Box 8527, Honolulu, 96815. **808-923-1811**

IDAHO

Division of Tourism and Industrial Development. Rm 108, State Capitol Bldg, Boise, 83720. **208-384-2470**

ILLINOIS

Illinois Office of Tourism, Department of Business and Economic Development. Rm 1100, 205 W Wacker Dr, Chicago, 60606.
312-793-4732

Chicago Convention and Tourism Bureau, Rm 2050, 332 S Michigan Ave, Chicago, 60604. **312-922-3530**

INDIANA

Tourism Development Division, Indiana Department of Commerce. Rm 336, State House, Indianapolis, 46204. **317-633-3376**

Community Information, Indianapolis Chamber of Commerce. 320 N Meridian Ave, Indianapolis, 46204. **317-635-4747**

IOWA

Travel Development Division, Iowa Development Commission. 250 Jewett Bldg, Des Moines, 50309. **515-281-3401**

Convention and Visitors' Bureau. 800 High St, Des Moines, 50307. **515-283-1777**

KANSAS

Tourist Division, Kansas Department of Economic Development. 6th Floor, 503 Kansas Ave, Topeka, 66603. **913-296-3487**

Wichita Area Chamber of Commerce. 350 W Douglas, Wichita, 67202. **316-265-7771**

KENTUCKY

Division of Advertising and Travel Promotion. Capitol Annex, Frankfort, 40601.
502-564-4930

Louisville Visitors' Bureau. Founders Sq, Louisville, 40202. **502-583-3377**

LOUISIANA

Louisiana Office of Tourism and Promotion. PO Box 44291, Capitol Station, Baton Route, 70804. **504-389-5981**

Greater New Orleans Tourist and Convention Commission. 334 Royal St, New Orleans, 70130. **504-522-8772**

Shreveport-Bossier Convention and Tourist Commission. PO Box 1761, Shreveport, 71166. **318-222-9391**

MAINE

Maine Publicity Bureau. 3 St John St, Portland, 04102. **207-773-7266**

Convention and Visitors' Bureau, Greater Portland Chamber of Commerce. 142 Free St, Portland, 04101. **207-772-2811**

MARYLAND

Division of Tourist Development, Department of Economic and Community Development.
1748 Forest Dr, Annapolis, 21401.
301-269-3517

MASSACHUSETTS

Division of Tourism, Massachusetts Department of Commerce and Development. 100 Cambridge St, Boston, 02202. **617-727-3201**

Greater Boston Convention and Tourist Bureau, Inc. 900 Boylston St, Boston, 02115.
617-536-4100

MICHIGAN

Michigan Travel Commission. PO Box 30226, Lansing, 48909. **517-373-0670** or
800-248-5456

Metropolitan Detroit Convention and Visitors' Bureau. Suite 1905, 100 Renaissance Ctr, Detroit, 48243. **313-259-4333**

MINNESOTA

Tourism Division, Minnesota Department of Economic Development. Hanover Bldg, 480 Cedar St, St Paul, 55101. **612-296-5027**

Minneapolis Convention and Tourism Commission. 15 S 5th St, Minneapolis, 55402.
612-348-4330

St Paul Convention and Visitors' Bureau, St Paul Area Chamber of Commerce. Suite 300, Osborn, Blvd, St Paul, 44102. **612-222-5561**

MISSISSIPPI

Travel and Tourism Department, Mississippi Agricultural and Industrial Board. 1504 Walter Sillers Bldg, Jackson, 39205.
601-354-6715

Natchez-Adams County Chamber of Commerce. PO Box 725, Natchez, 39120.
601-445-4611

MISSOURI

Missouri Division of Tourism. PO Box 1055, Jefferson City, 65101. **314-751-4133**

Convention and Visitors' Bureau. 1221 Baltimore Ave, Kansas City, 64105.
816-221-5242

Convention and Tourist Board of Greater St Louis. 500 N Broadway, St Louis, 63102.
314-421-1023

MONTANA

Travel Promotion Unit, Montana Department of Highways. Helena, 59601. **406-449-2654**

Great Falls Area Chamber of Commerce. PO Box 2127, Great Falls, 59403. **406-761-4434**

NEBRASKA

Division of Travel and Tourism, Nebraska Department of Economic Development. PO Box 94666, Lincoln, 68509. **402-471-3111**

Greater Omaha Chamber of Commerce. Suite 2100, 1620 Dodge St, Omaha, 68102.
402-341-1234

NEVADA

Tourism Division, Department of Economic Development. Capitol Complex, Carson City, 89701. **702-885-4322**

Las Vegas Chamber of Commerce. 2301 E Sahara Ave, Las Vegas, 89104. **702-457-4664**

NEW HAMPSHIRE

New Hampshire Office of Vacation Travel. PO Box 856, Concord, 03301. **603-271-2343**

NEW JERSEY

Division of Travel and Tourism, Department of Labor and Industry. PO Box 400, Trenton, 08625. **609-292-2470**

Greater Atlantic City Chamber of Commerce. 10 Central Pier, Atlantic City, 08401. **609-345-2251**

NEW MEXICO

Tourist Division, Department of Development. Bataan Memorial Bldg, Santa Fe, 87503. **505-827-3101** or **800-545-9876**

Convention and Visitors' Bureau, Greater Albuquerque Chamber of Commerce. 401 2nd St NW, Albuquerque, 87102. **505-842-0220**

NEW YORK

Travel Bureau, New York State Department of Commerce. 99 Washington Ave, Albany, 12245. **518-474-4116**

New York Convention and Visitors' Bureau. 90 E 42nd St, New York, 10017. **212-687-1300**

Niagara Falls Convention and Visitors' Bureau. PO Box 786, Falls St Station, Niagara Falls, 14303. **716-278-8010**

Syracuse Convention and Visitors' Bureau. 17th Floor, Mony Plz, Syracuse, 13202. **315-422-1343**

NORTH CAROLINA

Travel Development Section, North Carolina Department of Natural and Economic Resources. PO Box 27687, Raleigh, 27611. **919-829-4171**

NORTH DAKOTA

North Dakota Travel Division, State Highway Department. Capitol Grounds, Bismarck, 48401. **701-224-2525**

OHIO

Ohio Office of Travel and Tourism, Department of Economic and Community Development. PO Box 1001, Columbus, 43215. **514-466-5467**

Greater Cincinnati Chamber of Commerce. 120 W 5th St, Cincinnati, 45202. **513-721-3300**

Cleveland Convention and Visitors' Bureau. 511 Terminal Tower, Cleveland, 44113. **216-621-4110**

Columbus Convention and Visitors' Bureau. Suite 2540, 50 W Broad St, Columbus, 43215. **614-221-6623**

Dayton Area Chamber of Commerce. Rm 200, 111 W 1st St, Dayton, 45402. **513-226-1444**

OKLAHOMA

Tourism Promotion Division, Oklahoma Tourism and Recreation Department. 500 Will Rogers Bldg, Oklahoma City, 73105. **405-521-2406**

Oklahoma City Convention and Tourism Center. 3 Santa Fe Plz, Oklahoma City, 73102. **405-232-2211**

OREGON

Travel Information Section. 101 Highway Bldg, Salem, 97310. **503-378-6309** or **800-547-4901**

Portland Chamber of Commerce. 824 SW 5th Ave, Portland, 97204. **503-228-9411**

PENNSYLVANIA

Pennsylvania Bureau of Travel Development, Pennsylvania Department of Commerce. 206 South Office Bldg, Harrisburg, 17120. **717-787-5453**

Philadelphia Convention and Visitors' Bureau. 1525 John F Kennedy Blvd, Philadelphia, 19102. **215-864-1976**

Pittsburgh Convention and Visitors' Bureau. 200 Roosevelt Blvd, Pittsburgh, 15222. **412-281-7711**

Visitor Information Center. Gateway Ctr, 445 Liberty Ave, Pittsburgh, 15222. **412-281-9222**

PUERTO RICO

Puerto Rico Tourism Development Company. GPO Box BN, San Juan, 00936. **809-764-2390**

RHODE ISLAND

Tourist Promotion Division, Department of Economic Development. 1 Weybosset Hill, Providence, 02903. **401-277-2601**

Convention and Visitors' Bureau, Newport Chamber of Commerce. America Cup Ave, Newport, 02840. **401-847-1600**

SOUTH CAROLINA

Division of Tourism, South Carolina Department of Parks, Recreation, and Tourism. 1205 Pendleton St, Columbia, 29202. **803-758-2536**

Charleston Chamber of Commerce. PO Box 975, Charleston, 29402. **803-722-8338**

SOUTH DAKOTA

Division of Tourism. Joe Foss Bldg, Pierre, 57501. **605-224-3301.** or **800-843-1930**

Rapid City Chamber of Commerce. PO Box 747, Rapid City, 57701. **605-343-1744**

Sioux Falls Chamber of Commerce. PO Box 1425, Sioux Falls, 57101. **605-336-1620**

TENNESSEE

Tennessee Tourist Development Division. 1028 Andrew Jackson Bldg, Nashville, 37201. **615-741-2158**

Convention and Visitors' Bureau. Memorial Auditorium, 399 McCallie Ave, Chattanooga, 37402. **615-266-5716**

Communications and Conventions Department, Greater Knoxville Chamber of Commerce. PO Box 2229, Knoxville, 37901. **615-637-4550**

Memphis Area Chamber of Commerce. PO Box 224, Memphis, 38101. **901-523-2322**

TEXAS

Texas Tourist Development Agency. Box 12008, Capitol Station, Austin, 78711. **512-475-4326**

Travel and Information Division, State Department of Highways and Public Transportation. 11th and Brazos Sts, Austin, 78701. **512-475-3661**

Dallas Convention and Visitors' Bureau, Dallas Chamber of Commerce. 1507 Pacific Ave, Dallas, 75201. **214-651-1020**

El Paso Chamber of Commerce. 10 Civic Center Plz, El Paso, 79944. **915-544-7880**

Fort Worth Area Convention and Visitors' Bureau. 700 Throckmorton St, Fort Worth, 76102. **817-336-2491**

Greater Houston Convention and Visitors' Council. Suite 1101, 1006 Main St, Houston, 77002. **713-658-9201**

San Antonio Convention and Visitors' Bureau. PO Box 2277, San Antonio, 78298. **512-223-9133**

UTAH

Utah Travel Council. Council Hall, Capitol Hill, Salt Lake City, 84114. **801-533-5681**

Salt Lake Valley Convention and Visitors' Bureau. The Salt Palace, Salt Lake City, 84101. **801-521-2822**

VERMONT

Vermont Travel Division, Agency of Development and Community Affairs. 61 Elm St, Montpelier, 05602. **802-828-3236**

VIRGINIA

Virginia State Travel Service. 6 N 6th St, Richmond, 23219. **804-786-2051**

Norfolk Visitors' Bureau. PO Box 238, Norfolk, 23501. **804-441-5166**

VIRGIN ISLANDS

Division of Tourism. PO Box 1692, St Thomas, 00801. **809-774-2566**

WASHINGTON

Travel Development Division, Department of Commerce and Economic Development. General Administration Bldg, Olympia, 98504. **206-753-5610**

Seattle-King County Convention and Visitors' Bureau. 1815 7th Ave, Seattle, 98101. **206-622-5022**

Spokane Area Convention and Visitors' Bureau. W 1020 Riverside, PO Box 2147, Spokane, 99210. **509-624-1341**

WEST VIRGINIA

Governor's Office of Economic and Community Development, Travel Section. Rm B-504, Bldg 6, Charleston, 25305. **304-348-2286**

WISCONSIN

Division of Tourism, Department of Business Development. 123 W Washington Ave, Madison, 53702. **608-266-2161**

Green Bay Visitors' and Convention Bureau, Inc. Brown County Arena, PO Box 3278, Green Bay, 54303. **414-494-9507**

Greater Milwaukee Convention and Visitors' Bureau, Inc. 828 N Broadway, Milwaukee, 43202. **414-273-3950**

WYOMING

Wyoming Travel Commission. Frank Norris, Jr, Travel Center, Cheyenne, 82002. **307-777-7777**

Jackson Hole Chamber of Commerce. Box E, Jackson Hole, 83001. **307-733-3316**

STATE ARTS AGENCIES

ALABAMA STATE COUNCIL ON THE ARTS AND HUMANITIES. 449 S McDonough St, Montgomery, 36130. **205-832-6758.** M J Zakrzewski, executive director

ALASKA STATE COUNCIL ON THE ARTS. Suite 240, 619 Warehouse Ave, Anchorage, 99501. **907-279-1558.** Roy H Helms, executive director

AMERICAN SAMOA ARTS COUNCIL. Office of the Governor, Pago Pago, 96799. Palauni M Tuiasosopo, chairman

ARIZONA COMMISSION ON THE ARTS AND HUMANITIES. 6330 N 7th St, Phoenix, 85014. **602-271-5884.** Louise Tester, executive director

OFFICE OF ARKANSAS STATE ARTS AND HUMANITIES. 500 Continental Bldg, Markham and Main Sts, Little Rock, 72201. **501-371-2539** or **2530.** Dr R Sandra Perry, executive director

CALIFORNIA ARTS COUNCIL. 115 I St, Sacramento, 95817. **916-445-1530.** Clark Mitze, executive director

COLORADO COUNCIL ON THE ARTS AND HUMANITIES. 770 Pennsylvania St, Denver, 80203. **303-892-2617.** Robert N Sheets, executive director

CONNECTICUT COMMISSION ON THE ARTS. 340 Capitol Ave, Hartford, 06106. **203-566-4770.** Anthony S Keller, executive director

DELAWARE STATE ARTS COUNCIL. Room 803, Wilmington Tower, 1105 Market St, Wilmington, 19801. **302-571-3540.** Sophie Consagra, executive director

DISTRICT OF COLUMBIA COMMISSION ON THE ARTS AND HUMANITIES. 1023 Munsey Bldg, 1329 E St NW, Washington, 20004. **202-724-5613.** Larry Neal, executive director

FINE ARTS COUNCIL OF FLORIDA, DIVISION OF CULTURAL AFFAIRS, DEPARTMENT OF STATE. Capitol Bldg, Tallahassee, 32304. **904-487-2980.** Dr John K Urice, executive director

GEORGIA COUNCIL FOR THE ARTS AND HUMANITIES. Suite 1610, 225 Peachtree St NE, Atlanta, 30303. **404-656-3990.** Larry Stevens, public information specialist

INSULAR ARTS COUNCIL OF GUAM. PO Box EK (University of Guam), Agana, 96910. **729-2466.** Mrs Louis Hotaling, director

HAWAII STATE FOUNDATION ON CULTURE AND THE ARTS. Rm 310, 250 S King St, Honolulu, 96813. **808-548-4145.** Alfred Preis, executive director

IDAHO STATE COMMISSION ON ARTS AND HUMANITIES. c/o State House, Boise, 83720. **208-384-2119.** Suzanne Taylor, executive director

ILLINOIS ARTS COUNCIL. Rm 1610, 111 N Wabash Ave, Chicago, 60602. **312-435-6750.** Marianne Coplan, public information officer

INDIANA ARTS COMMISSION. Suite 614, Union Title Bldg, 155 E Market, Indianapolis, 46204. **317-633-5649.** Janet I Harris, executive director

IOWA STATE ARTS COUNCIL. State Capitol Bldg, Des Moines, 50319. **512-281-4451.** Jack E Olds, executive director

KANSAS ARTS COMMISSION. Suite 100, 117 W 10th St, Topeka, 66612. **913-296-3335.** Jonathan Katz, executive director

KENTUCKY ARTS COMMISSION. 100 W Main St, Frankfort, 40601. **502-564-3757.** Ms Nash Cox, executive director

LOUISIANA STATE ARTS COUNCIL. c/o Department of Education, State of Louisiana, PO Box 44064, Baton Rouge, 70804. **504-389-6991.** Lucile Blum, president

MAINE STATE COMMISSION ON THE ARTS AND THE HUMANITIES. State House, Augusta, 04330. **207-289-2724.** Alden C Wilson, director

MARYLAND ARTS COUNCIL. 15 W Mulberry, Baltimore, 21201. **301-685-6740.** Kenneth Kahn, executive director

MASSACHUSETTS COUNCIL ON THE ARTS AND HUMANITIES. 1 Ashburton Pl, Boston, 02108. **617-727-3668.** *Press contact.* Clem VanBuren

MICHIGAN COUNCIL FOR THE ARTS. Executive Plaza, 1200 6th Ave, Detroit, 48226. **313-256-3735.** Martha Gibiser, public information, **313-256-3495**

MINNESOTA STATE ARTS BOARD. 314 Clifton Ave, Minneapolis, 55403. **612-874-1335.** Mary Sulerud, executive director

MISSISSIPPI ARTS COMMISSION. 301 N Lamar St (PO Box 1341), Jackson, 39205. **601-354-7336.** Lida Rogers, executive director

MISSOURI STATE COUNCIL ON THE ARTS. Suite 410, 111 S Bemiston, St Louis, 63102. **314-721-1672.** Emily Rice, executive director

MONTANA ARTS COUNCIL. 235 E Pine, Missoula, 59801. **406-543-8386.** David E Nelson, executive director

NEBRASKA ARTS COUNCIL. 8448 W Center Rd, Omaha, 68124. **402-554-2111.** Robert C Pierle, executive director

NEVADA STATE COUNCIL ON THE ARTS. 506 Mill St, Reno, 89502. **702-784-6231** or **6232.** James Deere, executive director

NEW HAMPSHIRE COMMISSION ON THE ARTS. Phoenix Hall, 40 N Main St, Concord, 03301. **603-271-2789.** Susan Taylor, program information officer

NEW JERSEY STATE COUNCIL ON THE ARTS. 27 W State St, Trenton, 08625. **609-292-6130.** Brann J Wry, executive director

NEW MEXICO ARTS COMMISSION. Lew Wallace Bldg, State Capitol, Santa Fe, 87503. **505-827-2061.** Bernard Blas Lopez, executive director

NEW YORK STATE COUNCIL ON THE ARTS. 80 Centre St, New York, 10013. **212-488-3642.** *Press contact.* Jerrold Weitzman, **212-488-2866**

NORTH CAROLINA ARTS COUNCIL. North Carolina Department of Cultural Resources, Raleigh, 27611. **919-733-7897.** Mary B Regan, executive director

NORTH DAKOTA COUNCIL ON THE ARTS AND HUMANITIES. 309D Minard Hall, North Dakota State University, Fargo, 58102. **701-237-7674.** Glenn W Scott, executive director, **701-237-4917**

OHIO ARTS COUNCIL. Suite 3600, 50 W Broad St, Columbus, 43215. **614-466-2613.** Diane Wondisford, public information officer, **614-466-2613**

OKLAHOMA ARTS AND HUMANITIES COUNCIL. 640 Jim Thorpe Bldg, 2101 N Lincoln Blvd, Oklahoma City, 73105. **405-521-2931.** Betty Price, public information officer

OREGON ARTS COMMISSION. 328 Oregon Bldg, 494 State St, Salem, 97301. **503-378-3625.** Peter de C Hero, executive director

COMMONWEALTH OF PENN-SYLVANIA COUNCIL ON THE ARTS. 2001 N Front St, Harrisburg, 17102. **717-787-6883.** Otis B Morse, executive director

INSTITUTE OF PUERTO RICAN CULTURE. Apartado Postal 4184, San Juan, 00905. **809-723-2115.** Luis M Rodriguez Morales, executive director

RHODE ISLAND STATE COUNCIL ON THE ARTS. 334 Westminster Hall, Providence, 02903. **401-277-3880.** Channing Gray, director, public relations

SOUTH CAROLINA ARTS COMMISSION. 829 Richland St, Columbia, 29201. **803-758-3442.** Mary K Teague, public information officer, **803-758-3442** or **803-787-5725**

SOUTH DAKOTA STATE FINE ARTS COUNCIL. 108 W 11th St, Sioux Falls, 57102. **605-339-6646.** Charlotte Carver, executive director

TENNESSEE ARTS COMMISSION. 222 Capitol Hill Bldg, Nashville, 37219. **615-741-1701.** Norman Worrell, executive director

TEXAS COMMISSION ON THE ARTS AND HUMANITIES. PO Box 13406, Capitol Station, Austin, 78711. **512-475-6593.** Maurice D Coats, executive director

UTAH STATE DIVISION OF FINE ARTS. 609 E South Temple St, Salt Lake City, 84102. **801-533-5895.** Ruth Draper, director

VERMONT COUNCIL ON THE ARTS. 136 State St, Montpelier, 05602. **802-828-3291.** Ellen McCulloch-Lovell, executive director

VIRGINIA COMMISSION OF THE ARTS AND HUMANITIES. 400 E Grace St, Richmond, 23219. **804-786-4492.** Jerry T Haynie, executive director

VIRGIN ISLANDS COUNCIL ON THE ARTS. Caravelle Arcade, Christiansted, St Croix, 00820. **809-773-3075**, Ext 3. Stephen J Bostic, executive director

WASHINGTON STATE ARTS COMMISSION. 1151 Black Lake Blvd, Olympia, 98504. **206-753-3860.** James L Haseltine, executive director

WEST VIRGINIA DEPARTMENT OF CULTURE AND HISTORY, ARTS AND HUMANITIES DIVISION. Science and Culture Ctr, Capitol Complex, Charleston, 25305. **304-348-0240.** James B Andrews, executive director

WISCONSIN ARTS BOARD. 123 W Washington Ave, Madison, 53702. **608-266-0190.** Jerrold Rouby, executive director. Rena Gelman, public information officer

WYOMING COUNCIL ON THE ARTS. 200 W 25th St, Cheyenne, 82002. **307-777-7742.** John Buhler, executive director

REGIONAL ARTS COORDINATORS

NORTHEASTERN STATES (Connecticut, Maine, Massachusetts, New Hampshire, New York, Rhode Island, Vermont). 30 Savoy St, Providence, RI 02906. **401-274-4754.** Rudy Nashan, regional coordinator

MID-ATLANTIC STATES (Delaware, District of Columbia, Maryland, New Jersey, Ohio, Pennsylvania, Puerto Rico, Virginia, Virgin Islands, West Virginia). 5312 Allandale Dr, Bethesda, MD 20016. **301-656-2841.** Lara Mulholland, regional coordinator

SOUTHEASTERN STATES (Alabama, Florida, Georgia, Kentucky, Mississippi, North Carolina, South Carolina, Tennessee, Virginia). Southern Arts federation, 225 Peachtree St NE, Atlanta, GA 30303. **404-577-7244.** Adrian King, director, communications

SOUTH CENTRAL STATES (Arkansas, Kansas, Louisiana, Missouri, Nebraska, Oklahoma, Texas). 2440 Pershing Rd, Kansas City, MO 64108. **816-421-1388.** Henry Moran, executive director. Chad Milton, public information director

NORTH CENTRAL STATES (Illinois, Indiana, Iowa, Michigan, Minnesota, North Dakota, South Dakota, Wisconsin). 4200 Marine Dr, Chicago, IL 60613. **312-525-6748** or **312-782-7858** (service). Bertha Masor, regional coordinator

ROCKY MOUNTAIN STATES (Arizona, Colorado, Idaho, Montana, New Mexico, Oregon, Utah, Washington, Wyoming). Suite 201, 428 E 11th Ave, Denver, CO 80203. **303-832-7979.** Richard Harcourt, regional coordinator

PACIFIC STATES (Alaska, California, Hawaii, Nevada, Oregon, American Samoa, Washington). PO Box 15187, San Francisco, CA 94115. **415-921-9008.** Dale Kobler, regional coordinator

REGIONAL ARTS ORGANIZATIONS

NORTHEASTERN STATES (New Hampshire, Vermont). The Arts Exchange, Regional Center, Wilson Hall, Hanover, NH 03755. **603-646-2653.** Myra MacCuaig, executive director

SOUTHEASTERN STATES (Alabama, Arkansas, Florida, Georgia, Kentucky, Louisiana, Mississippi, North Carolina, South Carolina, Tennessee). Southern Federation of State Arts Agencies, 138 N Hawthorne Rd, Winston-Salem, NC 27104. **919-723-2523.** Howard R Hall, executive director

SOUTH CENTRAL STATES (Kansas, Missouri, Nebraska, Oklahoma). Mid-America Arts Alliance, 2440 Pershing, Kansas City, MO 64108. **816-421-1388.** Henry Moran, executive director

NORTH CENTRAL STATES (Iowa, Minnesota, North Dakota, South Dakota, Wisconsin). Affiliated State Arts Agencies of the Upper Midwest, Butler Sq-349, 100 N 6th St, Minneapolis, MN 55403. **612-338-1158.** Dean Myhr, executive director

ROCKY MOUNTAIN STATES (Arizona, Colorado, Idaho, Montana, Nevada, New Mexico, Oregon, Washington, Wyoming). Western States Arts Foundation, 1517 Market St, Denver, CO 80202. **303-571-1561.** Richard Collins, president

MAJOR SKI AREAS

Northeast

Maine

EVERGREEN VALLEY. East Stoneham, ME 04231. **207-928-3300**

SADDLEBACK. Rangeley, ME 04970. **207-864-3380**

SQUAW MOUNTAIN. Greenville, ME 04441. **207-695-2272**

SUGARLOAF. Kingfield, ME 04947. **207-237-2000**

Massachusetts

BERKSHIRE EAST. Charlemont, MA 01339. **413-339-6617**

EASTOVER. Lenox, MA 01240. **413-637-0625**

JUG END. South Egremont, MA 01258. **413-528-0434**

New Hampshire

ALPINE RIDGE. Gilford, NH 03246. **603-293-4304**

BRETTON WOODS. Bretton Woods, NH 03575. **603-278-1000**

CROTCHED MOUNTAIN. Francestown, NH 03043. **603-588-6345**

LOON MOUNTAIN. Lincoln, NH 03251. **603-745-8111**

MITTERSILL. Franconia, NH 03580. **603-823-5511**

MOUNT WASHINGTON VALLEY ASSOCIATION (Attitash, Black Mountain, Mount Cranmore, Tyrol, and Wildcat). North Conway, NH 03860. **603-356-5524**

PAT'S PEAK. Henniker, NH 03242. **603-428-3245**

WATERVILLE VALLEY. Waterville Valley, NH 03223. **603-236-8311**

WILDERNESS. Dixville Notch, NH. **603-255-3400**

New York

BIG BIRCH. Patterson, NY 12563. **914-878-9303** or **3181**

CATSKILL SKI CENTER. Andes, NY 13731. **914-676-3143**

CORTINA VALLEY. Haines Falls, NY 12436. **518-589-6500**

GREEK PEAK. Cortland, NY 13045. **607-835-6111**

HIDDEN VALLEY. Lake Luzerne, NY 12846. **518-696-2431**

HUNTER MOUNTAIN SKI BOWL. Hunter Mountain, NY 12442. **518-263-4223**

LABRADOR. Truxton, NY 13158. **607-842-6221**

LAKE MOHONK. New Paltz, NY 12561. **914-255-1000**

LAKE PLACID CLUB. Lake Placid, NY 12946. **518-523-3361**

PALEFACE SKI CENTER. Jay, NY 12941. **518-946-2272**

PEEK 'N PEAK. Clymer, NY 14724. **716-355-4141**

SONG MOUNTAIN. Tully, NY 13159. **315-696-5711**

WEST MOUNTAIN. Glens Falls, NY 12801. **518-793-6606**

WINDHAM MOUNTAIN CLUB. Windham, NY 12496. **518-734-4300**

Vermont

BOLTON VALLEY. Bolton Valley, VT 05477. **802-434-2131**

BROMLEY. Manchester, VT 05254. **802-824-5522**

HAYSTACK. Wilmington, VT 05363. **802-464-5321**

JAY PEAK. Jay Peak, North Troy, VT 05859. **802-988-2611**

KILLINGTON. Killington, VT 05751. **802-422-3333**

MAPLE VALLEY. West Dummerston, VT 05357. **802-254-6083**

MOUNT ASCUTNEY. Brownsville, VT 05037. **802-484-7711**

MOUNT SNOW. Mount Snow, West Dover, VT 05356. **802-464-3333**

OKEMO. Ludlow, VT 05149. **802-228-4041**

ROUND TOP MOUNTAIN. Rutland, Vt 05701. **802-672-3366**

SMUGGLERS' NOTCH. Jeffersonville, VT 05464. **800-451-3222** or **802-644-5355**

STOWE. Stowe, VT 05672. **802-253-7321**

STRATTON. Stratton, South Londonderry, VT 05155. **802-297-2200**

SUGARBUSH. Warren, VT 05674. **802-583-2381**

WOODSTOCK. Woodstock, VT 05091. **802-457-1100**

Middle Atlantic

New Jersey

CRAIGMEUR. Newfoundland, NJ 07435.
201-697-4501

VERNON VALLEY/GREAT GORGE.
Vernon, NJ 07462. **201-827-2000**

North Carolina

APPALACHIAN. Blowing Rock, NC 28605.
704-295-7828

CATALOOCHEE. Maggie Valley, NC
28751. **704-926-1401**

SEVEN DEVILS. Banner Elk, NC 28604.
704-963-5665

WOLF LAUREL. Mars Hill, NC 28754.
704-689-4111

Pennsylvania

BIG BOULDER. Lake Harmony, PA 18624.
717-722-0101

CAMELBACK. Tannersville, PA 18372.
717-629-1661

HIDDEN VALLEY. Somerset, PA 15501.
814-445-6014

JACK FROST. White Haven, PA 18661.
717-443-8425

TANGLEWOOD. Tafton, PA 18464.
717-226-9500

Virginia

BRYCE MOUNTAIN. Basye, VA 22810.
703-856-2121

MASSANUTTEN. Harrisonburg, VA 22801.
703-289-2711

WINTERGREEN. Wintergreen, VA 22958.
804-361-2200

West Virginia

CANAAN VALLEY. Davis, WV 26260.
304-866-4121

SNOWSHOE. Slatyfork, WV 26291.
304-799-6600

South

Georgia

SKY VALLEY. Dilard, GA 30537.
404-746-5301

Kentucky

BLACK MOUNTAIN. Lynch, KY 40855.
606-848-2656

Tennessee

GATLINBURG. Gatlinburg, TN 37738.
615-436-4117

Midwest

Arkansas

MARBLE FALLS. Dogpatch, AR 72648.
501-743-1111

Illinois

PLUMTREE. Shannon, IL 61078.
815-493-2881

VILLA OLIVIA. Bartlett, IL 60103.
312-742-5200

Michigan

BIG POWDERHORN. Bessemer, MI 49911.
906-932-4838

CABERFAE. Cadillac, MI 49601.
616-862-3300

CRYSTAL MOUNTAIN. Thompsonville,
MI 49683. **616-438-6000**

INDIANHEAD MOUNTAIN. Wakefield,
MI 49968. **906-229-5181**

SCHUSS MOUNTAIN. Mancelona, MI
49659. **616-587-9162**

SHANTY CREEK. Bellaire, MI 49615.
616-533-8621

SUGAR LOAF VILLAGE. Cedar, MI
49621. **616-228-5461**

TIMBERLEE. Traverse City, MI 49684.
616-946-2600

Minnesota

BUCK HILL. Burnsville, MN 55337.
612-435-7187

LUTSEN. Lutsen, MN 55612. **218-663-7212**

QUADNA MOUNTAIN. Hill City, MN
55748. **218-697-2324**

SPIRIT MOUNTAIN. 9500 Spirit Mountain
Dr, Duluth, MN 55810. **218-628-2891**

SUGAR HILLS. Country Rd 17, Grand
Rapids, MN 55744. **218-326-9859**

Wisconsin

ALPINE VALLEY. East Troy, WI 53120.
414-642-7374

DEVILS HEAD. Merrimac, WI 53561.
608-493-2251

SCOTSLAND. Oconomowoc, WI 53066.
414-567-0311

TELEMARK. Cable, WI 54821.
715-798-3811

Rocky Mountains

Colorado

A-BASIN. US Hwy 6, Dillon, CO 80435.
303-468-2608

ASPEN. 406 S Mill, Aspen, CO 81611.
303-925-4000

ASPEN HIGHLANDS. Aspen, CO 81611.
303-925-5300

BRECKENRIDGE. Breckenridge, CO 80424.
303-453-2368

COPPER MOUNTAIN. Copper Mountain,
CO 80443. **303-668-2882**

CRESTED BUTTE. Crested Butte, CO
81224. **303-349-6611**

GENEVA BASIN. Georgetown, CO 80444.
303-569-9872

HIDDEN VALLEY. Estes Park, CO 80517.
303-627-4887

KEYSTONE. Keystone, CO 80435.
303-468-2316

LOVELAND. Georgetown, CO 80444. **303-569-2288**

SNOWMASS. Aspen, CO 81611. **303-925-1220**

STEAMBOAT SPRINGS. Steamboat Springs, CO 80477. **303-879-2220**

TELLURIDE. Telluride, CO 81435. **303-728-3856**

VAIL. Vail, CO 31657. **303-476-5677**

WINTER PARK. Winter Park, CO 80482. **303-726-5514**

Idaho

SUN VALLEY. Sun Valley, ID 83353. **208-622-4111**

TARGHEE. Driggs, ID 83422. **307-353-2308**

Montana

BIG MOUNTAIN. Whitefish, MT 59937. **406-862-3511**

SKI YELLOWSTONE. West Yellowstone, MT 59758. **406-646-9364**

TETON PASS. Choteau, MT 59422. **406-466-2189**

Utah

BRIAN HEAD. Cedar City, UT 84720. **801-586-4636**

PARK CITY. Park City, UT 84060. **801-649-8111**

SNOWBIRD. Snowbird, UT 84070. **801-742-2222**

SUNDANCE. Provo, UT 84601. **801- 225-4100**

Wyoming

JACKSON HOLE. Teton Village, WY 83025. **307-733-4005** or **800-443-6931**

SNOW KING MOUNTAIN. Jackson Hole, WY 83001. **307-733-5200**

West Coast

Alaska

MOUNT ALYESKA. Girdwood, AL 99587. **907-783-6000**

California

ALPINE MEADOWS. Tahoe City, CA 95730. **916-583-4232**

NORTHSTAR. Truckee, CA 95734. **916-562-1111**

SQUAW VALLEY. Olympic Valley, CA 95730. **916-583-4211**

BADGER PASS. Yosemite Park, CA 95389. **209-372-4691**

CHINA PEAK. Lakeshore, CA 93734. **209-893-3316**

HEAVENLY VALLEY. South Lake Tahoe, CA 95705. **916-541-1330**

KIRKWOOD. Kirkwood Meadows, CA 95705. **209-258-6000**

JUNE MOUNTAIN. June Lake, CA 93529. **714-648-7794**

MAMMOTH MOUNTAIN. Mammoth Lakes, CA 93546. **714-934-2571**

MOUNT REBA. Bear Valley, CA 95223. **209-753-2301**

SNOW SUMMIT. Big Bear Lake, CA 92315. **714-866-4621**

SNOW VALLEY. Running Springs, CA 92382. **714-867-2434**

TAHOE DONNER. Truckee, CA 95734. **916-587-2551**

Nevada

INCLINE VILLAGE. Incline Village, NV 89450. **702-831-1821**

New Mexico

ANGEL FIRE. Eagle Nest, NM 87718. **505-377-2301**

RED RIVER VALLEY. Red River, NM 87558. **505-754-2223**

SANDIA PEAK. 10 Tramway Loop NE, Albuquerque, NM 87122. **505-296-9585**

SIERRA BLANCA. Ruidoso, NM 88345. **505-336-4356**

SIPAPU. Vadito, NM 87579. **505-587-2240**

TAOS SKI VALLEY. Taos, NM 87571. **505-776-2206**

Oregon

MOUNT BACHELOR. Bend, OR 97701. **503-382-2442**

MOUNT HOOD. Timberline, OR 97031. **503-272-3311**

Washington

CRYSTAL MOUNTAIN. Crystal Mountain, WA 98022. **206-663-2265**

MOUNT BAKER. Bellingham, WA 98225. **206-734-6771**

WHITE PASS. Yakima, WA 98907. **509-453-8731**

Canada

Alberta

LAKE LOUISE. Lake Louise, Alberta. **403-261-6574**

MOUNT NORQUAY. Banff, Alberta. **403-261-6574**

British Columbia

BIG WHITE. Kelowna, BC. **604-762-0402**

GROUSE MOUNTAIN. Vancouver, BC. **604-988-6151**

MOUNT SEYMOUR. Vancouver, BC. **604-988-3326**

TOD MOUNTAIN. Kamloops, BC. **604-578-7151**

WHISTLER MOUNTAIN. Alta Lake, BC. **604-685-2205**

Ontario

HURONIA. Barrie, Ont. **705-726-0932**

Quebec

MONT ORFORD. Orford, Que. **819-843-6548**

MONT STE MARIE. Lac Ste Marie, Que. **819-467-5200**

MONT TREMBLANT. Sutton, Que. **514-861-6165**

STE ADELE. Ste Adele, Que. **514-866-6661** or **514-229-3511**

SPORTS

THE MAJOR LEAGUES

Big League Baseball

75 Rockefeller Plz, New York, NY 10019. **212-586-7400.** Bowie Kuhn, commissioner of baseball. *Information Department.* Bob Wirz, **212-765-2177.** (h) **203-762-9302;** Art Berke, **212-856-7400.** (h) **914-835-1841;** Rick Cunningham, **212-856-7400.** (h) **914-761-1856.** *Major League Promotion Corporation.* Joe Podesta, Seth Abraham, Joe Reichler, **212-581-4990**

American League of Professional Baseball Clubs

280 Park Ave, New York, NY 10017. **212-682-7000**
President. Leland S MacPhail, Jr
Public Relations Directors. Bob Fishel, **212-682-7084.** (h) **212-355-2433.** Rick White, **212-682-7000.** (h) **914-235-6897**

Teams

BALTIMORE ORIOLES. Memorial Stadium, Baltimore, MD 21218. **301-243-9800**
Public Relations Director. Bob Brown, **301-235-9710.** (h) **301-825-8560**
Assistant Public Relations Director. Mac Barrett, **301-235-9710.** (h) **301-377-0360**

BOSTON RED SOX. Fenway Park, 24 Jersey St, Boston, MA 02215. **617-267-9440**
Public Relations Director. Bill Crowley, **617-267-2890.** (h) **617-444-8366**
Assistant Public Relations Director. Dick Bresciani, **617-267-2890.** (h) **617-899-1202**

CALIFORNIA ANGELS. Anaheim Stadium, 2000 State College Blvd, Anaheim, CA 92806. **714-634-2000** or **213-625-1123.** Mailing address: PO Box 2000, Anaheim, CA 92803

Public Relations Director. Tom Seeberg, **714-634-1044.** (h) **714-586-2211**
Assistant Public Relations Director. Mel Franks, **714-634-2000.** (h) **714-997-3362**

CHICAGO WHITE SOX. Comiskey Park, Dan Ryan at 35th St, Chicago, IL 60616. **312-924-1000**
Public Relations Director. Don Unferth, **312-924-1412.** (h) **312-598-7439**

CLEVELAND INDIANS. Municipal Stadium, Boudreau Blvd, Cleveland, OH 44114. **216-861-1200**
Public Relations Director. Randy Adamack, **216-861-4454.** (h) **216-731-7369**

DETROIT TIGERS. Tiger Stadium, Michigan and Trumbull Aves, Detroit, MI 48216. **313-962-4000**
Public Relations Director. Hal Middlesworth, **313-962-0825.** (h) **313-963-3922**
Assistant Public Relations Director. Bill Brown, **313-962-4000.** (h) **313-272-4832**

KANSAS CITY ROYALS. PO Box 1969, Kansas City, MO 64141. **816-921-8000**
Public Relations Director. Dean Vogelaar, **816-921-8000.** (h) **816-229-6446**
Assistant Public Relations Director. Bruce Carnanan, **816-921-8000.** (h) **816-229-8969**

MILWAUKEE BREWERS. County Stadium, Milwaukee, WI 53214. **414-933-9000**
Vice-President, Marketing, and Public Relations Director. Dick Hackett, **414-933-9000.** (h) **414-786-3286**
Publicity, Assistant Public Relations Director. Tom Skibosh, **414-933-6975.** (h) **414-781-0157**

MINNESOTA TWINS. Metropolitan Stadium, 8001 Cedar Ave, Bloomington, MN 55420. **612-854-4040**
Public Relations Director. Tom Mee, **612-854-3670.** (h) **612-447-2065**

NEW YORK YANKEES. Yankee Stadium, Bronx, NY 10451. **212-293-4300**
Public Relations Director. Mickey Morabito, **212-293-1720.** (h) **212-737-2883**
Assistant Public Relations Director. Larry Wahl, **212-293-1720.** (h) **914-237-3712**

OAKLAND A'S. Oakland Coliseum, Oakland, CA 94621. **415-762-3100**
Public Relations Director. Carl Finley, **415-635-3927.** (h) **415-444-6292**
Assistant Public Relations Director. Ed Munson, **415-635-7280.** (h) **415-562-5311**

SEATTLE MARINERS. 2nd Ave at S King St (PO Box 4100), Seattle, WA 98104. **206-628-3555**
Public Relations Director. Hal Childs, **206-628-3319.** (h) **206-453-0348**
Assistant Public Relations Director. Dave Szen, **206-628-3319.** (h) **206-283-8366**

TEXAS RANGERS. Arlington Stadium, 1500 Copeland Rd (PO Box 1111), Arlington, TX 76010. **817-265-9101**
Public Relations Director. Burt Hawkins, **817-265-8162.** (h) **817-265-8708**
Assistant Public Relations Director. Jeff Wolfskill, **817-265-9101.** (h) **817-277-0927**

TORONTO BLUE JAYS. Exhibition Stadium, Exhibition Pl, Toronto, Ont, Canada. **416-595-0077.** Mailing address: Box 7777, Adelaide St PO, Toronto, Ont, Canada M5C 2K7
Public Relations Director. Howard Starkman, **416-595-0077.** (h) **416-622-6245**
Assistant Public Relations Director. Joe Bodolai, **416-595-0077.** (h) **416-979-1922**

National League of Professional Baseball Clubs

Suite 1602, 1 Rockefeller Plz, New York, NY 10020. **212-582-4213**
President. Charles S Feeney
Public Relations Director. Blake Cullen

Teams

ATLANTA BRAVES. Fulton County Stadium, Atlanta, GA 30312. **404-522-7630**

Director, Public Relations. Bob Hope, (h) **404-292-6560**

Publicity Manager. Randy Donaldson, (h) **404-351-4533**

CHICAGO CUBS. Wrigley Field, Clark and Addison Sts, Chicago, IL 60613. *Administrative offices.* **312-281-5050.** Group sales: **312-327-1919**

Manager, Information and Services. Buck Peden, **312-281-4787.** (h) **312-271-4134**

Statistician. James Davidovich, (h) **312-833-7785**

CINCINNATI REDS. 100 Riverfront Stadium, Cincinnati, OH 45202. **513-421-4510.** Audio feed line (recorded interviews and accounts of the day's game): **513-421-3432**

Director, Publicity. Jim Ferguson, (h) **513-232-7590**

Director, Publications. Bob Rathgeber, (h) **513-521-1395**

HOUSTON ASTROS. Astrodome, PO Box 288, Houston, TX 77001. **713-749-9500.** Audio feed line (recorded interviews and accounts of the day's game): **713-748-1314.** Hot line (short game story, schedule information, etc): **713-748-3333**

Director, Public Relations. Donald Davidson, **713-749-9595.** (h) **713-729-5413**

Assistant Director, Public Relations. Paul Darst, (h) **713-668-3340**

LOS ANGELES DODGERS. Dodger Stadium, 1000 Elysian Park Ave, Los Angeles, CA 90012. **213-224-1500.** Audio feed lines (recorded interviews and accounts of the day's game): **213-221-5163** (home games, am feed); **213-670-2247** (home games, pm feed); **213-670-2247** (away games)

Vice-President, Public Relations and Promotions. Fred Claire, **213-224-1306.** (h) **714-624-9383**

Director, Publicity. Steve Brener, **213-224-1301.** (h) **213-996-2493**

MONTREAL EXPOS. PO Box 500, Station M, Montreal, Que, Canada H1V 3P2. **514-253-3263** or **3434**

Director, Public Relations. Larry Chiasson, (h) **514-365-7280**

NEW YORK METS. Shea Stadium, 126th St and Roosevelt Ave, Flushing, NY 11368. **212-672-2000**

Public Relations Director. Arthur Richman, (h) **212-675-5388**

Assistant Public Relations Director. Tim Hamilton, (h) **212-688-9183**

PHILADELPHIA PHILLIES. Veterans Stadium, Broad St and Pattison Ave, Philadelphia, PA 19148. **215-463-6000.** Audio feed line (recorded interviews and accounts of the day's game): **215-463-9443**

Director, Publicity and Public Relations. Larry Shenk, (h) **302-798-4205**

Assistant Director, Publicity and Public Relations. Chris Wheeler, (h) **215-483-7563**

PITTSBURGH PIRATES. Three Rivers Stadium, 600 Stadium Cir, Pittsburgh, PA 15212. **412-323-1000**

Director, Publicity and Public Relations. William J Guilfoile, (h) **412-833-0169**

ST LOUIS CARDINALS. Busch Memorial Stadium, 250 Stadium Plz, St Louis, MO 63102. **314-421-3060**

Vice-President, Public Relations. Jim Toomey, (h) **314-821-7126**

Assistant Director, Public Relations. Marty Hendin, (h) **314-569-0595**

SAN DIEGO PADRES. San Diego Stadium, 9449 Friars Rd, San Diego, CA 92120. **714-283-4494.** Audio feed line (recorded interviews and accounts of the day's game): **714-280-6652**

Director, Public Relations. Mike Ryan, (h) **714-272-6486**

SAN FRANCISCO GIANTS. Candlestick Park, San Francisco, CA 94124. **415-467-8000**

Director, Publicity. Stu Smith, (h) **415-573-6054**

Assistant Director, Publicity. Ralph Nelson, (h) **408-746-6191**

Big League Basketball

National Basketball Association

Olympic Tower, 645 5th Ave, New York, NY 10022. **212-826-7000.**

Director, Media Information. Matt Winnett

Public Relations department. Gail Torres and Roberta Ringer,

Director, Communications. Don Molinelli

Teams

ATLANTA HAWKS. The Omni, 100 Techwood Dr NW, Atlanta, GA 30303. **404-681-2100**

Public relations director. John Marshall

BOSTON CELTICS. Boston Garden at North Station, Boston, MA 02114. **617-523-6050**

Public Relations Directors. Howie McHugh and Jeff Cohen

BUFFALO BRAVES. Memorial Auditorium, Main and Terrace, Buffalo, NY 14202. **716-856-3131**

Public relations director. Mike Shaw

CHICAGO BULLS. 333 N Michigan Ave, Chicago, IL 60601. **312-346-1122**

Public Relations director. Mike McClure

CLEVELAND CAVALIERS. The Coliseum, 2923 Streetsboro Rd, Richfield, OH 44286. **216-659-9100**

Public Relations Director. Steven Jay Levine, **216-659-9100** or **216-864-9306**

DENVER NUGGETS. PO Box 4286, Denver, CO 80204. **303-893-6700**

Vice-president, Public Relations. Bob King

DETROIT PISTONS. Suite 3000, Cobo Hall, Detroit, MI 44286. **313-962-7844**

Public relations director. Brian Hitsky

GOLDEN STATE WARRIORS. Oakland Coliseum Arena, Oakland, CA 94621. **415-638-6000**

Public Relations Director. Bob Bestor

HOUSTON ROCKETS. The Summit, Houston, TX 77046. **713-627-0600**

Public relations director. Jim Foley

INDIANA PACERS. Lower concourse, Market Square Ctr, 151 N Delaware, Indianapolis, IN 46204. **317-632-3636**

Publicity Director. Lee Daniel

KANSAS CITY KINGS. 1800 Genessee St, Kansas City, MO 64102. **816-421-3131**

Public relations director. Dave Busch

LOS ANGELES LAKERS. PO Box 10, Inglewood, CA 90306. **213-674-6000**

Public Relations Director. Shep Goldberg

MILWAUKEE BUCKS. 901 N 4th St, Milwaukee, WI 53203. **414-272-6030**

Public Relations Director. Bill King

NEW ORLEANS JAZZ. PO Box 53213, New Orleans, LA 70153. **504-587-4263**
Public Relations Director. Dave Fredman

NEW YORK KNICKERBOCKERS. Madison Square Garden, 4 Pennsylvania Plz, New York, NY 10001. **212-563-8056**
Public Relations Director. Jim Wergeles

NETS. 30 Park Ave, Rutherford, NJ 07070. **201-935-8888**
Public Relations Director. Ted Pase

PHILADELPHIA 76ERS. Veterans Stadium, PO Box 25040, Philadelphia, PA 19147. **215-339-7630**
Public Relations Director. Harvey Pollack

PHOENIX SUNS. PO Box 1369, Phoenix, AZ 85001. **602-258-5753**
Public Relations Director. Tom Ambrose

PORTLAND TRAIL BLAZERS. Lloyd Bldg, Suite 380, 700 NE Multnomah St, Portland, OR 97232. **503-234-9291**
Public Relations Director. John White

SAN ANTONIO SPURS. HemisFair Arena, PO Box 530, San Antonio, TX 78292. **512-224-4611**
Public Relations Director. Wayne Witt

SEATTLE SUPERSONICS. 221 W Harrison St, Seattle, WA 98119. **206-281-3450**
Public Relations Director. Rick Welts

WASHINGTON BULLETS. Capital Ctr, 1 Harry S Truman Dr, Landover, MD 20786. **301-350-3400**
Public Relations Director. Marc Splaver

Big League Football

National Football League

410 Park Ave, New York, NY 10022. **212-758-1500**
Commissioner. Pete Rozelle
Executive Director. Don Weiss
Director, Public Relations. Jim Heffernan
Public relations. Betsy Colleran and Susan McCann

American Conference Teams

BALTIMORE COLTS. Executive Plz III, Hunt Valley, MD 21031. **301-667-4400**
Public Relations Director. Wilt Browning
Assistant Public Relations Director. Marge Blatt

BUFFALO BILLS. 1 Bills Dr, Orchard Park, NY 14127. **716-648-1800**
Public Relations Director. Budd Thalman
Assistant Public Relations Director. Rusty Martin

CINCINNATI BENGALS. 200 Riverfront Stadium, Cincinnati, OH 45202. **513-621-3550**
Public Relations Director. Al Heim

CLEVELAND BROWNS. Cleveland Stadium, Cleveland, OH 44114. **216-696-5555**
Public Relations Director. Nate Wallack

DENVER BRONCOS. 5700 Logan St, Denver, CO 80216. **303-623-8778**
Public Relations Director. Bob Peck
Assistant Public Relations Director. Dave Frei

HOUSTON OILERS. Box 1516, Houston, TX 77001. **713-797-9111**
Public Relations Director. Jack Cherry

KANSAS CITY CHIEFS. 1 Arrowhead Dr, Kansas City, MO 64129. **816-924-9300**
Public Relations Director. Bob Sprenger
Assistant Public Relations Director. Doug Kelly

MIAMI DOLPHINS. 330 Biscayne Blvd, Miami, FL 33132. **305-379-1851**
Public Relations Director. Bob Kearney
Publicity. Charlie Callahan

NEW ENGLAND PATRIOTS. Schaefer Stadium, Route 1, Foxboro, MA 02035. **617-543-7911**
Public Relations Director. Pat Horne

NEW YORK JETS. 598 Madison Ave, New York, NY 10022. **212-421-6600**
Public Relations Director. Frank Ramos
Assistant Public Relations Director. Ed Wisneski

OAKLAND RAIDERS. 7811 Oakport St, Oakland, CA 94621. **415-562-5900**
Executive Assistant. Al Lo Casale

PITTSBURGH STEELERS. Three Rivers Stadium, 300 Stadium Cir, Pittsburgh, PA 15212. **412-323-1200**
Public Relations Directors. Joe Gordon and Ed Kiely

SAN DIEGO CHARGERS. San Diego Stadium, PO Box 20666, San Diego, CA 92120. **714-280-2111**
Public Relations Director. Rick Smith

SEATTLE SEAHAWKS. 5305 Lake Washington Blvd, Kirkland, WA 98033. **206-827-9777**
Public Relations Director. Don Andersen
Publicity. Gary Wright

National Conference Teams

ATLANTA FALCONS. 521 Capitol Ave SW, Atlanta, GA 30312. **404-588-1111**
Public Relations Director. Charlie Dayton

CHICAGO BEARS. 55 E Jackson Blvd, Chicago, IL 60604. **312-663-5100.** Night line: **312-663-5103**
Public Relations Director. Ted Haracz
Assistant Public Relations Director. Pat McCaskey

DALLAS COWBOYS. 6116 N Central Expy, Dallas, TX 75206. **214-369-8000**
Public Relations Director. Doug Todd
Assistant Public Relations Director. George Heddleston

DETROIT LIONS. Pontiac Silverdome, 1200 Featherstone Rd (Box 4200), Pontiac, MI 48057. **313-335-4131**
Public Relations Director. Don Kremer
Assistants. Brian Muir and Val Tangert

GREEN BAY PACKERS. 1265 Lombardi Ave, Green Bay, WI 54303. **414-494-2351**
Public Relations. Chuck Lane
Publicity. Lee Remmel

LOS ANGELES RAMS. 10271 W Pico Blvd, Los Angeles, CA 90064. **213-277-4700**
Public Relations Directors. Jerry Wilcox and Jack Geyer

MINNESOTA VIKINGS. 7110 France Ave, S Edina, MN 55435. **612-920-4805**
Public Relations Director. Merrill Swanson
Assistant Public Relations Director. Jeff Diamond

NEW ORLEANS SAINTS. 944 St Charles Ave, New Orleans, LA 70130. **504-524-1421**
Public Relations Director. Jerry Wynn
Assistant Public Relations Director. Greg Suit

NEW YORK GIANTS. Giants Stadium, East Rutherford, NJ 07073. **201-935-8111**
Public Relations Director. Ed Croke
Assistant Public Relations Director. Tom Power

PHILADELPHIA EAGLES. Philadelphia Veterans Stadium, Broad St and Pattison Ave, Philadelphia, PA 19148. **215-463-2500**
Public Relations Director. Jim Gallagher
Assistant Public Relations Director. Chick McElrone

ST LOUIS CARDINALS. 200 Stadium Plz, St Louis, MO 63102. **314-421-0777**
Public Relations Director. Kevin Byrne

SAN FRANCISCO 49ERS. Candlestick Park, San Francisco, CA 94124. **415-468-1149**
Public Relations Director. George McFadden
Assistant Public Relations Director. Jim Muldoon

TAMPA BAY BUCCANEERS. 1 Buccaneer Pl, Tampa, FL 33607. **813-870-2700**
Public Relations Director. Dick Maxwell
Assistant Public Relations Director. Thom Meredith

WASHINGTON REDSKINS. Redskin Park, PO Box 17247, Dulles International Airport, Washington, DC 20041. **703-471-9100**
Assistant Public Relations Director. Charley Taylor

Big League Hockey

National Hockey League

920 Sun Life Bldg, Montreal, Que, Canada H3B 2W2. **514-871-9220**
President. John A Ziegler
Director, Information. Ron Andrews
Public Relations Staff. Mike Griffin
Public Relations Director. Bob Casey. Suite 2480, 2 Pennsylvania Plz, New York, NY 10001. **212-695-3600.** (National Hickey League Services, Inc)

Teams

ATLANTA FLAMES. 100 Techwood Dr NW, Atlanta, GA 30303. **404-681-2100**
Media Relations Director. Jiggs McDonald

BOSTON BRUINS. 150 Cswy, Boston, MA 02114. **617-227-3209**
Public Relations Director. Nate Greenberg

BUFFALO SABRES. Memorial Auditorium, PO Box 56, Buffalo, NY 14202. **716-856-7300**
Public Relations Director. Paul Wieland

CHICAGO BLACK HAWKS. 1800 W Madison St, Chicago, IL 60611. **312-733-5300**
Public Relations Director. Don Murphy

CLEVELAND BARONS. The Coliseum, Richfield, OH 44286. **216-659-9100**
Public Relations Director. Ron McGrath

COLORADO ROCKIES. McNichols Sports Arena, Denver, CO 80204. **303-573-1800**
Public Relations Director. Kevin O'Brien

DETROIT RED WINGS. 5920 Grand River Ave, Detroit, MI 48208. **313-895-7000**
Public Relations Director. Budd Lynch

LOS ANGELES KINGS. PO Box 10, Inglewood, CA 90306. **213-674-6000**
Public Relations Director. Mike Hope

MINNESOTA NORTH STARS. Metropolitan Sports Ctr, Bloomington, MN 55420. **612-854-4411**
Public Relations Director. Dick Dillman

MONTREAL CANADIENS. 2313 St Catherine St W, Montreal, Que, Canada. **514-932-6131**
Public Relations Director. Claude Mouton

NEW YORK ISLANDERS. 1155 Conklin St, Farmingdale, NY 11735. **516-694-5522.** *Nassau Coliseum.* **516-794-9510**
Public Relations Director. Hawley T Chester

NEW YORK RANGERS. 4 Pennsylvania Plz, New York, NY 10001. **212-563-8000**
Public Relations Director. John Halligan

PHILADELPHIA FLYERS. The Spectrum, Pattison Pl, Philadelphia, PA 19148. **215-465-4500**
Public Relations Directors. John Brogan and Joe Kadlec

PITTSBURGH PENGUINS. Gate 7, Civic Arena, Pittsburgh, PA 15219. **412-434-8911**
Public Relations Director. C Terry Schiffhauer

ST LOUIS BLUES. 5700 Oakland Ave, St Louis, MO 63110. **314-644-0900**
Public Relations Director. Susie Mathieu

TORONTO MAPLE LEAFS. 60 Carlton St, Toronto, Ont, Canada. **416-368-1641**
Public Relations Director. Stan Obadiac

VANCOUVER CANUCKS. Pacific Coliseum, Vancouver, BC, Canada. **604-254-5141**
Public Relations Director. Norm Jewison

WASHINGTON CAPITALS. Capital Ctr, Landover, MD 20786. **301-350-3400**
Public Relations Director. Pierce Gardner

World Hockey Association

1 Financial Plz, Hartford, Ct 06103. **203-278-4240**
President. Howard Baldwin
Public Relations Director. Gary Clark. (h) **203-521-4812**

Teams

BIRMINGHAM BULLS. 1 Civic Center Plz, Birmingham, AL 35203. **205-251-2855**
Marketing Manager. Bob Lachamy
Public Relations Director. Joe W Reid, Jr

CINCINNATI STINGERS. Cincinnati Riverfront Coliseum, Cincinnati, OH 45202. **513-241-1818**
Public Relations Director. John A Hewig

HOUSTON AEROS. The Summit, 10 Greenway Plz, Houston, TX 77046. **713-629-5555**
Public Relations Director. Terry Leiweke

EDMONTON OILERS. Edmonton Coliseum, 7424 118th Ave, Edmonton, Alta, Canada T5B 4M9. **403-474-8561**
Director, Publicity and Marketing. Doug Wenschlag

INDIANAPOLIS RACERS. 151 N Delaware St, Indianapolis, IN 46204. **317-635-3131**
Public Relations Director. Don Wahle

NEW ENGLAND WHALERS. 1 Civic Center Plz, Hartford, CT 06103. **203-728-3366**
Public Relations Director. Dennis Randall

QUEBEC NORDIQUES. Le Colisee de Quebec, Quebec, Que, Canada G1L 4W7. **418-529-4161**
Public Relations Director. Paul Le Francois

WINNEPEG JETS. 15-1430 Maroons Rd, Winnepeg, Man, Canada R3G OL5. **204-772-9491**
Public Relations Director. Norm Coston

SPORTS ORGANIZATIONS

Listed here are the many professional sports teams and leagues other than the six major leagues (American League, National League, National Basketball Association, National Football League, National Hockey League,

World Hockey Association). They are inter-filed alphabetically with amateur and professional sports associations, collegiate conferences, regulatory bodies, players' associations, and miscellaneous organizations of potential value to the sports writer.

AMATEUR ATHLETIC UNION OF THE UNITED STATES (AAU). 3400 W 86th St, Indianapolis, IN 46268. **317-297-2900.** Ollan C Cassell, executive director. Martin E Weiss, director, public relations and publications. Pete Cava, director, press relations

AMATEUR SOFTBALL ASSOCIATION OF AMERICA (ASA). PO Box 11437, Oklahoma City, OK 73111. **405-424-5266.** D E Porter, executive director

AMERICAN AMATEUR BASEBALL CONGRESS (AABC). 212 Plaza Bldg, 2855 W Market St, Akron, OH 44313. **216-836-6424.** Lincoln Hackim, president

AMERICAN BOWLING CONGRESS (ABC). 5301 S 76th St, Greendale, WI 53129. **414-421-6400.** Albert R Matzelle, executive secretary-treasurer

AMERICAN CANOE ASSOCIATION (ACA). 4260 E Evans Ave, Denver, CO 80222. **303-758-8257.** Chuck Tummonds, commodore. Eric Leaper, executive director

AMERICAN CONTRACT BRIDGE ASSOCIATION. 2200 Democrat Rd, Memphis, TN 38131. **901-332-5586**

AMERICAN GREYHOUND TRACK OPERATORS ASSOCIATION (AGTOA) (DOG RACING). 139 SE 14th Ln, Miami, FL 33131. **305-373-5588.** George D Johnson, Jr, executive director

AMERICAN HOCKEY LEAGUE. 31 Elm St, Springfield, MA 01103. **413-781-2030.** Jack A Butterfield, president and treasurer. Gordon C Anziano, vice-president and secretary. Night line: **413-533-3004.** Promotes professional ice hockey at the minor league level

AMERICAN HORSE SHOWS ASSOCIATION, INC. 598 Madison Ave, New York, 10022. **212-759-3070**

AMERICAN KENNEL CLUB(AKC). 51 Madison Ave, New York, NY 10010. **212-481-9200**

AMERICAN LEGION BASEBALL. PO Box 1055, Indianapolis, IN 46206.

317-635-8411. George Rulon, national director, (h) **317-255-3908**

AMERICAN MOTORCYCLIST ASSOCIATION (AMA). PO Box 141, Westerville, OH 43081. **614-891-2425.** Gene Wirwahn, acting executive director. Dave Despain, communications director. Steve Fordyce, public relations manager

AMERICAN PROFESSIONAL SLO-PITCH LEAGUE (softball). 5150 E Main St, Columbus, OH 43213. **614-868-8530.** Whitey Ford, commissioner. Bill Byrne, president. Tim Koelble, vice-president and public relations director. Dave Almstead, vice-president, licensing

Teams

Baltimore Monuments. 4335 Ebenezer Rd, Baltimore, Md 21236. **301-256-6722**

Chicago Storm. 7257 W Touhy Ave, Chicago, IL 60648. **312-631-6171**

Cincinnati Suds. 801-B W 8th St, Cincinnati, OH 45203. **513-421-0800**

Cleveland Jaybirds. 1st Floor, Leader Bldg, Cleveland OH 44144. **216-781-4400**

Columbus All Americans. 5150 E Main St, Columbus, OH 43213. **614-864-4062**

Detroit Caesars. 23455 Telegraph Rd, Southfield, MI 48075. **313-354-0990**

Kentucky Bourbons. 1815 Gardiner Ln, Louisville, KY 40205. **502-459-1600**

Milwaukee Copper Hearth. 5951 N Teutonia, Milwaukee, WI 53209. **414-461-4740**

Minnesota Goofy's. 32 Glenwood Ave, Minneapolis, MN 55403. **612-333-3376**

New York Clippers. 555 Broadhollow Rd, Melville, NY 11746. **516-694-7720**

Pittsburgh Hard Hats. 1119 S Braddock Ave, Pittsburgh, PA 15218. **412-371-6150**

Trenton's New Jersey Statesmen. 1300 Princeton Ave, Trenton, NJ 08638. **609-392-1191**

AMERICAN RACING DRIVERS' CLUB. 325 Otter St, Bristol, PA 19007. **215-788-0776.** Lawrence McCoy, president

AMERICAN SKI ASSOCIATION. 1190 S Colorado Blvd, Denver, CO 80222. **303-753-9356**

ASSOCIATION FOR INTERCOLLEGIATE ATHLETICS FOR WOMEN (AIAW). 1201 16th St NW, Washington, DC 20036. **202-833-5540.** Joan Warrington, executive secretary

ASSOCIATION OF TENNIS PROFESSIONALS. PO Box 58144, World Trade Ctr, Dallas, TX 75258. **214-747-9948.** Bob Briner, executive director. Doug Tkachuk, executive assistant. Alan Taylor (Padilla, Speer, and Newsome 950 3rd Ave, New York, NY 10022), public relations director, **212-752-8338**

ATLANTIC COAST CONFERENCE. PO Box 6271, Summit Station, Greensboro, NC 27405. **919-275-3269.** Robert C James, commissioner. Marvin A Francis, service bureau director, **919-273-3149.** Headquarters for the operation of the seven schools that make up the Atlantic Coast Conference

Member universities. Clemson University, Duke University, University of Maryland, University of North Carolina, North Carolina State University, University of Virginia, Wake Forest University

BABE RUTH LEAGUE (baseball). PO Box 5000, Trenton, NJ 08638. **609-695-1434.** Richard W Case, president

BIG EIGHT CONFERENCE. River Hills/Mark 1, 600 E 8th St, Kansas City, MO 64106. **816-471-5088.** Steve Hatchell, public relations, (h) **913-888-7437.** Mike Scott, assistant, (h) **913-888-1704**

BIG SKY CONFERENCE. Box 1736, Boise, ID 83701. **208-345-5393.** Steve Belko, commissioner. Paul J Schneider, sports information director, (h) **208-342-3876** (also night line)

Schools included in the conference. Boise State, Idaho State, Montana, Montana State, Gonzaga, Weber State, Northern Arizona

BIG TEN CONFERENCE (formally known as Intercollegiate Conference of Faculty Representatives). Big Ten Service Bureau, 1111 Plaza Dr, Schaumburg, IL 60195. **312-885-3933.** Wayne Duke, commissioner, (h) **312-381-9096.** Jeff Elliot, service bureau director, (h) **312-529-0529**

CAROLINAS CONFERENCE. High Point College, High Point, NC 27262. **919-885-2448.** Dr Murphy M Osborne, Jr, commissioner. Horace Billings, information director, **704-636-4231.** (h) **704-636-3128**

COLLEGE SPORTS INFORMATION DIRECTORS OF AMERICA (COSIDA). c/o Phil Langan, Athletic Department, Cornell University, Ithaca, NY 14850. **607-256-3752.** Bill Esposito, Sports Information Director (St John's University), president, **212-969-8000,** Ext 365

EAST COAST CONFERENCE.
1 Markle Hall, Lafayette College, Easton, PA 18042. **215-253-8802.** Night line: **215-352-1184.** Composed of 12 college and universities conducting competition in 10 sports. Ernest C Casale (athletic director, Temple University), commissioner, **215-787-7447.** Andy Dougherty, SIP (St Joseph's College), publicity director

EASTERN COLLEGES ATHLETIC CONFERENCE.
PO Box 3, Centerville, MA 02632. **617-771-5060.** Robert (Scotty) Whitelaw, commissioner. Richard J Hussey, assistant to commissioner, (h) **617-771-5437**
The ECAC is composed of over 200 eastern colleges. The purpose of the organization is to provide professional management and guidance of intercollegiate athletics in the East.

FANS (FIGHT TO ADVANCE NATION'S SPORTS).
PO Box 19312, Washington, DC 20036. **202-466-4980.** Peter Gruenstein, executive director. Nader's entry into the sports organizations field

FOOTBALL INFORMATION BUREAU.
6140 Longford Rd, Dayton, OH 45424. **513-233-8276.** A M "Tony" Ulrich, director "We operate on a "fee" basis—just trying to make a small living." The bureau provides statistics, facts, and lore, mostly in the field of college football.

GOLDEN GLOVES ASSOCIATION OF AMERICA
(boxing). 8801 Princess Jeanne NE, Albuquerque, NM 87112. **505-298-9286.** Stan Gallup, executive secretary-treasurer

GREAT LAKES INTERCOLLEGIATE ATHLETIC CONFERENCE.
Big Rapids, MI 49307. Bill Taylor, information director, **616-796-9711,** Ext 503, (h) **616-796-5517**

GULF SOUTH CONFERENCE.
101 N Oak St (PO Box 1659), Hammond, LA 70404. **504-345-4320.** Night line: **504-345-1724.** Stanley Galloway, commissioner. Langston Rogers, public relations director, **601-843-4226**
Member schools. Nicholls State, Jacksonville State University, North Alabama, Troy State University, Southeastern Louisiana College, Tennessee-Martin, Delta State College, Mississippi College, Livingston University

INDEPENDENT COLLEGE ATHLETIC ASSOCIATION.
Ithaca College, Ithaca, NY 14850. James Erickson, information director, **607-274-3233.** (h) **607-257-2565**

INDIANA ATHLETIC COMMISSION.
1021 State Office Bldg, Indianapolis, IN 46204. **317-633-4284.** Night line: **317-353-9046.** Kelse G McClure, administrative officer

INTERNATIONAL CYCLISTS' UNION.
Michal Jekiel, secretary general, 8 rue Charles-Humbert, 1205 Geneva, Switzerland. Telephone: **26.36.11.C**

INTERNATIONAL GOLF ASSOCIATION.
Rm 4018, Time and Life Bldg, New York, NY 10020. **212-581-2220.** James A Linen, chairman. Fred J Corcoran, tournament director. Sponsors of the World Cup golf tournament

INTERNATIONAL TENNIS FEDERATION.
Palliser Rd, Barons Court, London, W14, 9EG, England. Telephone: **London 385-8441.** David Gray, general secretary. Night line: **London 788-4809.** Organizes and promotes international tennis

INTERNATIONAL OLYMPIC COMMITTEE (IOC).
Lord Killanin, president, Chateau de Vidy, 1007 Lausanne, Switzerland. Telephone: **25.32.71.C** c/o Lausanne. Promotes and regulates the Olympics

INTERNATIONAL VOLLEYBALL ASSOCIATION.
1901 Avenue of the Stars, Los Angeles, CA 90067. **213-553-3005.** Wilt Chamberlain, president. Charles T Nelson, vice-president. *Press contact.* Nicholas P Curran, vice-president, (h) **213-836-3836**

IVY LEAGUE.
c/o Sports Information Office, Cornell University, Ithaca, NY 14850. David P Wohlhueter, information coordinator, **607-256-3752**
Individual Sports Contacts
Baseball. Columbia University, New York, NY 10027. **212-280-2534.** Kevin De Marrais
Basketball. Princeton University, Princeton, NJ 08540. **609-452-3568.** John Humenik
Football. Columbia University, New York, NY 10027. **212-280-2534.** Kevin De Marrais
Hockey. Harvard University, Cambridge, MA 02138. **617-495-2206.** Dave Matthews
Lacrosse. Yale University, New Haven, CT 06520. **203-436-1646.** Peter Easton
Soccer. University of Pennsylvania, Philadelphia, PA 19174. **215-243-6128.** Herb Hartnett
Jockey Club (JC) (horse racing). 300 Park Ave, New York, NY 10022. **212-355-6146.** Calvin S Rainey, executive secretary

JUNIOR COLLEGE ATHLETIC BUREAU/NATIONAL COMMUNITY COLLEGE INFORMATION SERVICE.
PO Box 5401, San Mateo, CA 94402. Fred Baer, director, **415-345-4114**

LADIES PROFESSIONAL GOLF ASSOCIATION.
919 3rd Ave, New York, NY 10022. **212-751-8181.** Ray Volpe, commissioner. Chip Campbell, director, public relations. Paula Marafino, public relations assistant. Jeff Adams, publicity coordinator

LITTLE LEAGUE BASEBALL, INC.
PO Box 3485, Williamsport, PA 17701. **717-326-1921.** Dr Creighton J Hale, president. Preston H Hadley, assistant public relations director. Sponsors youth baseball and softball programs, tournaments, and Little League World Series

LONE STAR CONFERENCE OF TEXAS.
500 Franklin Dr, San Marcos, TX 78666. **512-245-2263** or **512-392-9917.** Elton Chaney, president, **713-569-3100.** Gordon McCullough, news director, **512-245-2263** or **512-392-9917.** An organization of eight Texas universities for athletics
Member universities. Abilene Christian, Angelo State, East Texas State, Howard Payne, Sam Houston State, Southwest Texas State, SF Austin, Texas A & I

MID-AMERICAN ATHLETIC CONFERENCE.
Suite 230, 2000 W Henderson Rd, Columbus, OH 43220. **614-457-3183.** Fred Jacoby, commissioner, (h) **614-451-3111.** Bill Linson, assistant to commissioner, **614-457-3191.** (h) **614-457-8894.** An athletic conference with ten members
Member universities. Ball State, Muncie, IN; Bowling Green State, Bowling Green, OH; Central Michigan, Mount Pleasant, MI; Eastern Michigan, Ypsilanti, MI; Kent State, Kent, OH; Miami, Oxford, OH; Northern Illinois, De Kalb, IL; Ohio, Athens, OH; Toledo, Toledo, OH; Western Michigan, Kalamazoo, MI

MIDDLE ATLANTIC STATES COLLEGIATE ATHLETIC CONFERENCE.
David B Eavenson (Dickinson College, Carlisle, PA 17013), executive director, **717-243-5121,** Ext 320. Bill Hough, director, publicity bureau, **717-867-4411**

MID-EASTERN ATHLETIC CONFERENCE.
PO Box 1087, Durham, NC 27702. **919-682-1121.** Earl Mason, assistant commissioner (h) **919-596-7240**

MINOR LEAGUE RESEARCH COMMITTEE (MLRC) (baseball). c/o William Shlensky, 3015 E Belvoir Oval, Shaker Heights, OH 44122. **206-751-6680**

MISSOURI VALLEY CONFERENCE. Suite 702, 6111 E Skelly Dr, Tulsa, OK 74135. **918-664-9245**. Mickey Holmes, commissioner. Gary Griffith, director, public relations. A collegiate athletic conference

Universities included in the conference. Bradley, Creighton, Drake, Indiana State, New Mexico State, Southern Illinois, Tulsa, West Texas State, Wichita State

NATIONAL ACADEMY OF SPORTS. 220 E 63rd St, New York, NY 10021

NATIONAL ASSOCIATION OF AMATEUR OARSMEN. 31552 Waltham Rd, Birmingham, MI 48009

NATIONAL ASSOCIATION OF COLLEGIATE DIRECTORS OF ATHLETICS (NACDA). 21330 Center Ridge Rd, Cleveland, OH 44116. **216-331-5773**. Michael J Cleary, executive director. (h) **216-333-1098**. Tom Hathaway, information director, (h) **216-228-2507**. A voluntary professional association of college and university athletic directors

NATIONAL ASSOCIATION OF INTERCOLLEGIATE ATHLETICS. 1221 Baltimore, Kansas City, MO 64105. **816-842-5050**. Harry Fritz, executive director, **816-842-5051**. Charlie Eppler, public relations director, **816-842-5050**. (h) **816-229-4426**. Abe Goteiner, assistant public relations director, statistical services, **816-842-5050**

NAIA is a autonomous association currently administering programs of intercollegiate athletics in 525 fully accredited four-year colleges and universities in the US and two institutions in Canada. The fundamental tenet of the association is that intercollegiate athletics are an integral aspect of the total educational program of the institution. NAIA organizes and administers all areas of intercollegiate athletics at the national level, including rules and standards, and district and national sports competitions. It administers 16 national championship events for its member institutions and coordinates 32 district programs, which include about 230 championship events each year. It includes 15 coaches' associations and sports sections.

NATIONAL ASSOCIATION OF JAI ALAI FRONTONS. 9999 NE 2nd Ave, Miami Shores, FL 33138. **305-758-2524**. Pat McCann, director

NATIONAL ASSOCIATION OF PROFESSIONAL BASEBALL LEAGUES. PO Box A, St Petersburg, FL 33731. **813-822-6937**. Robert R Bragan, president. John P Dittrich, assistant to president. Acts as the commissioner's office for minor league baseball

NATIONAL ASSOCIATION FOR STOCK CAR AUTO RACING, INC (NASCAR). PO Box K Daytona Beach, FL 32015. **904-253-0611**. Bill France, Jr, president. Alexis Leras, news bureau manager

NATIONAL ATHLETIC TRAINERS ASSOCIATION. PO Drawer 1865, 112 S Pitt St, Greenville, NC 27834. **919-752-1725**. Otho Davis, (Philadelphia Eagles Football, Veterans Stadium, Philadelphia, PA 19148), executive director, **215-463-2500**

NATIONAL COLLEGIATE ATHLETIC ASSOCIATION. PO Box 1906, Shawnee Mission, KS 66222. **913-384-3220** (also night line). Walter Byers, executive director. David E Cawood, director, public relations, (h) **913-492-7533**. Administers intercollegiate athletics in all its phases for 841 member institutions

NATIONAL FIELD ARCHERY ASSOCIATION (NFAA). Box 514, Route 2, Redlands, CA 92373. **714-794-2133**. Ervin W Belt, executive secretary

NATIONAL FOOTBALL FOUNDATION AND HALL OF FAME (NFF). 17 E 80th St, New York, NY 10021. **212-879-7000**. James L McDowell, Jr, executive director

NATIONAL FOOTBALL FOUNDATION'S COLLEGE FOOTBALL HALL OF FAME. PO Box 300, Kings Mills, OH 45034. **513-421-5410**. Jack Wyant, general manager, (h) **513-232-5113**. Dave Kempton, director, media relations, (h) **513-398-3223**

NATIONAL FOOTBALL LEAGUE PLAYERS ASSOCIATION. 1300 Connecticut Ave NW, Washington, DC 20036. **202-833-3335**. Ed Garvey, executive director. Bob Epstein, staff writer

The association serves as the collective bargaining agent for the NFL players. It also provides them with legal advice and information

NATIONAL HOT ROD ASSOCIATION. 10639 Riverside Dr, North Hollywood, CA 91602. **213-985-6472**. Wally Parks, president. David Densmore, public relations director

NATIONAL JUNIOR COLLEGE ATHLETIC ASSOCIATION. PO Box 1586, Hutchinson, KS 67501. **316-663-5445**. George E Killian, executive director

NATIONAL RIFLE ASSOCIATION. 1600 Rhode Island Ave NW, Washington, DC 20036. **202-783-6505**.

The association sponsors teams for international competition and maintains competition records, in addition to its broader activities. *See also* **SPECIAL INTERESTS.**

NATIONAL SKEET SHOOTING ASSOCIATION. PO Box 28188, San Antonio, TX 78228. **512-688-3371**. Carroll E Bobo, executive director

NATIONAL STEEPLECHASE AND HUNT ASSOCIATION (NSHA) (riding). Box 308, Elmont, NY 11003. **516-437-6666**. John E Cooper, executive secretary

NEW YORK YACHT CLUB. 37 W 44th St, New York, NY 10036. **212-682-0001**. Sponsors America's Cup yacht race

NORTH AMERICAN SOCCER LEAGUE. Suite 3500, 1133 Avenue of the Americas, New York, NY 10036. **212-575-0066**. Phil Woosnam, commissioner. Bill Flak, director, public relations. Amy Oakley, assistant. Bob Ehlinger, deputy commissioner. Ted Howard, director, administration

This professional sports organization governs all teams and operations within the NASL. It is the major league of professional soccer in North America, encompassing teams in major cities throughout the US and in Canada. The NASL season runs from early April through August and is climaxed by the annual Soccer Bowl, the league's championship game.

Teams

Chicago Sting. Suite 1525, 333 N Michigan Ave, Chicago, IL 60611. **312-332-2292**. Steven C Weaver, public relations director. Nancy L Howard, assistant public relations director

Connecticut Bicentennials. c/o B L McTeague and Associates, 1 Constitution Plz, Hartford, CT 06103. **203-789-0365**. Rudi Schiffer, public relations director, (h) **203-658-9433**

The Cosmos. 75 Rockefeller Plz, New York, NY 10019. **212-484-6010**. Jim Trecker, public relations director, **212-484-6044**. (h) **201-967-0635**. Janie Slevens, secretary, assistant public relations director

Dallas Tornado. 6116 N Central Expy, Dallas, TX 75206. **214-750-0900.** Paul Ridings, public relations director, (h) **214-692-0574.** Sheila Barnes, assistant public relations director

Fort Lauderdale Strikers. Suite 405, 5100 N Federal Hwy, Fort Lauderdale, FL 33308. **305-491-5140.** Steve Rankin, public relations director, (h) **305-565-3261**

Team Hawaii. Suite 602, 745 Fort St, Honolulu, HI 96813. **808-536-2334.** John Fink, public relations director, **808-531-5702.** (h) **808-947-6622**

Las Vegas Quicksilvers. 3121 S Maryland Pkwy, Las Vegas, NV 89109. **702-733-8326.** Jerry Kissel, public relations director, **702-733-0305.** (h) **702-876-3715**

Los Angeles Aztecs. 1700 S Pacific Coast Hwy, Redondo Beach, CA 90277. **213-373-8522.** Bill Hanson, public relations director, (h) **213-375-9896**

Minnesota Kicks. Suite 128, 7200 France Avenue S, Minneapolis, MN 55435. **612-831-8871.** Dave Ferroni, public relations director, (h) **612-377-3721**

Portland Timbers. Suite 101, 10151 SW Barbur Blvd, Portland, OR 97219. **503-245-6464.** John Hahn, public relations director, (h) **503-636-5469**

Rochester Lancers. 812 Wilder Bldg, Rochester, NY 14614. **716-232-2420.** Jerry Epstein, public relations director, (h) **716-663-2563.** Gail Cullinane, secretary

St Louis Stars. Suite 317, 940 W Port Plz, St Louis, MO 63141. **314-878-6300.** Steve Weaver, public relations director. Debi Stewart, assistant public relations director

San Jose Earthquakes. Suite 272, 2025 Gateway Pl, San Jose, CA 95110. **408-998-5425.** Tom Mertens, public relations director, (h) **408-275-8305.** Steve Des Georges, assistant public relations director

Seattle Sounders. 300 Metropole Building, Seattle, WA 98104. **206-628-3551.** Keith Askenasi, public relations director, (h) **206-747-6684**

Tampa Bay Rowdies. Suite 109, 1311 N Westshore Blvd, Tampa, FL 33607. **813-870-1122.** Francisco Marcos, vice-president, public relations (h) **813-733-3311.** Marcia Schallert, assistant director, public relations (h) **813-855-5847**

Toronto Metros. Croatia Suite 202, 1678 Bloor St W, Toronto, Ont, Canada M6P 1A8. **416-766-1103.** Rick Matthew, public relations director, (h) **416-925-4716**

Vancouver Whitecaps. Suite 110, 885 Dunsmuir St, Vancouver, BC, Canada V6C 1N5. **604-683-2255.** Sam Lenarduzzi, public relations director, (h) **604-461-5065.** John Good, media, (h) **604-926-9192**

Washington Diplomats. Robert F Kennedy Stadium, 22 and E Capital Sts NE, Washington, DC 20003. **202-544-5425.** Norb Ecksl, public relations director, (h) **301-736-8049**

NORTHERN ILLINOIS INTERCOL-LEGIATE CONFERENCE. Box 307, Rockford College, Rockford, IL 61101. **815-226-4085.** Night line: **815-874-7017.** Changes president each year between NIIC teams on rotating alphabetical basis. Walter H Wells, Jr, sports information director

Member colleges. Aurora, Aurora, IL 60507. **312-892-6431**; Concordia Teachers, River Forest, IL 60305. **312-771-8300**; Illinois Benedictine, Lisle, IL 60532. **312-968-7270**; Judson, Elgin, IL 60120. **312-695-2500**; Olivet Nazarene, Kankakee, IL 60901. **815-939-5372**; Rockford, Rockford, IL 61101. **815-226-4085**; Trinity, Deerfield, IL 60015. **312-945-6700**

OHIO ATHLETIC CONFERENCE. 21330 Center Ridge Rd, Cleveland, OH 44116. **216-331-5773.** Michael J Cleary, commissioner, (h) **216-333-1098.** Tom Hathaway, information director, (h) **216-228-2507.** A conference of 14 small (900-2600 enrollments) private colleges, serving as a governing or regulatory body for intercollegiate athletics of the member institutions while providing the scheduling and competitive framework for the league's sports championships

OHIO VALLEY CONFERENCE. Suite 304B, 4205 Hillsboro Rd, Nashville, TN 37215. **615-383-6380.** Bob Vanatta, commissiner, (h) **615-353-0595.**

Member universities. Austin Peay State, East Tennessee State, Eastern Kentucky, Middle Tennessee State, Morehead State, Murray State, Tennessee Technical, Western Kentucky

PACIFIC COAST ATHLETIC ASSOCIA-TION. Suite 820, 9800 S Sepulveda Blvd, Los Angeles, CA 90045. **213-645-2570.** Jesse T Hill, commissioner

Member universities. California State University, Fullerton; California State University, Long Beach; Fresno State University; San Diego State University; San Jose State University; University of California, Santa Barbara; University of the Pacific

PACIFIC-8 CONFERENCE. Suite 400, 800 S Broadway, Walnut Creek, CA 94596. **415-932-4411.** Wiles Hallock, executive director. David Price, assistant executive director, (h) **415-937-5730**

The organization serves as the executive office of the eight-member college athletic conference, assigns and trains officials, and prepares conference schedules. It also issues news releases and statistics for all sports and audits the eligibility and financial aid records of member institutions

POLICE ATHLETIC LEAGUE, INC (New York City). $34\frac{1}{2}$ E 12th St, New York, NY 10003. **212-677-1400**

PROFESSIONAL ARCHERS ASSOCIA-TION. 1500 N Chatsworth St, St Paul, MN 55117. **612-774-1899.** Sam H Fudenberg, executive secretary

PROFESSIONAL BOWLERS ASSOCIA-TION. 1720 Merriman Rd, Akron, OH 44313. **216-836-5568.** Joseph R Antenora, commissioner

THE PROFESSIONAL GOLFERS' ASSOCIATION OF AMERICA. Box 12458, 804 Federal Hwy, Lake Park, FL 33403. **305-848-3481.** Mark H Cox (at headquarters), executive director. Earl Collings, director, communications, Ext 40. *PGA Tour.* 5101 River Rd, Washington, DC. **301-986-1550**

PROFESSIONAL RODEO COWBOYS ASSOCIATION. 2929 W 19th Ave, Denver, CO 80204. **303-629-0657** or **0658.** Hugh Chambliss, rodeo administrator. Bob Eidson, general manager

RODEO NEWS BUREAU. 2929 W 19th Ave, Denver, CO 80204. **303-455-3270.** Bob Eidson, general manager. Harla Dedrick, supervisor. Karen Morrison, editorial coordinator

Rodeo Sports News. 2929 W 19th Ave, Denver, CO 80204. **303-455-4135** or **303-477-5895.** Ken Stemler, publisher, chief executive officer of PRCA properties

SOUTH ATLANTIC CONFERENCE. PO Box 1986, Carson-Newman College, Jefferson City, TN 37760. Carl K Tipton, information director, **615-475-9061.** (h) **615-475-4365**

SOUTH ATLANTIC CONFERENCE. PO Box 2046, Statesboro, GA 30458. J B Scearce, commissioner. Ellwood Moyer (PO Box 361, Columbus, GA 31902), information director, **404-324-4761** or **404-322-3411.** (h) **404-561-2802**

SOUTHEASTERN CONFERENCE. 1214 Central Bank Bldg, Birmingham, AL 35233. **205-252-7415.** Boyd McWhoter, commissioner. Elmore ("Scoop") Hudgins, assistant commissioner, public relations, (h) **205-879-8024.** Headquarters for the organization of intercollegiate athletics for the ten universities properly named the Southeastern Conference

Member universities. Alabama, Auburn, Florida, Georgia, Kentucky, Louisiana State, Mississippi, Mississippi State, Tennessee, Vanderbilt

SOUTHERN CONFERENCE. Suite 106, 5 Woodlawn Green, Charlotte, NC 28210. **704-527-0314.** Kenneth G Germann, commissioner. J Dallas Shirley (1620 Valencia Way, Reston, VA 22090), assistant to commissioner, **703-471-1779** (also night line)

SOUTHWEST ATHLETIC CON-FERENCE (SWC). 4310H Westside Dr, Dallas, TX. **214-528-3131.** Mailing Address: PO Box 7185, Dallas, TX 75209. Cliff Speegle, commissioner. Bill Morgan, information director, (h) **214-381-3789** (also night line). Administers the intercollegiate athletic programs in eight varsity sports for member institutions

Member universities. University of Arkansas, Baylor University, University of Houston, Rice University, Southern Methodist University, University of Texas, Texas A & M University, Texas Christian University, Texas Technical University.

SPORTS INFORMATION CENTER. 1776 Heritage Dr, North Quincy, MA 02171. *Press contact.* Joe Costanza, **617-328-4674.** (h) **617-245-3055**

THOROUGHBRED RACING ASSOCIA-TIONS OF NORTH AMERICA (TRA). 300 Marcus Ave, Lake Success, NY 11040. **516-328-2660.** J B Faulconer, executive vice-president

THOROUGHBRED RACING PROTEC-TIVE BUREAU. 5 Dakota Dr, New Hyde Park, NY 11040. **516-328-2010.** Spencer J Dravton, president. Investigates violations of the rules of thoroughbred racing and conducts background investigations concerning individuals participating in the sport; accepts press inquiries

UNITED STATES AMATEUR JAI ALAI PLAYERS ASSOCIATION. 2 Biscayne Blvd-2670, Miami, FL 33131. **305-377-3333.** Robert H Grossberg, executive director

UNITED STATES AUTO CLUB (USAC). 4910 W 16th St, Indianapolis, IN 46224. **317-247-5151.** Richard H King, president

UNITED STATES COLLEGIATE SPORTS COUNCIL. Suite 102, 7250 State Ave, Kansas City, KS 66112. **913-788-5885.** Glen G Davies, executive director, (h) **912-299-4837.** The US franchise holder for world university games; sponsors international intercollegiate athletic competition

UNITED STATES GOLF ASSOCIATION. Golf House, Far Hills, NJ 07931. **201-234-2300.** P J Boatwright, Jr, executive director

UNITED STATES OLYMPIC COM-MITTEE. 57 Park Ave, New York, NY 10016. **212-686-1456.** F Don Miller, executive director. Bob Paul, director, communications

US SKI ASSOCIATION. 1726 Champa St-300, Denver, CO 80202. **303-825-9183.** T Mark O'Reilly, director, public relations, (h) **303-733-9549**

UNITED STATES TENNIS ASSOCIA-TION. 51 E 42nd St, New York, NY 10017. **212-953-1020.** Michael J Burns, executive secretary. Edwin S Fabricius, director, public relations

UNITED STATES TRACK AND FIELD FEDERATION. 30 N Norton Ave, Tucson, AZ 85719. **602-624-7475.** Carl W Cooper, executive director. Marilyn S Anderson, administrative assistant. Night line: **602-884-9893**

US TROTTING ASSOCIATION. 750 Michigan Ave, Columbus, OH 43215. **614-224-2291.** Edward F Hackett, executive vice-president. Donald P Evans, vice-president, publicity and public relations. Harness racing hotline (recorded message with major race results and important news, updated daily): **614-228-1821.** *New York office.* 1270 Avenue of the Americas, New York, NY 10020, Joe Goldstein, **212-265-1680**

The association is the rules-making, record-keeping body for harness racing. It also serves as the national press and promotion outlet for the sport.

US YACHT RACING UNION. PO Box 209, Goat Island, Newport, RI 02840. **401-849-5200.** Kenneth B Weller, director, services

WEST COAST ATHLETIC CON-FERENCE. 51 Oak Knoll Loop, Walnut Creek, CA 94596. **415-939-6235.** G B

("Jerry") Wyness, commissioner. Bill Fusco, director of publicity, **415-666-6161.** Night line: **415-922-9367**

WESTERN ATHLETIC CONFERENCE. Suite 300, 1515 Cleveland Pl, Denver, CO 80202. **303-534-0217.** Stan Bates, commissioner. Nordy Jensen, director, information, (h) **303-238-2733.** Serves as the administrative arm for the intercollegiate athletic programs of eight member universities

WOMEN'S INTERNATIONAL BOWLING CONGRESS (WIBC). 5301 S 76th St, Greendale, WI 53129. **414-421-9000.** Flora E Mitchell, executive secretary-treasurer

WOMEN'S PROFESSIONAL FAST PITCH LEAGUE (softball). 899 Merimac Station Rd, Fenton, MO 63026. **314-225-4922.** Gayle Harrawood, commissioner

WOMEN'S TENNIS ASSOCIATION. 1604 Union St, San Francisco, CA 94123. **415-673-2018**

WORLD BOXING ASSOCIATION

Important Officials

President. Dr Elias M Cordova, Jr, Apartado 273, Calle 58, No 17, (Urb Obarrio), Panama 1, Panama. Telephone: **23-0868**

Executive Secretary. Arch Hindman, 5935 Granville Dr, Sylvania, OH 43560. **419-691-2440.** (h) **419-882-8145**

International Legal Advisor and Convention Site Chairman. Bernard Shankman, Esq, 1511 K St NW, Washington, DC 20015. **202-783-2838**

International Commissioner. Abe J Greene, 362 17th Ave, Paterson, NJ 07509. **201-272-2161**

Treasurer. Nick P Kerasiotis, 412 Colorado Ave, Aurora, IL 60506. **312-897-4765**

Championships Committee Chairman. Fernando Mandry Galindez, Calle "El Mango Coromoto," San Antonio, Caracas 105, Venezuela. Telephone: **72-5919**

Batinas Committee Chairman. Rodrigo C Sanchez E, Association Mundial de Boxeo, Apartado 470, Panama 1, Panama. Telephone: **64-6937.** (h) **26-1448**

WORLD BOXING COUNCIL. Jose Sulaiman (Apartado postal 75-254, Mexico City, Mexico 14 D F), president, **905-569-1911.** Robert Turley (1021 O St, Sacramento, CA 95814), chairman, ratings committee, **916-445-7898**

WORLD CHESS FEDERATION. Central Office, Lignbaansgracht 231, Amsterdam C, Netherlands

WORLD JAI ALAI, INC. 3500 NW 37th Ave, Miami, FL 33142. **305-633-6400.** Fred McKenna, director, public relations. Milt Roth, public relations consultant, **305-633-1155.** The largest pro sponsor, with five frontons (stadia), of the sport in the US

WORLD TEAM TENNIS, INC. Suite 1838, 7733 Forsyth, St Louis, MO 63105. **314-727-7211.** Commissioner: Earl (Butch) Buchholz, Jr, **314-727-7211.** Richard Koster, director, public relations

Teams

The Boston Lobsters. 1 Boston Pl, Boston, MA 02108. **617-227-8205.** Betsy R Hickey, public relations director, (h) **617-581-7864**

Cleveland Nets. 29525 Chagrin Blvd, Pepper Pike, OH 44122. **216-464-7780.** 234 Forbes Ave, Pittsburgh, PA 15222. Sally Fayad, general manager

Golden Gaters. 110 Watergate Towers, Emeryville, CA 94608. **415-652-8404.** Denise Moya, public relations director

Indiana Loves. 2441 Production Dr, Indianapolis, IN 46241. **317-243-7377.** Jep Cadou, publicity director, (h) **317-844-7035**

Los Angeles Strings. 2116 Wilshire Blvd, Santa Monica, CA 90403. **213-829-5391.** Randy Perla, publicity, (h) **213-829-5245**

New York Apples. 230 Park Ave, New York, NY 10017. **212-661-8070.** Alan Taylor, Padilla, Speer, and Newsome, 950 3rd Ave, New York, NY 10022, public relations director, **212-752-8338.** (h) **212-581-6622**

Phoenix Racquets. Suite 404, 1130 E Missouri, Phoenix, AZ 85014. **602-263-5312.** Brenda Bricklin, public relations director

San Diego Friars. Suite 624, 1660 Hotel Circle N, Lion Plz, San Diego, CA 92108. **714-298-9855.** Irv Grossman, (11772 Sorrento Valley Rd, San Diego, CA 92121), publicity director, (h) **714-452-8640**

Sea Port Cascades. 210 Queen Anne Ave N, Seattle, WA 98111. **206-285-2744.** Also 1208 SW 13th St, Portland, OR 97205. **503-227-1460.** George Hill, public relations director, (h) **206-285-2744.** Sonya Reedy, assistant public relations director, (h) **503-227-1460**

The Soviets. 1660 S Amphlett Blvd, San Mateo, CA 94402. **415-574-4626**

YANKEE CONFERENCE. Field House, University of New Hampshire, Durham, NH 03824. Andrew Mooradian, commissioner, **603-862-1850.** (h) **603-868-2604**

COLLEGE SPORTS INFORMATION DIRECTORS

ABILENE CHRISTIAN UNIVERSITY. Abilene, TX 79601. Garner Roberts. **915-677-1911.** (h) **915-692-9250**

ADAMS STATE COLLEGE. Alamosa, CO 81102. David Green. **303-589-7121.** (h) **303-589-9587**

UNIVERSITY OF AKRON. Akron, OH 44325. Ken MacDonald. **216-375-7468.** (h) **216-928-7546**

UNIVERSITY OF ALABAMA. Tuscaloosa, AL 35486. Charley Thornton. **205-348-6084.** (h) **205-553-1731.** Kirk McNair, assistant (h) **205-556-4980**

UNIVERSITY OF ALABAMA. Huntsville, AL 35807. Larry Eakes. **205-895-6144.** (h) **205-852-7609**

ALBANY STATE COLLEGE. Albany, GA 31705. Alvin L Benson. **912-439-4078.** (h) **912-435-4624**

ALBION COLLEGE. Albion, MI 49224. Steve Drake. **517-629-6725.** (h) **517-629-9661.** Jean Taylor, assistant, (h) **517-629-6502**

ALBRIGHT COLLEGE. Reading, PA 19603. Alex Campbell. **215-921-2381** Ext 221, (h) **215-376-0386**

ALCORN STATE UNIVERSITY. Lorman, MS 39096. John I Hendricks. **601-877-3711.** (h) **601-877-2909**

ALLEGHENY COLLEGE. Meadville, PA 16335. Beth Giese. **814-724-2369.** (h) **814-724-6370**

AMERICAN UNIVERSITY. Washington, DC 20016. Ray Murphy. **202-686-2560.** (h) **703-450-4897**

AMHERST COLLEGE. Amherst, MA 01002. David E Downs. **413-542-2321.** (h) **413-542-2000**

ANDERSON COLLEGE. Anderson, IN 46011. Terry L Murawski. **317-644-0951** Ext 428. Aprille Rigsby. **317-644-0951,** Ext 309 or 386

APPALACHIAN STATE UNIVERSITY. Boone, NC 28607. Pat Gainey. **704-262-3080.** (h) **704-264-5688**

ARIZONA STATE UNIVERSITY. Tempe, AZ 85281. Dick Mullins. **602-965-3659.** (h) **602-967-3016**

UNIVERSITY OF ARIZONA. Tucson, AZ 85720. Frank W Soltys. **602-884-1919.** (h) **602-326-5697.** Ray McNally, assistant, (h) **602-326-3973**

ARKANSAS COLLEGE. Batesville, AR 72501. Mike Hendricks. **501-793-9813,** Ext 238. (h) **501-698-1364**

ARKANSAS POLYTECHNIC UNIVERSITY. Russellville, AR 72801. James R Staggs. **501-968-0242.** (h) **501-293-4577**

ARKANSAS STATE UNIVERSITY. AR 72467. Jerry Schaeffer. **501-972-2077.** (h) **501-972-0243**

UNIVERSITY OF ARKANSAS. Fayetteville, AR 72701. Butch Henry. **501-575-2751.** (h) **501-521-8018**

UNIVERSITY OF ARKANSAS. Little Rock, AR 72204. Harold Coggins. **501-569-3219.** (h) **501-227-4892**

UNIVERSITY OF ARKANSAS. Monticello, AR 71655. Larry G Smith. **501-367-6811,** Ext 32, (h) **501-367-5810**

ASHLAND COLLEGE. Ashland, OH 44805. Chuck Mistovich. **419-289-4135.** (h) **419-289-2274**

ASSUMPTION COLLEGE. Worcester, MA 01609. Steve Morris. **617-752-5615,** Ext 240 or 279, (h) **617-842-6372**

AUBURN UNIVERSITY. Auburn, AL 36830. Buddy Davidson. **205-826-4750.** (h) **205-887-7160**

AUSTIN COLLEGE. Sherman, TX 75090. Al Younts. **214-892-9101,** Ext 377, (h) **214-893-2344**

BALL STATE UNIVERSITY. Muncie, IN 47306. Earl Yestingsmeier. **317-285-4925.** (h) **317-282-4678**

UNIVERSITY OF BALTIMORE. Baltimore, MD 21201. Billy Woodard. **301-727-6350,** Ext 315

BATES COLLEGE. Lewiston, ME 04240. Joseph M Gromelski. **207-782-6321.** (h) **207-784-1403**

BELLARMINE COLLEGE. Louisville, KY 40205. Nanette Schuhmann. **502-452-8381.** (h) **502-451-8404**

BELMONT COLLEGE. Nashville, TN 37203. Bill Bandy. **615-383-7001,** Ext 306, (h) **615-361-0323**

BENEDICTINE COLLEGE. Atchison, KS 66002. Roger Swafford. **913-367-5340,** Ext 207, (h) **913-367-2936**

BENTLEY COLLEGE. Waltham, MA 02154. Dick Lipe. **617-891-2256.** (h) **617-893-6329**

BETHANY COLLEGE. Bethany, WV 26032. R. L. Westlake. **304-829-7221.** (h) **304-829-7760**

BETHEL COLLEGE. St Paul, MN 55112. David Klostreich. **612-641-6392.** (h) **612-645-8734**

BIRMINGHAM-SOUTHERN COLLEGE. Birmingham, AL 35204. Greg Walcavich. **205-328-5250,** Ext 340, (h) **205-328-5250,** Ext 342

BISCAYNE COLLEGE. Miami, Florida 33054. Roy H Slanhoff. **305-625-1561,** Ext 160, (h) **305-652-3714**

BISHOP COLLEGE. Dallas, TX 75241. John Lark. **214-376-4311,** Ext 202, (h) **214-374-3923**

BLACKBURN COLLEGE. Carlinville, IL 62626. Wayne King. **217-854-3231,** Ext 271, (h) **217-854-8624**

BLUEFIELD STATE COLLEGE. Bluefield, WV 24701. Barry Blizzard. **304-325-7102.** (h) **304-248-8213**

BOISE STATE UNIVERSITY. Boise, ID 83725. Jim Faucher. **208-385-1288.** (h) **208-345-4164**

BOSTON COLLEGE. Chestnut Hill, MA 02167. Reid P Oslin. **617-969-0100,** Ext 3004, (h) **617-964-5856**

BOWIE STATE COLLEGE. Bowie, MD 20715. Willie Mason. **310-262-3350,** Ext 313, (h) **301-341-3296**

BOWLING GREEN STATE UNIVERSITY. Bowling Green, OH 43403. Robert C Moyers. **419-372-2401,** Ext 54, (h) **419-352-6397**

BRADLEY UNIVERSITY. Peoria, IL 61625. Joe Dalfonso. **309-676-7611,** Ext 316, (h) **309-673-5248**

UNIVERSITY OF BRIDGEPORT. Bridgeport, CT 06602. Richard P Ondek. **203-576-4524.** (h) **203-268-5049**

BRIDGEWATER COLLEGE. Bridgewater, VA 22812. Steve Broache. **703-828-2501,** Ext 577, (h) **703-828-2391**

BRIGHAM YOUNG UNIVERSITY. Provo, UT 84601. David Schulthess. **801-374-1211,** Ext 4511, (h) **801-225-6566**

BROWN UNIVERSITY. Providence, RI 02912. Rosa Gatti. **401-863-2219.** (h) **401-438-0025**

BRYAN COLLEGE. Dayton, TN 37321. Jeff Tubbs. **615-775-2041.** (h) **615-775-9220**

BRYANT COLLEGE. Smithfield, RI 02917. John Gillooly. **401-231-1200.** (h) **401-941-7186**

BUCKNELL UNIVERSITY. Lewisburg, PA 17837. Dennis R O'Shea. **717-524-1221.** (h) **717-966-1832**

BUTLER UNIVERSITY. Indianapolis, IN 46208. Chris Theofanis. **317-283-9351.** (h) **317-849-0440**

CALIFORNIA STATE COLLEGE. Bakersfield, CA 93309. Craig Holland. **805-833-3071.** (h) **805-834-4291**

CALIFORNIA STATE POLYTECHNIC COLLEGE. San Luis Obispo, CA 93407. Wayne F Shaw. **805-546-2355.** (h) **805-489-2056**

CALIFORNIA STATE POLYTECHNIC UNIVERSITY. Pomona, CA 91768. Jim McConnell. **714-598-4614.** (h) **714-622-7393**

CALIFORNIA STATE UNIVERSITY. Chico, CA 95926. Art Thompson. **916-895-5308.** (h) **916-891-0312**

CALIFORNIA STATE UNIVERSITY. Fullerton, CA 92634. John Culwell. **714-870-3970.** (h) **714-529-7189**

CALIFORNIA STATE UNIVERSITY. Long Beach, CA 90840. Terry Ross. **213-498-4667.** (h) **213-597-3113**

CALIFORNIA STATE UNIVERSITY. Northridge, CA 91324. Lou Riggs. **213-885-3243.** (h) **213-886-1851**

CALIFORNIA STATE UNIVERSITY. Sacramento, CA 95825. Pete Dufour. **916-454-6481**

UNIVERSITY OF CALIFORNIA. Berkeley, CA 94720. John McCasey. **415-642-5363.** (h) **415-278-4252**

UNIVERSITY OF CALIFORNIA. Davis, CA 95616. Jim Doan. **916-752-3505.** (h) **916-756-2190**

UNIVERSITY OF CALIFORNIA. Irvine, CA 92717. Jim Brochu. **714-833-5814.** (h) **714-754-1749**

UNIVERSITY OF CALIFORNIA. Los Angeles, CA 90024. Vic Kelley. **213-825-3732.** (h) **213-784-3865.** Marc Dellins, assistant, (h) **213-766-1306**

UNIVERSITY OF CALIFORNIA. Riverside, CA 92502. Bill Scott. **714-787-5438.** (h) **714-687-5715**

UNIVERSITY OF CALIFORNIA. San Diego La Jolla, CA 92037. Margie Smith. **714-452-4211**

UNIVERSITY OF CALIFORNIA. Santa Barbara, CA 93106. Bob Vazquez. **805-961-3428.** (h) **805-967-2587**

CALVIN COLLEGE. Grand Rapids, MI 49506. Dave Tuuk. **616-949-4000,** Ext 2181, (h) **616-243-3001**

CAPITAL UNIVERSITY. Columbus, OH 43209. Harry Paidas. **614-236-6196.** (h) **614-231-7944**

CARLETON COLLEGE. Northfield, MN 55057. Gregg Hague. **507-645-4431,** Ext 506, (h) **507-645-4431,** Ext 491. J. G. Preston. **507-645-4431,** Ext 506, (h) **507-645-4431,** Ext 389

CARNEGIE-MELLON UNIVERSITY. Pittsburgh, PA 15213. Dennis Morabito. **412-621-2600,** Ext 8760

CATAWBA COLLEGE. Salisbury, NC 28144. Chip Williams. **704-637-4393.** (h) **704-636-9819**

UNIVERSITY OF CENTRAL ARKANSAS. Conway, AR 72032. Jim Schneider. **501-329-2931.** (h) **501-329-3653**

CENTRAL COLLEGE. Pella, IA 50219. Terry Beck. **515-628-4151,** Ext 294, (h) **515-628-4892**

CENTRAL MICHIGAN UNIVERSITY. Mount Pleasant, MI 48859. Jere T Craig. **517-774-3277.** (h) **517-772-5370**

CENTRAL MISSOURI STATE UNIVERSITY. Warrensburg, MO 64093. Stephen Weller. **816-429-4312.** (h) **816-747-3004**

CENTRAL STATE UNIVERSITY. Wilberforce, OH 45384. Ed Powell. **513-376-6318.** (h) **513-878-8833**

CENTRAL WASHINGTON UNIVERSITY. Ellensburg, WA 98926. Greg S Kummer. **509-963-1491**

COLLEGE OF CHARLESTON. Charleston, SC 29401. Steve Overton. **803-722-0181,** Ext 2057, (h) **803-795-3768**

CHEYNEY STATE COLLEGE. Cheyney, PA 19319. Anthony F Pinnie. **215-399-6911.** (h) **215-872-5469**

CHICAGO STATE UNIVERSITY. Chicago, IL 60628. Katherine Northrup. **312-995-2016.** (h) **312-493-2842**

UNIVERSITY OF CHICAGO. Chicago, IL 60637. Mike Krauss. **312-753-4431.** (h) **312-753-3257**

UNIVERSITY OF CINCINNATI. Cincinnati, OH 45221. Jerry Kissel. **513-475-5091.** (h) **513-475-3570.** Mike Ricciardi, assistant, (h) **513-621-6828.** Chris Stubbins, assistant, (h) **513-861-8439**

THE CITIDEL. Charleston, SC 29409. Jimmy Wilder. **803-577-6900,** Ext 2070, (h) **803-577-7337**

CLARK UNIVERSITY. Worcester, MA 01610. **617-793-7162**

CLEMSON UNIVERSITY. Clemson, SC 29631. Bob Bradley. **803-656-2101.** (h) **803-654-5419**

CLEVELAND STATE UNIVERSITY. Cleveland, OH 44115. Merle J Levin. **216-687-4818.** (h) **216-942-4590**

COLGATE UNIVERSITY. Hamilton, NY 13346. Robert D Cornell. **315-824-1000**

COLORADO COLLEGE. Colorado Springs, CO 80903. Fred Bluhm. **303-473-2233,** Ext 221, (h) **303-635-2139**

COLORADO STATE UNIVERSITY. Fort Collins, CO 80523. Tim Simmons. **303-491-5067.** (h) **303-482-3295**

UNIVERSITY OF COLORADO. Boulder, CO 80309. Mike Moran. **303-492-6128.** (h) **303-499-1920**

COLUMBIA UNIVERSITY. New York, NY 10027. Kevin G De Marrais. **212-280-2534.** (h) **201-692-0261.** Bill Steinman, assistant

COLUMBUS COLLEGE. Columbus, GA 31902. R Ellwood Moyer. **404-324-4761.** (h) **404-561-2802**

UNIVERSITY OF CONNECTICUT. Storrs, CT 06268. Joseph J Soltys. **203-486-3531.** (h) **203-429-4004**

CORNELL UNIVERSITY. Ithaca, NY 14850. Dave Wohlhueter. **607-256-3752.** (h) **607-273-5891**

CREIGHTON UNIVERSITY. Omaha, NE 68178. Dan Offenburger. **402-536-2720.** (h) **402-393-6908**

CULVER-STOCKTON COLLEGE. Canton, MO 63435. David Williford. **314-288-5221.** (h) **314-288-3598**

DAKOTA STATE COLLEGE. Madison, SD 57042. John Walsh. **605-256-3551,** Ext 270, (h) **605-256-6748**

DAKOTA WESLEYAN UNIVERSITY. Mitchell, SD 57301. Evalyn A Durfee. **605-996-6511,** Ext 229, (h) **605-996-7997**

DARTMOUTH COLLEGE. Hanover, NH 03755. Art Petrosemolo. **603-646-2468.** (h) **603-298-5028.** Kathy Slattery, assistant, (h) **603-448-2103**

DAVIDSON COLLEGE. Davidson, NC 28036. Emil Parker. **704-892-2000.** (h) **704-892-0607**

DAVIS AND ELKINS COLLEGE. Elkins, WV 26241. Public relations office. **304-636-1900,** Ext 222

UNIVERSITY OF DAYTON. Dayton, OH 45469. Gene Schill. **513-229-4421.** (h) **513-298-3310**

DELAWARE STATE COLLEGE. Dover, DE 19901. Elizabeth C Dix. **302-678-4924.** (h) **302-337-7265**

UNIVERSITY OF DELAWARE. Newark, DE 19711. Benjamin M Sherman. **302-738-2186.** (h) **302-737-3379.** Radio beeper telephone: **302-738-8139**

DELTA STATE UNIVERSITY. Cleveland, MS 38733. Langston Rogers. **601-843-4226.** (h) **601-843-9665**

UNIVERSITY OF DENVER. Denver, CO 80210. Bill Scharton. **303-753-2339.** (h) **303-722-4702**

DE PAUL UNIVERSITY. Chicago, IL 60614. Marty Hawkins. **312-321-8010.** (h) **312-281-1688**

DE PAUW UNIVERSITY. Greencastle, IN 46135. Patrick Aikman. **317-653-9721,** Ext 480, (h) **317-653-4798**

UNIVERSITY OF DETROIT. Detroit, MI 48221. Bill Kreifeldt. **313-927-1158.** (h) **313-547-6560**

DICKINSON COLLEGE. Carlisle, PA 17013. Jeff Wiles. **717-243-5121,** Ext 310, (h) **717-243-7085**

DRAKE UNIVERSITY. Des Moines, IA 50311. Steve Hellyer. **515-271-3740.** (h) **515-223-0461**

DREW UNIVERSITY. Madison, NJ 07940. Steve Goodrich. **201-377-3000,** Ext 235, (h) **201-377-3698**

DREXEL UNIVERSITY. Philadelphia, PA 19104. John Shiffert. **215-895-2551.** (h) **215-732-5798**

DRURY COLLEGE. Springfield, MO 65802. Roland Shultz. **417-865-8731.** (h) **417-753-2701**

UNIVERSITY OF DUBUQUE. Dubuque, IA 52001. Clifford D Gold. **319-557-2234.** (h) **319-583-7000**

DUKE UNIVERSITY. Durham, NC 27706. Tom Mickle. **919-684-2633.** (h) **919-929-1844.** Johnny Moore, assistant

DUQUESNE UNIVERSITY. Pittsburgh, PA 15219. Nellie King. **412-434-6564.** (h) **412-341-9062**

EAST CAROLINA UNIVERSITY. Greenville, NC 27834. Ken Smith. **919-757-6491.** (h) **919-758-2254**

EAST CENTRAL OKLAHOMA STATE UNIVERSITY. Ada, OK 74820. Dean Painter. **405-332-8000,** Ext 249

EAST STROUDSBURG STATE COLLEGE. East Stroudsburg, PA 18301. Pete Nevins. **717-424-3312.** (h) **717-421-4146**

EAST TENNESSEE STATE UNIVERSITY. Johnson City, TN 37601. John Cathey. **615-929-4220.** (h) **615-926-5302**

EAST TEXAS BAPTIST COLLEGE. Marshall, TX 75670. Richard Warren McKinney. **214-938-3711.** (h) **214-938-8233**

EAST TEXAS STATE UNIVERSITY. Commerce, TX 75428. Lou Margot. **214-468-2263.** (h) **214-886-2337**

EASTERN CONNECTICUT STATE COLLEGE. Willimantic, CT 06226. Del Dixon. **203-456-2231,** Ext 464, (h) **203-568-8170**

EASTERN ILLINOIS UNIVERSITY. Charleston, IL 61920. Dave Kidwell. **217-581-2920.** (h) **217-345-4166**

EASTERN KENTUCKY UNIVERSITY. Richmond, KY 40475. Karl Park. **606-622-2301.** (h) **606-623-3961**

EASTERN MICHIGAN UNIVERSITY. Ypsilanti, MI 48197. John C Fountain. **313-487-2323.** (h) **313-434-0083**

EASTERN NEW MEXICO UNIVERSITY. Portales, NM 88130. Mike Slinker. **505-562-2131.** (h) **505-356-4648**

EASTERN WASHINGTON STATE COLLEGE. Cheney, WA 99004. Robert W Polski. **509-359-7069.** (h) **509-235-8003**

ELIZABETHTOWN COLLEGE. Elizabethtown, PA 17022. Richard C Lytle. **717-367-1151.** (h) **717-367-1064**

EMPORIA STATE COLLEGE. Emporia, KS 66801. Bob Ecklund. **316-343-1200,** Ext 455, **316-342-1216**

ERSKINE COLLEGE. Due West, SC 29639. Dick Haldeman. **803-379-8858.** (h) **803-379-8354**

UNIVERSITY OF EVANSVILLE. Evansville, IN 47702. Greg Khipping. **812-479-2261.** (h) **812-422-9562**

FAIRFIELD UNIVERSITY. Fairfield, CT 06430. Ray Van Stone. **203-255-5411,** Ext 209, (h) **203-333-3680**

FAIRLEIGH DICKINSON UNIVERSITY. Madison, NJ 07940. Ted Bruning. **201-377-4700,** Ext 292, (h) **201-546-5089**

FAIRLEIGH DICKINSON UNIVERSITY. Teaneck, NJ 07666. Jay Horwitz. **201-836-6300,** Ext 397, (h) **201-546-5089**

FLORIDA A & M UNIVERSITY. Tallahassee, FL 32307. Roosevelt Wilson. **904-224-2475.** (h) **904-222-2821**

FLORIDA SOUTHERN COLLEGE. Lakeland, FL 33802. William H ("Skip") Boyer. **813-683-5521.** (h) **813-687-9455**

FLORIDA TECHNOLOGICAL UNIVERSITY. Orlando, FL 32816. Neil La Bar. **305-275-2504**

UNIVERSITY OF FLORIDA. Gainesville, FL 32604. Norm Carlson. **904-392-0641.** (h) **904-372-7822**

FORDHAM UNIVERSITY. Bronx, NY 10458. Jim O'Connell. **212-733-6052.** (h) **212-343-8198**

FRAMINGHAM STATE COLLEGE. Framingham, MA 01701. Jeffrey A Stone. **617-872-3501,** Ext 258, (h) **617-881-1392**

FRANCIS MARION COLLEGE. Florence, SC 29501. Bob Ward. **803-669-4121,** Ext 201, (h) **803-665-8619**

FRANKLIN AND MARSHALL COLLEGE. Lancaster, PA 17604. Bruce G Holran. **717-291-3981.** (h) **717-291-4423**

FRESNO STATE UNIVERSITY. Fresno, CA 93740. Tom Kane. **209-487-2509.** (h) **209-291-4515**

FURMAN UNIVERSITY. Greenville, SC 29613. Art Black. **803-294-2061.** (h) **803-246-5978**

GEORGETOWN COLLEGE. Georgetown, KY 40324. Mr Robin Oldham. **502-863-7326.** (h) **502-863-0106**

GEORGETOWN UNIVERSITY. Washington, DC 20057. Fran Connors. **202-625-4182.** (h) **703-820-5560**

GEORGIA INSTITUTE OF TECHNOLOGY. Atlanta, GA 30332. Jim Schultz. **404-894-5445.** (h) **404-433-0281**

GEORGIA SOUTHERN COLLEGE. Statesboro, GA 30458. Larry Albright. **912-681-5522.** (h) **912-764-9359**

UNIVERSITY OF GEORGIA. Athens, GA 30603. David Storey. **404-542-1621.** (h) **404-546-5321**

GLENVILLE STATE COLLEGE. Glenville, WV 26351. Jim Riffle. **304-462-7361,** Ext 281, (h) **304-462-5468**

GRAMBLING COLLEGE. Grambling, LA 71245. Collie J Nicholson. **318-247-8345.** (h) **318-247-3770**

GRAND VALLEY STATE COLLEGE. Allendale, MI 49401. Don Thomas. **616-895-6611,** Ext 222, (h) **616-245-4930**

COLLEGE OF GREAT FALLS. Great Falls, MT 59405. Ray Dodds. **406-761-8210,** Ext 277, (h) **406-452-7831**

GUILFORD COLLEGE. Greensboro, NC 27410. Cliff Hunsucker. **919-292-5511.** (h) **919-852-0474**

HANOVER COLLEGE. Hanover, IN 47243. Dolores A Long. **812-866-2151**

HARDING COLLEGE. Searcy, AR 72143. Stan Green. **501-268-6161,** Ext 316, (h) **501-268-8731**

UNIVERSITY OF HARTFORD. West Hartford, CT 06117. John (Jack) Repass. **203-243-4340.** (h) **203-646-7638**

HARVARD UNIVERSITY. Cambridge, MA 02138. Dave Matthews. **617-495-2206.** (h) **617-275-1943.** Joe Bertagna, assistant, (h) **617-484-9580**

HAVERFORD COLLEGE. Haverford, PA 19041. Robert J Tatar. **215-649-9600,** Ext 233, (h) **215-896-7759**

UNIVERSITY OF HAWAII. Honolulu, HI 96822. Ed Inouye. **808-948-7523.** (h) **808-955-2368**

HILLSDALE COLLEGE. Hillsdale, MI 49242. Charles Chandler. **517-437-7364.** (h) **517-439-1107**

HOFSTRA UNIVERSITY. Hempstead, NY 11550. John H Frew. **516-560-3578.** (h) **212-380-5515**

HOLY CROSS COLLEGE. Worcester, MA 01610. Rich Lewis. **617-793-2583.** (h) **617-832-4728**

UNIVERSITY OF HOUSTON. Houston, TX 77004. Ted Nance. **713-748-6844.** (h) **713-353-4663**

HOWARD UNIVERSITY. Washington, DC 20059. Cureton L Johnson. **202-636-7182.** (h) **202-575-4176.** Phil Maness, assistant, (h) **202-584-7625**

HUMBOLDT STATE UNIVERSITY. Arcata, CA 95521. Mike O'Brien. **707-826-3631** or **3666.** (h) **707-822-8126**

HUNTER COLLEGE. New York, NY 10021. Andrew Furman. **212-996-2200.** (h) **212-236-4589**

HUNTINGDON COLLEGE. Montgomery, AL 36106. Wayne Mitchell. **205-263-1611,** Ext 63, (h) **205-272-0975**

IDAHO STATE UNIVERSITY. Pocatello, ID 83209. Glenn Alford. **208-236-3651.** (h) **208-233-0516**

UNIVERSITY OF IDAHO. Moscow, ID 83843. J David Kellog. **208-885-7091.** (h) **208-233-0516**

ILLINOIS COLLEGE. Jacksonville, IL 62650. Mark J Schwartz. **217-245-7126.** (h) **217-245-8453**

ILLINOIS STATE UNIVERSITY. Normal, IL 61761. Roger Cushman. **309-438-5631.** (h) **309-452-5170**

UNIVERSITY OF ILLINOIS. Urbana-Champaign, IL 61820. Tab Bennett. **217-333-1390.** (h) **217-359-4784**

UNIVERSITY OF ILLINOIS AT CHICAGO CIRCLE. Chicago, IL 60680. Dave Jovanovic. **312-996-3131.** (h) **312-524-0898**

ILLINOIS WESLEYAN UNIVERSITY. Bloomington, IL 61701. Ed Alsene. **309-556-3181.** (h) **309-663-1261**

INDIANA CENTRAL UNIVERSITY. Indianapolis, IN 46227. Dr Kenneth Borden. **317-788-3298.** (h) **317-787-8028**

INDIANA STATE UNIVERSITY. Terre Haute, IN 47809. Ed McKee. **812-232-6311,** Ext 2587, (h) **812-299-4207**

INDIANA UNIVERSITY. Bloomington, IN 47401. Tom Miller. **812-337-2421.** (h) **812-332-9880**

INDIANA UNIVERSITY OF PENNSYL-VANIA. Indiana, PA 15701. Randy L Jesick. **412-357-2233.** (h) **412-465-5970**

IOWA STATE UNIVERSITY. Ames, IA 50011. Tom Starr. **515-294-3372.** (h) **515-292-4139**

UNIVERSITY OF IOWA. Iowa City, IA 52242. George Wine. **319-353-3038.** (h) **319-337-3933**

IOWA WESLEYAN COLLEGE. Mount Pleasant, IA 52641. Larry Marlow. **319-385-8021.** (h) **319-385-8667**

ITHACA COLLEGE. Ithaca, NY 14850. Robert Marx. **607-274-3233.** (h) **607-257-3295**

JACKSON STATE UNIVERSITY. Jackson, MS 39217. Sam Jefferson. **601-968-2274.** (h) **601-362-0119**

JACKSONVILLE STATE UNIVERSITY. Jacksonville, AL 36265. Rudy Abbott. **205-435-9820.** (h) **205-820-1650**

JACKSONVILLE UNIVERSITY. Jacksonville, FL 32211. Bill Coulthart. **904-744-3950,** Ext 284, (h) **904-744-1072**

JOHNS HOPKINS UNIVERSITY. Baltimore, MD 21218. Lee Horowitz. **301-338-7487**

JUNIATA COLLEGE. Huntingdon, PA 16652. Charles R Pollock. **814-643-4310,** Ext 17, (h) **814-643-2118**

KALAMAZOO COLLEGE. Kalamazoo, MI 49007. Maggie Haas. **616-383-8466**

KANSAS NEWMAN COLLEGE. Wichita, KS 67213. Randy Betzen. **316-942-4291,** Ext 48, (h) **316-943-9994**

KANSAS STATE UNIVERSITY. Manhattan, KS 66506. Glen Stone. **913-532-5855.** (h) **913-537-1077**

UNIVERSITY OF KANSAS. Lawrence, KS 66045. Don Baker. **913-864-3417.** (h) **913-842-2314**

KEARNEY STATE COLLEGE. Kearney, NE 68847. Donald K Briggs. **308-236-4192.** (h) **308-237-7113**

KENT STATE UNIVERSITY. Kent, OH 44242. Terry L Barnard. **216-672-2110.** (h) **216-325-7664**

KENTUCKY STATE UNIVERSITY. Frankfort, KY 40601. Kenny Snelling. **502-564-5971.** (h) **502-695-4671**

UNIVERSITY OF KENTUCKY. Lexington, KY 40508. Russell Rice. **606-257-3838.** (h) **606-277-5639**

THE KING'S COLLEGE. Briarcliff Manor, NY 10510. Douglas Ellenberger. **914-941-7200,** Ext 224

LAFAYETTE COLLEGE. Easton, PA 18042. Doug Elgin. **215-253-6281,** Ext 238

LAMAR UNIVERSITY. Beaumont, TX 77710. Joe Lee Smith. **713-838-7317.** (h) **713-892-5315**

LA SALLE COLLEGE. Philadelphia, PA 19149. W Lawrence Eldridge, Jr. **215-951-1080.** (h) **215-664-0324**

LEHIGH UNIVERSITY. Bethlehem, PA 18015. Joe Whritenour. **215-691-7000,** Ext 304, (h) **215-866-3672**

LEWIS AND CLARK COLLEGE. Portland, OR 97219. Chuck Charnquist. **503-244-6161.** (h) **503-644-9685**

LEWIS UNIVERSITY. Lockport, IL 60441. Victor J Reato. **815-838-0500,** Ext 294

LINCOLN UNIVERSITY. Lincoln University, PA 19352. Tom Varella. **215-932-8300,** Ext 427, (h) **302-453-0100**

LINFIELD COLLEGE. McMinnville, OR 97128. Phil Bond. **503-472-4121,** Ext 257, (h) **503-472-9985**

LIVINGSTON UNIVERSITY. Livingston, AL 35470. Dee Outlaw. **205-652-9661,** Ext 222, (h) **205-652-9925**

LOCK HAVEN STATE COLLEGE. Lock Haven, PA 17745. E Ross Nevel, Jr. **717-748-5351,** Ext 464, (h) **717-748-4592**

LONG BEACH STATE UNIVERSITY. Long Beach, CA 90840. Tim Taylor. **213-498-4667.** (h) **213-433-1432**

LONG ISLAND UNIVERSITY. Brooklyn, NY 11201. Bob Gesslein. **212-834-6090.** (h) **516-741-5810**

LOUISIANA STATE UNIVERSITY. Baton Rouge, LA 70893. Paul Manasseh. **504-388-8226.** (h) **504-769-0164**

LOUISIANA TECH UNIVERSITY. Ruston, LA 71270. Keith Prince. **318-257-3144.** (h) **318-255-7769**

UNIVERSITY OF LOUISVILLE. Louisville, KY 40208. Gary Tuell. **502-636-4105.** (h) **502-363-0989**

LOYOLA MARYMOUNT UNIVERSITY. Los Angeles, CA 90045. Ben Garcia. **213-642-3063.** (h) **213-396-2782**

LUTHER COLLEGE. Decorah, IA 52101. Rollie Dain. **319-387-1025.** (h) **319-382-5929**

LYNCHBURG COLLEGE. Lynchburg, VA 24504. HL Massie. **804-845-9071.** (h) **804-847-8759**

MCMURRY COLLEGE. Abilene, TX 79605. Johnnie Ray. **915-692-4130,** Ext 231, (h) **915-698-3550**

MCNEESE STATE UNIVERSITY. Lake Charles, LA 70601. Louis C Bonnette, Jr. **318-477-2520.** (h) **318-477-4182**

JAMES MADISON UNIVERSITY. Harrisonburg, VA 22801. Rich Murray. **703-433-6154.** (h) 703-433-1591

UNIVERSITY OF MAINE. Machias, ME 04654. Ed Seneff. **207-255-3313,** Ext 245

UNIVERSITY OF MAINE. Orono, ME 04473. Robert Creteau. **207-581-7376.** (h) **207-827-4816**

UNIVERSITY OF MAINE. Presque Isle, ME 04769. Ruth Mraz. **207-764-0311**

MARIETTA COLLEGE. Marietta, OH 45750. Phil Mazzara. **614-373-4643**

MARION COLLEGE. Marion, IN 46952. Thomas A Carr. **317-674-6901**

MARQUETTE UNIVERSITY. Milwaukee, WI 53233. Greg Sbaraglia. **414-224-7447.** (h) **414-771-8255**

MARSHALL UNIVERSITY. Huntington, WV 25715. John Evenson. **304-696-3190.** (h) **304-736-3773**

UNIVERSITY OF MARYLAND. College Park, MD 20740. Jack Zane. **301-454-2123.** (h) **301-322-3265**

UNIVERSITY OF MARYLAND, BALTIMORE COUNTY. Baltimore, MD 21228. Dan O'Connell. **301-455-2905.** (h) **301-323-4804**

MARYMOUNT COLLEGE. Salina, KS 67401. George Carroll. **913-823-6317,** Ext 20, (h) **913-827-6970**

MARYVILLE COLLEGE. Maryville, TN 37801. Mrs Clyde Ussery. **615-982-6412.** (h) **615-573-5728**

MASSACHUSETTS INSTITUTE OF TECHNOLOGY. Cambridge, MA 02139. Jill A Gilpatric. **617-253-7946.** (h) **617-623-6497**

UNIVERSITY OF MASSACHUSETTS. Amherst, MA 01002. Richard H Page. **413-545-2439.** (h) **413-253-7863**

MEMPHIS STATE UNIVERSITY. Memphis, TN 38152. Jack Bugbee. **901-454-2337.** (h) **901-452-9648**

MERCER UNIVERSITY. Macon, GA 31207. Jack Pigott. **912-745-6811,** Ext 335, (h) **912-743-7398**

MERRIMACK COLLEGE. North Andover, MA 01845. Edward F Coffey. **617-683-7111.** (h) **617-685-5856**

MIAMI UNIVERSITY. Oxford, OH 45056. Dave Young. **513-529-4327.** (h) **513-523-8709**

UNIVERSITY OF MIAMI. Coral Gables, FL 33124. George Gallet. **305-284-5802.** (h) **305-661-2391**

MICHIGAN STATE UNIVERSITY. East Lansing, MI 48824. Fred Stabley. **517-355-2271.** (h) **517-332-2334.** Nick Vista, assistant, (h) **517-482-8946.** Claudia Dinges, assistant, (h) **517-394-1443**

MICHIGAN TECHNOLOGICAL UNIVERSITY. Houghton, MI 49931. Dennis Hanks. **906-487-2350.** (h) **906-482-5032**

UNIVERSITY OF MICHIGAN. Ann Arbor, MI 48104. Will Perry. **313-763-1381.** (h) **313-971-6438**

MIDDLEBURY COLLEGE. Middlebury, VT 05753. Max P Peterson. **802-388-2046.** (h) **802-388-7021**

MIDDLE TENNESSEE STATE UNIVERSITY. Murfreesboro, TN 37132. Jim Freeman. **615-898-2450.** (h) **615-893-7344**

MIDWESTERN STATE UNIVERSITY. Wichita Falls, TX 76308. D L Ligon. **817-692-6611,** Ext 301, (h) **817-767-3513**

MILLERSVILLE STATE COLLEGE. Millersville, PA 17551. Don Bird. **717-872-5411,** Ext 313, (h) **717-898-7889**

MILLIKIN UNIVERSITY. Decatur, IL 62522. Reggie Syrcle. **217-424-6350.** (h) **217-422-2371**

UNIVERSITY OF MINNESOTA. Duluth, MN 55812. Bruce M McLeod. **218-726-8191.** (h) **218-525-4068**

UNIVERSITY OF MINNESOTA. Minneapolis, MN 55455. Bob Peterson. **612-373-5236.** (h) **612-757-1538**

UNIVERSITY OF MINNESOTA. Morris, MN 56267. Ron Hamm. **612-589-4322.** (h) **612-589-3332**

MISSISSIPPI COLLEGE. Clinton, MS 39058. Norman H Gough. **601-924-5131,** Ext 239, (h) **601-924-5115**

MISSISSIPPI STATE UNIVERSITY. Mississippi State, MS 39762. Bob Hartley. **601-325-4430.** (h) **601-323-3071**

UNIVERSITY OF MISSISSIPPI. University, MS 38677. Bobo Champion. **601-232-7345.** (h) **601-234-9293**

MISSISSIPPI VALLEY STATE UNIVERSITY. Itta Bena, MS 38941. Charles Prophet. **601-254-2321,** Ext 212, (h) **601-453-9580**

UNIVERSITY OF MISSOURI. Columbia, MO 65201. Bill Callahan. **314-882-6501,** Ext 201 or 211, (h) **314-442-5826**

UNIVERSITY OF MISSOURI. Kansas City, MO 64110. Bill Ross. **816-276-2714.** (h) **816-942-9560**

UNIVERSITY OF MISSOURI. Rolla, MO 65401. Ed Murphy. **314-341-4259.** (h) **314-364-6647**

UNIVERSITY OF MISSOURI. St Louis, MO 63121. Steve Hornbostel. **314-453-5121.** (h) **314-355-6697**

MISSOURI WESTERN STATE COLLEGE. St Joseph, MO 64507. Jerry Myers. **816-233-7192,** Ext 480, (h) **816-279-5721**

MOBILE COLLEGE. Mobile, AL 36613. Gene Perkins. **205-675-5990,** Ext 25, (h) **205-342-2079**

MONMOUTH COLLEGE. West Long Branch, NJ 07764. EJ Truppa. **201-222-6600,** Ext 322, (h) **201-222-2781**

MONTANA STATE UNIVERSITY. Bozeman, MT 59715. Arnie Sgalio. **406-994-2721.** (h) **406-587-8132**

UNIVERSITY OF MONTANA. Missoula, MT 59801. Bob Rosenthal. **406-243-2522.** (h) **406-728-0406**

MONTCLAIR STATE COLLEGE. Upper Montclair, NJ 07043. Stan Gorlick. **201-893-5238** or 5249 (h) **201-228-4330**

MORAVIAN COLLEGE. Bethlehem, PA 18018. Clifford O Koch. **215-865-0741,** Ext 265, (h) **215-282-3924**

MOREHEAD STATE UNIVERSITY. Morehead, KY 40351. Randy Stacy, men's sports information director, **606-783-3325.** (h) **606-784-9560.** Gary Grider, women's sports information director, **606-783-3325.** (h) **606-784-8438**

MOREHOUSE COLLEGE. Atlanta, GA 30314. James E Nix. **404-681-2800,** Ext 348, (h) **404-524-1805**

MORGAN STATE UNIVERSITY. Baltimore, MD 21239. Joseph McIver. **301-444-3266.** (h) **301-448-1238**

MURRAY STATE UNIVERSITY. Murray, KY 42071. Joe Tom Erwin. **502-762-4270.** (h) **502-436-2467**

UNIVERSITY OF NEBRASKA. Lincoln, NE 68588. Don Bryant. **402-472-2263** or **2264** (h) **402-423-6563**

UNIVERSITY OF NEBRASKA. Omaha, NE 68101. Tim Schmad. **402-554-2305.** (h) **402-571-8815**

UNIVERSITY OF NEVADA. Las Vegas, NV 89154. Dominic Clark. **702-739-3207.** (h) **702-870-6987**

NEWBERRY COLLEGE. Newberry, SC 29108. Gordon C Henry. **803-276-5010,** Ext 240, (h) **803-276-6072**

NEW HAMPSHIRE COLLEGE. Manchester, NH 03104. **603-668-2211,** Ext 291

UNIVERSITY OF NEW HAMPSHIRE. Durham, NH 03824. Bill Knight. **603-862-1850.** (h) **603-868-2906**

UNIVERSITY OF NEW HAVEN. West Haven, CT 06516. Peter H Vander Veer. **203-934-6321.** (h) **203-387-3105**

NEW MEXICO INSTITUTE OF MINING AND TECHNOLOGY. Sororro, NM 87801. Jim McCarthy. **505-835-5131.** (h) **505-835-2062**

NEW MEXICO STATE UNIVERSITY. Las Cruces, NM 88003. Dave Lopez. **505-646-3929.** (h) **505-522-3964**

UNIVERSITY OF NEW MEXICO. Albuquerque, NM 87131. John Gonzales. **505-277-2026.** (h) **505-836-1541**

UNIVERSITY OF NEW ORLEANS. New Orleans, LA 70122. Robert Steckel. **504-283-0239.** (h) **504-895-3649**

CITY COLLEGE OF NEW YORK. New York, NY 10031. Charles DeCicco. **212-690-5310.** (h) **914-776-6171**

STATE UNIVERSITY OF NEW YORK. Albany, NY 12222. Robert Rice. **518-457-4901.** (h) **518-371-5891**

STATE UNIVERSITY OF NEW YORK. Buffalo, NY 14214. Richard E Baldwin. **716-831-2935.** (h) **716-632-7227**

STATE UNIVERSITY OF NEW YORK COLLEGE AT BUFFALO. Buffalo, NY 14222. Randall W Schultz. **716-862-6533.** (h) **716-751-6537**

STATE UNIVERSITY OF NEW YORK COLLEGE AT CORTLAND. Cortland, NY 13045. Norbert W Haley. **607-753-2518.** (h) **607-756-2323**

STATE UNIVERSITY OF NEW YORK COLLEGE AT GENESEO. Geneseo, NY 14454. Art Hatton. **716-245-5516.** (h) **716-243-2746**

STATE UNIVERSITY OF NEW YORK COLLEGE AT ONEONTA. Oneonta, NY 13820. John Wright. **607-431-3595.** (h) **607-432-0186**

STATE UNIVERSITY OF NEW YORK COLLEGE AT OSWEGO. Oswego, NY 13126. Ross Aldrich. **315-341-2265.** (h) **315-343-8836**

STATE UNIVERSITY OF NEW YORK COLLEGE AT PLATTSBURGH. Plattsburgh, NY 12901. Donald L Garrant. **518-564-2090.** (h) **518-563-5259**

STATE UNIVERSITY OF NEW YORK COLLEGE AT POTSDAM. Potsdam, NY 13676. John Oliphant. **315-268-3651.** (h) **315-265-7501**

NIAGARA UNIVERSITY. Niagara University, NY 14109. Tom Hohensee. **716-285-1212,** Ext 344, (h) **716-689-8071**

NICHOLLS STATE UNIVERSITY. Thibodaux, LA 70301. Al Suffrin. **504-447-8111,** Ext 317, (h) **504-447-5843**

UNIVERSITY OF NORTH ALABAMA. Florence, AL 35630. Ronnie Thomas. **205-766-4100,** Ext 225, (h) **205-764-6839**

NORTH CAROLINA STATE UNIVERSITY. Raleigh, NC 27607. Ed Seaman. **919-737-2102.** (h) **919-829-9186**

UNIVERSITY OF NORTH CAROLINA. Asheville, NC 28804. Pete Gilpin. **704-258-0200.** (h) **704-254-0445**

UNIVERSITY OF NORTH CAROLINA. Chapel Hill, NC 27514. Rick Brewer. **919-933-2123.** (h) **919-929-2721**

UNIVERSITY OF NORTH CAROLINA. Charlotte, NC 28223. David R Taylor. **704-597-2354.** (h) **704-596-8954**

UNIVERSITY OF NORTH CAROLINA. Wilmington, NC 28401. John Justus. **919-791-4330,** Ext 265, (h) **919-791-7805**

NORTH DAKOTA STATE UNIVERSITY. Fargo, ND 58102. George A Ellis. **701-237-8321.** (h) **701-282-7929**

UNIVERSITY OF NORTH DAKOTA. Grand Forks, ND 58202. Lee Bohnet. **701-777-2234.** (h) **701-775-2858**

NORTH TEXAS STATE UNIVERSITY. Denton, TX 76203. Fred O Graham. **817-788-2278.** (h) **817-382-3325**

NORTHEAST LOUISIANA UNIVERSITY. Monroe, LA 71209. Bob Anderson. **318-342-3190.** (h) **318-343-2343**

NORTHEAST MISSOURI STATE UNIVERSITY. Kirksville, MO 63501. William Cable. **816-665-5121,** Ext 7215, (h) **816-665-6373**

NORTHEASTERN ILLINOIS UNIVERSITY. Chicago, IL 60625. Larry Bernstein. **312-583-4050,** Ext 481, (h) **312-539-0008**

NORTHEASTERN OKLAHOMA STATE UNIVERSITY. Tahlequah, OK 74464. Jim Patterson. **918-456-5511,** Ext 213, (h) **918-456-5328**

NORTHEASTERN UNIVERSITY. Boston, MA 02115. Jack Grinold. **617-437-2691.** (h) **617-782-5268**

NORTHERN ARIZONA UNIVERSITY. Flagstaff, AZ 86001. Wylie Smith. **602-523-2282.** (h) **602-774-9037**

UNIVERSITY OF NORTHERN COLORADO. Greeley, CO 80639. Gary Morgan. **303-351-2331.** (h) **303-353-2458**

NORTHERN ILLINOIS UNIVERSITY. De Kalb, IL 60115. Bud Nangle. **815-753-1706.** (h) **815-758-0798**

UNIVERSITY OF NORTHERN IOWA. Cedar Falls, IA 50613. James W Shaffer. **319-273-2761.** (h) **319-268-0324**

NORTHERN MICHIGAN UNIVERSITY. Marquette, MI 49855. Gil Heard. **906-227-2720.** (h) **906-226-8880**

NORTHWEST MISSOURI STATE UNIVERSITY. Maryville, MO 64468. Mike Kiser. **816-582-7141,** Ext 138, (h) **816-582-8879**

NORTHWESTERN COLLEGE. Orange City, IA 51041. Lillian Drake. **712-737-4821,** Ext 26, (h) **712-737-2250**

NORTHWESTERN OKLAHOMA STATE UNIVERSITY. Alva, OK 73717. S Floyd Sibley. **405-327-1700,** Ext 210, (h) **316-825-4897**

NORTHWESTERN STATE UNIVERSITY. Natchitoches, LA 71457. Dan McDonald. **318-357-6466.** (h) **318-352-5499**

NORTHWESTERN UNIVERSITY. Evanston, IL 60201. Jerry Ashby. **312-492-7503.** (h) **312-398-0318**

NORWICH UNIVERSITY. Northfield, VT 05663. George R Turner. **802-485-5011.** (h) **802-485-7450**

UNIVERSITY OF NOTRE DAME. Notre Dame, IN 46556. Roger O Valdiserri. **219-283-7516.** (h) **219-277-0695.** Robert P Best, Assistant, (h) **219-272-5096**

OAKLAND UNIVERSITY. Rochester, MI 48063. Nancy Liese. **313-377-3180.** (h) **313-651-2339**

OBERLIN COLLEGE. Oberlin, OH 44074. Marc Kaiser. **216-774-1221,** Ext 2295. J Kay. **216-774-1221,** Ext 2295, (h) **216-775-1254**

OHIO NORTHERN UNIVERSITY. Ada, OH 45810. Dave Fried. **419-634-9921,** Ext 230, (h) **419-634-7846**

OHIO STATE UNIVERSITY. Columbus, OH 43210. Marv Homan. **614-422-6861.** (h) **614-885-5611**

OHIO UNIVERSITY. Athens, OH 45701. Frank Morgan. **614-594-5031.** (h) **614-593-7175**

OHIO WESLEYAN UNIVERSITY. Delaware, OH 43015. Mike Welch. **614-369-4431,** Ext 257, (h) **614-369-6948**

OKLAHOMA CITY UNIVERSITY. Oklahoma City, OK 73106. John Gray. **405-521-5301,** (h) **405-524-9186**

OKLAHOMA STATE UNIVERSITY. Stillwater, OK 74074. Pat Quinn. **405-624-5749.** (h) **405-377-4654**

UNIVERSITY OF OKLAHOMA. Norman, OK 73069. John Keith. **405-325-3751.** (h) **405-329-6950**

OREGON STATE UNIVERSITY. Corvallis, OR 97330. John Eggers. **503-754-2611.** (h) **503-753-6178**

UNIVERSITY OF OREGON. Eugene, OR 97403. George Beres. **503-686-5494.** (h) **503-344-0282.** Ron Paradis, assistant, **503-686-5486.** (h) **503-747-6989**

COLLEGE OF THE OZARKS. Clarksville, AR 72830. Robert Owens. **501-754-8607.** (h) **501-754-8620**

PACE UNIVERSITY. New York, NY 10038. Barry Neuberger. **212-285-3671.** (h) **212-835-8871**

PACIFIC LUTHERAN UNIVERSITY. Tacoma, WA 98447. Jim Kittilsby. **206-531-6900.** (h) **206-531-9582**

PACIFIC UNIVERSITY. Forest Grove, OR 97116. Lono Waiwaiole. **503-357-6151,** Ext 365

UNIVERSITY OF THE PACIFIC. Stockton, CA 95211. Jay Goldberg. **209-946-2472.** (h) **209-957-0568**

PAN AMERICAN UNIVERSITY. Edinburg, TX 78539. Jim McKone. **512-381-2228.** (h) **512-682-5319**

PEMBROKE STATE UNIVERSITY. Pembroke, NC 28372. Gene Warren. **919-521-4214,** Ext 249, (h) **919-739-5007**

PENNSYLVANIA STATE UNIVERSITY. University Park, PA 16802. John Morris. **814-865-1757.** (h) **814-237-6321.** David L Baker, men's assistant, (h) **814-237-1821.** Mary Jo Haverbeck, women's assistant, (h) **814-237-2951**

PENNSYLVANIA STATE UNIVERSITY, THE CAPITOL CAMPUS. Middleton, PA 17057. Francine Z Taylor. **717-787-7737.** (h) **717-653-2890**

UNIVERSITY OF PENNSYLVANIA. Philadelphia, PA 19104. Herb Hartnett. **215-243-6128.** (h) **215-687-6390.** David Lanute, assistant

UNIVERSITY OF PITTSBURGH. Pittsburgh, PA 15213. Dean Billick. **412-624-4588.** (h) **412-531-7701.** Vince Di Nardo, assistant (h) **412-621-7837.** Joyce Aschenbrenner, assistant, (h) **412-881-7999**

PORTLAND STATE UNIVERSITY. Portland, OR 97207. Larry Sellers. **503-229-4400.** (h) **503-648-2326**

UNIVERSITY OF PORTLAND. Portland, OR 97203. Dan Friedhoff. **503-283-7117.** (h) **503-288-8743**

PRINCETON UNIVERSITY. Princeton, NJ 08540. John Humenik. **609-452-3568.** (h) **609-921-1564.** Tom Odjakjiah, assistant, (h) **609-799-8248**

PROVIDENCE COLLEGE. Providence, RI 02918. Mike Tranghese. **401-865-2272.** (h) **401-353-6842**

UNIVERSITY OF PUGET SOUND. Tacoma, WA 98416. Matthew J McCully. **206-756-3140.** (h) **206-759-1741**

PURDUE UNIVERSITY. West Lafayette, IN 47907. Greg Knipping. **317-494-8561.** (h) **317-463-0247**

QUEENS COLLEGE. Flushing, NY 11367. Mark Peters. **212-520-7124.** (h) **212-379-7941**

QUINCY COLLEGE. Quincy, IL 62301. Bob Kivisto. **217-222-8020,** Ext 213, (h) **217-224-4215**

UNIVERSITY OF REDLANDS. Redlands, CA 92373. Jack Flora. **714-793-2121,** Ext 259, (h) **714-793-2121, Ext 309**

RENSSELAER POLYTECHNIC INSTITUTE. Troy, NY 12181. Jim Greenidge. **518-270-6536.** (h) **518-273-6227**

RHODE ISLAND COLLEGE. Providence, RI 02908. Mike Scandura. **401-456-8007.** (h) **401-437-0198**

UNIVERSITY OF RHODE ISLAND. Kingston, RI 02881. Jim Norman. **401-792-2409.** (h) **401-789-9530**

RICE UNIVERSITY. Houston, TX 77001. Bill Whitmore. **713-527-4077.** (h) **713-782-7928**

UNIVERSITY OF RICHMOND. Richmond, VA 23173. Bob Dickinson. **804-285-6360**

RICKS COLLEGE. Rexburg, ID 83440. Denton Y Brewerton. **208-356-2927.** (h) **208-356-3765**

RIDER COLLEGE. Lawrenceville, NJ 06848. Earle Rommel. **609-896-0800,** Ext 338, (h) **609-771-0133**

ROANOKE COLLEGE. Salem, VA 24153. **703-389-2351**

ROCHESTER INSTITUTE OF TECHNOLOGY. Rochester, NY 14623. J Roger Dykes. **716-464-6154.** (h) **716-436-4682**

UNIVERSITY OF ROCHESTER. Rochester, NY 14627. Alan W Valoris. **716-275-4307.** (h) **716-442-5271**

ROCKFORD COLLEGE. Rockford, IL 61101. Walter H Wells, Jr. **815-226-4085.** (h) **815-874-7017**

RUTGERS UNIVERSITY. New Brunswick, NJ 08903. Robert E Smith. **201-545-4126.** (h) **201-932-7971.** James Lampariello, assistant (h) **201-263-8693**

SAGINAW VALLEY STATE COLLEGE. University Center, MI 48710. R Kevin Brazell. **517-793-9800,** Ext 521

ST ANSELM'S COLLEGE. Manchester, NH 03102. W Stephen McMahon. **603-669-1030,** Ext 210, (h) **603-668-2832**

SAINT AUGUSTINE'S COLLEGE. Raleigh, NC 27611. Thelma M Keck. **919-828-4451,** Ext 216, (h) **919-833-3566**

ST BONAVENTURE UNIVERSITY. St Bonaventure, NY 14778. Thomas P McElroy. **716-375-2319,** or **2304.** (h) **716-372-2952**

ST CLOUD STATE UNIVERSITY. St Cloud, MN 56301. Bill Lynch. **612-255-2141.** (h) **612-251-9159.** (Telecopier): **612-255-2141**

ST JOHN'S UNIVERSITY. Collegeville, MN 56321. Matt Wilch. **612-363-2593**

ST JOSEPH'S COLLEGE. Philadelphia, PA 19131. Andy Dougherty. **215-879-7447.** (h) **215-352-1184**

ST LAWRENCE UNIVERSITY. Canton, NY 13617. Walter H Johnson. **315-379-5586.** (h) **315-386-2638**

ST LOUIS UNIVERSITY. St Louis, MO 63108. Dick O'Connor. **314-535-3300,** Ext 247, (h) **314-965-6722**

SAINT PAUL'S COLLEGE. Lawrenceville, VA 23868. Stanley W Johnson. **804-848-3111,** Ext 243, (h) **804-447-3463**

ST PETER'S COLLEGE. Jersey City, NJ 07306. Pete Wevurski. **201-333-4400,** Ext 359, (h) **201-861-5751**

SALISBURY STATE COLLEGE. Salisbury, MD 21801. Gregory de F Islan. **301-546-3261.** (h) **301-742-8247**

SAMFORD UNIVERSITY. Birmingham, AL 35209. William A Nunnelley. **205-870-2921.** (h) **205-879-7237**

SAM HOUSTON STATE UNIVERSITY. Huntsville, TX 77340. Mike Davis. **713-295-6211,** Ext 2968, (h) **713-291-1477**

SAN DIEGO STATE UNIVERSITY. San Diego, CA 92182. John Maffei. **714-286-5547.** (h) **714-287-2404**

UNIVERSITY OF SAN DIEGO. San Diego, CA 92110. Paul Mendes. **714-291-6480,** Ext 357, (h) **714-291-4291**

SAN FRANCISCO STATE UNIVERSITY. San Francisco, CA 94132. Jenny Rae Rolen. **415-469-1579**

UNIVERSITY OF SAN FRANCISCO. San Francisco, CA 94117. Bill Fusco. **415-666-6161.** (h) **415-922-9367**

SAN JOSE STATE UNIVERSITY. San Jose, CA 95192. Jerry Walker. **408-277-3296.** (h) **415-968-0242**

UNIVERSITY OF SANTA CLARA. Santa Clara, CA 95053. Dick Degnon. **408-984-4063.** (h) **408-269-6912**

COLLEGE OF SANTA FE. Santa Fe, NM 87501. Leslie L Raschko. **505-982-6502.** (h) **505-471-6271**

SAVANNAH STATE COLLEGE. Savannah, GA 31404. Augustus George Howard. **912-356-2191.** (h) **912-236-5303**

SEATTLE UNIVERSITY. Seattle, WA 98122. Pat Hayes. **206-626-5305.** (h) **206-284-3971**

SETON HALL UNIVERSITY. South Orange, NJ 07079. Larry Keefe. **201-762-9000,** Ext 436, (h) **201-731-7026**

SHIPPENSBURG STATE COLLEGE. Shippensburg, PA 17257. John Alosi. **215-532-9121.** (h) **717-532-4435**

UNIVERSITY OF SOUTH ALABAMA. Mobile, AL 36688. Garry Summers. **205-460-7121.** (h) **205-666-4535**

SOUTH CAROLINA STATE COLLEGE. Orangeburg, SC 29117. William P Hamilton. **803-536-7060.** (h) **803-534-1814**

UNIVERSITY OF SOUTH CAROLINA. Columbia, SC 29208. Tom Price. **803-777-5204.** (h) **803-787-2395**

SOUTH DAKOTA SCHOOL OF MINES AND TECHNOLOGY. Rapid City, SD

57701. Jim Morrison. **605-394-2335.** (h) **605-342-1684**

SOUTH DAKOTA STATE UNIVERSITY. Brookings, SD 57006. Ron Lenz. **605-688-4623.** (h) **605-692-4600**

UNIVERSITY OF SOUTH DAKOTA. Springfield, SD 57062. Jim Hastings. **605-369-2681.** (h) **605-369-5570**

UNIVERSITY OF SOUTH DAKOTA. Vermillion, SD 57069. Mike Mahon. **605-677-5331.** (h) **605-624-8866**

UNIVERSITY OF SOUTH FLORIDA. Tampa, FL 33620. John Renneker. **813-974-2125.** (h) **813-576-7784**

SOUTHEAST MISSOURI STATE UNIVERSITY. Cape Girardeau, MO 63701. Wayne A Norton. **314-651-2256.** (h) **314-335-7143**

SOUTHEASTERN LOUISIANA UNIVERSITY. Hammond, LA 70402. Larry Hymel. **504-549-2244.** (h) **504-345-6442**

SOUTHEASTERN MASSACHUSETTS UNIVERSITY. North Dartmouth, MA 02747. William E Gathright. **617-997-9321,** Ext 577, (h) **617-998-3184**

SOUTHERN ARKANSAS UNIVERSITY. Magnolia, AR 71753. Dr Jack Harrington. **501-234-5120,** Ext 223, (h) **501-234-1688**

SOUTHERN CALIFORNIA COLLEGE. Costa Mesa, CA 92626. Fred Keener. **714-545-1473.** (h) **714-545-6268**

UNIVERSITY OF SOUTHERN CALIFORNIA. Los Angeles, CA 90007. Jim Perry. **213-746-2224.** (h) **213-797-2435**

UNIVERSITY OF SOUTHERN COLORADO. Pueblo, CO 81001. **303-549-2219**

SOUTHERN CONNECTICUT STATE COLLEGE. New Haven, CT 06515. Richard P Leddy. **203-397-2101,** Ext 223, (h) **203-288-0900**

SOUTHERN ILLINOIS UNIVERSITY. Carbondale, IL 62901. Tom Simons. **618-453-5311.** (h) **618-457-7302**

SOUTHERN ILLINOIS UNIVERSITY. Edwardsville, IL 62025. Alvin T Barnes, Jr. **618-692-3600.** (h) **618-931-3733**

SOUTHERN METHODIST UNIVERSITY. Dallas, TX 75275. Bob Condron. **214-692-2883.** (h) **214-424-2233**

UNIVERSITY OF SOUTHERN MISSISSIPPI. Hattiesburg, MS 39401. Ace Cleveland. **601-266-7324.** (h) **601-544-0927**

SOUTHERN OREGON STATE COLLEGE. Ashland, OR 97520. Mike Mendiburu. **503-482-6238.** (h) **503-482-5878**

SOUTHERN STATE COLLEGE. Magnolia, AR 71753. George M Henry. **501-234-5120,** Ext 223, (h) **501-234-5142**

SOUTHERN UNIVERSITY. Baton Rouge, LA 70813. Jess Peters. **504-771-3170.** (h) **504-357-6305**

SOUTHWEST MISSOURI STATE UNIVERSITY. Springfield, MO 65802. Mark Stillwell. **417-836-5139.** (h) **417-883-5452**

SOUTHWEST TEXAS STATE UNIVERSITY. San Marcos, TX 78666. Gordon McCullough. **512-245-2263.** (h) **512-392-9917**

UNIVERSITY OF SOUTHWESTERN LOUISIANA. Lafayette, LA 70504. George Foster. **318-233-0655.** (h) **318-981-1660**

SOUTHWESTERN OKLAHOMA STATE UNIVERSITY. Weatherford, OK 73096. Chuck Cole. **405-772-6611,** Ext 5218 or 5396, (h) **405-772-3562**

SPRINGFIELD COLLEGE. Springfield, MA 01109. Howard M Davis. **413-787-2380.** (h) **413-525-6117**

STANFORD UNIVERSITY. Stanford, CA 94305. Gary Cavalli. **415-497-4418.** (h) **415-497-4418.** Nancy Peterson, assistant, (h) **415-961-5679.** Mark Fitzpatrick, staff writer, (h) **415-967-2073**

STANISLAUS STATE COLLEGE. Turlock, CA 95380. Will Keener. **209-633-2131.** (h) **209-634-7937**

STEPHEN F AUSTIN STATE UNIVERSITY. Nacogdoches, TX 75961. Wayne King. **713-569-2606.** (h) **713-564-1470**

STONEHILL COLLEGE. North Easton, MA 02356. Bob O'Connor. **617-238-1081,** Ext 384, (h) **617-583-4165**

SUFFOLK UNIVERSITY. Boston, MA 02114. Lou Connelly. **617-723-4700.** (h) **617-665-0316**

SWARTHMORE COLLEGE. Swarthmore, PA 19081. Jonathan P Andrews. **215-544-7900,** Ext 426

SYRACUSE UNIVERSITY. Syracuse, NY 13210. Larry Kimball. **315-423-2608.** (h) **315-682-6002**

UNIVERSITY OF TAMPA. Tampa, FL 33606. Robert Shearer. **813-253-8861,** Ext 287

TAYLOR UNIVERSITY. Upland, IN 46989. Sheldon J Bassett. **317-998-2751,** Ext 372, (h) **317-998-2857**

TEMPLE UNIVERSITY. Philadelphia, PA 19122. Al Shrier. **215-787-7445.** (h) **215-561-5656.** John Everts, assistant, (h) **609-858-2824**

TENNESSEE TECHNOLOGICAL UNIVERSITY. Cookeville, TN 38501. J Mark Carlson. **615-528-3214.** (h) **615-528-5026**

UNIVERSITY OF TENNESSEE. Chattanooga, TN 37401. William O Patrick. **615-755-4148.** (h) **615-875-0842**

UNIVERSITY OF TENNESSEE. Knoxville, TN 37916. Haywood Harris. **615-974-3373.** (h) **615-584-3347**

UNIVERSITY OF TENNESSEE. Martin, TN 38238. Bob Carroll. **901-587-7504.** (h) **901-587-9683**

TEXAS A & I UNIVERSITY. Kingsville, TX 78363. Fred Nuesch. **512-595-3908.** (h) **512-592-6579**

TEXAS A & M UNIVERSITY. College Station, TX 77843. Spec Gammon. **713-845-5725.** (h) **713-846-5925**

TEXAS CHRISTIAN UNIVERSITY. Fort Worth, TX 76129. Jim Garner. **817-924-1181.** (h) **817-295-4346**

TEXAS SOUTHERN UNIVERSITY. Houston, TX 77004. Billy Morris. **713-527-7270.** (h) **713-524-2030**

TEXAS TECH UNIVERSITY. Lubbock, TX 79409. Ralph Carpenter. **806-742-3355.** (h) **806-797-2541**

UNIVERSITY OF TEXAS. Arlington, TX 76019. LeRoy Ramsey. **817-273-2263.** (h) **817-274-8780**

UNIVERSITY OF TEXAS. Austin, TX 78712. Jones Ramsey. **512-471-7437.** (h) **512-836-7383**

UNIVERSITY OF TEXAS. El Paso, TX 79968. Scott Binning. **915-747-5330.** (h) **915-584-5971**

UNIVERSITY OF TOLEDO. Toledo, OH 43606. Max E Gerber. **419-537-2675.** (h) **419-475-6959**

TOWSON STATE COLLEGE. Towson, MD 21204. Peter Schlehr. **301-321-2232.** (h) **301-838-9221**

TRENTON STATE COLLEGE. Trenton, NJ 08625. Tony Ianiero. **609-771-2368.** (h) **609-771-0599**

TRINITY COLLEGE. Hartford, CT 06106. Gerry La Plante. **203-527-3151,** Ext 217 or 370, (h) **203-527-3449**

TRI-STATE COLLEGE. Angola, IN 46703. B J Holloway. **219-665-3141,** Ext 256, (h) **219-665-2766**

TROY STATE UNIVERSITY. Troy, AL 36081. Gary Stogner. **205-566-5821.** (h) **205-566-5033**

TUFTS UNIVERSITY. Medford, MA 02155. Pete Kearin. **617-628-5000,** Ext 247, (h) **617-391-1379**

TULANE UNIVERSITY. New Orleans, LA 70118. M L Lagarde. **504-865-4394.** (h) **504-885-7967**

UNIVERSITY OF TULSA. Tulsa, OK 74104. Jeff Hurd. **918-939-6351,** Ext 395, (h) **918-622-7552**

TUSKEGEE INSTITUTE. Tuskegee Institute, AL 36088. Bernice Robertson. **205-727-8335.** (h) **205-264-5505**

US AIR FORCE ACADEMY. Air Force Academy, CO 80840. Hal Bateman. **303-472-2313.** (h) **303-475-0344**

US COAST GUARD ACADEMY. New London, CT 06320. Charlie Hennegan. **203-443-8463,** Ext 670, (h) **203-442-6869**

US MARINE CORPS ACADEMY. Quantico, VA 22134. Captain James L Pritchard. **703-640-2003.** (h) **703-221-7213**

US MERCHANT MARINE ACADEMY. Kings Point, NY 11024. Dennis T O'Donnell. **516-482-8200,** Ext 456

US MILITARY ACADEMY. West Point, NY 10996. Bob Kinney. **914-938-3303.** (h) **914-564-0696**

US NAVAL ACADEMY. Annapolis, MD 21402. Tom Bates. **301-268-6226.** (h) **301-647-5977**

UPPER IOWA UNIVERSITY. Fayette, IA 52142. Rosemary Nicholls. **319-425-3311,** Ext 231

UPSALA COLLEGE. East Orange, NJ 07019. Jacob Schaad, Jr. **201-266-7164.** (h) **201-427-4144**

URBANA COLLEGE. Urbana, OH 43078. Robert Cawley. **513-652-1301,** Ext 316

URSINUS COLLEGE. Collegeville, PA 19426. Michael T Cash. **215-489-4111,** Ext 251 or 282

UTAH STATE UNIVERSITY. Logan, UT 84322. Craig Hislop. **801-752-4100,** Ext 7434, (h) **801-752-7101**

UNIVERSITY OF UTAH. Salt Lake City, UT 84112. Bruce Woodbury. **801-581-3510.** (h) **801-531-0898**

UTICA COLLEGE. Utica, NY 13502. Nancy A Melsom. **315-792-3026.** (h) **315-792-3710**

VALDOSTA STATE COLLEGE. Valdosta, GA 31601. Steve Roberts. **912-247-3317.** (h) **912-244-6560**

VALPARAISO UNIVERSITY. Valparaiso, IN 46383. Gregory C Smith. **219-464-5232.** (h) **219-462-5945**

VANDERBILT UNIVERSITY. Nashville, TN 37215. Lew Harris. **615-322-4727**

UNIVERSITY OF VERMONT. Burlington, VT 05401. Richard P Whittier. **802-656-2005.** (h) **802-862-9412**

VILLANOVA UNIVERSITY. Villanova, PA 19085. Ted Wolff. **215-527-2100,** Ext 200, (h) **215-646-1582**

VIRGINIA COMMONWEALTH UNIVERSITY. Richmond, VA 23284. Earl McIntyre. **804-770-6773.** (h) **804-643-5657**

VIRGINIA MILITARY INSTITUTE. Lexington, VA 24450. Mike Strickler. **703-463-6251.** (h) **703-463-7555**

VIRGINIA STATE COLLEGE. Petersburg, VA 23803. Ronald Davis. **804-526-5111,** Ext 417, (h) **804-526-5111,** Ext 417

VIRGINIA POLYTECHNIC INSTITUTE. Blacksburg, VA 24061. Wendell Weisend. **703-951-6726.** (h) **703-552-5401**

UNIVERSITY OF VIRGINIA. Charlottesville, VA 22903. Barney Cooke. **804-924-3011.** (h) **804-293-6791**

WABASH COLLEGE. Crawfordsville, IN 47933. Wendy Tucker. **317-362-1400,** Ext 368, (h) **317-362-5355.** Mike Maloney. **317-362-1400,** Ext 368

WAKE FOREST UNIVERSITY. Winston Salem, NC 27109. Bruce Herman. **919-761-5640.** (h) **919-377-9141**

WASHBURN UNIVERSITY. Topeka, KS 66621. Bernie Richstatter. **903-295-6337**

WASHINGTON AND LEE UNIVERSITY. Lexington, VA 24450. Bill Schnier. **703-463-9111,** Ext 225, (h) **703-463-3600**

WASHINGTON COLLEGE. Chestertown, MD 21610. Mary U Skelton. **301-778-2800,** Ext 276, (h) **301-348-5459**

WASHINGTON STATE UNIVERSITY. Pullman, WA 99164. Rod Commons. **509-335-7758.** (h) **509-564-6271**

UNIVERSITY OF WASHINGTON. Seattle, WA 98105. Mike Wilson. **206-543-6441.** Chuck Niemi, assistant, **206-543-2230**

WAYNE STATE UNIVERSITY. Detroit, MI 48202. Paul Viglianti. **313-577-2150**

WESLEYAN UNIVERSITY. Middletown, CT 06457. Jack McCain. **203-347-9411,** Ext 584, (h) **203-346-5187**

WEST CHESTER STATE COLLEGE. West Chester, PA 19380. Nevin Morris. **215-436-3316.** (h) **215-383-4398**

WEST TEXAS STATE UNIVERSITY. Canyon, TX 79016. Jim Gustafson. **806-656-3701**

WEST VIRGINIA STATE COLLEGE. Institute, WV 25112. Robert W Craigo. **304-766-3163.** (h) **304-744-1081**

WEST VIRGINIA UNIVERSITY. Morgantown, WV 26505. Ron Steiner. **304-293-2821.** (h) **304-599-9096**

WESTERN CAROLINA UNIVERSITY. Cullowhee, NC 28723. Jim Rowell. **704-293-7171.** (h) **704-293-9687**

WESTERN CONNECTICUT STATE COLLEGE. Danbury, CT 06810. Alan Thomas. **203-792-1400,** Ext 212

WESTERN ILLINOIS UNIVERSITY. Macomb, IL 61455. Larry L Heimburger. **309-298-1993.** (h) **309-837-9134**

WESTERN KENTUCKY UNIVERSITY. Bowling Green, KY 42101. Ed Given. **502-745-4295.** (h) **502-842-4661**

WESTERN MICHIGAN UNIVERSITY. Kalamazoo, MI 49008. John Beatty. **616-383-1930.** (h) **616-349-8932**

WESTERN MONTANA COLLEGE. Dillon, MT 59725. Charles Stauffer. **406-683-2701.** (h) **406-683-2253**

WESTERN WASHINGTON STATE COLLEGE. Bellingham, WA 98225. Paul W Madison. **206-676-3105.** (h) **206-734-1804**

WESTMINSTER COLLEGE. New Wilmington, PA 16142. Charles K Henderson. **412-946-8761,** Ext 319 or 320, (h) **412-946-8565**

WHITTIER COLLEGE. Whittier, CA 90608. John Strey. **213-693-0771.** (h) **213-965-7792**

WHITWORTH COLLEGE. Spokane, WA 99251. Paul J Merkel. **509-489-3550,** Ext 301, (h) **509-487-5712**

WICHITA STATE UNIVERSITY. Wichita, KS 67208. Joe Yates. **316-689-3265.** (h) **316-685-9520**

WILLAMETTE UNIVERSITY. Salem, OR 97301. Bob Woodle. **503-370-6231.** (h) **503-362-1614**

WILLIAM AND MARY. Williamsburg, VA 23185. Bob Sheeran. **804-229-3111.** (h) **804-229-6550**

WILLIAMS COLLEGE. Williamstown, MA 01267. Ray Boyer. **413-597-2277.** (h) **413-499-2471**

WILMINGTON COLLEGE. Wilmington, OH 45177. Dick Kubik. **513-382-6661.** (h) **513-426-8460**

WINSTON-SALEM STATE UNIVERSITY. Winston-Salem, NC 27102. Charlie B Hauser. **919-725-3563,** Ext 76, (h) **919-722-8708**

UNIVERSITY OF WISCONSIN. Eau Claire, WI 54701. Tim Petermann. **715-836-2427.** (h) **715-834-8363**

UNIVERSITY OF WISCONSIN. Green Bay, WI 54302. Tim R Quigley. **414-465-2145.** (h) **414-336-1710**

UNIVERSITY OF WISCONSIN. La Crosse, WI 54601. Ken Dischler. **608-785-8493.** (h) **609-785-1653**

UNIVERSITY OF WISCONSIN. Madison, WI 53706. Jim Mott. **608-262-1811.** (h) **608-233-5009**

UNIVERSITY OF WISCONSIN. Milwaukee, WI 53201. Steve Rowbottom. **414-963-5150.** (h) **414-476-7078**

UNIVERSITY OF WISCONSIN. Oshkosh, WI 54901. John Wilusz. **414-424-0365.** (h) **414-233-2971**

UNIVERSITY OF WISCONSIN/STOUT. Menomonie, WI 54751. Charles L Buelow. **715-232-2425.** (h) **715-235-7255**

UNIVERSITY OF WISCONSIN. Superior, WI 54880. Mertz Mortorelli. **715-392-8101,** Ext 371, (h) **715-392-1802**

WITTENBERG UNIVERSITY. Springfield, OH 45501. Donald R Perkins. **513-327-6114.** (h) **513-323-6929**

WOOSTER, THE COLLEGE OF. Wooster, OH 44691. Keith R Gibson. **216-264-1234,** Ext 373, (h) **216-264-7773**

WORCESTER POLYTECHNIC IN-STITUTE. Worcester, MA 01609. Stephen Raczynski. **617-753-1411,** Ext 328, (h) **617-853-3803**

WORCESTER STATE COLLEGE. Worcester, MA 01602. Mack Hill. **617-752-7700,** Ext 179 or 288, (h) **617-757-2091**

WRIGHT STATE UNIVERSITY. Dayton, OH 45431. David Stahl. **513-873-2771.** (h) **513-296-1005**

UNIVERSITY OF WYOMING. Laramie, WY 82071. Kevin M McKinney. **307-766-2256.** (h) **307-742-3181**

XAVIER UNIVERSITY. Cincinnati, OH 45207. Daniel W Weber. **513-745-3416.** (h) **606-431-8219**

YALE UNIVERSITY. New Haven, CT 06520. Peter Easton. **203-436-1646.** (h) **203-248-2546.** Kim Scala, assistant

YOUNGSTOWN STATE UNIVERSITY. Youngstown, OH 44555. Dick Sapara. **216-746-1851.** (h) **216-843-8294**

COLLEGE FOOTBALL BOWL GAMES

ASTRO BLUE BONNETT BOWL. 1701 Chamber of Commerce Bldg, Houston, TX 77002

President. R. E. Hardister. **713-229-4681.** (h) **713-465-6796**

COTTON BOWL. PO Box 7185, Dallas, TX 75209

Information Director. Jim Brock. **214-528-5141.** (h) **214-691-0559**

FIESTA BOWL. 3410 E Van Buren, Phoenix, AZ 85008. **602-267-1477**

Executive Director. John Reid. (h) **602-949-8873**

Information Director. Bruce Skinner. (h) **602-838-6884**

GATOR BOWL ASSOCIATION. 11 E Forsyth, Jacksonville, FL 32202. **904-353-9072**

Executive Vice-President and General Manager. George R Olsen. (h) **904-249-4135**

Information Director. Ted Emery. (h) **904-249-2470**

LIBERTY BOWL. 4272 Gwynne Rd, Memphis, TN 38117

Executive Director. A F ("Bud") Dudley. **901-767-7700.** (h) **901-683-9501**

Information Director. T J Foley, Jr. **901-767-7700**

ORANGE BOWL FESTIVAL. Orange Bowl Committee, PO Box 350748, Miami, FL 33135. **305-642-1515**

Executive Director. Dan McNamara. (h) **305-667-7367**

Information Director. Ed Goss. (h) **305-221-3545**

PEACH BOWL. PO Box 1336, Atlanta, GA 30301. **404-525-2971**

Executive Director. George Crumbley

Information Director. Tommy Crumbley. (h) **404-294-7154**

ROSE BOWL. Pasadena Tournament of Roses Association, 391 S Orange Grove Blvd, Pasadena, CA 91105. **213-449-4100**

Information Director. Forest W ("Frosty") Foster. (h) **213-792-8037**

SENIOR BOWL. PO Box 2527, Mobile, AL 36622

Vice-President and General Manager. Rea Schuessler. **205-438-2276.** (h) **205-342-9045**

SUGAR BOWL. Suite 510, International Bldg, 611 Gravier St, New Orleans, LA 70130

Executive Director. Carl James. **504-523-4666.** (h) **504-831-7537**

SUN BOWL. PO Box 95, El Paso, TX 79941

Executive Director. Sonny Yates. **915-533-4416**

Information Director. Paul Brocker. **915-533-4416**

WEATHER

NATIONAL WEATHER SERVICE FIELD OFFICES BY STATES

ALABAMA. National Weather Service Forecast Office. Dannelly Field, RFD 2, Montgomery, 36108. **205-332-7460**

ALASKA. National Weather Service Forecast Office. Hill Bldg, Area 3-D, 632 6th Ave, Anchorage, 99501. **907-265-4701**

ARIZONA. National Weather Service Office. Rm 135, 2800 Sky Harbor Blvd, Phoenix, 85034. **602-261-4000**

ARKANSAS. National Weather Service Office. Adams Field, Little Rock, 72202. **501-771-0971**

CALIFORNIA. National Weather Service Office. 1641 Resources Bldg, 1416 9th St, Sacramento, 95814. **916-442-1468**

COLORADO. National Weather Service Forecast Office. 2520 Galena St, Aurora, 80010. **303-837-4393**

CONNECTICUT. National Weather Service Office. Bradley Field, Windsor Locks, 06096. **203-623-3888**

DELAWARE. National Weather Service Office. Airport Terminal Bldg, 151 N Dupont Pkwy, New Castle, 19720. **302-328-7596**

DISTRICT OF COLUMBIA. National Weather Service Forecast Office. Washington National Airport, Washington, DC 20001. **202-557-2648.** Recording Number: **703-920-3820.** Locator Number: **301-443-8910**

FLORIDA. National Weather Service Office. PO Box 8286, Coral Gables, 33124. **305-666-0413.** *National Hurricane Center, travel information office.* **305-665-0429**

GEORGIA. National Weather Service Forecast Office. Atlanta Airport, Atlanta, 30320. **404-762-0636**

HAWAII. National Weather Service Office. PO Box 3650, Honolulu, 96813. **808-845-2102**

IDAHO. National Weather Service Forecast Office. PO Box 4345, Boise, 83705. **208-384-9861**

ILLINOIS. National Weather Service Office. 214 Facilities Bldg, Capital Airport, Springfield, 62702. **217-522-8941**

INDIANA. National Weather Service Office. Weir Cook Municipal Airport, Indianapolis, 46241. **317-269-5444**

IOWA. National Weather Service Office. Municipal Airport, Des Moines, 50321. **515-284-4000**

KANSAS. National Weather Service Forecast Office. Municipal Airport, Topeka, 66616. **913-295-2630**

KENTUCKY. National Weather Service Office. PO Box 21256, Standiford Station, Louisville, 40221. **502-582-5230**

LOUISIANA. National Weather Service Forecast Office. 701 Loyola Ave, New Orleans, 70113. **504-525-8831**

MAINE. National Weather Service Office. Federal Bldg, 151 Forest Ave, Portland, 04101. **207-755-7781**

MARYLAND. National Weather Service Office. Friendship International Airport, Baltimore, 21240. **301-761-6036**

MASSACHUSETTS. National Weather Service Forecast Office. General Aviation Administration Bldg, Logan International Airport, Maverick St, East Boston, 02128. **617-567-4670**

MICHIGAN. National Weather Service Office. Capital City Airport, Lansing, 48906. **517-321-7604**

MINNESOTA. National Weather Service Forecast Office. Federal Aviation Bldg, 6301 34th Ave S, Minneapolis, 55450. **612-725-6090** (recording answers; then weatherman will pick up phone)

MISSISSIPPI. National Weather Service Office. PO Box 5779, Municipal Airport, Allen C Thompson Field, Jackson, 39208. **601-936-2189**

MISSOURI. National Weather Service Office. Route 1, Columbia, 65201. **314-443-1214**

MONTANA. National Weather Service Office. Box 1711, Helena, 59601. **406-449-5204**

NEBRASKA. National Weather Service Office. General Aviation Bldg, Municipal Airport, Lincoln, 68524. **402-432-6436**

NEVADA. National Weather Service Office. Reno Municipal Airport, 2601 E Plumb Ln, Reno, 89502. **702-784-5402**

NEW HAMPSHIRE. National Weather Service Office. Municipal Airport, Concord, 03301. **603-225-5191**

NEW JERSEY. National Weather Service Office. National Aviation Facilities Experimental Ctr, Atlantic City, 08405. **609-641-8200,** Ext 3475

NEW MEXICO. National Weather Service Forecast Office. PO Box 9025, Municipal Airport, Albuquerque, 87119. **505-243-0702**

NEW YORK. National Weather Service Office. Albany County Airport, Albany, 12211. **518-869-7891**

NORTH CAROLINA. National Weather Service Forecast Office. Box 627, Raleigh, 27602. **919-781-2710**

NORTH DAKOTA. National Weather Service Forecast Office. Box 1016, Bismarck, 58501. **701-223-4582**

OHIO. National Weather Service Office. Port Columbus International Airport, Columbus, 43219. **614-231-5212**

OKLAHOMA. National Weather Service Forecast Office. Will Rogers World Airport, 7100 Terminal Dr, Oklahoma City, 73159. **405-685-5759**

OREGON. National Weather Service Forecast Office. 5420 NE Marine Dr, Portland, 97218. **503-281-1911**

PENNSYLVANIA. National Weather Service Office. Harrisburg State Airport, New Cumberland, 17070. **717-782-4432** (recording answers; then weatherman will pick up phone)

PUERTO RICO. National Weather Service Forecast Office. Isla Verde International Airport, San Juan, 00913. **809-791-0376**

RHODE ISLAND. National Weather Service Office. TF Green Airport, Warwick, 02886. **401-737-5100**

SOUTH CAROLINA. National Weather Service Forecast Office. Columbia Metropolitan Airport, West Columbia, 29169. **803-794-2409**

SOUTH DAKOTA. National Weather Service Office. Administration Bldg, Foss Field, Sioux Falls, 57104. **605-336-3454**

TENNESSEE. National Weather Service Office. Berry Field, Nashville, 37217. **615-361-4887**

TEXAS. National Weather Service Office. Airport Administration Bldg, 3600 Manor Rd, Austin, 78723. **512-476-4993**

UTAH. National Weather Service Forecast Office. Rm 118, FAA-Weather Bureau Bldg, 175 North 23rd St West, Salt Lake City, 84116. **801-524-5133**

VERMONT. National Weather Service Office. Burlington International Airport, Burlington, 05401. **802-862-9883**

VIRGINIA. National Weather Service Office. Box A-63, Richmond, 23231. **804-222-7411**

WASHINGTON. National Weather Service Forecast Office. 7121 Federal Bldg, Seattle, 98104. **206-284-4300**

WEST VIRGINIA. National Weather Service Office. Kanawha Airport, Charleston, 25311. **304-342-7771**

WISCONSIN. National Weather Service Office. 3606 Stoughton Rd, Madison, 63704. **608-249-6645** (recording answers; then weatherman will pick up phone)

WYOMING. National Weather Service Forecast Office. Box 2238, Cheyenne, 82001. **307-635-9901** (recording answers; then weatherman will pick up phone)

NATIONAL WEATHER SERVICE REGIONAL OFFICES

EASTERN REGION OFFICE (Connecticut, Delaware, Maine, Maryland, Massachusetts, New Hampshire, New Jersey, New York, North Carolina, Ohio, Pennsylvania, Rhode Island, South Carolina, Vermont, Virginia, West Virginia). 585 Stewart Ave, Garden City, NY 11530. **516-222-2102**

SOUTHERN REGION OFFICE (Alabama, Arkansas, Florida, Georgia, Louisiana, Mississippi, New Mexico, Oklahoma, Tennessee, Texas).10E09 Federal Office Bldg, 819 Taylor St, Fort Worth, TX 76102. **817-334-2660**

CENTRAL REGION OFFICE (Colorado, Illinois, Indiana, Iowa, Kansas, Kentucky, Michigan, Minnesota, Missouri, Nebraska, North Dakota, South Dakota, Wisconsin, Wyoming). Rm 1836, 601 E 12th St, Kansas City, MO 64106. **816-374-5464**

WESTERN REGION OFFICE (Arizona, California, Idaho, Montana, Nevada, Oregon, Utah, Washington). Box 11188, Federal Bldg, 125 S State St, Salt Lake City, UT 84111. **801-524-5135 or 5122**

ALASKA REGION OFFICE (Alaska). 632 6th Ave, Anchorage, AK 99501. **907-272-5561**, Ext 4701, or **907-265-5701**

PACIFIC REGION OFFICE (Hawaii). PO Box 3650, Rm 516, 1149 Bethel St, Honolulu, HI 96813. **808-546-5680**

NATIONAL OCEANIC AND ATMOSPHERIC ADMINISTRATION

6010 Executive Blvd, Rockville, MD 20852. **301-443-8910**. Locator Numbers: **301-443-8910, 202-377-3521, 301-427-7616.** Communications support section (24-hour telephone): **301-763-8120**

ADMINISTRATOR. Richard A Frank. **202-377-3567**. (h) 3405 Lowell St NW, Washington, DC 20016. **202-966-3233**

NOAA PUBLIC AFFAIRS. 301-443-8243
Director. Stanley B Eames (h) 21708 Glendalough Rd, Gaithersburg, MD 20760. **301-460-3245**
Oceanic Programs. Roland D Paine
News. William J Brennan, chief
TV Services. Jeff Baker, chief
Radio Services. John Guinan, chief

NATIONAL OCEAN SURVEY PUBLIC AFFAIRS. Rockville, MD 20852. **301-443-8708.** *Contact.* John G Stringer

NATIONAL WEATHER SERVICE PUBLIC AFFAIRS. 8060 13th St, Silver Spring, MD 20910. **301-427-7622.** *Contact.* Edwin P Weigel
Director. George P Cressman. **301-427-7689.** (h) 9 Old State Ct, Rockville, MD 20852. **301-881-0131**

NATIONAL MARINE FISHERIES SERVICE PUBLIC AFFAIRS. 3300 Whitehaven St, Washington, DC 20235. **202-634-7281.** *Contact.* Gerald Hill

OFFICE OF SEA GRANT PUBLIC AFFAIRS. 3300 Whitehaven St, Washington, DC 20235. **202-634-4034.** *Contact.* James Elliot

COASTAL ZONE MANAGEMENT PUBLIC AFFAIRS. 2001 Wisconsin Ave, Washington, DC 20235. **202-634-6791.** *Contact.* James D Jacobsen

ENVIRONMENTAL RESEARCH LABORATORIES PUBLIC AFFAIRS. Boulder, CO 80302. **303-499-1000,** Ext 6286. *Contact.* Carl A Posey

Specialized NOAA and NWS Facilities

AIR RESOURCES LABORATORIES (Environmental Research Laboratories). Silver Spring, MD 20910. **301-427-7645.** Lester Machta, director

ARCTIC PROJECT OFFICE (Environmental Research Labortories). Fairbanks, AK 99701. **907-479-7371.** Gunter Weller, project manager

ATLANTIC OCEANOGRAPHIC AND METEROLOGICAL LABORATORIES (Environmental Research Labortories). 15 Rickenbacker Cswy, Virginia Key, Miami, FL 33149. **303-350-1300.** H Stewart, Jr, director

ATMOSPHERIC PHYSICS AND CHEMISTRY LABORATORY (Environmental Research Laboratories). Boulder, CO 80302. **303-499-1000,** Ext 6382

CENTER FOR CLIMATIC AND ENVIRONMENTAL ASSESSMENT (Environmental Data Service). 600 E Cherry St, Columbia, MO 65201. **314-443-3261.** Norton D Strommen, director

ENVIRONMENTAL RESEARCH LABORATORIES. Boulder, CO 80302. **303-499-1000,** Ext 6357. Wilmot N Hess, director

ENVIRONMENTAL SCIENCE INFORMATION CENTER (Environmental Data Service). Washington, DC 20235. **202-634-7399.** Joseph F Caponic, director

GREAT LAKES ENVIRONMENTAL RESEARCH LABORATORY (Environmental Research Laboratories). 2300 Washtenaw Ave, Ann Arbor, MI 48104. **313-994-5253.** Eugene J Aubert, director

NATIONAL CLIMATIC CENTER (Environmental Data Service). Federal Bldg, Asheville, NC 28801. **704-254-0236** Daniel B Mitchell, director

NATIONAL ENVIRONMENTAL SATELLITE SERVICE. Suitland, MD 20233. **301-763-7190.** David S Johnson, director

NATIONAL GEOPHYSICAL AND SOLAR TERRESTRIAL DATA CENTER (Environmental Data Service). Boulder, CO 80302. **303-499-1000,** Ext 6215. A H Shapley, director

NATIONAL HURRICANE AND EXPERIMENTAL METEOROLOGY LABORATORY (Environmental Research Laboratories). PO Box 248265, 1365 Memorial Dr, University of Miami Computing Center, Center Bldg, Coral Gables, FL 33124. **305-350-4150.** Noel E La Seur, director

NATIONAL METEOROLOGICAL CENTER. Camp Springs, MD 20233. **301-763-8016.** Frederick G Shuman, director
Long-Range Prediction Group. 301-763-8155. Donald L Gilman, chief
Forecast Division. 301-763-8097. James F O'Connor, deputy chief

NATIONAL OCEANOGRAPHIC DATA CENTER (Environmental Data Service). Washington, DC 20235. **202-634-7232.** Robert Ochinero, director

NATIONAL SEVERE STORMS FORE-CAST CENTER. Rm 1826, 601 E 12th St, Kansas City, MO 64106. **816-374-3428.** Allen D Pearson, director. Frederick P Ostby, deputy director, **816-374-3427**

NATIONAL SEVERE STORMS LABORA-TORY. 1313 Halley Cir, Norman, OK 73069. **405-329-4916.** Edwin Kessler, director

OUTER CONTINENTAL SHELF EN-VIRONMENTAL ASSESSMENT PRO-GRAM OFFICE (Environmental Research Laboratories). Boulder, CO 80302. **303-499-1000,** Ext 6562. Rudolf J Engelmann, director

PACIFIC MARINE ENVIRONMENTAL LABORATORY (Environmental Research Laboratories). 3711 15th Ave NE, Seattle, WA 98105. **206-422-0199.** John Apel, director

RESEARCH FACILITIES CENTER (Environmental Research Laboratories). Box 480197, 3400 NW 59th Ave, Miami, FL 33148. **305-350-2936.** C B Emmanuel, director

WEATHER MODIFICATION PROGRAM OFFICE (Environmental Research Laboratories). Boulder, CO 80302. **303-499-1000,** Ext 6455. Merlin C Williams, director

HIGH-VOLUME WEATHER INFORMATION NUMBERS

The National Weather Service provides the tapes for special high-volume telephone lines connected to tape-recorded weather messages in many cities, and it encourages out-of-town press to use such numbers, where available, rather than the National Weather Service numbers for the cities in question.

Alabama

BIRMINGHAM. 205-322-9222

MONTGOMERY. 205-269-0555

Alaska

ANCHORAGE. 907-936-2525, 2526, 2527, or 2528

California

FRESNO. 209-442-1212

LOS ANGELES. 213-554-1212

OAKLAND. 415-936-1212

SAN DIEGO. 714-289-1212

SAN FRANCISCO. 415-936-1212

WESTERN SONOMA COUNTY. 707-785-2311

District of Columbia

WASHINGTON. 202-936-1212

Connecticut

ALL CITIES. 203-936-1212

Florida

FORT MEYERS. 813-334-8111

ORLANDO. 305-422-1611

WEST PALM BEACH. 305-675-1212

WINTER PARK. 305-646-3131

Georgia

ALBANY. 912-883-4610

ATLANTA. 404-871-1212

CORNELIA. 404-778-2345

ROME. 404-295-1212

Illinois

BLOOMINGTON. 309-827-7111

CHICAGO. 312-936-1212

EL PASO. 309-527-4554

GALESBURG. 309-342-5300

HIGHLAND. 618-654-8711

HOOPESTON. 217-283-2345

JACKSONVILLE. 217-243-0111

JOLIET. 815-722-3456

QUINCY. 217-223-7750

RANTOUL. 217-893-1776

ST JACOB. 618-644-5533

TOLEDO. 217-849-2424

WONDER LAKE. 815-278-8123

Indiana

EVANSVILLE. 812-385-4801

INDIANAPOLIS. 317-222-2362

KOKOMO. 317-457-9211

PRINCETON. 812-385-4801

Iowa

DES MOINES. 515-244-4500

Kentucky

LEXINGTON. 606-293-1616

LOUISVILLE. 502-482-1212

OWENSBORO. 502-926-8121

Louisiana

HOUMA. 504-868-6670

MINDEN. 318-371-1776

LA ROSE. 504-693-8463

SHREVEPORT. 318-425-0211

Maryland

BALTIMORE. 301-936-1212

Massachusetts

BOSTON. 617-936-1212

Michigan

DETROIT. 313-932-1212

MUSKEGON. 616-726-1212

Mississippi

MERIDIAN. 601-693-5311

Missouri

COLUMBIA. 314-442-5171

ST LOUIS. 314-936-1212

Montana

KALISPELL. 406-755-2345

Nebraska

LINCOLN. 402-432-9211

New Jersey

NORTHERN CITIES. 201-936-1212

SOUTHERN CITIES. 609-936-1212

New York

BUFFALO. 716-643-1234

LONG ISLAND. 516-936-1212

NEW YORK. 212-936-1212

WESTCHESTER. 914-936-1212

North Carolina

RALEIGH. 919-829-1111

Ohio

CHILLICOTHE. 614-774-2151

CLEVELAND. 216-931-1212

COLUMBUS. 614-231-5212

TOLEDO. 219-931-1212

Pennsylvania

PHILADELPHIA. 215-936-1212

PITTSBURGH. 412-936-1212

South Carolina

BEAUFORT. 803-524-3333

COLUMBIA. 803-355-1212

HILTON HEAD. 803-785-8585

Tennessee

ATHENS. 615-745-0250

JACKSON. 901-423-4600

MEMPHIS. 521-521-1500

Virginia

HAMPTON. 804-936-1212

LYNCHBURG. 804-239-0344

NEWPORT NEWS. 804-936-1212

NORFOLK. 804-936-1212

RICHMOND. 804-936-1212

Washington

SEATTLE. 206-662-1111

Wisconsin

MILWAUKEE. 414-936-1212

RHINELANDER. 715-369-1010

PILOTS' WEATHER INFORMATION NUMBERS

The following is a list, by cities, areas, and major airports, of the Flight Service Station and National Weather Service telephone numbers that give detailed weather information to all pilots, and in some cases to others who call. Some of the numbers have automatic recordings, similar in operation to the standard Bell Telephone weather information service available in many cities, but much more detailed in content. Others give information directly to pilots after they describe their flight plans (time of departure, direction, destination, etc)

Alabama

ANNISTON. 205-831-2303

BIRMINGHAM. 205-595-6151;
205-595-2101 (automatic)

DOTHAN. 205-983-3551

HUNTSVILLE. 205-772-3521

MOBILE. 205-344-3610

MONTGOMERY. 205-832-7516

MUSCLE SHOALS. 205-383-6541;
205-381-2500 (automatic)

TUSCALOOSA 205-758-3628

Arizona

DOUGLAS. 602-364-8458

FLAGSTAFF. 602-774-2851; 602-774-1424;
602-774-0475

PHOENIX. 602-261-4295; (eastbound)
602-267-7239 (automatic); (westbound)
602-267-1181 (automatic)

PRESCOTT. 602-445-2160; (Grand Canyon)
602-638-2943; (Kingman) 602-753-5659

TUCSON. 602-792-6359; 602-898-8549
(automatic); (eastbound) 602-889-9588 (automatic); (westbound) 602-889-9638 (automatic)

WINSLOW. 602-289-3592

YUMA. 602-726-2601

Arkansas

EL DORADO. 501-863-5128

FAYETTEVILLE. 501-442-8277

FORT SMITH. 501-646-7885

HARRISON. 501-365-3433

JONESBORO. 501-935-3471

LITTLE ROCK. 501-376-0721;
501-835-7626

TEXARKANA. 501-774-4151

California

ARCATA. 707-839-1545

BAKERSFIELD. 805-399-1787

BISHOP. 714-873-3213

BLYTHE. 714-922-6151

CRESCENT CITY. 707-464-2514

DAGGETT. 714-254-2958; 714-254-2959

EUREKA. 707-442-2171

FRESNO. 209-251-8269

IMPERIAL. 714-352-8740

LANCASTER. 805-948-5385

LONG BEACH. 213-429-0337

LOS ANGELES INTERNATIONAL.
213-776-2727; (north) 213-466-4116; (south)
213-263-6776; (basin forecast)
213-776-8803 (automatic); (route forecast)
213-776-1640 (automatic)
Van Nuys. 213-781-5213 ;(basin forecast)
213-787-6580 (automatic); (route forecast)
213-787-4911 (automatic)
Burbank. 213-841-3904; (basin forecast)
213-843-6911 (automatic); (route forecast)
213-841-0034 (automatic)
Long Beach. 213-639-2618; 213-429-0337;
(basin forecast) 213-639-4200 (automatic);
(route forecast) 213-639-2647 (automatic)
Orange County. 714-542-3585; (basin forecast) 714-546-1610 (automatic); (route forecast) 714-546-0595 (automatic)
El Monte. 213-728-9957; (basin forecast)
213-442-3113 (automatic); (route forecast)
213-442-7800 (automatic)

MARYSVILLE (Yuba County)
916-742-8852

MONTAGUE (Siskiyou County)
916-459-3003

MOUNT SHASTA. 916-926-2227

NEEDLES. 714-326-3511

OAKLAND INTERNATIONAL.
415-562-7807; 415-569-0313 (automatic);
(East Bay) 415-638-5773; (South Bay)
415-295-6611
Condord. 415-933-8990
Fremont. 415-656-5093
Palo Alto. 415-326-2941
Redwood City. 415-364-2828 (automatic)
South San Francisco. 415-588-8623;
415-589-6711 (automatic)
San Jose. 408-248-8912; 408-263-0123 (au-
tomatic)
San Mateo. 415-342-8626

ONTARIO. 714-983-2618; 714-986-2006
(automatic)
Colton. 714-825-0749
Corona. 714-734-0280
El Monte. 714-728-9957

Hemet. 714-925-9230
Santa Ana. 714-836-0776

PASO ROBLES. 805-238-2448 (Paso Ro-
bles-San Luis Obispo-Arroyo Grande route)
805-544-6323

RED BLUFF. 916-527-0242

REDDING. 916-246-1556 (automatic)

SACRAMENTO. 916-428-6500;
916-428-4027 (automatic)

SALINAS. 408-422-4723

SAN DIEGO. 714-291-6381; 714-291-0750
(automatic)

SAN FRANCISCO. 415-588-8623;
415-589-6711 (automatic)

SANTA BARBARA. 805-967-2305

SANTA MARIA. 805-925-0246

SANTA ROSA (Sonoma County)
707-545-3724

STOCKTON. 209-982-4284

THERMAL. 714-399-5155; 714-345-1612

UKIAH. 707-462-8877

Colorado

AKRON. 303-345-2271

ALAMOSA. 303-589-2547

COLORADO SPRINGS. 303-837-3276,
303-634-1561

DENVER. 303-321-0031; 303-388-3653 (automatic)

DENVER-CHEYENNE-NORTH
PLATTE-AKRON AREA. 303-398-3967
(automatic)

DENVER-COLORADO SPRINGS-
PUEBLO-LA JUNTA AREA. 303-398-3967
(automatic)

DENVER-ALBUQUERQUE. 303-321-0564

DENVER-DALLAS. 303-321-0676

DENVER-KANSAS CITY. 303-398-5394
(automatic)

DENVER-PHOENIX. 303-321-0685

DENVER-SALT LAKE CITY. 303-398-5392

DENVER-BILLINGS ROUTE.
303-398-5393 (automatic)

DENVER-GRAND JUNCTION ROUTE.
303-398-5391 (automatic)

EAGLE. 303-328-6575

GRAND JUNCTION. 303-242-1801

LA JUNTA. 303-384-4311

PUEBLO. 303-948-3368

TRINIDAD. 303-846-2623

Connecticut

BRIDGEPORT. 203-378-2344

WINDSOR LOCKS. 203-623-2416

Delaware

WILMINGTON. 302-571-6360; (Millville)
302-652-3479

District of Columbia

BALTIMORE. (Local area) 301-766-0757
(automatic); (northerly routes) 301-768-6510
(automatic); (southerly routes) 301-768-6650
(automatic); (IFR flight plans only)
301-521-7333

WASHINGTON DULLES INTERNA-
TIONAL. (International flight briefing)
703-661-8526

WASHINGTON NATIONAL.
202-347-4040; (local area)
202-347-4950 (automatic); (northerly routes)
202-920-4000 (automatic); (southerly routes)
202-920-3603 (automatic); (IFR flight plans
only) 202-521-7333

Florida

APALACHICOLA. 904-653-3171

CRESTVIEW. 904-682-2795

DAYTONA BEACH. 904-252-3112;
904-253-6131

FORT LAUDERDALE LOCAL AREA.
305-463-2402 (automatic)

FORT MYERS. 813-936-1857; 813-332-5595

GAINESVILLE. 904-376-7515; 904-376-7516

JACKSONVILLE. 904-641-8333; 904-641-8055 (automatic)

KEY WEST INTERNATIONAL AIRPORT. 305-296-2042; 305-296-2741

LAKELAND. 813-682-4221

MELBOURNE. 305-723-6151; 305-783-7833; 305-269-2022

MIAMI. 305-233-2600
From Fort Lauderdale. 305-524-0233
From West Palm Beach. 305-655-3725

MIAMI LOCAL AREA. 305-233-2616 or 305-233-2617 (automatic)

MIAMI-BIMINI-NASSAU BAHAMAS ROUTE. 305-238-0694 or 305-238-0695 (automatic)

MIAMI-FORT MYERS-TAMPA ROUTE. 305-238-1107 or 305-238-1108 (automatic)

MIAMI-FREEPORT BAHAMAS ROUTE. 305-238-1496 (automatic)

MIAMI-KEY WEST ROUTE. 305-238-1435 (automatic)

MIAMI-ORLANDO ROUTE. 305-238-0821 or 305-238-0822 (automatic)

MIAMI-PALM BEACH-DAYTONA BEACH ROUTE. 305-238-0703 or 305-238-0704 (automatic)

ORLANDO. 305-894-0861

PENSACOLA. 904-438-4390; 904-432-3037; 904-453-2488

ST PETERSBURG. 813-531-1495; 813-531-1496; 813-531-1497; 813-531-8200 (automatic)

TALLAHASSEE. 904-576-3141; 904-576-6318; 904-575-1811

TAMPA. 813-229-1708; 813-879-3907

VERO BEACH. 305-562-2321; 305-562-2322; 305-464-1817; 305-287-8021

WEST PALM BEACH. 305-683-3032

Georgia

ALBANY. 912-435-6201

ALMA. 912-632-4422

ATHENS. 404-548-7318

ATLANTA. 404-691-2240; 404-691-0282; 404-755-6608 (automatic)

AUGUSTA. 404-793-6610

BRUNSWICK. 912-638-8641

COLUMBUS. 404-327-1153

MACON. 912-788-5064

ROME. 912-232-6801

SAVANNAH. 912-964-7730

VALDOSTA. 912-244-2361

Idaho

BOISE. 208-343-2525; 208-345-6163 or 208-345-6164 (automatic)

BURLEY. 208-678-8361; 208-678-8362

IDAHO FALLS. 208-522-9024

LEWISTOWN. 208-743-3841

POCATELLO. 208-233-0143

Illinois

CHICAGO. 312-626-8266; 312-584-5010; 312-686-2155; 312-584-5830 or 312-626-8629 (automatic)

DECATUR. 217-429-2311

MOLINE. 319-762-5528; (local vicinity) 309-762-7338 (automatic); (route forecast) 309-762-0394 (automatic); (IFR flight plans only) 309-762-7724

MOLINE (Davenport, IA). 319-326-1322

QUINCY. 217-885-3251

ROCKFORD. 815-965-6758

SPRINGFIELD. 217-575-3867

Indiana

EVANSVILLE. 812-426-2987

FORT WAYNE. 219-747-3139

INDIANAPOLIS. 317-244-3316; 317-247-2209 (automatic)

LAFAYETTE. 317-743-1802; 317-743-1803

SOUTH BEND. 219-232-5858

TERRE HAUTE. 812-232-0984

Iowa

AMES. (50 NM radius) 515-233-3651 (automatic); (easterly routes) 515-233-3668 (automatic); (westerly routes) 515-233-3670 (automatic)

BURLINGTON. 319-753-1626

CEDAR RAPIDS. 319-364-0237; (local vicinity) 319-364-0237 (automatic); (route forecast) 319-364-0598 (automatic); (IFR flight plans only) 319-365-1940

DAVENPORT. 319-326-1322

DES MOINES. 515-285-4640; (50 NM radius) 515-285-3280 (automatic); (easterly routes) 515-285-1793 (automatic); (westerly routes) 515-285-4793 (automatic)

DUBUQUE. 319-582-3171

IOWA CITY. 319-338-9852; (local vicinity) 319-354-4980 (automatic); (route forecast) 319-354-4981 (automatic)

MASON CITY. 515-423-7512

OTTUMWA. 515-682-3492

SIOUX CITY. 712-255-3944; (Omaha) 712-258-4593; (route forecast) 712-255-0620 (automatic); (50 NM radius) 712-255-0617 (automatic)

WATERLOO. 319-234-5711; 319-234-1602; (local vicinity) 319-232-8431 (automatic)

Kansas

CHANUTE. 316-431-4450

CONCORDIA. 913-243-3141

DODGE CITY. 316-225-0218; 316-225-0219

EMPORIA. 316-342-7475

GARDEN CITY. 316-275-9208

GOODLAND. 913-899-7154

HILL CITY. 913-674-5642

MANHATTAN. 913-539-4606

RUSSELL. 913-483-2165

SALINA. 913-825-0506; 913-825-0507

WICHITA. 316-942-4131; 316-942-3284 (automatic); (50 NM radius) 316-945-0234; (north) 316-945-0345; (south) 316-945-9381; (IFR flight plans only) 316-945-9326

Kentucky

BOWLING GREEN. 502-843-1152

ERLANGER. 606-371-6681

LONDON. 606-878-6122; 606-254-2743 (Lexington exchange); 606-679-6159 (Somerset exchange)

LOUISVILLE. 502-451-5344

PADUCAH. 502-442-6828

Louisiana

ALEXANDRIA. 318-445-3663

LAFAYETTE. 318-233-4952

LAKE CHARLES. 318-477-1784

MONROE. 318-322-3157

NEW ORLEANS. 504-241-2935; 504-241-2351 (automatic)

SHREVEPORT. (Downtown) 318-221-2211; (Greater Shreveport) 318-631-3558; 318-635-7769 (automatic)

Maine

AUGUSTA. 207-622-6491

BANGOR. 207-947-4028

CARIBOU. 207-489-3377

HOULTON. 207-532-2475

PORTLAND. 207-775-3071

Maryland

BALTIMORE. 301-761-1333; (Washington) 301-766-0757 (automatic); 301-766-3420

SALISBURY. 301-742-8719

Massachusetts

BOSTON. 617-223-6447; 617-567-7420; 617-569-1773 (automatic)

BOSTON AREA. 617-569-6520

BEVERLEY AREA. 617-927-7166

WORCESTER. 617-755-6083; 617-798-3815

Michigan

ALPENA. 517-354-8733

BATTLE CREEK. 616-962-7878

DETROIT. 313-372-3737; 313-729-2111; 313-372-1711 (automatic)

FLINT. 313-234-3987

GRAND RAPIDS. 616-456-2268; 616-949-2580 (automatic)

HOUGHTON. 906-482-0380

HOUGHTON LAKE. 517-366-5392

JACKSON. 517-782-0355

LANSING. 517-371-1150

MARQUETTE. 906-475-4197; 906-226-8642

PELLSTON. 616-539-8401

SAGINAW. 517-695-2511

SAULTE STE MARIE. 906-635-1551; 906-632-7751; (Traverse City) 906-635-1381

TRAVERSE CITY. 616-947-5056

YPSILANTI. 313-729-2111

Minnesota

ALEXANDRIA. 612-763-6593

DULUTH. 218-722-7982; 218-722-1737 (automatic)

HIBBING. 218-262-3826; 218-263-8981 (automatic)

INTERNATIONAL FALLS. 218-285-5151; 612-283-8425; 612-283-9471 (automatic)

MINNEAPOLIS-ST PAUL INTERNATIONAL AIRPORT (Wold-Chamberlain). 612-726-1130; (50 NM radius) 612-726-1104 (automatic)

REDWOOD FALLS. 507-637-8530

ROCHESTER. 507-288-7576

ST CLOUD. 612-253-2540

Mississippi

GREENWOOD. 601-453-2631

JACKSON. 601-939-5212; 601-939-2046 (automatic)

MCCOMB. 601-684-7070

MERIDIAN. 601-482-5556; 601-483-5270

Missouri

CAPE GIRARDEAU. 314-334-2803

COLUMBIA. 314-449-3836

JOPLIN. 417-623-6868

KANSAS CITY. 816-471-7565; (IFR flight plans only) 816-471-7570; (50 NM radius) 816-421-3288 (automatic); (easterly) 816-421-7747 (automatic); (southerly) 816-421-7492 (automatic)

ST LOUIS. 314-532-1011; (50 NM radius) 314-532-1238; (St Louis metropolitan area) 314-576-1108 (automatic); (Alton, IL) 618-465-0861 (automatic); (East St Louis, IL) 618-874-2670 (automatic); (St Charles, MO) 314-724-5577 (automatic)

(Easterly) (St Louis metropolitan area) 314-576-1503 (automatic); (Alton, IL) 618-465-0623 (automatic); (East St Louis, IL) 618-874-2713 (automatic); (St Charles, MO) 314-724-5897 (automatic)

(Westerly) (St Louis metropolitan area) 314-576-1556 (automatic); (East St Louis, IL) 618-974-2732 (automatic); (Alton, IL) 618-465-0529 (automatic); (St Charles, MO) 314-724-7534 (automatic)

SPRINGFIELD. 417-862-3588; (Springfield area) 417-831-1503 (automatic); (Joplin area) 417-624-1011 (automatic)

VICHY. 314-299-3911

Montana

BILLINGS. 406-259-4545

BOZEMAN. 406-388-4242

BUTTE. 406-494-3004

CUT BANK. 406-938-4522

DILLON. 406-683-5651

GLASGOW. 406-228-4042

GREAT FALLS. 406-761-7110

HAVRE. 406-265-6424

HELENA. 406-442-9902; 406-442-7312

KALISPELL. 406-756-4829

LEWISTOWN. 406-538-3639

LIVINGSTON. 406-222-2411

MILES CITY. 406-232-1503

MISSOULA. 406-542-2230

Nebraska

CHADRON. 308-432-3153

GRAND ISLAND. 308-382-5196

LINCOLN. 402-477-3929

NORTH PLATTE. 308-532-4034

OMAHA. 402-422-6866; (route forecast) 402-422-1052 (automatic); (50 NM radius) 402-422-1067 (automatic); (IFR flight plans only) 402-422-1063

SCOTTSBLUFF. 308-635-2615

SIDNEY. 308-254-3130

VALENTINE. 402-376-3442

Nevada

ELKO. 702-738-7222

ELY. 702-289-3051

LAS VEGAS. 702-736-1573; 702-736-1574; (Los Angeles route) 702-739-7863, 702-739-7864, or 702-739-7865 (automatic)

LOVELOCK. 702-273-2448

RENO. 702-784-5414; 702-786-7787 (automatic)

TONAPAH. 702-482-6421

WINNEMUCA. 702-623-2203

New Hampshire

CONCORD. 603-224-7474

LEBANON. 603-298-8360

New Jersey

ATLANTIC CITY. 609-645-2345

MILLVILLE. 609-825-1173; 609-825-1983; 609-327-1255; 609-825-2182 (automatic)
Dover. 302-653-8274; 302-674-8605 (automatic)
Hammonton. 609-561-6060; 609-561-7079; 609-561-6599 (automatic)
Pitman. 609-589-2596; 609-489-8096; 609-489-5551 (automatic)
South Jersey shore. 609-399-8096; 609-398-1162; 609-398-6565 (automatic)
Toms River. 201-341-8220; 201-341-1409 (automatic)
Wilmington. 302-652-3470; 302-652-3088; 302-652-1653 (automatic)

NEWARK. 201-624-7272 (automatic)

TETERBORO. 201-288-9092; 212-898-5256; 914-352-4535; 201-288-6436; 201-288-6437
Newark. 201-624-5352; 201-624-5353
Caldwell. 201-266-7077
Morristown. 201-539-1581

New Mexico

ALBUQUERQUE. 505-243-7831; 505-242-2661 (automatic)

CARLSBAD. 505-885-2042

CLAYTON. 505-374-9511

DEMING. 505-546-2726

FARMINGTON. 505-327-4479

GALLUP. 505-722-4308

HOBBS. 505-393-6143

LAS VEGAS. 505-425-7411

ROSWELL. 505-347-5400

TRUTH OR CONSEQUENCES. 505-894-3277

TUCUMCARI. 505-461-2900

New York

ALBANY. 518-869-9225; 518-869-2037 (automatic); 518-869-9173

BINGHAMTON. 607-797-0784

BUFFALO. 716-842-5790; 716-632-5042 (automatic)

ELMIRA. 607-739-2471

GLENS FALLS. 518-793-2593

MASSENA. 315-769-2033

NEW YORK. 212-639-5690; 212-476-5950 (automatic)
LaGuardia. 212-898-2323; 212-898-2339; (from New York City) 212-656-5898; 212-656-5899; 212-995-8657; 212-995-8658; (from Westchester County) 914-723-3862; 914-723-3863; 914-723-4330; 914-723-4331; 914-723-4332; 914-723-4333; 914-723-4334; (from Long Island) 516-737-3617; 516-737-3618; 516-737-3535; 516-737-3536; 516-737-3537; 516-737-3595; 516-737-3596; (International Flight Planning: from New York City) 212-656-8558; 212-995-8659

LOCAL NEW YORK CITY AREA (New York City) 212-476-8800 (automatic); (northern New Jersey) 201-288-3100 (automatic). Routes northbound: (from New York City) 212-426-8300 (automatic); (from northern New Jersey) 201-288-5570 (automatic). Routes south and westbound: (from New York City) 212-426-9300 (automatic); (from northern New Jersey) 201-288-9250 (automatic)

POUGHKEEPSIE. 914-462-3400

ROCHESTER. 716-325-3320; 716-328-7361

ROCKLAND COUNTY. 914-352-2569

SYRACUSE. 315-455-1214

UTICA. 315-736-9023; (from Rome) 315-337-0115; (from Syracuse) 315-475-9904; 315-475-9905; (other) 315-962-5667

WATERTOWN. 315-639-6228

North Carolina

ASHEVILLE. 704-684-3787

CAPE HATTERAS. 919-995-2321

CHARLOTTE. 704-399-6000

ELIZABETH CITY (Coast Guard Air Station). 919-338-3808

GREENSBORO. 919-294-4800; 919-668-0789

HICKORY. 704-328-5656

NEW BERN. 919-638-3133

RALEIGH-DURHAM. 919-755-4306; 919-596-2446; (local area) 919-787-3665 (automatic); (northeast) 919-787-3681 (automatic); (northwest) 919-787-3683 (automatic); (southwest) 919-787-3675 (automatic); (south) 919-787-3668; 919-781-1510; (Greensboro) 919-273-8660

ROCKY MOUNT. 919-442-7171

WILMINGTON. 919-763-8331

WINSTON-SALEM. 919-725-6882

North Dakota

BISMARCK. 701-223-0920

DICKINSON. 701-225-2989

FARGO. 701-232-1584

GRAND FORKS. 701-772-7201

JAMESTOWN. 701-252-4350

MINOT. 701-852-3696

WILLISTON. 701-572-3198

Ohio

AKRON. 216-896-2246

CINCINNATI. 513-871-8220; 513-871-6200 (automatic); 606-371-6681

CLEVELAND. 216-267-3700; (50 NM radius) 216-579-0220 (automatic); (Akron 50 NM radius) 216-535-6153 (automatic)

COLUMBUS. 614-237-7461; 419-526-2132; 614-236-8555 (automatic)

DAYTON. 513-898-7033

FINDLAY. 419-422-6176; 419-422-6177

MANSFIELD. 419-526-2132; 419-522-7070; 419-526-5920 (automatic)

SPRINGFIELD. 513-324-2942

TOLEDO. 419-865-8859

YOUNGSTOWN. 216-539-5121; 216-759-2117; 216-856-1993; 216-545-1755

ZANESVILLE. 614-453-0649

Oklahoma

GAGE. 405-923-2601

HOBART. 405-726-5234

MCALESTER. 918-423-4091

OKLAHOMA CITY. 405-787-9323; 405-787-9060 or 405-787-9061 (automatic)

PONCA CITY. 405-765-5485

TULSA. 918-836-3505; 918-336-5833; 918-683-1204; 918-835-2364 (automatic)

Oregon

ASTORIA. 503-861-2722

BAKER. 503-523-2961

EUGENE. 503-687-6407

KLAMATH FALLS. 503-882-4641; 503-882-9474

MEDFORD. 503-779-3241; 503-773-1525

NORTH BEND. 503-756-4916

PORTLAND. 503-222-1699; 503-648-2111

REDMOND. 503-548-2522

SALEM. 503-363-9829

THE DALLES. 509-767-1187

Pennsylvania

ALLENTOWN. 215-264-1944

ALTOONA. 814-793-3113

BRADFORD. 814-362-8860

CARLISLE. 717-243-2700

DU BOIS. 814-328-2231

ERIE. 814-833-1345; 814-838-1010

GETTYSBURG. 717-334-4833; 717-334-7818

HARRISBURG. 717-782-3777; 717-774-1818; 717-774-3626; 717-774-3626 (automatic)

JOHNSTOWN. 814-535-3088

LANCASTER. 717-394-4955; 717-394-8337

LE BANON. 717-273-9076; 717-273-9076

PHILADELPHIA. 215-673-8020; 215-677-9070 or 609-883-3882 (automatic); 215-673-5657; 609-771-0363

PHILIPSBURG. 814-342-0830

PITTSBURGH. 412-462-3707; 412-573-9166; 412-644-2887; 412-462-5558 or 412-462-5559 (automatic); (Butler) 412-282-2974; 412-282-6520 (automatic); (Hookstown) 412-462-5585 (automatic); 412-462-5586 (automatic); 412-462-5307 (automatic); 412-462-5334 (automatic)

READING. 717-376-5865; 717-376-1358

SHIPPENSBURG. 717-532-3898

WILKES-BARRE. 717-346-4512; 717-982-4301; 717-457-5650

WILLIAMSPORT. 717-368-8547; 717-286-2770; 717-368-1866

YORK. 717-854-2924; 717-854-0406; 717-782-3775

Puerto Rico

SAN JUAN. 791-1780; 791-3490

Rhode Island

PROVIDENCE. 401-737-3171

South Carolina

ANDERSON. 803-224-2573; 803-224-2574

CHARLESTON. 803-747-5293; 803-747-5778 (automatic)

COLUMBIA. 803-794-2593; 803-796-8710 or 803-796-8711 (automatic)

FLORENCE. 803-662-8197; 803-662-5382

GREER. 803-271-8930

MYRTLE BEACH. 803-272-6903

South Dakota

ABERDEEN. 605-225-5264

HURON. 605-352-3806

PIERRE. 605-224-5894

RAPID CITY. 605-342-2302

WATERTOWN. 605-886-4581

Tennessee

CHATTANOOGA. 615-892-6302

CROSSVILLE. 615-484-9541

DYERSBURG. 901-285-4842

JACKSON. 901-423-0252

KNOXVILLE. 615-577-6651; 615-983-4000

MEMPHIS. 901-398-9268; 901-398-2347 (automatic); (North-Cape Girardeau-St Louis) 901-398-6125 (automatic); (east—Nashville) 901-398-6959 (automatic); (south—Jackson) 901-398-4252 (automatic); (west—Little Rock) 901-398-7071 (automatic); (IFR flight plans only) 901-398-6235; 901-398-6236

NASHVILLE. 615-749-5378; 615-361-0737 (automatic); (northeast) 615-367-2990 615-367-2991 (automatic); (southeast) 615-367-0808 or 615-367-0809 (automatic); (southwest) 615-367-1040 or 615-367-1041 (automatic); (northwest) 615-367-2857 or 615-367-2858 (automatic); (from Nashville) 615-367-2757 or 615-367-2758 (automatic)

TRI-CITY. 615-323-6204

Texas

ABILENE. 915-677-4336; 915-677-4337

ALICE. 512-664-0184

AMARILLO. 806-335-1608

AUSTIN. 512-478-6695

BEAUMONT. 713-722-0288; 713-722-7011

BROWNSVILLE. 512-546-6421; 512-425-1115; 512-542-8231

CHILDRESS. 817-937-3892

COLLEGE STATION. 713-846-8784; 713-846-8785

CORPUS CHRISTI. 512-888-8061

COTULLA. 512-879-2417

DALHART. 806-249-2006

DALLAS. 214-350-3311; 214-357-4343 or 214-357-4344 (automatic)

DEL RIO. 512-775-2115

EL PASO. 915-778-6448; 915-778-4487 (automatic)

FORT WORTH. 817-624-8471; 817-626-3071 or 817-626-3072 (automatic)

GALVESTON. 713-744-3255; 713-765-5448

GREGG COUNTY. 214-643-2266; 214-443-2267

HOUSTON. 713-644-8361; (local area) 713-641-3000 (automatic); (Houston-New Orleans) 713-641-3001 (automatic); (Houston-Dallas) 713-641-3002 (automatic); (Houston-Midland) 713-641-3003 (automatic)

LUBBOCK. 806-762-0511

LUFKIN. 713-634-3319

MCALLEN. 512-682-2878; 512-682-2879

MIDLAND. 915-563-2611

MINERAL WELLS. 817-325-5922

PALACIOS. 512-972-2559

PORT ARTHUR. 713-722-0476

SAN ANGELO. 915-944-3322

SAN ANTONIO. 512-826-9561

TYLER. 214-597-8051

VICTORIA. 512-575-3182

WACO. 817-754-3126

WICHITA FALLS. 817-855-5574

WINK. 915-527-3351

Utah

BRYCE CANYON. 801-834-5331

CEDAR CITY. 801-586-3806

SALT LAKE CITY. 801-524-5183; 801-364-5571 (automatic)

SALT LAKE CITY TO BOISE AND IDAHO FALLS ROUTES. 801-531-8554 (automatic)

SALT LAKE CITY TO DENVER ROUTES. 801-531-8445 (automatic)

SALT LAKE CITY TO LAS VEGAS AND RENO ROUTES. 801-531-8523 (automatic)

Vermont

BURLINGTON. 802-862-9883

MONTPELIER. 802-223-2376

Virginia

BRISTOL. 615-323-8242

CHARLOTTESVILLE. 804-973-4316

DANVILLE. 804-793-1163

LYNCHBURG. 804-239-5811

NEWPORT NEWS. 804-877-0209

NORFOLK. 804-855-3029

RICHMOND. 804-222-7203; 800-572-6000; 800-572-6001

ROANOKE. 703-362-1668

Washington

BELLINGHAM. 206-734-6400

EPHRATA. 509-754-2361

HOQUIAM. 206-533-3432

OLYMPIA. 206-357-6169

SEATTLE. 206-767-2726; 206-767-4002 (automatic)

SPOKANE. 509-456-4546

TOLEDO. 206-864-2371

WALLA WALLA. 509-529-1413

WENATCHEE. 509-884-6656

YAKIMA. 509-453-8975

West Virginia

BECKLEY. 304-252-3171

BLUEFIELD. 304-325-6521

CHARLESTON. 304-343-8919

ELKINS. 304-636-0810

HUNTINGTON. 304-453-3951

MARTINSBURG. 304-263-9353

MORGANTOWN. 304-292-9489

PARKERSBURG. 304-485-6421

WHEELING. 304-277-1252

Wisconsin

EAU CLARE. 715-835-2269

GREEN BAY. 414-494-7417

LACROSSE. 608-784-3170; 507-452-1046

LONE ROCK. 608-583-2661

MILWAUKEE. 414-481-1060; 414-744-7810 (automatic)

WAUSAU. 715-845-7396

Wyoming

CASPER. 307-235-1555

CHEYENNE. 307-638-6437

DENVER. 307-635-4187

LANDER. 307-332-2718

LARAMIE. 307-745-4845

RAWLINS. 307-324-3241

ROCK SPRINGS. 307-362-2121

SHERIDAN. 307-674-7426

WORLAND. 307-347-4122

WORLD

MAJOR INTERNATIONAL ORGANIZATIONS

AMERICAN LATVIAN ASSOCIATION IN THE UNITED STATES, INC. 400 Hurley Ave, PO Box 432, Rockville, MD 20850. **301-340-1914.** Janis Riekstins, president, (h) **212-497-3766**

AMNESTY INTERNATIONAL. International Secretariat, 53 Theobald's Rd, London, England. Telephone: **01-404-5831.** A respected worldwide human rights campaigning organization; particularly interested in the treatment of political prisoners

ANTI-APARTHEID MOVEMENT. 89 Charlotte St, London W.1, England. Telephone: **01-580-5311.** Mike Terry, executive secretary

The organization campaigns "against British support for white minority regimes in Southern Africa and [for] support [of] Southern African liberation movements." It lobbies in parliament and publishes *Anti-Apartheid News.*

ANTI-SLAVERY SOCIETY FOR THE PROTECTION OF HUMAN RIGHTS. 60 Weymouth St, London, W1N 4DX, England. Telephone: **01-935-6498.** Colonel Patrick Montgomery, MC, secretary. A society whose purpose is "the eradication of slavery in all its forms; the abolition of all forms of forced labor resembling slavery;

protection and advancement of indigenous peoples"

THE ASIA FOUNDATION. 550 Kearny St, San Francisco, CA 94108. **415-982-4640.** Mailing address: PO Box 3223, San Francisco, CA 94119. Haydn Williams, president, Ext 222 or 223. Robert J Hill, director, communications and public relations, Ext 210. An organization that seeks to strengthen educational, civic, and cultural institutions in Asia by providing cash grants and books to Asian individuals and institutions

ASIAN DEVELOPMENT BANK. Roxas Blvd 2330, Metropolitan Manila, Philippines. Telephone: **80-72-51, 61,** or **71, 80-22-81,** or **80-26-61.** Toroicha Yoshida, president. P S Hariharan, chief, information office, **80-26-61.** An international development finance institution with 42 regional member countries

ASSEMBLY OF CAPTIVE EUROPEAN NATIONS. 29 W 57th St, New York, NY 10019. **212-751-3850.** Feliks Gadomski, secretary general. *European office.* 34 Rue de Wattignies, Paris 75012, France. Edmund Rehak, director. Represents, in the free world, the "aspirations for freedom" of nine Communist-dominated or controlled East European nations

ATLANTIC COUNCIL OF THE US. 1616 H St NW, Washington, DC 20006. **202-347-9353.** Francis O Wilcox, principal

official. A voluntary, nonpartisan organization that seeks to influence the policies of intergovernmental organizations, particularly NATO, in a private advisory capacity. *See also* SPECIAL INTERESTS.

BALTIC WORLD CONFERENCE. c/o President, Ilgvars Spilners, 119 Alleyne Dr, Pittsburgh, PA 15215. **412-781-2016**

CARE. Wrold Headquarters, 660 1st Ave, New York, NY 10016. **212-686-3110.** CARE Europe, Wesselstrasse 12, 53 Bonn, Germany, Telephone: **(02221) 639863.** CARE Canada, 1312 Bank St, Ottawa, Ont K1S 5Hz. Telephone: **613-521-7081.** *See also* SPECIAL INTERESTS.

CARNEGIE ENDOWMENT FOR INTERNATIONAL PEACE. 11 Dupont Cir, Washington, DC 20036. **202-797-6400.** Thomas L Hughes, president, **202-797-6411** (in New York: **212-557-0703**). Diane Bendahmane, assistant director, publications, **202-797-6425.** *New York office.* 345 E 46th St, New York, NY 10017. **212-557-0700.** Ruth Jett, assistant secretary, **212-557-0717**

COMMON MARKET. *See* The European Community.

COUNCIL OF ARAB ECONOMIC UNITY. *See* League of Arab States.

COUNCIL OF EUROPE. Avenue de l'Europe, 67-Strasbourg, Cedex, France. Telephone: **(88) 35-70-35.** *Paris office.* 55 Avenue Kiéber, 75784 Paris Cedex 16. Telephone: **704-38-65.** A public affairs, intergovernmental organization of Western European countries seeking to enhance unity and common purpose

COUNCIL FOR MUTUAL ECONOMIC ASSISTANCE. Kalinin Prospect 56, Moscow G-205, USSR. Telephone: **290-91-11** or **290-93-11.** N V Faddeyev, secretary. An organization of Eastern European countries and Russia

EURATOM (Communauté Européenne de l'énergie atomique). 200 Rue de la Loi, 1040 Brussels, Belgium. Telephone: **35-80-40**

EUROCONTROL. 72 Rue de la Loi, 1040 Brussels, Belgium. Telephone: **(02) 513-83-00.** The central air traffic control for Europe

THE EUROPEAN COMMUNITY (Common Market). 200 Rue de la Loi, 1040 Brussels, Belgium Telephone: **35-00-40.** Roy Jenkins, commission president.

The Common Market is technically a federation of three intergovernmental organizations: EURATOM, the European Economic Community, and the European Coal and Steel Community. Member nations are Belgium, Germany, Luxembourg, Denmark, Ireland, Netherlands, France, Italy, and England.

Delegation of the Commission of the European Communities. 2100 M St NW, Washington, DC 20037. **202-872-8350.** Ambassador Fernand Spaak, chief.

The delegation represents the Common Market in the US. Its press office is known as the European Community Information Service (see below).

European Community Information Service. 2100 M St NW, Washington, DC 20037. **202-872-8350.** Andrew Mulligan, chief, **202-872-8350** or **8375.** Night line: **202-244-3860.** John Shearer, deputy director, press and information. Walter Nicklin, editor, *European Community.* Webster Martin, news unit

Library and reference service. Ella Krucoff, Barbara Sloan, and Shannon Anderson, information specialist; Marie-Claude Carrere, library assistant

Scientific research and development. Luigi Massimo, first secretary

New York press and information service. 1 Dag Hammarskjold Plz, 245 E 47th St, New York, NY 10017. **212-371-3804.** Barbara

Jacob, head of service. Martin Haworth, press officer. Kerrie Buitrago, chief information specialist. Denise Sinclair, information specialist.

The ECIS has an active information program, issuing a weekly bulletin and many other publications. It maintains an extensive library on the Common Market.

EUROPEAN SPACE AGENCY. 8-10 Rue Mario Nikis, 75738, Paris, Cedex 15, France. Telephone: **567-5578.** *Washington office.* Suite 1404, 955 L'Enfant Plz N, SW, Washington, DC 20024. WJ Mellors, head of office, **202-488-4158**

European Space Research and Technology Centre. Domein weg, Noordwijk, Netherlands. Telephone: **(1719) 86555**

European Space Operations Centre. Robert Boschstrasse 5, Darmstadt, Germany. Telephone: **(6151) 8861**

Space Documentation Service. Casella Postale 64, Via Galileo Galilei, 00044 Frascati, Rome, Italy. Telephone: **(6) 942-2401**

FOOD AND AGRICULTURE ORGANIZATION OF THE UNITED NATIONS. *See* UNITED NATIONS.

INTER-AMERICAN DEFENSE BOARD. 2600 16th St, Washington, DC 20441. **202-387-7860.** Lieutenant General Gordon Sumner, Jr, USA, chairman, **202-387-1505.** Lieutenant Colonel Manuel J Baca, Jr, USAF, deputy secretary for liaison, protocol, and public relations

INTER-AMERICAN DEFENSE COLLEGE. Fort Lesley J McNair, P St between 3rd and 4th Sts, Washington, DC 20319. **202-693-8059**

INTER-AMERICAN DEVELOPMENT BANK (Banco Interamericano de Desarrollo). 808 17th St NW, Washington, DC 20577. **202-634-8000.** Antonio Ortiz Mena, president. Joseph U Hinshaw, associate chief, office of information, **202-634-8152.** Extends loans from funds provided by its member countries and raised in the capital markets for economic and social development projects in its Latin American member countries

INTER-AMERICAN TROPICAL TUNA COMMISSION. Headquarters office: Scripps Institution of Oceanography, La Jolla, CA 92037. **714-453-2820.** Dr James Joseph, director, investigations

INTERGOVERNMENTAL COMMITTEE FOR EUROPEAN MIGRATION. 16, Avenue Jean Trembley, PO Box 100,

Geneva, Switzerland. *Washington office.* 1346 Connecticut Ave, Washington, DC 20036. **202-785-1909.** *New York office.* 60 E 42nd St, New York, NY 10017. **212-697-4880.** John F Thomas, director. G Maselli, deputy director

INTERNATIONAL ATOMIC ENERGY AGENCY (Agence Internationale de l'Energie Atomique). Kärntner Ring 11, PO Box 590, A-1011, Vienna, Austria. Telephone: **52-45-11** or **25.** Dr Sigvard Eklund, director general. Georges Delcoigne, chief, public information section, division of external relations, Ext 292. Promotes the peaceful use of atomic energy and intergovernmental cooperation for the exchange of information and data

INTERNATIONAL BANK FOR RECONSTRUCTION AND DEVELOPMENT (World Bank). 1818 H St, Washington, DC 20433. **202-393-6360.** Robert S McNamara, president. John E Merriam, director, information and public affairs, **202-477-2468.** Mr Kyaw Htun, news coordinator, information and public affairs, **202-477-5728.** The first and the largest bank using member-country contributions and money raised in capital markets to aid developing countries

INTERNATIONAL BAR ASSOCIATION. 14 Waterloo Pl, London SW1Y 4AR, England. Telephone: **930-6432.** US headquarters: 180 E Post Rd, White Plains, NY. **914-428-1095.** A federation of national bar associations

INTERNATIONAL CHAMBER OF COMMERCE. 1212 Avenue of the Americas, New York, NY 10036. **212-582-4850.** *Geneva liaison office.* 57 Rue de Chêne, 1208 Geneva, Switzerland Telephone: **35-10-44**

INTERNATIONAL COMMISSION OF JURISTS. PO Box 120, 109 Rue de Chêne, 1224 Chêne-Bougeries, Geneva, Switzerland. Telephone: **(022) 49-35-45.** Niall MacDermot, secretary general. An influential organization that has as its purpose "the promotion of the rule of law and [the] legal protection of human rights in all parts of the world"

INTERNATIONAL COURT OF JUSTICE. *See* United Nations.

INTERNATIONAL CRIMINAL POLICE ORGANIZATION (INTERPOL). 26 Rue Armengaud, 92210 Saint-Cloud, France. Telephone: **603-82-30.** Jean Nepote, secretary-general. The intergovernmental society that provides cooperation and coordination between police agencies in more than 110 member countries

INTERNATIONAL FINANCE CORPORA-TION. 1818 H St, Washington, DC 20433. **202-393-6360.** *See* International Bank for Reconstruction and Development.

INTERNATIONAL JOINT COMMIS-SION, UNITED STATES AND CANADA. Rm 203, 1717 H St NW, Washington, DC 20440. **202-296-2142.** Henry P Smith III, chairman. Herman Gordon, public information officer

INTERNATIONAL LABOUR ORGANISA-TION. CH 1211, Geneva 22, Switzerland. Telephone: **32-62-00.** Francis Blanchard (France); director general. *Washington branch office.* 1750 New York Ave, Washington, DC 20006. **202-634-6335.** Edward B. Persons, director. *United Nations liaison office.* 345 E 46th St, New York, NY 10017. *Press contact.* Irvin S Lippe, public information officer, **212-697-0150** or **202-634-6335.** Night line: **215-297-5962**

The purpose of the organization is to raise the standard of life for workers. To this end it seeks to eliminate social inequity and to improve working conditions

INTERNATIONAL LEAGUE FOR HU-MAN RIGHTS. Suite 6F, 777 United Nations Plz, New York, NY 10017. **212-972-9554.** Roberta Cohen, executive director. An international league of affiliated national organizations in countries throughout the world working in the broad area of human rights

INTERNATIONAL MONETARY FUND. 700 19th St, Washington, DC 20431. **202-393-6362.** H Johannes Witteveen, managing director. Jay H Reid, director, information office

INTERNATIONAL PRESS TELECOM-MUNICATIONS COUNCIL. 184 Fleet St, London, England. Telephone: **405-2608.** Serves as a clearinghouse of information on technical developments of interest to the press in all countries

INTERNATIONAL TELECOMMUNICA-TIONS SATELLITE ORGANIZATION (INTELSAT). 490 L'Enfant Plz SW, Washington, DC 22204. **202-488-2300.** Santiago Astrain, director general, **202-488-2403.** Jose Alegrett, director, external relations, **202-488-2300.** An organization whose purpose is "the design, development, construction, establishment, operation, and maintenance of the space segment of the global commercial telecommunications satellite system"

INTERNATIONAL UNION FOR CON-SERVATION OF NATURE AND NA-TURAL RESOURCES. 1110 Morges, Switzerland. Telephone: **(021) 71-44-01.** Dr Duncan Poore, acting director general. Robert Allen, director, external affairs. An independent scientific organization of governments, government agencies, and private organizations devoted to conservation, particularly the preservation of endangered species

IUCN Commission on National Parks and Protected Areas. PO Box 19027, Washington, DC 20036. **202-523-5250.** Fred M Packard, secretary

LEAGUE OF ARAB STATES. Manmed Riod, Midan Al Tahrir, Cairo, Egypt. Telephone: **811960.** Includes the Council of Arab Economic Unity Ibrahimx Shukrallah, information director *US office.* 747 3rd Ave, New York, NY 10017. **212-838-8700**

LIGUE BELGE POUR LA DÉFENSE DES DROITS DE L'HOMME (Belgian League for the Defense of the Rights of Man). 1, Avenue de la Toison d'Or, 1060 Brussels, Belgium Telephone: **(02) 511-60-88.** Mrs Marc de Kock, president, **771-01-86**

LEAGUE OF RED CROSS SOCIETIES. 17 Chemin des Crêts, Petit-Saconnex, 1211 Geneva, Switzerland. Telephone: **345580.** A federation of Red Cross organizations throughout the world. *See also* POLICE AND EMERGENCY AGENCIES.

MIDDLE EAST INSTITUTE. 1761 N St NW, Washington, DC 20036. **202-785-1141.** L Dean Brown, president. *Press contact.* Dr Malcolm C Peck, assistant to president

The purpose of the institute is "to inform Americans about the Middle East" without taking a stand on any of the conflicts in the area. It also provides a business advisory service.

MINORITY RIGHTS GROUPS. 36 Craven St, London WCaN 5NG, England. Telephone: **(01) 930-6659.** Ben Whitaker, principal official. An antiracism research, public interest, and advocacy group whose principal activity is to issue detailed reports on the treatment of minorities

NATIONAL COMMITTEE ON US-CHINA RELATIONS. Suite 9B, 777 United Nations Plz, New York, NY 10017. **212-682-6848.** Arthur H Rosen, president. Jan Berris, program director

The committee is nonpartisan and nonideological. Its purpose is to carry out educa-tional, cultural, civic, and sports exchanges with Red China, and to increase public knowledge of the People's Republic.

NEAR EAST FOUNDATION. 54 E 64th St, New York, NY 10021. **212-838-3500.** David S Dodge, president. A voluntary agency concerned with providing agricultural technical assistance to developing countries in the Near East and Africa

NOBEL FOUNDATION. Sturbeatan 14, 11436 Stockholm, Sweden. Telephone: **630920.** Awards the Nobel prizes in physics, chemistry, physiology or medicine, and literature, and provides the money for the peace prize

Nobel Foundation. Drrammensveien 19, Oslo, Norway. Telephone: **443-3489.** Awards the Nobel peace prize

NORTH ATLANTIC TREATY ORGANI-ZATION (NATO). 1110 Brussels, Belgium. Telephone: **41-00-40.** An intergovernmental mutual defense and military body composed of Belgium, Canada, Denmark, England, France, Iceland, Italy, Luxembourg, The Netherlands, Norway, Portugal, and the US

NUCLEAR PUBLIC RELATIONS CON-TACT GROUP. Forum Italiano dell'Energia Nucleare, Via Paisello 26-28, 00198 Rome, Italy. Telephone: **868-291.** A group of representatives from major international organizations interested in the promotion of nuclear energy

ORGANIZATION OF AFRICAN UNITY (OAU). PO Box 3243, Addis Ababa, Ethiopia. Telephone: **47-480.** The intergovernmental organization representing most of black Africa

ORGANIZATION OF AMERICAN STATES. Pan American Union Bldg, 17th St and Constitution Ave NW, Washington, DC 20006. **202-331-1010.** *Department of Public Information.* Miquel Aranguren, deputy director; Wilson Velloso, senior editor; Stephen Banker, editor

Secretary-general. Ambassador Alejandro Orfila

Important Officials

Assistant Secretary-General. Jorge Luis Zelaya-Coronado

Executive Secretary for Education, Science, and Culture. Eduardo Gonzalez Reyes

Executive Secretary for Economic and Social Affairs. Annibal V Villela

Assistant Secretary for Management. L Ronald Scheman

Assistant Secretary for Development Cooperation. Santiago Meyer Picón

ORGANIZATION FOR ECONOMIC COOPERATION AND DEVELOPMENT. Chateau de la Muette, 2 Rue André-Pascal 75775, Paris, Cedex 16, France. Telephone: **524-8200.** *US center.* Suite 1207, 1750 Pennsylvania Ave, Washington, DC 20006. **202-298-8755**

ORGANIZATION OF THE PETROLEUM EXPORTING COUNTRIES (OPEC). Karl Lueger-Ring 10, 1010 Vienna 1, Austria. Telephone: **63-97-80.** An intergovernmental organization representing countries whose economies are based largely on oil revenues; acts as a cartel that sets worldwide prices, at least among its 11 members

OVERSEAS DEVELOPMENT COUNCIL. 1717 Massachusetts Ave NW, Washington, DC 20036. **202-234-8701.** James P Grant, president. Anthony Pearce-Batten, media relations.

The council was established to provide information and analysis for educators, journalists, public policy makers, and others on US relations with underdeveloped countries and on other issues involving the developing nations. It provides an annual assessment of these issues, containing analysis and statistical material. "Inquiries from journalists regarding the work of ODC are always welcome."

OXFAM. 274 Banbury Rd, Oxford, England. Telephone: **(0865) 56777.** An international relief and research organization concerned with major calamities, with special emphasis on famine and starvation

PACIFIC AREA TRAVEL ASSOCIATION. 288 Grant Ave, San Francisco, CA 94108. **415-986-4646.** Edward E Johnston, executive vice-president, **415-986-4545.** Robert W Warren, director, publicity and information. Promotes tourism in 31 countries, including Pacific islands

PAN AMERICAN HEALTH ORGANIZATION. 525 23rd St NW, Washington, DC 20037. **202-223-4700.** Dr Héctor R Acuña, director. César A Portocarrero, chief, public information office, **202-331-4402** or **4403**

The organization provides expertise, education, and direct assistance to public health projects throughout the Western Hemisphere, particularly in Latin America. Through its affiliate, the Pan American Sanitary Bureau (525 23rd St NW, Washington, DC 20037. **202-223-4700**), which serves as a regional office of the World Health Organization, the Pan-American organization is also affiliated with the United Nations.

PUBLICITY CENTRE OF THE INTERNATIONAL UNION OF RAILWAYS. 9 Via Marsala, 00185 Rome, Italy. Telephone: **461634**

RADIO FREE EUROPE/RADIO LIBERTY, INC. 1201 Connecticut Ave NW, Washington, DC 20036. **202-457-6900.** Sig Mickelson, president, **202-457-6910.** Gretchen S Brainerd, director, information services, **202-457-6920.** (h) **703-533-2876**

Programming headquarters. Oettingenstrasse 67, am Englischen Garten, 8000 Munich 22, Germany. Telephone: **21021.** *Press contact.* Robert Redlich, director, public affairs

New York program production center. 30 E 42nd St, New York, NY 10017. **212-867-5200** (There are also news and programming bureaus in London and Paris.)

RFE/RL is a nonprofit corporation that operates on congressional grants and under Presidential direction through appointments to the Board for International Broadcasting. Its stated purpose is to "encourage a constructive dialogue with the peoples of Eastern Europe and the Soviet Union by enhancing their knowledge of developments in the world at large and in their own countries." Though essentially a propoganda organ of the US government, RFE/RL is widely recognized in the West for its attempts to make balanced presentations in its broadcasts within, as it states, "the broad foreign policy objectives of the United States."

RED CROSS. *See* League of Red Cross Societies.

UNITED SCHOOLS INTERNATIONAL. USO House, Arya Samaj Rd, New Delhi, 5, India. Telephone: **52644.** An educational organization that encourages school exchange programs between countries, and seeks to increase knowledge about the United Nations

US-CHINA PEOPLES FRIENDSHIP ASSOCIATION. Suite 102, 2700 W 3rd St, Los Angeles, CA 90057. **213-388-9569.** Susan Dasso, executive secretary. *Press contact.* Frank S Pestana, chairman, **213-484-8140.** Night line: **213-388-9569.** Ann J Perry, tour coordinator, **213-388-9569.** A pro-Peking organization, the goal of which is "to build active and lasting friendship based on mutual understanding between the people of the United States and the people of [Red] China"

WAR RESISTERS' INTERNATIONAL. 3 Caledonian Rd, London, England. Telephone: **837-3860.** Seeks to promote pacifism

and specifically the right of people to conscientiously object to military service; maintains records on the status of conscientious objector and peace organizations in all nations.

WARSAW TREATY ORGANIZATION. Ministry of Defense, Warsaw, Poland. The Communist counterpart of NATO

WORLD BANK. *See* International Bank for Reconstruction and Development.

WORLD COUNCIL OF CHURCHES. 150 Route de Ferney, 1211 Geneva, 20, Switzerland. Telephone: **33-34-00.** *US office.* 475 Riverside Dr, New York, NY 10027. **212-870-2533**

WORLD COURT. *See* UNITED NATIONS: International Court of Justice.

WORLD FEDERATION OF FREE LATVIANS. 400 Hurley Ave, PO Box 432, Rockville, MD 20850. **301-340-1914.** Ilgvars Spilners, president, (h) **412-781-2016**

WORLD FUTURE SOCIETY. PO Box 30369, Bethesda, MD 20014. **202-656-8274**

WORLD INSTITUTE. 777 United Nations Plz, New York, NY 10017. **212-661-0884.** Night line: **212-383-5000.** Julius Stulman, president. A nonprofit educational and research organization that counsels government bodies and educational institutions on "the urgent problems facing mankind"

WORLD MEDICAL ASSOCIATION. 10 Columbus Cir, New York, NY 10019. **212-265-2190.** An educational and research organization seeking to promote and protect the medical profession worldwide

WORLD PEACE COUNCIL. Lönnrotinkatu 25 A-VI, 00180, Helsinki, Finland. Telephone: **649004**

WORLD WILDLIFE FUND. 1318 19th St NW, Washington, DC 20036. **202-466-2160.** Thomas E Lovejoy, program administrator

UNITED NATIONS

System of Organization

United Nations Plz, New York, NY 10017. **212-754-1234**

SECRETARY GENERAL. Kurt Waldheim

EXECUTIVE OFFICE OF THE SECRETARY-GENERAL.
Mr Rafeeuddin Ahmed, assistant secretary-general, executive assistant to the secretary-general

OFFICE OF PUBLIC INFORMATION.
212-754-7160. Genichi Akatani, Assistant Secretary-General. *Spokesman.* Francois Giulian

Director, Press and Publications Division. William C Powell

Director, Radio and Visual Services Division. Marcel Martin

Director, External Relations Division. Alexander Churlin

Director, Centre for Economic and Social Information. Leonardus Mazairac

Deputy Director, Press and Publications. Rudolf Stajduhar

UNITED NATIONS INFORMATION CENTRE.
2101 L St NW, Washington, DC 20037. 202-296-5370. Marcial Tamayo, director. A helpful and cooperative office that handles inquiries of a broad nature from press and public, and also maintains a public reference library for UN publications. (There are UN Information Centres in most member nations' capitals)

DEPARTMENT OF POLITICAL AND SECURITY COUNCIL AFFAIRS.
Arkady N Shevchenko, Under Secretary-General

Director, Security Council and Political Committees Division. Heinrich A Gleissner

Chief, Outer Space Affairs Division. Lubos Perek

Chief, Political Affairs Division. James S Sutterlin

Director, Centre against Apartheid. Enuga S Reddy

DEPARTMENT OF ECONOMIC AND SOCIAL AFFAIRS.
Gabriel van Laethem, Under Secretary-General

Director, Centre for Housing, Building, and Planning. Eliel P Mwaluko

Director, Division of Public Administration and Finance. Tse-chun Chang

Director, Population Division. Leon Tabah

Director, Centre for Natural Resources, Energy, and Transport. Vladimir Baum

Chief, Office for Ocean Economics and Technology. Jean-Pierre Levy

Director, Office for Science and Technology. Klaus Heinrich Standke

DEPARTMENT OF ADMINISTRATION AND MANAGEMENT.
George F Davidson, Under Secretary-General

UNITED NATIONS CENTRE FOR DISARMAMENT.
Rolf G Bjornerstedt, Assistant Secretary-General

UNITED NATIONS CENTRE ON TRANSNATIONAL CORPORATIONS.
Klaus Aksel Sahlgren, Assistant Secretary-General

UNITED NATIONS OFFICE AT GENEVA.
Palais des Nations, 1211 Geneva 10, Switzerland. Telephone: 34-60-11 or 31-02-11

Director General. Vittorio Winspeare Guicciardi, Under Secretary-General

Director, Information Service. Charles E Bourbonniere

Director, Division of Human Rights. Theodoor C van Boven

OFFICE OF THE COMMISSIONER FOR NAMIBIA.
Martti Ahtisaari, Assistant Secretary-General, commissioner

Important UN Agencies

ECONOMIC COMMISSION FOR EUROPE.
Palais des Nations, 1211 Geneva 10, Switzerland. Telephone: 34-60-11

Executive Secretary. Janez Stanovnik

Information Officer. Anthony Curnow

ECONOMIC AND SOCIAL COMMISSION FOR ASIA AND THE PACIFIC.
United Nations Bldg, Rajdamnern Ave, Bangkok, Thailand. Telephone: 2829161

Executive Secretary. Johan B P Maramis

Chief, Information Service. B Dorkenoo

ECONOMIC COMMISSION FOR LATIN AMERICA.
Edificio Naciones Unidas, Avenida Dag Hammarskjold, Vitacura, Santiago, Chile. Mailing address: Casilla 179-D, Santiago, Chile. Telephone: 485051, 485061, or 485071

Executive Secretary. Enrique V Iglesias

Chief, Information Service. Luis Carlos Sanchez

Regional Offices

Mexico. Mazaryk 29, Mexico, D F. Mailing address: Apartado Postal 6-718, Mexico 5, D F. Telephone: 250-12-78. Gert Rosenthal, director of office, 250-12-56

The Caribbean. Rm 312, Salvatori Bldg, 2 Frederick St, Port-of-Spain. Telephone: 62-35595. Silbourne St A Clarke, chief of office

Washington. Suite 1261, 1801 K St, Washington, DC 20006. 202-296-0822

Montevideo. Calle Soriano 791, 50 Piso, Montevideo, Uruguay. Telephone: 87473. Rene E Ortuno, chief of office

Bogota. Carrera 10(A) 70-48, Bogota, Colombia. Mailing address: Apartado Aereo 17603, Bogota, Colombia. Telephone: 492257. Alejandro Power, chief of office

Buenos Aires. Cerrito 264, 50 Piso, Buenos Aires, Argentina. Telephone: 356115. A Eric Calcagno, chief of office

ECONOMIC COMMISSION FOR AFRICA.
PO Box 3001, Addis Ababa, Ethiopia. Telephone: 44-72-00

Executive Secretary. Adebayo Adedeji

Chief, Information Service. Dube Kingsley

Acting Chief, Transport, Communications, and Tourism Division. W F Coleman

ECONOMIC COMMISSION FOR WESTERN ASIA.
Samer Hamza Bldg, Bir Hassan, Beirut, Lebanon. Telephone: 278803. Temporary address: Sakr Bldg, Jabal Hussein, Amman, Jordan. Temporary mailing address: PO Box 35099, Amman, Jordan. Temporary telephone: 63163-7

Executive Secretary. Mohamed Said Al-Attar

Chief, Information Service. Samir Sanbar

UNITED NATIONS RESEARCH INSTITUTE FOR SOCIAL DEVELOPMENT.
Palais des Nations, 1211 Geneva 10. Telephone: 34-22-00

Director. D V McGranahan

UNITED NATIONS SOCIAL DEFENCE RESEARCH INSTITUTE.
Via Giulia 52, 00186 Rome, Italy. Telephone: 65-53-01

OFFICE OF THE UNITED NATIONS DISASTER RELIEF COORDINATOR.
Palais des Nations, 1211 Geneva 10, Switzerland. Telephone: 31-02-11

Disaster Relief Coordinator. Faruk N Berkol, Under Secretary-General

New York liaison office. Rm LX-1256, United Nations, New York, NY 10017. 212-754-8120 or 8121. Henry Hunt McKee, chief

WORLD FOOD COUNCIL.
Via delle Terme, di Caracalla, Rome, Italy. Telephone: 5795

Executive Director. John A Hannah

Information Officer. S Apollonio

New York liaison office. Rm 2920A, United Nations, New York, NY 10017. 212-754-5693

UNITED NATIONS CONFERENCE ON THE LAW OF THE SEA. Bernardo Zuleta, Under Secretary-General

UNITED NATIONS CONFERENCE ON TRADE AND DEVELOPMENT. Palais des Nations, 1211 Geneva 10, Switzerland. Telephone: **34-60-11.** Gamani Corea, Secretary-General

Chief, Information Unit. Ramses Nassif

Director, Manufactures Division. Rangaswami Krishnamurti

Director, Shipping Division. Abid Al-Jadir

Chief, Transfer of Technology Division. Surendra Patel

Director, Division for Trade with Socialist Countries. Mikhail Davydov

New York office. Rm 927, United Nations, New York, NY 10017. **212-754-6893.** Gerassimos Arsenis, director

UNITED NATIONS INDUSTRIAL DE-VELOPMENT ORGANIZATION. Lerchenfelderstrasse 1, A-1070 Vienna, Austria. Mailing address: UNIDO, PO Box 707, A-1011 Vienna, Austria. Telephone: **4350-0**

Executive Director. Abd-El Rahman Khane

Director, Division of Conference Services, Public Information, and External Relations. Almamy Sylla

New York liaison office. Rm 2766, United Nations, New York, NY 10017. **212-754-5794.** Aron J Aizenstat, chief

UNITED NATIONS ENVIRONMENT PROGRAMME. PO Box 30552, Nairobi, Kenya. Telephone: **333930**

Executive Director. Mostafa K Tolba

Chief, Division of Communications and Public Information. A Matheson

Geneva liaison office. Palais des Nations, 1211 Geneva 10, Switzerland. Telephone: **342200. 985850** Petit Saconnex. Peter S Thacher, director

New York liaison office. 485 Lexington Ave, New York, NY 10017. **212-754-8139.** Noel Brown, chief

UNITED NATIONS CHILDREN'S FUND (UNICEF). 6th Floor, 866 United Nations Plz, New York, NY 10017. **212-754-1234**

Executive director. Henry R Labouisse, Under Secretary General

Director, Public Information Division. J C S Ling

Regional Directors

Ahmed Mostefaoui. Boite Postale 443, Abidjan Plateau, Ivory Coast. Telephone: **32-31-31**

Aida Gindy. PO Box 44145, Nairobi, Kenya. Telephone: **520671-2-3**

Sigurd Norberg. PO Box 1282, Lagos, Federated Republic of Nigeria. Telephone: **21926, 21743,** or **24969**

Carlot Martinez-Sotomayor. Casilla 13970, Santiago, Chile. Telephone: **289515, 289575,** or **289606**

Roberto Esguerra-Barry. PO Box 2-154, Bangkok, Thailand. Telephone: **282-3121** through **8**

T Glan Davies. House 11, Jor Bagh, New Delhi 110003, India. Telephone: **618371-75**

Deputy Regional Director, UNICEF/Area Representative, UNICEF. Rachid Koleilat, c/o UNDP, PO Box 565, Amman, Jordan. Telephone: **22169, 41202** through **6**

Director for Europe, UNICEF. Gordon Carter, Office For Europe, Palais des Nations, 1211 Geneva 10, Switzerland, Telephone: **34-60-11** or **31-02-11**

UNITED NATIONS DEVELOPMENT PROGRAMME. 1 United Nations Plz, New York, NY 10017. Telephone: **212-754-1234**

Administrator. Bradford Morse, Under Secretary-General

Director, Division of Information. Erskine Childers

Geneva office. 16 avenue Jean Trembley, Petit-Saconnex, Geneva, Switzerland. Leonce Bloch, director

WORLD FOOD PROGRAMME (a joint United Nations/FAO program). Via delle Terme, di Caracalla, Rome Italy. Telephone: **5797**

Executive Director. Thomas C M Robinson

Public Reiations Officer. D B Craig

OFFICE OF THE UNITED NATIONS HIGH COMMISSIONER FOR REF-UGEES. Palais des Nations, 1211 Geneva 10, Switzerland. Telephone: **34-60-11** or **31-02-11**

High Commissioner. Sadruddin Aga Khan

Information Officer. A G Shanley

New York office. Rm C.301-A, United Nations, New York, NY 10017. **212-754-7602.** V Dayal, regional representative

UNITED NATIONS RELIEF AND WORKS AGENCY FOR PALESTINE REFUGEES IN THE NEAR EAST. Museitbeh Quarter, Beirut, Lebanon. Telephone: **300986.** Temporary address: PO Box 484, Amman, Jordan. Temporary telephone: **44461** through **5.**

Commissioner-General. Sir John Rennie

Director, Public Information and Contributions Office. John F Defrates

Director, UNRWA Affairs, Jordan. J W Tanner

Director, UNRWA Affairs, Lebanon. R J Prevot

Director, UNRWA Affairs, Syrian Arab Republic. W af Sillen

Director, UNRWA Operations, Gaza. A M Ehrenstrom

Director, UNRWA Operations, West Bank. Georges Galipeau

Geneva office. Palais des Nations, 1211 Geneva 10, Switzerland. Telephone: **34-60-11** or **31-02-11.** Marcel Beroudiaux, UNRWA representative

New York office. Rm 1801A, United Nations, New York, NY 10017. **212-754-6420.** Jean van Wijk, director

UNITED NATIONS UNIVERSITY. 29th Floor, Toho Seimei Bldg, 15-1 Shibuya 2-chome, Shibuya-ku, Tokyo 150, Japan. Telephone: **(03) 499-2811**

Rector. James M Hester

New York liaison office. Rm DC-1177, United Nations, New York, NY 10017. **212-754-5610** or **5611.** Mrs Momoyo Ise, in charge of office

INTERNATIONAL COURT OF JUSTICE. Peace Palace, The Hague 2012, The Netherlands. Telephone: **070-392344**

President. Eduardo Kimenez de Arechaga

FOOD AND AGRICULTURE ORGANI-ZATION OF THE UNITED NATIONS. Via delle Terme di Caracalla, 00100 Rome, Italy. Telephone: **5797**

Director-General. Edouard Saouma

Agriculture Department. D F R Bommer, assistant director-general

Development Department. J F Yriart, assistant director-general

Economic and Social Policy Department. DJ Walton, officer-in-charge

Fisheries Department. H Watzinger, assistant director-general

Forestry Department. K F S King, assistant director-general

Department of General Affairs and Information. H W Mandefield, assistant director-general. C K Mackenzie, acting director, information division, P Savary, director, publications division

North American liaison office. 1776 F Street NW, Washington, DC 20437. **202-634-6215.** Don C Kimmel, director, **202-634-6200.** Peter Hendry, regional information advisor, **202-634-6215.** Jay J Levy, information officer, **202-634-6215.** (The liason office responds to general questions about the world agricultural situation. Black and white photograph service is available.)

Liason office with the United Nations. **212-754-6161, 6162** or **6164.** C H Weitz, representative

UNITED NATIONS EDUCATIONAL, SCIENTIFIC, AND CULTURAL ORGANIZATION. Headquarters: 7, Place de Fontenoy, F 75700 Paris, and 1, Rue Miollis, 75015 Paris. Telephone: **577-16-10**

Director-General. Amadou-Mahtar M'Bow

Assistant Director-General for Culture and Communication. Makaminan Makagiansar

Acting Director, Office of Public Information. Leon Davico, **677-16-10,** Ext 36, 37, or 38

Education Sector. Harold Foecke, deputy assistant director-general

Science Sector. Yri Novozhilov, deputy assistant director-general

Social Sciences Sector. Division for the Study of Development. Nicholas Bodart, Director Division of Human Rights and Peace. Karel Vasak, director

Culture and Communication Sector. Gerard Bolla, deputy assistant director-general

Liaison office with the United Nations. Rm 2201, United Nations, New York, NY 10017. **212-754-6112.** Andre Varchaver, director. *Press contact.* Yemi Lijadu

International Bureau of Education. Palais Wilson, Rue des Paquis, CH 1211 Geneva 13, Telephone: **31-37-35.** Leo Fernig, assistant director-general in charge

International Institute for Educational Planning. 9 Rue Eugene Delacroix, F 75016, Paris. Telephone: **504-28-22.** Hans Weiler, director

Regional offices

Africa (Science). PO Box 30592, Nairobi, Kenya. Telephone: **25861** or **25868.** Lawrence O Ibukun, head of office

Africa (Science). BP 3311, Dakar, Senegal. Telephone: **237-72** or **73.** M Bakari Kamian, director

Arab States (Science). 8, Abdel Rahman Fahmy St, Garden City, Cairo, Egypt. Telephone: **23036** or **25599.** M Chaudhuri Kemal Reheem, head of office

South and Central Asia (Science). 40 B, Lodhi Estate, New Delhi 5, India. Telephone: **618092** or **618093.** Viacheslav Podoinitsin, director

Southeast Asia (Science). United Nations Bldg, Jalan Thamrin 14, Tromolpos 273/JKT, Jakarta, Indonesia. Telephone: **51113.** James McDivitt, director

Asia (Education). "Darakarn Bldg," 920 Sukhumvit Rd, PO Box 1425, Bangkok 11, Thailand. Telephone: **910577, 910686, 910703,** or **910815.** Raja Roy Singh, director

Latin America and the Caribbean. Casilla 3187, Santiago de Chile, Chile. Telephone: **398289**

Latin America and the Caribbean (Culture). Apartado Postal 4158, Vedado, La Habana, Cuba. Telephone: **349-59, 353-22.** Cesar Fernandez Moreno, head of office

Latin America and the Caribbean (Science). Bulevar Artigas 1320-24, PO Box 859, Montevideo, Uruguay. Telephone: **411-807.** Gustavo Malek, head of office

WORLD HEALTH ORGANIZATION. Headquarters: 1211 Geneva 27, Switzerland. Telephone: **34-60-61**

Director-General. Dr Halfdan Mahler

Deputy Director-General. Dr Thomas Lambo

Director, Division of Public Information. F Tomiche

Liaison office with the United Nations. Rm 2235, United Nations, New York, NY 10017. **212-754-6138.** S A Malafatopoulos, director

International Agency for Research on Cancer. 150 Cours Albert Thomas, F-69372 Lyon, Cedex 2, France. Telephone: **(78) 75-81-81.** Dr J Higginson, director

INTERNATIONAL CIVIL AVIATION ORGANIZATION. PO Box 400, Succursale, Place de l'Aviation Internationale, 1000 Sherbrooke St W, Montreal, Que, Canada H3A 2R2.

President of the council. Assad Kotaite. **514-285-8011**

Director, Air Transport Bureau. R Bickley. **514-285-8055**

Chief, Public Information Office. E Sochor. **514-285-8220**

Regional offices

Europe. 3 bis, Villa Emile-Bergerat, 92200, Neuilly-sur-Seine, France. Telephone: **747-95-73.** J F Montgomerie, ICAO representative

Far East and Pacific. Sala Santitham, Rajadamnoen Avenue, Bangkok, Thailand. Telephone: **815366** or **815571.** P C Armour, ICAO representative

Middle East and Eastern Africa. 16 Hassan Sabri, Zamalek, Cairo, Egypt. Telephone: **801806** or **7,** or **803511.** G Wills, ICAO representative

North America and the Caribbean. 5th Floor, Avenida Thiers 251, Mexico 5, D F, Mexico.

Telephone: **5-31-93-78** or **9,** or **5-45-73-43.** R A Stewart, ICAO representative

South America. Edificio CORPAC, Zona Commercial, Aeropuerto Internacional Jorge Chavez, Lima (Callao), Peru. Telephone: **29-4523** or **5.** E Pol, ICAO representative

Africa. 15 Boulevard de la Republique, Dakar, Senegal. Telephone: **250-71.** A Merabet, acting ICAO representative

UNIVERSAL POSTAL UNION. Welpoststrasse 4, Berne, Switzerland. Telephone: **(031) 43-22-11**

Director-General. Mohamed Ibrahim Sobhi

Counsellor, Information and Documentation Section. Leon Koster

INTERNATIONAL TELECOMMUNICATION UNION. Palais des Nations, 1211 Geneva 10, Switzerland. Telephone: **34-60-21**

Secretary-General. Mohamed Mili

Chief, Information Division. Rene Fontaine

WORLD METEOROLOGICAL ORGANIZATION. 41 Avenue Giuseppe-Motta, Geneva, Switzerland. Mailing address: Case postale 5, 1211 Geneva 20, Switzerland. Telephone: **34-64-00.** D A Davies, Secretary-General

Administration, Conference, and Publications Department. Dr H Voss, director

Hydrology and Water Resources Department. Professor J Nemec, director

Meteorological Applications and Environment Department. N L Veranneman, director

Research and Development Department. N K Kljukin, director

World Weather Watch Department. G K Weiss, director. F Pimenta Alves, chief, Observing System Division.

WORLD INTELLECTUAL PROPERTY ORGANIZATION. 32 Chemin des Colombettes, Geneva, Switzerland. Telephone: **34-63-00**

Director General. Dr Arpad Bogsch

Copyright and Public Information Department. Claude Masouye, director

Liaison office with the United Nations. Rm U-404, 801 United Nations Plz, New York, NY 10017. **212-754-8647**

INTERNATIONAL TRADE CENTER. Palais des Nations, 1211 Geneva 10, Switzerland. Telephone: **34-60-11**

Director. Victor E Santiapillai

FOREIGN EMBASSIES IN THE US

All addresses are in Washington, DC.

AFGHANISTAN. *Chancery.* 2341 Wyoming Ave NW, 20008. **202-234-3770, 3771,** or **3772**
Charge d'Affairs ad Interim. Mohammed Siddiq Saljooque. **301-942-2742**

ALGERIA. *Chancery.* 2118 Kalorama Rd NW, 20008. **202-234-7247**
Ambassador. Abdelazig Maoui. **202-234-7246**

ARGENTINA. *Chancery.* 1600 New Hampshire Ave NW, 20009. **202-332-7100** through **7109**
Ambassador. Jorge A Aja Espil. **202-387-0247**

AUSTRALIA. *Chancery.* 1601 Massachusetts Ave NW, 20036. **202-797-3000**
Ambassador. Alan Philip Renouf
Information Secretary. Douglas J Cook. **202-797-3175**

AUSTRIA. *Chancery.* 2343 Massachusetts Ave NW, 20008. **202-483-4474**
Ambassador. Karl Herbert Schober
Press Counselor. Franz Cyrus. **202-965-1456**

BAHAMAS. *Chancery.* Suite 865, 600 New Hampshire Ave NW, 20037. **202-338-3940**
Ambassador. Livingston B Johnson. **301-654-2132**

BAHRAIN. *Chancery.* Suite 715, 2600 Virginia Ave NW, 20037. **202-965-4930** or **4931**
Ambassador. Abdulaziz Abdulrahman Buali. **202-244-0282**

BANGLADESH. *Chancery.* 3420 Massachusetts Ave NW, 20007. **202-337-6644, 6645,** or **6646**
Ambassador. Mustafizur Rahman Siddiqi. **301-320-5022**
Press Counselor. Mn syed Nuruddin. **703-527-7810**

BARBADOS. *Chancery.* 2144 Wyoming Ave NW, 20008. **202-387-7373, 7374,** or **3232**
Ambassador. Oliver H Jackman. **202-387-7374**

BELGIUM. *Chancery.* 3330 Garfield St NW, 20008. **202-333-6900**
Ambassador. Willy Van Cauwenberg. **202-338-2320**
Press Attache. Philippe Nieuwenhuys. **202-333-6900**

BENIN. *Chancery.* 2737 Cathedral Ave NW, 20008. **202-232-6656**
Ambassador. Thomas Setondji Boya. **301-299-2858**

BOLIVIA. *Chancery.* Suite 600, 1625 Massachusetts Ave NW, 20036. **202-483-4410, 4411,** or **4412**
Ambassador. Alberto Crespo. **202-244-7315**

BOTSWANA. *Chancery.* Suite 404, 4301 Connecticut Ave NW, 20008. **202-244-4990** or **4991**
Ambassador. Bias Mookodi. **202-686-9405**

BRAZIL. *Chancery.* 3006 Massachusetts Ave NW, 20008. **202-797-0100**
Ambassador. Joao Baptista Pinheiro
Press Attache. Guilherme N Correa de Araujo. **202-363-2825**

BULGARIA. *Chancery.* 2100 16th St NW, 10009. **202-387-7969**
Ambassador. Lubomir D Popov. **202-723-2560**

BURMA. *Chancery.* 2300 S St NW, 20008. **202-332-9044, 9045,** or **9046**
Ambassador. U Tin Lat. **202-234-6086**

BURUNDI. *Chancery.* 2717 Connecticut Ave NW, 20009. **202-387-4477, 4478, 4479,** or **4480**
Ambassador. Laurent Nzeyimana. **202-362-2565**

CAMEROON. *Chancery.* 2349 Massachusetts Ave NW, 20008. **202-265-8790** through **8794**
Ambassador. Benoit Bindzi. **202-265-8790**

CANADA. *Chancery.* 1746 Massachusetts Ave NW, 20036. **202-785-1400**
Ambassador. Peter M Towe
Press Officer. Robert J McGavin

CAPE VERDE. *Chancery.* Suite 300, 1120 Connecticut Ave NW, 20036. **202-659-3148** or **3149**
Ambassador. Dr Raul Querido Varela. **202-659-3148**

CENTRAL AFRICAN EMPIRE. *Chancery.* 1618 22nd St NW, 20008. **202-265-5637** or **4907**
Ambassador. Christophe Maidou. **202-882-4921**

CHAD. *Chancery.* Suite 410, 2600 Virginia Ave NW, 20037. **202-331-7696** or **7697**
Ambassador. Pierre Toura Gaba. **202-882-2999**

CHILE. *Chancery.* 1732 Massachusetts Ave NW, 20036. **202-785-1746**
Ambassador. Jorge Cauas
Press Attaché. Marcelo Maturana. **301-986-0643**

CHINA. *Chancery.* 2311 Massachusetts Ave NW, 20008. **202-667-9000** through **9005.** *Office of press counselor.* 552 National Press Bldg, 14th and F Sts NW, 20045. **202-347-4000** or **4001**
Ambassador. James C H Shen. **202-363-1815**
Press Counselor. Frank C H Tao. (h) **301-320-3595**
Press Attache. Samson Hsiang-chang Kuo. **202-347-4000** or **4001**
Assistant Press Attache. Steve Chi-ming Hsu. (h) **301-460-3669**

COLUMBIA. *Chancery.* 2118 Leroy Pl NW, 20008. **202-387-5828**
Councelor. Federico Clarkson. **202-337-5831**

COSTA RICA. *Chancery.* 2112 S St NW, 20008. **202-234-2945** or **2947**
Ambassador. Rodolfo Silva. **202-332-9325**

CYPRUS. *Chancery.* 2211 R St NW, 20008. **202-462-5772**
Ambassador. Nicos G Dimitriou. **202-232-7217**

CZECHOSLOVAKIA. *Chancery.* 3900 Linnean Ave NW, 20008. **202-363-6315** or **6316**
Charge. Dr Jaromir Johanes. **202-966-4317**
Cultural and Press Counselor. Zdenek Havlicek. **202-363-6317**

DENMARK. *Chancery.* 3200 Whitehaven St NW, 20008. **202-234-4300**
Ambassador. Otto R Borch
Counselor, Political and Press Affairs. Bent Skou. **301-656-4857**

DOMINICAN REPUBLIC. *Chancery.* 1715 22nd St NW, 20008. **202-332-6280**
Ambassador. Dr Horacio Vicioso-Soto. **202-667-3178** or **3179**

ECUADOR. *Chancery.* 2535 15th St NW, 20009. **202-234-7200**
Ambassador. Gustavo Ycaza Borja. **202-667-4372**
Counselor, Cultural and Press Affairs. Mrs Piedad De Suro. **301-652-6836**

EGYPT. *Chancery.* 2310 Decatur Pl NW, 20008. **202-232-5400.** *Office of press and information.* 2300 Decatur Pl NW, 20008. **202-234-0980** or **0981**

Ambassador. Ashraf A Ghorbal. **202-232-8721**

Minister Counselor, Press and Information. Mohamed I Hakki. **703-790-9726**

Counselor, Press and Information. Ahmed M Abushadi. **703-573-0727**

Press attaché. Fathalla Mahmoud El-boghdady. **703-379-7468**

EL SALVADOR. *Chancery.* 2308 California St NW, 20008. **202-265-3480, 3481,** or **3482**

Ambassador. Dr Francisco Bertrand Galindo. **301-299-4833**

ESTONIA. *Office of consulate general.* 9 Rockefeller Plz, New York, NY 10020. **212-247-1450**

Consul General in New York City in Charge of Legation. Ernst Jaakson. **914-337-5702**

ETHIOPIA. *Chancery.* 2134 Kalorama Rd NW, 20008. **202-234-2281** or **2282**

Counselor, Charge d'Affaires ad Interim. Ghebeyehou Mekbib. **202-234-2281**

FIJI. *Chancery.* Suite 520, 1629 K St NW, 20006. **202-296-3928**

Ambassador. Berenado Vunibobo

FINLAND. *Chancery.* 1900 24th St NW, 20008. **202-462-2224**

Ambassador. Jaako Iloniemi

Counselor, Press and Cultural Affairs. Jaakko Bergqvist. **202-966-3792**

FRANCE. *Chancery.* 2535 Belmont Rd NW, 20008. **202-234-0990**

Ambassador. Jacques Kosciusko-Morizet. **202-387-2666**

GABON. *Chancery.* 2210 R St NW, 20008. **202-797-1000**

Ambassador. Guy Rene Kombila. **301-365-0091**

GERMAN DEMOCRATIC REPUBLIC. *Chancery.* 1717 Massachusetts Ave NW, 20036. **202-232-3134**

Ambassador. Rolf Sieber

First Secretary, Press and Information Affairs. Frank Teutschbein

GERMANY, FEDERAL REPUBLIC OF. *Chancery.* 4645 Reservoir Rd NW, 20007. **202-331-3000**

Ambassador. Berndt Von Staden

Counselor, Press and Public Affairs. Karl Th. Paschke

GHANA. *Chancery.* 2460 16th St NW, 20009. **202-462-0761**

Ambassador. Samuel Ernest Quarm. **202-462-5711**

GREAT BRITAIN. *Chancery.* 3100 Massachusetts Ave NW, 20008. **202-462-1340**

Ambassador. Sir Peter Ramsbothom. **202-462-6040** or **6041**

GREECE. *Chancery.* 2221 Massachusetts Ave NW, 20008. **202-667-3168, 3169** or **3170.** *Office of press and information.* 2211 Massachusetts Ave NW, 20008. **202-332-2727**

Ambassador. Menelas D Alexandrakis. **202-667-3168**

Press Counselor. Alexander G Phylactopoulos. **202-244-1203**

GRENADA. *Chancery* (temporary). c/o Mission of Grenada to the United Nations, Suite 503, 866 2nd Ave, New York, NY 10017. **212-759-9675**

Ambassador E and P. Marie J McIntyre

GUATEMALA. *Chancery.* 2220 R St NW, 20008. **202-332-2865** or **2866**

Ambassador. Abundio Maldonado. **202-232-4253**

GUINEA. *Chancery.* 2112 Leroy Pl NW, 20008. **202-483-9420**

Ambassador. Daouda Kourouma. **202-332-8927**

GUINEA-BISSAU. *Chancery* (temporary). c/o Permanent Mission of Guinea-Bissau to the United Nations, Suite 604, 211 E 43rd St, New York, NY 10017. **212-661-3977**

Ambassador. Gil Vicente Vaz Fernandes

GUYANA. *Chancery.* 2490 Tracy Pl NW, 20008. **202-265-6900** through **6903**

Ambassador. Laurence E Mann. **301-469-7050**

Press Attache. Cicely Gouveia. **202-362-3115**

HAITI. *Chancery.* 4400 17th St NW, 20011. **202-723-7000** or **7001**

Ambassador. Georges Salomon. **301-657-8138**

HONDURAS. *Chancery.* Suite 408, 4301 Connecticut Ave NW, 20008. **202-966-7700, 7701** or **7702**

Ambassador. Dr Roberto Lazarus. **301-229-8139**

HUNGARY. *Chancery.* 3910 Shoemaker St NW, 20008. **202-362-6730**

Ambassador. Ferenc Esztergalyos

Second Secretary, Press. Istvan Fazekas. **202-966-3006**

ICELAND. *Chancery.* 2022 Connecticut Ave NW, 20008. **202-265-6653, 6654** or **6655**

Ambassador. Hans G Andersen. **202-332-3040**

INDIA. *Chancery.* 2107 Massachusetts Ave NW, 20008. **202-265-5050**

Ambassador. N A Palkhiwala. **202-362-1471**

Press Counselor. Mr O N Sheopuri. **202-265-2221.** (h) **703-379-7659**

INDONESIA. *Chancery.* 2020 Massachusetts Ave NW, 20036. **202-293-1745**

Ambassador. Roesmin Nurjadin. **202-363-4523**

IRAN. *Chancery.* 3005 Massachusetts Ave NW, 20008. **202-797-6500**

Ambassador. Ardeshir Zahedi

Press and Information Affairs Counselor. Manoutchehr Ardalan. **301-986-1382**

Press Attaché. Ali Akbar Tabatabai

Press Attaché. Nasrollah Soltani. **703-560-8567**

IRELAND. *Chancery.* 2234 Massachusetts Ave NW, 20008. **202-483-7639**

Ambassador. John G Molloy. **202-232-5510**

ISRAEL. *Chancery.* 1621 22nd St NW, 20008. **202-483-4100**

Ambassador. Simcha Dinitz

Information and Press Minister. Benyamin Navon

Press Counselor. Avierzer Pazner

ITALY. *Chancery.* 1601 Fuller St NW, 20009. **202-234-1935** through **1938**

Ambassador. Roberto Gaja. **202-234-1935**

IVORY COAST. *Chancery.* 2424 Massachusetts Ave NW, 20008. **202-483-2400**

Ambassador. Timothee N'Guetta Ahoua. **202-966-6514**

JAMAICA. *Chancery.* 1666 Connecticut Ave NW, 20009. **202-387-1010**

Ambassador. Alfred A Rattray. **301-654-5863**

Counsellor. Daphne E Ihnerarity

JAPAN. *Chancery.* 2520 Massachusetts Ave NW, 20008. **202-234-2266**
Ambassador. Fumihiko Toto
Counselor. Taizo Watanbz

JORDAN. *Chancery.* 319 Wyoming Ave NW, 20008. **202-265-1606**
Ambassador. Abdullah Salah. **301-652-5486**
First Secretary, Press. Michael Hamarneh. **703-893-0739**
Second Secretary, Press. Shehab A Madi. **202-265-1606**

KENYA. *Chancery.* 2249 R St NW, 20008. **202-387-6101**
Ambassador. John P Mbogua
Third Secretary, Press. Frank O Maina. **301-320-4915**

KOREA. *Chancery.* 2320 Massachusetts Ave NW, 20008. **202-483-7383.** *Ambassador's office.* 2370 Massachusetts Ave NW, 20008
Ambassador. Yong Shik Kim

KUWAIT. *Chancery.* 2940 Tilden St NW, 20008. **202-966-0702**
Ambassador. Khalid M Jaffar. **202-966-3613**

LAOS. *Chancery.* 2222 S St NW, 20008. **202-332-6416** or **6417**
First Secretary, Charge d'Affaires ad Interim. Somphong Vanitsaveth. **202-265-0403**

LATVIA. *Chancery.* 4325 17th St NW, 20011. **202-726-8213** or **8214**
Charge d'Affaires. Dr Anatol Dinbergs. **202-362-6920**

LEBANON. *Chancery.* 2560 28th St NW, 20008. **202-332-0300** through **0303**
Ambassador. Najati Kabbani. **202-667-6666**

LESOTHO. *Chancery.* Suite 300, Caravel Bldg, 1601 Connecticut Ave NW, 20009. **202-462-4190, 4191** or **4192**
Ambassador. Thabo Makeka. **301-656-0931**

LIBERIA. *Chancery.* 5201 16th St NW, 20011. **202-723-0437** through **0440.** *Office of the press and cultural counselor.* 1050 17th St NW, 20036. **202-331-0136**
Ambassador. Francis A Dennis. **202-333-6580**
Press and Cultural Counselor. Temynors Kla-Williams. **301-869-4228**

LIBYA. *Chancery.* 1118 22nd St NW, 20037. **202-452-1290** through **1295**
Counselor, Charge d'Affaires ad Interim. Shaban F Gashut

LITHUANIA. *Chancery.* 2622 16th St NW, 20009. **202-234-5860**
Charge d'Affaires. Dr Stasys A Backis. **202-234-2639**

LUXEMBOURG. *Chancery.* 2200 Massachusetts Ave NW, 20008. **202-265-4171**
Ambassador. Adrien Meisch. **202-244-2536**

MADAGASCAR. *Chancery.* 2374 Massachusetts Ave NW, 20008. **202-265-5525** or **5526**
Counselor, Charge d'Affaires ad Interim. Norbert Rakotomalala. **301-530-8905**

MALAWI. *Chancery.* Bristol House, 1400 20th St NW, 20036. **202-296-5530**
Ambassador. Jacob T X Muwamba

MALAYSIA. *Chancery.* 2401 Massachusetts Ave NW, 20008. **202-234-7600, 7601** or **7602**
Ambassador. Zain Asraai. **202-234-0400**
Information Officer. G N Nair. **202-234-7600**

MALI. *Chancery.* 2130 R St NW, 20008. **202-332-2249** or **2250**
Ambassador. Ibrahima Sima. **202-332-2287**

MALTA. *Chancery.* 2017 Connecticut Ave NW, 20008. **202-462-3611** or **3612**
Counselor, Charge d'Affaires ad Interim. Victor Gauci. **202-462-3611**

MAURITANIA. *Chancery.* 2129 Leroy Pl NW, 20008. **202-232-5700**
Ambassador. Mohamed Nassim Kochman. **202-483-6642**

MAURITIUS. *Chancery.* Suite 134, 4301 Connecticut Ave NW, 20008. **202-244-1491** or **1492**
Ambassador. Pierre Guy Girald Balancy, C B E. **301-652-6359**

MEXICO. *Chancery.* 2829 16th St NW, 20009. **202-234-6000**
Ambassador. Hugo B Margain. **202-265-5112** or **5133**

MOROCCO. *Chancery.* 1601 21st St NW, 20009. **202-462-7979** through **7982**
Ambassador. Ali Bengelloun. **202-462-7979**
Attaché. Abdelkader Kadiri

NEPAL. *Chancery.* 2131 Leroy Pl NW, 20008. **202-667-4550**
Ambassador. Padma Bahadur Khatri. **202-333-3389**

NETHERLANDS. *Chancery.* 4200 Linnean Ave NW, 20008. **202-244-5300** through **5309.** After 7 pm: **202-244-5300**
Ambassador. Age R Tammenoms Bakker. **202-234-1136**
Press and Cultural Affairs Counselor. Andries Ekker. **301-365-2955**
First Secretary. M Hetty De Bruijn. **202-686-1946**
Second Secretary, Press and Cultural Affairs. W Joris Witkam. **301-365-4268**

NEW ZEALAND. *Chancery.* 19 Observatory Cir NW, 20008. **202-265-1721** through **1724**
Ambassador. Lloyd White. **202-265-1721**
Press Officer. Rauru Kirikiri. **202-265-1721**

NICARAGUA. *Chancery.* 1627 New Hampshire Ave NW, 20009. **202-387-4371** or **4372**
Ambassador. Dr Guillermo Sevilla-Sacasa. **202-362-7448**

NIGER. *Chancery.* 2204 R St NW, 20008. **202-483-4224** through **4227**
Ambassador. Andre Wright. **202-882-1219**

NIGERIA. *Chancery.* 2201 M St NW, 20037. **202-223-9300**
Ambassador. Edward Olusola Sanu. **202-338-5574**

NORWAY. *Chancery.* 4200 Wisconsin Ave NW, 20016. **202-966-9550**
Ambassador. Soren Christian Sommerfelt. **202-965-9809**
Press and Cultural Affairs Counselor. Mr Harald Svanoe Midttun. **301-657-3529**

OMAN. *Chancery.* 2342 Massachusetts Ave NW, 20008. **202-387-1980, 1981,** or **1982**
Ambassador. Ahmed Macki. **202-363-0412**

PAKISTAN. *Chancery.* 2315 Massachusetts Ave NW, 20008. **202-332-8330**
Ambassador. Sahabzada Yaqub-Khan

PANAMA. *Chancery.* 2862 McGill Ter NW, 20008. **202-483-1407**
Ambassador. Gabriel Lewis

PAPUA NEW GUINEA. *Chancery.* 3122 Davenport St NW, 20008. **202-833-3510**
Charge d'Affaires. Paulias Nguna Matane, OBE. **202-686-0350**

PARAGUAY. *Chancery.* 2400 Massachusetts Ave NW, 20008. **202-483-6960**
Ambassador. Mario Lopex Escobar

PERU. *Chancery.* 1700 Massachusetts Ave NW, 20036. **202-833-9860** through **9869**
Ambassador. Carlos Garcia-Bedoya. **202-363-4808**

PHILIPPINES. *Chancery.* 1617 Massachusetts Ave NW, 20036. **202-483-1414**
Ambassador. Eduardo Z Romualdez
Press Counselor. Abelardo L Valencia. **202-966-4023**

POLAND. *Chancery.* 2640 16th St NW, 20009. **202-234-3800, 3801,** or **3802**
Ambassador. Dr Witold Trampczynski. **202-234-3800**
First Secretary, Press. Dr Zbigniew Bako. **301-234-3800**

PORTUGAL. *Chancery.* 2125 Kalorama Rd NW, 20008. **202-265-1643** or **1644**
Ambassador. Joao Hall Themido. **202-483-7075**
Press Counselor. Luis Amorim de Sousa. **301-656-1654**

QATAR. *Chancery.* Suite 1180, 600 New Hampshire Ave NW, 20037. **202-338-0111**
Ambassador. Abdullah Saleh Al-Mana. **202-244-5101**

ROMANIA. *Chancery.* 1607 23rd St NW, 20008. **202-232-4747, 4748,** or **4749**
Ambassador. Nicolae M Nicolae. **202-232-3694**

RWANDA. *Chancery.* 1714 New Hampshire Ave NW, 20009. **202-232-2882**
Ambassador. Bonaventure Ubalijoro. **202-726-2426**

SAUDI ARABIA. *Chancery.* 1520 18th St NW, 20036. **202-483-2100**
Ambassador. Ali Abdallah Alireza

SENEGAL. *Chancery.* 2112 Wyoming Ave NW, 20008. **202-234-0540** or **0541**
Ambassador. Andre Coulbary. **202-337-6483**
Press Attaché. Mr Emile J Senghor. **301-593-7740**

SIERRA LEONE. *Chancery.* 1701 19th St NW, 20009. **202-265-7700**
Ambassador. Philip J Palmer. **202-726-9010**

SINGAPORE. *Chancery.* 1824 R St NW, 20009. **202-667-7555**
Ambassador. Punch Coomaraswamy. **202-338-0290**

SOMALIA. *Chancery.* Suite 710, 600 New Hampshire Ave NW, 20037. **202-234-3261**
Ambassador. Dr Abdullahai Ahmed Addou. **202-726-0036**

SOUTH AFRICA. *Chancery.* 3051 Massachusetts Ave NW, 20008. **202-232-4400**
Ambassador. Donald B Sole
Minister, Charge d'Affaires ad Interim. Jeremy B Shearar. **202-362-5185**
Press Attaché. Hugo H Villiers

SPAIN. *Chancery.* 2700 15th St NW, 20009. **202-265-0190** or **0191**
Ambassador. Juan Jose Rovira. **202-265-1084, 202-265-3393,** or **202-347-6777**
Press Attaché. Guillermo Una. **202-362-1256**

SRI LANKA. *Chancery.* 2148 Wyoming Ave NW, 20008. **202-483-4025** through **4028**
Ambassador. Neville Kanakaratne. **202-387-0601**

SUDAN. *Chancery.* Suite 400, 600 New Hampshire Ave NW, 20037. **202-338-8565** through **8568**
Ambassador. Omer Salih Eissa. **202-332-5790**
Press Information. J Dhanapala. **202-483-4025**

SURINAM. *Chancery.* Suite 711, 2600 Virginia Ave NW, 20037. **202-338-6980** through **6984**
Ambassador. Roel F Karamat. **202-265-5309**

SWAZILAND. *Chancery.* 4301 Connecticut Ave NW, 20008. **202-362-6683**
Ambassador. Simon M Kunene

SWEDEN. *Chancery.* Suite 1200, 600 New Hampshire Ave NW, 20037. **202-965-4100** through **4108**
Ambassador. Count Wilhelm Wachtmeister. **202-362-3270** or **3271**
Press Counselor. Lars Arno. **301-299-5453**
Press Attaché. Lars Georgsson. **301-229-8237**

SWITZERLAND. *Chancery.* 2900 Cathedral Ave NW, 20008. **202-462-1811**
Ambassador. Raymond Probst. **202-462-4247**

SYRIA. *Chancery.* 2215 Wyoming Ave NW, 20008. **202-232-6313**
Ambassador. Dr Sabah Kabbani

TANZANIA. *Chancery.* 2010 Massachusetts Ave NW, 20036. **202-872-1005**
Ambassador. Paul Bomani. **301-229-8945**

THAILAND. *Chancery.* 2300 Kalorama Rd NW, 20008. **202-667-1446** through **1449**
Ambassador. Arun Panupong. **202-667-1446**

TOGO. *Chancery.* 2208 Massachusetts Ave NW, 20008. **202-234-4212** or **4213**
Ambassador. Messanvi Kokou Kekeh. **202-723-7703**

TRINIDAD and TOBAGO. *Chancery.* 1708 Massachusetts Ave NW, 20036. **202-467-6490**
Ambassador. Victor C McIntyre. **202-723-0077**

TUNISIA. *Chancery.* 2408 Massachusetts Ave NW, 20008. **202-234-6644**
Ambassador. Ali Hedda. **202-362-6337**

TURKEY. *Chancery.* 1606 23rd St NW, 20008. **202-667-6400, 6401, 7581,** or **1024.** *Office of press counselor.* 2523 Massachusetts Ave NW, 20008. **202-662-3134**
Ambassador. Melih Esenbel. **202-667-6400**
Press Counselor. Emin Hekimgil. **301-656-6308**
Assistant Press Counselor. Hasbi Akal. **703-354-2384**

UGANDA. *Chancery.* 5909 16th St NW, 20011. **202-716-7100, 7101,** or **7102**
Second Secretary, Charge d'Affaires ad Interim. Mahmud Musa. **202-244-2343**

UNION OF SOVIET SOCIALIST REPUBLICS. *Chancery.* 1125 16th St NW, 20036. **202-628-7551** or **8548**
Ambassador. Anatoliy F Dobrynin. **202-628-7551**
Press Counselor. Valentin M Kamenev. **202-628-7551. 202-347-1347**

UNITED ARAB EMIRATES. *Chancery.* Suite 740, 600 New Hampshire Ave NW, 20037. **202-338-6500**
Ambassador. Hamad Abdul Rahman Al Madfa

UPPER VOLTA. *Chancery.* 5500 16th St NW, 20011. **202-726-0992** or **0993**
Ambassador. Telesphore Yaguibou. **202-726-8531**

URUGUAY. *Chancery.* 1918 F St NW, 20006. **202-331-1313** through **1316**
Ambassador. Jose Perez Caldas. **301-365-0507**

VENEZUELA. *Chancery.* 2445 Massachusetts Ave NW, 20008. **202-265-9600**
Ambassador. Ignacio Iribarren. **202-232-9187**

YEMEN. *Chancery*. Suite 860, 600 New Hampshire Ave NW, 20037. **202-965-4760** or **4761**

Ambassador. Yahya M. Al-Mutawakel. **202-362-0296**

YUGOSLAVIA. *Chancery*. 2410 California St NW, 20008. **202-462-6566**

Ambassador. Dimce Belovski

Press and Culture Counselor. Dusan Trifunovic

ZAIRE. *Chancery*. 1800 New Hampshire Ave NW, 20009. **202-234-7690, 7691,** or **7617**

Ambassador. Asal B Idzumbuir. **202-234-7690**

ZAMBIA. *Chancery*. 2419 Massachusetts Ave NW, 20008. **202-265-9717** through **9721**

Counselor, Charge d'Affaires ad Interim. Fidelis F Bwalya. **202-723-4906**

Press and Information Attaché. Cosmo A Mlongoti. **301-229-0563**

UNITED STATES EMBASSIES ABROAD

AFGHANISTAN. Kabul (embassy), Wazir Akbar Khan Mina. Telephone: **24230** through **24239**

Ambassador. Theodore L Eliot, Jr

Public Affairs Officer. Roger M Lydon

ALGERIA. Algiers (embassy), 4 Chemin Cheikh Bachir Brahimi (ex Beaurepaire). Telephone: **601425, 601255, 601186, 601716, 601828** or **603670**. *Telex*: **52064**

Ambassador. Ulric St Clair Haynes, Jr

Public Affairs Officer. Christopher W R Ross

ANGOLA. Luanda, (consulate general), 13th and 14th Floors, 42, Avenida Paulo Dias de Novais. Telephone: **72494** or **73155**

ARAB REPUBLIC OF EGYPT. *See* Egypt.

ARGENTINA. Buenos Aires (embassy), Saramiento 663 (1613). Telephone: **46-32-11**

Ambassador. Paul H Caspro (nominee)

Public Affairs Officer. John R Higgins

AUSTRALIA. Canberra (embassy), Moonah Pl, Canberra, A C T 2600; APO San Francisco 96404. Telephone: **062-73-3711**. *Telex*: **AA62104**

Ambassador. Philip H Alston, Jr

Public Affairs Officer. Robert W Mount

AUSTRIA. Vienna (embassy), IX Boltzmangasse 16 a-1091. Telephone: **222-346611** or **347511**. *Telex*: **73634**

Ambassador. Milton A Wolf

Public Affairs Officer. Arthur A Bardos

BAHAMAS. Nassau (embassy), Mosmar Bldg, Queen St. Telephone: **809-322-1700** or **1181**. *Telex*: **20-138**

Ambassador. William B Schwartz, Jr (nominee)

BAHRAIN. Manama (embassy), Shaikh Isa Rd; PO Box 431, FPO New York 09526. Telephone: **714151**. *Commercial office*. **713323**

Ambassador. Wat Tyler Cluverius IV

Public Affairs Officer. Larry R Taylor

BANGLADESH. Dacca (embassy), 5th Floor, Adamjee Court Bldg, Montijheel Commercial Area, GPO Box 323, Ramna. Telephone: **244220** through **244229**

Ambassador. Edward E Masters

Public affairs officer. James L Meyer

BARBADOS. Bridgetown (embassy), PO Box 302, FPO New York 09553. Telephone: **63574** through **63577**. *Telex*: **259 USEMB BG1 WB**

Ambassador. Frank V Ortiz

BELGIUM. Brussels (embassy), 27 Boulevard de Regent; APO New York 09667. Telephone: **513-3830**. *Telex*: **846-21446**

Ambassador. Anne Cox Chambers

Public Affairs Officer. James C McIntosh

BELIZE. Belize City (consulate general), Gabourel Ln and Hutson St. Telephone: **3261**

Consul General. John L Gawf

BENIN. Cotonou (embassy), Rue Caporal Anani Bernard, Boite Postale 2012. Telephone: **31-26-92** or **93**

Charge d'Affaires. W Kenneth Thompson

Public Affairs Officer. Frederick E V La Sor

BERMUDA. Hamilton (consulate general), Vallis Bldg, Front St; FPO New York 09560. Telephone: **5-1342**

Consul General. S Richard Rand

BOLIVIA. La Paz (embassy), Banco Popular Del Peru Bldg, corner of Calles Mercado y Colon; APO New York 09867. Telephone: **50251**. *Telex*: **BX5240**

Ambassador. Paul H Boker (nominee)

Public Affairs Officer. John C Scafe

BOTSWANA. Gaborone (embassy), PO Box 90. Telephone: **2944** through **2947**

Ambassador. Donald R Norland

Public Affairs Officer. Clement Don Jones

BRAZIL. Brasilia (embassy), Lote 3, Avenida das Nocoes; APO New York 09676. Telephone: **0612-230120**. *Telex*: **061-1091**

Ambassador. John H Crimmins

Public Affairs Officer. Lyle D Copmann

BRITAIN. *See* United Kingdom.

BULGARIA. Sofia (embassy), 1 Stamboliiski Blvd. Telephone: **88-48-01** through **05**. *Telex*: **22690 BG**

Ambassador. Martin F Herz

Press and Cultural Officer (USIA). John J Karch

BURMA. Rangoon (embassy), 581 Merchant St. Telephone: **18055**

Ambassador. David L Osborn

Public Affairs Officer. Frank W Scotton

BURUNDI. Bujumbura (embassy), Chaussee Prince Louise Rwagasore, Boite Postale 1720. Telephone: **34-54**

Ambassador. David E Mark

CAMEROON. Yaounde (embassy), Rue Nachtigal, Boite Postale 817. Telephone: **221633** or **220512**. *Telex*: **8223**

Ambassador. Mabel M Smythe

Public Affairs Officer. Jerry L Prillaman

CANADA. Ottawa (embassy), 100 Wellington St. Telephone: **613-238-5335**. *Telex*: **533582**

Ambassador. Thomas O Enders

Public Affairs Officer. Ben F Fordney

CENTRAL AFRICAN EMPIRE. Bangul (embassy), Place de la Republique Centrafricaine. Telephone: **2050** or **2051**. *Telex*: **5216**

Ambassador. Anthony C E Quainton

CEYLON. *See* Sri Lanka

CHAD. N'Djamena (embassy), Rue du Lt Col Colonna D'Oranano, Boite Postale 413. Telephone: **30-91** through **94**. *Telex*: **5203 KD**

Ambassador. William G Bradford

Public Affairs Officer. Stanley N Schrager

CHILE. Santiago (embassy), Codina Bldg, 1343 Agustinas. Telephone: **82801** through **82804**. *Telex*: **40957-USIS-CL**

Public Affairs Officer. Brian Bell

CHINA (Taiwan). Taipei (embassy), 2 Chung Hsiao W Rd, Second Section; APO San Francisco 96263. Telephone: **331-3551** through **331-3559**. *Telex:* **23890**

Ambassador. Leonard Unger

Public Affairs Officer. William Ayers

COLOMBIA. Bogota (embassy), Calle 37, 8-40; APO New York 09895. Telephone: **329-100**. *Telex:* **44843**

Public Affairs Officer. Donald Y Gilmore

DEMOCRATIC REPUBLIC OF THE CONGO. *See* Zaire

COSTA RICA. San Jose (embassy), Avenida 3 and Calle 1; APO New York 09883.. Telephone: **22-55-66**

Ambassador. Marvin Weissman

Public Affairs Officer. Gordon W Murchie

CYPRUS. Nicosia (embassy), Therissos and Dositheos Sts; FPO New York 09530. Telephone: **65151** through **65155**

Ambassador. William R Crawford, Jr

Public Affairs Officer. Marie L Telich

CZECHOSLOVAKIA. Prague (embassy), Trziste 15-12548 Praha; Amembassy, Prague, c/o Amcongen, APO New York 09757. Telephone: **53-66-41** through **48**. *Telex:* **121196 AMEMBC**

Ambassador. Thomas R Byrne

Press and Cultural Officer (USIA). Eugene F Quinn

DAHOMEY. *See* Benin

DENMARK. Copenhagen (embassy), Dag Hammarskjolds Alle 24; APO New York 09170. Telephone: **12-31-44**. *Telex:* **22216**

Ambassador. John Gunther Dean

Public Affairs Officer. Deirdre M Ryan

DOMINICAN REPUBLIC. Santo Domingo (embassy), corner of Calle Cesar Nicolas Pensen and Calle Leopoldo Navarra; APO New York 09899. Telephone: **682-2171**. *Telex:* **3460013**

Ambassador. Robert A Hurwitch

Public Affairs Officer. Barbara A Hutchison

ECUADOR. Quito (embassy), 120 Avenida Patria. Telephone: **230-020**

Ambassador. Richard J Bloomfield

Public Affairs Officer. Holley Mack Bell

ECUADOR. Guayaquil (consulate general), Casilla X. Telephone: **511570**

Consul General. Robert A Bishton

Public Affairs Officer. John A Mason, Jr

EGYPT (Arab Republic of). Cairo (embassy), 5 Sharia Latin America; Box 10, FPO New York 09527. Telephone: **28211** through **28219**

Ambassador. Herman F Eilts

Public Affairs Officer. William A Rugh

EL SALVADOR. San Salvador (embassy), 1230, 25 Avenida Norte; APO New York 09889. Telephone: **25-7100**

Ambassador. Frank J Derine (nominee)

Public Affairs Officer. Vytautas Dambrava

ENGLAND. *See* United Kingdom

ETHIOPIA. Addis Ababa (embassy), Entoto St, PO Box 1014; APO New York 09319. Telephone: **110666**

Charge. Arthur T Tienkin

FIJI. Suva (embassy), 7th Floor, Ratu Sukuna House, MacArthur St, PO Box 218. Telephone: **25-304, 305,** or **306.**. *Telex:* **2255 AMEMBASSY FJ**

Charge. Robert L Flanegin

FINLAND. Helsinki (embassy), Itainen Puistotie 14A; APO New York 09664. Telephone: **171931**. *Telex:* **121644 USEMB SF**

Ambassador. Rozanne L Ridgway

Public Affairs Officer. Robert C Voth

FRANCE. Paris (embassy), 2 Avenue Gabriel, 75382 Paris, Cedex 08; APO New York 09777. Telephone: **265-74-00**. *Telex:* **65-221**

Ambassador. Arthur A Hartman

Public Affairs Officer. Burnett F Anderson

FRENCH WEST INDIES. Martinque (consulate), 14 Rue Blenac, Boite Postale 561, Fort de France 97206. Telephone: **71-93-01** or **71-93-03**

Consul (consular section). Robert G Shackleton

GABON. Libreville (embassy), Boulevard de la Mer, Boite Postale 4000. Telephone: **72-20-03** or **04, 72-13-37,** or **72-03-48**. *Telex:* **5250 GO**

Ambassador. Andrew L Steigman

Public Affairs Officer. Elton Stepherson, Jr

THE GAMBIA. Banjul (embassy), 16 Buckle St, PO Box 596. Telephone: **526** or **527**. *Telex:* **229 BJL GV**

Ambassador. Herman J Cohen

FEDERAL REPUBLIC OF GERMANY (West Germany). Bonn (embassy),

Mahlemer Ave, 5300 Bonn-Bad Godesberg; APO New York 09080. Telephone: **02221-89-55**. *Telex:* **885-452**

Ambassador. Walter J Stoessel, Jr

Public Affairs Officer. Alexander A Klieforth

GERMAN DEMOCRATIC REPUBLIC (East Germany). Berlin (embassy), 108 Berlin, Neustaedtische Kirchstrasse 4-5. Telephone: **2202741**

Ambassador. David E Bolen

Press and Cultural Officer (USIA). Edward Alexander

GHANA. Accra (embassy), Liberia and Kinbu Rds, PO Box 194. Telephone: **66811**. *Commercial Office.* **66125**

Ambassador. Robert P Smith

Public Affairs Officer. Kenneth Bache

GREECE. Athens (embassy), 91 Vasilissis Sophias Blvd; APO New York 09253. Telephone: **712951** or **718401** (area Code from US: 01130-1). *Telex:* **21-5548**

Ambassador. William E Schaufk, Jr

Public Affairs Officer. Mourad W Haratunian

GUATEMALA. Guatemala City (embassy), 7-01 Avenida de la Reforma, Zone 10; APO New York 09891. Telephone: **61542, 61543, 61544,** or **66205** through **66209**

Ambassador. Davis E Boster

Public Affairs Officer. Jack W Gallagher

GUINEA. Conakry (embassy), 2d Blvd and 9th Ave, Boite Postale 603. Telephone: **415-20** through **24**

Ambassador. William C Harrop

Public Affairs Officer. Stuart Halpine

GUINEA-BISSAU. Bissau (embassy), Avenida Domingos Ramos, CP 297. Telephone: **28-16** or **17**

Ambassador. Edward Marks

GUYANA. Georgetown (embassy), 31 Main St. Telephone: **62687**, Ext 26

Ambassador. John R Burke (nominee)

Public Affairs Officer. Stepney Kibble

HAITI. Port-Au-Prince (embassy), Harry Truman Blvd. Telephone: **20200**. *Telex:* **0157 EMPAP**

Ambassador. Heyward Isham

Public Affairs Officer. Francis D Gomez

HONDURAS. Tegucigalpa (embassy), Avenido la Paz; APO New York 09887. Telephone: 22-3121 through 3127

Ambassador. Ralph E Becker

Public Affairs Officer. Ernesto Uribe

HONG KONG. Hong Kong (consulate general), 26 Garden Rd; FPO San Francisco 96659. Telephone: 239011

Consul general. Charles T Cross

Public Affairs Officer. Jack Friedman

HUNGARY. Budapest (embassy), V Szabadsag Ter 12; APO New York 09757. Telephone: 329-375. *Telex:* 224-222

Ambassador. Philip Mayer Kaiser

Public Affairs Officer. G Michael Eisenstadt

ICELAND. Reykjavik (embassy), Laufasvegur 21; FPO New York 09571. Telephone: 24083

Ambassador. James J Blake

Public Affairs Officer. Irving E Rantanen

INDIA. New Delhi (embassy), Shanti Path, Chanakyapuri 21. Telephone: 690351

Ambassador. Robert F Goheen

Public Affairs Officer. Jay W Gildner

INDONESIA. Jakarta (embassy), Medan Merdeka Selatan 5; APO San Francisco 96356. Telephone: 40001 through 40009. *Telex:* 44218 AMEMB JKT

Ambassador. David D Newsom

Public Affairs Officer. Bernard J Lavin

IRAN. Tehran (embassy), 260 Takhte Jamshid Ave, PO Box 50; Box 2000, APO New York 09205. Telephone: 820-091 through 099, 824-001, or 829-051

Ambassador. William H Sullivan

Public Affairs Officer. Jack H Shellenberger

IRAQ. Baghdad (US interests section), Belgian Embassy, 52/5/35 Masbah (opposite Foreign Ministry Club), PO Box 2447 Alwiyah, Baghdad. Telephone: 96138 or 96139. *Telex:* 2287 1K

Principal Officer. Charles E Marthinsen

IRELAND. Dublin (embassy), 42 Elgin Rd, Ballsbridge. Telephone: 688777. *Telex:* 5240

Ambassador William Shannon

Public Affairs Officer. Joseph I Krene

ISRAEL. Tel Aviv (embassy), 71 Hayarkon St. Telephone: 54338. *Telex:* 03-2476

Ambassador. Samuel W Lewis

Public Affairs Officer. Stanley D Moss

ITALY. Rome (embassy), Via V Veneto 119/A, 00187-Rome; APO New York 09794. Telephone: 06-4674. *Telex:* 61450 Amembro. *US Information Service.* Via Boncompagril 2, 00187-Rome

Ambassador. Richard N Gardner

Public Affairs Officer. Robert C Amerson

IVORY COAST. Abidjan (embassy), 5 Rue Jesse Owens, Boite Postale 1712. Telphone: 32-46-30. *Telex:* 660

Ambassador. Monteagle Stearns

Public Affairs Officer. Sherman H Ross

JAMAICA. Kingston (embassy), 43 Duke St. Telephone: 932-6340

Ambassador. Frederick Irving

Public Affairs Officer. John L Sandstrom

JAPAN. Tokyo (embassy), 13-go, 14, Akasaka 1-chome Minato-ku; APO San Francisco 96503. Telephone: 583-7141. *Telex:* 2422118

Ambassador. Michael J Mansfield

Public Affairs Officer. William D Miller

JERUSALEM. Jerusalem (consulate general). 18 Agron Rd. Telephone: 226312. Also Nablus Rd. 282231 or 272681. (Both offices via Israel.)

Consul General. Michael H Newlin

JORDAN. Amman (embassy), Jebel Amman PO Box 354. Telephone: 44371 through 44376. *Commercial office.* 2nd Floor, Madi Bldg, King Faisal St. 38930 or 38724

Ambassador. Thomas R Pickering

Public Affairs Officer. John P Foster

KENYA. Nairobi (embassy), Cotts House, Wabera St, PO Box 30137. Telephone: 334141

Ambassador. Wilbert J Le Melle

Public Affairs Officer. Irwin K Teven

KOREA. Seoul (embassy), Sejong-Ro; APO San Francisco 96301. Telephone: 72-2601 through 2619

Ambassador. Richard L Sneider

Public Affairs Officer. Clyde G Hess

KUWAIT. Kuwait (embassy), PO Box 77 Safat. Telephone: 424156, 424157, or 424158

Ambassador. Frank E Maestrone

Public Affairs Officer. Edmund A Bator

LAO PEOPLE'S DEMOCRATIC REPUBLIC. Vientiane (embassy), Rue Bartholonie, Boite Postale 114; Box V, APO San Francisco 96346. Telephone: 3126 or 3570

LEBANON. Beirut (embassy), Corniche at Rue Ain Mreisseh. Telephone: 361-800

Ambassador. Richard B Parker

LESOTHO. Maseru (embassy), PO Box MS 333. Telephone: 2666 or 3954

Ambassador. Donald R Norland (resident in Gaborone)

Public Affairs Officer. Peter B Bielak

LIBERIA. Monrovia (embassy), United Nations Dr; APO New York 09155. Telephone: 22991 through 22994

Ambassador. W Beverly Carter

Public Affairs Officer. Charles M McGee

LIBYA. Tripoli (embassy), Shari Mohammad Thabit, PO Box 289. Telephone: 34021 through 34026

LUXEMBOURG. Luxembourg (embassy), 22 Boulevard Emmanuel Servais; APO New York 09132. Telephone: 40123 through 40127

Ambassador. James G Lowenstein

MADAGASCAR. Antananarivo (embassy), 14 and 16 Rue Rainitovo, Antsohavola, Boite Postale 620. Telephone: 212-57. *Telex:* TANA 22202

Charge d'Affaires. Robert S Barett

Public Affairs Officer. G Michael Razi

MALAWI. Lilongwe (embassy), PO Box 30016. Telephone: 30396 or 30166. *Telex:* 4183

Ambassador. Robert A Stevenson

Public Affairs Officer. Louis E Polichetti

MALAYSIA. Kuala Lumpur (embassy), AIA Bldg, Jalan Ampang, PO Box 35. Telephone: 26321

Ambassador. Robert H Miller

Public Affairs Officer. F Weston Fenhagen

MALI. Bamako (embassy), Rue Testard and Rue Mohamed V. Telephone: 246-63 or 64, 248-34 or 45

Ambassador. Patricia M Byrne

Public Affairs Officer. Alan L Gilbert

MALTA. Valletta (embassy), 2d Floor, Development House, St Anne St, Floriana; FPO New York 09534. Telephone: 623653, 620424, or 623216

Ambassador. L Bruce Laingen

Public Affairs Officer. Harold F Radday

MAURITANIA. Nouakchott (embassy), Boite Postale 222. Telephone: **52660** or **52663.** *Telex:* **AMEMB 558 MTN**
Ambassador. Holsey G Handyside

MAURITIUS. Port Louis (embassy), 6th Floor, Anglo-Mauritius House, Intendance St. Telephone: **2-3218** or **3219**
Ambassador. Robert V Keeley

MEXICO. Mexico, DF (embassy), Paseo de la Reforma 305, Mexico 5, DF. Telephone: **553-3333.** *Telex:* **017-73-091** or **017-75-685**
Ambassador. Patrick J Lucey
Public Affairs Officer. Leonard J Baldyga

MOROCCO. Rabat (embassy), 2 Avenue de Marrakech; Box 99, FPO New York 09544. Telephone: **30361** or **30362.** *Telex:* **31005**
Ambassador. Robert Anderson
Public Affairs Officer. James M Rentschler

MOZAMBIQUE. Maputo (embassy), 2nd Floor, 35 Rua da Mesquita. Telephone: **26051, 26052,** or **26053**
Ambassador. Willard A De Pree

NEPAL. Kathmandu (embassy), Pani Pokhari. Telephone: **11199, 12718, 11603,** or **11604**
Ambassador. L Douglas Heck
Public Affairs Officer. Diane Stanley

THE NETHERLANDS. The Hague (embassy), 102 Longe Voorhout; APO New York 09159. Telephone: **62-49-11.** *Telex:* **31016**
Ambassador. Robert J McCloskey
Public Affairs Officer. Victor L Stier

NETHERLANDS ANTILLES. Curacao (consulate general), St Anna Blvd 19, PO Box 158, vice John B Gorsirawea l. Telephone: **13066**
Consul General. Grover W Penberthy

NEW GUINEA. *See* Papau.

NEW ZEALAND. Wellington (embassy), IBM Centre, 155-157, The Terrace, PO Box 1190. Telephone: **722-068.** *Telex:* **NZ3305**
Ambassador Armistead I Selden, Jr
Public Affairs Officer. Kenneth D Koch

NICARAGUA. Managua (embassy), Km 4½ Carretera Sur; APO New York 09885. Telephone: **23061** through **23068,** or through **23887**
Ambassador. Mauricio Solaun
Public Affairs Officer. James M Fitzgerald

NIGER. Niamey (embassy), Boite Postale 201. Telephone: **72-26-61** through **64** or **72-26-70**
Ambassador. Charles A James
Public Affairs Officer. Thomas P Crawford

NIGERIA. Lagos (embassy), 1 King's College Rd, PO Box 554. Telephone: **57320**
Ambassador. Donald B Easum
Public Affairs Officer. Arthur W Lewis

NORWAY. Oslo (embassy), Drammensveien 18, Oslo 1; APO New York 09085. Telephone: **56-68-80.** *Telex:* **18470**
Ambassador. Louis A Lerner
Public Affairs Officer. Flemming E Nyrop

OMAN. Muscat (embassy), PO Box 966. Telephone: **722021**
Ambassador. William D Wolle

PAKISTAN. Islamabad (embassy), Diplomatic Enclave Ramna 4. Telephone: **26161-26179.** *Telex:* **952-5-864**
Ambassador. Arthur W Hummel, Jr
Public Affairs Officer. David G Briggs

PANAMA. Panama (embassy), Apartado 6959, Avenida Balboa Y Calle 38, RP 5. Telephone: **25-3600**
Ambassador. William J Jorden
Public Affairs Officer. Stephen F Dack

PAPUA NEW GUINEA. Port Moresby (embassy), Armit St, PO Box 3492. Telephone: **211455, 211594, 211654.** *Telex:* **70322189**
Ambassador. Mary S Olmsted
Public Affairs Officer. Frank L Albert

PARAGUAY. Asuncion (embassy), 1776 Mariscal Lopez Ave; APO 09881. Telephone: **2104** through **2109**
Ambassador. George W Landau
Public Affairs Officer. Thomas G Charouhas

PERU. Lima (embassy), corner Avenidas Inca Garcilaso de la Vega and Espana, PO Box 1995. Telephone: **286000**
Ambassador. Harry W Shlaudeman
Public Affairs Officer. Allen C Hansen

PHILIPPINES. Manila (embassy), 1201 Roxas Blvd; APO San Francisco 96528. Telephone: **598-011.** *Telex:* **722-7366**
Public Affairs Officer. Maurice E Lee

POLAND. Warsaw (embassy), Aleje Ujazdowskie 29/31; AmEmbassy Warsaw, c/o AmConGen, APO New York 09757.

Telephone: **283041** through **283049.** *Telex:* **813304**
Ambassador. Richard T Davis
Press and Cultural Officer (USIA). James E Bradshaw

PORTUGAL. Lisbon (embassy), Avenida Duque de Loule 39; APO New York 09678. Telephone: **555141.** *Telex:* **12528 Amemb**
Ambassador. Frank C Carlucci
Public Affairs Officer. Robert F Jordan

QATAR. Doha (embassy), Farig Bin Omran (opposite television station), PO Box 2399. Telephone: **87701, 87702,** or **87703**
Ambassador. Robert P Paganelli

ROMANIA. Bucharest (embassy), Strada Tudor Arghezi 7-9; AmConGen (Buch), APO New York 09757. Telephone: **12-40-40.** *Telex:* **11416**
Ambassador. Harry G Barnes, Jr
Public Affairs Officer. Norris D Garnett

RUSSIA. *See* Union of Soviet Socialist Republics.

RWANDA. Kigali (embassy), Boulevard Central. Telephone: **5601.** *Telex:* **16 AMEMB RW**
Ambassador. T Frank Crigier

SAUDI ARABIA. Jidda (embassy), Palestine Rd, Ruwais; APO New York 09697. Telephone: **53410, 54110, 52188, 52396,** or **52589.** *Commercial office.* Palestine Rd (opposite embassy), PO Box 149. **51553**
Ambassador. John C West
Public Affairs Officer. H Eugene Bovis

SENEGAL. Dakar (embassy), BIAO Bldg, Place de L'Independence, Boite Postale 49. Telephone: **26344.** *Telex:* **517 AMEMB SG**
Ambassador. Herman J Cohen
Public Affairs Officer. Vincent Rotundo

SEYCHELLES. Victoria (embassy), Box 148, APO New York 09030. Telephone: **23921** or **23922**
Ambassador. Wilbert J Le Melle (resident in Nairobi)

SIERRA LEONE. Freetown (embassy), corner Walpole and Siaka Stevens Sts Telephone: **26481.** *Telex:* **3210**
Ambassador. John Andrew Linehan

SINGAPORE. Singapore (embassy), 30 Hill St; FPO San Francisco 96699. Telephone: **30251**
Ambassador. John H Holdridge
Public Affairs Officer. Gerald Stryker

SOMALIA. Mogadiscio (embassy), Corso Primo Luglio. Telephone: **2811**

Ambassador. John L Loughran

Public Affairs Officer. Clathan McClain Ross

SOUTH AFRICA. Pretoria (embassy), Thibault House, 225 Poretorius St. Telephone: **48-4266.** *Telex:* **3-751**

Ambassador. William G Bowdler

Public Affairs Officer. Harry L Hughes

SPAIN. Madrid (embassy), Serrano 75; APO New York 09285. Telephone: **276-3400** or **276-3600.** *Telex:* **27763**

Ambassador. Wells Stabler

Public Affairs Officer. George A Rylance

SRI LANKA. Colombo (embassy), 44 Galle Rd, Colombo 3, PO Box 106. Telephone: **26211** through **26218**

Ambassador. W Howard Wriggins

Public Affairs Officer. Richard A von Glatz

SUDAN. Khartoum (embassy), Gamhouria Ave, PO Box 699. Telephone: **74611** or **74700**

Ambassador. Donald C Bergus.

Public Affairs Officer. Sterlyn B Steele

SURINAM. Paramaribo (embassy), Dr Sophie Redmondstraat 13, PO Box 1821. Telephone: **73024** or **75620.** *Telex:* **137**

Ambassador. J Owen Zurhellen, Jr

SWAZILAND. Mbabane (embassy), Embassy House, Allister Miller St, PO Box 199. Telephone: **2272, 2273,** or **2274**

Ambassador. Donald R Norland (resident in Gaborone)

SWEDEN. Stockholm (embassy), Strandvagen 101. Telephone: **(08) 63-05-20.** *Telex:* **12060 AMEMB S**

Ambassador. Rodney O'Gliasain Kennedy-Minot

Public Affairs Officer. Michael Weyl

SWITZERLAND. Bern (embassy), Jubilaeumstrasse 93, 3005 Bern. Telephone: **(031) 43-00-11.** *Telex:* **32128**

Ambassador. Marvin Warner

Public Affairs Officer. Elinor Green

SYRIA. Damascus (embassy), Abu Rumaneh, Al Monsur St 2, PO Box 29. Telephone: **332315** or **332814**

Ambassador. Richard W Murphy

Public Affairs Officer. Kenton W Keith

TANZANIA. Dar Es Salaam (embassy), National Bank of Commerce Bldg, City Dr, PO Box 9123. Telephone: **22775.** *Telex:* **41002**

Ambassador. James W Spain

Public Affairs Officer. Frederic S Mabbatt

THAILAND. Bangkok (embassy), 95 Wireless Rd; APO San Francisco 96346. Telephone: **252-5040** or **252-5171.** *Commercial office.* R Floor, Shell Bldg, 140 Wireless Rd. **251-9260, 9261,** or **9262**

Ambassador. Charles S Whitehouse

Public Affairs Officer. James A McGinley III

TOGO. Lome (embassy), Rue Pelletier Caventou and Rue Vouban, Boite Postale 852. Telephone: **29-91**

Ambassador. Ronald D Palmer

Public Affairs Officer. Ray Peppers

TRINIDAD AND TOBAGO. Port-of-Spain (embassy), Queen's Park W, PO Box 752. Telephone: **62-26371.** *Telex:* **230 Port of Spain**

Ambassador. Richard K Fox, Jr

Public Affairs Officer. Dennis Askey

TUNISIA. Tunis (embassy), 144 Avenue de la Liberte. Telephone: **282-566**

Ambassador. Edward W Mulcahy

Public Affairs Officer. William F Gresham

TURKEY. Ankara (embassy), 110 Ataturk Blvd; APO New York 09254. Telephone: **26-54-70**

Ambassador. Ronald I Spiers

Public Affairs Officer. Charles E Courtney

UNION OF SOVIET SOCIALIST REPUBLICS. Moscow (embassy), Ulitsa Chaykovskogo 19/21/23; APO New York 09862. Telephone: **252-00-11** through **252-00-19.** *Telex:* **7429 USEMB SU.** *Commercial office.* Ulitsa Chaykovskogo 15. **255-48-48** or **255-46-60.** *Telex:* **7805**

Ambassador. Malcolm Toon

Press and Cultural Officer (USIA). Raymond E Benson

UNITED ARAB EMIRATES. Abu Dhabi (embassy), Shaikh Khalid Bldg, Corniche Rd, PO Box 4009. Telephone: **61534** or **61535.** *Telex:* **2229 AMEMB AH**

Ambassador. Francois M Dickman

Public Affairs Officer. George A Naifeh

UNITED KINGDOM

England. London (embassy), 24/31 Grosvenor Sq, W 1A 1AE; Box 40, FPO New York 09510. Telephone: **(01) 499-9000.** *Telex:* **266777**

Ambassador. Kingman Brewster, Jr

Public Affairs Officer. Michael T F Pistor

Northern Ireland. Belfast (consulate general), Queen's House, 14 Queen St, BT1 6EQ. Telephone: **(0232) 28239**

Charge. Peter R Spicer

Scotland. Edinburgh (consulate general), 3 Regent Ter EH 7 5BW. Telephone: **031-556-8315**

Consul General. Theodore B Dobbs

UPPER VOLTA. Ouagadougou (embassy), Boite Postale 35. Telephone: **35442, 35444** or **35446**

Ambassador. Pierre R Graham

Public Affairs Officer. Gerald E Huchel

URUGUAY. Montevideo (embassy), Calle Lauro Muller 1776; APO New York 09879. Telephone: **40-90-51** or **40-91-26**

Ambassador. Lawrence A Pezzullo

Public Affairs Officer. Lewis W Pate

VENEZUELA. Caracas (embassy), Avenida Francisco de Miranda and Avenida Principal de la Floresta; APO New York 09893. Telephone: **284-7111.** *Telex:* **25501 AMEMB VEN**

Ambassador. Viron P Vaky

Public Affairs Officer. Richard M Key

YEMEN ARAB REPUBLIC. Sana (embassy), Box 33, FPO New York 09545

Ambassador. Thomas J Scotes

Public Affairs Officer. Marjorie Ann Ransom

YUGOSLAVIA. Belgrade (embassy), Kneza Milosa 50. Telephone: **645655.** *Telex:* **11529**

Ambassador. Lawrence S Eagleburger

Public Affairs Officer. Terrence Catherman

ZAIRE. Kinshasa (embassy), 310 Avenue des Aviateurs; APO New York 09662. Telephone: **25881** through **25886.** *Telex:* **386**

Ambassador. Walter L Cutler

Public Affairs Officer. James D Conley

ZAMBIA. Lusaka (embassy), PO Box 1617. Telephone: **50222**

Ambassador. Stephen Low

Public Affairs Officer. John T Burns

STATE DEPARTMENT DESKS AND COUNTRY OFFICERS

AFGHANISTAN (Kabul). Michael Austrian. **202-632-9552**

ALBANIA. Robert A Mosher. **202-632-1457**

ALGERIA. Donald L Jameson. **202-632-1714**

ANDORARA. Michael Durkee. **202-632-2633**

ANGOLA (Luanda). Edward F Fugit. **202-632-1637**

ANZUS. Thomas J Wadja. **202-632-9690**

ARGENTINA. (Buenos Aires). Fernando Rondon. **202-632-9166**

AUSTRALIA (Canberra). Thomas J Wadja. **202-632-9690**

AUSTRIA (Vienna). Susan M Kingaman. **202-632-2005**

BAHAMAS (Nassau). James Thyden. **202-632-2620**

BAHRAIN. John Plyle. **202-632-0304**

BALTIC STATES. Thomas H Gerth. **202-632-1739**

BANGLADESH (Dacca). Douglas B Archard. **202-632-0466**

BARBADOS (Bridgetown). Giovanni Palazzolo. **202-632-2115**

BELGIUM (Brussels). Katherine H Shirley. **202-632-0498**

BELIZE (Belize City). George Gowen. **202-632-3381**

BENIN (Cotonou). Brian S Kirkpatrick. **202-632-0842**

BERMUDA (Hamilton). John P Shumate, Jr. **202-632-2622**

BHUTAN. David R Telleen. **202-632-0653**

BOLIVIA (La Paz). Robert S Pace. **202-632-3076**

BOTSWANA (Gaborone). Robert C Perry. **202-632-0916**

BRAZIL (Brasilia). Regina Eltz. **202-632-1245**

BRITISH HONDURAS. *See* Belize

BRITISH INDIAN OCEAN TERRITORY (BIOT). **202-632-8851**

BRITISH SOLOMON ISLANDS PRO-TECTORATE. *See* Solomon Islands

BRUNEI. William S Shepard. **202-632-8202**

BULGARIA (Sofia). Robert A Mosher. **202-632-1457**

BURMA (Rangoon). Richard M Gibson. **202-632-9367**

BURUNDI (Bujumbura). David L Cardwell. **202-632-1418**

CAMBODIA (Phnom Penh). Timothy M Carney. **202-632-3132**

CAMEROON (Yaounde). John Blodgett. **202-632-0996**

CANADA (Ottawa). John H Rouse, Jr. **202-632-2170**

CANAL ZONE. *See* Panama

CAPE VERDE. Roger A McGuire. **202-632-8436**

CENTO. Larry Semakis. **202-632-3121**

CENTRAL AFRICAN REPUBLIC (Bangul). David L Cardwell. **202-632-1418**

CENTRAL AMERICA (ROCAP). Thomas Mehen. **202-632-9287**

CEYLON (Colombo). *See* Sri Lanka

CHAD (N'Djamena). George Dies. **202-632-3066**

CHILE (Santiago). Robert S Driscoll. **202-632-2575**

CHINA, REPUBLIC OF (Taiwan) (Nationalist China). David G Brown, Jr. **202-632-2012**

CHINA, PEOPLE'S REPUBLIC OF (Red China). Richard R Hart. **202-632-6300**

COLOMBIA (Bogota). David W Cox. **202-632-2360**

COMOROES. Richard C Castrodale. **202-632-3040**

CONGO (Brazzaville). Michael F Gallagher. **202-632-2216**

CONGO (Kinshasa). *See* Zaire, Republic of

COOK ISLANDS. Harold T Nelson, Jr. **202-632-9690**

COSTA RICA (San Jose). Michele M Bova. **202-632-2205**

COUNCIL OF EUROPE. William R Salisbury. **202-632-0740**

CUBA. Emery P Smith. **202-632-9272**

CYPRUS (Nicosia). Nuel L Pazdral. **202-632-1429**

CZECHOSLOVAKIA (Prague). Kent N Brown. **202-632-2140**

DAHOMEY (Colonou). *See* Benin

DENMARK (Copenhagen). Charles W Schaller. **202-632-1194**

DOMINICAN REPUBLIC (Santo Domingo). Gerald de Santillana. **202-632-2130**

EAST AFRICAN COMMUNITY. Harvey Ames. **202-632-3228**

EAST-WEST CENTER. Virginia G Cooper. **202-632-0896**

ECONOMIC AND SOCIAL COMMISSION FOR ASIA AND THE PACIFIC. Birney Stokes. **202-632-1655**

ECONOMIC COMMISSION FOR AFRICA. Louis Kahn. **202-632-0600**

ECONOMIC COMMISSION FOR EUROPE. David H Swartz. **202-632-0315**

ECONOMIC COMMISSION FOR LATIN AMERICA. Birney Stokes. **202-632-1655**

ECUADOR (Quito). James Alliho. **202-632-8440**

EGYPT, ARAB REPUBLIC OF (Cairo). Gordon R Beyer. **202-632-1169**

EL SALVADOR (San Salvador). **202-632-8148**

EQUATORIAL GUINEA (Malabo). John Blodgett. **202-632-0996**

ESTONIA. Thomas H Gerth. **202-632-1739**

ETHIOPIA (Addis Ababa). Robert S Barrett. **202-632-8852**

EUROPEAN ATOMIC ENERGY COMMISSION (Euratom). David Swartz. **202-632-0315**

EUROPEAN COAL AND STEEL COMMUNITY (ECSC). Robert O Homme. **202-632-0531**

EUROPEAN COMMUNITIES. Robert O Homme. **202-632-0531**

EUROPEAN ECONOMIC COMMUNITY (EFC). Robert O Homme. **202-632-0531**

EUROPEAN FREE TRADE ASSOCIATION (EFTA). Ralph E Bressler. **202-632-0457**

EUROPEAN LAUNCHER DEVELOPMENT ORGANIZATION (ELDO). David Swartz. **202-632-0315**

EUROPEAN PROGRAMS. George A Laudato. **202-632-9246**

EUROPEAN SPACE RESEARCH ORGANIZATION (ESRO). David Swartz. **202-632-0315**

FIJI (Suva). Harold T Nelson, Jr. **202-632-9690**

FINLAND (Helsinki). Ronald E Woods. **202-632-0529**

FRANCE (Paris). James F Dobbins. **202-632-0751**

FRENCH ANTILLES Yvonne Thayer. **202-632-3673**

FRENCH GUIANA. *See* French Antilles

FRENCH POLYNESIA. Harold T Nelson, Jr. **202-632-9690**

FRENCH TERRITORY OF AFARS AND ISSAS. Gerald W Scott. **202-632-0849**

GABON (Libreville). John S Blodgett. **202-632-0996**

GAMBIA, THE (Banjul). Dalton V Killion. **202-632-2865**

GERMANY, FEDERAL REPUBLIC OF (Bonn)(West Germany). Kenneth A Kurze. **202-632-3020**

Berlin. George Chester. **202-632-2717**

GERMAN DEMOCRATIC REPUBLIC (Berlin)(East Germany). John Kendall Ward. **202-632-2135**

GHANA (Accra). Roger A McGuire. **202-632-8436**

GIBRALTAR. John P Shumate, Jr. **202-632-2622**

GILBERT AND ELLICE ISLANDS. Harold T Nelson, Jr. **202-632-9690**

GREAT BRITAIN. *See* United Kingdom

GREECE (Athens). James H Morton. **202-632-1563**

GREENLAND. Charles W Schaller. **202-632-1194**

GRENADA. James E Thyden. **202-632-2620**

GUADELOUPE. Giovanni Palazzolo. **202-632-2115**

GUATEMALA (Guatemala). Mark J Platt. **202-632-0815**

GUINEA (Conakry). Brian S Kirkpatrick. **202-632-0842**

GUINEA-BISSAU. Roger A McGuire. **202-632-8436**

GUYANA (Georgetown). Frank Tumminia. **202-632-3449**

HAITI (Port-au-Prince). Gerald de Santillana. **202-632-2130**

HONDURAS (Tegucigalpa). **202-632-8148**

HONG KONG. Mary von Briesen. **202-632-1436**

HORN OF AFRICA. *See* Ethiopia *and* Somalia

HUNGARY (Budapest). Thomas H Gerth. **202-632-1739**

ICELAND (Reykjavik). Don J Donchi. **202-632-1774**

INDIA (New Delhi). Robert F Ober, Jr. **202-632-1289**

INDONESIA (Jakarta). David T Kenney. **202-632-3590**

IRAN (Tehran). Myles Greene. **202-632-0574**

IRAQ. David Reuther. **202-632-0695**

IRELAND (Dublin). Charles W Schaller. **202-632-1194**

ISRAEL (Tel Aviv). Walter B Smith II. **202-632-2647**

ITALY (Rome). Brunson McKinley. **202-632-8210**

IVORY COAST (Abidjan). Brian S Kirkpatrick. **202-632-0842**

JAMAICA (Kingston). James Thyden. **202-632-2620**

JAPAN (Tokyo). Edward M Featherston. **202-632-3152**

JORDAN (Amman). Thomas J Carolan. **202-632-1018**

KENYA (Nairobi). Richard W Baker. **202-632-0857**

KHMER REPUBLIC. *See* Cambodia

KOREA, NORTH. John S Boardman. **202-632-9330**

KOREA, REPUBLIC OF (Seoul)(South Korea). Philip R Mayhew. **202-632-2210**

KUWAIT (Kuwait). John P Lyle. **202-632-0304**

LAOS (Vientiane). Judith R Johnson. **202-632-3132**

LATVIA. Thomas H Gerth. **202-632-1739**

LEBANON (Beirut). W Nathaniel Howell. **202-632-1019**

LESOTHO (Maseru). Robert C Perry. **202-632-0916**

LIBERIA (Monrovia). Eric E Svendsen. **202-632-8354**

LIBYA (Tripoli). Marguerite L King. **202-632-0666**

LIECHTENSTEIN. Susan M Klingaman. **202-632-2005**

LITHUANIA. Thomas H Gerth. **202-632-1739**

LUXEMBOURG (Luxembourg). Katherine H Shirley. **202-632-0498**

MACAO. Mary von Briesen. **202-632-1436**

MADAGASCAR, REPUBLIC OF (Tananarive). Richard C Castrodale. 202-632-3040

MALAGASY REPUBLIC. *See* Madagascar, Republic of

MALAWI (Lilongwe). Peter G Smith. 202-632-8851

MALAYSIA (Kuala Lumpur). William S Shepard. **202-632-8202**

MALDIVES. Albert A Thibault, Jr. 202-632-2351

MALI REPUBLIC (Bamako). Dalton V Killion. **202-632-2865**

MALTA (Valletta). Joan V Smith. 202-632-1726

MARTINIQUE. Giovanni Palazzolo. 202-632-2115

MAURITANIA. Dalton V Killion. 202-632-2865

MAURITIUS (Port Louis). Peter G Smith. 202-632-8851

MEXICO (Mexico, DF). George Falk. 202-632-0661

MICRONESIA. *See* Trust Territory of the Pacific Islands

MONACO. Joan V Smith. **202-632-1726**

MONGOLIA. Mary von Briesen. 202-632-1436

MOROCCO (Rabat). Stanley T Escudero. 202-632-2030

MOZAMBIQUE (Maputo). Jeffrey S Davidow. **202-632-8434**

NAMIBI (South West Africa). **202-632-8434**

NAURU. Harold T Nelson, Jr. **202-632-9690**

NEPAL (Kathmandu). David Tellenn. 202-632-0653

NETHERLANDS (The Hague). Katherine H Shirley. **202-632-20498**

NETHERLANDS ANTILLES (Curacao). Giovanni Palazzol. **202-632-2115**

NEW CALEDONIA AND NEW HEBRIDES. Harold T Nelson, Jr. 202-632-9690

NEW ZEALAND (Wellington). Harold T Nelson, Jr. **202-632-9690**

NICARAGUA (Managua). George Gowen. 202-632-3381

NIGER (Niamey). George A Dies. 202-632-3066

NIGERIA (Lagos). Edward W Lollis II. 202-632-3406

NORTH ATLANTIC TREATY ORGANI-ZATION (NATO). Henry A Holmes. 202-632-1626

NORWAY (Oslo). Don J Donchi. 202-632-1774

ORGANIZATION FOR ECONOMIC COOPERATION AND DEVELOPMENT (OECD). Paul A Laase. **202-632-0326**

OMAN (Muscat). Frederick H Gerlach. 202-632-1139

PACIFIC ISLANDS (General). Harold T Nelson, Jr. **202-632-9690**

PAKISTAN (Islamabad). Richard K McKee. **202-632-2441**

PANAMA (Panama). John P Becker. 202-632-2240

PAPUA NEW GUINEA (Port Moresby). Thomas J Wadja. **202-632-9690**

PARAGUAY (Asuncion). Aurelia E Brazeal. 202-632-1552

PERU (Lima). Alexander S C Fuller. 202-632-9282

PHILIPPINES (Manila). Daniel P Sullivan. 202-632-1221

POLAND (Warsaw). Alan R Thompson. 202-632-0575

PORTUGAL (Lisbon). William P Kelly. 202-632-0718

PORTUGUESE GUINEA. *See* Guinea-Bissau

QATAR. John P Lyle. **202-632-0304**

REUNION. Joan V Smith. **202-632-1726**

ROMANIA (Bucharest). Ints M Silins. 202-632-3298

RWANDA (Kigali). David L Cardwell. 202-632-1418

SAMOA. *See* Western Samoa

SAN MARINO. Brunson McKinley. 202-632-2453

SAO TOME AND PRINCIPE. John Blodgett. **202-632-0996**

SAUDI ARABIA (Jidda). Charles O Cecil. 202-632-9373

SENEGAL (Dakar). Dalton V Killion. 202-632-2865

SEYCHELLES. Richard W Baker. 202-632-0857

SIERRA LEONE (Freetown). Eric E Swendsen. **202-632-8354**

SINGAPORE (Singapore). William S Shepard. **202-632-8202**

SOLOMON ISLANDS. Thomas J Wadja. **202-632-9690**

SOMALIA (Mogadiscio). Gerald W Scott. 202-632-0849

SOUTH AFRICAN REPUBLIC (Pretoria). Frank B Crump. 202-632-3274

SOUTHEAST ASIA TREATY ORGANI-ZATION (SEATO), William L Gallagher. 202-632-1200

SOUTHERN RHODESIA (Salisbury). George Moose. 202-632-8252

SOUTH PACIFIC COMMISSION. Harold T Nelson, Jr. **202-632-9690**

SOUTH WEST AFRICA. *See* Nambia

SPAIN (MADRID). Michael Durkee. 202-632-2633

SPANISH GUINEA. *See* Equatorial Guinea

SPANISH SAHARA. *See* Western Sahara

SRI LANKA (Ceylon) (Colombo). Albert A Thibault, Jr. **202-632-2307**

SUDAN (Khartoum). Robert F Illing. 202-632-3355

SURINAM (Paramaribo). Giovanni Palazzolo. **202-632-2115**

SWAZILAND (Mbabane). Robert C Perry. 202-632-0916

SWEDEN (Stockholm). Ronald E Woods. 202-632-0529

SWITZERLAND (Bern). Susan M Klingaman. **202-632-2005**

SYRIAN ARAB REPUBLIC (Damascus). Thomas J Carolan, Jr. **202-632-1018**

TANGANYIKA. *See* United Republic of Tanzania

THAILAND (Bangkok). Lucian L Rocke, Jr. **202-632-1741**

TOGO (Lome). Brian S Kirkpatrick. **202-632-0842**

TONGA (Nuku'alofa). Harold T Nelson. **202-632-9690**

TRINIDAD and TOBAGO (Port-of-Spain). Frank Tumminia. **202-632-3449**

TRUCIAL STATES. *See* United Arab Emirates

TRUST TERRITORY OF THE PACIFIC ISLANDS (Spain). Richard L Williams. **202-632-9690**

TUNISIA (Tunis). Theodore S Wilkenson. **202-632-2294**

TURKEY (Ankara). Elaine D Smith. **202-632-1562**

UGANDA (Kampala). Richard W Baker. **202-632-0857**

UNION OF SOVIET SOCIALIST REPUBLICS (Moscow). Melvyn Levitsky. **202-632-8671**

UNITED ARAB EMIRATES (Abu Dhabi). John P Lyle. **202-632-0304**

UNITED KINGDOM (London). John P Shumate, Jr. **202-632-2622**

UNITED REPUBLIC OF TANZANIA (Dar es Salaam). Richard Castrodale. **202-632-3040**

UPPER VOLTA (Ouagadougou). George A Dies. **202-632-3066**

URUGUAY (Montevideo). Aurelia E Brazeal. **202-632-1551**

VATICAN. Brunson McKinley. **202-632-2453**

VENEZUELA (Caracas). Thomas W Sonandres. **202-632-3338**

VIETNAM. David C Harr. **202-632-3132**

WEST BANK (Jerusalem). Edward Springer. **202-632-3444**

WESTERN EUROPEAN UNION (WEU). James H Madden. **202-632-2097**

WESTERN SAHARA. Dalton V Killion. **202-632-2865**

WESTERN SAMOA (Apia). Harold T Nelson, Jr. **202-632-9690**

YEMEN ARAB REPUBLIC (Sana). Frederick H Gerlach. **202-632-1139**

YEMEN, PEOPLE'S DEMOCRATIC REPUBLIC OF. Frederick H Gerlach. **202-632-1139**

YUGOSLAVIA (Belgrade). Jack M Seymour. **202-632-3655**

ZAIRE, REPUBLIC OF (Kinshasa). Edward Marks. **202-632-1706**

ZAMBIA (Lusaka). Peter G Smith. **202-632-8851**

ZANZIBAR. *See* United Republic of Tanzania

PART THREE
THE MEDIA

MEDIA ORGANIZATIONS

ACADEMY OF HOSPITAL PUBLIC RELATIONS. Suite 2701, 2650 N Lakeview, Chicago, IL 60614. **312-871-5800**

ACCURACY IN MEDIA, INC. 777 14th St NW, Washington, DC 20005. **202-783-4406.** Reed J Irvine, chairman of the board. Bernard Yoh, communications director. John R Van Evera, national director. C C Clinkscales III, executive assistant

This organization monitors the news media to check balance, fairness, and accuracy; it is concerned with public-interest coverage. If the organization receives complaints from the public about reporting, it may go back to the newspaper, magazine, or radio or television station involved to report the complaint. It is a nonprofit corporation funded by individual and business contributions

THE ADVERTISING COUNCIL, INC. 825 3rd Ave, New York, NY 10022. **212-758-0400.** Robert P Keim, president. Benjamin S Greenberg, director, public affairs, (h) **212-859-5905.** Night line: **212-758-0539**

Branch Offices and Contacts

Washington. 1730 Rhode Island Ave NW, Washington, DC 20036. **202-331-9153.** Lewis W Schollenberger

Los Angeles. 1717 N Highland Ave, Los Angeles, CA 90028. **213-462-0988.** Richard Dwan

The council was formed in 1942, and one of its first projects was to persuade Americans to buy war bonds. Since then, it has offered free public-service advertising in more than 20 campaigns annually.

The board of directors of the council has 85 members selected from American Business Press, the Association of National Advertisers, the Magazine Publishers Association, the National Association of Broadcasters, and the Outdoor Advertising Association of America. The board has a 24-member executive committee and standing committees on certain topics.

Its pronounced policy is to

"Accept no subsidy from government and remain independent of it...Conduct campaigns of service to the nation at large...Accept no campaign with a commercial interest unless the public interest is obviously overriding"

THE AMERICAN ADVERTISING FEDERATION. 1225 Connecticut Ave NW, Washington, DC 20036. **202-659-1800.** Howard Bell, president. Cathy Denk, manager, information and educational services

The federation is an organization of advertising agencies, television networks, and other advertising associations formed to lobby against advertising regulations. There are 328 national corporate members of the federation. It has 164 professional clubs and 41 collegiate clubs

AMERICAN ASSOCIATION OF SCHOOLS AND DEPARTMENTS OF JOURNALISM. 102 Reavis Hall, Northern Illinois University, De Kalb, IL 60150. **815-753-0150.** Quintus C Wilson, executive secretary

AMERICAN JEWISH PUBLIC RELATIONS SOCIETY. 60 Glenwood Ave, East Orange, NJ 07017. **201-673-6800.** William Pages, president. An organization "dedicated to the advancement of professional standards for public information and interpretation of Jewish affairs in the United States and abroad"

AMERICAN NEWSPAPER PUBLISHERS ASSOCIATION. PO Box 17407, Dulles International Airport, Washington, DC 20041 (Reston, VA). **703-620-9500.** Jerry Friedheim, general manager. William Schabacker, manager, public affairs

ANPA is an organization of more than 1200 daily newspapers in the US with more than 90 percent of the nation's circulation. It offers advice, seminars, and printed information on a number of topics affecting newspapers, including research, training, government relations, labor relations, and insurance. The association is the chief representative group for the newspaper industry and concerns itself with all phases of newspaper operation. It has a full-time headquarters in Reston, VA, and a research institute in Easton, PA.

ANPA offers two major conventions a year: a general membership meeting in the spring (usually April or May), and a production conference in June.

It has an extensive library, a credit bureau, and a foundation that provides grants and scholarships. ANPA offers direct help with its own insurance program, debt collection service, and research center. It also provides

publications dealing with nearly every aspect of newspaper operations

AMERICAN RADIO RELAY LEAGUE, INC. 225 Main St, Newington, CT 06111. **203-666-1541** (also night line). Richard Baldwin, general manager. Peter O'Dell, public information. *Other contact.* Bobbie (Roberta) Chamalian

The league provides coordination of ham radio operators for emergency communications. It is the national membership organization for US and Canadian ham radio operators

AMERICAN SOCIETY OF JOURNALISM SCHOOL ADMINISTRATORS. Journalism Department, Northern Illinois University, Dekalb, IL 60115. **815-953-1925.** Night line: **815-756-6690.** Dr Donald R Grubb, executive director

The society was organized in 1944 to help both large and small departments and schools of journalism maintain high standards of journalism instruction. Among other functions, it helps journalism instructors find employment during the summer months

AMERICAN SOCIETY OF NEWSPAPER EDITORS. Box 551, 1350 Sullivan Tri, Easton PA 18042. **215-252-5502.** Gene Giancarlo, executive secretary

AMERICAN THEATRE CRITICS ASSOCIATION. Suite 1012, 1860 Broadway, New York, NY 10023

ASSOCIATED PRESS MANAGING EDITORS ASSOCIATION. 50 Rockefeller Plz, New York, NY 10020. **212-262-4000**

ASSOCIATION OF AMERICAN PUBLISHERS. 1 Park Ave, New York, NY 10016. **212-689-8920.** Townsend W Hoopes, president. Mary McNulty, director, public relations, Ext 205. Richard Kleeman (1707 L St NW, Washington, DC 20036), Washington representative, **202-293-2585**

The association, with more than 300 member publishing houses, is the major organization of publishers in the US. It provides a lobby for book publishers and monitors threats to the First Amendment, copyright changes, postal regulations, and literary education. Policy is established by a 25-member board of directors, and the organization has a full-time staff of about 28 persons. AAP provides informational services, surveys, and a group insurance plan

ASSOCIATION OF SECOND CLASS MAIL PUBLICATIONS. 1518 K St NW, Washington, DC 20005. 202-628-7220

THE AUTHORS GUILD, INC. 234 W 44th St, New York, NY 10036. 212-398-0838. Peter Heggie, executive secretary. A corporate member of the Authors League of America, Inc (212-391-9198); the national society of professional authors

AVIATION/SPACE WRITERS ASSOCIATION (formerly the Aviation Writers Association). Cliffwood Rd, Chester, NJ 07930. 201-879-5667. William F Kaiser, executive secretary. Promotes "accuracy and veracity in reporting and writing on aviation and space matters"

BASEBALL WRITERS ASSOCIATION OF AMERICA. 36 Brookfield Rd, Huntington Station, NY 11746. 516-421-5270. Jack Lang, secretary-treasurer. An organization of sports writers for daily newspapers in major league cities whose specific duty is covering major league baseball

BROADCAST PIONEERS LIBRARY. 1771 N St NW, Washington, DC 20036. 202-223-0088. Catharine Heinz, director. A research library devoted to the history of radio and television, and a referral center to other sources of broadcast history

CABLE TELEVISION INFORMATION CENTER. The Urban Institute, 2100 M St NW, Washington, DC 20037. 202-872-8888

CODE AUTHORITY OF THE NAB. 7060 Hollywood Blvd, Hollywood, CA 90028. 213-462-6909. Roger G Feld, manager

COMMUNICATION COMMISSION. 475 Riverside Dr, New York, NY 10027. 212-870-2567. J Warren Day, news and information director. An agency of the National Council of Churches of Christ in the US that monitors movies and television

THE COMMUNITY FILM WORKSHOP COUNCIL. 17 W 60th St, New York, NY 10023. 212-247-3192. Cliff Frazier, executive director. An organization seeking to increase the participation of minority groups in film making and broadcasting

CORPORATION FOR PUBLIC BROADCASTING. 1111 16 St, Washington, DC 20036. 202-293-6160. Henry Loomis, president. S L Harrison, public affairs

This private corporation was created by Congress to further the development of educational radio and television stations. Although a nongovernmental agency, it is funded through public funds and some private donations. It helped to establish, and supports, the Public Broadcasting System (PBS) and provides grants to local radio and television stations

COUNCIL ON CHILDREN, MEDIA, AND MERCHANDISING. Suite 523, 1346 Connecticut Ave, Washington, DC 20036. 202-466-2583. Robert Choate, president. Pamela C Engle, assistant

The council acts as a watchdog on the effects of television viewing on children and has produced a number of studies on the subject. The latest, released in June 1977, was entitled "Edible TV: Your Child and Food Commercials "

DEPARTMENT OF STATE CORRESPONDENTS ASSOCIATION. c/o State Department Office of Press Relations, Main State Bldg, Washington, DC 20520. 202-632-2706

THE EDUCATION WRITERS ASSOCIATION. PO Box 281, Woodstown, NJ 08098. 609-769-1552. Charles H Harrison, executive director

The association consists of a group of education writers for newspapers, magazines, radio, and television whose aims are to see that trends and problems in education are reported, and to generally improve education coverage. The group holds seminars on a regional and a national basis and tries to attract top-notch writers and reporters to education coverage

EDUCATIONAL BROADCASTING CORP. 356 W 58th St, New York, NY 10019. 212-262-4200

FINANCIAL PUBLIC RELATIONS ASSOCIATION. 309 N Washington St, Chicago, IL 60606. 317-782-1442

FREEDOM OF INFORMATION CENTER. PO Box 858, Columbia, MO 65201. 314-882-4856. Dr Paul Fisher, director, 314-882-7495. Karen Siegert, administrative assistant, 314-882-4856

The center's primary function is to "collect and disseminate materials relating to the free flow of information." It publishes the

bimonthly *FOI Digest*, as well as the *FOI Report* 18 times a year. Topics covered by the FOI Center include press councils, freedom of information legislation, shield laws, government secrecy, privacy, libel, and other legal and social problems related to communications.

Individuals and organizations can subscribe to the Center's list of publications

THE FUND FOR INVESTIGATIVE JOURNALISM, INC. 1346 Connecticut Ave NW-1021, Washington, DC 20036. 202-462-1844. Howard Bray, executive director

The fund's basic function is giving grants, primarily to free-lancers, to cover the costs of investigative journalism. Since 1969 the fund has awarded more than 300 grants totaling about $300,000, and two of its grantees have won Pulitzer prizes

INTERNATIONAL PUBLIC RELATIONS ASSOCIATION. 1776 F St NW, Washington, DC 20006. 202-833-1800. *Contact.* William H McGaughey

INVESTIGATIVE JOURNALISM PROGRAM. Urban Policy Research Institute, Suite W, 321 S Beverly Dr, Beverly Hills, CA 90212. 213-553-4161. Dan Noyes, director. A service program for journalists in California and elsewhere in the West on how to find information from public records and how to pursue investigative stories

INVESTIGATIVE REPORTERS AND EDITORS, INC. 307 N Pennsylvania St, Indianapolis, IN 46206. 317-633-9273. Myrta Pulliam, treasurer. Robert W Greene (*Newsday*, 550 Stewart Ave, Garden City, NY 11530), president, 516-737-4466

IRE is "an educational organization designed to aid reporters and editors," and is best known for the team investigation it conducted of corruption in Arizona after the death of Phoenix reporter Don Bolles, a charter member of the organization. Although that investigation has been completed, IRE plans to continue in existence and is trying to broaden its base with increased membership among journalists—"membership is for those substantially engaged in reporting and/or editing" and journalism educators

JOURNALISM EDUCATION ASSOCIATION. Treasurer's address and telephone: St Rose Convent, 912 Market St, La Crosse, WI 54601. 608-782-5610. Publications program: Tomahawk Tri, Shabbona, IL 60550. Paula Simons, president, 913-682-8653.

Night line: **913-651-5241.** An organization of junior high, high school, and college journalism and communications teachers seeking to promote high professional standards through publications, conventions, and workshops

MAGAZINE PUBLISHERS ASSOCIATION, INC. 575 Lexington Ave, New York, NY 10022. **212-752-0055.** Stephen E Kelly, president. Gloria R Dixon, director, public relations, (h) **212-580-7120** (also night line). Chapin Carpenter (1629 K St NW, Washington, DC 20006), vice president, government relations, **202-296-7277**

This is a national organization of 125 concerns that publish a total of 450 magazines. "The magazine industry's major communications resource"

MEDIA ACCESS PROJECT. 1609 Connecticut Ave NW, Washington, DC 20009. **202-785-2613**

MEDIA COALITION, INC. 342 Madison Ave, New York, NY 10024. **212-687-2288.** Night line or emergency number: **212-687-2289.** Susan Clark, national coordinator. A group of seven trade associations (publishers, booksellers, wholesalers, college stores, motion picture producers) that follows the actions of state legislatures to monitor activity affecting the media

MUSIC CRITICS ASSOCIATION, INC., and MCA EDUCATIONAL ACTIVITIES, INC. 6201 Tuckerman Ln, Rockville, MD 20852. **301-530-9527.** Patrick J Smith, president. Richard D Freed, executive secretary

Organized in 1957, the association promotes high standards of music criticism and provides a forum for self-criticism and the exchange of ideas. The group provides seminars, workshops, and an exchange program, and seeks to establish a set of professional standards

NATIONAL ADVERTISING REVIEW BOARD. 845 3rd Ave, New York, NY 10028. **212-832-1321.** Kenneth A Cox, chairman

The board "functions as the advertising industry's self-regulatory mechanism" and is "primarily concerned with the truth and accuracy of specific claims made in a national advertisement." The primary sponsors of the board are the American Advertising Federation, the American Association of Advertising Agencies, the Association of National Advertisers, and the Council of Better Business Bureaus.

In 1977 the organization issued a summary report of its organization and the complaints

that it had handled. In the first 5 years of its existence since 1971, the board handled 31 appeals out of 1174 initial complaints

NATIONAL ASSOCIATION OF BROADCASTERS. 1771 N St NW, Washington, DC 20036. **202-293-3500.** Vincent T Wasilewski, president, **202-293-3516.** Candace L Greene, director, media relations, **202-293-4956.** Bob Hallahan, news bureau director, **202-293-3585**

NAB is the primary organization for broadcasters in the US, and has a widely observed code of operation and ethics for the industry. In addition, it monitors legislative, bureaucratic, and legal activities as they affect the industry. NAB provides a lobby; public relations department; legal department; engineering, management, and research advice; publications; and group insurance.

Its avowed purposes are

"to foster and promote the development of broadcasting in all its forms; to protect its members from injustices and unjust demands, and to encourage customs and practices that will strengthen the broadcast industry so that it can best serve the public"

NATIONAL ASSOCIATION OF BUSINESS AND EDUCATIONAL RADIO, INC. 1330 New Hampshire Ave NW, Washington, DC 20036. **202-639-8334.** Val Williams, president and general manager. Mays Browning, junior editor. Mary Zitello, public relations. A national trade organization representing radio licensees, suppliers, and others interested in radio

NATIONAL ASSOCIATION OF SCIENCE WRITERS, INC. PO Box H, Sea Cliff, NY 11579. **516-671-1734.** Rosemary Arctander, administrative secretary

This organization, founded in 1934, has a membership of about 950 full-time science writers, who must have at least 2 years in the field to join. Membership classes include actives, who are staff members of a publication and either write or edit science material, and associates, who write about science on behalf of their employers but whose output is directed to the public

NATIONAL ASSOCIATION OF STATE EDUCATION DEPARTMENT INFORMATION OFFICERS. 1801 N Moore St, Arlington, VA 22209

THE NATIONAL BLACK MEDIA COALITION. 2027 Massachusetts Ave NW, Washington, DC 20036. **202-797-7473.** Pluria Marshall, principal official. An advocate group for black minority access to the media

NATIONAL BOARD OF REVIEW OF MOTION PICTURES, INC. 210 E 68th St, New York, NY 10021. **212-988-4916.** Charles P Reilly, executive director

NATIONAL CABLE TELEVISION ASSOCIATION. 918 16th St NW, Washington, DC 20006. **202-457-6700.** Robert L Schmidt, president, **202-457-6740.** Lucille Larkin, vice-president, public affairs, **202-457-6760.** A national trade association representing some 1400 cable television companies in the US

NATIONAL CITIZENS COMMITTEE FOR BROADCASTING. Suite 402, 1028 Connecticut Ave NW, Washington, DC 20036. **202-466-8407.** Nicholas Johnson, chairperson. Elinor Koch, editor, *Access Magazine.* Melinda Halpert, lobby director. Formed in 1967; works toward "reform of broadcasting media, representation of public interest in broadcasting issues, and oversight of Congressional and regulatory issues affecting public interest in media"

NATIONAL FREE-LANCE PHOTOGRAPHERS ASSOCIATION. 4 E State St, Doylestown, PA 18901. **215-348-2990**

NATIONAL MEDIA. 301 E 48th St, New York, NY 10017. **212-371-8040**

THE NATIONAL NEWS COUNCIL. 1 Lincoln Plz, New York, NY 10023. **212-595-9411.** Norman Isaacs, chairman. William B Arthur, executive director. Ned Schnuman, associate director. A self-appointed organization that considers and reports on complaints concerning fair or ethical news coverage; publishes findings in *Columbia Journalism Review*

NATIONAL NEWSPAPER ASSOCIATION. 1627 K St NW, Washington, DC 20006. **202-466-7200.** William G Mullen, executive vice-president

NNA serves 5500 weekly and 950 daily newspapers in the US. It provides legislative, governmental, and industry information through its Washington staff and *Publishers' Auxiliary*, a weekly newspaper to inform newspaper executives of current events, trends, issues, and developments in the newspaper industry

NATIONAL NEWSPAPER PUBLISHERS ASSOCIATION. National Press Bldg, 529 14th St NW, Washington, DC 20045. **202-638-4473**

NATIONAL PRESS PHOTOGRAPHERS ASSOCIATION. Box 1146, Durham, NC

27702. **919-489-3700.** Charles Cooper, executive secretary

NATIONAL PUBLIC RADIO. 2025 M St NW, Washington, DC 20036. **202-785-5400.** Night line or emergency number: **202-785-5380.** Frank Mankeiwicz, president, **202-785-5522.** James P Barrett, director, public information, **202-785-5353.** Eva Archer, assistant director, public information, **202-785-5355**

National Public Radio and the Association of Public Radio Stations were merged into the National Public Radio organization, a private, nonprofit group started in 1970. Funded primarily by the Corporation for Public Broadcasting, an agency established by Congress, National Public Radio also receives corporate and individual contributions.

National Public Radio provides programs for about 200 noncommercial stations. It operates with a staff of about 130 persons, its own studios, its own tape distribution system, and regional offices in New York, Chicago, and Los Angeles

NATIONAL SCHOOL PUBLIC RELATIONS ASSOCIATION. 1801 N Moore St, Arlington, VA 22209. **703-528-5840.** John H Wherry, executive director. Public relations officers for school districts, as well as teacher in educational communications

THE NEWSPAPER FUND. PO Box 300, Princeton, NJ 08540. **609-452-2000.** Thomas E Engleman, executive director.

The fund, besides providing internships for journalism students, offers an excellent guide to journalism schools and scholarships throughout the US. The nonprofit foundation promotes journalism careers and provides abundant information to that end

OFFICE FOR FILM AND BROADCASTING. Suite 1300, 1011 1st Ave, New York, NY 10022. **212-644-1880.** The Reverend Patrick J Sullivan, director. The Catholic church's organization monitoring movies and television

PACIFICA FOUNDATION (does business as KPFA-FM, Berkeley, CA; KPFK-FM, Los Angeles, CA; KPFT-FM, Houston, TX; WBAI-FM, New York; WPFW-FM, Washington, DC.) PO Box 8455, Universal City, CA 91608. **213-763-0700.** Joel Kugelmass, executive director. Kenneth V Jenkins, president

Member Stations' Addresses and Managers
KPFA-FM. 2207 Shattuck Ave, Berkeley, CA 94704. Elbert Sampson

KPFK-FM. 3729 Cahuenga Blvd, North Hollywood, CA 91604. Judy Richardson
KPFT-FM. 419 Lovett Blvd, Houston, TX 77006. Michael August
WBAI-FM. 359 62nd St, New York, NY 10021. Anna Kosof
WPFW-FM. 1030 15th St NW, Washington, DC 20005. Denise Oliver (acting)
Pacifica Program Service/Tape Library. 5316 Venice Blvd, Los Angeles, CA 90019. Bill Stein

The foundation operates FM radio stations in Berkeley and Los Angeles, CA; Houston, TX; New York, NY; and Washington, DC. The stations are educational, noncommercial, and listener-supported, and are operated as "an alternative voice to the commercial media "

PERIODICAL PRESS ASSOCIATION. Suite 508, 100 University Ave, Toronto, Ont, Canada M5J 1V6. **416-364-1497.** George Mansfield, manager. An association of specialized newspapers and magazines

PUBLIC RELATIONS SOCIETY OF AMERICA. 845 3rd Ave, New York, NY 10022. **212-826-1750.** Rea W Smith, vice-president, administrator. The major membership organization of public relations people; publishes *Public Relations Journal* and the annual *Public Relations Register*

PUBLISHERS PUBLICITY ASSOCIATION, INC. c/o Robert Dahlin (*Publishers Weekly*, 1180 Avenue of the Americas, New York, NY 10036), secretary, **212-764-5170**

RADIO FREE EUROPE/RADIO LIBERTY, INC. 1201 Connecticut Ave, NW, Washington, DC 20036. **202-457-6900.** Sig Mickelson, president, **202-457-6910.** Gretchen S Brainerd, director, information services, **202-457-6920.** (h) **703-533-2876.** For further details, see WORLD.

This nonprofit corporation was set up in 1950-51 to broadcast news and other information to eastern European and Soviet countries, "in a manner not inconsistent with the broad foreign policy objectives of the United States." It has 46 transmitters in Germany, Portugal, and Spain totaling about 4.5 million watts, and, for the fiscal year 1977, had a budget of $52.7 million. Until 1971 it was funded by the Central Intelligence Agency and is now supported by congressional appropriation, for the most part.

The corporation employs 1821 persons and broadcasts in 21 languages, including 16 of the languages spoken in the Soviet Union. It claims a listening audience of 16

million eastern Europeans and between three and four million listeners in the Soviet Union. RFE focuses on news of the world and of the areas to which it directs its broadcasts

RADIO TELEVISION NEWS DIRECTORS ASSOCIATION. 1735 De Sales St NW, Washington, DC 20036. **202-737-8657.** Len Allen, managing director. Ernie Schultz, director, information, KTVY-TV, **405-478-1212.** Works to promote high standards of broadcast journalism, defends broadcasters' right to access to news, promotes training for broadcast journalists, and present annual awards for outstanding broadcast news efforts

REPORTERS COMMITTEE FOR FREEDOM OF THE PRESS. Rm 1112, 1750 Pennsylvania Ave NW, Washington, DC 20006. **202-347-6888.** Jean Campbell, administrative assistant

THE SOCIETY OF PROFESSIONAL JOURNALISTS, SIGMA DELTA CHI. 35 E Wacker Dr, Chicago, IL 60601. **312-236-6577.** Russell E Hurst, executive officer, (h) **312-668-6684** (also night line and emergency number). Kathy Lieberman, director, information services

The major membership organization of journalists in the US, the society has developed a strong code of ethics and has long been active in defending the rights of journalists. As of 1977, there were 154 campus chapters and 140 professional chapters. The society has been operating since 1909 and has produced a monthly, *Quill*, since 1912. The 1977 membership numbered about 33,000 professional and campus members; SDX says that requirements for professional membership have been tightened in recent years

US SENATE PRESS SECRETARIES ASSOCIATION. 2107 Dirksen Senate Bldg, Washington, DC 20510. Jack Pridgen, president, **202-224-5274.** Primarily a social organization; also offers information and education on public relations procedures and national issues

WASHINGTON INDEPENDENT WRITERS. Suite 710, 1010 Vermont Ave NW, Washington, DC 20005. **202-347-4973**

THE WASHINGTON JOURNALISM CENTER. 2401 Virginia Ave NW, Washington, DC 20037. **202-331-7977.** Julius Duscha, director. Celia M Kay, administrative assistant

Founded in 1965, the center is independent and nonprofit and is supported by funds from foundations, news-gathering organizations, and private sources. Its purpose is "to encourage more responsible reporting of public affairs." The center sponsors a series of conferences with speakers ranging from academic experts to Cabinet members

WHITE HOUSE NEWS PHOTOGRAPHERS ASSOCIATION. PO Box 28274, 529 14th St NW, Washington, DC 20045. **202-483-1011.** *Press contact.* Joe Tomko

WOMEN IN COMMUNICATIONS, INC. PO Box 9561, Austin, TX 78766.

512-345-8922. Night Line or emergency number: **512-345-0784.** Mary E Utting, executive director. Ernestine Wheelock, public relations director

Women in Communications, Inc, was started in 1909 as Theta Sigma Phi and until 1970 was the only major membership society for women journalists, since women were not admitted to membership in Sigma Delta Chi. The group says that it has about 8,000 members—men and women—nationwide in all areas of communications, including journalism, broadcasting, public relations, advertising, free-lance writing, and communications education. According to the organization,

"WICI speaks out on important First Amendment issues, sponsors a variety of continuing education opportunities, has a national job information service for members, and works for ratification of ERA and other legislation to provide equal opportunity to professional women "

WOMEN'S INSTITUTE FOR FREEDOM OF THE PRESS. 3306 Ross Place NW, Washington, DC 20008. **202-966-7783.** Dr Donna Allen, director. A nonprofit, tax-exempt organization that conducts research on improvements in the nation's communications system, and publishes an annual directory of feminist media

DAILY NEWSPAPERS

The following lists of daily newspapers are arranged alphabetically by cities within each state. Where the city is not given as part of the newspaper's name, it is placed in parentheses

Alabama

ANNISTON STAR. Consolidated Publishing Co, 216 W 10th St, Anniston, 36201. **205-236-1551**

ATHENS NEWS COURIER. 410 W Green St (PO Box 670), Athens, 35611. **205-232-2720**

BIRMINGHAM POST-HERALD. Birmingham Post Co, 2200 N 4th Ave, Birmingham, 35202. **205-325-2222**

BIRMINGHAM NEWS. Birmingham Post Co, 2200 N 4th Ave, Birmingham, 35202. **205-325-2222**

CULLMAN TIMES. 300 4th Ave SE, Cullman, 35055. **205-734-2131**

DECATUR DAILY. Tennessee Valley Printing Co, Inc, 201 1st Ave SE (PO Box 1527), Decatur, 35601. **205-353-4612**

DOTHAN EAGLE. 203 N Oates St, Dothan, 36301. **205-792-3141**

ENTERPRISE LEDGER. Enterprise Alabama Ledger, Inc, 106 N Edwards St (PO Box 1140), Enterprise, 36330. **205-347-9533.** Roy Shoffner, publisher and editor

FLORENCE TIMES AND TRI-CITIES DAILY. Tri-Cities Newspapers, Inc, 219 W Tennessee St, Florence, 35631. **205-766-3434**

GADSEN TIMES. 401 Locust St (PO Box 188), Gadsen, 35902. **205-547-7521**

HUNTSVILLE NEWS. 2117 W Clinton Ave (PO Box 1007), Huntsville, 35804. **205-539-6512**

HUNTSVILLE TIMES. 2317 Memorial Pkwy, Huntsville, 35807. **205-534-2411**

JASPER MOUNTAIN EAGLE. Jasper Newspapers, Inc, PO Box 1469, Jasper, 35501. **205-221-2840**

(LANETT) WEST POINT VALLEY TIMES-NEWS. 220 N 12th St (PO Box 348), Lanett, 36863. **205-644-1101**

MOBILE PRESS. Mobile Press Register, Inc, 304 Government St (PO Box 2488), Mobile, 36630. **205-433-1551**

MOBILE REGISTER. Mobile Press Register, Inc, 304 Government St (PO Box 2488), Mobile, 36630. **205-433-1551**

MONTGOMERY ADVERTISER. Advertiser Co, 200 Washington St, Montgomery, 36102. **205-262-1611**

MONTGOMERY ALABAMA JOURNAL. Advertiser Co, 200 Washington St, Montgomery, 36102. **205-262-1611**

OPELIKA-AUBURN NEWS. Opelika-Auburn Publishing Co, Inc, 716 1st Ave (PO Drawer 2208), Opelika, 36801. **205-745-5761**

SCOTTSBORO SENTINEL. Scottsboro Newspapers, Inc, 704 E Laurel St (PO Box 220), Scottsboro, 35768. **205-574-1020**

SELMA TIMES-JOURNAL. 1018 Water Ave, Selma, 36701. **205-875-3403**

TALLADEGA HOME. Talladega Publishing Co, Inc, 4 Sylacauga Hwy (PO Box 977), Talladega, 35160. **205-362-1000**

TROY MESSENGER. Troy Publishing Corp, 113 N Market St (PO Box 727), Troy, 36081. **205-566-4270**

TUSCALOOSA NEWS. Tuscaloosa Newspapers Inc, 2001 6th St (PO Drawer 1), Tuscaloosa, 35401. **205-345-0505**

Alaska

ANCHORAGE DAILY NEWS. Northern Publishing Co, Inc, PO Box 1660, Anchorage, 99510. **907-272-8561**

ANCHORAGE TIMES. 820 4th Ave, Anchorage, 99501. **907-279-5622**

FAIRBANKS DAILY NEWS-MINER. Fairbanks Publishing Co, 200 N Cushman, Fairbanks, 99701. **907-456-6661**

(JUNEAU) SOUTHEAST ALASKA EMPIRE. 138 Main St, Juneau, 99801. **907-586-3740**

KETCHIKAN NEWS. Pioneer Publishing Co, 501 Dock St (PO Box 79), Ketchikan, 99901. **907-225-3157**

KODIAK DAILY MIRROR. PO Box 1307, Kodiak, 99615. **907-486-3227**

SITKA SENTINEL. Arrowhead Press, Box 799, Sitka, 99835. **907-747-3219**

Arizona

CASA GRANDE DISPATCH. 200 W 2nd St (PO Box 639), Casa Grande, 85222. **602-836-7461**

DOUGLAS DISPATCH. Douglas Dispatch, Inc, division of Thomson Newspapers, Inc, 530 11th St, Douglas, 85607. **602-364-3424**

(FLAGSTAFF) ARIZONA DAILY SUN. 417 W Santa Fe (PO Box 1849), Flagstaff, 86001. **602-774-4545**

KINGMAN MINER. PO Box 871, Kingman, 86401. **602-753-2121**

MESA TRIBUNE. Tribune Publishing Co, 120 W 1st Ave, Mesa, 85202. **602-833-1221**

NOGALES HERALD. A L Sisk, 134 Grand Ave, Nogales, 85621. **602-287-3622**

PHOENIX GAZETTE. Phoenix Newspapers, Inc, 120 E Van Buren St, Phoenix, 85004. **602-271-8000**

PHOENIX REPUBLIC. Phoenix Newspapers, Inc, 120 E Van Buren St, Phoenix, 85004. **602-271-8000**

PRESCOTT COURIER. Western Newspapers, Inc, 205 N Cortez, Prescott, 86301. **602-445-3333**

SCOTTSDALE DAILY PROGRESS. 7302 E Earll Dr, Scottsdale, 85252. **602-947-7544**

(TEMPE) TEMPE DAILY NEWS. 607 Mill Ave (Box 27087), Tempe, 85282. **602-967-3321**

(TUCSON) ARIZONA STAR. Tucson Newspapers, Inc, 4850 S Park Ave (PO Box 26887), Tucson, 85726. **602-294-4433**

TUCSON CITIZEN. Tucson Newspapers, Inc, 4850 S Park Ave (PO Box 26887), Tucson, 85726. **602-294-4433**

YUMA SUN. Sun Printing Co, 2055 Arizona Ave, Yuma, 85364. **602-783-3333**

Arkansas

ARKADELPHIA HERALD. Arkadelphia Publishing Co, 203 S 6th St (PO Box 10), Arkadelphia, 71923. **501-246-5151**

BATESVILLE GUARD. Guard-Record Co, Inc, 115 N 4th (PO Box 2036), Batesville, 72501. **501-793-2383.** Roy Ockert, Jr, managing editor

(BENTON) DAILY COURIER. 322 Main St (PO Box 207), Benton, 72015. **601-778-8228**

BLYTHEVILLE COURIER NEWS. Courier News Co, Inc, Broadway at Moultrie (PO Box 1108), Blytheville, 72316. **501-763-4461**

CAMDEN NEWS. Camden News Publishing Co, 113 Madison Ave, Camden, 71701. **501-836-8192**

(CONWAY) LOG CABIN DEMOCRAT. Conway Printing Co, 1318 Oak, Conway, 72032. **501-329-2921**

DE QUEEN CITIZEN. De Queen Bee Co, 404 De Queen Ave, De Queen, 71832. **501-584-2111**

EL DORADO NEWS-TIMES. News-Times Publishing Co, 111 N Madison, El Dorado, 71730. **501-862-6611**

(FAYETTEVILLE) NORTHWEST ARKANSAS TIMES. 212 N East St, Fayetteville, 72701. **501-442-6244**

FORREST CITY TIMES-HERALD. Times-Herald Publishing Co, Inc, 222 N Izard St, Forrest City, 72334. **501-633-3130**

(FORT SMITH) SOUTHWEST TIMES RECORD. Southwestern Operating Co, Donrey Media Group, 920 Rogers Ave, Fort Smith, 72901. **501-782-2011**

HARRISON TIMES. Times Publishing Co, 111 W Rush Ave, Harrison, 72601. **501-365-2325**

HELENA WORLD. Helena World Publishing Co, Helena, 72342. **501-338-3493**

HOPE STAR. Star Publishing Co, W 3rd and Grady Sts (PO Box 648), Hope, 71801. **501-777-8841**

HOT SPRINGS SENTINEL-RECORD. AAN-Southern Assn, 300 Spring St, Hot Springs, 71901. **501-623-7711**

JACKSONVILLE NEWS. 116 Hickory St, Jacksonville, 72076. **501-982-6506**

JONESBORO SUN. Troutt Brothers, 200 E Washington, Jonesboro, 72401. **501-935-5525**

(LITTLE ROCK) ARKANSAS DEMOCRAT. Little Rock Newspapers, Inc, Capitol Ave and Scott, Little Rock, 72203. **501-378-3400.** Jerry McConnell, managing editor

(LITTLE ROCK) ARKANSAS GAZETTE. 112 W 3rd Ave (PO Box 1821), Little Rock, 72203. **501-376-6161**

MAGNOLIA BANNER-NEWS. Banner-News Publishing Co, 134 S Washington (PO Box 100), Magnolia, 71753. **501-234-5130**

MALVERN RECORD. Malvern Daily Record, 133 Main St (PO Box 70), Malvern, 72104. **501-337-7523**

MENA STAR. Mena Star Co, Inc, 501-7 Mena St, Mena, 71953. **501-394-1900**

NEWPORT INDEPENDENT. 308 2nd St, Newport, 72112. **501-523-5855**

PARAGOULD PRESS. Daily Press, Inc, Hwy 1 at Hunt St (PO Box 38), Paragould, 72450. **501-239-8562**

PINE BLUFF COMMERCIAL. Commercial Printing Co, Box 6469, Pine Bluff, 71611. **501-534-3400.** Bill Musser, city editor

ROGERS NEWS. Northwest Arkansas Publishing Co, Donrey Media Group, 313 S 2nd, Rogers, 72756. **501-636-4411**

RUSSELLVILLE COURIER-DEMOCRAT. Arkansas Newspapers, Inc, PO Box 887, Russellville, 72801. **501-968-5252**

SEARCY CITIZEN. Citizen Publishing Co, 3000 E Race Ave, Searcy, 72143. **501-268-8621**

SPRINGDALE NEWS. Donrey Media Group, 514 E Emma Ave, Springdale, 72764. **501-751-6200**

(STUTTGARD) DAILY LEADER CO. Box 531, Stuttgart, 72160. **501-673-8555**

TEXARKANA GAZETTE. Texarkana Newspapers, Inc, 313-7 Pine St, Texarkana, 75501. **214-794-3311**

TEXARKANA NEWS. Texarkana Newspapers Inc, 313–7 Pine St, Texarkana, 75501. **214-794-3311**

WEST MEMPHIS TIMES. Crittenden Publishing Co, 111 E Bond St (PO Box 459), West Memphis, 72301. **501-735-1010**

California

ALAMEDA TIMES STAR. 1516 Oak St, Alameda 94501. **415-523-1200**

ANTIOCH LEDGER. Antioch Newspapers, Inc, 1700 Cavallo Rd (PO Box 70), Antioch, 94509. **415-757-2525**

BAKERSFIELD CALIFORNIAN. 1707 I St, Bakersfield, 93302. **805-323-7631**

BANNING RECORD-GAZETTE. Record-Gazette Publishing Co, 218 N Murray, Banning, 92220. **714-849-4586**

(BARSTOW) DESERT DISPATCH. Courier Enterprises, 130 Coolwater St, Barstow, 92313. **714-256-2257**

BERKELEY GAZETTE. Brown Newspaper Publishing Co, Inc, 2043 Allston Way Berkeley, 94704. **415-843-4800**

BRAWLEY NEWS. 135 S Plz, Brawley, 92227. **714-344-1220**

BURBANK REVIEW. Glendale Newspaper, Inc, Morris Newspaper Corp, 111 N Isabel St, Glendale, 91209. **213-241-4141**

(CAMARILLO) Daily News, 99 S Glenn Dr, Camarillo, 93010. **805-482-2701**

CHICO ENTERPRISE-RECORD. Enterprise Publishing Co, 700 Broadway, Chico, 95926. **916-891-1234**

COLUSA DAILY SUN-HERALD. 210 6th St, Colusa, 94932. **916-458-2121**

CONCORD TRANSCRIPT. East Bay Newspapers, Inc, 1741 Clayton Rd (PO Box 308), Concord, 94522. **415-682-6440**

(CORNING) DAILY OBSERVER. 710 5th St (PO Box 558), Corning, 96021. **916-824-5464**

(CORONA) DAILY INDEPENDENT. 823 S Main St, Corona, 91720. **714-737-1234**

DAVIS ENTERPRISE. Davis Enterprise, Inc, 302 G St (PO Box 1078), Davis, 96516. **916-756-0800**

(DOWNEY) SOUTHEAST NEWS AND DOWNEY CHAMPION. 12130 Paramount Blvd (PO Box 789), Downey, 90242. **213-923-1223**

EL CAJON CALIFORNIAN. El Cajon Publishing Co, 613 W Main St (PO Drawer 1565), El Cajon, 92022. **714-442-4404**

(EL CENTRO) IMPERIAL VALLEY PRESS. 205 N 8th St (PO Box 251), El Centro, 92243. **714-352-2211**

ESCONDIDO TIMES-ADVOCATE. 207 E Pennsylvania Ave, Escondido, 92025. **714-745-6611**

EUREKA TIMES-STANDARD. Humboldt Newspapers, Inc, PO Box 3580, Eureka, 95501. **707-442-1711**

FAIRFIELD REPUBLIC. Fairfield Publishing Co, 1250 Texas St (PO Box 47), Fairfield, 94533. **707-425-4646**

FONTANA HERALD-NEWS. Fontana Publishing Co, 16920 Spring St, Fontana, 92335. **714-822-2231**

FREMONT ARGUS. 37070 Fremont Blvd, Fremont, 94536. **415-797-5275**

FRESNO BEE. McClatchy Newspapers, 1626 E St, Fresno, 93789. **209-268-5221**

GLENDALE NEWS-PRESS. Glendale Newspapers, Inc, Morris Newspaper Corp, 111 N Isabel, Glendale, 91209. **213-241-4141**

GOLETA VALLEY TODAY. 6464 Hollister Ave (PO Box 388), Goleta, 93017. **805-968-2504**

GRASS VALLEY UNION. Nevada County Publishing Co, 151 Mill St, Grass Valley, 95945. **916-273-9561**

HANFORD SENTINEL. 418 W 8th (PO Box 9), Hanford, 93230. **209-582-0471**

HAYWARD DAILY REVIEW. Daily Review, Inc, PO Box 3127, Hayward, 94540. **415-783-6111**

HEMET NEWS. 123 S Carmalita St, Hemet 92343. **714-925-0555**

(HOLLISTER) FREE LANCE. 360 6th St, Hollister, 95023. **408-637-5566**. Millard Hoyle, publisher

HUNTINGTON PARK DAILY SIGNAL. 12130 Paramount Blvd, Downey, 90242. **213-862-4254**

INDIO NEWS. Associated Desert Newspapers, 45–140 Towne St (PO Drawer NNN), Indio, 92201. **714-347-3313**

LANCASTER LEDGER-GAZETTE. 44815 Fig Ave (PO Box 4048), Lancaster, 93534. **805-948-4701**

(LIVERMORE) TRI-VALLEY HERALD. 325 S I St (PO Box 31), Livermore, 94550. **415-447-2111**. Barry Schrader, editor

(LIVERMORE) VALLEY TIMES/PLEASANTON TIMES. 126 Spring St, Livermore, 94550. **415-443-4160**

LODI NEWS-SENTINEL. 125 N Church St, Lodi, 95240. **209-369-2761**

LOMPOC RECORD. Lompoc Record Publications, 115 N H St, Lompoc, 93438. **805-736-2313**

LONG BEACH INDEPENDENT. Twin Coast Newspapers, Inc, 604 Pine Ave, Long Beach, 90844. **213-435-1161**

LONG BEACH PRESS-TELEGRAM. Twin Coast Newspapers, Inc, 604 Pine Ave, Long Beach, 90844. **213-435-1161**

LOS ANGELES HERALD-EXAMINER. 1111 S Broadway (Box 2416), Los Angeles, 90051. **213-748-1212**

LOS ANGELES TIMES. Times Mirror Co, Times Mirror Sq, Los Angeles, 90053. **213-625-2345**. Paul Bertness, corporate public relations, **213-486-3923**

MADERA TRIBUNE. Madera Newspapers, Inc, 100 E 7th St, Madera, 93637. **209-674-2424**

MARTINEZ NEWS-GAZETTE. Gibson Radio and Publishing Co, 615 Estudillo St (PO Box 151), Martinez, 94554. **415-288-6400**

(MARYSVILLE) APPEAL-DEMOCRAT. Freedom Newspapers, Inc, 319 G St, Marysville, 95902. **916-742-6491**

MERCED SUN-STAR. Lesher Newspapers, Inc, 3033 N G St (PO Box 739), Merced 95340. **209-722-1511**

MODESTO BEE. McClatchy Newspapers, PO Box 3928, Modesto, 95352. **209-524-4041**. Michael G Kidder, executive editor, Ext 312

MONTEREY PENINUSLA HERALD. Pacific and Jefferson Sts, Monterey, 93940. **408-372-3311**

NAPA REGISTER. Napa Valley Publishing Co, 1615 2nd St, Napa, 94559. **707-226-3711**

OAKLAND TRIBUNE. Tribune Publishing Co, 401 13th St, Oakland, 94623. **415- 645-2000**

OCEANSIDE BLADE-TRIBUNE. South Coast Newspapers, Inc, 1722 S Hill (PO Box 90), Oceanside, 92054. **714-433-7333**

ONTARIO REPORT. Daily Report Co, 212 E B St, Ontario, 91764. **714-983-3511**

ORANGE COUNTY BULLETIN. Freedom Newspapers, Inc, 232 S Lemon St (PO Box 351), Anaheim, 92805. **714-774-7870**

ORANGE COUNTY COAST PILOT. Orange Coast Publishing Co, PO Box 1560, Costa Mesa, 92626. **714-642-4321**

ORANGE COUNTY NEWS TRIBUNE. Fullerton Publishing Co, 655 W Valencia Dr, Fullerton, 92632. **714-871-2345**

ORANGE COUNTY REGISTER. Freedom Newspapers, Inc, 625 N ̄Grand Ave, Santa Ana, 92711. **714-835-1234**

ORANGE COUNTY STAR-PROGRESS. Freedom Newspapers, Inc, 600 S Palm St, La Habra, 90631. **213-697-1734** or **714-529-2144**

ORLAND UNIT-REGISTER. 729 4th St (PO Box 847), Orland, 95963. **916-865-4433**

OROVILLE MERCURY-REGISTER. Oroville Mercury Co, 1740 Bird St (PO Box 651), Oroville, 95965. **916-533-3131**. Don Shaffer, editor

OXNARD PRESS-COURIER. Oxnard Publishing Co, 300 W 9th St, Oxnard, 93030. **805-483-1101**

PALM SPRINGS DESERT SUN. Desert Sun Publishing Co, The Evening News Assn, 611 S Palm Canyon Dr (PO Box 190), Palm Springs, 92262. **714-325-8666**

PALO ALTO TIMES. Peninsula Newspapers, Inc, 245 Lytton Ave, Palo Alto, 94302. **415-326-1200**

(PALO ALTO) WALL STREET JOURNAL (Pacific Coast Edition). Dow Jones and Co, Inc, 1701 Page Mill Rd, Palo Alto, 94304. **415-493-2800**. *News.* 220 Battery St, San Francisco, 94111. **415-433-3200**

PASADENA STAR-NEWS. Twin Coast Newspapers, 525 E Colorado Blvd, Pasadena, 91109. **213-796-0311**

(PASO ROBLES) DAILY PRESS. Paso Robles Newspapers, Inc, 1212 Pine St (PO Box 427), Paso Robles, 93446. **805-238-0330**

PETALUMA ARGUS-COURIER. Sonoma-Marin Publishing Co, PO Box 1091, Petaluma, 94952. **707-762-4541**

PITTSBURG POST DISPATCH. Post-Dispatch Co, 515 Railroad Ave, Pittsburg, 94565. **415-432-7336**

PLEASANTON TIMES. PO Box 607, Pleasanton, 94566. **415-462-4160**

POMONA PROGRESS-BULLETIN. Donrey Media Group, 300 S Thomas St (PO Box 2708), Pomona, 91766. **714-622-1201**

PORTERVILLE RECORDER. Porterville Publishing Co, Inc, 115 E Oak Ave, Porterville, 93257. **209-784-5000**

RED BLUFF NEWS. Red Bluff Daily News, Inc, Donrey Media Group, 710 Main St, Red Bluff, 96080. **916-527-2151**

REDDING RECORD SEARCHLIGHT. Redding Record, Inc, 1205 Placer St, Redding, 96001. **916-243-2424**

REDLANDS DAILY FACTS. 700 Brookside Ave, Redlands, 92373. **714-793-3221**

REDWOOD CITY TRIBUNE. Peninsula Newspapers, Inc, 901 Marshall St, Redwood City, 94063. **415-365-3111**

RICHMOND INDEPENDENT. Brown Newspaper Publishing Co, Inc, 164 10th St, Richmond, 94801. **415-234-5678**

RIDGECREST INDEPENDENT. Daily Independent, Ridgecrest, China Lake, 93555. **714-315-4481**

RIVERSIDE ENTERPRISE. Press-Enterprise Co, 3512 14th St, Riverside, 92501. **714-684-1200**

RIVERSIDE PRESS. Press-Enterprise Co, 3512 14th St, Riverside, 92502. **714-684-1200**

ROSEVILLE PRESS-TRIBUNE. 341 Lincoln, Roseville, 95678. **916-783-0451**

SACRAMENTO BEE. McClatchy Newspapers, 21st and Q (PO Box 15779), Sacramento, 95813. **916-442-5011**

SACRAMENTO UNION. 301 Capitol Mall, Sacramento, 94812. **916-442-7811**

SALINAS CALIFORNIAN. Salinas Newspapers, Inc, Gannett West, 123 W Alisal St, Salinas, 93901. **408-424-2221**

SAN BERNARDINO SUN-TELEGRAM. Sun Co, Gannett Group, 399 D St, San Bernardino, 92401. **714-889-9666**

SAN CLEMENTE SUN-POST. Coastline Publishers, Inc, 1542 N El Camino Real (PO Box 367), San Clemente, 92672. **714-492-5121**

SAN DIEGO TRIBUNE. Copley Press, Inc, Union-Tribune Publishing Co, 350 Camino de la Reina, San Diego, 92108. **714-299-3131**

SAN DIEGO UNION. Copley Press, Inc, Union-Tribune Publishing Co, 350 Camino de la Reina, San Diego, 92108. **714-299-3131**

SAN FRANCISCO CHRONICLE. Chronicle Publishing Co, 901 Mission St, San Francisco, 94103. **415-777-1111**

SAN FRANCISCO EXAMINER. San Francisco Newspaper Printing Co, Hearst Corp, 110 5th St, Stan Francisco, 94103. **415-777-2424**

SAN GABRIEL VALLEY DAILY TRIBUNE. 1210 N Azusa Canyon Rd, West Covina, 91790. **213-962-8811**. Mailing address: PO Box 1259, Covina, 91722. Fred Downing, managing editor

SAN JOSE MERCURY. Northwest Publications, Inc, 750 Ridder Park Dr, San Jose, 95190. **408-289-5000**

SAN JOSE NEWS. Northwest Publications, Inc, 750 Ridder Park Dr, San Jose, 95190. **408-289-5000**

SAN LUIS OBISPO TELEGRAM-TRIBUNE. Telegram-Tribune Co, 1321 Johnson Ave (PO Box 112), San Luis Obispo, 93406. **805-543-1901**

SAN MATEO TIMES & NEWS LEADER. Amphlett Printing Co, 1080 S Amphlett Blvd, San Mateo, 94402. **415-348-4321**

SAN PEDRO NEWS-PILOT. Southern California Associated Newspapers, 362 7th St, San Pedro, 90731. **213-832-0221**. Mailing address: PO Box 191, San Pedro, 90733

SAN RAFAEL INDEPENDENT-JOURNAL. PO Box 330, San Rafael, 94902. **415-454-3020**

SANTA BARBARA NEWS-PRESS. News-Press Publishing Co, Inc, Drawer NN, Santa Barbara, 93102. **805-966-3911**

SANTA CRUZ SENTINEL. Santa Cruz Sentinel Publishers, Inc, 207 Church St (PO Box 638), Santa Cruz, 95060. **408-423-4242**

SANTA MARIA TIMES. Santa Maria Times, Inc, 3200 Skyway Dr, Santa Maria, 93454. **805-925-2691**

SANTA MONICA OUTLOOK. United Western Newspapers, Inc, 1540 3rd St, Santa Monica, 90406. **213-394-6731**

SANTA PAULA CHRONICLE. Santa Paula Daily Chronicle Publishing Co, 116 N 10th St, Santa Paula, 93060. **805-525-5555**

SANTA ROSA PRESS DEMOCRAT. Press Democrat Publishing Co, 427 Mendocino Ave (PO Box 569), Santa Rosa, 95402. **707-546-2020**

(SONORA) UNION DEMOCRAT. Union Democrat, Inc, 84 S Washington St, Sonora, 95370. **209-532-7151**

SOUTH BAY BREEZE. Southern California Associated Newspapers, 5215 Torrence Blvd, Torrence, 90503. **213-540-5511** or **213-772-6281**

(SOUTH LAKE TAHOE) TAHOE TRIBUNE. Tahoe Daily Tribune, Inc, 3079 Harrison Ave (PO Box 1358), South Lake Tahoe, 95705. **916-541-3880** or **702-831-2344**

STOCKTON RECORD. Stockton Newspapers, Inc, Gannett West, 530 E Market St, Stockton, 95202. **209-466-2652**

(TAFT) MIDWAY DRILLER. Midway Driller, Inc, 800 Center St (PO Box Z), Taft, 93268. **805-763-3171**

THOUSAND OAKS NEWS-CHRONICLE. John P Scripps Newspapers, PO Box 3129, Thousand Oaks, 91359. **805-495-7401** or **213-889-8221**

TULARE ADVANCE-REGISTER. Tulare Newspapers, Inc, 388 E Cross Ave, Tulare, 93274. **209-688-0521**

TURLOCK DAILY JOURNAL. 138 S Center, Turlock, 95380. **209-634-9141**

UKIAH JOURNAL. Ukiah Daily Journal, Inc, 590 S School St, Ukiah, 95482. **707-462-1421**

VALLEJO TIMES-HERALD. Times Herald, Inc, 500 Maryland St, Vallejo, 94590. **707-644-4121**

(VAN NUYS) VALLEY NEWS AND GREEN SHEET. 14539 Sylvan St, Van Nuys, 91411. **213-997-4132**

VENTURA COUNTY STAR FREE PRESS. John P Scripps Newspapers, 567 E Santa Clara St, (PO Box 171), Ventura, 93001. **805-643-9901**

VICTORVILLE DAILY PRESS. 13891 Park Ave (PO Drawer AC), Victorville, 92392. **714-245-7744**

VISALIA TIMES-DELTA. Visalia Newspapers, Inc, 330 N West St, Visalia, 93277. **209-734-5821**

VISTA PRESS. Morris Newspaper Corp, 425 Vista Way, Vista, 92083. **714-724-7161**

(WALNUT CREEK) CONTRA COSTA TIMES. 2640 Shadelands Dr, Walnut Creek, 94598. **415-935-2525**

(WATSONVILLE) REGISTER-PAJARONIAN & SUN. Watsonville Newspapers, Inc, 1000 Main St, Watsonville, 94076. **408-724-0611**

WHITTIER NEWS. Owens Publications, Inc, 7037 S Comstock Ave, Whittier, 90608. **213-698-2571**

WILLOWS JOURNAL. Willows Publishing Co, 236 W Sycamore, Willows, 95988. **916-934-5411**

WOODLAND DEMOCRAT. Court and 2nd Sts, Woodland, 94695. **916-662-5421**

YREKA SISKIYOU NEWS. Foss Publishing Co, Inc, 309 S Broadway (PO Box 129), Yreka, 96067. **916-842-5777**

Colorado

ALAMOSA VALLEY COURIER. Courier Publishing Co, 401–7 State Ave, Alamosa, 81101. **303-589-6661**

(BOULDER) THE CAMERA. Boulder Publishing, Inc, 1048 Pearl St, Boulder, 80306. **303-442-1202**. J Edward Murray, publisher

CANON CITY RECORD. 523 Main St, Cannon City, 81212. **303-275-2323**

COLORADO SPRINGS GAZETTE-TELEGRAPH. Freedom Newspapers, 30 Prospect St (PO Box 1779), Colorado Springs, 80901. **303-632-4641**

COLORADO SPRINGS SUN. 103 W Colorado Ave (PO Box 130), Colorado Springs, 80901, **303-633-3881**

(CRAIG) NORTHWEST COLORADO PRESS-TABLOID. Northwest Colorado Publishing Co, Box 1115, Craig, 81625. **303-824-5888** or **5269**. Bob Sweeney, editor and publisher

DENVER POST. 650 15th St, Denver, 80202. **303-297-1010**

(DENVER) ROCKY MOUNTAIN NEWS. Denver Publishing Co, 400 W Colfax Ave, Denver, 80204. **303-892-5000**

DURANGO HERALD. 1275 Main Ave, Durango, 81301. **303-247-3504**

FORT COLLINS COLORADOAN. Fort Collins Newspapers, PO Box 1577, Fort Collins, 80522. **303-493-6397**

FORT MORGAN TIMES. Times Publishing Co, 329 Main, Fort Morgan, 80701. **303-867-5651**

GLENWOOD POST. A division of Stauffer Communications, Inc, 201 8th St (PO Box 550), Glenwood Springs, 81601. **303-945-8515**

(GOLDEN) DAILY TRANSCRIPT. 1000 10 St, Golden, 80401. **303-279-5541**

GRAND JUNCTION SENTINEL. Sentinel Publishing Co, 730 S 7th St (PO Box 668), Grand Junction, 81501. **303-242-5050**

GREELEY TRIBUNE & REPUBLICAN. Tribune Republican Publishing Co, 714 8th St, Greeley, 80631. **303-352-0211**

LA JUNTA TRIBUNE-DEMOCRAT. Democrat Publishing Co, 422 Colorado Ave (PO Box 480), La Junta, 81050. **303-384-4475**

(LAMAR) TRI-STATE NEWS. Betz Publishing Co, 310 S 5th (PO Box 1217), Lamar, 81052. **303-336-2266**

LEADVILLE HERALD DEMOCRAT. Continental Divide Press, Inc, Box 980, Leadville, 80461. **303-486-0461**

LONGMONT TIMES-CALL. Times-Call Publishing Co, 717 4th Ave, Longmont, 80501. **303-776-2244**

LOVELAND REPORTER-HERALD. Loveland Publishing Co, 450 Cleveland, Loveland, 80537. **303-669-2879**

MONTROSE PRESS. Press Publishing Co, 535 S 1st St (PO Box 850), Montrose, 81401. **303-249-3445**

PUEBLO CHIEFTAIN. Star-Journal Publishing Corp, PO Box 36, Pueblo, 81002. **303-544-3520**

PUEBLO STAR-JOURNAL. Star-Journal Publishing Corp, PO Box 36, Pueblo, 81002. **303-544-3520**

ROCKY FORD GAZETTE. Rocky Ford Publishing Co, 912 Elm Ave, Rocky Ford, 81067. **303-254-3351**

SALIDA MOUNTAIN MAIL. 121–31 E 2nd, Salida, 81201. **303-539-6691**

STERLING JOURNAL-ADVOCATE. Sterling Newspapers, Inc, 504 N 3rd St (PO Box 1272), Sterling, 80751. **303-522-1990**

TRINIDAD CHRONICLE-NEWS. 200 W Church St, Trinidad, 80182. **303-846-3311.** Ed Swartley, editor

Connecticut

ANSONIA SENTINEL. Thomson Newspaper Publishing Co, Inc, 241 Main St, Ansonia, 06401. **203-734-2546**

BRIDGEPORT POST. Post Publishing Co, 410 State St, Bridgeport, 06602. **203-333-0161**

BRIDGEPORT TELEGRAM. Post Publishing Co, 410 State St, Bridgeport, 06602. **203-333-0161**

BRISTOL PRESS. 99 Main St, Bristol, 06010. **203-584-0501**

DANBURY NEWS-TIMES. Danbury Publishing Co, Ottaway Newspapers, Inc, 333 Main St, Danbury, 06810. **203-744-5100**

GREENWICH TIME. Greenwich Publishing Co, 20 E Elm St, Greenwich, 06830. **203-869-8300**

GROTON NEWS. PO Box 1126, Groton, 06340. **203-446-1560**

HARTFORD COURANT. 285 Broad St, Hartford, 06115. **203-249-6411**

HARTFORD TIMES. 10 Prospect St, Hartford, 06101. **203-249-8211**

MANCHESTER EVENING HERALD. Manchester Publishing Co, Scripps League Newspapers, Herald Sq, Manchester, 06040. **203-643-2711**

(MERIDEN) JOURNAL. Meriden Record Co, 11–9 Crown St, Meriden, 06450. **203-235-1661**

(MERIDEN) RECORD. Meriden Record Co, 11–9 Crown St, Meriden, 06450. **203-235-1661**

MIDDLETOWN PRESS. 472 Main St, Middletown, 06457. **203-347-3331**

MILFORD CITIZEN. 117 Broad St, Milford, 06450. **203-874-1691**

NAUGATUCK NEWS. 195 Water St, Naugatuck, 06770. **203-729-2228**

(NEW BRITAIN) HERALD. Herald Publishing Co, 1 Herald Sq, New Britain, 06050. **203-225-4601.** R F Conway, managing editor

NEW HAVEN JOURNAL-COURIER. Register Publishing Co, Inc, 367 Orange St, New Haven, 06503. **203-562-3131**

NEW HAVEN REGISTER. Register Publishing Co, Inc, 367 Orange St, New Haven, 06503. **203-562-1121**

NEW LONDON DAY. Day Publishing Co, 47 Eugene O'Neill Dr, New London, 06320. **203-443-2882**

NORWALK HOUR. Hour Publishing Co, 2 Knight St, Norwalk, 06852. **203-866-2511**

NORWICH BULLETIN. Bulletin Co, 66 Franklin St, Norwich, 06360. **203-887-9211**

STAMFORD ADVOCATE. Gillespie Brothers, Inc, 258 Atlantic St, Stamford, 06904. **203-327-1600**

TORRINGTON REGISTER. Torrington Register Publishing Corp, 190 Water St, Torrington, 06790. **203-489-3121**

(VERNON) JOURNAL INQUIRER. 306 Progress Dr, Manchester, 06040. **203-646-0500**

WATERBURY AMERICAN. American-Republican, Inc, 389 Meadow St (PO Box 2090), Waterbury, 06720. **203-754-0141**

WATERBURY REPUBLICAN. American-Republican, Inc, 389 Meadow St (PO Box 2090), Waterbury, 06720. **203-754-0141**

WILLIMANTIC CHRONICLE. Chronicle Printing Co, Chronicle Rd, Willimantic, 06226. **203-423-8466**

WINSTED CITIZEN. Citizen Printing Co, 448 Main St, Winsted, 06098. **203-379-3333**

Delaware

DOVER DELAWARE STATE NEWS. Independent Newspapers, Inc, PO Box 737, Dover, 19901. **302-674-3600**

(WILMINGTON) EVENING JOURNAL. News-Journal Co, 831 Orange St, Wilmington, 19899. **302-573-2000**

(WILMINGTON) MORNING NEWS. News-Journal Co, 831 Orange St, Wilmington, 19899. **302-573-2000**

District of Columbia

WASHINGTON POST. 1150 15th St NW, Washington, 20071. **202-223-6000**

WASHINGTON STAR. Evening Star Newspaper Co, 225 Virginia Ave SE, Washington, 20061. **202-484-5000**

Florida

BOCA RATON NEWS. 34 SE 2nd St (PO Box 580), Boca Raton, 33432. **305-395-8300**

BRADENTON HERALD. 401 13th St W, Bradenton, 33505. **813-748-0411**

CLEARWATER SUN. Clearwater Newspapers, Inc, 301 S Myrtle, Clearwater, 33517. **813-448-2011**

(COCOA) TODAY. Gannett Group, PO Box 1330, Cocoa, 32922. **305-632-8700**

(DADE CITY) PASCO NEWS. 306 N 7th St (PO Box 187), Dade City, 33525. **904-567-5671**

DAYTONA BEACH JOURNAL. News-Journal Corp, 901 6th St, Daytona Beach, 32015. **904-252-1511**

DAYTONA BEACH NEWS. News-Journal Corp, 901 6th St, Daytona Beach, 32015. **904-252-1511**

DELAND SUN-NEWS. General Newspapers, Inc, Morris Newspaper Corp, 119 S Alabama Ave, Deland, 32720. **904-734-3661**

FORT LAUDERDALE NEWS. Gore Newspapers Co, 101 N New River Dr E, Fort Lauderdale, 33020. **305-527-4311**

FORT MYERS NEWS-PRESS. News-Press Publishing Co, Gannett Group, PO Box 10, Fort Myers, 33902. **813-334-2351**

FORT PIERCE NEWS TRIBUNE. Florida Freedom Newspapers, Inc, PO Box 69, Fort Pierce, 33450. **305-461-2050**

(FORT WALTON BEACH) PLAYGROUND DAILY NEWS. Florida Freedom Newspapers, Inc, PO Box 1307, Fort Walton Beach, 32548. **904-863-1111.** Scott Fischer, publisher

GAINESVILLE SUN. 101 SE 2nd Pl, Gainesville, 32602. **904-378-1141**

HOLLYWOOD SUN-TATTLER. 2600 N 29th Ave, Hollywood, 33020. **305-922-1511.** Edward Wentworth, editor, Ext 201

HOMESTEAD NEWS-LEDGER. 15–7 NE 1st St (PO Box 339), Homestead, 33030. **305-247-2321**

(JACKSONVILLE) FLORIDA TIMES-UNION. Florida Publishing Co, 1 Riverside Ave, Jacksonville, 32202. **904-791-4282**

(JACKSONVILLE) JOURNAL. Florida Publishing Co, 1 Riverside Ave, Jacksonville, 32202. **904-791-4282**

KEY WEST CITIZEN. 515 Green St, Key West, 33040. **305-294-6641**

KISSIMMEE SUN. Florida Sunpapers, Inc, 700 W Vine St, Kissimmee, 32741. **305-847-5227**

LAKE CITY REPORTER. 226 E Duval St (PO Box 1709), Lake City, 32055. **904-752-1297**

LAKELAND LEDGER. Lakeland Ledger Publishing Corp, PO Box 408, Lakeland, 33802. **813-688-6011**

LAKE WALES HIGHLANDER. Lake Wales Publishing Co, 33 W Orange Ave (PO Box 872), Lake Wales, 33853. **813-676-2571**

(LEESBURG) COMMERCIAL. 212 E Main St (PO Box 7), Leesburg, 32478. **904-787-4515**

(MARIANNA) JACKSON COUNTY FLORIDAN. Marianna Newspapers, Inc, 104 E Lafayette St (PO Box 520), Marianna, 32446. **904-526-3614**

MIAMI BEACH SUN-REPORTER. 1771 West Ave (PO Box 420), Miami Beach, 33139. **305-532-4531**

MIAMI HERALD. Miami Herald Publishing Co, Knight-Ridder Newspapers, Inc, Herald Plz, Miami, 33101. **305-350-2111**

MIAMI NEWS. 1 Herald Plz, Miami, 33101. **305-350-2200**

NAPLES DAILY NEWS. 1075 Central Ave, Naples, 33940. **813-262-3161**

OCALA STAR-BANNER. 819 SE 1st Ter, Ocala, 32670. **904-629-0011**

(ORANGE PARK) CLAY TODAY. Clay County Publishing Co, Inc, 1564 Kingsley Ave (PO Box 1209), Orange Park, 32073. **904-264-4537**

ORLANDO SENTINEL-STAR. 633 N Orange Ave, Orlando, 32801. **305-420-5000**

PALATKA NEWS. 1825 St Johns Ave, Palatka, 32077. **904-328-2721**

PALM BEACH NEWS. Palm Beach Newspapers, Inc, 265 Royal Poinciana Way, Palm Beach, 33480. **305-655-5755**

PANAMA CITY NEWS-HERALD. Florida Freedom Newspapers, Inc, 123–5 W 5th St, Panama City, 32401. **904-763-7621**

PENSACOLA JOURNAL. Pensacola News-Journal, Inc, Gannett Group, 101 E Romana St, Pensacola, 32501. **904-433-0041**

POMPANO SUN-SENTINEL. Gore Newspapers Co, 2501 N Federal Hwy, Pompano Beach, 33061. **305-941-7800**

(PUNTA GORDA) DAILY HERALD-NEWS. PO Box 1808, Punta Gorda, 33950. **813-639-2151.** Jeffrey Lytle, managing editor

ST AUGUSTINE RECORD. 158 Cordova St, St Augustine, 32084. **904-829-6562**

ST PETERSBURG INDEPENDENT. Times Publishing Co, PO Box 1121, St Petersburg, 33731. **813-893-8111**

ST PETERSBURG TIMES. Times Publishing Co, PO Box 1121, St Petersburg, 33731. **813-893-8111.** Robert J Haiman, executive editor

(SANFORD) EVENING HERALD. 300 N French Ave, Sanford, 32771. **305-322-2611**

SARASOTA HERALD-TRIBUNE. Lindsay Newspapers, Inc, 801 S Tamiami Tri (PO Box 1719), Sarasota, 33578. **813-958-7755**

SARASOTA JOURNAL. Lindsay Newspapers, Inc, 801 S Tamiami Tri (PO Box 1719), Sarasota, 33578. **813-958-7755**

STUART NEWS. 111 E Ocean Blvd (PO Box 396), Stuart, 33494. **305-287-1550**

TALLAHASSEE DEMOCRAT. 277 N Magnolia Dr, Tallahassee, 32302. **904-599-2100**

TAMPA TIMES. Tribune Co, 202 Parker St, Tampa, 33602. **813-272-7711.** Mailing address: PO Box 191, Tampa, 33601

TAMPA TRIBUNE. Tribune Co, 202 Parker St, Tampa, 33602. **813-272-7711.** Mailing address: PO Box 191, Tampa, 33601

TAMPA TRIBUNE & TIMES. Tribune Co, 202 Parker St, Tampa, 33602. **813-272-7711.** Mailing address: PO Box 191, Tampa, 33601

(WEST PALM BEACH) PALM BEACH TIMES. Palm Beach Newspapers, Inc, 2751 S Dixie Hwy (PO Drawer T), West Palm Beach, 33402. **305-833-7411**

WEST PALM BEACH POST. Palm Beach Newspapers, Inc, 2751 S Dixie Hwy (PO Drawer T), West Palm Beach, 33405. **305-833-7411**

WINTER HAVEN NEWS-CHIEF. Winter Haven Publishing Co, Inc, PO Box 1440, Winter Haven, 33880. **813-293-2191**

Georgia

ALBANY HERALD. Albany Herald Publishing Co, Inc, 138 Pine Ave, Albany, 31702. **912-435-4511**

AMERICUS TIMES-RECORDER. Times-Recorder Co, Inc, Vienna Rd, Americus, 31709. **912-924-2751** or **2752**

ATHENS BANNER-HERALD. Athens Newspapers, Inc, 1 Press Pl, Athens, 30603. **404-459-0123**

(ATHENS) THE DAILY NEWS. 1 Press Pl, Athens, 30603. **404-549-0123**

ATLANTA CONSTITUTION. Atlanta Newspapers, 72 Marietta St NW, Atlanta, 30303. **404-572-5151**

ATLANTA JOURNAL. Atlanta Newspapers, 72 Marietta St NW, Atlanta, 30303. **404-572-5151**

ATLANTA WORLD. 145 Auburn Ave, Atlanta, 30303. **404-659-1110**

AUGUSTA CHRONICLE. Augusta Chronicle & Herald, 725 Broad St, Augusta, 30903. **404-724-0851**

AUGUSTA HERALD. Augusta Chronicle & Herald, 725 Broad St, Augusta, 30903. **404-724-0851**

BRUNSWICK NEWS. 3011 Atlanta Ave (PO Box 1557), Brunswick, 31520. **912-265-8320**

CARTERSVILLE TRIBUNE NEWS. Cartersville Newspapers, Inc, 251 S Tennessee St, Cartersville, 30120. **404-382-4545**

COLLEGE PARK TODAY. Neighbor Newspapers, Inc, College Park, 30349. **404-763-3200**

COLUMBUS ENQUIRER. R W Page Corp, 17 W 12th St, Columbus, 31902. **404-322-8831**

COLUMBUS LEDGER. R W Page Corp, 17 W 12th St, Columbus, 31902. **404-322-8831**

CORDELE DISPATCH. Cordele Publishing Co, Inc, 13th Ave W, Cordele, 31015. **912-273-4398**

DALTON CITIZEN-NEWS. Thompson Newspapers, Inc, 308 S Thornton Ave (PO Box 1167), Dalton, 30720. **404-278-1001**

DUBLIN COURIER-HERALD DISPATCH & PRESS. Courier-Herald Publishing Co, Dublin, 31021. **912-272-0545**

GAINESVILLE TIMES. Southland Publishing Co, 345 Green St NW (PO Box 838), Gainesville, 30501. **404-532-1234**

GRIFFIN NEWS. News Corp, 323 E Solomon, Griffin, 30223. **404-227-3276**

JONESBORO NEWS DAILY. PO Box 368, Jonesboro, 30286. **404-478-5753**

LA GRANGE NEWS. Mid-South Management Co, Inc, 112 Hines St, La Grange, 30240. **404-884-7311**

(LAWRENCEVILLE) GWINNETT NEWS. News Co, 394 Clayton St NE, Lawrenceville, 30245. **404-963-0311**

(MABLETON) SOUTH COBB TODAY. Neighbor Newspapers, Inc, 1598 Bankhead Hwy, Mableton, 30059. **404-944-9400**

MACON NEWS. Macon Telegraph Publishing Co, 120 Broadway, Macon, 31208. **912-743-2621**. Joseph Parham, editor

MACON TELEGRAPH. Macon Telegraph Publishing Co, 120 Broadway, Macon, 31208. **912-743-2621**

MARIETTA JOURNAL. Times-Journal, Inc, 580 Fairground St, Marietta, 30060. **404-428-9411**

MOULTRIE OBSERVER. Observer Publishing Co, 25 N Main St, Moultrie, 31768. **912-985-4545**

ROME NEWS-TRIBUNE. 305 E 6th Ave, Rome, 30161. **404-232-1511**

(ROSWELL) NORTH FULTON TODAY. Neighbor Newspapers, Inc, 603 Atlantic St, Roswell, 30075. **404-993-7400**

SAVANNAH NEWS. Savannah News-Press Division, Southeastern Newspapers Corp, 105-111 W Bay St, Savannah, 31402. **912-236-9511**

SAVANNAH PRESS. Savannah News-Press Division, Southeastern Newspapers Corp, 105-111 W Bay St, Savannah, 31402. **912-236-9511**

STATESBORO HERALD. Statesboro Herald Publishing Co, Morris Newspaper Corp, 8 N Walnut St, Statesboro, 30458. **912-764-6146**

THOMASVILLE TIMES-ENTERPRISE. 119 N Madison St (PO Box 650), Thomasville, 31792. **912-226-2400**

TIFTON GAZETTE. Gazette Publishing Co, 211 N Tift Ave, PO Box 708, Tifton, 31794. **912-382-4321**

VALDOSTA DAILY TIMES. Thomson Newspapers, Inc, Valdosta, 31601. **912-244-1880**

WARNER ROBINS SUN. 1553 Watson Blvd (PO Drawer A), Warner Robins, 31093. **912-923-6432**

WAYCROSS JOURNAL-HERALD. 402 Isabella St (PO Box 685), Waycross, 31501. **912-283-2244**

Hawaii

HAWAII HOCHI. Hawaii Hochi, Ltd, 912 Kokea St, Honolulu, 96817. **808-845-2255**

HAWAII TIMES. Hawaii Times Co, Ltd, 916 Nuuanu Ave (PO Box 1230), Honolulu, 96807. **808-536-1091**

HAWAII TRIBUNE-HERALD. Donrey Media Group, 355 Kinoole St (PO Box 767), Hilo, 96720. **808-935-6621**

HONOLULU ADVERTISER. Advertiser Publishing Co, 605 Kapiolani Blvd (PO Box 3110), Honolulu, 96802. **808-525-8090**

HONOLULU STAR-BULLETIN. Gannett Pacific Corp, 605 Kapiolani Blvd (PO Box 3080), Honolulu, 96802. **808-525-8000**

Idaho

BLACKFOOT NEWS. Bulletin Publishing Corp, 27 NW Main, Blackfoot, 83221. **208-785-1100**

BOISE IDAHO STATESMAN. Federated Publications, Inc, a wholly owned subsidary of Gannett Co, Inc, 1200 N Curtis Rd (PO Box 40), Boise, 83707. **208-376-2121**

(BURLEY) SOUTH IDAHO PRESS. South Idaho Newspapers, Inc, 230 E Main St, Burley, 83318. **208-678-2201**

CALDWELL NEWS-TRIBUNE. Treasure Valley Publishing Co, 819 Main St, Caldwell, 83605. **208-459-4664**

COEUR D'ALENE PRESS. Coeur D'Alene Press, Inc, 201 2nd Ave, Coeur d'Alene, 83814. **208-664-8176**

IDAHO FALLS POST REGISTER. Post Co, 333 Northgate Mile, Idaho Falls, 83402. **208-522-1800**

KELLOGG NEWS. Kellogg News, Inc, 401 Main St, Kellogg, 83837. **208-784-0201**

LEWISTON TRIBUNE. Tribune Publishing Co, PO Box 957, Lewiston, 83501. **208-743-9411**

MOSCOW IDAHONIAN. News Review Publishing Co, Inc, 409 S Jackson (PO Box 8187), Moscow, 83843. **208-882-5561**

(NAMPA) IDAHO FREE PRESS. Canyon Publishing Co, 316 10th Ave, South Nampa, 83651. **208-466-7891**

(POCATELLO) IDAHO STATE JOURNAL. 305 S Arthur, Pocatello, 83201. **208-232-4161**

SANDPOINT DAILY BEE. Pend Orielle Printers, Inc, 310 Church St (PO Box 579), Sandpoint, 83864. **208-263-5151**

TWIN FALLS TIMES-NEWS. 132 3rd St W, Twin Falls, 83301. **208-733-0931**

(WALLACE) NORTH IDAHO PRESS. North Idaho Publishing Co, 507 Cedar St, Wallace, 83873. **208-752-1212**

Illinois

(ALTON) WOOD RIVER TELEGRAPH. Alton Telegraph Printing Co, 111 E Broadway, Alton, 62002. **618-463-2500**

(ARLINGTON HEIGHTS) DAILY HERALD. Paddock Publications, PO Box 280, Arlington Heights, 60006. **312-394-2300**

AURORA BEACON-NEWS. Copley Press, Inc, 101 S River St, Aurora, 60506. **312-897-4241**

(BEARDSTOWN) ILLINOISAN-STAR. Beardstown Newspapers, Inc, 1210 Wall St, Beardstown, 62618. **217-323-1010**

BELLEVILLE NEWS-DEMOCRAT. 120 S Illinois St, Belleville, 62222. **618-234-1000**

BELVIDERE REPUBLICAN. Belvidere Daily Republican Co, 401 Whitney Blvd, Belvidere, 61008. **815-543-9811**

BENTON NEWS. Benton Evening News Co, 111 E Church St, Benton, 62812. **618-438-5611**

(BLOOMINGTON) PANTAGRAPH. Evergreen Communications, Inc, 301 W Washington, Bloomington, 61701. **309-829-9411**

CAIRO CITIZEN. Cairo Newspapers, Inc, 711 Washington Ave, Cairo, 62914. **618-734-4244**

(CALUMET) DAILY CALUMET. Chicago, 60617. **312-375-2000**

CANTON LEDGER. Canton Daily Ledger Co, 53 W Elm St, Canton, 61520. **309-647-1849**

(CARBONDALE) SOUTHERN ILLINOISAN. Southern Illinoisan, Inc, 710 N Illinois Ave, Carbondale, 62901. **618-549-5391**

CARMI TIMES. Carmi Times Publishing Co, 323-325 E Main St (PO Box 409), Carmi, 62821. **618-382-4176**

CASEY DAILY REPORTER. 104 S Central (PO Box 158), Casey, 62420. **217-932-5211**

(CENTRALIA) SENTINEL. Centralia, 62801. **618-532-5601**

CHAMPAIGN-URBANA COURIER. 110 W University, Champaign, 61820. **217-367-5461**

CHAMPAIGN-URBANA NEWS GAZETTE. Champaign News Gazette, Inc, 48-52 Main St, Champaign, 61820. **217-352-5252**

(CHARLESTON) COLES COUNTY TIMES-COURIER. PO Box 559, Mattoon, 61938. **217-235-5656**

CHICAGO DEFENDER. Robert S Abbott Publishing Co, 2400 S Michigan, Chicago, 60616. **312-225-2400**

CHICAGO DAILY NEWS. Field Enterprises, Inc, 401 N Wabash Ave, Chicago, 60611. **312-321-2000.** Ceased publication March 4, 1978

CHICAGO SUN-TIMES. Field Enterprises, Inc, 401 N Wabash Ave, Chicago, 60611. **312-321-3000**

CHICAGO TRIBUNE. 435 N Michigan Ave, Chicago, 60611. **312-222-3232.** Stephen G Crews, public relations manager. **312-222-3345**

(CHICAGO) WALL STREET JOURNAL (Midwest Edition). Dow Jones and Co, Inc, 200 W Monroe St, Chicago, 60606. **312-648-7600**

CLINTON JOURNAL-PUBLIC. 100 W Main St, Clinton, 61727. **217-935-3184**

DANVILLE COMMERCIAL-NEWS. Northwestern Publishing Co, Gannett Group, 17 W North, Danville, 61832. **217-446-1000**

DECATUR HERALD. Decatur Herald and Review, Inc, 601 E William St, Decatur, 62525. **217-429-5151**

DECATUR REVIEW. Decatur Herald and Review, Inc, 601 E William St, Decatur, 62525. **217-429-5151**

DE KALB DAILY CHRONICLE. Sycamore and Barber Green Rd, De Kalb, 60115. **815-756-4841**

DIXON TELEGRAPH. B F Shaw Printing Co, 113-5 Peoria Ave, Dixon, 61021. **815-284-2222**

DU QUOIN CALL. Call Publishing Co, 9 N Division St, Du Quoin, 62832. **618-542-2133**

(EAST ST LOUIS) METRO-EAST JOURNAL. 425 Missouri Ave, East St Louis, 62201. **618-874-2500**

EDWARDSVILLE INTELLIGENCER. 117 N 2nd St, Edwardsville, 62025. **618-656-4700**

EFFINGHAM NEWS. Effingham Daily News Co, 201 N Banker St, Effingham, 62401. **217-347-7151**

ELDORADO DAILY JOURNAL. 1200 Locust St, Eldorado, 62930. **618-273-3379**

ELGIN COURIER-NEWS. Copley Press, Inc, 300 Lake St, Elgin, 60120. **312-741-1800**

FLORA NEWS RECORD. Flora Record Publishing Co, 105 W North Ave (PO Box 519), Flora, 62839. **618-662-2108**

FREEPORT JOURNAL-STANDARD. 27 S State Ave, Freeport, 61032. **815-232-1171**

GALESBURG, REGISTER-MAIL. Galesburg Printing and Publishing Co, 140 S Prairie, Galesburg, 61401. **309-343-7181**

HARRISBURG REGISTER. Register Publishing Co, 35 S Vine (PO Box 248), Harrisburg, 62946. **618-253-7146**

HOOPESTON CHRONICLE-HERALD. Mills Publication, Inc, 206-10 1st Ave, Hoopeston, 60942. **217-283-5111**

JACKSONVILLE COURIER. Jacksonville Journal Courier Co, 235 W State St, Jacksonville, 62650. **217-245-6121**

JACKSONVILLE JOURNAL. Jacksonville Journal Courier Co, 235 W State St, Jacksonville, 62650. **217-245-6121**

(JOLIET) HERALD-NEWS. Copley Press, Inc, 300 Caterpillar Dr, Joliet, 60436. **815-729-6033**

KANKAKEE JOURNAL. Kankakee Daily Journal Co, PO Box 632, Kankakee, 60901. **815-937-3300**

KEWANEE STAR-COURIER. Lee Enterprises, Inc, 105 E Central Blvd, Kewanee, 61443. **309-852-2181**

(LA SALLE) NEWS-TRIBUNE. Daily News-Tribune, Inc, 426 2nd St, LaSalle, 61301. **815-223-3200**

LAWRENCEVILLE RECORD. Lawrenceville Publishing Co, 1209 State St (PO Box 559), Lawrenceville, 62439. **618-943-2331**

LINCOLN COURIER. Logan County Publishing Co, McLean and Pulaski Sts, Lincoln, 62656. **217-732-2101**

LITCHFIELD NEWS-HERALD. 112 E Ryder, Litchfield, 62056. **217-324-2121.** David A Jackson, editor

MACOMB JOURNAL. Macomb Daily Journal, Inc, 128 N Lafayette St, Macomb, 61455. **309-833-2114**

MARION REPUBLICAN. Marion Publishing Co, Inc, 111–115 Franklin Ave, Marion, 62959. **618-993-2626**

MATTOON JOURNAL-GAZETTE. Coles Publishers, Inc, 100 Broadway, Mattoon, 61938. **217-235-5656**

MOLINE DAILY DISPATCH. 1720 5th Ave, Moline, 61265. **309-764-4344**

MONMOUTH REVIEW ATLAS. Review Atlas Printing Co, 400 S Main St, Monmouth, 61462. **309-734-3176**

MORRIS HERALD. Morris Publishing Co, 124 E Washington St, Morris, 60450. **815-942-3221**

MOUNT CARMEL REPUBLICAN-REGISTER. Mount Carmel Register Co, 115 E 4th St, Mount Carmel, 62863. **618-262-5144**

MOUNT VERNON REGISTER-NEWS. Mount Vernon Register-News Co, Mount Vernon, 62864. **618-242-0117**

OLNEY MAIL. Olney Daily Mail Publishing Co, 206 Whittle Ave (PO Box 340), Olney, 62450. **618-393-2931**

OTTAWA TIMES. Ottawa Publishing Co, 110 W Jefferson St, Ottawa, 61350. **815-433-2000**

PARIS BEACON-NEWS. Paris Beacon Publishing Co, 218 N Main St, Paris, 61944. **217-465-6424**

PAXTON RECORD. Stevens Printing Co, 218 N Market St, Paxton, 60957. **217-379-4313**

PEKIN TIMES. 22 S 4th St, Pekin, 61554. **309-346-1111**

PEORIA JOURNAL-STAR. 1 News Plz, Peoria, 61601. **309-686-3000**

PONTIAC LEADER. Pontiac Leader Publishing Co, 318 N Main St, Pontiac, 61764. **815-842-1153**

QUINCY HERALD-WHIG. Quincy Newspapers, 130–8 S 5th (PO Box 909), Quincy, 62301. **217-223-5100**

ROBINSON NEWS. Larry H Lewis, 302 S Cross St, Robinson, 62454. **618-544-2101**

ROCKFORD REGISTER-REPUBLIC. Rockford Newspapers, Inc, Gannett Group, 99 E State St, Rockford, 61105. **815-962-4433**

ROCKFORD STAR. Rockford Newspapers, Inc, Gannett Group, 99 E State St, Rockford, 61105. **815-962-4433**

ROCK ISLAND ARGUS. J W Potter Co, 1724 4th Ave, Rock Island, 61201. **309-786-6441**

SHELBYVILLE UNION. Union Publishing Co, 100 W Main St, Shelbyville, 62565. **217-774-2161**

(SPRINGFIELD) STATE JOURNAL-REGISTER. A division of Copley Press, Inc, 313 S 6th St, Springfield, 62705. **217-544-5711**

STERLING GAZETTE. Sterling Gazette Co, 312 2nd Ave, Sterling, 61081. **815-625-3600**

STREATOR TIMES-PRESS. 122 S Bloomington St, Streator, 61364. **815-672-2111**

TAYLORVILLE BREEZE-COURIER. Breeze Printing Co, Inc, 212 S Main St, Taylorville, 62568. **217-824-2233**

WATSEKA TIMES-REPUBLIC. Iroquis County Times, 313 E Walnut St, Watseka, 60970. **815-432-4926**

WAUKEGAN NEWS-SUN. Keystone Printing Service, Inc, 100 W Madison St, Waukegan, 60085. **312-689-7000**

WEST FRANKFORT AMERICAN. American Daily Publishing Corp, 111–15 S Emma St, West Frankfort, 62896. **618-932-2416**

WHEATON JOURNAL. Copley Newspapers, Inc, 362 S Schmale Rd (PO Box 360), Wheaton, 60187. **312-653-1100**

WOODSTOCK SENTINEL. Woodstock Publishing Co, 109 S Jefferson, Woodstock, 60098. **815-338-1300**

Indiana

ANDERSON BULLETIN. Anderson Newspapers, Inc, 1133 Jackson St, Anderson, 46015. **317-643-5371**

ANDERSON HERALD. Anderson Newspapers, Inc, 1133 Jackson St, Anderson, 46015. **317-643-5371**

ATTICA LEDGER TRIBUNE. Fountain-Warren Publishers, Inc, 217 S Perry St, Attica, 47918. **317-762-2411**

AUBURN STAR. Auburn Evening Star, 118 W 9th St, Auburn, 46706. **219-925-2611**

BEDFORD SUNDAY HERALD-TIMES. Bedford Times-Mail, 813 16th St, Bedford, 47421. **812-275-3355**

BEDFORD TIMES-MAIL. 813 16th St, Bedford, 47421. **812-275-3355**

(BICKNELL) THE KNOX COUNTY DAILY NEWS. 310 N Main St, Bicknell, 47512. **812-785-2222**

(BLOOMFIELD) THE EVENING WORLD. 29 W Main St, Bloomfield, 47424. **812-384-4579**

BLOOMINGTON HERALD-TELEPHONE AND HERALD-TIMES. 1900 S Walnut St, Bloomington, 47401. **812-332-4401**

BLUFFTON NEWS-BANNER. News-Banner Corp, 125 N Johnson St, Bluffton, 46714. **219-824-0224**

BRAZIL TIMES. 100 Times Sq, Brazil, 47834. **812-446-2216**

CHESTERTON TRIBUNE. 143 S Calumet Rd, Chesterton, 46304. **219-926-1131**

(CLINTON) THE DAILY CLINTONIAN. 422 S Main St, Clinton, 47842. **317-832-2443**

COLUMBIA CITY COMMERCIAL MAIL. Post & Mail Publishing Co, Inc, 116 N Chauncey, Columbia City, 46725. **219-244-5153**

COLUMBIA CITY POST. Post & Mail Publishing Co, Inc, 116 N Chauncey, Columbia City, 46725. **219-244-5153**

COLUMBUS REPUBLIC. 333 2nd St (PO Box 10), Columbus, 47201. **812-372-7811**

CONNERSVILLE NEWS-EXAMINER. News-Examiner Co, Inc, 406 Central Ave, Connersville, 47331. **317-825-1571**

CRAWFORDSVILLE JOURNAL-REVIEW. Journal-Review, Inc, 119 N Green, Crawfordsville, 47933. **317-362-1200**

DECATUR DEMOCRAT. Decatur Publishing Co, 141 S 2nd St, Decatur, 46733. **219-724-2121.** Robert W Shraluka, managing editor

ELKHART TRUTH. Truth Publishing Co, Inc, Communicana Bldg, Elkhart, 46514. **219-294-1661**

ELWOOD CALL-LEADER. Elwood Publishing Co, Inc, 317 S Anderson St (PO Box 85), Elwood, 46036. **317-522-3355**

EVANSVILLE COURIER AND EVANSVILLE PRESS. Evansville Courier, Inc, Evansville Press Co, 201 NW 2nd St, Evansville, 47702. **812-424-7711**

(FORT WAYNE) JOURNAL-GAZETTE. Journal-Gazette Co, 600 W Main St, Fort Wayne, 46802. **219-423-3311**

FORT WAYNE NEWS-SENTINEL. News Publishing Co, 600 W Main St, Fort Wayne, 46802. **219-743-0111**

FRANKFORT TIMES. Frankfort Times, Inc, 251 E Clinton, Frankfort, 46041. **317-659-3311**

FRANKLIN JOURNAL. Daily Journal, PO Box 366, Franklin, 46131. **317-736-7101**

(GARY) POST-TRIBUNE. Knight-Ridder Newspapers, Inc, 1065 Broadway, Gary, 46402. **219-886-5000**

GOSHEN NEWS. News Printing Co, 114 S Main, Goshen, 46526. **219-533-2151**

GREENCASTLE BANNER-GRAPHIC. LuMar Newspapers, Inc, 20 N Jackson St, Greencastle, 46135. **317-653-5151**

(GREENFIELD) DAILY REPORTER. 212 E Main, Greenfield, 46140. **317-462-5528**

GREENSBURG NEWS. Worrell Newspapers of Indiana, Inc, 135 S Franklin, Greensburg, 47240. **812-633-3111**

HAMMOND TIMES. Howard Publications, Inc, 417 Fayette St, Hammond, 46320. **219-932-3100**

HARTFORD CITY NEWS TIMES. 123 Jefferson, Hartford City, 47348. **317-348-0110**

HUNTINGTON HERALD-PRESS. Huntington Newspaper, Inc, 7 N Jefferson, Huntington, 46750. **219-356-6700**

INDIANAPOLIS NEWS. Indianapolis Newspapers, Inc, 307 N Pennsylvania St, Indianapolis, 46206. **317-633-9070**

INDIANAPOLIS STAR. Indianapolis Newspapers, Inc, 307 N Pennsylvania St, Indianapolis, 46206. **317-633-1240**

(JASPER) HERALD. 216 E 4th St (PO Box 31), Jasper, 47546. **812-482-2424**

JEFFERSONVILLE NEWS & JOURNAL. 225 Spring St, Jeffersonville, 47130

KENDALLVILLE NEWS-SUN. Kendallville Publishing Co, 112 N Main St, Kendallville, 46755. **219-347-0400**

KOKOMO TRIBUNE. 300 N Union, Kokomo, 46901. **317-459-3121**

(LAFAYETTE) JOURNAL & COURIER. Federated Publications, Inc, Gannett Group, 217 N 6th St, Lafayette, 47901. **317-423-5511**

LA PORTE HERALD-ARGUS. La Porte Publishing Corp, 701 State St, La Porte, 46350. **219-362-2161**

LEBANON REPORTER. Lebanon Newspapers, Inc, 117 E Washington, Lebanon, 46052. **317-482-4650**

LINTON CITIZEN. Hammell Newspapers of Indiana, Inc, 79 S Main St (PO Box 151), Linton, 47441. **812-847-4487**

LOGANSPORT TRIBUNE. Logansport Newspapers, Inc, 517 E Broadway, Logansport, 46947. **219-753-7511**

MADISON COURIER. 310 Courier Sq, Madison, 47250. **812-265-3641**

MARION CHRONICLE-TRIBUNE. 610 S Adams, Marion, 46952. **317-664-5111**

MARTINSVILLE REPORTER. Reporter-Times, Inc, 60 S Jefferson St, Martinsville, 46151. **317-342-3311**

MICHIGAN CITY NEWS-DISPATCH. Dispatch Publishing Co, 121 W Michigan Blvd, Michigan City, 46360. **219-874-7211**

MONTICELLO HERALD-JOURNAL. Monticello Herald Co, 114 S Main St, Monticello, 47960. **219-583-5121**

MOUNT VERNON DEMOCRAT. Mount Vernon Publishing Co, Inc, 430 Main St, Mount Vernon, 47620. **812-838-4811**

MUNCIE PRESS. Muncie Newspapers, Inc, 125 S High, Muncie, 47302. **317-747-5700**

MUNCIE STAR. Muncie Newspapers, Inc, 125 S High, Muncie, 47302. **317-747-5700.** *City desk.* **317-747-5754**

NEW ALBANY LEDGER & TRIBUNE. New Albany Tribune Co, 303 W 2nd St, New Albany, 47150. **812-944-6481**

NEW ALBANY TRIBUNE. New Albany Tribune Co, 303 W 2nd St, New Albany, 47150. **812-944-6481**

NEW CASTLE COURIER-TIMES. 201 S 14th St, New Castle, 47362. **317-529-1111**

NOBLESVILLE DAILY LEDGER. PO Box K, Noblesville, 46060. **317-773-1210**

PERU DAILY TRIBUNE. 26 W 3rd St, Peru, 46970. **317-473-6641**

PLYMOUTH PILOT-NEWS. Pilot Co, 217-223 N Center St, Plymouth, 46563. **219-936-3101**

PORTLAND COMMERCIAL REVIEW.
Graphic Printing Co, Inc, 309 W Main St, Portland, 47371. **317-726-8141**

PRINCETON CLARION. Cochrane News-papers, Inc, PO Box 321, Princeton, 47670. **812-385-2525**

RENSSELAER REPUBLICAN. 117 N Van Rensselaer St, Rensselaer, 47978. **219-866-5111**

(RICHMOND) PALLADIUM ITEM.
Palladium Publishing Corp, 19 N 9th St, Richmond, 47374. **317-962-1575**

ROCHESTER SENTINEL. Sentinel Corp, 118 E 8th St, Rochester, 46975. **219-223-2111**

RUSHVILLE REPUBLICAN. Rushville Newspapers, Inc, 219 N Perkins St, Rush-ville, 46173. **317-932-2222**

SEYMOUR TRIBUNE. 1215 E Tipton, Seymour, 47274. **812-522-4871**

SHELBYVILLE NEWS. Shelbyville News-papers, Inc, 123 E Washington St, Shelby-ville, 46176. **317-398-6631**

SOUTH BEND TRIBUNE. 225 W Colfax, South Bend, 46626. **219-233-6161**

SPENCER WORLD. 114 E Franklin, Spencer, 47460. **812-829-2255**

SULLIVAN DAILY TIMES. 115 W Jackson Ave, Sullivan, 47882. **812-268-6356**

TERRE HAUTE STAR. Tribune-Star Pub-lishing Co, Inc, 721 Wabash Ave, Terre Haute, 47808. **812-232-0581**

TERRE HAUTE TRIBUNE. Tribune-Star Publishing Co, Inc, 721 Wabash Ave, Terre Haute, 47808. **812-232-0581**

TIPTON TRIBUNE. Elwood Publishing Co, PO Box 248, Tipton, 46072. **317-675-2115**

VALPARAISO VIDETTE-MESSENGER.
1111 Glendale Blvd, Valparaiso, 46383. **219-462-5151**

VINCENNES SUN-COMMERCIAL.
Central Newspapers, Inc, 702 Main St, Vincennes, 47591. **812-882-2310**

WABASH PLAIN DEALER. Wabash Plain Dealer Co, Inc, 123 W Canal St, Wabash, 46992. **219-563-2131**

WARSAW TIMES-UNION. Reub Williams and Sons, Inc, Times Bldg, Warsaw, 46580. **219-267-3111**

WASHINGTON TIMES-HERALD. Donrey Media Group, 102 E Vantress St, Washing-ton, 47501. **812-254-0480**

WINCHESTER NEWS-GAZETTE. Gazette Publishing Co, 224 W Franklin St, Winchester, 47394. **317-622-4501**

Iowa

AMES TRIBUNE. Ames Daily Tribune Times Co, 317 5th St (PO Box 380), Ames, 50010. **515-232-2160**

ATLANTIC NEWS-TELEGRAPH. News-Telegraph Publishing Corp, 410 Walnut St, Atlantic, 50022. **712-243-2624**

BOONE NEWS-REPUBLICAN. 812–4 Keeler St, Boone, 50036. **515-432-1234**

BURLINGTON HAWK EYE. 800 S Main (PO Box 10), Burlington 52601. **319-754-8461**

CARROLL TIMES HERALD. Herald Pub-lishing Co, 508 N Court St (PO Box 357), Carroll, 51401. **712-792-3573**

CEDAR FALLS RECORD. Cedar Falls Publishing Co, Inc, 124 E 18th St, Cedar Falls, 50613. **319-266-2611**

(CEDAR RAPIDS) GAZETTE. Gazette Co, 500 3rd Ave SE, Cedar Rapids, 52401. **319-398-8211**

CENTERVILLE IOWAGIAN & CITIZEN.
Iowagian Printing Co, Centerville, 52544. **515-856-6336**

CHARLES CITY PRESS. Mid-American Publishing Co, 100 N Main St, Charles City, 50616. **515-228-3211**

CHEROKEE TIMES. Times Publishing Co, Times Bldg, Cherokee, 51012. **712-225-5111**

CLINTON HERALD. PO Box 31, Clinton, 52732. **319-242-7101**

COUNCIL BLUFFS NONPAREIL. Thom-son Newspapers, Inc, 117 Pearl St, Council Bluffs, 51501. **712-328-1811**

CRESTON NEWS-ADVERTISER. Creston Publishing Co, 503 W Adams St, Creston, 50801. **515-782-2141**

(DAVENPORT) QUAD-CITY TIMES.
Davenport Newspapers, 124 E 2nd (PO Box 3828), Davenport, 52808. **319-383-2200**

DES MOINES REGISTER. Des Moines Register and Tribune Co, 715 Locust St, Des Moines, 50304. **515-284-8000**

DES MOINES TRIBUNE. Des Moines Register and Tribune Co, 715 Locust St, Des Moines, 50304. **515-284-8000**

(DUBUQUE) TELEGRAPH-HERALD.
Telegraph-Herald, Inc, W 8th and Bluff St (PO Box 668), Dubuque, 52001. **319-588-5611**

ESTHERVILLE DAILY NEWS. Mid-America Publishing Corp, 10 N 7 St, Estherville, 51334. **712-362-2622**

FAIRFIELD DAILY LEDGER. 112 E Broadway, Fairfield, 52556. **515-472-4129**

FORT DODGE MESSENGER. Ogden Newspapers, Inc, 713 Central Ave, Fort Dodge, 50501. **515-573-2141**

FORT MADISON DEMOCRAT. 1226 Ave H, Fort Madison, 52627. **319-372-6421**

IOWA CITY PRESS-CITIZEN. Speidel Newspapers, Inc, 319 E Washington St (PO Box 2480), Iowa City, 52240. **319-337-3181**

(KEOKUK) THE GATE CITY. 1016 Main St, Keokuk, 52632. **319-524-8300**

(LE MARS) DAILY SENTINEL. 41 1st Ave NE, Le Mars, 51031. **712-546-7031**

MARSHALLTOWN TIMES-REPUBLICAN. Times-Republican Printing Co, 135 W Main St, Marshalltown, 50158. **515-753-6611**

MASON CITY GLOBE-GAZETTE. Lee Enterprises, Inc, 300 N Washington, Mason City, 50401. **515-423-4270**

MOUNT PLEASANT NEWS. 215 W Monroe St, Mount Pleasant, 52641. **319-385-3131**

MUSCATINE JOURNAL. 301 E 3rd St, Muscatine, 52761. **319-263-2331**

NEVADA JOURNAL. 1133 6th St, Nevada, 50201. **515-382-2161**

NEWTON NEWS. News Printing Co, 200 1st Ave E, Newton, 50208. **515-792-3121**

OELWEIN REGISTER. Register Publishing Co, Inc, 16 E Charles St, Oelwein, 50662. **319-283-2144**

OSKALOOSA HERALD. Oskaloosa Newspapers, Inc, 123 N Market, Oskaloosa, 52577. **515-672-2581**

OTTUMWA COURIER. Lee Enterprises, Inc, 213 E 2nd St, Ottumwa, 52501. **515-684-4611.** Gerald G Moriarity, publisher

PERRY CHIEF. Chief Printing Co, 1323 2nd St, Perry, 50220. **515-465-4666**

SHENANDOAH SENTINEL. Sentinel Publishing Co, 118 S Elm St, Shenandoah, 51601. **712-246-1100**

SIOUX CITY JOURNAL. Sioux City Newspapers, Inc, Scripps-Hagadone, 6th and Pavonia, Sioux City, 51105. **712-255-8991**

SPENCER DAILY REPORTER. Mid-America Publishing Corp, 416 1st Ave, Spencer, 51301. **712-262-6610**

(VINTON) CEDAR VALLEY TIMES. Vinton, 52349. **319-472-2311**

WASHINGTON JOURNAL. Elder, Shannon, and Co, 111 N Marion Ave, Washington, 52353. **319-653-2191**

(WATERLOO) COURIER. W H Hartman Co, 501 Commercial St, Waterloo, 50704. **319-234-3551**

WEBSTER CITY FREEMAN-JOURNAL. Ogden Newspapers, Inc, 720 2nd St, Webster City, 50595. **515-832-4350**

Kansas

ABILENE REFLECTOR-CHRONICLE. Reflector Chronicle Publishing Corp, 303 Broadway, Abilene, 67410. **913-263-3110**

ARKANSAS CITY TRAVELER. Traveler Publishing Co, 200 E 5th Ave, Arkansas City, 67005. **316-442-4200**

ATCHISON GLOBE. Globe Publishing Co, 1015-25 Main St, Atchison, 66002. **913-367-0583**

AUGUSTA GAZETTE. Gazette Publishing Co, Inc, 413 State St, Augusta, 67010. **316-775-2218**

BELOIT CALL. Beloit Call Publishing Co, 122 E Court St, Beloit, 67420. **913-738-2711.** Gary W Hilt, publisher

BURLINGTON DAILY REPUBLICAN. 324 Hudson St, Burlington, 66839. **316-364-5325**

CHANUTE TRIBUNE. Chanute Publishing Co, 15 N Evergreen. Chanute, 66720. **316-431-4000**

CLAY CENTER DISPATCH. Clay Center Publishing Co, 805 5th, Clay Center, 67432. **913-632-2127**

COFFEYVILLE JOURNAL. Coffeyville Publishing Co, Inc, 80th and Elm, Coffeyville, 67337. **316-251-3300**

COLUMBUS ADVOCATE. Columbus Publishing Co, Inc, 215 S Kansas, Columbus, 66725. **316-429-2733**

CONCORDIA BLADE-EMPIRE. Blade-Empire Publishing Co, 510 Washington St, Concordia, 66901. **913-243-2424**

COUNCIL GROVE REPUBLICAN. 208 W Main St, Council Grove, 66846. **316-767-5124**

DERBY REPORTER. Derby, 67037. **316-788-1831**

(DODGE CITY) DAILY GLOBE. Globe Publishing Co, 705 2nd, Dodge City, 67801. **316-225-4151.** Lee Finch, editor

EL DORADO TIMES. 114 N Vine, El Dorado, 67042. **316-321-1120**

EMPORIA GAZETTE. White Corp, Inc, 517 Merchant St, Emporia, 66801. **316-342-4800**

FORT SCOTT TRIBUNE. Tribune-Monitor Co, 6 E Wall St. Fort Scott, 66701. **316-223-1460**

FREDONIA HERALD. Scanlan Publishing Co, 635 Monroe St, Fredonia, 66736. **316-378-2154.** Ed L Kessinger, publisher

GARDEN CITY TELEGRAM. Telegram Publishing Co, 310 N 7th St, Garden City, 67846. **316-275-7105.** Frederic T Brooks, editor and publisher

GOODLAND NEWS. McCants Publishing Co, Inc, 1205 Main, Goodland, 67735. **913-899-2338**

GREAT BEND TRIBUNE. Morris Newspaper Corp, 2012 Forest St, Great Bend, 67530. **316-793-3521** or **3546**

HAYS NEWS. News Publishing Co, 507 Main St, Hays, 67601. **913-628-1081**

HAYSVILLE REPORTER. Daily Reporter, Haysville, 67060. **316-788-2311**

HIAWATHA WORLD. World Publishing Co, 607 Utah St, Hiawatha, 66434. **913-742-2111**

HUTCHINSON NEWS. Hutchinson Publishing Co, 300 W 2nd St, Hutchinson, 67501. **316-662-2311**

INDEPENDENCE REPORTER. Reporter Publishing Co, Inc, 320 N 6th St (Box 869), Independence, 67301. **316-331-3550**

IOLA REGISTER. Iola Register Publishing Co, 302 S Washington St, Iola, 66749. **316-365-2111**

JUNCTION CITY UNION. John G Montgomery Publishing, 814 N Washington St, Junction City, 66441. **913-762-5000**

KANSAS CITY KANSAN. 901 N 8th St, Kansas City, 66101. **913-371-4300**

LARNED TILLER & TOILER. 115 W 5th St (PO Box 206), Larned, 67550. **316-285-3111.** Jack Zygmond, publisher

LAWRENCE JOURNAL-WORLD. World Co, 6th and New Hampshire Sts, Lawrence, 66044. **913-843-1000**

LEAVENWORTH TIMES. Thomson Newspapers, Inc, 416-22 Seneca, Leavenworth, 66048. **913-682-0305**

LIBERAL SOUTHWEST TIMES. Liberal Newspapers, Inc, 16 S Kansas Ave, Liberal, 67901. **316-624-2541**

LYONS DAILY NEWS. Lyons Publishing Co, Inc, 210 W Commercial, Lyons, 67554. **316-257-2368**

MANHATTAN MERCURY. Seaton Publishing Co, Inc, 5th and Osage, Manhattan, 66503. **913-776-8805**

MCPHERSON SENTINEL. McPherson Sentinel, Inc, 301 S Main, McPherson, 67460. **316-241-2422**

NEODESHA SUN. Tucker Publishing Co, 108 N 5th St, Neodesha, 66757. **316-325-2727**

NEWTON KANSAN. Stauffer Communications, Inc, 121 W 6th, Newton, 67114. **316-283-1500**

NORTON TELEGRAM. Telegram Publishing Co, 215 S Kansas St, Norton, 67654. **913-927-3361**

OLATHE NEWS. Harris Enterprises, Inc, 514 S Kansas, Olathe, 66061. **913-764-2211**

OTTAWA HERALD. 104 S Cedar St, Ottawa, 66067. **913-242-4700**

PARSONS SUN. Sun Publishing Co, 220 S 18th, Parsons, 67357. **316-421-2000**

PITTSBURG SUN. Pittsburg Publishing Co, 701 N Locust St, Pittsburg, 66762. **316-231-2600**

PRATT TRIBUNE. Tribune Publishing Co, 319 S Ninnescah, Pratt, 67124. **316-672-5511**

RUSSELL DAILY NEWS. Russell Publishing Co, Inc, 802 Maple St, Russell, 67665. **913-483-2116.** Russell T Townsley, publisher

SALINA JOURNAL. 333 S 4th St, Salina, 67401. **913-823-6363**

TOPEKA DAILY CAPITAL. Stauffer Communications, Inc, 6th and Jefferson, Topeka, 66607. **913-295-1111**

TOPEKA STATE JOURNAL. Stauffer Communications, Inc, 6th and Jefferson, Topeka, 66607. **913-295-1111**

WELLINGTON NEWS. Mitchell Publications, Inc, 115 W Harvey, Wellington, 67152. **316-326-3326**

WICHITA BEACON. Wichita Eagle and Beacon Publishing Co, Inc, 825 E Douglas Ave, Wichita, 67202. **316-268-6000**

WICHITA EAGLE. Wichita Eagle and Beacon Publishing Co, Inc, 825 E Douglas Ave, Wichita, 67202. **316-268-6000**

WINFIELD COURIER. Winfield Publishing Co, Inc, 201 E 9th St, Winfield, 67156. **316-221-1050**

Kentucky

ASHLAND INDEPENDENT. Ashland Publishing Co, 224 17 St, Ashland, 41101. **606-324-2136**

BOWLING GREEN NEWS. News Publishing Co, 813 College St, Bowling Green, 42101. **502-843-4231**

CORBIN TIMES-TRIBUNE. Kentucky and Monroe Sts, Corbin, 40701. **606-528-2464.** John L Crawford, publisher

(COVINGTON) KENTUCKY POST. E W Scripps Co, 421 Madison Ave, Covington, 41011. **606-292-2643**

(DANVILLE) ADVOCATE-MESSENGER. Advocate-Messenger Co, W Walnut St, Danville, 40422. **606-236-2551**

(ELIZABETHTOWN) NEWS-ENTER-PRISE. 408 W Dixie, Elizabethtown, 42701. **502-769-2312**

(FRANKFORT) STATE JOURNAL. Frankfort Publishing Co, 321 W Main St (PO Box 368), Frankfort, 40601. **502-227-4556**

FULTON LEADER. Fulton Publishing Co, State Line and Washington St, Fulton, 42041. **502-472-1121**

GLASGOW TIMES. Glasgow Publishing Corp, 301 S Green St, Glasgow, 42141. **502-651-5171**

HARLAN ENTERPRISE. Harlan Newspapers, Inc, Central St, Harlan, 40831. **606-573-4510**

HENDERSON GLEANER-JOURNAL. Gleaner and Journal Publishing Co, 216 N Elm, Henderson 42420. **502-826-7100**

(HOPKINSVILLE) KENTUCKY NEW ERA. 1618 E 9th St, Hopkinsville, 42240. **502-886-4444.** Cecil Herndon, Executive editor

LEXINGTON HERALD. Lexington Herald Leader Co, 229–39 W Short St, Lexington, 40507. **606-254-6666**

LEXINGTON LEADER. Lexington Herald Leader Co, 229–39 W Short St, Lexington, 40507. **606-254-6666**

LOUISVILLE COURIER-JOURNAL. Courier-Journal and Louisville Times Co, 525 W Broadway, Louisville, 40202. **502- 582-4011**

LOUISVILLE TIMES. Courier-Journal and Louisville Times Co, 525 W Broadway, Louisville, 40202. **502-582-4011**

MADISONVILLE MESSENGER. 221 S Main St, Madisonville, 42431. **502-821-6833**

MAYFIELD MESSENGER. Messenger Newspapers, Inc, 206 W Broadway, Mayfield, 42066. **502-247-1515**

MAYSVILLE LEDGER-INDEPENDENT. Maysville Publishing Corp, 43 W 2nd St (PO Box 518), Maysville, 41056. **606-564-3341**

MIDDLESBORO NEWS. Kentucky Newspapers, Inc, 120 N 11th St (PO Box 579), Middlesboro, 40965. **606-248-1010**

MURRAY LEDGER & TIMES. Murray Newspapers, Inc, 103 N 4th, Murray, 42071. **502-753-1916**

OWENSBORO MESSENGE-INQUIRER. Owensboro Publishing Co, 1401 Frederica, Owensboro, 42301. **502-685-3911**

PADUCAH SUN-DEMOCRAT. Paducah Newspapers, Inc, 408 Kentucky Ave, Paducah, 42001. **502-443-1771**

PARIS ENTERPRISE. 23 E 4th St, Paris, 40361. **606-987-2340**

RICHMOND REGISTER. Richmond Publishing Corp, S 2nd St, Richmond, 40475. **606-623-1669**

SOMERSET COMMONWEALTH JOURNAL. 102 N Maple St, Somerset, 42501. **606-678-8191**

WINCHESTER SUN. Wall and Cleveland Sts, Winchester, 40391. **606-744-3123**

Louisiana

(ALEXANDRIA) TOWN TALK. McCormick and Co, Inc, Main at Washington Sts (PO Box 7558), Alexandria, 71301. **318-442-1331**

BASTROP ENTERPRISE. Bastrop Enterprise Publishing Co, 119 E Hickory, Bastrop, **318-281-4421**

BATON ROUGE ADVOCATE. Capital City Press, 525 Lafayette St, Baton Rouge, 70821. **504-383-1111**

BATON ROUGE STATE TIMES. Capital City Press, 525 Lafayette St, Baton Rouge, 70821. **504-383-1111**

BOGALUSA NEWS. Bogalusa Daily News, Inc, 525 Ave V (PO Box 820), Bogalusa, 70427. **504-732-2565**

CROWLEY POST SIGNAL. 602 N Parkerson Ave, Crowley, 70526. **318-783-3450**

FRANKLIN BANNER-TRIBUNE. 111 Wilson St, Franklin, 70538. **318-828-3707**

HAMMOND DAILY STAR. 200 SW Railroad Ave (PO Box 1319), Hammond, 70401. **504-345-2333.** Larry Hitchcock, managing editor

HOUMA DAILY COURIER AND THE TERREBONNE PRESS. PO Box 2717, Houma, 70360. **504-879-1557**

JENNINGS DAILY NEWS. Newspaper Service Co, Inc, 238 Market St, Jennings, 70546. **318-824-3011**

LAFAYETTE ADVERTISER. The Independent, Inc, PO Box 3268, Lafayette, 70501. **318-235-8511**

LAKE CHARLES AMERICAN PRESS. 327 Broad (PO Box 2893), Lake Charles, 70601. **318-439-2781**

MINDEN PRESS-HERALD. 109 Dixie St, Minden, 71055. **318-377-1866**

MONROE NEWS-STAR. News-Star World Publishing Corp, 411 N 4th St, Monroe, 71201. **318-322-5161**

MONROE WORLD. News-Star World Publishing Corp, 411 N 4th St, Monroe, 71201. **318-322-5161**

(MORGAN CITY) THE DAILY REVIEW. PO Box 948, Morgan City, 70380. **504-384-8370**

(NEW IBERIA) IBERIAN. Teche Publishing Co, 926 E Main St, New Iberia, 70560. **318-364-1801**

NEW ORLEANS STATES-ITEM. Times-Picayune Publishing Corp, 3800 Howard Ave, New Orleans, 70140. **504-586-3650**

NEW ORLEANS TIMES-PICAYUNE. Times-Picayune Publishing Corp, 3800 Howard Ave, New Orleans, 70140. **504-586-3650**

OPELOUSAS WORLD. World News Co, Inc, Hwy 167 S (PO Box 1179), Opelousas, 70570. **318-942-4971**

RUSTON LEADER. Ruston Publishers, Inc, 208 W Park Ave, Ruston, 71270. **318-255-4353**

SHREVEPORT JOURNAL. Journal Publishing Co, Inc, 222 Lake St, Shreveport, 71130. **318-424-0373**

SHREVEPORT TIMES. Times Publishing Co, Ltd, 222 Lake St, Shreveport, 71130. **318-424-0373**

(SLIDELL) DAILY SENTRY-NEWS. 3648 Pontchartrain Dr, Hwy 11 S (PO Box 910), Slidell, 70458. **504-643-4918**

SLIDELL DAILY TIMES. 1701 3rd St (PO Box 490), Slidell, 70458

(THIBODAUX) THE DAILY COMET. 704 W 5th St (PO Box 550), Thibodaux, 70301

Maine

(AUGUSTA) KENNEBEC JOURNAL. 274 Western Ave, Augusta, 04330 (Guy Gannett Publishing Co, Portland). **207-623-3811**

BANGOR NEWS. Bangor Publishing Co, 491 Main, Bangor, 04401. **207-942-4881**

(BIDDEFORD) JOURNAL TRIBUNE. Journal Publishing Corp, Alfred Rd, Biddeford, 04005. **207-282-1535.** Brian Thayer, executive editor

BRUNSWICK TIMES RECORD. Brunswick Publishing Co, Industry Rd, Brunswick, 04011. **207-792-3311**

LEWISTON DAILY SUN. 104 Park St, Lewiston, 04240. **207-784-5411**

(LEWISTON) EVENING JOURNAL. Lewiston Daily Sun, 104 Park St, Lewiston, 04240. **207-784-5411**

PORTLAND EXPRESS. Guy Gannett Publishing Co, 390 Congress St, Portland, 04111. **207-775-5811**

(PORTLAND) MAINE SUNDAY TELEGRAM. Guy Gannett Publishing Co, 390 Congress St, Portland, 04111. **207-775-5811**

PORTLAND PRESS HERALD. Guy Gannett Publishing Co, 390 Congress St, Portland, 04111. **207-775-5811**

WATERVILLE SENTINEL. Guy Gannett Publishing Co, 25 Silver St, Waterville, 04901. **207-873-3341**

Maryland

ANNAPOLIS CAPITAL. Capital-Gazette Newspapers, Inc, 213 West St (PO Box 911), Annapolis, 21404. **301-268-5011**

BALTIMORE NEWS AMERICAN. Hearst Corp, Inc, Lombard and South Sts, Baltimore, 21203. **301-752-1212**

BALTIMORE SUN. A S Abell Co, Calvert and Centre Sts, Baltimore, 21203. **301-332-6000**

CAMBRIDGE BANNER. Banner Corp, 302 High St, Cambridge, 21613. **301-228-3131**

CUMBERLAND NEWS. Times and Alleghenian Co, 7–9 S Mechanic St, Cumberland, 21502. **301-722-4600**

CUMBERLAND TIMES. Times and Alleghenian Co, 7–9 S Mechanic St, Cumberland, 21502. **301-722-4600**

EASTON STAR-DEMOCRAT. N Hanson St (PO Box 600), Easton, 21601. **301-822-1500**

FREDERICK POST AND NEWS. Great Southern Printing and Manufacturing Co, 200 Patrick St, Frederick 21701. **301-662-1177.** George B Delaplaine, Jr, president-publisher. Tom Mills, managing editor

HAGERSTOWN HERALD. Herald-Mail Co, 25–31 Summit Ave, Hagerstown, 21740. **301-733-5131**

HAGERSTOWN MAIL. Herald-Mail Co, 25–31 Summit Ave, Hagerstown, 21740. **301-733-5131**

SALISBURY TIMES. Times Sq, Salisbury, 21801. **301-749-7171**

Massachusetts

ATHOL NEWS. Athol Press, Inc, 225 Exchange St, Athol, 01331. **617-249-3535**

ATTLEBORO SUN CHRONICLE. Attleboro Sun Publishing Corp, 34 S Main St, Attleboro, 02703. **617-222-7000**

BEVERLY TIMES. Beverly Evening Times, Inc, Times Park, Beverly, 01915. **617-922-1234**

(BOSTON) CHRISTIAN SCIENCE MONITOR. Christian Science Publishing Society, 1 Norway St, Boston, 02115. **617-262-2300**

BOSTON GLOBE. Globe Newspaper Co, 135 Morrissey Blvd, Boston, 02107. **617-929-2000**

BOSTON HERALD AMERICAN. Hearst Corp, 300 Harrison Ave, Boston, 02106. **617-426-3000**

BROCKTON ENTERPRISE & TIMES. Enterprise Publishing Co, 60 Main St, Brockton, 02403. **617-586-6200**

CHELSEA EVENING RECORD. 18 4th St, Chelsea, 02150. **617-884-2416**

CLINTON ITEM. W J Coulter Press, Inc, 156 Church St, Clinton, 01510. **617-365-2422**

(DEDHAM) THE DAILY TRANSCRIPT. Transcript Newspapers, Inc, 420 Washington St, Dedham, 02026. **617-329-5000**

FALL RIVER HERALD-NEWS. Northeast Publishing, Inc, 207 Pocasset St, Fall River, 02722. **617-676-8211**

FITCHBURG-LEOMINSTER SENTINEL AND ENTERPRISE. Thomson Newspapers, Inc, 808 Main St, Fitchburg, 01420. **617-343-6911**

FRAMINGHAM NEWS. News Publishing Co of Framingham, 375 Cochituate Rd, Framingham, 01701. **617-872-4321**

GARDNER NEWS. 309 Central St, Gardner, 01440. **617-632-8000**

GLOUCESTER TIMES. Essex County Newspapers, Inc, Whittenmore St, Gloucester, 01930. **617-283-7000**

GREENFIELD RECORDER. Recorder Publishing Co, Inc, 14 Hope St, Greenfield, 01301. **413-772-0261**

HAVERHILL GAZETTE. 447 W Lowell Ave, Haverhill, 01830. **617-374-0321.** Donald J Byrne, publisher. Steven M Harry, managing editor

HOLYOKE TRANSCRIPT-TELEGRAM. 120 Whiting Farms Rd, Holyoke, 01040. **413-536-2300**

HUDSON DAILY SUN. 5 Pope St, Hudson, 01749. **617-562-5200**

(HYANNIS) CAPE COD TIMES. Ottaway Newspapers, Inc, 319 Main St, Hyannis, 02601. **617-775-1200**

LAWRENCE EAGLE-TRIBUNE. Eagle-Tribune Publishing Co, PO Box 100, Lawrence, 01842. **617-685-1000**

LOWELL SUN. Lowell Sun Publishing Co, 15 Kearney Sq, Lowell, 01852. **617-455-5671**

LYNN ITEM. Hastings and Sons, 38 Exchange St, Lynn, 01903. **617-593-7700**

MALDEN NEWS. Malden Publications, Inc, 22 Ferry St, Malden, 02148. **617-322-0054**

MARLBOROUGH ENTERPRISE. Enterprise-Sun, Inc, Marlborough, 01752. **617-485-5200**

MEDFORD MERCURY. Medford Publications, Inc, Governors Ave, Medford, 02155. **617-395-0045**

MELROSE NEWS. Eastern Middlesex Press Publications, Inc, 458 Main St, Melrose, 02176. **617-662-5800**

MILFORD NEWS. Milford Daily News Co, 159 S Main St, Milford, 01757. **617-473-1111**

NEW BEDFORD STANDARD-TIMES. Standard Times Publishing Co, Ottaway Newspapers, Inc, 555 Pleasant St, New Bedford, 02742. **617-997-7411**

NEWBURYPORT DAILY NEWS. Essex County Newspapers, Inc, 23 Liberty St, Newburyport, 01950. **617-462-6666**

NORTH ADAMS TRANSCRIPT. Transcript Publishing Assn, Inc, PO Box 473, North Adams, 01247. **413-663-3741**

(NORTHAMPTON) HAMPSHIRE GAZETTE. H S Gere and Sons, Inc, 115 Conz St, Northampton, 01060. **413-584-5000**

(PITTSFIELD) BERKSHIRE EAGLE. Eagle Publishing Co, 33 Eagle St, Pittsfield, 01201. **413-447-7311**

QUINCY PATRIOT LEDGER. Geo W Prescott Publishing Co, 13-19 Temple St, Quincy, 02169. **617-472-7000**

SALEM NEWS. Salem News Publishing Co, 155 Washington St, Salem, 01970. **617-744-0600**

(SOUTHBRIDGE) EVENING NEWS. Nanlo, Inc, 25 Elm St, Southbridge, 01550. **617-764-4325**

SPRINGFIELD NEWS. Republican Co, 1860 Main St, Springfield, 01101. **413-787-2411**

SPRINGFIELD REPUBLICAN. Republican Co, 1860 Main St, Springfield, 01101. **413-787-2411**

SPRINGFIELD UNION. Republican Co, 1860 Main St, Springfield, 01101. **413-787-2411**

TAUNTON DAILY GAZETTE. Thomson Newspaper Publishing Co, Inc, 5–9 Cohannet St, Taunton, 02780. **617-822-7121**

WAKEFIELD ITEM. 26 Albion St, Wakefield, 01880. **617-245-0080**

WALTHAM NEWS-TRIBUNE. Waltham Publishing Co, 18 Pine St, Waltham, 02154. **617-893-1670**

WESTFIELD NEWS. Westfield News Advertiser, Inc, 62 School St, Westfield, 01085. **413-568-2427**

WOBURN TIMES. Woburn Daily Times, Inc, 25 Montvale Ave, Woburn, 01801. **617-933-3700**

WORCESTER GAZETTE. Worcester Telegram and Gazette, Inc, 20 Franklin St, Worcester, 01613. **617-755-4321**

WORCESTER TELEGRAM. Worcester Telegram and Gazette, Inc, 20 Franklin St, Worcester, 01613. **617-755-4321**

Michigan

ADRIAN TELEGRAM. Thomson Newspapers, Inc, 133 N Winter St, Adrian, 49221. **517-265-5111**

ALBION RECORDER. Albion Evening Recorder, Inc, 111 W Center St, Albion, 49224. **517-629-3984**

ALPENA NEWS. Alpena News Publishing Co, 130 Park Pl, Alpena, 49707. **517-354-3111**

ANN ARBOR NEWS. Booth Newspapers, Inc, 340 E Huron St, Ann Arbor, 48106. **313-994-6989**

(BAD AXE) HURON DAILY TRIBUNE. 211 N Heisterman, Bad Axe, 48413. **517-269-6461**

BATTLE CREEK ENQUIRER AND NEWS. Federated Publications, Inc, Gannet Co, Inc, 155 W Van Buren St, Battle Creek, 49016. **616-964-7161**

BAY CITY TIMES. Booth Newspapers, Inc, 311 5th St, Bay City, 48706. **517-895-8551**

(BENTON HARBOR) HERALD-PALLADIUM. Palladium Publishing Co, Michigan and Oaks Sts, Benton Harbor, 49022. **616-925-0022**

BIG RAPIDS PIONEER. Conine Publishing Co, 502 N State St, Big Rapids, 49307. **616-796-7624**

CADILLAC EVENING NEWS. Evening News Bldg, PO Box 640, Cadillac, 49601. **616-775-6564**

CHEBOYGAN TRIBUNE. Cheboygan Publishing Co, 310–2 N Main St, Cheboygan, 49721. **616-MA7-7144**

COLDWATER REPORTER. 15 W Pearl St, Coldwater, 49036. **517-278-2318**

DETROIT FREE PRESS. Knight-Ridder, Inc, 321 W Lafayette Blvd, Detroit, 48231. **313-222-6400**

DETROIT NEWS. Evening News Assn, 615 Lafayette Blvd, Detroit, 48231. **313-222-2000**

DOWAGIAC DAILY NEWS. 205 Spaulding St, Dowagiac, 49047. **616-782-2101**

ESCANABA PRESS. Panox Corp, 600–2 Ludington, Escanaba, 49829. **906-786-2021**

FLINT JOURNAL. Booth Newspapers, Inc, 200 E 1st St, Flint, 48502. **313-234-7611**

GRAND HAVEN TRIBUNE. Grand Haven Publishing Corp, 101 N 3rd St, Grand Haven, 49417. **616-842-6400.** Robert E Pifer, publisher. Fred VandenBrand, managing editor

GRAND RAPIDS PRESS. Booth Newspapers, Inc, Press Plz-Vandenberg Ctr, Grand Rapids, 49502. **616-459-1400**

GREENVILLE NEWS-BANNER. Greenville News, Inc, 109 N Lafayette St, Greenville, 48838. **616-754-5641**

HILLSDALE DAILY NEWS. Hillsdale Daily News Co, 33 McCollum, Hillsdale, 49242. **517-437-7351**

HOLLAND SENTINEL. Sentinel Printing Co, 54–6 W 8th St, Holland, 49423. **616-392-2311**

(HOUGHTON) MINING GAZETTE. 65 N Isle Royale St, Houghton, 49931. **906-482-1500**

IONIA SENTINEL-STANDARD. 114–6 N Depot, Ionia, 48846. **616-527-2100**

(IRON MOUNTAIN) NEWS. Panax Corp, 215 E Ludington, Iron Mountain, 49801. **906-774-2772**

IRONWOOD GLOBE. Globe Publishing Co, 118 E McLeod Ave, Ironwood, 49938. **906-932-2211**

JACKSON CITIZEN PATRIOT. 214 S Jackson St, Jackson, 49204. **517-787-2300**

KALAMAZOO GAZETTE. 401 S Burdick St, Kalamazoo, 49003. **616-345-3511**

LANSING STATE JOURNAL. Federated Publications, Inc, Gannett Group, 120 E Lenawee St, Lansing, 48919. **517-487-4611**

LUDINGTON DAILY NEWS. Ludington Daily News, Inc, 202 N Rath Ave, Ludington, 49431. **616-845-5181**

MANISTEE NEWS-ADVOCATE. J B Publishing Co, 75 Maple St, Manistee, 49660. **616-723-3593**

(MARQUETTE) MINING JOURNAL. Panax Corp, 249 Washington St, Marquette, 49855. **906-226-2554**

MARSHALL CHRONICLE. 115 S Grand St, Marshall, 49068. **616-781-3943**

MENOMINEE HERALD-LEADER. Menominee Publishing Co, 122 6th Ave, Menominee, 49858. **906-863-5544**

MIDLAND NEWS. 124 S McDonald St, Midland, 48640. **517-835-7171**

MONROE NEWS. Monroe Publishing Co, 20–2 W 1st, Monroe, 48161. **313-242-1100**

(MOUNT CLEMENS) MACOMB DAILY. Panax Newspapers, Inc, 67 Cass Ave (PO Box 707), Mount Clemens, 48043. **313-463-1501**

MOUNT PLEASANT-ALMA TIMES NEWS. 215 N Main St, Mount Pleasant, 48858. **517-772-2971**

MOUNT PLEASANT MORNING SUN. 215 N Main St, Mt Pleasant, 48858. **517-772-2971**

MUSKEGON CHRONICLE. Booth Newspapers, Inc, 981 3rd St, Muskegon, 49443. **616-722-3161**

NILES STAR. Star Publications Co, 217 N 4th St, Niles, 49120. **616-683-2100**

(OWOSSO) ARGUS-PRESS. 201 E Exchange St, Owosso, 48867. **517-725-5136**

PETOSKY NEWS-REVIEW. Northern Michigan Review, Inc, 319 State St, Petosky, 49770. **616-347-2544**

(PONTIAC) OAKLAND PRESS. PO Box 9, 48 W Huron St, Pontiac, 48056. **313-332-8181**

PORT HURON TIMES HERALD (Gannet). 907 6th St, Port Huron, 48060. **313-985-7171**

ROYAL OAK TRIBUNE. Tribune Publishing Co, 210 E 3rd St, Royal Oak, 48068. **313-541-3000**

SAGINAW NEWS. Booth Newspapers, Inc, 203 S Washington Ave, Saginaw, 48605. **517-752-7171**

SAULT STE MARIE NEWS. Sault News Publishing Co, 109 Arlington St, Sault Ste Marie, 49783. **906-632-2235**

SOUTH HAVEN TRIBUNE. South Haven Daily Tribune Co, 259 Kalamazoo St, South Haven, 49090. **616-637-1104**

STURGIS JOURNAL. 209 John St, Sturgis, 49091. **616-651-5407**

THREE RIVERS COMMERCIAL. Three Rivers Publishing Co, 124 N Main St, Three Rivers, 49093. **616-279-7488**

TRAVERSE RECORD-EAGLE. Herald and Record Co, 120 W Front St, Traverse City, 49684. **616-946-2000**

WAYNE EAGLE. Associated Newspapers, 35540 W Michigan Ave, Wayne, 48184. **313-729-4000.** David J Willett, publisher. Dennis G Fassett, managing editor

YPSILANTI PRESS. Harte-Hanks Newspapers, Inc, 20 E Michigan Ave, Ypsilanti, 48197. **313-482-2000**

Minnesota

ALBERT LEA TRIBUNE. Albert Lea Publishing Co, 808 W Front St, Albert Lea, 46007. **507-373-1411**

AUSTIN DAILY HERALD. Thomson Newspapers, Inc, 310 NE 2nd St, Austin, 44912. **507-433-8851**

(BEMIDJI) THE PIONEER. Scripps, Nielson and Pioneer Sts, Bemidji, 56601. **218-751-3740**

BRAINERD DISPATCH. Brainerd Dispatch Newspapers, 215 S 6th St, Brainerd, 56401. **218-829-4705**

CROOKSTON TIMES. Crookston Times Printing Co, 124 S Broadway, Crookston, 56716. **218-281-2730**

DULUTH HERALD. NW Publications, Inc, 424 W 1st, Duluth, 44801. **218-722-8333**

DULUTH NEWS TRIBUNE. NW Publications, Inc, 424 W 1st, Duluth, 55801. **218-722-8333**

FAIRMONT DAILY SENTINEL. 114 S North Ave, Fairmont, 56031. **507-235-3303**

FARIBAULT DAILY NEWS. 514 Central Ave, Faribault, 55021. **507-334-4383**

FERGUS JOURNAL. Fergus Journal Co, 914 E Channing, Fergus Falls, 56537. **218-736-7513**

HIBBING TRIBUNE. HTC, Inc, 2142 1st Ave, Hibbing, 55746. **218-262-1011**

INTERNATIONAL FALLS JOURNAL. North Star Publishing Co, Inc, International Falls, 56649. **218-283-8411**

LITTLE FALLS TRANSCRIPT. Transcript Publishing Co, 50 E Broadway, Little Falls, 56345. **612-632-6627**

(MANKATO) FREE PRESS. Free Press Co, 418 S 2nd St, Mankato, 56001. **507-625-4451**

MARSHALL INDEPENDENT. PO Box 411, Marshall, 56258. **507-532-4431**

MINNEAPOLIS STAR. Minneapolis Star and Tribune Co, 425 Portland Ave, Minneapolis, 55488. **612-372-4141**

MINNEAPOLIS TRIBUNE. Minneapolis Star and Tribune Co, 425 Portland Ave, Minneapolis, 55488. **612-372-4141**

MOORHEAD FORUM. Fargo ND Forum (Minnesota edition), 19 S 4th St, Moorhead, 56560. **701-235-7311**

NEW ULM JOURNAL. 508 North 3rd St, New Ulm, 56073. **507-354-2114**

OWATONNA PEOPLE'S PRESS. Free Press Co, 135 W Pearl St, Owatonna, 55060. **507-451-2840**

RED WING REPUBLICAN-EAGLE. Red Wing Publishing Co, 433 3rd St, Red Wing, 55066. **612-388-3535**

ROCHESTER POST BULLETIN. 18 1st Ave SE, Rochester, 55901. **507-288-2441**

ST CLOUD TIMES. St Cloud Newspapers, Inc, 3000 7th St N, St Cloud, 56301. **612-351-3121**

ST PAUL DISPATCH. Northwest Publications, Inc, 55 E 4th St, St Paul, 55101. **612-222-5011**

ST PAUL PIONEER PRESS. Northwest Publications, Inc, 55 E 4th St, St Paul, 55101. **612-222-5011**

STILLWATER GAZETTE. 102 S 2nd St, Stillwater, 44082. **612-439-3130**

(VIRGINIA) MESABI NEWS. Mesabi Publishing Co, 704 7th Ave S, Virginia, 55792. **218-741-5544**

WASECA JOURNAL. 203 3rd Ave NW, Waseca, 56093. **507-835-2220**

(WILLMAR) WEST CENTRAL TRIBUNE. Tribune Printing Co, 311 W 4th St, Willmar, 56201. **612-235-1151**

WINONA NEWS. Republican and Herald Publishing Co, 601 Franklin St, Winona, 55987. **507-452-7820**

WORTHINGTON GLOBE. Worthington Daily Globe, Inc, 300 11th St, Worthington, 56187. **507-376-4121**

Mississippi

(BILOXI) DAILY HERALD. Gulf Publishing Co, Inc, De Buys Rd, Gulfport, 39531. **601-896-2333.** James Lund, editor, **601-896-2301**

(BILOXI) SOUTH MISSISSIPPI SUN. Gulf Publishing Co, Inc, PO Box 4567, Gulfport, 39531. **601-896-2340.** Pic Firmin, editor, **601-896-2345**

BROOKHAVEN LEADER. Southwest Publishers, Inc, Brookhaven, 39601. **601-833-6961**

CLARKSDALE PRESS REGISTER. Delta Press Publishing Co, 123 2nd St, Clarksdale, 38614. **601-627-2201**

(CLEVELAND) BOLIVAR COMMERCIAL. 106 N Pearman St, Cleveland, 38732. **601-843-4241**

COLUMBUS COMMERCIAL DISPATCH. 516 Main St, Columbus, 39701. **601-328-2424**

(CORINTH) CORINTHIAN. Corinthian Newspapers, 808 Waldron, Corinth, 38834. **601-286-3366**

(GREENVILLE) DELTA DEMOCRAT-TIMES. Times Publishing Co, 988 N Broadway, Greenville, 38701. **601-335-1155**

GREENWOOD COMMONWEALTH. Commonwealth Publishing Co, Inc, 207–9 W Market, Greenwood, 38930. **601-453-5312**

GRENADA SENTINEL-STAR. 159 Green St, Grenada, 38901. **601-226-4321**

GULFPORT. *See* Biloxi

HATTIESBURG AMERICAN. 825 N Main St, Hattiesburg, 39401. **601-582-4321**

JACKSON CLARION-LEDGER. Mississippi Publishers Corp, PO Box 40, Jackson, 39205. **601-969-3700**

JACKSON NEWS. Mississippi Publishers Corp, PO Box 40, Jackson, 39205. **601-969-3700**

LAUREL LEADER-CALL. The Independent, Inc, 130 Beacon St, Laurel, 39440. **601-428-0551**

(MCCOMB) ENTERPRISE-JOURNAL. 129 N Broadway, McComb, 39648. **601-684-2421**

MERIDIAN STAR. 810–2 22nd Ave (PO Box 1591), Meridian, 39301. **601-693-1551**

NATCHEZ DEMOCRAT. Natchez Newspapers, Inc, 503 N Canal St, Natchez, 39121. **601-442-9101**

OXFORD EAGLE. Oxford Eagle Publishing Co, 916 Jackson Ave (PO Box 111), Oxford, 38655. **601-234-4331**

(PASCAGOULA) MISSISSIPPI PRESS REGISTER. Mississippi Press Register, Inc, 405 Delmas Ave, Pascagoula, 39567. **601-762-1111**

STARKVILLE DAILY NEWS. 316 University Dr, Starkville, 39759. **601-323-1643**

TUPELO JOURNAL. Journal Publishing Co, 1655 S Green (PO Box 909), Tupelo, 38801. **601-842-2611**

VICKSBURG POST. Vicksburg Printing and Publishing Co, 920 South St, Vicksburg, 39181. **601-636-4545**

(WEST POINT) DAILY TIMES LEADER. Harris Newspapers, Inc, 227 Court St (PO Box 1176), West Point, 39773. **601-494-1422**

Missouri

AURORA ADVERTISER. 32 W Olive St, Aurora, 65605. **417-678-2115**

BOONVILLE NEWS AND ADVERTISER. Boonville Daily News, 412 E High, Boonville, 65233. **816-882-5335**

BROOKFIELD NEWS-BULLETIN. Brookfield Publishing Co, 308 N Main, Brookfield, 64628. **816-258-4237**

CAMERON CITIZEN OBSERVER. PO Box 70, Cameron, 64429. **816-632-2131**

CAPE GIRARDEAU SOUTHEAST MISSOURIAN. Naeter Brothers Publishing Co, 301 Broadway, Cape Girardeau, 63701. **314-335-6611**

CARROLLTON DEMOCRAT. Carrollton Newspapers, Inc, Hwy 65-24 S, Carrollton, 64633. **816-542-0881**

CARTHAGE PRESS. Carthage Publishing Co, 527 S Main, Carthage, 64836. **417-358-2191**

CHILLICOTHE CONSTITUTION-TRIBUNE. Chillicothe Newspapers, Inc, 818 Washington, Chillicothe, 64601. **816-646-2411**

CLINTON DEMOCRAT. Democrat Publishing Co, Inc, 212 S Washington, Clinton, 64735. **816-885-2281**

COLUMBIA MISSOURIAN. Missourian Publishing Assn, 301 S 9th St, Columbia, 65201. **314-442-3161**

COLUMBIA TRIBUNE. Tribune Publishing Co, 4th and Walnut Sts, Columbia, 65201. **314-449-3811**

(CRYSTAL CITY) NEWS-DEMOCRAT. Twin Cities Newspapers, Inc, 301 Main St, Festus, 63028. **314-937-3636**

(DEXTER) DAILY STATESMAN-MESSENGER. 200 W Stoddard St, Dexter, 63841. **314-624-4545**

EXCELSIOR SPRINGS STANDARD. Standard Publishing Co, 417 Thompson St, Excelsior Springs, 64024. **816-637-3147**

FARMINGTON PRESS. Farmington Evening Press, PO Box 70, Farmington, 63640. **314-756-4523**

FESTUS. See Crystal City.

FLAT RIVER JOURNAL. Eastern Missouri Publishing Co, 1513 St and Joe Dr, Flat River, 63601. **314-431-2010**

FORT GATEWAY. See Waynesville.

(FULTON) KINGDOM NEWS. 307 Court, Fulton, 65251. **314-642-7272**

FULTON SUN-GAZETTE. Sun Communications, Inc, 115 E 5th St, Fulton, 65251. **314-642-2234**

HANNIBAL COURIER-POST. Hannibal Publishing Co, 200 N 3rd, Hannibal, 63401. **314-221-2800**

INDEPENDENCE EXAMINER. Examiner Publishing Co, PO Box 458, Independence, 64051. **816-254-8600**

JEFFERSON CITY DAILY CAPITAL NEWS. News Tribune Co, 210 Monroe St, Jefferson City, 65101. **314-636-3131.** Donald S Norfleet, editor

JEFFERSON CITY POST-TRIBUNE. News Tribune Co, 210 Monroe St, Jefferson City, 65101. **314-636-3131.** Donald S Norfleet, editor

JOPLIN GLOBE. Joplin Globe Publishing Co, 117 E 4th St, Joplin, 64801. **417-623-3480**

KANSAS CITY STAR. Kansas City Star Co, 1729 Grand Ave, Kansas City, 64108. **816-421-1200**

KANSAS CITY TIMES. Kansas City Star Co, 1729 Grand Ave, Kansas City, 64108. **816-421-1200**

KENNETT DEMOCRAT. Daily Dunklin Democrat, 212-4 N Main St, Kennett, 63857. **314-888-4505**

(KIRKSVILLE) DAILY EXPRESS & NEWS. Express Publishing Co, Inc, 110 E McPherson, Kirksville, 63501. **816-665-2808**

LAMAR DEMOCRAT. Lamar Publishing Co, Inc, 108 W 10th, Lamar, 64759. **417-682-5529**

LEBANON DAILY RECORD. 290 S Madison St, Lebanon, 65536. **417-532-3581.** Dalton Wright, publisher. Rich Brown, editor

(LEE'S SUMMIT) EXAMINER. Lee's Summit, 64063. **816-524-1700**

LEXINGTON ADVERTISER-NEWS. 906 Main St, Lexington, 64067. **816-259-2266**

MACON CHRONICLE-HERALD. Chronicle-Herald Publishing Co, 217 W Bourke St, Macon, 63552. **816-385-3121**

MARSHALL DEMOCRAT-NEWS. Marshall Publishing Co, The Democrat-News, 121 N Lafayette, Marshall, 65340. **816-886-2233**

MARYVILLE FORUM. Maryville Publishing Co, 101-11 E Jenkins St (PO Box 188), Maryville, 64468. **816-582-3161**

MEXICO LEDGER. Ledger Newspapers, Inc, Ledger Plz, Mexico, 65265. **314-581-1111**

MOBERLY MONITOR-INDEX & DEMOCRAT. Donrey Media Group, 218 N Williams, Moberly, 65270. **816-263-4123**

MONETT TIMES. Monett Newspapers, Inc, 505 Broadway, Monett, 65708. **417-235-3135**

NEOSHO NEWS. Neosho Publishing Co, 1006 W Harmony St, Neosho, 65850. **417-451-1520**

NEVADA HERALD. Nevada Publishing Co, 131 S Cedar, Nevada, 64772. **417-667-3344**

NEVADA MAIL. Nevada Publishing Co, 131 S Cedar, Nevada, 64772. **417-667-3344**

(POPLAR BLUFF) AMERICAN REPUBLIC. Poplar Bluff Printing Co, 206 Poplar St, Poplar Bluff, 63901. **314-785-1414**

RICHMOND NEWS. Richmond 64085. **816-776-5454**

ROLLA NEWS. Edward W Sowers, 101 W 7th, Rolla, 65401. **314-364-2468**

ST CHARLES BANNER-NEWS. Ogden Newspapers, 2431 Raymond Dr (PO Box 280), St Charles, 63301. **314-723-7800**

ST JOSEPH GAZETTE. News-Press and Gazette Co, 9th and Edmond Sts, St Joseph, 64502. **816-279-5671**

ST JOSEPH NEWS-PRESS. News-Press and Gazette Co, 9th and Edmond Sts, St Joseph, 64502. **816-279-5671**

ST LOUIS GLOBE-DEMOCRAT. Globe Democrat Publishing Co, 12th Blvd at Convention Plz, St Louis, 63101. **314-421-1212**

ST LOUIS POST-DISPATCH. Pulitzer Publishing Co, 900 N 12th Blvd, St Louis, 63101. **314-621-1111**

ST ROBERT. *See* Waynesville.

SEDALIA CAPITAL. Sedalia Democrat Co, 7th St and Massachusetts Ave, Sedalia, 65301. **816-826-1000**

SEDALIA DEMOCRAT. Sedalia Democrat Co, 7th St and Massachusetts Ave, Sedalia, 65301. **816-826-1000**

SIKESTON STANDARD. Sikeston Publishing Co, 205 S New Madrid, Sikeston, 63801. **314-471-1137**

SPRINGFIELD LEADER & PRESS. Springfield Newspapers, Inc, 651 Boonville, Springfield, 65801. **417-869-4411**

SPRINGFIELD NEWS. Springfield Newspapers, Inc, 651 Boonville, Springfield, 65801. **417-869-4411**

TRENTON REPUBLICAN-TIMES. W B Rogers Printing Co, Inc, PO Box 548, Trenton, 64683. **817-359-2212**

WARRENSBURG STAR-JOURNAL. Star-Journal Publishing Co, Inc, 135 E Market St, Warrensburg, 64093. **817-747-8123**

(WAYNESVILLE) DAILY GUIDE. Sowers Publishing Co, Waynesville, 65583. **314-336-3711**

WEST PLAINS QUILL. Quill Press, Inc, 125 N Jefferson St, West Plains, 65775. **417-256-9191**

Montana

BILLINGS GAZETTE. Lee Enterprises, Inc, 401 Broadway, Billings, 59103. **406-245-3071**

BOZEMAN CHRONICLE. Gallatin Publishing Co, 32 S Rouse (PO Box 1188), Bozeman, 59715. **406-587-4491**

(BUTTE) MONTANA STANDARD. Lee Enterprises, Inc, 25 W Granite St, Butte, 59701. **406-792-8301**

(HAMILTON) RAVALLI REPUBLICAN. 232 Main St, Hamilton, 59840. **406-363-3300**. John Barrows, editor and general manager. Night line: **406-363-4118**

HAVRE DAILY NEWS. 119 2nd St, Havre, 59501. **406-265-6796**

HELENA INDEPENDENT RECORD. Lee Enterprises, Inc, 317 Allen St, Helena, 59601. **406-442-7190**

(KALISPELL) THE INTER LAKE. Inter Lake Publishing Co, 300 1st Ave W, Kalispell, 59901. **406-755-7000**

LIVINGSTON ENTERPRISE. 220 S Main, Livingston, 59047. **406-222-2000**

MILES CITY STAR. Star Printing Co, 13 N 6th St, Miles City, 59301. **406-232-0450**

(MISSOULA) THE MISSOULIAN. Lee Enterprises, Inc, 502 N Higgins Ave, Missoula, 59801. **406-542-0311**

Nebraska

ALLIANCE TIMES-HERALD. Alliance Publishing Co, Inc, 114 E 4th, Alliance, 69301. **308-762-3060**

BEATRICE DAILY SUN. 7th and Ella (PO Box 847), Beatrice, 68310. **402-223-5233**

COLUMBUS TELEGRAM. Freedom Newspapers, 1254 27th Ave, Columbus, 68601. **402-564-2741**

FALLS CITY JOURNAL. Journal Publishing Co, 1810 Harlan St, Falls City, 68355. **402-245-2431**

FREMONT TRIBUNE. Fremont Newspapers, Inc, Speidel Newspapers, Inc, Tribune Triangle, PO Box 9, Fremont, 68025. **402-721-5000**

GRAND ISLAND INDEPENDENT. Stauffer Publications, 1st and Cedar Sts, Grand Island, 68801. **308-382-1000**

HASTINGS TRIBUNE. Seaton Publishing Co, 908 W 2nd St, Hastings, 68901. **402-462-2131**

HOLDREGE CITIZEN. Holdrege Daily Citizen, Inc, 418 Garfield St, Holdrege, 68949. **308-995-4441**

KEARNEY HUB. Kearney Hub Publishing Co, 13 E 22nd, Kearney, 68847. **308-237-2152**

LINCOLN STAR. Journal-Star Printing Co, 926 P St (PO Box 81609), Lincoln, 68501. **402-477-8902**

MCCOOK GAZETTE. Gazette Publishing Co, W 1st and E Sts, McCook, 69001. **308-345-4500**

NEBRASKA CITY NEWS-PRESS. Press Printing Co, 123 S 8th, Nebraska City, 68410. **402-873-3334**

NORFOLK NEWS. Huse Publishing Co, 525 Norfolk Ave, Norfolk, 68701. **402-371-1020**

NORTH PLATTE TELEGRAPH. Western Publishing Co, 315 E 5th, North Platte, 69101. **308-532-6000**

OMAHA WORLD-HERALD. 14th and Dodge Sts, Omaha, 68102. **402-444-1000**

SCOTTSBLUFF STAR-HERALD. Star-Herald Printing Co, 1405 Broadway, Scottsbluff, 69361. **308-632-6116**

YORK NEWS-TIMES. York Publishing Co, 327 Platte Ave (PO Box 279), York, 68467. **402-362-4478**

Nevada

(CARSON CITY) NEVADA APPEAL. Donrey Media Group, 200 Bath St (PO Box 2288), Carson City, 89701. **702-882-2111**

ELKO DAILY FREE PRESS. Box 1330, Elko, 89801. **702-738-3119**

ELY DAILY TIMES. Donrey Media Group, 655 Aultman, Ely, 89301. **702-289-4491**

FALLON DAILY EAGLE STANDARD. 40 E Williston St (PO Box 311), Fallon, 89406. **702-423-3101**

LAS VEGAS REVIEW-JOURNAL. Donrey Media Group, PO Box 70, Las Vegas, 89101. **702-385-4241**

LAS VEGAS SUN. 121 S Highland Ave, Las Vegas, 89106. **702-385-3111**. H M (Hank) Greenspun, publisher

(NORTH LAS VEGAS) VALLEY TIMES. PO Box 3936, North Las Vegas, 89030. **702-642-2567**

(RENO) NEVADA STATE JOURNAL. Reno Newspapers, Inc, Spiedel Newspapers, 401 W 2nd St, Reno, 89504. **702-786-8989**

New Hampshire

(CLAREMONT) EAGLE-TIMES. Eagle Publications, Inc, 19 Sullivan St, Claremont, 03743. **603-542-5121**

CONCORD MONITOR & NEW HAMP-SHIRE PATRIOT. Monitor Publishing Co, Inc, 3 N State St, Concord, 03301. **603-224-5301**

(DOVER) FOSTER'S DAILY DE-MOCRAT. George J Foster and Co, Inc, 333 Central Ave, Dover, 03820. **603-742-4455**

HANOVER. *See* White River Junction, Vermont.

KEENE SENTINEL. Keene Publishing Corp, 60 West St, Keene, 03431. **603-352-1234**

LACONIA CITIZEN. Citizen Publishing Co, Fair St, Laconia, 03246. **603-524-3800**

LEBANON VALLEY NEWS. *See* White River Junction, Vermont.

(MANCHESTER) NEW HAMPSHIRE SUNDAY NEWS. Union Leader Corp, 35 Amherst St, Manchester, 03105. **603-668-4321**

MANCHESTER UNION LEADER. Union Leader Corp, 35 Amherst St, Manchester, 03105. **603-668-4321**

NASHUA TELEGRAPH. Telegraph Publishing Co, 60 Main St, Nashua, 03060. **603-882-2741**

PORTSMOUTH HERALD. A division of Thomson Newspapers, Inc, 111 Maplewood Ave, Portsmouth, 03801. **603-436-1800**

New Jersey

ASBURY PARK PRESS. Press Plz, Asbury Park, 07712. **201-774-7000**

(ATLANTIC CITY) THE PRESS. South Jersey Publishing Co, 1900 Atlantic Ave, Atlantic City, 08401. **609-345-1111**

BERGEN RECORD. Bergen Evening Record Corp, 150 River St, Hackensack, 07602. **201-646-4000**

BRIDGETON NEWS. Evening News Co, 100 E Commerce St, Bridgeton, 08302. **609-451-1000**

BRIDGEWATER COURIER-NEWS. Gannett Group, 1201 Route 22 (PO Box 6600), Bridgewater, 08807. **201-722-8800**

CAMDEN COURIER-POST. Southern New Jersey Newspapers, Inc, Gannett Group, Camden, 08101. **609-663-6000**

DOVER ADVANCE. Daily Advance, 87 E Blackwell St, Dover, 07801. **201-366-3000**

ELIZABETH JOURNAL. Broad St, Elizabeth, 07207. **201-354-5000**

(JERSEY CITY) JERSEY JOURNAL. Evening Journal Assn, 30 Journal Sq, Jersey City, 07306. **201-653-1000**

(LAKEWOOD) OCEAN COUNTY TIMES. Ocean County Publishing Co, 121 2nd St, Lakewood, 08701. **201-363-0230**

MILLVILLE DAILY. 129 E Main St, Millville, 08332. **609-825-3456**

MORRISTOWN DAILY RECORD. Morristown Daily Record, Inc, 55 Park Pl, Morristown, 07960. **201-538-2000**. *Newsroom.* 800 Jefferson Rd, Parsippany, 07054. **201-386-0200**

NEWARK STAR-LEDGER. Newark Morning Ledger Co, Star Ledger Plz, Newark, 07101. **201-877-4141**

NEW BRUNSWICK HOME NEWS. Home News Publishing Co, 123 How Ln, New Brunswick, 08903. **201-246-5500**

(NEWTON) NEW JERSEY HERALD. PO Box 10, Newton, 07860. **201-383-1500**

(PASSAIC) HERALD-NEWS. Passaic Daily News, 988 Main Ave, Passaic-Clifton, 07055. **201-365-3000**

PATERSON MORNING/EVENING NEWS. News Printing Co, News Plz and Straight St, Paterson, 07509. **201-274-2000**

PERTH AMBOY-WOODBRIDGE NEWS TRIBUNE. Middlesex County Publishing Co, 1 Hoover Way, Woodbridge, 07095. **201-442-0400**

(RED BANK) THE DAILY REGISTER. Red Bank Register, 1 Register Plz, Shrewsbury, 07701. **201-542-4000**

(SALEM) TODAY'S SUNBEAM. Salem, 08079. **609-935-1500**

TOMS RIVER DAILY AND SUNDAY OBSERVER. Precision Publications, 8 Robbins St, Toms River, 08753. **201-349-3000**

TRENTON TIMES. 500 Perry St, Trenton, 08605. **609-396-3232**

(TRENTON) THE TRENTONIAN. Capitol City Publishing Co, Inc, 600 Perry St, Trenton, 08602. **609-989-7800**

(UNION CITY) THE DISPATCH. 400 38th St, Union City, 07087. **201-863-2000**. Robert L Boyle, publisher. Bertram J Kersen, executive editor

VINELAND TIMES-JOURNAL. 7 S 7th St, Vineland, 08360. **609-691-5000**

(WILLINGBORO) BURLINGTON COUNTY TIMES. Bristol Printing Co, Route 130, Willingboro, 08046. **609-877-1600**

(WOODBURY) GLOUCESTER COUNTY TIMES. Woodbury Daily Times Co, Inc, 309 S Broad St, Woodbury, 08096. **609-845-3300**

New Mexico

ALAMOGORDO DAILY NEWS. Alamogordo Daily News, Inc, 24th and Eudora Sts, Alamogordo, 88310. **505-437-7120**

ALBUQUERQUE JOURNAL. Journal Publishing Co, 7th and Silver SW, Albuquerque, 87103. **505-842-2300**

ALBUQUERQUE TRIBUNE. New Mexico State Tribune Co, 7th and Silver SW, Albuquerque, 87103. **505-842-2300**

ARTESIA DAILY PRESS. Valley Newspapers, Inc, 503 W Main St Artesia, 88210. **505-746-3524**. James K Green, publisher. Scott Eaton, editor, (h) **505-746-4520**

CARLSBAD CURRENT-ARGUS. Carlsbad Publishing Co, 101 W Mermond St, Carlsbad, 88220. **505-887-5501**

CLOVIS NEWS-JOURNAL. 6th and Pile Sts, Clovis, 88101. **505-763-3431**

FARMINGTON TIMES. New Mexico Newspapers, Inc, 201 N Allen (PO Box 450) Farmington, 87401. **505-325-4545**

GALLUP INDEPENDENT. 103 W Aztec, Gallup, 87301. **505-863-6811**

GRANTS BEACON. Grants Publishing Co, Inc, 300 N 2nd, Grants, 87020. **505-287-4411**

HOBBS NEWS-SUN. Sun Publishing Corp, 201 N Thorp, Hobbs, 88240. **505-393-2123**

LAS CRUCES SUN-NEWS. Sunshine Press, Inc, 256 W Las Cruces Ave, Las Cruces, 88001. **505-523-4581**

LAS VEGAS OPTIC. Las Vegas Publishing Co, 612 Lincoln, Las Vegas, 87701. **505-425-6796**

LOS ALAMOS MONITOR. 256 DP Rd (PO Box 899), Los Alamos, 87544. **505-662-4185**

LOVINGTON LEADER. 14 W Ave B (PO Box 1686), Lovington, 88260. **505-396-2844**

PORTALES NEWS-TRIBUNE. 101 E 1st St, Portales, 88130. **505-356-4481**

RATON DAILY RANGE. 208 S 3rd, Raton, 87740, **505-445-2721**

ROSWELL DAILY RECORD. PO Box 1897, Roswell, 88201. **505-622-7710**

SANTA FE NEW MEXICAN. 202 E Marcy, Santa Fe, 87501. **505-983-3303**

SILVER CITY PRESS & INDEPENDENT. Independent Publishing Co, 300 W Market, Silver City, 88061. **505-388-1576**

TUCUMCARI NEWS. Bar Two B Corp, 902 S 1st St (PO Box 1066), Tucumcari, 88401. **505-461-0110**

New York

ALBANY KNICKERBOCKER NEWS-UNION-STAR. Hearst Corp, 645 Albany-Shaker Rd, Albany, 12201. **518-453-5454**

ALBANY TIMES-UNION. Hearst Corp, 645 Albany-Shaker Rd, Albany, 12201. **518-453-5454**

(AMSTERDAM) THE RECORDER. Wm J Kline and Son, Inc, 1 Venner Rd, Amsterdam, 12010. **518-843-1100**

AUBURN CITIZEN. Auburn Publishers, Inc, 25 Dill St, Auburn, 13021. **315-253-5311**

BATAVIA NEWS. Griswold and McWain, Inc, 2 Apollo Dr, Batavia, 14020. **716-343-8000**

BINGHAMTON PRESS. Binghamton Press Co, Gannett Group, E Vestal Pkwy, Binghamton, 13902. **607-798-1234**

BINGHAMTON SUN-BULLETIN. Binghamton Press Co, Gannet Group, E Vestal Pkwy, Binghamton, 13902. **607-798-1234**

BUFFALO COURIER-EXPRESS. 787 Main St, Buffalo, 14240. **716-847-5353**

BUFFALO NEWS. Buffalo Evening News, Inc, 1 News Plz, Buffalo, 14240. **716-849-4444**

CANANDAIGUA DAILY MESSENGER. 73 Buffalo St, Canandaigua, 14424. **315-394-0770**

CATSKILL MAIL. Catskill Daily Mail, Inc, 391 Main St, Catskill, 12414. **518-943-2100**

CORNING LEADER. Corning Publishers, Inc, 149 E Pulteney St, Corning, 14830. **607-936-4651**

CORTLAND STANDARD. Cortland Standard Printing Co, Inc, 110 Main St, Cortland, 13045. **607-756-5665**

DUNKIRK OBSERVER. Dunkirk Printing Co, 8-10 E 2nd St, Dunkirk, 14048. **716-366-3000**

ELMIRA STAR-GAZETTE. Elmira Star-Gazette, Inc, Gannett Group, 201 Baldwin St, Elmira, 14902. **607-734-5151**

ELMIRA TELEGRAM. Elmira Star-Gazette, Inc, Gannett Group, 201 Baldwin St, Elmira, 14902. **607-734-5151**

(GENEVA) FINGER LAKES TIMES. Geneva Printing Co, 218 Genesee St, Geneva, 14456. **315-789-3333**

GLENS FALLS POST-STAR & TIMES. Glens Falls Newspapers, Inc, Lawrence and Cooper Sts, Glens Falls, 12801. **518-792-3131**

GLOVERSVILLE LEADER-HERALD. William B Collins Co, 8 E Fulton St, Gloversville, 12078. **518-725-8616**

HERKIMER EVENING TELEGRAM. Thomson Newspapers, Inc, 111 Green St, Herkimer, 13350. **315-866-2222**

HICKSVILLE NEWS. Litmor Corp, 22 W Nicholai St, Hicksville, 11801. **516-931-0012**

HORNELL SUNDAY SPECTATOR. W H Greenhow Co, 85 Canisteo St, Hornell, 14843. **607-324-1425**

HORNELL TRIBUNE. W H Greenhow Co, 85 Canisteo St, Hornell, 14843. **607-324-1425**

HUDSON REGISTER-STAR. Record Printing and Publishing Co, 336 Warren St, Hudson, 12534. **518-828-7726**. News: **518-828-4355**. Advertising: **518-828-9436**

ITHACA JOURNAL. Ithaca Journal-News, Inc, Gannett Group, 123 W State St, Ithaca, 14850. **607-272-2321**. Night line: **607-272-2327**

JAMESTOWN POST-JOURNAL. Ogden Newspapers, Inc, 11–21 W 2nd St, Jamestown, 14701. **716-487-1111**

KINGSTON FREEMAN. Mid-Hudson Publications, Inc, 79–97 Hurley Ave, Kingston, 12401. **914-331-5000**

LITTLE FALLS TIMES. Crowley Publishing Co, 347 S 2nd St, Little Falls, 13365. **315-823-3680**

LOCKPORT UNION SUN & JOURNAL. 459–91 S Transit St, Lockport, 14094. **716-433-3811**

(LONG ISLAND) NEWSDAY. 550 Stewart Ave, Garden City, NY 11530. **516-222-5527**. William Attwood, president and publisher, **516-222-5488**. Jack Squire, promotion and public affairs director, **516-222-5555**

LONG ISLAND PRESS. Publication suspended on March 25, 1977.

MALONE TELEGRAM. 136 E Main St, Malone, 12953. **518-483-4700**

MAMARONECK TIMES. Westchester Rockland Newspapers, Inc, Gannett Group, 126 Library Ln, Mamaroneck, 10543. **914-698-5500**

MEDINA DAILY JOURNAL-REGISTER. Medina Daily Journal-Register Publishing Co, Inc, 409–13 Main, Medina, 14103. **716-798-1400**

MIDDLETOWN TIMES HERALD-RECORD AND SUNDAY RECORD. Ottaway Newspapers, Inc, 40 Mulberry St, Middletown, 10940. **914-343-2181**

(MOUNT VERNON) ARGUS. Westchester Rockland Newspapers, Inc, Gannett Group, 147 Gramaton Ave, Mount Vernon, 10550. **914-558-3000**

NEWBURGH BEACON NEWS. 85 Dickson St, Newburgh, 12550. **914-561-3000**

NEW ROCHELLE STANDARD-STAR. Westchester Rockland Newspapers, Inc, Gannett Group, 92 North Ave, New Rochelle, 10802. **914-636-8900**

(NEW YORK—BROOKLYN) NEW YORK DAILY CHALLENGE. 1368 Fulton St, Brooklyn, 11207. **212-636-9500**

(NEW YORK—MANHATTAN) JOURNAL OF COMMERCE. Twin Coast Newspapers, Inc, a division of Knight-Ridder Newspapers, Inc, 99 Wall St, New York, 10005. **212-425-1616**

(NEW YORK—MANHATTAN) NEW YORK DAILY NEWS. 220 E 42nd St, New York, 10017. **212-949-1234**

(NEW YORK—MANHATTAN) THE DAILY WORLD. Long View Publishing Co, 239 W 23rd St, New York, 10011. **212-924-2523**

(NEW YORK—MANHATTAN) THE NEW YORK POST. New York Post Corp, 210 South St, New York, 10002. **212-349-5000**

(NEW YORK—MANHATTAN) THE NEW YORK TIMES. The New York Times Co, 229 W 43rd St, New York, 10036. **212-556-1234.** *See also* BUSINESS.

(NEW YORK—MANHATTAN) WALL STREET JOURNAL. Dow Jones and Co, Inc, 22 Cortland St, New York, 10007. **212-285-5000.** *See also* BUSINESS.

(NEW YORK—QUEENS) EVENING NEWS. Sylbea Printing, Inc, 41-11 45th St, Long Island City, 11104. **212-937-1234**

(NEW YORK—RICHMOND) STATEN ISLAND ADVANCE. Advance Publications, Inc, 950 Fingerboard Rd, Staten Island, 10305. **212-981-1234**

NEWSDAY. *See* Long Island.

NIAGARA FALLS GAZETTE. Niagara Falls Gazette Publishing Co, Inc, Gannett Group, 310 Niagara St, Niagara Falls, 14302. **716-282-2311**

(NORTH TONAWANDA) TONAWANDA NEWS. Tonawanda Publishing Corp, 435 River Rd, North Tonawanda, 14120. **716-693-1000**

NORWICH (CHENANGO COUNTY) THE EVENING SUN. 45-7 Hale St, Norwich, 13815. **607-334-3276**

(NYACK) ROCKLAND JOURNAL-NEWS. Westchester Rockland Newspapers, Inc, Gannett Group, 53-5 Hudson Ave, Nyack, 10960. **914-358-2200**

OGDENSBURG ADVANCE-NEWS. Park Newspapers of St. Lawrence, Inc, PO Box 409, Ogdensburg, 13669. **315-393-1000**

OLEAN TIMES-HERALD. 639 Norton Dr, Olean, 14760. **716-372-3121**

ONEIDA DISPATCH. 102 Dispatch Pl, Oneida, 13422. **315-363-5100**

ONEONTA STAR. Ottaway Newspapers, Inc, 102 Chestnut St, Oneonta, 13820. **607-432-1000**

OSSINING CITIZEN-REGISTER. Westchester Rockland Newspapers, Inc, Gannett Group, 109 Croton Ave, Ossining, NY 10562. **914-941-8000**

(OSWEGO) PALLADIUM-TIMES. 140 W 1st St, Oswego, 13126. **315-343-3800**

PEEKSKILL STAR. Ogden Newspapers, Inc, 824 Main St, Peekskill, 10566. **914-737-1200**

PLATTSBURGH PRESS-REPUBLICAN. Plattsburgh Publishing Co, Ottaway Newspapers, Inc, 170 Margaret St, Plattsburgh, 12901. **518-561-2300**

PORT CHESTER ITEM. Westchester Rockland Newspapers, Inc, Gannett Group, 33 New Broad St, Port Chester, 10573. **914-939-0800**

PORT JERVIS UNION-GAZETTE. Tri-States Publishing Co, 84-88 Fowler St, Port Jervis, 12771. **914-856-5383**

POUGHKEEPSIE JOURNAL. Poughkeepsie Newspapers, Inc, Gannett Group, Memorial Sq, Poughkeepsie, 12602. **914-454-2000**

ROCHESTER DEMOCRAT & CHRONICLE. Gannett Co, Inc, 55 Exchange St, Rochester, 14614. **716-232-7100**

ROCHESTER TIMES-UNION. Gannett Co, Inc, 55 Exchange St, Rochester, 14614. **716-232-7100**

ROME SENTINEL. 333 W Dominick St, Rome, 13440. **315-337-4000**

SALAMANCA REPUBLICAN-PRESS. 36-42 River St, Salamanca, 14779. **716-945-1644**

(SARANAC) LAKE ADIRONDACK ENTERPRISE. Adirondack Publishing Co, Inc, 61 Broadway, Saranac Lake, 12983. **518-891-2600**

(SARATOGA SPRINGS) SARATOGIAN-TRI-COUNTY NEWS. The Saratogian, Inc, Gannett Group, 20 Lake Ave, Saratoga Springs, 12866. **518-584-4242**

SCHENECTADY GAZETTE. Daily Gazette Co, 334 State St, Schenectady, 12301. **518-374-4141**

SYRACUSE HERALD-AMERICAN. The Post-Standard Co, PO Box 4915, Clinton Sq, Syracuse, NY 13221. **315-473-7700**

SYRACUSE HERALD-JOURNAL. PO Box 4915, Clinton Sq, Syracuse, 13221. **315-473-7700**

TARRYTOWN NEWS. Westchester Rockland Newspapers, Inc, Gannett Group, 111 Old White Plains Rd, Tarrytown, 10591. **914-631-5000**

TONAWANDA. See North Tonawanda.

TROY TIMES RECORD. Troy Publishing Co, Inc, Broadway and 5th Ave, Troy, 12181. **518-272-2000**

UTICA OBSERVER-DISPATCH. Observer-Dispatch, Inc, Gannett Group, 221 Oriskany Plz, Utica, 13503. **315-792-5000**

UTICA PRESS. Observer-Dispatch, Inc, Gannett Group, 221 Oriskany Plz, Utica, 13503. **315-792-5000**

WATERTOWN TIMES. Brockway Co, 260 Washington St, Watertown, 13601. **315-782-1000**

WELLSVILLE DAILY REPORTER. W H Greenhow Co, 159 N Main St, Wellsville, 14895. **716-593-5300**

WELLSVILLE SPECTATOR. W H Greenhow Co, 159 N Main St, Wellsville, 14895. **716-593-5300**

WHITE PLAINS REPORTER DISPATCH. Westchester Rockland Newspapers, Inc, Gannett Group, 1 Gannett Dr, White Plains, NY 10604. **914-694-9300**

YONKERS HERALD STATESMAN. West-chester Rockland Newspapers, Inc, Gannett Group, Larkin Plz, Yonkers, 10702. **914-965-5000**

North Carolina

ASHEBORO COURIER-TRIBUNE. PO Box 340, Asheboro, 27203. **919-625-2102**

ASHEVILLE CITIZEN. Asheville Citizen-Times Publishing Co, 14 O'Henry Ave, Asheville, 28802. **704-252-5611**

ASHEVILLE TIMES. Asheville Citizen-Times Publishing Co, 14 O'Henry Ave, Asheville, 28802. **704-252-5611**

BURLINGTON TIMES-NEWS. Times News Publishing Co, 707 S Main, Burlington, 27215. **919-227-0131**

CHAPEL HILL NEWSPAPER. Chapel Hill Publishing Co, 505 W Franklin St (PO Box 870), Chapel Hill, 27514. **919-967-7045**

CHARLOTTE OBSERVER. Knight-Ridder Publishing Co, 600 S Tryon St (PO Box 2138), Charlotte, 28233. **704-374-7215**

CONCORD TRIBUNE. 125 Union St, South Concord, 28025. **704-782-3155**

DUNN DAILY DISPATCH. S Railroad Ave, PO Box 7401, Dunn, 28334. **919-892-3142**

DUNN RECORD. Record Publishing Co, E Canary St, PO Box 811, Dunn, 28334. **919-892-3117**

DURHAM HERALD. Durham Herald Co, Inc, 115 Market St, Durham, 27702. **919-682-8181**

DURHAM SUN. Durham Herald Co, Inc, 115 Market St, Durham, 27702. **919-682-8181**

ELIZABETH CITY ADVANCE. Advance Publications, Inc, 216 S Poindexter St, Elizabeth City, 27909. **919-335-0841**

FAYETTEVILLE OBSERVER. Fayetteville Publishing Co, PO Box 849, Fayetteville, 28302. **919-485-2121**

FAYETTEVILLE TIMES. Fayetteville Publishing Co, 512 Hay St, Fayetteville, 28301. **919-485-2121**

GASTONIA GAZETTE. 2500 Wilkinson Blvd, Gastonia, 28052. **704-864-3293**

GOLDSBORO NEWS-ARGUS. Wayne Printing Co, 310 N Berkeley Blvd, Goldsboro, 27530. **919-778-2211**

GREENSBORO NEWS. Greensboro News Co, PO Box 20848, Greensboro, 27420. **919-373-1000**

GREENSBORO RECORD. Greensboro News Co, PO Box 20848, Greensboro, 27420. **919-373-1000**

GREENVILLE DAILY REFLECTOR. Daily Reflector, Inc, 209 Cotanche St, Greenville, 27834. **919-752-6166**

HENDERSON DISPATCH. Henderson Dispatch Co, 304 Chestnut St, Henderson, 27536. **919-492-4001**

HENDERSONVILLE TIMES-NEWS. Times-News Printing Co, Inc, 1717 Four Seasons Blvd, Hendersonville, 27839. **704-692-0505**

HICKORY RECORD. Hickory Publishing Co, 116 3rd St NW, Hickory, 28601. **704-322-4510**

HIGH POINT ENTERPRISE. High Point Enterprise, Inc, 210 Church Ave, High Point, 27261. **919-885-2161**

JACKSONVILLE DAILY NEWS. PO Box B, Jacksonville, 28540. **919-353-1171**

KANNAPOLIS INDEPENDENT. Kannapolis Publishing Co, 123 N Main, Kannapolis, 28081. **704-933-2181**

KINSTON FREE PRESS. 114 E North St, Kinston, 28501. **919-527-3191**

LENOIR NEWS-TOPIC. Lenoir Newspapers, Inc, Pennton Ave, Lenoir, 28645. **919-758-7381**

LEXINGTON DISPATCH. Dispatch Publishing Co, 30 E 1st Ave, Lexington, 27292. **704-249-3981**

LUMBERTON ROBESONIAN. Robesonian, Inc, 121 W 5th St, Lumberton, 28358. **919-739-4322**

MONROE ENQUIRER-JOURNAL. PO Box 70, Monroe, 28110. **704-289-1541**

MORGANTON NEWS-HERALD. News-Herald Publishing Co, Inc, 301 Collett St, Morganton, 28655. **704-437-2161**

NEW BERN SUN-JOURNAL. 226 Pollock St, New Bern, 28560. **919-638-8101**

(NEWTON) OBSERVER-NEWS-ENTER-PRISE. Catawba, 28658. **704-464-0221**

RALEIGH NEWS AND OBSERVER. News and Observer Publishing Co, 215 S McDowell St, Raleigh, 27601. **919-821-1234**

RALEIGH TIMES. News and Observer Publishing Co, 215 S McDowell St, Raleigh, 27601. **919-821-1234**

REIDSVILLE REVIEW. Reidsville Newspapers, Inc, 116 N Scales St, Reidsville, 27320. **919-349-4331**

ROANOKE RAPIDS HERALD. Herald Printing Co, Inc, 916 Roanoke Ave, Roanoke Rapids, 27870. **919-537-2505**

(ROCKINGHAM) RICHMOND COUNTY DAILY JOURNAL. 105 Washington St, Rockingham, 28379. **919-997-3111**

ROCKY MOUNT TELEGRAM. Rocky Mount Publishing Co, Thomson Newspapers, Inc, 150 Howard St, Rocky Mount, 27801. **919-446-5161**

SALISBURY POST. Post Publishing Co, Inc, 131 W Innes St, Salisbury, 28144. **704-636-4231**

SANFORD HERALD. Herald Publishing Co, 208 St Clair Ct, Sanford, 27330. **919-776-0535**

SHELBY STAR. Star Publishing Co, 315 E Graham St, Shelby, 28150. **704-482-3811**

STATESVILLE RECORD & LANDMARK. Statesville Daily Record, Inc, 220 E Broad St, Statesville, 28677. **704-872-5251**

TARBORO SOUTHERNER. Tarboro Printing Co, 504 W Wilson St, Tarboro, 28776. **919-823-3106**

THOMASVILLE TIMES. High Point Enterprise, Inc, 19 Trade St, Thomasville, 27360. **919-475-2151**

TRYON DAILY BULLETIN. Tryon Daily Bulletin, Inc, PO Box 790, Tryon, 28782. **704-852-1445**

WASHINGTON DAILY NEWS. Washington News Publishing Co, 217 Market St, Washington, 27889. **919-946-2145**

WILMINGTON STAR. Star-News Newspapers, Inc, PO Box 840, Wilmington, 28401. **919-343-2000**

WILMINGTON STAR-NEWS. Star-News Newspapers, Inc, PO Box 840, Wilmington, 28401. **919-343-2000**

WILSON TIMES. Wilson Daily Times, Inc, 117 N Goldsboro, Wilson, 27893. **919- 243-5151**

WINSTON-SALEM JOURNAL. Piedmont Publishing Co, Inc, an affiliate of Media General, Inc, 416–20 N Marshall, Winston-Salem, 27102. **919-727-7211**

WINSTON-SALEM SENTINEL. Piedmont Publishing Co, Inc, an affiliate of Media General, Inc, 416–20 N Marshall, Winston-Salem, 27102. **919-727-7394**

North Dakota

BISMARCK TRIBUNE. 220 4th St (PO Box 1498), Bismarck, 58501. **701-233-2500**

DEVILS LAKE JOURNAL. 3rd St and 4th Ave, Devils Lake, 48301. **701-662-2127**

DICKINSON PRESS. 127 1st St W, Dickinson, 58601. **701-225-8111**

FARGO-MOORHEAD FORUM. Forum Publishing Co, 101 5th St, North Fargo, 48102. **701-235-7311**

GRAND FORKS HERALD. Grand Forks Herald, Inc, 114 N 4th St, Grand Forks, 48201. **701-774-4211**

JAMESTOWN SUN. Hansen Bros, Inc, 122 2nd St NW, Jamestown, 58401. **701-252-3120**

MINOT DAILY NEWS. 301–4 4th St SE, Minot, 48701. **701-838-3341**

VALLEY CITY TIMES-RECORD. Mid-America Publishing Corp, 146 3rd St NE, Valley City, 48072. **701-845-0463**

(WAHPETON) TRI-STATE DAILY NEWS. 601 Dakota Ave (PO Box 1018), Wahpeton, 48075. **701-642-8585**

WILLISTON HERALD. Williston Herald, Inc, 14 W 4th St, Williston, 58801. **701-572-2165**

Ohio

AKRON BEACON JOURNAL. Beacon Journal Publishing Co, Knight-Ridder Newspapers, Inc, 44 E Exchange St, Akron, 44328. **216-375-8111**

ALLIANCE REVIEW. Alliance Publishing Co, Inc, 40 S Linden Ave, Alliance, 44601. **216-821-1200**

ASHLAND TIMES GAZETTE. Ashland Publishing Co, 40 E 2nd St, Ashland, 44805. **419-323-1581**

ASHTABULA STAR-BEACON. Ashtabula Printing Co, 4626 Park Ave, Ashtabula, 44004. **216-998-2323**

ATHENS MESSENGER. Messenger Publishing Co, Route 33 N and Johnson Rd, Athens, 45701. **614-592-6612**

BELLEFONTAINE EXAMINER. Hubbard Publishing Co, 127 E Chillicothe Ave, Bellefontaine, 43311. **513-592-3060**

BELLEVUE GAZETTE. Gazette Publishing Co, 107 N Sandusky St, Bellevue, 44811. **419-483-4190**

BOWLING GREEN SENTINEL-TRIBUNE. Sentinel Co, 300 E Poe Rd (PO Box 88), Bowling Green, 43402. **419-352-4611**

BRYAN TIMES. Bryan Publishing Co, 127 S Walnut St, Bryan, 43506. **419-636-1111.** Ford Cullis, publisher

BUCYRUS TELEGRAPH-FORUM. Freedom Newspapers, Inc, 119 W Rensselaer St, Bucyrus, 44820. **419-562-5881**

(CAMBRIDGE) THE DAILY JEFFERSONIAN. Jeffersonian Co, 821 Wheeling Ave, Cambridge, 43725. **614-439-3531**

CANTON REPOSITORY. Thomson-Brush-Moore Newspapers, Inc, 500 S Market Ave, Canton, 44702. **216-454-5611**

(CELINA) THE DAILY STANDARD. Standard Printing Co, E Market St, Celina, 45822. **419-586-2371**

(CHARDON) GEAUGA TIMES LEADER. 111 Water St, Chardon, 44024. **216-286-6101**

CHILLICOTHE GAZETTE. Chillicothe Newspapers, Inc, 50 W Main St, Chillicothe, 45601. **614-773-2111**

CINCINNATI ENQUIRER. 617 Vine St, Cincinnati, 45201. **513-721-2700**

CINCINNATI POST. E W Scripps Co, 800 Broadway, Cincinnati, 45202. **513-352-2727**

CIRCLEVILLE HERALD. Circleville Publishing Co, 210 N Court St, Circleville, 43113. **614-474-3131**

CLEVELAND PLAIN DEALER. Plain Dealer Publishing Co, 1801 Superior Ave, Cleveland, 44114. **216-523-4500**

CLEVELAND PRESS. E W Scripps Co, 901 Lakeside Ave, Cleveland, 44114. **216-623-1111**

COLUMBUS CITIZEN-JOURNAL. E W Scripps Co, 34 S 3rd St, Columbus, 43216. **614-461-5000**

COLUMBUS DISPATCH. Dispatch Printing Co, 34 S 3rd St, Columbus, 43216. **614-461-5000**

CONNEAUT NEWS-HERALD. Conneaut Printing Co, 182–4 Broad St, Conneaut, 44030. **216-593-1166**

COSHOCTON TRIBUNE. 115 N 6th St, Coshocton, 43812. **614-622-1122**

DAYTON JOURNAL HERALD. Dayton Newspapers, Inc, 4th and Ludlow Sts, Dayton, 45401. **513-225-2421**

DAYTON NEWS. Dayton Newspapers, Inc, 4th and Ludlow Sts, Dayton, 45401. **513-223-2112**

DEFIANCE CRESCENT-NEWS. Defiance Publishing Co, Perry and 2nd Sts, Defiance, 43512. **419-784-5441**

DELAWARE GAZETTE. 18 E William St, Delaware, 43015. **614-363-1161**

DELPHOS HERALD. 405–9 N Main, Delphos, 45833. **419-692-5050**

(DOVER) TIMES-REPORTER. Mansfield Journal Co, 629 Wabash Ave, New Philadelphia, 44663. **216-364-5577**

(EAST LIVERPOOL) THE EVENING REVIEW. 210 E 4th St, East Liverpool, 43920. **216-385-4545**

EAST PALESTINE LEADER. Leader Press Publishing Co, 78 N Market St, East Palestine, 44413. **216-426-9481**

ELYRIA CHRONICLE-TELEGRAM. Lorain County Printing and Publishing Co, 225 East Ave, Elyria, 44035. **216-323-3321**

FAIRBORN HERALD. Miami Valley Publishing Co, 579 E Xenia Dr, Fairborn, 45324. **513-878-3993**

FINDLAY COURIER. Findlay Publishing Co, 701 W Sandusky, Findlay, 45840. **419-422-5151**

FOSTORIA REVIEW-TIMES. 113 E Center St (PO Drawer C), Fostoria, 44830. **419-435-6641**

FREMONT NEWS-MESSENGER. Gannett Group, 107 S Arch St (PO Box 311), Fremont, 43420. **419-332-5511**

GALION INQUIRER. Inquirer Printing Co, 378 N Market St, Galion, 44833. **419-468-1117**

GALLIPOLIS TRIBUNE. Ohio Valley Publishing Co, 825 3rd Ave, Gallipolis, 45631. **614-446-2342**

GENEVA FREE PRESS. Geneva-Madison Printing Co, 23 S Forest St, Geneva, 44041. **216-466-1121**

GREENVILLE DAILY ADVOCATE. Thomson Newspapers, Inc, 309–11 S Broadway, Greenville, 45331. **513-548-3151**

GREENFIELD TIMES. Greenfield Times Publishing Co, 345 Jefferson, Greenfield, 45123. **513-981-2141**

HAMILTON JOURNAL-NEWS. Journal Publishing Co, Court and Journal Sq, Hamilton, 45012. **513-863-8200**

HILLSBORO PRESS GAZETTE. Hillsboro Publishing Co, 209 S High St, Hillsboro, 45133. **513-393-3456**

IRONTON TRIBUNE. 2903 S 5th St, Ironton, 45638. **614-532-1441**

(KENT) RECORD-COURIER. Record Publishing Co, N Chestnut St, Ravenna, 44266. **216-296-6438**

KENTON TIMES. Hardin County Publishing Co, 201 E Columbus St, Kenton, 43326. **419-674-4066**

LANCASTER EAGLE-GAZETTE. 138 W Chestnut St (PO Box 848), Lancaster, 43130. **614-654-1321**

LIMA NEWS. Lima News Publishing Co, 121 E High St, Lima, 45802. **419-223-1010**

(LISBON) MORNING JOURNAL. Buckeye Publishing Co, 308 Maple St, Lisbon, 44432. **216-424-9541**

LOGAN NEWS. Wayne Newspaper Co, 72 E Main St, Logan, 43138. **614-385-2109**

LONDON MADISON PRESS. Central Ohio Printing Corp, 30 S Oak St, London, 43140. **614-852-1616**

LORAIN JOURNAL. Horvitz Newspapers, 1657 Broadway, Lorain, 44052. **216-245-6901**

MANSFIELD NEWS JOURNAL. 70 W 4th St, Mansfield, 44901. **419-522-3311**

MARIETTA TIMES. 700 Channel Ln, Marietta, 45750. **614-373-2121**

MARION STAR. 150 Court St, Marion, 43302. **614-382-1101**

MARTINS FERRY TIMES-LEADER. 200 S 4th St, Martins Ferry, 43935. **614-633-1131**

MARYSVILLE JOURNAL-TRIBUNE. Marysville Newspapers, Inc, 207 N Main St, Marysville, 43040. **513-642-2015**

MASSILLON INDEPENDENT. Massillon Publishing Co, 50 North Ave NW, Massillon, 44646. **216-833-2631**

MEDINA COUNTY GAZETTE. Medina County Publications, Inc, 885 W Liberty, Medina, 44256. **216-725-4166**

MENTOR. *See* Willoughby

MIDDLETOWN JOURNAL. News Journal Publishing Co, 1st and Broad, Middletown, 45042. **513-422-3611**

MOUNT VERNON NEWS. Republican Publishing Co, 18–20 E Vine St (PO Box 791), Mount Vernon, 43050. **614-397-5333**

NAPOLEON NORTHWEST-SIGNAL. Napoleon, Inc, E Riverview, Napoleon, 43545. **419-592-5055**

NEWARK ADVOCATE. Advocate Printing Co, Inc, 25 W Main St, Newark, 43055. **614-345-4053**

NEW PHILADELPHIA. *See* Dover

NILES DAILY TIMES. Phoenix Publications, Inc, 35 W State St, Niles, 44446. **216-652-5841**

NORWALK REFLECTOR. Reflector-Herald, Inc, 61 E Monroe St, Norwalk, 44857. **419-668-3771**

PAINESVILLE TELEGRAPH. Lake Geauga Printing Co, 84 N State St, Painesville, 44077. **216-354-4333**

PIQUA CALL. Piqua Call Publishing Co, Spring and Ash, Piqua, 45356. **513-773-2721**

POMEROY TIMES-SENTINEL. Ohio Valley Publishing Co, 111 Court St (PO Box 729), Pomeroy, 45769. **614-922-2156**

PORT CLINTON NEWS-HERALD. Port Clinton News-Herald Publishing Co, 115 W 2nd St, Port Clinton, 43452. **419-734-3141**

PORTSMOUTH TIMES. 637 6th St, Portsmouth, 45662. **614-353-3101**

ST MARY'S LEADER. Leader Printing Co, 102 E Spring St, St Mary's, 45885. **419-394-5127**

SALEM NEWS. 161 N Lincoln Ave, Salem, 44460. **216-332-4601**

SANDUSKY REGISTER. Sandusky Newspapers, Inc, Market and Jackson Sts, Sandusky, 44870. **419-625-5500**

SHELBY GLOBE. 37 W Main St, Shelby, 44875. **419-342-4276**

SIDNEY NEWS. Amos Press, Inc, 911 S Vandemark Rd (PO Box 150), Sidney, 45365. **513-492-4141**

SPRINGFIELD NEWS-SUN. Springfield Newspapers, Inc, 202 N Limestone, Springfield, 45501. **513-323-3731**

SPRINGFIELD NEWS. Springfield Newspapers, Inc, 202 N Limestone, Springfield, 45501. **513-323-3731**

SPRINGFIELD SUN. Springfield Newspapers, Inc, 202 N Limestone, Springfield, 45501. **513-323-3731**

STEUBENVILLE HERALD-STAR. 401 Herald Sq, Steubenville, 43952. **614-282-5311**

TIFFIN ADVERTISER-TRIBUNE. Tiffin Publishing Co, 120 N Nelson St, Tiffin, 44883. **419-447-4455**

TOLEDO BLADE. 541 Superior St, Toledo, 43660. **419-259-6000**

TROY DAILY NEWS. Troy Daily News, Inc, 224 S Market St, Troy, 45373. **513-335-5634**

UHRICHSVILLE CHRONICLE. 109 N Water, Uhrichsville, 44683. **614-922-1321**

UPPER SANDUSKY DAILY CHIEF-UNION. Daily Chief Co, 111 W Wyandot Ave, Upper Sandusky, 43351. **419-294-2332**

URBANA CITIZEN. Brown Publishing Co, 220 E Court St, Urbana, 43078. **513-652-1331**

VAN WERT TIMES-BULLETIN. Van Wert Publishing Co, 700 Fox Rd, Van Wert, 45891. **419-238-2285**

WAPAKONETA DAILY NEWS. Daily News Printing Co, 8 Willipic St, Wapakoneta, 45895. **419-738-3318**

WARREN TRIBUNE CHRONICLE. Tribune Co, 240 Franklin St SE, Warren, 44482. **216-393-2521**

(WASHINGTON COURT HOUSE) RECORD-HERALD. Washington News Publishing Co, 138 S Fayette St, Washington Court House, 43160. **614-335-3611**

(WILLOUGHBY) NEWS-HERALD. Lorain Journal Co, 38879 Mentor Ave, Willoughby, 44094. **216-951-0000**

WILMINGTON NEWS-JOURNAL. 47 S South St, Wilmington, 45177. **513-382-2574**

WOOSTER RECORD. Wooster Republican Printing Co, 210–2 E Liberty St, Wooster, 44691. **216-264-1125**

XENIA DAILY GAZETTE. Chew Publishing Co, S Detroit St, Xenia, 45385. **513-372-4444**

YOUNGSTOWN VINDICATOR. Vindicator Printing Co, Vindicator Sq, Youngstown, 44501. **216-747-1471**

ZANESVILLE TIMES RECORDER. 34 S 4th St, Zanesville, 43701. **614-452-4561.** Jack E Budd, managing editor

Oklahoma

ADA NEWS. News Publishing and Printing Co, 112–20 N Broadway, Ada, 74820. **405-332-4433**

ALTUS TIMES-DEMOCRAT. 218–20 W Commerce St, Altus, 73521. **405-482-1221**

ALVA REVIEW-COURIER. Alva Newspapers, Inc, 622 Choctaw (PO Box 688), Alva, 73717. **405-327-2200**

ANADARKO DAILY NEWS. Joe W McBride, Jr, publisher, 117–9 E Broadway, Anadarko, 73005. **405-247-3331**

(ARDMORE) ARDMOREITE. Ardmoreite Publishing Co, 117 W Broadway (PO Box 1328), Ardmore, 73401. **405-233-2200**

BARTLESVILLE EXAMINER-ENTERPRISE. Western Publishing Co, Donrey Media Group, 300 EFPB, Bartlesville, 74003. **918-336-1600**

BLACKWELL JOURNAL-TRIBUNE. Midway Publishing Co, Donrey Media Group, 113 E Blackwell Ave, Blackwell, 74631. **405-363-3370**

CHICKASHA EXPRESS. Central Publishers, Ltd, Donrey Media Group, 302 N 3rd St, Chickasha, 73018. **405-224-2600**

CLAREMORE PROGRESS. Progress Printing, 315 W Will Rogers Blvd, Claremore, 74017. **918-341-1101**

CLINTON NEWS. Clinton Daily News Co, PO Box 158, Clinton, 73601. **405-323-5151**

CUSHING CITIZEN. Cushing Newspapers, Inc, 115 S Cleveland, Cushing, 74023. **918-225-3333**

DUNCAN BANNER. 10th and Elm Sts (PO Box 1268), Duncan, 73533. **405-255-5354**

DURANT DEMOCRAT. Durant Publishing-Broadcasting Co, PO Box 250, 200 W Beech St, Durant, 74701. **405-924-4388**

ELK CITY NEWS. News-Journal Publishing Co, 200 W Broadway, Elk City, 73644. **405-225-3000**

EL RENO TRIBUNE. Tribune Corp, 201 N Rock Island, El Reno, 73036. **405-262-5180**

ENID EAGLE. Enid Publishing Co, 227 W Broadway (PO Box 1192), Enid, 73701. **405-233-6600**

ENID NEWS. Enid Publishing Co, 227 W Broadway (PO Box 1192), Enid, 73701. **405-233-6600**

FREDERICK LEADER. Frederick Leader Publishing Co, Donrey Media Group, 304 W Grand, Frederick, 73542. **405-335-2188**

GUTHRIE DAILY LEADER. Logan Publishing Co, 107 W Harrison, Guthrie, 73044. **405-282-2222**

GUYMON HERALD. Panhandle Empire Publishing Co, Donrey Media Group, 515 N Ellison St, Guymon, 73942. **405-338-3355**

HENRYETTA FREE LANCE. Donrey Media Group, 812 W Main St, Henryetta, 74437. **918-652-3311**

HOBART DEMOCRAT-CHIEF. Democrat-Chief Publishing Co, 216 W 4th St, Hobart, 73651. **405-726-3333**

HOLDENVILLE NEWS. Donrey Media Group, 112 S Creek St (PO Box 751), Holdenville, 74848. **405-379-5411**

HUGO NEWS. Hugo Publishing Co, 128 E Jackson St, Hugo, 74743. **405-326-3311**

(IDABEL) MCCURTAIN DAILY GAZETTE. 107 S Central St, Idabel, 74745. **405-286-3321**

LAWTON CONSTITUTION. Lawton Publishing Co, 3rd St and A Ave, Lawton, 73501. **405-353-0620**

LAWTON PRESS. Lawton Publishing Co, 3rd St and A Ave, Lawton, 73501. **405-353-0620**

MCALESTER DEMOCRAT. Southeastern Publishers, Inc, McAlester, 74501. **918-423-6141**

MCALESTER NEWS CAPITAL. McAlester Publishing Co, 500 S 2nd (PO Box 987), McAlester, 74501. **918-423-1700**

MIAMI NEWS-RECORD. Miami Newspapers, Inc, 14 1st Ave (PO Box 940), Miami, 74354. **918-542-5533**

MUSKOGEE PHOENIX & TIMES DEMOCRAT. Oklahoma Press Publishing Co, 214 Wall St, Muskogee, 74401. **918-682-3311**

NORMAN TRANSCRIPT. 215 E Comanche, Norman, 73069. **405-321-1800**

NOWATA STAR. Daily Star Publishing Co, 215 N Maple, Nowata, 74048. **918-273-2446**

(OKLAHOMA CITY) OKLAHOMA JOURNAL. Oklahoma City, 73110. **405-737-8811**

(OKLAHOMA CITY) OKLAHOMAN. Oklahoma Publishing Co, 500 N Broadway (PO Box 25125), Oklahoma City, 73125. **405-232-3311**

OKLAHOMA CITY TIMES. Oklahoma Publishing Co, 500 N Broadway (PO Box 25125), Oklahoma City, 73125. **405-232-3311**

OKMULGEE TIMES. Times Publishing Co, Donrey Media Group, 114 E 7th St (PO Box 1218), Okmulgee, 74447. **918-756-3600**

PAULS VALLEY DEMOCRAT. Democrat Printing Co, Inc, Donrey Media Group, 108 S Willow, Pauls Valley, 73075. **405-238-6464**

PAWHUSKA DAILY JOURNAL-CAPITAL, OSAGE JOURNAL-NEWS. Western Publishing Co, Donrey Media Group, 700 Ki-he-kah (PO Box 238), Pawhuska, 74056. **918-287-3421** or **4138**

PERRY JOURNAL. 714 Delaware, Perry, 73077. **405-336-2222**

PONCA CITY NEWS. Ponca City Publishing Co, PO Box 191, Ponca City, 74601. **405-765-3311**

PRYOR TIMES. Pryor Publishing Co, 105 S Adair, Pryor, 74361. **918-825-3292**

SAPULPA HERALD. 16 S Park St, Sapulpa, 74066. **918-224-5185**

SAYRE JOURNAL. 110 N 4th St, Sayre, 73662. **405-928-3372**

SEMINOLE PRODUCER. 121 N Main St, Seminole, 74868. **405-382-1100**

SHAWNEE NEWS-STAR. Shawnee News Co, 215 N Bell, Shawnee, 74801. **405-273-4200**

STILLWATER NEWS-PRESS. Stillwater Publishing Co, 211 W 9th St, Stillwater, 74074. **405-372-5000**

TULSA TRIBUNE. 315 S Boulder Ave, Tulsa, 74102. **918-582-1101**

TULSA WORLD. World Publishing Co, 315 S Boulder Ave, Tulsa, 74102. **918-583-2161**

VINITA JOURNAL. Vinita Printing Co, Inc, 138–40 S Wilson, Vinita, 74301. **918-256-6422**

WEATHERFORD NEWS. Daily News, 118 S Broadway, Weatherford, 73096. **405-772-3301**

WEWOKA TIMES. Donrey Media Group, 210 S Wewoka Ave (PO Box 61), Wewoka, 74884. **405-257-3341**

WOODWARD DAILY PRESS. Woodward Daily Press, Inc, 1023 Main St (PO Box 129), Woodward, 73801. **405-256-3311**

Oregon

ALBANY DEMOCRAT-HERALD. Democrat-Herald Publishing Co, 138 W 6th Ave, Albany, 97321. **503-926-2211**

ASHLAND TIDINGS. Ashland Publishing Co, Inc, 1661 Siskiyou Blvd, Ashland, 97520. **503-482-3456**

(ASTORIA) THE DAILY ASTORIAN. Astorian-Budget Publishing Co, 949 Exchange (PO Box 210), Astoria, 97103. **503-325-3211**

BAKER DEMOCRAT-HERALD. La Grande Publishing Co, 1915 1st St (PO Box 807), Baker, 97314. **503-523-3673**

(BEND) THE BULLETIN. 1526 Hill St, Bend, 97701. **503-382-1811**

COOS BAY WORLD. Southwestern Oregon Publishing Co, 350 Commercial St (PO Box 779), Coos Bay, 97420. **503-269-1222**

CORVALLIS GAZETTE-TIMES. Gazette-Times Publishing Co, 600 SW Jefferson Ave, Corvallis, 97330. **503-753-2641**

EUGENE REGISTER-GUARD. Guard Publishing Co, 975 High St (PO Box 10188), Eugene, 97401. **503-485-1234**

GRANTS PASS COURIER. Courier Publishing Co, 409 SE 7th, Grants Pass, 97526. **503-476-4414**

KLAMATH FALLS HERALD AND NEWS. Klamath Publishing Co, PO Box 788, Klamath Falls, 97601. **503-884-8111**

LA GRANDE OBSERVER. La Grande Publishing Co, 1710 6th St (PO Box 1500), La Grande, 97850. **503-963-3161**

MEDFORD MAIL TRIBUNE. An Ottaway Newspaper, 33 N Fir St (PO Box 1108), Medford, 97501. **503-779-1411**

NORTH BEND. *See* Coos Bay

(ONTARIO) DAILY ARGUS OBSERVER. Daily Argus Observer, 310 SW 5th Ave (PO Box 130), Ontario, 97914. **503-889-5387**

OREGON CITY ENTERPRISE-COURIER. Enterprise-Courier Publishing Co, Scripps League, 10th and Main, Oregon City, 97405. **503-656-1911**

(PENDLETON) EAST OREGONIAN. East Oregonian Publishing Co, 211 SE Byers St, Pendelton, 97801. **503-276-2211**

(PORTLAND) DAILY JOURNAL OF COMMERCE. 2014 NW 24th Ave (PO Box 10127), Portland, 97210. **503-226-1311.** Dorothy Haugston Smith, publisher. A legal and commercial newspaper

PORTLAND OREGONIAN. Oregonian Publishing Co, 1320 SW Broadway, Portland, 97201. **503-221-8327**

(PORTLAND) OREGON JOURNAL. Oregonian Publishing Co, 1320 SW Broadway, Portland, 97201. **503-221-8327**

ROSEBURG NEWS-REVIEW. News-Review Publishing Co, 345 NE Winchester St, Roseburg, 97470. **503-672-3321**

SALEM CAPITAL JOURNAL. Statesman-Journal Co, Gannett Group, 280 Church St NE (PO Box 13009), Salem, 97308. **503-399-6767**

(SALEM) OREGON STATESMAN. Gannett Group, 280 Church St NE (PO Box 13009), Salem, 97309. **503-399-6677**

THE DALLES CHRONICLE. Mid-Columbia Publishing Co, Scripps League, Fourth and Federal, The Dalles, 97058. **503-296-2141**

Pennsylvania

ALLENTOWN CALL. Call-Chronicle Newspapers, Inc, 6th and Linden Sts, Allentown, 18105. **215-820-6502**

ALLENTOWN CHRONICLE. Call-Chronicle Newspapers, Inc, 6th and Linden Sts, Allentown, 18105. **215-820-6510**

ALTOONA MIRROR. Mirror Printing Co, 1000 Green Ave, Altoona, 16603. **814-944-7171.** Marjorie A Helsel, president-publisher

BANGOR DAILY NEWS. 13–5 S Main St, Bangor, 18103. **215-588-2196**

BEAVER COUNTY TIMES. PO Box 400, Beaver, 15009. **412-775-3200**

BEAVER FALLS NEWS-TRIBUNE. Tribune Printing Co, 715 13th St, Beaver Falls, 15010. **412-846-2560**

BEDFORD GAZETTE. Gazette Publishing Co, Inc, PO Box 571, Bedford, 15522. **814-623-1151**

BELLEFONTE. *See* State College

BERWICK ENTERPRISE. 106 E Front St, Berwick, 18603. **717-752-3645**

BETHLEHEM GLOBE-TIMES. Bethlehems' Globe Publishing Co, 202 W 4th St, Bethlehem, 18015. **215-867-7571**

BLOOMSBURG PRESS. Press-Enterprise, Inc, 111 W Main St, Bloomsburg, 17815. **717-784-2121**

BRADFORD ERA. Bradford Publications, Inc, 43 Main St, Bradford, 16701. **814-368-3173**

BRISTOL. *See* Levittown

BROWNSVILLE TELEGRAPH. Brownsville Publishing Corp, 16–8 Bridge St, Brownsville, 15417. **412-785-5000**

BUTLER EAGLE. Eagle Printing Co, 114 W Diamond St, Butler, 16001. **412-287-5771**

(CANONSBURG) THE DAILY NOTES. Scripps Pennsylvania Inc, 23 N Central Ave, Canonsburg, 15217. **412-745-6400.** J E Schiffer, publisher. Robert Kaminski, managing editor

CARLISLE SENTINEL. Cumberland Publishers, Inc, 457 E North St, Carlisle, 17013. **717-243-2611**

CHAMBERSBURG PUBLIC OPINION. McClure Newspapers, Inc, Gannet Group, 77 N 3rd St, Chambersburg, 17201. **717-264-6161**

(CHESTER) DELAWARE COUNTY DAILY TIMES. Peerless Publications Inc, Brookhaven, 19015. **215-284-7200**

CLEARFIELD PROGRESS. Progressive Publishing Co, Locust St, Clearfield, 16830. **814-765-5581**

COATESVILLE RECORD. Coatesville Record, Inc, 204 E Lincoln Hwy, Coatesville, 19320. **215-384-4900**

COLUMBIA NEWS. 341 Chestnut St, Columbia, 17512. **717-684-2125**

CONNELLSVILLE COURIER. 127 W Apple St, Connellsville, 15425. **412-628-2000**

CORRY EVENING JOURNAL. 28 W South St, Corry, 16407. **814-665-8291**

DANVILLE NEWS. Progressive Publishing Co, 14 E Mahoning St, Danville, 17821. **717-275-3235**

DONORA. *See* Monessen

DOYLESTOWN INTELLIGENCER. 333 N Broad St, Doylestown, 18901. **215-348-8171**

DUBOIS COURIER-EXPRESS. Courier-Express Publishing Co, Long and High Sts, DuBois, 15801. **814-371-4200**

EASTON EXPRESS. Easton Publishing Co, 30 N 4th St, Easton, 18042. **215-258-7171**

ELLWOOD CITY LEDGER. Citizens Publishing and Printing Co, 835 Lawrence Ave, Ellwood City, 16117. **412-758-7529**

ERIE TIMES-NEWS. Times Publishing Co, 205 W 12th St, Erie, 16512. **814-456-8531**

FRANKLIN NEWS-HERALD. News-Herald Printing Co, Inc, 631 12th St, Franklin, 16323. **814-432-3141**

GETTYSBURG TIMES. Times and News Publishing Co, Carlisle St, Gettysburg, 17325. **717-334-1131**

GREENSBURG TRIBUNE-REVIEW. Tribune Review Publishing Co, Cabin Hill Dr, Greensburg, 15601. **412-834-1151**

GREENVILLE RECORD-ARGUS. 10 Penn Ave, Greenville, 16125. **412-588-5000**

HANOVER EVENING SUN. 135 Baltimore St, Hanover, 17331. **717-637-3736**

HARRISBURG NEWS. Patriot-News Co, 812 Market St, Harrisburg, 17105. **717-255-8160**

HARRISBURG PATRIOT. Patriot-News Co, 812 Market St, Harrisburg, 17105. **717-255-8160**

(HATBORO) TODAY'S SPIRIT. Montgomery Publishing Co, 101 N York Rd, Hatboro, 19040. **215-675-3430**

HAZLETON STANDARD-SPEAKER. 21 N Wyoming St, Hazleton, 18201. **717-455-3636**

(HOMESTEAD) MESSENGER. Spenley Newspapers, Inc, 139 E 8th Ave, Homestead, 15120. **412-462-2500**

HUNTINGDON NEWS. Joseph F Biddle Publishing Co, 325 Penn St, Huntingdon, 16652. **814-643-4040**

INDIANA GAZETTE. Indiana Printing and Publishing Co, 899 Water St, Indiana, 15701. **412-465-5555**

JEANNETTE NEWS-DISPATCH. Jeannette Newspapers, Inc, 227 S 4th St (PO Box 101), Jeannette, 15644. **412-523-5541**

JOHNSTOWN TRIBUNE-DEMOCRAT. Johnstown Tribune Publishing Co, Locust St, Johnstown, 15907. **814-536-0711**

KANE REPUBLICAN. 200 N Fraley St, Kane, 16735. **814-837-6000**

(KING OF PRUSSIA) TODAY'S POST. Montgomery Publishing Co, 750 Moore Rd, King of Prussia, 19406. **215-337-1700.** After 9:30 pm: **215-646-5101**

KITTANNING LEADER-TIMES. Simpsons' Publishing Co, 115–21 N Grant Ave, Kittanning, 16201. **412-542-2541**

LANCASTER INTELLIGENCER JOURNAL. Lancaster Newspapers, Inc, 8 W King St, Lancaster, 17604. **717-397-5251**

LANCASTER NEW ERA. Lancaster Newspapers, Inc, 8 W King St, Lancaster, 17604. **717-397-5251**

LANCASTER SUNDAY NEWS. Lancaster Newspapers, Inc, 8 W King St, Lancaster, 17604. **717-397-5251**

(LANSDALE) NORTH PENN REPORTER. Equitable Publishing Co, 307 Derstine Ave, Lansdale, 19446. **215-855-8440**

LATROBE BULLETIN. Latrobe Printing and Publishing, 1211 Ligonier St, Latrobe, 15650. **412-537-3351**

LEBANON NEWS. Lebanon News Publishing Co, S 8th and Poplar Sts, Lebanon, 17042. **717-272-5611**

(LEHIGHTON) THE TIMES NEWS. First and Iron Sts, Lehighton, 18235. **215-377-2051.** Fred Masenheimer, general manager

(LEVITTOWN) BUCKS COUNTY COURIER TIMES. Bristol Printing Co, Route 13, Levittown, 19058. **215-943-1000**

LEWISTOWN SENTINEL. 6th St at Summit Dr, Lewistown, 17044. **717-248-6741**

LOCK HAVEN-JERSEY SHORE EXPRESS. Lock Haven Express Printing Co, 9–11 W Main St, Lock Haven, 17745. **717-748-6791**

MCKEESPORT-DUQUESNE-CLARTON NEWS. Daily News Publishing Co, 409 Walnut St, McKeesport, 15134. **412-664-9161**

MEADVILLE TRIBUNE. Tribune Publishing Co, 947 Federal Ct, Meadville, 16335. **814-724-6370**

MILTON STANDARD. Standard Printing Co, 21 Arch St, Milton, 17847. **717-742-9671**

(MONESSEN) THE VALLEY INDEPENDENT. Thomson Newspaper Publishing Co, Inc, Eastgate 19, Monessen, 15062. **412-684-5200.** Robert W Conroy, publisher and general manager

MONOGAHELA HERALD. Scripps Pennsylvania, Inc, 442 W Main St, Monogahela, 15063. **412-258-7000**

NEW CASTLE NEWS. The News Co, 27-35 N Mercer St, New Castle, 16103. **412-654-6651**

(NEW KENSINGTON) VALLEY NEWS DISPATCH. 4th Ave and Wood Sts (PO Box 311), Tarentum, 15084; 1100 4th Ave, New Kensington, 15068; PO Box 359, Route 66, Vandergrift, 15690. **412-224-4321**

NORRISTOWN TIMES-HERALD. Norristown Herald, Inc, 410 Markley, Norristown, 19404. **215-272-2500**

OIL CITY DERRICK. Derrick Publishing Co, Oil City, 16301. **814-645-1221**

PHILADELPHIA DAILY NEWS. Philadelphia Newspapers, Inc, Knight-Ridder Newspapers, 400 N Broad St, Philadelphia, 19101. **215-854-2600**

PHILADELPHIA EVENING AND SUNDAY BULLETIN. 30th and Market Sts, Philadelphia, 19101. **215-662-7550**

PHILADELPHIA INQUIRER. Philadelphia Newspapers, Inc, Knight-Ridder Newspapers, 400 N Broad St, Philadelphia, 19101. **215-854-2500**

PHILIPSBURG JOURNAL. Moshannon Publishing Co, Inc, 220 Prequeisle St, Philipsburg, 16866. **814-342-2770**

(PHOENIXVILLE) EVENING PHOENIX. Phoenixville Publishing, 225 Bridge St, Phoenixville, 19460. **215-933-8926**

PITTSBURGH POST-GAZETTE. Post-Gazette Publishing Co, 50 Boulevard of the Allies, Pittsburgh, 15222. **412-263-1100**

PITTSBURGH PRESS. 34 Boulevard of the Allies, Pittsburgh, 15222. **412-263-1441**

POTTSTOWN MERCURY. Peerless Publications, Inc, Hanover and King Sts, Pottstown, 19466. **215-323-3000**

POTTSVILLE REPUBLICAN. J H Zerbey Newspapers, Inc, 111-3 Manhantongo St, Pottsville, 17901. **717-622-3456**

PUNXSUTAWNEY SPIRIT. Spirit Publishing Co, Inc, 107-9 N Findley, Punxsutawney, 15767. **814-938-8740**

QUAKERTOWN FREE PRESS. 312 W Broad, Quakertown, 18951. **215-536-6820**

READING EAGLE. Reading Eagle Co, 345 Penn St, Reading, 19601. **215-373-4221**

READING TIMES. Reading Eagle Co, 345 Penn St, Reading, 19601. **215-373-4221**

RIDGWAY RECORD. Ridgway Publishing Co, PO Box T, Ridgway, 15853. **814-773-3151**

(ST MARYS) THE DAILY PRESS. Daily Press Publishing Co, Inc, 245 Brussells, St Marys, 15857. **814-781-1596**

SAYRE-ATHENS-WAVERLY TIMES. Sayre Printing Co, 99 W Packer, Sayre, 18840. **717-883-9241**

(SCRANTON) THE SCRANTONIAN. Scrantonian Publishing Co, 338 N Washington Ave, Scranton, 18501. **717-344-7221**

SCRANTON TIMES. Penn and Spruce Sts, Scranton, 18501. **717-342-9151**

(SCRANTON) THE TRIBUNE. Scranton Tribune Publishing Co, 338 N Washington Ave, Scranton, 18501. **717-344-7221**

SHAMOKIN & MOUNT CARMEL NEWS-ITEM. News Publishing and Printing Co, 701-9 N Rock, Shamokin, 17872. **717-648-4641**

SHARON HERALD. Sharon Herald Co, Ottaway Newspapers, Inc, S Dock St, Sharon, 16146. **412-981-6100**

SHENANDOAH HERALD. Shenandoah Valley Publishing Corp, Ringtown Rd, Shenandoah, 17976. **717-462-2777**

SOMERSET AMERICAN. Somerset Newspapers, Inc, 334 W Main St, Somerset, 15501. **412-445-9621**

(STATE COLLEGE) CENTRE DAILY TIMES. Nittany Print and Publishing Co, PO Box 89, State College, 16801. **814-237-4964**

(STROUDSBURG) POCONO RECORD. 511 Lenox St, Stroudsburg, ·18360. **717-421-3000**

(SUNBURY) THE DAILY ITEM. Daily Item Publishing Co, Ottaway Newspapers, Inc, 2nd and Market Sts, Sunbury, 17801. **717-286-5671**

TITUSVILLE HERALD. 209 W Spring St, Titusville, 16354. **814-827-3634**

TOWANDA REVIEW. Towanda Printing Co, 116 Main St, Towanda, 18848. **717-265-2151**

TYRONE HERALD. 1018 Pennsylvania Ave, Tyrone, 16686. **814-684-4000**

UNIONTOWN HERALD. Uniontown Newspapers, 8-18 E Church St (PO Box 848), Uniontown, 15401. **412-438-2501**

UNIONTOWN STANDARD. Uniontown Newspapers, 8-18 E Church St (PO Box 848), Uniontown, 15401. **412-438-2501**

VALLEY FORGE. *See* King of Prussia

VANDERGRIFT NEWS-CITIZEN. Vandergrift News Publishing Co, Inc, 203 Walnut St, Vandergrift, 15690. **412-567-5656**

WARREN TIMES OBSERVER. Central Publishing Co, 205 Pennsylvania Ave (PO Box 188), Warren, 16365. **814-723-8200**

WASHINGTON OBSERVER-REPORTER. Observer Publishing Co, 122 S Main St, Washington, 15201. **412-222-2200**

WAYNESBORO RECORD HERALD. Record-Herald Publishing Co, 30 Walnut St, Waynesboro, 17268. **717-762-2151**

WAYNESBURG DEMOCRAT MESSENGER. Pioneer Newspapers, 32 Church St, Waynesburg, 15370. **412-627-6166**

(WEST CHESTER) DAILY LOCAL NEWS. Daily Local News Co, 250 N Bradford Ave (PO Box 517), West Chester, 19380. **215-696-1775**

WILKES-BARRE TIMES-LEADER-NEWS RECORD. Wilkes-Barre Publishing Co, 15 N Main St, Wilkes-Barre, 18711. **717-822-2121**

WILLIAMSPORT SUN-GAZETTE. 252 W 4th St, Williamsport, 17701. **717-326-1551**

YORK DAILY RECORD. Scoggins Publishing Co, 1750 Industrial Hwy, York, 17402. **717-757-4842**

YORK DISPATCH. Dispatch Publishing Co, 15–21 E Philadelphia St, York, 17405. **717-854-1575.** Robert L Young, publisher. Henry R Merges, editor

Rhode Island

NEWPORT NEWS. Edward A Sherman Publishing Co, 101 Malbone Rd, Newport, 02840. **401-849-3300**

PAWTUCKET TIMES. New England Newspapers, Inc, 23 Exchange St, Pawtucket, 02862. **401-722-4000**

PROVIDENCE BULLETIN. Providence Journal Co, 75 Fountain St, Providence, 02902. **401-277-7000**

PROVIDENCE JOURNAL. Providence Journal Co, 75 Fountain St, Providence, 02902. **401-277-7000**

WESTERLY SUN. Utter Co, 56 Main St, Westerly, 02891. **401-596-7791**

(WEST WARWICK) PAWTUXET VALLEY DAILY TIMES. Pawtuxet Valley Times, Inc, 1353 Main St, West Warwick, 02893. **401-821-7400**

WOONSOCKET CALL. Evening Call Publishing Co, 75 Main St, Woonsocket, 02895. **401-762-3000**

South Carolina

AIKEN STANDARD. Aiken Communications, Inc, 124 Rutland Dr, Aiken, 29801. **803-648-2311**

ANDERSON INDEPENDENT. Independent Publishing Co, 1000 Williamston Rd, Anderson, 29621. **803-224-4321**

ANDERSON MAIL. Independent Publishing Co, 1000 Williamston Rd, Anderson, 29621. **803-224-4321**

BEAUFORT GAZETTE. 1556 Salem Rd (PO Box 320), Beaufort, 29902. **803-524-3183**

CHARLESTON EVENING POST. Evening Post Publishing Co, 134 Columbus St, Charleston, 29402. **803-577-7111**

(CHARLESTON) THE NEWS & COURIER. Evening Post Publishing Co, 134 Columbus St, Charleston, 29402. **803-577-7111**

COLUMBIA RECORD. Columbia Newspapers, Inc, Stadium Rd, PO Box 1333, Columbia, 29202. **803-771-6161**

COLUMBIA STATE. Columbia Newspapers, Inc, Stadium Rd, PO Box 1333, Columbia, 29202. **803-771-6161**

FLORENCE MORNING NEWS. Florence Morning News, Inc, 141 S Irby, Florence, 29501. **803-669-1771**

GREENVILLE NEWS. Greenville News-Piedmont Co, Multimedia, Inc, 305 S Main St, Greenville, 29601. **803-298-4100**

GREENVILLE PIEDMONT. Greenville News-Piedmont Co, Multimedia, Inc, 305 S Main St, Greenville, 29601. **803-298-4100**

MYRTLE BEACH SUN NEWS. Hwy 317, 10th and North (PO Box 406), Myrtle Beach, 29577. **803-448-8351**

ORANGEBURG TIMES & DEMOCRAT. Sims Co, Inc, 211 Broughton St, Orangeburg, 29115. **803-534-3352**

ROCK HILL HERALD. Herald Publishing Co, 132–6 W Main, Rock Hill, 29730. **803-327-7161**

SPARTANBURG HERALD. Newspaper Management-Production Co, Inc, Herald Sq, Spartenburg, 29301. **803-582-4511**

SPARTANBURG JOURNAL. Newspaper Management-Production Co, Inc, Herald Sq, Spartenburg, 29301. **803-582-4511**

SUMTER ITEM. Osteen Publishing Co, Inc, 20 N Magnolia St, Sumter, 29150. **803-773-3660**

UNION TIMES. PO Drawer 749, Union, 29379. **803-427-3636**

South Dakota

ABERDEEN AMERICAN NEWS. PO Box 430, Aberdeen, 57401. **605-225-4100**

BELLE FOURCHE POST. Northwest Publishers, 1004 5th Ave, Belle Fourche, 57717. **605-892-2528**

BROOKINGS REGISTER. Stauffer Publications, Inc, 306 4th St, Brookings, 57006. **605-692-6271**

HURON PLAINSMAN. Huron Publishing Co, 49 E 3rd, Huron, 57350. **605-352-6401**

LEAD DAILY CALL. Seaton Publishing Co, 7 S Main St (PO Box 876), Lead, 57754. **605-584-2303.** Larry A Weiers, managing editor

(LEAD) THE DEADWOOD PIONEER-TIMES. Seaton Publishing Co, 7 S Main St (PO Box 876), Lead, 57754. **605-584-2303.** Larry A Weiers, managing editor

MADISON LEADER. Hunter Publishing, Inc, 218 S Egan, Madison, 57042. **605-256-4555**

MITCHELL REPUBLIC. Thomson Newspapers, Inc, Mitchell, 57301. **605-996-5514**

(PIERRE) DAILY CAPITAL JOURNAL. Hipple Printing Co, Inc, 415 S Pierre St, Pierre, 57501. **605-224-7301**

RAPID CITY JOURNAL. 507 Main, Rapid City, 57701. **605-342-0280.** James W Swan, publisher

SIOUX FALLS ARGUS-LEADER. Speidel Newspapers, Inc, 200 S Minnesota, Sioux Falls, 57102. **605-336-1130**

WATERTOWN PUBLIC OPINION. 120 3rd Ave NW, Watertown, 57201. **605-886-6901**

YANKTON PRESS & DAKOTAN. Yankton Printing Co, 319 Walnut St, Yankton, 57078. **605-665-7811**

Tennessee

(ATHENS) DAILY POST-ATHENIAN. 320 S Jackson St, Athens, 37303. **615-745-5664**

BRISTOL HERALD COURIER. Worrell Newspapers, Inc, 320 Morrison Blvd, Bristol, 24201. **703-669-2181**

BRISTOL VIRGINIAN-TENNESSEAN. Worrell Newspapers, Inc, 320 Morrison Blvd, Bristol, 24201. **703-669-2181**

CHATTANOOGA NEWS-FREE PRESS. 400 E 11th St, Chattanooga, 37401. **615-756-6900**

CHATTANOOGA TIMES. Times Printing Co, 117 E 10th St, Chattanooga, 37401. **615-756-1234**

CLARKSVILLE LEAF CHRONICLE. 2nd and Commerce, Clarksville, 37040. **615-648-2261**

CLEVELAND BANNER. Cleveland Newspapers, Inc, 1505 25th St NW, Cleveland, 37311. **615-472-5041**

(CLEVELAND) THE MORNING SUN. Cleveland, 37311. **615-476-5518**

COLUMBIA HERALD. 1115 S Main St, Columbia, 38401. **615-388-6464**

COOKEVILLE HERALD CITIZEN. 145 S Jefferson St (PO Box 10), Cookeville, 38501. **615-526-9715**

DYERSBURG STATE GAZETTE. Dyersburg Newspapers, Inc, Hwy 51 By-pass, PO Box 647, Dyersburg, 38024. **901-285-4091**

ELIZABETHTON STAR. Elizabethton Newspapers, Inc, Sycamore St, Elizabethton, 37643. **615-542-4151**

GREENEVILLE SUN. Greeneville Publishing Co, 200 S Main St, Greeneville, 37743. **615-638-4181**

(HARRIMAN) TODAY'S NEWS. PO Box 261, Harriman, 37748. **615-882-1313**

JACKSON SUN. 245 W Lafayette, Jackson, 38301. **901-427-3333**

JOHNSON CITY PRESS-CHRONICLE. 204 W Main St (PO Box 1717), Johnson City, 37601. **615-929-3111**

KINGSPORT DAILY NEWS. 320 E Sullivan St, Kingsport, 37660. **615-246-4800**

KNOXVILLE JOURNAL. Roy N Lotspeich Publishing Co, Inc, 210 W Church Ave, Knoxville, 37901. **615-522-4141**. Charles H Smith III, publisher. William F Childress, editor. Tom Sweeten, managing editor

KNOXVILLE NEWS-SENTINEL. 204 W Church Ave, Knoxville, 37901. **615-523-3131**

LEBANON DEMOCRAT. 402 N Cumberland St (PO Box 430), Lebanon, 37087. **615-444-3952**

MARYVILLE-ALCOA TIMES. Maryville-Alcoa Newspapers, Inc, 307 E Harper, Maryville, 38701. **615-983-0260**

MEMPHIS COMMERCIAL APPEAL. Memphis Publishing Co, 495 Union Ave, Memphis, 38101. **901-526-2141**

MEMPHIS PRESS-SCIMITAR. Memphis Publishing Co, 495 Union Ave, Memphis, 38101. **901-526-2141**

MORRISTOWN CITIZEN TRIBUNE. 1609 W 1st St (PO Box 625), Morristown, 37814. **615-581-5630**

MURFREESBORO NEWS-JOURNAL. Mid South Publishing Co, Morris Newspaper Corp, 224 N Walnut St, Murfreesboro, 37101. **615-893-5860**

NASHVILLE BANNER. Nashville Banner Publishing Co, Gannett Group, 1100 Broadway, Nashville, 37202. **615-255-5401**

NASHVILLE TENNESSEAN. 1100 Broadway, Nashville, 37202. **615-255-1221**

(OAK RIDGE) OAK RIDGER. 101 E Tyrone Rd, Oak Ridge, 37830. **615-482-1021**

PARIS POST-INTELLIGENCER. Paris Publishing Co, Inc, 208 E Wood, Paris, 38242. **901-642-1162**

SHELBYVILLE TIMES-GAZETTE. Shelbyville Publishing Co, Inc, PO Box 380, 323 E Depot St, Shelbyville, 37160. **615-684-1200**

UNION CITY MESSENGER. Messenger Publishing Co, 613 Jackson St, Union City, 38261. **901-885-0744**

Texas

ABILENE REPORTER NEWS. Reporter Publishing Co, 100 block, Cypress St, Abilene, 79604. **915-673-4271**

ALICE ECHO-NEWS. 405 E Main St, Alice, 78332. **512-664-6588**

AMARILLO GLOBE TIMES. Southwestern Newspaper Corp, 900 Harrison St, Amarillo, 79166. **806-376-4488**

AMARILLO NEWS. Southwestern Newspaper Corp, 900 Harrison St, Amarillo, 79166. **806-376-4488**

AMARILLO NEWS-GLOBE. Southwestern Newspaper Corp, 900 Harrison St, Amarillo, 79166. **806-376-4488**

ARLINGTON DAILY NEWS. PO Box 1087, Arlington 76010. **817-274-8241**

ATHENS REVIEW. Athens Printing Co, 201 S Prairieville, Athens, 75751. **214-675-5626**

AUSTIN AMERICAN-STATESMAN. Texas Newspapers, Inc, Cox Enterprises, Inc, 308 Guadalupe, Austin, 78767. **512-397-1212**

BAY CITY TRIBUNE. Bay City Newspapers, Inc, 3013 7th St (PO Box 1551), Bay City, 77414. **713-245-5555**

BAYTOWN SUN. Southern Newspapers, Inc, 1301 Memorial Dr (PO Box 90), Baytown, 77520. **713-422-8302**

BEAUMONT ENTERPRISE. Enterprise Co, 380 Walnut St (PO Box 3071), Beaumont, 77704. **713-833-3311**

BEAUMONT JOURNAL. Enterprise Co, 380 Walnut St (PO Box 3071), Beaumont, 77704. **713-833-3311**

BIG SPRING HERALD. Harte-Hanks Newspapers, Inc, 710 Scurry, Big Spring, 79720. **915-263-7331**

BONHAM FAVORITE. Bonham Newspapers, Inc, 314 N Center, Bonham, 75418. **214-583-2124**

BORGER NEWS-HERALD. Panhandle Publishing Co, 207-9 N Main, Borger, 79007. **806-273-5611**

BRENHAM BANNER-PRESS. 204 W Vulcan St, Brenham, 77833. **713-836-3643**

BROWNSVILLE HERALD. Freedom Newspapers, 1135 E Van Buren (PO Box 351), Brownsville, 78521. **512-542-4301**

BROWNWOOD BULLETIN. Brownwood Publishing Co, 700 Carnegie (PO Box 1188), Brownwood, 76801. **915-646-2541**

BRYAN EAGLE. Eagle Printing Co, 124 E 26th St, Bryan, 77801. **713-822-3707**

CLEBURNE TIMES-REVIEW. 108 S Anglin, Cleburne, 76031. **817-645-2441**

(CONROE) THE DAILY COURIER. 100 Avenue A (PO Drawer 609), Conroe, 77301. **713-756-6671**

CORPUS CHRISTI CALLER. Caller Times Publishing Co, 820 Lower Broadway, Corpus Christi, 78401. **512-884-2011**

CORPUS CHRISTI TIMES. Caller-Times Publishing Co, 820 Lower Broadway, Corpus Christi, 78401. **512-884-2011**

CORSICANA SUN. Sun-Light Publishing Co, 405 E Collin, Corsicana, 75110. **214-872-2551**

DALHART TEXAN. Dalhart Publishing Co, 410 Denrock St, Dalhart, 79022. **806-249-4511**

DALLAS NEWS. A H Belo Corp, Communications Ctr, Dallas, 75222. **214-745-8222**

DALLAS TIMES HERALD. Times Herald Printing Co, 1101 Pacific, Dallas, 75202. **214-744-6111**

(DALLAS) WALL STREET JOURNAL. (Southwest Edition) Dow Jones and Co, Inc, 1233 Regal Row, Dallas, 75247. **214-631-7250**

DEL RIO NEWS-HERALD. 321 S Main St, Del Rio, 78840. **512-775-1551**

DENISON HERALD. 329 W Woodard, Denison, 75020. **214-465-7171**

DENTON RECORD-CHRONICLE. Denton Publishing Co, 314 E Hickory, Denton, 76201. **817-387-3811**

EDINBURG REVIEW. Hidalgo Publishing Co, Inc, 215 E University (PO Box 148), Edinburg, 78539. **512-DU3-2705**

EL PASO HERALD-POST. Herald Post Publishing Co, 401 Mills St, El Paso, 79901. **915-532-1661**

EL PASO TIMES. 401 Mills Ave, El Paso, 79901. **915-532-1661**

ENNIS NEWS. United Publishing Co, Inc, 213 N Dallas St, Ennis, 75119. **214-875-3801**

FORT WORTH STAR-TELEGRAM. Carter Publications, Inc, PO Box 1870, Fort Worth, 76101. **817-336-9271**

(FREEPORT) BRAZOSPORT FACTS. Review Publishers, 307 E Park (PO Box 1055), Freeport, 77541. **713-233-3511**

GAINESVILLE REGISTER & MESSENGER. Register Publishing Co, Donrey Media Group, 306 E California, Gainesville, 76240. **817-655-5511**

GALVESTON NEWS. Galveston Newspaper, Inc, 8522 Teichman Rd, Galveston, 77551. **713-744-3611**

GARLAND DAILY NEWS. 613 State, Garland, 75040. **214-272-6591**

GONZALES INQUIRER. Inquirer Publishing Co, Inc, 620 N St Paul, Gonzales, 78629. **512-672-2861**

GRAND PRAIRIE DAILY NEWS. PO Box 1289, Grand Prairie, 75050. **214-262-5141**

GREENVILLE HERALD-BANNER. Herald-Banner Publishing Co, 2305 King St, Greenville, 75401. **214-455-4220**

(HARLINGEN) VALLEY STAR. Freedom Newspapers, 1310 S Commerce, Harlingen, 78550. **512-423-5511**

HENDERSON DAILY NEWS. Henderson Daily News, Inc, 1703 S Hwy 79 (PO Box 61), Henderson, 75652. **214-657-2501**

HOUSTON CHRONICLE. Houston Chronicle Publishing Co, 801 Texas Ave, Houston, 77002. **713-220-7171**

HOUSTON POST. Houston Post Co, 4747 Southwest Fwy, Houston, 77001. **713-621-7000**

HUNTSVILLE ITEM. 1409 10th St, Huntsville, 77340

(HURST) MID-CITIES NEWS. News-Texan, Inc, PO Box 517, Hurst, 76053. **817-282-2571**

IRVING NEWS. News-Texan, Inc, 1622 W Irving Blvd, Irving, 75060. **214-254-6161**

JACKSONVILLE PROGRESS. Progress Publishing Co, corner at 201 Austin St, Jacksonville, 75766. **214-586-2236**

KERRVILLE DAILY TIMES. 325–7 Earl Garrett St (PO Box 1428), Kerrville, 78028. **512-257-6060**

KILGORE NEWS HERALD. 610 E Main St, Kilgore, 75662. **214-984-2593**

KILLEEN HERALD. Kileen Publishing Co, 2nd and Ave A, Killeen, 76541. **817-634-2125**

LAREDO TIMES. PO Box 29, Laredo, 78040. **512-723-2901**

(LEAGUE CITY) NEWS CITIZEN. 200 Hwy 3 N, League City, 75573. **713-332-4502**

LEVELLAND SUN NEWS. Kenley Publishing Co, 711 Austin St, Levelland, 79336. **816-894-3121**

LEWISVILLE DAILY LEADER. PO Box 308, Lewisville, 75067. **214-436-3566.** Robert L Savage, publisher

LONGVIEW JOURNAL. Longview News Co, Inc, 310–6 East Methvin, Longview, 75601. **214-757-3311**

LUBBOCK AVALANCHE-JOURNAL. 8th St and Ave J, Lubbock, 79408. **806-762-8844**

LUFKIN NEWS. PO Box 1089, Lufkin, 75901. **713-632-6631**

MARLIN DAILY DEMOCRAT. 337 Coleman St, Marlin, 76661. **817-883-2554**

MARSHALL NEWS MESSENGER. Marshall Publishing Co, 309 E Austin, PO Box 730, Marshall, 75670. **214-935-7914**

MCALLEN MONITOR. Freedom Newspapers, 1100 Ash St, McAllen, 78501. **512-686-4343**

MCKINNEY COURIER-GAZETTE. Courier-Gazette Publishing Co, 102 S McDonald, McKinney, 75069. **214-542-2631**

MESQUITE DAILY NEWS. 303 N Galloway Ave (PO Box 136), Mesquite, 75149. **214-285-6301.** Weldon Lacy, editor and publisher

MEXIA NEWS. News Publishing Co, 214 Railroad (PO Box 431), Mexia, 76667. **817-562-2868**

MIDLAND REPORTER-TELEGRAM. Reporter-Telegram Publishing Co, PO Box 1650, Midland, 79702. **915-682-5311**

MINERAL WELLS INDEX. Index Printing Co, 207 NW 1st Ave, Mineral Wells, 76067. **817-325-4466**

MT PLEASANT TRIBUNE. 111 E 2nd St (PO Drawer 1177), Mount Pleasant, 75455. **214-572-8701**

(NACOGDOCHES) REDLAND HERALD. Herald Publishing Co, Inc, PO Box 68, Nacogdoches, 75961. **713-564-8361**

NACOGDOCHES SENTINEL. Herald Publishing Co, Inc, PO Box 68, Nacogdoches, 75961. **713-564-8361**

ODESSA AMERICAN. 222 E 4th, Odessa, 79760. **915-337-4661**

ORANGE LEADER. 200 Front Ave (PO Box 1028), Orange, 77630. **713-883-3571**

PALESTINE HERALD-PRESS. PO Box 379, Palestine, 75801. **214-729-0281**

PAMPA NEWS. 403 W Atchison (PO Box 2198), Pampa, 79065. **806-669-2525**

PARIS NEWS. North Texas Publishing Co, 122–38 Lamar Ave, Paris, 75460. **214-784-4323**

PASADENA NEWS CITIZEN. News Citizen Newspapers, Inc, PO Drawer 6192, Pasadena, 77506. **713-477-0221**

PECOS ENTERPRISE. 324 S Cedar St, Pecos, 79772. **915-445-5475**

PLAINVIEW HERALD. Allison Communications, Inc, 820 Broadway, Plainview, 79072. **806-293-1343**

PLANO DAILY STAR-COURIER. 1301 19th St, Plano, 75074. **214-424-6565**

PORT ARTHUR NEWS. Texas Newspapers, Inc, 549 4th St, Port Arthur, 77640. **713-985-5541**

PORT LAVACA DAILY WAVE. 301 S Colorado St, Port Lavaca, 77979. **512-552-9788.** Cliff B Allen, publisher

RICHARDSON DAILY NEWS. 101 W Main St (PO Box 630), Richardson, 75080. **214-234-1131**

ROSENBERG HERALD-COASTER. Texco Newspapers, Inc, 1115 Mile St (PO Box 1088), Rosenberg, 77471. **713-232-3737**

SAN ANGELO STANDARD. San Angelo Standard, Inc, 34 W Harris, San Angelo, 76901. **915-653-1221**

SAN ANGELO TIMES. San Angelo Standard, Inc, 34 W Harris, San Angelo, 76901. **915-653-1221**

SAN ANTONIO EXPRESS. Express-News Corp, Ave E and 3rd St, San Antonio, 78205. **512-225-7411**

SAN ANTONIO LIGHT. Hearst Corp, McCullough and Broadway, San Antonio, 78206. **512-226-4271**

SAN ANTONIO NEWS. Express-News Corp, Ave E and 3rd St, San Antonio, 78205. **512-225-7411**

(SAN MARCOS) THE DAILY RECORD. San Marcos, 78660. **512-392-2458**

SHERMAN DEMOCRAT. Red River Valley Publishing Co, 600 S Sam Rayburn Exwy, Sherman, 75090. **214-893-8181**

SNYDER NEWS. Feather Printing and Publishing, Inc, 2107 25th St, Snyder, 79549. **915-573-5486**

STEPHENVILLE EMPIRE-TRIBUNE. 110 S Columbia, Stephenville, 76401. **817-965-3124**

SULPHUR SPRINGS NEWS-TELEGRAM. Echo Publishing Co, 401 Church St, Sulphur Springs, 75482. **214-885-3141**

SWEETWATER REPORTER. Donrey Media Group, 112 W 3rd St, Sweetwater, 79556. **915-236-6677**

TAYLOR PRESS. 211 W 3rd St, Taylor, 76574. **512-352-3621**

TEMPLE DAILY TELEGRAM. Bell Publishing Co, 118 W Ave A, Temple, 76501. **817-778-4444**

TERRELL TRIBUNE. 1125 S Virginia, Terrell, 75160. **214-563-6476**

TEXARKANA GAZETTE. Texarkana Newspapers, Inc, 313–7 Pine St, Texarkana, 75501. **214-794-3311**

TEXARKANA NEWS. Texarkana Newspapers, Inc, 313–7 Pine St, Texarkana, 75501. **214-794-3311**

(TEXAS CITY) THE DAILY SUN. 624 4th Ave (PO Box 2249), Texas City, 77590. **713-945-3441**

TYLER COURIER-TIMES. T B Butler Publishing Co, 410 W Erwin St (PO Box 2030), Tyler, 75710. **214-597-8111**

TYLER TELEGRAPH. T B Butler Publishing Co, 410 W Erwin St (PO Box 2030), Tyler, 75710. **214-597-8111**

VERNON RECORD. 1531 Cumberland (PO Box 1979), Vernon, 76384. **817-552-5454**

VICTORIA ADVOCATE. 311 E Constitution, Victoria, 77901. **512-575-1451**

WACO TRIBUNE-HERALD. Cox Enterprises, Inc, 900 Franklin, Waco, 76703. **817-753-1511**

WAXAHACHIE LIGHT. Waxahachie Publishing Co, division of Craco, Inc, 215 S College (PO Box 877), Waxahachie, 75165. **214-937-3310**

WEATHERFORD DEMOCRAT. Southwestern Operation Co, Inc, Donrey Media Group, Weatherford, 76086. **817-594-7447**

WICHITA FALLS RECORD-NEWS. Times Publishing Co, 1301 Lamar St, Wichita Falls, 76307. **817-767-8341**

WICHITA FALLS TIMES. Times Publishing Co, 1301 Lamar St, Wichita Falls, 76307. **817-767-8341**

Utah

LOGAN HERALD JOURNAL. Cache Valley Publishing Co, 75 W 3rd North St, Logan, 84321. **801-752-2121**

OGDEN STANDARD-EXAMINER. Standard Corp, 455 23rd St, Ogden, 84401. **801-394-7711**

(PROVO) THE DAILY HERALD. 1555 N 200 W, Provo, 84601. **801-373-5050**

(SALT LAKE CITY) THE DESERET NEWS. Deseret News Publishing Co, 30 E 1st South St, Salt Lake City, 84110. **801-237-2100.** William B Smart, editor and general manager. Jay Livingood, community relations director

SALT LAKE (CITY) TRIBUNE. Kearns-Tribune Corp, 143 S Main St, Salt Lake City, 84101. **801-524-2800**

Vermont

(BARRE) TIMES-ARGUS. Times-Argus Assn, Inc, 540 N Main St, Barre, 05646. **802-479-0191**

BENNINGTON BANNER. 425 Main St, Bennington, 05201. **802-447-7567**

BRATTLEBORO REFORMER. Reformer Publishing Corp, 71 Main St, Brattleboro, 05301. **802-254-2311**

BURLINGTON FREE PRESS. McClure Newspapers, Inc, Gannett Group, 191 College St, Burlington, 05401. **802-863-3441**

MONTPELIER. *See* Barre

NEWPORT DAILY EXPRESS. Scripps League Newspapers, 9 Central St (PO Box 347), Newport, 05855. **802-334-6568**

RUTLAND HERALD. Herald Assn, Inc, 27 Wales St, Rutland, 05701. **802-775-5511**

ST ALBANS MESSENGER. Vermont Publishing Corp, 281 N Main St, St Albans, 05478. **802-524-2104**

ST JOHNSBURY CALEDONIAN-RE-CORD. Caledonian-Record Publishing Co, Inc, 25 Federal St, St Johnsbury, 05819. **802-748-8121**

(WHITE RIVER JUNCTION) LEBANON VALLEY NEWS. Valley Publishing Corp, PO Box 877, White River Junction, 05001. **603-298-8711**

Virginia

ALEXANDRIA GAZETTE. Columbia Newspapers, Inc, 717 N St Asaph St, Alexandria, 22314. **703-549-0004**

(ARLINGTON) NORTHERN VIRGINIA SUN. 1227 N Ivy St, Arlington, 22210. **703-524-3000**

BRISTOL HERALD-COURIER. Worrell Newspapers, Inc, 320 Morrison Blvd, Bristol, 24201. **703-669-2181**

(BRISTOL) VIRGINIAN-TENNESSEAN. Worrell Newspapers, Inc, 320 Morrison Blvd, Bristol, 24201. **703-669-2181**

CHARLOTTESVILLE PROGRESS. Charlottesville Newspapers, Inc, 413 E Market St, Charlottesville, 22902. **703-295-0822**

(CLIFTON FORGE) THE DAILY REVIEW. 421 W Ridgeway, Clifton Forge, 24422. **703-862-4139**

COVINGTON VIRGINIAN. 343 Monroe Ave, Covington, 24426. **703-962-2121**

CULPEPER STAR-EXPONENT. 122 Spencer St, Culpeper, 22701. **703-825-0771**

DANVILLE REGISTER. Register Publishing Co, Inc, Paton and Union Sts, Danville, 24541. **804-793-2311**

FREDERICKSBURG FREE LANCE-STAR. Free Lance-Star Publishing Co, 616 Amelia St (PO Box 617), Fredericksburg, 22401. **703-373-5000**

HARRISONBURG NEWS-RECORD. Rockingham Publishing Co, 213 S Liberty, Harrisonburg, 22801. **703-433-2702**

HOPEWELL NEWS. 206 S Randolph Rd, Hopewell, 23860. **704-458-8511**

LYNCHBURG ADVANCE. Carter Glass and Sons, Publishers, Inc, Wyndale Dr, Lynchburg, 24502. **804-237-2941**

LYNCHBURG NEWS. Carter Glass and Sons, Publishers, Inc, Wyndale Dr, Lynchburg, 24502. **804-237-2941**

MANASSAS JOURNAL MESSENGER. 9009 Church St (PO Box 431), Manassas, 22110. **703-368-3101**

MARTINSVILLE BULLETIN. 204 Broad St, Martinsville, 24112. **703-638-8801**

NEWPORT NEWS DAILY PRESS. Daily Press, Inc, 7505 Warwick Blvd, Newport News, 23607. **804-244-8421**

NEWPORT NEWS TIMES-HERALD. Daily Press, Inc, 7505 Warwick Blvd, Newport News, 23607. **804-244-8421**

NORFOLK LEDGER-STAR. Landmark Communications, Inc, 150 W Brambleton Ave, Norfolk, 23501. **804-446-2000**

(NORFOLK) VIRGINIAN-PILOT. Landmark Communications, Inc, 150 W Brambleton Ave, Norfolk, 23501. **804-446-2000**

PETERSBURG PROGRESS-INDEX. The Independent, Inc, 15 Franklin St, Petersburg, 23803. **703-732-3456**

PORTSMOUTH. *See* Norfolk

PULASKI SOUTHWEST TIMES. New River Newspapers, 223 N Washington Ave (PO Box 391), Pulaski, 24301. **703-980-5220**

RADFORD NEWS JOURNAL. Radford Publishing Co, New River Newspapers, Inc, Grove and 1st Aves (PO Box 772), Radford, 24141. **703-639-2436**

RICHMOND NEWS LEADER. Richmond Newspapers, Inc, 333 E Grace St, Richmond, 23213. **804-649-6000**

RICHMOND TIMES-DISPATCH. Richmond Newspapers, Inc, 333 E Grace St, Richmond, 23213. **804-649-6000**

ROANOKE TIMES AND WORLD NEWS. Times-World Corp, 201-9 W Campbell Ave (PO Box 2491), Roanoke, 24010. **703-981-3000**

STAUNTON NEWS-LEADER. Staunton Leader Publishing Co, Inc, 13-7 N Central Ave, Staunton, 24401. **703-885-7266**

STRASBURG NORTHERN VIRGINIA DAILY. Shenandoah Publishing House, Inc, 120 Holliday St, Strasburg, 22657. **703-465-5137.** Winchester: **703-662-5868.**

Front Royal: **703-635-2214.** Woodstock: **703-459-3729.** John F Horan, Jr, editor

SUFFOLK NEWS-HERALD. 130 S Saratoga St, Suffolk, 23434. **804-539-3437**

WAYNESBORO NEWS-VIRGINIAN. Waynesboro Publishing Corp, 544 W Main St, Waynesboro, 22980. **703-942-8213**

WINCHESTER EVENING STAR. Winchester Evening Star, Inc, 2 N Kent St, Winchester, 22601. **703-667-3200**

Washington

(ABERDEEN) THE DAILY WORLD. Donrey Media Group, 315 S Michigan (PO Box 269), Aberdeen. **206-532-4000**

BELLINGHAM HERALD. Federated Publications, Inc, Gannett Group, 1155 State St (PO Box 1277), Bellingham, 98225. **206-734-3900**

BREMERTON SUN. Bremerton Sun Publishing Co, 545 5th St (PO Box 259), Bremerton, 98310. **206-377-3711**

THE CENTRALIA-CHEHALIS CHRONICLE. Pearl and Maple Sts, Centralia, 98531. **206-736-3311.** Jack Britten, publisher. Hal D Steward, executive editor

ELLENSBURG DAILY RECORD. 4th and Main Sts, Ellensburg, 98926. **509-925-1414**

EVERETT DAILY HERALD. Daily Herald Co, Grand and California, Everett, 98201. **206-259-5151**

LONGVIEW NEWS. Longview Publishing Co, 11th and Douglas Sts, Longview, 98632. **206-577-2500**

(MOSES LAKE) COLUMBIA BASIN HERALD. Columbia Basin Publishing Co, 813 W 3rd Ave (PO Box 910), Moses Lake, 98837. **509-765-4561**

(MOUNT VERNON) SKAGIT VALLEY HERALD. Skagit Valley Publishing Co, PO Box 578, Mount Vernon, 98273. **206-424-3251**

(OLYMPIA) THE DAILY OLYMPIAN. Federated Publications, Inc, Gannett Group, 1268 4th Ave E (PO Box 407), Olympia, 98507. **206-754-5423**

(PASCO) TRI-CITY HERALD. Scott Publishing Co, PO Box 2608, Tri-Cities, 99302. **509-586-2121**

PORT ANGELES DAILY NEWS. 305 W 1st, Port Angeles, 98362. **206-452-2345**

SEATTLE DAILY JOURNAL OF COMMERCE AND NORTHWEST CONSTRUCTION RECORD. Daily Journal of Commerce, Inc, Journal Bldg, 83 Columbia St, Seattle, 98104. **206-622-8272**

SEATTLE TIMES. Fairview Ave N and John St (PO Box 70), Seattle, 98111. **206-464-2200**

SPOKANE CHRONICLE. Spokane Chronicle Co, 926 Sprague, Spokane, 99210. **509-455-7130**

TACOMA NEWS TRIBUNE. Tribune Publishing Co, 1950 S State St, Tacoma, 98411. **206-597-8686**

TACOMA NEWS TRIBUNE & SUNDAY LEDGER. Tribune Publishing Co, 1950 S State St, Tacoma, 98411. **206-597-8686**

TRI-CITIES. *See* Pasco.

VANCOUVER COLUMBIAN. PO Box 180, Vancouver, 98666. **206-694-3391**

WALLA WALLA UNION-BULLETIN. 1st and Poplar Sts, Walla Walla, 99362. **509-525-3300**

WENATCHEE WORLD. World Publishing Co, 14 N Mission St (PO Box 1511), Wenatchee, 98801. **509-663-5161**

YAKIMA HERALD-REPUBLIC. Republic Publishing Co, 114 N 4th St, Yakima, 98907. **509-248-1251.** James E Tonkin, publisher

West Virginia

BECKLEY POST-HERALD. Beckely Newspapers Corp, 341 Prince St, Beckley, 25801. **304-253-3321**

(BECKLEY) THE RALEIGH REGISTER. Beckley Newspapers Corp, 341 Prince St, Beckley, 25801. **304-253-3321**

BLUEFIELD DAILY TELEGRAPH. Daily Telegraph Printing Co, 412 Bland St, Bluefield, 24701. **304-327-6171**

CHARLESTON DAILY GAZETTE. Daily Gazette Co, 1001 E Virginia St, Charleston, 25301. **304-348-5140**

CHARLESTON DAILY MAIL. Daily Mail Publishing Co, 1001 E Virginia St, Charleston, 25301. **304-348-4830**

CLARKSBURG EXPONENT. Clarksburg Publishing Co, 324–6 Hewes Ave, Clarksburg, 26301. **304-624-6411**

CLARKSBURG TELEGRAM. Clarksburg Publishing Co, 324–6 Hewes Ave, Clarksburg, 26301. **304-624-6411**

ELKINS INTER-MOUNTAIN. Elkins, 26241. **304-636-2121**

FAIRMONT TIMES & WEST VIRGINIAN. Quicny and Ogden, Fairmont, 26554. **304-363-5000**

GRAFTON MOUNTAIN STATESMAN. Scripps of West Virginia, Inc, 914 W Main St, Grafton, 26354. **304-265-3333**

HINTON DAILY NEWS. 210 2nd Ave, Hinton, 25951. **304-466-0005**

HUNTINGTON ADVERTISER. Huntington Publishing Co, Gannett Group, 946 5th Ave, Huntington, 25701. **304-696-5678**

HUNTINGTON HERALD-DISPATCH. Huntington Publishing Co, Gannett Group, 946 5th Ave, Huntington, 25701. **304-696-5678**

KEYSER NEWS-TRIBUNE. Mineral Daily News Tribune, Inc, 24 Armstrong, Keyser, 26726. **304-788-3333**

(LEWISBURG) WEST VIRGINIA DAILY NEWS. 114-A Washington St (PO Box 471), Lewisburg, 24901. **304-645-1206**

LOGAN BANNER. 439 Strafton St, Logan, 25601. **304-752-6950**

MARTINSBURG EVENING JOURNAL. Evening Journal Publishing Co, 207 W King St, Martinsburg, 25401. **304-263-8931**

MORGANTOWN DOMINION-POST. West Virginia Newspaper Publishing Co, Greer Bldg, Morgantown, 26505. **304-292-6301**

MOUNDSVILLE ECHO. 715 Lafayette Ave (PO Box 369), Moundsville, 26041. **304-845-2660**

PARKERSBURG NEWS. Ogden Newspapers, Inc, 519 Juliana, Parkersburg, 26101. **304-485-5521**

PARKERSBURG SENTINEL. Ogden Newspapers, Inc, 519 Juliana, Parkersburg, 26101. **304-485-5521**

POINT PLEASANT REGISTER. 200 Main St, Point Pleasant, 25550. **304-675-1333**

WEIRTON DAILY TIMES. 114 Lee Ave, Weirton, 26062. **304-748-0606**

WELCH DAILY NEWS. 125 Wyoming St, Welch, 24801. **304-436-3144**

WHEELING INTELLIGENCER. Ogden Newspapers, Inc, 1500 Main St, Wheeling, 26003. **304-233-0100**

WHEELING NEWS-REGISTER. Ogden Newspapers, Inc, 1500 Main St, Wheeling, 26003. **304-233-0100**

WILLIAMSON DAILY NEWS. East 3rd Ave, Williamson, 25661. **304-235-4242**

Wisconsin

ANTIGO JOURNAL. Berner Brothers Publishing Co, Inc, 612 Superior St, Antigo, 54409. **715-623-4191**

APPLETON POST-CRESCENT. Post Corp, 306 W Washington St, Appleton, 54911. **414-733-4411**

ASHLAND DAILY PRESS. 122 W 3rd St, Ashland, 54806. **715-682-2313**

BARABOO NEWS-REPUBLIC. Baraboo News Publishing Co, 408 Oak St, Baraboo, 53913. **608-356-4808**

BEAVER DAM CITIZEN. Citizen Publishing Co, 805 Park Ave, Beaver Dam, 53916. **414-885-3321**

BELOIT DAILY NEWS. Daily News Publishing Co, 149 State St, Beloit, 53511. **608-365-8811**

CHIPPEWA FALLS HERALD-TELEGRAM. Chippewa Publishing Co, Inc, 20–2 Central St, Chippewa Falls 54729. **715-723-5515**

EAU CLAIRE LEADER-TELEGRAM. Eau Claire Press Co, 701 S Farwell St, Eau Claire, 54701. **715-834-3471**

FOND DU LAC REPORTER. A subsidiary of Thomson Newspapers Wisconsin, Inc, 33 W 2nd St, Fond du Lac, 54935. **414-922-4600**

(FORT ATKINSON) JEFFERSON COUNTY UNION. W D Hoard and Sons, 28 W Milwaukee Ave, Fort Atkinson, 53538. **414-563-5551**

(GREEN BAY) THE DAILY NEWS.
Washington and Walnut Sts (PO Box 2467),
Green Bay, 54306. **414-432-2941**

GREEN BAY PRESS-GAZETTE. Green
Bay Newspaper Co, 435 E Walnut St (PO
Box 430), Green Bay, 54305. **414-435-4411**

JANESVILLE GAZETTE. Gazette Printing
Co, 1 S Parker Dr, Janesville, 53545.
608-754-3311

KENOSHA NEWS. Kenosha News Publishing Corp, 715 58th St, Kenosha, 53141.
414-657-5121

LA CROSSE TRIBUNE. 401 N 3rd St, La
Crosse, 54601. **608-782-9710**

(MADISON) THE CAPITAL TIMES.
Madison Newspapers, Inc, 1901 Fish
Hatchery Rd (PO Box 8060), Madison,
53713. **608-252-6420**

**(MADISON) WISCONSIN STATE
JOURNAL.** Madison Newspapers, Inc, 1901
Fish Hatchery Rd, Madison, 53713.
608-252-6120

**MANTIOWOC HERALD-TIMES-
REPORTER.** Thomson Newspapers, Inc,
902 Franklin, Manitowoc, 54220.
414-684-4433

MARINETTE EAGLE-STAR. Eagle Printing Co, 1809 Dunlap Ave, Marinette, 54143.
715-735-6611

MARSHFIELD NEWS-HERALD. A division of Forward Communications Corp, 111
W 3rd, Marshfield, 54449. **715-384-3131**

MILWAUKEE JOURNAL. The Journal Co,
333 W State St, Milwaukee, 53201.
414-224-2000

MILWAUKEE SENTINEL. The Journal
Co, 918 N 4th St, Milwaukee, 53201.
414-224-2000

MONROE TIMES. Monroe Publishing Co,
Inc, 901 16th Ave, Monroe, 53566.
608-328-5101

OSHKOSH NORTHWESTERN. 224 State
St, Oshkosh, 54901. **414-235-7700**

PORTAGE REGISTER. Register Publishing
Corp, 309 De Witt St, Portage, 53901.
608-742-2111

RACINE JOURNAL-TIMES. 212 4th St,
Racine, 53403. **414-634-3322**

RHINELANDER NEWS. Northern Lakes
Publishing Co, 314 Courtney St, Rhinelander, 54501. **715-362-6397**

SHAWANO EVENING LEADER. Shawano
Evening Leader Co, 107–13 E Green Bay St,
Shawano, 54166. **715-526-2121**

SHEBOYGAN PRESS. Press Publishing
Co, 632 Center Ave, Sheboygan, 53081.
414-457-7711

STEVENS POINT JOURNAL. Journal
Printing Co, 1200 3rd St, Stevens Point,
54481. **715-344-6100**

SUPERIOR EVENING TELEGRAM. Evening Telegram Co, 1226 Ogden Ave, Superior,
54880. **715-394-4411**

WATERTOWN TIMES. Times Publishing
Co, 113–5 W Main St, Watertown, 53094.
414-261-4949

WAUKESHA FREEMAN. Freeman Printing Co, 200 Park Pl, Waukesha, 53186.
414-542-2501

WAUSAU HERALD. Green Bay Newspaper
Co, 800 Scott St, Wausau, 54401.
715-842-2101

WEST BEND NEWS. Post Corp, 100 S 6th
Ave (PO Box 478), West Bend, 53095.
414-338-0622

WISCONSIN RAPIDS TRIBUNE. 220 1st
Ave S, Wisconsin Rapids, 54494.
715-423-7200

Wyoming

CASPER STAR-TRIBUNE. Howard Publications, Inc, 111 S Jefferson St, (PO Box
80), Casper, 82602. **307-237-8451.** Thomas
W Howard, publisher and editor. Phil
McAuley, managing editor

(CHEYENNE) WYOMING EAGLE.
Cheyenne Newspapers, Inc, 110 E 17th St,
Cheyenne, 82001. **307-634-3361**

**(CHEYENNE) WYOMING STATE TRIB-
UNE.** Cheyenne Newspapers, Inc, 110 E
17th St, Cheyenne, 82001. **307-634-3361**

LARAMIE BOOMERANG. Laramie Newspapers, Inc, 314 S 14th St, Laramie, 82070.
307-742-2176

RAWLINS TIMES. Rawlins Newspapers,
Inc, 6th and Buffalo Sts, Rawlins, 82301.
307-324-3411

RIVERTON RANGER. Times-Review Publishing Co, PO Box 993, Riverton, 82501.
307-856-2244

ROCK SPRINGS ROCKET-MINER. Rock
Springs Newspapers, Inc, 215 D St, Rock
Springs, 82901. **307-362-3737**

SHERIDAN PRESS. Sheridan Newspapers,
Inc, Sheridan, 82801. **307-672-2431**

**(WORLAND) NORTHERN WYOMING
DAILY NEWS.** Big Horn Basin Newspapers, Inc, 723 Robertson Ave, Worland,
82401. **307-347-3241**

LEADING MAGAZINES

The following list of major magazines is
selected from two classes of periodicals
among the thousands published in the US:
(1) magazines that publish mainstream
journalism on a regular basis, with particular
emphasis on including those that serve as
important outlets for journalistic free-
lancers, and (2) magazines that are of a
specialty, trade, esoteric, or technical nature,
but are so influential, or so important in
their fields, that they are likely to be
important resources for the journalist. Included also are any mass-circulation magazines falling outside these classes, as well
as leading city magazines and major Sunday
newspaper supplements.

ADVERTISING AGE. 740 Rush St,
Chicago, IL 60611. **312-649-5200.** L E
Doherty, managing editor

AFTER DARK. 10 Columbus Cir, New York, NY 10019. **212-399-2410.** William Como, editor

AMERICAN BAR ASSOCIATION JOURNAL. 77 Wacker Dr, Chicago, IL 60606. **312-621-9200.** Richard Allen, editor

AMERICAN BIBLE SOCIETY RECORD. Box 3575, Grand Central Station, New York, NY 10017. **212-581-7400.** C P MacDonald, editor

AMERICAN LEGION MAGAZINE. 1608 K St NW, Washington, DC 20006. **202-393-4811.** Raymond McHugh, editor

AMERICAN OPINION. 395 Concord Ave, Belmont, MA 02178. **617-489-0600.** Scott Stanley, Jr, managing editor

AMERICAN RIFLEMAN. 1600 Rhode Island Ave NW, Washington, DC 20036. **202-783-7505.** Ken Warner, editor

ARGOSY. 420 Lexington Ave, New York, NY 10017. **212-687-1234.** Lou Sahadi, editor

ATLANTIC. 8 Arlington St, Boston, MA 02116. **617-536-9500.** Robert Manning, editor-in-chief

ATLAS WORLD PRESS REVIEW. 230 Park Ave, New York, NY 10017. **212-697-6162.** Alfred Balk, editor

AUDUBON. 950 3rd Ave, New York, NY 10022. **212-832-3200.** Les Line, editor

AVIATION WEEK & SPACE TECHNOLOGY. 1221 6th Ave, New York, NY 10020. **212-997-4971**

BARRON'S. 22 Cortlandt St, New York, NY 10007. **212-285-5243.** Robert Bleiberg, editor

BETTER NUTRITION. 6 E 43rd St, New York, NY 10017. **212-949-0800.** Frank Murray, editor

BILLBOARD. 9000 Sunset Blvd, Hollywood, CA 90069. **213-273-7040.** Lee Zhito, editor

BLACK SPORTS. 31 E 28th St, New York, NY 10016. **212-725-9196.** Les Carson, editor

BON APPETIT. 5900 Wilshire Blvd, Los Angeles, CA 90036. **213-937-1025.** Paige Rense, editor-in-chief

BOSTON MAGAZINE. 1050 Park Square Bldg, Boston, MA 02116. **617-357-4000.** D Herbert Lipson, publisher

BROADCASTING MAGAZINE. 1735 De Sales St NW, Washington, DC 20036. **202-639-1022.** Sol Taishoff, editor

BULLETIN OF ATOMIC SCIENTISTS. 1020 24 E 58th St, Chicago, IL 60637. **312-363-5225**

BUSINESS WEEK. 1221 6th Ave, New York, NY 10020. **212-997-2641**

CALIFORNIA LIVING MAGAZINE. *Examiner and Chronicle.* 925 Mission St, San Francisco, CA 94103. **415-421-1111**

CAR AND DRIVER. 1 Park Ave, New York, NY 10016. **212-725-3500.** David E Davis, editor

CARTE BLANCHE. 3460 Wilshire Blvd, Los Angeles, CA 90010. **213-480-3328.** Margaret M Volpe, editor

CHANGING TIMES. 1729 H St NW, Washington, DC 20006. **202-298-6400.** Sidney Sulkin, editor

CHICAGO. 500 N Michigan Ave, Chicago, IL 60603. **312-751-7151.** Allen H Kelson, editor-in-chief

CHICAGO TRIBUNE MAGAZINE. 435 N Michigan Ave, Chicago, IL 60611. **312-222-3573**

CHRISTIANITY TODAY. Carol Stream, IL, 60187. **312-682-3020.** Harold Lindsell, editor

CHRONICLE OF HIGHER EDUCATION. 1717 Mass Ave NW, Washington, DC 20036. **202-667-3344.** Corbin Gwaltney, editor

CLEVELAND MAGAZINE. 1621 Euclid Ave, Cleveland, OH 44115. **216-771-2833.** Judith Kish, editor

COLUMBIA JOURNALISM REVIEW. Columbia University Graduate School of Journalism, New York, NY 10027. **212-280-3872.** James Boylan, editor

COMMENTARY. 165 E 56th St, New York, NY 10022. **212-751-4000.** Norman Podhoretz, editor

COMMONWEAL. 232 Madison Ave, New York, NY 10016. **212-683-2042.** James O'Gara, editor

CONNECTICUT MAGAZINE. 831 Black Rock Tpke, Fairfield, CT 06430. **203-576-1205.** Prudence Brown, editor

CONSUMERS DIGEST. 6316 N Lincoln Ave, Chicago, IL 60659. **312-286-7606.** Arthur Darack, editor

CONSUMER REPORTS. 256 Washington St, Mount Vernon, NY 10550. **914-664-6400.** Irwin Landau, editor

COSMOPOLITAN. 224 W 57th St, New York, NY 10019. **212-262-5700.** Helen Gurley Brown, editor

COUNTRY GENTLEMAN. 1100 Waterway Blvd, Indianapolis, IN 46202. **317-634-1100.** Michael New, managing editor

COUNTRY MUSIC MAGAZINE. 475 Park Ave S, New York, NY 10016. **212-685-8200.** Michael Bane, editor

CRAWDADDY MAGAZINE. 72 5th Ave, New York, NY 10011. **212-924-3000.** Peter Knobler, editor

CUE. 545 Madison Ave, New York, NY 10022. **212-371-6900**

CYCLE. 1 Park Ave, New York, NY 10016. **212-725-3766.** Cook Nielson, editor

D-MAGAZINE OF DALLAS. 2902 Carlisle St, Dallas, TX 75204. **214-748-9166.** Wick Allison, editor and publisher

DAWN MAGAZINE. Afro-American Newspapers, 628 N Eutaw, Baltimore, MD 21201. **301-728-8200.** Art Carter, editor

DISCOVER. *Philadelphia Bulletin*, 30th and Market Sts, Philadelphia, PA 19101. **215-662-7620** through **7623.** Jack Wilson, editor

EBONY. 820 S Michigan Ave, Chicago, IL 60605. **312-786-7600.** John H Johnson, editor

ELKS MAGAZINE. 425 W Diversey Pkwy, Chicago, IL 60614. **312-528-4500.** Jeffrey Ball, editor

ENCORE. 515 Madison Ave, New York, NY 10022. **212-593-2223.** Ida Lewis, editor

ESQUIRE. 488 Madison Ave, New York, NY 10022. **212-644-5605.** Clay Felker, publisher

ESSENCE MAGAZINE. 1500 Broadway, New York, NY 10036. **212-730-4260.** Edward Lewis, publisher

FAMILY CIRCLE. 488 Madison Ave, New York, NY 10022. **212-593-8000.** Arthur Hettich, editor

FAMILY WEEKLY MAGAZINE. 641 Lexington Ave, New York, NY 10022. **212-980-0300.** Scott De Gaumo, executive editor

FARM JOURNAL. 230 W Washington Sq, Philadelphia, PA 19105. **215-574-1200.** Lane Palmer, editor

FLYING. 1 Park Ave, New York, NY 10016. **212-725-3799.** Robert Parke, editor

FOOTBALL DIGEST. 1020 Church St, Evanston, IL 80201. **312-491-6440.** M K Herbert, editor

FOOTBALL NEWS. 19380 Mack Ave, Grosse Pointe, MI 48236. **313-881-9554.** Roger Stanton, editor

FORBES MAGAZINE. 60 5th Ave, New York, NY 10011. **212-675-7500**

FOREIGN AFFAIRS QUARTERLY. Council on Foreign Relations, 58 E 68th St, New York, NY 10021. **212-734-0400**

FORTUNE MAGAZINE. 1271 6th Ave, New York, NY 10020. **212-586-1212**

GLAMOUR. 350 Madison Ave, New York, NY 10017. **212-692-5500.** Ruth Whitney, editor

GOLF DIGEST. 495 Westport Ave, Norwalk, CT 06850. **203-847-5811.** Nick Seitz, editor

GOOD HOUSEKEEPING. 959 8th Ave, New York, NY 10019. **212-262-5700.** Wade Nichols, editor

GRIT. 208 W 3rd St, Williamsport, PA 17701. **717-326-1771**

HARPER'S BAZAAR. 717 5th Ave, New York, NY 10022. **212-481-5233.** Lewis Lapham, editor

HARPER'S MAGAZINE. 2 Park Ave, New York, NY 10016. **212-686-8710.** Lewis Lapham, editor

HARVARD MAGAZINE. 1341 Massachusetts Ave, Cambridge, MA 02138. **617-495-5746**

HOLLYWOOD REPORTER. 6715 Sunset Blvd, Hollywood, CA 90028. **213-464-7411.** Tichi Wilkerson Miles, editor and publisher

HONOLULU MAGAZINE. Box 80, Honolulu, HI 96810. **808-524-7400.** Jeri Bostwick, editor

HOT ROD MAGAZINE. 8490 Sunset Blvd, Los Angeles, CA 90069. **213-657-5100.** Dick Day, editor

HUMAN EVENTS. 422 1st St SE, Washington, DC 20003. **202-546-0856**

JET. 820 S Michigan Ave, Chicago, IL 60605. **312-786-7600.** John H Johnson, editor

JOURNAL OF THE AMERICAN MEDICAL ASSOCIATION. 535 N Dearborn St, Chicago, IL 60610. **312-751-6000**

LADIES' HOME JOURNAL. 641 Lexington Ave, New York, NY 10022. **212-935-4100.** Lenore Hershey, editor-in-chief

LONG ISLAND MAGAZINE. 437 Ward Ave, Mamaroneck, NY 10543. **914-698-8203.** Vita Nelson, editor

LONG ISLAND MAGAZINE. *Newsday*, 550 Stewart Ave, Garden City, NY 11530. **212-222-5722**

LOS ANGELES MAGAZINE. 18888 Century Park E, Los Angeles, CA 90067. **213-552-1021.** Geoff Miller, editor

LA TIMES HOME MAGAZINE. *Los Angeles Times.* Times Mirror Sq, Los Angeles, CA 90053. **213-625-2345**

MADEMOISELLE. 350 Madison Ave, New York, NY 10017. **212-692-5500.** Edith Locke, editor

MADISON AVENUE. 750 Madison Ave, New York, NY 10017. **212-682-5250.** Jenny Greenberg, editor

MAGAZINE OF VIRGINIA. 611 E Franklin St, Richmond, VA 23219. **804-643-7491.** J S Wamsley, editor

MCCALL'S MAGAZINE. 230 Park Ave, New York, NY 10017. **212-983-3200**

MEDICAL ECONOMICS. 680 Kinderkamack Rd, Oradell, NJ 07649. **201-262-3030.** A J Vogl, editor

MIDWEST-COLOR GRAVURE MAGAZINE. *Chicago Sun-Times.* 401 N Wabash Ave, Chicago, IL 60611. **312-321-3000**

MONEY. Time-Life Bldg, New York, NY 10020. **212-586-1212.** William Rukeyser, managing editor

MONEYSWORTH. 251 W 57th St, New York, NY 10019. **212-581-2000**

MOOSE MAGAZINE. 100 E Ohio St, Chicago, IL 60611. **312-337-3090**

MORE. 40 W 57th St, New York, NY 10019. **212-752-3040.** Robert Friedman, editor

MOTHER EARTH NEWS. PO Box 70, Hendersonville, NC 28739. **704-693-0211**

MS. 370 Lexington Ave, New York, NY 10017. **212-725-2666.** Patricia Carbine, editor

NATION. 333 6th Ave, New York, NY 10014. **212-242-8400.** Blair Clark, editor

NATIONAL CATHOLIC REPORTER. PO Box 281, Kansas City, MO 64141. **816-531-0538.** Paul Levy, managing editor

NATIONAL ENQUIRER. 600 S E Coast Ave, Lantana, FL 33464. **305-586-1111.** Paul Levy, managing editor

NATIONAL GEOGRAPHIC. 17th and M Sts NW, Washington, DC 20036. **202-857-7000.** Gilbert Grosvenor, editor

NATIONAL JOURNAL REPORTS. 1730 M St NW, Washington, DC 20036. **202-857-1400**

NATIONAL LAMPOON. 635 Madison Ave, New York, NY 10022. **212-688-4070**

NATIONAL REVIEW. 150 E 35th St, New York, NY 10016. **212-679-7330.** William F Buckley, Jr, editor-in-chief

NATION'S BUSINESS. 1615 H St NW, Washington, DC 20062. **202-659-6010.** Kenneth Medley, editor

NATURAL HISTORY. Central Park W and 79th St, New York, NY 10024. **212-873-1300.** Alan Ternes, editor

NEW DAWN. 99 Park Ave, New York, NY 10016. **212-679-5152**

NEW MEXICO MAGAZINE. Bataan Memorial Bldg, Santa Fe, NM 87503. **505-827-2642.** Sheila Tryk, editor

NEW ORLEANS MAGAZINE. PO Box 26215, New Orleans, LA 70126. **504-246-2700.** Bonnie Crone, editor

NEW REPUBLIC. 1244 19th St NW, Washington, DC 20036. **202-331-7494**

NEW TIMES. 1 Park Ave, New York, NY 10016. **212-889-6900.** Jonathan Larsen, editor

NEW WEST MAGAZINE. 9565 Wilshire Blvd, Beverly Hills, CA 90212. **213-273-7516**

NEW WORLDS. PO Box 1, Newport Beach, CA 92663. **714-833-3469.** Frank McGee, editor

NEW YORKER. 25 W 43rd St, New York, NY 10036. **212-695-1414.** William Shawn, editor

NEW YORK MAGAZINE. 755 2nd Ave, New York, NY 10017. **212-986-4600**

NEW YORK NEWS MAGAZINE. 220 E 42nd St, New York, NY 10017. **212-949-3762.** Richard C Lemon, editor

NEW YORK TIMES MAGAZINE. 229 W 43rd St, New York, NY 10036. **212-556-1234**

NEWSWEEK. 444 Madison Ave, New York, NY 10022. **212-350-2000**

ORGANIC GARDENING AND FARMING. 33 E Minor St, Emmaus, PA 18049. **215-967-5171.** Robert Rodale, editor

OUTDOOR LIFE. 380 Madison Ave, New York, NY 10017. **212-687-3000.** John Fry, editorial director

PALM SPRINGS LIFE. 250 E Palm Canyon Dr, Palm Springs, CA 92262. **714-325-2333.** Milton Jones, editor

PARADE MAGAZINE. 733 3rd Ave, New York, NY 10017. **212-953-7500**

PARENT'S MAGAZINE. 52 Vanderbilt Ave, New York, NY 10017. **212-661-9080.** Genevieve Millet Landan, editor-in-chief

PENTHOUSE. 909 3rd Ave, New York, NY 10022. **212-593-3301.** Bob Guccione, editor

PEOPLE. Time-Life Bldg, New York, NY 10020. **212-586-1212**

PHILADELPHIA MAGAZINE. 1500 Walnut St, Philadelphia, PA 19102. **215-545-3500.** Alan Halpern, editor

PHOENIX MAGAZINE. 4707 N 12th St, Phoenix, AZ 85014. **602-248-8900.** Anita J Welsh, editor

PLAYBILL. 151 E 50th St, New York, NY 10022. **212-751-9950**

PLAYBOY. 919 N Michigan Ave, Chicago, IL 60611. **312-751-8000.** Hugh M Hefner, editor

POTOMAC MAGAZINE. Washington Post, 1150 15th St NW, Washington, DC 20071. **202-223-6000**

PROGRESSIVE FARMER. PO Box 2581, Birmingham, AL 35209. **205-870-4440**

PSYCHOLOGY TODAY. 1 Park Ave, New York, NY 10016. **212-725-3900.** Jack Nessel, editor

QUILL. 35 E Wacker Dr, Chicago, IL 60601. **312-236-6577.** Charles Long, editor

READER'S DIGEST. Pleasantville, NY 10570. **914-769-7000.** Edward T Thompson, editor-in-chief

REDBOOK MAGAZINE. 230 Park Ave, New York, NY 10017. **212-983-3200.** Sey Chassler, editor

RING MAGAZINE. 120 W 31st St, New York, NY. **212-564-0354**

ROAD & TRACK. 1499 Monrovia, Newport Beach, CA 92663. **714-646-4451.** Tony Hogg, editor

SACRAMENTO VALLEY MAGAZINE. 2620 La Mesa Way, Sacramento, CA 95825. **916-482-3700.** Gary Brown, editor

SAN FRANCISCO MAGAZINE. 631 Howard St, San Francisco, CA 94105. **415-777-5555.** Thomas Shess, editor

SCIENCE MAGAZINE. 1515 Massachusetts Ave NW, Washington, DC 20005. **202-467-4430.** P H Abelson, editor

SCIENTIFIC AMERICAN. 415 Madison Ave, New York, NY 10017. **212-754-0500**

SIERRA CLUB BULLETIN. 530 Bush St, San Francisco, CA 94108. **415-981-8634.** Frances Gendlin, editor

SIGNATURE MAGAZINE. 260 Madison Ave, New York, NY 10016. **212-689-9020.** Robin Nelson, editor

SMITHSONIAN. 900 Jefferson Dr, Washington, DC 20560. **202-381-6195.** Edward K Thompson, editor and publisher

SOUTHERN LIVING. PO Box 523, Birmingham, AL 35209. **205-870-4440**

SPORT. 641 Lexington Ave, New York, NY 10022. **212-935-4100**

SPORTING NEWS. 1212 N Lindbergh Blvd, St. Louis, MO 63166. **314-997-7111.** C C Johnson Spink, editor

SPORTS ILLUSTRATED. Time, Inc. 1271 6th Ave, New York, NY 10020. **212-556-3117.** Robert W Creamer, articles editor

STAR. 730 3rd Ave, New York, NY 10017. **212-557-9200.** Peter Faris and George Gordon, aritcles editors

SUBURBAN WEEK. *Chicago Daily News.* Elk Grove Village, IL 60001. **312-956-6940.** 411 Busse Rd, Richard Honack, editor

SUCCESSFUL FARMING. 1716 Locust St, Des Moines, IA 50336. **515-284-9011**

SUNDAY MAGAZINE. Metropolitan Sunday Newspapers, 260 Madison Ave, New York, NY 10016. **212-689-8200**

TENNIS. 495 Westport Ave, Norwalk, CT 06856. **203-847-5811.** Shepherd Campbell, editor

TEXAS MONTHLY. PO Box 1569, Austin, TX 78767. **512-476-7085.** William Broyles, editor

TIME. 1271 6th Ave, New York, NY 10020. **212-586-1212**

TODAY. *Philadelphia Inquirer.* 400 N Broad St, Philadelphia, PA 19101. **215-854-2090.** David Boldt, editor

TODAY'S EDUCATION. 1201 16th St NW, Washington, DC 20036. **202-833-4110.** Walter Graves, editor

TOWN AND COUNTRY. 717 5th Ave, New York, NY 10022. **212-935-5900**

TRAVEL. *Holiday Magazine.* Travel Bldg, Floral Park, NY 11001. **516-352-9700.** Stephen A Maguire, assistant editor

TRAVEL & LEISURE. 1350 Avenue of the Americas, New York, NY 10019. **212-399-2500.** Pamela Fiori, editor

TUESDAY. Tuesday Publications, 625 N Michigan Ave, Chicago, IL 60611. **312-751-1755**

TUESDAY AT HOME. Tuesday Publications, 625 N Michigan Ave, Chicago, IL 60611. **312-751-1755**

TV GUIDE. Radnor, PA 19088. **215-688-7400**

US NEWS & WORLD REPORT. 2300 N St NW, Washington, DC 20037. **202-333-7400.** Marvin L Stone, editor

VARIETY. 154 W 46th St, New York, NY 10036. **212-582-2700.** Syd Silverman, executive editor

VFW MAGAZINE. 406 W 34th St, Kansas City, MO 64111. **816-756-3390.** John Smith, editor

VOGUE. 350 Madison Ave, New York, NY 10017. **212-692-5500**

WASHINGTONIAN MAGAZINE. 1828 L St NW, Washington, DC 20036. **202-296-3600.** Laughlin Phillips, editor-in-chief

WASHINGTON MONTHLY. 1028 Connecticut Ave NW, Washington, DC 20036. **202-659-4866.** Charles Peters, editor-in-chief

WOMEN'S WEAR DAILY. 7 E 12th St, New York, NY 10003. **212-741-4033**

WOMEN SPORTS. Foundation Magazine. Suite 266, 1660 S Amphlett Blvd, San Mateo, CA 94402. **415-574-1600.** Larry King, publisher

WORKING WOMAN. 600 Madison Ave, New York, NY 10022. **212-750-0020.** Beatrice Buckler, editor-in-chief

WRITER'S DIGEST. 9933 Alliance Rd, Cincinnati, OH 45242. **513-984-0717.** John Brady, editor

BOOK PUBLISHERS

ABINGDON PRESS. 201 8th Ave S, Nashville, TN 37202. **615-749-6000.** Mary Ellen Rist, advertising and publicity

HARRY N ABRAMS, INC. 110 E 59th St, New York, NY 10022. **212-758-8600.** Carol Schneider, public relations director

ACE BOOKS. 1120 Avenue of The Americas, New York, NY 10036. **212-867-5050.** Judith Neale, publicity director

ACROPOLIS BOOKS, LTD. 2400 17th St NW, Washington, DC 20009. **202-387-6800.** Sandra Trupp, publicity director

ADDISON-WESLEY PUBLISHING COMPANY, INC. Jacob Way, Reading, MA 01867. **617-944-3700,** Ext 389. Joyce Copland, public relations director

APPLETON-CENTURY-CROFTS. 292 Madison Ave, New York, NY 10017. **212-532-1700.** Deborah Vezzi, publicity director

ARBOR HOUSE. 641 Lexington Ave, New York, NY 10022. **212-832-3810.** Eden Collinsworth, director, publicity and promotion

ARLINGTON HOUSE. 165 Huguenot St, New Rochelle, NY 10801. **212-597-5050.** Maureen McCaffrey, publicity director

ASSOCIATION PRESS. 291 Broadway, New York, NY 10007. **212-374-2000.** Robert Hill, editorial director

ATHENEUM PUBLISHERS. 122 E 42nd St, New York, NY 10017. **212-661-4500.** Mrs Bennett Hargrove, publicity director

AVON BOOKS. 959 8th Ave, New York, NY 19000. **212-262-5700.** Diane O'Connor, publicity director

BANTAM BOOKS. 666 5th Ave, New York, NY 10016. **212-765-6500.** Esther Margolis, vice-president, promotion and public relations

BASIC BOOKS. 10 E 53rd St, New York, NY 10016. **212-593-7075.** Bart De Castro, vice-president and director, market advertising and promotion

BOBBS-MERRILL COMPANY, INC. 4 W 58th St, New York, NY 10019. Bonnie Ammer, director, advertising and publicity

R R BOWKER COMPANY. 1180 Avenue of the Americas, New York, NY 10036. **212-764-5100.** Shirley Soffer, publicity and public relations manager

BOYD & FRASER PUBLISHING CO. 3627 Sacramento St, San Francisco, CA 94118. **415-346-0686.** *Press contact.* Joan Parsons

CAMBRIDGE UNIVERSITY PRESS. 32 E 57th St, New York, NY 10022. **212-688-8885.** Lucy M Holmes, publicity manager

CHARTER COMMUNICATIONS, INC. 1120 Avenue of the Americas, New York, NY 10036. **212-867-5050.** Judith Neale, publicity director

CHILTON BOOK COMPANY. Radnor, PA 19089. **215-687-8200.** Alan Glass, advertising and promotion manager

THE CITADEL PRESS. 120 Enterprise Ave, Secaucus, NJ 07094. **212-736-0007.** Carole Livingston, publicity director

COLUMBIA UNIVERSITY PRESS. 562 W 113th St, New York, NY 10025. **212-678-6777.** Andirenne McAuley, publicity director

CORNELL UNIVERSITY PRESS. 124 Roberts Pl, Ithaca, NY 14850. **607-257-7000.** William Hendrick, advertising manager

COWARD-MCCANN & GEOGHEGAN, INC. 200 Madison Ave, New York, NY 10016. Risa Kaufman, publicity director

THOMAS CROWELL, INC. 75 Rockefeller Plz, New York, NY 10019. **212-489-2200.** Mayme Saunders, publicity director

CROWN PUBLISHERS, INC. 1 Park Ave, New York, NY 10016. **212-532-9200.** Marian Behrman, publicity director

CURTIS BOOKS. 600 3rd Ave, New York, NY 10016. **212-975-4321**

DELL PUBLISHING COMPANY. 1 Dag Hammarskjold Plz, New York, NY 10017. **212-832-7300.** Jane Heller, publicity director

DIAL PRESS. 1 Dag Hammarskjold Plz, New York, NY 10017. **212-832-7300.** Donna Schrader, publicity director

DODD, MEAD & CO. 79 Madison Ave, New York, NY 10016. **212-685-6464.** Sue Ellen Taub, publicity director

DOUBLEDAY & COMPANY, INC. 245 Park Ave, New York, NY 10017 .

212-953-4561. Anne Brown, associate publicity manager, 212-953-4493. Carole Gross, director, advertising, publicity, and promotion, 212-953-4499

Group and Other Publicists

General Trade Publishing Group. Olivia Blumer. **212-953-4574**

Basic/Special Interest Group. Anne Brown. **212-953-4493**

Anchor Press. Reid Boates. **212-953-4491**

Religious Books. Karen Lunstead. **212-953-4483**

Dolphin Books. Allison Clark. **212-953-4587**

Books for Young Readers. Pat Hinkley. **212-953-4489**

DOVER PUBLICATIONS, INC. 180 Varick St, New York, NY 10014. **212-255-3755.** Sue Ellen Taub, publicity director

DRAKE PUBLISHERS. 801 2nd Ave, New York, NY 10022. **212-986-5100.** Irene Gershon, publicity director

E P DUTTON & COMPANY. 2 Park Ave, New York, NY 10016. **212-725-1818.** Judith Goldfield, publicity manager

ENCYCLOPEDIA BRITANNICA, INC. 425 N Michigan Ave, Chicago, IL 60611. **312-321-7000**

FARRAR, STRAUS, & GIROUX, INC. 19 Union Sq W, New York, NY 10003. **212-741-6900.** Anita Halton, publicity director

FAWCETT PUBLICATIONS, INC. 1515 Broadway, New York, NY 10036. **212-869-3000.** Belle Blanchard, publicity director

FLEET PRESS. 160 5th Ave, New York, NY 10010. **212-243-6100.** C B Scott, publicity director

SAMUEL FRENCH, INC. 25 W 45th St, New York, NY 10010. **212-582-4700.** Peter La Beck, publicity director

FUNK & WAGNALLS COMPANY. 53 E 77th St, New York, NY 10021. **212-734-5502.** Sebastian Fiore, advertising manager

GOLDEN PRESS. 850 3rd Ave, New York, NY 10022. **212-753-8500.** Dee Brown, publicity manager

GROSSET & DUNLAP, INC. 51 Madison Ave, New York, NY 10010. **212-689-9200.** Jane Wesman, publicity director

GROSSMAN PUBLISHERS. 625 Madison Ave, New York, NY 10022. **212-755-4330.** Julia C Colman, publicity and promotion director

GROVE PRESS. 196 W Houston St, New York, NY 10014. **212-242-4900.** Kent Carroll, public relations director

HAMMOND INCORPORATED. 515 Valley St, Maplewood, NJ 07040. **212-763-600.** Dana L Hammond, publicity director

HARCOURT, BRACE, & JOVANOVICH, INC. 757 3rd Ave, New York, NY 10017. **212-888-4444.** Adam Borgenson, public relations manager

HARPER & ROW. 10 E 53rd St, New York, NY 10022. **212-593-7000.** Stuart Harris, public relations director. Sally Williams, press relations

HARVARD UNIVERSITY PRESS. 79 Garden St, Cambridge, MA 02138. **617-495-2600.** Betty J Zirnite, promotions manager. Joy A W Pratt, publicity director. Gayle A Treadwell, advertising director. Janie Bittinger, direct mail director

HAWTHORNE BOOKS, INC. 260 Madison Ave, New York, NY 10016. **212-725-7740.** Peggy Tagliarino, publicity director

HOLT, RINEHART, & WINSTON, INC. 383 Madison Ave, New York, NY 10017. **212-688-9100.** Karen Minder, publicity director

HOUGHTON, MIFFLIN CO. 551 5th Ave, New York, NY 10017. **212-867-8050.** Carolyn Amussen, public relations director

INDIANA UNIVERSITY PRESS. 10th and Morton Sts, Bloomington, IN 47401. **812-337-4203.** Kathleen Ketterman, publicity director

ALFRED A KNOPF, INC. 201 E 50th St, New York, NY 10022. **212-751-2600.** William T Loverd, publicity director

LATHUM PUBLISHERS. 41 E 42nd St, New York, NY 10017. **212-953-1800**

J B LIPPINCOTT COMPANY. 521 5th Ave, New York, NY 10017. Dianitia Hutcheson, publicity manager

LITTLE, BROWN, & COMPANY. 747 3rd Ave, New York, NY 10017. **212-688-8380.** Seldon Sutton, publicity relations

LIVERIGHT. 500 5th Ave, New York, NY 10036. **212-354-5500.** Joseph Santagato, publicity director

MCGRAW-HILL BOOK COMPANY. 1221 Avenue of the Americas, New York, NY 10020. **212-997-1221.** Victor de Keyserling, public information and publicity, **212-997-2486.** (h) **212-392-1233.** *See also* BUSINESS

DAVID MCKAY COMPANY, INC. 750 3rd Ave, New York, NY 10017. **212-949-1500.** Lynette Bieler, publicity director

THE MACMILLAN COMPANY. 866 3rd Ave, New York, NY 10017. **212-949-1524.** Gail Rentsch, publicity director

MIT PRESS. 28 Carleton St, Cambridge, MA 02142. **617-253-5646.** Tom McCorkoe, media director

WILLIAM MORROW AND COMPANY. 105 Madison Ave, New York, NY 10016. **212-889-3050.** Julia Knickerbocker, publicity director

NEW AMERICAN LIBRARY. 1301 Avenue of the Americas, New York, NY 10019. **212-956-3800.** Margaret Ternes, sales promotion manager

NEWBURY HOUSE PUBLISHERS, INC. 68 Middle Rd, Rowley, MA 01969. **617-465-9533.** Gilliam P Ingram, publicity director

NEW DIRECTIONS. 333 6th Ave, New York, NY 10014. **212-255-0230.** Griselda Ohannessian, publicity director

NEW YORK UNIVERSITY PRESS. 21 W 4th St, New York, NY 10003. **212-598-2886.** Cathy Curry, advertising and promotion manager

W W NORTON & CO. 500 5th Ave, New York, NY 10036. Lisl Cade, publicity director

OHIO STATE UNIVERSITY PRESS. 2070 Neil Ave, Columbus, OH 43210. **614-422-6930.** Weldon A Kefauver, director

OXFORD UNIVERSITY PRESS. 200 Madison Ave, New York, NY 10016. **212-679-7300.** Dana Cutie, publicity director

PINNACLE BOOKS. 2029 Century Park E, Los Angeles, CA 90067. **213-552-9111.** Linda K Brown, director, promotion, publicity, and advertising

PLAYBOY PRESS. 747 3rd Ave, New York, NY 10017. **212-688-3030.** Mickie MacKay, publicity chairman

POTOMAC BOOKS, INC, PUBLISHERS. Box 40604, Palisades Station, Washington, DC 20016. **202-338-5774.** Cary T Grayson, Jr, president and associations editor

FREDERICK A PRAEGER, INC. 200 Park Ave, New York, NY 10017. **212-949-8700.** Mrs Jessie Bourneuf, publicity director

PRENTICE HALL, INC. Route 9-W, Englewood Cliffs, NJ 07632. **201-592-2000.** Robert Shaw, publicity director

PRICE, STERN, SLOANE PUBLISHERS, INC. 401 N La Cienega Blvd, Los Angeles, CA 90048. **213-657-6100.** John Dickinson, publicity director

G P PUTNAM'S SONS. 200 Madison Ave, New York, NY 10016. **212-576-8900**

Publicity Directors

Corporate Publicity and Public Relations. Barbara J Hendra. **212-576-8970**

The Berkley Publishing Corp and Richard Marek Publishers. William Parkhurst. **212-576-8971**

G P Putnam's Sons. Susan O'Connell. **212-576-8973**

RAND MC NALLY & COMPANY. Box 7600, Chicago, IL 60076. **312-267-6868.** Conroy Erickson, public relations director

RANDOM HOUSE, INC. 201 E 50th St, New York, NY 10022. **212-572-2296.** Harriet Algrant, publicity director

ST MARTIN'S PRESS. 175 5th Ave, New York, NY 10010. **212-674-5151.** Arlynn Greenbaum, publicity director

SCHOCKEN BOOKS, INC. 200 Madison Ave, New York, NY 10016. **212-685-6500.** Jill Danzig, publicity director

CHARLES SCRIBNER'S SONS. 597 5th Ave, New York, NY 10017. **212-486-2700.** Susan Richman, publicity director

SIMON & SCHUSTER. 630 5th Ave, New York, NY 10020. **212-245-6400.** Dan Green, vice-president, promotion and marketing. Emily Boxer, director, public relations

STANFORD UNIVERSITY PRESS. Stanford, CA 94305. **415-323-9471.** Wesley Peverieri, promotion director

STATE UNIVERSITY OF NEW YORK PRESS. 99 Washington Ave, Albany, NY 12246. **518-474-6050.** Elnora Carrino, promotion and advertising manager

STEIN & DAY. 122 E 42nd St, New York, NY 10017. **212-697-6606.** Lesleigh Lad, publicity director

STRAIGHT ARROW (division of Rolling Stone). 625 3rd St, San Francisco, CA 94107. **415-362-4730.** Diane Cleaver, managing editor

TIME BOOKS, INC. 3 Park Ave, New York, NY 10016. **212-725-2050.** Maggie Goeghegan, publicity director

TIME-LIFE BOOKS INC. Alexandria, VA 22314. **703-960-5048.** Nicholas Benton, vice-president and public relations director

UNIVERSITY OF CALIFORNIA PRESS. 2223 Fulton St, Berkeley, CA 94720. **415-642-4247.** Becky Bishop, publicity manager

UNIVERSITY OF ILLINOIS PRESS. Urbana, IL 61801. **217-333-0950.** Christie B Schuetz, promotion manager

UNIVERSITY OF MINNESOTA PRESS. 2037 University Ave SE, Minneapolis, MN 55455. **612-373-3266.** Miriam Butwin, publicity director, **612-373-3880**

UNIVERSITY OF TEXAS PRESS. Box 7819, University Station, Austin, TX 78712. **512-471-7233.** Christine Gray, publicity manager

UNIVERSITY OF WISCONSIN PRESS. Box 1379, Madison, WI 53701. **608-262-7756.** Jerry A Minnich, director, marketing

UNIVERSITY PRESSES OF FLORIDA. 15 NW 15th St, Gainesville, FL 32603. **904-392-1351.** Clay L Morgan, sales promotion

VANGUARD PRESS. 424 Madison Ave, New York, NY 10017. **212-753-3906.** Evelyn Shrifte and Tom Woll, public relations

VAN NOSTRAND REINHOLD COMPANY. 450 W 33rd St, New York, NY 10001. **212-594-8660.** Robert Baird, publicity director

VIKING PRESS, INC. 625 Madison Ave, New York, NY 10022. **212-755-4330.** A Richard Barber, director, public relations. May P Hornby, director, publicity. Marcia Burch, director, publicity, Penguin Books

WARNER BOOKS. 75 Rockefeller Plz, New York, NY 10019. **212-484-8000.** Deloris Ferrell, publicity director, **212-484-8677**

FRANKLIN WATTS, INC. 730 5th Ave, New York, NY 10019. **212-757-4050.** Madeline Nierman, publicity director

JOHN WILEY & SONS, INC. 605 3rd Ave, New York, NY 10016. **212-867-9800.** Lizanne Adams, manager, public relations, (h) **212-753-5732**

WORKMAN PUBLISHING CO. 231 E 51st St, New York, NY 10022. **212-421-8050.** Jennifer Rogers, publicity director

WORLD PUBLISHING COMPANY. 2080 W 117th St, Cleveland, OH 44111. **216-941-6930.** John Horner, public relations

YALE UNIVERSITY PRESS. 92-A Yale Station, New Haven, CT 06520. **203-432-4979.** Christine Rago, publicity director

WIRE SERVICES

ASSOCIATED PRESS

Headquarters: 50 Rockefeller Plz, New York, NY 10020. **212-262-4000**

Executive Department

PRESIDENT AND GENERAL MANAGER. Wes Gallagher

VICE-PRESIDENT AND DEPUTY GENERAL MANAGER. Keith Fuller

VICE-PRESIDENTS

James F Tomlinson. Treasurer

Stanley M Swinton. Assistant general manager and director, world services

Conrad C Fink. Assistant general manager, newspaper membership

David L Bowen. director, communications

Louis D Boccardi. Assistant general manager and executive editor

Thomas F Pendergast. Assistant general manager and director, personnel and labor relations

Roy Steinfort. Assistant general manager, broadcasting

GENERAL NEWS EDITOR. Rene J Cappon

EXECUTIVE NEWSPHOTO EDITOR. Harold G Buell

Directors

TERM EXPIRES 1977

Richard C Steele. *Worcester* (MA) *Telegram and Sunday Telegram*

J Kelly Sisk. *Greenville* (SC) *Piedmont*

Robert M White II. *Mexico* (MO) *Ledger*

W H Cowles III. *Spokane* (WA) *Spokesman-Review*

Katharine Graham. *Washington* (DC) *Post*

James F Chambers, Jr. *Dallas* (TX) *Times Herald*

TERM EXPIRES 1978

Paul Miller. *Rochester* (NY) *Times-Union*

J M McClelland, Jr. *Longview* (WA) *Daily News*

Frank Batten. *Norfolk* (VA) *Ledger-Star*

Stanton R Cook. *Chicago* (IL) *Tribune*

Arthur Ochs Sulzberger. *New York* (NY) *Times*

Daniel H Ridder. *Long Beach* (CA) *Independent*

TERM EXPIRES 1979

David R Bradley. *St Joseph* (MO) *News-Press and Gazette*

Jack Tarver. *Atlanta* (GA) *Constitution and Journal*

G Gordon Strong. *Canton* (OH) *Repository*

Robert L Taylor. *Philadelphia* (PA) *Evening and Sunday Bulletin*

W S Morris III. *Augusta* (GA) *Chronicle and Herald*

Charles S Rowe. *Fredericksburg* (VA) *Free Lance-Star*

Domestic Bureaus

Alabama: Control Bureau Atlanta, GA

BIRMINGHAM. News Bldg, 4th Ave and 22nd St N, Birmingham, 35203. **205-251-4221**

Correspondent. Hoyt Harwell

MOBILE. Press Register Bldg, 304 Government St, Mobile, 36601. **205-433-1551**

Correspondent. Kendall M Weaver

MONTGOMERY. Advertiser-Journal Bldg, 101 S Lawrence St (PO Box 950), Montgomery, 36102. **205-262-5947**

Correspondent. Rex N Thomas

Alaska: Control Bureau Seattle, WA

ANCHORAGE. Suite 502, Carr-Gottstein Bldg, 310 K St (PO Box 2175, Federal Station), Anchorage, 99501. **907-272-1131.** Photos: **907-278-4162**

Chief of Bureau. Warren Robert Weller

JUNEAU. PO Box 209, State Capitol, Juneau, 99801. **907-586-1515**

Correspondent. G Michael Harmon

Arizona: Control Bureau Phoenix

PHOENIX. Republic and Gazette Bldg, 120 E Van Buren St, Phoenix, 85504. **602-258-8934**

Chief of Bureau. Gavin Scott

Chief of Communications. Ralph W Keibler

TUCSON. Tucson Newspapers, Inc, 4850 S Park Ave (PO Box 26807), Tucson, 85726. **602-294-4433**

Correspondent. Michael A Chihak

Arkansas

LITTLE ROCK. Suite 115, 115 E Capitol Ave (PO Box 789), Little Rock, 72220. **501-374-5536**

Chief of Bureau. Robert P Dalton

Chief of Communications. William E Knox

California

FRESNO (Control Bureau San Francisco). Rm 235, 1626 E St, Fresno, 93786. **209-264-3000** or **3009**

Correspondent. Joseph A Bigham

LOS ANGELES. Rm 263, 1111 S Hill St, Los Angeles, 90015. **213-746-1200.** Photos: **213-746-1231**

Chief of Bureau. Paul H Finch

Chief of Communications. Herb Kelley

Regional Membership Executive. Mark Thayer

SACRAMENTO (Control Bureau San Francisco). Suite 320, 925 L St, Sacramento, 94814. **916-445-6196**

Correspondent. Douglas R Willis

SAN DIEGO (Control Bureau Los Angeles). Union-Tribune Bldg, 350 Camino de la Reina (PO Box 191), San Diego, 92108. **714-298-9671** or **714-299-3131**, Ext 1721 or 1722

Correspondent. Daniel O Tedrick

SAN FRANCISCO. 318 Fox Plz (PO Box 3554), Rincon Annex, San Francisco, 94102. **415-621-7432.** Wirephotos: **415-621-7474.** Traffic: **415-621-7478**

Chief of Bureau. Martin C Thompson

Chief of Communications. Fred L England

Regional Membership Executive. John Morrison

Colorado

DENVER. 304 Denver Post Bldg, 650 15th St, Denver, 80202. **303-825-0123**
Chief of Bureau. Richard W Daw
Chief of Communications. Arthur Loomis
Regional Membership Executive. Robert T Kerr

Connecticut: Control Bureau Hartford

HARTFORD. 196 Trumbull St, Hartford, 06103. **203-246-6876**
Chief of Bureau. Ambrose B Dudley
Chief of Communications. William Dawson

NEW HAVEN. Register Bldg, 367 Orange St, New Haven, 06511. **203-624-9825**
Correspondent. Daniel W Hall

Delaware: Control Bureau Baltimore, MD

(Traffic control for Wilmington is Philadelphia, PA.)

DOVER. PO Box 934, State Capitol, Dover, 19901. **302-674-3037**
Correspondent. Kristin Goff

District of Columbia

WASHINGTON. Rm 606, 2021 K St NW, Washington, 20006. **202-833-5300**
Chief of Bureau. Marvin L Arrowsmith
Assistant Chief of Bureau. Burl Osborne
Chief of Communications. Larry Stephens
Regional Membership Executive. Tony Catella
Associated Press Radio. Rm 615, 1825 K St NW, Washington, 20006. **202-833-5910**. WATS line, incoming feeds: **800-424-8804**. Edward De Fontaine, managing editor. Bill McCloskey, assistant managing editor. George Mayo, chief engineer

Florida: Control Bureau Miami

JACKSONVILLE. 1 Riverside Ave, Jacksonville, 32202. **904-356-2829**
Correspondent. Fred T MacFeely

MIAMI. IBM Bldg, 2125 Biscayne Blvd, Miami, 33137. **305-573-7230**. Wirephotos: **305-573-6421**
Chief of Bureau. Reid G Miller
Chief of Communications. Charles W Bruce

ORLANDO. Sentinel-Star Bldg, 633 N Orange Ave, Orlando, 32801. **305-425-4547** or **4548**
Correspondent. Isaac M Flores

TALLAHASSE. State Capitol, Monroe St, Tallahasse, 32304. **904-224-1211**
Correspondent. John Van Gieson

TAMPA. Tampa Tribune Bldg (PO Box 2972), Tampa, 33601. **813-223-3270**
Correspondent. Patricia Leisner

Georgia

ATLANTA. Title Bldg, 30 Pryor St SW, Atlanta, 30303. **404-522-8971** or **8972**
Chief of Bureau. Ronald Autry
Chief of Communications. Edson R Sharp
Regional Membership Executive. Doug Kienitz

Hawaii

HONOLULU. Hawaii Newspaper Agency News Bldg (PO Box 2956), Honolulu, HI 96802. **808-536-5510** or **808-533-2422**. *AP Telex RCA*, **723372**
Chief of Bureau. Michael M Short

Idaho: Control Bureau Salt Lake City, UT

BOISE. Statesman Bldg, 1200 N Curtis Rd (PO Box 327), Boise, 83704. **208-376-2061**
Correspondent. Robert J Leeright

Illinois: Control Bureau Chicago

CENTRALIA. Evening Sentinel Bldg, 232 E Broadway, Centralia, 62801. **618-533-2259**
Correspondent. Charles D Roberts

CHICAGO. Rm 215, Randolph Tower Bldg, 188 W Randolph St, Chicago, 60601. **312-781-0500**. Newsphotos: **312-781-0523**. Wide world photos: **312-781-0519**
Chief of Bureau. Thomas J Dygard
Chief of Communications. Michael Smith
Regional Membership Executive. James Farrell

PEORIA. Journal Star Bldg, 1 News Plz, Peoria, 61601. **309-682-0141**
Correspondent. John W Prater

SPRINGFIELD. Lincoln Tower Plz, Springfield, 62704. **217-789-2700**
Correspondent. T Lee Hughes

Indiana

INDIANAPOLIS. Star-News Bldg, 307 N Pennsylvania St (PO Box 1950-B), Indianapolis, 46204. **317-639-5501**
Chief of Bureau. John T Marlow
Chief of Communications. Walter M Tabak

Iowa

DES MOINES. 715 Locust St, Des Moines, 50309. **515-284-8324, 515-282-7393, 515-243-3281,** or **515-243-6460**
Chief of Bureau. George Zucker
Chief of Communications. David Young

Kansas: Control Bureau Kansas City, MO

TOPEKA. Capital-Journal Bldg, 616 Jefferson, Topeka, 66607. **913-234-5654**
Correspondent. Lewis L Ferguson

WICHITA. Wichita Eagle-Beacon, 825 E Douglas, Wichita, 67202. **316-263-4601**
Correspondent. David G Bartel

Kentucky: Control Bureau Louisville

FRANKFORT. Rm 243, State Capitol, Frankfort, 40601. **502-223-3222**
Correspondent. Sy Ramsey

LEXINGTON. 146 Market St, Lexington, 40507. **606-254-2070**
Correspondent. Robert J Cooper

LOUISVILLE. Rm 407-A, Courier-Journal and Times Bldg, 525 W Broadway, Louisville, 40202. **502-583-7718**
Chief of Bureau. William L Winter (h) **502-459-8994**
Chief of Communications. R V Jenkins

Louisiana: Control Bureau New Orleans

BATON ROUGE. PO Box 44395, Press Room, Ground Floor, State Capitol Bldg, Baton Rouge, 70804. **504-343-1325** (day) or **0151** (night)
Correspondent. Jerry Estil

NEW ORLEANS. Times-Picayune-States Bldg, 3800 Howard Ave, New Orleans, 70140. **504-821-3946**
Chief of Bureau. Dorman E Cordell
Chief of Communications. Wayne Parrack

Maine: Control Bureau Concord, NH

AUGUSTA. State House, Augusta, 04333. 207-289-2671 or 207-622-3018
Correspondent. Steven P Rosenfeld

PORTLAND. Press Herald Bldg, 390 Congress St (PO Box 617), Portland, 04104. 207-772-4157 or 6321
Correspondent. Jerome Harkavy

Maryland: Control Bureau Baltimore

ANNAPOLIS. PO Box 1471, State House, State Cir, Annapolis, 21404. 301-269-0196
Correspondent. Tom C Stuckey

BALTIMORE. 210 N Calvert St, Baltimore, 21202. 301-539-3524
Chief of Bureau. John A Woodfield
Chief of Communications. Kenneth Berger

Massachusetts: Control Bureau Boston

BOSTON. 260 Summer St, Boston, 02210. 617-357-8100
Chief of Bureau. Joe A McGowan, Jr
Chief of Communications. Donald H Barry
Regional Membership Executive. James Smith

SPRINGFIELD. Rm 201, 292 Worthington St, Springfield, 01103. 413-781-0217
Correspondent. Martin J Waters

Michigan: Control Bureau Detroit

DETROIT. Rm 600, 320 W Lafayette St, Detroit, 48226. 313-965-9500. Communications: 313-965-9505. Wirephotos: 313-965-9504
Chief of Bureau. James Wilson
Chief of Communications. Herman Delidow
Regional Membership Executive. George Otwell

GRAND RAPIDS. Press Bldg, 155 Michigan NW, Grand Rapids, 49502. 616-458-8853
Correspondent. Pieter D Bennett

LANSING. Rm 1112, Bank of Lansing Bldg, 103 N Washington, Lansing, 48933. 517-482-8011. State House. 517-373-0254
Correspondent. Patrick J Connolly

Minnesota: Control Bureau Minneapolis

MINNEAPOLIS. 426 Portland Ave, Minneapolis, 55415. 612-335-6741
Chief of Bureau. Joe Dill
Chief of Communications. Howard Kaspen

ST PAUL. Rm B-28, State Capitol, Aurora and Park, St Paul, 55155. 612-296-6561
Correspondent. Gerald D Nelson

Mississippi: Control Bureau New Orleans, LA

JACKSON. Clarion-Ledger. Daily News Bldg, 311 E Pearl St (PO Box 446), Jackson, 39201. 601-948-5897 or 601-353-2421

Correspondent. Robert L Shaw
Regional Membership Executive. Paul Freeman

Missouri: Control Bureau Kansas City

JEFFERSON CITY. PO Box 272, Jefferson City, 65101. 314-636-9415. Capitol Press Room. 314-636-6732
Correspondent. Terrence Ganey

KANSAS CITY. Star Bldg, 1715 Grand Ave, Kansas City, 64108. 816-421-4844. Kansas City carrier transmission office. 816-471-2078
Chief of Bureau. Fred W Moen
Chief of Communications. Herbert G Mundt
Regional Membership Executive. H Laurens Genuchi
Technical Service Manager. R G Hall

ST LOUIS. (Day) Post-Dispatch Bldg, 900 N 12th St, St Louis, 63101. 314-241-2496
Correspondent. Roger D Jolley

Montana

HELENA. Independent Record Bldg (PO Box 178), Helena, 59601. 406-442-7440
Chief of Bureau. Hugh Van Swearingen, Jr

Nebraska: Control Bureau Des Moines, IA

LINCOLN. Journal-Star Bldg, 926 P St (PO Box 82061), Lincoln, 68508. 402-432-2525
Correspondent. Edward W Howard

OMAHA. Rm 252, World-Herald Bldg, World-Herald Sq (PO Box 838, Downtown

Station), Omaha, 68102. 402-341-4963
Correspondent. Edward C Nicholls
Chief of Communications. Joseph Ambort

Nevada: Control Bureau Los Angeles, CA

CARSON CITY. Rm 32, State Capitol, Carson City, 89701. 702-885-4190
Correspondent. Brendan Riley

LAS VEGAS. Review-Journal Bldg, Las Vegas, 89101. 702-382-7440
Correspondent. Jerome P Curry

RENO. Gazette-Journal Bldg, 401 W 2nd St (PO Box 280), Reno, 89503. 702-322-3639
Correspondent. William R Martin

New Hampshire

CONCORD. Monitor Bldg, 3 N State St (PO Box 1296), Concord, 03301. 603-224-3327
Chief of Bureau. David L Swearingen
Chief of Communications. Lawrence Kananen

New Jersey: Control Bureau Newark

ATLANTIC CITY. c/o The Press, Devins Lane, Pleasantville, 08232. 609-645-2063 or 609-45-1111, Ext 59
Correspondent. Peter Matise

NEWARK. Suite 933, 50 Park Pl, Newark, 07102. 201-642-0151
Chief of Bureau. Hal McClure
Chief of Communications. Bernie Schlueter

TRENTON. State House, Trenton, 08625. 609-292-5176. Mailing address: PO Box 3407, Cherry Hill, NJ 08034
Correspondent. Carl Zeitz
Regional Membership Executive. Joseph Bradis

New Mexico: Control Bureau Albuquerque

ALBUQUERQUE. Tribune Bldg, 7th and Silver SW (PO Box 1845), Albuquerque, 87103. 505-243-7857
Chief of Bureau. Howard Graves
Chief of Communications. Gaylord L Reaser

SANTA FE. PO Box 2326, Rm 202, State Capitol, Santa Fe, 87501. 505-982-1012
Correspondent. Joseph W Feather

New York

ALBANY. Capital Newspapers Bldg, 645 Albany-Shaker Rd (PO Box 11010), Albany, 12211. **518-458-7821**

COMMUNICATIONS: 518-458-7824
Chief of Bureau. Howard E Staats
Chief of Communications. William Welch
Regional Membership Executive. Richard Shafer

BUFFALO. (Control Bureau Albany). (Day). *Buffalo Evening News.* 1 News Plz; (night) Courier-Express Bdg, 787 Main St, Buffalo, 14240. **716-852-1051**
Correspondent. Benjamin B De Forest

NEW YORK. 50 Rockefeller Plz, New York, 10020. **212-262-4000**
Correspondent. Craig Ammerman
Chief of Communications. Edward Fornel. AP Telex: RCA, 224728 or **224729**; ITT, **2420049** or **2420061**; WU, **126079**; WUI, **62368UW**. *United Nations Bureau.* Secretariat Bldg, New York, 10017. **212-262-6227**
Chief Correspondent. George Bria. *AP-Dow Jones.* 22 Cortland St, New York, NY 10007. **212-285-5284**. **Telex: 232911.** William R Clabby, managing editor

SYRACUSE. (Control Bureau Albany). *Syracuse Herald-Journal*, Clinton Sq, Syracuse, 13201. **315-471-6471**
Correspondent. Michael B Hendricks

North Carolina: Control Bureau Charlotte

CHARLOTTE. 531 S Tryon St, Charlotte, 28202. **704-334-9115** or **4624**
Chief of Bureau. John O Lumpkin
Chief of Communications. Frank E Turner
Regional Membership Executive. Ben Avery
General Broadcast Executive. Jay C Bowles, Box 630, Route 6, Mooresville, 28115. **704-663-5262**

RALEIGH. 215 S McDowell St (PO Box 1311), Raleigh, 27602. **919-833-8687**
Correspondent. Robert B Cullen

North Dakota: Control Bureau Minneapolis, MN

BISMARCK. Tribune Bldg (PO Box 814), Bismarck, 58501. **701-223-8450**
Correspondent. John W Schweitzer

FARGO. Forum Bldg, 101 N 5th St, Fargo, 58102. **701-235-1908**
Correspondent. James D Wilson

Ohio: Control Bureau Columbus

CINCINNATI. Enquirer Bldg, 617 Vine St (PO Box 206), Cincinnati, 45202. **513-241-2386**
Correspondent. Andrew Lippman

CLEVELAND. Forest City Publishing Co, 1801 Superior Ave NE, Cleveland, 44114. **216-771-2172**
Correspondent. Neil Bibler
Chief of Communications. William Lewis

COLUMBUS. 4th Floor, Dispatch Bldg, 34 S Third St (PO Box 1812), Columbus, 43215. **614-228-4306**
Chief of Bureau. James C Lagier
Chief of Communications. Gerald E Mowery
Regional Membership Executive. George Otwell

Oklahoma: Control Bureau Oklahoma City

OKLAHOMA CITY. Old Daily Oklahoman Bldg, 500 N Broadway, Oklahoma City, 73102. **405-236-0663**
Chief of Bureau. Charles K Siner
Chief of Communications. Doyle Taylor

TULSA. 315 S Boulder (PO Box 1770), Tulsa, 74103. **918-584-4346**
Correspondent. D Dayton Blair

Oregon: Control Bureau Portland

PORTLAND. 1320 SW Broadway, Portland, 97201. **503-228-2169**
Chief of Bureau. Frank R Wetzel
Chief of Communications. Robert T Colburn

SALEM. Press Room, State Capitol, Salem, 97310. **503-378-4155** (day) or **503-364-6811** (night)
Correspondent. James A Church

Pennsylvania: Control Bureau Philadelphia

HARRISBURG. Rm 526, E Floor, 408–9 Payne-Shoemaker Bldg, 240 North St, Main Capitol, Harrisburg, 17120. **717-238-9413**
Correspondent. William G Williams
Regional Membership Executive. Anthony Rizzo

PHILADELPHIA. Bulletin Bldg, 30th and Market Sts (PO Box 7784), Philadelphia, 19101. **215-382-5571.** Newsphotos: **215-386-0169**
Chief of Bureau. George Zucker
Chief of Communications. Regis Goergen

PITTSBURGH. 1111 Clark Bldg, 717 Liberty Ave, Pittsburgh, 15222. **412-281-3747**
Correspondent. D Byron Yake

Rhode Island: Control Bureau Boston, MA

PROVIDENCE. 10 Dorrance St, Providence, 02903. **401-274-2270**
Correspondent. John C Shurr

South Carolina

COLUMBIA. State and Record Bldg, Corner Stadium and Key Roads (PO Box 1435), Columbia, 29201. **803-771-6161**, Ext 314 or **803-799-5510**
Chief of Bureau. George E Rowland

South Dakota: Control Bureau Minneapolis, MN

PIERRE. PO Box 368, Capitol Bldg, Pierre, 57501. **605-224-7811**
Correspondent. Terry R Woster

SIOUX FALLS. Argus-Leader Bldg, 200 S Minnesota (PO Box 1125), Sioux Falls, 57102. **605-332-3111** or **2111**
Correspondent. James A Carrier
Regional Membership Executive. Terry De Vine

Tennessee: Control Bureau Nashville

CHATTANOOGA. 400 E 11th St, Chattanooga, 37403. **615-266-4600**
Correspondent. Eric Newhouse

KNOXVILLE. (Day) News Sentinel Bldg, 204 W Church St; (night) Journal Bldg; Knoxville, 37901. **615-522-3963**
Correspondent. Matthew L Yancey

MEMPHIS. Press-Scimitar and Commercial Appeal Bldg, 495 Union Ave (PO Box 326), Memphis, 38103. **901-525-1972**
Correspondent. Lester W Seago, Jr

NASHVILLE. Banner-Tennessean Bldg, 1100 Broadway (PO Box 22990), Nashville, 37203. **615-244-2205** or **615-255-1221**, Ext 323. Photos: **615-256-0552**

Chief of Bureau. William M Di Mascio

Chief of Communications. Charles D Gibson

Regional Membership Executive. Nancy Shipley

Texas: Control Bureau Dallas

AUSTIN. PO Box 12247, Capitol Station, State Capitol, Austin, 78711. **512-472-4004**

Correspondent. Garth Jones

DALLAS. Times Herald Bldg, Herald Sq, 1101 Pacific St, Dallas, 75202. Photos: Rm 353, Dallas News Bldg, **214-742-3447**. News photos: **214-742-8853**. Communications: **214-748-2378**

Chief of Bureau. James W Mangon

Chief of Communications. Emmett Renfrow

Regional Membership Executive. William F Greer

FORT WORTH. Fort Worth Star-Telegram Bldg, 7th and Taylor, Fort Worth, 76101. **817-336-9271**

Correspondent. Mike Cochran

HARLINGEN. KGBT Bldg, 1519 W Harrison, Harlingen, 78550. **512-423-7790** or **7407**

Correspondent. Miller H Bonner, Jr

HOUSTON. c/o. *Chronicle*, Houston, 77002. **713-220-7391** or **713-227-2475**. (day) **713-621-7000**, Ext 457. (night) News photos: **713-220-7470**. eCommunications: **713-220-7392**

Correspondent. Max B Skelton

Regional Membership Executive. Thomas B De Cola. **713-220-7391**

SAN ANTONIO. Express Publishing Co, Ave E and 3rd St, San Antonion, 78206. **512-222-2713**

Correspondent. Richard H Scott

Utah

SALT LAKE CITY. Rm 323, Annex, 143 S Main, Salt Lake City, 84111. **801-322-3405**

Chief of Bureau. Larry D Kurtz

Chief of Communications. L Mike Wood

Regional Membership Executive. Timothy Madden

Vermont: Control Bureau Concord, NH

MONTPELIER. Thrush Tavern, 2nd Floor, 107 State St (Box 866), Montpelier, 05602. **802-223-7638**

Correspondent. Diane L Minarcin

Virginia: Control Bureau Richmond

NORFOLK. c/o Norfolk Newspapers, Inc, 150 W Brambleton Ave, Norfolk, 23501. **804-625-2047**

Correspondent. Larry McDermott

RICHMOND. Richmond Newspapers Bldg, 333 E Grace St (PO Box 27603), Richmond, 23261. **804-643-6646**

Chief of Bureau. Robert S Gallimore. **804-272-9771**

Chief of Communications. Bobby E Baker

Washington: Control Bureau Seattle

OLYMPIA. PO Box 607, Legislative Bldg, Olympia, 98501. **206-753-7222**

Correspondent. John E White

SEATTLE. 201 Boren N (PO Box 2144), Seattle, 98111. **206-682-1812**. Traffic Department: **206-682-6662**

Chief of Bureau. John M Armstrong

Chief of Communications. Charles A Price, Jr

Regional Membership Executive. Al Dean Beste

SPOKANE. PO Box 2173, Spokane, 99210. **509-624-1258**

Correspondent. John W Kuglin

West Virginia: Control Bureau Charleston

CHARLESTON. Rm 206, Charleston Newspapers Bldg, 1001 Virginia St E, Charleston, 25301. **304-346-0897**

Chief of Bureau. Richard W Buholz

Chief of Communications. William C Crouch

HUNTINGTON. Huntington Publishing Co, PO Box 445, Huntington, 25709. **304-523-8721**

Correspondent. Stratton L Douthat

Wisconsin: Control Bureau Milwaukee

MADISON. 1901 Fish Hatchery Rd, Madison, 53713. **608-252-6297**

Correspondent. Arthur L Srb

MILWAUKEE. Journal Square, 918 N 4th St, Milwaukee, 43203. **414-271-0158**

Chief of Bureau. Dion W Henderson

Chief of Communications. Ray Hilbert

Wyoming: Control Bureau Denver, CO

CHEYENNE. 2003 Central Ave (PO Box 1323), Cheyenne, 82001. **307-632-9351**

Correspondent. Warren E Wintrode

Foreign Service Bureaus

Headquarters: 50 Rockefeller Plz, New York, NY 10020. **212-262-4000**

ARGENTINA. Buenos Aires. Calle San Martin 344. Mailing address: Casilla de Correo 1296. Telephone: **49-6688, 6689,** or **1784**. *Cable:* **Associated**. *Telex:* **121053**

Chief of Bureau. William F Nicholson

AUSTRALIA. Sydney, New South Wales, 364 Sussex St, Sydney 2001. Mailing address: GPO Box 3978. Telephone: **211-2033** or **2140**. *Cable:* **Associated**. *Telex:* **21181-APWORLD AA21181**

Chief of Bureau. Peter O'Loughlin

AUSTRIA. Vienna. International Press Center (IPZ), 1190 Vienna, Gunoldstrasse 14. Telephone: **36-41-58** or **59**. *AP Telex:* **03/5930**

Chief of Bureau. Eric Waha

BELGIUM. Brussels. International Press Centre-B.49, Boulevard Charlemagne 1, Karel de Grote Laan 1, 1041 Brussels. Telephones: **736-06-63** (news), **736-09-75** (photos)

Chief of Bureau. Alfred Cheval

Correspondent. Carl Hartman

NATO and Common Market. 129A Avenue Louise, Brussels 5 (Control Bureau London). **736-12-29**

AP-Dow Jones Correspondent. John Fiehn

BOLIVIA. La Paz. Casilla 4364. Telephone: **40125** or **40460**. *Cable:* **Associated**

Correspondent. Harold Olmos

BRAZIL. Brasilia. Caixa Postal 14-2260, Brasilia, DF Telephone: **23-9492**. *Telex*: **(061) 1454**
Correspondent. Richard W Foster

BRAZIL. Rio De Janeiro. Avenida Rio Branco, 25, 13 Andar. Mailing address: Clixa Postal 72-ZC-00. Telephone: **233-6133** or **5085**. *Cable*: **Associated**. *Telex*: **RIO (021) 21888**
Chief of Bureau. Edgar H Miller, Jr

BRAZIL. Sao Paulo. Rua Major Quedinho 28, 6° Andar, 01000 Sao Paulo, SP. Mailing address: Caixa Postal 3815. Telephone: **256-4135** or **0520**. *Cable*: **Associated**. *Telex*: **(011) 21595**

BURMA. Rangoon. U Sein Win. Mail from US bureaus *only*: 283 U Wisara Rd, Dagon, PO *Cable*: **Associated**

CHILE. Santiago. Calle Tenderini 85, Piso 10-Oficina 101. Mailing address: Casilla 2653, Tenderini 85. Telephone: **3-5015** or **4934**. *Cable*: **Associated**. *Telex*: **3520234**
Chief of Bureau. William R Long

COLOMBIA. Bogota. Edificio Condiminio Parque Santander, Carrera 6, No 14–98, Office 902. Mailing address: Apartado Aereo 4231. Telephone: **41-88-08** or **42-91-44**. *Cable*: **Associated**. *Telex*: **44641**
Chief of Bureau. Jorge S Canelas

CYPRUS. Nicosia. Andreas Zakos St 4, Engomi-Nicosia, Cyprus. Telephone: **47086** or **47142**. *Telex*: **2459**
Chief of Middle East Service. Nicholas S Ludington

CZECHOSLOVAKIA. Prague. Iva Drapalova, Prague 1-Ruzova 7, Prague 110. Telephone: **243592**

DENMARK. Copenhagen. 2nd Floor, Kristen Bernikows Gade 4, DK-1105. Telephone: **(01) 11-15-94**. Photos: **(01)-11-36-17**. *AP Telex*: **22381**. *Telex*: **22200**
Chief of Bureau. George J F Boultwood

GERMANY. Berlin. Mailing address: Kurfurstendamm 26a, Berlin, W. 15. Telephone: **8818386** or **8818387**. *Cable*: **Associated Press**. *AP Telex*: **0183495**
Correspondent. Hubert J Erb

GERMANY. Bonn. Pressehaus 1/101, An der Heussalle 2-10. Mailing address: Postfach 120147 53, Bonn 12. Telephone: **224093** or **224094**. *Cable*: **Associated Press**. *AP Telex*: **08 86301 (AP Bonn)**

News Editor, Germany. Otto C Doeling
AP-Dow Jones Correspondent. James Furlong

GERMANY. Frankfurt-Main. Moselstrasse 27, Frankfurt-Main (FK). Telephone: **231271** or **239181**. *Cable*: **Associated Press**. *AP Telex*: **41 1320** or **41 1388**
Chief of Bureau. Henry Hartzenbusch
AP-Dow Jones Correspondent. Tom Hielle

GERMANY. Hamburg. Katharinenstrasse 3/111, Hamburg, 11. Telephone: **367086** or **367087**. *Cable*: **Associated Press**. *Telex*: **02 13203**
Correspondent. Eduard Spiess

GREECE. Athens. Akadimias 27A Athens, 124. Telephone: **602-755** or **604-550**. *Cable*: **Associated**. *AP Telex*: **215133**
Correspondent. Philemon Dopoulos

EGYPT. Cairo. 33 Kasr El Nil. Mailing address: PO Box 1077. Telephone: **54687, 977089,** or **971796**. *Cable*: **Associated**. *Telex*: **2211**
Chief of Bureau Harry A Dunphy

ENGLAND. London. Associated Press Bldg, 83–6 Farringdon St, London, EC 4A, 4BR. Telephone: **353-1515**. Photos: **583-1691**. *Cable*: **Associated Londonps 4**. *AP Telex*: **262887**
Chief of Bureau. Richard O'Regan
News Editor. Fred Coleman
AP-Dow Jones Administrative Director. Frank N Hawkins, Jr
AP-Dow Jones Assistant Managing Editor. Robert Muller. *Cable*: **APDOW PS4**. *Telex*: **267215**

FINLAND. Helsinki. Mannerheimvagen 18, 00100 Helsinki 10. Telephone: **64-68-83**. *Cable*: **Associated**
Correspondent. Risto Maenpaa

FRANCE. Paris. 21 Rue de Berri, Paris (PS) 75008. Telephone: **359-8676**. *Cable*: **Associated**. *AP Telex*: **280770**
Chief of Bureau. Morris W Rosenberg
AP-Dow Jones Correspondent. Jack Aboaf. **25-60-972**

HONG KONG. Rm 1282, Floor 12, News Mercury House, Waterfront Rd. Telephone: **5-274-324**. *Copy dictation*: **5-274-316**. *AP Telex*: **73265**
Chief of Bureau. Robert Liu

INDIA. New Delhi. 19 Narendra Pl, Parliament St. Telephone: **310377** or **312467**.

Cable: **Apworld Newdelhi**. *Telex*: **2232**
Chief of Bureau. Myron Belkind

INDONESIA. Jakarta (Control Bureau Singapore). Flat 30, Dj Kebon Sirih 40. Mailing address: PO Box 2056. Telephone: **50234**. *Cable*: **Associated Jakarta**
Correspondent. Ghafur Fadyl

IRAN. Tehran. 5 5th St and Park Ave (Abass-Abad). Mailing address: PO Box 698. Telephone: **627-376**. *Cable*: **Telex Associated Tehran**. *AP Telex*: **212 470 APTIR**
Correspondent. Parviz Raein

ISRAEL. Jerusalem. PO Box 20102. Telephone: **68745**. *AP Telex*: **2340, AP JLM ILO**
Correspondent. Marcus Eliason

ISRAEL. Tel Aviv. 49 Petach Tikva Rd. Mailing address: PO Box 20220. Telephone: **287128** or **287129**. Photos: **287120**. *Telex*: **Tel Aviv 33532**
Chief of Bureau. Frank Crepeau

ITALY. Milan. Pizza Cavour 2, Milan 20121. Telephone: **792-500**
Correspondent. Franco Giani

ITALY. Rome. 5 Piazza Grasioli, Rome 00186. *Cable*: **Associated**. *AP Telex*: **RM 61196**
Chief of Bureau. Dennis F Redmont
AP-Dow Jones Correspondent. Barth Healey. **68 87 65**

JAPAN. Tokyo. Asahi Shimbun Bldg, 6-1, Yurakucho 2-Chome, Chiyoda-ku, Tokyo 100. Mailing address: Central PO Box 607, Tokyo 100-91. Telephone: **201-2801**. *Cable*: **Associated**. *Wide-world cable*: **Wideworldphotos**. *AP Telex*: **J 22260**
Chief of North Asia Services. Roy K Essoyan
AP-Dow Jones Correspondent. Fowler Martin

KENYA. Nairobi. Nation House, Tom Mboya St. Mailing address: PO Box 47590. Telephone: **21449**. Cable: **AP News**. *Telex* (shared): **NAIROBI 22239**
Correspondent. Brian Jeffries

KOREA. Seoul. Hapdong New Agency Bldg, 108-4, Susong-dong, Chongro-ku. Mailing address: Central PO Box 1869. Telephone: **74-3908** or **3909**. *Cable*: **Associated**
Correspondent. K C Hwang

LEBANON. Beirut. Kings Hotel, Rauche, Beirut. Telephone: **297501, 297502,** or **297503**. *AP Telex*: **21389**

MALAYSIA. Kuala Lumpur (Control Bureau Singapore). 174 Tuanku Abdul Rahman Rd. Mailing address: GPO Box 2219. Telephone: **22374** or **22375.** *Cable*: **Associated Kualalumpur**
Correspondent. Hari Subramanian

MEXICO. Mexico, DF 6th Floor, Paseo de Reforma 46. Mailing address: Apartado Postal 1181. Telephone: **905-566-3488.** *Cable*: **Associated.** *Telex*: **Assopress Mex 017-71-064**
Chief of Bureau. Charles H Green

NEPAL. Katmandu. Thapathali Panchayan, Post Box 513, Katmandu, Nepal. Telephone: **12767.** *Cable*: **AP World Katmandul**
Correspondent. Binaya Guruacharya

NETHERLANDS. Amsterdam C Keizersgracht 205, PO Box 1016, Amsterdam 02. Telephone: **235057, 231420,** or **235074.** *AP Telex*: **12218**
Chief of Bureau. John Gale

NIGERIA (West Africa). Lagos. 24 Keffi St. Mailing address: PO Box 2454. Telephone: **25859.** *Telex*: **21388**
Correspondent. Brian Jeffries

NORWAY. Oslo. Fr Nansens Plass 5. V. 201. Telephone: **41-29-55.** *AP Telex*: **1019**
Chief of Bureau. Erik Wold

PARAGUAY. Asuncion. Avenida San Martin 1836, Villa Guarani. Mailing address: Casilla de Correo 264. Telephone: **5762** or **1316.** *Cable*: **Associated**
Correspondent. Nestor A Verdina

PERU. Lima. Jiron Cailloma 377. Mailing address: Apartado Postal 119. Telephone: **27-7775** or **28-8959.** *Cable*: **Associated.** *AP Telex*: **WLA-5245**
Chief of Bureau. Henry S Ackerman
Correspondent. Diego Gonzalez

PHILIPPINES. Manila. L and S Bldg, 1515 Rox Blvd. Mailing address: PO Box 2274. Telephone: **59-49-69, 59-62-29,** or **59-63-39.** *Cable*: **Associated.** *AP Telex*: RCA, **722571**; Mackay, **742 0021**
Chief of Bureau. Arnold Zeitlin

POLAND. Warsaw. Rm 302, Ulica Piekna 68. Mailing address: PO Box 108. Telephone: **389-159.** *Cable*: **APPRESS.** *AP Telex*: **81 3440**
Correspondent. George Brodzki

PORTUGAL. Lisbon 2. Praca da Alegria 58, 3A. Telephone: **370-967** or **968.** *Cable*: **Associated.** *Telex*: **12530**
Chief of Bureau. Andrew Jorchia

PUERTO RICO. San Juan, 00906. 400 Ponce De Leon Ave. Mailing address: PO Box 5829. Telephone: **809-724-2424** or **6610.** *Cable*: **Associated San Juan.** *AP Telex*: RCA, **325354**; ITT, **3450480**
Chief of Caribbean Services. Edith M Lederer

RHODESIA. Salisbury. c/o Inter-African News Agency, PO Box 785, Salisbury, Rhodesia. Telephone: **28245** or **76622.** *Telex*: **Salisbury 2128**
Correspondent. John Edin

ROMANIA. Bucharest. St Corbeni 30, Ap 4, Sector 2. Telephone: **116-599**
Representative. Viorel Urma

SINGAPORE. Rm 1001, 10th Floor, Robina House, Shenton Way, Singapore 1. Mailing address: PO Box 44. Telephone: **2201849** or **2202336.** *Cable*: **Associated Singapore.** *Telex*: **RS 21232**
Chief of Bureau. Kenneth L Whiting

SOUTH AFRICA. Johannesburg. 701-3 Union Ctr, 31 Pritchard St. Telephone: **838-7871** or **7872.** *Cable*: **APnews.** *AP Telex*: **J 7617**
Chief of Bureau. Larry E Heinzerling

SPAIN. Madrid. Carrera de San Jeromino 16. Mailing address: PO Box 844. Telephone: **2-22-60-02** or **2-22-79-21.** *Cable*: **Associated.** *AP Telex*: **27771**
Chief of Bureau. John Fenton Wheeler

SWEDEN. Stockholm, C. Vattugatan 12. Mailing address: Box 1625 S-111 86. Telephone: **11-12-80.** *Cable*: **Associated.** *AP Telex*: **1195**
Chief of Bureau. Rolf Ulvestam

SWITZERLAND. Geneva. Palais des Nations. Telephone: **34-72-22.** *Cable*: **Associated.** *AP Telex*: **22127**
Chief of Bureau. Hanns Neuerbourg
AP-Dow Jones Correspondent. Adrian Lithi. **32-49-27**

TAIWAN. Taipei. Central News Agency Bldg, 209 Sungkiang Rd. Telephone: **521-6651** or **5805.** *Cable*: **Associated.** *Telex*: **Taiwan 21835**
Correspondent. George Chu

THAILAND. Bangkok. 10th Floor, Sivadon Bldg, 1 Convent Rd. Mailing address: PO Box 775. Telephone: **2345553, 2333085,** or **2332857.** *Cable*: **Associated.** *Telex*: **AP Press TH 2606**
Correspondent. Denis D Gray

TURKEY. Ankara. 16 Konur Sokak, Kirilay-Ankara. Telephone: **170847.** *Telex*: **Ankara 40**
Correspondent. Mrs Emel Anil

TURKEY. Istanbul. Catalcesme Sokak 5, Cesme Han Kat 3, Cagaloglu. Mailing address: PO Box 724. Telephone: **223052.** *Cable*: **Associated.** *AP Telex*: **305**
Administrative Director. Thalia Donas

URUGUAY. Montevideo (Control Bureau Buenos Aires)

UNION OF SOVIET SOCIALIST REPUBLICS. Moscow. Kutuzovsky Prospekt 7-4, Korpus 5, Ku.33. Telephone: **243-5692** or **7014.** *Cable*: **Associated.** *Telex*: **Moscow 7422**
Chief of Bureau. David Mason

VENEZUELA. Caracas. Apto 46, Edificio El Nacional, Puerto Escondido a Puente Nuevo. Mailing address: Apartado de Correo 1015. Telephone: **41-6343** or **6342.** *Cable*: **Associated.** *Telex*: **22840 ASO Press**
Chief of Bureau. William H Heath

YUGOSLAVIA. Belgrade 11000. Dositijeva 12. Telephone: **631-553.** *Cable*: **Associated.** *AP Telex*: **11264**
Correspondent. Boris Boskovic

UNITED PRESS INTERNATIONAL

Headquarters: 220 E 42nd St, New York, NY 10017. **212-682-0400.** *Telex*: ITT, **420546** or **420548**; RCA, **224369**; WUI, **620444**; WU, **14-7203**

Executive Officers

CHAIRMAN EMERITUS OF THE BOARD. Frank H. Bartholomew. **415-626-6313**

PRESIDENT and CHIEF EXECUTIVE OFFICER. Roderick W Beaton. **212-682-0419**

VICE-PRESIDENT, BROADCAST SERVICES. William B Ketter. **212-682-0231**

VICE-PRESIDENT, NEWSPICTURES. F W Lyon. **212-682-0173**

VICE-PRESIDENT, GENERAL MANAGER, and SUPERINTENDENT OF BUREAU OPERATIONS. Robert E Page. **212-682-2084**

VICE-PRESIDENT and EDITOR-IN-CHIEF. H L Stevenson. **212-682-5493**

Departments

NEWSPICTURES DEPARTMENT. 220 E 42nd St, New York, NY 10017. **212-682-0400, 0471, 6329** or **1353.** Cable: **PIXUNIT NEW YORK**

BROADCAST SERVICES. Audio, New York, receiving: **212-867-3995.** Audio, Chicago, receiving: **312-467-5055**

COMMUNICATIONS DEPARTMENT. Ernest F Price, communications manager. **212-682-5086**

Domestic Bureaus

ALBANY, NY (KT). 2nd Floor, Capital Newspapers Bldg, 645 Albany Shaker Rd, Colonie, NY. Mailing address: 645 Albany Shaker Rd, Albany, NY 12211. **518-458-7833**
News Editor for New York State. John J Maloy
Bureau Manager. William Stevens
Albany Capitol Bureau (CX). Mailing address: PO Box 7271, Capitol Station, Albany, NY 12224. **518-472-8496** or **7569**
Newspictures (KTP). **518-458-7833**
Bureau Manager. Joseph W Paeglow

ALBUQUERQUE, NM (AQ). Albuquerque Tribune Bldg, 701 Silver Ave SW, Albuquerque, NM 87103. Mailing address: PO Drawer U, Albuquerque, NM 87103. **505-247-4196** or **4197**
Bureau Manager and State News Editor. Philip Bradley Smith, Montano NW,

ANNAPOLIS, MD (CB). Maryland-Delaware State Headquarters, State House, Annapolis, MD. Mailing address: PO Box 347, Annapolis MD 21404. **301-269-5518**
Bureau Manager and State News Editor. Mary Ellen Haskett

ATLANTA, GA (AJ). United Press Bldg, 1211 Williams St NW, Atlanta, GA 30309. **404-875-7631.** Telex: **54-2571**
General News Editor. Glen R Carpenter

News Center Editor. Jack E Wilkinson
Bureau Manager and State News Editor. Willion O Tome
Night Manager. Martin Murphy
Overnight Manager. A O'Neil Hendrick
General Communications Manager. William H Smith
General Sports Editor. David M Moffit
Office Manager. Rounelle Martin
Newspictures (AJP). **404-875-7635**
General Editor. J L Shields
Bureau Manager. Russell H Yoder
Regional Telephoto Engineer. J W Hodges

AUGUSTA, ME (ME). Rm 421, State House, Augusta, ME 04330. **207-623-9275**
Bureau Manager and State News Editor. Arthur P Bushnell

AUSTIN, TX (US). State House, Austin, TX 78711. Mailing address: PO Box 12187, Capitol Station, Austin, TX 78711. **512-472-2471**
Bureau Manager. James R Lindsey
Newspictures (USP). **512-476-5960**
Bureau Manager. Robert Thomas

BALTIMORE, MD (BR). News-American Bldg, Lombard and South Sts, Baltimore, MD 21203. **301-539-6446** or **6447**
Bureau Manager. Richard S Newcombe

BATON ROUGE, LA (BG). Press Room, State Capitol, Baton Rouge, LA 70804. Mailing address: PO Box 44132, Baton Rouge, LA 70804. **504-344-0870**
Bureau Manager. Royal Brightbill

BIRMINGHAM, AL (BX). News-Post Herald Bldg, 2200 4th Ave, N Birmingham, AL 35203. **205-328-4242** or **205-325-2490**
Bureau Manager and State News Editor. Thomas P Brooks

BOISE, ID (BE). 430 N 9th St, Boise, ID 83701. Mailing address: PO Box 413, Boise, ID 83701. **208-342-6621**
Bureau Manager and State News Editor. R Richard Charnock, Jr

BOSTON, MA (BH). 20 Ashburton Pl, Massachusetts Teachers Association Bldg, Boston, MA 02108. **800-225-6210** or **617-227-4000.** Telex: **94-6245**
General News Editor. Donald A Davis
NewsCenter Editor. Ronald W Reichmann
Bureau Manager and State News Editor. Warren Talbot
New England Broadcast News Editor. Ronald W Reichmann

General Sports Editor. Gilbert H Peters
Newspictures (BHP). **617-227-4000** or **617-523-1587**
General Editor. David Wurzel

BUFFALO, NY (BF). Buffalo Evening News Bldg, 1 News Plz, Washington and Scott Sts, Buffalo, NY 14240. **716-852-2085**
Bureau Manager. Herbert Y Weber

CARSON CITY, NV (CC). State Capitol Bldg, Carson City, NV 89701. **702-882-7629**
Bureau Manager. Robert E Ryan

CHARLESTON, WV (CW). 401 Nelson Bldg, Kanawha Blvd and Broad St, Charleston, WV 25330. Mailing address: PO Box 2946, Charleston, WV 25330. **304-343-7560**
Bureau Manager and State News Editor. William A Shearer

CHARLOTTE, NC (CT). Rm 1203, 12th Floor, Bank of North Carolina Bldg, 112 S Tryon St, Charlotte, NC 28284. **704-334-4691**
Bureau Manager. Jerry L Mitchell

CHEYENNE, WY (TM) Eagle Tribune Bldg, 110 E 17th St, Cheyenne, WY 82001. **307-634-2850**
Bureau Manager. Richard Olive

CHICAGO, IL (HX). 360 N Michigan Ave, Chicago, IL 60601. **312-781-1600**
General News Editor. Don Reed
NewsCenter Editor. James R Quinn
General News Executive. Ian Westergren
Chicago News Editor. David Smothers
Bureau Manager and State News Editor. Robert Kieckhefer
Night Manager. Everett R Irwin
General Sports Editor. Edward P Sainsbury
General Communications Manager. W F Kimbrough
General Communications Chief. Charles Ziegler
Newspictures (HXP). **312-332-7472** or **7473**
General Editor. Remo G Macchini
Bureau Manager. Bruno Torres
Regional Chief Telephoto Engineer. Jack C Harenberg
Commercial Photography Department Manager, Midwest Region. Louis G Tepke. **312-346-1922**
Broadcast Services (HXR)
Vice-President. William B Ketter. **212-682-0231**
National Broadcast Department Editor. Bill G Ferguson

Associate News Director, Production. Thomas L McGann

Associate News Director, Operations. John I Pelletreau

Executive Editor, Broadcast Services. Robert S Huntley

News Editors. Barbara May Hillebrand, Robert S Huntley, James Pecora

Cable Television Editor. Robert Gately

Broadcast Sports Editor. Walter W Martin

Broadcast Feature Editor. Weber F Trout

CINCINNATI, OH (PO). Post and Times-Star Bldg, 800 Broadway, Cincinnati, OH 45202. **513-721-0345**

Bureau Manager. Frederick W Van Sant

CLEVELAND, OH (SM). Press Bldg, Press Plz, Cleveland, OH 44114. **216-771-3455**

Bureau Manager. J Robert Penick

Newspictures (SMP). 216-771-3455

Bureau Manager. Ronald F Kuntz

COLUMBIA, SC (CA). Suite 201, Columbia Bldg, Columbia, SC 29201. **803-254-2738.** Mailing address: PO Box 11298, Columbia, SC 29211

Bureau Manager. Fred McNesse

Newspictures (CAP). 803-254-2738

Bureau Manager. John E (Jack) Young

COLUMBUS, OH (CZ). Suite 1801, Le Veque-Lincoln Tower, 50 W Broad St, Columbus, OH 43215. **614-221-4291**

News Editor for Ohio and Kentucky. Edward V Di Pietro

Bureau Manager. John T Kady

Night Manager. Mason V Blosser

Newspictures (CZP). 614-221-4291 or **614-224-7940**

Bureau Manager. Terry C Bochatey

CONCORD, NH (HM). 88 N Main St, Concord, NH 03301. Mailing address: PO Box 27, Concord, NH 03301. **603-224-2351**

Bureau Manager and State News Editor. Brenda Warner Rotzell

DALLAS, TX (DA). Suite 901, 8585 N Stemmons Fwy, Dallas, TX 75247. **214-630-3560.** *Telex*: **73-2371**

General News Editor. Bruce B Bakke. **214-630-3566**

NewsCenter Editor. Judson J Dixon

Bureau Manager and State News Editor. Edward Fulton

General Sports Editor. Mike Rabun

General Communications Manager. James T Tolbert. **214-630-0688**

Office Manager. Margaret A Boatright

Newspictures (DAP). 214-630-1730

General Editor. Craig L Mailloux

Regional Chief Telephoto Engineer. Max Van Duser

Commercial Photography Department. 214-630-0049

Manager, Longhorn Region. Jack Klinge

DENVER, CO (DX). Suite 220, 3665 E Dakota, Denver, CO 80209. **303-321-2234**

Bureau Manager and State News Editor. Peter M Kelly

Newspictures (DXP). Mailing address: 3665 E Dakota, Denver, CO 80209. **303-321-4307.** Engineering: **303-321-4306**

Bureau Manager. Joseph C Marquette

DES MOINES, IA (NW). Securities Bldg, 418 7th St, Des Moines, IA 50309

Bureau Manager and State News Editor. William C Hoop

Newspictures (NWP). 515-244-5185

Bureau Manager. Thomas C Peterson

DETROIT, MI (DU). Rm 945, Free Press Bldg, 321 W Lafayette Blvd, Detroit, MI 48226. **313-965-7950** or **800-572-7680**

Bureau Manager and State News Editor. Paul W Varian

Newspictures (DUP). 313-961-9561

Bureau Manager. Daniel Dmitruk

FRANKFORT, KY (FY). Frankfort State Journal Bldg, 321 W Main St, Frankfort, KY 40601. **502-223-8286**

Bureau Manager and State News Editor. Randy Minkoff

FRESNO, CA (FZ). Fresno Bee Bldg, 1626 E St, Fresno, CA 93786. **209-237-7469**

Bureau Manager. William P Coleman

GRAND RAPIDS, MI (HP). Waters Bldg, Grand Rapids, MI 49502. Mailing address: PO Box 2162, Grand Rapids, MI 49501. **616-459-5519**

Bureau Manager. Jeffrey L Sheler

HARRISBURG, PA (HG). Rm 810, Payne-Shoemaker Bldg, 240 N 3rd St, Harrisburg, PA 17101. **717-234-4189**

Bureau Manager. David A Milne

Newspictures (HGP). 717-238-1993

Bureau Manager. Susan Klemens

Hartford, CT (HF). 770 Asylum Ave, Hartford, CT 06105. **203-249-5659**

Bureau Manager and State News Editor. James V Healion

Newspictures (HFP). 203-249-5659

Bureau Manager. Frank Lorenzo

HELENA, MT (HN). 2021 11th Ave, Helena, MT 59601. Mailing address: PO Box 1141, Helena, MT 59601. **406-442-6470**

Bureau Manager and State News Editor. A F ("Bud") Iwen

HONOLULU, HI (HONO). News Bldg, 605 Kapiolani Blvd, Honolulu, HI 96813. Mailing address: PO Box 3110, Honolulu, HI 96813. **808-533-1828.** Direct line: **808-537-2977,** Ext 210. *Cable*: **UNIPRESS HONOLULU.** *Telex*: RCA, **723-395**

Bureau Manager and State News Editor. Robert C Miller

HOUSTON, TX (HS). Suite 952, Houston Chronicle Bldg, 801 Texas Ave, Houston, TX 77002. Main numbers: **713-227-2171** or **0036.** Day: **713-220-7788.** Night after 6 pm, CST: **713-621-7000,** Ext 455. *Astrodome press box.* **713-747-2432.** *Spaceflight office* (during manned spaceflights only). **713-488-5214**

Bureau Manager. James L Overton

Newspictures (HSP). Suite 820, Houston Chronicle Bldg, Houston, TX 77002. **713-223-0500**

Bureau Manager. Walter L Frerck

INDIANAPOLIS, IN (IA). 113 N Capitol Ave, Indianapolis, IN 46204. **317-634-6592**

Bureau Manager and State News Editor. Duston Harvey

Assistant Bureau Manager. Kurt Freudenthal

Newspictures (IAP). Star-News Bldg, 307 N Pennsylvania St, Indianapolis, IN 46206 . **317-631-8931.** Telephoto engineering line: **317-368-5835**

Bureau Manager. James H Schweiker

JACKSON, MS (JK). Rm 603, Bankers Trust Plaza Bldg, 112 Congress St, Jackson, MS 39205. Mailing address: PO Box 1124, Jackson, MS 39205. **601-353-2907**

Bureau Manager and State News Editor. Andrew J Reese, Jr.

Newspictures (JKP)

Bureau Manager. William C Womack

JACKSONVILLE, FL (JX). Times Union and Journal Bldg, 1 Riverside Dr, Jacksonville, FL 32202. **904-356-2877**

Bureau Manager. J Paul Wyatt

JEFFERSON CITY, MO (JC). Rm 200, State Capitol, Jefferson City, MO. Mailing address: PO Box 1, Jefferson City, MO 65102. **314-636-6921**

Bureau Manager. Andrew A Yemma

KANSAS CITY, MO (KP). 220 W 11th St, Kansas City, MO 64105. **816-471-2070**
Bureau Manager and State News Editor. James F Wieck
Newspictures (KPP)
Bureau Manager. Jose M More

KNOXVILLE, TN (KI). News-Sentinel Bldg, Knoxville, TN 37902. **615-525-3162**
Bureau Manager. Carl Vines, Jr

LANSING, MI (NS). Senate Press Room, State Capitol Bldg, Lansing, MI 48904. **517-482-1923.** Mailing address: PO Box 15055, Lansing, MI 48904
Bureau Manager. Joanna Firestone
Newspictures (NSP). UPI, 1510 Bank of Lansing Bldg, 101 Washington Sq, Lansing, MI 48933. **517-482-7793**
Bureau Manager. Edward A Persons

LAS VEGAS, NV (LV). Las Vegas Sun Bldg, 121 S Highland Ave, Las Vegas, NV. Mailing address: PO Box 1088, Las Vegas, NV 89101. **702-384-4915**
Bureau Manager. Myram Borders

LINCOLN, NE (SR). Journal Bldg, Lincoln, NE 68501. Mailing address: PO Box 80696, Lincoln, NE 68501. **402-432-0381**
Bureau Manager and State News Editor. Earl F Flowers

LITTLE ROCK, AR (CK). Rm 302, Gazette Bldg, Little Rock, AR 72201. **501-375-5559**
Bureau Manager and State News Editor. Robert D Carey

LOS ANGELES, CA (HC). Suite 808, Civic Center Law Bldg, 205 S Broadway, Los Angeles, CA 90012. Mailing address: PO Box 2231, Main Office Station, Los Angeles, CA 90053. **213-620-1230.** *Telex*: 67-7131
Bureau Manager. John D Lowry
Night Manager. Stewart Slavin
Overnight Manager. Terrance McGarry
Senior Editor. Vernon Scott
Newspictures (HCP). Rm 438, 1543 W Olympic Blvd, Los Angeles, CA 90015. **213-387-7221** or **9088**
Bureau Manager. Carlos A Schiebeck
Commercial Photography Department. 1265 S Cochran Ave, Los Angeles, CA 90019. **213-933-5741**
Pacific Manager. Ed Yotka

LOUISVILLE, KY (SV). WKLO Radio Station, 307 W Walnut St, Louisville, KY. Mailing address: PO Box 537, Louisville, KY 40201. **502-587-1217**
Bureau Manager. Robert T Weston

LUBBOCK, TX (LU). Avalanche-Journal Bldg, 8th St and Ave J, Lubbock, TX. Mailing address: PO Box 491, Lubbock, TX 79408. **806-765-8289**
Bureau Manager. Robert M Patterson

MADISON, WI (MD). 1901 Fish Hatchery Rd, Madison, WI 53713. **608-255-6779** or **6770.** *State capital subbureau (MDC).* **608-266-7599**
Bureau Manager and State News Editor. Gene W Hintz

MARION, IL (LE). Republican Bldg, Marion, IL 62959. **618-993-5796**
Bureau Manager. Samuel O Hancock

MEMPHIS, TN (MP). Commercial Appeal and Press-Scimitar Bldg, Memphis, TN 38101. **901-525-0611** or **0612**
Bureau Manager. Susan White

MIAMI, FL (MH). Miami Herald Bldg, 1 Herald Plz, Miami, FL 33132. **305-373-7685**
Bureau Manager and State News Editor. Stanley Brown
Newspictures (MHP). **305-358-8860**
Bureau Manager. Douglas L Roberts

MILWAUKEE, WI (UC). Rm 214, 918 N 4th St, Milwaukee, WI 53203. **414-271-6588**
Bureau Manager. Lance J Herdegen
Newspictures (UCP). **414-271-5334**
Bureau Manager. Ralph G Schauer

MINNEAPOLIS, MN (MS). 416 Portland Ave, Minneapolis, MN 55415. **612-338-7547**
Bureau Manager. Richard McFarland
State News Editor. Arnold Dibble
Newspictures (MSP). **612-338-7547**
Bureau Manager. James Hubbard

MONTGOMERY, AL (MG). Suite 1E, 304 Dexter Ave, Montgomery, AL 36102. Mailing address: PO Box 1306, Montgomery, AL 36102. **205-262-1951** or **1952.** Capitol phone: **205-263-0671**
Bureau Manager. Bessie Ford

MONTPELIER, VT (VT). Lower Arcade, Tavern Motor Inn, 100 State St, Montpelier, VT 05602. Mailing address: PO Box 611, Montpelier, VT 05602. **802-223-7201**
Bureau Manager and State News Editor. William H Poole

NASHVILLE, TN (NV). Banner-Tennessean Bldg, 1100 Braodway, Nashville, TN 37202. Mailing address: PO Box 942, Nashville, TN 37202. **615-242-7348** or **7349**
Bureau Manager and State News Editor. Duren Cheek

Newspictures (NVP). **615-242-6250**
Bureau Manager. Samuel W Parrish

NEWARK, NJ (NK). Press Room, Federal Courthouse, Main Post Office Bldg, Federal Sq, Newark, NJ. Mailing address: PO Box 739, Main Post Office, Newark, NJ 07101. **201-643-1887**
Bureau Manager. Judith Hasson

NEW ORLEANS, LA (NE). Suite 811, 1440 Canal St, New Orleans, LA 70112. **504-581-6371**
Bureau Manager and State News Editor. Joseph A Reaves
Newspictures (NEP). 520 Royal St, New Orleans, LA 70130. **504-581-4042**
Bureau Manager. Patrick Benic

NEW YORK, NY (NX). 220 E 42nd St, New York, NY 10017. **212-682-0400.** *Telex*: ITT, **420546** or **420548**; RCA, **224369**; WUI, **620444**; WU, **14-7203**
Chairman Emeritus, of the Board. Frank H Bartholomew. **415-626-6313.** *Cable*: **UNIBART NEW YORK**
President and Chief Executive Officer. Roderick W Beaton. **212-682-0419**
Senior Vice-President. Frank Tremaine
Vice President, Comptroller, and Secretary. A P Bock. **212-682-1816**
Vice President, Systems Development. James F Darr. **212-682-0174**
Vice President, Broadcast Services. William B Ketter. **212-682-0231**
Vice President, Newspictures. F W Lyon. **212-682-0173**
Vice President, General Manager, and Super-intendent of Bureau Operations. Robert E Page. **212-682-2084**
Vice President and Editor-in-Chief. H L Stevenson. **212-682-5493**
Vice President, Marketing. H Calvin Thornton. **212-682-0749**

Administrative Assistant to President. Norman A Cafarell

News Department
Managing Editor. Paul G Eberhart
Assistant Managing Editor. Donald P Myers
Assistant Managing Editor/Administration. William R Barrett
Assistant Managing Editor/Enterprise. Frederick Winship
International Editor. Kenneth Braddick
Business Editor. Dorothea Brooks
Manager/Unistrox Services. S Richard Brown
Executive Sports Editor. Joseph Carnicelli
General News Editor. Lucien Carr
Overnight Cables Editor. Janet Cawley
Lively Arts Editor. Glenne Currie

International Services Editor. Donald Dillon

Latin American Department Editor. Enrique Durand

World Horizons Editor. Fred T Ferguson

General News Editor. John G Griffin

Night Cables Editor. Wilborn R Hampton

Television Writer. Joan Hanauer

General News Editor. Bartholomew M Kinch

General News Editor/Enterprise. William D Laffler

Food and Family Living Editor. Jeanne Lesem

Foreign Editor. Walter Logan

Day Cables Editor. John Martinco

Office Manager for New York Newsservices. Paul McNeece

General News Editor. Bobby Ray Miller

UN Bureau Manager. Bruce W Munn

Life Style Editor. Lillian O'Connell

Senior Editor. Gay Pauley

Senior Editor. H D ("Doc") Quigg

Sports Editor. Milton S Richman

Newspictures (NXP). 212-682-0400, 0471, 6329 or **1353.** *Cables:* **PIXUNIT NEW YORK**

Vice President, Newspictures. F W Lyon. **212-682-0173**

Executive Picture Editor. Edward T Majeski

Managing Editor. Larry De Santis

Foreign Newspictures Editor. Robert Schnitzlein

Newspictures Editors. Salvatore J Acerra, William M Hudson, Leo J Stoecker

New York Chief Day Telephoto Engineer. Wilfred J Brazeau

Newspicture Editor. Walter Ehlers

Manager of Library Sales. Daniel J Gallagher

Chief Photographer. Harry Leder

Business Manager. G P Panarotto

Director of Library Sales and Services. Al Whalen

Newspictures Engineering Laboratory. 48 Essex St, Hackensack, NJ 07601. Mailing address: PO Box 2347, South Hackensack, NJ 07606. **201-343-7331**

Director of Engineering. Jerome J Callahan

Director of Facsimile Development. Dewey Frezzolini

Broadcast Services. Audio, New York, receiving: **212-867-3995.** Audio, Chicago, receiving: **312-467-5055**

Vice-President, Broadcast Services. William B Ketter

Editor, National Radio. Bill G Ferguson

Program Director and New York Audio Bureau Manager. Frank Sciortino

Coordinator, Broadcast Services. Stan Sabik

Chief Engineer. William E Wilson

News Editor. Art McAloon

Communications Department

Vice-President, Systems Development. James F Darr

Communications Manager. Ernest F Price

International Telecommunications Chief. Ted R Brady

Superintendent of Telecommunications Systems. Frank Duzenski

Superintendent of Telegraph Production and Personnel. Reynold A DiCuia

Supervisor, Communications Operations. Breck Slossman

Marketing

Vice-President, Marketing. Calvin H Thornton. **212-682-0749**

Director, North American Sales, and General Manager, Marketing Administration. James P Buckner. **212-682-0422**

General Executive for Special Projects. Travis M Hughs

General Manager, International Features. George H Pipal

Sales Executive, Computer Services. C Robert Woodsum

Promotion and Public Relations Manager. Kenneth Smith

Director, Commercial Photography Department. Roy Mehlman

Editor, International Film and Television Features Service. David L Dugas

Film Sales Manager. Thomas Hawley

Account Executive for Marketing. John Nagel

Marketing Administration

General Manager, Marketing Administration and Director, North American Sales. James P Buckner **212-682-0422**

General Administrative Supervisor. Chris Tortosa

Administrative Supervisor. Robert J Ricca

Administrative Supervisor, Communications. Alexander Baker

Manager, Customer Relations and Communication and Credit Departments. Stephen P Warga

Systems Manager. William E O'Brien, Jr

Office of the Comptroller and Secretary

Vice-President, Comptroller, and Secretary A P Bock **212-682-1816**

Assistant Comptroller. Fred J Greene

Accounting Department

Chief Accountant and Assistant Treasurer. Arthur C Becker

Assistant Secretary and Office Manager, Accounting and Credit Departments. Joseph F Frigenti

Chief Auditor, International Department. Charles J Dolansky

Chief Accountant, UFS and UPITN. Roy A Kimmett

Credit Department

Credit Manager. William E O'Brien

Personnel Relations

Director, Personnel Relations. Dale M Johns. **212-682-1598**

Assistant Director, Personnel Relations. Albert E Kaff

Assistant Director, Personnel Administration. Robert J Sinclair

Manager, Personnel Recruiting. Miriam S Shakter

Manager, Pension and Contract Administration. Raymond P Ayres

Office Manager, Personnel Department. Claudia Diaz

Automated Data Processing

Vice-President, Automated Data Processing. Michael Williams. **212-986-2766**

Manager of Advanced Systems. Andrew J Fedich

Manager of News Systems. John Astranis

Manager of Operations. Stephen M Budd

Chief Programmer, News Systems. John M Connors

Chief Programmer, News Systems. Michael Howell

Manager of Commercial Systems. John S McDonnell

Manager of Computer Communications. Leonard B Murray, Jr

Manager of Financial (Stocks) Systems. Stewark Skolnick

Office of the Superintendent of Bureaus

Vice-President and Superintendent of Bureau Operations. Robert E Page. **212-682-2084**

Assistant Superintendent of Bureau Operations. Deborah L Nolan

Purchasing

Purchasing Manager. Marjorie Sbano

Mailroom

Manager, Mailroom Services. George Muldowney

Cable Television Services

General Sales Executive. Roy Mehlman

UPITN Corporation (NXT). 321 W 44th St, New York, NY 10036. **212-682-0400,** Ext 481-5. Direct line: **212-246-1957.** *Telex:* **223059**

Bureau Manager. Roy Berke

Chief Librarian. Vincent O'Reilly

New York-New Jersey News Editor. Richard A Hughes

New York City Editor. Scott Latham

OKLAHOMA CITY, OK (KO). 3601 N Lincoln Blvd, Oklahoma City, OK 73105. **405-524-3344**

Bureau Manager and State News Editor. James R Campbell

OLYMPIA, WA (YM). Rm 104, Insurance Bldg, Capitol Campus, Olympia, WA. Mailing address: PO Box 1697, Olympia, WA 98507. **206-753-6534**

Bureau Manager. Gordon Schultz

OMAHA, NE (WH). World Herald Bldg, Omaha, NE 68101. Mailing address: PO Box 1336, Omaha, NE 68101. **402-346-6868**

Bureau Manager. Jonathan Sweet

ORLANDO, FL (OR). Suite 12, 501 N Magnolia Ave, Orlando, FL 32801. **305-422-8051**

Bureau Manager. Douglas C Monroe

PHILADELPHIA, PA (NA). 6 Penn Center Plz, Philadelphia, PA 19103. **215-567-1373**

Bureau Manager. Edward J McFall

Newspictures (NAP). 215-563-8076

Bureau Manager. Michael Feldman

Commercial Photography Department. 215-567-1373

Regional Manager. Robert McCann

PHOENIX, AZ (IX). 20 E Jefferson, Phoenix, AZ 85004. Mailing address: PO Box 4066, Commerce Station, Phoenix, AZ 85030. **602-252-5641**

Bureau Manager and State New Editor. Herbert F Surrett

PIERRE, SD (PR). Rm 427, State Capital, Pierre, SD 57501. Mailing address: PO Box 459, Pierre, SD 57501. **605-224-8843** or **8844**

Bureau Manager. J Patrick Little

PITTSBURGH, PA (PS). 13th Floor, Manor Bldg, 564 Forbes Ave, Pittsburgh, PA 15219. **412-566-1011**

News Editor for Pennsylvania-West Virginia. Malcolm Hughes

Bureau Manager. John H Rutherford

General Communications Manager. G H Briggs

Newspictures (PSP). 412-566-1205

General Editor. James P Dever

Commercial Photography Department. 412-281-0848

Manager, Keystone Region. Warren B Dana

PORTLAND, OR (JO). Oregonian Bldg, 1320 SW Broadway, Portland, OR 97201. **503-226-2644**

Bureau Manager and State News Editor. B J (Bill) McFarland

Assistant Bureau Manager. Howard V Applegate

Newspictures (JOP). 503-226-2644

Bureau Manager. Max Gutierrez

PROVIDENCE, RI (RI). Rm 108A, State House, Providence, RI 02903. **401-351-5955**

Bureau Manager and State News Editor. Kenneth D Franckling

RALEIGH, NC (RA). 3rd Floor, News and Observer Bldg, 213 S McDowell St, Raleigh, NC 27601. **919-833-3685**

Bureau Manager and State News Editor. Glenn A Stephens

Newspictures (RAP). 213 S McDowell St, Raleigh, NC 27601. **919-833-3685**

Bureau Manager. William F Cranford, Jr

RENO, NV (MC). Nevada State Journal Bldg, Reno, NV 89503. **702-322-1142**

Bureau Manager and State News Editor. Russell R Nielsen

RICHMOND, VA (RV). Suite 507, Heritage Bldg, 1001 E Main St, Richmond, VA 23213. Mailing address: PO Box 1578, Richmond, VA 23213. **804-644-0701**

Bureau Manager and State News Editor. Robert P Lambert

Newspictures (RVP). 804-644-0701

Bureau Manager. A Mitchell Koppelman

ROCHESTER, NY (DV). WHAM, 350 E Ave, Rochester, NY 14604. **716-454-4444**

Bureau Manager. Michael R Franco

SACRAMENTO, CA (BC). Suite 1185, Park Executive Bldg, 925 L St, Sacramento, CA 95814. **916-443-5685**

Bureau Manager. Carl Ingram

Newspictures (BCP). 916-445-7755

Bureau Manager. Karl J Kramer

ST LOUIS, MO (X). Post Dispatch Bldg, 1133 Franklin Ave, St Louis, MO 63101. **314-241-5111** or **5112**

Bureau Manager. Donald Berns

Newspictures (XP). 314-241-0629. *Post Dispatch autofoto overhead line:* **314-621-1111,** Ext 542

Bureau Manager. Arthur F Phillips

ST PAUL, MN (WS). Rm 200, State Capital, St Paul, MN 55101. **612-296-6561**

Bureau Manager. William J Fox

SALEM, OR (GP). Rm 10, Capitol Bldg, Salem, OR 97310. **503-363-1918**

Bureau Manager. Robert Shepard

SALT LAKE CITY, UT (AG). 802 Tribune Bldg, 143 S Main St, Salt Lake City, UT 84110. Mailing address: PO Box 1375, Salt Lake City, UT 84110. **801-328-8866**

Bureau Manager and State News Editor. Peter Gillins

SAN ANTONIO, TX (AL). San Antonio Light Bldg, 420 Broadway, San Antonio, CA

78206. Mailing address: PO Box 2161, San Antonio, TX 78297. **512-222-1816**

Bureau Manager. Mack Sisk

SAN DIEGO, CA (KM). Union Tribune Bldg, 350 Camino de la Reina, San Diego, CA 92108. Mailing address: PO Box 191, San Diego, CA 92112. **714-299-3131,** Ext 1751

Bureau Manager. Clarence Zaitz

SAN FRANCISCO, CA (SX). Suite 1212, Grosvenor Plz, 9th and Market Sts, San Francisco, CA 94102. Mailing address: PO Box 4329, San Francisco, CA 94102. **415-626-6300.** *Cable:* **UNIPRESS SAN FRANCISCO.** *Telex:* RCA, **SER-207;** ITT, **470060;** WU, **34-0564**

General News Editor. Reeve L Hennion

NewsCenter Editor. Jeffrey L Field

Bureau Manager and State News Editor. Max Vanzi

General Sports Editor. Joseph P Sargis

Overnight Manager. Michael Hudson

General Communications Manager. William B Rector

Newspictures (SXP). 415-626-2500 or **6300**

General Editor. Raymond P Maroney

Bureau Manager. Jack Holper

Regional Chief Telephoto Engineer. James Cifelli

SANTA FE, NM (FR). Press Room, 3rd Floor, State Capitol, Santa Fe, NM 87501. Mailing address: PO Box 1798, Santa Fe, NM 87501. **505-983-3122**

Bureau Manager. E Michael Myers

SEATTLE, WA (AR). Post-Intelligencer Bldg, 6th and Wall Sts, Seattle, WA 98111. **206-622-2505**

Bureau Manager and State News Editor. Martin A Heerwald

SPOKANE, WA (SP). W 500 Boone Ave, Spokane, WA. Mailing address: PO Box 37, Spokane, WA 99210. **509-328-9483**

Bureau Manager. Gerald A McGinn

SPRINGFIELD, IL (GX). Ridgely Bldg, 500 E Monroe, Springfield, IL 62701. **217-525-2326.** Mailing address: UPI Box 238, Springfield, IL 62705. Capitol phones: **217-782-2157** (press room). **217-525-5458** (House). **217-525-5329** (Senate)

Bureau Manager. Thomas Lave

Newspictures (GXP). 217-525-2656

Bureau Manager. Michael Smeltzer

TALLAHASSEE, FL (TA). State Capitol, Tallahassee, FL 32304. Mailing address: PO Box 164, Tallahassee, FL 32302. **904-222-1317**

Bureau Manager. Barbara L Frye

Newspictures (TAP). 904-222-7404

Bureau Manager. Donald G Dughi

TAMPA, FL (TP). Tampa Tribune-Times Bldg, Tampa, FL. Mailing address: PO Box 191, Tampa, FL 33601. **813-228-8752**

Bureau Manager. Orval E Jackson

TOPEKA, KS (AC). Press Room, 135N Statehouse, Topeka, KS 66612. **913-233-8555**

Bureau Manager and State News Editor. John C Braden

TRENTON, NJ (TR). Trenton Times Bldg, 500 Perry St, Trenton, NJ. Mailing address: PO Box 710, Trenton, NJ 08604. **609-392-0700.** Also Statehouse Bldg, Trenton, NJ 08625. **609-292-5182.** Weekends and after 7 pm: **609-392-0700**

Bureau Manager and State News Editor. William M Coombe

Newspictures (TRP). Rm 124, Statehouse Bldg, Trenton, NJ 08625. **609-292-5182.** Overhead transmitting line: **609-292-4668**

Bureau Manager. Mitchell Toll

TUCSON, AZ (TC). 100 W Broadway, La Placita (42A), Tucson, AZ 85701. Mailing address: PO Box 2868, Tucson, AZ 85702. **602-623-6409**

Bureau Manager. Arthur J Lingle

TULSA, OK (TW). Suite 913, 324 Main Mall, Tulsa, OK 74103. **918-587-3788**

Bureau Manager. George W Boosey

WASHINGTON, DC (WA). Rm 315, National Press Bldg, 529 14th St NW, Washington, DC 20045. **202-393-3430**

Vice-President and Washington Manager. Grant Dillman. **202-393-8337**

International Department Editor. Henry Keys

Editor, Washington Capital News Service. John M Vogt

Senior Editor. Arnold B Sawislak

Senior Editor. Richard Growald

News Editor. Ronald E Cohen

Enterprise Editor. Robert M Andrews

Overnight Editor. Elizabeth A Wharton

Day Editor. David A Wiessler

General Communications Manager. James Hennessy

White House Bureau. 202-638-2760

Bureau Manager and White House Reporter. Helen Thomas

Audio (WAA). 202-393-3450

Bureau Manager. Denis Gulino

Newspictures (WAP). Rm 506, National Press Bldg, 529 14th St NW, Washington, DC 20045. **202-347-1124**

Bureau Manager. Hugo L Wessels

Editor. James Southerland

Regional Chief Telephoto Engineer. Alan Michaels

Middle Atlantic Region

News Editor, Delaware, Virginia, Maryland, and Washington, DC. Daniel C Riker

NewsCenter Editor. Joseph H Chapman

Caribbean Division

MEXICO, DF, MEXICO. Avenida Morelos 110, Despacho 1107, Mexico, DF, Mexico. Mailing address: Apartado Postal 91-Bis, Mexico 1, DF. Telephone: **905-546-9188, 9189, 1189,** or **5075.** Domestic photo lines: LD 94, **905-546-5076.** International photo line: LD 208, **905-546-5075.** Telex: **017-73957**

Manager, Mexico-Central America Division. John F Virtue

Division News Editor. Carol Cook

Night Editor. Stephen J Downer

PANAMA, REPUBLIC OF PANAMA. Correspondent. Tomas Cupas, Altos de Miraflores 4-H Panama. (h) **61-9613.** Mailing address: Apartado Postal 393, Panama 9A. Telex: WUI, **368772**

SAN JUAN, PR. 164 Avenida Ponce de Leon, Puerta de Tierra, PR 00901. Mailing address: Apartado 5315, Puerta de Tierra, San Juan, 00906. Telephone: **809-725-4460** or **4468.** Cable: UNIPRESS via ITT or RCA. Cable and Wireless: WUI, **3654262.** Telex: ITT, **385252**

Manager, Caribbean Division. Daniel Drosdoff

Division News Editor. Pieter Van Bennekom

Day Editor. Pedro Bonetti

SANTO DOMINGO, DOMINICAN REPUBLIC. All mail for Santo Domingo to be sent to:

Chief Correspondent for the Dominican Republic. Miguel Guerrero. Avenida Mexico Prolongacion 147, Santo Domingo. (h) **682-0202.** Telex: ITT, **3460001**

South America

ASUNCION, PARAGUAY. Presidente Franco 787, Asuncion, Paraguay. Telephone: **4-6661**

News Correspondent. German Chaves

BOGOTA, COLOMBIA. Carrera 5a, 16-14, Oficina 502, Bogota, Colombia. Mailing address: Apartado Aereo 3516, Bogota. Telephone: **41-5333** or **9974, 43-5854** or **7892.** Office. **81-1948.** Telephotos: **43-7892.** Telex: **044-892**

Manager, Colombia. Rafael Bermudez

News Editor. Hector Menoni

Night Editor. Henry Maldonado

BRASILIA DF, BRAZIL. Edificio Gilberto Salomao, Sala 813, Setor Comercial Sul (SCS), Brasilia DF. Telephone: **24-6413** or **4213**

Correspondent. Antonio Praxedes

BUENOS AIRES, ARGENTINA. Avenida Belgrano 271, 1092 Buenos Aires. Letters only: Casilla de Correo 796, Correo Central, 1000 Buenos Aires. Telephone: **34-5501** through **5506** (administration). **33-6706** or **34-5501** through **5505** (news). International photo line: **30-7479** or (night calls only) **34-5505.** Telex: ITT, RCA, and CYT: **350-1225**

Manager, Argentina, and Regional Executive (Peru, Bolivia, Uruguay, Chile, Paraguay). Alberto J Schazin

South American News Editor. Martin D McReynolds

CARACAS, VENEZUELA. Residencias Avilanes B Penthouse, Avilanes a Rio, Candelaria. Mailing address: Apartado 667, Caracas, Venezuela. Telephone: **51-34-19, 51-23-31,** or **51-22-31.** Telephotos: **51-34-19.** Telex: **22591**

Manager, Venezuela, and Regional Executive (Colombia, Ecuador, Guianas). Martin D Houseman

News Editor. Kim Fuad

GUYAQUIL, ECUADOR. Mailing address: c/o El Universo, Guayaquil, Ecuador. Telephone: **51-1530.** Cable: UNIPRESS

News Correspondent. Ricardo Polit

LA PAZ, BOLIVIA. Mailing address: Casilla 1219, La Paz, Bolivia. Telephone: **26-868** or **25-553.** Cable: UNIPRESS

News Correspondent. Alberto Zuazo Nathes

Newspictures and UPITN. Mailing address: Casilla 3202, La Paz, Bolivia. Telephone: **23-891.** Cable: FOTOCAPRI

Correspondent. Freddy Alborta

LIMA, PERU. Jiron Puno 271, Oficina 601, Lima, Peru. Mailing address: Casilla 1536, Lima, Peru. Telephone: **27-3537** or **4827** or **28-3481.** Telex: **20094**

Manager, Peru and Bolivia. Stephen Morrow

Assistant Bureau Manager. Hubert Cam

MARACAIBO, VENEZUELA. Edificio Panorama, Calle 96, No 3-55, Maracaibo, Zulia. Telephone: **25-117**

Correspondent. Jesus Anex Navas

MONTEVIDEO, URUGUAY. Avenida 18 de Julio 1224, 2 Piso, Montevideo. Telephone: **80-121** or **122**. *Telex*: **398-707**

Manager, Uruguay. Jorge Brinseki Hector Menoni

QUITO, ECUADOR

News and Pictures Correspondent. Jorge Ribadeneira. "El Comercio," PO Box 57. Telephone: **21-0151.** *Telex*: **393022246**

RIO DE JANEIRO, BRAZIL. Avenida Brasil 500-6° Andar, Rio de Janeiro. Mailing address: Caixa Postal 719-ZC 20000, Rio De Janeiro. Telephone: **254-2032, 2033,** or **2034.** *Telex*: **391-31453**

General Manager, Brazil. Luis Menezes

News Editor. Robert E Sullivan

SANTIAGO, CHILE. 9th Floor, Calle Nataniel 47, Santiago. Mailing address: Casilla 71-D, Santiago. Telephone: **6-0162, 6-0163,** or **8-4447.** *Telex*: **40570**

Chief Correspondent. Charles E Padilla

Night Editor. Roberto Mason

SAO PAULO, BRAZIL. Rua Major Quedinho 28, Sobre-loja, Sao Paulo. Mailing address: Caiza Postal 2280, Sao Paulo. Telephone: **256-1624, 1549** or **8313.** *Telex*: **391-21565**

Bureau Manager. Stanley H Lehman

Editor (Brazilian desk). Joao Stelzer

Editor (Brazilian desk) Mario Leite Fernandes

Europe, Middle East, and Africa

ABIDJAN, IVORY COAST. Contact Paris

ALGIERS, ALGERIA. Contact Paris

ATHENS, GREECE. Valaoritu 12, Athens 134. Telephone: **627242** or **637941.** *Cable*: **UNIPRESS ATHENS.** *Telex*: **215572**

Bureau Manager. John N Rigos

BEIRUT, LEBANON. Press Cooperative Bldg, Rue Hamra, Beirut. Mailing Address: PO Box 9180, Beirut. Telephone: **343015, 346204** or **349631.** *Cable*: **UNIPRESS BEIRUT.** *Telex*: **20724**

Bureau Manager. David Pearce

BELGRADE, YUGOSLAVIA. Generala Zdanova 19, 11000 Belgrade. Telephone: **342490.** *Telex*: **11250**

Bureau Manager. Doyle McManus

BONN, GERMANY. Heuss Allee 2-10, Pressehaus 1, 5300 Bonn. Telephone: **(02221) 221631.** *Telex*: **886-538**

Manager, Germany. Wellington Long

Correspondent. Joseph B Fleming

BRUSSELS, BELGIUM. (For European Division executive office see London.) 34 Rue de la Loi, Box 14, B-1040, Brussels. Telephone: **5138470** through **5138475.** *Cable*: **UNIPRESS BRUSSELS.** *Telex*: **26997** or **26998**

Editor, Europe, Middle East and Africa. Leon Daniel

European News Editor. Charles W Ridley

European Diplomatic Correspondent. Barry James

Chief Engineer. John Minting

Newspictures. Telephone: **5138476** through **5138479.** *Telex*: **26997** or **26998**

European Editor. Charles J McCarty

Brussels Editor. Leslie H Sintay

BUDAPEST, HUNGARY. Contact Vienna

CAIRO, EGYPT. 4 Sharia Eloui, Cairo. Mailing address: PO Box 872, Cairo. Telephone: **49300, 53106** or **972533.** *Cable*: **UNIPRESS CAIRO**

Bureau Manager. Maurice Guindi

COPENHAGEN, DENMARK. Contact Stockholm

DUBLIN, IRELAND. 18 Zion Rd, Rathgar, Dublin. Telephone: **970139**

Bureau Manager. Donal P O'Higgins

FRANKFURT/MAIN, GERMANY

Newspictures. Baselerstrasse 33-37, D-6000 Frankfurt/Main. Mailing address: D-6000, Frankfurt/Main 16, Postfach 766. Telephone: **(0611) 251276** or **(0611) 253912.** *Telex*: **(041) 21 46.** Editor for Germany. Dieter Hespe.

UPITN. Kaiserstrasse 16, D-6000 Frankfurt/Main 1. Telephone: **(0611) 293441** or **(0611) 293873.** *Telex*: **(041) 3981**

Vice-President. Gernot Anderle

GENEVA, SWITZERLAND. Rm 76, Palais des Nations, Geneva. Telephone: **341740, 340095,** or **346011,** Ext 3782. *Telex*: **22300.** *Cable*: **UNIPRESS GENEVA**

Staff Correspondent. John A Callcott

THE HAGUE, NETHERLANDS. Parkstraat 32, The Hague. Telephone: **460035.** *Cable*: **UNIPRESS HAGUE.** *Telex*: **32178**

Correspondent. Willem Vuur

HELSINKI, FINLAND. Ludviginkatu 3-5, Helsinki 13. Telephone: **605701** or **605643.** *Cable*: **UNIPRESS HELSINKI.** *Telex*: **12403**

ISTANBUL, TURKEY. Turk Haberler Ajansi, Basin Sarayi Kat-4, Cagaloglu, Istanbul. Telephone: **272906** or **285060.** *Cable*: **UNIPRESS ISTANBUL.** *Telex*: **22304**

Stringer Correspondent. Kadri Kayabal

JERUSALEM, ISRAEL. Apt 25, 3 Bar Kochba St, French Hill, Jerusalem. Telephone: **223463**

Correspondent. Allen Alter

JOHANNESBURG, SOUTH AFRICA. 129 Corlett Dr, Bramley, Johannesburg. Mailing address: PO Box 2385, Johannesburg. Telephone: **40-2018.** *Cable*: **UNIPRESS JOHANNESBURG.** *Telex*: **43-3142**

Regional Executive for Southern and East Africa and Johannesburg, and Bureau Manager. John Platter

KAMPALA, UGANDA. Contact Nairobi.

KINSHASHA, ZAIRE. Contact Brussels.

LAGOS, NIGERIA. Contact Brussels.

LENINGRAD, USSR

Bureau Manager. Emil R Sveilis (contact Moscow)

LISBON, PORTUGAL. 4th Floor, Praca da Alegria 58, Lisbon 2. Telephone: **324160** or **366627.** *Cable*: **UNIPRESS LISBOA.** *Telex*: **12524**

Bureau Manager. Nathan C Gibson

LONDON, ENGLAND. (For European Divison news, newspictures, and communications center, see Brussels.) 8 Bouverie St, London EC4Y 8BB. News telephone: **353-2282** or **2284.** Administration: **353-5832** or **5833.** Accounts: **353-8143** or **8144.** *Telex*: **28829**

Vice President and General Manager, Europe, Middle East, and Africa. Julius B Humi

Business Manager, Europe, Middle East, and Africa. Eugene Blabey

Financial Controller and Auditor, Europe, Middle East, and Africa. Charles S Curmi

Syndicated Features Manager. Elsie Aspman

Bureau Manager. Michael Keats

Senior Editor. Robert S Musel

Chief European Correspondent. Joseph W Grigg

Division Sports Editor. Alex Frere

Newspictures. 8 Bouverie St, London EC4Y 8BB. Telephone: **353-3671** or **3672**. *Cable*: **UNIPIX LONDON**. *Telex*: **28829**

Sales Executive. Reginald J Spencer

Bureau Manager. Gary Bartlett

Audio. Telephone: **353-0526, 1787,** or **1788.** *Telex*: **28829**

European Audio Manager. Edwin Smith

UPITN. ITN House, 48 Wells St, London W1. Telephone: **637-2424**. *Cable*: **UNITELLY LONDON**. *Telex*: **23915**

President. C E ("Dusty") Rhodes

Vice-President and General Manager. Kenneth A Coyte

Managing Editor. A Trevor Jones

News Editor. Derek Langsdon

Manager, Special Services. Eric C Jessup

MADRID, SPAIN. Plaza de las Cortes 3, Madrid 14. Telephone: **221-9532** or **9533, 232-1278** or **4861.** Mailing address: Apartado de Correos 993, Madrid. *Cable*: **UNIPRESS MADRID.** *Telex*: **27757**

Bureau Chief and Chief Correspondent for Iberia. Peter Uebersax

NEWSPICTURES. 221-9532 or **9533.** *Telex*: **27757**

Editor for Spain. John C Anderson

MALTA. Contact Brussels

MONROVIA, LIBERIA. Contact Brussels

MOSCOW, USSR. Apt 67-68, Kutuzovsky Prospekt 7/4, Moscow. Telephone: **243-1170** or **6829.** Audio: **243-1182.** *Cable*: **UNIPRESS MOSCOW.** *Telex*: **A/B 7424 UNIPRS SU**

Bureau Manager. Joseph Galloway

NAIROBI, KENYA. Nation House, Tom Mboya St, Nairobi. Mailing address: PO Box 42249, Nairobi. Telephone: **24548** or **27691.** *Cable*: **UNIPRESS NAIROBI.** *Telex*: **22239**

Bureau Manager. Raymond P Wilkinson

NICOSIA, CYPRUS. Contact Brussels

OSLO, NORWAY. Contact Stockholm

OUAGADOUGOU, UPPER VOLTA. Contact Paris

PARIS, FRANCE. 2 Rue des Italiens, Paris 75009. Telephones: **770-91-70** (news). **770-15-18** (photos). **770-20-41** (technical service). *Telex*: **650 547.** *Cable*: **UNIPRESS PARIS**

Bureau Manager. Arthur L Higbee

Business Manager. Albert Fontan

Feature Sales. Robert Ahier

Newspictures. Telephone: **770-1518.** *Cable*: **UNIPIX PARIS.** *Telex*: **65547**

Editor for France. Louis Garcia

UPITN. Telephone: **824-61-76**: *Cable*: **UNIPRESS PARIS.** *Telex*: **65547**

Manager. Henri Brzoska

PRAGUE, CZECHOSLOVAKIA. Contact Vienna

RABAT, MOROCCO. Contact Paris

ROME, ITALY. Via Della Dataria 94, Rome 00187. **679-5747** or **4463.** *Cable*: **UNIPRESS ROME**: *Telex*: **61046**

Bureau Manager. Jack R Payton, Jr

Feature Sales. Massimo Ascani

Newspictures. Telephone: **679-3525.** *Cable*: **UNIPIX ROME.** *Telex*: **61046**

Editor for Italy. Enzo I Brizzi

UPITN. Telephone: **679-5747.** *Cable*: **UNIPRESS ROME.** *Telex*: **61046**

Manager. Orazio Nocco

SALISBURY, RHODESIA. Contact Johannesburg

SOFIA, BULGARIA. Contact Vienna.

STOCKHOLM, SWEDEN. Master Samuelsgatan 44, S-111 84 Stockholm. Telephone: **208290, 208830,** or **208850.** *Cable*: **UNIPRESS STOCKHOLM.** *Telex*: **19130**

Bureau Manager. Philip M Stone

TEHERAN, IRAN. 15 Iranyad Ave, Maelk St, Old Sherman Rd, Teheran 15. Telephone: **821670.** *Telex*: **21-3303**

Bureau Manager. Sadji Rizvi

TEL AVIV, ISRAEL. 138 Petah Tikva Rd, Tel Aviv. Mailing address: PO Box 16176, Tel Aviv. Telephone: **297287** or **297288.** *Telex*: **33587**

Bureau Manager. Richard C Gross

TRIPOLI, LIBYA. Contact Rome.

TUNIS, TUNISIA. Contact Paris.

VIENNA, AUSTRIA. Opernringhof 1/E/620, A-1010 Vienna. Telephone: **573646, 573647,** or **573648.** *Cable*: **UNIPRESS VIENNA.** *Telex*: **1-1662** or **1-3497**

Bureau Manager. Terrence J Andrew

Newspictures. Telephone: **561150**

WARSAW, POLAND. Rm 306, Piekna St 68, Warsaw. Telephone: **216795.** *Telex*: **813417**

Correspondent. Boguslaw Turek

Asia

BANGKOK, THAILAND. 2nd Floor, U Chuliang Bldg, 986 Rama 4 Rd, Bangkok. Mailing address: GPO Box 608, Bangkok. Telephone: **234-9753, 9902,** or **8802.** *Cable*: **UNIPRESS BANGKOK**

Correspondent. Alan Dawson

Business Manager. Khauv Bun Kheana

HONG KONG AND MACAO. (Direct all inquiries for Macao to the Hong Kong Bureau.) 1260 New Mercury House, 22 Fenwick St, Hong Kong. Mailing address: GPO Box 15692, Hong Kong. Telephone: **273221.** *Telex*: **HX 3418**

Vice-President and General Manager, Asia. Frank W Beatty

General Asian News Editor. Leon Daniel

General Asian Newspictures Editor. Philip K Elliott

Senior Editor. Charles R Smith

Deputy News Editor for Asia. Bert W Okuley

Comptroller, Asia. Lemmy Pinna

UPITN Manager, Asia. Nick Quinn

Business Manager. David Young

JAKARTA, INDONESIA. Jalan Cilacap 6, Jakarta Pusat, Indonesia. *Cable*: **UNIPRESS JAKARTA**

Correspondent. Hari Hartojo

KARACHI, PAKISTAN. *Cable*: **UNIPRESS KARACHI**

Correspondent. Asrar Ahmed

KATMANDU, NEPAL. PO Box 802, Katmandu. *Cable*: **UNIPRESS KATMANDU**

Stringer Correspondent. Bhola Bikrum Rana. **15-684**

KUALA LUMPUR, MALAYSIA. 95 Jalan Travers, Brickfields, Kuala Lumpur. Telephone: **24646**

Correspondent. Wee Sin Chuan

MANILA, PHILIPPINES. 4th Floor, Globe-Mackay ITT Bldg, 669 United Nations Ave, Ermita, Manila. Mailing address: PO Box 374, Manila. Telephone: **50-10-08, 10-22, 28-20,** or **28-48.** *Cable*: **UNIPRESS MANILA.** *Telex*: **ITT, 7420206; RCA, 7222272**

Correspondent. Vicente Maliwanag

Business Manager. Lino Anupol

NEW DELHI, INDIA. Himalaya House 23, Kasturba Gandhi Marg, New Delhi 110001. Telephone: **40000.** *Cable:* **UNIPRESS NEW DELHI.** *Telex:* **ND 2374**

Manager, India, Pakistan, and Bangladesh. John F Needham

Business Manager. Ramesh C Pande

RANGOON, BURMA. *Cable:* **UNIPRESS RANGOON**

Stringer Correspondent. U Maung Chit Tun. 55 Kalagar St, Kemmendine, Rangoon. (h) **32849**

SEOUL, KOREA. Orient Press Bldg, 188 Chongjin-Dong, Jongro-Ku, Seoul. Mailing address: KPO Box 178. Telephone: **72-2941.** *Cable:* **UNIPRESS SEOUL.** *Telex:* **22605**

Correspondent. James Kim

SINGAPORE. Suite 69-B, Raffles Hotel, Beach Rd, Singapore 7. Telephone: **327836, 327837,** or **328041.** *Cable:* **UNIPRESS SINGAPORE**

Manager, Southeast Asia. Charles Bernard

Business Manager. Ong Beng Chuan

TAIPEI, TAIWAN. Central News Agency, 209 Sung Kiang Rd, Taipei. Telephone: **581-5364.** *Cable:* **UNIPRESS TAIPEI**

Correspondent. Shullen Shaw

TOKYO, JAPAN. Palaceside Bldg, 1-1-1 Hitotsubashi, Chiyoda-Ku, Tokyo. Mailing address: Central PO Box 665, Tokyo, 100-91. Telephone: **212-7911.** *Telex:* **TK 2364.** *Cable:* **UNIPRESS TOKYO**

Manager, North Asia. Frederick Marks Robert Crabbe

News Editor. Ted Shimizu

Business Manager. Robert H Tanji

Newspictures Editor, North Asia. Rikio Imajo

Tokyo Newspictures Editor. Toshiyuki Aizawa

Pacific

SYDNEY, AUSTRALIA. 1st Floor, News House, 2 Holt St, Sydney. Mailing address:

GPO Box 5336, Sydney 2001. Telephone: **212-3899.** *Cable:* **UNIPRESS SYDNEY.** *Telex:* **20578**

Manager, Australia and New Zealand. Brian Dewhurst

Newspictures Manager. Joe Hilgar

Canada

MONTREAL, QUE (MR). Suite 1475, 550 Sherbrooke St W, Montreal, Que. Telephone: **514-284-1035**

General Manager, Canada. Patrick Harden. **514-866-5113**

Executive Assistant, Sales and Administration. John Chartier

News Editor, Canada. Dale Morsch

Communications Manager. John McCaskill

Newspictures (MRP). Telephone: **514-284-1035**

Bureau Manager. Robert W Carroll

OTTAWA, ONT (OA). Suite 711, National Press Bldg, 150 Wellington St, Ottawa, Ont. Mailing address: Parliament Press Gallery, Ottawa KIA OA8. Telephone: **613-236-5715**

Bureau Manager. Claude Henault

Newspictures (OAP). Telephone: **613-233-1141.** 24-hour service: Pagette 39, **613-237-6160**

Bureau Manager. Rod C MacIvor

TORONTO, ONT (JN). Suite 50-51, 171 Yonge St, Toronto, Ont M5C 1X9. Telephone: **416-363-8834** or **8835**

Bureau Manager. Kenneth M Becker

Newspictures (JNP). Telephone: **416-363-8834**

Bureau Manager. Julien Le Bourdais

VANCOUVER, BC (SU). Pacific Press Bldg, 1465 W 7th Ave, Vancouver, BC 9. Telephone: **604-736-9423**

Bureau Manager. Ransome Holmes

OTHER WIRE SERVICES

AGENCE FRANCE-PRESSE. 50 Rockefeller Plz, New York, NY 10020. **212-757-6712**

CHICAGO DAILY NEWS/SUN-TIMES NEWS SERVICE. 401 Wabash St, Chicago, IL 60611. **312-321-2801**

CHRISTIAN SCIENCE MONITOR NEWS SERVICE. PO Box 4994, Des Moines, IA 50306. **515-284-8250**

DOW JONES NEWS SERVICE. 22 Cortland St, New York, NY 10007. **212-285-5182**

KNT NEWS WIRE (Knight-Ridder papers, *New York Daily News, Chicago Tribune*). 1195 National Press Bldg, Washington, DC 20045. **202-637-3642.** Dean H Schoelkopf, editor

LOS ANGELES TIMES/WASHINGTON POST NEWS SERVICE. Times Mirror Sq, Los Angeles, CA 90053. **213-625-2345**

NEWSPAPER ENTERPRISE ASSOCIATION. 230 Park Ave, New York, NY 10017. **212-679-3600**

NEW YORK TIMES NEWS SERVICE. 229 W 43rd St, New York, NY 10036. **212-556-7087**

NORTH AMERICAN NEWSPAPER ALLIANCE. 200 Park Ave, New York, NY 10017. Sidney Goldberg, executive editor. Sheldon Engelmayer, editor

REUTERS, LTD. 1700 Broadway, New York, NY 10019. **212-582-4030**

WIDE WORLD. 50 Rockefeller Plz, New York, NY 10020. **212-262-6300**

BROADCASTING NETWORKS

THE BIG THREE

American Broadcasting Companies, Inc

1330 Avenue of the Americas, New York, NY 10019. **212-581-7777**

Chairman of the Board and Chief Executive Officer. Leonard H Goldenson

President and Chief Operating Officer. Elton H Rule

President, ABC News. Roone Arledge

Public Relations—Corporate

New York. 212-581-7777

Vice-President, Public Relations. Ellis O Moore. Ext 7717. Responsible for the creation, direction, and supervision of public relations activities for all departments and divisions of the corporation

Manager, Administration and Business Affairs. Asa Hoff. Ext 8016. Responsible for public relations financial planning and control, personnel, facilities, and administration

Director, Public Relations Planning. Thomas Madden. Responsible for long-range, corporate public relations planning

Manager, Editorial Services. Roann Levinsohn. Ext 6955. Responsible for preparing special research and writing assignments pertaining to corporate and industry matters

Public Relations—Broadcasting

New York. 212-581-7777

Vice-President, Public Relations, Broadcasting. Richard J Connelly. Ext 6077. Responsible for all broadcasting public relations activities for ABC, which include the ABC Television and Radio divisions, ABC News, and ABC Sports

Director, Program Information. Tom Mackin. Ext 6214. Responsible for the direction of publicity for ABC television programming

Manager, Entertainment Publicity. David Horowitz. Ext 7842. Responsible for the initiation and supervision of publicity for all ABC entertainment programming and supervision of New York publicity staff

Director, Business Information, Broadcasting. Patricia Matson. Ext 8925. Responsible for development and placement of publicity with broadcasting, advertising, and other trade publications, as well as the business and advertising pages of the consumer press

Director, News Information. Steve Strassberg. Ext 8761. Responsible for publicity in all areas of ABC News

Manager, News Information. Ron Najman. Ext 6156. Responsible for press contact and public information for ABC News

Manager, Sports Information. Irv Brodsky. Ext 8198. Responsible for press contact and public information for ABC Sports

Manager, Newspaper Publicity. Charles Franke. Ext 7276. Responsible for contact with national television editors plus wire service and syndicated television writers

Manager, Magazine Publicity. Vic Ghidalia. Ext 7297. Responsible for publicity placement and contact with all general interest and specialty magazines

Manager, Audience Information. Dan Rustin. Ext 7231. Directs department responsible for analyzing and responding to communications from the television viewing public; responsible for ABC Speakers' Bureau, coordinating the appearance of ABC executives before community, industry, and educational groups

Awards Manager. Gene Matalene. Ext 7565. Prepares and coordinates submissions of awards presentations to national organizations that seek to recognize and honor excellence in fields of radio, television, graphic design and printing, and leisure activities

Supervisor, Broadcast Publicity. Ilene Berg. Ext 7276. Responsible for placement of ABC broadcast and leisure division personalities on television and radio outlets and for liaison with affiliate promotion managers; contacts television editors to arrange interviews

Supervisor, Service Division. Barbara Cronin. Ext 7126. Responsible for all public relations internal and external mailing lists and for press release files

Listings Editor. Cheryl Glick. Ext 8088. Responsible for preparation of all listings of ABC Television Network programs

Washington. 202-393-7700

Director, News Information. Mary Fifield. Ext 240. Responsible for publicity in all areas of ABC News and its placement with the Washington press

Los Angeles. 213-553-2000

Vice-President, Public Relations, Broadcasting, West Coast. Phil Kriegler. Ext 601. Responsible for all broadcast public relations originating in Los Angeles

Manager, Press Relations, West Coast. Joe Maggio. Ext 603. Responsible for television program publicity operations of ABC Press Relations, West Coast, including the movement of press information to New York, and supervision of all press contacts located in Los Angeles

Manager, Business Information, West Coast. Bob Wright. Ext 605. Responsible for trade and business publicity on behalf of ABC's broadcast operations and for support of business and trade press activity for the company's leisure operations, West Coast

Manager, Special Projects, West Coast. Jerry Hellard. Ext 676. Responsible for the development of all areas of publicity and public relations not directly related to print media for all divisions of the corporation

Supervisor, Special Projects, West Coast. (Ext 473). Assists manager, special projects, West Coast, in all publicity and public relations areas not directly related to print media

Public Relations—Leisure Activities

New York. 212-581-7777

Vice-President, Public Relations, Leisure Activities. William J Liss. Ext 6848. Responsible for all public relations activities of ABC leisure divisions, including ABC Records, Inc, ABC Record and Tape Sales Corp, ABC Entertainment Center, ABC Farm Publications, ABC Leisure Magazines, Word, Inc, ABC Scenic Attractions, and ABC Theatres

Manager, Public Relations, Leisure Activities. Carmen Anthony. Ext 5089. Responsible for writing all news and feature publicity material; assists in coordination of publicity efforts for leisure activities of ABC, Inc

Editor, Company Newsletter. Karen Hurley. Ext 6797. Responsible for all phases of the newsletter circulated to all ABC employees

Photography Department

New York. 212-581-7777

Director of Photography. Rick Giacalone. Ext 7236. Responsible for the creation and direction of photographic coverage of all broadcast and leisure activities of ABC, Inc, and the dissemination of photographs to affiliated stations and print and broadcast media

Manager, Still Photography. Deborah Pierce. Ext 6709. Responsible for the creation of photographic coverage of all broadcast and leisure activities of ABC, Inc, and for the editing, production, and dissemination of these photographs to affiliated stations and the print and broadcast media

Editor, Color Photographs. Ext 6719. Responsible for the editing and dissemination of color photographs to affiliated stations and to the print and broadcast media

Assistant Editor, Color Photographs. Vika Zahn. Ext 6710. Assists in the editing and dissemination of color photographs to affiliated stations and to the print and broadcast media

Editor, Black and White Photographs. Ext 8043. Responsible for the editing and dissemination of black and white photographs to affiliated stations and to the print and broadcast media

Research Editor. Gloria Nappi. Ext 8046. Responsible for liaison between the ABC photographic group and affiliated stations, clients, and corporate divisions of the broadcast and leisure divisions

Staff Photographer. Steve Fenn. Ext 8043. Responsible for the creation of photographic coverage of all East Coast broadcast and leisure activities of ABC, Inc

Los Angeles. 213-553-2000

Manager of Photographic Operations, West Coast. Hal Garb. Ext 607. Responsible for the creation of photographic coverage of West Coast broadcast and leisure activities of ABC, Inc, and for dissemination to the print and broadcast media

Supervisor, Photographic Operations, West Coast. Bill Kobrin. Ext 691. Responsible for the supervision of photographic coverage of West Coast broadcast and leisure activities of ABC, Inc

Staff Photographer. Jim Britt. Ext 629. Responsible for the creation of photographic coverage of all West Coast broadcast and leisure activities of ABC, Inc

CBS, Inc

51 W 52 St, New York, NY 10019.
212-975-4321

Chairman. William S Paley
President. John D Backe
Senior Vice-President. Peter A Derow
Senior Vice-President and General Executive. John A Schneider
Vice-President, Corporate Affairs. E K Meade, Jr. **212-975-2895**
Vice-President, Investor Relations. J Garrett Blowers. **212-975-6075**
Vice-President, Corporate Information. Leonard Spinrad. **212-975-3895**
CBS Washington. 1800 M St NW, Washington, DC 20036. **202-457-4321, Ext 4505.** John A Loftus, director, information services
CBS Technology Center. 227 High Ridge Rd, Stamford, CT 06905. **203-327-2000** Ext 236. Sherman Levin, director, information services

CBS/Broadcast Group

President. Gene F Jankowski. **212-975-8060**
Vice-President and Assistant to President. Gene P Mater. **212-975-5416**

CBS Television Network. James H Rosenfield, president, **212-975-3956** Barrie D Richardson, vice-president, press information, **212-975-3131**
CBS Television Stations. Thomas F Leahy, president, **212-975-2661** Alan R Morris, director, communications, **212-975-5678**
CBS Radio. Sam Cook Digges, president, **212-975-4421.** W Thomas Dawson, vice-president, division services, **212-975-3205**
CBS News. 524 W 57 St, New York, NY 10019. Richard S Salant, president, **212-975-2988.** Ellen Ehrlich, director, information services, **212-975-5461**
CBS Entertainment Division. Robert A Daly, president, **213-651-2345**
CBS Sports Division. Robert J Wussler, president, **212-975-4221**

CBS/Records Group

President. Walter R Yetnikoff. **212-975-5383**
Vice-President, Press and Public Affairs. Robert Altchuler. **212-975-5047**
CBS Records. Bruce G Lundvall, president **212-975-4977.** Judy Paynter, national director, press and public information, **212-975-5054.** Susan Blond, director, press and public information, epic, portrait, and associated labels, **212-975-5154.** Win Wilford, director, press information and artist affairs, special markets, **212-975-5483**
CBS Records International. M Richard Asher, president, **212-975-5955.** Perry Chasen, director, international publicity, **212-975-5357**

CBS/Columbia Group

President. John Phillips. **212-975-5371**
Columbia House. Cornelius F Keating, president, **212-975-4621**
CBS Musical Instruments. 100 Wilmot Rd, Deerfield, IL 60015. Robert G Campbell, president, **312-948-5800**
CBS Retail Stores. 1313 53rd St, Emeryville, CA 94608. Thomas C Andersen, president, **415-653-9983**
CBS Toys. Edinburg Rd, Cranbury, NJ 08512. Seymour L Gartenberg, president, **609-488-2221,** Ext 214

CBS/Publishing Group

President. John R Purcell. **212-975-4093**
CBS Educational Publishing. 383 Madison Ave, New York, NY 10017. Stanley D Frank, president, **212-688-9100,** Ext 203
CBS Consumer Publishing. 1515 Broadway, New York, NY 10036. John S Suhler, president, **212-975-7201**

CBS Professional Publishing. W Washington Sq, Philadelphia, PA 19105. Thomas M Kirwan, president, **215-574-4700,** Ext 4884
CBS International Publishing. 383 Madison Ave, New York, NY 10017 **212-975-6558**

National Broadcasting Company, Inc

(subsidiary of RCA Corporation). 30 Rockefeller Plz, New York, NY 10020. **212-664-4444**

Chairman of the Board. Julian Goodman
President, NBC News. Richard C Wald.
Executive Vice-President, NBC News. Robert Mulholland
Executive Vice-President, Television News. Lester M Crystal. **212-664-2554**
Vice-President, Television News. G Joseph Bartelme. **212-664-5601**
Vice-President, News Operation. Richard Rischer. **212-664-5253**
Executive Producer, "NBC Nightly News" Joseph Angotti. **212-664-4971**
Executive Producer, "Today" Program. Paul Friedman. **212-664-3236**
Director, News Information. Joseph J Derby. **212-664-3431**

OTHER NETWORKS

CANADIAN BROADCASTING CORP (CBC). 1500 Bronson Ave (PO Box 8478), Ottawa, Ont K1G 3J5, Canada. **613-731-3111**

EDUCATIONAL BROADCASTING CORP. 304 W 58th St, New York, NY 10019. **212-262-4200**

HUGHES TELEVISION NETWORK. 133 Avenue of the Americas, New York, NY 10036. **212-765-6600**

NATIONAL BLACK NETWORK. 1350 Avenue of the Americas, New York, NY 10019. **212-586-0610**

NATIONAL PUBLIC RADIO. 2025 M St NW, Washington, DC 20036. **202-785-5400**

PUBLIC BROADCASTING SERVICE. 485 L'Enfant Plz W, SW, Washington, DC 20024. **202-488-5000.** Also 75 Rockefeller Plz, New York, NY 10019. **212-489-0945**

TVS TELEVISION NETWORK. 280 Park Ave, New York, NY 10017. **212-697-0660**

WESTINGHOUSE BROADCASTING CO. 90 Park Ave, New York, NY 10016. **212-983-6500**

ALL-NEWS RADIO STATIONS

Alabama

WATV-AM (900). 3025 Ensley Ave, Broadcast Plz, Birmingham, 35208. **205-780-2014**

Arizona

KTAR-AM (620). Box 711, Phoenix, 85001. **602-257-6600** (ABC Mutual, APR)

KTUC-AM (1400). Box 4009, Tucson, 85717. **602-622-3344** (ABC)

Arkansas

KFPW-AM (1230). Box 4150, Fort Smith, 72901. **501-783-4105** (CBS)

California

KFWB-AM (980). 6419 Hollywood Blvd, Los Angeles, 90028. **213-463-5151**

KNX-AM (1070). 6121 Sunset Blvd, Los Angeles, 90028. **213-469-1212** (CBS)

KPRO-AM (1440). Box 1440, Riverside, 92502. **714-686-0917** (CBS)

KCRA-AM (1320). 310 10th St, Sacramento, 95814. **916-441-5272** (NBC, ABC)

KFBK-AM (1530). 21st and Q Sts, Sacramento, 95813. **916-442-0476** (CBS)

KGB-AM (1360). 4141 Pacific Coast Hwy, San Diego, 92138. **714-295-7373**

KGB-FM (101.5). 4141 Pacific Coast Hwy, San Diego, 92138. **714-297-2201**

KSDO-AM (1130). 1450 7th Ave, San Diego, 92101. **714-234-8361** (CBS, MBS)

KGO-AM (810). 277 Golden Gate Ave, San Francisco, 94102. **415-863-0077** (ABC)

KYUV-FM (99.7). 1700 Montgomery St, San Francisco, 94111. **415-546-2214** (NBC)

KXRX-AM (1500). Box 167, San Jose, 95103. **408-292-5080**

KDEN-AM (1340). 5660 S Syracuse Cir, Denver, 80237. **303-935-3525**

Connecticut

WPOP-AM (1410). Box 11-1410, Newington Branch, Hartford, 06111. **203-666-1411** (NBC/NIS)

Delaware

WILM-AM (1450). 1215 French St, Wilmington, 19801. **302-656-9800**

District of Columbia

WRC-AM (980). 4001 Nebraska Ave, Washington, DC 20016. **202-686-4000** (NBC/NIS)

WTOP-AM (1500). Broadcast House, Washington, 20016. **202-686-6000** (CBS)

Florida

WINZ-AM (940). 100 Biscayne Blvd, Miami, 33132. **305-371-6641** (NBC/NIS)

WQSA-AM (1220). Box 7700, Sarasota, 33578. **813-366-0424**

WMEN-AM (1330). Box 1695, Tallahassee, 32303. **904-877-5116** (NBC/NIS)

WPOM-AM (1600). 4286 Upthegrove Ln, West Palm Beach, 33407. **305-686-8000**

Hawaii

KHVH-AM (1040). 1060 Bishop St, Honolulu, 96813. **808-524-3111** (CBS)

Idaho

KSPD-AM (790). Box 2298, Boise, 83701. **208-345-3790** (NBC/NIS)

Illinois

WBYS-AM (1560). Box 60, Canton, 61520. **309-647-1560** (ABC)

WBBM-AM (780). 630 N McClurg, Chicago, 60611. **312-944-6000** (CBS)

WFRL-AM (1570). Box 200, Freeport, 61032. **815-235-4113**

Indiana

WNTS-AM (1590). 4800 E Raymond St, Indianapolis, 46203. **317-359-5591** (ABC)

Iowa

KRLS-FM (92.1). 1610 N Lincoln, Knoxville, 50138. **515-842-3161**

Kansas

KCNW-AM (1380). 6230 Eby, Shawnee Mission, 66202. **816-722-2866** (NBC, MBS, ABC)

KBUL-AM (1410). Box 486, Wichita, 67201. **316-838-7744** (NBC)

Kentucky

WNNS-FM (97.5). Box 1084, Louisville, 40202. **502-582-7317** (CBS)

Louisiana

KJOE-AM (1480). 526 Lane Bldg, Shreveport, 71101. **318-222-0732** (NBC/NIS)

KWKH-AM (1130). Box 21130, Shreveport, 71120. **318-222-8711** (CBS)

Maine

WLBZ-AM (620). 861 Broadway, Bangor, 04401. **207-942-4656** (NBC)

WBAL-FM (97.9). 3800 Hooper Ave, Baltimore, 21211. **301-467-3000** (NBC/NIS)

Massachusetts

WEEI-AM (590). 4450 Prudential Tower, Boston, 02199. **617-262-5900** (CBS)

Michigan

WWJ-AM (950). 622 Lafayette Blvd, Detroit, 48231. **313-222-2406** (NBC)

WMAX-AM (1480). 205-B Waters Bldg, Grand Rapids, 49503. **616-458-3793** (NBC/NIS)

WMPL-AM (920). 326 Quincy St, Hancock, 49930. **906-482-3700** (NBC)

WMPL-FM (93.5). 326 Quincy St, Hancock, 49930. **906-482-3700** (NBC)

Minnesota

KSJR-FM (90.1). c/o William H Kling, Collegeville, 56321. **612-363-7702** (NPR)

KDAN-AM (1370). 3092 Military Rd, Newport, 55055. **612-459-7000**

WWTC-AM (1280). 609 2nd Ave S, Minneapolis, 55402. **612-333-2363** (NBC/NIS)

Mississippi

WRBC-AM (1300). Box 9801, Jackson, 39206. **601-956-4151** (NBC/NIS)

Missouri

KMOX-AM (1120). 1 Memorial Dr, St Louis, 63102. **314-621-2345** (CBS)

Nebraska

KLNG-AM (1490). 3516 Dodge St, Omaha, 68131. **402-345-8380** (CBS/ABC)

Nevada

KBMI-AM (1400). Box 15223, Las Vegas, 89114. **702-732-7753** (NBC/NIS)

New Jersey

WBUD (1260). Box 551, Trenton, 08601. **609-882-7191** (NBC/NIS)

New Mexico

KZIA-AM (1580). Box 25166, Albuquerque, 87125. **505-262-1733** (ABC, MBS)

New York

WABY-AM (1400). 80 Braintree St, Albany, 12205. **518-459-2111** (ABC)

WEBR-AM (970). 23 North St, Buffalo, 14202. **712-886-0970** (APR, NPR)

WCBS-AM (880). 51 W 52nd St, New York, 10019. **212-765-4321** (CBS)

WINS-AM (1010). 90 Park Ave, New York, 10016. **212-557-1010**

WNWS-FM (97.1). 30 Rockefeller Plz, New York, NY 10020. **212-247-8300** (NBC)

North Carolina

WSOC-AM (930). Box 2536, Charlotte, 28201. **704-372-0930** (NBC)

WKBX-AM (1500). 3066 Trendwest Dr, Winston-Salem, 27103. **919-765-1551** (MBS)

Ohio

WERE-AM (1300). 1500 Chester Ave, Cleveland, 44114. **216-696-1300** (ABC, MBS)

WAVI-AM (1210). 1400 Cincinnati St, Dayton, 45408. **513-224-1137** (ABC)

WBBW-AM (1240). 418 Knox St, Youngstown, 44502. **216-744-4421** (ABC)

Oklahoma

KRMA-AM (1220). PO Box 32097, Oklahoma City, 73132. **405-672-5577**

Oregon

KYXI-AM (1520). Box 22125, Portland, 97222. **503-656-1441** (NBC, CBS)

Pennsylvania

WVCC-FM (101.7). Box 307, Linesville, 16424. **814-683-4000** (MBS)

KYW-AM (1060). Independence Mall E, Philadelphia, 19106. **215-238-4984**

WCAU-AM (1210). City Line and Monument Aves, Philadelphia, 19131. **215-839-7000** (CBS)

KQV-AM (1410). 411 7th Ave, Pittsburgh, 15219. **412-281-9100** (ABC)

WBRE-AM (1340). 62 S Franklin St, Wilkes-Barre, 18703. **717-823-0117** (NBC)

Rhode Island

WEAN-AM (790). 10 Dorrance St, Providence, 02903. **401-277-7411** (MBS)

WERI-AM (1230). Colonial Office Bldg, Westerly, 02891. **401-596-7728**

WERI-FM (103.7). Colonial Office Bldg, Westerly, 02891. **401-596-7728**

South Carolina

WSCQ-FM (100.1). Box 888, West Columbia, 29169. **803-796-9060** (NBC/NIS)

Texas

KLBJ-AM (590). Box 1209, Austin, 78767. **512-474-6543** (CBS)

WRR-AM (1310). Fair Park Station, Dallas, 75226. **214-823-1310** (NBC/NIS)

KURV-AM (710). Box 1638, Edinburg, 78539. **512-383-2777** (NBC, MBS)

KTSM-AM (1380). 801 N Oregon St, El Paso, 79925. **915-532-5421** (NBC)

KLYX-FM (102.1). 3100 Richmond Ave, Houston, 77006. **713-527-9545** (NBC/NIS)

KEYH-AM (850). Suite 501, 3130 Southwest Fwy, Houston, 77098. **713-527-9363** (MBS, AP)

WOAI-AM (1200). 1031 Navarro St, San Antonio, 78205. **512-226-9331** (NBC, CBS)

Utah

KBBX-AM (1600). PO Box 338, Salt Lake City, 84110. **801-290-1142**

Virginia

WSIG-AM (790). Box 425, Mount Jackson, 22842. **703-477-2937** (MBS)

Washington

WGDN-AM (630). 19303 Fremont Ave N, Seattle, 98133. **206-546-7350**

Wisconsin

WRIT-AM (1340). 5407 W McKinley Dr, Milwaukee, 53208. **414-453-4130** (NBC/NIS)

WIBU-AM (1240). Route 2, Poynette, 53955. **608-635-4532**

WCOW-FM (97.1). 209 E Main St, Sparta, 54656. **608-269-3307** (MBS)

TV STATIONS

This list includes all US Commercial VHF *television stations.*

Alabama

WAPI-TV (Channel 13). Box 10502, Birmingham, 35202. **205-933-2720** (NBC)

WBRC-TV (Channel 6). Box 6, Birmingham, 35201. **205-322-4701** (ABC)

WTVY (Channel 4). Box 1089, Dothan, 36301. **205-792-3195** (CBS)

WALA-TV (Channel 10). Box 1548, Mobile, 36601. **205-433-3753** (NBC)

WKRG-TV (Channel 5). Box 2367, Mobile, 36601. **205-432-5501** (CBS)

WSFA-TV (Channel 12). Box 2566, Montgomery, 36105. **205-281-2900** (NBC)

WEAR-TV (Channel 3). Box 12278, Pensacola, 32581. **904-455-7311** (ABC)

WSLA (Channel 8). Box 1888, Selma, 36701. **205-875-2240** (CBS)

Alaska

KIMO (Channel 13). 3910 Seward Hwy, Anchorage, 99503. **907-279-9437** (ABC)

KFAR-TV (Channel 2). 516 2nd Ave, Fairbanks, 99701. **907-452-2125** (ABC)

KTVF (Channel 11). Box 950, Fairbanks, 99707. **907-452-5121** (CBS)

KINY-TV (Channel 8). 231 S Franklin St, Juneau, 99801. **907-586-1800** (NBC)

KIFW-TV (Channel 13). Box 299, Sitka, 99835. **907-747-6626**

Arizona

KOAI (Channel 2). Box 1843, Flagstaff, 86001. **602-774-1818** (NBC)

KOOL-TV (Channel 10). 511 W Adams, Phoenix, 85016. **602-257-1234** (CBS)

KTAR-TV (Channel 12). Box 711, Phoenix, 85001. **602-258-7333** (NBC)

KTVK (Channel 3). 3435 N 16th St, Phoenix, 85010. **602-266-5691** (ABC)

KGUN-TV (Channel 9). Box 5707, Tucson, 85703. **602-792-9933** (ABC)

KOLD-TV (Channel 13). 115 W Drachman St, Tucson, 85705. **602-624-2511** (CBS)

KVOA-TV (Channel 4). Box 5188, Tucson 85703. **602-623-2555** (NBC)

KBLU-TV (Channel 13). Box 1501, Yuma, 85364. **602-782-3881** (NBC)

Arkansas

KTVE (Channel 10). Box 791, 400 W Main, El Dorado, 71730. **501-862-3488** (ABC)

KFSM-TV (Channel 5). 318 N 13th St, Fort Smith, 72901. **501-783-3131** (NBC)

KAIT-TV (Channel 8). Box 790, Jonesboro, 72401. **501-932-4288** (ABC)

KARK-TV (Channel 4). 10th and Spring Sts, Little Rock, 72203. **501-376-2481** (NBC)

KATV (Channel 7). 401 Main (Box 77), Little Rock, 72203. **501-374-1691** (ABC)

KTHV (Channel 11). Box 269, Little Rock, 72203. **501-374-3764** (CBS)

California

KNBC (Channel 4). 3000 W Alameda Ave, Burbank, 91523. **213-845-7000** (NBC)

KHSL-TV (Channel 12). Box 489, Chico, 95926. **916-342-0141** (CBS)

KECC-TV (Channel 9). Box 29, El Centro, 92243. **714-352-9670** (CBS)

KIEM-TV (Channel 3). Box 3E, Eureka, 95501. **707-443-3123** (CBS)

KVIQ-TV (Channel 6). Box 1019, Eureka, 95501. **707-443-3061** (ABC)

KABC-TV (Channel 7). 4151 Prospect Ave, Los Angeles, 90027. **213-663-3311** (ABC)

KNXT (Channel 2). 6121 Sunset Blvd, Los Angeles, 90028. **213-469-1212** (CBS)

KTLA (Channel 5). 5800 Sunset Blvd, Los Angeles, 90028. **213-469-3181**

KTTV (Channel 11). 5746 Sunset Blvd, Los Angeles, 90028. **213-462-7111**

KTVU (Channel 2). 1 Jack London Sq, Oakland, 94607. **415-834-2000**

KRCR-TV (Channel 7). Box 7R, Redding, 96001. **916-243-7777** (ABC)

KCRA-TV (Channel 3). 310 10th St, Sacramento, 95814. **916-444-7300** (NBC)

KOVR (Channel 13). 1216 Arden Way, Sacramento, 95815. **916-927-1313** (ABC)

KXTV (Channel 10). Box 10, Sacramento, 95801. **916-441-4041** (CBS)

KSBW-TV (Channel 8). Box 1651, Salinas, 93901. **408-422-6422** (NBC)

KFMB-TV (Channel 8). 1405 5th Ave, San Diego, 92101. **714-232-2114** (CBS)

KGTV (Channel 10). Box 81047, San Diego, 92138. **714-262-2421** (NBC)

KGO-TV (Channel 7). 277 Golden Gate Ave, San Francisco, 94102. **415-863-0077** (ABC)

KPIX (Channel 5). 2655 Van Ness Ave, San Francisco, 94109. **415-776-5100** (CBS)

KRON-TV (Channel 4). Box 3412, 1001 Van Ness Ave, San Francisco, 94119. **415-441-4444** (NBC)

KNTV (Channel 11). 645 Park Ave, San Jose, 95110. **408-286-1111** (ABC)

KSBY-TV (Channel 6). Box 1368, San Luis Obispo, 93406. **805-543-0920** (NBC)

KEYT (Channel 3). Drawer X, Santa Barbara, 93102. **805-965-8533** (ABC)

KCOY-TV (Channel 12). 1503 N McClelland, Santa Maria, 93454. **805-922-1943** (CBS)

Colorado

KKTV (Channel 11). 3100 N Nevada Ave, Colorado Springs, 80901. **303-634-2844** (CBS)

KRDO-TV (Channel 13). Box 1457, Colorado Springs, 80901. **303-632-1515** (ABC)

KBTV (Channel 9). 1089 Bannock St, Denver, 80217. **303-825-5288** (ABC)

KMGH-TV (Channel 7). 123 Speer Blvd, Denver, 80217. **303-832-7777** (CBS)

KOA-TV (Channel 4). 1044 Lincoln St, Denver, 80217. **303-861-8111** (NBC)

KWGN-TV (Channel 2). 550 Lincoln St, Denver, 80203. **303-832-2222**

KREZ-TV (Channel 6). Box 789, Grand Junction, 81501 (ABC)

KREX-TV (Channel 5). Box 789, Grand Junction, 81501. **303-242-5000** (CBS)

KREY-TV (Channel 10). Box 49, Montrose, 81401. **303-249-9601** (CBS)

KOAA-TV (Channel 5). Box 876, Pueblo, 81002. **303-544-5782** (NBC)

KTVS (Channel 3). 204½ Main St, Sterling, 80751. **303-522-5743** (CBS)

Connecticut

WFSB-TV (Channel 3). Broadcast House, 3 Constitution Plz, Hartford, 06115. **203-525-0801** (CBS)

WTNH-TV (Channel 8). Box 1859, New Haven, 06508. **203-777-3611** (ABC)

District of Columbia

WMAL-TV (Channel 7). 4461 Conecticut Ave NW, Washington, 20008. **202-686-3000** (ABC)

WRC-TV (Channel 4). 4001 Nebraska Ave NW, Washington, 20016. **202-686-4000** (NBC)

WTOP-TV (Channel 9). 40th and Brandywine Sts NW, Washington, 20016. **202-686-6000** (CBS)

WTTG (Channel 5). 5151 Wisconsin Ave NW, Washington 20016. **202-244-5151**

Florida

WESH-TV (Channel 2). Box 1551, Daytona Beach, 32015. **904-253-7616** (NBC)

WINK-TV (Channel 11). Box 1060, Fort Myers, 33902. **813-334-1131** (CBS)

WJXT (Channel 4). Box 5270, Jacksonville, 32207. **904-399-4000** (CBS)

WTLV (Channel 12). Box 1212, Jacksonville, 32201. **904-354-1212** (NBC)

WCIX-TV (Channel 6). 1111 Brickwell Ave, Miami, 33131. **305-377-0811**

WCKT (Channel 7). 1401 79th St, Cswy, Miami, 33141. **305-751-6692** (NBC)

WPLG-TV (Channel 10). 3900 Biscayne Blvd, Miami, 33137. **305-573-7111** (ABC)

WTVJ (Channel 4). 316 N Miami Ave, Miami, 33128. **305-377-8241** (CBS)

WDBO-TV (Channel 6). Box 1833, Orlando, 32802. **305-843-0006**

WFTV (Channel 9). Box 999, Orlando, 32802. **305-841-9000** (ABC)

WLCY-TV (Channel 10). Box 14000, St Petersburg, 33733. **813-577-111** (ABC)

WDTB (Channel 13). Box 1340, Panama City, 32401. **904-769-2313** (NBC)

WJHG-TV (Channel 7). Box 2349, Panama City, 32401. **904-234-2125** (ABC)

WPTV (Channel 5). Box 510, Palm Beach, 33480. **305-655-5455** (NBC)

WCTV (Channel 6). Box 3048, Tallahassee, 32303. **904-385-2121** (CBS)

WFLA-TV (Channel 8). Box 1410, Tampa, 33601. **813-229-7781** (NBC)

WTVT (Channel 13). Box 22013, Tampa, 33622. **813-876-1313** (CBS)

WPEC (Channel 12). Fairfield Dr, West Palm Beach, 33407. **305-848-7211** (ABC)

Georgia

WALB-TV (Channel 10). Box 3130, Albany, 31706. **912-435-8386** (NBC)

WAGA-TV (Channel 5). Box 4207, Atlanta, 30302. **404-875-5551** (CBS)

WSB-TV (Channel 2). 1601 W Peachtree St NE, Atlanta, 30309. **404-897-7000** (NBC)

WXIA-TV (Channel 11). 1611 W Peachtree St NE, Atlanta, 30309. **404-892-1611** (ABC)

WJBF (Channel 6). Box 1404, Augusta, 30903. **404-722-6664** (ABC)

WRDW-TV (Channel 12). Drawer 1212, Augusta, 30903. **803-278-1212** (CBS)

WRBL-TV (Channel 3). Box 270, Columbus, 31902. **404-322-0601** (CBS)

WTVM (Channel 9). Box 1848, Columbus, 31902. **404-324-6471** (ABC)

WMAZ-TV (Channel 13). Box 5008, Macon, 31208. **912-746-7311** (CBS)

WSAV-TV (Channel 3). Box 2429, Savannah, 31402. **912-236-0303** (NBC)

WTOC-TV (Channel 11). Box 8086, Savannah, 31402. **912-232-0127** (CBS)

Hawaii

KGMB-TV (Channel 9). Box 581, Honolulu, 96809. **808-941-3011** (CBS)

KHON-TV (Channel 2). 1170 Auahi St, Honolulu, 96814. **808-531-8585** (NBC)

KIKU-TV (Channel 13). 150 B Puuhale Rd, Honolulu, 96819. **808-847-1178**

KITV (Channel 4). 1290 Ala Moana Blvd, Honolulu, 96814. **808-537-3991** (ABC)

KMAU-TV (Channel 3). Box 1574, Kahului, 96732. **808-244-5348**

Idaho

KBCI-TV (Channel 2). Box 2600, Boise, 83701. **208-342-9331** (CBS)

KTVB (Channel 7). Box 7778, Boise, 83701. **208-375-7277** (NBC)

KID-TV (Channel 3). Box 2008, Idaho Falls, 83401. **208-522-5100** (CBS)

KIFI-TV (Channel 8). Box 2148, Idaho Falls, 83401. **208-523-1171** (NBC)

KIVI (Channel 6). 1866 E Chisholm Dr, Nampa, 83651. **208-467-3301**

KPVI (Channel 6). Box 4909, 421 Fredregill Rd, Pocatello, 83201. **208-233-6667** (ABC)

KMVT (Channel 11). Box 547, Twin Falls, 83301. **208-733-1280** (ABC)

Illinois

WCIA (Channel 3). 509 S Neil, Champaign, 61820. **217-356-8333** (CBS)

WBBM-TV (Channel 2). 630 N McClurg Ct, Chicago, 60611. **312-944-6000** (CBS)

WGN-TV (Channel 9). 2501 Bradley Pl, Chicago, 60618. **312-528-2311**

WLS-TV (Channel 7). 190 N State St, Chicago, 60601. **312-263-0800** (ABC)

WMAQ-TV (Channel 5). Merchandise Mart, Chicago, 60654. **312-644-8300** (NBC)

WSIL-TV (Channel 3). 21 W Poplar St, Harrisburg, 62946. **618-253-7837**

WQAD-TV (Channel 8). 3003 Park 16th St, Moline, 61265. **309-764-9694** (ABC)

KHQA-TV (Channel 7). 510 Main St, Quincy, 62301. **217-222-6200** (CBS)

WGEM-TV (Channel 10). Box 769, 513 Hampshire, Quincy, 62301. **207-222-6840** (NBC)

WREX-TV (Channel 13). Auburn and Winnebago Rds, Rockford, 61105. **815-968-1813** (ABC)

WHBF-TV (Channel 4). 231 18th St, Rock Island, 61201. **309-786-5441** (CBS)

Indiana

WTVW (Channel 7). 477 Carpenter St, Evansville, 47736. **812-422-1121** (ABC)

WISH-TV (Channel 8). 1950 N Meridian St, Indianapolis, 46202. **317-924-4381** (CBS)

WRTV (Channel 6). 1330 N Meridian St, Indianapolis, 46206. **317-635-9788** (NBC)

WTHR (Channel 13). 1401 N Meridian St, Indianapolis, 46202. **317-639-2311** (ABC)

WTTV (Channel 4). 3490 Bluff Rd, Indianapolis, 46217. **317-787-2211**

WTHI-TV (Channel 10). 918 Ohio St, Terre Haute, 47808. **812-232-9481** (CBS)

WTWO (Channel 2). Box 299, Terre Haute, 47808. **812-232-9504** (NBC)

Iowa

WOI-TV (Channel 5). WOI Bldg, Ames, 50010. **515-294-5555** (ABC)

KCRG-TV (Channel 9). 2nd Ave at 5th St SE, Cedar Rapids, 52406. **319-398-8422** (ABC)

WMT-TV (Channel 2). Broadcast Park, Cedar Rapids, 52406. **319-393-8200** (CBS)

WOC-TV (Channel 6). 805 Brady St, Davenport, 52808. **319-324-1661** (NBC)

KCCI-TV (Channel 8). 9th and Pleasant, Des Moines, 50308. **515-243-4141** (CBS)

WHO-TV (Channel 13). 1100 Walnut St, Des Moines, 50308. **515-288-6511** (NBC)

KGLO-TV (Channel 3). 112 N Pennsylvania Ave, Mason City, 50401. **515-423-2540** (CBS)

KTVO (Channel 3). 211 E 2nd St, Ottumwa, 52501. **515-682-4535** (ABC)

KCAU-TV (Channel 9). 7th and Douglas Sts, Sioux City, 51101. **712-277-2345** (ABC)

KTIV (Channel 4). Box 87, Sioux City, 51102. **712-258-0545** (NBC)

KWWL-TV (Channel 7). 500 E 4th, Waterloo, 50703. **319-234-4401** (NBC)

Kansas

KUPK-TV (Channel 13). Box 216, Copeland, 67837

KTVC (Channel 6). Box 157, Dodge City, 67801. **316-227-3121**

KGLD (Channel 11). Box 1076, Garden City, 67846. **316-276-2311** (NBC)

KCKT (Channel 2). Box 689, Great Bend, 67530. **316-793-7868**

KAYS-TV (Channel 7). Box 817, Hays, 67601. **913-625-2578** (CBS)

KOAM-TV (Channel 7). Box 659, Pittsburg, 66762. **316-231-0400** (NBC)

WIBW-TV (Channel 13). Box 119, Topeka, 66601. **913-272-3456** (CBS)

KAKE-TV (Channel 10). Box 10, Wichita, 67201. **316-943-4221** (ABC)

KARD-TV (Channel 3). 833 N Main, Wichita, 67201. **316-265-5631** (NBC)

KTVH (Channel 12). Box 12, Wichita, 67201. **316-838-1411** (CBS)

Kentucky

WBKO (Channel 13). Box 1198, Bowling Green, 42101. **502-781-1313** (ABC)

WAVE-TV (Channel 3). Box 1000, Louisville, 40201. **502-585-2201** (NBC)

WPSD-TV (Channel 6). Box 1037, Paducah, 42001. **502-442-8214** (NBC)

Louisiana

KALB-TV (Channel 5). 605-11 Washington St, Alexandria, 71301. **318-445-2456** (NBC)

WAFB-TV (Channel 9). 929 Government St, Baton Rouge, 70821. **504-348-4921** (CBS)

WBRZ (Channel 2). Box 2906, Baton Rouge, 70821. **504-344-2641** (NBC)

KATC (Channel 3). Box 3347, Lafayette, 70501. **318-232-6111** (ABC)

KLFY-TV (Channel 10). Box 3687, Lafayette, 70501. **318-233-2152** (CBS)

KPLC-TV (Channel 7). Box 1488, Lake Charles, 70601. **318-439-9071** (NBC)

KNOE-TV (Channel 8). Box 4067, Monroe, 71201. **318-322-8155** (CBS)

WDSU-TV (Channel 6). 520 Royal St, New Orleans, 70130. **504-588-9378** (NBC)

WVUE (Channel 8). Box 13847, New Orleans, 70185. **504-486-6161** (ABC)

WWL-TV (Channel 4). 1024 N Rampart St, New Orleans, 70116. **504-529-4444** (CBS)

KSLA-TV (Channel 12). Box 4812, Shreveport, 71104. **318-424-8101** (CBS)

KTAL-TV (Channel 6). 3150 N Market St, Shreveport, 71107. **318-425-2422** (NBC)

KTBS-TV (Channel 3). 312 E Kings Hwy (Box 4367), Shreveport, 71104. **318-868-3644** (ABC)

Maine

WABI-TV (Channel 5). 35 Hildreth St, Bangor, 04401. **207-947-8321** (CBS)

WEMT (Channel 7). 41 Farm Rd, Bangor, 04401. **207-945-6457**

WLBZ-TV (Channel 2). Box 934, Bangor, 04401. **207-942-4822** (NBC)

WCSH-TV (Channel 6). 579 Congress St, Portland, 04101. **207-772-0181** (NBC)

WGAN-TV (Channel 13). 390 Congress St, Portland, 04111. **207-772-4461** (CBS)

WMTW-TV (Channel 8). Lafayette Towne House, 638 Congress St, Portland, 04101. **207-773-5664** (ABC)

WAGM-TV (Channel 8). Box 1149, Presque Isle, 04769. **207-764-4461** (CBS)

Maryland

WBAL-TV (Channel 11). Maryland Broadcasting Ctr, Baltimore, 21211. **301-467-3000** (NBC)

WMAR-TV (Channel 2). 6400 York Rd, Baltimore, 21212. **301-377-2222** (CBS)

Massachusetts

WBZ-TV (Channel 4). 1170 Soldiers Field Rd, Boston, 02134. **617-254-5670** (NBC)

WNAC-TV (Channel 7). Government Ctr, Boston, 02114. **617-742-9000** (CBS)

WCVB-TV (Channel 5). 5 TV Pl, Needham, 02192. **617-449-0400** (ABC)

Michigan

WBKB-TV (Channel 11). Box 35, Alpena, 49707. **517-354-8216** (CBS)

WWTV (Channel 9). Box 627, Cadillac, 49601. **616-775-3478** (CBS)

WJBK-TV (Channel 2). 2 Storer Pl, Detroit, 48075. **313-557-9000** (CBS)

WWJ-TV (Channel 4). 622 Lafayette Blvd, Detroit, 48231. **313-222-2000** (NBC)

WJRT-TV (Channel 12). 2302 Lapper Rd, Flint, 48503. **313-239-6611** (ABC)

WOTV (Channel 8). Box B, Grand Rapids, 49501. **616-459-4125** (NBC)

WZZM-TV (Channel 13). Box Z, Grand Rapids, 49501. **616-364-9551**

WILX-TV (Channel 10). Box 380, Jackson, 49204. **517-783-2621** (NBC)

WKZO-TV (Channel 3). 590 W Maple St, Kalamazoo, 49001. **616-345-2101** (CBS)

WJIM-TV (Channel 6). 2820 E Saginaw, Lansing, 48904. **517-372-8282** (CBS)

WLUC-TV (Channel 6). Box 460, Marquette, 49855. **906-475-4161** (CBS)

WNEM-TV (Channel 5). 5700 Becker Rd, Saginaw, 48606. **517-755-8191** (NBC)

WXYZ-TV (Channel 7). 20777 W Ten Mile Rd, Southfield, 48075. **313-444-1111**

WTOM-TV (Channel 4). Paul Bunyan Bldg, Traverse City, 49684. **616-947-7675** (NBC)

Minnesota

KCMT (Channel 7). 720 Hawthorne St, Alexandria, 56308. **808-763-5166**

KAAL (Channel 6). Box 577, Austin, 55912. **507-433-8836** (ABC)

KBJR-TV (Channel 6). 230 E Superior St, Duluth, 55802. **218-727-8484** (NBC)

KDAL-TV (Channel 3). 425 W Superior St, Duluth, 55802. **218-727-8911** (CBS)

WDIO-TV (Channel 10). 10 Observation Rd, Duluth, 55811. **218-727-6864** (ABC)

KEYC-TV (Channel 12). Box 128, Mankato, 56001. **507-387-7905** (CBS)

WCCO-TV (Channel 4). 50 S 9th St, Minneapolis, 55402. **612-338-0552** (CBS)

WTCN-TV (Channel 11). 441 Boone Ave N, Minneapolis, 55427. **612-546-1111**

KMSP-TV (Channel 9). 6975 York Ave, Minneapolis-St Paul, 55435. **612-925-3300** (ABC)

KROC-TV (Channel 10). 601 1st Ave SW, Rochester, 55901. **507-288-4444** (NBC)

KSTP-TV (Channel 5). 2415 University Ave, St Paul, 55114. **612-645-2724** (NBC)

Mississippi

WLOX-TV (Channel 13). Box 4596, Biloxi, 39531. **601-896-1313** (ABC)

WCBI-TV (Channel 4). Box 271, Columbus, 39701. **601-328-5631** (CBS)

WABG-TV (Channel 6). Drawer 720, Greenville, 38930. **601-453-4001**

WDAM-TV (Channel 7). Box 1978, Hattieburg, 39402. **601-544-4730** (NBC)

WJTV (Channel 12). Box 8887, Jackson, 39204. **601-372-6311** (CBS)

WLBT (Channel 3). Box 1712, Jackson, 39205. **601-948-3333** (NBC)

WTOK-TV (Channel 11). Southern Bldg, Meridian, 39302. **601-483-1441** (CBS)

WTWV (Channel 9). Box 350, Tupelo, 38801. **901-842-7620** (NBC)

Missouri

KFVS-TV (Channel 12). 324 Broadway, Cape Girardeau, 63701. **314-335-5511** (CBS)

KOMU-TV (Channel 8). Highway 63 S, Columbia, 65201. **314-442-1122** (NBC)

KRCG (Channel 13). Box 659, Jefferson City, 65101. **314-636-6188** (CBS)

KODE-TV (Channel 12). 1928 W 13th St, Joplin, 64801. **417-623-7260** (ABC)

KCMO-TV (Channel 5). 125 E 31st St, Kansas City, 64108. **816-531-6789** (CBS)

KMBC-TV (Channel 9). 11th and Central Sts, Kansas City, 64105. **816-421-2650** (ABC)

WDAF-TV (Channel 4). Signal Hill, Kansas City, 64108. **816-753-4567** (NBC)

KQTV (Channel 2). 40th and Faraon Sts, St Joseph, 64506. **816-233-2528** (ABC)

KMOX-TV (Channel 4). 1 Memorial Dr, St Louis, 63102. **314-621-2345** (CBS)

KPLR-TV (Channel 11). 4935 Lindell Blvd, St Louis, 63108. **314-367-7211**

KSD-TV (Channel 5). 1111 Olive St, St Louis, 63101. **314-421-5055** (NBC)

KTVI (Channel 2). 5915 Berthold Ave, St Louis, 63110. **314-647-7777** (ABC)

KOLR (Channel 10). Box 1716, Springfield, 65805. **417-862-7474** (CBS)

KYTV (Channel 3). 999 W Sunshine, Springfield, 65804. **417-866-2766** (NBC)

Montana

KTVQ (Channel 2). Box 2557, Billings, 59103. **406-252-5611** (CBS)

KULR-TV (Channel 8). Box 2512, Billings, 59103. **406-252-4676** (ABC)

KXLF-TV (Channel 4). Box 3500, Butte, 59701. **406-792-9111**

KXGN-TV (Channel 5). 210 S Douglas, Glendive, 59330. **406-365-3377** (CBS)

KFBB-TV (Channel 5). Box 1139, Great Falls, 59403. **406-453-4377** (ABC)

KRTV (Channel 3). Box 1331, Great Falls, 59403. **406-453-2433** (NBC)

KTCM (Channel 12). 2433 N Montana Ave, Helena, 59601. **406-443-5050** (NBC)

KCFW-TV (Channel 9). Box 857, Kalispell, 59901. **406-756-9051**

KYUS-TV (Channel 3). Box 760, Miles City, 59301. **406-232-3540**

KGVO-TV (Channel 13). Drawer M, Missoula, 59801. **406-543-8313**

KTVM (Channel 6). Drawer M, Missoula, 59801. **406-728-9318** (NBC)

Nebraska

KGIN-TV (Channel 11). Box 1069, Grand Island, 68801. **308-382-6100** (CBS)

KHAS-TV (Channel 5). Box 578, Hastings, 68901. **402-463-1321** (NBC)

KDUH-TV (Channel 4). Box 250, Hay Springs, 69347. **308-638-2741** (NBC)

KHGI-TV (Channel 13). NTV Network, Kearney, 68847. **308-743-2494** (ABC)

KCNA-TV (Channel 8). Kearney, 68847. **308-743-2494** (ABC)

KOLN-TV (Channel 10). Box 30350, Lincoln, 68503. **402-467-4321** (CBS)

KOMC (Channel 8). Box 184, Oberlin, 67749. (NBC)

KNOP-TV (Channel 2). Box 749, North Platte, 69101. **308-532-2222** (NBC)

KETV (Channel 7). 27th and Douglas Sts, Omaha, 68131. **402-345-7777** (ABC)

KMTV (Channel 3). 2615 Farnam St, Omaha, 68131. **402-345-3333** (NBC)

WOWT (Channel 6). 3501 Farnam St, Omaha, 68131. **402-346-6666** (CBS)

KSTF (Channel 10). Box 731, Scottsbluff, 69361. **308-632-6107** (CBS)

Nevada

KVVU-TV (Channel 5). 1800 Boulder Hwy, Henderson, 89015. **702-565-9755**

KLAS-TV (Channel 8). Box 15047, Las Vegas, 89114. **702-735-7511** (CBS)

KORK-TV (Channel 3). Box 550, Las Vegas, 89101. **702-451-7600** (NBC)

KSHO-TV (Channel 13). 3355 Valley View Blvd, Las Vegas, 89102. **702-876-1313** (ABC)

KCRL-TV (Channel 4). Box 7160, Reno, 89510. **702-322-9145** (NBC)

KOLO-TV (Channel 8). Box 2610, Reno, 89505. **702-786-8880** (ABC)

KTVN (Channel 2). Box 2111, Reno, 89505. **702-786-2212** (CBS)

New Hampshire

WMUR-TV (Channel 9). 1819 Elm St, Manchester, 03105. **603-623-8061** (ABC)

New Mexico

KGGM-TV (Channel 13). Box 1294, Albuquerque, 87103. **505-243-2285** (CBS)

KOAT-TV (Channel 7). 1377 University Blvd NE, Albuquerque, 87106. **505-247-0101** (ABC)

KOB-TV (Channel 4). Box 1351, Albuquerque, 87103. **505-243-4411** (NBC)

KAVE-TV (Channel 6). Box 219, Carlsbad, 88220. **505-885-3931** (ABC)

KIVA-TV (Channel 12). Box 1620, Farmington, 87401. **505-327-9881** (NBC)

KFDW-TV (Channel 12). Box 922, Portales, 88130. **505-276-8444** (CBS)

KBIM-TV (Channel 10). Box 910, Roswell, 88201. **505-622-2120** (CBS)

New York

WAST (Channel 13). Box 4035, Albany, 12204. **518-436-4791** (ABC)

WTEN (Channel 10). 341 Northern Blvd, Albany, 12204. **518-436-4822** (CBS)

WBNG-TV (Channel 12). 50 Front St, Binghamton, 13905. **607-723-7311** (CBS)

WBEN-TV (Channel 4). 2077 Elmwood Ave, Buffalo, 14207. **716-876-0930** (CBS)

WGR-TV (Channel 2). 259 Delaware Ave, Buffalo, 14202. **716-856-1414** (NBC)

WKBW-TV (Channel 7). 1420 Main St, Buffalo, 14209. **716-883-0770** (ABC)

WABC-TV (Channel 7). 1330 Avenue of the Americas, New York, 10019. **212-581-7777** (ABC)

WCBS-TV (Channel 2). 51 W 52d St, New York, 10019. **212-765-4321** (CBS)

WNBC-TV (Channel 4). 30 Rockefeller Plz, New York, 10020. **212-247-8300** (NBC)

WNET (Channel 13). 304 W 58th St, New York, 10019. **212-262-4200** (PBS)

WNEW-TV (Channel 5). 205 E 67th St, New York, 10021. **212-535-1000**

WOR-TV (Channel 9). 1440 Broadway, New York, 10018. **212-764-7000**

WPIX (Channel 11). 220 E 42d St, New York, 10017. **212-883-1100**

WPTZ (Channel 5). 357 Cornelia St, Plattsburgh, 12901. **518-561-5555**

WHEC-TV (Channel 10). 191 East Ave, Rochester, 14604. **716-546-5670** (CBS)

WOKR (Channel 13). 4225 W Henrietta Rd, Rochester, 14623. **716-334-8700** (ABC)

WROC-TV (Channel 8). 201 Humboldt St, Rochester, 14601. **716-288-8400** (NBC)

WRGB (Channel 6). 1400 Balltown Rd, Schenectady, 12309. **518-377-2261** (NBC)

WHEN-TV (Channel 5). 980 James St, Syracuse, 13203. **315-474-8511** (CBS)

WNYS-TV (Channel 9). Box 9, Syracuse, 13214. **315-446-4780** (ABC)

WSYR-TV (Channel 3). 1030 James St, Syracuse, 13203. **315-474-3911** (NBC)

WKTV (Channel 2). Box 2, Utica, 13503. **315-733-0404** (NBC)

WWNY-TV (Channel 7). Box 211, Watertown, 13601. **315-788-3800** (CBS)

North Carolina

WBTV (Channel 3). 1 Julian Price Pl, Charlotte, 28208. **704-374-3500** (CBS)

WSOC-TV (Channel 9). Box 2536, Charlotte, 28234. **704-372-0930** (NBC)

WFMY-TV (Channel 2). Drawer 22047, Greensboro, 27420. **919-274-0113** (CBS)

WGHP-TV (Channel 8). 400 N Main St, High Point, 27260. **919-883-7131** (ABC)

WCTI (Channel 12). Box 2325, New Bern, 28560. **919-637-2111** (ABC)

WRAL-TV (Channel 5). Box 12000, Raleigh, 27605. **919-828-2511** (ABC)

WITN (Channel 7). Box 468, Washington, 27889. **919-946-3131** (NBC)

WECT (Channel 6). 322 Shipyard Blvd, Wilmington, 28401. **919-791-8070** (NBC)

WWAY-TV (Channel 3). Box 2068, Wilmington, 28401. **919-762-8581** (ABC)

WXII (Channel 12). Box 11847, Winston-Salem, 27106. **919-723-9241** (NBC)

North Dakota

KFYR/TV (Channel 5). Box 1738, Bismarck, 58501. **701-223-0900** (NBC)

KMOT (Channel 10). Box 1738, Bismarck, 58501. **701-852-4101** (NBC)

KXMB-TV (Channel 12). Box 1617, Bismarck, 58501. **701-223-9197** (CBS)

KDIX-TV (Channel 2). Box 1368, Dickinson, 58601. **701-225-5133** (CBS)

KTHI-TV (Channel 11). Box 1878, Fargo, 58102. **701-237-5211** (ABC)

KXJB-TV (Channel 4). Box 2926, 4000 W Main Ave, Fargo, 58102. **701-282-0444**

WDAY-TV (Channel 6). 207 N 5th St, Fargo, 58102. **701-237-6500** (NBC)

WDAZ-TV (Channel 8). Box 638, Grand Forks, 58201. **701-775-2511**

KXMC-TV (Channel 13). Box 1686, KXMC-TV Bldg, Minot, 58701. **701-838-2104** (CBS)

KUMV-TV (Channel 8). Box 1287, Williston, 58801. **701-875-4311** (NBC)

Ohio

WCPO-TV (Channel 9). 500 Central Ave, Cincinnati, 45202. **513-721-9900** (CBS)

WKRC-TV (Channel 12). 1906 Highland Ave, Cincinnati, 45219. **513-651-1200** (ABC)

WLWT (Channel 5). 140 W 9th St, Cincinnati, 45202. **513-241-1822** (NBC)

WEWS (Channel 5). 3001 Euclid Ave, Cleveland, 44115. **216-432-1500** (ABC)

WJW-TV (Channel 8). 5800 S Marginal Rd, Cleveland, 44103. **216-431-8888** (CBS)

WKYC-TV (Channel 3). 1403 E 6th St, Cleveland, 44114. **216-696-1000** (NBC)

WBNS-TV (Channel 10). 62 E Broad St, Columbus, 43215. **614-224-7121** (CBS)

WLWC (Channel 4). Box 4, Columbus, 43216. **614-263-5441** (NBC)

WTVN-TV (Channel 6). 753 Harmon Ave, (Box 718), Columbus, 43216. **614-228-5801** (ABC)

WHIO-TV (Channel 7). 1414 Wilmington Ave, Dayton, 45401. **513-254-5311** (CBS)

WLWD (Channel 2). 4590 Avco Dr, Dayton, 45401. **513-293-2101** (NBC)

WSTV-TV (Channel 9). Broadcast Ctr, Steubenville, 43952. **614-282-0911** (CBS)

WSPD-TV (Channel 13). 136 Huron St, Toledo, 43604. **419-255-1313** (NBC)

WTOL-TV (Channel 11). 604 Jackson St, Toledo, 43604. **419-244-7411** (CBS)

KTEN (Channel 10). Box 10, Ada, 74820. **405-332-3311** (ABC)

KSWO-TV (Channel 7). Box 708, Lawton, 73501. **405-355-7000** (ABC)

KOCO-TV (Channel 5). Box 32325, Oklahoma City, 73132. **405-848-3311** (ABC)

KTVY (Channel 4). Box 14068, Oklahoma City, 73114. **405-478-1212** (NBC)

KWTV (Channel 9). Box 14159, Oklahoma City, 73114. **405-843-6641** (CBS)

KOTV (Channel 6). 302 S Frankfort, Tulsa, 74120. **918-583-9223** (CBS)

KTEW (Channel 2). 3701 S Peoria, Tulsa, 74105. **918-742-5561** (NBC)

KTUL-TV (Channel 8). Box 8, Tulsa, 74101. **918-446-3351** (ABC)

Oregon

KCBY-TV (Channel 11). Box 1156, Coos Bay, 97420. **503-269-1111** (NBC)

KEZI-TV (Channel 9). 2225 Coburg Rd, Eugene, 97401. **503-343-3301** (ABC)

KVAL-TV (Channel 13). Box 1313, Eugene, 97401. **503-342-4961** (NBC)

KOTI (Channel 2). Box 2K, Klamath Falls, 97601. **503-884-8131** (CBS)

KMED-TV (Channel 10). Box 10, Medford, 97501. **503-773-7373** (NBC)

KOBI (Channel 5). Box 5M, Medford, 97501. **503-779-5555**

KATU (Channel 2). 2153 NE Sandy Blvd, Portland, 97208. **503-233-2422** (ABC)

KGW-TV (Channel 8). 1501 SW Jefferson St, Portland, 97201. **503-224-8620** (NBC)

KOIN-TV (Channel 6). 140 SW Columbia St, Portland, 97201. **503-228-3333** (CBS)

KPTV (Channel 12). Box 3401, Portland, 97208. **503-222-9921**

KPIC (Channel 4). Box 1345, 655 N Umpqua, Roseburg, 97470. **503-672-4481**

KVDO-TV (Channel 3). 3000 Portland Rd NE, Salem, 97303. **503-581-6300**

Pennsylvania

WTAJ-TV (Channel 10). Commerce Park, Altoona, 16603. **814-944-2031** (CBS)

WICU-TV (Channel 12). 3514 State St, Erie, 16508. **814-454-5201** (NBC)

WJAC-TV (Channel 6). Hickory Ln, Johnstown, 15905. **814-255-5831** (NBC)

WGAL-TV (Channel 8). Lincoln Hwy W, Lancaster, 17604. **717-393-5851** (NBC)

KYW-TV (Channel 3). Independence Mall E, Philadelphia, 19106. **215-238-4700** (NBC)

WCAU-TV (Channel 10). City Line and Monument Aves, Philadelphia, 19131. **215-839-7000** (CBS)

WPVI-TV (Channel 6). 4100 City Line Ave, Philadelphia, 19131. **215-878-9700** (ABC)

KDKA-TV (Channel 2). 1 Gateway Ctr, Pittsburgh, 15222. **412-391-3000** (CBS)

WIIC-TV (Channel 11). 341 Rising Main Ave, Pittsburgh, 15214. **412-321-8700** (NBC)

WTAE-TV (Channel 4). 400 Ardmore Blvd, Pittsburg, 15230. **412-242-4300** (ABC)

Rhode Island

WTEV (Channel 6). TV Ctr, New Bedford, 02741. **617-993-2651** (ABC)

WJAR-TV (Channel 10). 176 Weybosset St, Providence, 02902. **401-751-5700** (NBC)

WPRI-TV (Channel 12). 25 Catamore Blvd, East Providence, 02914. **401-438-7200** (CBS)

South Carolina

WLOS-TV (Channel 13). Box 2150, 288 Macon Ave, Asheville, 28802. **704-255-0013** (ABC)

WCBD-TV (Channel 2). Box 879, Charleston, 29402. **803-884-4141** (ABC)

WCSC-TV (Channel 5). Box 186, Charleston, 29402. **803-723-8371** (CBS)

WFBC-TV (Channel 4). Box 788, Greenville, 29602. **803-233-4601** (NBC)

WCIV (Channel 4). Hwy 703, Mount Pleasant, 29464. **803-884-8513** (NBC)

WSPA-TV (Channel 7). Box 1717, Spartanburg, 29304. **803-585-7777** (CBS)

South Dakota

KABY-TV (Channel 9). Box 1520, Aberdeen, 57401. **605-225-4350**

KDLO-TV (Channel 3). Florence

KXON-TV (Channel 5). Box 1049, Mitchell, 57301. **605-996-7501** (ABC)

KOTA-TV (Channel 3). Box 1760, Rapid City, 57701. **605-342-2000** (NBC)

KRSD-TV (Channel 7). 1116 Jackson Blvd, Rapid City, 57701. **605-342-6050** (CBS)

KELO-TV (Channel 11). Phillips at 13th, Sioux Falls, 57102. **605-336-1100** (CBS)

KSFY-TV (Channel 13). 6th and Dakota, Sioux Falls, 57102. **605-336-1300** (NBC)

Tennessee

WDEF-TV (Channel 12). 3300 Broad St, Chattanooga, 37408. **615-267-3392** (CBS)

WRCB-TV (Channel 3). 900 Whitehall Rd, Chattanooga, 37405. **615-267-5412** (NBC)

WTVC (Channel 9). Box 1150, Chattanooga, 37401. **615-756-5500** (ABC)

WBBJ-TV (Channel 7). Box 2387, Jackson 38301. **901-424-4515** (ABC)

WJHL-TV (Channel 11). Box 1130, Johnson City, 37601. **615-926-2151** (CBS)

WATE-TV (Channel 6). 1306 NE Broadway, Knoxville, 37901. **615-637-9666** (NBC)

WBIR-TV (Channel 10). 1513 Hutchison Ave, Knoxville, 37917. **615-637-1010** (CBS)

WHBQ-TV (Channel 13). 485 S Highland Ave, Memphis, 38111. **901-323-7661** (ABC)

WMC-TV (Channel 5). 1960 Union Ave, Memphis, 38104. **901-274-8515** (NBC)

WREG-TV (Channel 3). Hotel Peabody, Memphis, 38103. **901-525-1313** (CBS)

WNGE (Channel 2). 441 Murfreesboro Rd, Nashville, 37210. **615-259-2200** (ABC)

WSM-TV (Channel 4). Box 100, Nashville, 37202. **615-749-2244** (NBC)

WTVF (Channel 5). 474 James Robertson Pkwy, Nashville, 37219. **615-244-5000** (CBS)

Texas

KRBC-TV (Channel 9). 4510 S 14th St, Abilene, 79604. **915-692-4242** (NBC)

KTXS-TV (Channel 12). Box 2997, Abilene, 79604. **915-677-2281** (ABC)

KAMR-TV (Channel 4). Box 751, Amarillo, 79105. **806-383-3321** (NBC)

KFDA-TV (Channel 10). Box 1400, Amarillo, 79105. **806-383-2226** (CBS)

KFDO-TV (Channel 8). Box 1400, Amarillo, 79105. **405-928-3233**

KVII-TV (Channel 7). Box 13000, Amarillo, 79101. **806-373-1787** (ABC)

KTBC-TV (Channel 7). Box 2223, Austin, 78767. **512-472-2424** (CBS)

KBMT (Channel 12). Box 1550, Beaumont, 77704. **713-833-7512** (ABC)

KFDM-TV (Channel 6). Beaumont, 77704. **713-892-6622** (CBS)

KBTX-TV (Channel 3). Drawer 3730, Bryan, 77801. **713-846-7777** (ABC)

KIII (Channel 3). Box 6669, Corpus Christi, 78411. **512-854-4733** (ABC)

KRIS-TV (Channel 6). Box 840, Corpus Christi, 78403. **512-883-6511** (NBC)

KZTV (Channel 10). Show Room Bldg, Corpus Christi, 78401. **512-884-1616** (CBS)

KDFW-TV (Channel 4). 400 N Griffin, Dallas, 75202. **214-742-5711** (CBS)

WFAA-TV (Channel 8). Communications Ctr, Dallas, 75202. **214-748-9631** (ABC)

KDBC-TV (Channel 4). Box 1799, El Paso, 79999. **915-532-6551** (CBS)

KELP-TV (Channel 13). Box 12277, El Paso, 79912. **915-533-5911** (ABC)

KTSM-TV (Channel 9). 801 N Oregon St, El Paso, 79902. **915-532-5423** (NBC)

KTVT (Channel 11). Box 2495, Fort Worth, 76101. **817-738-1951**

KXAS-TV (Channel 5). Box 1780, Fort Worth, 76101. **817-429-1550** (NBC)

KGBT-TV (Channel 4). Box 711, Harlingen, 78550. **512-423-3910** (CBS)

KHOU-TV (Channel 11). Box 11, Houston, 77001. **713-526-8811** (CBS)

KPRC-TV (Channel 2). Box 2222, Houston, 77001. **713-771-4631** (NBC)

KTRK-TV (Channel 13). Box 13, Houston, 77001. **713-666-0713** (ABC)

KGNS-TV (Channel 8). Box 1378, Laredo, 78040. **512-723-7457** (NBC)

KVTV (Channel 13). Box 735, Laredo, 78040. **512-723-2923** (CBS)

KCBD-TV (Channel 11). Box 2190, Lubbock, 79408. **806-744-1414** (NBC)

KSWS-TV (Channel 8). Box 2190, Lubbock, 79408. **806-744-1414** (NBC)

KLBK-TV (Channel 13). 7400 University Ave, Lubbock, 79408. **806-744-2345** (CBS)

KTRE-TV (Channel 9). Drawer 729, Lufkin, 75901. **713-634-7771** (NBC)

KMID-TV (Channel 2). Drawer B, Midland, 79701. **915-563-2222** (NBC)

KMOM-TV (Channel 9). Drawer N, Monahans, 79756. **915-943-3231** (ABC)

KOSA-TV (Channel 7). Box 4186, 1211 N Whitaker, Odessa, 79760. **915-337-8301** (CBS)

KENS-TV (Channel 5). Box TV5, San Antonio, 78299. **512-225-5211** (CBS)

KMOL-TV (Channel 4). Box 2641, San Antonio, 78299. **512-226-4251** (NBC)

KSAT-TV (Channel 12). Box 2478, San Antonio, 78298. **512-226-7611** (ABC)

KXII (Channel 12). Box 1175, Sherman, 75090. **214-892-8123**

KCEN-TV (Channel 6). Box 188, Temple, 87601. **817-773-6868** (NBC)

KLTV (Channel 7). Box 957, Tyler, 75701. **214-592-3873** (ABC)

KWTX-TV (Channel 10). Box 7528, Waco, 76710. **817-776-1330** (CBS)

KRGV-TV (Channel 5). Box 626, Weslaco, 78596. **512-968-3131** (NBC)

KAUZ-TV (Channel 6). Box 2130, Wichita Falls, 76307. **817-322-6957** (CBS)

KFDX-TV (Channel 3). Box 4000, Wichita Falls, 76308. **817-692-4530** (NBC)

Utah

KSL-TV (Channel 5). 145 Social Hall Ave, Salt Lake City, 84111. **801-524-2500** (CBS)

KTVX (Channel 4). 1760 Fremont Dr, Salt Lake City, 84104. **801-486-3392** (ABC)

KUTV (Channel 2). 179 Social Hall Ave, Salt Lake City, 84111. **801-322-2505** (NBC)

Vermont

WCAX-TV (Channel 3). Box 608, Burlington, 05401. **802-862-5761** (CBS)

Virginia

WCYB-TV (Channel 5). Box 100., Bristol, 24201. **703-699-4161**

WVEC-TV (Channel 13). Box 400, Hampton, 23669. **804-722-6331**

WSVA-TV (Channel 3). Box 752, Harrisonburg, 22801. **703-434-0331** (ABC)

WLVA-TV (Channel 13). Box 238, Lynchburg, 24505. **804-845-1242** (ABC)

WTAR-TV (Channel 3). 720 Boush St, Norfolk, 23510. **804-625-6711** (CBS)

WAVY-TV (Channel 10). 801 Wavy St, Portsmouth, 23704. **804-397-3441** (NBC)

WTVR-TV (Channel 6). 3301 W Broad St, Richmond, 23230. **804-355-8611** (CBS)

WWBT (Channel 12). 5710 Midlothian Tpke, Richmond, 23201. **804-233-5461** (NBC)

WXEX-TV (Channel 8). Box 888, Richmond, 23207. **804-643-0166** (ABC)

WDBJ-TV (Channel 7). Box 7, Roanoke, 24022. **703-343-8031** (CBS)

WSLS-TV (Channel 10). Box 2161, Roanoke, 24009. **703-344-9226** (NBC)

Washington

KVOS-TV (Channel 12). 115 Ellis St, Bellingham, 98225. **206-734-4101** (CBS)

KING-TV (Channel 5). 320 Aurora Ave, Seattle, 98109. **206-223-5000** (NBC)

KIRO-TV (Channel 7). 3rd and Broad, Seattle, 98121. **206-624-7077** (CBS)

KOMO-TV (Channel 4). 100 4th Ave N, Seattle, 98109. **206-223-4000** (ABC)

KHQ-TV (Channel 6). 4202 S Regal St, Spokane, 99203. **509-534-0511** (NBC)

KREM-TV (Channel 2). 4103 S Regal St, Spokane, 99203. **509-534-0423** (ABC)

KXLY-TV (Channel 4). 500 W Boone Ave, Spokane, 99201. **509-328-9084** (CBS)

KSTW (Channel 11). Box 11411, Tacoma, 98411. **206-572-5789**

West Virginia

WHIS-TV (Channel 6). Broadcast Ctr, E Cumberland Rd, Bluefield, 24701. **304-327-7114** (NBC)

WDTV (Channel 5). Box 480, Bridgeport, 26330. **304-842-3558**

WCHS-TV (Channel 8). 1111 Virginia St E, Charleston, 25324. **304-342-8131** (CBS)

WBOY-TV (Channel 12). 912 W Pike St, Clarksburg, 26301. **304-624-7573** (NBC)

WOWK-TV (Channel 13). 625 4th Ave, Huntington, 25701. **304-525-7551** (ABC)

WSAZ-TV (Channel 3). 645 5th Ave, Huntington, 25721. **304-697-4780** (NBC)

WOAY-TV (Channel 4). Box 251, Oak Hill, 25901. **304-469-3361** (ABC)

WTRF-TV (Channel 7). 96 16th St, Wheeling, 26003. **304-232-7777** (NBC)

Wisconsin

WEAU-TV (Channel 13). Box 47, Eau Claire, 54701. **715-832-3474** (NBC)

WBAY-TV (Channel 2). 115 S Jefferson, Green Bay, 54301. **414-432-3331** (CBS)

WFRV-TV (Channel 5). 1181 E Mason St (Box 1128), Green Bay, 54305. **414-437-5411** (NBC)

WLUK-TV (Channel 11). Box 7711, Green Bay, 54303. **414-494-8711** (ABC)

WKBT (Channel 8). 141 S 6th St, La Crosse, 54601. **608-782-4678** (CBS)

WISC-TV (Channel 3). 4801 W Beltline Hwy, Madison, 53711. **608-271-4321** (CBS)

WISN-TV (Channel 12). Box 420, Milwaukee, 53201. **414-342-8812** (CBS)

WITI-TV (Channel 6). 5445 N 27th St, Milwaukee, 53209. **414-462-6666** (ABC)

WTMJ-TV (Channel 4). 720 E Capitol Dr, Milwaukee, 53211. **414-332-9611** (NBC)

WAEO-TV (Channel 12). Box 858, Rhinelander, 54501. **715-369-4700** (NBC)

WAOW-TV (Channel 9). 1908 Grand Ave, Wausau, 54401. **715-842-2251** (ABC)

WSAU-TV (Channel 7). 1114 Grand Ave, Wausau, 54401. **715-845-4211** (CBS)

Wyoming

KTWO-TV (Channel 2). Box 2720, Casper, 82602. **307-237-3711** (NBC)

KYCU-TV (Channel 5). 2923 E Lincolnway, Cheyenne, 82001. **307-634-7755** (CBS)

KWRB-TV (Channel 10). 500 Arapahoe, Thermopolis, Riverton, 82443. **307-864-2351**

PUBLIC RELATIONS

O'DWYER'S LIST OF LARGEST PUBLIC RELATIONS FIRMS

The following agencies are those listed in *O'Dwyer's Directory of Public Relations Firms* as the 40 largest public relations operations, independent and ad agency affiliated. The determination is based on annual net fee income as shown in documentation submitted to O'Dwyer's.

AYER PUBLIC RELATIONS SERVICES. 1345 Avenue of the Americas, New York, NY 10019. **212-974-7400.** A P Galli, senior vice-president and director, public relations

BARKIN, HERMAN, SOLOCHEK, AND PAULSEN. 777 E Wisconsin Ave, Milwaukee, WI 53202. **414-271-7434**

SYDNEY S BARON AND CO, INC. 540 Madison Ave, New York, NY 10022. **212-751-7100.** Jessie M Canning, president. Margaret Maese, media

BROOKE AND CO. 919 3rd Ave, New York, NY 10022. **212-593-8600.** Dear R Erickson, president

BURSON MARSTELLER. 866 3rd Ave, New York, NY 10022. **212-752-8610.** Elias Buchwald, vice-chairman

CARL BYOIR AND ASSOCIATES. 800 2nd Ave, New York, NY 10017. **212-986-6100.** Robert J Wood, president

CREAMER DICKSON BASFORD, INC. 1301 Avenue of the Americas, New York, NY 10019. **212-956-5200.** Sally Dickson, president

CUNNINGHAM AND WALSH, PUBLIC RELATIONS DIVISION. 260 Madison Ave, New York, NY 10016. **212-683-4900.** Edgar A Falk, vice-president and director, public relations

AARON D CUSHMAN AND ASSOCIATES. 333 N Michigan Ave, Chicago, IL 60601. **312-263-2500.** Aaron D Cushman, president

DOREMUS AND CO. 120 Broadway, New York, NY 10005. **212-964-0700.** Wesley E Truesdell, senior vice-president and director, public relations department

DUDLEY-ANDERSON-YUTZY. 40 W 57th St, New York, NY 10019. **212-977-9400.** Jean Way Shoanover, president

DANIEL J EDELMAN. 221 La Salle St, Chicago, IL 60601. **312-368-0400.** Daniel J Edelman, president

FLEISHMAN-HILLARD. 1 Memorial Dr, St Louis, MO 63102. **314-231-1733.** John D Graham, president

FOOTE, CONE, AND BELDING, PUBLIC RELATIONS. 401 N Michigan Ave, Chicago, IL 60611. **312-467-9200.** Thomas L Harris, vice-president and director, public relations

ANTHONY M FRANCO. 28 W Adams Ave, Detroit, MI 48226. **313-962-4510.** Anthony M Franco, president. Ronald Hingst, media relations

GIBBS AND SOELL. 117 E 38th St, New York, NY 10010. **212-679-2630.** Richard L Gibbs, president

GOLIN COMMUNICATIONS. 500 N Michigan Ave, Chicago, IL 60611. **312-836-7100.** Alvin Golin, president

GRAY AND ROGERS. 1234 Market St E, Philadelphia, PA 19107. **215-864-6800.** David L Ferrell, executive vice-president and director, public relations

GROSS AND ASSOCIATES. 592 5th Ave, New York, NY 10036. **212-221-2267.** Sidney Gross, president

HARSHE-ROTTMAN AND DRUCH. 300 E 44th St, New York, NY 10017. **212-661-3400.** Morris B Rottman, chairman

HILL AND KNOWLTON. 633 3rd Ave, New York, NY 10017. **212-697-5600.** William A Durbin, chairman. Toney File, media, **212-697-5614** or **5611**

EDWARD HOWARD AND CO. 1021 Euclid Ave, Cleveland, OH 44115. **216-781-2400.** John T Bailey, president

ICPR. 9255 W Sunset Blvd, Los Angeles, CA. **213-874-0204.** Rupert Allan, executive officer

WOODY KEPNER ASSOCIATES. 3361 W 3rd Ave, Miami, FL 33145. **305-854-4765.** Woody Kepner, president

KETCHUM, MACLEOD, AND GROVE. 4 Gateway Ctr, Pittsburgh, PA 15222. **412-261-5100.** Robert E Shafer, acting supervisor

MANNING, SELVAGE, AND LEE, INC. 6th Floor, 666 5th Ave, New York, NY 10019. **212-586-2600.** Robert N Schwartz, president

ROBERT MARSTON AND ASSOCIATES. 645 Madison Ave, New York, NY 10022. **212-593-1914.** Robert A Marston, president

HANK MEYER ASSOCIATES. 2990 Biscayne Blvd, Miami, FL 33137. **305-576-5700.** Hank Meyer, president

PADILLA AND SPEAR. 244 Franklin Ave, West Minneapolis, MN 55404. **612-871-8900.** Donald G Padilla, president

PUBLIC COMMUNICATIONS. 35 E Wacker Dr, Chicago, IL 60601. **312-726-9766.** James B Strenski, chairman

ROGERS AND COWAN. 3 E 54th St, New York, NY 10017. **212-486-7100.** Kathie Berlin, vice-president

THE ROWLAND CO. 415 Madison Ave, New York, NY 10017. **212-688-1200.** Herbert L Rowland, president

RUDER AND FINN. 110 E 59th St, New York, NY 10022. **212-593-6400.** David Finn, president

THE SOFTNESS GROUP. 3 E 54th St, New York, NY 10022. **212-752-7700.** John Softness, president

SONTHEIMER AND CO. 445 Park Ave, New York, NY 10022. **212-688-8350.** Morton Sontheimer, president

J WALTER THOMPSON. 420 Lexington Ave, New York, NY 10017. **212-686-1383.** Jack Raymond, president

UNDERWOOD, JORDAN ASSOCIATES. 230 Park Ave, New York, NY 10017. **212-686-4700.** Don Underwood, chairman

RICHARD WEINER. 888 7th Ave, New York, NY 10019. **212-582-7373.** Richard Weiner, president

PUBLIC RELATIONS WIRE SERVICES

All these services reach major news media in their cities via teleprinter or similar means. They serve largely to distribute company and government handouts by wire.

ATLANTA. Southeastern Press Relations News Wire. Suite 417, 161 Peachtree St, Atlanta, GA 30303. **404-523-2515**

CHICAGO. PR News Service. 188 W Randolph St, Chicago, IL 60601. **312-782-9655**

DALLAS (HOUSTON). Southwest Press Relations Newswire. 1355 Mercantile Dallas Bldg, 1807 Commerce St, Dallas, TX 77030. **214-748-1943.** Also 1303 Fannin Bank Bldg, 1020 Holcombe Blvd, Houston, TX 77025. **713-795-0631**

DETROIT. Press Relations Newswire. 24500 Southfield Rd, Southfield, MI 48075. **313-557-7474.** James O Brams, manager

MINNEAPOLIS. Newswire Central, 224 Franklin Ave W, Minneapolis, MN 55404. **612-871-7201**

NEW YORK. PR Newswire, 150 E 58th St, New York, NY 10022. **212-832-9400**
Regional Offices
Boston. 225 Franklin St, Boston, MA 02101. **617-482-5355**
Miami. 3892 Biscayne Blvd, Miami, FL 33137. **305-576-5020**
Los Angeles. 900 Wilshire Blvd, Los Angeles, CA 90017. **213-626-5501**
San Francisco. 145 Montgomery St, San Francisco, CA 94104. **415-781-7210**

PHILADELPHIA. Mediawire, 1530 Chestnut St, Philadelphia, PA 19102. **215-568-2961**

SAN FRANCISCO. Business Wire, 235 Montgomery St, San Francisco, CA 94104. **415-986-4422.** WATS: **800-227-0845**
Regional Offices
Boston. 10 Post Office Sq, Boston, MA 02109. **617-426-1320**
Los Angeles. 3600 Wilshire Blvd, Los Angeles, CA 90010. **213-380-8383**
Seattle. 905 Tower Bldg, Seattle, WA 98101. **206-622-1632**

TORONTO (Canada). Canada News Wire. 25 Adelaide St W, Toronto, Ont, Canada. **416-863-9380.** Coast to coast in Canada, or Montreal, Toronto, and Ottawa

WASHINGTON. Press Relations Wire, Inc, 979 National Press Bldg, Washington, DC 20045. **202-347-5155**

NATIONAL JOURNALISM AWARDS

The awards are listed in the order of approximate final entry date, which may be subject to change.

MIKE BERGER AWARD. January 10. Open to all New York reporters. Nominating letter; biographical sketch. Dean, Graduate School of Journalism, Columbia University, New York, NY 10027

HEYWOOD BROUN AWARD. January 14. Accompanying letter on circumstances and ingenuity; mounted copy of article. Newspaper Guild, 1125 15th St NW, Washington, DC 20005

ERNIE PYLE MEMORIAL AWARD. January 15. Nominating letter; biographical sketch; mounted copy of article. Scripps-Howard Foundation, 200 Park Ave, New York, NY 10017

ENGINEERING JOURNALISM AWARDS PROGRAM. January 15. Original copy. National Society of Professional Engineers, 2029 K St NW, Washington, DC 20006

SIDNEY HILLMAN AWARDS. January 15. Accompanying letters; do not mount. Amalgamated Clothing Workers, 15 Union Sq, New York, NY 10003

SIGMA DELTA CHI, NATIONAL CHAPTER—DISTINGUISHED SERVICE AWARD. January 25. Nomination form; biographical sketch; photo of author; fee; mounted in booklet form, not larger than 20×24 inches. Sigma Delta Chi, Suite 3108, 35 E Wacker Dr, Chicago, IL 60601

ROBERT F KENNEDY AWARD. January 28. Entry form; four copies, mounted, not larger than 15×24 inches. Journalism Awards Committee, 1035 30th St NW, Washington, DC 20007. **202-338-7444**

JOHN HANCOCK AWARDS FOR EXCELLENCE IN BUSINESS JOURNALISM. January 31. Entry form; six copies, unmounted, whole pages. Awards for Excellence, John Hancock Mutual Life Insurance Co, PO Box 111, Boston, MA 02117

CECIL AWARDS (ARTHRITIS). January 31. Entry form; five copies (original, showing name and date of publication), unmounted. The Arthritis Foundation, 3400 Peachtree Rd NE, Atlanta, GA 30326 (Attention: Roy Scott)

CATHERINE O'BRIEN AWARDS. January 31. Entry blank; one unmounted copy; up to three news stories. Ruder and Finn, 110 E 59th St, New York, NY 10022

SCIENCE WRITING AWARD. January 31. Entry blank; nine copies; up to three entries per author. American Institute of Physics, 335 E 45th St, New York, NY 10017

RELIGION NEWSWRITERS ASSN—JAMES O SUPPLE AWARD. February 1. Clippings of 10 articles; mounted ($8\frac{1}{2} \times 11$ inches), showing date published, name of publication, and writer. W A Reed, *Nashville Tennessean*, 1100 Broadway, Nashville, TN 37203

RELIGION NEWSWRITERS ASSN—HAROLD J SCHAHERN MEMORIAL AWARD. February 1. Clippings of five sections of newspaper on religion (loose). W A Reed, *Nashville Tennessean*, 1100 Broadway, Nashville, TN 37203

PULITZER PRIZE. February 1. Biographical sketch and photo of nominee; 1–2 page summary and background; one mounted copy. Advisory Board on the Pulitzer Prizes, 702 Journalism, Columbia University, New York, NY 10027. **212-280-3841**

THOMAS L STOKES AWARD. February 1. Letter summarizing work; one unmounted copy. Washington Journalism Center, 2401 Virginia Ave NW, Washington, DC 20037

EDWARD WILLIS SCRIPPS AWARD. February 1. Sponsoring letter; one mounted copy. Scripps-Howard Foundation, 200 Park Ave, New York, NY 10017

BOB CONSIDINE MEMORIAL AWARD. February 2. Mounted entry, supplemented by three copies of 200-word biography and three photos; classification designated on outside; fee. Overseas Press Club, Biltmore Hotel, Madison Ave and 43rd St, New York, NY 10017

MARK OF EXCELLENCE CONTEST (college journalism). February 10. Sigma Delta Chi, 35 E Wacker Dr, Chicago, IL 60601

CLAUDE BERNARD SCIENCE JOURNALISM AWARDS. February 15. Two copies, separate cover sheet. National Society for Medical Research, 1000 Vermont Ave NW, Washington, DC 20005

NATIONAL HEADLINER AWARD. February 15. Entry blanks; background letter of accomplishments and results; clippings can be included. National Headliners Club, Convention Hall, Atlantic City, NJ 08401

CLARION AWARDS. February 15. Entry blank; objectives, approach, rationale; fee. Women in Communications, PO Box 9561, Austin, TX 78766

EDWARD J MEEMAN CONSERVATION AWARD. February 15. Sponsoring letter; mounted entry. Scripps-Howard Foundation, 200 Park Ave, New York, NY 10017

PAUL TOBENKEN AWARD. February 15. Four copies (one mounted, three tearsheets); letter from editor; biographical resume, plus accompanying letter in summary. Graduate School of Journalism, Columbia University, New York, NY 10027

GERALD LOEB AWARD. February 15. Entry blank; eight copies (unmounted). Gerald F Corrigan, Graduate School of Management, UCLA, 405 Hilgard Ave, Los Angeles, CA 90024

EDWARD WEINTAL JOURNALISM PRIZE. March 1. Letter of introduction. School of Foreign Service, Georgetown University, Washington, DC 20007

SILVER GAVEL AWARDS. March 1. (Books: February 1). Entry blank; biographical sketch; introductory letter of objectives and achievements; letter of summary; three copies plus one original (mounted, $8\frac{1}{2} \times 11$ inches). American Bar Association, 1155 E 60th St, Chicago, IL 60637

ROY HOWARD PUBLIC SERVICE AWARD. March 1. Sponsoring letter from a colleague; brief history; one mounted copy. Scripps-Howard Foundation, 200 Park Ave, New York, NY 10017

GRADY AWARD. March 1. Nomination by member of American Chemical Society; biographical sketch; introductory letter with

identification and evaluation; six copies (mounted, $8\frac{1}{2} \times 11$ inches). American Chemical Society, 1155 16th St NW, Washington, DC 20036

DEEMS TAYLOR AWARD. March 1. Letter of introduction; five copies. American Society of Composers and Authors, 1 Lincoln Plz, New York, NY 10023

AMERICAN SOCIETY OF PLANNING OFFICIALS AWARD. March 1. Sponsoring letter; entry form; background data on article; brief factual statements by planning officials, or civil association, on the effect of the article (if appropriate); article mounted, 15×24 inches. American Society of Planning Officials, 1313 E 60th St, Chicago, IL 60637

INTERNATIONAL ASSOCIATION OF FIRE FIGHTERS AWARDS CONTEST. March 15. International Association of Fire Fighters, 1750 New York Ave NW, Washington, DC 20006

MARIA MOORS CABOT PRIZES. March. Graduate School of Journalism, Columbia University, New York, NY 10027

HOWARD BLAKESLEE AWARD. May 1. Entry blank; statement of objectives and intended audience; unmounted copy. American Heart Association, 7320 Greenville Ave, Dallas, TX 75231

SCIENCE IN SOCIETY JOURNALISM AWARD. May 1. Entry blank; 10 copies (one original tearsheet plus nine copies; mount one); article must explain why its materials matter. National Association of Science Writers, PO Box H, Sea Cliff, NY 11579

BUSINESS JOURNALISM AWARD. May. Entry blank; six copies (two originals plus four copies); tearsheets only. Neff Hall, School of Journalism, University of Missouri, Columbia, MO 65201

AMERICAN PSYCHOLOGICAL ASSOCIATION NATIONAL MEDIA AWARD. May. Entry blank; two copies. American Psychological Association, 1200 17th St NW, Washington, DC 20036

APME FREEDOM OF INFORMATION AWARD. July. Narrative of courageous acts. Associated Press Managing Editors, c/o The Associated Press, 50 Rockefeller Plz, New York, NY 10020

PACEMAKER AWARDS (college journalism). July. Associated Collegiate Press, 720 Washington Ave SE, Minneapolis, MN 55414

PUBLIC SERVICE AWARDS. August 10. Letter of background and accomplishments (all mounted). Associated Press Managing Editors, c/o The Associated Press, 50 Rockefeller Plz, New York, NY 10020

MENTAL HEALTH BELL AWARDS. August. Apply by letter to the Pennsylvania Mental Health Association; supplemental materials are welcome; mounted copy. National Association for Mental Health, 1800 N Kent St, Arlington, VA 22209

AMERICAN ACADEMY OF PEDIATRICS AWARD. August. Covering letter; two copies. American Academy of Pediatrics, 1801 Hinman Ave, Evanston, IL 60204

GEORGE JEAN NATHAN DRAMA AWARD (criticism and reviews). September. Entry blank. George Jean Nathan Trust, Manufacturers Hanover Trust Co, 350 Park Ave, New York, NY 10022

FORUM AWARD. September. Entry blank; six copies. Atomic Industrial Forum, Inc, 7101 Wisconsin Ave, Washington, DC 20014

AMERICAN CANCER SOCIETY MEDIA AWARDS. September. Two copies of article; tape or summary of broadcast. American Cancer Society, Suite 1900, 40 W 57th St, New York, NY 10019

REAL ESTATE JOURNALISM ACHIEVEMENT COMPETITION. October 1. National Association of Realtors, 430 N Michigan Ave, Chicago, IL 60611

PENNEY-MISSOURI AWARDS, (Lifestyle Section Entry). October 31 (May 1 for articles). Entry blank; four sets of each entry (three daily papers in one week); full pages, unmounted. School of Journalism, University of Missouri, Columbia, MO 65201

UNIVERSITY OF MISSOURI JOURNALISM HONOR AWARDS. November 1.

Letter of nomination. Dean, School of Journalism, University of Missouri, Columbia, MO 65201

WESTINGHOUSE SCIENCE AWARDS. November. Entry blank; five copies. American Association for the Advancement of Science, 1515 Massachusetts Ave NW, Washington, DC 20005

DREW PEARSON PRIZE. November. Drew Pearson Foundation, 1156 15th St NW, Washington, DC 20005

AMERICAN INSTITUTE OF ARCHITECTS AWARD. November. American Institute of Architects, 1735 New York Ave NW, Washington, DC 20006

EPILEPSY FOUNDATION OF AMERICA AWARD. December. Epilepsy Foundation of America, 1828 L St NW, Washington, DC 20036

PRESS CLUBS

At the turn of the century, press clubs were such a universal institution that there even existed an International League of Press Clubs. Virtually every city big enough to have a couple of daily newspapers had its club. Every respectable club had a bar open to the wee hours; most had restaurants, apartments for weary toilers (inebriated and otherwise), telegraph lines, and other amenities. But as the number of daily newspapers encountered the great post-World War II decline, so did the press clubs. Many folded; others just atrophied.

Today those that survive are a select few, but they remain an important resource for both local and visiting press. Most of them welcome visiting journalists, although some require membership in another club that grants reciprocal privileges. In most cases reciprocity, if it does not already exist, is easily established by an exchange of correspondence between officers of the clubs in question. Some clubs maintain work spaces for journalists and provide access to transmission facilities. Most have local newspapers on hand. And all are likely to offer that most important resource: a wagging tongue at the brass rail.

There are welcome signs of growth among press clubs today; many of the clubs surveyed reported plans of expansion. In some cities where the press club of yore has folded, a paper organization lives on in the hopes of restarting the club, and there are reports of plans for new clubs in several cities. Press clubs are undoubtedly profiting from the renewed respectability of the profession today, and the growing sense of camaraderie that has resulted.

Because of this resurgence, the following list of bona fide press clubs is undoubtedly incomplete. It is as comprehensive as any list around, however, because there is no other list, and most major cities are represented. The great exception is New York City, where the lack of a true press club is probably a statement in itself. Candidates for inclusion in future editions are invited.

In the survey upon which this list is based, an attempt was made to weed out organizations that are not truly press clubs, that is, clubs run basically by and for working press. Where possible, each listing includes details on officers, types of membership and dues, bar and restaurant hours, special facilities, club policy on visiting press and members

of other clubs, person to contact to obtain access, and club publications.

ALASKA PRESS CLUB. 4808 Sund Dr, Anchorage, AK 99502. **907-265-4412.** Cliff Cernick, president. Membership open to working press ($10) and others with press interests ($15). Founded 1954. Meets in existing hotels. Out-of-town press welcome. Reciprocal privileges to members of other clubs. *Contact.* President. Newsletter. *Polar Bear*

ALBUQUERQUE PRESS CLUB. 201 Highland Park Cir SE (PO Box 644), Albuquerque, NM 87103. **505-766-5327.** Tomas Martinez, president. Membership open to working press ($15), professional associates ($17.50), and social members ($20). Founded 1966. Usual bar hours: Wed and Fri, 9 pm to 2 am. Kitchen facilities Reciprocal privileges to out-of-town press and members of other clubs; also, guest privileges to visiting journalists. *Contact.* Martinez, assistant state editor of *Albuquerque Journal.* Monthly newsletter

ARKANSAS PRESS ASSOCIATION. 212 Wallace Bldg, Little Rock, AK 72201. Louise Bowker, manager. "We do not have a press club in Arkansas, haven't had for years. We maintain a listing in the hope we can re-establish some day."

ATLANTA PRESS CLUB. PO Box 615, Atlanta, GA 30301. **404-659-3954** (answering service). Zeke Segal, chief, CBS News Southeastern Bureau, president. Larry Keller, executive secretary, **404-523-2515.** Working press ($20), public relations and news sources ($40), students ($5), and nonresidents ($10). Founded 1964 to 1965. Visiting journalists and members of other clubs welcome. *APC News Notes*

BIRMINGHAM PRESS CLUB. Suite 228, Clark Bldg, Corner of 4th Ave and 20th St N, Mailing address: PO Box 2493, Birmingham, AL 35201. **205-325-2109.** Ralph Cassell Palmer, president. Working press, non-news persons working in support functions for news media, nonprofit public relations and students ($30); commercial public relations, advertising, and allied fields ($50). Founded 1968. Bar hours: Mon to Wed, 4:30 pm to 10:30 pm; Thurs and Fri, 4:30 pm to midnight. Serves light food. Telephones and file of local newspapers. Out-of-town press welcome; reciprocal club members and all active members of Sigma Delta Chi welcome. "Alabama law requires that guests in licensed private clubs be in company of a club member. However, this law has never caused a problem with visiting journalists, whether on assignment or not." *Contact* by phoning city desk of *Birmingham News* or *Post-Herald*. Monthly newsletter

DENVER PRESS CLUB. 1330 Glenarm Pl, Denver, CO 80200. **303-255-2591.** Ernie Azlein, president. Active members ($43.20), associate members ($86.40). Chartered 1890. Bar hours: 11 am to 2 am. Restaurant hours: 11 am to 11 pm
Out-of-town journalists welcome, but "must pay cash." Members of other press clubs also welcome. *Contact.* Manager. Issues a regular publication

PRESS CLUB OF EL PASO. Box 20, Kansas and Mills Sts, El Paso, TX 79999. **915-747-6900.** Robert J McBrinn, president. Working press ($7.50), public relations ($10), honorary ($15). Founded about 25 years ago. Club activities held at Empire Club (private club)
Members of other press welcome to attend functions

HONOLULU PRESS CLUB. 12 S King St, Honolulu, HI 96800. **808-523-1222.** Harry Lyons, president. Elva Johnson, club manager. Working press ($15), public relations and journalism students ($25), sustaining members such as politicians, attorneys, and business people ($40). Founded 1946. Bar hours: 11:30 am to 7:30 pm weekdays (also, special Friday programs, hours until 11 pm). Restaurant: 11:30 am to 2 pm. Public telephones and public address system. Out-of-town press "very welcome"; need only show credentials. Members of other press clubs welcome. "Try to be commercial but end up nonprofit." *Contact.* Elva Johnson at club number. Twice monthly newsletter

PRESS CLUB OF HOUSTON. Suite 601, 2016 Main St, Houston, TX 77002. **713-659-4309.** Michael G Harris, manager. Working press, electronic media, public relations (active, $60; associate, $120). Founded 1949. Bar hours: 11 am to 9 pm daily. Restaurant: 11 am to 3 pm. Public telephones and press conference meeting areas. Visiting journalists welcome on cash basis with press credentials. Members of other press clubs welcome. *Contact.* Manager

IDAHO PRESS CLUB. PO Box 2221, Boise, ID. Quane Kenyon. Journalists ($5). No facilities at present. "There's usually a bottle around. We'd be happy to share" with visiting press and members of other clubs. *Contact.* Tim Woodward, *The Idaho Statesman*

INDIANAPOLIS PRESS CLUB. 150 W Market St, Indianapolis, IN, 46204. **317-636-2343.** Ralph L Darling, general manager. Working press, public relations, lobbyists, and state government members ($30 to $85). Founded 1933. Bar hours: 11 am to 11 pm Mon to Fri. Restaurant hours 11 am to 8 pm.
File of local newspapers, library, pool, and card and social rooms; available from 11 am to 8 pm. Out-of town journalists welcome on cash basis. Members of other press clubs welcome. *Contact.* General manager. Monthly newsletter

LAS VEGAS PRESS CLUB. 1724 E Charleston Blvd, Las Vegas, NV 89104. **702-385-2898.** Charles A Fleming, president. John Cartwright, steward. Newsroom ($20), regular ($30), associate ($50). "Associate membership open to just about anyone." Founded 1948. Bar hours: 3 pm to 11 pm Mon to Sat

Work space with typewriters, public telephones, small library, meeting room. "Immediately adjacent to a large branch of the Clark County library." Out-of-town journalists and members of other press clubs welcome. *Contact.* President or steward. Monthly newsletter

GREATER LOS ANGELES PRESS CLUB. 600 N Vermont Ave, Los Angeles, CA 90004. **213-665-1141.** Alberto C Diaz, president. Joe Sorrentino, manager. Journalists, public relations, students, professors, "contributors to media" (from $43 for newsmen to $246 for corporate members). Bar hours: usually 10 am to 10 pm Mon to Fri. Restaurant hours: 11:30 am to 3:00 pm daily Work space with typewriters, public telephones, and library; available 10 am to 10 pm. Out-of-town journalists and members of other press clubs welcome. Club is commercial; rents space for press conferences. *Contact.* Manager. Monthly newsletter, *Eight Ball*, and yearbook

MADISON PRESS CLUB. PO Box 33, Madison, WI 53701. **608-257-0711.** Mickey McLinden, president. Working press, public relations, students, and communicators. Dues: working press ($20), nonresident ($15), associate ($25). Founded 1957. No permanent quarters
Meets for dinner programs monthly; members of other press clubs or visiting press welcome. *Contact.* Local newspaper city desk. Monthly newsletter

MILWAUKEE PRESS CLUB. 125 E Wells St, Milwaukee, WI 53201. **414-273-7375.** John Thompson, president. William Griesemer, manager. Journalists, public relations, students, advertising executives. Founded November 1, 1885. Bar hours: Mon, Tues, Thurs, 11 am to 7 pm; Wed and Fri, 11 am to 2 am. Restaurant hours: Mon to Fri, 11 am to 2 pm; plus, on Wed and Fri, 5:30 pm to 10 pm
Public telephones, library, limited work space with typewriters, small meeting rooms. Out-of-town press welcome, but "no credit extended"; members of other press clubs welcome. *Contact.* Manager. Monthly newsletter and yearbook

MINNESOTA PRESS CLUB. Radisson Hotel, 45 S 7th St, Minneapolis, MN 55402. **612-338-4466.** Don W Larson, president. Richard Holter, chairman. Jan Claseman, manager. Working press and others (active, $55; associate, $60); students and apprentices ($10). Founded 1959. Bar and restaurant hours: 11:30 am to 7:30 pm

Public telephones, file of local newspapers, library, news conference facilities. Out-of-town journalists and members of other press clubs admitted if they belong to reciprocal press clubs. *Contact.* Manager

MONTREAL PRESS CLUB/CERCLE DES JOURNALISTES DE MONTREAL. Sheraton-Mount Royal Hotel, Montreal, Que, Canada. **514-849-2281.** Axel Thogerson, president. Rene Beaulieu, chief steward. Working press ($45), public relations ($90). Founded 1948. Bar hours: 11:30 am to 2:30 am (and sometimes 4 am) Mon. to Fri. Club has its own facilities in the hotel. Public telephones, file of local newspapers. Those seeking access must belong to another bona fide press club, except that visiting journalists with no press club in their own hometowns are welcome (but may not bring guests other than an escort). *Contact.* Duty steward at the bar

NATIONAL PRESS CLUB. National Press Bldg, 529 14th St NW, Washington, DC 20045. **202-737-2500.** Frank A Aukofer, president. Working press, public relations, students, professors, and associate members "who are a source of news." No information submitted on dues. Founded March 1908. Utilizes the top two floors of the National Press Building, of which it owns 78% of the stock. Bar hours: Mon to Fri, 11:30 am to 2:00 am; Sat, to 8 pm. Restaurant hours: Mon to Fri, 11:30 am to 8:30 pm; Sat, to 3:30 pm
Transmission facilities, work space with typewriters, public telephones, file of local newspapers, library, ballroom; available 24 hours on weekdays, closed 8 pm Sat to Mon morning. Out-of-town journalists admitted with a guest card, or if they belong to a club with established reciprocal privileges. Members of other press clubs admitted if their clubs have formal reciprocity. *Contact for a guest card.* A member or, "in extraordinary circumstances," the manager. Weekly house organ

PRESS CLUB OF NEW ORLEANS. Suite 210, 301 Camp St, New Orleans, LA, 70130. **504-524-1131,** Ext 288. Ed Anderson, Jr, president. Working press, public relations, students, professors, employees of media organizations ($15 to $75). Founded 1958. Permanent office, but no bar or restaurant at present. "Every effort is being made to find a permanent home as soon as possible." Out-of-town press and members of other clubs welcome. *Contact.* Bonnie A Morris, executive secretary, **504-523-1010.** Monthly newsletter

PRESS CLUB OF OHIO. 62 E Broad St, Columbus, OH 43215. **614-464-1856.** Phil Jenkins, club manager. Working press and others, $21 to $48. Bar hours: Mon to Fri, 11 am to 1 am. Restaurant hours: Mon to Fri, 11 am to 2 pm
Out-of-town journalists welcome up to three times a year; members of other press clubs welcome. "Ring door bell."

OMAHA PRESS CLUB, INC. 22nd Floor, First National Ctr, 17th and Dodge Sts, Omaha, NE, 68102. **402-345-8008.** Al Crounse, president. Hans Luthi, executive director. Unrestricted membership: working press ($30), public relations ($60), others ($180). Bar hours: 11:30 am to 1 am daily. Restaurant hours: 11:30 am to 2 pm and 6:30 pm to 9:30 pm daily
Public telephone. Out-of-town journalists and members of other press clubs admitted if they belong to reciprocal clubs. Monthly newsletter

PEN & PENCIL CLUB. 2nd Floor, 1600 Chancellor St, Philadelphia, PA 19102. *Bar.* **215-545-9604.** *Office.* **215-545-0907.** Arthur R H Morrow, president. Working press ($10), public relations and other associates ($15). Chartered 1892; founded circa 1865. Bar hours: Mon to Fri, 6 pm to 3 am; Sat, 7 pm to 3 am; Sun, 11 am to 3 am. No restaurant, but light snacks
Public telephones, work space with typewriter, file of local newspapers, limited library, meeting room; available 24 hours, 7 days a week. Out-of-town press welcome; also members of other clubs with reciprocal privileges. *Contact.* Bartender or president. Monthly newsletter; yearbook

PHOENIX PRESS CLUB. Valley National Bank Ctr, Concourse, Phoenix AZ 85001. **602-252-9280.** Joe Gacioch, president. Roy Rivers, manager. Working press ($48), allied news fields ($72), others ($108), nonresidents ($12). Founded 1949. Club occupies penthouse floor of hotel. Bar hours: Mon, Tues, and Wed, 11 am to 6 pm; Thurs and Fri, 11 am to 1 am; plus other hours for special events. Restaurant hours: 11 am to 2 pm Mon to Fri, plus other hours for special events
Work space with typewriters, and public telephones; available during business hours. Out-of-town journalists welcome as guests of members, or with membership in a reciprocal club. Members of other press clubs welcome with reciprocal privileges or as guests of members. *Contact for guest pass information.* Club manager. Weekly bulletin

PITTSBURGH PRESS CLUB. 300 6th Ave, Pittsburgh, PA 15222. **412-471-4644.** Adolph J Donadeo, CCM, general manager. Alfonso X Donalson, president. News associates ($45), working press ($45), public relations associates ($90), news sources affiliates ($140), nonresidents ($22.50 to $80). Organized in 1881. Occupies the penthouse in the 6th Ave building. Bar hours: Mon to Fri, 11:30 am to 1:00 am; Sat. 4:30 pm to 1 am. Restaurant hours: 11:30 am to 2:30 pm Mon to Sat.; also 5 pm to 10 pm Mon to Fri, and 5 pm to 11:15 pm Sat
Visiting journalists admitted if they have a current card showing membership in a club with established reciprocity. Monthly newsletter

SAINT JOHN PRESS, RADIO, TV CLUB INC. PO Box 6673, Station (a) Hilyard Pl, Saint John, NB, Canada. **506-652-9458**

PRESS CLUB OF METROPOLITAN ST LOUIS. 335 Mansion House Ctr, St Louis, MO 63102. **314-241-6397.** Wilma Draper, manager. Journalists, public relations, and others ($72 to $120). Founded 1960. Shares facilities with Washington University Alumni Club. Restaurant and bar hours: Mon to Thurs, 11 am to 5 pm; Fri and Sat, 11 am to 10 pm; later for parties
Out-of-town journalists welcome if they belong to another press club and pay cash. Members of other press clubs admitted. *Contact.* Manager

PRESS CLUB OF SAN FRANCISCO. 555 Post St, San Francisco, CA 94102. **415-775-7800.** Syd Kossen, president. Hans Fallant, general manager. Membership open to all professions; dues from $100 to $350. Founded 1888. Club owns a seven-story building in downtown area. Bar hours: 11 am to 11 pm daily. Restaurant hours: 7 am to 10 am; noon to 2 pm; 6 to 8 pm
Work space with typewriters, public telephones, library, sleeping quarters, press conference area; available 24 hours a day, 7 days a week. Out-of-town journalists admitted only if they belong to a club with reciprocal privileges. *Contact.* Jon Fox, program coordinator. Weekly newsletter

PRESS CLUB OF TOLEDO. PO Box 921, Toledo, OH 43660. **419-246-7131.** Don Wolfe, president. Laura Stamos, manager. Journalists and public relations ($15 to $55). Founded 1972. Bar hours: Mon to Fri, 11 am to 7:30 pm, with extended evening hours on special occasions. Restaurant hours: 11 am to 2:30 pm

Transmission facilities and public telephones; available 9 am to 7:30 pm. Out-of-town journalists and members of other press clubs welcome, with press identification. Monthly newsletter

TOPEKA PRESS CLUB. 616 Jefferson, Topeka, KS 66600. Elon M Torrence, president. Journalists and Sigma Delta Chi members ($5). No permanent quarters at present

TORONTO PRESS CLUB. 3rd Floor, 73 Richmond St W, Toronto, Ont, Canada. **416-362-4266** Tony Prawl, manager. Journalists, public relations, students, and others ($74 to $110). Founded 1949. Bar hours: noon to 1 am. Restaurant hours: noon to 2:30 pm

Out-of-town journalists and members of other press clubs welcome with credentials

VALLEY PRESS CLUB. PO Box 541, Van Nuys, CA 91408. Anne Parlapiano, president. Journalists, public relations, students, professors, and associates ($15). Founded 1960. Meets at the Sportsmen's Lodge, Studio City, CA. *Contact.* Viivi Piirisild, **213-765-2587**

WASHINGTON PRESS CLUB. 505 National Press Bldg, Washington, DC 20045. **202-393-3417.** William J Eaton, president. June Kelley, executive secretary. Journalists and government press information officers

($45). Founded 1919. Club has its own office in National Press Bldg and operates the Club Pub in the Sheraton-Carlton Hotel. Bar and restaurant hours: noon to 3 pm

Out-of-town journalists may use Club Pub for luncheon by obtaining a courtesy card from the office. Monthly newsletter

WINNIPEG PRESS CLUB. Mezzanine Floor, Delta's Marlborough Inn, 331 Smith St, Winnipeg, Man, Canada. **204-957-1188.** Ernest Nutimer, president. Journalists and public relations ($25). Club has its own facilities in the hotel. Bar hours: noon to 11 pm. Restaurant service in hotel.

Public telephones and library. Out-of-town journalists and members of other press clubs welcome. Publication: *Mossback*

INDEX